THE DEVELOPMENT OF CHILDREN

THE
DEVELOPMENT
OF
CHILDREN

...

MICHAEL COLE
University of California, San Diego

SHEILA R. COLE

SCIENTIFIC
AMERICAN
BOOKS

Distributed by W. H. Freeman and Company

A series of books in psychology

Editors: Richard C. Atkinson
Gardner Lindzey
Richard F. Thompson

Cover photograph: Imre Benkó, copyright © Eastfoto.

Library of Congress Cataloging-in-Publication Data

Cole, Michael, 1938–
    The development of children / Michael Cole and Sheila R. Cole.
        p.   cm.
    Bibliography: p.
    Includes index.
    ISBN 0-7167-1864-2
    1. Child development.   I. Cole, Sheila R.   II. Title.
RJ131.C585 1989   88-15768
155.4—dc19   CIP

Printed in the United States of America

Scientific American Books is a subsidiary of Scientific American,
Inc. Distributed by W. H. Freeman and Company, 41 Madison Avenue,
New York, New York 10010 and 20 Beaumont Street, Oxford OX1 2NQ, England

1 2 3 4 5 6 7 8 9 0   KP   7 6 5 4 3 2 1 0 8 9

For our parents and our children,
who have served as the medium of our development, and
for Jonathan Cobb, loyal intellectual midwife whose
experience of these birth pangs has brought a deeper
understanding of development than he ever imagined.

BRIEF CONTENTS

...

• • •

• • •

CONTENTS

...

CHAPTER 17   THE PSYCHOLOGICAL ACHIEVEMENTS OF ADOLESCENCE   559

CHAPTER 18   DEVELOPMENT AND LATER LIFE   597

PREFACE

• • •

What sets this book apart from all the other human development texts that beckon teachers and students? There are chronological books, which describe developmental changes from conception to adulthood and beyond; topical books, which concentrate on one aspect of development at a time; and books that combine these two approaches. There are books that emphasize research, others that focus on issues of concern to future child-care professionals, and still others that address students as prospective parents.

Our goal in writing this book has been to provide a broad foundation for understanding child development. In preparing this foundation we have attempted to build on the natural interest students have in human nature and on their own experience. We have been guided in our effort by the belief that in attempting to achieve such understanding it is a mistake to make sharp distinctions in developmental psychology between practical, theoretical, and research orientations. Truly fundamental knowledge in developmental psychology, we believe, must draw on and illuminate all three orientations if it is to serve the broad range of interests that students bring to this topic.

Practical Orientation

The authors of *The Development of Children* are two people who have known each other since adolescence, who have shared an interest in children's development from the time they were teenagers working as camp counselors, and who have raised their own children. Each of us also has a professional interest in child development. Sheila Cole is a journalist who has written articles about children and books for children. Michael Cole is a psychologist who has specialized in the study of children's learning and cognitive development. In our personal and professional lives our interest in children has been closely linked to practical activities to foster their development.

Reflecting this orientation, we include many discussions of practical problems in child development: for example, how to design effective environments for premature infants; how to promote children's intellectual skills, self-control, and participation with other children at play; and how to help children to recover from traumatic experiences. We also include many examples drawn from the everyday lives of children that illustrate how beliefs about children influence children's development by shaping both the laws and the norms that govern child-rearing practices.

Many child-care issues will be familiar to readers, either from their own experience or from stories they have heard or read. We believe that such experience, combined with good common sense and a lively interest in children's behavior, is an essential starting point for the deeper understanding of development that we seek to foster in this book.

Theoretical Orientation

There is a lot of truth in the idea that nothing is so practical as a good theory. A deep understanding of development requires familiarity not only with its phenomena but also with theories that provide coherent interpretations of the facts, allowing one to anticipate the consequences of various courses of action.

The major difficulty in introducing readers to the theoretical underpinnings of child development is the absence of a single, broadly accepted theoretical framework for understanding development. We have adopted two strategies to deal with this problem. First, we frame our presentation in terms of the enduring issues that all theories of development must resolve; how biological and environmental contributions (nature and nurture) are woven together and the extent to which the interaction of these factors results in discontinuities in the nature of the organism during the dynamic process of development. Second, we present competing theories in a constant dialogue with one another and with the practical issues that they were designed to address. Rather than gloss over differences among theories, we have attempted to build an appreciation of the basis for their competing interpretations. Then we have tried to move beyond them to show how each perspective contributes to an overall understanding of development.

Research Orientation

The dialogue between theory and practice leads naturally to disputes about the facts of development and efforts to marshal facts in support of one or another theory. Research is the process by which scholars gather new facts to challenge or support existing theories.

It is essential to understand research methods not only as a means of gaining a firm grasp of the basic facts but also as a means of thinking critically about the conclusions. Is it true that sparing the rod spoils the child? Do boys and girls play different kinds of games because they have been shaped to do so by social pressure or do such differences reflect deep-seated biological predispositions? Does watching violent programs on television increase children's aggressive behavior? And why is it so difficult for psychologists to answer enduring questions about development once and for all? Only through an awareness of the logic, methods, and indeed the shortcomings of psychological research can students come away from a course on development with the ability to evaluate the relative merits of different kinds of evidence that scientists offer in trying to answer such questions.

The kind of critical thinking needed to evaluate evidence and to appreciate the process of research does not develop spontaneously. It requires careful study and experience. Consequently, we have endeavored to keep the nature of developmental psychology as *disciplined* knowledge based on principled research practices in the forefront of our presentation.

Attention to Culture

Our work has taken us to live in many parts of the world: West Africa, Mexico, the Soviet Union, Israel, Japan, and Great Britain. Within the United States we have lived and worked in affluent suburbs and inner-

city ghettos. Often our children have accompanied us, providing rich opportunities for getting to know children from many walks of life.

Anyone who has spent time living among people in different parts of the world cannot help but be impressed by the incredible variety of circumstances in which children grow up. Such experiences have led us to believe that a full theory of development must incorporate the factor of culture as a fundamental constituent. In order to accomplish such a goal, it is necessary to overcome the ethnocentrism in our view of children's development in other cultures.

This task is by no means an easy one. One's initial reaction to daily life in an African village, an Asian metropolis, or the slums of a large U.S. city is likely to be "culture shock," a sense of disorientation that stems from the difficulty of understanding why people in other cultures behave the way they do. Very often, culture shock is accompanied by a sense of cultural superiority; the way "we" do it (prepare our food, build our houses, care for our children) seems superior to the way "they" do it. With time and patience, both the disorientation and the sense of superiority diminish.

Recognizing how difficult it is to think objectively about the nature of development in unfamiliar cultures, we have tried to keep before the reader the diversity of human child-rearing practices and their impact on the lives of children. Only by considering our culture as but one design for living among many can we arrive at a valid understanding of the principles that guide development for all human beings. According to this view, an appreciation of culture's contribution to development requires more than attention to ways that people far away raise their children. Culture must be considered a constituent of children's experience in *any* society — not something added on to the process of development but an essential characteristic of human beings.

Attention to Biology

It may seem surprising that authors who espouse a special interest in culture would simultaneously underscore, as we do, the importance of biology to human development; often the two sources of human variability are set in opposition to each other, as if somehow, by virtue of using culture, human beings ceased to be biologically evolving creatures. In our opinion, this is a false opposition. Not only is the ability to create and use culture one of the most striking biological facts about our species, but there would be no development at all without biological maturation. Advances in the biological sciences have profoundly influenced human development through improved health care and advanced medical procedures. In addition, the biological sciences have increased our understanding of development by shedding light on important issues such as the intimate links between biological changes in the brain and changes in children's cognitive capacities. The importance of such scientific contributions is made clear throughout this book, not just in the early chapters where biological influences on development are typically summarized only to be put into the background later.

The Story of Development and the Organization of This Book

The Development of Children combines traditional chronological and topical approaches to make as clear as possible the idea that development is a process involving *the whole child*. The book is chronological in its overall structure, describing development from conception to adulthood, as befits our understanding of development as a process that unfolds over time. It also adopts traditional stage boundaries for each of its major sections.

The organization of the text is topical in two respects. First, within broad, conventionally defined stages, it traces interwoven developments in the biological domain, the social domain, and the psychological domain (including affect and cognition). Second, it focuses on the way in which stagelike changes emerge from the convergence of events in different developmental domains, the traditional focus of topical accounts.

The chronological and topical perspectives correspond to the warp and the woof of development. The pattern that is woven from their combination is the story of development. It is that story we have attempted to tell in this book.

In the first chapter we introduce our main themes: the grounding of scientific concern about children in practical experience; the perennial questions of the field; the nature of developmental psychology as a discipline; and the interweaving of research methods, theories, and practice.

Part I is titled "In the Beginning," and describes three types of beginnings: the genetic basis of behavior and mechanisms of inheritance (Chapter 2), prenatal development (Chapter 3), and the process of birth, including a description of the capacities with which children emerge from the womb (Chapter 4).

Part II covers infancy. Chapters 5, 6, and 7 correspond to three widely recognized transition points within the first several years after birth — the first $2\frac{1}{2}$ months, the period from 3 to 12 months, and the second year of life. By dividing the period of infancy in this way, we attempt to focus on the process of developmental change, to highlight the issue of continuity and discontinuity in development, and to retain a picture of the whole developing child. The last chapter of Part II examines an enduring issue in the study development: is the pattern of development that is established during infancy fixed and unchangeable or can it be significantly influenced by the maturational changes and experiences that occur during childhood and adolescence?

Part III describes the major achievements of early childhood. The four chapters in this section cover the acquisition of language (Chapter 9), cognitive development (Chapter 10), social and personality development (Chapter 11), and the influence of varied contexts on children's development in the years from 3 to 6 (Chapter 12).

The first chapter in Part IV describes the biological and cognitive changes that contribute to making middle childhood, the years from 6 to 12, a distinctive stage of development in societies around the world. The next two chapters concentrate on the two contexts of particular importance in most children's lives in these years: school and peer groups. Chapter 14 discusses the relationship between schooling and development; Chapter 15 covers the new social relations that emerge during middle childhood, particularly among peers.

Part V covers the transition from childhood to adulthood, a great watershed in development not only because those formerly considered "children" are now biologically capable of becoming parents but also because this biological change coincides with a fundamental transition in the developing person's responsibilities and power. Although this transition is conventionally thought of as a distinct period of development called adolescence, the existence of major cultural and historical variations in the way it is organized have led us to question the senses in which adolescence should be considered a universal, distinctive stage of development. Chapter 16 highlights biological and social changes; Chapter 17 examines the psychological achievements of this period and critically re-examines the cultural and historical conditions under which adolescence appears as a stage of development.

Chapter 18 completes our narrative by considering both the changes that occur when a child reaches adulthood and the light these changes sheds on basic questions of development throughout life.

A Note to Instructors

The Development of Children has been designed to be taught within either in a quarter or a semester system. For classes taught on the quarter system in which the curriculum is restricted to childhood, the final two sections of the book can be left to students to read or not, as they choose, and the remainder can be fit comfortably into a 10-week course. For those who include adolescence and some treatment of adulthood in their courses, sections rather than whole chapters in Part I could be read; Chapter 8 (on the way infant experience shapes later development) and Chapter 9 (on language) could also be skipped or assigned selectively without disrupting the general flow of the presentation.

For those who prefer to organize this course in a topical fashion, decisions about Chapters 2 to 4 remain the same, and the natural sequence of chapters then becomes 5, 6, 10, 13, 17, which emphasize cognitive development, and 7, 11, 15, and 16, which emphasize social and personality development.

Pedagogical Features

Several pedagogical features will aid students in reading and learning from the text. Each chapter begins with an outline of the chapter's main sections and ends with a succinct summary of the major points. Key terms are set in boldface type in the text and listed at the end of each chapter. Their definitions are brought together in the glossary at the end of the text. Finally, the Part Introductions provide a synthetic framework for reading the individual chapters. We recommend

that students be urged to read these introductions from time to time as a reminder of the overall framework.

The text itself can be supplemented with an *Instructor's Manual,* which contains teaching suggestions, ideas for student projects, a resource guide to films and books, essay and multiple choice questions, and a review of each chapter's main points. An extensive *Computerized Test Bank* provides materials for examinations. There is also a *Study Guide,* which, in addition to reviewing the main points of each chapter, provides practice questions, excercises that help to integrate themes that cut across chapters, and information about how to make observations of children and how to write research papers.

Acknowledgments

A book of this scope and complexity could not be produced without the help of others. A great many people gave generously of their time and experience to deepen our knowledge of different areas of development.

Inger Bernth (University of Copenhagen), Joe Campos (University of Illinois), Klaus Grossman (University of Regensburg), Paul Harris, (Oxford), Jerome Kagan (Harvard University), Jean Mandler (University of California, San Diego), and John Morton (Child Development Unit, London) all contributed in various ways to enrich our understanding of infancy. In our presentation of language development we have been especially fortunate in obtaining ongoing advice and criticism from Peg Griffin and Carol Padden, both of whom are at the University of California, San Diego; and the help of Annette Karmiloff Smith and Richard Cromer (Child Development Unit, London).

A number of people assisted us in various ways in gathering together the materials on childhood and adolescence. We have been greatly influenced in our thinking about childhood by Vivian Paley, whose powers of observation and analytic methods are unsurpassed in the field. Pierre Dasen (University of Geneva), Giyoo Hatano (Dokkyo University), Robert LeVine (Harvard University), Barbara Rogoff (University of Utah), Diane Rubel (New York University), Beatrice and John Whiting (Harvard University), and James Youniss (Catholic University) all made helpful suggestions about drafts of these chapters.

In addition, we wish to thank the following people for their helpful reviews of various chapters of the manuscript.

Kathryn N. Black, Purdue University
Patricia C. Broderick, Villanova University
Urie Bronfenbrenner, Cornell University
Ann L. Brown, University of Illinois at Urbana-
    Champaign
Andrew C. Coyne, Ohio State University
Frank Curcio, Boston University
Judy S. DeLoache, University of Illinois at Urbana-
    Champaign
Don Devers, North Virginia Community College,
    Annandale
Shari Ellis, Virginia Commonwealth University
Sylvia Farnham-Diggory, University of Delaware
Mark Feldman, Stanford University
Sam Glucksberg, Princeton University
Mark Grabe, University of North Dakota
Patricia M. Greenfield, University of California, Los
    Angeles
Harold D. Grotevant, University of Texas at Austin
William S. Hall, University of Maryland, College Park
Janis E. Jacobs, University of Nebraska, Lincoln
Claire Kopp, University of California, Los Angeles
Alan W. Lanning, College of DuPage
Shitala P. Mishra, University of Arizona

Frank B. Murray, University of Delaware
Nora Newcombe, Temple University
Herbert L. Pick, Jr., University of Minnesota
Ellen F. Potter, University of South Carolina, Co-
    lumbia
Thomas M. Randall, Rhode Island College
LeRoy P. Richardson, Montgomery County Com-
    munity College
Barbara Rogoff, University of Utah
Sylvia Scribner, City University of New York
Stephanie Stolarz-Fantino, San Diego State University
Lawrence J. Walker, University of British Columbia
Harriet S. Waters, State University of New York at
    Stony Brook
Patricia E. Worden, California State University at
    Fullerton

Joe Campos (University of Illinois), Carol Izard (University of Delaware), and Larry Nucci (University of Illinois, Chicago) each contributed valuable illustrative material from their research.

We would also like to thank Julia De Rosa, Philip McCaffrey, Lynn Pieroni, and Anna Yip for the help they gave us with the arduous process of production.

MICHAEL COLE
SHEILA R. COLE
Solana Beach, California

THE DEVELOPMENT OF CHILDREN

THE STUDY OF HUMAN DEVELOPMENT

. . . .

A CHILD OF NATURE?

Early one morning in the cold winter of 1800, a naked, dirty boy wandered into a hut at the edge of a tiny French hamlet in the province of Aveyron to beg for food. Some of the people in the area had caught glimpses of the boy in the months before as he dug for roots, climbed trees, swam in streams, and ran at great speed on all fours. They said he was a wild beast. Word spread quickly when the boy appeared in the village, and everyone came to see him.

Among the curious was a government commissioner, who took the boy home and fed him. The child, who appeared to be about 12 years old, seemed ignorant of the civilized comforts that were offered to him. When clothes were put on him, he tore off whatever garments he could not slip off. He would not eat meat, preferring raw potatoes, roots, and nuts instead. He rarely made a sound and seemed indifferent to human voices. In his report, the government commissioner concluded that the boy had lived alone since early childhood, "a stranger to social needs and practices. . . . [T]here is . . . something extraordinary in his behavior, which makes him seem close to the state of wild animals" (quoted in Lane, 1976, pp. 8–9).

When the commissioner's report reached Paris it caused a sensation. Newspapers hailed the child as the "Wild Boy of Aveyron." It was thought that the boy would provide the means for resolving questions about the nature of human beings that had been the focus of philosophical and political disputes for many decades. Put in modern terms, these questions were

- What distinguishes us from other animals?

- What would we be like if we grew up totally isolated from human society?

- In making us who we are, what do we owe to our education and what to the characteristics with which we are born?

Many people hoped that the boy would have a noble character, which would support their claims that children are born good, only to be corrupted by society. But instead of a noble child of nature, examining physicians saw a disheveled, pathetic creature who was unable to speak and who often moved about on all fours. He looked and acted like children who were locked away in wards for the mentally defective and insane at that time. The physicians diagnosed the boy as mentally deficient and suggested that he had been put out to die by his parents for that reason. They recommended that he be put in an asylum.

One person who disputed the diagnosis of retardation was a young physician, Jean-Marc Itard (1774–1838). Itard argued that the boy appeared to be defective only because his years of isolation from society had not allowed him to develop normal social skills. Perhaps as many as one in three normal children born in France in the late eighteenth century were aban-

(Left) Victor, the Wild Boy of Aveyron. (Right) Jean-Marc Itard, who tried to transform the Wild Boy of Aveyron into a civilized Frenchman.

doned by parents who were often too poor to support them (Kessen, 1965). Itard maintained that what made the Wild Boy different was not innate mental deficiency but his remarkable ability to survive on his own.

Itard took personal charge of the boy, believing that he could teach him to become a full-fledged Frenchman, master of the best of civilized knowledge. France had recently overthrown its monarchy and had embraced the political ideals of equality, liberty, and brotherhood. Itard and other supporters of the republic wanted to demonstrate by educating peasant children and improving the conditions of their lives that it was possible to shape the process of development itself. The elaborate training program Itard devised for the Wild Boy would be a test of his faith in science and his theory that the environment of human beings shapes their development (Itard, 1801/1932).

Victor, as Itard named the Wild Boy, made rapid progress at first. He learned to communicate simple needs and to recognize and write several words. He also developed affection for those who took care of him. But Victor never learned to speak. And contrary to Europeans' notions of what a "savage" would be like, he never displayed strong sexual interests. When Itard took Victor out on walks, he was agile, sensitive to his surroundings, and happy. But when Victor was in public for long stretches of time, he became frustrated and angry or simply mischievous. On one occasion Itard took Victor to a fashionable salon so that the guests could meet a "child of nature." Victor wolfed down the food on his plate, stuffed his pockets with desserts, and slipped out of the room to the front yard. There he shed his clothing and climbed a tree, to be lured down only by a gardener offering him a basket of peaches.

After 5 years of intense work, Itard abandoned his experiment. Victor had not made enough progress to satisfy Itard's superiors, and Itard himself was unsure what more he might do. Victor was sent to live with a woman who was paid to care for him. He died in 1828, still the Wild Boy of Aveyron, leaving unsettled the large questions about human nature and the influence of civilized society that had aroused so much interest in him. Most physicians and scholars of the time eventually concluded that Victor had indeed been mentally defective from birth. But doubts remain to this day. Victor spent many of his formative years alone. When found, he had already passed the age after which it may be impossible to learn to use language normally. It is also possible that Itard's methods of teaching were

inadequate. For these and other reasons, some modern scholars believe that Itard may have been right in his belief that Victor was normal at birth but was stunted in his development as a result of his social isolation (Lane, 1976).

THE LEGACY OF ITARD

At the time of Itard, there was no scientific specialty called developmental psychology; in fact, there was relatively little scientific interest in children altogether. The modern science of developmental psychology did not arise until the century following that of Itard. But when it did, it adopted many of Itard's specific techniques as well as his overall faith in science as a means of bettering the human condition.

Despite many differences of philosophy and method, scholars who identify themselves as developmental psychologists share an interest in the study of **human development,** the sequence of changes in human beings that begins with conception and continues throughout life. As applied to human psychological processes, the strategy for developmental research rests on a very ancient intuition about personal understanding and self-discovery: If we can discover our roots and the history of changes that led us to the present moment, we can learn who and what we are and how we got to be this way. If we then combine insight into the past with information about our present circumstances, we are in a better position to anticipate the future and to prepare to meet it on our own terms.

The legacy of Itard was to show not only that science can be applied to human behavior but also that scientific research on human development can reach beyond personal issues to inform broad philosophical and political debates and, in doing so, yield practical applications. In his work with Victor, Itard created methods for diagnosing mental and linguistic abilities. He combined these diagnostic procedures with a program of instruction that served simultaneously as a test of his scientific, social, and political theories and as a means for bettering the life of the individual child he was studying.

The fusion of science, philosophy, and public policy in developmental concerns remains as relevant now as it was in Itard's day. From one family and community to the next, decisions on issues affecting children's development will be influenced by different assumptions about human nature and the factors that influence it: Will preschoolers be harmed if both parents work? Is it better to place handicapped children in the same schools with everyone else or in separate facilities where they may feel isolated but can obtain special help? Should children be taught to read as soon as they learn to talk to give them a headstart on their education, or should instruction be delayed until they begin school? How does divorce influence children's development at different ages? When are children old enough to testify in a court case or to be left at home without a baby-sitter? Although these questions range well beyond the issues Itard studied, they illustrate the kinds of questions that he believed could be investigated fruitfully using the methods of science. The answers provided by the research of developmental psychologists reverberate far beyond the lives of individual children. They affect the policies of federal, state, and local governments, school boards, and the judicial system. They are also the subject of intense political debate (see Figure 1.1).

FIGURE 1.1 *Daily newspaper headlines make clear the ways in which ideas about development are linked to important social and political issues.*

The Rise of a New Discipline

The growth of scientific concern about children in the decades following Itard's work with Victor was linked to the broad social changes in Europe and America that came with the industrial revolution. During the nineteenth century, industrialization transformed the basic economic activities by which people earned their livelihoods. It also transformed the role of children in society and the environments within which they developed. No longer did almost all children grow up on farms where they were cared for by their parents and contributed their labor. Instead, many were employed in factories, alongside and sometimes in place of their parents (Hiner & Hawes, 1985).

Industrialization also fueled urbanization, and huge slums grew up in sprawling, industrialized cities. When they were not at work, urban children were a liability to their parents, who had little space to accommodate them and little money with which to feed them. They were also a liability to the community, which perceived them as a rowdy nuisance. As much for social control as for any academic reasons, public schools arose as a place to supervise children's development when neither parents nor employers were supervising them.

Many children worked long hours in factories and mines from an early age under conditions that were dangerous and unhealthy. These conditions eventually became a matter of social concern, and gradually philanthropic, medical, and scientific attention began to focus on children. The close links between social concerns and scientific research are illustrated by early studies of children's growth. The Factories Inquiries Committee in England, for instance, conducted a study in 1833 to discover whether children could work 12 hours a day without suffering physical damage. The majority of the commission decided that 12 hours was an acceptable workday for children. Those who thought a 10-hour workday would be preferable were not concerned about the effects of long work hours on small children's intellectual or emotional well-being but about their morals; these committee members recommended that 2 hours of religious and moral education a day replace 2 of the hours spent working in mine, factory, or shop (Lomax, Kagan, & Rosenkrantz, 1978).

As they addressed concerns arising from changes in society, the nineteenth-century pioneers of developmental psychology continued to attend to general

Children at work in a factory near the turn of the century. The money they earned was usually a vital part of their family's income.

questions about human nature and methods for its study. For example, the early studies of growth and work capacity showed that children working in textile mills were shorter and lighter than local nonworking children of corresponding ages. Surveys of intellectual growth, which eventually led to IQ testing, showed wide variations in children's achievements that seemed to depend upon family background and individual experience. Both these lines of investigation fueled the continuing debates about the factors that influence development.

A crucial event that spurred scientists to view the process of development as a topic of serious study was the publication of Charles Darwin's *The Origin of Species* in 1859. Wide acceptance of Darwin's thesis that human beings have evolved from earlier species fundamentally changed the way people thought about children. Instead of an imperfect adult to be seen and not heard, the child came to be viewed as a microcosm for

the study of development of all kinds. By carefully observing the sequence of changes that occur in individual development, scientists hoped to confirm Darwin's ideas about the evolution of human beings from lower species. As William Kessen (1965) remarks in his historical account of the study of child development, Darwin initiated "a riot of parallel-drawing between animal and child, between primitive man and child, between early human history and child" (p. 113).

Late in the nineteenth century, developmental psychologists began to form organizations to promote their work. Important scientific landmarks were the formation in the 1890s of the Child-Study Association by G. Stanley Hall and the publication of the first journal devoted to child development, *Pedagogical Seminary.* During the same period, various child welfare organizations were formed to raise money for hospitals and orphanages and to support social reforms that would benefit the lives of children. A land-

A group of boys living in the slums of New York at the turn of the century.

mark in the institutionalization of concern about children was the creation in 1912 of the U. S. Children's Bureau to monitor the working conditions of children and to disseminate information about effective child-rearing practices. In addition, special institutes and departments devoted to the study of development began to spring up in major universities.

Modern Developmental Psychology

In the decades since psychologists began to concern themselves with the study of human development, they have accumulated a great deal of knowledge about the behavior of human beings at every age level, starting even before birth. They have developed a variety of research methods for learning about children, and they have devoted intensive effort to explaining the causes of the age-related changes they study.

Developmental psychologists are also active in applying their knowledge to furthering development. They serve in hospitals, childcare centers, schools, recreational facilities, and clinics. They assess children's developmental status and prescribe measures for assisting children in difficulty. They design special environments for development such as cribs for premature babies or more effective techniques for teaching children to read. Modern developmental psychol-

ogists, recognizing that change is a lifelong process, also take an active role in enhancing the development of adolescents and people of middle age, and in caring for the elderly.

The detailed knowledge developmental psychologists have accumulated in doing research and implementating development-enhancing programs is important, and this book will describe many aspects of it. But in learning about the techniques and skills of developmental psychology it is just as important to keep firmly in mind the more general goal of the psychological sciences, which is to increase our understanding of human nature and its development.

THE CENTRAL QUESTIONS OF DEVELOPMENTAL PSYCHOLOGY

Despite great variety in the work they do and the theories they use to guide their work, psychologists who study development share two fundamental concerns:

1. Is the course of development best understood as a continuous process of change or as a series of transformations that produce sharp discontinuities in the organization of a person's behavior?

2. Is development primarily guided by the genetic program locked into the body's cells or is it fundamentally directed by forces in the external environment?

Psychologists are deeply divided on many aspects of these two fundamental issues. The assumptions they make about continuity and sources of change shape their interpretations of what they observe and their proposals for fostering development.

Questions about Continuity

Questions about continuity arise in several different guises, each of which will be considered in turn. How similar are we to other species in our mental capacities, in our emotional responses, and in other important respects? Is our development gradual or do we undergo a series of transformations in the course of our development? Lastly, are there periods in a person's life during which specific events must occur for development to proceed normally?

Are human beings distinctive?   For centuries, people have debated to what extent we are different from other creatures and to what extent we are subject to the same natural laws as are all other living forms. Questions about the uniqueness of human beings concern **phylogeny,** the evolutionary history of a species. Answering them is important to developmental psychologists because they imply different possibilities for and potential constraints on human development.

When Charles Darwin (1809–1882) published *The Origin Of Species*, the idea of evolution was already a subject of speculation. Darwin's great achievement was to convince most of the Western scientific world, and eventually other people as well, that "the innumerable species, genera and families, with which this world is peopled, are all descended, each within its own class or group, from common parents, and all have been modified in the course of descent" (Darwin, 1859/1958, p. 425).

Darwin was a firm believer in continuity among species. To test his claim that our species evolved gradually and continuously as a part of the natural order, scientists have searched, with some success, for evidence of evolutionary links that connect us with other forms of life and have compared our genetic makeup and behavior with that of other organisms.

While accepting Darwin's major claim that the origin of new species is a natural process, many modern evolutionary theorists reject the idea that evolution is a continuous process (Eldredge & Gould, 1972). They claim instead that new species have arisen quite rapidly in relatively isolated environments and have subsequently been able to survive momentous environmental changes that have destroyed other species. Stephen Gould (1980), a champion of the theory of discontinuous evolution, likens the process of evolutionary change to the boiling of water:

> change occurs in large leaps following a slow accumulation of stresses that a system resists until it reaches a breaking point. Heat water and it eventually boils. (pp. 184–185)

On the side of continuity between ourselves and other animals, it has been established that we share as much as 90 percent of our genetic material with chimpanzees (King & Wilson, 1975). However, it is also clear that there is something distinctive about the pattern of our species' characteristics. The difficult question is: what is that something?

One obvious characteristic of *Homo sapiens* is that we develop in an environment that has been shaped by countless prior generations of people in their struggle for existence (White, 1949). This special environment consists of artifacts, such as tools and clothing, knowledge about how to construct and use those artifacts, beliefs about the world, and values about what is worthwhile, all of which guide people in the ways they behave. Anthropologists call this accumulation of knowledge, beliefs, values, and artifacts **culture.** It is the "man-made" part of the environment that greets us at birth (Herskovitz, 1948) and the "design for living" that we acquire from our community (Kluckhohn & Kelly, 1945).

A key feature of culture is that it is transmitted from generation to generation through language. Thus, it is not surprising that, since antiquity, language has been proposed as a defining characteristic of our species. In

Although chimpanzees and human beings share more than 90 percent of their genetic material, the differences between the two species are profound.

the seventeenth century, the philosopher René Descartes stated the traditional view eloquently:

> Language is in effect the sole sure sign of latent thought in the body; all men use it, even those who are dull or deranged, who are missing a tongue, or who lack the voice organs, but no animal can use it, and this is why it is permissible to take language as the true difference between man and beast. (Quoted in Lane, 1976, p. 23)

In recent years, scientists have demonstrated that claims for culture and language as uniquely human qualities have been overstated. Rudiments of culture and languagelike behavior can be found in chimpanzees and other primates (Kawai, 1965; Lieberman, 1984; Premack & Premack, 1983; Goodall, 1986). Still, as we will see in later chapters, human culture and language-using capacities appear to be qualitatively different from similar phenomena exhibited by any other species.

The evidence that there are both important continuities and significant discontinuities between human beings and other species complicates the task of understanding human development. In so far as the relation of *Homo sapiens* to other species is continuous, the study of other animals can provide useful suggestions about the processes of development in human beings. To the extent that *Homo sapiens* are distinctive, research that describes the processes of individual growth and change in other species may not apply to our development. The existence of continuities and discontinuities means that we must use caution when considering the applicability of studies with other animals to human development.

Is individual development continuous?

The second major question about continuity concerns **ontogeny**, the course of development during an individual's lifetime. Is ontogeny gradual and continuous or do we progress through a series of qualitatively different stages of development? (See Figure 1.2.)

To the extent that development is discontinuous, the way in which the child experiences the world and the way in which the world influences the child are likely to change as the child progresses from one stage to the next. For example, infants are especially sensitive to the sounds of language (Butterfield & Siperstein, 1972), but once they begin to understand and produce language themselves, the way they learn about the world appears to change fundamentally. According to several prominent theories, the discontinuity that accompanies the onset of language marks the boundary between infancy and early childhood (Flavell, 1985).

In everyday conversations the concept of a developmental stage is sometimes misused as a way of explaining behavior. Suzy, we may be told, "behaves wildly because she is an adolescent." We would not be satisfied by an explanation that butterflies fly because they are in the butterfly and not the caterpillar stage. Instead we would want to know what it is about butterflies that enables them to fly. The same applies to human behavior. We need to know what it is about being an adolescent that may cause Suzy's "wild" behavior. Without a careful specification of the processes that give rise to a person's behavior in different stages, explanations of behavior solely as a characteristic of a stage add nothing to our understanding. Sensitive to this problem, psychologists who use the stage concept attempt to specify exactly what they mean by a stage and how the psychological processes that they believe are distinctive to each stage are related to the behaviors that are characteristic of it.

John Flavell (1971) suggests that four criteria are central to the concept of a developmental **stage:**

1. Stages of development are distinguished by changes that are qualitative. Asked to memorize a set of words, adolescents not only remember more than 8-year-olds do, they remember *differently,* by grouping words according to accepted categories and employing sophisticated strategies of memorization.

2. The transition from one stage to the next is marked by simultaneous changes in a great many, if not all, aspects of a child's behavior. For example, about the time of their second birthday, children not only begin to imitate adults in a new way; they also begin to talk about themselves as distinct individuals, and they start to use objects to represent other objects in their play.

3. When the change from one stage to the next occurs, it is rapid. Periods of relative stability in a person's physical and behavioral characteristics are followed by periods of rapid transition.

4. The numerous behavioral and physical changes that mark the appearance of a stage form a pattern. The new forms of reasoning that arise dur-

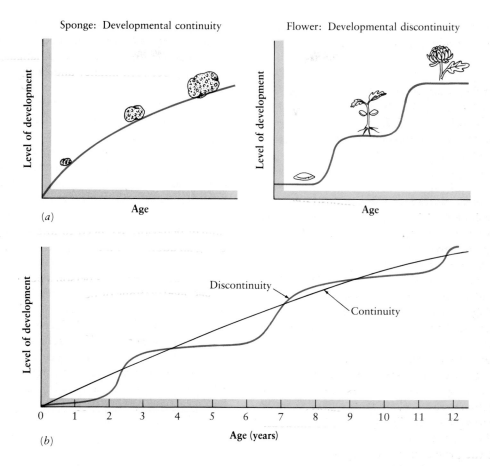

FIGURE 1.2 *(a) The contrasting courses of development of sponges and flowers provide idealized examples of continuous and discontinuous development. (b) According to the continuity view, development is a process of gradual growth, whereas according to the discontinuity view it is a series of stagelike transformations. Human beings appear to exhibit a mixture of the two types of development.*

ing middle childhood (approximately ages 6 to 12), for example, are closely linked to new forms of social interaction that appear at the same time.

Some psychologists deny that the stage concept is crucial to understanding development. A leading behavior theorist, Albert Bandura (1977), for example, argues that the mechanisms by which people learn new behaviors are the same at all ages, so there is considerable continuity in the process of developmental change. According to this view, discontinuities in development are relatively rare occurrences that follow abrupt alterations in "social-training and other relevant biological or environmental variables" (Bandura & Walters, 1963, p. 25). Robert Siegler, a psychologist

who specializes in studying the development of children's thinking, makes a similar argument: "Children's thinking," he writes, "is continually changing, and most of the changes seem to be gradual rather than sudden" (1986, p. 11).

During most of the twentieth century, stage theories of development have been more numerous and more influential than continuity theories. Yet stage theories are confronted with a variety of facts that appear to violate one or more of the criteria for developmental stages proposed by Flavell.

One acute problem facing modern stage theories is that some aspects of a child's behavior appear to vary according to circumstances. For example, 4-year-olds often have difficulty taking another's point of view, but when they are speaking to a 2-year-old, they simplify their speech appropriately; they also frequently become solicitous when the younger child appears to be emotionally upset (Hoffman, 1981; Shatz & Gelman, 1973). Such simultaneous occurrences of behaviors thought to be characteristic of two different stages seem incompatible with the idea that stages provide general characterizations of an individual's psychological makeup.

Another challenge to the idea that development is a process of qualitative stage transformations comes from the belief that some behaviors remain stable over long periods of time. For example, parents often try to read their newborn baby's behavior for hints of things to come. If baby Sam is fussy, perhaps it means he will be an irritable child. If baby Georgia has a large appetite, maybe she will be a big eater as a teenager.

Although the notion that some of our psychological characteristics remain constant over extended periods of time has intuitive appeal, demonstrating it scientifically has proven difficult. The problem is that the indicators of, say, a good memory or an easy-going temperament that seem appropriate for an infant are not likely to be appropriate for an 8-year-old or a teenager. Perhaps for this reason, many studies have failed to support the idea of psychological continuity over time (Kopp & McCall, 1982). However, the refinement of research techniques in recent years has allowed some investigators to find support for developmental continuity. For example, children who are shy and uncertain when tested at 21 months are likely to be timid and cautious when tested again at 5½ years (Reznick, Kagan, Snidman, Gersten, Baak, & Rosenberg, 1986). Similarly, infants who rapidly adapt to novel visual stimuli have been found to score well on tests of mental development 4 or 5 years later (Bornstein & Sigman, 1986).

The stability of children's psychological characteristics over time also depends on stability in their environment. A number of studies have found that children who remain in an orphanage that provides only minimal care from infancy through adolescence are at risk for intellectual and emotional difficulties as adults (Dennis, 1973). But if the environment of these children is improved—that is, if they are given extra care and stimulating attention by the orphanage staff or if they are adopted into caring families—their condition improves markedly and many of them become intellectually and emotionally normal adults (Dennis, 1973; Koluchova, 1976; Tizard & Rees, 1976; Rutter, 1981).

As with human similarities to other species, it seems clear that there are both distinctive discontinuities and conspicuous similarities in a child's development over time. An important task of developmental psychology is to distinguish characteristics that undergo stagelike transformations from those that remain relatively constant as children grow older.

Are there critical periods of development? A question closely related to that about the continuity of individual development is whether or not there are **critical periods** of development—periods in the growth of an organism during which specific environmental or biological events must occur for development to proceed normally. The existence of critical periods has been firmly established for some animals (see Figure 1.3) and for some aspects of human physi-

FIGURE 1.3 *Ethologist Konrad Lorenz proposed the existence of a critical period in the development of ducklings. These ducklings would not have followed Lorenz had he not been the first moving thing they saw as soon as they were able to walk.*

cal development. If the newly formed gonads (sex glands) do not produce male hormones at about 7 weeks following conception in human beings, for example, the development of female genitalia is irreversibly set, even in embryos with genes for maleness (Austin & Short, 1972). The strongest evidence for critical periods in human behavioral development comes from studies of the development of language (Curtiss, 1977; Goldin-Meadow, 1982; Lenneberg, 1967). Children who, like Victor, have for some reason not had sufficient exposure to language to acquire one prior to the age of 6 or 7 years may never acquire a language.

Questions about the Sources of Development

The second major issue that preoccupies developmental psychologists is the way in which biological factors directed by the genes interact with environmental factors in human development. During much of the twentieth century, this problem has been posed in the form of a choice between "nature" and "nurture." **Nature** refers to the inborn biological capacities and limitations of the individual; **nurture** refers to the influences of the social environment on the individual, particularly those of the family, the community, and the school. Much of the argument about Victor was essentially about nature and nurture: Was Victor incapable of speech and other behaviors normal for his age because of defective biological endowment (nature) or because of inadequate nurturing? (See Box 1.1, "Philosophical Forefathers of Developmental Psychology," for early formulations of this issue.)

The way nature-nurture questions are answered can have far-reaching effects on how children are treated by society. For example, if it is assumed that girls, by nature, lack interest and ability in mathematics and science, they are not likely to be encouraged to become scientists or mathematicians. If, on the other hand, it is assumed that mathematical and scientific talent is largely a result of nurture, a society may train girls and boys equally in these activities.

Modern psychologists emphasize that development cannot be adequately described by considering either nature or nurture in isolation because the organism and its environment constitute a single life process (Freedman, 1974). Nonetheless, it is common practice to study living systems by separating definable influences and analyzing them independently. The prob-

lem, then, is twofold: (1) to determine the relative contributions of nature and nurture to various kinds of behavior and (2) to discover how nature and nurture interact to create the developing child.

Disagreements among developmental psychologists about the relative influences of nature and nurture on development and about how nature and nurture interact have contributed to the formation of different schools of thought, or theoretical perspectives, that attempt to explain the developmental process. Four of these perspectives will be discussed repeatedly in this book: the biological-maturation perspective, the environmental-learning perspective, the interactional perspective, and the cultural-context perspective (see Figure 1.4). What follows here is only a brief overview of

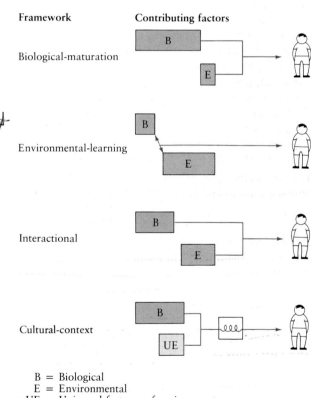

B = Biological
E = Environmental
UE = Universal features of environment
ℓℓℓ = Culture (historically specific features of environment)

FIGURE 1.4 *Four frameworks for interpreting the influence of nature and nurture on individual development. In the first three frameworks, biological and environmental factors directly shape the individual. In the fourth, the cultural-context framework, biological inheritance and universal features of the environment act through the medium of culture.*

BOX 1.1

PHILOSOPHICAL FOREFATHERS OF DEVELOPMENTAL PSYCHOLOGY
• • •

When Europeans first became conscious of the peoples of Africa and Asia in the fifteenth and sixteenth centuries, they debated the source of the obvious physical and behavioral differences between themselves and the peoples they encountered. Were these creatures human, they wondered. Were they also the children of God, and if so, why did they look and act so differently? Stated in modern terms, were they different in their basic *nature*, or were they different because of the conditions of their *nurture*?

Europeans asked similar questions about one another. Were peasants and princes different because God willed it so? Or were they different because they had been exposed to different experiences after they entered the world? These were not abstract questions of interest only to philosophers. They were questions of deep political significance. For centuries kings and nobles had claimed that they had a God-given right to rule over others because they were naturally superior by virtue of their births.

At the beginning of the modern era, two philosophers whose writings were to have an important influence on the history of child development, John Locke and Jean-Jacques Rousseau, challenged the view that human differences were determined primarily by birth. Their views of human differences and social inequality were directly connected to their beliefs about children's development.

JOHN LOCKE

The English philosopher John Locke (1632–1704) proposed that the child's mind is a *tabula rasa*, a blank slate upon which experience writes its story. In *Some Thoughts Concerning Education* (1699/1938), Locke expressed the central intuition that guided his thinking:

> The little, and almost insensible Impressions on our tender Infancies, have very important and lasting Consequences: And there 'tis, as in the Fountains of some Rivers, where a gentle Application of the Hand turns the flexible waters into Chanels, that make them take quite contrary Courses, and by this little Direction given them at first in the Source, they receive different Tendencies, and arrive at last, at very remote and distant Places. (pp. 1–2)

Locke did not deny that there are limits to what the "Application of the Hand" can achieve. One cannot make waters run uphill. He believed that children are born with different "temperaments and propensities," and he advised that instruction should be tailored to fit these differences, a view that remains central to modern theories of education. But Locke clearly asserted that nurture, in the form of adults "channeling" children's initial impulses, was the key factor in creating the main differences between people.

JEAN-JACQUES ROUSSEAU

The French philosopher Jean-Jacques Rousseau (1712–1778) also argued that differences among people were primarily the result of experience, but his view of children and the role of adult training of children was different from Locke's. Rousseau asserted that "natural man" was not born in sin but was corrupted by civiliza-

each of these major theoretical frameworks. They will be expanded on in subsequent chapters in conjunction with specific aspects of development.

The biological-maturation perspective The first principle of the biological-maturation view of the nature-nurture relationship is that every species exhibits its own distinctive form of physical organization and pattern of behavior traits. All the distinctive traits of individuals within a species fall within the biological constraints that define the species. From this perspective, biological factors are considered to be much more important than environmental factors in determining the course of individual development.

tion. In the state of nature all people were equal; inequality appeared with the rise of agriculture, industry, and property. According to this view, the native peoples encountered during the age of European exploration were more virtuous than the Europeans who took such pride in their civilization.

Rousseau claimed for the child at birth what he had claimed for natural man—a nature unspoiled by civilization. In *Emile* (1762/1911), a book that was part novel and part treatise on education, he indicated his opinion of adult attempts to bring the child "up" to virtue:

> God makes all things good. Man meddles with them and they become evil. He forces one soil to yield the products of another, one tree to bear another's fruit. He confuses and confounds time, place, and natural conditions. He mutilates his dog, his horse, and his slave. He destroys and defaces all things; . . . he will have nothing as nature made it, not even man himself, who must learn his paces like a saddlehorse, and be shaped to his master's taste like the trees in his garden. (p. 5)

In his tale of Emile's education, Rousseau provided a vision of childhood and education in which the role of the caretaker is to protect the child from the pressures of adult society. Emile, who stands for Every Child, is *not* an incomplete adult who must be perfected through instruction but a whole human being whose capabilities are suited to his age. Emile passes through several natural stages of development. In each, his activities are appropriate to his needs at the time, and they are guided by an adult using suitably paced educational practices. As William Kessen (1965) points out, these ideas about a stagelike character to development were later taken up by developmental psychologists, and they remain influential to this day.

LOCKE, ROUSSEAU, AND THE MODERN WORLD

Locke's notion of a *tabula rasa* and Rousseau's vision of the natural man have been rightly criticized and sometimes ridiculed in the centuries that have passed since the two philosophers died. Modern research makes it clear that we are not born with a *tabula rasa*; we enter the world with brains that are highly structured. Nor is it plausible that there ever existed a purely "natural" state of humankind, which the modern world corrupts. When Victor, the Wild Boy who really did grow up in a "state of nature," misbehaved outrageously during one of his outings with Itard, people joked, "If only Rousseau could see his noble savage now!"

The common wisdom underlying Locke's and Rousseau's views on the crucial role of experience in shaping human behavior remains valid, however. In 1776 the United States was founded as a republic based on a profound faith in the "self-evident" truth that "all men are created equal." In an earlier era, when kings and nobles ruled by "divine right," the open expression of such ideas would have been unthinkable. A clear indication of the political significance of the belief that human beings can shape the course of their development by arranging their environments is the fact that when the Bishop of Paris read *Emile* he sought to have Rousseau arrested, which caused Rousseau to flee from France.

With the acceptance of the idea that children are born good, or at least not evil, came a deep obligation to confront obvious inequalities in the conditions of life of developing children. Not only the newly formed United States, but France, and eventually England as well, came to respect the idea that children's welfare, indeed the welfare of persons of every age, is a concern for which society must accept some responsibility.

The crucial claim of the biological-maturation perspective is that the basic sequence of changes that characterize development are **endogenous**; they come from "inside" the organism and are the result of the child's biological heritage. The major cause of development from this viewpoint is **maturation**, which refers to genetically determined patterns of change that occur as individuals age from their immature starting point to full adulthood. Psychologists who adopt the biological-maturation perspective are likely to believe that psychological development is a progression of stagelike changes that accompanies (and is caused by) stagelike changes in the biological structure of the organism.

The influence of the environment in shaping the basic course of developmental change is decidedly secondary in the biological-maturation view. This point was made quite forcefully by Arnold Gesell (1880–1961), one of the most influential developmental psychologists of the early twentieth century:

Environment . . . determines the occasion, the intensity, and the correlation of many aspects of behavior, but it does not engender the basic progressions of behavior development. These are determined by inherent, maturational mechanisms. (1940, p. 13)

At midcentury, biological-maturation theories of human development were out of favor, but in more recent decades, they have enjoyed renewed attention. Modern studies of language acquisition, for example, suggest to some researchers that the environment plays only a "triggering" role in the realization of linguistic potential; the ability to use language appears to mature at a fixed pace and is inherited by all human beings (Piatelli-Palmerini, 1980). In addition, temperament and intelligence have been shown to have a significant inherited component (Plomin & DeFries, 1985), and several basic intellectual competencies appear to be present in embryonic form at or near birth, suggesting that they initially do not depend on interactions with the postnatal environment (Baillargeon, 1987).

Arnold Gesell testing a child in the observation room at the Yale Child Study Center.

The environmental-learning perspective   According to the environmental-learning perspective, biological factors provide the basic foundation for development, but the major causes of developmental change are predominantly **exogenous**, that is, they come from the environment, particularly from the adults in the environment who reward and punish the child's efforts. The major mechanism of development according to this perspective is **learning**, the process by which an organism's behavior is modified by experience. John B. Watson (1878–1958), an early behavior theorist, presented an extreme statement of this position:

Give me a dozen healthy infants, well-formed, and my own specified world to bring them up in and I'll guarantee to take any one at random and train him to become any type of specialist I might select — doctor, lawyer, artist, merchant-chief, and, yes, even beggar-man and thief, regardless of his talents, penchants, tendencies, abilities, vocations, and race of his ancestors. (1930, p. 104)

Modern psychologists who adopt an environmental-learning perspective no longer ignore biological differences among children so completely. However, they do believe that the environment, acting through learning mechanisms, is overwhelmingly important in shaping development. In support of their position, they point to evidence that enriching the experience of children who have lived in isolation or who have been brought up in orphanages with little intellectual stimulation dramatically improves their later social and cognitive development (Clarke & Clarke, 1986); that certain styles of parenting appear to promote children's competence (Baumrind, 1971); and that television can influence aggressive behavior (Bandura, 1973).

The interactional perspective   Those who adopt the interactional view of sources of development assert that nature and nurture play reciprocal roles and that it is inappropriate to attribute more importance to one factor or the other. Interactional theorists differ, however, in their focus on particular aspects of development and on the specific roles they assign to nature and nurture in particular cases.

For example, the Swiss developmental psychologist Jean Piaget (1896–1980), who began his scientific career as a biologist, paid close attention to processes common to the biological development of all organic

Jean Piaget, whose work has had a profound influence on developmental psychology, observing children at play.

life, much like a biological-maturation theorist. "Mental growth is inseparable from physical growth," he argued; "maturation of the nervous and endocrine systems, in particular, continues until the age of sixteen" (Piaget & Inhelder, 1969, p. vii). At the same time, Piaget, like supporters of the environmental-learning perspective, believed that the environment plays a role in development that goes well beyond triggering the child's innate potential:

The human being is immersed right from birth in a social environment which affects him just as much as his physical environment. Society, even more, in a sense, than the physical environment, changes the very structure of the individual. . . . Every relation between individuals (from two onwards) literally modifies them. . . . (Piaget, 1973, p. 156)

As practiced by Piaget, the interactional perspective attributes to children a greater role as active constructors of their own development than does either the environmental-learning or biological-maturation perspective. Piaget and his followers maintain that the

environment does not act in an automatic way that is the same for all children at all ages. Instead, the influences of the environment depend on the child's current stage of development.

According to Piaget, children, through their active striving to master their environments, *construct* higher levels of development from elements contributed by both maturation and environmental circumstances. This constructive process, as Piaget conceived of it, is fundamentally the same in all human groups. It can be speeded up or slowed down by variations in the environment, but the basic sequence of changes is universal.

Throughout his long career, Piaget concentrated his attention on the development of knowledge and thought. His studies of the way children's thought processes shape such things as moral reasoning and theories of how the physical world works were the foundation for his enormously influential stage theory of development.

Sigmund Freud (1856–1939), who is best known for his theories of personality formation and mental illness, is sometimes thought of as a biological theorist because he reduced all human drives to the need to reproduce the species. When considering the process of individual development, Freud was more of an interactionist, however. "The constitutional factor," he wrote, "must await experiences before it can make itself felt" (1905/1953, p. 239). In other words, the basic human drives are biologically determined, but the social environment directs the way in which these drives will be satisfied, thereby fundamentally shaping individual personalities.

The cultural-context perspective   Psychologists working within the three theoretical frameworks described thus far assume that development arises from the interaction of factors from two sources, biological heritage and the environment. Their disagreements focus on the relative weights that should be attributed to the two sources and how they interact to cause development. Scholars such as Urie Bronfenbrenner, Lev Vygotsky, Beatrice Whiting, and John Whiting who adopt the cultural-context perspective emphasize that the same biological or environmental factor may have quite different consequences for development, depending upon the specific context in which it occurs. The ways people organize the contexts of their activities depend upon the experiences of prior generations. Therefore, this perspective includes a third source, the history of the child's social group as brought into the present in the form of culture, as an important contributor to development (Bronfenbrenner, 1979; Vygotsky, 1978).

The technical term *culture* used in discussions of development should not be confused with the popular notion of being "cultured," which usually refers to people who have acquired refined manners or the ability to read thick books. As mentioned earlier, culture consists of human designs for living that are based on the accumulated knowledge of a people that has been encoded in their language and embodied in the physical artifacts, beliefs, values, and customs that have been passed down from one generation to the next.

The development of mathematical understanding provides an example of cultural influences on development. The kinds of mathematical thinking children develop depend not only on their ability to deal with abstractions and adult efforts to teach them mathematical concepts but also on the adults' own knowledge in the domain of numbers, which in turn depends on their cultural heritage. A child growing up among the Oksapmin of New Guinea appears to have the same universal ability to grasp basic number concepts as a child growing up in Paris or Pittsburgh. But the system of counting used in Oksapmin culture—counting by body parts—does not support the development of algebraic thinking (Saxe, 1981). Brazilian market children, who grow up in a country where modern mathematics is a part of the national cultural heritage but who do not attend school, develop remarkable mathematical skills in the context of everyday buying and selling, but they experience difficulties with the same problems if they are presented in a school-like format (Carraher & Carraher, 1981). Many U.S. high school students can solve certain physics problems, which they consider elementary, that confounded the Greek philosopher Aristotle in ancient times. In each of these cases, culture has shaped the course of development.

The cultural-context and interactional points of view are similar enough that on occasion it is difficult to classify a theorist as belonging in one camp or the other. For example, Erik Erikson (1902–   ), a student of Freud whose work will figure prominently in later chapters, is sometimes classified as an interactional theorist because he adheres to the view that nature sets the basic stage sequence while nurture shapes developmental processes within stages. However, Erikson draws on evidence from many cultures, and he emphasizes that the prior experience of the society into which children are born, embodied in its current culture, plays a major role in development (Erikson, 1963). In these respects he is similar in point of view to cultural-context theorists.

Although adherents of these competing perspectives have been attempting to explain development all during the twentieth century, the central issues of developmental psychology remain unresolved. There is still no generally accepted set of answers to the basic questions about human development. Nor is there agreement on a single "correct" perspective that should be used in searching for them. The modern discipline of developmental psychology is essentially a mechanism for organizing inquiry that allows scholars with different views to compare notes and learn from each other's work. The resulting discussions encompass every aspect of the field—the observations that are made, the methods for relating facts to theories, and the implications of facts and theories for the way we raise our children.

Cultural-context approaches pay special attention to variations in children's development arising from differences in the human-made parts of the environment.

THE DISCIPLINE OF DEVELOPMENTAL PSYCHOLOGY

Among the sciences that study development, psychology focuses on the individual human being whereas sociology and anthropology focus on human groups. The hundred-year-old division of scientific labor between these disciplines creates a paradox. On the one hand, psychologists seek to understand development in terms of the individual person; on the other, the natural-sciences tradition from which psychology springs insists that the relevant level of analysis is humankind, not the individual human (Gould, 1980). This paradox is eloquently described by novelist-philosopher Walker Percy:

> There is a secret about the scientific method which every scientist knows and takes as a matter of course, but which the layman does not know. . . . The secret is this: Science cannot utter a single word about an individual molecule, thing, or creature in so far as it is an individual but only in so far as it is like other individuals. (1975, p. 22)

The difference between these two ways of knowing— one based upon intimate knowledge of individual characteristics and biography, the other based upon characteristics common to many people—is the source of constant tension in psychologists' attempts to understand development. The more psychologists want to know about individuals, the more they need to know about people's histories and circumstances. But the more they concentrate on unique histories and patterns of influence, the less they can generalize their findings to other individuals.

This trade-off requires psychologists to vary their research methods depending upon their specific goals. If, for example, the goal is to create a beneficial environment for infants born prematurely or to create a system of education for blind children, methods that treat all children as equivalent *with respect to the issue in question* are appropriate. But if the goal is to help Johnny, who suddenly has started to fail his classes and misbehave at school, the psychologist will want to know about Johnny's *unique* history and current circumstances.

These complexities have led developmental psychologists to devote a great deal of attention to how they arrive at their conclusions about development. In order to accumulate useful scientific knowledge, they must pay close attention to the adequacy of their descriptions, their techniques for collecting data, and the way they design their research. Only by doing so can the data psychologists collect be related in meaningful ways to their theories, which in turn guide their practical activities on behalf of children.

Criteria of Scientific Description

In every society, commonsense beliefs about the nature of children and the course of their development abound. Many of them are contradictory; some are foolish, and some are wise. To arrive at useful knowledge based on scientific evidence rather than commonsense speculation, developmental psychologists, like all scientists, attempt to design their investigations in ways that allow others to check them. Psychologists use four general criteria to judge the descriptions derived from investigations of children's behavior: *objectivity*, *reliability*, *validity*, and *replicability*.

To be useful in constructing a disciplined account of human development, descriptions should be **objective**; that is, they should not be biased by the investigators' preconceptions about development. Total objectivity is impossible to achieve in practice because human beings come to the study of behavior with prior beliefs that influence their interpretations of what they see. But objectivity remains an important ideal toward which to work.

Descriptions should be **reliable** in two senses. First, the descriptions arrived at on each occasion when the same behavior is observed should be consistent with one another. Second, independent observers on the same occasion should agree in their descriptions of the behavior. Suppose that the behavior being observed is how upset infants become when a pacifier is taken from them while they are sucking on it (Goldsmith & Campos, 1982). Statements about an infant's behavior are considered reliable in the first sense if the level of upset (manifested as crying or thrashing about) is found to be more or less the same on successive occasions when the baby's sucking is interrupted. The statements are considered reliable in the second sense if independent observers agree on how upset the baby becomes when the pacifier is taken away.

Validity means that the behavior being studied is actually a reflection of the underlying psychological process that the researcher claims it is. Many psychologists, for example, believe that the level of upset infants display when their sucking is interrupted reflects their predisposition to become irritable (Kagan, 1984). One important test of validity is whether different ways of measuring the same characteristic agree. Children who become upset when their pacifier is removed should also become irritable when a rattle is taken away or when they are not fed on time. Another important test of validity is whether the behavior exhibited at one time can be used to predict future behavior. If the same infants who appear greatly upset when their pacifier is removed also become upset when interrupted in future situations (when recess ends in the middle of a game, for example), that is evidence to support the validity of the claim about a predisposition to irritability. If these same infants don't become upset easily in future situations, the original claim that the behavior is an indicator of an underlying temperamental predisposition to be irritable is suspect.

The fourth requirement of scientific descriptions is that they be open to **replication**. A study is replicated when other researchers use the same procedures as the initial investigators did and obtain the same results. In research on the ability to imitate, for example, some researchers report that newborns will imitate exaggerated facial expressions, whereas others report being unable to elicit imitation when they have attempted to observe the phenomenon. Only if the same findings are obtained repeatedly by different investigators are they likely to be considered firmly established by the scientific community.

In addition to these four basic criteria, it is important that the people studied be a **representative sample** of those about whom the psychologist draws conclusions. Conclusions drawn from data collected from one group of people may not be applicable to others with different characteristics. For example, a study of infants' distress when they are separated from their mothers among middle-class children in Denver may not yield the same results as a study using the same procedures among children from working-class homes in Denver or middle-class homes in Tokyo.

Techniques of Data Collection

Over the past hundred years, psychologists have refined a variety of techniques for gathering information on the development of children. These include self-reports, naturalistic observations, experiments, and clinical interviews. No one technique can answer all the questions that psychologists have about human development, but each has a strategic role in creating an understanding of development.

Self-reports   Perhaps the most direct way to obtain information about psychological development is through **self-reports**, in which people report about themselves. To obtain these, psychologists usually conduct interviews, but the use of written questionnaires is also common. Such far-flung topics as children's developing ideas about friendship and popularity (Youniss, 1980) or parents' ideas about child rearing (Sigel, 1985) have been investigated in this manner. In one study, which will be described in Chapter 16, researchers went so far as to provide teenagers with "beepers." When signaled at random intervals throughout the day, the teenagers filled out a questionnaire about what they were doing and feeling (Csikszentmihaly & Larson, 1984).

Self-reports can provide intimate accounts of people's life experiences, and they can reveal dynamics of thought and behavior that might otherwise escape notice. A major limitation of this method, however, is that the validity of what people report about themselves is often open to question.

Naturalistic observation   In the nineteenth century, several scientists began to write **baby biographies**, diaries in which they recorded observations of their children (Kessen, 1965). The most famous of these is Darwin's (1877) daily record of the early development of his eldest son (see Figure 1.5). By documenting characteristics shared by human beings and other species, Darwin hoped to support his thesis of human evolution. Some baby biographies, such as W. F. Leopold's (1949) record of his daughter's language development or Piaget's (1952, 1954) descriptions of his children's mental development, have proved to be of enduring scientific value. But currently they are rarely used outside the area of language development because even scientists usually cannot maintain objectivity when describing their own children. As Kessen comments, "no one can distort as convincingly as a loving parent" (1965, p. 117).

An example of how parents are likely to be selective in what they remember, or at least in what they are willing to report about themselves and their children,

FIGURE 1.5 *Naturalist Charles Darwin became famous for his theory of evolution. His observations of his son, which he recorded in a baby biography, provide one of the first systematic descriptions of infant development.*

comes from a study in which parents were asked to recall their child-rearing practices several years earlier, when their children were 3 years old (Robbins, 1963). The parents' reports could be checked against what they had actually done because they had participated in an earlier study in which their behavior had been observed. Parents' recall, Robbins found, was distorted to conform to the opinion of childcare experts. Some of the mothers, for example, claimed that their children had never sucked their thumbs, a practice disapproved of by experts at the time of the original observations, even though they were on record as having consulted with their physicians about their children's thumb sucking! To reduce such distortions in retrospective reports, researchers now often ask parents to focus on specific, on-going behaviors, such as temper tantrums, disobedience, or bedwetting, and ask for daily reports on these behaviors and the parents' responses to them (Patterson, 1982; Zahn-Waxler, & Radke-Yarrow, 1982).

Because of the problems that arise when adults report on their own children's behavior, psychologists prefer to rely on trained observers who do not have a personal stake in the children they study. The goal of these **naturalistic observations** is to obtain detailed evidence on children as they actually behave in the real world settings they inhabit, including the home, the school, and the community.

Observation in many contexts   An important goal of naturalistic observation is to describe the *ecology* of the child, a term derived from the Greek word meaning "home" or "homeland." In the biological sciences, the term refers to the habitats of a plant or animal and the plant's or animal's biological structure, functions, and characteristics as a population. In psychology, **ecology** has come to refer to the range of situations in which people are actors, the roles they play, the predicaments they encounter, and the consequences of those encounters (Bronfenbrenner, 1979). Ecological descriptions provide an overall picture of people's niches in the world (see Figure 1.6). With respect to children, they give us a sense of the whole child and the many influences that act on the child. We can thereby learn what predicaments loom largest in their lives and how circumstances might be changed to foster their development.

The most ambitious project seeking to determine the ecology of human development was conducted by Roger Barker and Herbert Wright (1951, 1955). These researchers spent hundreds of hours discovering, observing, and describing the natural ecology of school children in various communities in the United States and abroad. In one such study, they observed a single 7-year-old American boy from the time he awoke on April 26, 1949, until he went to sleep that night. They noted everything the boy did, everywhere he went, and everything that happened along the way. Barker and Wright found that this one child on just one day participated in approximately 1300 distinct activities in many different settings and involving hundreds of different objects and dozens of different people. These observations gave some idea of the wide range of skills children possess by the age of 7 and the many social expectations they encounter.

Barker and Wright made it a point of pride and principle to write down everything about a child's daily behavior and the contexts in which it occurred that they could notice and get on paper. Other investigators who study children across a range of contexts are more focused. They usually decide in advance on a particular type of behavior to observe in different contexts or they select a few important contexts within which to make extensive observations of the various behaviors that occur.

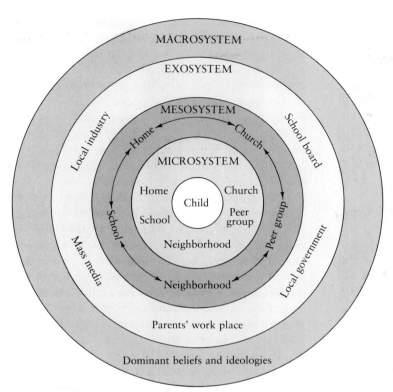

FIGURE 1.6 *The concentric circles with the child at the center illustrate the basic idea of ecological approaches to development, in which children are studied in relation to the nested contexts of their environments.*

In a study of 160 Mayan children between 1 and 14 years of age in a village in Guatemala, Barbara Rogoff (1978, 1981), for example, sampled brief time periods to provide a sort of "snapshot" of children's activities. Rogoff drew up a list of the observations she planned to make and worked out a schedule that allowed her or her assistant to observe each child for about 10 minutes several times a day on different days of the week. During these periods she noted whom a child was with and what the child was doing. Rogoff discovered that Mayan children, like U.S. children, spend much of their time separate from adults. When they do spend time with adults, however, their experiences are quite different from those of U.S. children. When Mayan children are with adults, they are expected to help with the grownups' usual jobs. In industrial societies like our own, children cannot (or are not allowed to) help with many adult jobs. Instead, when U.S. children are with adults, they are likely to be instructed by them, even outside school.

Observations in a single context The very breadth of the ecological approach means that it is time-consuming and expensive to apply. As a result, develop-mental psychologists often restrict their observations to a single social setting that is widely encountered and important in children's lives. They observe in minute detail the face-to-face interactions between children or between children and adults and how participants in these interactions tend to regulate their behavior together. A study from a widely studied context, the classroom, illustrates this approach.

Lisa Serbin and her colleagues (Serbin, O'Leary, Kent, & Tonick, 1973) wanted to determine whether classroom interactions between teachers and students might, unwittingly, foster aggressiveness in boys and dependence in girls. The researchers observed the relation between children's behavior and teachers' disciplinary actions in 15 preschool classrooms. They found that the teachers did not pay equal attention to the misbehavior of boys and girls. The teachers chastised the boys publicly for a greater proportion of their misdeeds than they did the girls for theirs. Often this selective treatment seemed to *increase* aggressiveness among the boys. In a parallel set of observations, the researchers discovered that the teachers rewarded dependent behavior among girls by paying more attention to those girls who were sitting closest to them;

they paid equal amounts of attention to all the boys no matter where they were sitting in the classroom. Once such social practices are made explicit, new patterns of interaction can be suggested to the teachers that might foster more effective behavior in schoolchildren of both sexes.

Limitations of naturalistic observations   Observational studies are a keystone of scientific research on children's development and a crucial source of data about children's social development. As with self-reports, there are some limits to what we can learn from them, however. Observers enter the scene with expectations about what they are going to see, and there is a natural tendency to observe selectively in line with those expectations. An observer cannot write down everything, so information is lost. Note-taking schemes help, but detail is still lost, and such schemes are not flexible if unexpected events occur. If time elapses between an event and note taking, further distortion may occur because people's selective remembering accentuates the problem of selective observing (D'Andrade, 1974). Tape recording, video recording, and filming are useful aids, but they are expensive and time-consuming to analyze.

Another difficulty with observational research is that people's behaviors change when they know they are being watched, creating a false impression of normal behavior (Zegiob, Arnold, & Forehand, 1975). A laboratory study of the interactions between mothers and their children illustrates the problem. Zoe Graves and Joseph Glick (1978) asked mothers to help their 18- to 25-month-old children put together a simple jigsaw puzzle. To determine the influence that being observed had on the behavior of the mothers, Graves and Glick told half of the mothers that the video equipment being used to record their interactions was not working. They found that these mothers acted less formally but that they were not as helpful to their children as were those who had been told that they were "on camera."

The major problem with naturalistic observation as a source of information about development is that it rarely allows one to establish the existence of causal relationships between phenomena, which is a basic aim of science. When observations are collated and compared, it can be established that two factors are *correlated*; when a **correlation** exists, changes in one factor vary with changes in another. But that doesn't tell us whether one factor causes the other or whether

both factors are caused by a third, undetermined factor (see Box 1.2, "Correlation Does Not Imply Causation"). In their ecological study, for example, Barker and Wright revealed many relationships between the settings in which children find themselves and the characteristics of children's behavior in those settings. Similarly, Serbin and her colleagues discovered interesting patterns of how teachers treat boys and girls in the classroom. These studies do not, however, pinpoint the causes of the different patterns they describe.

The difficulty in both these cases is that researchers have no means of telling from their observations alone which factors are causal. Did the children in Barker and Wright's study who acted more grownup in church than they did in a drugstore do so because church attendance evokes religious feelings or because their parents were there to observe them? In the study by Serbin and her colleagues, did the kind of attention the boys received arise because the teacher had stereotyped all of them as troublemakers wherever they might be or because there are important differences in the way the two sexes react to teacher discipline? Similar questions can be raised about almost any observational study of behavior. To attempt to resolve such questions, psychologists turn to experimental methods.

Experimental methods   Studies in which the investigator introduces some change in the child's experience and then measures the effect of the change on the child's behavior are called **experiments**. Ideally, all the other possible causal influences are "held constant" while the factor of interest is allowed to vary to determine if it makes a difference. If an experiment is well designed and executed, it should provide a means of confirming a scientific hypothesis about the causes of the behavior observed. A *scientific hypothesis* is an assumption that is precise enough to be tested and can be shown to be incorrect. If there is no way to disprove the hypothesis, it has little scientific value.

An investigation of the development of a fear of high places by Joseph Campos and his colleagues (Bertenthal, Campos, & Barrett, 1984) illustrates the main features of the experimental method and indicates how it can help resolve uncertainties about causal factors in development. For many years, it was believed that the fear of heights is innate in the human infant. According to this view, the fear of high places will become apparent when infants begin to *locomote*, or move about under their own steam, not because either locomotion or fear causes the other, but because both are the result of general maturational factors (Rader, Bausano, & Richards, 1980; Richards & Rader, 1981). Campos and his colleagues disagreed with this hypothesis. They believed that fear of heights is the result of experience, especially the experience that infants have once they start to crawl.

Initially, Campos and his colleagues studied a group of infants who were between 6 and 8 months old, beginning a week or two after they began to crawl. They discovered that, on the first few opportunities the infants were given, all would cross a *visual cliff*, a transparent platform that gives the illusion of a sharp drop off in elevation such as that shown in Figure 1.7. However, on subsequent trials, the infants became increasingly reluctant to cross over the visual cliff even though they had never experienced any unpleasantness when doing so. Something seemed to be building up in the infants' minds with experience. But what something and what experience? To begin to answer these questions, the investigators needed to conduct an experiment.

Campos and his colleagues designed an experiment to test the hypothesis that the onset of the fear of heights results from the experience of moving about (Bertenthal et al., 1984). They located 92 infants who were near the age when they might be expected to start

FIGURE 1.8 *Experience moving around the environment in a walker influences the onset of fear on the visual cliff.*

crawling and showing a fear of heights. The infants were randomly assigned to one of two groups. The first group was designated as the **experimental group** — the group in an experiment whose environment is changed. Over several days, the infants in this group were given more than 40 hours of experience moving about in special baby walkers prior to the time they learned to crawl (see Figure 1.8). The second group of children, called the **control group** — the group in an experiment that is treated as much as possible like the experimental group except that it does not participate in the experimental manipulation — were provided with no special experience in locomoting. If the hypothesis of Campos and his colleagues was correct, the difference in the amount of experience in moving around that the experimental and control groups had should lead to a difference in their responses to the visual cliff.

Although 40 hours of careening around a room in a walker might not seem like a lot of experience, it apparently made a big difference in how the infants in the experimental group responded when they were placed on the visual cliff. Although there was some variation from child to child, the infants in the experimental group as a rule showed fear on their *first* exposure to the visual cliff, whereas the infants in the control group, who had no locomoting experience, showed no fear in the initial trials.

FIGURE 1.7 *A baby hesitates at the edge of a visual cliff, a transparent platform that makes it appear to the baby that there is a sharp drop just ahead.*

BOX 1.2

CORRELATION DOES NOT IMPLY CAUSATION
• • •

In their attempts to discover factors that cause development, psychologists often begin by determining that different factors are related. Two factors are said to be *correlated* with each other when changes in one are associated with changes in the other. In later chapters, we will see many examples of correlation: As children grow older, they display increased ability to remember lists of words; that is, age is correlated with memory. The higher the social class of parents, the greater the achievement children display in school; that is, school achievement is correlated with social class. These relationships are important hints about causal factors in development, but they fall short of specifying the actual mechanisms involved.

A *correlation coefficient* (symbolized as r) provides a quantitative index of the degree of association between two factors that allows psychologists to distinguish between relationships that occur by chance and those that occur with significant regularity. A correlation coefficient indexing the relationship between Factor 1 and Factor 2 can vary in both magnitude and direction. When $r = 1.00$, there is a perfect positive correlation between the two factors: as Factor 1 changes, Factor 2 changes in the same direction and at the same rate. If every increase in age were accompanied by an increase in weight in a population, the correlation between age and weight would be 1.00. If instead, people always got smaller as they aged, the correlation would be -1.00. If there were no correspondence between age and weight, the correlation would be .00. Intermediate positive or

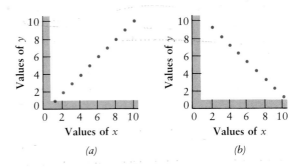

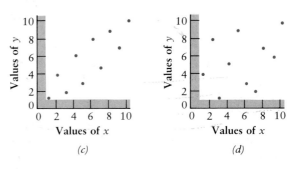

Four examples of different relationships between two variables: (a) As values of x increase, values of y increase, producing a correlation of 1.00. (b) As values of x increase, values of y decrease, producing a correlation of -1.00. (c) As values of x increase, values of y often increase, but there are some exceptions, producing a correlation of .84. (d) As values of x increase, values of y show a weak, but noticeable tendency to increase, producing a correlation of .33.

This experiment provided Campos and his associates with strong support for their hypothesis that the development of locomotion is an important contributor to the development of the fear of heights. Additional research would be useful to rule out possibilities that this research did not delve into. For example, if children were moved around in little vehicles that permitted them to explore the environment without locomotion, might they still become fearful when placed on the visual cliff? Uncertainties of this kind about research results are almost inevitable. A series of ex-

periments is often necessary to isolate specific causes because the complexities of behavior exceed the researcher's ability to control all the relevant factors in a single experiment (Cole & Means, 1981).

In general, the clear strength of the experimental method is that it can help isolate causal factors in a way no other method of investigation can. There are two main limitations to its usefulness as a source of information about development. One is that, for ethical reasons, many experiments should not be performed. The other is that the very control of the environment

negative values of a correlation coefficient indicate intermediate levels of association. For example, there is a correlation of approximately .50 between the heights of parents and their offspring, indicating that there is a tendency for taller parents to have taller offspring (Tanner, 1978).

A correlation may point to a causal relationship between two events, but correlation is not the same as *causation,* in which the occurrence of one event depends upon the occurrence of the other. The difficulty of distinguishing correlation from causation is often the source of scientific controversy. In the case of the heights of parents and their children, the problem is not serious. We can be pretty certain that the height of children does not cause the height of parents. Little confusion is likely to arise about the relationship between a child's age and weight either. Age by itself cannot cause increases in weight because age is simply another name for the time that has elapsed since an agreed-upon starting point. Certainly, weight cannot cause increases in age.

Other cases are less clear-cut. For example, among school children a correlation of about .30 between height and scores on tests of mental ability has been found; that is, taller children tend to have higher intelligence test scores (Tanner, 1978). Since nothing about height can plausibly be said to be a cause of intelligence, nor intelligence of height, some other factor must be the cause of both. One possibility is maturational forces. Taller children could be considered more mature and thus able to function at a higher level. But this explanation implies that the correlation between intelligence test scores and height should disappear in adulthood, when all individuals are considered mature, yet the correlation remains. Some other factor, perhaps nutritional status, perhaps general health, perhaps something altogether different, is the cause of both greater height and higher test scores.

The slipperiest cases to deal with are those in which a scientist has a strong theory about causal connections among the events under study but only correlational data to work with. In such cases, it is tempting to assume causation although the data can support only conclusions about correlation. For example, there is a correlation of .50 between children's current grades in school and their scores on standard IQ tests (Minton & Schneider, 1980). It might be tempting to conclude that intelligence causes cognitive development. This conclusion does not follow from the evidence, however, any more than the conclusion that age causes changes in weight does, although it fits many people's notion that intelligence causes school achievement. It could just as plausibly be argued that students who work hard get their schoolwork done more often and learn more, thereby boosting their IQ scores.

The use of correlation coefficients to describe relationships among phenomena is very important in the study of human development because so many of the factors of interest to psychologists (social class, ethnic origin, genetic constitution, and a host of other factors, including age itself) cannot be experimentally controlled. Because correlations often suggest causal relationships but do not provide crucial evidence of causation, controversies often arise that have no clear resolution, requiring developmental psychologists to exercise caution in the interpretation of their data.

that experiments often require may distort the validity of the results obtained.

Ethics and experimentation   The central ethical tenet of all psychological research is: if a research procedure may be harmful to a person, it should not be done.

The issues of ethics in psychological research are not always as clear cut as this tenet suggests, however. What is harmful and how do we assess the risks? Practically any intervention in another person's life *may* involve some risk, so the judgment can be a difficult one. Furthermore, the factors taken into account often differ from one culture to the next and from one historical era to another. In 1920, John B. Watson, the behavior theorist, and Rosalie Rayner published the results of an experiment to demonstrate that children's fears of animals are not innate but are shaped by the environment (Watson & Rayner, 1920). Today, the experiment would be considered potentially harmful, but it aroused little comment about ethics at the time.

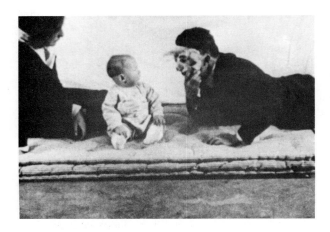

John B. Watson and Rosalie Rayner experimenting with infant fears. (Courtesy of Professor Benjamin Harris.)

Watson and Rayner showed a 9-month-old boy a white rabbit. According to these investigators, the baby played with the rabbit with no expression of fright. Then they hit a steel bar with a hammer behind the baby as he reached for the rabbit. The boy cried with fear at the loud noise. After several such experiences, the baby cried whenever he saw the rabbit. Watson and Rayner reported that his fear of the white rabbit extended to many white, fuzzy objects he was shown, including a dog, a fur coat, and even a Santa Claus mask. Fear of white rabbits, fur coats, and Santa Claus masks is not inherited, they claimed, it is learned.

Watson and Rayner's research has been severely criticized because it did not conform to important scientific principles of experimentation. They did not have an appropriate control group, they studied only one child and failed to replicate their results, and their reports of the procedures and results were inconsistent (Harris, 1979; Samelson, 1980). What is of interest here, however, is less Watson and Rayner's skill as experimenters than their apparent willingness to override ethical considerations about the baby's welfare in the name of science. Watson's doctrine of learning led him to believe that if fear could be created by events in the environment, it also could be removed. But Watson and Rayner never proved this point in their experiment. They made no attempt to help the child overcome the fears they had induced in him.

Psychologists' judgments of the ethics of Watson and Rayner's experiment would almost certainly be different today than they were in the 1920s. Psychologists now are less certain of their ability to turn psycho-logical processes on and off than Watson was, and they appreciate more fully that scientific knowledge is by no means certain knowledge. To protect the rights of children, modern researchers are closely monitored by their own institutions and by government agencies. In order to carry out their research, they must satisfy committees of their peers that they will not harm those who participate in their investigations. They must also demonstrate that the research promises, in the long run, some benefits to the people involved. (See Box 1.3, "Ethical Standards for Research with Children.")

Experiments and artificiality   When a researcher deliberately constructs a special experimental situation to test a hypothesis, the experiences and the resulting behaviors of the participants may be far different from those that occur in everyday life. This artificality can raise doubts about the generality of some experimental results. Indeed, the pervasiveness of the problem has led Urie Bronfenbrenner (1979) to describe many laboratory experiments as studies of "the strange behavior of children in strange situations with strange adults for the briefest possible periods of time" (p. 19).

Often, there is no simple solution to the problem of artificiality because the factors being studied in the experiment arise too seldom to be studied systematically in real life. However, in some cases researchers have partially overcome the problem by introducing experimental control in naturally occurring situations without significantly disrupting the usual course of events. For example, to investigate how young children add new words to their vocabularies, Elsa Bartlett (1977) and Susan Carey (1978) had a preschool teacher introduce an unusual color, olive, to her charges in the natural course of her classroom routine. To avoid the possibility that some children already knew the name of the color, the teacher referred to it as "chromium." When the new word was introduced casually — "Please pass the chromium crayon" — the researchers found that the children acquired it after very few exposures. In contrast, laboratory studies of word acquisition typically find that children require extensive instruction by an adult to learn a new word.

Clinical methods   All the research methods discussed thus far, with the exception of diary studies, attempt to apply uniform procedures of data collection to every individual observed. In this respect, clini-

BOX 1.3

ETHICAL STANDARDS FOR RESEARCH WITH CHILDREN

The following guidelines have been condensed from The Society for Research In Child Development's *Ethical Standards for Research with Children.*

• • •

Children as research subjects present ethical problems for the investigator different from those presented by adult subjects. Not only are children often viewed as more vulnerable to stress, but, having less knowledge and experience, they are less able to evaluate what participation in research may mean. Consent of the parent for the study of the child, moreover, must be obtained in addition to the child's consent. These are some of the major differences between research with children and research with adults.

- No matter how young the child, he has rights that supersede the rights of the investigator.

- The final responsibility to establish and maintain ethical practices in research remains with the individual investigator. He is also responsible for the ethical practices of collaborators, assistants, students, and employees, all of whom, however, incur parallel obligations.

- The investigator should inform the child of all features of the research that may affect his willingness to participate and he should answer the child's questions in terms appropriate to the child's comprehension.

- The investigator should respect the child's freedom to choose to participate in research or not, as well as to discontinue participation at any time. . . .

- The informed consent of parents or of those who act *in loco parentis* (e.g., teachers, superintendents of institutions) similarly should be obtained, preferably in writing. Informed consent requires that the parent or other responsible adult be told all features of the research that may affect his willingness to allow the child to participate. . . .

- The informed consent of any person whose interaction with the child is the subject of the study should also be obtained. . . .

- The investigator uses no research operation that may harm the child either physically or psychologically. . . .

- Although we accept the ethical idea of full disclosure of information, a particular study may necessitate concealment or deception. Whenever concealment or deception is thought to be essential to the conduct of the study, the investigator should satisfy a committee of his peers that his judgment is correct. . . .

- The investigator should keep in confidence all information obtained about research participants. . . .

- Immediately after the data are collected, the investigator should clarify for the research participant any misconceptions that may have arisen. The investigator also recognizes a duty to report general findings to participants in terms appropriate to their understanding. Where scientific or humane values may justify withholding information, every effort should be made so that withholding the information has no damaging consequences for the participant.

- When, in the course of research, information comes to the investigator's attention that may seriously affect the child's well-being, the investigator has a responsibility to discuss the information with those expert in the field in order that the parents may arrange the necessary assistance for their child.

- When research procedures may result in undesirable consequences for the participant that were previously unforeseen, the investigator should employ appropriate measures to correct these consequences, and should consider redesigning the procedure.

- The investigator should be mindful of the social, political, and human implications of his research and should be especially careful in the presentation of his findings. This standard, however, in no way denies the investigator the right to pursue any area of research or the right to observe proper standards of scientific reporting.

- When an experimental treatment under investigation is believed to be of benefit to children, control groups should be offered other beneficial alternative treatments, if available, instead of no treatment.

cal methods are fundamentally different. The essence of the **clinical method** is the tailoring of questions to the individual subject, with each question depending upon the answer to the one that precedes it.

As the term implies, clinical methods are often used to investigate the problems of persons who are unwell. When developmental psychologists use clinical methods in this way, they, like medical clinicians, seek a set of appropriate remedies. The most famous application of clinical methods in developmental psychology comes from the work of Sigmund Freud, who considered the early family history of the child to be essential to later personality development. From a patient's account, he sought to identify crucial events that produced the difficulty from which the person was suffering. In Freud's use of the clinical method, analysis was coupled with therapy; the analyst's theory was tested by the effectiveness of treatment in resolving the person's difficulty.

Clinical methods are not restricted to pathology, however. Jean Piaget often used clinical techniques to explore the reasoning behind the answers children gave when he asked them to solve intellectual problems. In a classic example of the clinical interview, Piaget put 20 wooden beads into a box while a 6-year-old boy named Bis watched. Two of the beads were white, the rest brown. The box lid was left open so that Bis could look at the beads while he answered Piaget's questions about them. The following dialogue ensued (1965a, p. 164):

Piaget: Are there more wooden beads or more brown beads?

Bis: More *brown* ones because there are two *white* ones.

Piaget: Are the white ones made of wood?

Bis: Yes. . . .

Piaget: Then are there more brown ones or more wooden ones?

Bis: More brown ones.

Piaget: What color would a necklace made of the wooden beads be?

Bis: Brown and white.

The last answer shows that Bis knew that all the beads were made of wood, and later answers showed that he understood the concepts of *more* and *less*. Nevertheless, he was unable to answer Piaget's questions correctly when they required him to include the class of brown beads in the class of wooden beads. Why couldn't Bis "be logical" and tell Piaget that, of course, there were more wooden beads than brown beads? Piaget answers that "Logic is the mirror of thought, and not visa versa." Unlike children a few years older, Bis could not simultaneously concentrate on the whole and its parts, so he mixed the logic that applies to the parts with the logic that applies to the whole. Piaget's careful probing revealed how the two systems of logic became confused in Bis's attempt to answer the initial question.

Alexander Luria (1902–1977), a Soviet psychologist, showed that the clinical method could also be used to uncover qualitative differences in thinking in different cultural environments. In one study, he presented people of varying ages who lived in a pastoral culture in Central Asia with drawings of four objects —a hammer, a saw, a log, and a hatchet—three of which could be grouped into the single category "tools." He then asked which of the objects did not fit with the others (1976, p. 58):

When reserachers conduct experiments in different cultural settings, they must adapt their methods to local conditions.

Subject: They all fit here! The saw has to saw the log, the hammer has to hammer it, and the hatchet has to chop it. And if you want to saw the log up really good, you need the hammer. You can't take any of these things away. There isn't any you don't need.

Luria: But one fellow told me that the log didn't belong here.

Subject: Why'd he say that? If we say the log isn't like the other things and put it off to one side, we'd be making a mistake. All these things are needed for the log.

Luria: But that other fellow said that the saw, hammer, and hatchet are all alike in some way, while the log isn't.

Subject: So what if they're not alike? They all work together and chop the log. Here everything works right, here everything's just fine.

Here we see a classic use of the clinical interview. The investigator probes the person's understanding by challenging various lines of reasoning and suggesting different (sometimes incorrect) alternatives depending upon the person's prior responses. In this case, Luria has encountered someone for whom "similar" seems to mean "enters into the same activity." By contrasting this subject's answers with the answers given by people from distinctly different cultural backgrounds, Luria was able to formulate plausible conclusions about the ways in which culture influences the development of intellectual functions.

The strong point of clinical methods is that they provide insight into the dynamics of individual behavior. But as Walker Percy warns (p. 18), the price of concentrating on the individual is a corresponding difficulty in generalizing to the group. Each adult psychoanalyzed by Freud, each child interviewed by Piaget, and each Central Asian pastoralist interviewed by Luria provided a somewhat different pattern of responses that corresponded to their individual experiences. To arrive at general conclusions, the clinician must ignore individual differences in order to distill the general pattern. But as the general pattern appears, the individual picture disappears.

Research Designs

In order to illuminate the process of developmental change, psychological research must be designed to reveal how possible factors work over time. There are two basic research designs that psychologists use to study behavioral development, longitudinal and cross-sectional, each of which takes time into account in a distinctive way. In the **longitudinal design**, the psychologist collects information about the same children at different ages. In the **cross-sectional design**, the researcher collects information about children of different ages at the same time. These designs can be used in conjunction with any of the techniques of data collection just discussed, and each design has its own advantages and disadvantages.

Longitudinal designs   In a longitudinal design, researchers select a sample of the population they want to study and gather data from them at more than one age. The longitudinal design thus traces change in persons over time, which is consistent with the basic definition of development as the changes that occur in the physical structure and behavior of the organism during its lifetime. For example, a research team at the Fels Research Institute in Yellow Springs, Ohio, studied personality development in 71 children from their birth until they reached their midteens (Kagan & Moss, 1962). Observations, tests of personality, and interviews repeated at different times allowed the Fels group to determine the stability of such characteristics as the tendency of particular children to become angry or upset when an ongoing activity is disturbed. Without longitudinal measurements, it would be impossible to discover if this particular behavior pattern remains constant or changes as children grow older. Other influential studies using a longitudinal design have focused on such varied topics as personality (Baumrind, 1971), mental health (Werner & Smith, 1982), and temperament and intelligence (Plomin & DeFries, 1985; Rutter, 1985).

Longitudinal designs would seem to be an ideal way to study development because they fit so closely the requirement that development be studied over time. Unfortunately, longitudinal research designs have some practical and methodological drawbacks that have restricted psychologists' reliance on them. They often require a lengthy commitment on the part of the researcher, and they are expensive to carry out, particularly if they are to be conducted over several years. In addition, some parents may refuse to allow their children to participate in a lengthy study. If such refusals are more frequent in one social, economic, or ethnic group, they may make the sample unrepresentative of

Longitudinal designs follow the same person at different ages.

the population as a whole. Of the children who do begin a study, some may drop out, further changing the sample in ways that weaken the conclusions that can be drawn from the study. To circumvent these problems, some researchers use special procedures to study children over a relatively short period in order to focus on specific mechanisms of developmental change (Werner, 1948; Vygotsky, 1978).

Another difficulty with longitudinal designs is that people may become used to the various testing and interviewing procedures; in other words, they may learn how they are expected to respond. As a consequence, it is difficult to know whether a change in a person's responses over time represents the influence of normal causal influences on development or simply practice in taking the tests.

Finally, longitudinal designs confound (mix together) the influence of age-related changes with other sources of change that relate specifically to the subjects' **cohort**—persons born at the same time who may therefore share experiences that are different from those of older or younger persons. For example, a longitudinal study of children's fears from birth onward that began in London in 1932 would coincide in its first years with a period of severe economic depression. At the age of 9 or 10, many of these children would have been sent away from their parents (one or both of whom may have later been killed in the war) to the countryside in order to avoid Hitler's nightly bombings of the city. If the results of such a study indicated that children's fears center on hunger in their first years and that later, around the age of 9, they begin to fear that they will lose their parents, it would

not be possible to determine whether the observed age trends reflected general laws of development true any time and any place or whether they were the result of growing up in a particular time and place or both (Baltes, Dittman-Kohli, & Dixon, 1984).

Cross-sectional designs The most widely used developmental research design is called the cross-sectional design because groups representing a "cross-section" of ages are studied at a single time. To study the development of memory, for example, one might first test the way that samples of 4-year-olds, 10-year-olds, 20-year-olds, and 60-year-olds remember a list of familiar words. By comparing how people at the different ages go about the task and what the results of their efforts are, one could then form hypotheses about developmental changes in this basic cognitive process. (See Figure 1.9 for a graphic comparison of longitudinal and cross-sectional research designs.) In fact, a great many such studies of memory development have been carried out using cross-sectional designs (Kail, 1984).

The advantages of the cross-sectional design are readily apparent. Because it samples several age levels at one time, this design takes less time and is less expensive than a longitudinal approach to the same question would be, but it can still yield important information. The limited time commitment required of the participants also makes it more likely that a representative sample will be recruited and that few participants will drop out of the study.

Despite these attractive features, cross-sectional designs also have drawbacks. Like longitudinal designs, cross-sectional designs can confound age-related changes and characteristics particular to a specific cohort. Only to the extent that people of different ages are equivalent in all relevant ways except for the factor of age will the study be likely to yield accurate information about development.

Consider the possibilities for the hypothetical study of memory development. Suppose that the study was conducted in 1985. Suppose further that the study showed that the 60-year-olds performed significantly more poorly than the 20-year-olds. These results might reflect a universal tendency for memory to decline in old age. But the differences might also be caused by differences in childhood nutrition, which has been claimed to affect intellectual development (Freeman, Klein, Townsend, & Lechtig, 1981); in 1925, when the 60-year-olds were babies, nutrition was generally not as good as it was in 1965, when the 20-year-olds were babies. Or it might be that memory performance is maintained by the constant practice provided by schooling. In this case, the 60-year-olds may not have performed as well because they have been out of school for a long time.

A second difficulty with cross-sectional designs is that, by sampling the behavior of *different* people at different ages, they inappropriately slice up the process of development, a process that occurs within individuals over time. For example, in contrasting the way that 4- and 10-year-olds remember a list of words, it may be possible to say how memory differs, on the average, for children at the two ages. But the developmental process by which one form of memory has changed into another is lost because the same children are not being studied. This limitation means that when formulating hypotheses about development on the basis of cross-sectional designs, developmental psychological theorists must do a good deal of extrapolation and guesswork.

Each design and each technique for data collection has its uses, but no single design or technique is likely to serve all purposes. *Longitudinal designs* sample behavior of the same individuals over time, but at the risk of confounding age with cohort and of bias in samples. *Cross-sectional designs* are more efficient, but at the expense of artificially breaking up the process of development. *Self-reports* provide unique insight into the

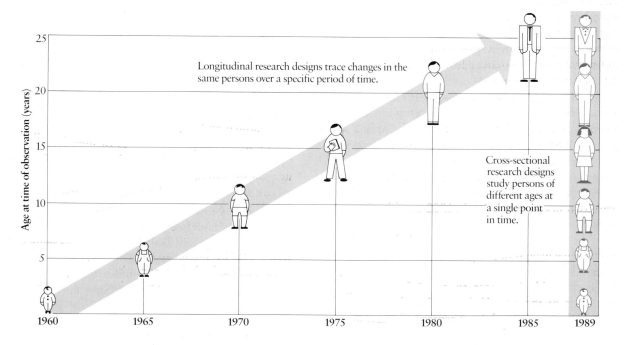

FIGURE 1.9 *A graphic representation of the difference between longitudinal and cross-sectional research designs.*

process of development from the perspective of the individual, but they are sometimes of questionable validity. Systematically collected *naturalistic observations* yield essential information about the real-life activities of people, but they are weak when it comes to justifying causal statements about development. *Experiments* can isolate causal factors in specific settings, but the results obtained may not be generalizable beyond the artificial boundaries of the experimental situation. *Clinical methods* can reveal the dynamics of individual thought and feelings, but they are difficult to generalize beyond the individual case. In the chapters that follow, the advantages and problems of the various research methods will be discussed time and again as they apply to specific aspects of development.

The Role of Theory

Each of the techniques of data collection and the two research designs are of practical use to psychologists in gathering facts about the development of children. However, those facts help us to understand development only if they are embedded in a **theory**, a broad framework or body of principles that can be used to interpret facts. Like heredity and environment, facts and theories go together. Neither comes "first"; they arise and exist together. Nor do facts "speak for themselves"; they speak through theories.

When a newborn infant cries, the physical fact of crying is plain enough. But what does it mean? Is crying a reflex response to gastric pain or is it an expression of the newborn's distress at being wrenched from the mother's womb? Is the infant asking for help or showing anger? Only an interpretation of crying within a theory gives meaning to the "facts" by providing a framework within which to investigate such questions through research and reason.

Speaking about our understanding of the physical world, Albert Einstein described the central role of theory in extending human knowledge. Observation of the world may be useful, he said:

> But on principle, it is quite wrong to try founding a theory on observable magnitudes alone. In reality the very opposite occurs. It is the theory which decides what we can observe. (Quoted in Sameroff, 1983, p. 243)

Einstein's point applies to psychologists' attempts to understand the human world just as forcefully as it applies to investigations of the physical world. A deeper understanding of human development will not automatically accrue from the continuous accumulation of facts. Rather, it will come through new attempts to make sense of the accumulating evidence on development in the light of some theory.

At the present time in the history of developmental psychology, there is no overarching theoretical framework that gives unity to the entire body of relevant scientific knowledge. The acquisition of knowledge in developmental psychology, as in other fields of science, results from attempts to resolve inconsistencies in existing theoretical interpretations of what has been observed. A new theory may win out temporarily by appearing to resolve the inconsistencies of existing views. But change in science is neverending. As new discoveries are made in light of an accepted theory, new inconsistencies will be found. The accepted theory will gradually lose its ability to direct and organize scientific activity, and a newer, more comprehensive theory will eventually arise to take its place (Kuhn, 1962).

THIS BOOK AND THE FIELD OF DEVELOPMENTAL PSYCHOLOGY

The lack of a comprehensive and widely accepted developmental theory creates difficulties for anyone seeking an integrated picture of the whole child in the dynamic processes of growth and change. Basic facts are interpreted differently within the various theoretical frameworks. In the face of these difficulties, this book takes a basically chronological approach to development, in keeping with the definition of development as a process that occurs over time. Within this chronological structure, the material is divided into broad periods; within each period, different aspects of development and their interrelationships are explored.

In any chronological account of development, two major issues must be resolved. First, there are the questions of where to draw the boundaries between different periods and how much significance should be attributed to them. Second, there is the problem of keeping track of all the different influences on development in a systematic way so that they are easy to remember and think about.

The issue of how to divide the sequence of development into periods is easily settled at the general level because adherents to all of the major theoretical approaches refer to the same five periods from conception to adulthood: the prenatal period between conception and birth, infancy, the preschool era, middle childhood, and adolescence.

Beyond a division of development into five periods, consensus among psychologists breaks down. Some theorists believe that these divisions are little more than verbal conventions, whereas others believe that the periods represent developmental stages that are both real and of essential importance for understanding the nature of development. Among stage theorists themselves there is disagreement about whether or not there are significant subperiods that must be distinguished in their content and length. (See Table 1.1 for a comparison of the ways different theories treat the basic periods of development.) At the same time, anthropological and historical studies suggest that the five developmental periods themselves may not be fixed characteristics of children in all cultures and all historical eras; many societies recognize no periods that correspond to the preschool era or adolescence (Ariès, 1962; Whiting, Burbank, & Ratner, 1982).

The organization adopted in this book follows psychological convention and divides the time between conception and adulthood into five broad periods, each of which has a major section of the text devoted to it. Within this chronological framework, the presentation is designed to make clear how the fundamental biological, social, behavioral, and cultural factors of development weave together in the process of change from one period to the next. It is also designed to show that developmental patterns are not restricted to one or another aspect of the child. In so far as development is characterized by stagelike changes, the new patterns that emerge at each stage should apply to broad areas of the child's functioning.

The text subdivides infancy, when change occurs at a particularly rapid rate, into three subperiods marked by important transition points where distinctively new and significant forms of behavior emerge. Robert Emde and his colleagues (Emde, Gaensbauer, & Harmon, 1976) refer to these transitions as *bio-behavioral shifts* because the resulting reorganization in the child's functioning emerges from the interaction of biological and behavioral factors. Modifying these researchers' ideas slightly, the text refers to such transitions in infancy, and in later development as well, as **bio-social-behavioral shifts**. The social dimension has been added because, as Emde and his colleagues themselves note, every bio-behavioral shift involves a change in the relationship between children and their social worlds. Not only do children experience the social environment in a new way as a result of the changes in their behavior and biological makeup, they are also treated differently by other people.

The cultural context of children's development is also an essential factor in the bio-social-behavioral

TABLE 1.1 Stages of development according to different theories

Conventional	Piaget	Freud	Erikson	Vygotsky
Infancy (Birth–2½ years)	Sensorimotor	Oral Anal	Trust vs. mistrust Autonomy vs. shame	Affiliation
Early childhood (2½–6 years)	Preoperations	Phallic	Initiative vs. guilt	Play
Middle childhood (6–12 years)	Concrete operations	Latency	Industry vs. inferiority	Learning
Adolescence (12–19 years)	Formal operations	Genital	Identity vs. role confusion Intimacy vs. isolation	Peer activity
Adulthood (19–65 years)			Generativity vs. stagnation	Work
Old Age (65–death)			Ego integrity vs. despair	Theorizing

shifts. From the earliest hours of life, differing cultural conceptions of what children are and what the future holds for them influence how parents shape their experience. For example, children raised by parents who believe that they are mischievous creatures who require strong discipline to keep them on the right path are likely to experience life differently from those whose parents believe that children are naturally good and will remain so unless corrupted by adults. Moreover, the timing and, in some cases, the essential character of a developmental period may be strongly influenced by cultural factors (Dasen, 1977; Whiting, Burbank, & Ratner, 1982).

The adoption of a bio-social-behavioral framework for the study of development does not imply a commitment to a strict stage theory; rather, it provides a systematic way to keep in mind the intricate play of different forces in creating development. Caution is required in embracing stage notions because stagelike shifts in the functioning of the organism are rarely all or nothing phenomena. Behaviors that characterize a new stage of development can almost always be found in embryonic form at an earlier age, and following the transition to a new stage, old forms of behavior crop up from time to time. Finally, the existence of important continuities in behavior over time and the significant diversity in a child's behavior at a given age in different circumstances are fundamental realities that dividing development into periods and subperiods should not be allowed to obscure.

TABLE 1.2 **Prominent bio-social-behavioral shifts in development**

Developmental Period	Shift Point	Prominent Changes at Point of Shift and Characteristics of Stages
	Conception	*Genetic material of parents combines to form unique individual*
Prenatal		Formation of basic organs
	Birth	*Transition to life outside the womb*
Early infancy (Birth–2½ months)		Becoming coordinated with the environment
	2½ months	*Cortical-subcortical brain connections form; social smiling; new quality of maternal feeling*
Middle infancy (2½–9 months)		Increased memory and sensorimotor abilities
	7–9 months	*Wariness of novelty; fear of strangers; attachment*
Late infancy (9–30 months)		Symbolic thought; distinct sense of self
	End of infancy (24–30 months)	*Grammatical language*
Early childhood (2½–6 years)		Strikingly uneven levels of performance; sex-role identity; sociodramatic play
	5–7 years	*Assigned responsibility for tasks outside of adult supervision; deliberate instruction*
Middle childhood (6–12 years)		Peer group activity; rule-based games; systematic instruction
	11–12 years	*Sexual maturation*
Adolescence (12–19 years)		Sex-oriented social activity; identity integration; formal reasoning
	19–21 years	*Shift toward primary responsibility for self*
Adulthood (19–)		

Table 1.2 outlines the bio-social-behavioral shifts that appear to be prominent in the development of the child from conception to adulthood. Not all of the shift points have been equally well established. Nevertheless, they provide a fruitful means of organizing discussions of development because they require us to consider both the sources of change and the evidence concerning developmental continuity and discontinuity in a systematic way.

Throughout the chapters that follow, the large questions of development that captivated Itard and his contemporaries will be constantly recurring themes: What makes us human? Can our natures be remolded by experience or must we be content with the characteristics inscribed in our genes at conception? Can we use our knowledge of development to help us plan for our futures and guide the growth of our children? Each chapter is designed to provide the basic facts, methods, and theories that will allow us to apply the research on these questions to an understanding of our own lives.

SUMMARY

1. Developmental psychology is a scientific discipline that studies the origins of human behavior and the laws of psychological change over the course of a lifetime.

2. The early history of developmental psychology is closely linked to social changes wrought by the industrial revolution, which fundamentally changed the nature of family life, education, and work.

3. Many scientific and social questions about development revolve around two fundamental concerns:
   a. Is the process of development gradual and continuous or is it marked by sharp stagelike discontinuities?
   b. How do nature and nurture interact to produce development?

4. Concerns about continuity branch into more specific questions:
   a. How alike and how different are we from our near neighbors in the animal kingdom?
   b. Are there qualitatively distinct stages of development?
   c. Are there critical periods in development?

5. Concerns about sources of development have given rise to competing theories about the contributions of biology and the environment to the process of development.
   a. The biological-maturation perspective holds that the sources of development are primarily endogenous, arising from the organism's biological heritage.
   b. The environmental-learning perspective holds that developmental change is primarily caused by exogenous factors.
   c. The interactional perspective holds that development arises from the active adaptation of the organism to the environment. Environmental and biological factors are given an equal role.

   d. The cultural-context perspective holds that the interactions out of which development emerges are crucially shaped by the prior history of the group as embodied in its culture.

6. Developmental psychologists use several data collection techniques in their efforts to connect abstract theories to the concrete realities of people's everyday experience. These techniques are used to ensure that the data used to explain development are objective, reliable, valid, and replicable.

7. Prominent among the techniques of data collection used by developmental psychologists are
   a. Self-reports — observations in the form of interviews or responses to a questionnaire
   b. Naturalistic observation — the systematic description of behavior in naturally occurring settings
   c. Experimentation — the introduction of a change in a person's experience to test causal hypotheses
   d. Clinical methods — interview techniques for determining the unique circumstances that influence the development of individual people

8. Research designs that include systematic comparisons among children of different ages enable researchers to establish relationships among developmental phenomena. Two basic research designs are
   a. Longitudinal designs — the same children are studied repeatedly over a period of time
   b. Cross-sectional designs — different children of different ages are studied at a single time

9. Theory plays an important role in developmental psychology by providing a broad conceptual framework within which facts can be interpreted.

10. No one method or research design can supply the answers to all the questions put to developmental psychology, just as no one theory can encompass all the questions.

11. The concept of the bio-social-behavioral shift highlights the ways biological, social, and behavioral factors interact in a cultural context to produce developmental change. Keeping these factors in mind helps us to maintain a picture of the whole developing child.

KEY TERMS

Baby biographies
Bio-social-behavioral shift
Clinical method
Cohort
Control group
Correlation
Critical periods
Cross-sectional design
Culture
Ecology
Endogenous causes

Exogenous causes
Experiments
Experimental group
Human development
Learning
Longitudinal design
Maturation
Nature
Naturalistic observations
Nurture
Objectivity

Ontogeny
Phylogeny
Reliability
Replication
Representative sample
Self-report
Stage
Theory
Validity

SUGGESTED READINGS

ARIÈS, PHILIPPE. *Centuries of Childhood.* New York: Vintage Books, 1962.

A history of the concept of childhood that reveals many of our unexamined assumptions about children and human nature. This influential book uses paintings, diaries, games, and school curricula dating back to the Middle Ages to show how current conceptions of children and childhood have developed.

KESSEN, WILLIAM. *The Child.* New York: Wiley, 1983.

A collection of original writings by experts of the past three centuries on children, supplemented by useful commentary by a leading contemporary developmental psychologist.

KESSEN, WILLIAM (Ed.). *History, Theory, and Methods,* Vol. 1 of P. H. Mussen (Ed.), *Handbook of Child Psychology.* New York: Wiley, 1983.

The essays in this authoritative handbook provide state-of-the-art accounts of the history of developmental psychology, summaries of the major theoretical positions, and discussions of the methods that psychologists use in their research with children.

LANE, HARLAN. *The Wild Boy of Aveyron.* Cambridge, Mass.: Harvard University Press, 1976.

A fascinating account of the famous wild child and his teacher, Itard, which makes clear the enduring importance of Itard's research for developmental psychology.

LOMAX, ELIZABETH M., KAGAN, JEROME, and **ROZEN-KRANTZ, BARBARA G.** *Science and Patterns of Child Care.* New York: W. H. Freeman, and Company, 1978.

An historically based discussion of the complex relationships among scientific knowledge about children, child-care practices, and public policy.

MILLER, PATRICIA H. *Theories of Developmental Psychology,* Second Edition. New York: W. H. Freeman and Company, 1989.

A readable discussion of the major approaches to the study of developmental psychology.

MILLER, SCOTT A. *Developmental Research Methods.* Englewood Cliffs, N.J.: Prentice-Hall, 1987.

A thorough survey of the basic research methods used in the study of human development. The author describes the pitfalls of different methods and illustrates general principles of research using concrete examples.

I

...

In the Beginning

The definition of development given in Chapter 1 says that the development of each human being starts with the formation of a single cell at the time of conception. In adopting conception as a useful starting point, however, it is important to keep in mind that it is only a convention. Each individual human life is but a tiny drop in the vast stream of life that reaches back through thousands of generations and unimaginable millenia of evolutionary time, the beginning of which remains a mystery. Human biological structure is a product of the evolutionary past of the species, and the environment each baby will experience is a product of the earth's history and the development of culture and society. Because human development is the result of the interaction between biological structure and environment, the entire history of life plays a role in shaping the course of every new human being.

Science views the life process as a constant interplay between forces that create order and pattern on the one hand and forces that create variation and disorder on the other. In the modern scientific view, the interaction of these competing forces is the engine of developmental change.

What are the forces that create order and diversity in human development? In Chapter 2, we will see that the beginning of an explanation can be found in our biological inheritance. Order, the ways in which all human beings are alike, initially arises from the limits on the common pool of genetic possibilities for our species. Variation initially arises through sexual reproduction, which in virtually every instance ensures that each individual conceived will inherit a unique combination of genes from the common pool.

If we are to understand development, we must understand our biological inheritance and the importance of genetic combinations to later life. And we cannot understand genetic mechanisms without considering the interactions of genes with the environment. Chapter 2 describes the basic mechanisms of genetic transmission, the processes of gene-environment interaction, and some of the diseases that result from genetic abnormalities. It also includes a discussion of the contribution of cultural evolution, a distinctly human mode of inheritance, to our development.

As soon as the new organism has been formed at conception, the basic materials provided by nature begin to interact with the surrounding environment. Once again the processes that create order and variation are very much in evidence. Chapter 3, which covers prenatal development, traces the changes that transform a single cell into an infant with millions of cells of different kinds, organized into an intricate system of coordinated body parts.

The process of prenatal development illustrates many principles of development that will recur in later chapters. For example, the changes in form and activity that distinguish the organism at 5 days from the organism at 5 weeks or 5 months provide excellent examples of the kinds of *qualitative* changes that stage theorists focus on to distinguish stages of development from *quantitative* increases in size. The great sensitivity of the embryo *at certain times* to the hormonal secretions that trigger organ development and to such external agents as drugs that can block organ development supports the idea of critical periods in development.

After 9 months of growth and nurturing within the mother's body, chemical changes initiate the birth process. The transition to life outside of the mother changes the conditions for continued development in fundamental ways. As we will see in Chapter 4, birth constitutes the first major bio-social-behavioral shift in development. No longer able to obtain life-giving oxygen and nutrients automatically from the mother's body, the baby must use biological capacities developed during the prenatal period in new ways in order to breathe and eat. The behavioral changes that occur are no less remarkable. Contrary to the common wisdom of earlier decades, modern research is demonstrating that babies are born with an impressive array of abilities to process information about their environment and to act upon that information. However, without the social support of parents who structure the baby's interactions with the environment according to culturally prescribed patterns, the baby would not survive. Parents must feed, clothe, and protect their offspring for many years before they are able to take care of themselves.

Thus begins the lifelong process in which the biological forces that created the new organism at conception interact with the forces of the culturally organized environment that greets the child at birth. Barring unforeseen calamities, in approximately two decades, the process will begin again with a new generation.

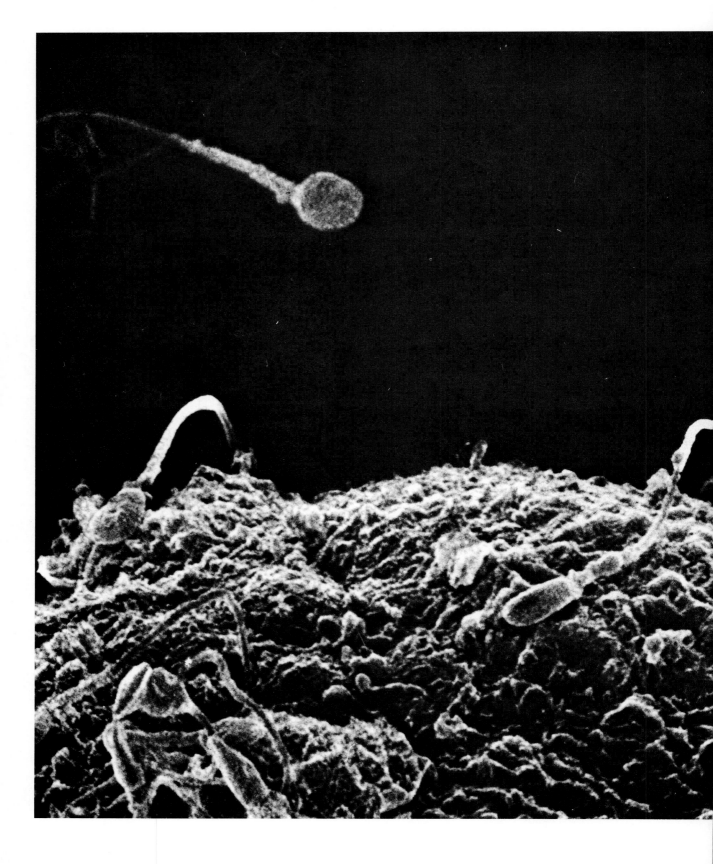

2

...

THE HUMAN HERITAGE: GENES AND ENVIRONMENT

Every child conceived by a given couple is the result of a genetic lottery. He is merely one out of a large crowd of possible children, any one of whom might have been conceived on the same occasion if another of the millions of sperm cells emitted by the father had happened to fertilize the egg cell of the mother—an egg cell which is itself one among many. . . . If we go to all the trouble it takes to mix our genes with those of somebody else, it is in order to make sure that our child will be different from ourselves and from all our other children.

—François Jacob, *The Possible and the Actual*

. . . .

A maternity ward nursery provides an interesting setting for thinking about the origins and development of human beings. In some communities, the babies may look so much alike that it is difficult to tell one from another. In other communities, they may be easily distinguished because some have dark skins and others have light skins. If we look at the grownups these infants will become in 30 years, the differences among them will have increased a great deal, making it much easier to tell them apart. Some will be men and some will be women; some will be tall, some short; some will have curly hair, some none at all. They may speak different languages, engage in different types of work, and enjoy different kinds of food. Some will often be morose, whereas others will usually be cheerful; some will be impulsive, others reflective; some will be gifted at mathematics, others at growing rice or selling stocks. Despite this great variation, none will be mistaken for any other species; all will clearly be *Homo sapiens*. Such observations raise a fundamental question about the sources of developmental change: What causes us to be so different from each other but, at the same time, more like each other than we are like members of any other species?

Both the similarities and differences among people come ultimately from the interaction between the environments in which they develop and the set of genes that they inherit from their parents. The similarities that make us members of a single species arise, on the one hand, because we inherit from other human beings our **genes,** the specialized molecules that contain the biological blueprints for the development of the individual. On the other hand, these similarities arise because human beings develop in the common environment of the planet earth.

Both genes and environment are also responsible for the great differences among people. Because of sexual reproduction, which mixes up the genes we inherit from our two parents, the particular combination of genes each of us inherits is, with rare exception, unique. The environment contributes to variations among people by determining which of their characteristics will prove to be successful in adapting to the specific conditions in which they live. For example, children born into families living deep in the forests of the Amazon basin, where people still live by hunting and gathering, must develop physical endurance and become close observers of nature. Conversely, children born into families living in a North American suburb must develop the ability to sit still for long hours in school and acquire the knowledge and skills they will need for economic success as adults. Furthermore, even within a particular family in a particular setting, each child occupies a unique position; thus, each child has a unique set of experiences that further shapes the characteristics he or she develops (Plomin, 1986; Whiting & Whiting, 1975).

We begin this chapter by discussing sexual reproduction, the mechanism for what François Jacob calls the "genetic lottery," and the basic laws of genetic inheritance to which that "lottery" is subject. Next, we will discuss the lifelong process of gene-environment interaction that begins once the specific genetic combination that defines the new organism has been created. The crucial importance of an individual's genetic constitution and the principles of gene-environment interaction will then be illustrated through a discussion of genetic abnormalities. Lastly, we will take a look at the way biology and culture interact in the process of human development.

SEXUAL REPRODUCTION AND GENETIC TRANSMISSION

At his climax during sexual intercourse, a man ejaculates about 350 million sperm into a woman's vagina. For the next several hours, the tiny tadpole-shaped sperm swim through the viscous fluid of the woman's uterus and fallopian tubes. The head of each sperm contains 23 **chromosomes**—threadlike structures consisting of approximately 20,000 genes each. These 23 chromosomes provide half the genetic information necessary for the development of a new individual. If one of the man's sperm penetrates the woman's ovum (egg), which provides the other half of the genetic information, conception occurs. The 23 chromosomes contained in the ovum and the 23 chromosomes from the sperm line up side by side in 23 pairs, each containing genes for the same characteristics. The chromosomes then merge to form a **zygote**, the single cell containing the 46-chromosome combination of the father's and mother's genetic material. From this single cell will ultimately come all the cells that the child will have at birth.

Mitosis: A Process of Cell Replication

The zygote creates new cells through **mitosis**, the process of cell duplication and division that generates all the individual's cells except sperm and ova. Mitosis begins within a few hours of conception. The 46 chromosomes move to the middle of the zygote, where, through replication, they produce exact copies of themselves. These chromosomes then separate into two sets, which migrate to opposite sides of the cell. The cell then divides in the middle to form two daughter cells, each of which contains identical pairs of the 46 chromosomes inherited at conception (see Figure 2.1). These two daughter cells go through the same process to create two new cells each, which themselves divide as the process repeats itself again and again. Mitosis is guided by the complex molecules of deoxyribonucleic acid (DNA) that make up each gene. The DNA also specifies precisely what kinds of chemical substances will be created by each cell, resulting eventually in the formation of bone cells, blood cells, nerve cells, and so on.

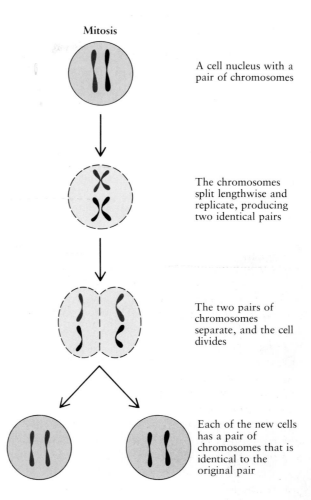

Mitosis

A cell nucleus with a pair of chromosomes

The chromosomes split lengthwise and replicate, producing two identical pairs

The two pairs of chromosomes separate, and the cell divides

Each of the new cells has a pair of chromosomes that is identical to the original pair

FIGURE 2.1 *Mitosis is the process of cell division that generates all the cells of the body except for the germ cells. During mitosis each pair of chromosomes replicates, creating two identical pairs, which then separate such that one pair is contributed to each new cell. In this way, the process ensures that identical genetic information is maintained in the body cells over the life of the organism.*

Mitosis continues throughout the life of an individual, creating new **somatic** (body) cells and replacing old ones. Each new somatic cell contains copies of the original 46 chromosomes inherited at conception. This ensures the biological continuity of the individual over the course of a lifetime. The genetic material carried by our chromosomes is not altered by the passage of time nor by the experiences that shape our minds and bodies under the ordinary conditions of

(a) Meiosis in the Male

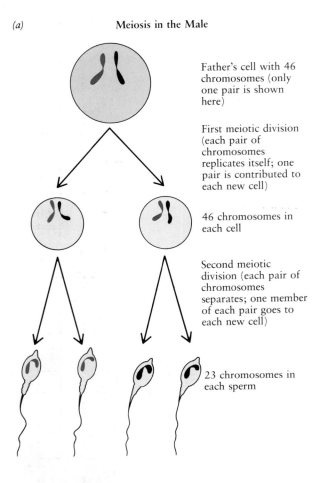

Father's cell with 46 chromosomes (only one pair is shown here)

First meiotic division (each pair of chromosomes replicates itself; one pair is contributed to each new cell)

46 chromosomes in each cell

Second meiotic division (each pair of chromosomes separates; one member of each pair goes to each new cell)

23 chromosomes in each sperm

(b) Meiosis in the Female

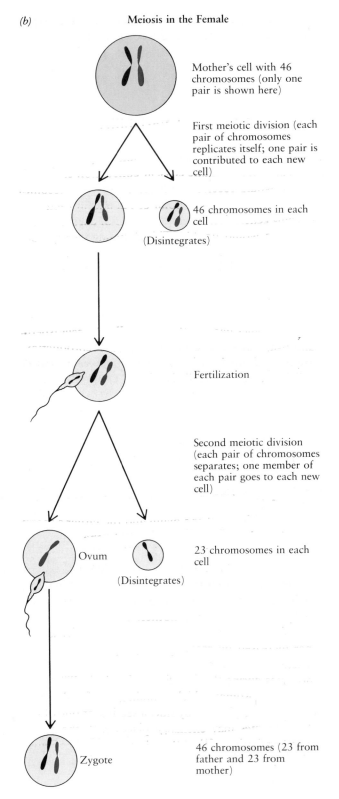

Mother's cell with 46 chromosomes (only one pair is shown here)

First meiotic division (each pair of chromosomes replicates itself; one pair is contributed to each new cell)

46 chromosomes in each cell

(Disintegrates)

Fertilization

Second meiotic division (each pair of chromosomes separates; one member of each pair goes to each new cell)

Ovum

(Disintegrates)

23 chromosomes in each cell

Zygote

46 chromosomes (23 from father and 23 from mother)

FIGURE 2.2 *(a) Formation of sperm. As meiosis in the male begins, the first division is like that of mitosis; the chromosome pairs replicate, and one of the resulting identical pairs is contributed to each new cell. A second division then occurs in which these pairs of chromosomes separate. The result is four sperm cells, each of which contains one member (or a copy) of each of the original pairs of chromosomes.*
(b) Formation of the ovum. Meiosis in the female differs slightly from meiosis in the male. When the first division occurs, the cytoplasm, the matter comprising most of the material of the cell, divides unequally such that the two resulting cells are unequal in size. The smaller of the two cells disintegrates. The large cell, the ovum, does not divide again unless it is fertilized. If fertilization occurs, the pairs of chromosomes in the ovum separate into two new cells. Again the cytoplasm divides unequally, and the smaller of the resulting cells disintegrates. The 23 chromosomes of the larger cell fuse with the 23 chromosomes of the sperm to form the zygote with its 46 chromosomes.

life. There is, however, increasing evidence that exposure to direct radiation and to certain chemicals may alter genes. As we will see later in this chapter, the consequences of such changes can be disastrous.

Meiosis: A Source of Variability

If mitosis governed the production of sperm and ova cells as well as somatic cells, at conception each individual would receive a full set of 46 chromosomes from each parent for a total of 92, and in each succeeding generation the total number of chromosomes inherited would double. This doubling clearly does not occur. Except in abnormal cases, the number of chromosomes inherited remains constant at 46 from one generation to the next for all members of the human species.

The zygote of each generation contains only 46 chromosomes because the **germ cells,** the cells (sperm and ova) that are specialized for sexual reproduction, are formed not by mitosis but by a different kind of cell division process called **meiosis.** In the first phase of this process, the 46 chromosomes in the germ-producing cells produce copies of themselves, just as in mitosis. But then the cell divides not once, as in mitosis, but *twice,* creating four daughter cells. Each of these daughter cells contains only 23 chromosomes — half of the parent cell's original set. Meiosis occurs somewhat differently in males and females, as can be seen in Figure 2.2.

Because the mother's ovum and the father's sperm contain only 23 chromosomes each, the zygote receives its full complement of 46 chromosomes when the two germ cells unite at conception. Because half of the zygote's chromosomes come from each parent, each individual conceived is genetically different from both the father and the mother. This creates genetic diversity across generations. Genetic diversity is further increased by **crossing over,** a process in which genetic material is exchanged between a pair of chromosomes during the first phase of meiosis. While the two chromosomes, which contain genes for the same characteristics, lie side by side, a section of one of the chromosomes may exchange places with the corresponding section of the other chromosome (see Figure 2.3). This exchange alters the genetic composition of

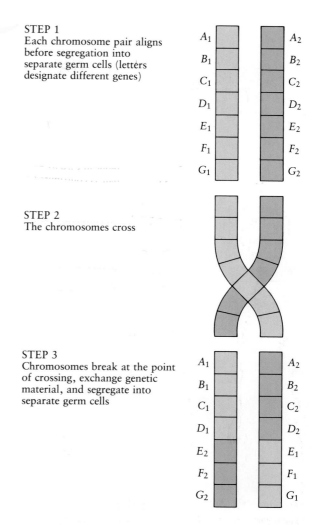

STEP 1
Each chromosome pair aligns before segregation into separate germ cells (letters designate different genes)

STEP 2
The chromosomes cross

STEP 3
Chromosomes break at the point of crossing, exchange genetic material, and segregate into separate germ cells

FIGURE 2.3 *The crossing-over process. (From Shaffer, 1985.)*

the two chromosomes; genes originally carried on one chromosome are now carried on the other.

We can now better appreciate the extreme improbability of any two children, even siblings, being exactly alike, except for the special case of identical twins (see Box 2.1, "Twinning"). Although we receive 23 chromosomes from each of our parents, it is a matter of chance which member of any pair of chromosomes ends up in a given germ cell during meiosis. According to the laws of probability, there are 2^{23}, or about 8

BOX 2.1

TWINNING

• • •

During the first few mitotic divisions following the formation of the zygote, the daughter cells occasionally separate completely and develop into separate individuals. When there are two of these individuals, they are called **monozygotic twins,** meaning that they come from one zygote. Having come from the same fertilized egg, "identical twins" inherit identical genetic information. Thus, they potentially have the same physical and psychological makeup, susceptibility to disease, and life expectancy. Monozygotic twins occur in about 1 of every 250 conceptions. It is not understood what leads to separation of the cells after the first few mitotic divisions; neither race, mother's age, the number of

children she has had previously, nor heredity seem to be factors.

Many twins do not originate from a single fertilized ovum but rather from the fertilization by two different sperm of two different eggs that are released at the same time. The two fertilized eggs develop into **dizygotic twins,** meaning that they come from two zygotes. Save for having shared the same uterus and being born at the same time, "fraternal twins" are no more alike at birth than are any other children of the same parents. The tendency to have dizygotic twins is influenced by race, heredity, maternal age, the number of prior pregnancies, and fertility drugs. Black women, mothers who are

Monozygotic twins not only look alike naturally, they are often dressed alike and treated similarily by others, which further accentuates their similarity.

million, possible genetic combinations whenever a sperm and ovum unite. When the additional possibilities from crossing over are added, it is estimated that there is only 1 chance in 64 trillion that a particular genetic combination will be repeated (Scheinfeld, 1972).

Sexual Determination: A Case of Variability

Of the 23 pairs of chromosomes found in human cells, 22 are similar in males and females. The twenty-third pair differs and determines a person's genetic sex, a crucial source of variety in our species. In the chromo-

themselves fraternal twins, women between 35 and 40 years of age, women who have had four or more children, and those who have taken fertility drugs are all more likely to give birth to fraternal twins.

Twins are of special interest to psychologists because studying their characteristics can help answer questions about the influences of nature and nurture. By comparing the similarities in certain characteristics between identical twins (who have the same genes) with the similarities between fraternal twins (whose genes are no more alike than those of any siblings), it is possible to obtain an estimate of the influence of hereditary factors for those characteristics. For example, Robert Plomin and his colleagues (Plomin & DeFries, 1985) compared identical and fraternal twins with respect to such temperamental characteristics as emotionality, level of activity, and sociability. They found that identical twins

These dizygotic twins illustrate the great potential for variety of two individuals conceived by the same parents at the same time.

were somewhat similar in their expression of these characteristics: the correlation was .55. For fraternal twins, the correlation was zero; thus, fraternal twins resembled each other in the expression of the characteristics no more than would any two children selected at random from the community. These findings indicate that inherited factors probably play a role in the development of temperament.

somes of normal females, both members of the twenty-third pair are the same and are called **X chromosomes.** The normal male has just one X chromosome and a much smaller Y chromosome. Since mothers are always XX, their eggs always contain an X chromosome. Sperm, however, may carry an X or a Y

chromosome. If a sperm containing an X chromosome fertilizes the egg, the resulting child will be XX, a female. If the sperm contains a Y chromosome, the child will be XY, a male (see Figure 2.4).

The existence of both X and Y chromosomes in the male might suggest that there would be a 50–50

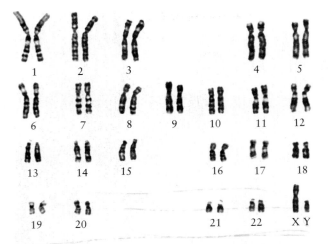

FIGURE 2.4 *Human chromosomes for a male arrayed in matched pairs, an arrangement called a karotype. Note that the two members (X and Y) of the twenty-third pair for a male differ markedly in size, whereas they would be the same for a female (X and X).*

TABLE 2.1 **Approximate sex ratios for U.S. whites**

Age	Ratio Male : Female
Conception	120 : 100
Birth	106 : 100
18 years	100 : 100
50 years	95 : 100
67 years	70 : 100
87 years	50 : 100
100 years	21 : 100

SOURCE: Lerner & Libby, 1976.

chance that a baby will be a boy, or a girl. However, as can be seen in Table 2.1, many more male than female zygotes are conceived, and slightly more boys than girls are actually born (McMillen, 1979). There is still uncertainty about the source of these differences. With respect to the greater proportion of male conceptions, the most likely explanation is that males have a tendency to produce more Y-bearing than X-bearing sperm. That fewer male babies are born than are conceived and that the ratio of males to females declines over the lifespan appear to reflect the greater vulnerability of males to genetic diseases and other problems that lead to death (McKusick, 1975).

A cultural factor that may increasingly influence the ratio of males to females at birth is parental preference for one sex or the other. With the recent development of methods for identifying the sex of the fetus, selective abortion has sometimes been used to prevent the birth of female babies. In South Korea, for example, the birth ratio in 1985 was 117 males to 100 females because, according to South Korean obstetricians, some mothers were aborting their female fetuses (Jameson, 1986).

THE LAWS OF GENETIC INHERITANCE

When the male and female germ cells come together at conception, the new organism acquires a unique combination of genetic material from its parents and ultimately from its distant ancestors. The mechanisms by which parents transmit their characteristics to the next generation were first studied scientifically by Gregor Mendel (1822–1884). On the basis of indirect evidence from experiments in which he cross-bred varieties of garden peas, Mendel proposed that parents transmitted their characteristics unchanged to their offspring via "characters." It was not until later that Mendel's hypothetical "characters" were shown to be actual physical structures—genes in the nucleus of the cell.

In the simplest form of hereditary transmission, a single pair of genes, one from each parent, determines a particular inherited characteristic. Genes that control a particular trait can have alternative forms called **alleles**. The gene that determines blood type, for example, comes in three allelic forms—A, B, and O. When the corresponding genes inherited from the two parents are of the same allelic form, the person is said to be **homozygous** for the trait. When the alleles are different, the person is said to be **heterozygous** for the trait. The distinction between homozygous and heterozygous is essential for understanding how different combinations of genes produce different characteristics.

Gregor Mendel, discoverer of the basic principles of genetics, experimenting with garden peas.

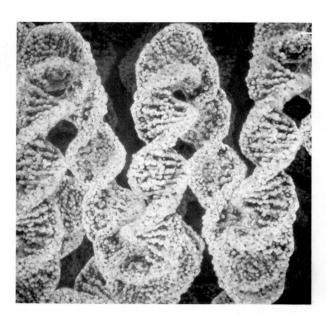

A photomicrograph of deoxyribonucleic acid (DNA). Each gene on a chromosome is either a whole molecule of DNA or a part of one. A DNA molecule consists of two strands twisted about each other and connected by cross steps to form a laddered spiral called a double helix. When a parent DNA molecule replicates to form two identical daughter molecules, the two strands of the double helix separate. Each serves as a template for the snythesis of a complementary strand.

When a child is homozygous for a trait that is controlled by a single pair of alleles, only one outcome is possible: the child will display the characteristic specified by the allele. When a child is heterozygous for a trait, one of three outcomes is possible:

1. The child will display the characteristic specified by only one of the two alleles. When this occurs, the allele whose characteristics are expressed is referred to as a **dominant allele,** and the allele whose characteristics are not expressed is called a **recessive allele.**

2. The child will show the effects of both alleles and will display a characteristic that is *intermediate* between those of children who are homozygous for either of the alleles.

3. The child will display a characteristic that is contributed to by both alleles, but rather than being intermediate, the characteristic will be distinctively different from that specified by either of the contributing alleles. This outcome is called **codominance.**

The inheritance of blood type illustrates the homozygous outcome and two of the heterozygous outcomes. There are three alleles for blood type — A, B, and O — and four basic blood types — A, B, AB, and O. If children receive two type A, two type B, or two type O alleles, they are homozygous for the trait and will have type A, type B, or type O blood, respectively. But if they inherit either the type A or type B allele from one parent and the type O allele from the other,

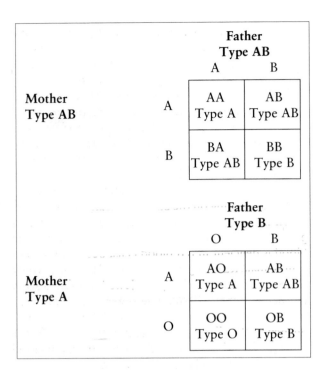

FIGURE 2.5 *Alternative forms of a gene for blood type inherited from parents produce different blood types.*

they will have type A or type B blood. Even though their genetic code for blood type is AO or BO, the O allele is recessive, so it does not affect the exhibited blood type. Finally, if children inherit one type A allele and one type B allele, they will exhibit a codominant outcome — type AB blood, which is qualitatively different from either type A or type B blood. Figure 2.5 shows some of the various outcomes for different combinations of the three alleles for blood type.

There is no intermediate outcome for blood type, but there is one for skin pigmentation. A light-skinned parent and a dark-skinned parent may have a child whose skin color falls between those of the parents.

Genotype and Phenotype

That an individual's genetic code for blood type may be AO or BO but only the A or B alleles are expressed in the blood type itself means that it is not possible to specify the individual's genetic code for blood type simply from knowing the person's actual blood type. Such differences between the genetic code for a trait and the actual expression of that trait occur for a great many characteristics. As a consequence, geneticists must study organisms on two levels to discover the effects of genes. One level is the **genotype,** the individual's genetic endowment or, in other words, the particular alleles that the individual has inherited. The genotype is constant over the lifetime of the individual. The second level is that of the **phenotype,** the observable characteristics of the individual that develop through interactions between the genotype and the environment. The study of genotypes focuses on the characteristics of genes and gene combinations, whereas the study of phenotypes focuses on actual organisms as they develop.

Discussions about genetic influences on development rely heavily upon inferences about genotypes based on observations of phenotypes. Making such inferences is a hazardous and often controversial enterprise because it is usually impossible to isolate genetic from environmental variables. We will discuss some of these controversies, such as those about the degree to which temperament and intelligence are fixed by the genotype, in later chapters.

Determining genetic influences is further complicated by the fact that most human traits are **polygenic,** that is, they are caused by the interaction of several genes. There is, for instance, no specific gene for height, which is believed to be controlled by many genes, each exerting a small effect (Tanner, 1978). Furthermore, a change in any one of the genes that contributes to the development of a given characteristic can lead to a change in the expression of that characteristic. What is more, most phenotypical characteristics determined by the interaction of a number of genes are also subject to considerable influence by the environment (Plomin, 1986).

Genes may interact with each other in several different ways. Some genes *modify* the action of other genes. Human eye color is often said to be controlled by a gene that has two allelic forms, a dominant allele for brown eyes and a recessive allele for blue eyes. If this were actually the case, there would be only two expressions of eye color: blue eyes and brown eyes. Our eyes can be a number of other colors (grey, black, green, or hazel, for example) because **modifier genes,** genes that influence the action or expression of other genes, influence eye color. These modifier genes affect the amount of pigment in the iris, the tone of the pigment (which may be "light," "yellow," or "dark-brown"), and the distribution of pigment (over the entire iris, in scattered spots, or in a ring around the outer edge) (Lerner & Libby, 1976).

Other genes are **complementary** to one another —that is, more than one gene is necessary for the expression of a characteristic. For example, purple color in pea flowers occurs only when both the dominant allele for a gene, C, and the dominant allele for another gene, P, are present together. In the absence of either of these alleles, the flowers are always white.

Still other genes may mask the normal expression of a gene; appropriately, they are referred to as **masking genes.** In the case of guinea pigs, for example, there are two genes that affect the animal's color. One determines whether melanin, the pigment that determines color, is produced; the other determines *how much* melanin is deposited. There are two alleles, one that causes a lot of melanin to be deposited which gives the guinea pig a black coat, and one that causes a moderate amount of melanin to be deposited, which gives the guinea pig a brown coat. If no melanin is produced, the guinea pig is an albino, and the gene that determines how much melanin is deposited cannot be expressed.

Sex-Linked Genetic Effects

Some inherited human characteristics are determined by genes that are found only on the X chromosome. These are called **sex-linked characteristics.** Because females receive two X chromosomes, they get two doses of sex-linked genes, one from each of their parents. Normal males receive only one X chromosome and therefore only one dose of sex-linked genes, which always comes from their mother. This asymmetry in genetic material leaves men susceptible to a number of genetic defects that ordinarily do not affect females. If a daughter has a harmful recessive gene on one X chromosome, she will usually have a dominant gene on the other X chromosome to override it. Thus, the recessive gene is not expressed. In sons there is no complementary allele to dominate the effects of a harmful recessive gene on the X chromosome, so the harmful gene is expressed.

Red-green color blindness is an example of a sex-linked recessive trait. For a daughter to exhibit this trait, she must be homozygous for it; that is, she must have a father who is red-green color blind and a mother who is either color blind or heterozygous for the trait. By contrast, if a son receives the gene for red-green color blindness on the X chromosome he inherits from his mother, he will be unable to distinguish red from green because there is no corresponding gene on the Y chromosome to counteract the recessive gene.

Other harmful sex-linked traits that primarily affect males include hemophilia (a disease in which the blood does not clot), certain types of night blindness, atrophy of the optic nerve, hypogammaglobulin (the inability of the body to produce the antibodies necessary to fight bacterial infections), brown teeth, vitamin-D resistance (which causes rickets), Duchenne's muscular dystrophy (a progressive wasting away of the muscles that leads to an early death), and some forms of diabetes (Jenkins, 1979).

The frequency of sex-linked abnormalities varies greatly depending on the particular trait and the population in which it occurs. For example, one form of genetically caused anemia, a condition in which the blood is deficient in red blood cells, occurs in 60 percent of male Kurdish Jews living in Israel, whereas only 0.5 percent of male European Jews have this disease (Lerner & Libby, 1976). The difference in the incidence of the disease reflects the difference in frequency of the allele that causes it in the two different **gene pools**—the total genetic information possessed by a sexually reproducing population.

GENES, THE ORGANISM, AND THE ENVIRONMENT

Knowledge about the laws of genetic inheritance is essential to answering questions about the influences of nature and nurture on development. But this knowledge alone will not allow us to understand genetic contributions to the development of an individual's characteristics because it leaves out an essential ingredient—the *environment,* which literally means "that which surrounds." Genes do not exist in isolation; they exist only within an environment. And only through the interactions of their genes with their environments do organisms develop.

Studying Gene-Environment Interactions

The relation of genes to their environment is complex and multileveled. Genes are merely chemical structures that provide the code for the amino acids produced by the cells. By so doing, they determine the form and functions of the cells. The cells, in turn, provide the immediate environment of the genes within them. Thus, the genes and the cell material are in constant interaction. The system of cells as a whole — the organism — is also in constant interaction with its environment. The outcomes of these organism-level interactions determine the conditions of the individual cells and, hence, the immediate environment of the genes (Lewontin, 1982).

Variations in the environment at any level can have profound effects on the development of the phenotype. This is vividly illustrated in a set of experiments using a rather unlikely subject, the Himalayan rabbit (Winchester, 1972). The Himalayan rabbit normally has a white body and black ears, nose, feet, and tail. If a patch of the white fur on the rabbit's back is removed and an ice pack is placed over the area, the new fur that grows there will be black (see Figure 2.6). This result shows that the fur-color phenotype depends upon the temperature at the specific site of hair growth. The gene for black color is expressed only at low temperatures. But simply specifying the temperature of the rabbit's general environment is not sufficient; the temperatures at specific sites on the rabbit are the relevant environments for the expression of the gene for black fur. The rabbit's extremities are normally colder than the rest of its body, and this uneven distribution of temperatures causes the typical variations in the color of the rabbit's fur. This experiment makes it clear that in investigating gene-environment interactions, the environment must be specified with as much care as the relevant genes.

In conducting research on gene-environment interactions, geneticists use two related approaches. In one, they attempt to keep the environment of various genotypes constant so that any variation in phenotype can be attributed to variations in the genes. In the other, the genotype is kept constant while the environment is varied so that variations in the phenotype can be attributed to variations in the environment. The first procedure highlights genetic influences on development; the second highlights the influences of the environment. Either approach by itself will give us only a partial picture of gene-environment interaction.

By charting the changes that occur in the phenotype as the environment of a particular genotype is varied, a **range of reaction** (also called a *norm of reaction*) for that genotype can be established. Ideally, this range will be based on all the possible gene-environment relationships that are compatible with sustaining the life of the organism so that it will include all the possible developmental outcomes. In the case of the Himalayan rabbit, the range of reaction for fur color would be bounded at one end by the temperature at which the rabbit would freeze to death and at the other end by the temperature that would be too hot for it to live. As the temperature approaches the lower boundary, we would expect the rabbit's fur to be predominantly black. As the temperature approaches the higher boundary, even the extremities might remain white. The variations in the phenotypic expression of fur color as the temperature is varied from one extreme to the other is the range of reaction for the Himalayan rabbit's genotype for fur color.

(a)   (b)   (c)

FIGURE 2.6   *The effect of the environment on the expression of a gene for fur color in the Himalayan rabbit. Under normal conditions (a) only the rabbit's feet, tail, ears, and nose are black. If fur is plucked from a patch on the rabbit's back and an ice pack is placed there (b), creating a cold local environment, the new fur that grows in is black (c). (Adapted from Winchester, 1972.)*

The Range of Reaction for Human Genotypes

Geneticists believe that the principles of gene-environment interactions they have derived from their experiments with plants, insects, and animals also apply to human beings. In actuality, however, there is little information about the ranges of reaction for human genotypes. Two major problems restrict the study of human genetic expression. First, to obtain a range of reaction, organisms with the same genotype must be exposed to a wide variety of environments, in principle the widest range in which the organism can survive. The degree of control over human beings and the risks to their lives that such experiments would require, however, is incompatible with moral precepts and standards of ethical research.

The second problem is as limiting as the first. To discover a range of reaction, we need many genetically identical individuals in order to determine how the genotype is expressed in different environments. The obvious difficulties here are that humans with identical genotypes (identical twins) are few and far between, and they normally live in the rather similar environments provided by their common family. Cases in which identical twins have been adopted by different families allow for the investigation of some environmental variation, but even in these cases, the family environments of the adopted children are likely to be similar (Scarr, 1981). Thus, the extent to which the children are similar can't be attributed entirely to the similarity of their genes; it may be due to the similarity of their environments.

These problems in establishing ranges of reaction for human characteristics have led geneticists concerned with human behavior to concentrate their efforts on kinship studies— studies in which members of the same biological family are compared to see how similar they are in one or more attributes (Plomin & DeFries, 1983; Scarr, 1981). If the attribute being studied is largely controlled by heredity, the similarity in that attribute between any two people living in the same environment should increase as the degree to which they share the same genes increases. According to the logic of kinship studies, identical twins should show the greatest degree of similarity for inherited traits because they have the same genotype. Fraternal twins and siblings, who are estimated to share, on the average, half their genetic material, should differ more

than identical twins but less than half-sisters and half-brothers, who have only one parent in common and therefore share only about 25 percent of their genetic material (Plomin, DeFries, and McClearn, 1980).

Kinship studies are not without problems. Although no two people live in precisely the same environment, the more closely related two people are, the more likely it is that they will be subject to similar environmental influences; this makes it very difficult to isolate genetic influences (Plomin, 1986; Plomin, DeFries, & McClearn 1980). Still, scientists comparing members of the same biological family have reported significant genetic influences for such varied characteristics as activity level and irritability (Goldsmith & Gottesman, 1981), intelligence test scores (Plomin & DeFries, 1983; Scarr & Weinberg, 1977, 1983), the tendency to respond empathetically to others (Matthews, Bateson, Horn, and Rosenbaum, 1981), and susceptibility to mental illness (Gottesman & Shields, 1973).

Feedback in Gene-Environment Interactions

When trying to determine how particular phenotypic characteristics develop, psychologists must take into consideration the existence of complex feedback mechanisms among children's genotypes, phenotypes, and environments. Sandra Scarr and Kathleen McCartney (1983) have proposed a model for understanding gene-environment interactions that encompasses a good deal of the current research on this topic.

The full Scarr-McCartney model is easiest to understand if we work up to it in steps. The simplest model, shown in Figure 2.7a, represents the common wisdom that the whole organism (the phenotype) is created through the interaction between its genes and its environment. For example, there is evidence that some people are genetically predisposed to "irritability." Figure 2.7a represents the idea that the actual expression of irritability in a child will depend on the degree to which the environment interacts with the genetic predisposition for irritability to create irritable behavior.

Figure 2.7b reminds us that the picture is more complicated because the parents' genes not only contribute to their child's genotype but also, through their phenotypic expression, contribute to their child's environment. If, for example, a baby has a mother and father for whom irritability is a highly expressed trait, their presence in the baby's environment may well

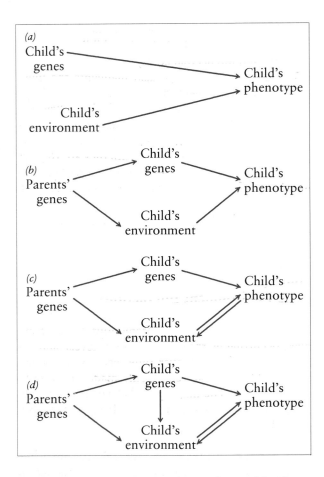

FIGURE 2.7　*The increasingly complex models of gene-environment interactions proposed by Scarr and McCartney.*

"boost" the expression of irritability in the baby. By contrast, if the parents maintain a calm environment in the home despite their own genetic predispositions for irritability, the expression of irritability in the baby may be reduced.

　The model in Figure 2.7c comes still closer to real life. It shows that the child's expressed characteristics feed back to influence the environment with which the child is interacting. Given enough provocation, even the most placid parents may become annoyed by an irritable baby and behave in a manner that will increase the baby's irritation. When this happens, the infant's genotype is interacting with an environment that is shaped in part by its own phenotypic characteristics.

　Finally, Scarr and McCartney add the possibility that the infant's genotype may influence how the child experiences the environment. An irritable child may become so upset that it experiences even a normally

soothing environment as irritating. When this possibility is included, we arrive at the gene-environment interactions of the full model depicted Figure 2.7d.

　An aspect of gene-environment interactions that is especially important to developmental psychologists, but is not explicitly taken into account by Scarr and McCartney, is that although the child's genotype is fixed for life, the environments with which the genotype interacts change over time. Plomin, DeFries, and Loehlin (1977) add a useful time perspective to Scarr and McCartney's model. Early in life, when children are still living largely within the family, gene-environment interaction is likely to be strongly affected by their parents, who determine both the genotypes and the environments of their children. Later, when children go to school and are given a larger voice in their own affairs — by choosing their own friends and leisure activities, for example — they play a more active role in determining the environments in which they develop.

Picturing Gene-Environment Interactions

The complexities of gene-environment relationships over the course of development have led scientists to try to represent the overall process in a single, easily comprehended picture. Such pictures are necessarily incomplete, but they can illustrate important aspects of the effects of gene-environment interactions. Biologist C. H. Waddington (1966) pictures the process by which a characteristic develops as a ball rolling through a landscape of valleys of differing depths, as illustrated in Figure 2.8. The varying depths of the valleys represent the degree to which a genetic trait is susceptible to different environmental influences.

　Deep valleys represent characteristics for which development is strongly controlled by the genes. Unless something highly unusual happens, all children will follow the same developmental path for these characteristics. They will, for example, develop two arms, two legs, two eyes, a nose, and a distinctive gender. Waddington refers to characteristics that are relatively invulnerable to environmental influence during their development as **canalized characteristics**. Shallow valleys represent traits for which genes do not strongly constrain the phenotype. In these cases, the inherited trait is more susceptible to environmental influences, which allows for a wider range of phenotypes. For example, the likelihood that a child will develop an

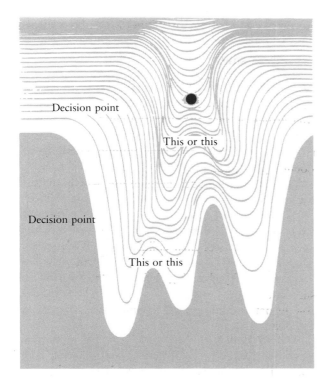

FIGURE 2.8 *Waddington's landscape. The rolling ball represents the developing organism. At each decision point, the organism can go forward along one of two diverging pathways. As development proceeds, it becomes increasingly difficult to move to a different pathway. (From Fishbein, 1976.)*

emotional disturbance is affected by such environmental events as the loss of a parent, moving to a new city, or the support of a sympathetic teacher (Rutter, 1979).

As individual children move through Waddington's landscape, they come upon points of transition, labeled "decision points" in the figure. At these decision points, relatively small differences in environmental influences can produce important differences in a child's phenotype, although the phenotype will still be constrained by the larger "valley" in which the decision point is located. For example, in many places in the world, a child's future occupation is greatly influenced by what happens when the child is between 6 and 8 years of age. Will the child become a doctor, a shepherd, a soldier, a shopkeeper, or a housewife? Environmental factors that influence this decision point include the range of adult occupations in the society in which the child lives, the availability of schools, and

the child's access to them. Important factors that are influenced by genes include the child's sex, size, strength, and intellectual ability.

Waddington's landscape also highlights the influences early developments have on later ones. The further one has traveled along a particular valley, the harder it is to "cross the hill" to a different path. For example, children who grow up in an area where formal schooling is not introduced until they are 16 years old are unlikely to embark on the new path of schooling; they are far more likely to follow a traditional path of their culture.

Four Questions about Gene-Environment Interactions

Because gene-environment interactions are so complex, occurring as they do on several levels simultaneously and changing over time, certain errors and oversimplifications are commonly made in trying to describe them. The major pitfalls have been summarized by Richard Lewontin (1982), from whose work the following discussion is drawn.

Is there a developmental program? An appealing analogy that is often encountered in discussions of development is that between the genetic code and a computer program. Computer programs are physical symbol systems that consist of instructions for processing the data the operator feeds in. It is tempting to think of the genetic code as a program that is specified at conception and determines the output — development — of the organism from then on.

The intricacies of gene-environment interactions indicated by the full Scarr-McCartney model (Figure 2.7*d*), however, should be sufficient to convince us that the computer-program analogy has only limited application. Unlike the case for computers, where program + data = outcome, the characteristics of living organisms are not strictly determined by the mechanical unfolding of preset instructions. Instead, they depend to a large extent upon the uncertain outcomes of the gene-environment interactions that occur along the way. Computer scientists may one day construct self-modifying machines. Until that time, the computer-program analogy for development should be used with great caution.

The kinds of gene-environment interaction that lead a child to perform well with a hoop greatly depend on the cultural context that specifies how it is to be used.

mostly

Do genes determine the phenotype? As implausible as it might seem after considering the complexities of gene-environment interaction discussed so far in this chapter, it is still common to encounter the idea that once the genotype is given, the phenotype is fixed. There are, to be sure, some traits that exhibit a one-to-one correspondence between genotype and phenotype for known ranges of reaction. Blood type is one such trait. Phenotypes, however, are generally *not* fixed by genotypes. Consider alcoholism. Data gathered by behavioral geneticists suggest that there is some genetic influence in alcoholism (Plomin, 1986). But no one becomes an alcoholic without consuming large quantities of alcohol. In an environment in which alcoholic beverages are not available at all or in which it is customary to drink only small amounts of alcohol, any genetic predisposition to alcohol abuse would not be expressed.

Do genes determine capacity? Another commonly encountered idea is that genes determine capacity. This idea can be illustrated by the hypothetical story of a young woman who wants nothing in the world so much as to be a track star. Through vigorous exercise on the high school track, she assures herself that she will not tire quickly and will have the necessary energy for the final push at the finish line. She practices endlessly at getting quickly off the starting blocks. She goes to sleep early every night and eats the healthiest foods. But despite all these efforts, she never achieves a running speed that allows her to be a champion. The set of genes she inherited have given her legs and a torso do not enable her to run as fast as many of her competitors.

It is true that for a given genotype there is going to be some greatest speed that the organism can achieve over the range of all possible environments. However, before concluding that our hypothetical runner has realized her full genetic capacity for running speed, we need to consider the influence of the environment more fully because hidden in the story is an unexamined assumption about the environment. High school tracks are a familiar environment in which North Americans develop their running capacities, but they do *not* represent the full range of environments within which human beings do their running. Had our runner grown up in the Himalayas or in the Amazon jungle, where the conditions of running are quite different,

A cinder track provides an excellent standard running surface, but it is only one of the many possible environments within which running abilities may develop, a fact that needs to be kept in mind when investigating the genetic contribution to running speed.

she might indeed be a champion precisely because her torso and legs are shaped in a way that is suited to running in those environments.

Discussions of the genetic determination of capacity routinely neglect the fact that the effectiveness of the phenotype is always relative to the environment in which it is expressed. The ancestor of a boy growing up in the Peruvian Andes today might have been highly accomplished in performing mathematical calculations in the conduct of business in the Inca empire. The modern boy may possess the same genes relevant to mathematical ability, but if he does not go to school and instead stays at home to help farm, there is likely to be little expression of his presumed mathematical capacity (Ascher & Ascher, 1981).

In everyday life, we often speak of more and less capacity related to a genotype's expression (running track in most U. S. high schools, doing mathematics in Peru). But in the absence of information about the physical and cultural environment of development, all such descriptions remain problematic because the extent of children's capacities stemming from their genotypes always depends upon the environments in which they are expressed.

Do genes determine tendencies? If genes by themselves do not fix capacities, might they determine tendencies? Perhaps the genetic contribution to excitability is a "tendency to become excited."

This simplification of gene-environment interaction is appealing because it seems to exhibit moderation and a tentative orientation that is consistent with real-world complexities. But, as in the case of claims about genes and capacity, statements about genes and tendencies often include narrow assumptions about the environments in which the tendency is expressed. For example, based upon a comparison of Sandy with boys of similar age and family background in some environments in which they all spend time, like the baseball field or the classroom, one might say that Sandy has a tendency to become excitable. And it may be true that in those settings, Sandy *is* more excitable than his peers by some objective measure. But Sandy may still not be *generally* more excitable than his peers. Is he more excitable when he is reading poetry? When he is talking to his girlfriend? When he is doing homework?

Underlying the proposition that genes determine tendencies is an implicit assumption that the individual's behavior in comparison to that of peers remains consistent across a variety of environments. If this assumption is not valid, if it is made on the basis of only a few environments that are assumed to be typical, the proposition is not really being tested.

MUTATIONS AND GENETIC ABNORMALITIES

Despite its fantastic power to produce diversity among human beings, sexual reproduction is restricted to recombining genes that are already present in the human gene pool. The source of new genes is **mutation,** an error in the process by which a gene is replicated that results in a change in the molecular structure of the genetic material itself. Mutations occur when there are qualitative changes in a particular gene or in the sequence of the genes on the chromosomes. They may also consist of additions or deletions in which part of a chromosome is duplicated or lost. Mutations change the overall set of genetic possibilities that sexual reproduction then rearranges.

Mutations sometimes occur in the somatic (body) cells—in skin, liver, brain, or bone cells, for example. The somatic cells that carry these mutations pass on the changed genetic instructions to the cells that descend from them by mitosis. These changes affect only the person in whom they occur; they are not passed on to following generations. However, when a mutation is present in a parent's sperm or ova, the changed genetic information may be passed on to the next generation.

Geneticists assume that spontaneous mutations have been occurring constantly on a random basis since life on earth began, pouring new genes into the gene pools of every species. Indeed, mutation is the driving force behind the evolutionary processes by which new subspecies and species are formed. The fact that mutations are a natural and fundamental part of life does not, however, mean that they benefit the individual organisms in which they occur. Each living organism is an intricate whole in which the functioning of every part influences the functioning of every other part. It is little wonder, then, that the introduction of even a small change in the genes can have serious repercussions for the individual.

Most mutations are not expressed in the phenotypes of the organisms that harbor them. Although it is estimated that as many as half of all human conceptions have some sort of genetic or chromosomal abnormality, the majority of these mutations are lethal and result in early spontaneous abortions (Plomin, De-Fries, & McClearn, 1980). Still, about 1 out of every 200 babies born has some kind of genetic aberration (Moore, 1982). These mutations tend to be recessive, so individuals who receive them from one parent usually receive normal genes or chromosomes from the other parent to counteract them. There are, though, a number of genetic abnormalities that affect human beings. Some of the more significant of these are described in Table 2.2.

Developmental psychologists are interested in mutations and genetic abnormalities for several reasons:

1. By disturbing the well-integrated mechanisms of development, mutations can help to reveal the intricate ways in which heredity and the environment interact.

2. If the existence of genetic abnormalities can be detected during very early stages of development, ways may be found to prevent or ameliorate the birth defects that would normally result.

3. When children are born with genetically related abnormalities, developmental psychologists are often responsible for finding ways to reduce their impact on the children and their families.

These concerns are illustrated in the following discussions of sickle-cell anemia, Down's syndrome, certain sex-linked chromosomal abnormalities, and phenylketonuria.

Sickle-Cell Anemia: An Example of Gene-Environment Interaction

In certain environments, some mutations can provide a selective advantage to people who are heterozygous for them. The recessive sickle-cell gene is a case in point. People who inherit this gene from both of their parents, making them homozygous for it, suffer from *sickle-cell anemia,* a serious abnormality of their red blood cells. Normally, red blood cells are round. In

TABLE 2.2 Common genetic diseases and conditions

Disease or Condition	Description	Mode of Transmission	Incidence	Prognosis	Prenatal Detection	Carrier Detection
Cleft palate, cleft lip (Hare lip)	The two sides of the upper lip or the palate are not joined	Causes include genetic defects, pre-natal injury, drugs, and malnutrition	Unknown because not always reported; varies with ethnic group	Correctable by surgery	No	No
Cystic fibrosis	Lack of enzyme causes mucous ob-struction, especially in the lungs and digestive tract	Recessive gene	1 in 21,000 live births in U.S.; most common in people of Northern European descent	Few victims survive to adulthood	No (possible in near future)	No
Diabetes melitus (ju-venile form)	Deficient metabolism of sugar because body does not produce adequate insulin	Thought to be polygenic	1 in 25 to 40 of all diabetics	Fatal if untreated; controllable by insulin and a restricted diet	No	No
Down's syndrome	Physical and intellectual retardation; distinctive physical appearance	Chromosomal abnormal-ity; extra chromo-some 21	1 in 600 to 700 births	Moderate to severe mental re-tardation; eye, ear, and heart problems	Yes	Possible in cases of chromo-somal rearrange-ment (only 5% of cases)
Hemophilia (bleeding disease)	Blood does not clot readily	X-linked gene; also spontaneous mutation	1 in 21,500 live births of males	Possible crippling and death from internal bleeding; transfusions are used to ameliorate effects	No	Yes
Huntington's chorea	Deterioration of the central ner-vous system and body in middle age	Dominant gene	Rare	Fatal	Yes	Yes
Klinefelter's syndrome	Affects males; failure to mature sexually at adolescence; sterility	Chromosomal abnormal-ity; an extra X chromo-some (XXY)	1 in 1000 white males in U.S.	Emotional and social problems; treated by administer-ing testos-terone	Yes	No

(Continued)

TABLE 2.2 Common genetic diseases and conditions (*Continued*)

Disease or Condition	Description	Mode of Transmission	Incidence	Prognosis	Prenatal Detection	Carrier Detection
Muscular dystrophy (Duchenne's type)	Weaking and wasting away of the muscles	X-linked gene	1 in 200,000 males under the age of 20	Crippling; often fatal by age of 20	Yes	Sometimes
Neural tube defects (anencephaly and spina bifida)	In anencephaly, part of the brain and skull is missing; in spina bifida, part of the spine is not closed over	Uncertain	1 in 1000 live births in U.S.	Babies with anencephaly die shortly after birth. Those with spina bifida may survive with surgery; their prognosis depends on the defect's severity	Yes	No
Phenylketonuria (PKU)	Lack of enzyme causes abnormal digestion of certain proteins	Recessive gene	1 in 15,000 white births; lower in blacks and Ashkenazi Jews	Mental retardation and hyperactivity; controllable in many through diet	Yes	Often
Sickle-cell anemia	Abnormal red blood cells	Recessive gene	1 in 625 births among U.S. blacks	Possible heart and kidney failure; many survive into adulthood	Yes	Yes
Tay-Sachs disease	Lack of an enzyme causes waste build-up in the brain	Recessive gene	1 in 3600 for Ashkenazi Jews in U.S.	Neurological degeneration leading to death before the age of 4	Yes	Yes
Thalassemia (Cooley's anemia)	Abnormal red blood cells	Recessive gene	1 in 100 births in populations from subtropical and tropical areas of Europe, Africa, and Asia	Listlessness, enlarged liver and spleen, occasionally death; treatable by blood transfusions	Yes	Yes
Turner's syndrome	Affects females; short stature, webbed neck, and broad chest; failure to produce the hormone estrogen; sterility	Chromosomal abnormality; single X chromosome (XO)	1 in 10,000 female births	Physical defect may lead to social and emotional problems; treated with hormone therapy	Yes	No

SOURCES: Bergsma, 1979, McKusick, 1986; Nightingale & Meister, 1987.

sickle-cell anemia, however, these cells take on a curved, sickle shape when the supply of oxygen to the blood is reduced, as may occur at high altitudes or during strenuous exercise (see Figure 2.9). These abnormal blood cells tend to clump together and clog the smaller blood vessels. Because sickle-cell anemia impairs circulation, people who suffer from the disease experience severe pains in their abdomen, back, head, and limbs. The disease causes the heart to enlarge and the brain cells to be deprived of blood. The deformed blood cells rupture easily, which may lead to severe anemia and, in some cases, to early death.

People who are heterozygous for the sickle-cell gene are said to have the *sickle-cell trait*. They usually do not suffer from the symptoms associated with sickle-cell anemia, although about 40 percent of their red blood cells may assume the sickle shape when the supply of oxygen to their blood is reduced, which may interfere with their circulation. As many as 40,000 blacks in the United States are estimated to suffer from sickle-cell anemia (Lerner & Libby, 1976).

Because many people who suffer from sickle-cell anemia die at an early age and therefore fail to reproduce, one would expect that this mutation would eventually die out. This is exactly what is occurring in the United States, where the incidence of the trait among blacks is about 10 percent (Lerner & Libby,

1976). But in West Africa, the area from which the ancestors of most black Americans were brought to this continent, the incidence of the sickle-cell trait is greater than 20 percent (Allison, 1954). For a long time these facts puzzled scientists. Then investigators noticed that the areas in which the sickle-cell trait was most common also tended to have a high incidence of malaria. This correspondence raised the possibility that there might be some connection between the two.

The link between the sickle-cell gene and malaria was established in 1954 by A. C. Allison of Oxford, England. Allison conducted a number of studies showing that heterozygous carriers of the gene have a much higher than normal resistance to the malaria parasite. This means that in malaria-infested areas like the West African coast, people who do not carry the sickle-cell gene are at a disadvantage because they are more likely to suffer from malaria, which can be deadly. Because of the selective advantage the sickle-cell gene affords, its high frequency has been maintained in the population despite the losses caused by the early death of homozygous carriers.

Down's Syndrome: An Example of a Chromosomal Error

Down's syndrome was the first human disease to be linked with a specific chromosomal disorder. More than 95 percent of the children born with Down's syndrome have 47 chromosomes, one more than normal. Instead of two chromosomes in the twenty-first position, they have three. (For this reason, the disorder is sometimes called *Trisomy 21.*) Children with Down's syndrome are mentally and physically retarded and have several distinctive physical characteristics: slanting eyes; a fold on the eyelids; a rather flat facial profile; lower than normal ears; a short neck; a protruding tongue; dental irregularities; short, broad hands; curved little fingers; a wider than normal space between the toes; and a simian crease across the palm (see Figure 2.10). Because of the slanting eyes and the fold on the eyelids of these children, British neurologist Langdon Down, who first described the syndrome in 1867, called it "Mongolism." On the average, children with this disorder are more likely to suffer from heart, ear, and eye problems than are other children, and they are more susceptible to leukemia and to respi-

FIGURE 2.9 *Normal red blood cells (upper left) and the sickle-shaped red blood cells (below and on right) of a person with sickle-cell anemia.*

FIGURE 2.10 *A Down's syndrome child.*

ratory infections. As a result, they are more likely to die at an early age (Bergsma, 1979).

Although over 10 percent of the people in institutions for the retarded suffer from Down's syndrome (Moore, 1982), how effectively Down's-syndrome children function as they grow depends both on the severity of the disorder and on the environment in which they are raised. Intense intervention by concerned adults can markedly improve the intellectual functioning of some of these children, which implies a wide range of reaction for this genotype.

Down's syndrome occurs in about 1 out of every 600 to 700 births in the United States (Edgerton, 1979). A strong relationship has been found between the incidence of Down's syndrome and the age of the parents, the mother in particular. The incidence of the disorder increases from 1 in every 1500 births for mothers below the age of 30 to 1 in every 130 births for those between the ages of 40 and 44 to 1 in every 65 births for those over the age of 45 (Plomin, DeFries, and McClearn, 1980) perhaps because at birth the human female carries all the potential egg cells that she will ever produce. The ova are especially vulnerable to such environmental agents as viruses, radiation, and chemicals, which can damage the chromosomes or interfere with the process of meiosis. The older a woman is, the more time she has had to be exposed to such harmful agents. This view is supported by the fact that other chromosomal anomalies, such as Klinefelter's syndrome (discussed next), also show increased incidence with greater maternal age.

Sex-Linked Chromosomal Abnormalities

Abnormalities of the chromosomes that determine sex are of special interest to developmental psychologists because they provide one means of obtaining information about the genetic basis of sex differences. The most common sex-linked chromosomal abnormality is *Klinefelter's syndrome,* in which a male is born with an extra X chromosome (XXY). Estimates are that among whites this abnormality occurs in about 1 out of every 1000 males in the United States (Bergsma, 1979). XXY males appear to develop normally until adolescence, but then, unlike normal males, their sex organs do not mature, they do not acquire facial hair, their voices do not change, they have low levels of the male hormone testosterone, and they are sterile.

The most common sex-linked abnormality in females is *Turner's syndrome.* About 1 out of every 10,000 females is born with only one X chromosome (XO) (Bergsma, 1979). These children have female genitals, although they differ from normal XX females in that they are often shorter than average and have stubby fingers and toes, a "webbed" neck, and a broad chest. At puberty, girls with Turner's syndrome fail to produce the female hormone estrogen. As a result they do not develop breasts or pubic hair, rarely menstruate, and are sterile. Children suffering from this abnormality were once thought to be mentally retarded, but more recent research has shown that this is not the case. Such girls, as a group, have been found to be about average in verbal ability, although they frequently score below average on tests of spatial ability and have difficulty with such tasks as following a road map or copying a geometric design (Rovet & Netley, 1982).

Phenylketonuria: A Treatable Genetic Disease

The modern history of *phenylketonuria* (PKU), an inherited metabolic disorder that often leads to severe mental retardation if not treated, provides a dramatic example of how human beings can change the environment of development to change the effects of a genetic defect. In the United States, it is estimated that 1 in every 15,000 white infants born each year has PKU and that 1 in 100 people of European descent is a carrier of the recessive mutant gene (Hsia, Driscoll, Troll, & Knox, 1956). The incidence of PKU among blacks is lower than that among whites (Bergsma, 1979).

PKU was discovered in 1934 in Norway after Dr. Ashborn Folling found that two mentally retarded children who had been brought to him had abnormal amounts of phenylpyruvic acid in their urine. Spurred by this discovery, Dr. Folling tested other retarded children in institutions and found that some of them also had this symptom. We now know that PKU is caused by a defective recessive gene that leads to the absence of an enzyme necessary to metabolize certain proteins. Because PKU children lack this enzyme, they accumulate phenylalanine and phenylpyruvic acid in the bloodstream, which in turn prevents their brain cells from developing normally.

Knowledge of the abnormal biochemistry of the condition led researchers to hypothesize that, if the accumulation of phenylalanine and phenylpyruvic acid could be prevented, infants with PKU might develop normally. This hypothesis has been tested by feeding PKU infants a diet low in phenylalanine. (Phenylalanine is highly concentrated in such basic foods as milk, eggs, bread, and fish.) It has been found that in many cases the mental retardation that characterizes PKU can be avoided through such dietary intervention. The timing of the intervention is crucial. If phenylalanine intake is not restricted by the time a PKU infant is 1 to 3 months of age, significant brain damage will occur that cannot be reversed.

In 1961, Dr. Robert Guthrie devised a test to screen for newborns with PKU so that preventive measures can be taken before phenylalanine and phenylpyruvic acid have a chance to accumulate. The test is now compulsory in most states. Hospital personnel draw blood from each baby's heel a few days after birth. The blood is then added to a bacterial culture that grows if the phenylalanine level in the baby's blood is high. The test is not always effective, however, so some PKU babies have not been identified.

Recently, a means has been developed to detect PKU prenatally (Nightingale & Meister, 1987). Researchers have also developed a test that can identify people who carry the recessive PKU gene. This test enables carriers of the gene to decide whether they want to risk having a child with the disease. (For further discussion of methods of detecting genetic problems, see Box 2.2, "Genetic Counseling.")

BIOLOGY AND CULTURE

Today we know that mutations are the source of biological variation among species, but at the time Darwin wrote *The Origin of Species* (1859), the genetic basis of hereditary transmission was unknown. Ignorance of genetics and a limited knowledge of the fossil record helped to fuel a fundamental confusion about precisely how hereditary transmission works. In attempting to account for the differences observed among species and among peoples past and present, many argued that the mechanisms that produce historical change and the differences between people living in different cultures were the same as those that produce biological change. An examination of this confusion can give us a broader perspective on the relation between our genetic and our environmental heritages and on why attempts to separate the influences of nature and nurture are so problematic.

Acquired Characteristics

In the absence of knowledge of genetics, many prominent biologists in the nineteenth and early twentieth centuries hypothesized that characteristics acquired

BOX 2.2

GENETIC COUNSELING

• • •

Thanks to recent advances in the field of genetics, many potential genetic problems can be avoided through genetic testing and counseling. The main responsibilities of genetic counselors are to test potential parents to learn whether they are carriers of a genetic disease and to determine the probabilities that a particular couple will bear a child with a genetic disease.

Genetic counselors are often called on by couples who have had one child with a genetic defect and who want to know the likelihood that a second child will have the abnormality. Genetic counselors also advise potential parents who have relatives with a genetic disease, who have physical anomalies they suspect are genetic, who have had several pregnancies that have ended in spontaneous abortion, or who are over the age of 35. Potential parents whose ancestors come from parts of the world where the incidence of a specific genetic disorder is high also use their services. Several inherited disorders in addition to sickle-cell anemia are likely to be found in specific groups of people. For example, the recessive allele for Tay-Sachs, a disease in which a missing enzyme inevitably leads to death before the age of 4, is carried by 1 in 30 Ashkenazi Jews in the United States. The recessive allele for Thalassemia, a blood disease, is carried by 1 in 10 Americans of Greek or Italian descent (Omenn, 1978).

Detecting the carriers of the gene for some genetic disorders is relatively simple. The allele for Tay-Sachs and the sickle-cell allele can be detected through a blood test. Carriers of chromosomal abnormalities, such as the translocation of chromosome 21 that causes Down's syndrome, can be detected through the analysis of a cell from their body. Female carriers of Lesch-Nyhan syndrome (a metabolic disorder affecting male children that leads to the overproduction of uric acid) can be detected through an analysis of their hair follicles. The carriers of certain chromosomal disorders are signaled by specific fingerprint, palm, and sole patterns.

On the basis of test results and family histories, the genetic counselor will try to determine whether there is a potential problem and what the odds are that a child of the couple will be affected by it. Such predictions can presently be made for diseases and traits that are caused by a single recessive or dominant gene or are sex-linked and, in some cases, by those caused by several genes acting together (polygenic defects). They cannot be made for defects caused by spontaneous mutations.

It must always be kept in mind that genetic theory generates statistical probabilities that apply to whole populations. Thus, the genetic counselor cannot say for certain in advance of conception that a particular couple will have a child that will suffer from a genetic

by individuals during their lifetimes are transmitted biologically to the next generation. This belief raised concerns that parents who, for example, engaged in criminal activity would pass on a tendency to criminality to their children in the same way that they passed on eye or hair color (Gould, 1979).

The erroneous idea that acquired characteristics can be biologically inherited is widely identified with Jean-Baptiste Lamarck (1744–1829), a French biologist who specialized in the analysis of fossils. Consider a Lamarckian explanation of how the giraffe came to

have such a long neck. In the beginning, giraffes had short necks. As they ate up the low-lying foliage, however, they tended to stretch their necks to reach the leaves of trees. This constant stretching changed their biological constitution, making their longer necks a characteristic that they could pass on biologically to their offspring. In this way, the giraffe's neck became longer and longer in succeeding generations.

Contrast such an explanation with modern evolutionary theory's Darwinian explanation (see Figure 2.11), which begins with the assumption that the an-

abnormality. Once potential parents have been informed of the risks, they must make their own decision.

After conception, the principal techniques used to determine whether a given fetus suffers from a genetic defect are amniocentesis, sampling of the chorionic villi, and alpha-fetoprotein tests. To perform an **amniocentesis,** the doctor first determines the position of the fetus by means of a *sonogram,* in which high frequency sound waves are bounced off of the fetus and are transformed into a detailed picture. The doctor then inserts a long, hollow needle into the mother's abdomen and extracts some of the amniotic fluid from the sac surrounding the fetus. Because the cells in the amniotic fluid are identical to all of the fetus's other cells, the fluid can be analyzed for chemical abnormalities and for the presence of certain genetic disorders. Amniocentesis can not be performed before the fourth month of pregnancy, and two additional weeks are needed to determine the results.

Another procedure for detecting chromosomal disorders involves sampling cells taken from the *villi* (hairlike projections) on the chorion, a tissue that forms the placenta. One advantage to such **chorionic villus sampling** is that it can be performed as early as the ninth week of pregnancy and its results are available within a few days; this allows for an earlier, safer abortion, should the woman make that choice. Some controversy still surrounds the procedure with regard to both its safety and the accuracy of the findings (Kolata, 1987).

The **alpha-fetoprotein test** is a blood test that is mainly used to detect the presence of defects in the neural tube, which forms the spinal column and brain. Defects caused by incomplete closure of the neural tube are the most common birth defects in the United States, occurring in 1 out of every 1000 live births. When a fetus has a neural-tube defect, large amounts of alpha-fetoprotein pour out of the open spine or skull into the amniotic fluid. From there it enters the mother's bloodstream, where it can be detected. The results of this blood test are only suggestive, however. Women whose alpha-fetoprotein levels are abnormally high are usually offered sonograms and amniocentesis to confirm that there is a problem.

When a genetic disorder is detected by any of these tests, parents usually have only two choices: the woman can carry the pregnancy to term and give birth to a child who is genetically defective in some way, or she can terminate the pregnancy. These are not easy choices, especially since the diagnosis often fails to predict the degree of disability the affected person will suffer or the quality of life that can be expected for it. The severity of a neural-tube defect, for example, can vary greatly, and many people who suffer from such defects have lived lives that are almost normal. In some cases, fetal surgery and other kinds of prenatal and postnatal interventions, such as special diets or blood transfusions, can ameliorate the effects of a defect.

cestors of present-day giraffes, like all creatures, displayed diversity in many characteristics, including neck length. In their competition with each other for food, relatively long-necked giraffes had a selective advantage. This increased the likelihood that the longer-necked giraffes in each generation would live to mate. Thus, the longer-necked giraffes thrived and the shorter-necked giraffes gradually died out.

Although the inheritance of acquired characteristics as a mechanism of *biological* evolution has been discredited, the idea behind it is not irrelevant to the

study of development. Consider, for example, that the ability of early human beings to make marks on objects has gradually evolved into symbol systems for writing and numerical calculation. Today, the millions of children all over the world who are learning to read and do arithmetic in school are mastering symbol systems that are vastly more complex than those used by any humans as little as 10,000 years ago. This increased ability is *not* the consequence of biological evolutionary change through the action of genes. Rather, it is the result of *cultural* evolution, in which the adaptations

Lamarck's Theory. Existing data do not support this theory.

Ancestral giraffes probably had short necks that were subjected to frequent stretching to enable the giraffes to reach the foliage of trees.

The offspring had longer necks that also were stretched frequently in the quest for food.

Eventually the continued stretching of the neck gave rise to modern giraffes.

Darwin's Theory. Existing data support this theory.

Ancestral giraffes probably had necks that varied in length. The variations were hereditary. (Darwin could not explain the origin of variations.)

Competition and natural selection led to survival of longer–necked offspring at the expense of shorter–necked ones.

Eventually only long–necked giraffes survived the competition.

FIGURE 2.11 *Lamarck's theory that characteristics acquired by parents during their lifetimes are transmitted biologically to offspring compared with Darwin's theory that evolution proceeds by natural selection. (From Fishbein, 1976.)*

that arose from the experience of prior generations— how to make tools for plowing fields, the theorems of geometry, and even the best way to cure a cold— accumulate, are added to by the present generation, and are passed on to succeeding generations through language and by example (White, 1959). The handing down of culture from one generation to the next is almost totally absent in nonhuman species.

Coevolution

For a great many years it was believed that the two forms of development that characterize *Homo sapiens,* biological and cultural, arose in a strict sequence; first the biological capacities we associate with humanity evolved to a critical point and then some biological change occurred that allowed *Homo sapiens* to use

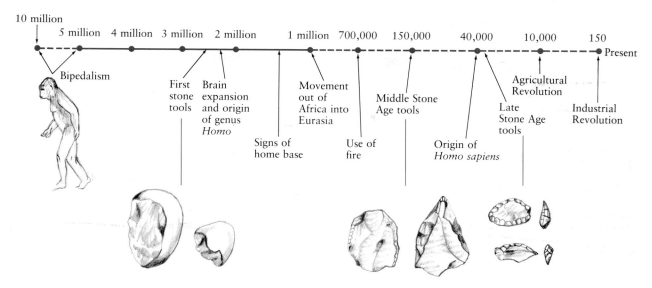

FIGURE 2.12   *The coevolution of tool-making abilities and Homo sapiens.*

language and generate culture. Contemporary paleontology and archeology present us with a far more complicated picture. It now appears that rudimentary forms of culture were already present during early phases of human evolution (see Figure 2.12). *Australopithecus* (one of our primitive ancestors who lived some 3 million years ago) domesticated fire, built shelters, engaged in organized hunting and used tools —flints, knives, cooking utensils, and notation systems (Tanner, 1981). Although no one can be certain, many scholars assume that *Australopithecus* also had some form of language (Bates & McWhinney, 1982; Geertz, 1973).

Biological evolution of the human line did *not* end with the appearance of cultural objects. The brain of modern people is about three times larger than the brain of *Australopithecus*. Most of this increase has occurred in the frontal lobes of the brain, those areas that govern complex, specifically human capacities (Jerrison, 1982; Luria, 1973). In so far as the capacity to engage in cultural activities and to reason using cultural tools—such as geometry, which permits navigation—confers a selective reproductive advantage, it is probable that the more effective users of culture have been more successful in passing on their genes to succeeding generations. In short, the two forms of evolution, biological and cultural, have interacted with each other in a process called **coevolution** (Lumesden & Wilson, 1981).

FIGURE 2.13   *The physical differences among people who live in different environments reflect evolutionary adaptations to those environments. The Eskimo, who lives in a cold climate, has a ratio of body surface area to body volume different from the Nilotic Negro, who lives in a warm climate. (From Howells, 1960.)*

As a consequence of the coevolution of human physical and cultural characteristics, attempts to separate the influences of nature and nurture in the development of contemporary children are even more problematic than our discussion of the range of reaction earlier in this chapter would suggest. People who have grown up in different parts of the world have lived in environments with very different physical demands (see Figure 2.13). Furthermore, their cultural histories have differed greatly for tens of thousands of years. There is a clear genetic contribution to the physical differences among people, but there is great uncertainty about the possible genetic basis of their mental differences. When Japanese children excel at mathematics, for example, what part of their performance should we attribute to genetically transmitted characteristics and what part to the way they were raised in their culture (Gardner, 1983)? Are the extraordinary navigational abilities of Micronesian sailors, who can cross many miles of ocean from one tiny island to another in small canoes without the aid of a compass, the result of genes or cultural tradition (Gladwin, 1970)? There are no general formulas for determining the relative contributions of culture and genes in shaping such human abilities.

The complex interactions between genetic heritage and the environment begin when genes in the zygote start to express themselves and guide the creation of new cells. Each new human being is a variant within the overall possibilities that define *Homo sapiens*. The next chapter takes up the course of gene-environment interaction from the moment the genetic material of the mother and father come together. In later chapters, we will see instances of gene-environment interactions, with culture playing a mediating role, repeatedly as we consider the development of children.

SUMMARY

1. The particular set of genes each human being inherits comes from the pool of genes that is common to the species. Sexual reproduction rearranges the genetic combinations in each new individual. With the exception of identical twins, every person inherits a unique combination of genes from the common pool, guaranteeing great diversity among people.

2. New body cells are created throughout the life cycle by *mitosis,* a copying process that replicates the genetic material inherited at birth.

3. The germ cells (sperm and ova) that unite at conception are formed by *meiosis,* a process of cell division that maintains a constant total of 46 chromosomes in each new individual.

4. The sexes differ genetically in the composition of one pair of chromosomes. In females, the two chromosomes making up the twenty-third pair are both X chromosomes. In males, there is one X and one Y chromosome.

5. The genes carried by the twenty-third chromosome give rise to sex-linked characteristics. Because females receive two X chromosomes, they get two doses of sex-linked genes, one from each parent. Normal males receive only one X chromosome, and therefore only one dose of sex-linked genes, which always comes from the mother. This leaves men susceptible to a number of genetic defects that usually do not affect females.

6. It is not possible to determine the genetic constitution of individuals from their visible characteristics. This makes it necessary to distinguish an individual's genetic constitution (genotype) from its expression through interaction with the environment (phenotype).

7. The overall relationship between genotype and phenotype can be established only by exposing the genotype to a variety of environments. By charting the changes that occur in the phenotype as the environment is varied, a *range of reaction* can be established. Ideally, such a range specifies all possible phenotypes that are compatible with life for a single genotype.

8. The range of reaction for most human characteristics has not been established because few humans have identical genotypes and because moral precepts and ethical standards make it impossible to carry out investigations that would expose people to dangerous environments.

9. Mutation is the ultimate source of variability in living organisms. In some cases mutations in human beings are compatible with normal life. Often, however, the changes brought about by mutation result in death or cause disorders.

10. The presence of culture provides human beings with a mode of adaptation that other species do not have. Cultural evolution occurs when adaptations arising in one generation are learned by the next.

11. Cultural and biological evolution of human beings have interacted with each other in a process called coevolution, greatly complicating attempts to separate the influences of nature and nurture in development.

KEY TERMS

Allele
Alpha-fetoprotein test
Amniocentesis
Canalized characteristics
Chorionic villus sampling
Chromosome
Coevolution
Complementary genes
Codominance
Crossing over
Dizygotic twins
Dominant allele

Genes
Gene pool
Genotype
Germ cells
Heterozygous
Homozygous
Kinship studies
Masking gene
Meiosis
Mitosis
Modifier gene
Monozygotic twins

Mutation
Phenotype
Polygenic traits
Range of reaction
Recessive allele
Sex-linked characteristics
Somatic cells
X chromosome
Y chromosome
Zygote

SUGGESTED READINGS

JACOB, FRANÇOIS. *The Possible and the Actual*. New York: Pantheon, 1982.

A brief, provocative inquiry into the sources of human diversity that combines philosophical speculation with a discussion of the mechanisms of human evolution.

JENSEN, ARTHUR. *Bias in Mental Testing*. New York: Free Press, 1980.

A leading proponent of the controversial theory that racial groups differ in their innate intelligence makes his case and answers his critics.

LERNER, MICHAEL I., and WILLIAM J. LIBBY. *Evolution, Heredity, and Society*. New York: W. H. Freeman and Company, 1976.

A general introduction to evolutionary theory that provides a thorough discussion of the many tangled issues that make up the nature-nurture controversy. Separate chapters deal with such important topics as natural selection, polygenic inheritance, mutation, population genetics, and the political implications of genetic research.

LEWONTIN, RICHARD C. *Human Diversity*. New York: Scientific American Books, 1982.

An excellent introduction to human genetics by a leading population geneticist. The topics covered range from the mechanisms of hereditary transmission to the historical migrations of whole nations and the intermixing of populations.

PERSAUD, T. V. N. *Problems of Birth Defects: From Hippocrates to Thalidomide and After*. Baltimore: University Park Press, 1977.

A compilation of important articles about birth defects that includes fascinating accounts of beliefs about birth defects throughout history.

PLOMIN, ROBERT. *Developmental Genetics and Psychology*. Hillsdale, N. J.: Erlbaum, 1986.

A major researcher on the genetic foundations of human behavior has written an introduction to this rapidly growing and important area of research on human development. Examples drawn from recent research studies are worked through in detail, helping the reader to gain a firm grasp of such important concepts as heritability and gene-environment interaction.

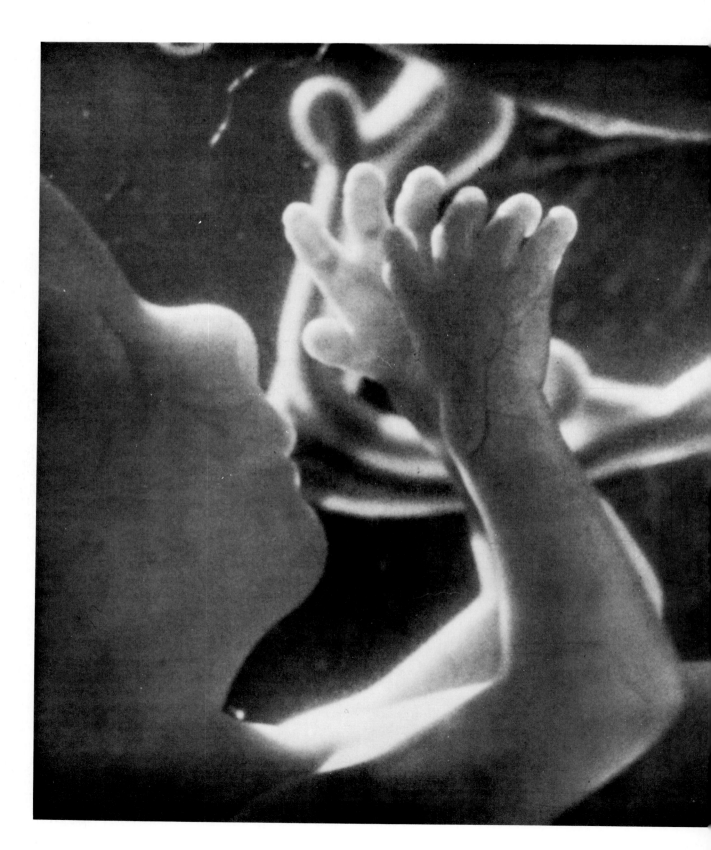

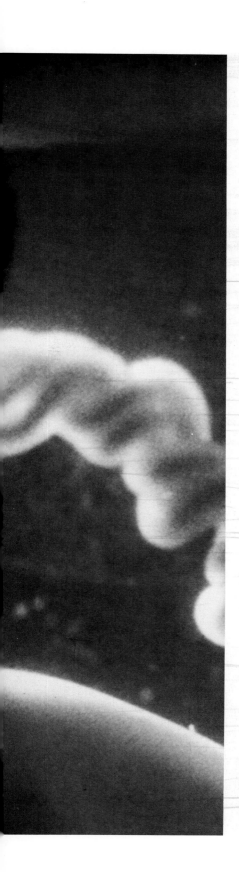

3

...

PRENATAL DEVELOPMENT

Every man is some months older than he bethinks him, for we live, move, have
being, and are subject to the actions of the elements and the malice of disease,
in that other world, the truest Microcosm, the womb of our mother.

—Sir Thomas Browne, *Religio Medici, 1642*

. . . .

Of all our existence, the 9 months we live hidden from view inside our mother's womb are the most eventful for our growth and development. At conception, we begin as a zygote, a single cell $\frac{1}{175}$ of an inch in diameter, about the size of a period on this page, weighing approximately fifteen-millionths of a gram. At birth, we consist of some 2 billion cells and weigh, on the average, 3250 grams, or 7 pounds. The changes that occur

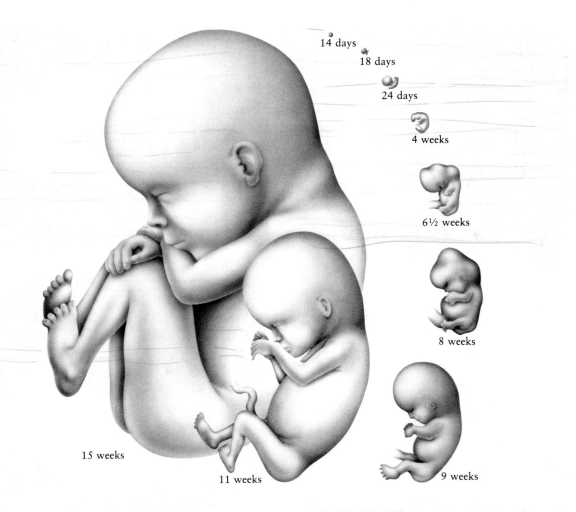

14 days

18 days

24 days

4 weeks

6½ weeks

8 weeks

15 weeks

11 weeks

9 weeks

in our form are no less remarkable than the increase in our size (see Figure 3.1). The first few cells to form from the zygote are all identical, but in a few weeks there will be many different kinds of cells arranged in intricately structured, interdependent organs. A basic task in the study of development is to explain how these prenatal changes in form and size take place.

Many developmental theorists look upon development during the prenatal period as a model for development during all subsequent periods, from birth to death, because many of the principles used to explain development after birth are first seen during the prenatal period. For example, Arnold Gesell (1945), a leading advocate of the biological-maturation perspective,

argued that the changes that occur during the prenatal period demonstrate the overwhelming importance of biological maturation as the basic process of development. In his view, the organism develops without significant shaping by its environment either in the womb or after birth.

Many psychologists who challenge the strong maturational view by proposing a larger role for the environment nonetheless believe that the prenatal period provides a model for later development. Jean Piaget, for example, who championed the view that development is a process of constructive interaction between the organism and the environment, claimed that understanding change in the prenatal period is a key to

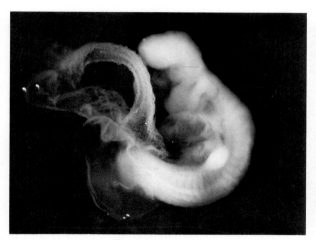

3 weeks

5 weeks

7 weeks

FIGURE 3.1 *Changes in the size and form of the human body from 14 days to 15 weeks. (Adapted from Arey, 1974.)*

understanding development after birth. "[C]hild psychology," he said, "must be regarded as the study of one aspect of embryogenesis [the organism's initial development], the embryogenesis of organic as well as mental growth, up to the beginning of . . . the adult level" (Piaget & Inhelder, 1969, p. vii).

Understanding the prenatal period is important for practical as well as theoretical reasons. The developing organism can be adversely affected by the mother's nutritional status, the state of her health, her drug and alcohol intake, her emotional responses to her situation, and by the surrounding environment. Considerable research has been devoted to understanding how to prevent damage to the growing organism during prenatal development.

In order to understand the relation of prenatal development to later development, we first must look at the changes that take place as the organism progresses from zygote to newborn. Then we can look at how the developing organism can be affected by the environment.

THE PERIODS OF PRENATAL DEVELOPMENT

Through a microscope, the fertilized ovum appears to be made up of small particles inside of larger ones. At the center of the cell, the chromosomes bearing the genes are contained within the nucleus. Surrounding the nucleus is the cell matter, which serves as the raw material for the first few cell divisions. The entire zygote is contained within the **zona pellucida**, a delicate envelope only a few molecules thick that forms its boundary.

No part of the zygote looks like a bone cell or a blood cell, let alone a newborn baby. Yet within the first few weeks following conception, this single cell will have subdivided many times to form many different kinds of cells. In approximately 266 days, it will have been transformed into a wiggling, crying infant. As a first step in trying to understand this process, scientists often divide prenatal development into three broad periods, each characterized by distinctive patterns of growth and interaction between the organism and its environment.

1. The **germinal period** begins when the mother's and father's germ cells are joined at conception and lasts until the developing organism is implanted in the wall of the uterus, about 8 to 10 days later.

2. The **period of the embryo,** which runs from the time of implantation to the end of the eighth week, is when all of the major organs take primitive shape.

3. The **period of the fetus** begins the ninth week after conception with the first signs of the hardening of the bones and continues until birth, an average of 30 weeks. During this period the primitive organ systems develop to the point where the baby can exist outside of the mother without medical support.

At any step in these prenatal periods, the process begun when the sperm penetrates the egg may come to an end. For example, an estimated 31 percent of the time that a sperm and egg unite, the genetic material that comes together proves to be incompatible with life and the zygote fails to develop at all (Wilcox et al., 1988). However, if all goes well at conception, the creation of a new human being is under way.

The Germinal Period

During the first 8 to 10 days following conception, the fertilized ovum moves slowly through the fallopian tube and into the uterus (see Figure 3.2). The timing of this journey is crucial. If the new organism enters the uterus before the chemistry of the uterine environment is conducive to its survival, it will be destroyed. If the new organism arrives too late, the proper uterine conditions for implantation will no longer be present, and it will pass out of the mother's body.

The first cells of life **Cleavage,** the initial mitotic divisions of the zygote into several cells, begins about 24 hours after conception, as the fertilized ovum travels down the fallopian tube. (Mitosis is described in Chapter 2, p. 43.) The single-celled zygote divides to produce two daughter cells, each of which subsequently divides to produce two more daughter cells, and so on (see Figure 3.3). Thanks to this periodic doubling, the developing organism will already consist of hundreds of cells by the time it reaches the uterus.

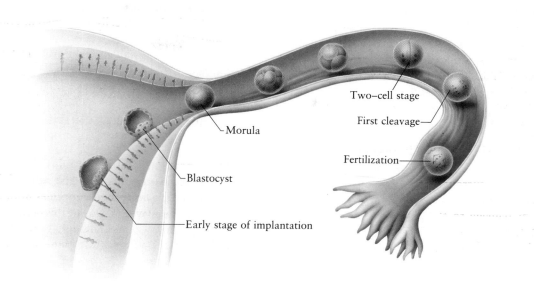

FIGURE 3.2 *Development of the human embryo in the mother's reproductive tract from fertilization to implantation. (Adapted from Tuchmann-Duplessis, David, & Haegel, 1971.)*

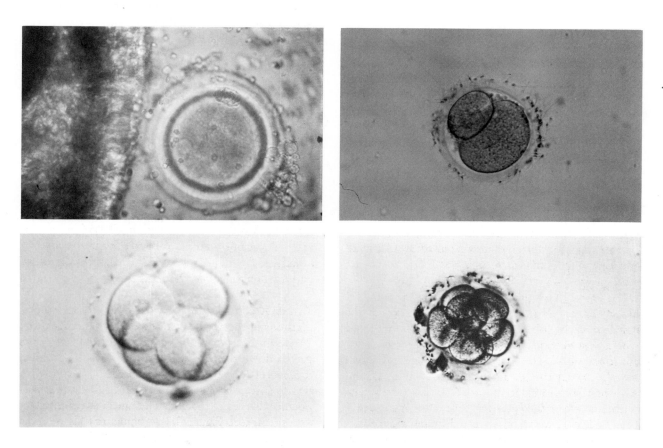

FIGURE 3.3 *The initial cleavages of the developing organism.*

An important characteristic of cleavage is that the cells existing at any given moment do not divide simultaneously. Instead of an orderly progression from a two-cell stage to a four-cell stage and so on, the cells divide at different rates (Austin & Short, 1972). Later in prenatal development and in development after birth, we will see similar instances in which development proceeds at different rates in different parts of an organism.

As the first several cleavages occur, a cluster of cells called the **morula** takes shape inside the zona pellucida. For the first 4 or 5 days following conception, the cells in the morula all look identical under a powerful microscope, much like a large number of Ping-Pong balls crowded into a balloon. The cells produced in each succeeding cleavage are smaller than the previous ones, until they are approximately the size of average adult cells. At this point, the cells must begin to interact with the environment outside the zona pellucida to take in nutrients. If they do not, cleavage will cease and the organism will die.

As the first interactions between the organism and its environment commence, a fluid-filled cavity appears within the morula. In the organism, which is now called the **blastocyst,** two distinct kinds of cells can be distinguished for the first time (see Figure 3.4). These different cells play different roles in development.

Lumped along one side of the central cavity is a knot of small cells called the **inner cell mass.** This mass will give rise to the organism itself. Around the outside of the cavity, a single layer of large, flat cells called the **trophoblast** forms a protective barrier between the inner cell mass and the environment. Later, the trophoblast will develop into the membranes that will protect the developing organism and through which it will be supplied with nutrients. (Appropriately, the term *trophoblast* is derived from the Greek word *trophos,* meaning "to nourish.")

As the cells of the blastocyst differentiate, the zona pellucida surrounding it disintegrates. The trophoblast layer now serves as a kind of pump, filling the inner cavity with energy-giving fluid from the uterus that allows the cells to continue to divide and the organism to grow.

The emergence of new forms With the emergence of the blastocyst, we first encounter one of the great puzzles about development. How can the single-celled zygote develop into different *kinds* of cells, and what causes those cells to arrange themselves into new forms?

During the eighteenth century, the leading scientists of the day favored the **preformationist hypothesis** to explain the development of human forms. It was as-

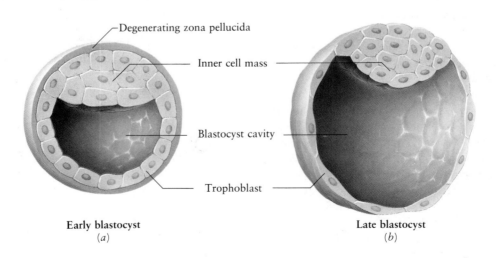

Degenerating zona pellucida

Inner cell mass

Blastocyst cavity

Trophoblast

Early blastocyst
(a)

Late blastocyst
(b)

FIGURE 3.4 *Two stages in the development of the blastocyst: (a) the formation of the inner cell mass in the early blastocyst stage, and (b) the differentiation of the trophoblast cells in the late blastocyst stage. By the late blastocyst stage, the zona pellucida has disappeared. (Adapted from Moore, 1982.)*

sumed that, in some way, adult forms—head, arms, legs, brain, liver, and heart—already exist in the very first cell created at conception. According to this view, no new forms really develop; all are there at the beginning.

Critics of the preformationists argued that a fertilized ovum does not look like a baby, so why claim that it "contains" the baby? They favored the **epigenetic hypothesis** (from the Greek expression meaning "at the time of generation") to explain the emergence of new forms during development. According to this view, later forms are *not* contained within preceding ones. Rather, the new forms emerge through the different kinds of interactions of the preceding forms with the environment.

The epigenetic explanation is now generally favored by embryologists, whose speciality is early organic development (Gottlieb, 1973). At first glance, though, it may not be clear how different kinds of interactions with the environment can explain, say, the emergence of the inner cell mass and the trophoblast from the morula. After all, the cells of the morula are all inside the zona pellucida, which is inside the mother's reproductive tract. How, then, can we say that these cells have differing kinds of contact with the environment?

The answer comes if we think of the environment of each cell individually rather than the environment of the morula as a whole. The cells in the morula do *not* all have the same surroundings, regardless of their location. The cells in the interior of the morula are surrounded by other morula cells. Those on the outside have some contact with other morula cells, but they are also in contact on one side with the zona pellucida, which is in turn in contact with the mother's reproductive tract and its fluids.

As a consequence of their different locations, the morula cells on the inside interact with a different environment than those on the outside. When the morula begins to take in nutrients, the nutrients must pass through the cells on the outside to reach those on the inside. According to this epigenetic explanation, the new forms are not there to begin with; they are assumed to be created in the process of interaction and growth. The result is the emergence of different kinds of cells (Austin & Short, 1972). This pattern of existing forms giving rise to new ones through differing interactions with the environment is repeated again and again throughout human development.

In the nineteenth and early twentieth centuries, preformationism was generally considered to be more appropriate as an object of caricature than as a reasonable scientific position (see Figure 3.5). Currently, however, it is being looked upon more favorably. As Stephen J. Gould (1977a; pp. 205–206) points out, in one respect, "the preformationists were . . . right in insisting that complexity cannot arise from formless raw material—that there must be something within the egg to regulate its development." That "something," however, is not the preformed parts the early preformationists thought were there, but rather, what is now understood to be the coded instructions contained in the genes.

Implantation   As the blastocyst moves further into the uterus, the trophoblast cells put out tiny branches that burrow into the spongy wall of the uterus until they come in contact with the maternal blood vessels. Thus begins implantation, the process by which the

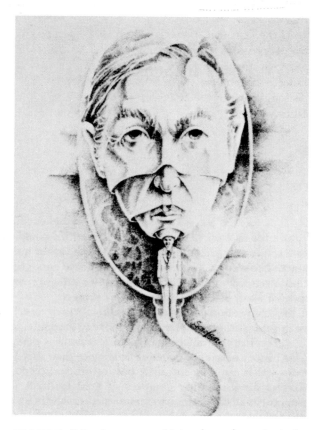

FIGURE 3.5   *A cartoon satirizing the performationist hypothesis.* (Joseph Scrofani, reproduced with permission, from Natural History *Magazine, August-September 1974,* © *The American Museum of Natural History, 1974*).

blastocyst becomes attached to the uterus. Like all of life's transitions (birth being an especially dramatic example), implantation, which marks the transition between the germinal and embryonic periods, is hazardous for the organism. In this case, the danger arises because the blastocyst, being formed from the genes of both the father and the mother, is genetically different from the mother. If, instead of the blastocyst, some other bit of genetically different tissue were introduced into the uterus, it would be rejected by the mother's immune system. But for reasons that are not well understood, the blastocyst is usually not rejected, despite its genetic uniqueness (Austin & Short, 1972).

The Embryonic Period

If implantation is successful, the developing organism enters the period of the embryo, which lasts for about 6 weeks. During this period, all of the basic organs of the body take shape and the organism begins to respond to direct stimulation. Rapid growth is facilitated by the efficient way the mother now supplies nutrition.

Sources of nutrition and protection The rapid growth of membranes from the trophoblast ensures that the requisites for the developing organism's survival — nutrients and protection from environmental trauma — are provided early in the embryonic period (see Figure 3.6). The **amnion,** a thin, tough, transparent membrane that holds the amniotic fluid (bag of water), surrounds the embryo. The amniotic fluid protects the organism from hard surfaces and jolts as the mother moves, provides liquid support for its weak muscles and soft bones, and gives it a medium in which it can move and change positions.

Surrounding the amnion is another membrane, the **chorion,** that becomes the fetal component of the **placenta,** a complex organ made up of tissue from both

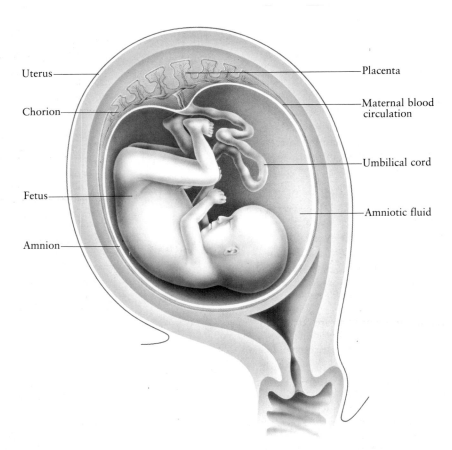

Uterus

Chorion

Fetus

Amnion

Placenta

Maternal blood circulation

Umbilical cord

Amniotic fluid

FIGURE 3.6 *The fetus in its protective environment. (Adapted from Curtis, 1979.)*

the mother and the embryo. The placenta and the embryo are linked by the **umbilical cord.** Until birth, the placenta acts simultaneously as a barrier that prevents the bloodstreams of the mother and infant from coming into direct contact and as a filter that allows nutrients, oxygen, and waste products to be exchanged. It converts nutrients carried by the mother's blood into food for the embryo. It also enables the embryo's waste products to be absorbed by the mother's bloodstream, from which they are eventually extracted by her kidneys. Thus, the mother literally eats, breathes, and urinates for two.

The growth of the embryo While the trophoblast is forming the placenta and the other membranes that will supply and protect the embryo, the growing num-

ber of cells in the inner cell mass begin to differentiate into the various kinds of cells that will eventually become all the organs of the body. The first step in this process is the separation of the inner cell mass into two layers. The **ectoderm,** the outer layer, gives rise to the outer surface of the skin, the nails, part of the teeth, the lens of the eye, the inner ear, and the central nervous system (the brain, the spinal cord, and the nerves). The **endoderm,** the inner layer, develops into the digestive system and the lungs. Shortly after these two layers form, a middle layer, the **mesoderm,** appears that eventually becomes the muscles, the bones, the circulatory system, and the inner layers of the skin (Moore, 1982).

The major events in the development of the embryo are given in Table 3.1. As can be seen from the table,

TABLE 3.1 Embryonic growth and development

Days 10–13 — Cells separate into ectoderm, endoderm, and mesoderm layers. The neural plate, which will eventually become the brain and the spinal cord, forms out of the ectoderm.

Third week — A cylindrical body forms. The neural plate closes except at the ends; it swells out at the brain end and the three major divisions of the brain — the hindbrain, the midbrain, and the forebrain — begin to differentiate by the end of the week. Primitive blood cells and blood vessels are present. The heart fuses into a tube and bends. By the end of the week it is beating; these movements are a property of the heart muscle and not a response to outside stimulation.

Fourth week — The body is flexed in a C shape. Limb buds are visible. Eyes and ears are forming. A digestive system with an esophogus, stomach, intestine, liver, ducts, and gall bladder begins to take form. The major veins are completed and the aorta fuses. Vertebrae are present in primitive form. Nerves begin to take form.

Fifth week — The body is curved and has a prominent tail. The umbilical cord takes shape. Bronchial buds, which will eventually become the lungs, take form. Premuscle masses are present in the head, trunk, and limbs. The hand plates are formed.

Sixth week — Head becomes dominant in size. The lower jaw is fused and the components of the upper jaw are present. The external ear makes its appearance. The limbs are easily recognizable. Pigment is visible in the retina of the eye. The three main parts of the brain are distinct.

Seventh week — The trunk of the body has begun to straighten. The face and neck are beginning to take form. Eyelids take shape. The stomach is taking its final shape and position. The tail has regressed. Muscles are rapidly differentiating throughout the body and are assuming their final shapes and relationships. Neurons are developing at the rate of thousands per minute. The foreward swelling of the brain is very large; it will become the cerebral cortex, the folded grey matter that forms the outside of the brain, as well as some of the brain's internal structures.

Eighth week — The growth of the gut makes the body evenly round. The head is elevated and the neck is distinct. The external, middle, and inner ear assume their final forms. Taste buds begin to form. Lungs become gland-like. By the end of this week the fetus is capable of some movement, and the first indication of ossification of the bones is present.

development takes place at a breathtaking pace. The sequence in which the parts of the body form follows two patterns that are maintained until the organism reaches adolescence. The first of these is the **cephalo-caudal pattern,** which means that development occurs from the head down. For instance, the arm buds appear before the leg buds. The second is the **proximo-distal pattern,** which means that development proceeds from the middle of the organism out to the periphery. For example, the spinal cord develops before the arm buds, the arm develops before the forearm, and the forearm develops before the hand. In general, the process of organ formation is the same for all human embryos, but in one major respect — sexual differentiation — it differs. This aspect of development is discussed in Box 3.1, "The Development of Sexual Differentiation."

The emergence of embryonic movement   When the essential organ systems and the nerve cells of the spine have formed, the embryo becomes capable of its first organized responses to the environment. Studies of embryos as they were being removed from the womb during therapeutic abortions indicate that the 8-week-old embryo will turn its head and neck in response to a light touch to the area around the mouth. Its arms will quiver, the upper body will flex, and in many cases its mouth will open (Hooker, 1952). Within the womb, such movements are not detected by the mother because an 8-week-old embryo is still exceedingly small.

The Fetal Period

The fetal period begins once the basic tissues and organs exist in rudimentary form and the tissue that will become the skeleton begins to harden, or **ossify** (Arey, 1966). During the fetal period, which lasts from the eighth or ninth week of pregnancy until birth, the

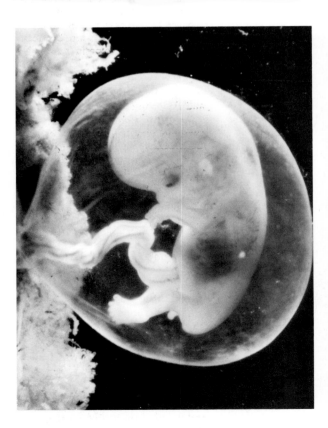 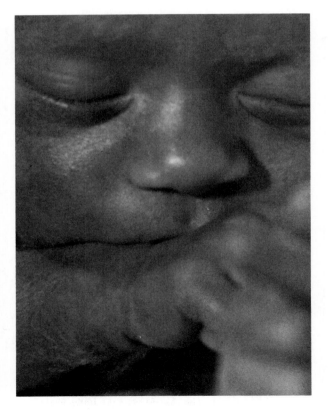

FIGURE 3.7   *Changes in the fetus from the beginning of the fetal period (approximately 9 weeks) to 7 months. The fetus on the left is less than 1 inch long, the one on the right more than 12 inches long.*

fetus becomes 10 times larger and its proportions change dramatically (see Figure 3.7). Each of the organ systems continues to become more complex and coordination of the parts of the body increases. The major events in fetal growth and development are detailed in Table 3.2.

Fetal activity During the fetal period, the marked increase in the complexity of the organism is associated with a change in the level of fetal activity. The fetus begins to move its arms and head. At 10 weeks the fingers will close fleetingly when the palm is stimulated and the toes will curl when the sole of the foot is touched. Over the next few weeks body movements become increasingly varied and smooth. Spontaneous movements begin to combine the jerks and thrusts of the limbs with slower squirming movements of the trunk. Toward the end of the fourth month the fetus is big enough for the mother to feel it moving.

At 17 or 18 weeks following conception, there is a marked decrease in fetal activity as a result of the development of the higher regions of the brain (see

TABLE 3.2 Fetal growth and development

Tenth week — The head is erect. The intestines have assumed their characteristic position within the body. The kidneys are able to secrete fluids. The spinal cord is a definite internal structure.

Twelfth week — The head is still dominant in size. The nose gains a bridge. Males and females are externally distinguishable from one another. Blood begins to form in the bone marrow. The eye takes final form. The fetus is capable of reflex response to being touched, first on the face and then on the body.

End of month 4 — The fetus looks human. Hair begins to appear. The body has grown larger in relation to the head. The kidney attains its final shape and plan. The uterus and vagina are recognizable in females. In males, the testes are in position for later descent into the scrotum. Most of the bones are distinct and the joints appear. The division between the two halves of the brain becomes visible. More reflexes become operational, including swallowing and sucking.

End of month 5 — Brown fat, which will help the newborn stay warm, begins to form. New divisions differentiate within the brain. All of the nerve cells that the person will ever have are present. The sheathing of the nerve fibers begins, but it will not be completed until several years after birth.

End of month 6 — The body is more evenly proportioned. The skin is usually wrinkled and translucent so that the blood in the capillaries is visible. The lungs begin to make surfactin, a chemical compound that prevents the lungs from collapsing. The fissure between the two sides of the brain is very marked.

End of month 7 — The lungs are capable of breathing air, and the central nervous system is sufficiently developed to direct rhythmic breathing movements. Considerable amounts of fat form, smoothing out the fetus' wrinkled skin. The eyes, which have been closed, open and can respond to light. The brain begins to lose its smoothness and to become wrinkled and fissured.

End of month 8 — The fetus's skin is smooth and the arms and legs have a chubby appearance. Many folds of the brain are present, although some will not form until after birth.

Month 9 — The fetus becomes plumper, adding 50 percent of its weight in the last month. As birth approaches, growth slows. The brain becomes considerably more convoluted. Although the fetus has many reflexes and is active, there is no evidence that the cerebral cortex has any influence on behavior yet.

BOX 3.1

THE DEVELOPMENT OF SEXUAL DIFFERENTIATION

•••

Sexual differentiation provides a striking example of the ways in which nature and nurture interact over the course of the organism's development. During the prenatal period, there are several stages of sexual differentiation (see figure). In each stage, a new configuration of the parts present during the preceding stage is created and new mechanisms appear that will regulate sexual development in the following stage (Moore, 1982).

The genetic influence on sexual determination is coded in the X and Y chromosomes inherited at conception. Zygotes with one X and one Y chromosome are *genetically male,* whereas zygotes with two X chromosomes are *genetically female.* For the first 6 weeks following conception, however, there is no physical difference between genetically male and genetically female embryos. Both have two ridges of tissues called *gonadal ridges* in the urogenital region that cannot be distinguished as male or female.

If the embryo is genetically male (XY), the process of sexual differentiation begins during the seventh week of life, when the gonadal ridges begin to form testes. If the embryo does not have a Y chromosome, no changes are apparent until several weeks later, when the ovaries begin to form. Thus, the genes inherited at the moment of conception determine whether the sex glands that develop from the gonadal ridges will be male testes or female ovaries. From this point on, though, it is not the presence of the Y chromosome itself but rather the presence or absence of male gonads that determines whether the embryo will develop male or female genital ducts. The male hormones, principally testosterone, produced by the male gonads determine maleness. Femaleness does not depend on the secretion of hormones by the ovaries, however, but on the absence of testosterone.

Like the gonads, the external genitalia pass through a stage in which it is impossible to tell male from female. At the end of seventh week following conception, genetically male and genetically female embryos have the same urogenital membrane and primitive phallus, the future penis or clitoris. Again, the presence or absence of testosterone determines subsequent differentiation. If testosterone is present, the membranes are transformed into the male penis and scrotum. In its absence, the female external genitalia are formed.

The role of testosterone in sexual differentiation is also evident in other species. If the testes are removed during the early stages of development, further sexual differentiation still occurs, but the embryo develops into a female. If the ovaries are removed, no such reversal occurs; the female genitalia still develop. As many researchers have commented, it appears as though nature requires that something be added in order for the embryo to become masculine (Halpern, 1986).

The influence of testosterone is not limited to the gonads and the genital tract. During the last 6 months of prenatal development, the presence of testosterone suppresses the natural rhythmic activity of the pituitary gland, located in the brain. If testosterone is absent, the pituitary gland establishes the cyclical pattern of hormone secretion that is characteristic of the female and eventually comes to control her menstrual cycle (Wilson, George, & Griffin, 1981).

Embryologists are still uncertain how the presence of testosterone creates differences in brain activity, but data from animal research suggest that it may shape the development of certain neural pathways in the brain (MacLusky & Naftolin, 1981). These studies show that a dose of testosterone given to a rat at a critical period in the development of its brain will cause it to be responsive to male hormones and insensitive to female hormones from then on, no matter what its genetic sex. If the brain does not receive testosterone at this critical period, it will be responsive to female hormones.

The predisposition to sensitivity to male rather than female hormones can apparently have a striking effect on the organism's later behavior. William Young and his colleagues (Young, Goy, & Phoenix, 1964) injected pregnant rhesus monkeys with testosterone. These females later gave birth to female offspring who behaved more like young male monkeys: they threatened other monkeys, failed to withdraw when approached by other monkeys, and played in a rough and tumble way. Their sexual behavior was also masculine in many respects. Other researchers have reported similar findings (Ehrhardt & Meyer-Bahlburg, 1981).

During the prenatal period, the development of sexual differences is under strict biological control that is determined directly or indirectly by the genetic code.

However, the genetic code does not rigidly control the development of sexual identity in later life. Once the baby is born and the parents learn what kind of genitals it has, powerful social, cultural, and psychological factors begin to influence the child's sexual development through a long sequence of interactions between the child and the environments it encounters (MacLusky & Naftolin, 1981; Money & Ehrhardt, 1972).

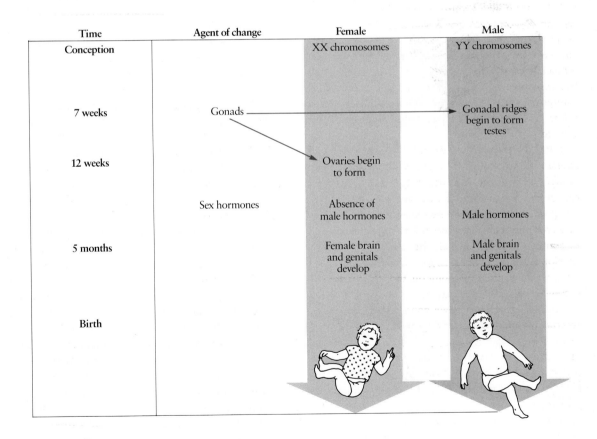

Time	Agent of change	Female	Male
Conception		XX chromosomes	YY chromosomes
7 weeks	Gonads		Gonadal ridges begin to form testes
12 weeks		Ovaries begin to form	
	Sex hormones	Absence of male hormones	Male hormones
5 months		Female brain and genitals develop	Male brain and genitals develop
Birth			

Schematic diagram of the stages of sexual differentiation that occur during prenatal development. (Adapted from Halpern, 1986.)

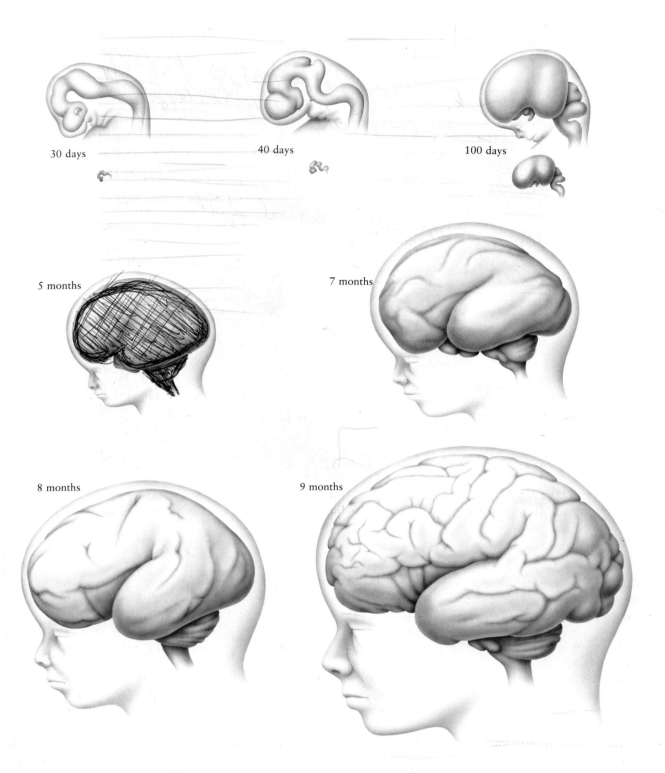

30 days   40 days   100 days

5 months   7 months

8 months   9 months

FIGURE 3.8 *The prenatal development of the brain. The primitive parts of the brain are present very early. The cerebral hemispheres, with their characteristic convolutions, do not make their appearence until the middle of pregnancy. (Adapted from Cowan, 1979.)*

FIGURE 3.9 *The fetus is active and sensitive to changes in its prenatal environment. Many of its activities, such as thumbsucking, foreshadow those that will be commonplace after birth.*

Figure 3.8) that eventually makes more complex control of activity possible (Hofer, 1981). As these brain regions mature, they begin to inhibit the primitive activity of the central nervous system characteristic of the less mature fetus. The thrusting and squirming movements of the fetus subside and it becomes less responsive to stimulation. This period of inhibited activity continues well into the sixth month, at which point the trend toward increasing fetal activity resumes.

As the time of birth draws near, the fetus becomes especially active, moving its limbs, changing its position, even sucking its finger (see Figure 3.9). In some cases, fetal activity appears to be *endogenous,* meaning that it arises directly from the maturation of the organism's tissues. This is the case with the activity of the heart mentioned in Table 3.1. In other cases, it is clearly *exogenous,* meaning that it arises in response to stimulation from the environment, as in a sudden movement of the fetus in response to a loud sound.

Functions of fetal activity Does fetal activity, whether the result of endogenous or exogenous factors, play a significant role in fetal development? Until recently, many embryological theorists answered a resounding "No" to this basic question about prenatal development. Consistent with the views of Gesell and other biologically oriented developmental psychologists, these theorists argued that as long as the genetic material encounters the environmental conditions that trigger its action, the organism develops "according to plan." The embryologist Viktor Hamburger, for example, claims that the structure of the nervous system and the behavior patterns it supports "result from self-generating growth and maturation processes that are determined entirely by inherited, intrinsic factors . . . (1957, p. 56). According to this view, fetal activity has no adaptive value whatsoever for the developing organism; it is simply a by-product of physical growth.

Because life-threatening experimentation on the human fetus is unethical, most of the data on fetal activity Hamburger and others cite in support of their views come from experiments on simple organisms such as *Amblystoma,* a small salamanderlike creature. Leonard Carmichael (1926) found that when a paralyzing substance was put in the water of *Amblystoma* embryos to prevent them from moving, they nonetheless began to move normally at the appropriate age after the substance was removed. Similar experiments with a variety of other simple organisms support the view that fetal activity is not necessary for normal development.

However, when embryos phylogenetically closer to human embryos have been studied, a different picture has emerged. For example, when chick embryos are immobilized using drugs that paralyze their muscles, they remain rigidly immobile even after the drug is removed (Pittman & Oppenheim, 1979). Like *Amblystoma,* their muscles develop normally, but unlike *Amblystoma,* their joints fuse into rigid structures that cannot move.

Other experiments with chick embryos suggest why their embryonic activity may be crucial to normal limb development. Under normal circumstances, the spinal cord sends out many more neurons — nerve cells — to connect the limbs to the brain than will be needed when the animal is fully coordinated. Many of these neurons die off while the remainder are connected to muscles in an efficient way. But the elimination of excess neurons that ordinarily accompanies neuromuscular development fails to occur in chick embryos that have been paralyzed by drugs. The results are disastrous. In as little as 1 or 2 days, the joints of the chick embryos became fixed into rigid structures, indicating that movement is necessary for articulation between the bones to develop (Bradley & Mistretta, 1975).

In sum, experiments with fetuses of other species suggest that fetal activity may be crucial to develop-

ment. However, gathering direct evidence from species similar to *Homo sapiens* has been impossible because such embryos are difficult or impossible to keep alive when their development is interfered with. Great uncertainties about the importance of human fetal activity therefore remain. What is clear, however, is that the fetus is both active and sensitive to its environment.

THE DEVELOPING ORGANISM IN THE PRENATAL ENVIRONMENT

The marvelous ways in which the mother's body provides a protective and supportive environment for the growth of the human fetus can blind us to the realization that even in the womb the fetus is not independent of the larger world. Modern research makes it clear that there are not only significant interactions between the organism and its immediate prenatal environment but between it and the world outside the womb as well.

The fetus can be influenced by its uterine environment in a number of ways. The mother's digestive system and heart are sources of noise, and the mother a source of motion stimuli. The fetus can also be influenced by the environment outside the mother. It not only comes in contact with its mother's surroundings through the wall of her abdomen, it is connected to the external world through the placenta and the umbilical cord. Nutrients, oxygen, some viruses, and some potentially harmful chemicals all cross the placenta to the fetus. Through these biologically mediated routes a mother's experiences, emotions, illnesses, diet, and social circumstances can affect the child prenatally (Hofer 1981).

Understanding the effect of the larger environment on the developing fetus is important for several reasons. First, stimulation coming from the environment may have a significant impact on fetal development. Second, fetal responses to the environment provide clues about the behavioral capacities that will be present at birth. Third, in those cases where the impact of the environment is detrimental to development, it is important for prospective parents to understand the dangers so that they can take preventive action.

The Fetus's Sensory Capacities

Using modern techniques of measurement and recording, researchers have begun to produce a detailed picture of the prenatal development of the human fetus's sensory capacities, which is essential to determining how it is influenced by its environment.

Motion The vestibular system of the middle ear, which controls the sense of balance, begins to function in the human fetus about 4 months following conception and is fully matured at birth (Patten, 1968). This early maturity means that the fetus is capable of sensing changes in the mother's posture as it floats inside the fluid-filled amniotic sac.

The amniotic sac gives the fetus room to move, protection from hard surfaces, and liquid support for its weak muscles and soft bones. The amniotic environment appears to be particularly conducive to fetal development. Researchers have attempted to simulate the "floating" quality of the fetal environment by placing babies born prematurely on a specially constructed waterbed, which was rocked periodically. The premature babies that were placed in waterbeds gained more weight and developed larger, rounder heads than the premature babies that were cared for in ordinary cribs (Kramer & Pierpont, 1976). Apparently, the waterbed supports the premature infant in a manner more like the amniotic sac and therefore offers a more appropriate environment for normal growth processes than normal cribs (Korner, Kraemer, Haffner, & Cosper, 1975; Kramer & Pierpont, 1976).

Vision Anatomical studies show that the visual system develops only partially during the prenatal period. Little is known for certain about the extent of the fetus's visual experience. However, babies born 7 months after conception show changes in brain-wave patterns when a light flashes, which indicates that they may be able to respond to light in the womb. Aidan Macfarlane (1977) suggests that toward the end of pregnancy, the fetus may be able to see light that has penetrated the mother's stretched stomach wall. He likens the fetus's visual experience to the glow seen when the palm of the hand covers a flashlight.

Sound The uterus is a noisy place, auditory analysis suggests. Studies in which tiny microphones have been inserted into the uterus adjacent to the fetus's head reveal that the average sound level is approximately 75

decibels, about the level we experience riding in a car. This background noise is punctuated by the sound of air passing through the mother's stomach and, every second or so, by the more intense sound of the mother's heartbeat (Birnholz & Benacerraf, 1983).

Because noises from the outside world are muted as they pass through the mother's body and the amniotic fluid, only distinct sounds can be discriminated from the normal background noise of the uterus. Mothers sometimes report an increase in fetal activity when they listen to music or there is a loud noise like that of a slammed door. Carefully controlled studies also suggest that the fetus responds to distinctive noises from the outside world. As early as the 1930s, Lester Sontag and Robert Wallace (1935) demonstrated that fetal reactions could be elicited by sounding a tone next to the mother's abdomen. Each time the tone generator was turned on, fetal activity increased and the fetus's heart rate accelerated.

James Grimwade and his associates (1970) added a useful control to the Sontag and Wallace experiment to ensure that the fetal response was to the tone itself rather than to the mother's reaction to the tone. They placed a tone generator on the abdomens of 14 pregnant women who were wearing headphones into which a sound was played constantly. This background noise prevented the women from hearing or feeling the high-frequency tones played by the generator, which precluded the possibility that the women themselves were indirectly causing the fetal reactions. Again fetal activity increased a few seconds after the tone was turned on, confirming the earlier findings that the fetus perceived the sound directly.

Sound consists of vibrations that can be felt by parts of the body other than the ear (an effect well known to devotees of rock music). It is possible that fetuses, immersed in amniotic fluid, may sense these vibrations with parts of their bodies other than their ears. However, recent research shows that the extent of fetal response to auditory stimuli can predict hearing deficits once the baby is born (Birnholz & Benacerraf, 1983). This evidence confirms that, however a fetus experiences sounds from outside the womb, its auditory system is somehow involved.

Fetal Learning

The folklore of many societies includes the belief that fetal experience has a significant effect on postnatal development: whatever the mother desires, fears, or admires, the fetus and then the child will come to desire, fear, or admire (Verny & Kelly, 1981). Although such beliefs have met with considerable skepticism during the twentieth century (Carmichael, 1970), there is evidence that at least some events originating both inside and outside the mother may result in some form of fetal learning.

One line of evidence for fetal learning comes from an unusual experiment by Lee Salk (1973). Working in a hospital where mothers and their newborn infants are customarily separated a good deal of the time, Salk arranged for different groups of infants to hear the sound of a human heart beating at different rates. One group was played the sound of a heart beating at a normal 80 times per minute, the rate they would have heard while in the womb, and another group was played a heart beating 120 times per minute. A third group heard no special sounds at all. The infants who were exposed to the accelerated heartbeat became so upset that Salk terminated their part in the experiment. However, the babies who heard the normal heartbeat gained more weight and cried less during the 4-day course of the experiment than did the group that heard no special sounds. The specific influence of the sound of the normal heartbeat suggests that the infants' prior experience in the womb had made this sound familiar and therefore reassuring. The rewarding nature of the sound of the mother's heartbeat to newborns was later confirmed by DeCasper and Sigafoos (1983).

Salk's experiment suggests that fetuses learn from experiences that originate *inside* the mother. Evidence of similar learning from stimuli originating *outside* the mother comes from a study by Anthony DeCasper and Melanie Spence (1986). DeCasper and Spence asked 12 pregnant women to read aloud a passage from *The Cat in the Hat,* a well-known rhyming children's story by Dr. Seuss, twice a day for the last month and a half before their babies were due. By the time the babies were born, the story had been read to them for a total of about $3\frac{1}{2}$ hours.

Two or three days after the babies were born, DeCasper and Spence tested them using a special pacifier that had been wired to record sucking rates (see Figure 3.10). First, the baby was allowed to suck for 2 minutes to establish a baseline sucking rate. Afterwards, changes in the rate of sucking turned a tape recording of a story on or off. For half the babies, the story was the one their mothers' had read and they had presumably heard many times from within the womb. For the other half, the story was new. The key finding

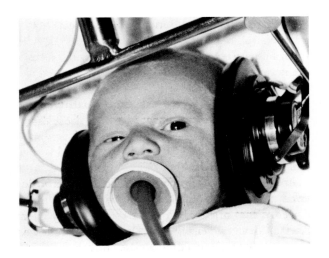

FIGURE 3.10 *This baby is listening to a recording of its mother reading a story. The apparatus permits recordings of changes in sucking to determine if newborns would react to stories read to them while in the womb.*

was that the children modified their rate of sucking when they heard *The Cat In The Hat* but not when they heard the new story. The investigators concluded that the infants had indeed heard the stories being read to them by their mothers and that their learning while in the womb influenced the sounds they found rewarding after birth.

The evidence that some kinds of learning occur in the womb is fascinating. Nevertheless, the demonstration of a baby's greater response to familiar sounds over unfamiliar ones does not in itself support claims that prenatal learning has a significant impact on later development.

Maternal Conditions and Prenatal Development

In addition to influences that impinge directly on its senses, the fetus is also affected by changes in the mother's situation. These influences are related to such factors as the mother's attitude toward having the baby, her emotional state, the food she eats, and her health. They are transmitted to the fetus biochemically through the placenta.

The effects of maternal attitudes and psychological stress Many physicians who care for preg-

nant women and newborn infants suspect that a woman's feelings of well-being and her attitudes toward her pregnancy affect the well-being of the fetus she is carrying and the child after its birth. Having a sympathetic mate (see Box 3.2, "Fathers and Pregnancy") and other family members, adequate housing, and steady employment — that is, having those things that provide a basic sense of security — all appear to influence positively the prospects for a healthy baby (Pritchard & McDonald, 1980).

An extensive investigation conducted in Czechoslovakia in the 1960s and 1970s provides the clearest evidence that negative attitudes can adversely affect prenatal development. Henry David (1981) followed up the lives of 220 children whose mothers indicated strong negative attitudes toward having them by *twice* asking for abortions to end the pregnancy. The refusal of the abortion was an indication that medical authorities believed these women to be capable of carrying through the pregnancy and raising the child.

The children were carefully matched with a control group of children whose mothers either planned for or accepted their pregnancies. The mothers in the two groups were matched for socioeconomic status and age; the children were matched for sex, birth order, number of siblings, and date of birth. In comparison with the control group, the unwanted children weighed less at birth and needed more medical help, even though their mothers had ready access to medical care and were judged to be in good health themselves. After birth, fewer of the unwanted children were breast fed, they had more difficulties in school, and they were referred for psychiatric help more often as teenagers.

Maternal stress can also influence prenatal development. A moderate amount of stress can be expected to accompany any major life transition, which clearly includes pregnancy (Holmes & Holmes, 1969). The expectant mother has to adjust her life to accommodate new responsibilities. A pregnant woman who decides to quit working may have to cope with a reduced income. Another may be working so hard that she feels she does not have enough time to take care of herself, let alone her expected child. And many pregnancies are unplanned, which often magnifies the normal stress that comes with pregnancy.

A number of studies have shown that a mother who is under stress or becomes emotionally upset secretes hormones, such as adrenaline and cortisone, that pass through the placenta and have a measurable effect on the fetus's motor activity. When a woman is under extreme stress for a significant amount of time during her pregnancy, she is at increased risk for such complications as miscarriage, long and painful labor, and premature delivery (Blomberg, 1980; Sameroff & Chandler, 1975). She is also more likely to give birth to a child that is irritable, hyperactive, and has eating, sleeping, and digestive problems (Friedman & Sigman, 1980; Sontag, 1941, 1944).

In the relatively favored circumstances of middle-class life in industrialized countries, many women may experience little stress during pregnancy. However, most of the world's women are poor, live in difficult circumstances, and must worry about how to provide for their child before and after its birth. Even with a sympathetic mate or relatives to ease the burden, stress seems unavoidable under such conditions and is indeed very much a part of a pattern of environmental circumstances that puts many women and their unborn children at risk.

Nutritional influences on prenatal development Babies in utero are totally dependent on their mothers for the nutrients that keep them alive and allow them to develop. Research indicates that a pregnant woman needs to consume at least 2700 calories daily in a well-balanced diet that includes all the essential vitamins and minerals (National Research Council,

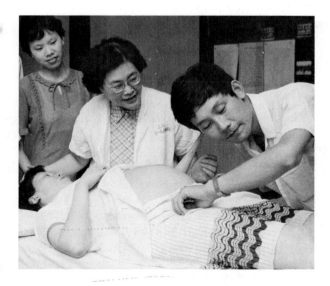

Listening for the fetal heartbeat. A prenatal examination in a Chinese hospital.

BOX 3.2

FATHERS AND PREGNANCY

• • •

"Pregnancy is a family affair," notes psychologist Ross Parke (1981, p. 13). Although it is the mother who undergoes the most profound physical and mental changes as the new organism grows inside her body, fathers can play a significant role during pregnancy. In light of research indicating that maternal stress can have negative effects on prenatal development, special attention has been focused on ways the father can help create favorable conditions for the mother and the baby-to-be.

Among the stress factors that are common during pregnancy, several directly or indirectly involve the father (Blomberg, 1980; Mowbray, Lanir, & Hulce, 1982). These include financial concerns, marital problems, and out-of-wedlock conception. Fathers who deny paternity or refuse to support the mother greatly increase her burden. On the other hand, fathers who are mature, flexible, supportive, and loving can greatly reduce maternal stress.

Harold Rausch and his colleagues report that many men try to react positively to their pregnant wives' needs for emotional as well as financial support (Rausch, Barry, Hertel, & Swain, 1974). The researchers observed the ways expectant couples settled minor disputes, such as deciding what television pro-

gram to watch. Some of these couples had been seen before the woman became pregnant, so the researchers were able to identify the changes in the ways the couple interacted caused by the pregnancy. They found that, generally, the expectant fathers had become more conciliatory than they had been previously. Many expectant fathers also show an increased interest in babies and parenting by taking childbirth and childcare classes with their wives and reading books about pregnancy and child rearing. They may also take on extra jobs to meet the increased financial obligations that come with having a child.

An important way in which the father can reduce both family tension and the mother's work load is to take a larger role in the care of the couple's other children. Many years ago, psychologist Alfred Baldwin (1947) observed that when women who already have children become pregnant, they tend to spend less time with their children and behave less warmly toward them. The father's help with older children not only makes life more pleasant for the mother, but it also sets up a pattern of family interaction that improves the way the older children will react to their new sibling after it is born (Legg, Sherick, & Wadland, 1974).

In some preindustrial cultures, men mark the transi-

1980). The importance of good maternal nutrition to normal prenatal development may seem obvious, but it is often difficult to demonstrate conclusively because maternal malnourishment is closely associated with a host of other factors that can also harm the fetus, such as poor maternal health.

Extreme malnutrition   The clearest evidence that insufficient maternal nutrition has a detrimental effect on fetal development comes from studies of sudden periods of famine. For example, during the fall and winter of 1944–1945, famine occurred in the large cities of western Holland. The famine was the result of an embargo imposed by the Nazi occupation forces

because Dutch railway workers had gone on strike to aid the advancing Allied armies. During and after the famine, spontaneous abortions, stillbirths, malformations, and deaths at birth increased markedly. For those babies who were born alive, birth weight was significantly lower than normal, as can be seen in Figure 3.11 (Stein, Susser, Saenger, & Marolla, 1975).

A more severe wartime famine occurred in the Soviet Union. In September of 1941, Leningrad was encircled by the German army, and no supplies were brought into the city until February of 1942. The standard daily ration during this period was 500 grams of bread made with poor quality rye flour, cellulose, and malt. The number of infants born in the first half of

tion to fatherhood with special rituals called *couvade* that are variously intended to deflect evil spirits that might harm the mother and baby and to establish paternity (Parke, 1981). As soon as the husbands hear that their wives are in labor, they take to their beds, where they simulate the agony of labor and birth. During the last century, for example, it was reported that when a woman of the Erickala-Vandu, a tribe in Southern India, went into labor

> [S]he informs her husband who immediately takes some of her clothes, puts them on, places on his forehead the mark the women usually place on theirs, retires into a dark room where there is only a dim lamp, and lies down on the bed, covering himself with a long cloth. When the child is born, it is washed and placed on a cot beside the father.
>
> (Cain, 1874, quoted in Parke, 1981, p. 15)

Expectant fathers in modern industrialized societies do not practice such formalized rituals as couvade. Still, an estimated 15 to 20 percent experience what British psychiatrist W. H. Trethowan and his colleague M. F. Conlon call the *couvade syndrome*: a set of physical symptoms that mimic some of those of the initial stages of pregnancy, including fatigue, backache, headache, loss of appetite, nausea, and vomiting (Trethowan & Conlon, 1965; Liebenberg, 1967). These physical symptoms are often accompanied by such psychological problems as depression, tension, insomnia, and irrita-

bility. All the symptoms disappear almost immediately after the mother gives birth.

Data collected by Bittman and Zalk (1978) show how difficult it can be for expectant couples to deal with pregnancy and the new responsibilities of parenthood. As a case in point, Bittman and Zalk describe Mr. A., a 28-year-old factory worker. Mr. A. described his wife's pregnancy of 7 months as "model." However, he admitted that he had been experiencing a great deal of physical discomfort from nausea, vomiting, alternating diarrhea and constipation, head and back pains, and leg cramps. In the course of the interview, he revealed that his wife felt that their apartment was too small for three people but was also concerned about the financial burden of a larger one. Because of worries about his ability to provide for the baby, Mr. A. was working overtime at a factory job he hated. The extra work meant that he did not get home until after ten o'clock in the evening, by which time his wife was usually exhausted and often asleep. Although his wife understood that the overtime would help pay for the baby furniture she wanted, she was unhappy about being left home alone. She complained bitterly, accused Mr. A. of not loving her, and turned away from his embraces. According to Bittman and Zalk, Mr. A. may be an extreme case, especially with regard to the physical symptoms he suffered, but his worries about being able to provide for his child and the conflicts and stresses he and his wife faced in adjusting to their impending parenthood are not at all unusual.

1942 was much lower than normal, and the incidence of stillbirths was double. Very few infants were born in the second half of 1942, all of them to women who had better access to food than did the rest of the population. These babies were, on the average, more than 500 grams lighter than babies born before the siege, and they were much more likely to be premature. They were also in very poor condition at birth; they had low vitality and were unable to maintain their body temperature adequately (Antonov, 1947).

The sudden famine in Leningrad produced nutritional variations so extreme that normal environmental influences on prenatal development were dwarfed by comparison. Consequently, the specific effects on

the developing fetus of maternal malnutrition during particular segments of the prenatal period could be isolated with a high degree of certainty. Severe nutritional deprivation during the first 3 months of pregnancy was most likely to result in abnormalities of the central nervous system, premature birth, and death. Deprivation during the last 3 months of pregnancy was more likely to retard fetal growth and result in low birth weights.

Undernourishment and associated factors Studies of the relation between maternal nutrition, prenatal development, and neonatal health suggest that lesser degrees of malnourishment also increase risks to the

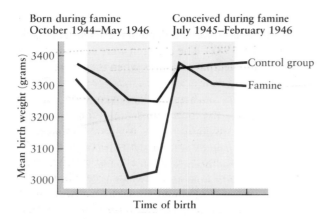

FIGURE 3.11 *Birth weight for children conceived or born in Rotterdam, Holland during a period of severe famine compared with birth weights for children from other parts of the country where conditions were less severe. (Adapted from Stein et al., 1975.)*

fetus. However, it is difficult to single out the effects of poor nutrition alone because malnourished mothers frequently live in impoverished environments where housing, sanitation, education, and medical care are all also inadequate (Evans, Moodie, & Hansen, 1971; Hurley, 1980) (Table 3.3 illustrates just how important prenatal care can be for low-income mothers and their children.) Expectant mothers with low incomes are more likely than women who live in materially more comfortable circumstances to suffer from diseases or simply to be in a weakened state. Their babies are more likely to suffer from a wide variety of birth defects and illnesses and to be born prematurely (Cravioto, De Licardie, & Birch, 1966). Low-income mothers are also more likely to have babies who die at birth or in the period immediately following birth, according to a variety of studies conducted in many parts of the world, including the United States (Dott & Fort, 1975a, 1975b; Macfarlane, 1977; Moore, Origel, Key, & Resnik, 1986).

Not all undernourishment results from food not being available. Research in both industrialized and nonindustrial societies demonstrates that cultural factors also play an important role in determining what foods expectant mothers eat. The Siriono of South America, for example, believe that the characteristics

of any animal a woman eats while pregnant will be transferred to her unborn child. Pregnant women are therefore not allowed to eat the meat of the owl monkey because their children might develop the tendency to stay awake at night. Jaguar meat is also forbidden for fear that the child will be "quietly born" (stillborn). In some societies, the banning of foods extends to staples, including meat, eggs, fish, and milk, which can lead to significant reductions in essential protein in the mother's diet and thereby put the unborn child at risk (Mead & Newton, 1967).

In the United States, food choices differ even among people from the same social class. One study comparing the health of babies born to low-income, rural women classified as having either "fair to good" or "poor to very poor" dietary habits found that expectant mothers who ate more nutritious food had markedly healthier babies (Jeans, Smith, & Stearns, 1955).

The possibility of preventing or at least reducing the damaging effects of malnutrition and impoverished environments has been demonstrated by several studies. The basic design of this type of research is to

TABLE 3.3 **Birth complications and prenatal medical care for low-income women in San Diego, California (per 100 births)**

Complication	Women Who Receive No Prenatal Care	Women Who Receive Prenatal Care
Premature rupture of membranes	13	2
Ominous fetal heart rate	10	5
Prematurity	13	2
Low birth weight (less than 2500 grams)	21	6
Low Apgar score (a measure of immediate risk)	8	2
Hospital stay more than 3 days	24	12
Prenatal death	4	1

SOURCE: Moore, Origel, Key, & Resnick, 1986.

compare expectant mothers and their offspring who receive supplemental food and medical attention with those who do not. One of these studies examined the effects of a massive supplemental food program for women, infants, and children — appropriately dubbed *WIC* — that was initiated by the U. S. government in 1972 (Kotelchuck, Schwartz, Anderka, & Finison, 1984). Low-income women in the program were given vouchers for such staples as milk, eggs, fruit juices, and dried beans. When infants born to mothers in the program were compared with infants born to mothers not in the program but otherwise matched with respect to age, race, education, and other factors, the program infants had significantly fewer health problems.

Similar findings resulted from a study of 1083 children born in a poor, rural area of Guatemala (Klein et al., 1976). The investigators found that giving calorie supplements to the poorer pregnant women of the population studied reduced the incidence of low birth weights among their babies from 18 percent to 9 percent. This study also underlined the close association between poverty and the need for nutritional supplements. Giving food supplements to the pregnant women from the better-off families in the area did not reduce the incidence of low birth weights among their babies; such cases were already rare.

Several studies indicate that maternal nutrition is important to the intellectual development as well as the physical health of the child (Kopp, 1983; Kopp & Parmalee, 1979). The basic findings of these studies are as follows:

- Many experiments with mammals other than humans point to brain size at birth as a strong predictor of the ease with which the organism learns, retains, and uses new information.

- Although the association is not strong, better-fed mothers have heavier babies with bigger brains.

- Although intellectual deficits are not invariably associated with maternal undernourishment, it is primarily the children of poor mothers who are at risk (Kopp, 1983).

In a study of children whose mothers had participated in the WIC program in Louisiana, marked differences in the intellectual development of the children were found depending on when their mothers began receiving food supplements (Hicks, Langham, & Takenaka, 1982). The children were evaluated on a variety of intellectual measures when they were 6 or 7 years of age and were already enrolled in school. Those children whose mothers had received food supplements during the last three months of their pregnancies — the period when the fetal brain undergoes especially rapid development — outperformed the children of mothers who did not receive food supplements until after their children were born.

As important as adequate maternal nutrition is to the growth of the fetus, the long-term effects of prenatal malnutrition are also heavily influenced by the adequacy of the child's diet after birth. The most devastating consequences befall prenatally malnourished children who live in economically impoverished conditions where nutrition remains inadequate (Cravioto, De Licardie, & Birch, 1966). Such children are subject to continued health problems as well as deficits in intellectual functioning.

The importance of postnatal care for determining the long-term consequences of prenatal undernourishment has been emphasized in a longitudinal study by Philip Zeskind and Craig Ramey (1978, 1981). These researchers note that children who are born malnourished are often apathetic and unresponsive and become irritable when stimulated. These characteristics make the babies unpleasant to interact with, a situation that can only intensify their already severe problems.

Zeskind and Ramey conducted an experiment in which 10 fetally malnourished children 3 months old were assigned at random to two postnatal treatment groups. In one group, the children received nutritional supplements and health care. In the other group, the children participated in a special day-care program in which they were not only provided with nutritional supplements and health care but were also taught basic language, cognitive, and social skills. At the start of the experiment, the two groups were indistinguishable with respect to indices of health and development. During the course of the experiment, however, the children in the special day-care program showed increases in their cognitive and social skills at a normal rate, whereas the children who received only supplemental food and medical care fell further and further behind the norms for their age. An important ancillary finding of this study was that the mothers of the day-care children became more and more responsive to their children over the course of the study, whereas the mothers of the other children became less responsive.

The results of Zeskind and Ramey's study make clear the desperate situation of the millions of children throughout the world who experience both prenatal and postnatal malnutrition. Most of these children do not receive food supplements, and even fewer receive high-quality educational help. Quite the opposite. The evidence points to a cascade of risk factors, in which malnutrition is associated with the lack of sanitary facilities, the lack of medical care, and the lack of educational opportunities (see Figure 3.12). The cumulative consequences of these conditions are high rates of infant mortality and short life expectancies (Kopp, 1983).

Teratogens: Environmental Sources of Birth Defects

Another source of threats to the prenatal organism are teratogens — environmental agents that can cause deviations in normal development that can lead to serious abnormalities or death. (The term comes from the Greek word *teras*, meaning "monster.") Common teratogens include drugs, infections, radiation, and pollution.

Drugs Pregnant women in the United States take an average of four drugs, excluding nutritional supplements and vitamins but including prescription drugs and such nonperscription drugs as aspirin, diuretics, and antihistamines (Golbus, 1980). Some of the drugs

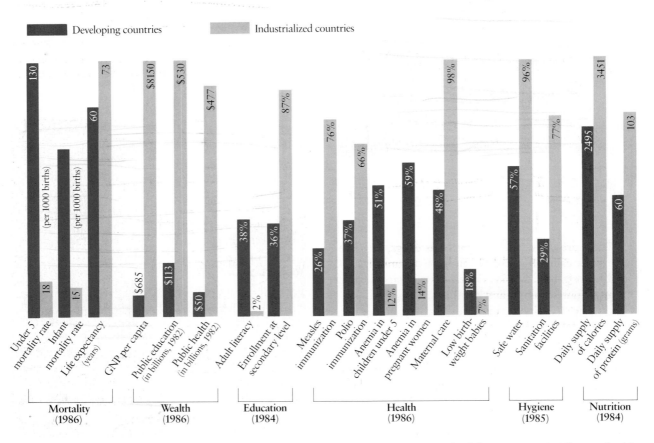

FIGURE 3.12 *In many countries of the world, poor economic conditions create a set of risk factors. For example, poor health conditions and lack of parents' education negatively influence child health and welfare. (Adapted from United Nations Children's Fund (UNICEF), 1987.)*

FIGURE 3.13 *The devastating effects of the drug thalidomide can be partially overcome by extensive training.*

they take are often not thought of as drugs, as is the case with caffeine, alcohol, and the chemical substances in cigarette smoke. Caffeine is not known to be harmful, but smoking and drinking alcoholic beverages have been shown to have a variety of adverse effects on fetal development.

Prescription and nonprescription drugs From 1956 until 1961, the prescription drug thalidomide was used in Europe as a sedative and to control nausea in the early stages of pregnancy. The women who took the drug were themselves unharmed by it, and many of them gave birth to children who suffered no ill effects. Some, however, had children who were born without arms and legs; their hands and feet were attached directly to their torsos like flippers (see Figure 3.13).

There were defects of sight and hearing, as well. About 8000 children were deformed by the drug before its effects were discovered and it was removed from the market (Persaud, 1977).

Since the disastrous effects of thalidomide were discovered, a number of other prescription drugs have been found to cause abnormalities in the developing organism, including the antibiotics streptomycin and tetracycline, anticoagulants, anticonvulsants, most artificial hormones, Thorazine (a drug used in the treatment of schizophrenia), and Valium (a tranquilizer). In large doses, aspirin can also cause abnormalities. Indeed, all drugs are capable of entering the bloodstream of the developing organism and only a few have been studied well enough to determine whether they are "safe" for expectant mothers. Therefore, pregnant women are advised to check with their physician before taking any nonprescription drugs, and physicians are advised to prescribe only the most necessary therapeutic drugs for their pregnant patients.

Smoking Smoking by pregnant women is not known to produce birth defects, but according to a British study of 150,000 births, mothers who smoke have a 28

This pregnant woman is putting her unborn child at risk for low birth weight and other complications.

TABLE 3.4 **Mean birth weights at various gestations in smokers and nonsmokers**

Maturity (weeks)	Mean Birth Weight (grams)		
		Cigarettes per Day	
	Nonsmokers	1–20	Over 20
31	2624	2415	1887
34	2798	2615	2488
37	3007	2848	2816
40	3341	3189	3188
43	3438	3274	3346

SOURCE: Naeye, 1978.

percent higher rate of stillbirths and deaths at birth than do women who do not smoke (Bolton, 1983). Smoking is also associated with lower birth weights (see Table 3.4). This effect appears to be specific to smoking during the pregnancy since mothers who smoke during one pregnancy and not during another have smaller babies from the pregnancies during which they smoke (Bolton, 1983).

Alcohol Alcohol is the most commonly abused drug, and about 2 percent of all women of childbearing age suffer from alcoholism (Golbus, 1980). Infants born to mothers who are heavy drinkers during pregnancy — that is, who have five or more drinks a day — have a 30 percent chance of suffering from *fetal alcohol syndrome*, a set of symptoms that includes abnormally small heads and underdeveloped brains, eye abnormalities, congenital heart disease, joint anomalies, and malformations of the face (see Figure 3.14). The physical growth and mental development of children with this syndrome are likely to be retarded throughout childhood (Hanson, Streissguth, & Smith, 1978). Women who drink heavily during the first trimester of pregnancy and then reduce their consumption of alcohol during the second and third trimesters do *not* reduce their risk of having children with this affliction (Vorhees & Mollnow, 1986).

The effects of alcohol on prenatal development depend on how much is consumed. However, even moderate consumption is believed to affect adversely prenatal development; drinking as little as two glasses of red wine daily during pregnancy is considered to place the fetus at risk (Bolton, 1983). For this reason, health

professionals advise women to stop drinking before they become pregnant.

Methadone and heroin Babies of mothers who are addicted to either heroin or methadone are born addicted themselves and must be given drugs shortly after birth if they are not to undergo withdrawal, which is often life-threatening. These babies are more likely to be premature, underweight, and vulnerable to respiratory illnesses. They are twice as likely to die following birth as are babies whose mothers come from the same socioeconomic class but who are not addicted (Bolton, 1983; Ostrea & Chavez, 1979).

While the addicted babies are being weaned from the drugs, they are irritable and have tremors, their cries are abnormal, their sleep is disturbed, and their motor control is impaired. Studies have found that the effects of the addiction are still apparent in their motor

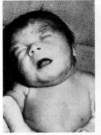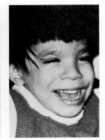
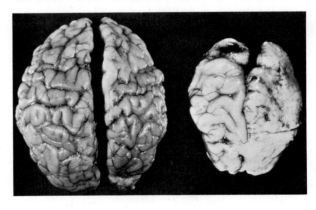

FIGURE 3.14 *Children suffering from fetal alcohol syndrome do not just look different; their brains are also underdeveloped, often resulting in severe retardation. The boy pictured here at birth, at 8 months, and at 4½ years had profoundly lower intelligence-test scores than normal. The picture of another child's brain who suffers from fetal alcohol syndrome, compared to the brain of a normal child, shows that characteristic convolutions have failed to develop.*

control 4 months later. Even at 1 year of age, they are not as able to pay attention as are babies who were not prenatally exposed to narcotics (Vorhees & Mollnow, 1986).

Infections   A variety of infection-causing microorganisms can endanger the embryo and the fetus. Most infections spread from the mother to the unborn child across the placental barrier. In a few instances, however, the baby may be infected directly when passing through the birth canal. Table 3.5 summarizes the effects of some of the more common maternal infections that may affect the developing human organism.

Rubella   In 1941 Dr. N. M. Gregg, an Australian opthomologist, noticed a sudden increase in the number of infants who were born blind. He interviewed their mothers and found that many of them recalled having had a mild rash, swollen lymph glands, and a low fever —all symptoms of *rubella,* or German measles — early in their pregnancies. Based on his findings, Gregg wrote an article suggesting that there might be some connection between the rubella epidemic of the summer of 1940 and the subsequent increase in the number of babies who were born blind that alerted the medical community to this danger for the first time (Gregg, 1941). Subsequently, researchers have found that rubella causes developmental defects in more than 50 percent of all babies born to mothers who suffer from the disease during the first months of pregnancy (Stevenson, 1977). Infection during the first 3 months of pregnancy often results in a syndrome of congenital heart disease, cataracts, deafness, and mental retardation. Infection during the second 3 months may lead to mental and motor retardation and to deafness. A rubella epidemic in the United States during the winter of 1964–1965 resulted in 30,000 stillbirths and 20,000 infants who suffered congenital defects (LaVigne, 1982).

The development of a vaccine for rubella in 1969 has greatly reduced the incidence of the disease, but it has not been eradicated. After receiving the vaccine, women are advised to avoid becoming pregnant for at least 6 months. In a few states, testing for immunity to rubella is available as part of the blood test given before a marriage license is issued.

Acquired Immune Deficiency Syndrome (AIDS) Transmission of the AIDS virus from the mother to her baby may occur either by the virus passing through the

placental barrier or through the exposure of the baby to the mother's infected blood during delivery (Weber, Redfield, & Lemon, 1986). The odds that a mother carrying the AIDS virus will transmit it to her baby or that a child thus infected will develop the disease are presently unknown. There is no known cure for AIDS, which invariably leads to death.

Rh incompatibility   Rh is a complex substance on the surface of the red blood cells. One of the components of Rh is determined by a dominant gene. People who have this component are said to be *Rh* positive. Less than one in five people inherit the recessive form of the gene, which makes them *Rh negative.* When an Rh-negative woman conceives a child with an Rh-positive man, the child is likely to be Rh positive. During the birth of the baby, some of its blood cells usually pass into the mother's bloodstream while the placenta is separating from the uterine wall. The mother's immune system creates antibodies to fight this foreign substance, and the antibodies stay in her bloodstream.

The first pregnancy of an Rh-negative mother with an Rh-positive child is usually normal because the baby is born before the mother has developed antibodies in her blood. However, if the mother again becomes pregnant with an Rh-positive child, the antibodies in her blood from the birth of the first child will pass into its bloodstream, where they will attack and destroy its red blood cells. This results in *Rh disease,* a complication that can lead to serious birth defects or even death. Fortunately, Rh disease can be prevented by giving the Rh-negative mother an injection of anti-Rh serum within 72 hours of the delivery of an Rh-positive child. The serum kills any Rh-positive blood cells in the mother's bloodstream so that she will not develop antibodies to them. Children who are born with Rh disease can be treated with periodic blood transfusions (Moore, 1982).

Radiation   Massive doses of radiation often lead to serious malformations of the developing organism and in many cases cause prenatal death or spontaneous abortion (Moore, 1982). Somewhat lesser doses may spare the life of the organism, but they may have a profound effect on its further development. These dangers were made tragically evident following the atomic blasts at Hiroshima and Nagasaki in 1945. Many of the pregnant women who were within 1500 meters of the blasts but survived later lost their babies.

TABLE 3.5   Maternal diseases and conditions that may affect prenatal development

Sexually Transmitted Diseases		*Other Diseases and Maternal Conditions (continued)*	
Gonorrhea	The gonococcus organism may attack the eyes while the baby is passing through the infected birth canal. Silver nitrate eye drops are administered immediately after birth to prevent blindness.	Diabetes	Diabetic mothers face a greater risk of having a stillborn child or one who dies shortly after birth. Babies of diabetics are often very large because of the accumulation of fat during the third trimester. Diabetic mothers require special care to prevent these problems.
Herpes simplex (genital herpes)	Infection with herpes simplex usually occurs at birth as the baby comes in contact with herpes lesions on the mother's genitals, although the virus may also cross the placental barrier to infect the fetus. Infection can lead to blindness and serious brain damage. There is no cure for the disease. Mothers with active genital herpes often have a cesarean delivery to avoid infecting their babies.	Hepatitis	Mothers who have hepatitis while giving birth are likely to pass it on to their newborn.
		Hyper-tension	Hypertension (chronic high blood pressure) increases the probability of miscarriage and infant death.
Syphilis	Before the twenty-first week of pregnancy, the syphilis spirochete cannot penetrate the placental membrane. The effects of syphilis on the fetus can be devastating. Stillbirth occurs an estimated one-fourth of the time. Deafness, mental retardation, and deformations may occur in those who survive. Syphilis can be diagnosed by a blood test and can be cured before the fetus is affected.	Influenza	The more virulent forms of influenza may lead to spontaneous abortion or may cause a number of abnormalities during the early stages of pregnancy.
		Mumps	Mumps are suspected of causing spontaneous abortions in the first trimester of pregnancy.
		Rubella	See text.
		Rh disease	See text.
Acquired Immune Deficiency Syndrome (AIDS)	See text.	Toxemia	About 5 percent of pregnant women in the United States are affected during the third trimester by this disorder of unknown origin. Most commonly occurring during first pregnancies, the condition mainly affects the mother. Symptoms are water retention, high blood pressure, rapid weight gain, and protein in urine. If untreated, toxemia may cause convulsions, coma, and even death in the mother. Death of the fetus is not uncommon when a mother suffers from this condition.
Other Diseases and Maternal Conditions			
Chicken pox	Chicken pox may lead to spontaneous abortion or premature delivery, but it does not appear to cause malformations.		
Cytomegalo-virus	The most common source of prenatal infection, cytomegalovirus produces no symptoms in adults, but it may be fatal to the embryo. Infection later in intrauterine life has been related to brain damage, deafness, blindness, and cerebral palsy (a motor coordination defect caused by brain damage).	Toxo-plasmosis	A mild disease in adults with symptoms similar to those of the common cold, toxoplasmosis is caused by a parasite that is present in raw meat and cat feces. It may cause spontaneous abortion or death. Babies who survive may have serious eye or brain damage.

SOURCES: Moore, 1982; Stevenson, 1977.

Of those babies that appeared to be normal at birth, 64 percent were later diagnosed as mentally retarded. The effects of radiation on the organism's developing central nervous system were found to be greatest during the eighth through the fifteenth week of the prenatal period, a time of rapid proliferation of the cortical neurons (Vorhees & Mollar, 1986). In cases in which the gonads receive doses of radiation, the germ cells may be affected, causing possible genetic damage to subsequent generations (Tuchmann-Duplessis, 1975).

The effects of low doses of radiation on human beings have not been firmly established. Because they may cause malformations in prenatal development, however, physicians are likely to be cautious about x-raying pregnant women.

Pollution   Most of the thousands of chemicals that are used in food, cosmetic, and industrial production have never been tested to see if they are harmful to prenatal development, although a number of these substances reach the organism through the placenta (Ames, 1979). Certain herbicides and pesticides have been shown to be harmful or, in some cases, fatal to unborn rats, mice, rabbits, and chicks. Several pollutants in the atmosphere and in the water we drink also appear to be teratogenic if exposure to them is great. Moreover, some of the effects are cumulative as concentrations of the chemicals build up in the body.

In 1953 it was discovered that the consumption of large quantities of fish from Minimata Bay in Japan was associated with a series of symptoms that have come to be known as *Minimata disease*. The symptoms include cerebral palsy (a central nervous system disorder), deformation of the skull and, in some cases, abnormally small heads. The bay was polluted by mercury from waste discharged into the Minimata river from nearby industrial plants. The mercury passed in increasingly concentrated amounts through the food chain from the fish to, among others, pregnant women and from them to their unborn babies. Minimata disease has since become a synonymous term for mercury poisoning (Tuchmann-Duplessis, 1975).

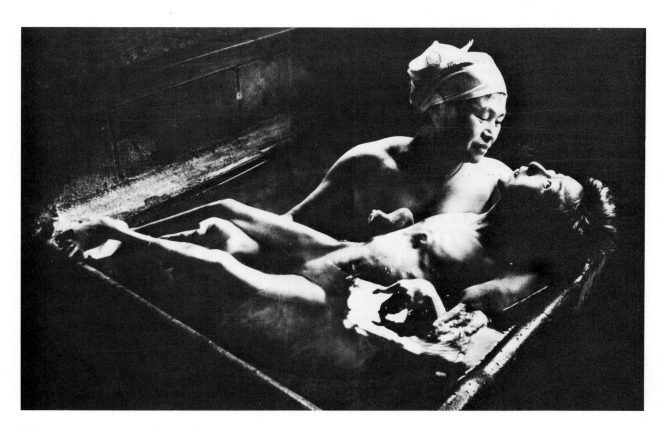

The tragic consequences of prenatal mercury poisoning.

The incidence of birth defects is also known to be abnormally high in areas of heavy atmospheric pollution. In the Brazilian industrial city of Cubata, for instance, the air pollution from petrochemical and steel plants exceeds that generated by all the combined industries in the Los Angeles Basin of California. In Cubata, 65 out of every 1000 babies die of a birth defect in which the brain fails to develop, double the rate for neighboring communities that are not as heavily polluted (Freed, 1983).

Atmospheric pollution in such U. S. cities as Los Angeles, Elizabeth (New Jersey), Chicago, and Denver is not as high as that in Cubata, but it is still high enough to cause concern about its effects on prenatal development. Similarly, what are the risks to pregnant women and their unborn children who live near chemical dumps? What should a pregnant woman do to minimize these risks? More research is necessary in order to answer such questions.

Principles of teratogenic effects   Although different teratogens affect the developing organism in different ways, there are several general principles that apply to their effects on prenatal development (Moore, 1982; Tuchmann-Duplessis 1975).

- *The susceptibility of a developing organism to a teratogenic agent varies with the developmental stage the organism is in at the time of exposure* Overall, the gravest danger to life is during the first 2 weeks, before the cells of the organism have undergone extensive differentiation (see Figure 3.15). During this critical period, a teratogenic agent may completely destroy the organism. Once the different body systems have begun to form, each is most vulnerable at the time of its initial growth spurt. For example, as can be seen in Figure 3.15, the most vulnerable period for the central nervous system is from 15 to 36 days whereas that for the upper and lower limbs is from 24 to 49 days.

- *Each teratogenic agent acts in a specific way on specific developing tissue and therefore causes a particular pattern of abnormal development.* Thalidomide, for example, causes deformation of the legs and arms, and mercury compounds cause brain damage that leads to cerebral palsy.

- *Not every organism will be equally affected by a given amount of exposure to a particular teratogen.* The way a developing organism responds to teratogenic agents depends to some degree on its genotype and the genotype of its mother. Less than one-quarter of the pregnant women who used thalidomide during the period when the organism's limbs were forming gave birth to malformed babies.

- *Susceptibility to teratogenic agents depends on the physiological state of the mother.* The mother's age, nutrition, uterine condition, and hormonal balance all affect the action of teratogens on the developing organism. The risk of malformations is highest in teenage mothers and those who are over 40. The precise reason for these differences isn't known. Maternal nutritional deficiencies intensify the adverse effects of certain teratogens. The impact of teratogens also appears to increase if the mother suffers from diabetes, toxemia, metabolic imbalances, or liver dysfunction, among other disorders.

- *In general, the greater the concentration of the teratogenic agents to which the organism has been exposed, the greater the risk of abnormal development.*

- *Levels of teratogens that can produce defects in the developing organism may affect the mother only mildly or not at all.* A number of diseases and several drugs that have little or only a temporary effect on the mother can lead to serious abnormalities in the developing organism.

PRENATAL DEVELOPMENT RECONSIDERED

As noted in the introduction to this chapter, the prenatal period is viewed by many developmental psychologists as a model for all subsequent development because many of the principles used to explain prenatal development are the same as those used to explain development after birth. In closing this chapter, it is therefore worthwhile to review these explanatory principles as they apply to the prenatal period.

- *Sequence is important.* There must be one cell before there are two. There must be muscles and bones before nerves can coordinate movement. Gonads must secrete testosterone before further sexual differentiation can occur.

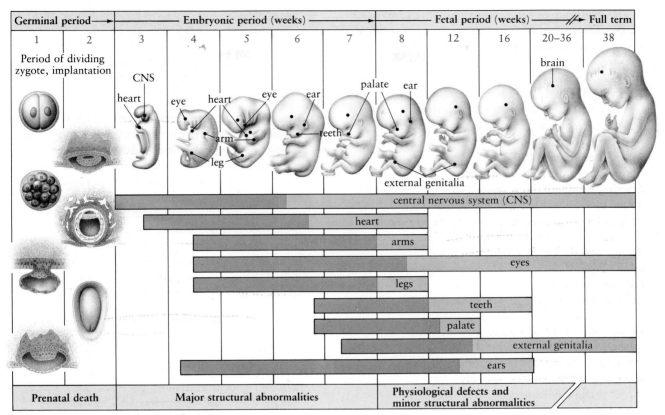

Germinal period→ | Embryonic period (weeks) | Fetal period (weeks) ──//→ Full term

Prenatal death | Major structural abnormalities | Physiological defects and minor structural abnormalities

• Indicates common site of action of teratogen

FIGURE 3.15 *Schematic illustration of the critical periods in human prenatal development when the organs and other body parts are forming and are therefore most vulnerable to teratogens. Before implantation, teratogens either damage all or most of the cells of the organism, resulting in its death, or they damage only a few cells, allowing the organism to recover without developing defects. The dark red portions of the bars represent periods of highest risk of major structural abnormalities; the pink portions of the bars represent periods of reduced sensitivity to teratogens. (Adapted from Moore, 1982.)*

- *Timing is important.* If the ovum moves too rapidly or too slowly down the fallopian tube, pregnancy is terminated. If thalidomide is encountered after the first 3 months, the fetus is unlikely to be affected, but if it is encountered during the first 2 to 3 months of pregnancy, it may have a disastrous effect on the organism. The importance of timing implies the existence of critical periods for the formation of basic organ systems.

- *Development consists of differentiation and integration.* The single cell of the zygote becomes the many, apparently identical cells of the morula. These cells then differentiate into two distinct kinds of cells, which are later integrated into a new configuration of cells called the blastocyst.

- *The course of development implies stages.* Discontinuities in the form of the organism and in the ways that it interacts with its environment suggest that development is characterized by a series of stage-like transformations. The embryo not only looks entirely different than the blastocyst, but it also interacts with its environment in a different way.

- *Development proceeds unevenly.* From the earliest steps of cleavage, different subsystems that make up the organism do not develop at the same rate. An important special case of such unevenness is physical development, which is cephalocaudal (from head to foot) and proximodistal (from the center of the organism to the periphery).

- *Regressions appear to occur during the course of development.* Although development generally progresses through time, there are also periods of apparent regression. Regressions often occur during periods of reorganization, such as when fetal activity decreases when the higher regions of the brain are beginning to become active.

- *Development is still a mystery.* The process by which the human organism develops from a single cell into a squalling newborn baby continues to mystify science. In one sense, the results of development are present at the beginning, coded in the genetic materials of the zygote, which constrain the kinds of forms that can emerge in the interactions between the organism and its environment. In this sense, the preformationist hypothesis is valid. But,

in a second sense, new forms are constantly emerging in the organism-environment interactions that sustain and propel development. Organism and environment are each the sea in which the other swims. In this sense, the epigenetic hypothesis is confirmed.

Following birth, the environmental circumstances of the organism will change dramatically. No longer will food and oxygen be filtered through the mother's body. The infant will be enveloped in a larger world. Parents who have tended indirectly to an unknown being will begin to relate to their child face to face. Despite these momentous changes, the basic principles of prenatal development will, in somewhat different form, be important for understanding the mechanisms of postnatal developmental change.

SUMMARY

1. Many developmental theorists look upon the prenatal period as a model for all periods of development from conception to death.

2. Prenatal development is often divided into three broad periods:
    a. The germinal period, when the zygote moves into the uterus and become implanted.
    b. The period of the embryo, which begins with implantation and ends with the first signs of ossification at the end of the eighth week. During this period the basic organs are formed.
    c. The period of the fetus, during which there is especially extensive growth of the brain and integration of the separate organ systems.

3. The growth of the organism from a single cell to a full-term, newborn child is characterized by the constant emergence of new forms. The preformationist hypothesis holds that all forms are already present in the organism's first cells. The epigenetic hypothesis emphasizes that different interactions between the cells and their environment generate the emergence of new forms.

4. At implantation, the organism becomes directly dependent on the mother's body for sustenance.

5. The embryo becomes active with the first pulses of a primitive heart, beginning about 1 month following conception.

6. The fetus is subject to environmental influences originating from outside as well as inside the mother. Outside influences are sometimes experienced directly by the fetus through its own sensory mechanisms, but often they exert their influences indirectly through their effects on the mother.

7. Fetuses appear to be capable of learning, as is indicated by their reactions following birth to events they first experienced while still in the womb.

8. The mother's reaction to her environment in the form of feelings and attitudes is associated with fetal well-being. Children born to mothers who do not want them or who are under stress are subject to developmental risk.

9. The nutritional status of the mother is an important factor in fetal development. Extreme maternal malnutrition has a devastating effect on reproduction. Lesser degrees of malnourishment associated with other forms of environmental deprivation also increase risks to fetal and postnatal development.

10. Teratogens (environmental agents that can cause deviations in fetal development) come from many sources. Drugs, infections, radiation, and pollution all pose threats to the developing organism.

11. There are several basic principles that apply to the effects of teratogens:
    a. Susceptibility varies according to the developmental stage of the organism.
    b. Teratogenic effects are likely to be specific to a particular organ.
    c. There is individual variation in susceptibility.
    d. The physiological state of the mother influences the impact of a teratogen.
    e. The greater the concentration of a teratogenic agent, the greater the risk.
    f. Teratogens that adversely affect the developing organism may affect the mother little or not at all.

KEY TERMS

Amnion
Blastocyst
Cephalocaudal pattern
Chorion
Cleavage
Ectoderm
Endoderm
Epigenetic hypothesis

Germinal period
Implantation
Inner cell mass
Mesoderm
Morula
Neurons
Ossify
Period of the embryo

Period of the fetus
Placenta
Preformationist hypothesis
Proximodistal pattern
Teratogens
Trophoblast
Umbilical cord
Zona pellucida

SUGGESTED READINGS

GESELL, ARNOLD. *The Embryology of Behavior.* New York: Harper & Row, 1945.

Although somewhat dated, Gesell's book provides an excellent introduction to the view that *all* of human development can be thought of as the embryology of behavior.

GOULD, STEPHEN J. "On Heroes and Fools in Science." *Ever Since Darwin.* New York: Norton, 1977.

In this lucid essay, Gould discusses the history of the preformationist and epigenetic theories of prenatal development and shows how knowledge of modern genetics is blurring the lines between them.

GUTTMACHER, ALAN F. *Pregnancy, Birth, and Family Planning.* Revised and updated by I. H. Kaiser. New York: Signet, 1984.

A prominent expert on conception and family planning provides a detailed account of pregnancy.

HURLEY, LUCILLE S. *Developmental Nutrition.* Englewood Cliffs, N.J.: Prentice-Hall, 1980.

A readable summary of the way that maternal nutrition influences the development of the fetus.

NILSSON, LENNART. *A Child Is Born: The Drama of Life before Birth.* With text by A. Ingelman-Sundberg and C. Wirsen. New York: Dell, 1981.

A collection of stunning photographs documenting prenatal development.

WALTERS, WILLIAM A. W., and PETER SINGER. *Test-Tube Babies.* New York: Oxford University Press, 1982.

This book explains the process of in vitro fertilization that allows a woman to bear children even though her fallopian tubes are obstructed, making natural fertilization impossible. In addition, the book contains a discussion of the controversial subject of surrogate motherhood, in which one woman agrees to bear a child for another woman who cannot bear children herself.

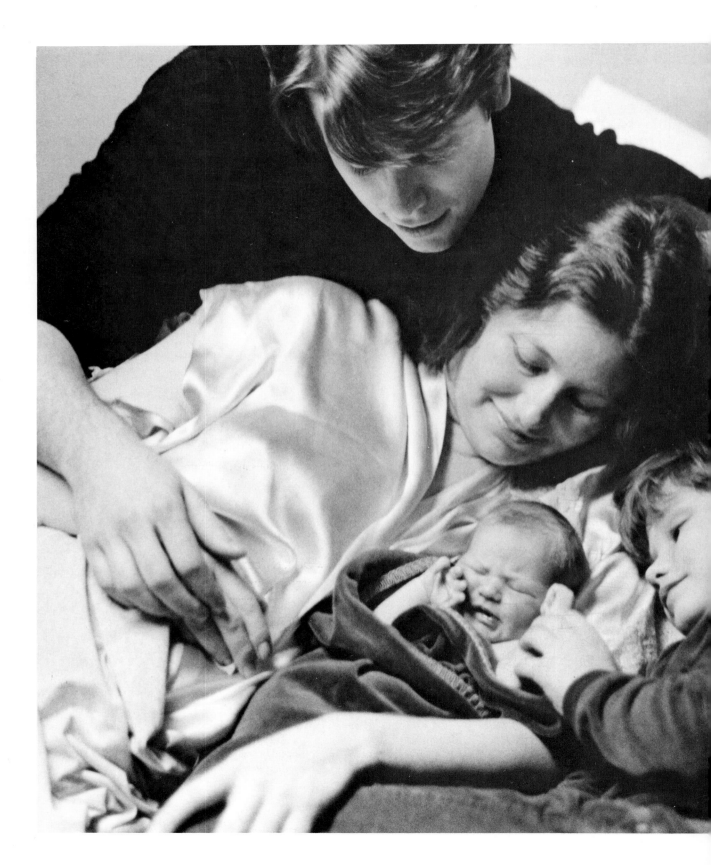

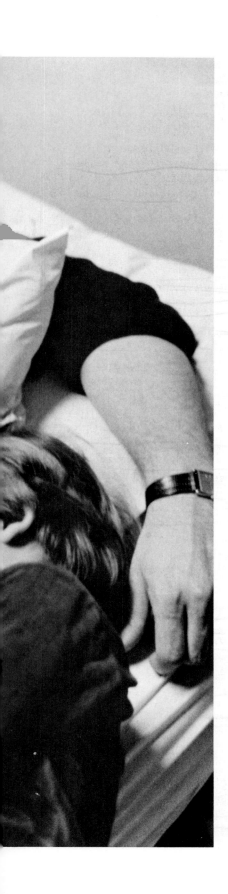

BIRTH: STARTING LIFE ON THE OUTSIDE

. . . there at the foot of the bed, in the deft hands of Lizaveta Petrovna, like a flickering

light in a lamp, lay the life of a human creature, which had never existed before, and which

would now with the same right, with the same importance to itself, live and create in its

own image. . . . In the midst of the silence . . . a voice quite unlike the subdued voices

speaking in the room [was heard]. It was the bold, clamorous self-assertive squall of the

new human being, who had so incomprehensibly appeared.

—Leo Tolstoy, *Anna Karenina*

. . . .

Among all of life's transitions, birth is the most dramatic. Before birth, the amniotic fluid provides a wet, warm environment and the fetus receives continuous oxygen and nourishment through the umbilical cord. The environment outside the womb that greets the newborn is dry and cold by contrast. When the umbilical cord is cut and tied, the automatic supply of oxygen and nourishment comes to an abrupt halt. The lungs inflate to take in oxygen and exhale carbon dioxide for the first time, which changes the pressure within the baby's circulatory system and causes the blood flow to reverse direction. Nourishment now comes only intermittently, and it must be worked for by sucking. The baby no longer has even the partial protection of the placenta against disease-causing organisms.

The social and behavioral changes that occur at birth are no less pronounced than the biological ones, marking it as the first major bio-social-behavioral shift in human development. The newborn encounters other human beings directly for the first time, and the parents get their first glimpse of their child. From the moment of birth neonates and parents begin to construct a social relationship. If babies are to survive, they must be actively cared for in ways that require changes in their parents' previous routines. To thrive, they should be accepted and loved. Parents bring to the task of child rearing the experience of years of participation in a larger social group and some knowledge of the child-rearing practices of their culture. Neonates, for their part, come into the world with remarkable sensory and behavioral capacities for perceiving and responding to their new environment.

This chapter begins with the transition to postnatal life, with special focus on childbirth practices in the United States. Next, the baby's earliest capacities will be described. Understanding these are of considerable practical importance because they provide the means of assessing whether the baby has come through the

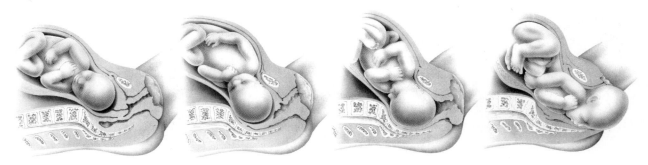

FIGURE 4.1 *During the first stage of labor, which usually lasts several hours, the cervix dilates. During the second stage, the birth canal widens, permitting the baby to emerge. The final stage (not shown) occurs when the placenta is delivered. (Adapted from Clarke-Stewart, 1983.)*

arduous birth process in a healthy state. They are also of theoretical importance because the baby's initial state must be known in order to answer fundamental questions about development. What aspects of a child's later characteristics are continuous with those present at birth? Which aspects of children's later characteristics are laid down by their genetic heritage and their experience in the womb? What difference will variations in the child's environment make in the future course of its development? Lastly, we will take a look at the initial relationship between parent and child.

GIVING BIRTH

The biological process of birth begins with a series of changes in the mother's body that forces the fetus through the birth canal. It ends when the mother expels the placenta after the baby has emerged. If all goes well, a healthy child enters the world to be greeted by its parents.

The Stages of Labor

Labor normally begins approximately 280 days after the first day of a woman's last menstrual period, or 266 days after conception. It is customarily divided into three overlapping stages (see Figure 4.1).

The *first stage of labor* lasts from the first regular, intense contractions of the uterus until the cervix, the opening of the uterus into the vagina, is fully dilated and the connections between the bones of the pelvis become more flexible. The length of this stage varies from woman to woman and from pregnancy to pregnancy: it may last anywhere from less than an hour to several days. The norm for first births is about 14 hours (Niswander, 1981). At the beginning, the muscle contractions come 15 to 20 minutes apart and last anywhere from 15 to 60 seconds. As labor proceeds, the contractions become more frequent, more intense, and are longer in duration.

Once the cervix is fully dilated, the baby's head, which is flexible because all of the bones of the skull have not yet fused, pushes through the cervix into the vagina, beginning the *second stage of labor*. The contractions now usually come no more than a minute apart and last about a minute. The pressure of the baby and the powerful contractions of the uterus typically cause the mother to bear down and push the baby out. Usually, the top of the baby's head and the brow are the first to emerge. Once the head has cleared the vaginal opening, the shoulders rotate and the head turns to the side. The top shoulder emerges next, and then the rest of the body quickly slides out. Occasionally, babies emerge in other positions, the most common being the *breech position*, in which the feet or buttocks come first.

The final, *third stage of labor* occurs as the baby is born. The uterus contracts around its diminished contents. The placenta buckles and separates from the uterine wall, pulling the other fetal membranes with it. Contractions quickly expel them, and they are delivered as the *afterbirth*.

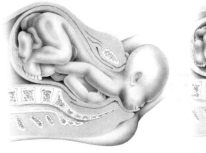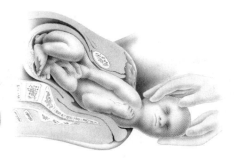

Cultural Variations in Childbirth

As a biological process, labor occurs in roughly the same way everywhere. The *experience* of giving birth, however, varies with the traditions of different cultures (see Figure 4.2). These traditions provide the mother and the community with a prescribed set of procedures to follow during birthing and a set of expectations about how they are going to feel (Mead & Newton, 1967).

In a few societies, giving birth is treated as a natural process that requires no special preparation. Consider, for example, the following description of birth among the !Kung, a hunting and gathering society in Africa's Kalahari desert:

> Mother's stomach grew very large. The first labor pains came at night and stayed with her until dawn. That morning, everyone went gathering. Mother and I stayed behind. We sat together for a while, then I went and played with the other children. Later, I came back and ate the nuts she had cracked for me. She got up and started to get ready. I said, "Mommy, let's go to the water well, I'm thirsty." She said, "Uhn, uhn, I'm going to gather some mongongo nuts." I told the children that I was going and we left; there were no other adults around.
>
> We walked a short way, then she sat down by the base of a large nehn tree, leaned back against it, and little Kumsa was born. . . .
>
> (Shostak, 1981, pp. 53–54)

Such unassisted birthing is relatively rare. A far more common pattern is to have several attendants present for labor and delivery. Often, a special house is built for childbearing. In Japan, in earlier periods, a special birth hut was built either by the family or the village; in our culture, most women give birth in a hospital. Special practices, such as having the woman lie in a particular posture while giving birth or keeping the laboring woman's husband and other children away, are used to see the mother and baby through the dangerous transition.

In many cultures, the specialists who assist the mother are called doctors, although there is wide variation in what people believe medicine to be. The Cuna Indians of Panama regard childbirth as an illness. The expectant mother makes daily visits to the medicine man throughout her pregnancy, and she receives constant medication during labor (Stout, 1947).

The Ngoni women of East Africa consider themselves to be the childbirth experts, and men are totally excluded from the process. The women even conceal the fact that they are pregnant from their husbands as long as they can. "Men are little children. They are not able to hear those things which belong to pregnancy," the women claim (Read, 1960/1968, p. 20). When the mother-in-law in an Ngoni village learns that her daughter-in-law's labor has begun, she and other female kin move into the woman's hut, banish the husband, and take charge of the preparations. They remove everything that belongs to the husband—clothes, tools, and weapons—and all the household belongings except old mats and pots to be used during labor. Men are not allowed back into the hut until after the baby is born.

Some cultures treat childbirth as a social event. The Navaho living in the southwestern United States 50 years ago, for example, opened their homes to the whole community when a child was being born. An anthropologist working among them at the time reported that "Anyone who comes and lends moral sup-

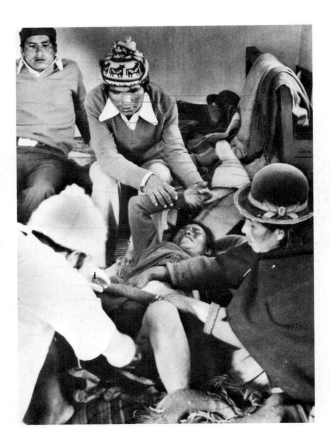

port is invited to stay and partake of what food is available" (quoted in Mead & Newton, 1967, p. 171).

Childbirth in the United States

In the United States today, most babies are born in a hospital, a place people go when they are sick. This emphasis on the medical aspects of childbirth represents a marked shift in cultural practices over the past century. In the nineteenth century, most births took place at home, attended only by a midwife, a woman recognized for her experience in assisting childbirth. By the middle of the twentieth century, 86 percent of all babies were born in hospitals and 95 percent were delivered by a physician (Gordon & Haire, 1981). Underlying this shift from home to hospital were two developments. First, many of drugs were developed to relieve the pain of childbirth; by law, these could be administered only by physicians. Second, hospitals became better equipped to provide both antiseptic surroundings and specialized help in case complications arose during labor and delivery (Ciafrani, 1960).

The lives of thousands of babies and mothers are saved each year by the intervention of doctors using modern drugs and special medical procedures. In 1915, approximately 100 out of every 1000 births resulted in the death of the baby within a year, and in almost 7 out of every 1000 births, the mother died. By 1985, infant deaths had been reduced to less than 11 out of every 1000 born (see Figure 4.3). In the same year, only 1 woman out of every 10,000 who gave birth in the United States died of causes related to pregnancy, childbirth, or after-birth complications (National Center for Health Statistics, 1987).

Nevertheless, in recent decades there has been much debate within the health care professions and among prospective parents about problems arising from medical intervention during normal, uncomplicated births (United States Congress, Senate Committee on Human Resources Research, 1978). These debates center on two questions: (1) What is the safest method for dealing with pain during childbirth? (2) What precautions are necessary to ensure the health of the mother and the baby?

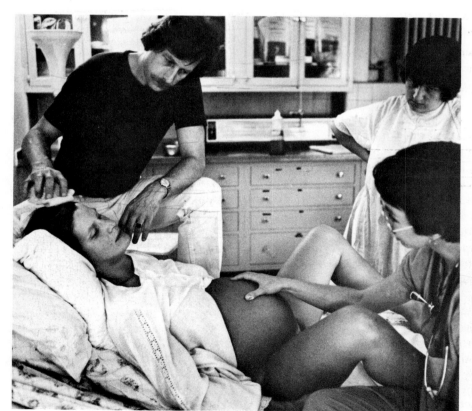

FIGURE 4.2 *Despite many differences in the particular circumstances of childbirth, in almost every culture the mother and child are helped through this difficult transition by others. The experience of childbirth, however, is quite different in, for example, a hut high in the Andes compared to that in a well-equipped U.S. hospital.*

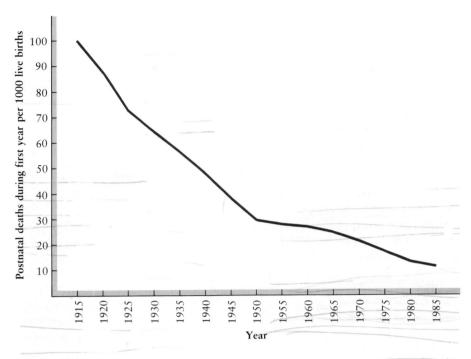

FIGURE 4.3 *During this century the death rate among children under 1 year of age has dropped dramatically in the United States.*

Childbirth pain and its medication The first medical technique used to reduce the pain of childbirth was to administer chloroform to women during labor (Cianfrani, 1960). When James Young Simpson, a Scottish physician, began using this technique in 1847, several clergymen objected. Citing Genesis 3:16, "in sorrow thou shalt bring forth children," they argued that childbirth should be painful. They were joined in their opposition by some physicians who questioned both the necessity and the safety of anesthetizing women during childbirth. Most of these objections were overridden, however, when England's Queen Victoria was given chloroform during the birth of her eighth child, Prince Leopold, and afterward announced her approval of the method.

Since the Victorian era, many different drugs have been used to lessen the pain of labor and delivery. These include anesthetics (which dull feeling), analgesics (which reduce the perception of pain), and sedatives (which relax the mother). Although there are no national data on the current use of drugs during childbirth, a 1974 poll of 18 large teaching hospitals in the United States found that almost 95 percent of the births in these institutions took place under some form of medication (Brackbill, 1979).

Recently, evidence has begun to mount that the drugs administered to the mother to control the pain of labor affect the baby when they pass through the placental barrier and enter the fetus's bloodstream (Abboud, Khoo, Miller, Doan, & Henriksen, 1982). These drugs tend to reduce the mother's oxygen intake and blood pressure, which in turn reduces the supply of oxygen to the fetus and may cause the baby to have breathing difficulties after birth. The baby's immature liver and kidneys are unable to rid the body of these drugs efficiently, allowing some of them to lodge in the neonate's brain (Wilson, 1977).

Obstetric medications are seldom life-threatening for healthy, full-term babies. But those drugs that have been tested have been found to affect neonatal behavior. The babies of mothers who receive one or another of a variety of drugs during labor and delivery are less

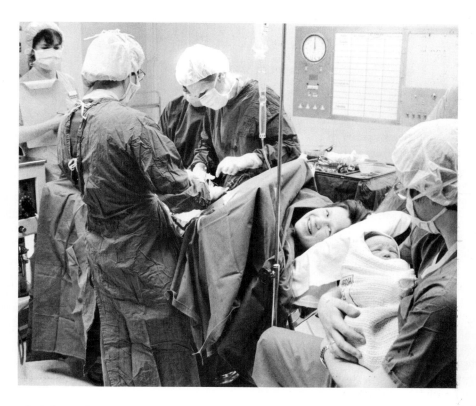

The baby in this picture has just been delivered by Cesarean section.

attentive, more irritable, have poorer muscle tone, and are weaker than those whose mothers do not receive medication (Aleksandrowicz, 1974; Brackbill, 1979; Sepkoski, 1985). The vigor of the newborn infant's sucking response has also been found to be reduced by some obstetric drugs (Brazelton, 1973). As one might imagine, the extent of these effects varies with the kind of drug, the strength of the dosage, and the point during labor when it is administered (Brackbill, McManus, & Woodward, 1985; Lester, Als, & Brazelton, 1982).

The evidence that obstetric drugs affect the neonate has caused concern that they may have long-term effects on the child's development. Yvonne Brackbill and her colleagues claim, for example, that the heavy use of drugs during birth is implicated in a high incidence of learning disorders among U. S. school children (Brackbill, McManus, & Woodward, 1985). Most of the existing evidence indicates, however, that low levels of medication do not significantly affect healthy babies. It is only when substantial levels of medication are used in births of babies who are at risk for other reasons that medication may have longer-term effects (Brazelton, Nugent, & Lester, 1987).

Because of their concern about the possible adverse side effects of drugs on the neonate, many women in the United States and Western Europe are seeking alternative methods of controlling the pain of labor. Box 4.1, "Prepared Childbirth," discusses the most prominent of these methods.

Medical interventions during childbirth In addition to administering drugs to ease the pain of labor, doctors may use a number of medical procedures to safeguard the lives of mother and child. One common practice when the baby is significantly overdue or when the mother is confronted with some life-threatening situation is to *induce labor,* either by rupturing the membranes of the placenta or by giving the mother some form of the hormone oxytocin. Another commonly used procedure is *cesarean section,* in which the

BOX 4.1

PREPARED CHILDBIRTH

• • •

Among the most widely used methods to control the pain of labor without drugs is **prepared childbirth**—special training in which pregnant women learn about the process of labor and are taught various techniques intended to reduce the sensation of pain. Two competing schools of thought about pain reduction underlie the techniques usually taught:

The Dick-Read Approach   In *Childbirth without Fear*, English obstetrician Grantley Dick-Read (1933, p. 131) argues that the *natural* state of childbirth is painless: "There is no physiological function in the body that gives rise to pain in the normal course of health." In Dick-Read's view, women experience pain during childbirth because fear and tension disrupt the normal interactions among the crucial muscles involved. He proposed that women be prepared for labor by teaching them about its physiological mechanisms and by instructing them in a series of exercise and breathing techniques to help them relax.

The Lamaze Approach   In 1951 Fernand Lamaze, a French physician, attended an obstetrical confer-

ence in Leningrad, where he saw women give birth apparently painlessly without medication. Soviet researchers had developed a method of childbirth training based not on the idea that labor was naturally painless but on the idea that the experience of pain could be blocked. According to the researchers, an expectant mother can learn to control voluntarily her breathing and attention and to relax her muscles during labor. This reorganizes her brain activity and thereby blocks the incoming signals from the pain receptors in the areas affected by labor and delivery. Lamaze's version of the method was imported to the United States a few years later, where it is often called the *Lamaze method* (Lamaze, 1970).

Despite their differences, both approaches agree that the woman in labor requires the constant support and help of those around her to carry out the required activities. They recommend that she not be left alone. Someone—her physician, a midwife, her husband, or a friend—should be constantly at her side to provide emotional comfort, monitor her labor, encourage her

baby is surgically removed from the mother's uterus. This procedure is typically used in cases of difficult labor, when the baby is in distress during delivery, or when the baby is in other than a head-first position. The use of cesarean section grew in popularity during the 1970s, and by the end of that decade it accounted for 10 to 15 percent of the deliveries at many hospitals (Brackbill, 1979).

Although modern medical techniques have made childbirth a great deal safer than it was in the past, some medical personnel claim that they are used more often than they should be (United States Congress, Senate Committee on Human Resources Research, 1978). These critics argue, for example, that many of the cesarean operations performed in the United States are unnecessary. Furthermore, these operations raise the cost of childbirth, expose the mother to the risk of postoperative infection, and cause mothers to be sepa-

rated from their infants while they heal from surgery. They may also change babies' conditions at birth in ways that are detrimental to their well-being (see Box 4.2, "The Baby's Experience of Birth"). Concerns about unnecessary medical intervention also extend to other procedures, such as induced labor and the electronic monitoring of the vital signs of the fetus during labor.

THE BABY'S CONDITION

To first-time parents, especially those who imagine that newborn infants look like those pictured on jars of baby food, the real neonate may cause alarm and disappointment. The baby's head is large in propor-

to maintain control, see to her comfort, and ensure the conditions necessary for her to concentrate on the techniques that will allow her to deliver her baby with little or no pain.

Problems of Evaluation

Despite numerous positive self-reports about prepared childbirth, some members of the scientific community still have doubts about its effectiveness. One reason for these doubts is the nature of pain itself. The sensation of pain depends on several factors: the nerve messages sent to the brain from the part of the body that is affected; the person's expectations, fears, and anxieties; and how fatigued or preoccupied the person is. Uncertainty also arises because pain cannot be measured directly. Responses to the same pain stimuli vary widely. One person may become quiet and withdrawn; another may grimace, scream, and writhe; a third may pass out. It is therefore difficult for an observer to know the severity of the pain another person is feeling. Finally, it is not understood specifically why labor is painful (Pritchard & MacDonald, 1980). These factors make it impossible to be certain when particular techniques, such as those suggested by Dick-Read or Lamaze, are effective.

An additional problem in evaluating prepared childbirth is that, for ethical reasons, most studies designed to determine its effectiveness are not true experiments in which subjects are randomly assigned to different treatments (Beck & Hull, 1978; Widman & Singer, 1984). Expectant mothers cannot be coerced into practices they do not believe in for experimental purposes. Consequently, participants in these studies are self-selected. This leaves open the logical possibility that the women studied are naturally less susceptible to pain. It is also possible that when the techniques work, they do so because of the attention the women receive from their husbands and others and not because of the techniques themselves. Furthermore, the obstetricians involved in the delivery are aware of the kind of preparation that their patients have had. As a result, they may treat mothers who have been through prepared childbirth programs differently than other mothers.

The fact that there are doubts about the scientific validity of prepared childbirth does not mean that such programs should be dismissed. It seems reasonable that the information and training women receive in prepared childbirth classes help some of them to cope more effectively with the pain, anxiety, and excitement that are part of labor and childbirth. An additional benefit of many prepared childbirth programs is that they allow the father to play a role in the childbirth process and thus become directly involved with the baby in its first moments of life.

tion to the rest of the body, and the limbs are relatively small and tightly flexed. Unless the baby has been delivered by cesarean section, the head may look misshapen from being squeezed through the birth canal. (The head usually regains its symmetry by the end of the first week after birth.) Upon birth, the baby's skin may be covered with *vernix caseosa,* a white, cheesy substance that protects the skin against bacterial infections, and it may be spotted with blood.

Medical personnel, accustomed to the way newborns look, are not distracted by their temporarily unattractive appearance. The baby is checked for indications of danger so that they can take immediate action if something is wrong. They consider the size of the baby, check its vital signs, and look for evidence of normal capacities.

In the United States, neonates weigh an average of 3200 to 3400 grams (7 to 7½ pounds), although babies weighing anywhere from 5½ to 10 pounds are considered to fall in the normal range. During their first days of life, most babies lose about 7 percent of their initial weight, primarily due to the loss of fluid. They usually gain back this weight by the time they are 10 days old.

The average length of a neonate is 20 inches. To a large extent, length at birth is determined by the size of the maternal uterus. It does not reflect the baby's genetic inheritance because the genes that control height do not begin to express themselves until shortly after birth (Tanner, 1978).

Assessing the Baby's Viability

To assess the neonate's physical state and behavioral condition, a number of tests, typically referred to as *scales,* have been developed. The basic procedure in

BOX 4.2

THE BABY'S EXPERIENCE OF BIRTH

• • •

What is the experience of birth like for the baby? During the childbirth process, the fetus is squeezed through the birth canal for several hours, where it is subjected to considerable pressure and occasional oxygen deprivation. Finally, the newborn infant is delivered from the warm, dark, sheltered environment of the womb into a cold, bright hospital room, where it is held upside down and slapped on the buttocks. From the perspective of adults, it is difficult to imagine this experience as anything other than traumatic.

Psychiatrist Otto Rank (1929), one of Sigmund Freud's first and most-valued students, believed that the birth trauma is the cardinal source of adult neurotic anxiety. Rank further believed that he could cure his patients by getting them to analyze and thereby overcome this "primal trauma." Freud (1937/1953) had reservations about this aspect of his former student's work. He declared that "Rank's argument was bold and ingenious, but it did not stand the test of critical examination" (p. 316). Although Freud's judgment has generally been sustained (Pratt, 1954), concern over the possible long-term effects of the traumatic birth experience continues.

Modern research on the baby's experience of birth has focused on the biological mechanisms that equip the baby to cope with the stress involved. Hugo Lagercrantz and Theodore Slotkin (1986) have suggested that, as the birth process begins, the fetus produces adrenaline and other "stress" hormones that protect it from the adverse conditions — the pressure on the head and the deprivation of oxygen — it experiences. They go on to suggest that the events that cause the production of stress hormones are of vital importance because these hormones prepare the infant to survive outside of the womb.

In support of their hypothesis, Lagercrantz and Slotkin cite the fact that infants delivered by cesarean section often have difficulties breathing because they do not produce adrenaline and other hormones in the hours before birth. These hormones facilitate the absorption of liquid from the lungs and the production of surfactin, which allow the lungs to function well. In addition, they appear to accelerate the infant's meta-bolic rate at birth. This speeds up the breakdown of energy stored in the infant's fat cells to provide nourishment once the infant is no longer receiving a steady supply of nutrients through the umbilical cord.

Lagercrantz and Slotkin also believe that the stress hormones are instrumental in restricting the flow of blood to the periphery of the baby's body and thereby increase blood flow to such vital organs as the heart, lungs, and brain. This especially increases the chances of survival of a baby who is experiencing breathing difficulties. Furthermore, these researchers speculate that the hormonal surge during the birth process causes the newborn to be alert, which facilitates the attachment between mother and infant during its first hour of life (see the photo below).

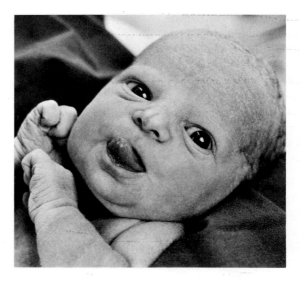

This infant is alert 5 to 6 minutes after birth and has dilated pupils in spite of the strong light. These effects appear to be the result of the surge of stress hormones that occurs during a vaginal delivery. By causing the infant to be alert, the hormonal surge may facilitate attachment between mother and child during the first hour of life.

constructing such scales is first to identify those characteristics that are essential to the newborn's immediate well-being and later development. Ratings are then collected from a large number of infants to establish norms for comparison. These norms are then used to assess the relative condition of individual babies.

Physical state   In the 1950s, Virginia Apgar (1953), an anesthesiologist who worked in the delivery room of a large metropolitan hospital, developed the **Apgar Scale,** a quick and simple method of diagnosing the physical state of newborns. Her test is now widely used throughout the United States to determine if a baby requires emergency care.

The Apgar Scale is used to rate babies 1 minute after birth and again 5 minutes later on five vital signs: heart rate, respiratory effort, muscle tone, reflex responsivity, and color. The criteria for scoring each of the signs are given in Table 4.1. The individual scores are totaled to give a measure of the baby's overall physical condition. A baby with a score of less than 4 is considered to be in poor condition and to require immediate medical attention to survive.

Behavioral condition   During the past half century, many scales have been constructed to assess the more subtle behavioral aspects of the newborn's condition (Brazelton, 1973, 1978; Gesell & Amatruda, 1947; Graham, Matarazzo, & Caldwell, 1956). One of the most widely used is the **Brazelton Neonatal Assessment Scale,** developed by pediatrician T. Berry Brazelton and his colleagues. A major purpose of this scale is to assess the newborn's neurological condition after the stress of labor and delivery. It is also used to assess

the progress of premature infants, to compare the functioning of newborns from different cultures, and to evaluate the effectiveness of interventions designed to alleviate developmental difficulties (Brazelton, Nugent, & Lester, 1987; Zeskind, 1983).

Included in the Brazelton scale are tests of infants' reflexes, motor capacities, muscle tone, capacity for responding to objects and people, and capacity to control their own behavior and attention. The only equipment the tests require are a rattle, a bell, a flashlight, and a pin. When scoring newborns on such tests, the examiners must be aware of the infant's degree of alertness and, if necessary, repeat the tests when the baby is wide awake and calm. The following are some typical items on the Brazelton scale:

Orientation to animate objects — visual and auditory: The examiner calls the baby's name repeatedly in a high-pitched voice while moving his head up and down and from side to side. Does the baby focus on the examiner? Does she follow the examiner with her eyes smoothly?

Pull-to-sit: The examiner puts a forefinger in each of the infant's palms and pulls him to a sitting position. Does the baby try to right his head when he is in a seated position? How well is he able to do this?

Cuddliness: The examiner holds the baby against her chest or up against her shoulder. How does the baby respond? Does she resist being held? Is she passive or does she cuddle up against the examiner?

Defensive movements: The examiner places a cloth over the baby's face and holds it there. Does the

TABLE 4.1   **The Apgar scoring system**

Vital Sign	Ratings		
	0	1	2
Heart rate	Absent	Slow (below 100)	Over 100
Respiratory effort	Absent	Slow, irregular	Good, crying
Muscle tone	Flaccid	Some flexion of extremities	Active motion
Reflex responsivity	No response	Grimace	Vigorous cry
Color	Blue, pale	Body pink, extremities blue	Completely pink

SOURCE: Apgar, 1953.

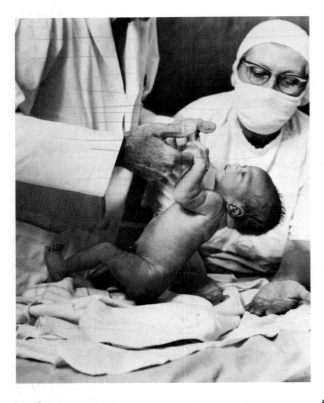

This newborn is demonstrating the ability to hold tight while being pulled to a sitting position.

baby try to remove the cloth from his face by turning his head away or by swiping at it?

Self-quieting activity: The examiner notes what the baby does to quiet herself when she is in a fussy state. Does she suck her thumb, look around?

A lively controversy has developed about the usefulness of scales such as Brazelton's (Brazelton, Nugent, & Lester, 1987; Francis, Self, & Horowitz, 1987; Sameroff, 1978). Most of these scales are designed with two purposes in mind: (1) to screen for infants at risk and (2) to predict newborns' future development. Research over the past decade shows that they are satisfactory guides for determining when medical intervention is necessary (Francis, Self, & Horowitz, 1987). However, they appear to be useful for predicting later development only when newborns are tested repeatedly during the early days and weeks of life so that a reliable estimate of the baby's early developmental

progress can be obtained (Brazelton, Nugent, & Lester, 1987). Even when this is done, the predictions are accurate only to a modest degree.

Problems and Complications

Though most babies are born without any serious problems, some are in such poor physical shape that they die soon after birth. Others are at risk for later developmental problems, sometimes fatal ones. Newborns are considered to be at risk if they suffer from any of a variety of problems, including asphyxiation or head injury during delivery (either of which may result in brain damage), acute difficulty breathing after birth, or difficulty digesting food owing to an immature digestive system (Korner, 1987). These are the kinds of problems that are likely to result in low scores on the Apgar Scale. Most of the newborns who are at risk are premature, abnormally underweight, or both (Kopp, 1983; Korner, 1987).

Prematurity The normal gestational age—the elapsed time between conception and birth—is 37 to 43 weeks. Babies born before the thirty-seventh week are considered to be **premature,** or *preterm.* In the United States, 5 to 7 percent of all births are premature (Korner, 1987). Disorders related to premature birth are the fourth leading cause of infant mortality. With the expert care now available in modern hospitals, mortality rates for premature infants are decreasing (see Figure 4.4). Eighty percent of those who weigh more than 1020 grams ($2\frac{1}{4}$ pounds) now survive (Goldberg & DiVitto, 1983).

The most critical problem for preterm infants is the functional immaturity of their lungs. If the lung's tiny air sacs are not sufficiently well developed, they do not produce enough *surfactin,* a substance that prevents the air sacs from collapsing, and the baby may have severe problems breathing. This condition, known as *respiratory distress syndrome,* is the leading cause of death among preterm infants (Evans & Glass, 1976).

The other main obstacles to the survival of preterm infants are immaturities of their digestive and immune systems. Even babies of normal gestational age sometimes have difficulties coordinating sucking, swallowing, and breathing in the first few days after birth. In preterm infants these difficulties are likely to be more serious. Their coordination may be so poor that they

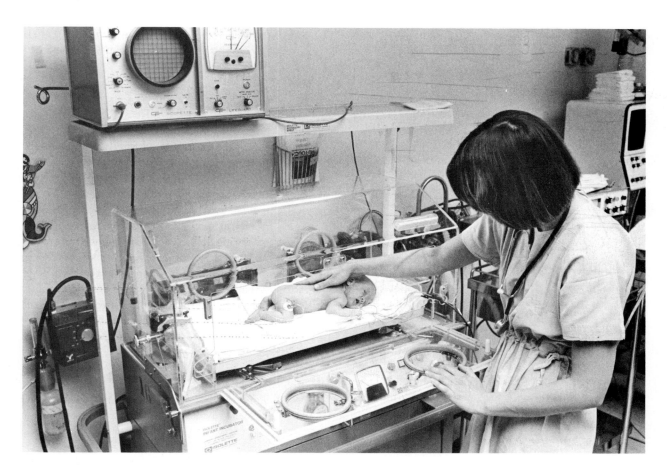

FIGURE 4.4 *Babies born prematurely may require intensive care in an incubator to sustain their early development.*

cannot be fed directly from breast or bottle and must be fed using special equipment. Moreover, their immature digestive systems often cannot handle normal baby formulas, so special formulas must be made.

A few of the factors that can lead to prematurity have been identified. Twins are likely to be born about 3 weeks early; triplets and quadruplets, even earlier. Very young women whose reproductive systems are immature and women who have had many pregnancies close together are more likely to have premature babies. So are women who smoke, who are in poor health, or who have intrauterine infections. The chances of giving birth to a premature infant also vary with socioeconomic status (Goldberg & DiVitto, 1983; Niswander, 1981). Poor women are twice as likely to give birth to small or preterm infants as are

women who are more affluent. This can be explained by the fact that poor women are more likely to be undernourished or chronically ill, to have inadequate health care before and during pregnancy, to suffer from infections, and to experience complications during pregnancy.

Many of the causes of prematurity, however, are still not well understood. At least half of all premature births are not associated with any of the identified risk factors. These premature babies are born following otherwise normal pregnancies to healthy women who are in their prime childbearing years and have had good medical care (Goldberg & DiVitto, 1983).

Low birth weight Although premature babies tend to be small, not all small babies are premature. Babies are considered to have a **low birth weight** if they weigh 2500 grams or less, whether or not they are premature. Newborns whose birth weights are especially low for their gestational age are said to suffer from **fetal growth retardation**, which simply means that they have not grown at the normal rate. Multiple births, intrauterine infections, chromosomal abnormalities, maternal smoking or narcotic use, maternal malnutrition, and abnormalities of the placenta or umbilical cord have all been identified as probable causes of fetal growth retardation (Niswander, 1981).

Developmental consequences   Intensive research has been conducted on the developmental consequences of prematurity and low birth weight (Goldberg & DiVitto, 1983; Kopp & Krakow, 1983). Although both premature and low-birth-weight babies are at risk for later developmental problems, the probable course of their development differs.

Low birth weight increases the risk of developmental difficulty whether the baby is premature or full-term. The smaller the baby, the more likely it is to have some sort of congenital abnormality, such as neurological impairment or a permanent impairment of

growth potential (Evans & Glass, 1976). Small babies are also more likely to die in the first year of life than are infants of the same gestational age who are of normal size (U.S. Department of Health and Human Services, 1982).

The developmental consequences of prematurity can appear quite different depending on how the age of the infant is calculated and what capacities are measured. Figure 4.5 contrasts the progress of premature and full-term infants toward such early developmental milestones as babbling, sitting up, and coordinating the thumb and forefinger to pick up objects based on two different ways of calculating the babies' ages. In Figure 4.5a, the scores reflecting the growth of these capacities are plotted from *birth*. Two results stand out: (1) the scores of the different groups all increase at similar rates, and (2) the more premature a baby is, the lower its score, which suggests that, in comparison to babies born at the normal gestational age, premature infants are developmentally delayed.

In Figure 4.5b, all the curves in Figure 4.5a have been adjusted to reflect the babies' gestational ages by subtracting the amount of prematurity from the time-scale. When this adjustment is made, the scores of the

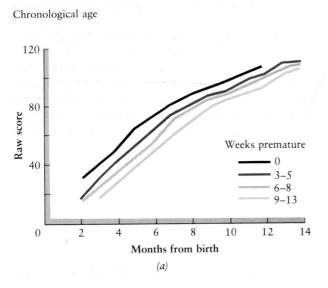

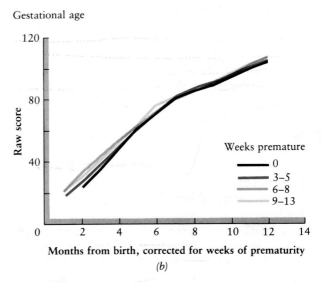

FIGURE 4.5   *(a) Performance on the Bayley scales of infant achievement for infants grouped according to age calculated from birth. Note that premature infants appear to be developmentally delayed. (b) Performance on the Bayley scales of infant achievement for infants grouped according to age from conception. When age is calculated in this manner, premature infants do not appear to be developmentally delayed. (Adapted from Hunt & Rhodes, 1977.)*

different groups are virtually equal. Thus, the extent of developmental delay among the premature babies turns out to be equal to the number of weeks they were born before term. A baby born a month early reaches each new postnatal milestone about one month later than a full term baby.

Figure 4.5b seems to indicate that experiencing the environment outside the womb has little effect on the rate at which babies develop. Such findings lend support to the contention of Gesell and other biologically oriented theorists that early development depends almost exclusively on maturation. However, research on the development of some other behavioral capacities suggests that premature infants may develop more slowly than full-term infants even when gestational age is taken into account. Premature babies have been found to experience delays in the acquisition of early language skills, for example (Crnic, Ragozin, Greenberg, Robinson, & Basham, 1983). They also appear to develop the ability to recognize something that they have seen before more slowly than full-term babies (Rose, 1983). Findings such as these would seem to indicate that environment does play a role in the rate at which premature babies develop.

Many premature babies catch up with full-term babies during infancy, but some do not (Cohen & Parmalee, 1983). Two factors appear to be central in determining what happens to a premature baby in the long run: (1) whether the premature infant is also low in birth weight for its gestational age, and (2) what environmental conditions greet the infant after birth. Premature babies who are of normal size for their gestational age are the most likely to catch up with full-term babies. It is those who are also low in birth weight who are most at risk for future developmental difficulties (Goldberg & DiVitto, 1983). Among premature babies who are particularly light for their gestational age, those with very small head size at birth and slow head growth during the first 6 weeks of postnatal life are especially likely to suffer long-term developmental problems (Eckerman, Sturm, & Gross, 1985).

Among the environmental factors that may contribute to the comparatively slow development of some capacities among premature infants are the effects that prematurity has on the parents. Premature babies are tiny and fragile in appearance; they are also less responsive and more irritable than full-term infants (Brazelton, Nugent, & Lester, 1987). These characteristics may make it more difficult for parents initially to be-

come attached to them. Furthermore, premature infants must often spend their first few weeks in the hospital in heated isolettes that maintain their body temperature and protect them from infection, which means that they and their parents are separated. Although parents are encouraged to visit their babies often and to establish emotional relationships with them, these visits are just that, visits, after which the parents go home and leave the babies alone. Once the mothers of premature infants are able to take them home, they spend as much or more time with their babies as do mothers of full-term babies. But their interactions tend to be disturbed. One study (Crnic et al., 1983) found, for example, that mothers and their premature babies have difficulty maintaining eye contact with one another. The mothers in this study also seemed to have difficulty finding an appropriate level of stimulation for their premature infants, who tended to become overexcited or bored when their mothers attempted to engage them. Other studies have found that a disproportionate number of premature babies are later abused by their parents (Egeland & Brunquette, 1979; Stern, 1973).

As premature and low-birth-weight infants grow older, environmental factors become increasingly more important to their development. Children who are raised in comfortable socioeconomic circumstances with an intact family and a mother who has a good education are less likely to suffer negative effects from their condition at birth than are children who are raised without these benefits (Sameroff & Chandler, 1975; Sigman & Parmalee, 1979).

Once the crisis of birth is past, parents can turn their attention to the baby's future. Crucial in constructing that future are the wide range of sensory and response capacities that children exhibit at birth. These elementary capacities are the basic building blocks for later psychological development.

NEWBORN BEHAVIOR

No issue has fired the curiosity of developmental psychologists more strongly than the question of the extent of babies' psychological capacities when they emerge from the womb. How prepared are these newcomers to perceive the sights, smells, and sounds of the world around them? Is the newborn mind a *tabula rasa* (blank slate) upon which the environment writes, as John Locke proposed? (See Box 1.1.) Or do infants come into the world already equipped with highly structured nervous systems, primed to experience an environment for which they have been shaped by their particular genetic endowment?

At the beginning of this century, psychological opinion leaned in Locke's direction. This view was summarized by the philosopher-psychologist William James (1890) in his famous statement that the newborn child experiences the world as a "buzzing, blooming, confusion." The new circumstances that greet the infant at birth may well be confusing, but as we will see, the research of recent decades has demonstrated that infants are born with remarkable capacities to experience the world and to behave in ways that promote their own survival.

Sensory Capacities

The sensory systems of an organism are the primary means by which it receives information from the environment. Normal, full-term newborns enter the world with all sensory systems functioning, but their sensory capacities are not all at the same level of maturity. In Chapter 3, we saw that organ systems develop at different rates during the fetal period; this continues following birth (Werner & Lipsitt, 1981).

The basic method developmental psychologists use to determine infant sensory capacities is to introduce some change into the child's environment and observe its effect on the child's physiological processes or behavior (Gottlieb & Krasnegor, 1985). For example, an investigator might present a tone or a flashing light and watch for an indication—a turn of the head, a variation in brain waves, or a change in the rate at which the baby sucks on a nipple—that it has been sensed by the newborn. In some cases, the researcher will present two stimuli at once to determine if babies will attend to one longer than to the other. If they do, it presumably shows that they can tell the stimuli apart, and it may also indicate that the one attended to longer is preferred.

Another widely used technique is to present a stimulus repeatedly until the infant stops paying attention to it. This response pattern is called **habituation**. Then, some aspect of the stimulus is changed: the frequency

of the tone, the language being spoken, or the arrangement of elements within a visual array. If the infant continues to ignore the stimulus despite the change, the investigator can conclude that the change is not psychologically significant to the baby. But if the infant's interest is renewed, the investigator can conclude that the infant did sense the change. To begin paying attention again when some aspect of the stimulus situation has been changed is called **dishabituation**.

Hearing Make a loud noise and infants minutes old will startle and may even cry. They will also turn their heads toward the source of the noise, which indicates that they perceive sound as being localized in space (Muir & Field, 1979). Newborns appear to be sensitive to the same range of sound frequencies as older children. There is even evidence that they are especially sensitive to very high-pitched sounds but lose this sensitivity as they grow older (Aslin, 1987). However, newborn hearing is not as acute as hearing among older children and adults (Hecox & Deegan, 1985). In the days following birth, the acuity of newborn hearing improves rapidly as the amniotic fluid left in the ears is absorbed, and it continues to improve for several months.

Infants appear to be able to distinguish the sound of the human voice from other kinds of sounds, and they seem to prefer it. Infants only a few days old will learn to suck on an artificial nipple to turn on recorded speech or vocal music, but they will not suck as readily to hear a rhythmic nonspeech sound or instrumental music (Butterfield & Siperstein, 1972). One of the most striking discoveries about the hearing of very young infants is that they can perceive sound categories in human speech (Eimas, 1985), a capacity that appears to be essential for the acquisition of language (see Box 4.3, "The Categorical Perception of Speech Sounds"). There is also evidence that some babies have formed a preference for the language spoken around them over a foreign language by the time they are 4 days old (Mehler, Lambertz, Jusczyk, & Amiel-Tison, 1986).

Vision The basic elements of the visual system are present at birth, but they are not fully developed and they are not well coordinated (Gottlieb & Krasnegor, 1985). The lens of the eye is still somewhat immature; it focuses images several millimeters behind the retina instead of on the retina as it should, causing the images to be blurred. Also, the movements of the baby's eyes are not coordinated well enough to make the images on the two retinas sufficiently complementary to form a clear composite image. The newborn's visual capacities are further limited because some of the neural pathways that relay information from the retina to the brain are still immature (Atkinson & Braddick, 1982).

Color perception There is currently uncertainty about newborns' color perception. While it appears that they possess all, or nearly all, of the physiological prerequisites for seeing color, psychologists disagree about whether or not neonates perceive color in the same way that adults do (Aslin, 1987; Bornstein, 1976; Teller, Peeples, & Sekel, 1978; Werner & Wooten, 1985).

Visual acuity A basic question about infant vision is how nearsighted or farsighted the newborn is. To determine newborns' visual acuity, Robert Fantz and his colleagues (Fantz, Ordy, & Udelf, 1962) developed a test based on the fact that when a striped visual field moves in front of the eyes, the eyes start to move in the same direction as the pattern. If the gaps between the stripes are so small that they cannot be perceived, the eyes do not move. By varying the width of the gaps and comparing the results obtained from newborns with those obtained from adults, these researchers were able to estimate that neonates have 20/300 vision — that is, they can see at 20 feet what an adult with normal vision can see at 300 feet. Other researchers estimate the visual acuity of newborns to be closer to the 20/800 range (Cornell & McDonnell, 1986). Although these estimates differ a good deal, they are alike in suggesting that the newborn is very nearsighted.

Poor visual acuity is probably not as much of a problem for newborns as it is for older children and adults. After all, newborns are unable to move unless carried, and they cannot hold their heads erect without support. However, their visual system is well enough tuned to allow them to see objects that are at the same distance as their mother's face when they are nursing. This level of acuity allows them to make eye contact, which is important in establishing the social relationship between mother and child (Stern, 1977). By 7 or 8 months of age, when infants are able to crawl on their own, their visual acuity is close to the adult level (Banks & Salapatek, 1983; Cornell & McDonnell, 1986).

Visual scanning Although newborns are nearsighted and have difficulty focusing, studies by Marshall Haith and his associates (Haith, 1980; Haith, Berman, & Moore, 1977) have shown that they actively scan their surroundings from the earliest days of life. These investigators developed an infrared recording technique that allowed them to determine precisely where infants were looking and to monitor infants' eye movements in the dark. Using it, they discovered that neonates scan with short eye movements about twice a second, even in a completely darkened room. Since there is no light entering their eyes, this kind of scanning cannot be caused by the visual environment. It must therefore be endogenous, originating in the neural activity of the central nervous system. Endogenous eye movements seem to be an initial, primitive basis for looking behavior.

Haith's studies also found that neonates exhibit an early form of exogenous looking, that is, looking that is stimulated by the external environment. When the lights are turned on after infants have been in the dark, they pause in their scanning when their gaze encounters an object or some change of brightness in the visual field. This very early sensitivity to changes in illumination, which is usually associated with the edges and angles of objects, appears to be an important component of the baby's developing ability to perceive visual forms (Haith, 1980).

Pattern perception What do babies see when their eyes encounter an object? Do they perceive only a jumbled, formless play of light? Or are they able to see objects much as adults do?

In the early 1960s, Robert Fantz (1961, 1963) dealt a severe blow to the then commonly accepted view that neonates perceive only a formless play of light by demonstrating that babies less than 2 days of age can distinguish among visual forms. The technique he used was very simple. Babies were placed on their backs in a specially designed "looking chamber" (see Figure 4.6) and shown various forms. An observer looked down through the top of the chamber and recorded how long the infants looked at each form. Because the infants spent more time looking at some forms than at others, it was assumed that they could tell the forms apart and that they preferred the ones they looked at the longest. Fantz found that neonates would rather look at patterned figures, such as faces or concentric circles, than at plain figures (see Figure 4.7).

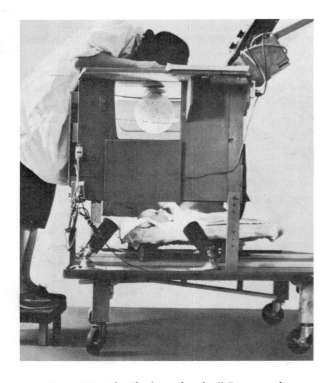

FIGURE 4.6 *The "looking chamber" Fantz used to test newborns' visual interests. The infant lies in a crib in the chamber, looking up at the stimuli attached to the ceiling. The observer, watching through a peephole, determines how long the infant looks at each stimulus.*

Fantz's conclusions set off a search to determine the extent of newborn capacities to perceive form and the reasons they prefer some forms over others. The resulting research has confirmed that infants visually perceive the world as more than random confusion, but it has also provided evidence that infants do not enter the world prepared to see it in the same way adults do. Philip Salapatek and William Kessen (1966), for example, studied the way newborns scan outline drawings of simple figures, such as triangles, on a lighted visual field. When adults are shown such figures, they scan the entire boundary. In contrast, Salapatek and Kessen found that babies 1 month of age do not scan the entire figure but instead appear to focus on areas of high contrast, such as lines and angles (see Figure 4.8a). This kind of looking behavior is clearly not random, but it does not provide evidence that children are born able to perceive basic patterns. At 2 months of age, infants scan more of the figure, but their scanning movements are still incomplete and still

seem to be captured by areas of high contrast (see Figure 4.8b) (Salapatek, 1975).

Salapatek also discovered another important limitation to neonates' visual perception. When newborns are presented with a pattern consisting of one contour inside another, they fixate only on the external contour. By 2 or 3 months of age, however, they begin to notice and concentrate more on the internal contours. This finding, which may seem insignificant by itself, is important for interpreting evidence concerning infant perception of the human face.

Face perception In Fantz's early studies, one of the complex forms presented to the babies was a schematic human face. The fact that infants looked longer at this form than at any of the others suggested that newborn infants can perceive faces and prefer to look at them. When Fantz (1961, 1963) tested infants using a schematic face and a form in which facial elements had been scrambled, he found that the infants could apparently distinguish the schematic face from the

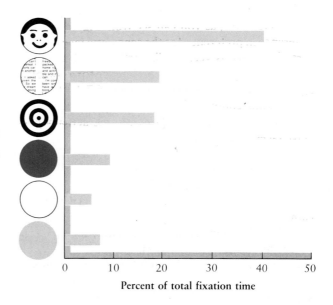

FIGURE 4.7 *Infants tested during the first weeks of life show a preference for patterned stimuli over plain stimuli. The length of each bar indicates the relative amount of time the babies spent looking at the corresponding stimulus. (Adapted from Fantz, 1961.)*

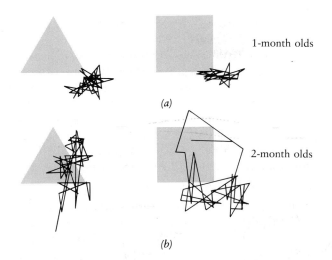

1-month olds

(a)

2-month olds

(b)

FIGURE 4.8 *Visual scanning of triangles and squares by young infants. (a) Note that 1-month-olds concentrate their gaze on a point of high contrast, whereas (b) 2-month-olds visually explore the figures more fully. (Adapted from Salapatek, 1975.)*

begin to distinguish between schematic facelike forms and forms in which facial elements have been scrambled.

Still, there is tantalizing evidence that under the right conditions of viewing newborns are especially sensitive to the sight of human faces. In Fantz's studies and in many that followed, researchers used only stationary and schematic representations of faces. These figures were convenient for the researchers, but their use appears to have resulted in a misunderstanding about early human visual perception. Several more recent studies indicate that when newborns see representations of the human face under more natural conditions, they are especially responsive to them. Babies only 9 *minutes* old will turn their heads to gaze at a schematic face if it moves in front of them, for example (Goren, Sarty, & Wu, 1975). But they do not turn their heads if the moving "face" is scrambled or if a featureless outline of a head is used. A complementary

jumbled face (see Figure 4.9). Such a strong suggestion that newborns have an unlearned preference for a biologically significant form naturally attracted great interest. However, as you can see from Figure 4.9, the difference in preference for the schematic face and the scrambled face is very small, particularly when contrasted with the difference in preference for a complex figure over a plain one shown in Figure 4.7. In the years since Fantz conducted his studies, there has been much debate about whether newborns actually perceive faces or are simply visually attracted to complex figures (Aslin, 1987; Banks & Salapatek, 1983).

The evidence from early follow ups of Fantz's studies ran against the idea that neonates are primed to respond to "faceness." Lonnie Sherrod (1979) replicated Fantz's research using both schematic faces and scrambled faces. He controlled carefully for such factors as the degree of brightness, the contrast between the forms and their background, and the number of turns and angles within each form. His conclusion, supported by others (Haaf, Smith, & Smitely, 1983), was that the presence of highly contrasting elements or many turns and angles, not "faceness" itself, accounted for Fantz's results. In a recent review of this line of research, Aslin (1987) concluded that it is not until at least the third month after birth that infants

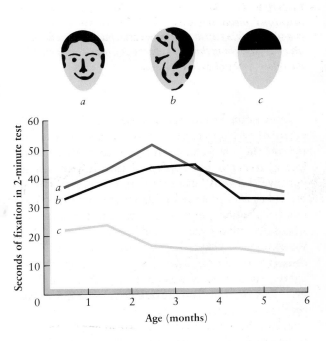

FIGURE 4.9 *Visual preferences of infants for (a) a schematic face, (b) a scrambled schematic face, and (c) a nonfacelike figure, all having equal amounts of light and dark areas. Both facelike forms were preferred over the nonfacelike form, with the "real" face receiving slightly more attention than the scrambled face. (Adapted from Fantz, 1961.)*

BOX 4.3

THE CATEGORICAL PERCEPTION OF SPEECH SOUNDS

• • •

As anyone who has tried to learn a foreign language knows, one of the essential tasks involved is learning to segment the complex sounds of the language into the basic sounds that are put together to make up words. These basic language sounds are called **phonemes.** Making the task more difficult is the fact that phonemes differ from language to language. In English, for example, /s/ and /z/ are phonemes; *sap* and *zap* sound different and have different meanings. (Linguists denote phonemes and other language sounds by enclosing them in slashes.) In Spanish, however, there is no

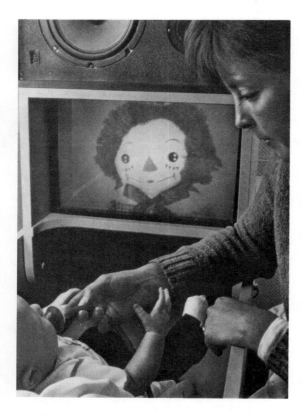

Apparatus for presenting artificially manipulated speech sounds to young infants. The infant sucks on a pacifier connected to recording instruments as speechlike sounds are presented from a loudspeaker just above the Raggedy Ann display.

distinction between these phonemes. Similarly, /r/ and /l/ are different phonemes in English but not in Japanese. No wonder learning a new language often seems such a formidable undertaking.

Now consider the even more difficult problem newborn babies confront. Except for possibly having picked up a sense of the basic rhythms of their native language while in the womb (as suggested by a few studies discussed in Chapter 3, p. 88), babies are born into the world with no experience of language at all. Yet within a year, and with no formal training, they will be making speechlike sounds and may even have begun to produce their first words. What underlies the prodigious ability human infants have to acquire language?

Part of the answer comes from studies by Peter Eimas and his colleagues that indicate the ability to perceive basic language sounds is an innate skill that is present at birth (Eimas, Siqueland, Jusczyk, & Vigorito, 1971). These researchers had neonates suck on a nipple that was attached to a recording device in a special apparatus they set up for their study (see figure at left). After establishing a baseline rate of sucking for each baby, they presented the speech sound /pa/ to the babies each time they sucked. At first the babies' rate of sucking increased as if they were excited by each presentation of the sound. But after a while, they settled back to their baseline rate of sucking. When the infants had become thoroughly habituated to the sound of /pa/, a new sound, /ba/, was presented that differed from the original sound only in its initial phoneme — /b/ versus /p/. The neonates began sucking rapidly again when the change was made, indicating that they perceived the difference (see top figure on page 125).

Further studies showed that infant perception of phonemic distinctions is based upon an innate categorizing ability that appears to be shared by newborn infants and adults. The English phonemes /b/ and /p/ are both generated by first blocking the flow of air through the vocal tract and then releasing it. The only difference between these two phonemes is the time required for the vocal chords to start into motion once the air has been released. This brief time delay is called the *voice-onset-time*. The phoneme /b/ has a voice-onset-time of 0 milliseconds because there is no delay; /p/ has a voice-onset-time greater than 30 milliseconds. Eimas and his colleagues found that the ability to perceive differences in voice-onset-times is the critical feature in infants' (and adults') ability to distinguish among these phonemes (Eimas, 1985). In general, the ability to distinguish between variations in some aspect of otherwise similar stimuli is called *categorical* perception.

Other studies have shown that newborns are able to perceive all the categorical sound distinctions used in all the world's various languages. Japanese babies, for example, can perceive the difference between /r/ and /l/ even though adult speakers of Japanese cannot. The ability to make phonemic distinctions apparently begins to narrow to just those distinctions that are present in one's native language at about 6 to 8 months of age (see bottom figure at right), the same age at which the baby's first halting articulations of languagelike sounds are likely to begin (Aslin, 1987; Eimas, 1985).

Although it is tempting to conclude from these findings that human infants are born with perceptual skills that are specially pretuned to the properties of human speech, studies indicate that other species can make similar distinctions (Kuhl & Miller, 1978). The difference is that humans use this ability as a stepping stone to the mastery of language, an achievement that is beyond the capacities of other animals.

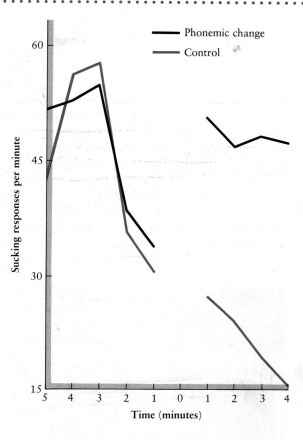

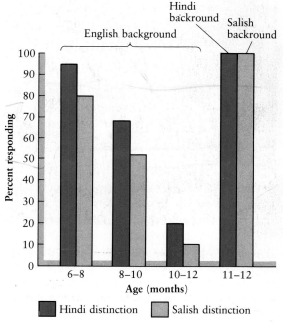

(Above) The rate of sucking following the repetition of a particular consonant sound. For the curve labelled "phonemic change" the consonant is changed following the time marked "0." Note that the rate of sucking sharply increases. For the curve labelled "control," there was no change in the consonant presented, and the rate of sucking continued to decrease. (Below) The narrowing of the ability of infants to make phonemic distinctions among contrasting language sounds that are foreign to their native language. The proportion of infants from an English-speaking background who responded to consonant contrasts from Hindi (a language of the Indian subcontinent) and Salish (a North American Indian language) fell rapidly with age. In contrast, 1-year-old Hindi and Salish infants retain the capacity to perceive the linguistic contrasts native to their respective languages. (Adapted from Eimas, 1985.)

study has demonstrated that 45-hour-old infants prefer to look at their mother's face rather than the face of a strange woman (Field, Cohen, Garcia, & Greenberg, 1984).

Neonates' abilities to respond to "faceness" and to distinguish their mothers' faces from those of strangers appear to be based on the influence of two factors. The first is the existence of areas of high contrast, which is suggested by the evidence discussed earlier of neonates' tendency to concentrate their gaze on lines, angles, or light-dark transitions (Haith, 1980; Haith, Berman, & Moore, 1977). This suggests that newborns may recognize their mother's face by using the light-dark patterns created by her hairline and the outline of her face.

The second factor is motion. Both movement of the whole face (as in the study by Goren, Sarty, and Wu, described above) and movement of the eyes or mouth within the face appear to be important. I. W. R. Bushnell (1982) presented a group of 1- to 2-month-olds with stationary compound figures, such as a triangle within a circle. The figure was shown repeatedly until the infant stopped looking at it for more than a brief period. When the outside element was changed (the circle in our example), the infants stared longer at the figure, but when the inside element was changed (the triangle), they did not. Bushnell then arranged his apparatus so that the inside element oscillated back and forth instead of remaining motionless and repeated the experiment. With these figures, which are analogous to faces in which the eyes or mouth are moving, neonates responded to changes in both the external and internal elements.

In real life, people move both their heads and the features of their faces. The experimental evidence shows that this movement improves the ability of newborns to perceive the internal features as well as the outlines of faces.

Taste and smell   Neonates have a well-developed sense of smell (Engen, Lipsitt, & Kaye, 1963; Steiner, 1977, 1979). Trygg Engen and his colleagues demonstrated that newborns have this sensory capacity by placing 2-day-old infants on a "stabilometer," an apparatus that measures how physically active a baby is. The experimenters held either an odorless cotton swab or a swab soaked in a solution having a distinctive odor under the newborns' noses. Babies were judged to react to an odor if their level of activity increased over what it had been when they were pre-

sented with the odorless cotton swab. The infants reacted strongly to some odors, such as garlic and vinegar, and less strongly to others, such as licorice and alcohol. Their responses indicated not only that they were sensitive to odors but also that they could tell one odor from another.

Newborns' sense of taste, like their sense of smell, is acute. They prefer sweet to sour tastes (Lipsitt, 1977). They will suck on a bottle longer and pause for shorter periods when they are fed sweet substances than when they are given plain water. In response to different tastes, they also make characteristic facial expressions that look remarkably like the facial expressions of adults when they encounter the same tastes, suggesting that these expressions are unlearned (see Figure 4.10).

Touch, temperature, and position   The abilities to detect a touch to the skin, changes in temperature, and changes in physical position develop very early in the prenatal period. Although these sensory capacities have not received as much attention as vision and hearing, they are no less important to the baby's survival. Newborns show that they sense they have been touched by making a distinctive movement, such as withdrawing the part touched or turning toward the touch. Some evidence suggests that neonatal sensitivity to touch increases in the days following birth (Lipsitt & Levy, 1959). However, little is known about whether neonates can distinguish between different tactile stimuli or tell what part of the body is being touched or about how such capacities might develop.

Neonates indicate that they are sensitive to temperature changes by becoming more active if there is a sudden drop in temperature (Pratt, 1954). They respond to abrupt changes in their physical position, such as being suddenly tipped up or dropped, with distinctive, reflex-like movements. Such responses indicate that the mechanism for detecting changes in position, which is located in the middle ear, is operating.

Overall, there is extensive evidence that babies come into the world with sensory capacities in good working order and far more structured than was once thought. This brings us to the next question about newborn behavior: What capacities do infants have for acting on the world? By studying the ability of infants to take in information from the environment and their ability to act upon that information, researchers can gather the data they need to determine the starting point of postnatal psychological development.

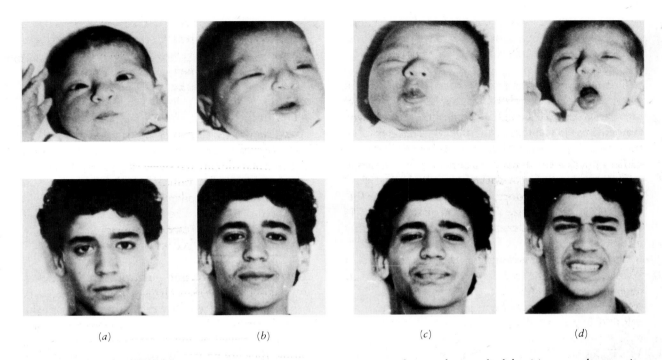

FIGURE 4.10 *Facial expressions evoked by different tastes are very similar in infants and adults: (a) a neutral expression follows the presentation of distilled water; (b) a hint of a smile follows the presentation of a sweet stimulus; (c) the pucker is in response to a sour stimulus; (d) a bitter stimulus evokes a distinctive grimace.*

Response Capacities

Infants are born with a number of ways of responding to, and thereby acting on, the world around them. Here, we will examine three important aspects of infant response capacities—reflexes, emotions, and temperament.

Reflexes Newborn babies come equipped with a variety of **reflexes**—specific, well-integrated responses to specific types of stimulation that are automatic, or involuntary. A number of the reflexes with which infants are born are described in Table 4.2. Virtually all psychologists agree that reflexes are the elemental building blocks out of which the complex behavioral capacities of later life are constructed. They disagree, however, about the nature of reflexes themselves and how those complex capacities develop.

Some reflexes are clearly part of the baby's elementary "survival kit." The eyeblink reflex, for example, has a clear function: it protects the eye from overly bright lights or foreign objects that might damage it. The same is true of the sucking and swallowing reflexes, which are essential to feeding. Others, however, such as the grasping reflex (closing fingers around an object that is pressed against the palm) and the Moro reflex (grasping with the arms when suddenly dropped), appear to have no particular function. This raises questions both about the developmental significance of these reflexes and about how they evolved in the first place. Some biologically oriented developmental theorists believe that these reflexes are not now functional but were during early evolutionary stages, when infants needed to cling to their mothers in order to survive (Peiper, 1963). Others, such as John Bowlby (1973), believe that they may still be functional because they now promote a close relationship between mother and infant.

Emotions Emotion—the feeling tone, sometimes referred to as *affect,* with which individuals respond to their circumstances—is an important aspect of

TABLE 4.2 Reflexes present at birth

Reflex Name	Description	Developmental Course	Significance
Babinski	When the bottom of the baby's foot is stroked, the toes fan out and then curl	Disappears in 8 to 12 months	Presence at birth and normal course of decline are a basic index of normal neurological condition
Breathing	Repetitive, rhythmic inhalation and exhalation	Permanent	Provides oxygen and removes carbon dioxide
Crawling	When baby placed on stomach and pressure applied to the soles of the feet, rhythmic movements of the arms and legs are elicited	Disappears after 3 to 4 months; possible reappearance at 6 to 7 months as component of voluntary crawling	Uncertain
Eyeblink	Rapid closing of eyes	Permanent	Protection against aversive stimuli such as bright lights or foreign objects
Grasping	When a finger or some other object is pressed against the baby's palm, the baby's fingers close around it	Disappears in 3 to 4 months; replaced by voluntary grasping	Presence at birth and later disappearance is a basic sign of normal neurological development
Moro	If the baby is allowed to drop unexpectedly while being held, or there is a loud noise, the baby will throw her arms outward while arching her back, and then bring the arms together as if grasping something	Disappears in 6 to 7 months (although startle to loud noises is permanent)	Disputed; its presence at birth and later disappearance are a basic sign of normal neurological development; possibly functions as facilitator of mother-infant bonding
Rooting	Turning the head and opening the mouth when touched on the cheek	Disappears between 3 and 6 months	Component of nursing
Stepping	When the baby is held upright over a flat surface, he will make rhythmic leg movements	Disappears in first 2 months	Disputed; it may be only a kicking motion, or it may be a component of later voluntary walking
Sucking	Sucking elicited by putting something into the baby's mouth	Permanent	Fundamental component of nursing

human psychological functioning. Beyond the coloration emotions give to experience, they serve two basic adaptive functions — they motivate and they communicate (Barrett & Campos, 1987). Emotions motivate by energizing us, alerting us to certain information in the environment and preparing us to respond in particular ways. For example, when something frightens us, our senses become heightened and we become tense, ready to fight or flee. Emotional expressions also communicate to other people how we are responding to

situations, which is important for the helpless and inarticulate newborn.

In interviews, mothers of infants as young as 4 weeks old reported a high incidence of distinct emotional expressions, which they used to interpret the needs of their babies. Among the emotions the mothers claimed their babies expressed were interest (99%), joy (95%), surprise (74%), fear (58%), and sadness (34%) (Johnson, Emde, Pannabecker, Stenberg, & Davis, 1982).

The behaviorist J. B. Watson (1930), an early champion of the idea that infants are born ready to feel emotions, claimed that the newborn has three primitive emotions—fear, anger, and love. According to Watson, these emotions are reflected in the way the baby responds to particular events. Fear is aroused by threatening stimuli, and it causes babies to cry and clutch; anger is aroused when the baby's ongoing behaviors are blocked, causing babies to stiffen their bodies and hold their breath; love is aroused by soothing stimulation, which makes babies smile.

In their modern version of Watson's idea, Joseph Campos and his co-workers claim that the emotions present at birth include pleasure, anger, disgust, surprise, and possibly fear and sadness (Campos, Barrett, Lamb, Goldsmith, & Stenberg, 1983). They define emotions as central nervous system states associated with characteristic configurations of feeling tone and external expression (facial pattern, intonation, and body movements). In their view, emotions are responses to particular relationships between the baby's goals and the events the baby encounters. If babies are given something sour when they are hungry, for example, they will be surprised, and they may also be disgusted and angry. If they are given something exceptionally sweet instead, their surprise will be accompanied by pleasure.

The evidence that newborns experience emotions is indirect. It depends on the assumption that the crucial defining elements—feelings and goals—can be validly inferred from the infant's facial expressions, noises, and movements (see Figure 4.11). For this rea-

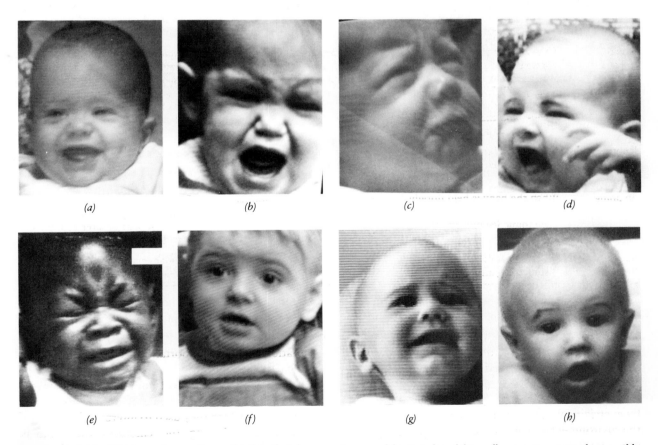

(a) (b) (c) (d)

(e) (f) (g) (h)

FIGURE 4.11 *Videotaped recordings of infant facial expressions used by Izard and his colleagues to assess the possible universal relation between emotion and facial expression. What emotion do you think each facial expression represents? The responses most of Izard's adult subjects gave are printed upside down:*

(a) joy, (b) anger, (c) sadness, (d) disgust, (e) distress/pain, (f) interest, (g) fear, (h) surprise

son, some researchers have attempted to establish the existence of emotions in newborns by studying the extent to which facial expressions in response to various events have the same meaning for everyone (Izard, 1977). For example, Carroll Izard and his colleagues videotaped infants' responses to such events as being inoculated at the doctor's or being reunited with their mothers after a brief separation (Izard, Huebner, Risser, McGinnes, & Dougherty, 1980). They then showed the videotapes or stills from them to college students and nurses. All the subjects agreed fairly consistently on the facial expressions they identified as showing interest, joy, surprise, and sadness and to a somewhat lesser extent on the expressions they identified as showing anger, disgust, or contempt.

Psychologists who accept the findings of Izard and his co-workers as evidence of infant emotion reason that adults agree on the meanings of infant expressions because the ways in which emotions are expressed facially are universal. Support for this idea comes from the cross-cultural research of Paul Ekman and his associates (Ekman & Friesen, 1972; Ekman, Sorenson, & Friesen, 1969). These researchers asked people in five literate and two nonliterate cultures to pose expressions to such events as the death of a loved one or being reunited with a close friend. Both literate and nonliterate adults configured their faces in the same way to express each emotion. The researchers also showed the subjects photographs that had been posed by actors and asked them to choose the ones that expressed the emotions they had posed. The literate and nonliterate adults agreed on the photographs that represented happiness, sadness, anger, and disgust. The nonliterate adults did not distinguish fear and surprise from one another, although they did distinguish them from the other expressions.

Despite the evidence gathered in support of the idea of emotion in the newborn, there is need for caution. Facial expressions, however universal their meanings are among adults, may not be reliable indicators of the same emotion among neonates. Newborns may frown simply because they are hungry or cold. Their emotion is a response to immediate physical circumstances. An adult may frown, however, because she has just lost her job and is worried how she will support herself. Her emotion involves the synthesis of information about her current circumstances and her anticipation of future events. This synthesis occurs in the higher brain centers, which are not yet active at birth. Conse-

quently, the facial expressions of newborns may have different meanings from the same facial expressions in adults. Although Campos, Izard, and others acknowledge that such criticisms have some merit, they maintain that the evidence for the existence of emotions in the neonate is nevertheless convincing.

Temperament A commonly held intuition about human nature is that people exhibit stable differences in the way they respond to the world around them and in the quality of their dominant mood. These differences are referred to as temperament (Allport, 1937; Bates, 1987; Goldsmith, 1987). Some people, for example, are easily upset and frustrated, whereas others seem imperturbable. A wide variety of infant characteristics have been taken as evidence of temperamental qualities. They include how active newborns are, the ease with which they become upset, the intensity of their reactions, and how sociable they are (see Bates, 1987, for an extensive discussion). Many developmental psychologists believe that these temperamental characteristics are present at birth and are an important source of continuity in development. These characteristics have proven difficult to pin down scientifically, however.

Pioneering studies of temperament and development were conducted by Alexander Thomas, Stella Chess, and their colleagues. Their work has had great influence over the years both because of the techniques used to assess temperament and because the researchers followed the children's development into early adulthood. They began their research in the late 1950s with a group of 141 middle- and upper-class children in the United States. Subsequently, they added 95 working-class Puerto Rican children and several groups of children suffering from disease, neurological impairment, and mental retardation to their longitudinal study (Thomas, Chess, Birch, Hertig, & Korn, 1963; Thomas & Chess, 1977, 1984). Initially, the researchers asked the parents of the children to fill out questionnaires periodically, beginning shortly after the birth of their child. Included were questions about such matters as how the children reacted to their first bath, to wet diapers, and to their first taste of solid food. As the children grew older, the parental questionnaires were supplemented through interviews with teachers and tests of the children.

When the researchers analyzed the data they obtained, they found they could identify nine different behavioral traits that, taken together, became their definition of temperament (see Table 4.3). After scoring the children on each of these nine traits using a three-point scale, they found that most of the children could be classified according to three broad temperamental categories. Those who were playful, were regular in their biological functions, and adapted readily to new circumstances were labeled *easy* babies. At the opposite extreme were the children who were irregular in their biological functions, who were irritable, and who often responded intensely and negatively to new situations, which they tried to withdraw from. They were classified as *difficult*. The third group of children

TABLE 4.3 Basic categories of temperament according to Chess and Thomas

Trait	Definition
Activity level	The motor component present in a given child's functioning and the proportion of inactive and active periods
Rhythmicity (regularity)	The degree of predictability of biological functions
Approach or withdrawal	The nature of the initial response to a new stimulus, such as food, a toy, or a person
Adaptability	The ease with which initial responses to a situation are modified
Threshold of responsiveness	The intensity level of a stimulus that is needed to evoke a response
Intensity of reaction	The energy level of a response
Quality of mood	The amount of joyful, pleasant, and friendly behaviors relative to unpleasant and unfriendly behaviors
Distractibility	The effectiveness of extraneous stimuli in disrupting or altering the direction of ongoing behaviors
Attention span and persistence	Two related indicators of the length of time an activity is pursued

SOURCE: Chess and Thomas, 1982.

were low in activity level and their responses were typically mild. They tended to withdraw from new situations, but in a mild way, and required more time than the "easy" babies to adapt to change. These children were categorized as *slow to warm up*.

A critical issue in the study of temperament is the degree to which temperamental characteristics are present at birth and are therefore presumed to be genetically determined. Some researchers require that a trait be demonstrably inherited for it to count as temperament (Buss & Plomin, 1984). Many others do not restrict the definition of temperament to inherited characteristics, although they acknowledge that there are genetic contributions to temperament (Goldsmith & Campos, 1982). These differing definitions are important because they influence how psychologists conceive of the extent to which temperament can be modified through experience.

The strongest evidence for the heritability of temperamental traits comes from twin studies. Arnold Buss and Robert Plomin (1975) found that ratings on emotionality, activity level, and sociability were strongly related for identical twins (who have identical genes) but not for fraternal twins (who inherit different mixes of genes from their parents). H. H. Goldsmith and Irving Gottesman (1981) obtained similar findings for individual differences in activity level.

Daniel Freedman (1974) has documented ethnic differences in excitability among newborn infants that suggest that excitability has a significant genetic component. He found that, during their first days of life, Chinese-American babies tend to be more placid and more difficult to perturb than Anglo-American or black-American babies. In one set of observations, Freedman placed a cloth over the babies' noses and observed their reactions. Most black-American and Anglo-American babies quickly turned their heads aside or swiped at the cloth with their hands. In contrast, the Chinese-American babies usually lay quietly with the cloth covering their noses and breathed through their mouths.

The possibility that temperamental traits are stable physiological "biases" in the way individuals respond to their environment suggests that, if the right measurements are taken, it should be possible to predict the characteristic style with which individuals will behave at later stages of development from observations of their temperamental characteristics at birth (Kagan, 1984). Some research suggests that this is in fact the case. For example, one study found that the degree of distress displayed by newborn boys when a pacifier they were sucking on was removed from their mouths predicted their attentiveness in nursery school (Bell, Weller, & Waldrop, 1971). Those infants who became the most upset were later the least likely to become absorbed in their nursery school lessons. Similar results were reported in a study in which temperament ratings for 110 newborn infants were compared with ratings collected when the children were 9 months old (Matheny, Riese, & Wilson, 1985). Using a measure of "emotional tone," which combined ratings for irritability, resistance to soothing, and adult judgments of how nice it was to be around the baby, the researchers found significant temperamental stability.

Despite these interesting findings on temperament, theories of infant temperament remain controversial. Many studies have failed to produce convincing evidence that there are stable temperamental traits (Goldsmith & Campos, 1982; Lewis & Starr, 1979). One reason for this is that the environment over the course of development is *not* always stable. As Thomas and Chess (1984) suggest, temperament may be no different from other psychological phenomena when it comes to stability over time. In any practical consideration of stability, the environment must also be taken into account.

When we begin to consider the environment as an important contributor to the stability of temperament and other aspects of the newborn's functioning, we need to turn first to the situation that greets the newborn following delivery. Babies are not born in isolation. As they emerge from the womb, they are greeted by their mother, sometimes by their father, and soon by other members of their family and community who have gathered to help the mother and welcome the newcomer.

BEGINNING THE PARENT-CHILD RELATIONSHIP

As impressive as newborns' sensory capacities and abilities to respond to their new environment may be, human infants are helpless creatures in many basic ways. Their very survival depends on the active sup-

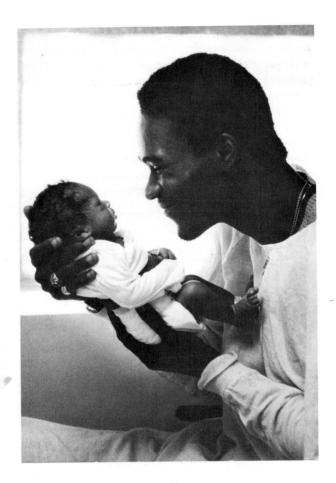

A young father greeting his newborn son.

port and protection of their caretakers. The development of a close relationship between infants and their parents is therefore crucial to infants' well-being. Unfortunately, love between parent and child is neither inevitable nor automatic. The large numbers of infants who are neglected, abused, abandoned, or even murdered the world over each year should convince even the most sentimental and optimistic observer of this harsh fact. In 1984, for example, more than 100,000 cases of child neglect and abuse were reported to local authorities in the United States (Statistical Abstract of the U. S., 1985). Many knowledgeable people believe that this is only the tip of the iceberg because the majority of cases are never reported.

Yet most parents love their babies. How, then, is the bond between parent and child formed? When no strong attachment develops, what goes wrong? These are large questions that will arise again and again in subsequent chapters because the formation of a close parent-child relationship is not a momentary event; it develops over many years after the birth of the child. Here we will examine the factors that come into play immediately following birth and set the stage for the future: the initial reactions of the parents to their baby's appearance, the first hours of contact between parent and infant, and the expectations parents have for their babies.

The Baby's Appearance

In their search for the sources of mother-infant love, some psychologists have turned to **ethology**—the study of animal behavior and its evolutionary bases. These psychologists believe that examining the factors that cause the mothers of various nonhuman species to protect and care for their young or to reject them can provide insight into some of the factors that may influence human mothers. One important factor that seems to influence how animals respond to their young is their offspring's appearance.

Konrad Lorenz (1943), a German ethologist, noted that the newborn of many animal species have physical characteristics that distinguish them from the mature animal. These characteristics include a large head relative to body size, a large and protruding forehead in relation to the rest of the face, large eyes relative to face size, eyes that are positioned below the horizontal midline of the face, and round, full cheeks (see Figure 4.12). According to Lorenz, this combination of features has the quality of **babyness,** which seems to appeal to adults and, more significantly, appears to evoke caregiving behaviors in them.

Evidence supporting Lorenz's hypothesis comes from a study by William Fullard and Ann Rieling (1976). These researchers asked people ranging from 7 years of age to young adulthood which of matched pairs of pictures, one depicting an adult and the other depicting an infant, they preferred. Some of the pictures were of human beings; others were of animals. They found that adults, especially females, were most likely to choose the pictures of infants over those of adults. Children between the ages of 7 and 12 preferred the pictures of adults. Between the ages of 12

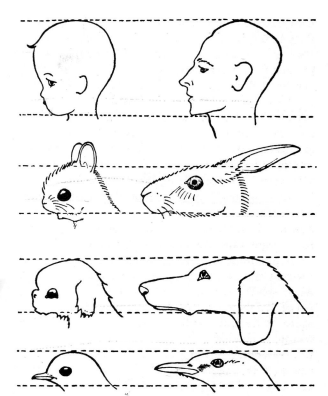

FIGURE 4.12 *Comparison of the shape of infant and adult heads for four species, illustrating the distinguishing features of "babyness." (From Lorenz, 1943.)*

and 14, the preference of girls shifted quite markedly from adults to children. A similar shift occurred for most boys when they were between 14 and 16. These shifts in preference coincide with the average ages at which girls and boys go through the physiological changes of puberty that make the body able to reproduce.

Patterned adult responses to the appearance of infants may explain why mothers find it difficult to care for malformed offspring. Mothers of dogs, cats, guinea pigs, and some other species will kill malformed offspring. While human parents usually do not kill their malformed babies, they do interact more frequently and more lovingly with infants they judge attractive than with those they judge homely (Parke & Sawin, 1975). They also attribute greater competence to attractive babies (Stephan & Langlois, 1984). Ross

BOX 4.4

THE PARENTS' RESPONSE TO THE BABY'S ARRIVAL
...

The following is a transcript of a delivery room conversation recorded by Aidan Macfarlane, an English pediatrician. It illustrates common maternal behaviors in the way the mother checks to see that the baby is physically sound. It also shows the powerful effect of cultural belief systems in shaping parents' initial responses to the newborn, in this case, a girl.

Transcript: Mrs. B, age 27, first baby (girl)

Doctor: Come on, junior. Only a lady could cause so much trouble. Come on, little one.

[A baby is delivered]

Mother: A girl.
D: Well, it's got the right plumbing.
M: Oh, I'm sorry darling.
Father: [laughs]
D: What are you sorry about?
M: He wanted a boy.
D: Well, you'll have to try again next week, won't you!
M: [laughs]
D: She looks great. Want to see her? Bloody and messy, but that's not from her.
M: Oh, she's gorgeous.
F: Looks like you.

[Mother kisses father]

M: Is she all right?
D: Why don't you ask her? She's quite capable of letting you know how she feels about the situation.
M: She's noisy, isn't she?
D: Yes, just like the modern generation.
F: Yes.
M: Well, Dr. Murphy, I was right. I had a sneaky feeling it was a girl, just because I wanted a boy.
F: Well, it will suit your mum, won't it?
M: [laughs]
D: Often tactically best to have a girl first—she can help with the washing up.

[Baby given to mother]

M: Hello darling. Meet your dad. You're just like your dad. *[Baby yells.]*
F: I'm going home!
M: Oh you've gone quiet. *[laughs]* Oh darling, she's just like you—she's got your little tiny nose.
F: It'll grow like yours.
M: She's big, isn't she? What do you reckon?
D: She's quite good-looking, despite forcep marks on her head—but don't worry about that. She'll have little bruises around her ears—well they usually have. I don't know if she does.
M: There's one—there. . . . Oh look, she's got hair. It's a girl—you're supposed to be all little.

Parke (1978) wryly comments on this finding: "to a parent some babies are more beautiful than others and a baby's face that may stop a clock may also stop a mother" (p. 80).

Early Parent-Infant Contact

Further evidence of biological influences on the process by which parents and infants establish relationships comes from studies of animal species in which early contact between mother and offspring is crucial to the formation of an emotional bond between them. For example, if a baby goat is removed from its mother

immediately after birth and is returned 2 hours later, the mother will attack it. But if the baby goat is allowed to stay with its mother for as little as 5 minutes after its birth before it is removed for a few hours, the mother will welcome its return (Klopfer, Adams, & Klopfer, 1964).

Marshall Klaus, John Kennell, and their co-workers claim that there is a similar sensitive period for maternal bonding with babies among humans (Klaus, Kennell, Plumb, & Zuehlke, 1970). These researchers divided 28 first-time mothers into an experimental and a control group. The mothers in the control group had the amount of contact with their newborn infants that

D: What do you think she weighs, Richard? I think about seven and a half.

M: Oh, she's gorgeous, she's lovely. She's got blue eyes. You hold her. Come on.

F: No.

M: Why not? *[laughs]* You're all of a tremble, aren't you?

D: I dropped the first one I held.

F: Charming!

M: Oh look, oh mine. Hello darling. Good lungs, hasn't she? She's got a dimple—where'd she get that from?

D: That's probably from the forceps. Actually, have you got dimples?

M: Oh no, neither of us have. Oh, you're lovely. Look. . . . she's lovely.

M: I thought she'd be all mauve and crinkly.

D: Oh, she's in great nick.

M: Yes. I was expecting her to be all mauve and shriveled, but she's not is she?

D: Not at all. In front of the cameras she's a real lady.

M: Oh dear. Having your photo taken darling? Oh.

D: Ma'am, can I ask you to drop your ankles apart?

M: She doesn't go much on this.

[Nurse attaches name-tag to baby]

F: Like British Rail, labeling her like a parcel.

M: Oh look, darling, look at the size of her feet. She's got no toenails.

D: What do you mean, she hasn't got any toenails?

M: She hasn't got any toenails.

M: They're soft.

D: I don't think you'd like it scratching around inside you.

M: Look—fabulous. Aren't you pleased with her.

F: Yes, of course.

D: I'm not putting her back.

M: You said that if it was a girl it could go back.

D: Back to the manufacturers, yes.

M: Well, it came from him in the first place.

D: Its' his spermatozoa that decides the sex.

M: Quite. *[kisses the baby and laughs]*

F: I shall be worried to death when she's eighteen.

M: You'll imagine her going out with all sorts of blokes like you were. *[laughs]* In a sort of odd way I was after his money really.

D: Yes?

M: All two quid. Go, go to dad.

(Macfarlane, 1977, pp. 61–67)

Mr. and Mrs. B are not the only parents who find they must quickly change their plans and make a virtue out of having a daughter instead of a son. In the United States, it is a fairly common occurrence. According to one survey, 80 percent of all Americans want their first child to be a son, and two-thirds of the women polled said that if they were to have only one child, they preferred that child to be a boy (Sanderson, 1982). Despite their initial hopes and expectations, most parents eventually accept the sex of their newborns.

was traditional in many hospitals in the late 1960s: a glimpse of the baby shortly after its birth, brief contact with it between 6 and 12 hours after birth, and then 20-to-30-minute visits for bottle feedings every 4 hours. In between these periods, the baby remained in the nursery. The mothers in the experimental group were given their babies to hold for 1 hour within the first 3 hours after delivery. The babies were undressed so that their mothers could feel them. In addition, the mother and child spent 5 hours together each afternoon for the 3 days following delivery. Many of the mothers reported that, although they were already excited by being able to fondle their newborn infants, their excitement reached a peak when they succeeded in achieving eye contact with them.

When the mothers and babies in both groups returned to the hospital 1 month later, the mothers in the experimental group were more reluctant to leave their infants with other caretakers. They also seemed more interested in the examination of their infants, were better at soothing them, and seemed to gaze at and fondle their babies more than did the mothers in the control group. Eleven months later, the extended-contact mothers still seemed more attentive to their babies and more responsive to their cries than were the mothers in the control group (Kennell et al., 1974).

Drawing an analogy with animal behavior, Klaus and Kennell (1976) subsequently suggested that if a mother and child are allowed to be in close physical contact immediately following birth, "complex interactions between mother and infant help to lock them together" (p. 51). The researchers speculate that hormones generated by the mother's body during the birth process may make her more receptive to forming an emotional bond with her baby. If these hormones dissipate before the mother has any extended contact with her newborn, she will presumably be less responsive to it (Kennell, Voos, & Klaus, 1979).

Klaus and Kennell's findings received a good deal of attention and prompted doctors and nurses at many hospitals to encourage mothers to have prolonged contact with their newborn babies. They also provoked a lot of criticism. Klaus and Kennell were attacked on methodological grounds because their experimental and control groups were quite small; there were only 14 mothers in each. Also, all the mothers were unmarried and black and had low incomes, which prompted some critics to claim they were not representative of mothers in general. Furthermore, the mothers in the experimental group were probably aware of the special treatment they received, and some critics suggested that this awareness, rather than the extended contact with their babies, may have been the source of their behavior. In the years since the study was conducted, some follow-up studies have replicated Klaus and Kennell's results, but others have failed to discover any long-lasting, significant differences between the relationships of mothers and infants who had extended early contact and the relationships of those who did not (Chess & Thomas, 1982; de Chateau, 1987; Lamb, 1982).

Most researchers today agree that immediate mother-infant contact is not crucial for the establishment of a long-term, positive emotional relationship between human mothers and normal infants. Parents who do not have immediate contact with their infants for whatever reasons are not forever estranged from them. Mothers who are anesthetized during delivery or suffer complications and who therefore do not see their babies for several hours or even days after their birth do not reject them; nor do mothers whose babies must be kept in incubators nor fathers who are not present for their children's birth (Rutter, 1979). In short, mothers and fathers form attachments to their babies under all sorts of circumstances (see de Chateau, 1987, or Lamb & Hwang, 1982, for a review).

Social Expectations

When a baby is born among the Ngoni of East Africa, the mother-in-law announces the baby's arrival by proclaiming, "A stranger has come!" In a certain sense, all newborn babies are strangers; they are newcomers no one has seen before. In important ways, however, babies are not total strangers.

While the mother is pregnant, most parents develop specific expectations about what their baby will be like. This is one reason the disappointment and grief parents feel if the baby dies or is deformed can be so devastating. But in cases of normal birth, no sooner do babies emerge from the womb than the parents begin to examine their looks and behaviors for hints of their futures. Will she have Grandmother Cameron's high, round forehead? Does his lusty cry mean that he will have his father's quick temper. Naturally, the actual baby will differ in some respects from the baby of the parents' prior imaginings. Usually, though, the parents begin to accommodate themselves to the reality of their child at the moment of its birth. According to Aidan Macfarlane (1977), adjusting to the actual sex of the child when the other sex was wanted is one of the most frequent parental adjustments that must be made. An example of the initial stages of such an adjustment can be seen in Box 4.4, "The Parents' Response to the Baby's Arrival."

No matter whether the baby is a boy or a girl, parents' beliefs and expectations begin to shape their responses to the baby even before the child displays any truly distinctive features. In one study, for example, first-time mothers and fathers were asked to choose words that described their newborn babies within 24 hours after their birth (Rubin, Provezano, & Luria, 1974). The babies did not differ in birth length or weight or in their scores on the Apgar Scale. Nevertheless, the parents described their daughters as "little," "beautiful," "pretty," or "cute" and as resembling their mothers. Sons, on the other hand, were described as "big" and as resembling their fathers. Fathers, the researchers found, were more likely to sex-type their babies than were mothers.

There is every reason for their baby's sex to be important to parents. Children's sex determines what they are named, how they are dressed, how they are treated, and what will be expected of them. Characterizing their baby according to its sex is one important way for parents to gain a sense of the child as a unique individual who belongs to them.

There is a disconcerting side to this process, too. We like to think of ourselves as individuals, and we want to be treated in terms of who we are, not just what others expect us to be. It therefore comes as something of a shock to learn that so many important aspects of our futures are shaped so early by parental expectations. But unless they are held so rigidly that they become destructive, parental expectations do not represent a parental failing.

Parental responses to their newborns reflect the fact that human infants are not just biological organisms but cultural entities as well. Infants have special meanings for their parents and other members of the community that are shaped by the culture's ideas about people and about the events that infants are likely to encounter as they grow to adulthood. These meanings, in turn, shape the ways adults construct the environmental contexts within which children develop. For example, there is a consistent difference in how boys and girls are treated not just because parents think that infant boys and girls are different to begin with,

but more importantly, because they believe that men and women have different roles to play (Sigel, 1985).

In this way, culturally organized beliefs act as powerful environmental sources of developmental continuity. As anthropologist Leslie White wrote some four decades ago, only among human beings does the world of ideas come

to have a continuity and permanence that the external world of the senses can never have. It is not made up of the present only, but of a past and a future as well. (1949, p. 372)

Just as infants arrive at childbirth with a set of genetically built-in capacities to learn about and to act upon the world, parents arrive at this moment with their own tendencies to respond in certain ways that have developed through their experience as members of their culture. The relationship between child and parents that begins at birth is an essential part of the foundation upon which later development builds.

SUMMARY

1. Birth is the first bio-social-behavioral shift in human development.

2. The process of birth begins approximately 266 days after conception when changes in the mother's body force the fetus through the birth canal.

3. Labor proceeds through three stages. It begins with the first regular, intense contractions of the uterus, and it ends when the baby is born, the umbilical cord is severed, and the afterbirth is delivered. Although the biological process of labor is roughly the same everywhere, there are marked cultural variations in the organization of childbearing.

4. The use of medication to reduce maternal pain became common toward the end of the nineteenth century. A possible negative outcome of the use of pain-reducing drugs is their impact on the neonate.

5. The infant's physical state at birth is usually assessed using the Apgar Scale, which rates the infant's heart rate, respiratory effort, reflex responsivity, muscle tone, and color. Babies with low Apgar scores require immediate medical attention to survive.

6. Scales have been developed to assess the neonate's behavioral capacities. These scales are satisfactory for identifying neonates who require medical intervention; they appear to be modestly useful, at best, for predicting later patterns of development.

7. Many premature babies who are normal-sized for their gestational age can catch up with full-term infants if they are well cared for. Those who have low birth weights and small head size are especially at risk for long-term developmental problems.

8. Infants are born with remarkable sensory and behavioral capacities with which to experience and respond to their postnatal circumstances.
   a. Hearing: Neonates are able to hear across the same frequency range as older children, and they display a special sensitivity to the basic sound categories of human language.
   b. Vision: Although they are nearsighted, infants systematically scan their surroundings and are sensitive to areas of light-dark contrast. They will track moving facelike forms at birth, and within a few days they seem to be able to distinguish their mother's face from other objects.

c. Taste and smell: Neonates can distinguish between different tastes and smells. They seem to prefer sweet tastes and pleasant smells.

d. Touch, temperature, and position: These senses are relatively mature at birth.

9. A variety of reflexes, which are automatic responses to specific environmental events, are present at birth.

10. It is widely believed that neonates are capable of experiencing such elementary emotions as pleasure, anger, disgust, surprise, and perhaps fear and sadness. Whether or not the quality of these emotions is the same as in older children and adults is doubtful.

11. There are individual variations in temperament, which refers to style of response and dominant mood, that are present at birth. Although findings about temperament remain controversial, it appears that temperamental variations among individuals are stable for long periods of time, constituting an important source of developmental continuity.

12. Neonatal appearance plays a significant role in how parents respond to their infants.

13. Some investigators believe that there is a critical period for emotional bonding between mothers and their infants shortly after birth. Attempts to replicate the study on which this claim is based have been only partially successful. Currently, most researchers believe contact shortly after birth is not essential to long term emotional attachment.

14. Parental expectations patterned by cultural belief systems are an important environmental source of developmental continuity.

KEY TERMS

Apgar Scale
Babyness
Brazelton Neonatal Assessment Scale
Dishabituation
Emotion

Ethology
Fetal growth retardation
Gestational age
Habituation
Low birth weight

Phonemes
Premature
Prepared childbirth
Reflexes
Temperament

SUGGESTED READINGS

APGAR, VIRGINIA, and JOAN BECK. *Is My Baby All Right?: A Guide to Birth Defects.* New York: Trident, 1972.

The originator of the most widely used neonatal assessment method and her coauthor provide an extremely useful summary of the genetic and environmental sources of birth defects.

BRAZELTON, T. BERRY. *Infants and Mothers: Differences in Development* (Rev. ed.). New York: Dell, 1983.

This book by the originator of a widely used neonatal assessment scale provides a solid foundation for thinking about the origins of individuality in early life.

KITZINGER, SHEILA. *Giving Birth: The Parents' Emotions at Birth.* New York: Taplinger, 1971.

The core of this book is a set of accounts by parents about their feelings surrounding the birth of their babies. Parents' relationships to each other and their initial reactions to their children are also described.

KOPP, CLAIRE B. "Risk Factors in Development." In P. H. Mussen (Ed.) *Handbook of Child Development* (Vol. 2) *Infancy and Developmental Psychobiology.* New York: Wiley, 1983.

A thorough summary of the risk factors that can endanger development, starting with conception and continuing through infancy. Major neonatal tests are described and compared, and methods for assessing their predictive power are carefully explained.

MACFARLANE, AIDAN. *The Psychology of Childbirth.* Cambridge, Mass.: Harvard University Press, 1977.

Pregnancy, birth, and the first days of life are described by a British pediatrician in a particularly lucid and sympathetic manner. Special emphasis is placed on the impact of common medical practices on the well-being of the baby and nature of early parent-infant interactions.

Infancy

Infancy is recognized as a distinct period of life in every culture. Its starting point is clear. It begins when the umbilical cord is severed and the child starts to breathe. The end of infancy is not so easily identified, however. According to the ancient Romans, an infant was "one who does not speak." Although the ability to speak is still considered an important indicator that infancy has ended, it is not a sufficient marker by itself. Modern developmental psychologists look for converging changes in several spheres of physical and psychological functioning to establish that one stage has ended and another has begun. The acquisition of language is not an isolated event in children's development. It is accompanied by changes in their social relations, their concepts of themselves, their modes of thought, and their physical capacities. This ensemble of changes, rather than any one of them by itself, is what transforms babies from relatively helpless infants into young children who, though still dependent upon adults, are on their way to independence.

The new psychological configuration that marks the end of infancy does not emerge all at once. It is the end result of a delicate interplay among the changes in the biological, behavioral, cultural, and social spheres of the infant's development that occur between birth and the age of $2\frac{1}{2}$ years. The chapters in Part II are organized to highlight the important sequences of changes in each sphere and the interactions among them.

Chapter 5 traces events in children's development from birth to the age of about $2\frac{1}{2}$ months. Although the period is relatively short, it provides an excellent introduction to the processes of developmental change. A major requirement of this earliest postnatal period is that the behaviors of infants and their caretakers become sufficiently coordinated for the adults to be able to provide the infants with enough food and warmth to support their continued growth. This requirement is met through a wide variety of different cultural systems of infant care that call upon the infant's basic capacity to learn from experience. If all goes well, the development of crucial brain structures that has occurred by the end of this period enables changes in infants' behavior that enhance their abilities to learn from experience and to reorder their interactions with their caretakers. This ensemble of changes is the first postnatal bio-social-behavioral shift.

Between about $2\frac{1}{2}$ and 12 months of age, the period covered in Chapter 6, the infant's capacities in several spheres progress markedly. Increases in size and strength are accompanied by increases in coordination and mobility: the ability to sit independently appears at about 5 or 6 months of age, crawling at about 7 or 8 months, and walking at about 1 year. Both memory and problem-solving abilities improve, providing infants with a firmer sense of their environment and their ability to act upon it. Sometime between the ages of 7 and 9 months, infants' increased physical ability and intellectual power bring about changes in their social relations. They become upset when left alone, they are likely to become wary of strangers for the first time, and they begin to form strong emotional attachments to their caretakers. They also begin to make their first speechlike sounds, heralding the beginning of language acquisition. These changes mark what appears to be a second bio-social-behavioral shift during infancy.

Chapter 7 describes the changes that occur between the ages of 12 months and 2½ years and culminate in the bio-social-behavioral shift that signals the end of infancy. Rapid growth in the baby's ability to use language is accompanied by the emergence of pretend play and more sophisticated forms of imitation and problem solving. Toward the end of infancy, children become more confident of their own abilities and less dependent on the immediate presence of their caretakers. They begin to show a concern for adult standards and to attempt to meet those standards. As infancy comes to an end, young children stand on their own two feet, turn aside the helping hands of their parents, and announce "I do it self." Parents, for their part, view these changes as a sign their children are no longer "babies." They can begin to reason with their children, explain things to them, and make demands on them.

The coverage of infancy ends with Chapter 8, which takes up an enduring question concerning human development: Is the pattern of development that is established during infancy fixed and unchangeable, or can it be significantly influenced by the maturational changes and experiences that occur during childhood and adolescence? Is there hope that children who have had traumatic early experiences can, with proper help recover to lead normal lives? Will a happy and healthy infancy enable children to develop the capacities they need to cope with later difficulties? These scientific questions have practical counterparts: Should society provide special supports for infants and their parents in order to reduce costly problems later on, or should infancy remain purely a family concern? As we will see, opinions about how these questions should be answered are sharply divided. Nevertheless, studying the efforts of psychologists to answer them makes clear the need to consider the whole child in the context of both the family and the community if we are to gain a scientific understanding of development and make informed decisions about social policies that affect children.

5

...

DEVELOPMENTAL CHANGE IN EARLY INFANCY

Babies control and bring up their families as much as they are controlled by them; in fact, we may say that the family brings up a baby by being brought up by him. Whatever reaction patterns are given biologically and whatever schedule is predetermined developmentally must be considered to be a series of *potentialities for changing patterns of mutual regulation.*

—Erik Erikson, *Childhood and Society*

· ·

Compared to guinea pigs and other creatures that are mature enough at birth to negotiate their environments almost as well as their parents, human beings are born in a state of marked immaturity. The capacities of children at birth are not adequate, by themselves, to ensure their survival. The sucking reflex, for example, is of no help in obtaining food unless the newborn's mouth is in touch with a source of milk, and newborns are incapable of arranging things alone so that the sucking reflex can come into play in an adaptive way. They must be physically aided to accomplish even such an elementary function as feeding. The relative helplessness of babies at birth has two obvious consequences. First, human newborns must depend upon their parents and other adults for many years after birth for their survival. Second, in order to survive on their own and eventually reproduce, humans must acquire a vast repertoire of knowledge and skills they do not possess at birth.

This chapter describes the processes of developmental change that occur in the initial period of infancy. This period begins immediately after birth with babies' first adjustments to the world and the parents' first adjustments to the responsibilities of bringing up a new human being. It ends some 2½ months later when the accumulated changes that occur in babies' central nervous systems and in what they have learned converge to make possible new kinds of behavior and a qualitatively different social relationship between infants and their caretakers. The convergence of changes in different domains is an example of the kind of qualitative reorganization in developing children that we have designated as a bio-social-behavioral shift. The explanations of developmental change that psychologists apply to this period will recur repeatedly in discussions of later infancy and subsequent periods of development.

BECOMING COORDINATED

The first task of parents and their baby is to coordinate their behaviors with each other so that the baby's basic needs are met. Each partner in this process comes partially prepared for the task. Parents come to this task equipped with a great deal of experience interacting with other human beings, rudimentary knowledge about how to care for newborn babies, and the support of their social group, which expects them to fulfill their roles as parents. Neonates, as we have seen, come equipped with reflexes and sensory capacities that give them an initial, tenuous grip on the world around them. The initial resources of each partner are essential to the process of development. But only through the mutual accommodation and coordination of the partners will development proceed successfully.

Parents cannot always be hovering over their baby, anticipating every need before it is expressed, for example. They must find a way to meet their infant's needs within the confines of their own rhythms of life and work. If parents work the land, they must be up with the sun. If they have to be at the office at 9 A.M., they need to sleep at night. If it is the custom to eat large meals during the middle of the day followed by a nap before returning to work, that is when the meal is scheduled. These circumstances cause parents to attempt to modify their babies' patterns of eating and sleeping so that they will fit into the life patterns of the household and the community.

In the United States this attempt to modify the infants' initial patterns of behavior is often referred to as "getting the baby on a schedule." Getting the baby on a schedule is more than a convenience. Through the coordination of activities that results, babies and par-

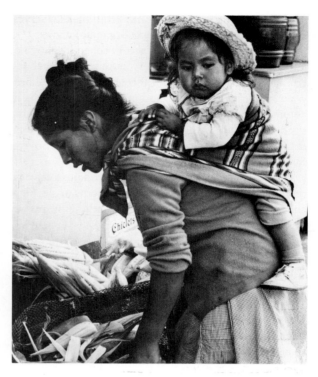

Every culture works out its own best way to transport babies.

ents create a system of mutual expectations that serves as the foundation for later developmental change.

Achieving a mutually satisfactory schedule is by no means easy or automatic. Every system of mutual accommodation causes some stress and strain. But when, eventually, families and newborns do achieve a common schedule and begin to coordinate smoothly, a general feeling of well-being is produced that helps to make the baby a welcome addition (Sprunger, Boyce, & Gaines, 1985).

Parental efforts to achieve a common schedule with their babies center on the infant's patterns of sleeping and eating. Babies' cries are their earliest means of signaling when these efforts fall short.

Sleeping

As with adults, the extent of newborns' arousal varies from complete rest to frantic activity. The patterns of their rest and activity are far different from those of adults, however, particularly in the first weeks after birth. To find out about newborn arousal patterns, Peter Wolff (1966) studied babies during their first weeks after birth. Based on such observable behaviors as muscle activity and eye movement, Wolff was able to distinguish seven states of arousal. These states are described in Table 5.1. Additional research has shown that there are distinctive patterns of brain activity associated with the different states of arousal (Berg &

Berg, 1987; Emde, Gaensbauer, & Harmon, 1976). In this kind of research, a device called an *electroencephalograph (EEG)* is used to record the tiny electrical currents generated by the brain's cells, which are detected by electrodes placed on the scalp.

EEG recordings of infant brain waves made shortly after birth distinguish two kinds of sleep that are the precursors of adult sleeping patterns: (1) an active pattern, called *rapid-eye-movement (REM) sleep,* that is characterized by uneven breathing; low-level, rapid brain-wave activity; and a good deal of eye and limb movement; and (2) a quiet pattern, called *non-rapid-eye-movement (NREM) sleep,* in which breathing is regular, brain waves are larger and slower, and the baby barely moves (see Figure 5.1). During the first 2 to 3 months of life, infants begin their sleep with active, REM sleep and only gradually fall into quiet, NREM sleep (Emde, Gaensbauer, & Harmon, 1976). After the first 2 or 3 months, the sequence reverses, and NREM sleep precedes REM sleep. Although this reversal is of little significance to parents, who are most concerned with their child's overall pattern of sleeping and waking, it is an important sign of developmental change in early infancy because it shows a shift in the brain basis of behavior toward the adult pattern.

Neonates spend most of their time asleep, though the amount of sleep they need gradually decreases. This trend is clearly evident from a study in which mothers were asked to keep a record of their babies' sleep time from birth until 4 months of age (Emde, Gaensbauer, & Harmon, 1976). Babies sleep about

TABLE 5.1 States of arousal in infants

State	Characteristics
Non-rapid-eye-movement sleep (NREM sleep)	Full rest; low muscle tone and motor activity; eyelids closed and eyes still; regular breathing (about 36 times per minute)
Rapid-eye-movement sleep (REM sleep)	Increased muscle tone and motor activity; facial grimaces and smiles; occasional eye movements; irregular breathing (about 48 times per minute)
Periodic sleep	Intermediate between REM and NREM sleep — bursts of deep, slow breathing alternating with bouts of rapid, shallow breathing
Drowsiness	More active then NREM sleep but less active than REM or periodic sleep; eyes open and close; eyes glazed when open; breathing variable but more rapid than in NREM sleep
Alert inactivity	Slight activity; face relaxed; eyes open and bright; breathing regular and more rapid than in NREM sleep
Active alert	Frequent diffuse motor activity; vocalizations; skin flushed; irregular breathing
Distress	Vigorous diffuse motor activity; facial grimaces; red skin; crying

SOURCE: Wolff, 1966.

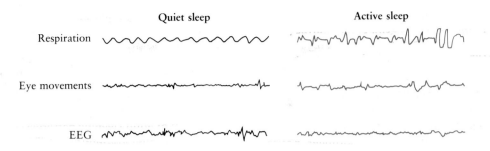

FIGURE 5.1 *The contrast between quiet and active sleep patterns in newborns is illustrated by the patterns of respiration, eye movements, and brain activity (EEG). Active sleep is characterized by irregular breathing, frequent eye movements, and continuous low-voltage brain activity. (Adapted from Parmelee, Akiyama, Schulte, Wenner, Schulte, & Stern, 1968.)*

16½ hours a day during the first week of life. By the end of 4 weeks, they sleep a little more than 15 hours a day; and by the end of 4 months, they sleep a little less than 14 hours a day.

If babies sleep most of the time, why do parents lose so much sleep? The reason is that newborns tend to sleep in snatches that last anywhere from a few minutes to several hours. Thus, they may be awake at any time of the day or night. As babies grow older, their sleeping and waking periods lengthen and begin to coincide with the night/day schedule common among adults (see Figure 5.2). A marked shift toward the night/day cycle occurs in the first weeks after birth among many babies born in the United States; by the end of the second week, their combined periods of sleep average 8½ hours between 7 P.M. and 7 A.M. (Kleitman, 1963). But the hours they are awake still result in some loss of sleep for their parents because the longest sleep period is only 4 or 5 hours.

Although babies' adoption of the night/day sleep cycle seems natural to those who live in industrialized countries and urban settings, studies of infants raised in other cultures suggest that it is at least partly a function of culturally patterned social influence on the infant. The role of social pressure in rearranging the newborn's sleep (such as putting the baby to bed at certain hours and not attending to waking periods during the night) can be seen by contrasting U.S. patterns with the development of babies' sleep-wake behavior in rural Kenya. Among the Kipsigi of rural Kenya, infants are almost always with their mothers. During the day they sleep when they can, often while being carried on their mothers' backs as their mothers go about their daily round of farming, household chores, and social activities. During the night they sleep with their mothers and are permitted to nurse

"on demand" whenever they wake up. Among Kipsigi infants, the longest period of sleep reported at 1 month is only about 3 hours; many shorter periods of sleep are sprinkled throughout the day and night. Eventually, Kipsigi infants begin to sleep through the night, but not until many months after American infants. Even as adults, the Kipsigi are more flexible in their sleeping hours than Americans (Super & Harkness, 1982).

In the United States, the length of the longest sleep period is often used as an index of the infant's maturation. It gradually increases from 4 or 5 to 8 hours in the typical, healthy American child in the first 16 weeks. Charles Super and Sara Harkness (1982) suggest that the lengthy period of sleep expected of American babies before they are 16 weeks old may be the limit of what young infants can adapt to. They report evidence that the many changes in a newborn's state of arousal

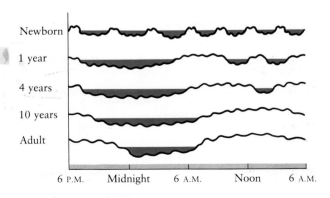

FIGURE 5.2 *The pattern of sleep-wake cycles among babies in the United States changes rapidly during infancy. A long period of sleep comes to replace many brief periods of alternating sleep and wakefulness. (From Kleitman, 1963.)*

that occur over a 24-hour period reflect the immaturity of the infant's brain, which sets a limit on how quickly children can conform to adult sleeping routines. This would explain why some infants do not adopt a night/day pattern of sleeping and waking as quickly or easily as parents in industrialized societies would like them to.

Feeding

Besides attempting to regulate their babies' sleeping patterns, parents also encourage their infants to adjust to a regular pattern of feeding. These have long been a favorite concern of pediatricians, whose recommendations as to when babies should be fed have changed significantly over the years. Today, pediatricians often recommend that newborns be fed as often as every 2 to 3 hours. From the early 1930s through the 1950s, mothers were advised to feed their babies only every 4 hours, whether they showed signs of hunger before then or not.

> Feed him at exactly the same hours every day.
> Do not feed him just because he cries.
> Let him wait until the right time.
> If you make him wait, his stomach will learn to wait.
> (Weill, 1930, p. 1)

For very small infants, 4 hours can be a long time to go without food. In a study in Cambridge, England, mothers were asked to keep records of their babies' behaviors and their own caretaking activities. Included were the time their babies spent in their cradles, the hours at which they were fed, the time the mothers spent bathing their babies and changing their diapers, and the time their babies spent crying. All the mothers were advised to feed their babies on a strict 4-hour schedule, but not all followed the advice. The less-experienced mothers tended to stick to the schedule, but the more-experienced mothers sometimes fed their babies as soon as 1 hour after a scheduled feeding. Not surprisingly, the reports of the less-experienced mothers showed that their babies cried the most (Bernal, 1972).

What happens if babies are fed "on demand"? In one study, the majority of newborn babies allowed to feed on demand preferred a 3-hour schedule (Aldrich & Hewitt, 1947). This interval gradually increased as the babies grew older. At 2½ months, most of the infants were feeding on a 4-hour schedule. By 7 or 8 months, the majority had come to approximate the normal adult schedule and were choosing to feed about four times a day. (Some parents reported this by saying that their children ate three meals and a snack.) It should be noted, however, that the figures given here are averages; at every age studied, about 40 percent of the babies did not fit the norm.

Crying

One of the most difficult problems parents face in establishing a pattern of care for their babies is interpreting their infants' needs. Parents can ask their newborn babies how they are feeling, but babies cannot answer. However, infants do have one important way of signaling that something is wrong — they can cry.

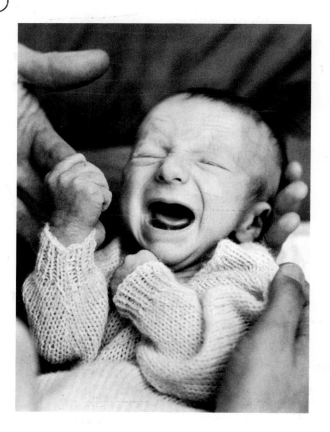

Even without the sound effects, it is clear that this infant's cries are likely to be taken as a preemptory command to anyone listening to do something quickly.

Babies' cries have a powerful effect on those who hear them. Both experienced parents and childless adults respond to infant cries with increases in heart rate and blood pressure, both physiological signs of increased anxiety (Bleichfeld & Moely, 1984; Frodi, Lamb, Leavitt, & Donovan, 1978). New parents react more strongly to infant cries than childless adults or experienced parents (Boukydis & Burgess, 1982). When nursing mothers hear babies' cries, even on recordings, their milk may start to flow (Newton & Newton, 1972).

When newborns cry, it is usually because something is causing discomfort. For the anxious parent, the problem is to figure out what that "something" is.

The cries themselves can sometimes indicate possible causes of distress. Electronic analysis has revealed that there are distinctive sound patterns for three types of crying: (1) the cries of a baby at birth who has been spanked on the bottom to start breathing; (2) the cries of an infant pricked by a pin; and (3) the cries of a hungry infant (see Figure 5.3). Although there is disagreement about how they do it, adult listeners, even those who are not regularly in contact with newborn babies, can distinguish among these different types of cries (Wasz-Höckert, Lind, Vuorenkoski, Partanen, & Valanné, 1968; Zeskind, Sale, Maio, Huntington, & Weiseman, 1985). Listeners in a variety of cultures can also distinguish the cries of infants who are at risk for a variety of developmental difficulties from the cries of normal infants (Lester & Zeskind, 1982; Zeskind, 1983; Zeskind, Sale, Maio, Huntington, & Weiseman, 1985). These findings have led Barry Lester (1984) to suggest that an unusual acoustic pattern of crying is a signal that special caretaking is urgently needed.

In spite of their ability to distinguish among types of crying, even experienced parents often cannot tell precisely why their baby is distressed. In part, this is because prolonged crying of all types eventually slips into the rhythmic pattern that characterizes the hunger cry. Thus, in many cases, only the intensity of the distress is evident. Hunger is, of course, a common reason for a newborn baby to cry. Studies of crying before and after feedings confirm that babies cry less after being fed (Dunn, 1977; Wolff, 1969). Circumstantial evidence suggests that some crying is the result of gastrointestinal pain. Babies will temporarily stop crying after they spit up, are burped, or have passed gas for example.

All these uncertainties make it difficult for parents to know what to do when their baby cries, especially

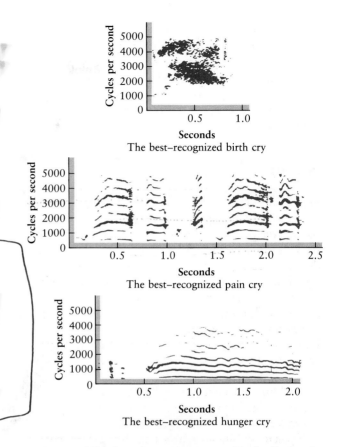

FIGURE 5.3 *Sound spectograms graphically display the physical differences among the cries that provide adults with information about the causes of babies' distress (From Wasz-Höckert, Lind, Vuorenkoski, Partanen, & Valanné, 1968.)*

when the cry does not signal acute pain (see Box 5.1, "Comforting Techniques for Fussiness"). A common concern of parents is that they will end up with a spoiled child if they pick up their baby in response to every cry. However, research discussed in Chapter 8 shows that this fear is unfounded. In any case, in the period from birth to 2½ months of age, crying gradually decreases in healthy babies who get enough to eat.

Coordinating infant and caretaker behaviors and getting babies on a schedule continue as the months go by. These accomplishments are so commonplace that it is easy to overlook their significance. However, they are crucially important for establishing the background against which the more obviously dramatic changes associated with the first months of life occur.

BOX 5.1

COMFORTING TECHNIQUES FOR FUSSINESS

• • •

All infants occasionally cry and seem to be mildly distressed for no readily identifiable cause, especially during the first 2½ months of life. Generally referred to as *fussiness*, this distress often peaks in the evenings for reasons not yet understood (Dunn, 1977). Sometimes, fussy babies can be soothed by nursing. If they have just been fed and still cry, their mothers often assume it is because their diapers are wet or they are cold. And, indeed, changing babies' diapers and wrapping them up warmly does tend to quiet them.

To find out just what it is about having their diapers changed that comforts babies, Peter Wolff (1969) had maternity ward nurses change the diapers of crying babies right after they had been fed, a time when a wet diaper is likely. For half the babies, the nurses changed the diapers as usual. For the other half the nurses went through all the motions of changing a diaper, but they put the wet diapers back on the babies. Significantly, most of the babies in both groups stopped crying. This suggests that it was the handling and attention the babies received rather than the change from a wet to a dry diaper that made the difference.

Mothers and others who care for babies all over the world have long known that babies quiet down when they are being handled or moved. Studies by Annaliese Korner and her associates have confirmed this common knowledge scientifically (Korner & Grobstein, 1966; Korner & Thoman, 1970). These researchers also compared the different ways that parents move and hold crying babies — by moving them so that they are lying prone, sitting them up, or picking them up and holding them to the shoulder or to the breast or in an embrace. They found that holding babies to the shoulder is by far the most effective way to make them stop crying. An added benefit when babies are held to the shoulder is that they are more likely to become attentive to their surroundings.

Other methods mothers use to calm crying infants include rocking, patting, cuddling, and swaddling them. Through her research, Yvonne Brackbill (1971) has found that the important features shared by these techniques are that they provide constant or rhythmic stimulation or that they reduce the amount of stimulation the babies receive from their own movements. Swaddling babies, which involves wrapping them tightly in a blanket so that they cannot move their arms and legs, does both (see the photo below). The blanket provides them with constant touch stimulation and, by restricting their movements, reduces the amount of stimulation they receive from those movements. Of all the techniques that provide continuous stimulation, Brackbill found that swaddling was overwhelmingly the most effective way to soothe a baby.

Another commonly used and very effective way to calm crying babies is to give them a pacifier to suck on. Sucking provides the baby with regular and rhythmic stimulation of the mouth. This apparently relaxes both the gut and the major muscles and reduces the baby's random thrashings (Dunn, 1977; Field & Goldson, 1984).

Among the techniques for soothing babies, swaddling, which is used in many cultures, is one of the most effective.

MECHANISMS OF DEVELOPMENTAL CHANGE

Almost immediately after birth, the behavioral repertoire of neonates begins to expand, allowing them to interact with the world around them with ever-increasing effectiveness. In part, the changes in behavior that occur during the first months of life are a matter of perfecting already existing capacities. For example, as infants become able to suck more effectively, they obtain more food, which allows them to go longer between feedings without distress. The perfecting of existing behaviors does not, however, explain how *new* behaviors arise. By the age of 2½ months, infants can raise their heads to look around, smile in response to the smiles of others, reach for objects, and shake rattles put into their hands. One task of developmental psychology is to explain how these new forms of behavior arise.

From Sucking to Nursing

A prime example of a new behavior that appears in early infancy is nursing. When we compare the way newborn infants feed with the nursing behavior of 6-week-old infants, a striking contrast is evident. Newborns possess several reflexes that are relevant to feeding: rooting (turning the head in the direction of a touch on the cheek), sucking, swallowing, and breathing. However, these component behaviors are not well integrated, so babies' early feeding experiences are likely to be discoordinated affairs. When first held to the breast, a touch to the cheek will make newborns turn their heads and open their mouths, but they root around in a disorganized way. When they take the nipple and begin to suck, they easily lose it and stop sucking. When they do suck, the upper lip may fold back and block their nostrils, eliciting a sharp head-withdrawal reflex (see Figure 5.4). Furthermore, breathing and sucking may not be well coordinated at first, so newborns are likely to have to stop sucking to come up for air.

By the time infants are 6 weeks old, their feeding behavior has changed noticeably. The infants anticipate being fed when they are picked up. More significantly, they have worked out the coordination of all the component behaviors of feeding—sucking, swallowing, and breathing—such that they can perform them in a smooth, integrated sequence (Bruner, 1968). Feeding has become nursing. In fact, babies become so efficient in their nursing that they can accomplish in less than 10 minutes what originally took them as long as an hour.

Nursing is clearly *not* a reflex. It is a new form of behavior that develops through the reorganization of the various reflexes with which infants are born. Although the acquisition of this behavior is commonplace, it raises in clear form the question of how developmental change comes about. Each of the four broad theoretical frameworks—the biological-maturation perspective, the environmental-learning perspective, the interactional perspective, and the cultural-context perspective—emphasizes different factors in attempting to explain development (see Chapter 1, pp. 12–17).

FIGURE 5.4 *In this sequence the infant's nostrils are blocked while he is nursing. As a consequence, his breathing is cut off, which elicits a head-withdrawal reflex that interferes with nursing.*

FIGURE 5.5   *A schematic drawing of how a simple reflex works. The heat of the candle flame sends a sensory message to the spinal cord. The spinal cord sends a message to the arm muscles to pull the hand from the heat. (Adapted from Church, 1974.)*

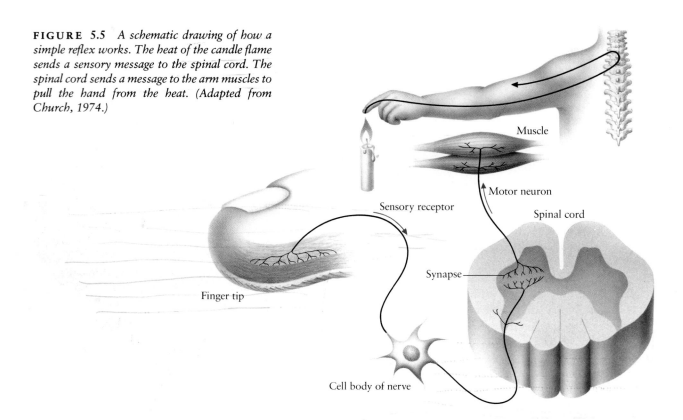

By examining the phenomena highlighted by each perspective and how theorists working within these perspectives attempt to explain the development of the seemingly "simple" behavior of nursing, we can gain a sense of how each perspective contributes to our understanding of the development of other behaviors during infancy and beyond.

The Biological-Maturation Perspective

Biologically oriented developmental theorists invoke precisely the same mechanism to explain the development of nursing and other new behaviors following birth that they use to explain all aspects of prenatal development—maturation. New behaviors, they say, arise from old behaviors owing to distinct maturational changes in the physical structures and physiological processes of the organism. This position was stated most forcefully by Arnold Gesell: "The child comes by his psychic [psychological] constitution through embryological processes" (Gesell, 1945,

p. 167). Consequently, the role of the organism's genetic inheritance is considered to be of paramount importance, and the role of the environment in development, is considered to be minimal, just as during the prenatal period.

Reflexes and the brain   The biological-maturation approach emphasizes the fact that neonatal reflexes must involve the central nervous system in some way. Figure 5.5 illustrates how a simple reflex works. When a child puts a finger in a candle flame, a *sensory receptor*—a neuron that is specialized to receive sensory input from the environment—in the finger tip is excited. The resulting electrical impulse travels from the finger to the spinal cord, where it comes to a **synapse**—a small gap between neurons. The impulse passes across the synapse to a *motor neuron*—a neuron that initiates muscle activity—and then back to the muscles in the arm. There it causes the muscles to contract, jerking the hand away from the flame.

For simple reflexes, the circuit that connects the sensory receptor and the motor neuron goes only as far

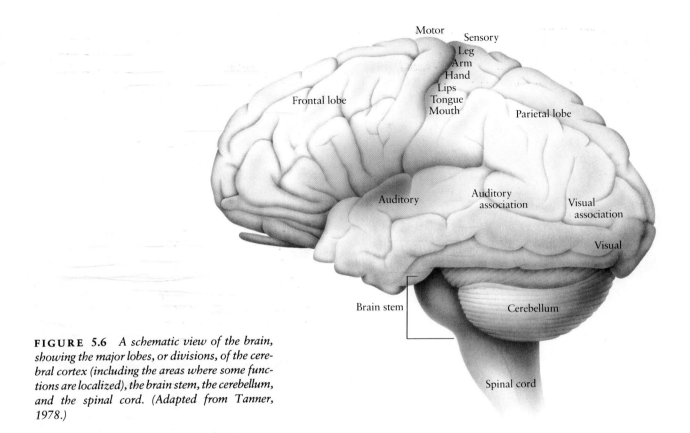

FIGURE 5.6 *A schematic view of the brain, showing the major lobes, or divisions, of the cerebral cortex (including the areas where some functions are localized), the brain stem, the cerebellum, and the spinal cord. (Adapted from Tanner, 1978.)*

as the spinal cord, so regions in the brain do not play a role. With such reflexes, the response may occur so quickly that the child does not feel pain or fear until afterwards. However, many reflex actions, including crying and the various feeding reflexes, have neural circuitry that is far more complicated and involves the more complex structures of the central nervous system in the brain. These reflexes, say the biological maturationists, can be expected to change simply because the associated structures themselves mature.

In human beings and some other species, the upper end of the spinal cord thickens to form the **brain stem.** Clusters of neurons within the brain stem begin to function during the fetal period. By birth the brain stem is one of the most highly developed areas of the brain. It controls such inborn reflexes as rooting and sucking, as well as such vital functions as breathing and sleeping. The brain stem also contains the neural structures that are associated with the emotions.

The nerves of the brain stem do not respond to specific forms of sensory input in a neat, one-to-one manner. The brain stem contains several distinct neural pathways that mix various sources of sensory input with impulses from other regions of the brain and the body. Stimulation from the environment that reaches the brain stem is modulated and reorganized. This allows for activities that are more complex and sustained than those that are characteristic of the simple reflexes that involve only the spinal cord.

In addition to the spinal cord and the brain stem, there is a third major area of the central nervous system that is important to consider in understanding early development—the **cerebral cortex** (see Figure 5.6). Stimulation from the environment that reaches the cerebral cortex travels through fields of interacting neurons so complex that scientists have thus far found it impossible to trace completely the fate of a single stimulus event such as a touch on the cheek. By permitting the integration of information from several sensory sources and memories of past experiences, the cerebral cortex plays a vital role in the development of new behaviors.

The cerebral cortex is the area of the brain that most clearly distinguishes human beings from other animals.

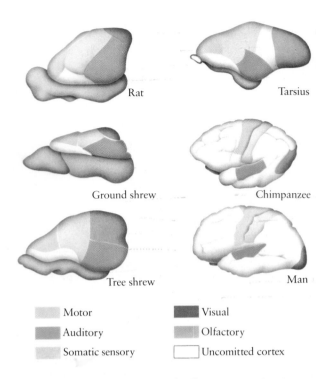

Motor — Visual

Auditory — Olfactory

Somatic sensory — Uncomitted cortex

FIGURE 5.7 *Comparison of different mammalian brains showing the approximate proportions of the brain mass that are devoted to different functions. The areas marked "uncommitted" are not dedicated to any particular sensory or motor functions and are available for integrating information of many kinds. (Adapted from Fishbein, 1976.)*

Within the cortex, certain regions are specialized for the analysis of time, space, and language as well as for motor functions and sensory discriminations. However, large areas of the cortical mass are not prewired to respond directly to external stimulation in any discernible way (see Figure 5.7). These "uncommitted" areas underpin the human capacity to synthesize sensory information in unique ways, making possible such higher psychological functions characteristic of the human adult as voluntary remembering and logical deduction (Luria, 1973).

The neonate's cortical brain structures undergo many changes after birth, continuing processes that began during the fetal period. There are increases in the number, size, complexity, and even the kinds of cells in the brain after birth (Lecours, 1982; Milner, 1967) (see Figure 5.8).

A cortical change that has received a great deal of attention in studies of development in the first postna-

tal months is **myelination,** the process by which the neurons become covered by **myelin,** a sheath of fatty cells that stabilizes the neurons and speeds transmission of nerve impulses along them (Conel, 1939–1963; Yakovlev & Lecours, 1967). Cortical nerve cells, including those that connect the cerebral cortex with the brain stem, are not myelinated at birth. Consequently, the circuitry of the cortex is only tenuously connected to the lower-lying parts of the nervous system that receive stimulation from the environment. At birth these lower-lying areas can mediate motor reflexes and visual responses without cortical involvement. As the nerve fibers connecting the cortex with regions below the cortex become myelinated, the infant's abilities expand.

Different parts of the cerebral cortex develop at different times throughout infancy and well into childhood and adolescence (Rabinowicz, 1979). Using such criteria as the number and size of neurons and the degree of myelination, scientists who study the anatomy of the nervous system estimate that the first area of the cerebral cortex to undergo important developmental change is the **primary motor area,** which controls voluntary movement (Kolb & Wishaw, 1985; Tanner, 1978). Within the primary motor area, the first cells to become functional are those that control the arms and the trunk. By about 1 month, the neurons in this area are becoming myelinated, allowing them to conduct neural impulses more efficiently. The region of the primary motor area that governs leg movements is the last to develop; it is not fully developed until sometime in the second year (Tanner, 1978).

Structural developments in the motor cortex are associated with increases in infants' voluntary movements. At the end of the first month, many infants can raise their heads while lying on their stomachs. At 3 months, they show more voluntary movement in the muscles that move the upper trunk, shoulders, arms, and forearms. Voluntary control of leg movements does not come until a few months later.

The **primary sensory areas** of the cortex, those areas that are responsible for the initial analysis of sensory information, are also maturing in the months following birth. The nerve fibers responsible for touch are the first to become active, followed by those in the primary visual area and then those in the primary auditory area. By 3 months, all the primary sensory areas are relatively mature (Tanner, 1978).

According to the biological-maturation perspective, the baby can be expected to engage in more complex

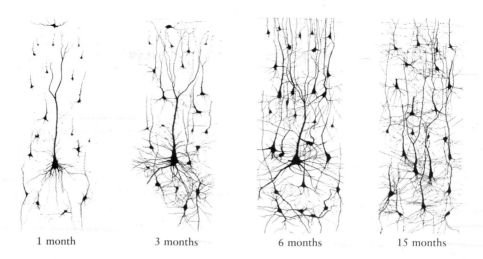

1 month   3 months   6 months   15 months

FIGURE 5.8 *These drawings from photomicrographs of infant brain tissue illustrate the marked increases in the size and number of cerebral neurons during the first 15 months of postnatal life. (From Conel, 1939–1963.)*

and refined interactions with the environment as the brain matures. In this view, the infant's increasing success at nursing, like the gradual lengthening of the intervals between feedings and the periods of sleep, would appear to depend at least in part upon the maturation of underlying brain structures. Two lines of evidence — one from studies of developmental abnormalities, the other from studies of the relation of reflexes to later behavior — support this view.

Evidence from studies of babies with abnormalities In rare cases, infants are born with cerebral cortexes that have failed to develop. Such babies may have normal reflexes at birth (see Figure 5.9). E. Gamper (1926/1959), for example, observed an infant who was born with an intact brain stem but little or no cerebral cortex. The baby could suck, yawn, stretch, cry, and follow a visual stimulus with his eyes.

Babies born without a cerebral cortex seldom live long. Those that do live for more than a few days fail to develop the complex, well-coordinated behaviors seen in normal babies. This strongly suggests that the cerebral cortex plays an essential role in the development of such coordinated actions as nursing (Emde & Harmon, 1972; Kolb & Wishaw, 1985).

Evidence from studies of reflexes and later behavior Within the first few months following birth, the Moro reflex and several of the other reflexes infants

are born with disappear, never to return. Others, such as the stepping reflex, disappear for awhile and then, reappear as part of a more mature behavior. Still others are transformed into more complex behaviors without first disappearing for a time. Many researchers

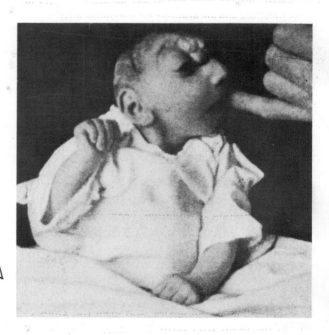

FIGURE 5.9 *Even babies born with little or no cerebral cortex display basic reflexes such as sucking. (Courtesy of the New York Academy of Medicine Library.)*

BOX 5.2

EXPERIENCE AND DEVELOPMENT OF THE BRAIN

... ∙ ∙ ∙

In attempting to understand the relationship between the brain and psychological development, it seems no more than common sense to expect that increases in the complexity of the brain will precede, or at least accompany, increases in behavioral complexity. An example of such a relationship is the development of social smiling described later in this chapter (p. 172): the cells of the visual cortex and connections between the visual cortex and the brain stem must become functional before children can see others smiling and so be able to smile in return. What this simplified account leaves out, though, is that the development of the brain cells themselves depends upon visual experience. The principle that development emerges from the interaction of the organism and the environment applies no less to the development of the brain than to the development of behavior (Greenough, Black, & Wallace, 1987; Rosenzweig, 1984).

Early demonstrations of the influence of experience on the brain were provided by the studies of Austin Riesen (1950), which were carried out with normal chimpanzees who were raised for the first 16 months of their lives in total darkness. When the chimpanzees were then placed in a normally lighted environment, they were unable to learn simple pattern and color discriminations, and their visual acuity was severely impaired. Eye examinations showed that their retinas had failed to develop normally. Subsequently, anatomical and biochemical analyses have shown that animals deprived of visual experience suffer disturbances of pro-

tein synthesis in the visual cortex; as a result, the visual cortex has neurons with fewer and shorter branches and up to 70 percent fewer synapses than normal (Blakemore & Mitchell, 1973; Coleman & Riesen, 1968). Significantly, the degree and duration of these effects depend on the age at which light deprivation occurs. If it ends early enough, recovery is possible, which is consistent with the idea of critical periods.

Additional animal research has shown that the nature of the visual experience plays a role in shaping the neural connections between the eyes and the visual cortex. Certain cells in a cat's brain, for example, normally respond best to horizontal lines whereas other cells respond best to vertical lines. Both kinds of cells are present in large numbers in kittens who have not yet opened their eyes (Hubel & Wiesel, 1979). When kittens are raised in an environment that allows them to see only horizontal lines for several months, they have far fewer of the nerve cells that respond to vertical lines than do normal kittens, so their ability to detect vertical lines does not develop normally (Hirsch & Spinelli, 1971).

Evidence that the visual cortex is not the only part of the brain that is affected by experience is provided by the pioneering studies of Mark Rosenzweig and his colleagues (summarized in Rosenzweig, Bennett, & Diamond, 1972). These researchers raised groups of young male laboratory rats from the same litter in three different environments. The first group was housed individually in standard laboratory cages. Members of the sec-

... ∙ ∙ ∙

see these changes in the structure of early reflexes as important evidence about the way in which the maturation of higher brain centers changes behavior (McGraw, 1943; Oppenheim, 1981).

In the **Moro reflex,** infants respond to a sudden noise or to the sensation of being dropped by flinging their arms out with their fingers spread and then bringing their arms back in toward their bodies with their fingers bent as if to hug something (see Figure

5.10). The Moro reflex usually disappears by the fifth or sixth month. It is seen again only if there is an injury to the central nervous system, which leads some researchers to conclude that its disappearance is the result of the maturation of higher brain centers. Injury to these centers shifts control of the limbs back to the brain stem (Prechtl, 1977).

The **stepping reflex** is the tendency newborns have to make rhythmic leg movements when they are held

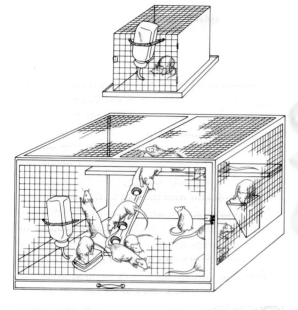

The standard laboratory cage in which laboratory rats are typically housed (top) provides little opportunity for complex interactions with the environment compared to cages that provide for an enriched environment (bottom). (Adapted from Rosenzweig, Bennett, & Diamond, 1972.)

At the end of the experimental period, which lasted anywhere from a few weeks to several months, behavioral tests and examinations of the animals' brains revealed many differences that favored the animals who were raised in enriched conditions. These included

- Increased rates of learning in standard laboratory tasks, such as learning a maze
- Increased overall weight of the cerebral cortex
- Increased amounts of acetylcholinesterase, a brain enzyme that enhances learning
- Larger neuronal cell bodies and glial (supportive) cells
- More synaptic connections

These findings confirm an earlier study that showed that when animals were housed singly in small cages within an enriched environment so that they could do no more than observe what was going on around them, their learning capacity was no different from that of the animals who were housed in the normal individual cages (Forgays & Forgays, 1952). Active interaction with the environment seems to be the crucial factor in producing these changes.

Although these results were obtained with nonhuman animal species, they are consistent with what is known about the importance of active involvement with the environment for human development. They show that behavioral changes should not be thought of as secondary consequences of changes that occur in the brain. Behavioral changes induced by environmental stimulation can themselves lead to changes in the brain that then support more complex forms of behavior.

ond group were housed together in standard laboratory cages. The third group was provided with enriched conditions. Its members were housed in a large cage that was furnished with a variety of objects they could play with. A new set of playthings, drawn from a pool of 25 objects, was placed in the cage every day. Often, the animals in this group were given formal training in a maze or were exposed to a toy-filled open field.

in an upright position with their feet touching a flat surface (see Figure 5.11). It ordinarily disappears at around 2 months of age. At about 1 year of age, babies use similar motions as a component in walking, a voluntary activity that is acquired with practice.

There is currently a lively debate about the reasons for the disappearance of the stepping reflex and its relation to later walking. According to Philip Zelazo (1983), the disappearance of this reflex is an example

of a lower, reflex action being suppressed as higher, cortical functions begin to mature. After a period of reorganization, he argues, the old reflex reappears in new form as a component of voluntary walking.

This explanation is criticized by Esther Thelan and her colleagues who believe that the stepping reflex is really a form of kicking (Thelan, 1986; Thelan & Fisher, 1982). According to these researchers, early kicking behavior disappears because of changes in

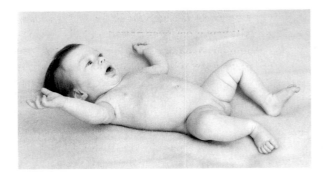

FIGURE 5.10 *Babies exhibit the Moro reflex when they are startled or experience a sudden loss of support.*

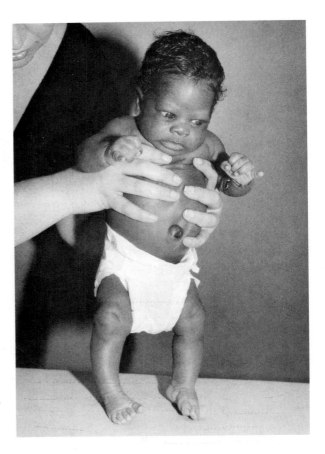

FIGURE 5.11 *Babies held upright with their feet touching the ground move their legs in a fashion that looks like walking. Called the stepping reflex, this form of behavior is currently the subject of debate concerning its origins and subsequent developmental history.*

the baby's muscle mass and weight, not because of changes in the cortex. They claim that the voluntary walking that appears later is not the same movement; it requires not only the maturation of the cortex but also a number of concurrent developments, including increased strength and the ability to balance upright.

A reflex that does not disappear but is instead transformed is **prereaching,** or *visually initiated reaching,* in which newborns reach toward an object that catches their attention and simultaneously make grasping movements (Bushnell, 1985; Trevarthan, 1982; Von Hofsten, 1984). Shortly after birth, reaching and grasping appear to be independently functioning reflexes because they are not coordinated. Often infants fail to grasp an object because their hands close too early or too late, even after repeated attempts.

Between 2 and 3 months of age, and coincident with maturational changes in the visual and motor areas of the cerebral cortex, the visually *initiated* reaching reflex is transformed into visually *guided* reaching, a new form of behavior in which reaching and grasping are coordinated. Although no one has yet pinpointed the cortical areas that underlie such new behaviors as visually guided reaching or nursing, it seems safe to say that the maturation of cortical structures, and probably of the musculature as well, must be accorded a significant role in their development. At the same time, it is not clear that all of the brain connections that are associated with coordinated reaching or nursing develop before those behaviors begin to appear or that they develop completely independent of environmental influence, as some biological maturationists seem to imply. It may be that some of these brain developments grow out of infants' interactions with their envi-

ronment (see Box 5.2, "Experience and Development of the Brain").

The Environmental-Learning Perspective

Whatever the biological contribution to the development of sucking and the other reflexes that are present at birth may be, some form of adaptation to the environment on the part of the infant is clearly necessary for nursing behavior to develop. A mother does not have to continue to be responsible for insuring that a bottle or breast is always presented in precisely the position required to elicit the sucking reflex throughout infancy. Before long infants begin to make the proper adjustments as soon as feeding begins.

Developmental psychologists working within the environmental-learning framework acknowledge that the brain is maturing during early infancy, but they deny that maturation alone could explain how innate reflexes become coordinated with each other and with appropriate eliciting stimuli in the environment, as is the case when nursing is elicited by the sight of a bottle or the mother's breast. They argue that such coordination requires *learning*, which is generally defined as a relatively permanent change in behavior brought about by the experience of events in the environment. Several types of learning are believed to operate throughout development, including habituation (which was described in Chapter 4, p. 120), classical conditioning, and operant conditioning. A fourth type of learning, imitation, is important in later infancy, but it may or may not be present shortly after birth. The current controversy surrounding imitation in early infancy is discussed in Box 5.3, "Imitation in the Newborn?"

Classical conditioning Classical conditioning is the process by which an organism learns which events in its environment go with each other. As Carolyn Rovee-Collier (1987), a researcher who has been influential in promoting the study of classical conditioning among infants, points out, "Because many events in nature occur in an orderly fashion, classical conditioning permits organisms to exploit this orderliness and anticipate events instead of simply reacting to them" (p. 107).

The existence of this very basic learning mechanism was demonstrated at the turn of the century by the Russian physiologist Ivan Pavlov (1849–1936). Pavlov (1927) showed that, after several experiences of hearing a tone just prior to having food placed in its mouth, a dog would begin to salivate in response to the tone, before the dog received the food. In everyday language, the dog began to expect food when it heard the tone and its mouth "watered at the thought."

In the terminology of environmental learning theories, Pavlov paired a conditional stimulus (CS)—a tone—with an unconditional stimulus (UCS)—food in the mouth. The food is called an **unconditional stimulus** because it "unconditionally" causes salivation, salivation being a reflex response to food in the mouth. Salivation, in turn, is called an **unconditional response** (UCR) because it is automatically and invariantly (that is, "unconditionally") elicited by food in the mouth. The tone is called a **conditional stimulus** because the behavior it elicits depends on ("is conditional on") the way it has been paired with the unconditional stimulus. When the unconditional response (salivation in response to food in the mouth) occurs in response to the CS (the tone), it is called a **conditional response** (CR) because it depends on the pairing of the CS (the tone) and the UCS (the food). The key indicator that learning has occurred is that the CS elicits the CR *before* the onset of the UCS (see Figure 5.12).

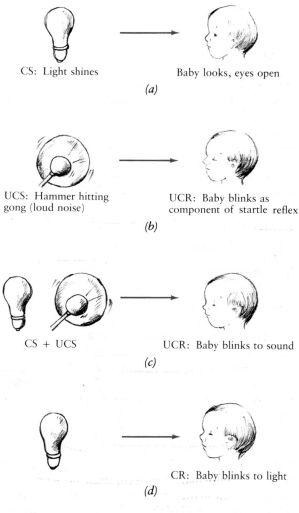

CS: Light shines   Baby looks, eyes open

(a)

UCS: Hammer hitting gong (loud noise)   UCR: Baby blinks as component of startle reflex

(b)

CS + UCS   UCR: Baby blinks to sound

(c)

CR: Baby blinks to light

(d)

FIGURE 5.12 *Classical conditioning. In the top panel (a) the sight of a light (CS) elicits no particular response. In (b) the loud sound of a gong (UCS) causes the baby to blink his eyes (UCR). In (c) the sight of the light (CS) is paired with the loud sound of the gong (UCS), which evokes an eyeblink (UCR). Finally, (d) the sight of the light (CS) is sufficient to cause the baby to blink (CR), demonstrating that learning has occurred.*

BOX 5.3

IMITATION IN THE NEWBORN?

• • •

When we consider newborns' limited visual capacities and the uncoordinated nature of their movements, the notion that neonates can imitate actions they see might seem farfetched. Yet several studies appear to show that babies are capable of rudimentary forms of imitation from birth (Gardner & Gardner, 1970; Meltzoff & Moore, 1977, 1983a, 1983b). These studies have generated intense interest among developmental psychologists because it has long been believed that imitation does not become possible until several months after birth (Abravanel, Levan-Goldschmidt, & Stevenson, 1976; Piaget, 1962). If true imitation does exist in newborns, it would provide them with an important avenue for learning about the world.

All that would seem necessary to determine whether newborns are capable of imitating would be for the researcher to present some behavior to newborns and then observe whether or not they repeat it. However, a good deal of research has failed to resolve the question of imitation in newborns definitively. Part of the prob-

lem is finding behaviors that are within newborns' capacities.

In research by Andrew Meltzoff and Keith Moore (1977, 1983a, 1983b), an adult loomed above an alert newborn baby and made distinctive facial expressions such as opening his mouth very wide or sticking out his tongue. Meltzoff and Moore reported that the infants often imitated the facial expression of the adult. Aware that their claims were going to be viewed sceptically, Meltzoff and Moore took special precautions to ensure that their results could not be attributed to procedural errors. As a check of their findings they photographed the infants and the adult model independently. They then asked judges who had not been present during the experimental sessions to look at the photographs of the infants and guess what sort of face the adult had made. The judges were successful at this unusual task at a greater-than-chance level, suggesting that the infants did, indeed, imitate the distinctive adult facial expressions they saw.

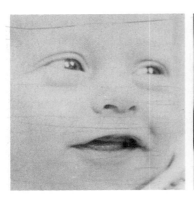  

Each pair of photos shows the expression of an infant after observing an adult; the correspondence between the infant's

Almost immediately, psychologists seized on Pavlov's demonstrations as a possible model for the way infants learn about their environments. One of Pavlov's co-workers demonstrated conditioned feeding responses in a 14-month-old infant (Krasnogorski, 1907/1967). The baby opened his mouth and made

sucking motions (CRs) at the sight of a glass of milk (CS). When a bell (a new CS) was sounded on several occasions just before the glass of milk was presented, mouth opening and sucking begin to occur at the sound of the bell, showing that classical conditioning would build expectations in the infant based on a

However, the results were not as clear-cut as the report of the findings might suggest. For example, on the 97 trials when the researcher stuck out his tongue, the babies "most often" stuck out their tongues in return. But the "most often" means that they stuck out their tongues 30 times; they opened their mouths 20 times, and they puckered their lips or moved their fingers on the remaining trials. The imitative response won out, but just barely.

The research of Meltzoff and Moore has generated many follow-up studies. Tiffany Field and her colleagues (Field, Woodson, Greenberg, & Cohen, 1982) found support for Meltzoff and Moore's conclusions using somewhat different procedures and responses (see the photos below). They arranged for an adult to model three facial expressions—happy, sad, and surprised—for babies who were an average of 36 hours old. The babies showed that they could distinguish among the model's different facial expressions by the fact that they habituated to the repeated presentation of a single expression but then began to pay close attention again when the model presented them with a different facial expression. Most important, the babies appeared to imitate these new expressions. An observer who could not see the model and who did not know what expressions were being presented to the babies was able to determine the facial expression of the model from the facial movements of the babies on a statistically reliable basis. These results are difficult to explain without assuming that the infants somehow matched what they did with what they saw the model doing. Precisely how infants accomplished this matching remains uncertain (Vinter, 1986).

Not everyone who has attempted to replicate Meltzoff and Moore's study has been successful, however. This has led some researchers to suggest that either there was some peculiarity in their procedures or the behavior they observed is a very special form of imitation (Abravanel & Sigafoos, 1984; Hayes & Watson, 1981). One possibility is that imitation in the newborn is a reflex behavior that disappears with time, unless it is specially maintained by operant conditioning.

Even if newborns are capable of imitation, it cannot be counted among the important learning mechanisms that are present at birth. It will, however, become an important mechanism of learning when it appears as a prominent part of infants' behavioral repertoire later in the first year of life.

 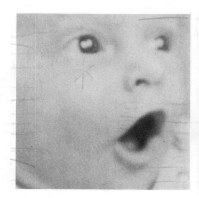 

expression and the adult's expression is taken as evidence that newborns are capable of imitation.

process of association. The crucial point to these observations is that there is no *biological* connection between the sight of a glass of milk or the sound of a bell and the mouth opening and sucking responses they elicited. Rather, the occurrence of these responses to the new stimuli shows that learning has occurred.

Pavlov's ideas soon won a large following in the United States and several studies intended to demonstrate the importance of classical conditioning as a mechanism of infant learning were conducted. In a study mentioned in Chapter 1 (p. 26), Watson and Rayner purported to show that infant fears are learned through the process of classical conditioning. Dorothy Marquis (1931), in one of the early studies of classical conditioning in newborn infants, showed that sucking motions could be conditioned to the sound of a buzzer by sounding the buzzer just before giving babies a bottle.

These early studies were criticized because they did not entirely rule out other possible causes for the babies' behavior. For example, the babies in Marquis's study may have opened their mouths and made sucking motions simply because they were excited by the buzzer and not because they had made a specific association between the buzzer and food. These criticisms took on additional force when several well-controlled experiments failed to show classical conditioning in newborn infants (Sameroff & Cavanaugh, 1979). Thus, as recently as a decade ago, it appeared that classical conditioning does not occur in infants until 2 or 3 months after birth. However, intensive research conducted during the past 10 years, in which stimuli that are biologically significant to an infant were chosen and great care was taken to make certain that the infant subjects were alert at the time the experiments were performed, has demonstrated with virtual certainty that classical conditioning can occur within hours of birth.

For example, Elliott Blass and his associates conditioned the sucking response to stroking of the forehead (Blass, Ganchrow, & Steiner, 1984). These researchers assumed that such tactile stimulation occurs naturally during feeding but that it does not ordinarily produce sucking. They used a pipette to give infants only a few hours old a small dose of sugar-water (sucrose) immediately after stroking the infants' foreheads. Infants in a control group were also stroked and given sugar-water, but the researchers performed the two acts independently and at variable intervals to preclude the possibility that the infants would form an association between them. The infants in the experimental group began to suck and pucker up their faces a response pattern the researchers dubbed a "pucker-suck"—when they were stroked on the forehead. The infants in the control group did not.

One of the most convincing bits of evidence that classical conditioning had occurred was the way the infants reacted when the investigators later stroked their foreheads but did not give them sugar-water. The first or second time this happened, the infants in the experimental group responded by frowning or making an angry face and then crying or whimpering. The researchers also stopped giving sugar-water to the infants in the control group, but when their foreheads were stroked, they did not express anger or cry. Rovee-Collier (1987) comments that this finding "suggests that infants in the experimental group had learned the predictive relation between stroking and sucrose delivery and cried because their *expectancy was violated*" (p. 113).

One kind of classical conditioning that does not seem to occur in newborns is **aversive conditioning,** in which the infant must learn to anticipate an unpleasant event such as a pin prick or a bright light shining in the eyes. Aversive conditioning is apparently not possible until a few months after birth. Why this is so is not clear. Rovee-Collier (1987) suggests that it may reflect an evolutionary adaptation to the environment human infants normally encounter. During their first months of life, infants are protected by their caretakers from things that can harm them. Thus, the ability to form expectations about aversive events becomes biologically relevant only when infants begin to move around on their own, which makes it possible for them to get themselves into serious trouble.

Operant conditioning   Classical conditioning is a process by which previously existing behaviors come to be elicited by new stimuli. It explains how infants begin to build up expectations about the connections between events in their environment, but it does little to explain how even the simplest changes take place in infants' behavioral repertoires. The kind of conditioning that gives rise to new and more complex behaviors is called *operant,* or *instrumental, conditioning,* emphasizing the way in which the learned response allows the organism to operate more effectively on its environment in an instrumental fashion.

The basic idea of **operant conditioning** is that changes in behavior occur as a result of the positive or negative consequences the behavior produces; that is, organisms will tend to repeat behaviors that lead to rewards and will tend to give up behaviors that fail to produce rewards or that lead to punishment (Skinner, 1938; Thorndike, 1911). In the terminology of operant conditioning, a consequence, such as receiving a reward, that increases the likelihood that the behavior that produces it will occur again is called **reinforcement.** According to an operant explanation of the development of nursing, such behaviors as turning the head away from the bottle or burying the nose in the mother's breast will become less probable because they do not result in the infant receiving milk. At the same time, such behaviors as well-coordinated breathing, sucking, and swallowing will increase in strength and probability because they are likely to be rewarded with milk.

Until the 1960s, it was generally believed that newborns were capable of only simple, reflexive behaviors, so there was no research on operant conditioning in young infants. Since that time, it has been demonstrated that newborn infants are indeed capable of operant learning, which can be reinforced by such varied stimuli as milk, sweet substances, an interesting visual display, a pacifier, and the sound of a heartbeat or the mother's voice (DeCasper & Fifer, 1980; DeCasper & Sigafoos, 1983; Rovee-Collier, 1987; Siqueland, 1968).

An experiment by Einar Siqueland (1968), for example, demonstrated that neonates can learn to turn their heads in order to suck on a pacifier. The key feature of operant learning is that a behavior has to occur before it can be reinforced. Head turning is ideal in this respect since it is something even the youngest neonates do. While the babies lay in laboratory cribs, Siqueland placed a band around their heads that was connected to a device that recorded the amount of head movement to either side (see Figure 5.13). A pacifier was given to the baby to suck on when the designated response occurred.

In the first phase of his study, Siqueland recorded how often the babies naturally turned their heads. Once this baseline rate was established, he set his apparatus to signal when the babies had turned their heads at least 10 degrees to either side. As soon as they did, they were given the pacifier to suck on. After only 25 occasions in which the head turning was reinforced with the pacifier, most of the babies had tripled the rate at which they turned their heads.

To make certain that the excitement of being placed in the crib was not sufficient to cause the babies' head turning, Siqueland included another group of infants in his experiment who were rewarded with a pacifier for holding their heads *still*. These infants learned to move their heads *less* during the course of the experiment.

In the view of environmental-learning theorists, operant conditioning is a major source of developmental change in early infancy and throughout life. Sidney Bijou and Donald Baer, two prominent environmental-learning theorists, summarize the developmental implications of operant conditioning as follows:

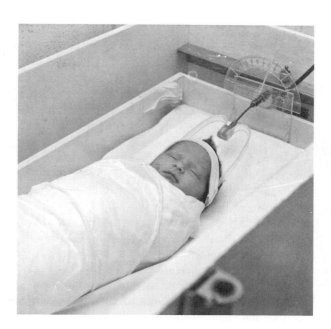

FIGURE 5.13 *A newborn with a specially designed headpiece that records head turning. Head turns of more than 10° were reinforced by the opportunity to suck on a pacifier.*

Operant conditioning is involved in a vast change in the form and complexity of the infant's responses which may be described as the stringing together of a collection of operants in a chain. An infant may be capable of a variety of arm motions. These may be linked in slightly different order to produce behavior described as a wave or a pat, making patti-cake, beating a drum, grabbing a cookie, fending off, sweeping away, etc. (1966, p. 83)

Support for the argument that behavioral development results from learning comes from studies that show infants are capable of remembering what they have learned from one testing session to the next from early in postnatal life (Rovee-Collier, 1984, 1987; Vander Linde, Morrongiello, & Rovee-Collier, 1985; Watson, 1984). These studies also suggest that memory for newly learned behaviors improves markedly between 2 and 3 months, a finding to which we will return at the end of this chapter and again in Chapter 6 (pp. 199 and 200).

The environmental-learning theorists' emphasis on the power of the environment to shape behavior provides an important counterweight to the biological-maturation theorists' emphasis on the primacy of genetic influences in determining the course of development. But, there are also some significant shortcomings in the environmental-learning explanations of developmental change. In effect, this approach makes no distinction between learning and development; it views development as simply the accumulation of learned modifications in behavior. It acknowledges no qualitative differences that distinguish older and younger children, only quantitative differences in the number and complexity of the behaviors they have acquired. It also has a difficult time dealing with the important issue of individual differences in behavior, including differences associated with sex and temperament. According to this perspective, such differences can only be accounted for by differences in the experiences of individuals; the effects of genetic variation are discounted. Contemporary research on individual differences has made this extreme view difficult to justify (Plomin, 1986).

The Interactional Perspective: Jean Piaget

The biological-maturation and environmental-learning perspectives can be considered interactional in the minimal sense that they accept the basic idea that nature and nurture are jointly responsible for development. But unlike the approaches referred to as interactional in Chapter 1 (pp. 14–16), they ascribe very unequal roles to these two developmental factors. The biologically oriented theories privilege nature over nurture. They take embryology as their model and minimize the degree to which development can be deliberately modified. By contrast, environmental-learning theories deny that embryology provides an appropriate model for postnatal development. Instead, they emphasize the crucial role of the environment both in determining babies' expectations about what follows what and in integrating babies' separate reflexes into new patterns of behavior.

Interactional theorists emphasize that the roles of nature and nurture in shaping development are balanced and complementary. Jean Piaget, the most prominent champion of interactionism during this century, whose views we will concentrate on here, objected to both the biological-maturation and environmental-learning theories of his day. Although he believed that embryology provides an important

model for later development, he criticized biological explanations for failing to spell out how the environment of human infants interacts with their biological capacities to permit development to occur (Piaget & Inhelder, 1969). At the same time, he was critical of environmental explanations for their assumption that the environment is the *originator* of developmental change. Piaget held that the ongoing activity of the child plays the crucial role in determining what effect the environment will have.

Piaget's theory of developmental change   The starting point of Piaget's theory of development is his view of the nature of early reflexes. To Piaget, a reflex is a primitive example of a *schema*, the basic unit of psychological functioning in his theory. The concept of a *schema* will appear frequently in subsequent chapters because it figures prominently in many modern approaches to development, often with slightly different meanings attached to it. For the present, a **schema** can be thought of as a psychological structure that provides an organism with a template for action in similar or analogous circumstances (Piaget & Inhelder, 1969).

During the first month of life, the "reflex schemas" with which babies are born provide them with a kind of skeleton for action that is gradually "fleshed out" by experience. These initial schemas are eventually strengthened and transformed into new schemas through *adaptation*, a twofold process comprised of what Piaget termed *assimilation* and *accommodation*.

During the **assimilation** part of adaptation, various experiences are taken in by the organism and are transformed to fit its existing schemas, strengthening the schemas and making them work more efficiently. Piaget used the process of digestion as a metaphor to help clarify what he meant by assimilation. Reflex schemas, he explained, assimilate experience in much the same way the human body assimilates food. Various kinds of food taken in by the body are assimilated through the process of digestion into such existing physical structures as bone, blood, and brain tissue (Piaget, 1952).

The first primitive schemas, the inborn reflexes such as sucking, are initially closely tied to specific eliciting stimuli, but they do not remain so for long. At some point, babies are likely to find, say, their thumb instead of a nipple touching their face and start sucking on it. Since a thumb is similar to a nipple, the infants can adjust the way the thumb is held so that they can suck on it in the same way they suck on the nipple. In other words, they assimilate the thumb, a new object, to their existing sucking schema.

Not every object babies encounter can be assimilated to an existing schema. For instance, when babies first encounter a blanket, they will often try to suck on it. However, because the qualities of the blanket — the satin binding, perhaps or the woolen interior — are so unlike the qualities of a nipple or a thumb their existing sucking schema may not allow them to assimilate the blanket as an object to suck on. They must therefore make some **accommodation;** that is, they must modify their existing schema so that they can apply it to the new environmental experience. If a baby encounters a toy truck and tries to suck on it, accommodation can be quite problematic!

Piaget and Inhelder (1969) expressed the two-sided nature of the process that leads in their view to developmental change in the following way:

> [Our] view of assimilation presupposes a reciprocity between S—R [stimulus and response]; that is to say, the input, the stimulus, is filtered through a structure that consists of the action schemes, . . . which in turn are modified and enriched when the subject's behavioral repertoire is accommodated to the demands of reality. The filtering or modification of the input is called *assimilation;* the modification of the internal schemes is called *accommodation.* (p. 6)

One way to summarize Piaget's theory is to view development as a constant tug-of-war between assimilation and accommodation. Piaget referred to this back-and-forth process of seeking a "fit" between the existing schemes of the child and new environmental experiences as **equilibration,** which is basically an attempt to achieve a balance, or equilibrium. At certain times, a balance between assimilation and accommodation is achieved, bringing the child to a new level of development. But during childhood the balance does not last for long because the process of biological maturation and the accumulation of experience lead to new imbalances, which cause the tug-of-war between assimilation and accommodation to begin again, pushing development to increasingly higher stages until adulthood is reached.

The sensorimotor period and its substages Piaget was a stage theorist who maintained that develop-

ment proceeds by a sequence of qualitative transformations in the global psychological structure of the child. Overall, he believed that there are four major developmental stages between birth and adulthood corresponding to infancy, early childhood, middle childhood, and adolescence. Piaget (1952) referred to infancy as the **sensorimotor stage** because the behaviors that develop during this period are based on coordinations between infants' sensory perceptions and simple motor behaviors, such as reaching for an object or starting to nurse at the mother's breast. It lasts from birth to about the age of 2 years. Within the sensorimotor period, Piaget identified six substages, each of which builds on the accomplishments of the one that precedes it. We will discuss the first two substages of the sensorimotor period here because they correspond to the early months of postnatal life. The remaining substages will be described in Chapters 6 and 7.

Substage 1 lasts from birth to approximately 1 month. It is the stage during which infants consolidate their reflexes. Piaget believed that the reflexes present at birth provide the initial connection between infants and their environments, but they do not, in themselves, add anything new to development because they have undergone very little accommodation and so still reflect the "preestablished boundaries of the hereditary apparatus" (Piaget & Inhelder, 1969, p. 7).

An important property of the initial reflex schemas is that they *produce* stimulation in addition to responding to it. For example, when infants suck, they experience tactile pressure on the roof of the mouth that stimulates further sucking, which tends to produce more tactile pressure, and so on. This stimulus-producing aspect of reflexes is the key to the development of the second sensorimotor substage because it results in the earliest extensions of already existing reflexes.

Substage 2 lasts from about 1 month to about 4 months. The first hints of new forms of behavior are found in the way existing reflexes are extended in time, such as sucking between feedings, or are applied to new objects. Piaget and Inhelder (1969) offered thumb sucking as an example of the extension of a reflex to accommodate a new object. They note that thumb sucking may occur accidentally as early as the first day of life. (We now know it can occur even before birth; see Chapter 3, Figure 3.9.) They believe, however that the systematic thumb sucking seen at 2 months of age and beyond is the result of sensorimotor accommodation, which extends the sucking reflex to a new object, since there exists no reflex for thumb sucking.

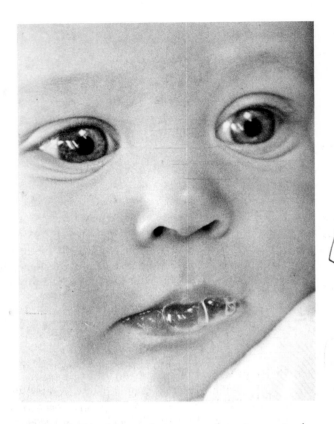

Blowing bubbles is an early instance of a primary circular reaction in which an accidental aspect of sucking is prolonged for the pleasure of continuing the sensation.

Substage 2 is characterized by what Piaget called **primary circular reactions,** reactions in which infants repeat a variety of pleasurable motions, such as waving their hands or kicking their feet, for their own sake. These actions are called *primary* because they are centered on the baby's own body; they are called *circular* because they lead only back to themselves. In substage 3, which we will discuss in Chapter 6 (p. 189), infants begin to engage in similar behaviors that are directed at the environment.

Piaget was a keen observer of his own infants, and evidence for many of his ideas about the earliest substages of the sensorimotor period can be seen in the notes he kept about their behavior. The following observations illustrate the kind of behaviors he referred to as primary circular reactions:

[A]fter having learned to suck his thumb, Laurent continues to play with his tongue and to suck, but

intermittently. On the other hand, his skill increases. Thus at 1 month, 20 days, I notice he grimaces while placing his tongue between gums and lips and in bulging his lips, as well as making a clapping sound when quickly closing his mouth after these exercises. . . .

[F]rom 2 months, 18 days Laurent plays with his saliva, letting it accumulate within his half-open lips and then abruptly swallowing it. About the same period he makes sucking-like movements, without putting out his tongue. . . . (1952, p. 65)

Piaget felt that such examples of primary circular reactions are very important because they are the first evidence of cognitive development. "The basic law of dawning psychological activity," he wrote, "could be said to be the search for the maintenance or repetition of interesting states of consciousness" (1977, p. 202).

Over the first few months of life, these circular reactions undergo *differentiation* — infants learn to use different grasps for different objects, they learn not to suck on toy trucks — and *integration* — infants can grasp their mother's arm with one hand while sucking in a coordinated way. All the while, infants' experiences are providing more nourishment for their existing schemas and are forcing them to modify those schemas, permitting them to master more of the world.

In contrast to the infants portrayed by biological-maturation and environmental-learning approaches, Piagetian infants are, virtually from the beginning, active, problem-solving organisms who are busy acting on the environment in the process of adapting to it. The starting point for development, reflexes, appears to be the same as in the alternative theories, but this appearance is somewhat misleading. Because Piaget conceives of reflexes as schemas for action, his approach downplays the role of the environment in evoking or reinforcing particular behaviors and instead emphasizes the constructive activity of the infant in shaping the way the environment will exert its effects.

Piaget's theory and the social environment Despite Piaget's avowal of the importance of the social environment for development, analysis of the social context for the early development of reflexes is virtually absent from his writings. Yet a closer look at the acquisition of new forms of behavior during the first $2\frac{1}{2}$ months of life reveals that changes in a baby's be-

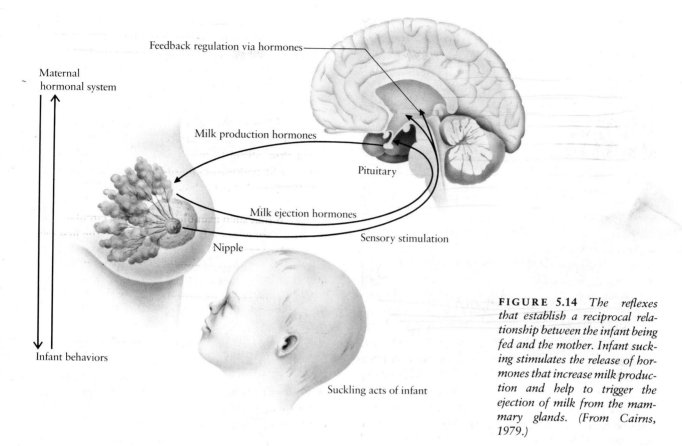

Feedback regulation via hormones

Maternal hormonal system

Milk production hormones

Pituitary

Milk ejection hormones

Sensory stimulation

Nipple

Infant behaviors

Suckling acts of infant

FIGURE 5.14 *The reflexes that establish a reciprocal relationship between the infant being fed and the mother. Infant sucking stimulates the release of hormones that increase milk production and help to trigger the ejection of milk from the mammary glands. (From Cairns, 1979.)*

havior are accompanied by changes in the mother's behavior. These changes in maternal behaviors appear to be just as essential to the infant's development as are the changes that occur in the infant's relationships to objects or brain functioning.

Nursing clearly illustrates the contributions of the mother's behaviors to the infant's development. In the beginning, the mother's nursing behavior may be not much more coordinated than her baby's. She must learn how to hold the baby and adjust herself so that the nipple is placed at exactly the right spot against the baby's mouth to elicit the sucking reflex. She must also learn not to press the baby so tightly to her breast that its breathing is disrupted and the head-withdrawal reflex is brought into play.

When the mother breast-feeds, maternal reflexes in response to the baby's sucking combine with the mother's voluntary efforts to maximize the amount of milk that the baby receives. This system of mutually facilitating reflexes between infant and mother, which changes the consequences of reflex sucking, is illustrated in Figure 5.14. The infant's sucking not only

transports milk from nipple to mouth, but it also stimulates the production of more milk, thereby *increasing the sucking reflex's adaptive value.*

A different type of mutual facilitation arises from the physical movements mothers make while they are feeding their children by either breast or bottle. Kenneth Kaye and his colleagues (Kaye, 1982) found that, even during the very first feeding, mothers occasionally jiggle their baby (or the bottle). These jiggles do not come at random intervals; rather, they are most likely to occur during the pauses between the infant's bursts of sucking. The jiggles increase the probability of sucking and prolong the feeding session, thereby increasing the amount of milk the neonate receives.

Sucking in response to jiggling is *not* a reflex in the sense that rooting is a reflex. Rooting is an automatic, involuntary response to being touched on the side of the mouth. There are no known neural connections that make sucking inevitable when a baby is jiggled. Yet it happens, it is to some extent automatic, and it has clear adaptive value. Scholars do not know for sure where such adaptive patterns come from. Kaye calls them "preadapted responses," implying that they may have arisen in the course of human evolution.

Kaye speculates that the mother's jiggle between her infant's bursts of sucking is her way of intuitively "conversing" with her baby by filling in her "turn" during the pauses in the baby's rhythmic sucking. Mothers' reports support Kaye's view. Although they are not aware that they are jiggling their babies in a systematic way, mothers report that they actively try to help their babies nurse. They notice and disapprove of the pauses between bursts of sucking. When mothers are asked about their jiggling behavior, a typical response is that the baby "gets lazy, or dozes off, so I jiggle her to get her back on task."

Kaye's demonstration that mothers play a crucial role in children's behavioral development by actively structuring the children's experiences adds an important ingredient to Piaget's analysis of the mechanisms of developmental change. But in one essential respect, the forms of interactionism advanced by Kaye and Piaget are the same; both investigators assumed that the interactional processes they described are *universal* features of human behavior and thus apply to children everywhere.

The Cultural-Context Perspective

The basic stages of sensorimotor development described by Piaget may well be universal (Dasen, 1977). But there is also abundant evidence of significant cultural variation in the way that adults arrange their interactions with their children. These variations encourage development along certain lines while discouraging it along others, thereby changing the resulting patterns of behavior (Laboratory of Comparative Human Cognition, 1983). This additional source of variation in the process of developmental change is the special concern of cultural-context theories.

In explaining one way cultural variations influence development, Margaret Mead and Frances Macgregor (1951) noted that cultures "differ from each other in the way in which the growth process is interwoven with learning" (p. 26). This principle, they went on to explain, first operates in the different ways adults of different cultures respond to such basic neonate capacities as the sucking reflex:

The existence of the sucking reflex at birth . . . will be taken advantage of in some cultures by putting the baby at once to the mother's breast, so

that the infant's sucking is used to stimulate the flow of the mother's milk while the infant itself remains hungry, or the infant may be put at the breast of a wet nurse with a well-established flow of milk, in which case the infant's sucking behavior is reinforced but the mother is left without the stimulation that it would have provided. As another alternative, the infant may be starved until the mother has milk, and as still another, the infant may be given a bottle with a different kind of nipple. . . . (p. 26)

These different feeding practices are equivalent in that they are all ways in which parents arrange for infants' innate sucking reflexes to become part of nursing. In this respect, nursing is universal—in every culture, *some* arrangement is made for the infant's sucking reflex to become a part of nursing (see Figure 5.15).

According to the cultural-context perspective, however, cultural variations in the actual arrangements made with regard to a neonate's initial capacities may have a direct effect on the infant's early experience. To continue with the example provided by Mead and Macgregor, if a baby is bottle fed until the mother's milk begins to flow, changes in the baby's sucking that are adaptive to bottle feeding may interfere with subsequent breast feeding. If this interference is great, breast feeding may be given up altogether, which will alter both the kind of milk that the infant receives and the forms of social interaction between infant and mother that are a part of feeding.

Specific cultural practices, such as bottle feeding or the use of a wet nurse, are likely to be linked to larger patterns of interaction that have significant influences on later development. For example, if a mother who stays at home gives her baby a bottle because she believes that bottled milk is more nutritious, the use of a bottle rather than breast feeding may have no differential impact on the development of social relations between mother and child. However, if a mother who is working in an office or factory without on-site child-care, bottle feeding may become part of a pattern in which there is a less exclusive relationship between the mother and baby, and the baby is likely to become accustomed from an early age to social interactions with peers and many caretakers. In either case, the immediate consequences of the specific feeding practice are less important than the larger patterns of life with which they are associated.

An important implication of the cultural-context perspective that is not captured by the example of

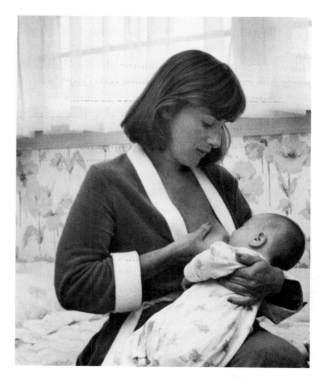

FIGURE 5.15 *Although babies are nursed in all cultures, there are wide variations in the way babies' nursing behavior is organized to fit in with their parents' other activities.*

nursing is that cultures provide people with a frame-work for interpreting their experiences, which include how they view their own babies. The way in which newborn babies are treated depends very much on what a culture defines babies to be. In the United States today, for example, well-educated, middle-class adults tend to have a higher opinion of the psychological capacities of young infants than do adults of many other cultures and even some subcultures within the United States (Super, 1981). When the behavioral consequences of this cultural belief are viewed in isolation from usual childcare contexts, they can be quite striking, as the following description from a study by pediatrician T. Berry Brazelton and his colleagues illustrates. In this study, 1-week-old infants were placed in infant seats in the laboratory, and their mothers were asked to spend several minutes interacting with them. Here's how the scene unfolded:

> Our mothers were faced with the problem of communicating with infants who, if they were not crying or thrashing, were often hanging limply in the infant seat with closed or semi closed eyes or, just as frequently, were "frozen" motionless in some strange and uninterpretable posture—staring at nothing. . . .
> Perhaps the most interesting response to the challenge of facing an unresponsive infant is this. The mother takes on facial expressions, motions, and postures indicative of emotion, as though the infant were behaving intentionally or as though she and he were communicating. Frequently, in response to a motionless infant, she suddenly acquires an expression of great admiration, moving back and forth in front of him with great enthusiasm; or again in response to an unmoving infant, she takes on an expression of great surprise, moving backward in mock astonishment; or in the most exaggerated manner, she greets the infant and, furthermore, carries on an animated extended greeting interchange, bobbing and nodding enthusiastically exactly as though her greeting were currently being reciprocated. . . .

> Most mothers, in sum, are unwilling or unable to deal with neonatal behaviors as though they were meaningless or unintentional. Instead, they endow the smallest movements with highly personal meaning and react to them affectively. They insist on joining in and enlarging on even the least possible

interactive behaviors, through imitation. And they perform *as if* highly significant interaction has taken place when there has been no interaction at all. (Brazelton, Koslowski, & Main, 1974, pp. 67–68)

The Kaluli, who live in the rain forests of Papua, New Guinea, have a far different set of beliefs about babies than middle-class Americans do, and they treat their babies quite differently as a result. As reported by Eleanor Ochs and Bambi Schieffelin (1984), the Kaluli see their babies as helpless creatures who have "no understanding." Although they may greet their infants by name, they do not talk to them in the way that middle-class American adults do. Nor do Kaluli mothers engage in extended eye contact with their babies, because the Kaluli believe that it is impolite to gaze at the person you are talking to. Kaluli mothers hold their infants facing outward so they can see, be seen by, and interact with other members of the social group. Instead of speaking *to* their infants, Kaluli mothers speak *for* their infants. As Ochs and Schieffelin point out, "in taking this role the mother does for the infant what the infant cannot do for itself, that is appear to act in a controlled and competent manner, using language" (p. 290).

Notice that the words Ochs and Schieffelin use to describe the intent of the Kaluli mothers could also be applied to the U.S. mothers, even though the specific actions involved are quite different. In both cultures, beliefs about what babies are, what they can do, and what they will need to do in the future affect how babies are treated by those around them and, thus, how they experience the environment. In short, different cultural patterns lead to different child-rearing practices, which have quite different effects on further development, as we will see in later chapters. It is therefore important to keep cultural factors constantly in mind when considering the mechanisms of developmental change.

INTEGRATING THE SEPARATE THREADS OF DEVELOPMENT

The complexities involved in accounting for how nursing develops during the first months of life provide some idea of the enormous difficulties facing anyone who seeks to explain human development. Even for this seemingly simple form of behavior, the contributions of biological and environmental factors as well as cultural influences and the specific circumstances in which infants find themselves must all be considered. The difficulties do not end here, however. A child's behaviors do not develop in isolation but rather as parts of an integrated system. Thus, psychologists must also study them in relation to each other. The requirement that developing organisms must be studied as a whole is expressed with particular clarity by the embryologist C. H. Waddington, whose ideas about nature-nurture interactions were introduced in Chapter 2.

> A new level of organization cannot be accounted for in terms of the properties of its elementary units as they behave in isolation, but is accounted for if we add to these certain other properties which the units only exhibit when in combination with one another. (1947, p. 145)

Nursing, for instance, must be understood as but one element in the system of developing infant behaviors that includes increasingly longer sleeping and waking periods and the buildup of elementary expectations about the environment.

In meeting this requirement that developing behaviors be considered both individually and in relation to one another, the analytical strategy developed by Robert Emde and his associates is especially useful (Emde, Gaensbauer, & Harmon, 1976). As mentioned in Chapter 1 (p. 33), this strategy involves tracing developments in the biological, behavioral, and social domains *as they relate to each other*. It allows the identification of bio-social-behavioral shifts, those periods when changes in the separate domains converge to create the kind of qualitative reorganization in the overall pattern of behaviors that signals the onset of a new stage of development. We can see the usefulness of this approach by examining the first bio-social-behavioral shift following birth, which occurs at about 2½ months of age in full-term babies.

The First Postnatal Bio-Social-Behavioral Shift

Emde and his co-workers contend that, although infants learn through active adaptation to their environments and reciprocal interaction with their caretakers during the first 2 months, there is a shift in the "modes and mechanisms" of their behavior during the third month of life (Emde et al., 1976). This shift arises from the convergence of developmental changes that previously have proceeded in relative isolation from each other. Table 5.2 lists in capsule form the changes in the separate domains that converge to create the first postnatal bio-social-behavioral shift. To appreciate the far-reaching significance of this and subsequent bio-social-behavioral shifts, we must visualize what it means for all of the changes listed in Table 5.2 to occur at about the same time. Emde and his colleagues convey the sense of this by tracing how changes in infant smiling are related to other aspects of the developing child.

TABLE 5.2 Elements of the first postnatal bio-social-behavioral shift (2½ months)

Biological domain

Central Nervous System

Myelination of cortical and subcortical neural pathways

Myelination of primary neural pathways in some sensory systems

Increased cortical control of subcortical activity

Increases in the number and diversity of brain cells

Psychophysiology

Increases in amount of wakefulness

Decreases in active (REM) sleep as a proportion of total sleep time

Shift in pattern of sleep; quiet (NREM) sleep begins to come first

Behavioral domain

Aversive conditioning clearly appears for the first time

Learning retained better between episodes

Increases in visual acuity

More complete visual scanning of objects

Onset of social smiling

Decreases in generalized fussiness and crying

Social domain

New quality of coordination and emotional contact between infants and caretakers

The Emergence of Social Smiling

During the earliest weeks of life, the corners of a baby's mouth often curl up in a facial expression that looks for all the world like a smile. Most experienced mothers do not pay much attention to these smiles, however, because they are most likely to come when the infant is asleep or very drowsy. Emde and his colleagues explain why these smiles occur. In conjunction with their extensive observations of infants' smiles, these researchers recorded the infants' brain waves. They found that the pattern of infant brain waves is characterized by frequent small oscillations that are punctuated by occasional bursts of high activity, even during the arousal states of drowsiness and rapid-eye-movement (REM) sleep. They also determined that these bursts accompany infants' early smiles and that they originate in the brain stem. Emde and Robinson (1979) call these endogenous smiles *REM smiles*.

Infants' social smiles evoke a ready response in their parents.

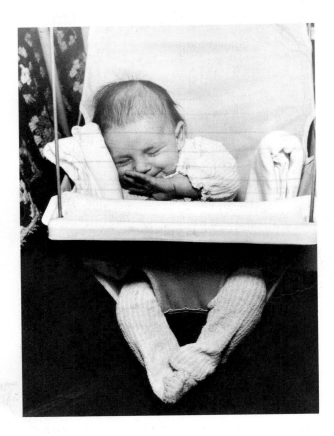

Smiling during REM sleep.

The frequency of the REM smile decreases rapidly in the early months of life. It is replaced by an exogenous smile, one that is a response to stimulation from the environment. The special characteristic of this early exogenous smile is that almost anything can elicit it. For about 6 weeks, between the ages of 1 month and $2\frac{1}{2}$ months, infants smile indiscriminately at things or people they see, touch, or hear. Thus, this earliest form of exogenous smiling is not really social even though it is stimulated from the outside.

To become truly social, babies' smiles must be reciprocally related to the smiles of others; that is, the babies must both smile in response to the smiles of others and elicit others' smiles. This is precisely what begins to happen for the first time at the age of $2\frac{1}{2}$ to 3 months as part of the first postnatal bio-social-behavioral shift. This new behavior depends on changes in the brain and the nervous system that result in marked increases in infants' visual acuity and in their ability to scan objects systematically. This improved visual capacity permits babies to focus their eyes, and thus their smiles, on *people*, making it possible for early exogenous smiling to become social smiling.

The changes in infant behavior that accompany the social smile are not lost on parents. Quite the opposite, as is indicated by the following observations of mothers on their feelings about their babies before the shift and a description of a mother interacting with her baby after the shift:

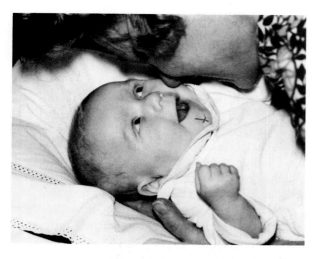

This 2½-month-old blind infant smiled and turned her face toward her mother upon hearing her mother's voice.

demonstrated by research conducted by Selma Fraiberg (1974) on the development of congenitally blind infants. Like sighted infants, blind babies exhibit REM smiles. But unlike sighted infants, they may not exhibit the shift to social smiling at 2½ months.

Under normal conditions of growth, the social smile is connected to visual exploration of the world. It depends upon increased visual capacity and visual feedback from people smiling back. Blind infants cannot explore the world visually and hence may not establish the feedback loop they need in order to develop social smiling.

The frequent failure of blind infants to make the expected shift toward social smiling also means that their sighted parents cannot use their baby's facial expressions as information by which to gauge their own efforts to help their infant. But it does *not* mean that blind infants receive no social feedback or that they

Before

I don't think there is interaction. . . . [T]hey are like in a little cage surrounded by glass and you are acting all around them but there is no real interaction. . . .

I realized I was doing things for him he couldn't do for himself but I always felt that anyone else could do them and he wouldn't know the difference. . . . (Robson & Moss, 1970, pp. 979–980)

After

His eyes locked on to hers, and together they held motionless. . . . This silent and almost motionless instant continued to hang until the mother suddenly shattered it by saying "Hey!" and simultaneously opening her eyes wider, raising her eyebrows further, and throwing her head up and toward the infant. Almost simultaneously the baby's eyes widened. His head tilted up . . . , his smile broadened. . . . Now she said, "Well hello! . . . heelló, . . . heeelloóoo!," so that her pitch rose and the "hellos" became longer and more stressed on each successive repetition. With each phrase the baby expressed more pleasure, and his body resonated almost like a balloon being pumped up. (Stern, 1977, p. 3)

The importance of feedback from the social world as a part of bio-social-behavioral shifts is dramatically

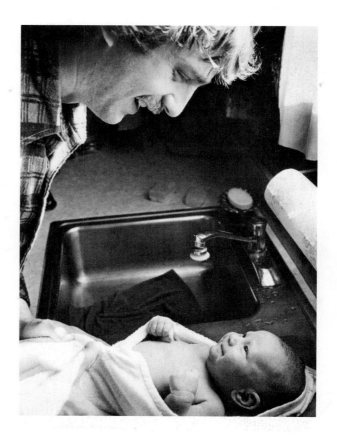

The moment parents and their babies make eye contact is pleasurable for both parties.

cannot acquire social smiling. After all, their brains are, like those of sighted children, maturing. The problem is that their increased capacities cannot be expressed in visually related ways. The absence of this major channel for social feedback means that parents must find alternate ways to interact with their blind children.

The intuitive solution that some parents of blind children work out is to establish communication through touching. Fraiberg noticed that they, far more than the parents of sighted children, often bounce, nudge, and tickle their children. At first, this struck Fraiberg as socially abnormal, but then she noticed that the touching made the children smile and realized that, for blind babies, tactile stimulation was a good substitute for the looming, smiling face that elicits the smiles of sighted babies. The touching made the infants smile, and the parents had found a way to get the feedback that *they* needed from their infants. Fraiberg used this observation to design a training program to help blind infants and their parents (Fraiberg, 1974). Parents were taught to attend carefully to the way their children used their hands to signal their intentions and reactions and how to organize their baby's environment to encourage interaction. Once the children of these parents were provided with appropriate feedback they began to develop social smiling.

The success of Fraiberg's training program indicates that social smiling does not arise simply from the fact that an infant's brain has matured to the point where social smiling is possible. For social smiling to emerge, appropriate interaction with others is necessary; when this new behavior does emerge, a new affective quality is able to develop between infants and their parents. As we will see in other periods of a child's life, development results from a complex interaction of biological, social and behavioral changes that the notion of bio-social-behavioral shifts helps us to understand.

Summing Up the First Two and a Half Months

Looking back over the first $2\frac{1}{2}$ months or so of postnatal life, we can see a remarkable set of changes in infants' behaviors. Babies are born with a rudimentary ability to interact with their new environment. They have a number of reflexes that enable them to take in oxygen and nutrients and expel waste products. They are able to perceive objects, including people, al-

though in a somewhat fragmentary way. They are sensitive to the sounds of human language, and they quickly develop a preference for the sound of their mother's voice. Although they sleep most of the time, they are occasionally quite alert.

From the moment of birth, infants interact with and are supported by their parents or other caretakers, who come equipped with the biological and cultural resources necessary to see that their babies receive food and protection. Despite these resources, babies and their caretakers interact in a tentative and a somewhat discoordinated way during the first few days after birth. Within a matter of days, however, a process of mutual adjustment has begun that will provide an essential framework for later development.

The developmental changes that characterize the first 10 to 12 weeks have clear origins in biology and in both the physical and social environments. In the domain of biology, there is rapid maturation of the central nervous system, particularly in the connections between the brain stem and the cerebral cortex. As a consequence of frequent feeding, the baby grows bigger and stronger. As a consequence of practice at feeding, such elementary feeding reflexes as sucking become more efficient, an accomplishment that owes a good deal to the complementary efforts of the baby's caretakers, primarily the mother.

Between the ages of $2\frac{1}{2}$ and 3 months, several different lines of development, which have been proceeding more or less independently, converge. The consequences are qualitatively different forms of infant behavior and a new type of social relationship between babies and their caretakers. The story of the development of the seemingly simple behavior of social smiling illustrates the intricate way in which these different lines of development must relate to each other for a transition to a qualitatively new level of development to occur. Maturation of the visual system enables a new level of visual acuity and a new ability to analyze the visual field. As a consequence, smiling, a seemingly unrelated behavior, may be transformed. However, this transformation will take place only if there is proper feedback from the infant's caretakers. Without appropriate feedback, as occurs in the case of some blind children, social smiling does not develop. And if social smiling does not develop, there may be a subsequent disruption in the development of social interactions.

In subsequent chapters, we will see versions of this same pattern repeated again and again. For a stretch of time, there is stability in the child's overall level of development while different systems undergo changes in relative isolation from each other. Then there is a brief period during which these separate lines of development converge, resulting in a new level of organization with regard to both the child's behaviors and child-caretaker interactions. It will not always be possible to identify the specific biological, social, and behavioral factors that contribute to the emergence of higher levels of development with equal certainty and rigor. But it will always be useful to consider the various domains that enter into the process of developmental change as a means of keeping the whole child in mind.

SUMMARY

1. The basic behavioral capacities with which infants are born are sufficient for their survival only if they are coordinated with adult caretaking activities.

2. "Getting the baby on a schedule" is more than a convenience. By coordinating schedules, babies and their parents create a system of mutual expectations that supports further development.

3. Initially, babies sleep approximately two-thirds of the time, but their sleep periods are relatively brief and are distributed across all 24 hours of the day. Babies in all cultures begin to follow the pattern of sleeping more at night than during the day within a few weeks, but there are wide cultural variations in how rapidly they begin to sleep through the night, depending upon the sleeping patterns of the adults who care for them.

4. Newborn babies tend to eat about every 3 hours if given constant access to food. Babies fed only every 4 hours may experience trouble adjusting to such a feeding schedule, although a 4-hour schedule is spontaneously adopted by most infants $2\frac{1}{2}$ months of age.

5. Crying is a primitive means of communication that evokes a strong emotional response in adults and alerts them that something may be wrong. There are differences among early cries that can help cue caretakers as to possible sources of distress in some situations.

6. In the beginning, feeding is based on primitive reflex mechanisms that are not well coordinated with each other. Within several weeks, this form of behavior is reorganized and becomes voluntary; the various constituent reflexes become integrated with each other and the baby becomes well coordinated with the mother.

7. The four basic perspectives on development can all be applied to the earliest forms of infant development; each emphasizes different ways in which biological and environmental factors contribute to early developmental change.

8. *Biological-maturation* approaches maintain that postnatal development follows the same principles as prenatal development. New structures are said to arise from endogenous (inherited) capabilities that unfold as the baby matures. Changes in nursing as well as in other behaviors, according to this view, result from such factors as the increased myelination of the neurons and the growth of muscles.

9. The maturation of brain structures contributes to the reorganization of early reflexes. Some of these early reflexes disappear completely within a few months of birth. Others may disappear and then reappear at a later time as an element in a new form of activity. Still others remain and are transformed into voluntary behaviors under cortical control.

10. *Environmental-learning* theories assign the environment a leading role in creating new forms of behavior through the mechanism of learning.

11. Infants' ability to learn from experience increases steadily during the first months of life. *Classical conditioning* permits infants to form expectations about the connections between events in their environment. *Operant conditioning* provides a mechanism whereby new behaviors arise as a consequence of the positive or negative events they produce.

12. *Interactional* theories assign equal weight to biological

and environmental factors in creating development. Reflexes, in this view, are coordinated patterns of action (schemas) that have differentiated from a more primitive state of global activity during the prenatal period.

13. In the view of Jean Piaget, the leading interactional theorist of the twentieth century, developmental change arises through the interplay of *assimilation* (modification of the input to fit existing schemas) and *accommodation* (modification of existing schemas to fit the input). The interplay of accommodation and assimilation continues until a new form of equilibrium between the two processes is reached. New forms of equilibrium constitute qualitatively new forms of behavior; they are new stages of development.

14. According to Piaget, infancy is characterized by sensorimotor ways of knowing. He divides the sensorimotor period into six substages, the first two of which occur during the first 10 to 12 weeks of postnatal life:
    a. Substage 1 is characterized by the exercise of basic reflexes.
    b. Substage 2 is characterized by the beginning of accommodation and the prolongation of pleasant sensations arising from reflex actions.

15. At the same time that infants are assimilating their environments and are accommodating their existing schemas to fit environmental demands, their caretakers are undergoing an analogous set of changes with respect to their role in the interactional process. Careful observations of mother-infant interaction reveal that some part of the work attributed by Piaget to infants is in fact contributed by those with whom they interact.

16. *Cultural-context* theories of development emphasize that all social interaction is subject to cultural influences.

17. There are significant and pervasive cultural variations in the way in which parents interact with their newborn children that influence both their short-term and long-term development.

18. At approximately $2\frac{1}{2}$ months of age, there is a bio-social-behavioral shift in the organization of infant behavior. Changes in brain function owing to maturation are accompanied by such changes as increased visual capacity, increased wakefulness, social smiling, and increased feelings on the part of caretakers that they can communicate with their babies.

KEY TERMS

Accommodation
Assimilation
Aversive conditioning
Brain stem
Cerebral cortex
Classical conditioning
Conditional response
Conditional stimulus
Equilibration

Moro reflex
Myelin
Myelination
Operant conditioning
Prereaching
Primary circular reaction
Primary motor area
Primary sensory areas
Reinforcement

Schema
Sensorimotor stage
Stepping reflex
Synapse
Unconditional response
Unconditional stimulus

SUGGESTED READINGS

BIJOU, SIDNEY W., and DONALD M. BAER. *Child Development,* Vol. 2: *The Universal Stage of Infancy.* New York: Appleton-Century-Crofts, 1966.

An introduction to the topic of developmental change in terms of the basic learning mechanisms of classical and operant conditioning.

DUNN, JUDITH. *Distress and Comfort.* Cambridge, Mass.: Harvard University Press, 1977.

A discussion of the earliest periods of postnatal development that focuses on the basic adjustments between mother and child.

EMDE, ROBERT N., THEODORE. J. GAENSBAUER, and ROBERT J. HARMON. "Emotional Expression in Infancy: A Behavioral Study." *Psychological Issues,* 1976, *10* (37), International Universities Press.

The basic statement of the concept of bio-behavioral developmental shifts, including a discussion of the changes in the social world that are a part of them.

KAYE, KENNETH. *The Mental and Social Life of Babies.* Chicago: University of Chicago Press, 1982.

This report of the author's research on early mechanisms of developmental change illustrates the way in which maternal behaviors help to construct "next steps" in infant development.

MEAD, MARGARET, and FRANCES C. MACGREGOR. *Growth and Culture.* New York: Putnam, 1951.

A study of the cultural organization of infant behaviors in Bali. This richly illustrated book is based on research carried out in collaboration with Arnold Gesell in an early attempt to reconcile maturational and cultural approaches to the explanation of developmental change.

PIAGET, JEAN. *The Origins of Intelligence in Children.* New York: International Universities Press, 1952.

Piaget's account of the earliest stages of development. Piaget's theoretical writings are never easy to read, but his descriptions of children's behavior are fascinating. Because these descriptions are the basic data upon which his theory rests, familiarity with them is an aid to understanding his more abstract statements.

ROSENBLITH, JUDY F., and JUDITH E. SIMS-KNIGHT. *In the Beginning: Development during the First Two Years.* Monterey, Cal.: Brooks/Cole, 1985.

An authoritative summary of current theories and research on infant development. An excellent resource for all the chapters in Part II of this book.

STERN, DANIEL. *The First Relationship.* Cambridge, Mass.: Harvard University Press, 1977.

Stern, a psychiatrist, used film and videotape to record parent-child interactions. Through analyses of the moment-by-moment patterns of coordination and discoordination, he demonstrates the importance of close observation for understanding the interpersonal basis of individual development.

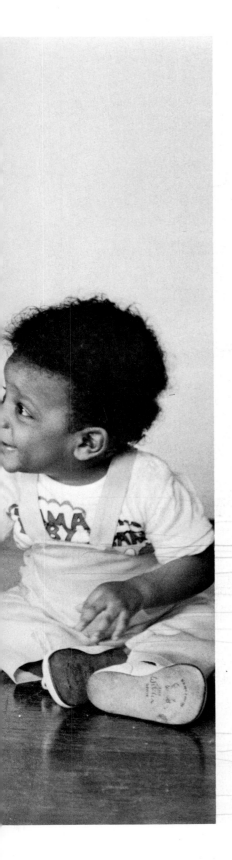

THE ACHIEVEMENTS OF THE FIRST YEAR

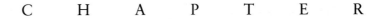

The question . . . is not where or when mind begins. Mind in some . . . form is there from the start, wherever "there" may be.

— Jerome Bruner, *In Search of Mind*

. . . .

Our neighbors Jake, who is about to celebrate his first birthday, and his mother, Barbara, have been out for a walk and have stopped by our house. Sheila is in the kitchen preparing dinner. Jake is sitting on his mother's lap at the kitchen table, drinking apple juice from a plastic cup while the two women chat.

Jake finishes his juice, some of which has dribbled onto his shirt, and puts the cup down on the table with a satisfied bang. He squirms around in his mother's lap so that he is facing her. He tries to get her attention by pulling at her face. When Barbara ignores him, Jake wriggles out of her lap to the floor, where he notices the dog.

"Wuff wuff," he says excitedly, pointing at the dog.

"Doggie," Barbara says. "What does the doggie say, Jake?"

"Wuff wuff," Jake repeats, still staring at the dog.

Following his pointing finger, Jake toddles toward the dog. His walk has a drunken, side-to-side quality, and he has a hard time bringing himself to a stop. Barbara grabs hold of Jake's extended hand, redirecting it from the dog's eyes.

"Pat the doggie, Jake."

Jake pats the dog's head.

The dog does not like the attention and escapes into the living room. Jake toddles after her like a pull toy on an invisible string. The dog leads him back into the kitchen, where Jake bumps into Sheila's legs and falls to a sitting position.

"Well hello, Jake," Sheila says, as she bends over and picks him up. "Did you fall down? Go boom?"

Jake, who has not till then taken his eyes off of the dog, turns, looks at Sheila with a smile, and points at the dog. "Wuff wuff," he repeats.

Suddenly Jake's body stiffens. He stares searchingly at Sheila's face for an instant, then turns his head away and holds his arms out to his mother.

Sheila hands Jake to Barbara, who says, "Did you get scared? It's only Sheila."

But Jake eyes Sheila warily and hides in his mother's arms for several minutes afterward.

At almost 1 year of age, Jake behaves far differently than he did at 2½ months. The contrast in Jake's behavior gives us a picture of some of the amazing developmental changes that occur in the first year of infancy and challenge psychologists who seek to explain them.

At 2½ months Jake's main activities were eating, sleeping, and gazing around the room. He could hold his head up, and turn it from side to side, but he could not readily reach out and grasp objects or move around on his own. He took an interest in mobiles and other objects when they were immediately in front of him, but he quickly lost interest in them when they disappeared. Although he seemed most comfortable with his mother, he was not unhappy when he was cared for by someone else. His communications were restricted to cries, frowns, and smiles.

Several kinds of changes appear to be crucial to the major developments that occurred in Jake's behavior in the period between 2½ months and 1 year. First, babies' mobility and coordination increase. At 3 months, infants are just beginning to be able to roll over. Their parents know that they will remain, more or less, wherever they are put down. At about 7 to 8 months they begin to crawl, and at about 1 year they begin to walk. They also become much more adept at reaching for and grasping objects. They prod, bang, squeeze, push, and pull almost anything they can get their hands on, and they often put objects into their mouths to find out about them. Their parents, afraid that they will either harm themselves or ruin the objects, must be constantly on guard.

As infants near their first birthday, they also exhibit important new cognitive abilities. They learn and remember with markedly greater ease and effectiveness, for example, and they have come to recognize the existence of categories of objects. They can anticipate the course of simple, familiar events, and they act surprised when their expectations are not met. This new level of understanding makes it possible for them to play simple games like peekaboo.

These changes in infants' motor and cognitive abilities are supported by developments in their biological structure (see Figure 6.1). Jake is visibly larger and stronger than he was at 2½ months. Invisible, but essential, maturation has also taken place in his cerebral cortex and other brain structures.

Finally, a new form of social and emotional relationship between infants and their caretakers emerges toward the end of the first year. Infants become upset when separated from their caretakers, and sometimes they are afraid of strangers, as Jake was when he noticed Sheila. They also begin to use their few newly acquired words to supplement their gestures, smiles, and cries as a way of communicating and maintaining contact with their caretakers.

This chapter covers children's development from the age of 2½ months to 1 year. A great deal of evidence suggests that important changes in the separate domains of biological functioning, behavior, and social relations occur about halfway through this period, sometime between the ages of 7 and 9 months. While not all psychologists would agree, we believe that these changes converge to create a new bio-social-behavioral shift and a qualitatively new stage of development.

Some specialists in infant behavior (Bretherton & Bates, 1985; Fischer, 1987; McCall, 1983) suggest that there is also a stagelike developmental shift at around 12 months of age. Two developmental changes are the bases for this view. First, most babies begin to walk on their own at approximately 12 months of age, greatly increasing their independence and the difficulties their caretakers experience in keeping them out of harm's way. Second, infants' communicative abilities expand noticeably about the same time. We will not treat these changes as a separate bio-social-behavioral shift, but there is no doubt that the increases in infants' mobility and communicative ability are central to later development.

BIOLOGICAL CHANGES

The extensive changes in babies' motor behavior and cognitive abilities that occur between the ages of 2½ months and 1 year depend upon changes in their body proportions, muscles, bones, and brain structures (Thelen, 1984).

Size and Shape

Most healthy babies triple in weight and grow approximately 10 inches during the first year (see Figure 6.2). As Figure 6.2 shows, the rate of physical growth is greatest in the first months after birth; it then gradually tapers off through the rest of infancy and childhood. Then there is a brief growth spurt at the onset of adolescence. There are, however, wide variations in the rates at which individual children normally grow as well as in the heights and weights they eventually attain (Tanner, 1978). Many factors contribute to this variation, including quantity and quality of food, family income level, exposure to sunlight (vitamin D), and genetic constitution (Howe & Schiller, 1952; Johnston, Borden, & MacVean, 1973).

FIGURE 6.1 *The differences in size, strength, shape, and motor control between small infants and babies in their second year are evident in the young infant lying on the bed and her older sibling, who has taken her bottle.*

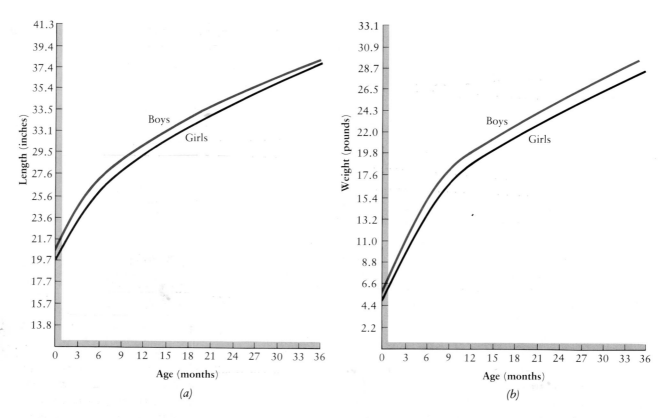

FIGURE 6.2 *Babies' length roughly doubles and their weight increases by 5 or 6 times during the first 3 years of life. (a) Average length by age. (b) Average weight by age. (From the U.S. Department of Health, Education, and Welfare. National Center of Health Statistics, 1976.)*

Increases in height and weight are accompanied by changes in body proportions (see Figure 6.3). At birth, the head is 70 percent of its adult size and comprises about 25 percent of total body length. At 1 year, the head will be 20 percent of the body's length, and in adulthood it will be 12 percent. Infants' legs at birth are not much longer than their heads. By adulthood, the legs will account for about half of a person's total length. Changes in body proportions produce a lower center of gravity by about 12 months of age, making it easier for the child to balance on two legs and begin walking (Thelen, 1984).

Muscle and Bone

As babies increase in size and weight, the bones and muscles needed to support their increasing bulk and mobility undergo corresponding changes. Most of a newborn's bones are relatively soft and only gradually harden as minerals are deposited in them in the months following birth. The bones in the hand and wrist are among the first to ossify (Tanner, 1978). They harden by the end of the first year, making it easier for a baby to grasp, pick up, and manipulate objects.

Although humans are born with all the muscle fibers they will ever have, their muscles change in length and thickness and increase in total mass throughout childhood and into late adolescence. In infancy, increases in muscle mass are closely associated with the development of the baby's ability to stand alone and walk.

The Brain

The entire nervous system—especially the cerebral cortex, which allows voluntary activity and higher psychological functions—continues to grow in size and complexity between 3 and 12 months (Lecours, 1982). Sometime between the ages of 7 and 9 months, the frontal lobe areas of the cortex begin to function more fully as a consequence of neuronal growth and myeli-

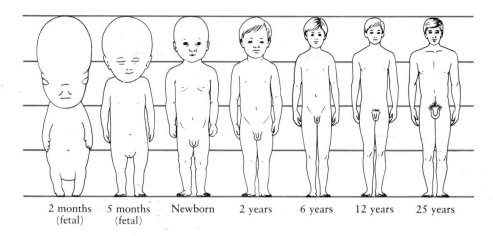

2 months (fetal)   5 months (fetal)   Newborn   2 years   6 years   12 years   25 years

FIGURE 6.3   *The proportions of body length accounted for by the head, trunk, and legs at different stages of development are very different. The disproportion is greatest during the fetal period, when the head accounts for as much as 50 percent of body length. The head decreases from 25 percent of body length at birth to 12 percent in adulthood. (From Robbins et al., 1928.)*

nation, and new patterns appear in the electrical activity of the cortex, indicating that it is functioning in a more mature way (Dreyfus-Brisac, 1978). These changes coincide with similar developments in lower-lying areas of the brain, especially the hippocampus, which plays an important role in memory, and the cerebellum, which is a key center of motor control. Several psychologists believe that these changes in brain structure provide the physical basis for more complex motor behavior and for increases in the ability to learn and solve problems (Diamond, 1985; Fischer, 1987; Goldman-Rakic, 1987; Milner, 1967). Babies begin to be able to compare present circumstances with past experience more effectively than they could in the first few months after birth, which allows them to discover common patterns and trends in their environment. Each of these changes contributes to the bio-social-behavioral shift that seems to occur between 7 and 9 months of age.

MOTOR DEVELOPMENT

One of the most dramatic developments of the first year of life is the enormous increase in infants' motor control. The resulting improvement in their ability to manipulate objects and to move around allows them to explore their environment in new, more effective ways. Infants do not develop control over all their muscle groups at the same time. Instead, motor development follows the proximodistal (from center to periphery) and cephalocaudal (from head to foot) patterns that we first saw in prenatal development (Chapter 3, p. 80).

Reaching and Grasping

The development of arm and hand movements proceeds in a proximodistal sequence. Babies can reach directly in front of them before they can reach to the side, and they gain control of their shoulder movements before they gain control over their fingers (Bruner, 1968).

At the time of the first postnatal bio-social-behavioral shift, which occurs about $2\frac{1}{2}$ months after birth, babies begin to guide their movements visually when reaching for an object, as was discussed in Chapter 5 (p. 158). At first, this requires concentration, and they are likely to glance back and forth between the objects they wish to grasp and their hands. With practice, their

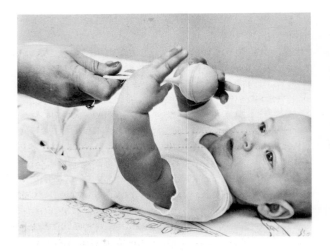

FIGURE 6.4   *(Left) In the first months after birth, babies' eye-hand coordination takes effort. (Right) Only after a number of months of attention and practice can infants perform more complex actions, such as eating with a spoon.*

eye-hand coordination gradually improves (see Figure 6.4). By the time they are 9 months old, most babies can guide their movements with a single glance. At about the same time, they begin to use their thumbs in opposition to their fingers when picking up objects rather than clutching them against the palm as they did in earlier months (see Figure 6.5). As their reaching and grasping become better coordinated and more precise, they can use these motions in more complicated action sequences, such as drinking from a cup or eating with a spoon.

By approximately 9 months of age, then, babies' arm and hand movements have taken on the automatic appearance of a reflex. But in contrast to the earlier reflex action seen shortly after birth, these movements are now under voluntary control (Von Hofsten, 1984). This sequence of changes from reflex to voluntary action suggests that reaching and grasping are at first controlled by areas of the brain that lie below the cortex and are later reorganized under cortical control, following the pattern of development discussed in Chapter 5 (p. 158).

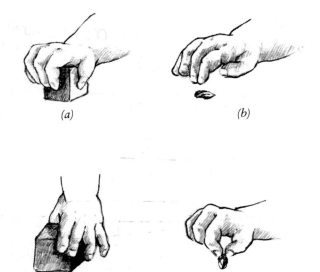

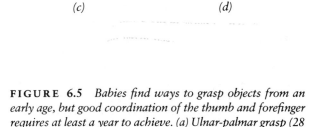

FIGURE 6.5   *Babies find ways to grasp objects from an early age, but good coordination of the thumb and forefinger requires at least a year to achieve. (a) Ulnar-palmar grasp (28 weeks). (b) Whole hand contact (28 weeks). (c) Thumb and finger grasp (36 weeks). (d) Scissors grasp (36 weeks). (e) Thumb and forefinger grasp (52 weeks). (f) Pincer grasp (52 weeks). (Adapted from Halverson, 1931.)*

Locomotion

[handwritten: learn to crawl]
[handwritten: head to foot]

Motor control of the body develops in a cephalocaudal pattern. Babies can raise their heads before they can sit up, they can sit up before they can stand, and they can stand before they can walk.

Before babies can move very far on their own, they must integrate the movements of many parts of the body. The development of crawling, babies' first effective mode of locomotion, takes several months and progresses through several phases (see Figure 6.6). During the first month of life, when movements appear to be controlled primarily by subcortical reflexes, infants may creep across a blanket, propelled by rhythmic pushing movements of their toes or knees. At about 2 months of age this reflexive pushing disappears. It will be 5 or 6 months before babies can really crawl about on their own. Although they can hold up their heads from about 2 months of age, young infants cannot move their arms in a coordinated way, so reaching forward with one arm is likely to land them on their noses. Some forward progress can be made by drawing one leg up underneath the body and lunging ahead, but until this lunging becomes coordinated with arm movements, the baby is likely to topple over. Once this coordination is achieved, babies can pull themselves along, but their legs drag behind uselessly. Slightly later, they can get on their hands and knees, but all they can do is rock back and forth because their arms and legs are not yet working together properly. Even in the final phase of crawling, which does not occur until approximately 8 months of age, babies may lack coordination until, with practice, the various movements are knit into the well-coordinated action of the whole body.

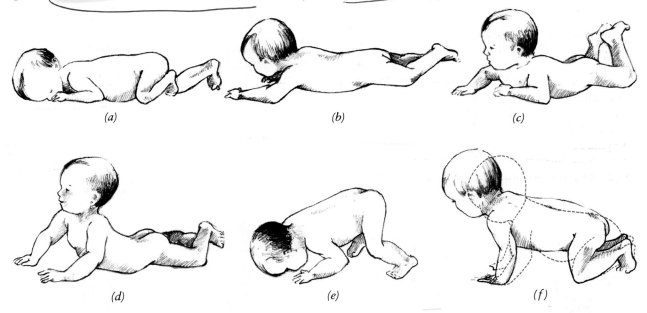

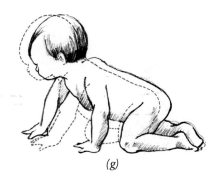

FIGURE 6.6 *Phases in the development of creeping and crawling: (a) Newborns creep using pushing movements of their knees or toes. (b) The head can be held up, but leg movements diminish. (c) Control over movement of head and shoulders has increased. (d) Ability to support the upper body with the arms improves. (e) Babies have difficulty coordinating shoulder and midsection regions; when the midsection is raised, the head lowers. (f) Babies can keep the midsection raised, but they are unable to coordinate arm and leg movements, so they tend to rock back and forth. (g) Coordinated arm and leg movements enable the baby to crawl. (From McGraw, 1975.)*

After they begin crawling, babies usually do not master walking for several more months. However, they do begin to stand by pulling themselves up, using furniture or people as props, between 7 and 9 months (see Figure 6.7).

Table 6.1 shows some of the results of a large-scale study of the ages at which children achieve various milestones in motor development that was conducted in Denver in the 1960s (Frankenburg & Dodds, 1967). Note the wide variations in the ages at which children are able to perform the various behaviors. For example, although 50 percent of the babies studied could walk by the time they were just over 1 year old, some 10 percent were still not walking 2 months later.

The Role of Practice in Motor Development

Studies of motor development were among psychologists' earliest attempts to discover the relative roles of nature and nurture in development. During the 1930s and 1940s, when Arnold Gesell's infant scales were in very wide use, it was commonly believed that learning and experience play little or no role in the development of such motor milestones as sitting or walking. One of the widely cited studies used to bolster this view was conducted by Wayne and Margaret Dennis (1940) among Hopi families in the southwestern United States. In traditional Hopi families, babies were wrapped up tightly and strapped to a flat cradle board for the first several months of life. They were unwrapped only once or twice a day so that they could be washed and their clothes could be changed. The wrapping permitted very little movement of the arms and legs and no practice of such complex movements as rolling over. The Dennises compared the motor development of traditionally raised babies with that of the babies of less traditional parents who did not use cradle boards. The two groups of babies did not differ in the age at which they began to walk unaided, which is consistent with the notion that this basic motor skill does not depend upon practice for its development.

In recent decades, however, psychologists have again begun to explore the possibility that experience, as well as maturation, plays a significant role in motor

FIGURE 6.7 *Babies who are just beginning to stand up find other people and furniture to be handy aids. In the photograph on the left a Balinese child is holding on to anthropologist Margaret Mead.*

TABLE 6.1 Age at which a given percentage of infants reach selected milestones in motor development

Motor Milestone	Age			
	25%	50%	75%	90%
Lifts head up	1.3 months	2.2 months	2.6 months	3.2 months
Rolls over	2.3	2.8	3.8	4.7
Sits without support	4.8	5.5	6.5	7.8
Pulls self to stand	6.0	7.6	9.5	10.0
Walks holding on furniture	7.3	9.2	10.2	12.7
Walks well	11.3	12.1	13.3	14.3
Walks up steps	14.0	17.0	21.0	22.0
Kicks ball forward	15.0	20.0	22.3	24.0

SOURCE: Frankenburg & Dodds, 1968.

development. For example, Philip Zelazo and his colleagues provided a group of 2-week-old babies with four 3-minute sessions of walking practice per day for 6 weeks. During these practice sessions, adults supported the infants' stepping activities by holding them erect. Infants trained in this way took their first unaided steps at approximately 10 months of age, 2 months earlier than control groups of babies who were not given equivalent practice (Zelazo, Zelazo, & Kolb, 1972).

Observations of babies among the Kipsigi, a group living in Kenya, provide further evidence that practice can have an effect on the age at which babies reach universal motor milestones. Kipsigi parents begin to teach their babies to sit up, stand, and walk shortly after birth (Super, 1976). In teaching their children to sit up, for example, Kipsigi parents seat their babies in shallow holes in the ground that have been dug so as to support the infants' backs, or they nestle blankets around them to hold them upright. Such procedures are repeated daily until the babies can sit up quite well by themselves. Walking is taught beginning in the eighth week. The babies are held under the arms with their feet touching the ground and are gradually propelled forward. Kipsigi babies reach the developmental milestones of sitting 5 weeks earlier and walking 3 weeks earlier, on the average, than babies in the United States. However, they are *not* advanced in skills they have not been taught or practiced. For example, they learn to roll over or crawl no faster than American

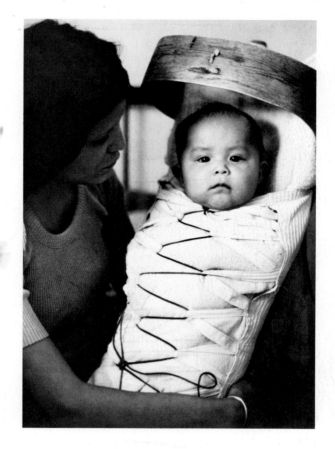

Like Hopi babies, Navaho babies spend a good deal of their early life on cradle boards, but they still learn to walk without significant delay.

Children whose houses have stairs learn to negotiate them earlier than those whose houses provide no opportunities for them to practice the skill.

children, and they lag behind American children in their ability to negotiate stairs.

Although special, early practice does not appear to have any long-term advantages in the development of basic motor skills, there is some evidence that early practice in culture-specific skills, such as boomerang throwing, tennis playing, roller skating, and typing, does make a lasting difference. In one of the classic early studies of the role of experience in motor development, Myrtle McGraw (1935/1975) trained one fraternal twin extensively in various activities that re-

quired specialized skills, such as riding a tricycle, swimming, and roller skating. When the first had attained proficiency, the second twin was given training in the same activities. McGraw reported that the twin given training later rather quickly caught up with the first twin in general skill level. However, when the twins were adolescents and young adults, the twin who received the special training earlier was more skilled in these activities and more enthusiastic about them (McGraw, 1977).

As anyone knows who has tried some unfamiliar sport, specialized motor skills are not acquired without extensive practice and, in some cases, years of instruction as well. In recognition of this fact, specialized training in highly valued skills, such as playing a musical instrument or dancing, is begun quite early in many cultures, producing high levels of proficiency (see Figure 6.8).

FIGURE 6.8 *At the tender age of 7 months, 29 days, young Parks Bonifay is the youngest person to water ski, according to The Guinness Book of Records. Water skiing is an example of a skill that requires practice to learn.*

COGNITIVE CHANGES

At the same time infants are becoming better able to move around and grasp objects, they also show an increase in their ability to understand their surroundings. Their new cognitive abilities include

- Understanding basic properties of objects and spatial relations

- Recognizing and responding appropriately to categories of things

- Comparing present experience with remembrances of past events

These new cognitive achievements enable infants to think more systematically and begin to use planning in their problem-solving.

In looking at cognitive development during the period from 2½ to 12 months, we will examine Piaget's theory in some detail, even though it is currently being challenged, because the phenomena he studied remain central to the formulation of a more comprehensive theory of infant development.

Piaget's Sensorimotor Substages

As we saw in Chapter 5, Piaget held that development emerges from children's own efforts to master their environments. In his terms, infants actively seek to *assimilate* their environmental experiences into their existing action schemas. When they are unable to do this, they *accommodate* their existing schemas to the environmental realities they encounter. During substage 1 of the sensorimotor period, which encompasses the first 1½ months of life, assimilation dominates accommodation as children exercise the action schemas—reflexes—with which they are born. During substage 2, which lasts from about 1½ months to about 4 months, the fact that reflexes create as well as respond to stimulation leads children to engage in *primary circular reactions*: they repeat actions they find pleasurable. Throughout both of these substages, however, infants appear to have only a vague realization that the environment is separate from their own actions.

Between the ages of 4 or 5 months and 12 months, infants gain a better grasp of external reality as they

complete two more substages of sensorimotor development. Especially important in this regard is the change that occurs at about 8 months of age, when, according to Piaget, infants begin to understand that objects have an existence apart from their own actions (see Table 6.2, p. 192).

Substage 3: secondary circular reactions (4 to 8 months) The basic characteristic of substage 3 is an increasing orientation of babies to the world beyond their own bodies. Instead of repeating actions for the sensual pleasure that results, babies now repeat actions that produce interesting changes in their environment. Piaget termed these actions **secondary circular reactions** because their focus is on objects external to themselves. For instance, when babies kick a bar suspended above their crib and a bell rings, they will kick the bar repeatedly to make the bell ring again and again. Similarly, when babies make a noise and their mother answers back, they will repeat the noise.

The change from primary circular reactions to secondary circular reactions indicated to Piaget that infants are beginning to realize that objects are more than extensions of their own actions. However, babies in this substage still have only rudimentary notions of objects and space, and their discoveries about the world seem to have an accidental quality to them.

Substage 4: coordination of secondary circular reactions (8 to 12 months) The hallmark of the fourth sensorimotor substage is infants' emerging ability to coordinate several of the secondary circular reactions acquired in substage 3 in order to achieve a goal. Piaget believed that such coordination is the earliest form of true problem solving because it requires that different schemas be combined to achieve a desired effect.

For an example, Piaget describes the behavior of his son, Laurent, when he was 10 months old. Piaget gave Laurent a small tin container, which Laurent dropped and picked up repeatedly (an example of a secondary circular reaction characteristic of substage 3 behavior). Piaget then placed a wash basin a short distance from Laurent and struck it with the tin, which made an interesting sound. From earlier observations, Piaget knew that Laurent would repeatedly bang on the basin to make the interesting sound occur (another typical example of a secondary circular reaction). This time Piaget wanted to see if Laurent would combine the newly acquired "dropping the tin box" schema with the previously acquired "make an interesting sound" schema. Here is his report of Laurent's behavior:

> Now, at once, Laurent takes possession of the tin, holds out his arm and drops it over the basin. I moved the latter as a check. He nevertheless succeeded, several times in succession, in making the object fall on the basin. Hence this is a fine example of the coordination of two schemas of which the first serves as a "means" whereas the second assigns an end to the action. . . . (Piaget, 1952, p. 255)

According to Piaget, the new way infants relate actions to objects in substage 4 indicates that they are developing a sense that objects have an existence independent of themselves.

Out of Sight, Out of Mind?

As adults, we believe that objects have substance, are external to ourselves, maintain their identity when they change location, and continue to exist when out of sight. Piaget referred to this understanding as **object permanence.** He believed it to be something young infants lack. Theirs, he claimed, is a world of discontinuous pictures that are constantly being "annihilated and resurrected," in which an object is "a mere image which reenters the void as soon as it vanishes, and emerges from it for no apparent reason" (Piaget, 1954, p. 11). Until objects are conceived of as having an existence of their own, "out of sight, out of mind" may be a literal description of children's thought processes.

Compelling evidence for Piaget's view that infants lack object permanence comes from observations such as the following of 5- and 6-month-old babies:

Observation 1: A baby seated at a table is offered a soft toy. He grasps it. While he is still engrossed in the toy, the experimenter takes it from him and places it on the table behind a screen. The baby may begin to reach for the toy, but as soon as it disappears from sight he stops short, stares for a moment, and then looks away without attempting to move the screen (see Figure 6.9) (Piaget, 1954).

Observation 2: A baby is placed in an infant seat in a bare laboratory room. Her mother, who has been playing with her, disappears for a moment. When the mother reappears, there are *three* images of her, an illusion the experimenter has

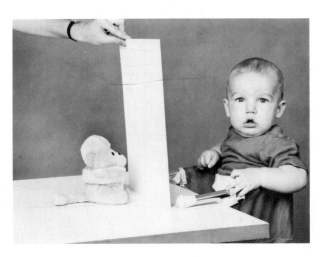

FIGURE 6.9 *Instead of searching behind the screen when his toy disappears, this infant looks dumbfounded. This kind of behavior led Piaget to conclude that objects no longer in view cease to exist for infants less than 8 months of age.*

created through the use of carefully arranged mirrors (see Figure 6.10). The baby displays no consternation as she babbles happily to her multiple mother (Bower, 1982).

Observation 3: From the comfort of his mother's lap, a baby follows a toy train with his eyes as it chugs along a track (see Figure 6.11). The baby watches as the train enters a tunnel, but instead of continuing to follow the train's progress with his eyes, his gaze remains fixed on the tunnel's entrance. When the train reappears at the tunnel's exit, it takes him a few seconds to catch up with it. He displays no surprise even when the train has changed color or shape while in the tunnel (Bower, 1982).

In line with his belief that babies' actions create their understanding, Piaget maintained that we cannot infer that babies understand that objects continue to exist when they are out of sight until they begin *actively* to

FIGURE 6.10 *A simple optical arrangement creates the illusion of three identical mothers. Unlike older infants, babies who do not yet search for a hidden object show no consternation when confronted with this situation.*

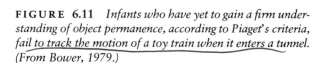

FIGURE 6.11 *Infants who have yet to gain a firm understanding of object permanence, according to Piaget's criteria, fail to track the motion of a toy train when it enters a tunnel. (From Bower, 1979.)*

search for an object they no longer see. Not all psychologists agree. Some suggest that infants may understand what objects are but simply do not know how to go about searching for an object that disappears. Others believe that babies quickly forget the location of objects and so become confused.

Stages of Object Permanence

Piaget's ideas concerning object permanence have generated substantial disagreements about the true nature of babies' understanding of objects and how that understanding can best be assessed. These disagreements have in turn generated a large body of research that sheds considerable light on the complex cognitive changes that occur in the first year of life. Before we address these disagreements, however, we need to take a look at Piaget's conception of the stagelike changes that occur in infants' understanding of objects and the observations on which his conception was based.

Piaget proposed six stages in the development of object permanence, which correspond roughly to the six substages of the sensorimotor period (see Table 6.2). We will discuss the first four of these stages in this chapter and the remaining two in Chapter 7.

Stages 1 and 2 (birth to 4 months) Piaget observed that during the first 4 months of life babies look toward the source of sounds they hear. He also reports that during this period his own children continued to stare at the place where he was last visible to them (Piaget, 1952). However, since they did not actively search for an object when it disappeared but instead seemed quickly to turn their attention elsewhere, he denied that these behaviors were evidence that they had a conception of objects.

Stage 3 (4 to 8 months) At about 4 or 5 months of age, babies begin to show more of a response to the disappearance of an object. Although they can sit up with some support and can reach out to grasp objects with reasonable accuracy, their ability to explore at this age is still relatively restricted. Furthermore, their attention to events around them is often fleeting. This is the stage the children in our three observations are in. Objects that disappear completely seem quickly to be forgotten, and the appearance of the same object in several places causes no visible consternation. However, when objects are only *partly* hidden, the child will reach for them (Piaget, 1954).

TABLE 6.2 Sensorimotor substages and the development of object permanence

Substage	Age Range (months)	Characteristics of Sensorimotor Substage	Developments in Object Permanence
1	$0-1\frac{1}{2}$	Reflex schemas exercised	Infant does not search for objects that have been removed from sight
2	$1\frac{1}{2}-4$	Primary circular reactions; repeated actions that are pleasurable	Infant does not search for objects that have been removed from sight
3	4–8	Secondary circular reactions; dawning awareness of relation of own actions to environment; extended actions that produce pleasant sensations	Infant will reach for partially hidden object but stops if it disappears
4	8–12	Coordination of secondary circular reactions; earliest form of problem solving	Infant will search for a completely hidden object; the infant keeps searching the original location of the object even if it is moved to another location in full view of the infant
5	12–18	Tertiary circular reactions; deliberate variation of problem-solving means; experimentation in order to see what the consequences will be	Infant will search for an object after seeing it moved but not if the object is secretly moved
6	18–24	Beginnings of symbolic representation; invention of new means of problem solving through symbolic combinations	Infant will search for a hidden object, certain that it exists somewhere

Stage 4 (8 to 12 months) At about 8 months of age, babies begin to show the first evidence, according to Piaget's criteria, that they know objects exist when they are out of sight because they begin to search for them. However, in searching for missing objects, babies in this stage tend to make what researchers have called the **A-not-B error** — babies who have found a missing object in one place will subsequently search the same place for the object even when they have seen that it has been moved to another place. This error can be illustrated as follows: First an object is hidden under cover A and the baby is allowed to retrieve it. Then, in full view of the baby, the object is placed under cover B. When allowed to retrieve the object this time, the baby will regularly look under cover A, where the object was found before, rather than under cover B (Piaget, 1954). Figure 6.12 shows another example of the A-not-B error. The tendency of infants to make this error continues until they are more than a year old, as we will see in Chapter 7.

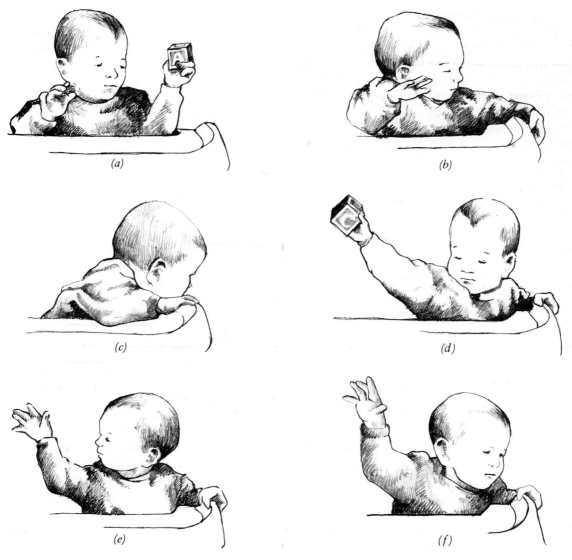

FIGURE 6.12 *An A-not-B error in spontaneous play behavior. These pictures are drawn from a movie sequence of an infant playing with his toys in his home. (a) The boy plays with a block as he sits in his high chair. (b) He drops the block over his left side (A) of the high chair. (c) He looks over his left side (A) of the high chair for the block he has just dropped. (d) He drops the block over his right side (B) of the high chair. (e) He looks at his empty hand as if noting the absence of the block. (f) He looks for the block over his left side (A) of the high chair rather than over his right side (B). (Adapted from Rosenblith & Sims-Knight, 1985.)*

The role of familiarity in object permanence On the basis of familiarity alone, it might be expected that the people who care for them would be among the first objects infants recognize as permanent. Research supports this conclusion. Infants *do* seem to understand that familiar adults and objects still exist when they are out of sight approximately 1 week earlier than they understand that unfamiliar adults and objects are permanent. However, there is no evidence to support the view that different rules apply to the development of infants' understanding of the permanence of people than to the development of their understanding of the permanence of other objects (Jackson, Campos, & Fischer, 1978).

There is an important difference between object permanence and person permanence, however. When objects disappear or fail to appear where they are expected, babies who have achieved stage 4 of object permanence do not seem to get upset. They simply lose interest. But when mothers or fathers disappear or appear in too many places at once, as in the case of the multiple mother, children do become upset. This emotional response is an important indication of the qualitatively distinct relationship that begins to develop between children of this age and their caretakers and that will become even more significant in the months ahead (Corter, Zucker, & Galligan, 1980).

Explaining the acquisition of object permanence
The sequence of changes in children's developing understanding of object permanence described by Piaget occurs so reliably that tests of object permanence have been standardized for use in assessing the development of children at risk because of disease, physical impairment, or extreme environmental deprivation (Decarie, 1969; Uzgiris & Hunt, 1975). Even so, recent research in which the experimental procedures used were designed to take into account young infants' limited abilities to remember and to act on their knowledge has indicated that they may understand object permanence earlier than Piaget suggested. For example, experiments conducted by Renée Baillargeon, Elizabeth Spelke, and Stanley Wasserman (1985) and by Baillargeon (1987) show that under some conditions 3½-month-old infants realize that objects continue to exist when they are hidden. This is fully 4½ months earlier than Piaget proposed and thus casts doubt on his explanation of the development of the object permanence stages.

Baillargeon and her colleagues arranged for babies to watch a screen as it rotated slowly back and forth through a 180 degree arc on a hinge attached to the floor of the viewing surface. In its upright position the screen was like a fence behind which an object might be hidden from view. The screen could rotate toward the babies until it was lying flat and away from them until it was again lying flat.

When the babies were first shown the rotating screen, they stared at it for almost a full minute, but after several trials, they seemed to lose interest in it and looked at it for only about 10 seconds. The experimenters then appeared to place a box behind the screen so that the screen obscured the "box" as it moved into its perpendicular position. (They arranged mirrors to create the illusion of the box.) Next, they did one of two things. For one group of babies, they rotated the screen until it reached the point where it should bump up against the box, after which it returned to its starting position. For the second group, they rotated the screen in its original 180 degree arc as though there were no box (see Figure 6.13).

Baillargeon and her colleagues reasoned that if the babies thought the box still existed even when it was obscured by the screen, they would stare at the screen longer when it seemed to pass through the box than they would when the screen seemed to bump into the box before returning to its starting point. This is just what the babies did. They showed no special interest when the screen seemed to bump into the box (even though this was a novel event), but they showed great interest when it appeared to pass right through the place where the obscured box was located. Their increased interest when the screen continued to rotate in its original manner is difficult to explain unless it is assumed that the babies expected it to bump into the hidden object.

Their responses to the rotating screen indicate that infants realize hidden objects do not cease to exist simply because they cannot be seen. But if they know this, why do they behave as they do on other tests of object permanence? A number of studies have been designed to test possible difficulties babies may have.

Problems associated with motor skills Some experimenters have suggested that babies in stage 3 of the development of object permanence (4 to 8 months of age) do not yet have sufficient motor coordination to retrieve an object that has been hidden, usually behind a handkerchief or a screen, and consequently they

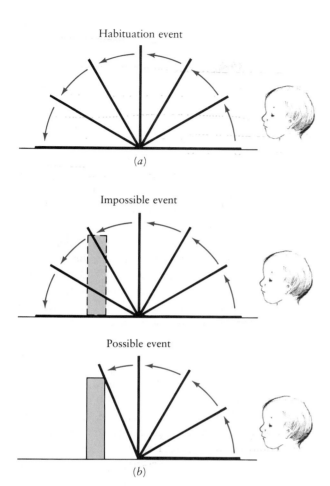

Habituation event

(a)

Impossible event

Possible event

(b)

FIGURE 6.13 *A schematic representation of the (a) habituation and (b) test events arranged for babies by Renée Baillargeon and her colleagues. In the impossible event, the rotating screen appears to pass through a box that the baby has previously seen behind it. (From Baillargeon, 1987.)*

appear to lose interest in the object. To test this hypothesis, T. G. R. Bower and Jennifer Wishart (1972) "hid" an object under a transparent cover. When the babies could see the object, they had no trouble retrieving it from underneath the cover, showing that inadequate motor skills, by themselves, are not the problem at this stage.

Problems remembering A factor that does seem to hinder stage-3 infants in a search for a hidden object is their limited memory span. If Piaget was correct in his assumption that the searching errors made during this stage are the result of a lack of understanding rather than a lack of memory, the likelihood that babies will

make a searching error ought not to depend upon the amount of time that passes between the hiding of an object and the start of the babies' search for it, within reasonable bounds. To test whether this was so, Adele Diamond (1985) carefully varied the time that the object in the test described in the discussion of the A-not-B error (page 193) was out of sight under cover B before the babies were allowed to begin searching for it. She found that the babies' errors *did* depend on the amount of delay. When they were allowed to search immediately, babies as young as $7\frac{1}{2}$ months looked correctly for the object under cover B. But with as little as a 2-second delay, they looked incorrectly under cover A. By the same token, babies as old as 12 months can be induced to make the A-not-B error if they are prevented from beginning their search for at least 10 seconds. These results indicate that stage-3 babies as well as stage-4 babies realize that the hidden objects still exist; they just quickly lose track of where to look for them.

Problems separating movement and location A longitudinal study of 24 babies conducted by Linda Acredolo (1978) helped to pin down the factors that lead young infants to forget the location of hidden objects. The infants were tested at 6, 11, and 16 months of age. Acredolo's purpose was to determine whether infants forget the locations of objects because they concentrate too narrowly on their own actions, as Piaget maintained, or simply because they are especially susceptible to forgetting about locations.

The baby was seated facing a round table in a small, plain room. To the right and to the left of the baby was a window in which the experimenter could appear and disappear. One window was surrounded by a giant star to make it a visually distinctive landmark. The experiment began with five trials in which a buzzer sounded and the experimenter appeared at the starred window. All the children quickly learned to anticipate her appearance. The babies were then wheeled around to the other side of the table so that the starred window was on the *opposite* side of the room with respect to their bodies. When the buzzer sounded again, would the baby look at the starred window, which would indicate remembrance of the correct location, or at the unstarred window, which would involve repeating the movements that had previously been successful?

Acredolo's results nicely support Piaget's notion that young infants rely primarily on their own actions to orient themselves and only slowly come to consider

BOX 6.1

ACTION AND UNDERSTANDING

• • •

Piaget's hypothesis that children's own activities are the driving force of their development has led many psychologists to study the developmental consequences of restricted or enhanced movement early in life. A basic intuition guiding such research is the idea that locomotion not only allows babies to learn how to move their bodies in space, but it also provides them with a different understanding of the objects that fill space. As Selma Fraiberg has written,

> Travel changes one's perspective. A chair, for example, is an object of one dimension when viewed by a six-month-old baby propped up on the sofa, or by an eight-month-old baby doing push-ups on a rug. It's even very likely that the child of this age confronted at various times with different perspectives of the same chair would see not one chair, but several chairs, corresponding to each perspective. It's when you start to get around under your own steam that you discover what a chair really is. . . . (Fraiberg, 1959, p. 52)

A classic study demonstrating a close link between locomotor experience and the understanding of spatial relations was carried out by Richard Held and Alan Hein (1963) with kittens who were raised from birth in

total darkness. When the kittens were old enough to walk, they were placed two at a time in an apparatus called a "kitten carousel" (see the illustration). One

The kitten carousel used in Held and Hein's classic experiment demonstrating the importance of active experience to development. (From Held, 1965.)

external landmarks. At 6 months of age, 83 percent of the infants looked at the unstarred window; that is, they made the same movements as before. At 11 months, 50 percent of the babies still looked at the unstarred window. At 16 months, however, only 17 percent of the infants repeated their prior movements; the rest looked at the starred window, indicating that they had come to rely on external landmarks.

Taken together, the data on the development of object permanence and motor skills between 4 and 12 months suggest the following general picture. By 4 months of age, many infants understand that objects do not cease to exist simply because they are out of

sight, but they are unable to act upon this understanding except to register their surprise when their expectations are not met (Baillargeon, Spelke, & Wasserman, 1985). At this early age, the act of reaching for and grasping an object is still effortful. Infants must monitor their movements carefully by looking back and forth between their hands and the object that they are trying to grasp. This diverts the infants' attention from an object that has been hidden from sight and causes them to forget about it. They remember their own movements instead of the object's location. By about 9 months, reaching and grasping have become well-integrated responses that no longer require spe-

kitten pulled the carousel. This kitten could use what it saw to control its movements, and its movements determined, to some extent, what it saw. The other kitten was carried in the gondola of the carousel and had no active interactions with the world it saw. The experiences of the passive kitten were largely controlled by the actions of the kitten pulling the carousel. Each pair of kittens was given 3 hours of visual experience in the carousel every day for 42 days. Between these sessions, they were returned to the dark. Thus, the only visual experience the kittens had, and hence the only opportunity they had for developing visual-motor coordination, was the time they spent in the carousel.

The influence of active versus passive movement on the kittens' responses to their environment became strikingly apparent when Held and Hein lowered them onto the surface of a visual cliff similar to the one shown in Figure 1.7 of Chapter 1 (p. 23). This apparatus had stripes painted on it like the stripes around the sides of the kitten carousel except that they were painted to look as if one side of the apparatus were far below the other. The kittens that had been active in the carousel shied away from the deep side of the visual cliff and appropriately stretched out their legs to land on it. The passive kittens did not try to avoid the deep side of the cliff, nor did they make appropriate adjustments in the positions of their legs in anticipation of landing on it.

This finding fits well with the results of the experiment by Joseph Campos and his co-workers described in Chapter 1 (p. 23) that confirmed the importance of movement in human cognitive development (Bertenthal, Campos, & Barrett, 1983). In that study, 5-month-old babies who had not yet begun to crawl did not seem to be afraid of a visual cliff when they first saw it. They began to be afraid of heights only after they had begun to move around on their own or after they had experience locomoting in baby walkers.

Campos and his co-workers have also shown that locomotion enhances the development of infants' memory for the location of hidden objects. Babies who had extensive experience moving around in baby walkers before they could move about on their own were more adept at locating hidden objects in standard object permanence tests than were children the same age who had no experience moving around on their own (Campos, Benson, & Rudy, 1987).

Finally, unusual support for the close connection between locomotion and development is provided by a study of the development of infants suffering from a neural tube defect that impedes locomotion (Telzrow, Campos, & Bertenthal, 1986). Such children were found to be delayed in their development of correct search behaviors for hidden objects by 5 to 6 months. They began to search correctly only after they had begun to move voluntarily. The results of these experiments on how locomotion affects development provide support for the belief that active engagement of the world makes a fundamental contribution to development.

cial attention and therefore no longer distract them. Thus, they can keep their knowledge of the location of a hidden object in mind long enough to act on it.

This overall picture of the development of infants' behaviors related to object permanence contradicts Piaget's belief that infants do not understand the continued existence of objects that are out of sight before 8 months of age. The data also seem to indicate the need for some modification of his strong emphasis on action as the essential motor of cognitive development. (See Box 6.1, "Action and Understanding," for further discussion of the role of activity in early cognition development.) However, Piaget appears to be correct in his contention that infants become better able to coordinate their sensory knowledge and their movements during substage 4 of the sensorimotor period.

Integrating the Different Properties of Objects

Understanding that objects continue to exist even when they are out of sight is by no means all that babies come to know about them. They also come to understand that the different pieces of information they

4

derive from the sight, sound, taste, smell, and feel of an object all go together. This helps them to infer the existence of the whole object from its individual characteristics. For example, they are eventually able to understand that the voice coming from the other room and the face they see a few moments later are two aspects of the same person and that the gold color of the stuff on the spoon goes with its awful taste.

For most of this century, developmental psychologists assumed that, at birth, babies respond to the sight, sound, and other sense impressions of objects as if they were completely separate (Harris, 1983; James, 1890). According to this view, infants must learn to integrate mentally the different aspects of an object as they occur together in the course of everyday experience. Recently, however, several ingenious studies have shown that, for some combinations of features, at least, the ability to integrate the different attributes of objects either does not have to be learned or is learned rapidly and quite early in infancy.

Compelling evidence that infants respond to certain features of objects as if they naturally go together has been collected by Elizabeth Spelke (1976, 1984). Spelke presented pairs of film strips to 4-month-old babies and tested to see if they knew what sort of sound should accompany each film. In one study she showed a film of percussion instruments being played alongside a film of a game of peekaboo. A loudspeaker located between the two screens sometimes played sounds appropriate to the percussion instruments and other times played sounds appropriate to the game of peekaboo. The infants looked most often at the film appropriate to the sounds being played. Using a similar setup, Spelke and Owsley (1979) demonstrated that 4-month-olds expected a male voice to go with a picture of a man and a female voice to go with a picture of a woman. These results indicate that infants understand the connections among different properties of objects by the time they are 4 months old. No techniques have yet been developed to determine if neonates have such an understanding, so the question of how early it develops is still unresolved.

Learning About Kinds of Things

By the time babies are 1 year old, they have learned to categorize; that is, they are able to perceive objects or events that differ in various ways as equivalent because they share certain common features. Infants come to understand, for example, that two somewhat different objects, a round, blue thing that makes noise when you shake it and a thin, shiny thing that makes noise when you shake it, are both rattles (Rovee-Collier, 1987). The ability to form categories is essential for the development of both language and memory capacity.

The ability of infants to form categories appears to develop between 6 and 9 months of age (Bertenthal, Campos, & Barrett, 1984; Kagan & Hamburg, 1981; Ruff, 1978; Younger & Cohen, 1986). Holly Ruff (1978), for example, found this when she compared the amount of time 6- and 9-month-old babies looked at objects that differed in form, size, and color. Each object consisted of a cylinder and a cube that had been glued to a rectangular base. Ruff began with familiarization trials in which she gave the babies the objects depicted in Figure 6.14a one at a time. The objects differed in color and size but not in form; that is, each

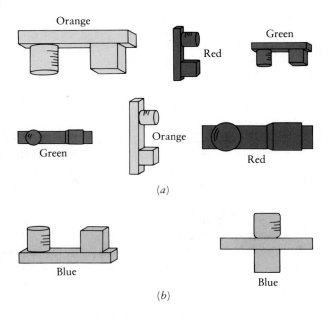

FIGURE 6.14 *(a) The familiarization objects in Holly Ruff's experiment are of different sizes and colors—orange, green, and red (depicted here in shades of red and gray)—but the same form. (b) The test objects in the experiment are of the same color—blue—and size but are different in form. The differences in color and size between the familiarization objects and the test object on the left did not interest the infants because they had learned those properties were irrelevant during the first phase of the experiment. (From Ruff, 1978.)*

of them had the cylinder and the cube glued to the same side of the rectangular base. The babies were allowed to touch each of the objects for 30 seconds. Then, in two test trials, the babies were shown the two objects depicted in Figure 6.14b. In the first test trial, the object was of a different color and size but the same form as the objects with which the babies had become familiar. Since form, not color or size, was the categorizing characteristic of the familiarization objects, the first trial object belonged to the same category. In the second test trial, the cylinder and the cube were glued to opposite sides of the rectangular base. Thus, the second trial object was of a new form and therefore belonged to a new category. The 6-month-olds did not respond differently to the two test objects, but the 9-month-olds did. They spent more time examining the object that differed from the familiarization objects in form than they did the object that differed in color and size. This indicates that they had formed a mental category based on the form of the objects during the familiarization trials.

David Starkey (1981) obtained similar results when he showed 6-, 9-, and 12-month-old infants four yellow plastic pillboxes and four blue clay balls mixed together on a tray. Almost all the 12- and 9-month-olds touched either all the pillboxes or all the clay balls one after the other before turning to the other kind of object. The 6-month-olds, however, touched the two kinds of objects in a completely haphazard manner, indicating that they were not responding to the categorical distinctions between them.

The ability to make categorical distinctions among objects and the ability to keep in mind the existence of an object that has disappeared from sight bespeak an increase in the infant's ability to structure information from past experience. This increase enables the infant to deal more effectively with current circumstances.

The Growth of Memory

The ability of infants to learn and to remember what they have learned improves significantly between $2\frac{1}{2}$ and 12 months of age (Rovee-Collier, 1984; Sullivan, Rovee-Collier, & Tynes, 1979).

Carolyn Rovee-Collier and her colleagues (Sullivan, Rovee-Collier, & Tynes, 1979) trained infants to make a mobile move by kicking one of their legs, which was

attached by a ribbon to the mobile (see Figure 6.15). They found that 3-month-olds could remember this experience for 1 week; the babies started to kick as soon as they were put in the crib and the ribbon was tied to their leg. However, after 2 weeks the babies seemed to have forgotten their training; they took just as long to start the mobile moving as they had when they were first trained to do so.

A second experiment revealed that the infants could, if they were given a brief visual reminder, remember their earlier training even after some time had elapsed. The researchers trained a group of 3-month-old babies to kick to activate a mobile. They then let a month elapse, more than enough time for the babies to

FIGURE 6.15 *This infant is being trained to make the mobile, which is attached to her leg by a ribbon, move by kicking her leg. Once learned, such responses can be used to test infants' memories over extended periods of time. (Courtesy of Carolyn Rovee-Collier.)*

forget their training, the researchers thought. On the day before they tested the infants' memory for how to make the mobile move, they showed the infants the mobile but did not allow the infants to kick. When the babies were tested the next day, they started kicking as soon as they were placed in the crib and the ribbon was tied to their leg (Rovee-Collier, Sullivan, Enright, Lucas, & Fagan, 1980).

Adults tend to forget the specific features of an event or an object and to retain only a generalized impression of it. To see if this is also the way babies remember, Rovee-Collier and Sullivan (1980) trained 3-month-olds to move a mobile. Once again, two groups of babies were trained. They were then tested on a different mobile. One group was tested only 1 day after being trained. They did *not* kick, indicating that they remembered the mobile they were trained on and realized they were seeing a new one. They had to learn all over again how to make the new mobile move. The second group was tested 4 days after being trained. They *did* kick. Apparently, they had forgotten the details of *the* mobile they had been trained on but remembered what to do when they saw *a* mobile. These results suggest that 3-month-olds, like adults, remember the general properties of objects or events even after they have forgotten the specifics.

Recall and Wariness

A number of investigators have suggested that infants become capable of a new kind of remembering between 7 and 9 months of age (Kagan, Kearsley, & Zelazo, 1978; Mandler, 1984; Schacter & Moscovitch, 1984; Schaffer, 1974). They begin to recall objects that are absent without being reminded of them. For example, Daniel Ashmead and Marion Perlmutter (1980) describe the recall memory of a 9-month-old girl who was accustomed to playing with ribbons that were kept in the bottom drawer of a bureau. On one occasion, the girl crawled to the bureau and opened the bottom drawer, only to discover that the ribbons were not there. She then opened all of the drawers until she found the ribbons, which had been placed in the top drawer. When she wanted the ribbons the next day, she crawled over to the bureau, immediately opened the top drawer, and removed the ribbons.

Some researchers believe that the advent of recall memory is an essential precondition for the changes in the way that infants behave when they are confronted

with a strange object or person that occur between 7 and 9 months. At this age, infants begin to become wary and even afraid when something out of the ordinary happens (see Figure 6.16). In an illustration of this, Rudolph Schaffer (1974) repeatedly presented babies between the ages of 4 and 9 months with a strange object until they became habituated to it. He then presented them with a new strange object, a plastic model of an ice cream sundae. The typical 4-month-old strained toward the sundae immediately, without any hesitation. Most 6-month-olds hesitated for a second or two and then reached for the sundae impulsively, often bringing it to their mouths. In contrast, 9-month-olds tended to hesitate for a relatively long time, and some of them even turned away or started to cry.

Nathan Fox, Jerome Kagan, and Sally Weiskopf (1979) hypothesize that the 9-month-olds' wariness is

FIGURE 6.16 *The wide-eyed look this child is giving her disguised mother is an example of the wariness that infants develop sometime between the ages of 7 and 9 months.*

caused by their newly acquired ability to compare current events with remembered past events in a systematic way. When the 4-month-olds see the strange sundae, they do not react to it as strange. 6-month-olds hesitate, indicating they have noted the change. The 9-month-olds not only note that it is unfamiliar, but they also search their memories to determine if it corresponds to any category of thing they have seen before. They become upset because it does not.

Considered as a whole, the data on object permanence, categorization, and the changing bases of remembering support the conclusion that the seemingly separate aspects of cognitive development that occur in the later part of the first year of life are separate neither from each other nor from the development of motor capacities and the biological maturation described earlier in this chapter. In addition, as the evidence presented in the following sections demonstrates, these new cognitive capacities are intimately linked with changes in the babies' social world, including their emotional relationships with their caretakers and their communicative abilities.

A NEW RELATIONSHIP TO THE SOCIAL WORLD

The development of infants' understanding of object permanence and their increasing ability to remember are reflected in their relationships with other people. Jake's wariness of Sheila at 12 months of age described at the start of this chapter is one of the social behaviors that results. When Jake was 10 weeks old, Sheila was an acceptable substitute for his mother. But 10 months later, Jake was genuinely upset when he looked up and saw Sheila where he expected his mother to be. In this and other ways Jake is displaying his attachment to his mother.

Many developmental psychologists agree that the fear of an unfamiliar adult and the attachment to their mothers expressed by children Jake's age are a result of infants' increasing ability to categorize and remember (Bertenthal, Campos, & Barrett, 1984; Emde, Gaensbauer, & Harmon, 1976; Kagan, 1984). No one is strange until the infant can categorize people as those who are familiar or those who are strange and can remember who is who.

The Role of Uncertainty in Wariness

In trying to discover why an understanding of object permanence and an improved memory should result in wariness and fear, it is important to remember the predicament confronting babies. They are constantly encountering new situations and new objects, but they have little past experience to guide their responses to them and little physical strength or coordination to draw upon even if they know what to do. They cannot feed, dress, or go to the toilet by themselves. What is more, since they do not talk at all or have a vocabulary of only a few words, they have no reliable system of communication. Therefore, to get through each day reasonably well fed and comfortable, they must depend on adults and older siblings to know what needs to be done and how to do it, as the following vignette illustrates:

Amy, almost four months old, sat in her father's lap in a booth at the coffee shop. He was talking to a friend. Amy was teething on a hard rubber ring he had brought along for her. Her father supported Amy's back with his left arm, keeping his hand free. Twice he used that hand to catch the ring when it fell to her lap or his own lap. When Amy dropped the ring for the third time, he interrupted his conversation, said "Klutz," picked it up and put it on the table. She leaned toward it, awkwardly reached out and touched it, but was not able to grasp it well enough to pick it up. Her father had returned to his conversation, and this time without interrupting it (though he was glancing back and forth between Amy's hand and his friend) he tilted the ring upward toward Amy so that she could get her thumb under it. She grasped the ring and pulled it away from him. Absorbed in chewing on the toy, Amy did not look at him. He went on talking and drinking his coffee, paying no further attention to her until he felt the toy drop into his lap once again. (Kaye, 1982, pp. 1–2)

There are countless ways, such as those just described, in which the adults who care for babies act for them and with them so that babies can function effectively despite their relative ineptness. The adult's actions must be finely coordinated with the baby's abilities and needs or the baby will experience some form of difficulty.

The kind of finely tuned adult support that permits children to accomplish with assistance actions that they will later learn to accomplish independently creates what cultural-context theorist Lev Vygotsky (1978) called a zone of proximal development. Vygotsky attributed great significance to such child-adult interactions throughout development. The zone referred to is the gap between what children can accomplish independently and what they can accomplish when they are interacting with others who are more competent. The term *proximal* (nearby) indicates that the assistance provided goes just slightly beyond the child's current competence, complementing and building on the child's existing abilities instead of directly teaching the child new behaviors. Notice, for example, that Amy's father did not put the teething ring in Amy's hand, nor did he hold it up to her mouth for her to teethe on. Instead, he tilted it upward so that she could grasp it herself, and he did this almost automatically while doing something else. To coordinate behaviors in this way requires that the adult know what the child is trying to do, and be sensitive to the child's abilities and signals.

The mundane ways in which adults provide a predictable and supportive environment for infants help to explain the onset of wariness during the seventh month of life. There are only certain people that babies can count on to arrange the environment appropriately and in accordance with their expectations. Prior to 7 months, infant capacities to classify people as "those who can be trusted to help" versus "unpredictable strangers" and to remember the likely implications for themselves may be very weak or absent. Once infants can form such categories and use them to compare their current circumstances with similar past experiences, strange people may become upsetting because babies realize that strangers do not have routines for interacting with them. They cannot be depended upon to notice and understand infants' signals or to do their part in making things go well.

A New Form of Emotional Relationship

An important result of children's new understanding of the vital role their primary caretakers play in their well-being is the emergence of a new, enduring emotional bond with their caretakers called attachment. Infants begin to form such bonds sometime between 7 and 9 months of age, usually with their mothers at first.

Eleanor Maccoby (1980) lists four signs of attachment among babies and young children:

1. They seek to be near their primary caretaker. Before the age of 7 to 8 months few babies make organized, planful attempts to achieve contact with the other person; after this age, babies often follow their mothers closely, for example.

2. They show distress if separated from their caretaker. Before attachment begins, infants show little disturbance when their mothers walk out of the room.

3. They are happy when they are reunited with the person they are attached to.

4. They orient their actions to the other person, even when he or she is absent. Babies listen for their mother's voice and watch her while they play.

The special emotional attachment between mothers and their babies is often written on their faces.

The special relationship to their mothers that babies begin to display between 7 and 9 months of age has been the subject of many studies because of its importance for understanding the cognitive and social development of children during infancy (Bretherton & Waters, 1985; Parkes & Stevenson-Hinde, 1982). Often these studies are carried out using a procedure called the **strange situation**, which was designed by Mary Ainsworth to observe babies' responses to a stranger when they are with their mothers, when they are left alone, and when they are reunited with their mothers (Ainsworth & Wittig, 1969). Although such situations are artificial and although there are difficulties in interpreting children's behavior in them when they are used in different cultural contexts (discussed further in Chapter 7), they give a clear sense of the new emotional reactions that children all over the world exhibit by about 9 months of age.

The following case study, which is summarized from research reported by Mary Ainsworth and Barbara Wittig (1969, pp. 116–118), illustrates the "strange-situation" procedure and how a typical 12-month-old, North American, middle-class child behaves in it.

An observer shows a mother and her baby into an experimental room that has toys scattered on the floor. "Brian had one arm hooked over his mother's shoulder as they came in the room. . . . He looked around soberly, but with interest at the toys and at the observer."

The observer leaves the room. "After being put down Brian immediately crept toward the toys and began to explore them [Figure 6.17a]. He was very active. . . . Although his attention fixed on the playthings, he glanced at his mother six times. . . ."

After three minutes the stranger enters, greets the mother, and sits down quietly in a chair. "[Brian] turned to look at the stranger . . . with a pleasant expression on his face. He played with the tube again, vocalized, smiled and turned to glance at his mother. . . . When the stranger and his mother began to converse, he continued to explore actively. . . . When the stranger began her approach by leaning forward to offer him a toy, he smiled, crept forward and reached for it" [Figure 6.17b].

The mother leaves the room, leaving her purse on the chair, while the stranger distracts Brian's attention. "He did not notice his mother leave. . . . He continued to watch the stranger and the toys. . . . Suddenly, he crept to his mother's chair, pulled himself to a standing position, and looked at the stranger. She tried to distract him with a pull toy . . . but he glanced again at his mother's empty chair. He was less active than he had been when alone with his mother and after two minutes his activity ceased. He sat chewing the string of the pulltoy and glancing from the stranger to his mother's chair. He made an unhappy noise, then a cry face, then he cried. The stranger tried to distract him by offering him a block; he took it, but threw it away."

"When his mother opened the door . . . Brian looked at her immediately and vocalized loudly . . . then crept to her quickly, and pulled himself up, with her help, to hold on to her knees. Then she picked him up, and he immediately put his arms around her neck, his face against her shoulder and hugged her hard [Figure 6.17c]. . . . He resisted being put down; he tried to cling to her and protested loudly. Once on the floor, he threw himself down, hid his face in the rug, and cried angrily [Figure 6.17d]. His mother knelt beside him and tried to interest him in the toys again. He stopped crying and watched. After a moment she disengaged herself and got up to sit on her chair. He immediately threw himself down and cried again."

Brian's mother gets up and leaves the room again. "As she said 'Bye-bye' and waved, Brian looked up with a little smile, but he shifted into a cry before she had quite closed the door. He sat crying, rocking himself back and forth [Figure 6.17e]. . . ."

The stranger, who had earlier left the room, reenters. "Brian lulled slightly when he saw the stranger enter, but he continued to cry. She first tried to distract him, then offered her arms to him. Brian responded by raising his arms; she picked him up and he stopped crying immediately. . . . Occasionally he gave a little sob, but for the most part he did not cry. But when she put him down, he screamed. She picked him up again, and he lulled."

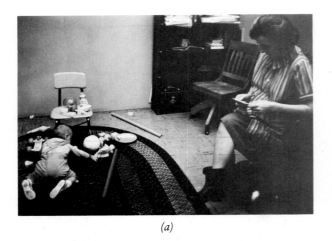

(a)   (b)

(c)   (d)

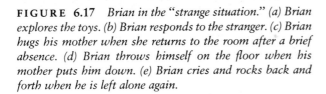

FIGURE 6.17 *Brian in the "strange situation." (a) Brian explores the toys. (b) Brian responds to the stranger. (c) Brian hugs his mother when she returns to the room after a brief absence. (d) Brian throws himself on the floor when his mother puts him down. (e) Brian cries and rocks back and forth when he is left alone again.*

(e)

"At the moment that his mother returned Brian was
   crying listlessly. He did not notice his mother.
   The stranger half-turned and pointed her out.
   Brian looked toward her, still crying, and then
   turned away. But he soon 'did a double take.' He
   looked back and vocalized a little protest. His
   mother offered her arms to him. He reached
   toward her, smiling, and leaned way out of the
   stranger's arms and his mother took him. . . . "

Extensive observation using the "strange situation"
in a variety of cultural settings indicates that the formation of strong attachments is a universal characteristic of children about the age of 12 months, unless
they are raised in extremely harmful circumstances
(Bretherton & Waters, 1985; Field, Sostek, Vietze, &

Liederman, 1981). Once established, attachments provide babies with a sense of security that helps to regulate their exploration of the world. Attachment undergoes extensive development during the second year of life. Because its significance can be seen more clearly in the context of this later development, an extended discussion of attachment has been postponed until Chapter 7.

The Changing Nature of Communication

As babies become mobile and begin to respond warily to novel objects and strange people, their ability to communicate with adults and adults' ability to communicate with them undergo important changes. Initially, this involves a new form of behavior that Joseph Campos and Craig Stenberg (1981) call **social referencing**: In social referencing, infants check the reactions of their care takers to see how to interpret an unusual event. For example, babies who have started to crawl may grow wary if they notice that their mothers look concerned in response to some event. But facial expressions provide only a crude means of communicating. As babies become able to wander out of their mother's reach and line of vision, expressions lose their power to communicate. A new means of communication that will allow babies to coordinate their actions with the caretaker at a distance becomes an urgent necessity.

At 9 months of age, children begin to understand certain words and expressions in highly specific, often ritualized, situations. For example, one little girl observed by Elizabeth Bates and her colleagues (Bates, 1979) touched her head when asked "Where are your little thoughts?" Another would bring her favorite doll when asked to "bring a dolly," but she did not understand the word "doll" to refer to any but that one object.

The development of the ability to produce language can be traced back to the cooing and gurgling noises babies begin to make at 10 to 12 weeks of age. Soon thereafter, babies with normal hearing not only coo on their own, but they begin to respond with gurgles and coos to the voices of others. When they are imitated, they will answer with another coo, thereby engaging in a "conversation" in which turns are taken at vocalizing. They are most likely to vocalize with their mothers and other familiar people.

This newcomer to the world of upright posture is looking back to see what her mother thinks of her exploits. Her inquiring gaze is an example of social referencing.

Babbling, a form of vocalizing that includes making consonant and vowel sounds like those used in speech, begins around 4 months of age (de Villiers & de Villiers, 1978). Initially, babbling amounts to no more than vocal play, as babies discover the wealth of sounds they can make with their tongue, teeth, palate, and vocal cords. They practice making these sound combinations endlessly, much as they practice grasping objects or rolling over. They even produce syllables they have never heard before and that they will not use when they learn to speak. Infant babbling during the first year of life is the same the world over, whether the baby is a member of a family that speaks English,

French, or Japanese (Oller, 1978). At about 9 months of age, babies begin to stop making sounds that are not in the language they will eventually speak. As babies often babble when playing alone, early babbling is not an attempt to communicate.

Toward the end of the first year, babies begin to vocalize strings of syllables that have the intonation and stress of actual utterances in the language they will eventually speak. Such vocalizations are called **jargoning**. John Dore (1978) found that, before the end of the first year, babies begin to use the same short utterances in particular situations, as if they mean something. For example, when Jake was about 10 months old, if he wanted the bottle of juice from the bag hanging on the back of his stroller, he would turn around in his seat, say "Dah, dah," and reach toward the bag while looking up at his mother in appeal. She immediately knew what he wanted and gave it to him.

The course of vocal babbling among deaf children provides an instructive contrast with that among hearing children. Like hearing babies, deaf babies start to coo at about 10 to 12 weeks and to babble at about 3 to 4 months, which indicates that cooing and babbling are initially reflex actions that do not depend on environmental feedback (Lenneberg, Rebelsky, & Nichols, 1965). However, instead of gradually acquiring intonation and expressiveness, their vocalizations begin to die out. By 1 year of age or so, deaf children rarely vocalize. By then a different kind of communication system has begun to show itself. At the same time the vocal babbling of hearing children begins to change, deaf children can be seen "babbling" with their *hands*, making the movements that will become the elements of sign language (Bonvillian, Orlansky, & Novack, 1983). We will consider the development of language more thoroughly in Chapter 9.

A NEW BIO-SOCIAL-BEHAVIORAL SHIFT

Table 6.3 summarizes the set of changes that converge in infants between 7 and 9 months of age to create a bio-social-behavioral shift that leads to a new level of development (Emde, Gaensbauer, & Harmon, 1976).

Whereas the crucial biological events at the 2½-month bio-social-behavioral shift centered on changes in the sensory pathways of the brain, the shift that occurs at 7 to 9 months involves changes in the cerebellum and other parts of the brain which control movement and balance, the hippocampus (which is important for memory), and the frontal lobes of the cerebral cortex (which are important for the organization of deliberate action). Also significant are increases in the strength of muscles and bones, which are necessary to support increasingly vigorous movement.

New motor skills help infants to discover the many characteristics of objects that we take for granted as adults. They become capable of picking up objects, feeling them, tasting them, moving around them, and attempting to use them for various purposes of their own. When babies learn that some of the objects "out there" move and respond to them, their interactions with people take on a whole new dimension. Sympathetic adults buffer them against discomfort and danger. These adults can be counted on to understand babies' signals, to complete their actions for them, and to arrange things so that they can act more effectively for themselves.

Even before babies can use words, they are likely to babble in response to adults when they are engaged by them.

TABLE 6.3 Elements of the bio-social-behavioral shift at 7 to 9 months

Biological domain

Growth of muscles and hardening of bones

Myelination of motor neurons to lower trunk, legs, and hands

Myelination of cerebellum, hippocampus, and frontal lobes

New forms of EEG activity in cortex

Behavioral domain

Onset of crawling

Fear of heights

Automated reaching and grasping

Action sequences coordinated to achieve goals

Object permanence displayed in actions

Memory based on categories

Wariness in response to novelty

Babbling

Social domain

Wariness of strangers

New emotional response to caretaker (attachment)

Social referencing

These experiences would not amount to much, however, if memories of them did not begin to accumulate in infants' minds. Once babies can move away from the immediate presence of watchful adults, they can no longer rely on the adults to help them complete their actions and to rescue them from their mistakes in the same manner as before. They must therefore remember their prior experiences with objects, including people, in order to behave appropriately.

Both the baby and the caretaker must accommodate to the uncertainties of their increasing separation. Caretakers arrange the environment so that the baby is likely to encounter no harm, and they keep a watchful eye (or ear) open for something amiss. Babies anticipate trouble, too. Once they begin to move about on their own (and before they can talk), they keep an eye on their caretakers' responses to the things they do. They become wary of strange events and people because they are not sure what unfamiliar adults will do.

Changes in infants' ability to communicate during the first year of life bring them to the threshold of being able to coordinate with other people at a distance. Even deaf children coo and babble like hearing babies, which indicates that the earliest stages of language are innate reflexes that require no special support from the environment. But about the time that babies can move away from their caretakers' arms, the crucial role of the environment in supporting further language development becomes apparent. Without environmental feedback, the child's budding language capacities begin to atrophy.

The pattern of adaptation that babies achieve by about 12 months of age is destined to change. They keep growing, keep exploring, and continue to gain a more and more reliable understanding of the world in which they find themselves. The first year of life is filled with a great many accomplishments, and it sets the stage for children's arrival at a new level of independence. As infants progress from crawling to walking, a new realm to explore becomes available. This, in turn, creates a whole new set of worries and pleasures for their caretakers.

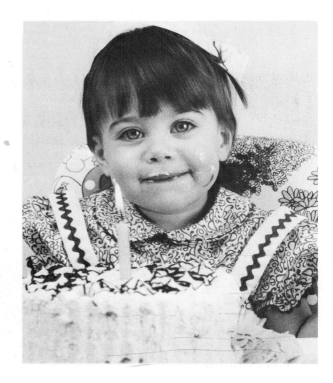

At 1 year of age, this pleased little girl has come a long way in just 12 months' time.

07

ARY

1. Although there is great individual variation, most healthy babies triple in weight during the first year of life. Changes in size are accompanied by changes in overall body proportions that are important to the eventual achievement of balanced walking.

2. Hardening of the bones and increases in muscle mass make possible the development of crawling, walking, and the coordinated movements of the arms and hands.

3. Brain development in several areas is important to the behavioral changes that occur between 2 and 12 months of age:
   a. Primary motor area—general coordination of movement
   b. Cerebellum—coordination and balance
   c. Hippocampus—memory
   d. Frontal lobes—voluntary control and planning

4. The development of motor control of the arms and hands follows a proximodistal pattern: it begins at the center of the body and moves toward the periphery. Poorly coordinated reaching and grasping, which are controlled by subcortical brain centers, is followed by a stage of visually guided reaching and grasping that gives way to rapid voluntary movements after several months of practice.

5. Important increases in the ability to grasp objects and locomote occur during the second half of the first year of life. Motor control of the body follows a cephalocaudal pattern: control begins at the head and neck and proceeds gradually to the trunk and legs. At 7 to 8 months, infants begin to locomote by crawling or creeping, using a combination of leg and arm movements. Walking is achieved a few months later, around the first birthday.

6. Motor development can be speeded up by extensive practice, but practice does not much influence the achievement of basic motor skills. Extensive early practice may influence the later performance of specialized motor skills such as dancing or swimming.

7. According to Piaget, infants progress through two additional sensorimotor substages before the end of the first year. Between 4 and 8 months they pay increased attention to external objects and prolong actions that produce interesting changes in their environment (substage 3). Between 8 and 12 months of age, they achieve the ability to coordinate separate actions to achieve goals (substage 4).

8. An important change occurs in infants' ability to keep in mind the continued existence of objects that are out of sight during the period between 2½ and 12 months:
   a. For the first 3 months of life, infants appear to forget objects not present to their senses.
   b. At 4 months, many infants seem to understand that objects exist even when out of sight but they are incapable of acting on this knowledge. The object and its location are quickly forgotten.
   c. At about 8 months of age, infants begin to search for hidden objects but quickly forget their location, often remembering their own movements instead.
   d. Memory for object locations and the ability to search for hidden objects continues to improve into the second year of life.

9. Infants develop an understanding of object permanence earlier for familiar objects and people than for unfamiliar objects and people.

10. By 4 months of age, infants are able to perceive the correspondence between such varied properties of objects as the way they look and the sounds they make. It is not known how early infant understanding of the connections among the properties of objects develops or what aspects of such understanding are present at birth.

11. The ability to perceive different objects as members of the same category appears to develop sometime after the age of 6 months.

12. Between the ages of 2½ and 12 months, there is a steady growth of memory. Provided with a specific reminder of earlier training, infants as young as 3 months of age will remember how to make a mobile move a month later.

13. At about the same time babies begin to categorize objects, their ability to remember undergoes a qualitative change: they can call to mind objects and people that are not present.

14. Changes in social and emotional behavior accompany changes in motor skills and cognition; infants become wary of strangers and upset when separated from their primary caretakers. Monitoring of the expression on their caretaker's face, called social referencing, helps them to evaluate their environment.

15. Late in the first year, as infants begin to explore their environments on a new scale, a new form of communication appears: infants begin to create their first genuine words.

16. Events in the major developmental domains converge between the ages of 7 and 9 months in a bio-social-behavioral shift that ushers in a qualitatively new stage of development.

KEY TERMS

A-not-B error
Attachment
Babbling
Categorizing

Jargoning
Object permanence
Secondary circular reactions

Social referencing
Strange situation
Zone of proximal development

SUGGESTED READINGS

FRAIBERG, SELMA H. *The Magic Years: Understanding and Handling Problems of Early Childhood.* New York: Scribner's, 1959.

A richly detailed account of early childhood that incorporates the ideas of Sigmund Freud in a highly readable and sympathetic manner.

HARRIS, PAUL L. "Infant Cognition." In P. H. Mussen (Ed.), *Handbook of Child Psychology,* Vol. 2: *Infancy and Developmental Psychobiology.* New York: Wiley, 1983.

A summary of evidence concerning early infant intellectual capacities, including an evaluation of the competing claims of different theorists.

KAGAN, JEROME, RICHARD B. KEARSLEY, and PHILLIP ZELAZO. *Infancy: Its Place in Human Development.* Cambridge, Mass.: Harvard University Press, 1978.

A rich source of data on the development of memory and cognition during the first year of life. This book is notable for its emphasis on experimental methods and its focus on the effects of variations in infants' experience, such as that provided by different cultural environments, on their development.

LAMB, MICHAEL E., and MICHAEL H. BORNSTEIN. *Development in Infancy: An Introduction,* Second Edition. New York: Random House, 1987.

A thorough, readable introduction to infant behavior and development.

MCGRAW, MYRTLE B. *Growth: A Study of Johnny and Jimmy.* New York: Arno, 1975.

This classic study of the growth of basic motor skills, which shows its sequential nature and the relative ineffectiveness of special training, was an important contribution to maturational accounts of development.

PIAGET, JEAN. *The Construction of Reality in the Child.* New York: Basic Books, 1954.

An account of the development of sensorimotor behaviors that includes particularly rich descriptions of the stages in the acquisition of object permanence.

TANNER, JOHN M. *Fetus into Man: Physical Growth from Conception to Maturity.* Cambridge, Mass.: Harvard University Press, 1978.

A thorough treatment of human growth that includes discussions of the genetic and environmental factors responsible for variability within and among populations.

THE END OF INFANCY

> The self and its boundaries are at the heart of philosophical speculation on human nature, and the sense of self and its counterpart, the sense of other, are universal phenomena that profoundly influence all our social experiences.
>
> — Daniel Stern, *The Interpersonal World of the Infant*

. . . .

Just before Jake's second birthday, his mother, Barbara, and his father and sisters went to Switzerland. Barbara's sister, Retta, said it would be no trouble to look after Jake while they were gone. Prior to the trip, Barbara arranged to spend a week at her sister's with Jake so that he would have a chance to become familiar with the household.

At first Jake ignored everyone at his aunt's house but his mother and his 4-year-old cousin, Linda. The first afternoon he was in the sandbox with Linda, he sat and watched with fascination as she conducted a tea party for her teddy bear and bunny rabbit. After a while, he placed several small containers in a row on the edge of the sandbox, filled a large container with sand, and then poured its contents into the smaller ones in perfect imitation of his cousin. Then Linda caught his eye. Calling "Beep, beep! Get out of my way!" she took a toy truck and ran it along the edge of the sandbox, knocking over the tea cups and stuffed animals. In an instant Jake was yelling "Beep, beep," and knocking over his containers with a toy car. Linda laughed wildly. Jake laughed too and chased her truck around the edge of the sandbox with his car.

From then on Jake followed Linda around the house. If she asked her mother for something to eat or drink, he was right behind her, waiting for his share. Jake did not talk to his aunt directly, and he would not permit her to change his diaper or help him. A lot of the time he would refuse help from anyone, but if he really couldn't manage, he would say, "Mommy do it."

Jake knew that Barbara was leaving. "You goin', Mommy?" he asked her several times during that week.

At the airport Jake held Linda's hand and he bravely watched as his mother disappeared into the plane. But that afternoon, he cried. Linda tried to distract him, but he would not join her in play. Finally, she brought him his favorite pillow, which he carried around for the next few days. Then he seemed to adjust to his mother's absence to the point that he began calling his aunt "Mommy."

When Jake's family returned almost a month later, there was much excitement at the airport. No one paid any attention when Jake sat on his aunt's lap on the ride back to her house.

That afternoon Jake fell and scraped his knee while he was kicking a ball. He ran crying to his father. His father, who was busy at that moment, suggested that he ask his mother to put a Band-Aid on his scrape. Jake ran into the kitchen where his aunt and his mother were sitting. "Mommy fix it," he said, showing his injured knee to his aunt and ignoring his mother. When Barbara offered to help, Jake refused.

Later, in the swimming pool, Jake was showing his father all the new things he had learned to do. "Show Mommy," his father said, suspecting something. His suspicions were confirmed when Jake turned and tried to get his aunt's attention.

Jake had called his uncle "Daddy" throughout his stay, but as soon as his father was on the scene again, his uncle became "Uncle Len" and his father became "Daddy." No such switch occurred for "Mommy." For the 3 days that Jake's family remained at his aunt and uncle's house, Jake ignored his mother and refused to allow her to do anything for him. When they were preparing to return to their own home, however, Jake looked up at his aunt and said, "Bye bye, Auntie Retta." Then, turning to his mother, he addressed her directly for the first time since she had returned. "Let's go, Mom," he said, raising his arms up as a signal for her to pick him up.

The changes that have occurred in Jake's behavior since his first birthday illustrate the new developments that mark the second year of life. At 12 months, Jake was just beginning to walk; at 24 months, he runs and climbs with ease. He is also far more skilled in manipulating small objects. His vocabulary at 12 months consisted primarily of single words and a few set phrases —"juice," "woof woof," "Mommy," "all gone"; now Jake's language skills enable him to communicate more effectively and to participate in imaginative play with another child. He is still wary of strange people and places, and he is still so strongly attached to his parents that it was difficult for him to adapt to being left at his aunt's home.

In this chapter, we will examine the events that complete the period of infancy and account for the increases in the complexity of children's behavior that occur between the ages of 12 and 30 months. These include changes in the brain and body; increased sophistication in reasoning about the world of objects and people; emerging abilities to imitate, to engage in pretend play, and to communicate; and changes in the form of social relationships between children and their caretakers. Each of these accomplishments is interesting in its own right. But more significantly, each is a single thread in a tapestry, creating a distinctive individual personality. About the time that infants celebrate their second birthday or soon thereafter, these individual changes converge to create a new bio-social-behavioral shift—the end of infancy—from which a new stage of development emerges.

BIOLOGICAL MATURATION

During the second and third years of life, children's bodies continue to grow rapidly, but their rate of growth is considerably slower than in the first year (Eichorn, 1979; Tanner, 1978). Children raised in the United States in recent decades have been found to grow, on the average, from 29 to 38 inches in height and to increase from 20 to 33 pounds in weight during their second and third years, although there is considerable variation from one child to the next. These increases in overall size are accompanied by important changes in the structure of the brain and by increases in neuromuscular control.

Changes in Brain Structure

Anatomical studies of the brains of children who have died at different ages during infancy have revealed that

This kind of precocious climbing is quite an achievement, as can be seen from the little boy's gleeful expression. At the same time, it clearly exposes him to new risks.

several changes occur in the brain during the second year (Lecours, 1975; Rabinowicz, 1979). This evidence has encouraged developmental psychologists to seek links between changes in the brain and the emergence of the new psychological capacities that are characteristic of the last year of infancy.

For example, during the second postnatal year, myelination of the connections among different parts of the cerebral cortex and between the brain stem and the cerebral cortex accelerates. As a consequence, the centers in the brain stem where emotional responses are generated and the cortical centers where sensory input is analyzed, such as the visual and auditory cortexes, become more closely linked to the functioning of the frontal lobes. This is important for the development of more complex psychological functions, including self-awareness, planful problem solving, voluntary control of behavior, and language acquisition, characteristics that are widely held to define late infancy (Fischer, 1987; Kagan, 1981; Luria, 1973).

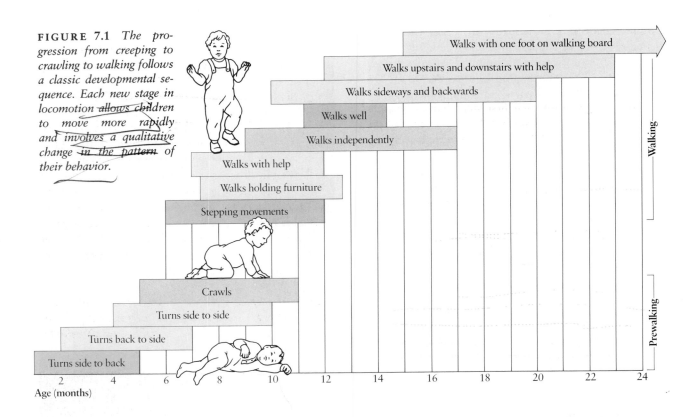

FIGURE 7.1 *The progression from creeping to crawling to walking follows a classic developmental sequence. Each new stage in locomotion allows children to move more rapidly and involves a qualitative change in the pattern of their behavior.*

Walks with one foot on walking board

Walks upstairs and downstairs with help

Walks sideways and backwards

Walks well

Walks independently

Walks with help

Walks holding furniture

Stepping movements

Crawls

Turns side to side

Turns back to side

Turns side to back

Walking

Prewalking

2   4   6   8   10   12   14   16   18   20   22   24

Age (months)

In the early stages of learning to walk, infants must pay close attention to what they are doing to avoid falling.

There is also evidence that toward the end of infancy the length and the degree of branching of the neurons in the cerebral cortex approach adult magnitudes, providing multiple connections among them. At this time, the different areas of the brain, which have been maturing at very different rates, reach similar levels of development. For the first time, the balance among the various brain systems begins to approximate that of adults (Lecours, 1975; Rabinowicz, 1979). Although the brain will continue to develop at a more modest pace for at least another decade, a great deal of the brain structure that will eventually support adult behavior appears to be present by the end of the second year. This suggests that later developments are largely refinements of already existing structures.

Motor Control

A major consequence of the developments in the neuronal foundations of behavior during late infancy is children's increased motor control over their legs, arms, bladders, and bowels.

Walking   Most babies do not have the neural basis for independent walking until they are about 12 months of age. With their first steps babies become *toddlers*, a word that describes the characteristic way they use their legs, toddling from side to side with their legs spread for stability. Most 1-year-olds are unbalanced and fall often, but it does not stop them. The ground is not far away. Besides, walking is too exciting to give up on, so they simply get up and rush ahead to the next tumble.

Walking brings about even more changes in babies' lives than crawling. As Selma Fraiberg so eloquently puts it, walking represents

a cutting of the moorings to the mother's body. . . . To the child who takes his first steps and finds himself walking alone, this moment must bring the first sharp sense of uniqueness and separateness of his body and his person, the discovery of the solitary self. (1959, p. 61)

After the first steps are taken, it takes many months before walking and other uses of the legs become well coordinated (see Figure 7.1). Most American children cannot walk up and down stairs until they are at least 17 months old, kick a ball forward until they are 20 months old or jump until they are almost 24 months old (Frankenburg & Dodds, 1967; Gesell, 1929).

Manual dexterity   Coordination of fine hand movements increases significantly between 12 and 30 months. Infants 1 year old can only roll a ball or fling it awkwardly; by the time they are 2½, they can throw it. They can also turn the pages of a book carefully without tearing or creasing them, snip with scissors, string beads with a needle, build a tower six blocks high with considerable ease, hold a cup of milk or a spoon of applesauce without spilling it, and dress themselves (as long as there are no buttons or shoelaces to be dealt with) (Gesell, 1929). Each of these accomplishments, minor in itself, increases infants' overall ability to behave competently when separated from their caretakers.

Control of elimination   Another important element in the growing ability of children to look after themselves is the acquisition of voluntary control over the muscles that control elimination. In the early

months of life, elimination is involuntary. When the baby's bladder or bowels are full, the appropriate sphincter muscles open automatically and empty them. Before a baby can control these muscles voluntarily, the sensory pathways from the bladder and bowels must be mature enough to transmit signals to the cortex of the brain. Children must then learn to associate these signals with the need to eliminate. They must also learn to tighten their sphincters to keep from eliminating and to loosen them to permit it. Children are usually not capable of voluntary control over elimination until they are at least 15 months of age but they can be taught to eliminate when placed on a potty at 5 to 6 months of age (deVries and deVries, 1977). As we will see later in the chapter, several major developmental theorists attribute special importance to the events surrounding toilet training.

In the nineteenth and early twentieth centuries, toilet training was begun as early as possible, not only for convenience in an era before washing machines and

One of the primary ways toddlers express independence is by taking their clothes off and, as their manual dexterity increases during the second year, by putting their clothes on by themselves.

Some children are not altogether happy with the regular potty-training sessions they receive to help them master control over the processes of elimination.

disposable diapers, but also because it was believed that early training would ensure bowel regularity, which was considered healthy. In the first edition of *Infant Care,* published by the United States Children's Bureau in 1914, for example, mothers were advised to begin bowel training by the third month or even earlier (Wolfenstein, 1953).

Because the neural basis for bladder and bowel control is still immature when children are very young, toilet training often takes a while to complete. One study found that toilet training begun before 5 months of age usually requires 10 months to complete; children learn in less than half that time when the start of training is delayed until 20 months of age. Most children are able to remain dry during the day by the time they are 2 years old (Oppel, Harper, & Reder, 1968). But many children do not achieve such control until they are 3 years old, and most children do not learn to stay dry while they are asleep until they are even older.

A NEW MODE OF THOUGHT

As toddlers are perfecting their ability to get around on their own two legs and are gaining control over their body functions during the second year of life, they also begin to display a qualitatively new mode of thinking. In Piaget's theory, this change signals the end of the sensorimotor period. Even psychologists who disagree with much of Piaget's theory agree that a number of important developments occur around the end of the second year that enable children to think in a new way (Fischer, 1980; Kagan, 1982; Kaye, 1982).

Completing the Sensorimotor Substages

The first four substages of the sensorimotor period were described in Chapter 5 (pp. 165–166) and Chapter 6 (pp. 189–190). As we have seen, babies are capable of repeating an action for its own sake during the first months of life, but they appear unaware of the relation of the action to the world beyond their own bodies. At about 4 months of age, they begin to focus their actions on objects in the external world. Between 8 and 12 months of age, they develop the ability to combine simple actions to achieve a simple goal. Piaget believed that all of the actions of the first four substages are very much tied to the here and now and that the ability of infants less than 1 year old to think about absent objects is very limited.

During the second year of life children complete the stage of sensorimotor development. As conceived by Piaget, their thinking becomes "mental" in a new way because they develop the ability to act on the world mentally without the need to carry out overt actions.

Substage 5: tertiary circular reactions (12–18 months) The fifth substage of the sensorimotor period is characterized by tertiary circular reactions. The term *tertiary* signals the fact that the infant's understanding is becoming more remotely tied to fixed actions, such as reflexes. Now, in addition to making interesting events last using already established secondary circular reactions, infants become capable of performing varied action sequences, thereby making their explorations of the world more complex. Piaget referred to tertiary circular reactions as "experiments in order to see" (1952, p. 272) because children seem to be experimenting in order to find out about the nature of objects. Piaget's observations of his son, Laurent, at the age of 10 months, 11 days illustrate this kind of behavior. Laurent is lying in his crib:

He grasps in succession a celluloid swan, a box, etc., stretches out his arm and lets them fall. He distinctly varies the positions of the fall. . . . Sometimes he stretches out his arm vertically, sometimes he holds it obliquely, in front of or behind his eyes, etc. When the object falls in a new position (for example, on his pillow), he lets it fall two or three times more on the same place, as though to study the spatial relations; then he modifies the situation. (Piaget, 1952, p. 269)

This kind of trial-and-error exploration distinguishes tertiary circular reactions from secondary circular reactions, which involve only previously acquired schemas. At the same time, this kind of behavior is different from that found in substage 6 because infants appear able to carry out such actions only when actually manipulating their physical environment.

Substage 6: representation (18–24 months) The sensorimotor period comes to an end when a baby displays an ability to carry out actions mentally and think about objects in the absence of any physical manipulation. Representation, the term Piaget used to characterize the new mental capacity characteristic of

children who have completed the peri[od] [of sensori]motor development, is the basic achiev[ement of this] substage. Prior to substage 6, children ca[n act] only on a "present" world. When they can "*re*-present the world to themselves" — that is, when they can present it to themselves mentally — they can be said to be engaging in true mental actions.

Chief among the new behaviors cited by Piaget as evidence for the appearance of representational thought are the abilities to think about the relations between objects without actually acting on them, to imagine objects that are not present, to imitate events that are not presently occurring, to engage in pretend play, and to use language. Each of these accomplishments illuminates a different aspect of the new mental capacities that mark the end of infancy.

The final substages of sensorimotor development, along with the earlier substages described in Chapters 5 (p. 165) and 6 (p. 189), are summarized in the left column of Table 7.1. The right column summarizes parallel developments in infants' understanding of object permanence.

TABLE 7.1 Sensorimotor substages and stages of object permanence

Substage	Age Range (months)	Characteristics of Sensorimotor Substage	Developments in Object Permanence
1	$0-1\frac{1}{2}$	Reflex schemas exercised	Infant does not search for objects that have been removed from sight.
2	$1\frac{1}{2}-4$	Primary circular reactions; repetition of actions that are pleasurable	Infant does not search for objects that have been removed from sight.
3	$4-8$	Secondary circular reactions; dawning awareness of relation of own actions to environment; extension of actions that produce interesting changes in the environment	Infant will reach for partially hidden object but stops if it disappears.
4	$8-12$	Coordination of secondary circular reactions; earliest form of problem solving	Infant will search for a completely hidden object; the infant keeps searching the original location of a hidden object even if the object is moved to another location in full view.
5	$12-18$	Tertiary circular reactions; deliberate variation of problem-solving means; "experiments in order to see"	Infant will search new location of a hidden object if its placement there is seen but will stop search if it is not seen.
6	$18-24$	Beginnings of symbolic representation	Infant will search for a hidden object, certain that it exists somewhere.

Mastery of Object Permanence

About the time they are 1 year old, babies stop making the A-not-B error; that is, they are no longer confused when an object is first hidden in one location and is then hidden in a second location while they are watching. They will now search for the object in its new location. This increased ability to keep track of an object's location marks stage 5 of the understanding of object permanence. However, if they have *not* seen the object moved to the new location, they will look for it where they last saw it, and when they do not find it, they are likely to become confused and stop searching.

This can be illustrated by pretending to hide an object in your hand while really hiding it behind your back; a stage-5 baby will continue to search for it in your hand, failing to reason that it must be somewhere else nearby. A version of this procedure used in many studies is shown in Figure 7.2.

Infants enter stage 6 of the understanding of object permanence between the ages of 18 and 24 months. From that time on, their search for a hidden object is no longer disrupted if the object is moved from one location to another without them seeing the change (Piaget, 1952). They appear to be able to reason, "Well, the toy wasn't where I expected, but it must be

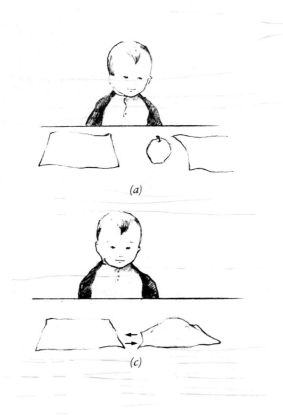

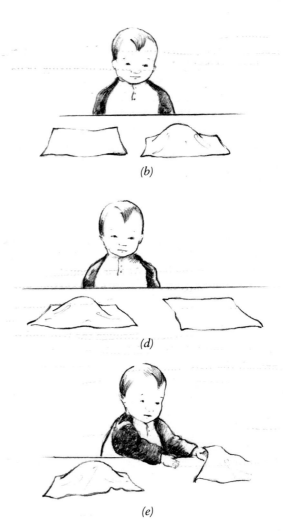

FIGURE 7.2 *Children in stage 5 of the development of object permanence cannot yet maintain a firm idea of the permanence of an object when its location is changed without their seeing the change. (a) The infant sees the apple. (b) The apple is hidden beneath the cloth on the right. (c) The position of the hidden apple is changed without the infant seeing it. (d) The infant is confused. (e) The infant searches for the apple under the wrong cloth. (From T. G. R. Bower, 1982.)*

here somewhere." Then, as they search, they systematically check possible locations until they find the object.

During stage 6, infants also begin to be able to anticipate the trajectory of a moving object and the location of its reemergence if it goes behind a barrier. When a ball rolls under a couch, for example, a 2-year-old will go around to the other side of the couch to look for it instead of looking under the couch. Piaget argued that in order to perform successfully when confronted with a hidden object or a moving object, babies must calculate the location of objects mentally. They can no longer rely solely on the immediate information given by their senses to guide their actions.

Problem Solving

The ability to reason about the locations of unseen objects is accompanied by marked increases in the planfulness of babies' other problem-solving behaviors. Two examples from Piaget's observations of his own children nicely illustrate how these transformations in children's knowledge about objects and events permit them to solve problems planfully instead of by trial and error. Both Jacqueline, at age 15 months, and Lucienne, at age 13 months, confront the same problem. Each wants to pull a stick from outside a playpen through the bars (see Figure 7.3), but there is a significant difference in how they solve the problem.

Jacqueline is seated in her playpen. Outside is a stick 20 centimeters long, the distance of about three spaces between the bars. At first Jacqueline tries to pull the stick into her playpen horizontally, but it will not go through the bars. The second time, she accidentally tilts the stick a little in raising it. She perceives this and reaches through the bars and tilts the stick until it is sufficiently vertical to pass through the bars. But several subsequent attempts make it clear that this is an accidental success; she does not yet understand the principle involved. On the next several tries she grasps the stick by the middle and pulls it horizontally, against the bars. Unable to get it in that way, she then tilts it up. It is not until the seventeenth try that she tilts the stick up before it touches the bars, and not until the twentieth that she does this systematically. (Adapted from Piaget, 1952, p. 305.)

FIGURE 7.3 *This child in substage 5 of the sensimotor period carries out deliberate problem solving but still relies on trial and error.*

Jacqueline seems to have a clear goal in mind and she is certainly persistent. She continues to work at the problem until it is solved. But her efforts are rather hit and miss. When she succeeds, she does not understand why. She "gets the idea" only after many trial-and-error experiences, which is typical of substage 5 of the sensorimotor period.

Although she is 2 months younger than Jacqueline was when she solved this problem, Lucienne's problem solving is more sophisticated than was Jacqueline's, a reminder that age norms associated with Piagetian stages, like other developmental norms, are only approximate.

Lucienne grasps the stick in the middle and pulls it horizontally. Noticing her failure, she withdraws the stick, tilts it up, and brings it through easily. When the stick is again placed on the floor, she grasps it by the middle and tilts it up before she pulls it through, or she grasps it by one end and brings it through easily. She does this with longer sticks and on successive days. Unlike her sister Jacqueline's long, groping efforts toward a solution, Lucienne profits from her failure at once. (Adapted from Piaget, 1952, p. 336.)

Lucienne's actions exemplify the essence of substage 6 sensorimotor behavior; she seems to be using information that is not immediately available to her senses to solve the problem. Instead of going through the slow process of trial and error as her sister did, Lucienne seems to have pictured a series of events in her mind before she acted. She imagined what would happen if she pulled the stick horizontally. She then inferred that if she turned the stick so that it was vertical and parallel to the bars, it would fit between them. Piaget singled out Lucienne's ability to infer that she could pull the stick through the bars if she reoriented it *without making any overt attempts* as the key evidence for the existence of a new form of thought separate from immediate action in substage 6.

Play

During the period from 12 to 30 months, the kinds of behaviors that lead psychologists to believe that new mental abilities are emerging can be seen in new forms of play (Belsky & Most, 1982; Bretherton & Bates, 1985; Fenson & Ramsay, 1980, 1981; Piaget, 1962;

Watson & Fischer, 1977). For example, in a series of observations of babies playing in a room that contained many toys, Jay Belsky and Robert Most (1982) found that at about 12 months babies begin to play with objects in ways that are increasingly similar to the ways these objects are conventionally used by adults. They put spoons in their mouths and bang hammers on the floor. Between the ages of 15 and 18 months, babies become more deliberate in their play. They investigate objects before doing anything with them, just as Lucienne did before she brought the stick through the bars of her playpen.

Belsky and Most observed a shift away from the conventional usage of objects sometime between the ages of 18 and 24 months, when babies begin to treat one thing as if it were another. They "stir their coffee" with a twig and "comb the doll's hair" with a toy rake or, as Jake and his cousin did, act as if the edge of a sandbox is a roadway. This kind of behavior is called **symbolic play** — play in which one object stands for another, as the rake stands for a comb.

Symbolic play becomes more complex and elaborate during the second year, according to the findings of Malcom Watson and Kurt Fischer (1977). From observations of 14-, 19-, and 24-month-olds, these researchers were able to distinguish four kinds of pretending that differed with respect to how the action was carried out (see Table 7.2). In the simplest case,

This child, who is playing with a peglike doll and a toy train, is engaging in the kind of complicated symbolic play that appears to emerge between the ages of 18 and 24 months.

TABLE 7.2 Four steps in the development of agent use in pretending

Type of Agent Use	Example
1. Self as agent	The infant puts his head on a pillow to pretend to go to sleep.
2. Passive other agent	The infant puts a doll on a pillow to pretend that it goes to sleep.
3. Passive substitute agent	The infant puts a block on a pillow to pretend that it goes to sleep.
4. Active other agent	The infant has the doll lie down on the pillow and go to sleep, as if the doll were actually carrying out the action itself.

SOURCE: Watson & Fischer, 1980.

which even many 14-month-olds could do, the infant was the agent of the action; in the most complicated case (active other agent), a doll manipulated by the infant was the agent of the action. As shown in Figure 7.4, the most complicated type of pretending, in which the toddlers have one pretend element operate as if it were totally autonomous, is impossible among the 14-month-olds, whereas half of the 19-month-olds were observed to engage in such elaborate pretending. It is not until they reach the age of 2 years that most of the toddlers could be observed to make such complex symbolic substitutions in their play.

Evidence that the key element in symbolic play, the ability to have one object or concept stand for another, continues to develop during the third year is provided in an experiment by Judy De Loache (1987). De Loache asked 2½- and 3-year-olds to watch while she hid an attractive toy within a scale model of the room they were in. Then the children were asked to find an analogous toy that had been hidden in the corresponding place in the room itself. The 2½-year-olds could not use the information from the model and were confused by the task; the 3-year-olds completed it rather easily. De Loache concluded that the younger children could not think of the scale model both as a symbol and as the thing itself.

Why all this scientific attention to something as seemingly frivolous as play? Developmental psychologists believe that, despite its appearance as "time out" from the serious business of living, play serves important functions for the growing organism (Bruner,

1972; Piaget, 1962; Rubin, Fein, & Vandenburg, 1983; Vygotsky, 1978). One of the most widely held speculations is that early forms of infant play provide practice in activities that will become important later, just as the movements of the embryo are a part of the process of fetal development although the embryo is not going anywhere. There is also widespread agreement that play allows exploration and invention without the possible negative consequences of the "real thing." So, for example, when children begin to play at having tea parties or taking care of a baby, they do so under circumstances in which no one is likely to get burned with hot water or jabbed with a diaper pin.

Peter Smith (1982) describes four major types of play that provide practice for later functions:

1. Locomotor play, such as actions that involve running, jumping, and leaping.

2. Object play, which includes pulling, tugging, and shaking things.

3. Social play, which can be divided into play that involves physical contact, such as chasing and wrestling, and play that does not, such as building with blocks.

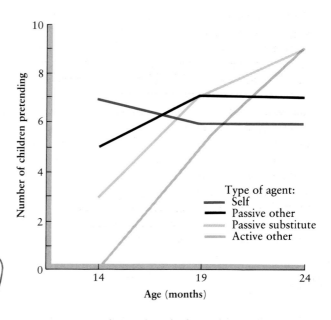

FIGURE 7.4 *The number of infants showing each type of agent use at each age in Watson and Fischer's study. During the second year of life, play with complex substitutions of one object or agent for another becomes common. (From Watson & Fischer, 1980.)*

4. Fantasy play, in which the meanings of objects and actions are transformed to fit an imaginary situation.

Often the different kinds of play are combined, as when children jump rope or play cards. Smith points out that the first three kinds of play are widely found among the young of many species but that clear examples of fantasy play are found exclusively among human beings.

Another hypothesis about play is that it facilitates the transition to higher levels of cognitive development because, when they are playing, children are allowed to interact with the world more or less on their own terms. In Piaget's words, play provides children with the opportunity to assimilate the external world to their own goals with little need to accommodate external realities (Piaget, 1962).

Lev Vygotsky (1978) emphasized that the social nature of symbolic play is important to development. He conceived of the imaginary situations created in play as zones of proximal development that operate as mental support systems. (For an earlier example of such a support system, see Chapter 6, p. 201, where a father supports his infant daughter's attempts to grasp a teething ring before she is able to pick it up on her own.) According to this interpretation, the "as if" nature of social play activity and the active collusion of other children allow individual children to perform actions that are developmentally more advanced than those they can perform on their own. Thus, Jake can "pour tea" in a make-believe game with his cousin in which the demands for precision are far more lenient than they would be if he were to try to pour himself a glass of milk.

Imitation

 Although there is great controversy about when infants first begin to imitate (see Box 5.3, Chapter 5, p. 160), psychologists generally agree that imitation can be observed by late in the first year of life and that new forms of imitation emerge between children's first and second birthdays (Kaye, 1982; Maccoby & Martin, 1983; Piaget, 1962). At 1 year of age, infants imitate only in response to immediate stimulation from the environment. For example, as babies watch Grandma wave goodby, they will modify the way they close their hand to match the way Grandma closes hers.

About the middle of the second year, a new kind of imitation, one that is *not* the simple copying of events that are being witnessed, makes its appearance. In **deferred imitation,** as this new kind of copying is called, children lift action sequences they observe out of their original contexts and repeat them at a later time in original ways. According to Piaget (1962), the appearance of deferred imitation is a central piece of evidence that the period of sensorimotor development is coming to a close and that a new mode of thought, reflected in children's ability to think about (represent) actions that are not presently occurring, is developing. The following example, taken from Piaget's work, illustrates both deferred imitation and the importance that he attributed to it as evidence that children are beginning to think in a new way. The example is taken from his observations of Jacqueline at the age of 16 months after a visit from an 18-month-old boy who got into a terrible temper in the course of the afternoon.

> He screamed as he tried to get out of his playpen and pushed it backwards, stamping his feet. J. stood watching him in amazement, never having witnessed such a scene before. The next day, she herself screamed in her playpen and tried to move it, stamping her foot lightly several times in succession. The imitation of the whole scene was most striking. Had it been immediate, [the imitation] would naturally not have involved representation, but coming as it did after an interval of more than twelve hours, it must have involved some representative or pre-representative element. (Piaget, 1962, p. 63)

A key part of Piaget's argument for the significance of deferred imitation was that it appears during the same period when symbolic play begins. He believed that the two processes are related and that they signal the same underlying change in cognitive capacities, constituting, in effect, two sides of the same developmental coin.

Recall that in Piaget's framework development results from the constant interplay between the *assimilation* of the environment into preexisting patterns of action (called schemas) and the *accommodation* of existing schemas to aspects of the environment. Piaget believed that imitation is closely linked to accommodation because it fits behavior to what is "out there" rather than molding the world to already existing, internal schemas, as play does.

This child is engaging in deferred imitation, the repetition of an act seen at an earlier time.

Imitation can also provide a zone of proximal development by allowing children to participate in activities in conjunction with someone else before they are competent to carry out those activities on their own (Kaye, 1982). This potential of imitation is easy to observe. It appears in Jake's sandbox play with Linda and in the familiar sight of a 2-year-old sitting at the table and trying to eat with a knife and fork like the grownups or putting marks on paper like an older brother. It is also illustrated by a number of studies that show children are able to imitate action sequences slightly before they become capable of incorporating them in symbolic play (Watson & Fischer, 1977).

The Growth of Categorizing Ability

Deferred imitation and symbolic play provide circumstantial evidence that children become able to engage in the psychological process called mental representation sometime around the middle of the second year. However, little is known about the content or form of these mental representations except that they provide children with a mental model of the world. Because mental representations are internal, they cannot be observed directly. The challenge for psychologists

seeking to study mental representations is to make good use of the clues provided by children's behaviors to gain insight into the content and structure of these hidden processes.

As we saw in Chapter 6 (p. 199), a rudimentary ability to *recognize* a common characteristic in an array of objects can be demonstrated during the first year of life. During the second year, this rudimentary capacity develops sufficiently for babies to be able to *generate* categories themselves and begin to use them.

The growth of the capacity to generate categories has been documented by Susan Sugarman (1983). She presented 12- to 30-month-old babies with eight objects that could be classified and subclassified in various ways. Figure 7.5 shows one such set of objects composed of boats and dolls, which can be grouped by color and form to yield four categories. While sitting on their mother's lap, the toddlers were urged to "fix up" the haphazard array of objects to determine if they would create the same categories as adults. If this didn't work, Sugarman showed them ways to group the objects and then urged them to do it.

Sugarman's results support the findings of David Starkey (1981), reported in Chapter 6, that 1-year-olds display only the most rudimentary knowledge of categorical distinctions that are obvious to adults. They did not, for example, place all of the boats or all of the red toys together. Instead, they picked up one of the toys, looked it over, and then touched it to the other toys one at a time. The only indication that they noticed the similarities between individual objects was

FIGURE 7.5 *The ability to categorize boats and dolls of two different colors and to subcategorize them according to color and form emerges slowly during late infancy. (From Sugerman, 1983.)*

that they were most likely to touch the toy they picked up to other toys that had the same shape. This subtle ordering of movements indicates that the 1-year-olds are aware of the similarities among the objects but express this awareness weakly in their behavior.

The 18-month-olds also concentrated their attention on objects of one kind. But instead of taking one object and touching the others with it, these older children created a little work space in front of them and put different objects of the same kind in it. The creation of the work space makes the beginning of representation visible in an interesting way. Once the children create the work space, they are able to concentrate on the properties of the objects that they select in a systematic fashion. In a literal sense, when the 18-month-olds were *presented* with a set of objects to act upon, they *represented* these objects to themselves, creating categories in the process. The objects in the work space apparently become the model *both* of the categorical nature of the contents of the array, which can be directly observed, and of the *mental* representation of that category, which cannot be directly observed.

The first categories the 18-months-olds in Sugarman's study created using this work-space representation were not yet adultlike. Adults quickly rearrange the objects according to their obvious standard categorical distinctions, as shown in Figure 7.5. By contrast, the categories the 18-month-olds generated consisted of only two or three items of one kind. For example, a child might select three boats, place them in the work space, and then stop. Such categorization does not explicitly represent the fact that there are two kinds of objects in the array — boats and dolls — nor that there are such subcategories as red boats or black dolls.

The 24-month-old toddlers divided the objects into *two* distinct categories. They did this by working on one category at a time, selecting, for example, all the boats first and then all the dolls. If Sugarman offered a boat to children of this age who were collecting dolls, they immediately set the boat aside and kept working on the dolls. It is as if they were saying, "Wait, I am working on dolls now. Don't confuse me." It is not clear if these children were aware that the "nondolls" also formed a category as they were completing the doll category. Perhaps the most they could manage was to form the concept of one category at a time, with everything that didn't fit into that category being viewed as some other, unanalyzed collection.

The 30-month-old children simultaneously coordinated their work on the two major categories and created subcategories as well. They began by making a work space in front of them and then creating two categories within it. They added new members to the categories according to whatever toy was nearest at hand. If these children were handed a doll right after they had placed a boat in its group, they put it with the other dolls.

Sugarman's results suggest that by the end of infancy, children are able to represent concepts. This capacity will be central to their mastery of language and the more mature forms of thinking that will emerge during early childhood. It also has important implications for understanding other activities, such as imitation, play, and problem solving, in which they begin to treat certain kinds of objects — teacups, beds, chairs, and so forth — as somehow "belonging together." However, Sugarman's careful analysis cautions us about overinterpreting the content of children's representations when play and deferred imitation first appear. When children between the ages of 18 and 24 months begin to operate on objects and to try out possible actions mentally, their representations may be narrowly focused on a single category because they still cannot hold two categories in mind at the same time.

First Words

One of the most obvious indicators that children are beginning to think representationally is the appearance of identifiable words that stand for (represent) people, objects, and events. Although many children begin to use a word or two in direct imitation of adults at about 8 or 9 months of age, the first use of words that are *not* direct imitations usually occurs around the first birthday. Babies this age respond selectively to their own names and will stop, or at least hesitate, if someone says "No!" (See Chapter 6, p. 205, for a discussion of the precursors of children's earliest words. Further discussion of language development appears in Chapter 9.)

Sometime between the ages of 14 and 18 months, toddlers are able to name a few objects when they are shown them and asked what they are, according to the findings of a large longitudinal study by Robert McCall, Dorothy Eichorn, and Pamela Hogarty

(1977). They can also remember the names of two or more objects that are shown to them one right after another. When pictures of common animals and objects on cards are shown to them, they can name one or more of them.

By 21 months of age, toddlers are able to follow relatively complex verbal instructions. When told to "Put the block *under* the doll's chair," for example, they can place the objects in the correct location relative to each other. They are also able to understand terms that are the opposites of one another. For instance, if a large spool and a small spool are set in front of a child and the child is told "Here is the big one" at the same time the large spool is pointed to, the child can comply with the request to "Give me the little one."

The use of words that stand for people, objects, and events is sufficient by itself to show that children are beginning to engage in mental representation. But what especially intrigues developmental psychologists is the association between children's use of representational words and the development of the other forms of mental representation — symbolic play and deferred imitation — discussed in this chapter (Bretherton & Bates, 1985; Bruner, 1968, 1972; McCall, Eichorn, & Hogarty, 1977; Piaget, 1962).

The link between deferred imitation and word acquisition is perhaps the most obvious, as a good deal of children's early word use is closely tied to words they have heard adults speak. For example, "more" was one of the first words used by our daughter Jenny. Earlier, when she finished drinking a cup of milk or juice, Jenny would bang the empty cup on the tray of her highchair. We would then ask her, "Do you want some more?" Shortly before her first birthday, she began to hold up her cup and say "More" before anyone asked her if that was what she wanted.

Likewise, there is a clear association between language and symbolic play, which are similar in that both involve the representation of absent persons, objects, or actions. In symbolic play, arbitrary objects are used to stand for other objects — a banana is treated as a telephone, for example, or a sandbox railing becomes a highway; in language, arbitrary sounds are the substitutes. In the earliest stages, children's fantasy play is restricted to single actions and their utterances are restricted to single words. But at about 18 months of age, they begin to combine two actions in play and to use two-word sentences (Bretherton & Bates, 1985; McCune-Nicolich & Bruskin, 1982; Watson &

Fischer, 1977). So, for example, about the same time children begin to say "Allgone milk," they also begin to pretend that they are pouring water into a cup *and* feeding the water to a baby.

Parallels between changes in word use and changes in mental representation were also found by Sugarman (1983) during her study of categorical classification. For example, a little girl 18 months old (the age at which Sugarman found children can begin to select different objects that belong to the same category from an array of objects) showed that she knew two different chairs belong to the same category of objects. She said "chair" as she was seated in a highchair and then pointed at Sugarman's chair and repeated the word "chair." Sugarman also recorded many examples in which 2- to 2½-year-olds explicitly noted that two objects belonged to the same category by saying "That's the same as that" or "That doll is like that doll." Furthermore, she found that when children are able to combine symbolic actions in play and say such two-word sentences as "Daddy shoe," they are also able to categorize objects according to two characteristics, such as shape and color.

McCall and his co-workers (McCall, Eichorn, & Hogarty, 1977) speculate that the flexible use of two-word utterances reflects children's ability to think about "two separate entities in symbolic form and place them in relation to each other" (p. 75). In other words, they can classify objects mentally by manipulating words in the same way they can classify arrays of objects such as those presented by Sugarman.

Children's new cognitive abilities, combined with their ability to communicate with others, create new conditions for their development. Although 2½-year-olds are by no means fully articulate, their caretakers can learn something of their thoughts and needs from the words they use. Furthermore, caretakers can begin to use words to teach their children about the world in a new and powerful way. These changes build upon the achievements that appeared at 7 to 9 months, when children began to show wariness at the appearance of strange people and objects and a strong attachment to their primary caretakers. They culminate in a new sense of self and a major reorganization in children's relationship to their social world at 24 to 30 months of age. All of these changes, working in concert with each other, bring about the bio-social-behavioral shift that marks the end of infancy and the transition to early childhood.

THE DEVELOPMENT OF CHILD-CARETAKER RELATIONS

During the second year of life, children find novelty and excitement everywhere. A walk to the corner drugstore with a 1½-year-old can take forever. Each step presents new and interesting sights to explore: a bottle cap lying by the edge of the sidewalk requires close examination; a pigeon waddling across a neighbor's lawn invites a detour; even the cracks in the sidewalk may prompt sitting down to take a closer look.

However, things that attract babies may also cause them to be wary. To toddlers, whizzing cars, strange people, and novel objects are often frightening as well as fascinating. Both interest and fear must be kept in bounds as infants continue to explore and learn about the world. They cannot spend their entire lives tied to their mothers' apron strings, but they cannot survive for long if they wander off on their own. Research with both simian and human mothers and babies has enabled us to begin to understand how the balance between exploration and safety is created and maintained in ways that allow continued development. A key element in this balance is the emotional bond, called *attachment*, that develops between children and their caretakers.

The Course of Attachment

As we saw in Chapter 6 (p. 202), children begin to show wariness in the presence of strangers and signs that they are actively attached to their caretakers sometime between the ages of 7 and 9 months. They keep very close track of the people to whom they are attached and seek to be near them. Like all psychological states, attachment cannot be studied directly; its characteristics must be inferred from behavior.

Behaviors that appear to signal strong feelings of attachment seem to emerge and then decline with great consistency among infants living in vastly different cultural settings all over the world. Figure 7.6 shows the changes in overt distress expressed by infants of different ages in four different cultures when left by their mothers in the "strange situation," the procedure widely used to measure attachment described in Chapter 6 (p. 203). As the figure indicates, 5-month-old babies did not seem to be distressed following the departure of their mothers, implying that attachment had not yet emerged. The first signs of

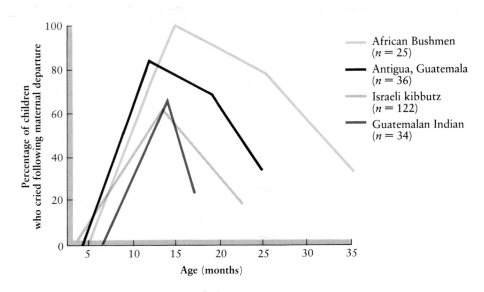

FIGURE 7.6 *The percentage of children at different ages from four different cultures who cried following their mother's departure from the room in the "strange situation." (From Kagan, Kearsley, & Zelazo, 1978.)*

attachment appear at about 7 months, the same time that children begin to search actively for objects that are out of sight. The proportion of children who become distressed builds for several months and then begins to wane during the second year. This changing pattern of distress indicates that the strong attachment relations established between 7 and 9 months of age are becoming integrated into a new psychological and social system, which has broad implications for children's development.

Explaining how the attachment of infants to their caretakers comes about has proven to be a major challenge to developmental psychologists.

Explanations of Attachment

The fact that children begin to become upset when they are separated from their primary caretakers at about the same age everywhere, even though their social experiences may differ in many respects, suggests that attachment is a universal feature of development. This possibility has led to a lively debate about the reasons for attachment, the causes of changes in attachment as children grow older, and the influence the quality of attachment has on children's later development. Three major explanations of the basis of attachment have dominated this debate: Sigmund Freud's suggestion that infants become attached to those who satisfy their need for food; Erik Erikson's idea that infants become attached to those they can trust to help them; and John Bowlby's somewhat similar hypothesis that infants become attached to those who provide them with a firm foundation for exploring the world.

Sigmund Freud's drive-reduction explanation
The process of attachment plays an important role in Sigmund Freud's theory of development. Freud held that the early interactions between children and their social environment, particularly the people who care for them, set the pattern for later personality and social development. He believed that human beings, like other organisms, are motivated in large part by **biological drives**—aroused states, such as hunger or thirst, that urge the organism to obtain the basic prerequisites for its survival. When a drive is aroused, the organism will seek to satisfy the need that gives rise to it. Pleasure occurs as the drive is reduced, the need is satisfied, and the organism returns to a more comfortable bio-

logical equilibrium. In this sense, then, pleasure seeking is a basic mode of adaptation.

Freud (1933/1961) identified the mouth as the primary locus of pleasure during the first year of life, which he dubbed the *oral stage* of development. During this stage, children become attached to the objects or persons that satisfy their hunger (Freud, 1940/1964). The first person infants become attached to is usually the mother, who is most likely to nourish them; "love has its origin in attachment to the satisfied need for nourishment" (p. 188). Freud believed that attachment to the mother is central to the formation of children's personalities as they progress through later stages of development. In adulthood, the relationship with the mother becomes "the prototype for all . . . love relations for both sexes" (p. 188).

According to Freud (1933/1961) there is a basic shift in the locus of children's pleasure seeking from the mouth to the anus during the second year after birth. In contrast with oral pleasures, which he characterized as receptive and dependent, Freud believed that anal satisfaction is basically expulsive and reflects a drive for self-control and independence.

Although Freud's theories offer insights into many aspects of development, his theory of early human attachment has not fared well. One major problem is that his notion that attachment is caused by the reduction of the hunger drive has not been substantiated, as we will soon see. Furthermore, this theory would seem to imply that children would begin to act more independently once they enter the anal stage. Thus, it fails to explain why children are increasingly likely to become distressed when they are separated from their mothers until well into the second year of life.

Erik Erikson's psychosocial explanation of attachment
A more promising explanation of attachment than Freud's, though one still within the Freudian tradition, was proposed by Erik Erikson, one of Freud's most influential students. Erikson (1963), whose theory of development will figure in many discussions throughout the remainder of this book, believes that there are eight stages in the human life cycle, each characterized by a different conflict that the individual must resolve. Through the resolution of the conflict at each stage of development, people acquire new skills, such as the ability to act independently of their parents or to do productive work, that open up new opportunities for them. These new opportunities, in turn, increase the demands made on them by

society and create new conflicts. Individuals who do not resolve the conflict at each stage satisfactorily will continue to struggle with that conflict later in life.

The conflicts of the first two stages in Erikson's theory provide an explanation for the increase in children's anxiety when they are separated from their mothers late in the first year of life and its decline during the second year. According to Erikson's scheme, during the first stage of development, which lasts from birth to roughly 1 year of age, babies must develop a favorable balance between *trust* and *mistrust:* Will my mother come when I call? Can I trust her to take care of me? In Erikson's view, children will become attached to the people who reliably minister to their needs and who foster a sense of trust. Once babies gain faith in their caretakers, they will be more likely to tolerate their absence because they understand that they will come back.

Erikson believes that some mistrust is necessary for self-protection at all ages because mothers and other caretakers cannot satisfy all of their baby's desires. However, if feelings of mistrust dominate children's relations with their caretakers because their needs are not met with reasonable consistency, they may become frustrated, withdrawn, suspicious, and lacking in self-confidence.

The second stage in Erikson's theory, which usually spans the ages of about 1 to 2½ years, is characterized by a conflict between *autonomy* and *shame* or *doubt.* During this stage children want to control their actions and their bodies. They are beginning to develop some notion of adult standards and rules of behavior (which will be discussed later in this chapter). When children fail to behave appropriately, adult displeasure and control cause them to have feelings of shame and doubt.

In the United States, this struggle for control often centers on toilet training. As long as adults changed their diapers whenever they were soiled, children were free to determine when and under what conditions they eliminated their body's waste products. But the situation changes dramatically once children are expected to use a toilet; their soiled pants and tell-tale puddles become sources of displeasure, leading to feelings of shame and guilt.

Children's struggle for self-control is by no means restricted to their processes of elimination. According to Erikson, the increased motor control that develops during the second and third years gives the young child "greater power over the environment in the ability to reach out and hold on, to throw and push away, to appropriate things and keep them at a distance" (1963, p. 82). Consequently, the conflict between the push toward autonomy and the struggle with shame and doubt may crop up in many different settings. Such everyday activities as eating, getting dressed, taking a bath, going to the store, or going on an outing become occasions for struggles between toddlers who want to do these things their way and parents who have their own ideas about the way they should be done.

Erikson's description of the conflicts of the first two stages of life fits nicely with the pattern of distress depicted in Figure 7.6. Distress at being separated begins when babies first realize how dependent they are on the person they have come to trust. As children develop, they gain an increasing sense of autonomy, built upon that initial trust. During the second year, as their feelings of autonomy increase and their feelings of trust are solidified through increased experience, children cease being distressed when they experience a brief separation from their mother, and the incidence of distress in the "strange situation" correspondingly decreases.

John Bowlby's evolutionary explanation   In the aftermath of the terrible destruction and loss of life of World War II, many public agencies became deeply concerned about the consequences of an early childhood deprived of normal maternal care. In 1950, the World Health Organization asked John Bowlby, a British psychiatrist, to undertake a study of the mental health problems of children who had been separated from their families and were cared for in institutions (Bowlby, 1969, 1973, 1980).

Bowlby reviewed observations of children in hospitals, nurseries, and orphanages who had either lost their parents or had been separated from them for long periods of time. He also looked at reports from clinical interviews with psychologically troubled or delinquent adolescents and adults. He found a similar sequence of behaviors described in these different sources. When first separated from their mothers, children become frantic with fear. They cry, throw tantrums, and try to escape their surroundings. Next, they go through a stage of despair and depression. If the separation continues and no new stable relationship is formed, these children seem to become indifferent to other people. Bowlby called this indifferent state *disattachment.*

In his attempt to explain the distress of young children when they are separated from their parents, Bowlby adopted a broad evolutionary perspective. His theory incorporated what was then known about mother-infant interactions among large, ground-living apes that share their environment with predators against whom they defend themselves by banding together. A special property of infancy among such primates is that it lasts for a long time, during which the growing infant is relatively helpless. This vulnerability means that the infants must remain close to their mothers to survive. Counteracting this need for safety through proximity is the infants' urge to explore and to play, which takes them away from their mothers.

Bowlby hypothesized that some mechanism must exist to provide a balance between infants' need for safety and their need for varied learning experiences. He termed this mechanism *attachment*. He hypothesized that attachment works in a fashion somewhat analogous to a furnace thermostat. In a thermostat, a switch is thrown to turn on the furnace whenever the temperature falls below a certain minimum. When the heat rises sufficiently, the switch is thrown again to turn the furnace off. As a result, temperature is maintained within comfortable limits.

Bowlby (1969) believes that attachment is a highly evolved system of regulation that normally develops during the first year of life to produce a "dynamic equilibrium between the mother-child pair" (p. 236). Whenever the distance between mother and child becomes too great, one or the other is likely to become upset and act to reduce the distance. Just as babies become upset if their mothers leave them, mothers become upset if their babies wander out of sight. Attachment provides the child with a feeling of security. The mother provides a **secure base** from which babies can make exploratory excursions, coming back every so often to renew contact before returning to their explorations.

At first, the mother bears the greatest responsibility for maintaining the equilibrium of the attachment system because the infant cannot. As the child becomes more mobile and increasingly spends time away from the mother, the pair enters a transitional state in which they share responsibility for maintaining the equilibrium of the system. Among humans, this transitional phase lasts for several years. Eventually, when the child has become a young adult, the mother leaves the maintenance of closeness almost entirely to the child and usually acts only in cases of emergency.

Bowlby's theory provides a logical explanation for

The knowledge that his mother is hovering nearby, ready to intervene should anything frightening happen, gives this little boy the courage to explore the world from the top of a table.

the increase and decline of children's distress in the "strange situation." The period during which distress increases reflects babies' increasing awareness of their vulnerability, which is brought on in part by the mobility that takes them away from their mothers. The decline of distress during the second and third years shows that, within the protected circumstances of the testing situation, children have gained confidence that they can make do on their own.

Evidence from animal models   Ethical considerations make it difficult, if not impossible, to test different hypotheses regarding the source and developmental dynamics of human attachment. Therefore, scientists have turned to experimental studies using our near evolutionary kin, monkeys, whose behavior is used as an **animal model** to learn more about the causes and consequences of apparently analogous human behaviors.

Throughout the first half of the twentieth century, most American scholars who studied learning believed it to be a process of associating objects and events in the world with pleasurable experiences that satisfy the basic needs associated with the survival of the individual and the species — food, drink, freedom from pain, procreation. This *drive-reduction theory* is similar to Freud's explanation of why the baby becomes attached to the mother (Miller & Dollard, 1941).

To test the drive-reduction theory of attachment, Harry Harlow and his co-workers (Harlow & Harlow, 1969) carried out an extensive series of studies with rhesus monkeys. In one of these studies, the researchers separated eight baby monkeys from their mothers 12 hours or less after birth and placed them in individual cages with two inanimate surrogate

FIGURE 7.7 *This baby monkey spent most of its time clinging to the terry cloth surrogate mother even when its nursing bottle was attached to the wire surrogate mother that can be seen in the background. Harlow concluded from this that bodily contact and the comfort it gives are important in the formation of the infant's attachment to its mother.*

mothers — one made of wire, the other of cloth. The wire mother was a wire-mesh cylinder with a wooden-block head; the cloth mother was a wooden cylinder covered by a terry cloth sheath that was also topped with a wooden-block head (see Figure 7.7). Four of the infant monkeys received milk from the wire mothers, four from the terry cloth mothers. The surrogate mothers were equally effective as sources of nutrition. The babies drank the same amount of milk and gained weight at the same rate whether they nursed at the wire mother or the cloth mother. Only the feel of the surrogate mothers differed.

Over the 165-day period that they lived with surrogate mothers, the baby monkeys showed a distinct preference for the cloth mothers. Even if they obtained all of their food from a wire mother, the babies would go to that surrogate only to feed and would then go back to cling to the terry cloth mother. Harlow concluded, "These results attest the importance — possibly the overwhelming importance — of bodily contact and the immediate comfort it supplies in forming the infant's attachment for its mother" (Harlow, 1959, p. 70). From the perspective of drive-reduction theory, the choice of the four infant monkeys who received their food from a wire mother to spend their time with a terry cloth mother (which might feel good but satisfied no apparent biological drive, like hunger or thirst) made no sense at all.

In subsequent investigations Harlow and his colleagues (Harlow & Harlow, 1969) sought to determine whether attachment to the surrogate mothers had the power to regulate the infants' explorations that was crucial to Bowlby's evolutionary theory. The researchers knew that normal human and monkey babies run to their mothers for comfort when they are confronted with a strange situation, so the researchers created such a situation for the monkeys who had surrogate mothers. They placed a mechanical teddy bear that marched forward while beating a drum in the cages with the baby monkeys who had received milk from wire mothers. The terrified babies fled to their *terry cloth* mothers, not to their wire mothers (see Figure 7.8). If, in its fear, one of the babies rushed blindly to the wire mother, it soon abandoned her for the cloth mother. However, once the babies had overcome their fear by rubbing their bodies against the cloth mother, they turned to look at the bear with curiosity. Some even left the protection of the mother to approach the object that had so terrified them only moments before.

FIGURE 7.8 *(Above) This baby monkey clings to its terry cloth surrogate mother and hides its eyes when it is frightened by the approach of a mechanical teddy bear. (Right) After gaining reassurance, the baby monkey looks at the strange intruder. That the terry cloth mother, which does not provide nourishment, acts as a secure base rather than the wire mother, which does provide nourishment, contradicts drive-reduction theories of attachment.*

Were the bonds the infant monkeys formed with their surrogate mothers strong enough to withstand a period of separation? Following separations of up to a year, the baby monkeys were placed in an apparatus in which pressing a lever would allow them to look at the terry cloth mother, the wire mother, or an empty box. The monkeys who had been raised with a wire mother that provided milk and a terry cloth mother that did not spent more time pressing the lever to get a glimpse of the terry cloth mother than the lever to see the wire mother. They were no more interested in the wire mother than in the empty box. Even monkeys who had been raised with only a wire mother showed no signs of attachment to it when given a chance to view it (Harlow & Zimmerman, 1959).

The studies of Harlow and his colleagues undermine the hypothesis that attachment is caused by drive reduction, which implies that infants should become attached to the people who feed them. The idea that receives the most support is that attachment is based on soothing tactile sensations that provide the baby with a sense of security.

Although a sense of security appears to be necessary for healthy development, it is not sufficient. From their observations of these monkeys as they grew older, the researchers found that they were either indifferent or abusive to other monkeys. None of them could copulate normally. The researchers concluded:

> [T]he nourishment and contact comfort provided by the nursing cloth covered mother in infancy does not produce a normal adolescent or adult. The surrogate cannot cradle the baby or communicate monkey sounds and gestures. It cannot punish for misbehavior or attempt to break the infant's bodily attachment before it becomes a fixation. . . . (Harlow & Harlow, 1962, p. 142)

The later social behavior of these monkeys is evidence that *social interaction* is a necessary condition for healthy development. Although the terry cloth mothers provided the infant monkeys with a secure base, they could not do their part in creating the "dynamic equilibrium" that Bowlby talks about as the key to attachment. In the absence of a live mother, all of the adjusting was left to the baby, so the "thermostat" of attachment did not work.

Patterns of Attachment

The maladaptive social behaviors of monkeys raised with inanimate surrogate mothers poses a pointed question: What patterns of attachment between mother and child provide the most effective basis for the development of healthy human social relations?

Because no two mother-infant pairs are alike and because the environmental conditions into which human babies are born vary enormously, we should not expect there to be "one right pattern" of attachment that meets the basic requirements for social development (Hinde, 1982). However, many investigators believe that it is possible to identify those patterns of mother-child interaction that are most conducive to development, as we will see in this and the following chapter.

Research on attachment has been greatly influenced by the studies of Mary Ainsworth, which were introduced in Chapter 6 (p. 203). Based on observations of mother-infant pairs in Africa and the United States, Ainsworth (1967, 1982) reports that there are consistent, qualitatively distinct patterns in the ways mothers and infants relate to each other during the second and

Many small children become strongly attached to a teddy bear, a blanket, or some other object. British psychiatrist D. W. Winnicott (1971) has called such objects "transitional objects." They are the first objects that children perceive to be their very own. They support children in their attempts to understand and deal with the reality that exists beyond their own bodies.

third years of infancy. Most of the mother-infant pairs she observed seemed to have worked out a comfortable, secure relationship, but some had relationships characterized by persistent tension and difficulties in regulating joint activities.

To study differences in attachment systematically, Ainsworth and her colleagues (Ainsworth, Bell, & Stayton, 1971; Ainsworth, Blehar, Waters, & Wall, 1978) worked out a method of categorizing infant responses in the "strange situation." It is based on the child's behaviors when the child and mother are alone in the playroom together, when the mother leaves the room, when a strange woman offers comfort, and when the mother returns. (See Chapter 6, p. 203, for a description of the basic procedures used in the "strange situation.") The researchers came up with the following three categories, in which the way the child reacts to the return of the mother is considered to be the key element:

Anxious/avoidant: During the time the mother and child are left alone together in the playroom, anxious/avoidant infants are more or less indifferent to where their mothers are sitting. They may or may not cry when their mothers leave the room. If they do become distressed, strangers are likely to be as effective at comforting them as their mothers. When the mother returns, these children may turn or look away from her instead of going to her to seek closeness and comfort. About 23 percent of U.S. middle-class children show this pattern of attachment.

Securely attached: As long as the mother is present, the securely attached child plays comfortably with the toys in the playroom and reacts positively to the stranger. These children become visibly and vocally upset when their mothers leave, and they are unlikely to be consoled by a stranger. However, when the mother reappears and they can climb into her arms, they quickly calm down and soon resume playing. This pattern of attachment is shown by about 65 percent of U.S. middle-class children.

Anxious/resistant: Anxious/resistant children have trouble from the start in the "strange situation." They stay close to their mothers and appear anxious even when their mothers are near. They become very upset when the mother leaves, but they are not comforted by her return. Instead,

In resisting her mother's attempt to leave her in someone else's arms, this little girl is showing the distress that babies experience at being separated from their mothers.

they *simultaneously* seek renewed contact with their mother and resist her efforts to comfort them. They may cry angrily to be picked up with their arms outstretched, but they will struggle to climb down once they are in their mother's arms. These children do not readily resume playing after their mother returns. Instead, they keep a wary eye on her. About 12 percent of U.S. middle-class children show this pattern of attachment.

Anxious/avoidant and anxious/resistant children are sometimes labeled as *insecurely attached* or simply *anxious*.

Accumulated experience has shown that the basic behaviors described by Ainsworth and her colleagues occur routinely in the "strange situation" and can be scored with reasonable reliability. Using this method of classifying modes of attachment, psychologists have spent more than two decades seeking to determine the causes of these different patterns of behavior (Ainsworth, 1982; Bretherton, 1985; Campos, Barrett,

Lamb, Goldsmith, & Stenberg, 1983). Most of this research has focused on the mother-infant relationship, although other attachments that are important in children's lives have also been studied (see Box 7.1, "Attachment to Fathers and Others").

As often happens when a new scientific technique is introduced, research using the "strange situation" has raised many new questions about social and emotional development. Two major questions have dominated the study of patterns of attachment. First, what are the causes of the different patterns? Second, do differences in patterns of attachment have important consequences for later development? We will concentrate on the first question here and postpone discussion of the long-term consequences of different patterns of attachment until Chapter 8.

The causes of different patterns of attachment

Research on what leads to the different patterns of attachment has focused on several factors. These include the behavior of the mother toward the child, the capacities and temperamental disposition of the child, and the child-rearing patterns of the cultural group to which the mother and child belong.

Maternal behaviors   In an early study of the antecedents of attachment, Ainsworth and Bell (1969) hypothesized that differences in the responsiveness of mothers to their infants would result in different patterns of attachment. They found that mothers who quickly responded to their children's cries when the children were 3 months old and were sensitive to their children's needs during feeding had children who were likely to be evaluated as securely attached in the "strange situation" at 12 months.

Attempts to replicate Ainsworth and Bell's study have met with mixed success. Some studies (Egeland & Sroufe, 1981; Grossmann, Grossmann, Spangler, Suess, & Unzer, 1985) have supported the finding that high ratings of maternal responsiveness predict secure attachment, whereas others have found only very weak relationships between ratings of maternal responsiveness and patterns of attachment or no relationship at all (see Lamb, Thompson, Gardner, Charnov, & Estes, 1984, for a review). It has been reliably found, however, that abusive or neglectful mothers are especially likely to have babies who are rated as anxious/avoidant or anxious/resistant (Egeland & Sroufe, 1981; Schneider-Rosen, Braunwald, Carlson, & Cicchetti, 1985).

BOX 7.1

ATTACHMENT TO FATHERS AND OTHERS

• • •

Mothers are not the only ones babies become attached to. They often become attached to their fathers, their sisters and brothers, baby-sitters, grandparents, and other people as well. How early they form these additional attachments depends upon the particular circumstances and cultural setting within which they are raised (Ainsworth, 1967; Schaffer & Emerson, 1964).

Does the attachment of infants to their fathers differ from their attachment to their mothers? To find out, Milton Kotelchuck (1976) used a variation of the "strange situation" to compare the attachment of babies between the ages of 6 months and 2 years to their mothers with that to their fathers. At all the ages he observed, the babies' play was likely to be disrupted when the mother left the room. Most of the babies did not respond to their fathers' leaving in the same way until they were about 15 months old. Kotelchuck concluded from this evidence that, among the U.S. families he studied, babies are slower to form an attachment to their fathers than to their mothers.

What seems to be the critical factor in determining when babies become attached to their fathers is the amount of time that they spend together. When their fathers were involved in their day-to-day care, even the youngest babies studied by Kotelchuck responded to their fathers' leaving in the "strange situation" in the same way they responded to their mothers' leaving: their play was disrupted. Since most fathers in the United States spend far less time interacting with their babies than do mothers, the slower development of attachment between fathers and their infants is understandable (Golinkoff & Ames, 1979; Lamb, 1978; Lewis & Weinraub, 1974).

Infants do eventually become attached to fathers who spend relatively little time with them. Here the excitement during the time they spend together and the predictableness of the father in the limited circumstances in which they interact seem to be important. The vast majority of exchanges between fathers and their babies are brief *play* episodes that come at marked periods of the day (Clarke-Stewart, 1978; Kotelchuck, 1976). Set aside as they are, these periods are likely to be memorable. If given a choice of whom to play with,

Children also form a strong attachment to their fathers, which provides them with an additional secure base for their continued development.

18-month-old infants will more often choose their fathers than their mothers, but in times of stress, mothers are generally preferred (Clarke-Stewart, 1978).

Babies also form attachments with peers and siblings. In some societies, such as the !Kung bushmen of the Kalahari desert, babies are cared for in multiaged groups of children beginning around the age of 1 year so that their mothers can resume their work (Konner, 1977). Under such circumstances, babies form strong cross-age attachments with many children in the group. In more industrialized settings, babies are less upset and more sociable in strange surroundings when an older sibling is present (Dunn, 1984).

Characteristics of the child   Some psychologists have criticized the initial research of Ainsworth and Bell for concentrating on the caretaker and ignoring the role of the child in the formation of attachment (Campos, Barrett, Lamb, Goldsmith, & Stenberg, 1983). These critics point out that, just as infants need a responsive mother to develop normally, mothers need responsive infants in order to achieve their full potential as caretakers.

The importance of a baby's responsiveness in the development of attachment can be seen in studies of deaf children with hearing parents. These children are, of course, less responsive than hearing children to orally communicated parental behaviors. Parents often fail to realize that their babies are deaf for many months, and it is not uncommon for deaf babies not to be diagnosed for as long as 2 years. Attachment between these undiagnosed deaf children and their mothers takes a long time to form and is often weak (Schlesinger, 1980).

Besides children's capacities, another possible source of variation in patterns of attachment is their temperamental disposition (Campos, Barrett, Lamb, Goldsmith, & Stenberg, 1983; Kagan, 1982). For example, Kazuo Miyake, Shing-jen Chen, and Joseph Campos (1985) found that newborns who became extremely distressed when their feeding was interrupted were more likely to be evaluated as insecurely attached at 1 year than newborns who did not become upset. This suggests that infant temperament does influence patterns of attachment. But the issue is controversial because some researchers have found no relationship between temperament and attachment (Bates, Maslin, & Frankel, 1985). An interesting resolution to the controversy is offered by Jay Belsky and Michael Rovine (1987). Based on a careful reanalysis of existing research, these researchers suggest that infant temperament affects the way babies express security or insecurity but that it does not directly affect the actual pattern of attachment.

Cultural influences   The pattern of attachment between children and their caretakers may also be influenced by the child-rearing practices of their culture. For example, children who grow up on Israeli kibbutzim (collective farms) are raised communally from an early age. Although they see their parents daily, the adults who look after them are usually not family members. When such communally raised children were placed in the "strange situation" at the ages of 11 to 14 months, many of them became very upset; half

were classified as anxious/resistant, and only 37 percent appeared to be securely attached (Sagi, Lamb, Lewkowicz, Shoham, Dvir, & Estes, 1985). As noted earlier, only about 12 percent of the middle-class U.S. children, who are cared for by their parents, are judged to be anxious/resistant (Ainsworth, Blehar, Waters, & Wall, 1978).

A low percentage of securely attached babies has also been observed among German children, although for apparently quite different reasons. One study (Grossmann, Grossmann, Spangler, Suess, & Unzer, 1985) found that 49 percent of the 1-year-olds tested were anxious/avoidant and only 33 percent were securely attached. From their extensive observations of German home life, the researchers were able to reject the possibility that a large proportion of German parents are insensitive or indifferent to their children. Rather, German parents adhere to a cultural value that calls for the maintenance of a relatively large interpersonal distance between individuals and a cultural belief that babies should be weaned from bodily contact as soon as they become mobile. The researchers suggest that among German mothers, "The ideal is an independent, nonclinging infant who does not make demands on the parents but rather unquestioningly obeys their commands" (p. 253).

Among traditional Japanese families, a high proportion of anxious/resistant infants has been found, but

This little boy's reaction is characteristic of children who are securely attached to their mothers and are happy to be reunited with them.

no anxious/avoidant infants at all (Miyake, Chen, & Campos, 1985). Kazuo Miyake and his colleagues explain this by pointing out that traditional Japanese mothers rarely leave their children in the care of another and behave toward them in ways that foster a strong sense of dependence. Consequently, the experience of being left alone with a stranger is unusual and upsetting to these Japanese children. This interpretation is supported by a study of nontraditional Japanese families in which the mothers were pursuing careers, which required them to leave their children in the care of others (Durrett, Otaki, & Richards, 1984). Among the children of these mothers, the distribution of the basic patterns of attachment was similar to that seen in the United States.

Systematic cross-cultural study of attachment is still relatively rare, and there is as yet no agreement about the significance of the different distributions of attachment patterns that have been found in different cultures. But the evidence from the existing studies strongly suggests that cultural factors are an important influence on child-caretaker relationships (Bretherton & Waters, 1985).

Stability of the patterns of attachment A number of studies that have included children from middle-class families in the United States and Germany have found that the patterns of attachment—anxious/avoidant, securely attached, or anxious/resistant—are likely to remain stable for at least several months (Connell, 1976; Grossmann, Fremmer-Bombik, Rudolph, & Grossmann, 1987; Main & Weston, 1981; Waters, 1978). However, evidence is accumulating that the stability of a pattern of attachment depends on the stability of the child's life circumstances. If the family is going through a difficult period because of unemployment, poverty, illness, or conflict between adult family members, there is a much greater chance that the pattern of attachment for children between the ages of 12 and 18 months will change. In a study of families living below the poverty level the pattern of attachment changed for about one-third of the infants (Vaughn, Egeland, Sroufe, & Waters, 1979). When there was a high level of family stress, the change was from more to less securely attached.

No single factor appears sufficient to account for the various patterns of attachment. The complicated interrelationships between caretaker behaviors, the innate characteristics of children, cultural influences, and life circumstances create many different developmental paths having many different outcomes. This point is made quite forcefully by Robert Hinde, an eminent British ethologist, in a recent summary of research on human attachment.

[W]e must accept that individuals differ and society is complex, and that mothers and babies will be programmed not simply to form one sort of relationship but a range of possible relationships according to circumstances. So we must be concerned not with normal mothers and deviant mothers but with a *range* of styles and a capacity to select appropriately between them.

At one level of approximation, there are general properties of mothering necessary whatever the circumstances. At a more precise level, the optimal mothering behavior will differ according to the sex of the infant, its ordinal position in the family, the mother's social status, caregiving contributions from other family members, the state of physical resources, and so on. *Natural selection must surely have operated to produce conditional maternal strategies, not stereotypy.* (Hinde, 1982, p. 71; italics in original)

Much the same type of complexity characterizes the long-term consequences of attachment. As we will see when we discuss this hotly debated topic in Chapter 8, there is conflicting evidence about the significance of the various patterns of attachment for later development.

A NEW SENSE OF SELF

Thus far, we have been tracing changes in different realms of children's development during the second year of life one by one. A most striking fact about 2-year-olds is the way that these separate threads of development come together to provide them with a new and distinctive sense of themselves as people.

The transition that marks the end of infancy is noted by people in many parts of the world. On the South Pacific island of Fiji, parents say that children gain *vakayalo*, sense, around their second birthday; they can be held responsible for their actions because they are supposed to be able to tell right from wrong. The Utku of the Hudson Bay say that the 2-year-old has gained *ihuma*, reason. Parents in the United States react to their infants' newly acquired independence and their accompanying decrease in control over them by labeling the change as the onset of the "terrible twos."

However it is described, the distinctive pattern of behavior that tells people in many cultures that children have entered a new stage of development seems to be comprised of several interconnected elements: a growing sensitivity to adult standards of what is good and bad, a new awareness of their ability to live up to adult standards, and an ability to create plans of their own that they then judge against adult standards (Kagan, 1981). All of these elements taken together mean that children can participate more adequately in many situations, which provides the basis for the sense of autonomy that Erikson (1963) says characterizes this time of life.

A Sense of Standards

As we have seen repeatedly in this and earlier chapters, infants are sensitive to unusual changes in their environment. Even in the first days of life, babies become habituated to events that occur repeatedly and pay attention to unexpected changes in their surroundings. But around the age of 2 years, children also become sensitive to events that violate the way things are "supposed to be." Children at this age become upset if the plastic eye of their teddy bear is missing or if there is mud on the hem of a new dress. When 14-month-olds are brought to a play room where some of the toys are damaged, they seem to be unaware of the flaws and they play as if nothing were wrong. But 19-month-olds comment disdainfully, "Yukky" or "fix it" (Kagan, 1981, p. 47). Apparently, their emerging ability to classify objects of different kinds includes an ability to classify events as proper and improper, according to adult standards.

Sensitivity to adult standards also expresses itself when children feel they are supposed to imitate an adult. In several studies, Jerome Kagan (1981) had an adult model various activities in a play setting. For example, the adult might make one toy monkey hug another monkey, or build a stack of blocks, or enact a small drama using toy blocks as animals. Many of the acts were too complex for 2-year-olds to imitate. Starting around 18 months of age, the children in Kagan's study seemed to feel that they were expected

When things are slightly out of order, the diligent 2-year-old will seek to put them right.

to do what the adult had done even when they couldn't. As a result, many of them started to fret, stopped playing, and clung to their mothers. Kagan concluded that their distress signaled a new ability to recognize adult standards and an associated sense of responsibility to live up to them.

Further evidence that toddlers develop a sense of standards comes from situations in which children set themselves a goal while playing and then work diligently to achieve it. It is not at all unusual to encounter 2½-year-old children struggling to build a tower using all the blocks in the room or to fit every available doll into a single toy baby carriage so that all the babies can go on a trip. However, such deliberate goal setting and self-motivated behavior is rare in children under 18 months of age. Until children are able to represent themselves symbolically in relation to a future goal — "I wash baby's face" — their problem solving is easily sidetracked.

Accompanying the emergence of children's ability to set a goal for themselves is the appearance of a new

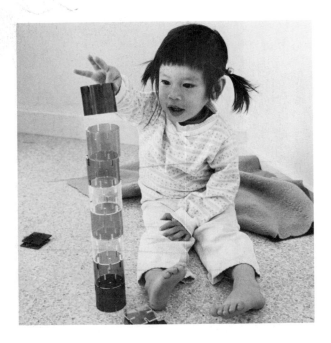

When they achieve a goal that they have set for themselves, 2-year-olds feel a sense of mastery and pleasure that leads them to smile.

kind of smile. As the topmost block is placed on the stack or the last doll is stuffed into the carriage, the child smiles with self-satisfaction. Kagan (1981) refers to this kind of smile as a *mastery smile.*

Once children can set goals for themselves and realize that there are standards of performance that they must meet, they begin to interact with their parents in a new way; they actively seek their parents' help in reaching the goals and meeting the standards. When confronted with a task that appeared too difficult, one child is reported to have said, while clinging to his mother, "It's mommy's turn to play" (Kagan, 1981, p. 49). More routinely, children around 20 months of age begin to tell adults what they want them to do. Their success varies, of course, depending upon the willingness of adults to let them have their way, which differs from family to family and culture to culture.

Self-Description

When speech first emerges, most one-word utterances name objects in the visual field. Children point at or pick up an object and say its name. These first descriptions include no explicit reference to the self. A child hitting pegs with a hammer says only "hit." Between the ages of 18 and 24 months, about the same time that children begin to use two-word utterances, they also begin to describe their own actions. A child completing a jigsaw puzzle exclaims, "Did it!" or "Becky finished." When blocks fall, a child exclaims, "Uh oh. I fix." In these utterances we see not only children's ability to refer to themselves explicitly but also the ability to represent two aspects of an event in words, —their recognition of adult standards and their desire to meet them.

Self-Recognition

Consciousness of self is among the major characteristics said to distinguish human beings from other species and 2-year-olds from younger children. This is an interesting idea, but finding a way to demonstrate it convincingly has been a problem.

In 1970, Gordon Gallup reported an ingenious series of mirror experiments with chimpanzees that has subsequently been repeated with children. Gallup showed adolescent, wild-born chimpanzees their images in a full-length mirror. At first the chimps acted as if another animal were in the room: they threatened, vocalized, and made conciliatory gestures to the "intruder." After a few days, however, they began to use the mirror to explore *themselves.* For example, they picked bits of food from places on their face that they could not see.

To make certain of the meaning of these reactions, Gallup anesthetized several chimps and painted a bright, odorless dye above one eye and on the ear on the opposite side of the head. When they woke up and looked in the mirror, these chimps immediately began to explore the marked spots with their hands. Gallup concluded that they had learned to recognize themselves in the mirror.

This kind of self-recognition is by no means universal to all simian species. Gallup gave a wild-born macaque monkey over 2400 hours of mirror exposure during more than 5 months, but it never showed any sign of self-recognition. The problem was not simply dealing with the mirror image; the monkey quickly learned to use the mirror to find food that was out of sight. The monkey could not recognize *itself.*

Gallup's procedure has been used with human infants between the ages of 3 and 24 months. The results fit nicely with the evidence from other studies of the development of self-awareness (Bertenthal & Fischer, 1978; Lewis & Brooks-Gunn, 1979). These studies reveal that there are several stages in learning to recognize oneself in a mirror. Prior to the age of 3 months, children held up to a mirror show little interest in their own image or in the images of anyone else. At about 4 months, if a toy or another person is reflected in the mirror, babies will reach out and touch the mirror image. At this stage, they clearly don't understand that they are seeing a reflection. Babies 10 months old will reach behind them if a toy is slowly lowered behind their back while they are looking in the mirror. However, they will not try to rub off a red spot that has been surreptitiously applied to their nose. Not until children are 18 months old will they reach for their own noses when they see the red spot. Some try to rub the spot off; others ask, "What's that?" Within a few months, however, the child will be able to answer unhesitatingly, "Me," whenever someone points to the child's mirror image and asks, "Who's that?"

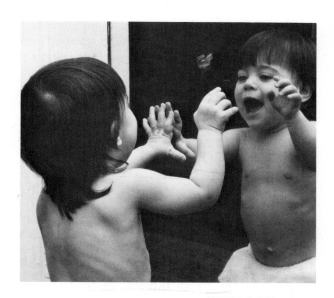

Children's ability to recognize themselves in a mirror attests to the emergence of a new sense of self at the end of infancy.

THE END OF INFANCY

The combined data on the changes in children's self-concept between the ages of 18 and 30 months—their declining distress when separated from their caretakers, and their increased ability to engage in symbolic play, to imitate absent events, and to express themselves in elementary words and phrases—indicate that they undergo a stagelike transition in the overall pattern of their capacities that we have identified as a bio-social-behavioral shift around their second birthday or soon thereafter. The changes that converge to create the transition from infancy to early childhood are summarized in Table 7.3. The table provides a timely reminder that the social and cognitive changes that have figured so prominently in this chapter are part and parcel of more mundane behavioral changes, such as coordinated walking and bladder control, and that all of these changes are dependent on the physical development of the body, most particularly the central nervous system.

The new configuration of characteristics that emerges during the second year and into the third does

TABLE 7.3 The bio-social-behavioral shift at the end of infancy

Biological domain

Myelination of connections among brain areas

Leveling off of brain growth

Roughly equal degrees of maturation of different brain areas

Behavioral domain

Walking becomes well coordinated

Manual dexterity becomes adequate to pick up small objects

Control over bladder and bowels

Planful problem solving

Symbolic play

Deferred imitation

Conceptual representations

Elementary vocabulary and the beginning of word combinations

Social domain

Decline of distress at separation

Distinctive sense of self

not, of course, mean that children can survive on their own. Far from it. But it does set the stage for a new form of interdependence and a new system of interactions between children and their environments. If all goes well, the individual aspects of development will undergo further modification and a new, distinctive stage of development will emerge in 3 to 4 years.

SUMMARY

1. Sometime between their second and third birthdays, children complete the period of development called infancy. Like all major stage transitions, the end of infancy is marked by changes in biological processes and physical and mental abilities, and by the appearance of a new relationship to the social world.

2. Important connections in the cerebral cortex and between the cortex and the brain stem become myelinated. Neurons in the brain begin to achieve adult length and density, and the rate of overall brain growth slows.

3. Children gain increasing control over several muscle systems, which makes it possible for them to walk upright, run, jump, and execute such movements as eating with a spoon or picking up small objects. They also gain voluntary control over elimination.

4. A new configuration of cognitive abilities is manifested in many domains: problem solving, play, imitation, categorization of objects, and communication.

5. Toddlers continue to search for objects that are hidden and then moved; they no longer give up when they cannot find something in the first place they think to look. Problem solving in general becomes more deliberate; solutions are reached without extensive overt trial and error.

6. Play evolves from a concentration on variation in patterns of movements to the pretend use of objects in imaginary situations. Pretend play itself evolves. Children 1 to 1½ years old can use themselves as agents and can carry out only a single pretend act at a time. By the time they are 2 years old, children can carry out a sequence of pretend actions in which objects such as dolls are used as the agents.

7. Late in the second year, children become capable of imitating actions seen many hours or even days earlier. This kind of behavior is called *deferred imitation.*

8. Coincident with the onset of pretend play and deferred imitation is the appearance of a new form of categorizing. Presented with a collection of objects to group, toddlers create a separate work space and categorize objects in accordance with adult criteria.

9. Toddlers' vocabularies begin to grow rapidly at the same time that they begin to play symbolically and to imitate the actions of others who are not present.

10. The ability to combine words to make elementary two-word sentences coincides with the ability to combine objects in pretend play and to categorize objects according to two characteristics.

11. Infants' distress when separated from their mothers is interpreted by developmental psychologists as an indicator of feelings of attachment. This distress increases steadily until sometime in the second year and then declines.

12. A variety of theories offer competing explanations for the onset of attachment.
    a. Freud believed attachment has its roots in the reduction of such biological drives as hunger.
    b. Erikson explains attachment as the establishment of a trusting relationship between parent and child.
    c. Bowlby hypothesizes that attachment serves to reduce fear by establishing a secure base of support from which children can explore their environments.

13. Research with monkeys has disproved the drive-reduction theory and has shown that infant monkeys can become attached to inanimate surrogate mothers that provide soothing tactile sensations.

14. The social incapacity of monkeys raised with inanimate surrogate mothers has focused research on the role of maternal responsiveness in the development of normal social interactions.

15. The "strange situation" has been widely used to assess distinctive patterns of attachment. Research has focused on the causes and consequences of three broad patterns of attachment: anxious/avoidant, securely attached, and anxious/resistant.

16. The best predictor of secure attachment is attentive, sensitive caretaking. Abusive, neglectful, and inconsistent caretaking are likely to lead to insecure attachment.

17. Children from families in which the mother is the primary caretaker also become attached to their fathers

and siblings, but these attachments usually occur later than their attachment to their mothers.

18. Children's characteristics are a contributing factor in the nature of their attachments. Children who are handicapped in communicating with their caretakers or who are easily upset when their ongoing activity is interrupted may experience difficulty in forming secure attachments.

19. There appear to be marked cultural variations in patterns of infant-caretaker attachments. Traditions both of exclusive mothering and of communal upbringing can result in manifestations of anxiety in the "strange situation."

20. A new sense of self accompanies the decline in distress at separation in the "strange situation." This new sense of self is manifested in the following:
   a. A growing sensitivity to adult standards
   b. Concern about living up to those standards
   c. A new ability to set one's own goals and standards
   d. Self-reference in language
   e. Immediate recognition of one's image in a mirror

KEY TERMS

Animal model
Biological drives
Deferred imitation

Representation
Secure base

Symbolic play
Tertiary circular reactions

SUGGESTED READINGS

BATES, ELIZABETH. *The Emergence of Symbols: Cognition and Communication in Infancy.* New York: Academic Press, 1976.

A summary of the evidence linking cognitive changes to the emergence of language during the second year of life.

BOWLBY, JOHN. *Attachment and Loss,* Vol. 1: *Attachment.* New York: Basic Books, 1969.

Bowlby's ideas have had an enormous and continuing impact on the study of infant development. This first volume in his trilogy provides the rationale and data upon which his concept of attachment is based.

BRETHERTON, INGE, and **EVERETT WATERS** (Eds.). *Growing Points in Attachment Theory. Monographs of the Society for Research in Child Development,* 1985, *50,* No. 209.

Reports from a wide spectrum of researchers on the current status of research on the growth of attachment.

HARLOW, HARRY. *Learning to Love.* San Francisco: Albion, 1971.

A summary of Harlow's research on the role of social interaction on the socioemotional development of monkeys. Although somewhat dated, this work continues to have a great impact on conceptions of emotional development in early childhood.

KAGAN, JEROME. *The Second Year.* Cambridge, Mass.: Harvard University Press, 1982.

A well-rounded description of the interlocking intellectual and social changes associated with the end of infancy. The book is unusual in its inclusion of cross-cultural data and for bringing together modern evidence concerning the biological changes that accompany the distinctive pattern of behaviors that mark the transition to early childhood.

PIAGET, JEAN. *Play, Dreams, and Imitation.* New York: Norton, 1962.

Piaget's account of the end of the sensorimotor stage of development, which makes the argument that different domains of infant behavior all point to a single underlying change in thought processes and provides many interesting observations that are classics in the study of this age period.

8

...

EARLY
EXPERIENCE
AND LATER LIFE

Two roads diverged in a yellow wood,
And sorry I could not travel both
And be one traveler, long I stood
And looked down one as far as I could
To where it bent in the undergrowth;

Then took the other, as just as fair,
And having perhaps the better claim,
Because it was grassy and wanted wear;
Though as for that the passing there
Had worn them really about the same,
And both that morning equally lay
In leaves no step had trodden black.
Oh, I kept the first for another day!
Yet knowing how way leads on to way,
I doubted if I should ever come back.

I shall be telling this with a sigh
Somewhere ages and ages hence:
Two roads diverged in a wood, and I —
I took the one less traveled by,
And that has made all the difference.

— Robert Frost, "The Road Not Taken"

• • •

One of the most fundamental processes in development consists in the closing of
doors . . . , in the progressive restriction of possible fates.

— Joseph Needham, *Order and Life*

• •

The poet and the scientist agree. Paths taken early in life launch one on a course that, once set, may be difficult to change. Insofar as children's possible fates are shaped by their experience in the world, it seems reasonable to conclude that their earliest experiences, the paths they first travel down, will be the most significant for determining their later development. This idea is called **primacy.** We can find it in our proverbs — "As the twig is bent, so grows the tree" — as well as in our heritage from the Greeks. For example, we can find an expression of this view in the writings of Plato (428 – 348 B.C.):

And the beginning, as you know, is always the most important part, especially in dealing with anything young and tender. That is the time when the character is being molded and easily takes any impress one may wish to stamp on it. (1945, p. 68)

During the twentieth century, primacy has become associated with the specific claim that children's experiences during infancy determine their future development. This line of thought was greatly influenced by Freud's claims that psychological illness in adulthood can be traced back to unresolved conflicts in the first years of life (Freud, 1940/1964). It is by no means restricted to Freudian theorists, however. In summarizing his research on intellectual development, psychologist Burton White (1975) argues that *"To begin to look at a child's educational development when he is two years of age is already much too late*, particularly in the area of social skills and attitudes" (p. 4, italics added). Similarly, Alan Sroufe and June Fleeson (1986) maintain that the nature of children's first attachments greatly influences the way they form subsequent relationships.

In this chapter, we will focus on the questions of whether and to what extent the experiences of infancy are more important than the experiences of later stages of life in determining development. The answers to these questions are important with regard to such issues as how society and parents can best provide for infants to ensure their optimal development and what can be done to improve the lives of children who suffer deprivation early in life. As we will see, there is no question that infant experiences are crucial to later development. But there is good reason to doubt extreme claims that the trends begun during the first $2\frac{1}{2}$ years of life are irreversible (Rutter, 1987).

OPTIMAL CONDITIONS FOR INFANT DEVELOPMENT

The widespread belief that the early experiences of infants are crucial to their later development has produced a continuing effort to identify the conditions that will best foster their early development. Information about these conditions serves as a guide for parents, who want to do all they can to ensure a happy and healthy life for their children, and policymakers, who must sometimes pass laws concerning children. In our society, the optimal conditions for development are usually thought to be those that will allow "as many doors as possible to remain open" for the child's continued growth.

It is often suggested that development is best fostered when the mother, or whoever else cares for the baby, is sensitive and responsive to the baby's signals and states. We have seen this in previous chapters — for example, in Kaye's descriptions of how mothers encourage nursing in Chapter 5 (p. 167) and in Ainsworth and Bell's research on the conditions that promote secure attachment in Chapter 7 (p. 233). A particularly powerful vision of the sensitive mother is provided by the Danish philosopher Søren Kierkegaard:

The loving mother teaches her child to walk alone. She is far enough from him so that she cannot actually support him, but she holds out her arms to him. She imitates his movements, and if he totters, she swiftly bends as if to seize him, so that the child might believe that he is not walking alone. . . . And yet, she does more. Her face beckons like a reward, an encouragement. Thus, the child walks alone with his eyes fixed on his mother's face, not on the difficulties in his way. He supports himself by arms that do not hold him and constantly strives towards the refuge in his mother's embrace, little suspecting that in the very same moment he is emphasizing his need for her, he is proving that he can do without her, because he is walking alone. (Kierkegaard, 1846, quoted in Sroufe, 1979, p. 462)

Kierkegaard's "loving mother" is so finely tuned to her child's needs that she creates the illusion of physical support where none exists. This illusion provides the child with a sense of individual achievement and self-confidence that encourages maximum effort and courage. These character traits are widely admired in Western European and North American cultures. Consequently, the child-rearing behaviors that foster them are often considered the optimal conditions of development.

Kierkegaard's maternal ideal seems to be embodied in what Burton White and Jean Carew Watts (1973) call A mothers. The children of these mothers were judged as more competent than their peers when they were in kindergarten, based on their performance on a battery of tests and the researchers' observations.

TABLE 8.1 Characteristics of competent 3-year-olds

Social abilities

Getting and holding attention of an adult in socially
  acceptable ways
Using adults as resources after concluding that they
  cannot handle the task themselves
Expressing affection and mild hostility
Engaging in role play

General intellectual skills

Understanding and communicating effectively
Engaging in complex problem solving, including finding
  materials and using them to make a product
Self-control in the absence of external constraints
Ability to plan for and prepare for an activity
Ability to explore novel objects and situations systematically

SOURCE: White & Watts, 1973.

(Table 8.1 lists some of the characteristics the researchers evaluated.) *A* mothers enjoyed being with their toddlers and talked to them on a level they could understand. They placed more importance on their children's happiness and learning than on the appearance of their homes, which were organized to be safe and interesting for toddlers. They allowed their children to take minor risks, but they set reasonable limits for them. For instance, they might allow their 1½-year-olds to negotiate stairs while holding on to the banister but not to climb up on the edge of the bathtub. Their close attention to their children was complemented by their dominant mood: they were busy and happy rather than unoccupied and depressed.

A mothers did *not* spend all day attending to their toddlers. In fact, they spent less than 10 percent of their time actually caring for them. Some had part-time jobs, and some had several other children. However, they were nearly always available for answering questions, setting up a new activity, or giving encouragement. The researchers found that neither a lot of money nor a lot of education was necessary to be an *A* mother, although poverty did make a mother's work more difficult. Some of the *A* mothers were on welfare, and some of them had not graduated from high school.

White and Watts' description of effective maternal behaviors tells us about the caretaking environments that foster optimal development in late infancy, as measured by successful early adaptations to a modern,

technologically advanced society in which the ability to behave oneself and perform well in school are basic demands. But it does not help answer many important questions that parents and other caregivers must face: What is the "right" kind of responsiveness? How much support is too much, and how much is not enough? What kind of support will prepare children to succeed in school? Will the same kind of responsiveness that prepares children to succeed in school also prepare them to cope with frustration, inadequate housing, discrimination, or extended periods of unemployment?

Answers to questions about what constitutes adequate preparation for later life depend upon the historical and cultural circumstances into which a child is born. For example, Japanese mothers, like mothers in the United States, aspire for their children to attain high levels of academic achievement. But in Japanese society, working together with others is valued more than individual achievement, and Japanese mothers stress this value in raising their children. By U.S. standards, Japanese mothers may seem too responsive to their children, thereby encouraging considerable emotional dependence (Azuma, Kashiwagi, & Hess, 1981). However, Japanese mothers' high level of responsiveness does not mean that they provide inappropriate environments for their children's development. Japanese society differs from American society. Therefore both the overall pattern of adult characteristics that Japanese mothers strive to foster in their children and their strategies for achieving this pattern differ.

A quite different situation exists for the people living in the poverty-stricken slums of towns in the northeast of Brazil (Scheper-Hughes, 1985). The environment into which their babies are born is extremely hostile to survival: the drinking water is contaminated, there is little food to eat, there are no sanitary facilities, and there is little medical care. Almost 50 percent of the children born in these communities die before the age of 5 years. For those that survive, success in later life is rarely influenced by academic abilities. Little schooling is available; later in life these children can look forward to laboring as unskilled farmworkers, which affords no hope of advancement or even of a comfortable living.

In response to these conditions, the mothers of this region studied by Nancy Scheper-Hughes have developed beliefs and behaviors about child rearing that seem harsh and uncaring by either middle-class American or Japanese standards. They are fatalistic about

In many parts of the world large numbers of children do not survive to celebrate their fifth birthday. Often they die of diseases that could be prevented with better sanitary conditions, nutrition, and health care.

their infants' well-being. Children who are developmentally delayed or who have a passive, quiet temperament may be neglected or simply left to die, with no attempt being made to give them special care. The favored children are those who are precocious, active, and demanding. If children survive to the age of 5 or 6 years, they are expected to begin contributing to the family's livelihood. The boys are allowed to roam the streets, searching for food and stealing if necessary. The girls are required to pick sugar cane or do housework. But as Scheper-Hughes makes clear, these mothers were simply being practical; they were preparing their children to survive in an environment where weakness means death.

Spoiling: Responding Too Much

Even among middle-class families in the United States, beliefs about proper parental behaviors differ. One mother may ignore her toddler's requests for a treat at the store or cries in the middle of the night in the belief that too much responsiveness will foster a false basis for dealing with the world and spoil the child. Another mother may respond to her children's every whim and whimper because she believes that she must buffer them against difficult circumstances until they are strong enough to cope on their own. Which mother is right? Is there a right answer to how much parents should cater to the desires and distresses of their infants? Is spoiling a problem?

The question of how to respond when infants cry is a useful example for considering the problem of spoiling. As we saw in Chapter 5 (p. 148), newborn cries are often ambiguous signals. Consequently, parents often worry that they will encourage fussiness if they pick up their babies each time that they start to cry.

There is evidence that parental concerns about spoiling their children by being too responsive to their crying is warranted. A study based on laboratory research shows that the duration of crying episodes can be decreased by ignoring infant cries and responding instead to other behaviors, such as smiling (Etzel & Gewirtz, 1967). However, observations in home situations suggest that crying may become more frequent if it is ignored, according to Silvia Bell and Mary Ainsworth (1972). These researchers studied the ways that 26 mothers responded to their infant's cries. A member of the research team visited each home for 4 hours, once every 3 weeks, for the first year of each baby's life. During the visits, the observer recorded how often the baby cried and how the mother responded. Contrary to common wisdom about spoiling babies, the results showed that mothers who responded quickly to their infant's cries had babies who cried relatively little. The mothers who ignored their baby's cries for long periods ended up with the babies that cried most often. Bell and Ainsworth suggest that the most important consequence of mothers' quick attention to their infants' cries is that it helps the babies to develop trust in the mother and trust in their own ability to control what happens to them.

Spoiling does not seem to be a serious risk factor during infancy. Perhaps there are some parents who cater to their children's every whim, thus giving them an exaggerated sense of their own power that will be maladaptive in the long run. However, in most cases, the everyday demands on parents to earn a living and maintain a household make it almost inevitable that children eventually learn that they cannot always have their own way.

Learned Helplessness: Responding Too Little

Parents' concerns that they will create a baby tyrant if they respond to their infant's every demand is balanced by the competing concern that if they never respond on the baby's terms, but only on their own, they will create children who believe that they cannot influence the world around them. Research on extreme forms of such **learned helplessness** indicates that when people are put in situations in which events are unaffected by their behavior they eventually become passive and lose the desire to act (Fincham & Cain, 1986; Seligman, 1975).

A number of studies show that infants are capable of learning about their ability to control events. In one, John S. Watson (not to be confused with John B. Watson, the founder of behaviorism mentioned in earlier chapters) set up an apparatus that allowed 8-week-old infants to move a mobile hanging above their cribs by pressing their heads against an air pillow. Because of the direct relationship between pressing down on the pillow and the movement of the mobile, the infants rapidly learned to make the mobile move (Watson, 1972).

Watson reports that once the infants learned to control the mobile, their daily levels of activity increased. They also began to smile delightedly and coo at the mobile. These observations led Watson to speculate that even very young infants find it pleasurable to control their environment because it gives them a feeling of personal effectiveness. On the basis of similar observations with infants and young children, psychiatrist Robert White (1959) concluded that human beings have a basic drive to be in control of their environments, which he called the *competence motive*.

In another study, Watson (1971) contrasted the behavior of two groups of children who were provided with mobiles for their cribs at home. One group could set the mobile in motion by pushing down on their pillows; the other group saw the mobile move equally often, but their own actions did not affect its move-

ment. Subsequently, both groups were given an opportunity to make a similar mobile move in the laboratory. The infants who had learned to control the mobile at home soon learned to make the laboratory mobile move. The infants who could not control the mobile at home did not learn to control the laboratory mobile. Consistent with the idea of learned helplessness, it seems that experiencing lack of control over an aspect of the environment in one situation impairs later learning in a similar situation.

Neal Finkelstein and Craig Ramey (1977) extended Watson's findings to show that babies who learn a particular behavior to control the environment in one situation may apply what they've learned to establish new behaviors. In the first stage of this study, the researchers placed 8-month-old babies in front of a panel that lit up and made interesting sounds. Half the babies could produce the interesting outcome by pushing on the panel; the others could push the panel or not, as they pleased, and still see and hear the same things. As expected, the babies whose actions caused the change learned to press the panel, whereas the others did not.

In the second stage of the experiment, *both* groups could make the sights and sounds occur by engaging in an entirely different kind of behavior, vocalizing. The babies who had learned to push the panel to produce the lights and sounds also learned to activate the panel by vocalizing. But the group who learned earlier that their behavior was irrelevant to producing the lights and sounds failed to learn this new way of accomplishing the same thing.

Findings such as Finkelstein and Ramey's suggest that even infants as young as 8 months of age learn more than the association between their own actions and specific outcomes, such as the connection between crying and being picked up or between sucking and obtaining nourishment. They also seem to learn something about their ability to control their environment. Although infants cannot tell us directly what they are feeling or thinking, such experiences seem to shape their sense of personal effectiveness, judging from their actions.

An important limitation of the research on spoiling and learned helplessness is that it does not indicate what mix of learning about their ability to control their environment and learning to accept external control provides infants with the optimum foundation for later development. This research is best viewed as indicating the boundaries within which parents and other caretakers must remain for healthy development to occur. There is no single recipe for the correct amount of responsiveness for every situation, which is why psychologists emphasize that parental sensitivity is a key factor in development.

EFFECTS OF SEPARATION

There are a variety of situations in which parents are separated from their children, making it impossible for them to fine-tune their children's upbringing. The need to earn a living often separates parents from their young children for many hours, several days a week. Family upheavals such as divorce, the death of a parent, or prolonged illness requiring hospitalization also separate children from their parents (Wolkind & Rutter, 1985). Similarly, major disasters such as war, flood, and famine, can often dislocate large populations.

Developmental psychologists have long been interested in the consequences of the separation of children from their parents. They seek to understand how separation influences development at the time it occurs and how it might affect later development. This can help them to devise effective therapies for children who have been adversely affected by these separations.

In the following discussion, we will concentrate on studies of children who were separated from their parents when their first attachment relationships would be expected to be forming (for a general review see Rutter & Hersov, 1985). We will consider children who have experienced one or another of a wide range of separations, including those involving day care, hospitalization, and residence in a foster home or orphanage. By assessing the impact of different types of early separation on children's later ability to form attachments and get along with others, this line of psychological research provides important clues concerning the impact of infancy on later development.

Temporary Separation from Parents

A relatively mild form of separation is experienced by children who spend part of each weekday being cared for by a nonfamily member while their parents work. Many researchers are convinced that high-quality day care has no lasting impact on infants' later development. Some, however, claim that no matter what its quality, extensive day care for babies under the age of 1 year has lasting, negative effects (see Box 8.1, "Out-of-Home Care in the First Year of Life"). We will return to the subject of day care in Chapter 12, where the focus will be on slightly older children.

Another form of separation occurs when young children must spend time in a hospital. Several studies have evaluated the consequences of hospitalization on later emotional development. Michael Rutter (1976), for example, studied 400 10-year-olds to see if early hospitalization had influenced their later psychological adjustment. He found that a single hospital stay before the age of 5 that lasted a week or less produced no emotional or behavioral disturbances that could be detected at the age of 10. On the other hand, several hospitalizations *were* found to be associated with behavior problems and delinquency in later childhood. However, Rutter suggests that these later psychological problems may have resulted from the stress of continued ill health rather than from the children's separation from their parents. Another possibility is suggested by subsequent research revealing that children who had been hospitalized repeatedly were more likely than children who had not been hospitalized to come from socially and economically disadvantaged families (Quinton & Rutter, 1976). The negative effect of repeated hospitalization may therefore be less a reflection of disturbed social relations owing to separation than it is a reflection of chronically difficult home circumstances or ill health.

A more traumatic form of family separation often occurs in time of war. In the early 1940s, the German air force carried out an intensive bombing campaign

The Vietnam War orphaned many children, leaving them with no home but the street.

BOX 8.1

OUT-OF-HOME CARE IN THE FIRST YEAR OF LIFE
···

A dramatic example of the ways in which questions about the primacy of infancy reach beyond scientific research into individual lives and the arena of public policy is the current controversy over the effects of placing infants in the care of someone other than their parents during the first year of life. According to some experts, this puts them at risk for long-term socioemotional difficulties. According to others, there is no risk associated with early high-quality child care (Belsky, 1986; Phillips, McCartney, Scarr, & Howes, 1987).

The issue of out-of-home care for infants potentially affects the lives of many people owing to two trends in American society: (1) the growing number of single-parent households and (2) the increasing economic need for both parents to work full time. At the present time, women constitute the fastest growing segment of the work force, and many of them have infants 1 year of age or younger (Ad Hoc Daycare Coalition, 1985). If current trends continue, by the year 2000 four out of every five infants under the age of 1 will have a mother in the labor force.

Prominent among those raising concerns about out-of-home care during the first year of life is Jay Belsky (1986, 1987). He bases his conclusions on evidence that children who have had extensive nonmaternal care (more than 20 hours a week) during the first year of life are more likely to exhibit insecure patterns of attachment in the "strange situation" and that such patterns have long-term negative consequences for children's emotional development and social behavior. For in-

stance, insecurely attached children have been found to be more likely to experience difficulties when they attend nursery school. These difficulties may take the form of heightened aggressiveness and low levels of compliance and cooperation.

With the majority of mothers returning to work within a year of the birth of their children, a growing number of babies are being cared for out of their homes before the age of 1. The effects of such care on their socioemotional development are the subject of intense debate among psychologists.

against the civilian population of London and other large English cities. Many English children were separated from their parents when they were sent to live in the safer countryside with relatives, sponsoring families, or other children in special group living arrangements. Dorothy Burlingham and Anna Freud (1942) studied the reactions of a group of such children who

ranged in age from a few months to 4 years. They found that many of these children were distressed at being separated from their parents. However, when a group of these children were examined 20 years later, the researchers found no instances of severe mental illness among them; their behavior as young adults fell within normal limits (Maas, 1963).

Belsky's concerns are supported by a recent study conducted by Peter Barglow, Brian Vaughn, and Nancy Molitor (1987). These researchers found that first-born children who had been placed in day-care arrangements before their first birthday were significantly more likely to display insecure forms of attachment when they were 12 to 13 months old than were children who stayed at home with their mothers.

Belsky's conclusions have been vigorously attacked on two grounds. First, the basic premise of his argument has been called into question because some studies have found no differences in the responses to the "strange situation" of children who have been cared for exclusively by their mothers and children who have had alternative forms of care. For example, Lindsay Chase-Landsdale and Margaret Owen (1987) studied the attachment behaviors of ninety-seven 1-year-olds whose mothers had returned to work by the time they were 6 months old, leaving them in a variety of alternative care situations. These researchers found no differences whatsoever between the attachment behaviors of the children whose mothers stayed at home and those whose mothers went back to work.

Second, Belsky's conclusions that early nonmaternal care causes insecure forms of attachment and behavioral difficulties in nursery school have been questioned. Deborah Phillips and her colleagues (Phillips, McCartney, Scarr, & Howes, 1987), for example, argue that Belsky's concern is misplaced. They maintain that "studies converge to suggest that early entry into day care may be less important than the kind and quality of care children receive while in day care" (p. 20).

In deciding such complex issues, the real-life circumstances of the people involved must be considered. If brief separations with high-quality care are the only disruptions in an otherwise secure family situation, the consequences might be quite different than they would be for a family under various stresses. Consistent with evidence on the cumulative impact of risk factors presented in this chapter, Gamble and Zigler (1986) conclude that in families that are facing a number of life stresses, substitute care during the first year of life increases the likelihood of insecure infant-parent attachments and that insecure attachments make the infant more vulnerable to stresses encountered later in life.

The stakes in the debate are very high. On the one hand, everyone is aware that it is in the interests not only of the children involved but also of society as a whole to ensure that children grow up to be emotionally stable and socially competent people. If they do not, society will incur huge costs in later social services required and economic productivity lost. On the other hand, there are pressing economic and social reasons that are bringing many mothers into the work force and keeping fathers there. The problem is how best to deal with these conflicting realities to maximize children's life chances. Belsky suggests that this goal could best be achieved if parents received support for staying home with their infants during their first year of life. Phillips and her colleagues argue that what is called for is better and more accessible day care.

Many millions of dollars will be spent dealing with the issue of infant child care in the decades to come, and millions of families, parents and children alike, will be affected by the policies that are eventually adopted. In fact, virtually everyone will be involved, if only in the role of taxpayers who must pay for whatever policies are eventually adopted.

Extended Separation from Parents

An extreme form of separation is experienced by children who spend their early lives in orphanages because their parents are dead or are unable to care for them. Because orphanages often keep good records of the children they care for, studies of orphanage-raised children provide some of the most systematic data on how multiple caretakers in suboptimal circumstances influence later social and intellectual development.

Children of the creche
A classic, long-range study of orphanage-raised children was carried out by Wayne Dennis and his colleagues in a creche (orphan-

age) in Lebanon (Dennis, 1973). The children were brought to the creche shortly after birth. Once there, they received little adult attention; there was only one caretaker for every 10 children. These caretakers had themselves been brought up in the creche until the age of 6, when they were transferred to another institution. According to Dennis, the caretakers showed little regard for the children's individual needs or temperaments. They rarely talked to the children, did not respond to their infrequent vocalizations, and seldom played with them while bathing, dressing, changing, or feeding them. Instead, they left the babies to lie on their backs in their cribs all day and the toddlers to sit in small playpens with only a ball to play with.

The harmful effects of this low level of stimulation and human contact were evident within a year. Although the children were normal at 2 months, as measured by an infant scale, Dennis found that they had developed intellectually at only half the normal rate when he tested them at the end of the first year.

The later developmental fates of these children depended on their subsequent care. Those who were adopted made a remarkable recovery. The children who were adopted before they were 2 years old were functioning normally when tested 2 to 3 years after their adoption, and those who were adopted within the next 4 years were only slightly retarded in their intellectual functioning.

The children who remained institutionalized fared less well. At the age of 6, the girls were sent to one institution and the boys to another. The girls' institution, like the creche, provided few stimulating experiences and virtually no personal attention. When these girls were tested at 12 to 16 years of age, they were found to be so retarded intellectually that they would be unable to function in modern society. They could barely read, they could not tell time, and they were not able to dial a seven digit telephone number or to make change in a store.

The outcome for the boys was quite different. The institution to which they were transferred provided far more intellectual stimulation and more varied experiences than did the creche. What is more, they came into frequent contact with the workers at the institution, who came from the surrounding communities. As a result, the boys showed a substantial recovery from their initial intellectual lag when they were tested at 10 to 14 years of age. Although their performance on standardized tests was below the norm and below the performance of the children who had been

adopted, it was within the range that would allow them to function in society.

Children reared in well-staffed orphanages   The grim picture painted by Dennis's research provoked further studies of orphanage-raised children in an effort to determine if the negative consequences he found were the result of particular forms of orphanage care. Barbara Tizard and her colleagues (Tizard & Rees, 1975; Tizard & Hodges, 1978) conducted one of these studies with 65 English children from working-class backgrounds who were raised in residential nurseries from just after birth until at least the age of 2 years. The nurseries were considered to be of high quality. There was enough to eat, the children were cared for by a trained staff, and toys and books were plentiful. However, the staff scheduling discouraged the formation of close personal relationships between adults and children. Tizard and Hodges estimated that some 24 different nurses had cared for each of the children by the time they were 2 years old. By the age of $4\frac{1}{2}$, each child had been cared for by as many as 50 nurses. This situation would certainly appear to preclude the kind of intimate knowledge and caring that presumably underlies sensitive caretaking.

Tizard and her colleagues evaluated the developmental status of the children when they were $4\frac{1}{2}$ years old and again when they were 8. They grouped the children into three categories:

1. Children who remained in the institutions during all 8 years

2. Children who had returned to their original families after the age of 2

3. Children who were adopted between the ages of 2 and 8 years

For comparison purposes, the researchers also evaluated a group of children from a similar working-class background who had always lived at home.

Leaving institutional care had a positive effect on the children, as might be expected from Dennis's research. But how much difference it made depended on what kind of environment they entered. One of the surprising results was that the children who were restored to their biological families did not fare as well as the children who were adopted. The adopted children scored higher on standardized tests of intellectual achievement, and they were able to read at a more advanced level. The quality of their relationships with their adoptive parents also appeared to be better. Almost all of the children who were adopted formed mutual attachments with their adoptive parents, no matter how old they were when they were adopted. This was not the case for the children who returned to their biological parents. The older they were when they left the nurseries, the less likely it was that mutual attachment developed.

One reason the adoptive homes may have been superior to the biological homes was that the families who took back their children were often not altogether happy to have them. Many of the mothers expressed misgivings, but they accepted the responsibility because the children were their own. Often these children returned to homes in which there were other children who required their mother's attention or a stepfather who was not interested in them. By contrast, most of the adoptive parents were older, childless couples who wanted the children and gave them a good deal of attention. Also, the adoptive families were often financially better off than the children's biological families had been (Tizard & Hodges, 1978).

The positive consequences of leaving institutional care speak against rigid early critical periods for forming emotional attachments. Although the environment of the nurseries prevented the children from forming emotional attachments with their caretakers, most of the children who were adopted formed attachments with their new parents even though they were all past their second birthdays when they left the institution. At the same time, the research of Tizard and her colleagues confirms the idea that the environment during *later* periods of life can be important in determining whether or not an early deficit will be overcome since the children who returned to indifferent biological parents were less likely to form attachments.

One area in which most of these institutionalized children were reported to have more difficulties than children who had always lived at home was in their social relations at school. The previously institutionalized children were seen to be "overly friendly." They had "an almost insatiable desire for adult attention, and a difficulty in forming good relationships with their peer group" (Tizard & Hodges, 1978, p. 114). Why these children experienced difficulties in social relations at school but not at home is not clear. Perhaps their early experiences in institutions left them with a deficit in their ability to form peer relationships. Alternatively, they may have learned styles of interaction that were adaptive in the institutions but were maladaptive outside them (Rutter & Garmezy, 1983).

Isolated Children

The most extreme cases of neglect on record are those of children who have been separated not only from their parents but from other human beings as well. During the past two hundred years, a number of these so-called feral children have been discovered, the most famous being the Wild Child, Victor, discussed in Chapter 1. Such children never fail to excite public interest because the idea of a little child fending for itself in nature is so dramatic. But the circumstances of such children's isolation and their condition before being isolated are usually unknown. As a result, it is rarely possible to draw firm conclusions about the effects of their experiences while isolated.

There are, however, a few well-documented modern cases of children who have been isolated early in life by sociopathic parents. Because public officials now keep good birth records and other health records, enough is known about the early lives of these children to permit more solidly based conclusions about the developmental impact of their bizarre circumstances (Skuse, 1984b).

Foster care provides an alternative to life in an orphanage. These children are shown with foster grandparents.

Jarmila Koluchová (1972, 1976) studied one of these cases that occurred in Czechoslovakia. Identical twin boys were born to a mother of normal intelligence who died shortly after their birth. Beginning at about the age of 1½ years, when their father remarried and their stepmother took an active dislike to them, the boys were forced to live in a closet. They were not allowed to enter those parts of the house where the other family members lived, and they were rarely visited. They spent most of their time in the small, bare closet, without adequate food, exercise, or sunshine.

The boys came to the attention of the authorities when they were 6 years old. They were abnormally small and suffered from rickets, a disease caused by a vitamin deficiency that leaves bones soft and bent. They could barely talk, they did not recognize common objects in photographs, and they were terrified of the new sights and sounds around them. The boys were taken to a children's home where they were housed with children younger than themselves in a nonthreatening environment and were well cared for. In these new circumstances, the twins soon began to gain weight, to take an active interest in their surroundings, and to learn to speak. When they were first tested at the age of 8 years, the boys' intelligence measured well below normal. But year by year their performance improved until, at the age of 14, they both manifested perfectly normal intelligence (see Figure 8.1).

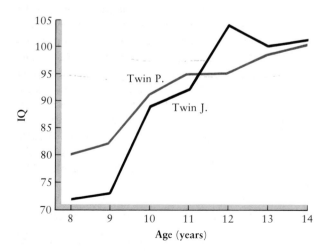

FIGURE 8.1 *Once the twins studied by Koluchová were released from isolation, their intellectual abilities showed gradual recovery until they were normal. (Adapted from Koluchová, 1976.)*

An example of an even more severely neglected child is Genie, a girl who was locked in a room by herself sometime before her second birthday (Curtiss, 1977). For more than 11 years, Genie lived chained by day to a potty and tied up by night in a sleeping bag. No one spoke to her. When her father came to tie her in for the night or to bring her food, he growled at her like a beast and scratched her with his fingernails.

Genie was a pitiful creature when she was liberated from these horrible circumstances. Although she was 13 years old, she weighed only 59 pounds and was only 4 feet, 6 inches tall. She rarely made a sound and was not toilet trained. She could not walk normally; instead, she shuffled her feet and swayed from side to side. Remarkably, when given a battery of psychological tests, Genie displayed an amazing ability to perceive and think about spatial relationships even though she could barely speak.

Genie did not recover as much as the twin boys did. She learned to control her bowels and to walk normally, but she never developed normal language, although she did expand her meager vocabulary. She also learned a variety of appropriate social behaviors. When first found, she would show no emotion at all when people left her; eventually, though, she became attached to people who lived in the same hospital rehabilitation unit. She developed ways to keep people from leaving after a visit and would become upset when they did leave.

Studies of isolated children leave little doubt that severe isolation can profoundly disrupt normal development, but they also show that extreme early deprivation of caretaking and normal interaction with the environment is not necessarily devastating to later development (Skuse, 1984a). Fortunately, such cases are too rare for us to know just how long and how severe isolation has to be before it causes irreversible damage. This rarity also makes it difficult to assess the impact of isolation on various aspects of development. Emotional, intellectual, and physical development may all be affected by isolation, but they are probably not all affected in the same way (Clarke & Clarke, 1986).

An important question raised, but not answered, by the studies of extreme isolation is the way that the conditions of the isolation environment and the predispositions of isolated children interact to determine the extent of later recovery. For example, is it important that the twins described by Koluchová had each other for company? Was Genie's great ability in spatial thinking a consequence of some special intellectual ability that would have shown up whether or not she had been isolated, or did it develop as a consequence of her immobility and her socially isolated environment? Answering such questions is important for understanding the vulnerability to developmental disorders of children raised in less extreme but still adverse circumstances and the factors that enable them to recover despite these circumstances.

VULNERABILITY AND RESILIENCE

Even in times of relative peace and prosperity many adults find life a struggle. In responding to their own pressing needs, they create less than optimal environments for their children. Precisely because these situations are *not* extreme, they may persist for years and become a permanent feature of the family environment that shapes the development of the children. They may eventually contribute to delinquent behavior, failure in school, and mental health problems.

Michael Rutter and his colleagues (Rutter, Yule, Quinton, Rowland, Yule, & Berger, 1975) conducted a large-scale study of the incidence of psychiatric disorders among 150 English families. They found four factors that, taken together, were strongly associated with childhood behavior problems and psychiatric disorders:

1. Family discord

2. Parental social deviance of either a criminal or a psychiatric nature

3. Social disadvantage, including low income, inadequate housing, and a large number of children close in age

4. A poor school environment, including high rates of turnover and absence among staff and pupils and a large proportion of pupils from economically depressed homes

None of these factors by itself was strongly associated with psychiatric disorders in childhood. But if as few as two of them were present at the same time — for example, if one parent had a personality disorder and the family had a low income — there was a 400 percent increase in the risk the child would suffer from a psychiatric disorder.

The emphasis Rutter and his colleagues place on the cumulative nature of risk factors is substantiated by a growing body of research. Many studies have demonstrated that a *combination* of biological, social, and ecological factors, interacting with each other over a considerable period of time, is required to cause serious developmental problems (Garmezy & Tellegen, 1984; Kopp, 1983; Rutter, 1985; Sameroff & Chandler, 1975; Werner & Smith, 1982). At the same time, a persistent finding in this research is that some children who live in stressful circumstances do not have developmental problems. They can apparently cope with their difficulties better than other children can. This observation has led psychologists to search for the sources of children's resilience in the face of hardship (Garmezy & Tellegen, 1984).

Family Characteristics

The family is the main support system for the child. We would expect, then, that variations in the kinds of support that families provide for children should be associated with children's abilities to withstand threats to their development. This idea is supported by a variety of research (see Bronfenbrenner, 1986, for a review). Many facets of the way family characteristics influence risk factors and resilience can be seen in the results of an important longitudinal study among a large, multiracial group of children born on the Hawaiian island of Kauai (Werner & Smith, 1982). Statistically, these children were especially likely to suffer developmental problems because they came from low-income families, had higher than average rates of prematurity and stress during the birth process, and were raised by mothers who had little formal education. The researchers found that the following circumstances reduced the risk of developmental difficulties:

• There were four or fewer children in the family.

• More than 2 years separated the child studied and the next younger or older sibling.

• Alternate caretakers were available to the mother within the household (father, grandparents, or older siblings).

- The workload of the mother, including employment outside the home, was not excessively heavy.

- The child had a substantial amount of caretaker attention during infancy.

- A sibling was available as a caretaker or confidant during childhood.

- During adolescence, the family provided structure and rules.

- The family was cohesive.

- There was an informal, multigenerational network of kin and friends during adolescence.

- The cumulative number of chronic stressful life events experienced during childhood and adolescence was not great.

Characteristics of the Community

In general, children from poor communities are more likely to suffer from developmental difficulties than are children from affluent communities (Rutter, 1987). The ecological circumstances in which children live also seem to make a difference in the likelihood that they will develop problems. Those who live in poor inner-city neighborhoods have a significantly higher risk of developing a psychological disorder than do those who live in relatively poor small towns or rural areas (Lavik, 1977).

One factor found to reduce the impact of negative community characteristics is the strength of social support networks provided by kin and social service agencies (Furstenberg & Crawford, 1978; Crockenberg, 1985). For example, Susan Crockenberg found that community-based social support services for parents provided by the National Health Service in England significantly increased the amount and quality of teenage mothers' interactions with their infants. These mothers behaved in ways predictive of healthier developmental outcomes according to the criteria described earlier in the chapter (p. 246).

At present, little is known about the factors outside the home that help to buffer children from stressful and depriving life circumstances. One factor that seems to make a difference is the school. Children from disadvantaged and discordant homes are less likely to develop psychological problems if they attended schools that have attentive personnel and good academic records (Rutter, 1987).

Characteristics of the Child

Temperamental disposition can be considered a factor "in" the child insofar as temperamental variations are strongly influenced by genetic factors (Goldsmith & Campos, 1982; Plomin, 1982). By itself, no single temperamental trait evident in infancy, such as level of activity or distractibility, has been shown to predict adult psychological adjustment. However, young adults who suffer from psychiatric disorders are likely to differ from psychologically healthy adults in their temperamental profiles as infants, according to the findings of a longitudinal study by Alexander Thomas and Stella Chess (1984). These researchers report that infants characterized as "difficult"—those who display traits that include irregularity of biological functions, negative responses to new situations and people, and frequent negative moods—are more likely to experience psychological problems as adults.

On the basis of records provided by health, mental health, and social service agencies and educational institutions, as well as personal interviews and personality tests, Emmie Werner and Ruth Smith (1982) report complementary results from their study of disadvantaged Hawaiian children. They found that the children who were able to cope best with their life circumstances during their first two decades were those described by their mothers as "very active" and "socially responsive" when they were infants. The mothers' reports were verified by independent observers, who noted that these children displayed "pronounced autonomy" and a "positive social orientation." When they were examined during their second year of life, these children scored especially well on a variety of tests, including measures of motor and language development.

Transactional Models of Development

Although the evidence about developmental risk shows that several different factors may lead to long-term developmental damage, it also shows that to consider any one factor in isolation from the others would be a mistake. The various influences on development seem to work in combination. One study, for example, found that infants characterized as "difficult" were more likely to suffer developmental problems when there was discord between their parents and other stresses acting on the family than were children who were characterized as "easy" (Graham, Rutter, & George, 1973). The researchers suggest that temperamentally "difficult" children draw a lot of flak from their families during periods of stress, making their already difficult situation worse, whereas "easy" children are able to stay out of the line of fire. Alternatively, "easy" children may simply fail to become upset by such experiences as family disputes that severely affect "difficult" children.

In recent years, several researchers have developed models that emphasize the interplay among the factors that may influence development (Clarke & Clarke, 1986; Sameroff & Chandler, 1975). These **transactional models** trace the ways in which the characteristics of the child and the characteristics of the child's environment interact *across time* to determine developmental outcomes.

Thomas and Chess (1984) used a transactional model to explain the developmental implications of early temperamental patterns. The following example focuses on how the influence of a child's temperamental traits on development depends on the way those traits are interpreted by the child's parents.

One girl had severe [neurotic] symptoms starting in her preschool years. She was temperamentally a difficult child, and her father responded with rigid demands for quick, positive adaptation and hostile criticisms and punishment when the girl could not meet his expectations. The mother was intimidated by both her husband and daughter and was vacillating and anxious in her handling of the child. With this extremely negative parent-child interaction, the girl's symptoms grew worse. Psychotherapy was instituted, with only modest improvement. But when she was 9-10 years of age, the girl blossomed forth with musical and dramatic talent, which brought her favorable attention and praise from teachers and other parents. This talent also ranked high in her parents' own hierarchy of desirable attributes. Her father now began to see his daughter's intense and explosive personality not as a sign of a "rotten kid," his previous label for her, but as evidence of a budding artist. He began to make allowances for her "artistic temperament," and with this the mother was able to relax and relate positively to her daughter. The girl was allowed to adapt at her own pace, and by adolescence all evidence of her neurotic symptoms and functioning had disappeared. (p. 7)

Rutter and his colleagues used a transactional model to explain the range of mothering behaviors among young women who had spent significant parts of their infancy and childhood in childcare facilities (Quinton & Rutter, 1985; Rutter, 1985). As youngsters, these women had been placed in institutions because their parents could not cope with child rearing, not because they had any behavioral problems. Many of them remained in institutions throughout their infancy and early childhood. When they were 21 to 27 years old, these women were compared with a group of young women of the same age from the same part of London. The "ex-care" women were found to have experienced a number of difficulties that were not shared by the comparison group. To begin with, 42 percent had become pregnant before the age of 19 years, and 39 percent of them were no longer living with the biological father of their children. One-third had experienced a relatively serious breakdown in their care of their own children. Only 5 percent of the women in the comparison group had become pregnant by the age of 19, all were living with the biological father of their children, and none had experienced a serious breakdown in the care of their children. When the women's current parenting practices were studied, the "ex-care" women were far more likely to receive poor ratings than were the women in the comparison group (see Table 8.2).

At first, these results may appear to be a straightforward example of the long-term effects of early misfortune. But looked at in terms of a transactional model, it becomes clear that the early misfortune set in mo-

TABLE 8.2 Child-care behaviors of mothers raised in institutions versus a comparison group of mothers

Child-care Difficulty	Ex-care Group ($n = 40$)	Comparison Group ($n = 43$)
Lack of expression of warmth to children	45%	19%
Insensitivity	65%	28%
Lack of play with children	33%	16%
At least two of the above	59%	23%

SOURCE: Quinton & Rutter, 1984.

tion a series of events that tended to perpetuate the early difficulty. Institutional care led first to the lack of strong attachments during infancy and childhood. This led to an increased likelihood of teenage pregnancy. The early pregnancy led to reduced likelihood of obtaining further education or job training. The ensuing economic pressures created a disadvantaged environment, which in turn created the stresses that were the immediate cause of poor parenting.

Early institutionalization did not necessarily lead to continual misfortune, however. Those women raised in institutions who had supportive husbands were found to be just as effective at parenting as were the women from the comparison group. These positive results led the researchers to conclude that institutionalization during infancy and childhood and the lack of strong personal attachments that goes with it do not necessarily doom women to become poor mothers. If the usual chain of consequences can be broken and favorable transactions can be established, normal behavior is likely to follow.

RECOVERY FROM DEPRIVATION

The mounting evidence that the long-term consequences of early social or intellectual deprivation depend to a significant degree upon later circumstances has spurred a search for principles of successful intervention. A key element in any effort to repair developmental damage is a change in the child's environment, but such a change alone is not sufficient. When the children from the creche in Lebanon were moved to different institutions, they did not reach normal levels of development. The girls showed virtually no improvement, and although the boys showed significant recovery, it was by no means complete. Similarly, when Genie was removed from her isolation, she recovered to some degree, but not to a level considered normal for her age.

These findings raise questions about what conditions are necessary to foster recovery from early deprivation. Would the Lebanese girls have recovered as much as the boys if they had been placed in an institution with a more stimulating environment? Might the boys from the creche have gained totally normal func-

tioning, like the twins described by Koluchová, if they had been treated even better? And what about Genie? Is it possible that some as yet undiscovered environmental conditions might have allowed her to regain normal functioning? Or did her isolation start too early and last too long for her ever to recover completely?

Such questions are impossible to answer completely because human babies cannot deliberately be forced to live in potentially damaging circumstances to satisfy the quest for scientific knowledge. However, research with monkeys, combined with scattered studies of human subjects, suggests what some of the factors that can facilitate recovery from early deprivation might be.

Harlow's Monkeys Revisited

In Chapter 7, we examined Harry Harlow's studies of infant monkeys raised in isolation with inanimate surrogate mothers. One of the important findings of that research was the difficulty the infant monkeys, even those who became attached to the terry cloth mothers, had developing normal social relations once they were introduced into cages with their peers. Harlow and his colleagues discovered that the severity of the behavioral disruption displayed by these monkeys depended upon both the duration of their isolation and the age at which it began (Suomi & Harlow, 1972). Monkeys who were totally isolated for the first 3 months of life, for example, did not seem to be permanently affected by the experience. When they were moved to a group cage, they were initially overwhelmed by the more complex environment, but within a month they had become accepted members of the social group.

When monkeys who were totally isolated for their first 6 months of life were placed in a cage with other monkeys, they rocked, bit, or scratched themselves compulsively. However, if the monkeys were isolated for the *second* 6 months of life, they became aggressive and fearful when put back with other monkeys.

The long-term behavior of monkeys isolated at birth or after 6 months also differed. Those who were isolated after 6 months of social interaction in the colony recovered quickly and were able to mate normally when they came of age. But those isolated for 6 months starting at birth recovered only partially and proved incapable of normal sexual behavior at 3 years of age, when they should have been able to mate:

Isolates may grasp other monkeys of either sex by the head and thrust aimlessly, a semi-erotic exercise without amorous achievement. Another erotic genuflection is that of grasping at another monkey, male or female, at the midline and thrusting across their bodies. This exercise leaves the early totally isolated monkey working at cross-purposes with reality. (Harlow & Novak, 1973, p. 468)

Total isolation for the entire first year of life produced full-fledged social misfits who showed no propensities for social play or social interchanges (Harlow & Novak, 1973). When placed in a group cage, these monkeys were often the targets of aggression by their peers. They showed no signs of spontaneous recovery.

Recovery from the Effects of Isolation

Initially, Harlow and his associates felt their observations of the effects of isolation suggested that birth to 6 months of age might be a critical period for social development in these monkeys. If this were true, recovery would be impossible for monkeys isolated for this period regardless of any subsequent changes in their environment. The researchers tried various ways of aiding the adaptation of such monkeys to their new social world. One technique they used was to punish the monkeys for inappropriate behaviors by administering a mildly painful shock. Another approach was to introduce changes slowly, based on the assumption that an abrupt change from total isolation to the busy environment of the group cage induced an "emergence trauma" that blocked recovery. All these efforts were basically ineffective, which seemed to support the idea that there was a critical period for social development. As it turned out, such was not the case at all.

The first hint that there might be an effective therapy for these monkeys came from observations of the maternal behaviors of the females, who had been artificially inseminated (Suomi, Harlow, & McKinney, 1972). The babies were often beaten and sat on by their mothers. Few lived through it. However, *if* their babies managed to survive, the mothers began to recover. Watching the babies with their mothers suggested to the researchers how this change came about. If the baby monkeys could manage to cling to their mother's chest, which is what newborn infant mon-

This mature female monkey, who was isolated for the first 6 months of life, finds it difficult to react to the baby monkey. But if the baby is sufficiently persistent in its attempts to interact, the older monkey may eventually learn to interact more or less normally with it.

keys normally do, they survived. While clinging, they not only had access to life-sustaining milk, but they could also usually escape their mothers' attempts to harm them. The longer they held on and the stronger they grew, the more time their mothers spent behaving in ways that were approximately normal, if not loving. By the end of the usual period of nursing, the mothers were no longer abusive and interacted more or less normally with their babies. Even more striking was the caretaking behavior of these mothers when they had a second baby. It was indistinguishable from that of their nondeprived peers. They had recovered normal social functioning.

Based on the recovery of these mothers, Harlow and his colleagues speculated that it might be possible to reverse the social pathologies of previously isolated monkeys if a pattern of dependence similar to that between mother and infant could be set up (Harlow & Novak, 1973; Suomi & Harlow, 1972). The researchers introduced 2- to 3-month-old monkeys, who were strong enough to survive the abuse they were likely to receive, into a cage with monkeys who had been isolated for 12 months. The immature, playful, love-hungry babies provided just what the older monkeys needed to learn appropriate social behaviors. Over a period of 18 weeks, the former isolates gradually stopped rocking and clasping themselves compulsively. They began to move around more, to explore their environments, and to engage in social play. In the end, all of the former isolates became so well adjusted that even experienced researchers could seldom differentiate between them and monkeys who had been raised normally.

Implications for Human Recovery

Harlow's research with monkeys suggests that placing previously isolated children in an environment in which they can interact with younger children may be therapeutic. This idea seems to be supported by the limited information available about the recovery of human children from extreme social deprivation. For example, when the twins Koluchová (1972, 1976) studied were removed from their isolation, they were at first placed in a special environment in which they lived with younger children. The twins recovered normal functioning despite their years of isolation.

Wyndol Furman, Donald Rahe, and Willard Hartup (1979) formally tested the therapeutic potential of interactions with younger children. Through observations in day-care centers, the researchers identified 24 children between the ages of 2½ and 5 years who interacted so little with their peers that they were judged to be "socially isolated." These children were randomly assigned to three groups of eight children each. The first group participated in one-on-one play sessions with children 1 to 1½ years old. The second participated in play sessions with children their own age. The final group served as a control and received no special treatment. There were 10 play sessions, lasting 20 minutes, over a 6-week period. During each session, the two children were placed together in a room in which there were blocks, puppets, clothes to dress up in, and other toys that might promote positive social interaction. An observer sitting in the corner of the room took notes but otherwise tried not to interfere with the children.

Following the play sessions, observers who did not know which children had participated in the study rated the social interactions of all the children in the day-care classrooms. The researchers found that the

This baby monkey is "comforting" an older monkey raised in isolation.

level of peer interaction of the group of socially isolated children who had played with the younger children almost doubled. Those who had played with age mates showed some improvement, but they did not differ statistically from the control group. Despite the relatively brief treatment period, these results show that interactions with younger children can be therapeutic in reducing social isolation.

Such evidence of successful therapeutic interventions suggests the intriguing possibility that many of the instances in which recovery does not occur reflect the psychologist's inability to arrange the proper environment rather than an irreversible change that has occurred *in* the child. The best environment for a formerly deprived or isolated child is not necessarily one in which only one or two concerned adults are present. Adults ordinarily have limited time to spend with children, and they may not provide the special forms of attention and playfulness that will allow deprived children to reorganize their patterns of social interaction.

THE PRIMACY OF INFANCY RECONSIDERED

The significant recovery of both young animals and children who have experienced extreme isolation or have lived in deprived environments means that practitioners cannot write off such a child; rather, a concerted effort should be made to create as therapeutic an environment as possible when a change in the child's circumstances becomes possible. However, it would be incorrect to conclude that experiences during infancy, especially those that are abnormal for the society in which they occur, have no detectable effects on later development. Even in those studies reviewed in this chapter that show remarkable recovery from potentially damaging experiences, there is evidence that scars remain. For example, the children in Dennis's study who were adopted after infancy continued to exhibit somewhat depressed levels of intellectual ability and the institutionalized children who were adopted in the studies of Tizard and her colleagues continued to display problems in social adjustment at school.

In attempting to arrive at an overall conclusion concerning the primacy of infancy, it is useful to think more deeply about the proverb "As the twig is bent, so grows the tree," mentioned at the beginning of the chapter. If forces in the environment bend a sapling long enough, the tree may become so bent to the ground that its leaves cannot get light, which means that it will fail to flower and reproduce. But if the forces bending the tree cease or if a gardener stakes the tree upright, the only lasting effect may be a slight bend in the trunk. The tree will flower and reproduce.

In applying this analogy to humans, we must take into account three factors that may attenuate the role of infant experiences on later development. The first, which this chapter has focused on, is changes in the environment. Whether these changes involve providing day care for the children of working mothers, a war, severe economic depression, or the death of a parent, they may create discontinuities in children's experiences that will set them on a new path of development.

The second, which was the focus of Chapter 7, is the organization of physical and psychological functions into qualitatively new patterns as infancy comes to completion. In the case of human babies (but not twigs!) such factors as the acquisition of language, new cognitive capacities, and a new relationship to the social world at the end of infancy result in a new way of dealing with the world. Hence, a 12-month-old who is easily frustrated when she cannot get her own way may become a placid preschooler once she has learned to

When single parents marry, conditions of development for their children undergo a significant change.

speak because she has acquired the ability to coordinate with her surroundings on her own terms. Alternatively, a placid baby who seems to take little interest in objects may suddenly display enormous curiosity and energy once he begins to walk.

The third factor is the changes in the way children experience their environments as a result of their increased capacities. For example, the separation anxiety shown by a 1-year-old when the caretaker is not present may be a realistic response for a helpless, relatively immobile infant because of the loss of crucial support that such separation entails. But 3-year-olds, who have a greater sense of autonomy because they can talk, walk, and run, are less dependent on their caretaker. Consequently, an experience that has a big effect on a 1-year-old will not affect a 3-year-old in the same way.

In recognition of the complicated interplay among the developing capacities of the child, the changes these capacities bring about in the way the environment is experienced, and changes in the environment itself, psychologists who study the effects of infant experience focus on the *degree* of discontinuity between infancy and later periods, the identification of significant threads of continuity, and the mechanisms by which characteristics evident in early life are transformed or preserved in the transition from infancy to early childhood. The following examples will illustrate some of the areas of psychological functioning that are currently at the heart of these inquiries.

Attachment

In research on the long-term consequences of the different patterns of attachment, the basic strategy is to assess children's attachment just before their first birthday and then again several years later (Bretherton & Waters, 1985). The evidence concerning later developmental outcomes is mixed. Using this research strategy, Leah Matas, Richard Arend, and Alan Sroufe (1978) found evidence that securely attached infants cooperate with their mothers in a difficult problem-solving task at the age of 2 years more effectively than children who manifest either anxious/avoidant or anxious/resistant attachment patterns. Babies who are securely attached also achieve higher scores on a scale of infant development (Main, 1973). Furthermore, they are more curious and play more effectively with their age mates when they are $3\frac{1}{2}$ years old (Erikson, Sroufe, & Egeland, 1985; Waters, Wippman, & Sroufe, 1979).

On the negative side, John Bates, Christine Maslin, and Karen Frankel (1985) failed to find a relation between attachment behavior in the "strange situation" at 12 months and behavior problems at 3 years. Even studies that have found a general relationship between insecure attachment and later behavior problems report significant numbers of exceptions (Erikson, Sroufe, & Egeland, 1985). These inconsistencies in the conclusions of different studies mirror complexities of predicting development in general.

Researchers who believe that patterns of attachment tend to remain consistent throughout development, as Freud suggested early in this century (see Chapter 7, p. 227), emphasize that children's attachment to their primary caretaker serves as the model for all later relationships. Inge Bretherton (1985), drawing on an earlier formulation by Bowlby (1969), has proposed that infants build up an *internal working model* of the way to behave toward other people. They then use this model to figure out what to do each time they enter a new situation. As long as the people with whom children interact behave in ways that allow them to apply their internal working model effectively, continuity in the way the children relate to others is to be expected.

In Chapter 7, (p. 232), we saw that anxious/resistant children tend to cling to their mothers. Suppose that we observe such children in a preschool setting. According to Sroufe and Fleeson (1986), the children will attempt to recapitulate the forms of interaction that are typical in the home or, in Bretherton's terms, to apply their internal working models. We would therefore expect these children to try to stay close to the teacher. If the teacher sees these children as polite, cooperative, and eager to learn, their internal working models are likely to be effective. Thus, their patterns of interaction are likely to continue and may even be reinforced by the teacher. However, suppose the teacher is concerned about the dependent aspects of the children's behavior. She might arrange for them to act as helpmates to younger, shyer children, thereby providing them with the experience of a new form of social interaction. As a result, the children's internal working models might change and their subsequent interactions with others might be discontinuous with their previous patterns.

The preceding example illustrates both how internal working models of relationships can produce continuity in social interactions over time and why it is difficult to predict whether infants' patterns of interaction will be maintained in later life. The degree of continuity depends upon both the nature of the initial internal working model and the extent to which it is adaptive in the many contexts children find themselves in later in life.

Psychological Functioning

Conflicting evidence from research on the predictive reliability of measures of infant psychological functioning (such as those discussed in Chapter 4, p. 115) illustrate the difficulty in specifying whether or not the patterns of functioning of infants will be maintained in later childhood. Evidence for the *dis*continuity of psychological functioning comes from studies showing that scores on infant developmental scales do not correlate highly with scores on childhood scales that are designed to tap the same functions. After reviewing many of these studies, Claire Kopp and Robert McCall (1982) reached the unequivocal conclusion that "Tests given during the first 18 months of life do not predict childhood IQ to any useful or interesting degree" (p.

35). Prediction from standardized psychological tests improves markedly after 24 months of age. Still, tests given at 3, 4, and 5 years of age are not sufficiently predictive of children's subsequent behavior to be useful unless their functioning deviates a great deal from the norm (McCall, 1981; Sameroff, 1978).

One objection to basing conclusions about developmental discontinuity on measures of infant psychological functioning is the suspicion that tests given in infancy do not in fact tap the same psychological processes as those given in childhood. Some psychologists argue that it is possible to demonstrate a modest degree of continuity from infancy into childhood when appropriate behaviors are sampled and are measured sensitively.

Support for continuity in the intellectual sphere comes from studies in which infants who habituate rapidly to repeated events and respond markedly when novel events subsequently occur have been found to display a number of characteristics that are associated with advanced intellectual development in early childhood. These children are, for instance, more likely to explore their environment rapidly, to play in relatively sophisticated ways, and to excel at various problem-solving and concept-formation tasks (Bornstein & Sigman, 1986).

Additional evidence of continuity comes from studies of temperament. Infants who respond in a frustrated and angry way when their sucking is interrupted are likely to become aggressive or upset whenever their activity is blocked as nursery school students (Bell, Weller, & Waldrop, 1971). Similarly, babies who become inhibited in novel circumstances are likely to be fearful when they enter nursery school (Kagan, Reznick, Clarke, Snidman, & Garcia-Coll, 1984).

Although such studies imply that there are significant continuities between infancy and later developmental periods, they do not imply total continuity. The correlations they produce are very modest in magnitude. Consequently, data showing marked recovery from early traumatic conditions (which suggest that there can be marked changes, or discontinuities, in psychological functioning following infancy) and data showing a moderate correlation in individual behavioral traits over time (which implies continuity of functioning) should not be seen as contradictory. Both provide evidence of the simultaneous existence of continuities and discontinuities in children's development.

Coming to Terms with Limited Predictability

Many years ago, Sigmund Freud pointed out that whether development seems continuous and predictable or discontinuous and uncertain depends to a certain extent on one's vantage point:

> So long as we trace the development [of a psychological process] from its final stage backwards, the connection appears continuous, and we feel we have gained an insight which is completely satisfactory or even exhaustive. But if we proceed the reverse way, if we start from the premises inferred from the analysis and try to follow these up to the final result, then we no longer get the impression of an inevitable sequence of events which could not be otherwise determined. We notice at once that there might have been another result. . . . (1920/1924, p. 226)

Figure 8.2 is a schematic representation of Freud's insight. If we start at some point in the future, E, and trace a life history back to its beginnings, A, we can

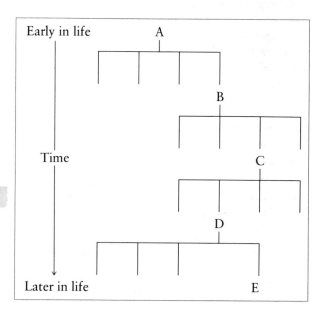

FIGURE 8.2 *It is relatively easy to trace development backwards to its origins. But the many decision points with uncertain outcomes that confront organisms during the lifespan defeat the precise prediction of their futures. (Adapted from: Emde, Gaensbauer, & Harmon, 1976).*

build a convincing case for why that precise life history proceeded as it did. At each decision point, we can sort out the various contributing factors and discern which had the most influence. Only one route leads into the past at each point. But standing at the beginning, A, and looking ahead to the future, we cannot foresee the choices that will be made at points B, C, and D. To borrow Robert Frost's metaphor, the bends in the diverging roads are hidden in the undergrowth.

For parents, the uncertainties of development during infancy are a natural source of anxiety. However, research on primacy shows us that this uncertainty has its good side. A perfectly predictable future holds no possibility of choice. Without the uncertainties that arise from changes in the environment and the changes in the child that accompany development, parents could not dream about influencing the course of their baby's future. It would be immutable. With these uncertainties come the possibility and the challenge of taking advantage of those changes to promote the child's welfare.

SUMMARY

1. There is widespread belief in the primacy of infancy in shaping later behavior.

2. Fostering optimal development in the sense of keeping as many doors open as possible for the child's future requires that the caretaker be sensitive and responsive to the infant's needs and signals. The amounts of sensitivity and responsiveness that are optimal in child rearing and the way they are expressed depend on the historical and cultural circumstances into which the child is born.

3. Evidence does not support the belief that parental responsiveness to infant's cries will spoil the child and cause unrealistic expectations that will result in antisocial behavior at a later time.

4. Paying too little attention to infants can result in *learned helplessness*, a state of mind that occurs when children believe that what they do does not matter. As a result of learned helplessness, babies will fail to take initiative on their own behalf.

5. Separation from parents is upsetting to babies. However, such separations have long-term negative consequences only when they are of long duration or are repeated.

6. The consequences of the short daily separations that result from out-of-home care during the first year of life are in dispute.

7. Extended residence in a poorly staffed orphanage retards both mental and social development. Residence in a well-staffed orphanage produces less pronounced developmental difficulties. The degree of recovery from such experiences depends on the subsequent environments of the children and the age at which they leave the institution.

8. Total isolation leads to severe mental and social retardation. If children are moved to a supportive environment before they are 6 or 7 years old, recovery is sometimes possible. If a change in circumstances is not brought about until adolescence, full recovery appears impossible.

9. Children raised in families in which there is a combination of high levels of discord, parental social deviance, or poverty and that live in communities in which the school environment is poor are at risk for later psychiatric disorders.

10. Children's vulnerability to stressful circumstances can be modified by:

   a. Variations in temperament
   b. Such family factors as the number of siblings, maternal workload, and the presence of a network of kin and friends
   c. Community characteristics, such as whether the neighborhood is in an urban slum or a rural area
   d. The quality of the local school

11. The processes that lead to various developmental outcomes can be thought of as transactions between child and environment that occur over extended periods of time.

12. Studies of monkeys suggest that recovery from early isolation can be accomplished later than previously thought possible if an adequate therapeutic environment can be arranged. Research has shown that similar principles can be applied to socially isolated children.

13. Discontinuities in psychological functioning between infancy and later ages limit the degree to which the psychological characteristics of older children and adults can be predicted from their characteristics as infants.

KEY TERMS

Learned helplessness   Primacy   Transactional models

SUGGESTED READINGS

CHESS, STELLA, and **ALEXANDER THOMAS.** *Origins and Evolution of Behavior Disorders: From Infancy to Early Adulthood.* Cambridge, Mass.: Harvard University Press, 1987.

A comprehensive summary of one of the major longitudinal studies of developmental changes in personality. Rich clinical case studies provide excellent illustrations of the transactions between the individual and the environment that regulate continuities and discontinuities in development.

CLARKE, ANN M., and **A. D. B. CLARKE.** *Early Experience: Myth and Evidence.* London: Open Books, 1976.

This important compendium of articles about the effects of early experience brings together a variety of evidence showing that even very severe forms of early deprivation may be overcome when environmental circumstances are changed.

CURTISS, SUSAN. *Genie: A Psycholinguistic Study of a Modern-Day "Wild Child."* New York: Academic Press, 1977.

The amazing case study of a child isolated from normal human contact for many years. It provides very

thought-provoking evidence about the limits of human plasticity and the role of the environment in development.

EMDE, ROBERT, and **ROBERT HARMON.** *Continuities and Discontinuities in Development.* New York: Plenum Press, 1984.

A wide-ranging discussion of the theoretical and methodological problems in specifying continuities and discontinuities in behavior. The contributors differ both in the specific phenomena they study and in the theories they favor and thereby provide a realistic picture of the difficulties involved in resolving this basic issue of developmental psychology.

KAGAN, JEROME. *The Nature of the Child.* New York: Basic Books, 1984.

Kagan, who has conducted several influential studies of developmental continuity and discontinuity, surveys recent research in the field. His discussion of "connectedness" in Chapter 3 is especially relevant to the themes of this chapter.

NICOL, A. R. *Longitudinal Studies in Child Psychology and Psychiatry: Practical Lessons from Research Experience.* New York: Wiley, 1985.

Evaluation of the long-term effects of infant experience generally require longitudinal research design. This collection of essays provides insights into the practice and pitfalls of longitudinal research applied to many of the issues raised in this and preceding chapters.

RUTTER, MICHAEL. *The Qualities of Mothering: Maternal Deprivation Reassessed.* New York: Aronson, 1974.

A British psychiatrist surveys research on the relationship between maternal behavior and child development. Particular emphasis is placed on problems associated with multiple caregivers, the role of the father, and the long-term consequences of various modes of child rearing.

WERNER, EMMIE E., and RUTH S. SMITH. *Vulnerable but Invincible: A Longitudinal Study of Resilient Children and Youth.* New York: McGraw Hill, 1982.

An important longitudinal study that tracked the development of a large sample of children from the Hawaiian island of Kauai. This research illustrates the strength of longitudinal methods for addressing basic issues of developmental theory and for providing realistic data upon which social policies affecting children can be based.

III

...

Early Childhood

By the age of 2½ or 3, children are clearly infants no longer. As they enter early childhood — the period between 2½ and 6 — they lose their baby fat, their legs grow longer and thinner, and they move around the world with a great deal more confidence than they did only 6 months earlier. Preschoolers (we will use this term for convenience, although many of the world's children never go to school) can usually ride a tricycle, control their bowels, and put on their own clothes. They can get out of bed quietly on Sunday morning and turn on the TV to amuse themselves while their parents sleep late. They can go over to a friend's house to play and participate as flower girls or ringbearers at a wedding. Most 3-year-olds can talk an adult's ears off, but they are also an avid audience when an interesting story is being told. They can be bribed with promises of a later treat, but they won't necessarily accept the terms that are offered, and may try to negotiate for a treat now as well as later. They develop theories about *everything,* which they constantly test against the reality around them.

Despite their developing independence, 3-year-olds need assistance from adults and older siblings in many areas. They cannot hold a pencil properly, string a loom, or tie their shoes. They do not yet have the ability to concentrate for long periods of time without a great deal of support. As a result they often go off on tangents in their games, drawings, and conversations. One minute a 3-year-old might be mommy in a game of house; the next, Cinderella; and the next a little girl in a hurry to go to the toilet. Children at this time still understand relatively little about the world in which they live and have little control over it. Thus they are prey to fears of monsters, the dark, dogs, and other apparent threats. They combat their awareness of being small and powerless by wishful, magical thinking that turns a little boy afraid of dogs into a big, brave, gun-toting cowboy who dominates the block.

Developmental change during early childhood seems to go more slowly than during infancy. Whereas infancy lasts only 2½ years, early childhood lasts 3½ years, until the next bio-behavioral-social shift — to middle childhood, when children are given new social responsibilities and new freedoms. On the one hand, they must start formal schooling or contribute to the family economy; on the other hand, they are permitted to gather with their peers beyond the immediate control of adults. Developments in early childhood provide the essential preparation for the new demands and opportunities to come.

We have divided our presentation of early childhood development into four chapters. Chapter 9 examines the nature of language and its development. Once children begin to acquire language, they can experience the world in an entirely new way. Language is the medium through which their parents instruct them about their roles in the world, acceptable behavior, and their culture's assumptions about how the world works. Simultaneously, language enables children to ask questions, to explain their thoughts and desires, and to make more effective demands on the people around them.

Chapter 10 examines the characteristics of preschool thinking. Leading theories are compared for their ability to explain how preschool children can behave in a logical, self-possessed manner at one moment only to become fanciful and dependent the next. The chapter considers whether their apparently illogical behavior is the result of their lack of experience or is actually governed by its own special logic.

Chapter 11 considers the social development and personality formation of preschoolers: their ideas about themselves, the way they think about rules of proper behavior, and their relations with the people around them. The chapter focuses on the acquisition of sex roles and on children's changing abilities to get along with each other, particularly as they learn to balance their own desires with the demands of their social group.

With these general characteristics of preschool children's development as background, Chapter 12 addresses the influence of different contexts on preschoolers' development. The presentation begins with the family, where children first come to learn about who they are and what adults expect of them. Then we examine the influence of various other institutions in our culture that affect children, including day-care centers, preschools, and the media.

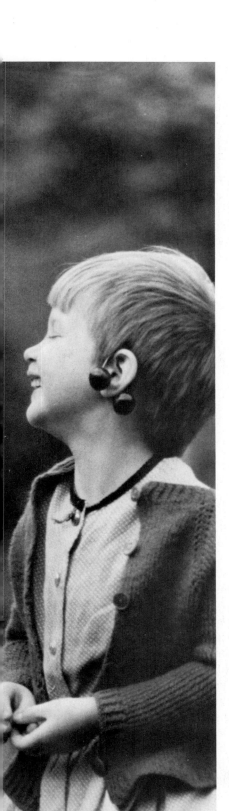

LANGUAGE ACQUISITION

A conversation between two 4-year-old children in a playroom:

Girl: [*on toy telephone*] David!
Boy: [*not picking up second phone*] I'm not home.
Girl: When you'll be back?
Boy: I'm not here already.
Girl: But *when will you be back?*
Boy: Don't you know if I'm gone already, I went *before* so I can't talk to you!

—George Miller, *Language and Speech*

• • •

The poet T. S. Eliot writes:

So here I am, in the middle way, having had twenty years—
Twenty years largely wasted, the years of *l'entre deux guerres*—
Trying to learn to use words, and every attempt
Is a wholly new start, and a different kind of failure
Because one has only learnt to get the better of words
For the thing one no longer has to say, or the way in which
One is no longer disposed to say it.

—"East Coker"

Both the real conversations of young children and the musings of a poet testify to the fact that learning to "say it right" is a lifelong process. As we have seen, precursors of language, such as the ability to distinguish among the different sounds of a language, to coo, and to babble, are evident in the first months after birth. The blossoming of language at the end of infancy, by which time children have accumulated a vocabulary of several hundred words and have begun to construct brief sentences, is a basic element in the bio-social-behavioral shift from infancy to early childhood. However, language development is by no means complete by age $2\frac{1}{2}$! An infant can express only very limited ideas and acquires new vocabulary at a relatively slow rate (McCall, 1979).

In the period between $2\frac{1}{2}$ and 6 years of age, however, children's mental and social lives are totally transformed by the explosive growth in their ability to use language. By the age of 6, children are estimated to be learning more than 15 words per day and their vocabularies have grown to anywhere between 8000 and 14,000 words (Smith, 1926; Carey, 1977). They can understand verbal instructions ("Go wash your face and don't come back until it's clean"), chatter excitedly about the tiger they saw at the zoo, and insult their sisters and brothers. Although linguistic nuances may take more time to acquire and vocabulary continues to grow, 6-year-old children have become competent language users, an achievement that transforms their mental processes and is essential to meeting the new responsibilities their society will assign them.

In this chapter we begin by examining the special properties of language in order to understand what it is that children must master. Then we look at the question of how children acquire language, the major milestones in their language-using capacity, and the relation of the development of language to children's social relations, as well as to their abilities to think.

THE PUZZLE OF LANGUAGE DEVELOPMENT

It is a strange fact that language, one of the most distinctive characteristics of our species, is still very poorly understood. *Linguists,* specialists in the study of language, can tell us a great deal about the structure of adult language, the history and meaning of different words, and the physical apparatus that transmits utterances from one person to another. But they have not been able to give definite answers to such basic questions as how children acquire language and how either children or adults produce and comprehend it. Two phenomena that are particularly difficult to explain are how children discover what words mean (the problem of reference) and how they learn to arrange words in comprehensible sequences (the problem of syntax).

The Problem of Reference

Perhaps the most common intuition about language is that words *refer.* They name real or fancied objects and relationships in the world. This idea seems so commonsensical that it is difficult to grasp the mystery it conceals, a mystery that no philosopher, linguist, or psychologist has ever been able to solve: How, among all the many things or relations to which any word or phrase might refer, do we ever learn to pick out its referent?

Figure 9.1 illustrates the problem of determining what a word refers to. Look at the picture and try to decide what the father is saying. Difficult, isn't it?

It might be objected that the example is unfair. The utterance is in a foreign language and we can't be certain what the father and son have been doing together previously. A little more reflection reveals that the example may be fair after all; in the beginning, all

"Smotri, sinockek, tam sidit ptitsa."

FIGURE 9.1 *For children just learning to talk, the problem of knowing what words refer to is particularly acute.*

languages are foreign to newborn children, who must somehow figure out that the sounds they hear are in fact meant to *refer* to something, to indicate an actual object or relation.

To make the case clearer, suppose that you know all of the words that the father says except one. For example, "Look, son, there sits a *ptitsa*." Even this additional information does not tell us which of the objects in the scene is a *ptitsa*. The cat sitting on the wall? The helicopter sitting on the building? Or the bird sitting on its nest? If you know Russian you know that the father is pointing at a bird. But the language-learning child, even the Russian language-learning child, is not born knowing the meaning of the sound package "ptitsa." Somehow the child must learn that when the father says "ptitsa" he is talking about the winged creature on the tree and not about any of the other objects.

The problem of how we come to know what words mean is further complicated by the fact that the same object can be referred to in a great many ways. The philosopher Gottlieb Frege (1960) provides a good illustration of the problem. On a clear morning we can look into the eastern sky and see a bright star, which we call the morning star. In the evening we can see the evening star. The morning star and the evening star are the same object, so the two names refer to the same thing. Yet we have no trouble believing that the words "morning star" and "evening star" do not have the same meaning. To make matters worse, the object is not a star at all: it's the planet Venus! Yet somehow, despite all the apparent confusion, children learn the meanings of "morning star" and "evening star."

The Problem of Syntax

When we combine words into a comprehensible sentence, the words must be related not only to objects and events but to one another. The rules that govern both the sequence of words in a sentence and the ordering of parts of words (prefixes such as *pre* begin words; suffixes such as *ing* end words) are called the **syntax** of a language.

One clear indicator that even children as young as $2\frac{1}{2}$ to 3 years old have some grasp of syntax comes from the errors they make when they string words together. When we hear a child make such statements as "Where Mommy is?" or "Mommy, Johnny camed

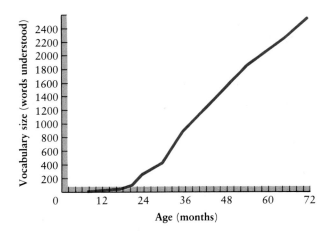

FIGURE 9.2 *Vocabulary growth as a function of age. The results of this early study of vocabulary growth show the rapid acceleration of development around 24 months of age. Estimates of actual vocabulary size vary depending on the techniques used to sample children's word knowledge, but the pattern of growth is impressive by all estimates. (From Smith, 1926)*

late" we know immediately that the child has confused one grammatical form with another. Such errors are so common that it is easy to overlook their significance. Children virtually never hear such incorrect sentences uttered; therefore they are unlikely to have learned them simply by imitating adult speech. How, then, do they learn to make such utterances?

No less impressive is the appearance in children's language of **recursion,** the ability to embed sentences within each other. Recursion is one of the central properties of syntax. It provides language with great economy and flexibility of expression. For example, the three sentences "The boy went to the beach," "He saw some fish," and "The boy got sunburned" can be easily combined to create "The boy who went to the beach saw some fish and got a sunburn": three sentences for the price of one. Only human communication exhibits this recursive capacity, and there is no evidence that it is ever consciously taught. How, then, do children develop it?

These examples illustrate the central puzzle of language acquisition. On the one hand, almost all children, even many who are mentally retarded, acquire the ability to speak and communicate with words, often at a phenomenal rate (see Figure 9.2), so language must be a fundamental human capacity. On the other hand, the complexity of language is so great that it is difficult to understand how word meanings could ever be formed or syntactic rules acquired.

Somehow, in the space of a very few years, children accomplish something denied the young of all other species. What do they do, and how do they manage to do it?

EXPLANATIONS OF LANGUAGE ACQUISITION

During much of the twentieth century, two widely divergent theories have organized most research on language acquisition. These theories correspond roughly to the polar positions on the sources of human development — nature versus nurture — discussed in Chapter 1. The *learning-theory* approach attributes language to "nurture"; it accords the leading role in language acquisition to children's environments, especially to the language environment and the teaching activities provided by adults. The *structural-innatist* approach attributes language acquisition largely to "nature"; it assumes that children are born ready to learn language, and that as they mature, their language-using capacity appears as naturally as walking or breathing, without the need for any special training.

In recent years, a third approach, the *interactionist*, has gained prominence. With language as with other areas of human development, interactionists emphasize that both nature and nurture play significant roles, stressing the relation between children's development of language and their overall mental development.

The Learning-Theory Explanation

The basic assumption of the learning-theory view is that a child's development of language is just like the development of other behaviors and conforms to the same laws of learning. According to this point of view, language acquisition depends on imitation and on learning by association through the mechanisms of classical and operant conditioning (Miller & Dollard, 1941; Skinner, 1957; Staats, 1968).

Classical conditioning As described in Chapter 5 (p. 159), classical conditioning begins when a pre-

viously neutral stimulus, which evokes no special response in a person, is paired with a stimulus that already causes a predictable reaction. After several pairings of the neutral and the "unconditional" stimulus, the response to the unconditional stimulus begins to occur in response to the previously neutral stimulus. The process is depicted in Figure 9.3 for the word "candy."

Upon first hearing the word "candy" a child cannot know what it means. But if the sound "candy" is reliably paired with a sweet taste, the child begins to associate the sound and the object, thereby learning part of what the sound "candy" means. According to learning theorists, the child grasps the meaning of "candy" as the sum of all the associations that the word evokes after having been paired to many different experiences (Mowrer, 1950).

Learning theorists use the classical conditioning model to account for how children learn to *understand* language, but this theory does not account for a child's ability to *produce* language. To explain this aspect of language acquisition, learning theorists point to the mechanism of operant conditioning.

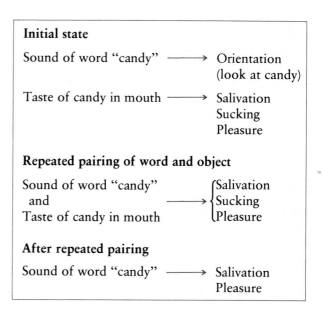

Initial state

Sound of word "candy" ⟶ Orientation (look at candy)

Taste of candy in mouth ⟶ Salivation Sucking Pleasure

Repeated pairing of word and object

Sound of word "candy" and ⟶ Salivation Sucking Taste of candy in mouth Pleasure

After repeated pairing

Sound of word "candy" ⟶ Salivation Pleasure

FIGURE 9.3 *The explanation of how word meaning is acquired through classical conditioning. After the word "candy" has been paired with the sight of candy and the taste of candy, the word "candy" begins to acquire the meaning "tastes good."*

Operant conditioning   The operant explanation begins with the observation, described in Chapter 5 (p. 162), that children emit a rich repertoire of sounds more or less at random during the early phases of babbling. These sounds represent the initial elements of spoken language, which are gradually shaped through reinforcement and refined through the child's practice. For example, a sound like "da" might be shaped into "dog," or "mo" might be shaped into "more" through a parent's praise and attention for the child's successively closer approximations to the sound of these words.

The process of language acquisition proposed by learning theorists applies to all societies at all times, but the particulars will differ from one language environment to another. An American child growing up in Boston will acquire a different way of pronouncing "Boston" ("Baaston") than a New Yorker ("Bawstin"). A Kpelle child growing up in West Africa will learn to be sensitive to the sound contour of words in order to pronounce the word *kali* with a rising tone on "a" to mean "hoe" and with a falling tone to mean "leopard"; while an American child, whose history of reinforcement has rendered rising and falling tones insignificant as meaning-bearing features, may not even hear the difference.

Imitation   It seems obvious that imitation is involved in language acquisition if only because children acquire the languages they hear around them, rather than inventing totally new languages that adults cannot understand. Moreover, modern research has shown that young children often learn to name things by hearing someone else name them and then repeating what they hear (Leonard, Chapman, Rowan, & Weiss, 1983). However, simple imitation does not appear to explain how children acquire complex patterns of syntax or the ability to express new ideas they have not previously heard. These complexities led Albert Bandura (1977; 1986), a leading learning theorist, to propose that language is acquired through a kind of imitation called **abstract modeling**. This kind of modeling is called abstract because, in Bandura's view, even when children imitate specific utterances, they abstract from them the general linguistic principles that underlie those utterances. Thus a child repeating "Juana walked home" abstracts the syntactic principle of adding *ed* to show past tense, and can then go on to say "Juana fixed the toy" without having to hear those exact words first.

A Structural-Innatist Explanation

The structural-innatist view of language acquisition has been dominated by the work of linguist Noam Chomsky (1965; 1975). In Chomsky's view, the fact that children produce sentences that they have never before heard makes it implausible that language could be acquired primarily through classical or operant conditioning. The fact that children's early original utterances often violate grammatical rules in a systematic way suggests to Chomsky that imitation of the kind Bandura described is likewise not crucial in language acquisition.

Chomsky proposes instead that the capacity to comprehend and generate language is innate, and that it is *not* like other human behaviors. Instead, he argues, the capacity to comprehend and generate language is more like a special human organ with its own structure and function.

Chomsky's strategy for discovering the nature of language and the conditions for its acquisition is to determine the grammatical rules common to many sentences despite variability from one utterance to the next. This restricted set of rules suggests the structure

Linguist Noam Chomsky, whose ideas about language have greatly influenced the study of language acquisition in recent decades.

of the language organ's innate capacities. For basic data, Chomsky uses the intuitions of native speakers about whether a sample sentence is grammatical or not. Of course, native speakers could not actually produce an entire language, which by definition consists of an infinite set of utterances. But native speakers can judge whether any given utterance is a legitimate part of their language because this ability is a basic part of every language user's competence. For example, an English speaker might or might not choose to *say* "Put the needles in the blue drawer" — this utterance is just one of an infinite number of sentences that can be spoken in English. However, any adult English speaker of average intelligence can say that "Put the needles in the blue drawer" is grammatical, while "Put the needles in the drawer blue" is not. No one teaches children *not* to choose this alternative word order (which, while not grammatical in English, would be perfectly acceptable in French or German); therefore, Chomsky reasons, they must have an innate capacity for grasping and using syntactical structures.

In line with the analogy of language-as-organ, Chomsky proposes that every child is born with a **"language acquisition device" (LAD)**, which Chomsky believes is programmed to recognize the universal rules that underlie any particular language that a child might hear. The LAD is like a genetic code for the acquisition of language. Although at birth the child's language is still in a completely primitive state, as the child matures and interacts with the environment, the LAD enables the child to acquire more complex language structures and eventually to develop the language-using abilities of adults.

A controversial aspect of Chomsky's view is the small role he ascribes to children's environment in the development of their language abilities. According to Chomsky, the essential structures that make language acquisition possible — the universals of grammar — are determined far more by the evolutionary history of the species than by the experiential history of particular children. Experience of language may be necessary, but according to Chomsky, this experience plays only a restricted role in shaping language. Experience does of course determine which of the many possible human languages a child actually acquires. A child without the experience of hearing Chinese spoken will not grow up speaking Chinese, even though he or she is genetically capable of learning this language. A child's experience of hearing a particular language also "triggers" his or her innate ability (LAD) to speak that

language. What the child's language experience does *not* do is to modify the way the LAD works once it is activated.

Interactionist Explanations

Interactionist approaches to language acquisition, like interactionist approaches to overall development, emphasize that higher levels of development emerge out of constructive interactions between innate and environmental factors (Bates, Benigni, Bretherton, Camioni, & Volterra, 1979; Bruner, 1983; Locke, 1980; Maratsos, 1983). Within this overall position, scholars differ over exactly how such interactions work.

According to the *cognitive hypothesis,* language grows out of the basic structures of sensorimotor thought as described by Piaget. For example, Elizabeth Bates and her colleagues claim that children develop three fundamental skills in the first two years of life, all of which combine to enable language development:

1. Conventionalized referential communication (the ability to point at an object in order to communicate something about that object)

2. Means-ends analysis (the ability to formulate goals and to develop more than one means to pursue them)

3. Delayed imitation (the ability to repeat actions experienced at earlier times or in other circumstances)

Bates and her colleagues believe that language acquisition is primarily a matter of learning how to "do things with words" rather than acquiring grammar. They treat the mastery of linguistic structures as a by-product of simply being able to use language to get things done.

To illustrate how complex structures such as grammar might arise from interactions that do not explicitly have the construction of those structures as their goal, Bates and Snyder (1987) point to the way in which bees build complex hives not out of direct intention but as a by-product of collecting and storing honey. As the individual bees deposit the wax that is carried in their heads, pushing their load up against the wax deposited by other bees, they create a honeycomb labyrinth made up of hexagonal cells. It might be tempting to assume that bees have a genetic predisposition to

A great deal of language learning takes place in contexts in which adults play an important role in structuring the activity.

make hexagons to carry out their hive-building functions. But in fact, as Bates and Snyder point out, hexagons are inevitably created whenever circles or spheres are packed together with pressure from all sides. That is, the hexagons emerge from the interaction between the bees and their environment, rather than being directly intended or predetermined.

Applying this same logic to linguistic structures, Bates and Snyder propose that grammatical structures are the inevitable result of "packing together" different people's communicative intentions within the highly constrained linguistic channel of language in such a way as to produce jointly usable communicative products.

A *cultural-context* version of the interactionist approach to language acquisition is offered by Jerome Bruner (1983), Andrew Locke (1980), and others who emphasize the role of adults in shaping the child's environment of communication. Bruner suggests that the manner in which adults structure the language input to children be considered a **"language acquisition support system"** (LASS), the necessary complement to Chomsky's LAD in the process of a child's acquisition of language. Locke (1980) titles his book *The Guided Reinvention of Language* in order to emphasize the two-sided nature of the process: each child

must reinvent language for himself or herself (i.e., language cannot simply be learned through memorizing principles), but this process is not a totally individual achievement because it must be guided by those who already know how to use language. Both Bruner's and Locke's proposals are similar in spirit to Vygotsky's idea of a "zone of proximal development" introduced in Chapter 6 (p. 202).

Theoretical Approaches Compared

Linguists and psychologists are still a long way from a complete theory of language acquisition. In addition to continuing uncertainties about the mechanisms by which children learn syntax, no existing theory offers an adequate solution to the problem of reference. Nor is there an account of all the important aspects of even one human language. (See Table 9.1 for a summary of the major theories of language acquisition.) Chomsky's structural theory, which currently enjoys great popularity, is strongest where the learning theory and interactional approaches are weakest; it provides a *formal* description of how syntax works. His view highlights the creative, generative nature of language because the LAD only constrains what language can

TABLE 9.1 Salient features of major approaches to language acquisition

Theory	Major Causal Factor	Mechanism	Major Phenomenon Explained
Learning	Environment	Imitation, conditioning	Word meaning
Structural–innatist	Heredity	Triggering	Syntax
Interactionist (cognitive hypothesis)	Interaction of social and biological	Assimilation–accommodation	Correlation of cognitive and linguistic developments
Interactionist (cultural-context approach)	Cultural mediation of social-biological interaction	Coordination in cultural scripts	Language–thought relationships

become, it does not cause language acquisition. However, Chomsky's approach provides almost no guidance for thinking about word meaning, the nature of the experiences necessary for language to be "triggered," or the role of other people in the overall process of language development, areas where learning theory and interactionist approaches have made more substantial contributions. (The current state of these controversies is presented in Piatelli-Palmerini, 1980; Wanner & Gleitman, 1982.)

Despite the absence of an overarching explanation, psychologists and linguists have learned a great deal about the process of language acquisition in recent decades. In the sections that follow we will review what is known about the development of major linguistic capacities. With this information as background we will return to examine the essential ingredients of language acquisition that the major theories describe.

FOUR SUBSYSTEMS OF LANGUAGE

Language, according to Webster's dictionary, is "the words, their pronunciation, and the methods of combining them used and understood by a considerable community." This definition identifies four central aspects of language: sounds, words, methods of combining words, and the communal uses that language serves. We will discuss the development of each of these aspects separately, but it is important to keep in mind the *systemic* nature of language: each of its different aspects is connected to all of the others, forming a unified, organic whole, and each aspect is itself made up of elements which constitute a distinctive subsystem.

Sounds

Evidence presented in Chapter 4 (p. 120) shows that newborn infants are sensitive to the sounds of human language and basic sound categories (DeCasper & Fifer, 1980; Eimas, 1985). Within a few months of birth they begin to produce a wide range of possible speech sounds in the gurgles and babbles that precede their first words (Chapter 6, p. 205) (Oller, 1978). These facts are important evidence that human children come into the world equipped to acquire language. From the beginning, however, the actual conditions of communication begin to select and shape children's further linguistic development.

Pronunciation In the change from babbling to pronouncing words late in the first year, children give up their relative freedom to play with sounds and begin to vocalize the particular sounds and sound sequences that make up words in their language community. This conformity to a restricted set of sounds brings with it both the ability to create meaningful distinctions between sounds and the freedom to speak rapidly. As adults, English speakers speak at an average rate of about 150 words per minute. The words they use contain an average of 5 *phones* (sounds) each. This means that adults can easily produce about $12\frac{1}{2}$ sounds per second, and with extra effort are capable of producing speech at rates as high as 25 to 30 sounds per second (Lieberman, 1984). According to Philip Lieberman, these rates would be impossible if the set of sounds and sound combinations were not organized, with permissible combinations drastically restricted. These same restrictions assist children in discovering the system of sounds in the language they hear.

It takes children several years to master the pronunciation of the separate sounds of their native language. Their first efforts may be no more than crude stabs at the right sound pattern, almost as if they are attempting to "get the tune right" at the same time that they are working on the words. One frequent simplification is to leave out parts of words ("ca" instead of "cat"). Multisyllable words are often turned into a repeating pattern. For example, a child might use the sound pattern "bubba" to say "button, butter, bubble," and "baby." A long word, such as "motorcycle," can come out sounding like most anything: "momo," "moto-kaka," or even "lomacity"!

Children's mastery of the sound system of their native language proceeds unevenly. Sometimes a particular sound will prove especially difficult, even after many words that employ that sound are well understood. For example, at the age of 2½ Alexander could not say /l/ sounds at the beginning of words, so he could not pronounce the name of his friend's dog, Lucky. Instead, he consistently pronounced the name "Yucky," much to the amusement of his family. This error didn't concern Alex at all; he knew who other people were talking about when they referred to Lucky, and Lucky didn't seem to notice any problem when Alex called him.

Neil Smith (1971) showed that such substitutions do not arise because children are incapable of pronouncing certain sounds. When he asked one young child to say the word "puddle" it came out as "puzzle," but when he asked for "puzzle" it became "puggle"! Another child would always say "fick" instead of "thick" but he had no difficulty in saying "thick" when he meant to say "sick." Both examples illustrate that the basic sounds of a language must be learned as part of the larger system into which they fit, rather than as isolated instances of pronunciation.

Sounds and Meaning Newborn children can evidently perceive the differences among the basic sounds, or phones, of their language. This does not mean, however, that *phonemes,* the categories of sound that are meaningful in a language, are "just there" at birth. It would be a mistake to believe that an English /l/ is only a sound-wave pattern that the child learns to reproduce by creating a particular mouth shape. In reality, /l/ is a phoneme (sound category) of English because in our language it contrasts with other phonemes like /y/ as part of meaningful words. We hear /l/ and /y/ as different *only* because they create different meanings: English speakers must learn that "lap" and "yap" or "lard" and "yard" are not simply pronunciation variations on a single word. Children's attention to the differences between sounds is not simply a mechanical skill, but develops along with children's growing understanding of the meaning of words.

The close connection between phonemes and meanings becomes clear when one is attempting to learn a foreign language. Native speakers of Spanish, for whom the difference between /b/ and /v/ does not correspond to a difference in word meaning, find it difficult to produce or to hear this difference. To native English speakers "boat" and "vote" sound quite different; to Spanish speakers, these two pronunciations sound the same and thus may be spoken interchangeably. Likewise, the English speaker frequently has difficulty hearing and producing the difference between the French "u" and "ou," because that difference does not exist in English.

Although it is often convenient to think of words as the basic units of meaning in language, many words contain more than one meaning-bearing part, or **morpheme**. A morpheme may be a whole word, or only a

Learning to make language sounds properly takes time and practice.

part of one. The word "implanted," for example, is made up of three morphemes. The root of the word is "plant," which means "to fix in place." The morpheme "im" is derived by rules of sound combination from the prefix "in," meaning "in, into, or toward," and the morpheme "ed" is a marker of past tense. We do not stop to ponder all of these relations when we say a sentence with the word "implanted" in it. In fact, until the rules are pointed out, we rarely stop to think about the parts of words or the way that we mold sounds (such as "in" to "im"). Yet every child must learn to decipher and reproduce just such intricate interweavings of sound and meaning.

Words

There is no difficulty in figuring out when children make their first sounds; a shrill cry at birth settles that question. More problematic is deciding when children first use not simply sounds, but actual words. Adults may be so anxious to claim the power of speech for their children that they discover "words" in early cooing and babbling. However, genuine words appear only late in the first year, after children have been babbling for some time and after the contours of their sounds have become gradually more speechlike (see Chapter 6).

In line with interactionist theories of language acquisition, the process of word formation is best thought of as a peculiar sort of collusion. Neither the adult nor the child *really* knows what the other is saying. Each tries to gather in a little meaning by supposing that the other's utterance fits a particular sound pattern that corresponds to a particular meaning. This joint effort, or collusion, may eventually result in something common, a word in a language that both can understand. This process may also fail. As the following examples make clear, the process can proceed in a number of different ways, depending upon how the parent interprets the relation between the child's sounds and actions.

At 8 months Pablo began to say "dahdee." This "first" word clearly did not mean "daddy," however, because Pablo used "dahdee" for commands and requests when daddy was nowhere to be seen. Adults interpreted "dahdee" to mean either "Take it from me" (when it was said while offering something to someone) or "Give it to me"; they ignored the fact that Pablo's first word sounded like *daddy*. At about the

age of 12 months, "dahdee" disappeared from Pablo's vocabulary (Shopen, 1980).

A different fate befell Brenan's first word, "whey." Around 1 year of age, Brenan began to say "whey" at the end of adult sentences. In this case, the adults had a ready interpretation that allowed them to incorporate the word into the way they spoke to Brenan. "Whey" not only sounded something like "why," it also came at a position in normal conversational turn-taking where "why" would be a possible (if not topically appropriate) thing to say. Brenan's parents therefore responded to "whey" as if Brenan had asked a question and rephrased what they had said in order to "answer his question," expanding on their original utterance. Over time, Brenan pronounced and used "whey" more and more like a true "why" until it became a genuine "why" in the English language (Griffin, 1983).

Many first words label familiar objects.

Yet another route to first word formation occurs in Samoa (Ochs, 1982). Samoan adults believe that once infants begin to walk, they become cheeky and willful. Consistent with this belief, the only word that Samoan parents acknowledge as a child's *first* word is "tae," which is a Samoan curse word meaning "shit." They explain this remarkable agreement among their children as confirmation for what every Samoan knows — that young children have defiant and angry characters. In fact, young Samoan children may make a number of sounds that *might* be interpreted as words, but Samoan adults choose to hear and acknowledge only "tae."

Each of these examples differs from the others in significant ways, but all share the characteristics of a process in which adults collude with each other and their children to create word meanings.

Words as mediators At some point, usually around 11 to 12 months of age, babies seem to discover that the sound sequences they make can recruit adult attention and help. What began as a process of sound matching that merely accompanied action becomes a process of sound production that anticipates, guides, and stimulates action. With the emergence of the capacity to use words, children acquire the ability to organize their activity in a new way.

This key feature of language is illustrated in observations that Elizabeth Bates made of a 13-month-old girl:

C. is seated in a corridor in front of the kitchen door. She looks toward her mother and calls with an acute sound *ha*. Mother comes over to her, and C. looks toward the kitchen, twisting her shoulders and upper body to do so. Mother carries her to the kitchen, and C. points toward the sink. Mother gives her a glass of water, and C. drinks it eagerly. (1976, p. 55)

Bates's example shows clearly that it is the relationship of the sound to action, and not just properties of the sound itself, that justifies the conclusion that a word has entered a person's vocabulary. Of course, in this case *ha*, the "word" in question, functions in a

These children are making clear the close connection between gestures and words.

very small community, the community of mother and child. Nonetheless, the child's use of it displays an important new ability. In order to use a communicative gesture or sound, the child shifts her orientation from the object of attention to another person. Instead of seeking to operate *directly* on the object (by, for example, attempting to toddle over to the sink), the child operates *indirectly* through an idiosyncratic sound that evokes the desired behavior from the mother.

In this and the remaining chapters of this book, we will refer to the property of language illustrated in Bates's example as the *mediated* character of language. Until words enter the organization of their activity, children's possibilities for operating on the world are restricted to *im-mediate*, or direct, actions. But with the advent of language, they can then act *in*-directly, in a *mediated* manner as well. The same principle applies to the way that children can be influenced by others; once they start to use words, children can be influenced by others both directly, via nonverbal actions, and indirectly, through the mediating power of words (see Figure 9.4).

Alexander Luria beautifully summarizes the new intellectual power that human beings obtain when their behavior begins to be mediated by words:

The enormous advantage is that their world doubles. In the absence of words, humans would have to deal only with those things which they could perceive and manipulate directly. With the help of language, they can deal with things which they have not perceived even indirectly and with things which were part of the experience of earlier generations. Thus, the word adds another dimension to the world of humans. . . . Animals have only one world, the world of objects and situations which can be perceived by the senses. Humans have a double world. (1981, p. 35)

The earliest vocabulary From the diaries kept by interested parents, we can obtain a fair picture of children's initial vocabulary. Katherine Nelson (1973) enlisted the aid of 18 families in keeping track of everything their infants said during the months they were acquiring their first words. She found that most early words (51%) are what she called **general nominals**—words that label things and classes of things at the same time—such as "doggie," "juice," or "ball." In the beginning, children may understand these labels only

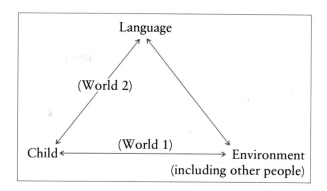

FIGURE 9.4 *Children experience the world in two distinctive ways once they acquire language: directly through their sensory contact with the physical environment (World 1); and indirectly (symbolically) through language (World 2).*

in a restricted way, as if orange juice was the only thing that qualified as juice. The next most common category (14 percent) of early words was **specific nominals**, such as "Mommy," "Daddy," and pet names; these nominals labeled particular objects, not categories of objects. Other important categories were action words ("bye-bye," "want"), modifiers ("dirty," "mine"), and personal-social words ("no," "yes," "please").

Nelson points out that the first words acquired are often closely linked to actions that the child can accomplish with the things named. "Hat" and "sock" are common in the initial vocabularies of American children, but "sweater" and "diapers" are not, perhaps because little children can act more or less effectively on hats and socks, but sweaters and diapers are "done to them." In addition, objects that can change and move (e.g., cars and animals) are likely to be named, whereas large, immobile objects like trees and houses are "just there" and are not likely to be named. First adjectives denote attributes that are transitory ("wet," "hot," "broken") or attributes that must be interpreted in reference to the things which they describe, such as "big" or "little" (Nelson, 1976). Children also tend to use words just at the moment when objects are changing and moving, suggesting a close link between words and actions in the young child's mind (Greenfield, 1982).

Early word meanings To understand the ways in which word meanings change during a child's development it is useful to think of words as *cultural objects*, patterns of sound—or visual patterns of print—that enable people to share each other's interpretation of the world around them. As cultural objects that mediate activity, words do not have unique or fixed meanings even for adults. The fact that words do not have unique references is illustrated by, for example, adults from different cultures discovering that they mean very different things by such terms as *freedom.* Moreover, the same principle applies even to people in the same culture and to common nouns. For example, "table" can refer to an article of furniture or to an abbreviated list. Nonetheless, the illusion that there is one word for each real-world referent remains strong. (See Jonathan Swift's satirical comment in Box 9.1.)

As the nature of children's activities gradually changes, the meanings they attribute to the words they use change correspondingly. Of course, the ambiguity inherent in words can never be completely eradicated, even for adults. But as children gain familiarity with the way that people around them use words, their own uses come to conform more and more to the general uses in their cultural group. The process of approximation occurs in two directions simultaneously: children narrow down the set of circumstances in which some words are used, while broadening the application of others (Kay & Anglin, 1982).

Overextensions Adults are amused when a 2-year-old wanders into a room full of adults and proceeds to name each of the men present "daddy." This form of mislabeling, in which many examples in a category are referred to by a single term that adults use to label only one of the examples, is called **overextension** (Rescorla, 1980).

Children's early overextensions appear to be strongly influenced by perceptual features of the items named as well as by the way that the things named function in children's actions (Clark, 1973). A word such as "kitty" may be extended to cover a wide variety of four-legged animals because of their common shape, or it might cover a variety of soft, furry objects because of their similar texture. (See Table 9.2.)

Underextensions Children also commit the error of **underextension,** using word meanings that are more restrictive than the adult usage. For example, the early meanings attributed to the word "animal" by American children are likely to be restricted to a small class of mammals. Young children may hotly deny that a lizard, a fish, or a mommy is an animal. They may also believe that "cat" applies only to their family's cat, not to cats in the neighborhood or on television.

Levels of abstraction In choosing how to refer to something, children must learn to deal with the fact that several words can be used to refer to the same object. In speaking of someone she sees at the supermarket, a child might point and say:

"Mommy, look at *Sally.*"

"Mommy, look at *that girl.*"

"Mommy, look at *her.*"

"Mommy, look at *that person.*"

Each of these methods of referring is equally accurate. But they are not each equally appropriate to the circumstances. If the girl being talked about is well known to the mother and daughter, it would be inappropriate to refer to her as "that person" or "that girl." It might be appropriate under some circumstances to

TABLE 9.2 Overextensions

Child's Word	First Referent	Extensions	Possible Common Property
Bird	Sparrows	Cow, dogs, cats, any moving animal	Movement
Mooi	Moon	Cakes, round marks on window, round shapes in books, tooling on leather book covers, postmarks, letter O	Shape
Fly	Fly	Specks of dirt, dust, all small insects, his own toes, crumbs, small toad	Size
Koko	Cock crowing	Tunes played on a violin, piano, accordion, phonograph, all music, merry-go-round	Sound
Wau-wau	Dogs	All animals, toy dog, soft slippers, picture of old man in furs	Texture

SOURCE: deVilliers & deVilliers, 1979.

refer to the girl as "her" instead of Sally, but to do so would change the meaning of the utterance. Children rapidly learn to distinguish among such nuances if the appropriate words are in their vocabularies.

An interesting characteristic of the early words that children say is that they tend to refer to objects at an intermediate level of abstraction. Only later do children acquire words that are at a higher or lower level of generality (Nelson, 1979). In terms of the adult **lexicon,** or basic store of words, these early vocabulary items classify the world into categories that are neither too big nor too small.

This point is illustrated by an experiment in which Jeremy Anglin (1977) showed children posters that contained four different pictures of objects that could be related at some level of abstraction and asked for a label that applied to the whole (see Figure 9.5). For example, one poster might have four pictures of roses, which could be labeled by the relatively specific category "roses;" another could have a rose, a daisy, a carnation, and a pansy, which could be labeled at the intermediate category of abstraction as "flowers;" while a third might have an elm, a rose, a rubber plant, and a cactus, which could be labeled at a higher level of abstraction as "plants." Anglin found that adults were able to vary the level of generality of their labels, as appropriate, whereas the children between the ages of 2 and 5 who were shown the posters tended to label all the sets at the same intermediate level of generality. They not only called the set containing the daisy, rose, carnation, and pansy "flowers," but they also called all four roses "flowers," and were unable to provide a single label for the four plants. Most 4- and 5-year-olds were able both to name specific flowers and to use the general term "plants," but they too tended to use the intermediate term "flowers" far more than the adults did. These same results were obtained with many other category hierarchies, such as food – fruit – apples and animals – dogs – collies.

Children's limitations in labeling specific objects and general categories do not mean that they fail to understand differences between objects. Even children who labeled all pictures of dogs and cats as "cat" in one study could still pick out the picture of the proper animal when asked to do so. (Fremgen & Fay, 1980).

The changing structure of the lexicon From what has been said above, it should be clear that the growth of children's lexicons involves more than a simple in-

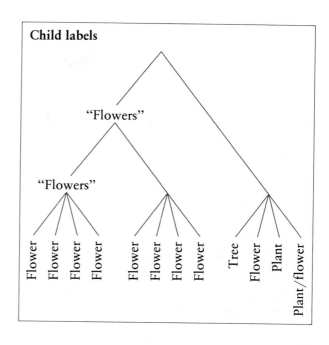

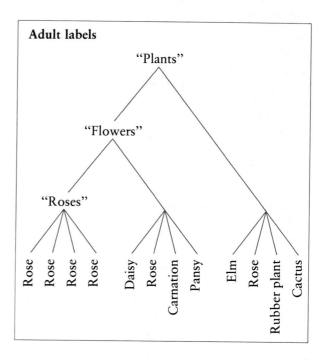

FIGURE 9.5 *Young children fail to differentiate levels of abstractness in the way they label sets of objects, using an intermediate level more frequently than adults. (Adapted from Anglin, 1977.)*

BOX 9.1

GULLIVER AMONG THE LAPUTANS

• • •

The commonsense idea that words can be identified only with things, and have fixed, unique meanings, is very difficult to overcome. In the following passage, Jonathan Swift highlights the absurdities to which such common sense leads. In the land of Laputa, the people have listened to their literal-minded philosophers too attentively. Swift's hero, Gulliver, tells us:

since Words are only names for *Things,* it would be more convenient for all Men to carry about them such *Things* as were necessary to express the particular Business they are to discourse on. . . . Many of the most Learned and Wise adhere to the new

Scheme of expressing themselves by *Things,* which hath only this Inconvenience attending it; that if a Man's Business be very great, and of various Kinds, he must be obliged in Proportion to carry a greater Bundle of *Things* upon his Back, unless he can afford one or two strong Servants to attend him. I have often beheld two of these Sages almost sinking under the Weight of their Packs, like Peddlers among us, who when they meet in the Streets, would lay down their Loads, open their Sacks, and hold Conversation for an Hour together; then put up their Implements, help each other to resume their Burthens, and take their Leave. (Swift, 1726/1970, p. 158)

crease in the number of individual words they know and more than a simple improvement in their ability to label objects. Growth in a child's lexicon also is accompanied by fundamental changes in the ways in which the child relates words to one another and in the contexts in which the child uses words, ultimately creating qualitatively new systems of meaning (Carey, 1985; Luria, 1981; Nelson, 1979).

The changing structure of word meaning can be illustrated by tracing the developmental course of a single word such as "dog." The first words and phrases children use are likely to represent the specific circumstances of the first time they associate the sound and its referent, with their feelings playing as important a role as their thoughts. For example, "dog" may mean something terrible if the child has just been bitten; the same word may mean something wonderful if the dog lies on the rug and allows the child to burrow in its fur.

Then, as the child accumulates experience with dogs, the word "dog" begins to evoke a range of different concrete situations in which "dog" is only one element: the structure of the lexicon at this stage is dominated by the pattern shown in Figure 9.6a. There, "dog" is a unifying element in several situations: dog growls, dog barks, dog is petted, dog runs away, dog fights. Each situation is connected to "dog" in a different way as part of a different kind of action.

As the child's experience increases it becomes apparent that dogs are not the only creatures that bite. Cats bite too, and so do babies. At the same time, it becomes clear that cats do not bark (seals do) and they rarely take walks (but mommies do). Some of the things you can say about dogs you can just as easily say about cats (or seals or mommies), but some you cannot. When children are familiar with a large number of concrete situations in which the same word is used in different ways, words begin to acquire *conceptual meanings* that do not depend upon any one context, or even on a real-world context. This aspect of language development is depicted in Figure 9.6b.

Once a word's meaning is influenced by the logical categories of the language, the word "dog" evokes more than the single emotion of fear or the single concrete image of Fido begging at the table. It has become part of an abstract system of word meanings independent of any particular situation. "Dog" becomes an example of the category "domestic animal," or the more general category "animal," or the still more general category "living thing."

These changes in the organization of word meanings can be tracked in many ways. One of the simplest is to ask children of different ages to say the first word that comes to mind in response to each of a set of stimulus words. Early in development, children respond to "dog" with "bites" or "run," depending upon the situation that the stimulus word evokes; later they respond to "dog" with "cat" or "animal" (Nelson, 1977).

Although new forms of word meaning reshape the child's lexicon, old forms do not disappear. Adults, no less than children, respond with fear, love, or some other emotion to "dog." A great deal of adults' use of language depends upon a fine-grained appreciation of the way that words relate to each other in particular contexts. What distinguishes the adult's lexicon from the child's, other than its greater size, is the presence of several alternative forms of meaning for each word, which provides a richer arsenal of linguistic tools for reasoning about dogs, cats, and everything else, and for talking about these entities with other people.

Words or sentences? The evidence presented so far about words indicates that children in early childhood know something about their individual meanings. But this does not imply that they appreciate the new meanings that can arise from combinations of words or the possible changes of meaning that can be achieved by changes in word order or syntax.

Several investigators believe that even when children can utter only single words, they are expressing whole ideas. These theorists use the term **holophrase** to refer to the way that these early one-word utterances may stand for whole sentences. By this account holophrases contain the germ of later, more differentiated language capacities (McNeil, 1970). As children's memory increases and as they become more familiar with language forms, they begin to use increasing numbers of words to articulate the concepts they had previously packed into one-word utterances.

Patricia Greenfield and Joshua Smith (1976) offer a quite different interpretation of single-word utterances. They do not believe that a single-word utterance stands for a whole sentence, but only for a particular element of the situation that the child wants to talk about. Greenfield and Smith point out that children's single words are almost always accompanied by nonverbal elements such as gestures and distinctive facial expressions. Thus the single word is not a holophrase, but rather one element in a whole complex of communication that also includes nonverbal actions.

It is difficult to decide between competing theories of children's linguistic understanding at the stage of single-word utterances because there is too little information available. Certainly, adults respond as if the child's single-word utterances are meaningful. For example, a child says "shoe" and the father responds by saying, "Oh, you want Daddy to tie your shoelace." But how much of this meaning is the child's, and how much of it is the adult's interpretation of the utterance

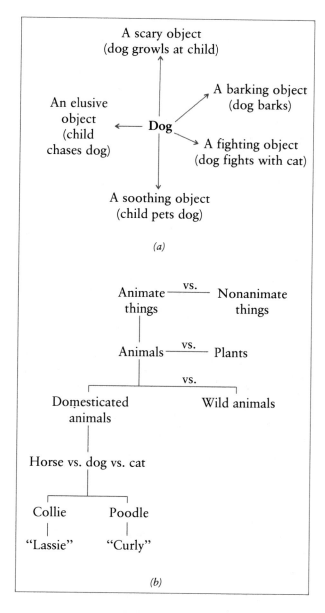

FIGURE 9.6 *(a) For the younger child, word meaning is dominated by the contexts of action in which the words have played a role. (b) As children acquire the formal conceptual categories of their language, the structure of word meanings changes accordingly. (Adapted from Luria, 1981).*

"That's a cloud, too. They're all clouds."

Drawing by Gahan Wilson; © *1984*
The New Yorker Magazine, Inc.

based on information gleaned from the context in which the child speaks? Until there is more to go on than a single word, it is especially difficult to determine where the child's word leaves off and the adult's interpretation begins. Although this problem of interpretation never completely disappears, it becomes less vexing when the child begins to string words together.

Sentences

As described in Chapter 7, an important watershed of language development is reached toward the end of infancy when children begin to utter two or more words within a single sound contour. Although these initial multiword utterances seldom form grammatical sentences, even two-word utterances carry more than twice as much information about the child's meaning than does a single-word utterance. Each of the two words provides hints about what the child is saying, just as the single word provided hints. But now the

relationship *between* the two words can also be used. With as few as two words children can indicate possession ("Daddy sock"), nonexistence ("all-gone cookie"), and a variety of other meanings. They can vary the order of the words to create different meanings (e.g., "Sock Daddy" and "Daddy sock"). This new potential for creating meaning by varying the arrangement of linguistic elements marks the birth of syntax. Syntactical expression undergoes a long period of development.

Two-word utterances   Table 9.3 contains a sample of two-word utterances recorded in one of the first attempts to discover the earliest syntactic rules evident in the speech of infants (Braine, 1963). Several features stand out in these early "protosentences."

1. *Explicitness.* A child who can say "See boy" instead of being limited to "see" or "boy" in isolation has a better chance of communicating effectively to a listening adult, especially when the context does not make one specific interpretation obvious.

2. *Ordering.* Part of the gain in explicitness comes from the order in which the two words are used. "Boy see" or "Do bunny" does not convey the same meaning as "See boy" or "Bunny do." The gains in meaning that result from the order of elements in the utterance are the crucial evidence that something like syntax is beginning to organize the child's talk.

3. *Telegraphic quality.* In these two-word utterances children appear to be coding only the most obvious and essential parts of their ideas, in much the same way that adults simplify their language when sending a telegram ("Mom. Cash low. All well. Send money. Love. Johnny"). Such

TABLE 9.3   Sample two-word utterances

See boy	Mail come
See sock	Mama come
Night night office	Bunny do
Night night boat	Want do
More care	Boat off
More sing	Water off

SOURCE: Braine, 1963.

When they are first beginning to speak, children are curious about the possible range of conversational partners.

utterances are more informative than single words, but they are often ambiguous.

The shortcomings of two-word utterances are illustrated in an amusing way by a series of incidents in *Higglety, Pigglety, Pop,* Maurice Sendak's tale of an adventurous dog who accepts a job as nanny for Baby, a child caught in the grip of the terrible twos. At first, the dog attempts to get the baby to eat, and the baby says "No eat!" In the second incident, the dog decides to eat the food himself, and the baby again says, "No eat!" Finally, the baby and dog find themselves confronted by a lion, the baby says for the third time "No eat!"

As adults, we have ready interpretations of what the baby *means* in each instance. In the first case he appears to mean "I won't eat," in the second case he means "Don't eat my food," and in the third case he means "Don't eat me" (or, if he is feeling generous, "Don't eat us"). The difficulty with these two-word utterances is clear: the same sound pattern ("Don't eat") has at least three different interpretations and there is no resource within the language itself to differentiate among them. The ambiguity in two-word utterances restricts effective communication to occasions when listeners can reliably interpret the context in which the child is operating. Thus, effective communication about absent or abstract subjects is not yet possible.

Increasing complexity As children begin to string more and more words together and consistently form complete sentences, they simultaneously increase the number, the complexity, and the variety of words and syntactic devices that they use. These changes are illustrated by the following prodigious sentence spoken by an excited 2-year-old:

> You can't pick up a big big kitty 'cos a big big kitty might bite! (de Villiers & de Villiers, 1978, p. 59)

This sentence is by no means typical of 2-year-olds, but it provides a good opportunity to assess how more complex utterances communicate more explicitly. The sentence makes clear not only that the little girl doesn't want to pick up the cat, but that no one should pick up the cat; it also conveys her understanding that cats sometimes bite but do not invariably do so. Such complex sentences communicate shades of meaning that assist adults in responding sensitively to the girl's experience.

As shown in Figure 9.7, 2-year-olds display an explosive growth in the length of their utterances, along

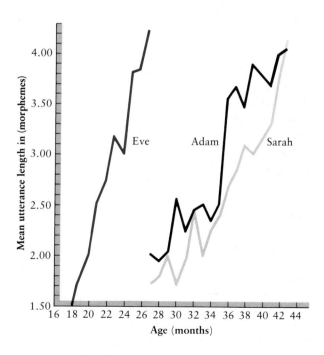

FIGURE 9.7 *This graph shows the rapid increase in the mean length of utterances for three children during the first four years of life. (From Brown, 1973)*

with growth in their vocabularies and syntactic abilities (Brown, 1973). Note that the growth of utterance length is graphed in terms of the average number of *morphemes* per utterance (or the so-called "mean length of utterance" [MLU]), rather than by the average number of words. For example, the phrase "that big bad boy plays ball" contains six words and seven morphemes while the phrase "boys aren't playing" contains only three words but six morphemes (words: *boys, aren't, playing;* morphemes: *boy, s, are, (not), play, ing*). This procedure of counting morphemes rather than words provides an index of a child's total potential for making meaning in a particular utterance.

Grammatical morphemes   In large measure, the complexity of the girl's long sentence is attributable to just those little words and word parts that are systematically absent in two-word utterances. The article *a* ("*a* big big kitty") indicates that it is big cats in general, not just this particular big cat, that is worrisome. The word *'cos* connects two propositions and indicates the causal relationship between them. The contraction *can't* specifies a particular relationship of negation.

These elements are called **grammatical morphemes** because they are units that create meaning by showing the relations between other elements within the sentence.

Whether the rate of language acquisition is fast or slow, the sequence in which grammatical morphemes appear is roughly the same for all children (at least, for all children acquiring English as a first language). As shown in Table 9.4, the morpheme likely to appear first is *ing*, indicating the present progressive verb case. This verb form allows children to describe their ongoing activity. Morphemes indicating location, possession, and number make their appearance next. Children have many opportunities to use these words in the course of play with toys; blocks are stacked one *on top of* another, dolls go *in* their cribs, and a little girl's lunch belongs *to her*. Morphemes that mark complex relations, such as "I'm going" (which codes a relation between the subject of the action and the time of the action), are generally slower to emerge.

The appearance of grammatical morphemes is a strong indicator that children are implicitly beginning to distinguish parts of speech, at least nouns and verbs, because their speech conforms to rules about which

TABLE 9.4   Usual order of acquiring grammatical morphemes

Morpheme	Meaning	Example
Present progressive	Temporary duration	I walk*ing*
In	Containment	*In* basket
On	Support	*On* floor
Plural	Number	Two ball*s*
Past irregular	Prior occurrence	It *broke*
Possessive inflection	Possession	Adam*'s* ball
Use of "to be" without contraction	Number; prior occurrence	There it *is*
Articles	Specific-nonspecific	That *a* book That *the* dog
Past regular	Prior occurrence	Adam walk*ed*
Third person regular	Number; prior occurrence	He walk*s*
Third person irregular	Number; prior occurrence	He *does* She *has*
Uncontractible progressive auxiliary	Temporary duration; number; prior occurrence	This *is going*
Contractible use of "to be"	Number; prior occurrence	That*'s* book
Contractible progressive auxiliary	Temporary duration; prior occurrence	*I'm* walking

SOURCE: Brown, 1973.

morphemes should be attached to which words in a sentence. Children demonstrate their intuitive grasp of the rules for using grammatical morphemes by the fact that they do not apply a past-tense morpheme to a noun (e.g., "girl*ed*"); nor do they place articles before verbs ("*a* walked"). By the time they are 5 or 6 years old, most children will have implicit command of all of the standard parts of speech they will use as adults.

Complex constructions Between the ages of 2 and 6, children will begin to use a great many syntactic devices, the "grammatical rules" that bedevil students in language classes throughout their school days. Some of these syntactic constructions obey rules of such subtlety that, although we follow them intuitively in our speech, we have great difficulty in making explicit the basis of our own judgments.

It might seem from examples that appear in small children's two- and three-word utterances that mastery of syntax requires no more than acquisition of a few ordering rules. But examples abound to demonstrate that more than surface ordering principles are needed to achieve language competence. Consider the following sentences:

1. John is easy to please.
2. John is willing to please.

Both sentences seem to follow a single ordering principle. But at some level the syntax of these sentences, despite their surface similarity, must be different. This difference can be illustrated by adding a single word to the end of each sentence while still preserving the order of elements. Compare the two new sentences:

3. John is willing to please Bill.
4. John is easy to please Bill.

Sentence 3 is just as acceptable in the English language as sentences 1 and 2, but sentence 4, despite the fact that surface ordering principles are unchanged, is not grammatically acceptable, and we cannot interpret it. Examples such as these are central to Noam Chomsky's claim that language acquisition is constrained by highly abstract rules that cannot be learned directly from experience. Yet such rules appear to be acquired by all normal children, regardless of the language they speak.

Children's difficulties in mastering the subtle syntactic constructions demanded by adult language, even after they know the meanings of the words in-

volved, have been studied by Carol Chomsky (1969). In one of her examples, Lisa, who is 6½ years old, is seated at a table on which there is a doll with a blindfold over its eyes.

Adult: Is this doll easy to see or hard to see?

Lisa: Hard to see.

Adult: Will you make her easy to see?

Lisa: If I can get this [blindfold] untied.

Adult: Will you explain why she was hard to see?

Lisa: [*to doll*] Because you had a blindfold over your eyes.

Adult: And what did you do?

Lisa: I took it off.

Before this interchange, Carol Chomsky had made certain that Lisa knew the meaning of "easy." Lisa knew that it is easy to sit in a chair but hard to climb a tree. What, then, was her difficulty in the case of the blindfolded doll? Chomsky argues that children like Lisa still assume that the person mentioned at the beginning of a sentence is the one who carries out the action (in this case, that it is the doll who does the seeing). This assumption is often true, but it is not true in the case of "easy to see"; children must learn to dig beneath the surface features of the sentence to find the true relationship it codes.

Young children take great delight in their ability to communicate using their rapidly developing linguistic skills.

The Uses of Language

All the while that children are acquiring new words and the rules for combining them, they are also learning complex ways to make their talk work for them (Shatz, 1983). In order to communicate effectively, children must master the **pragmatic uses of language,** that is, the ability to select words and word orderings that are appropriate to their actions in particular contexts. As children master the pragmatic aspects of language, they become able to use various types of speech to accomplish specific functions, as well as to say things in ways that are specifically designed for the person being spoken to.

Conversational acts   Language is more than a set of rules. It is also a form of action. A sentence such as "Is

TABLE 9.5   Major conversational acts

Requestives: solicit information or action
  Choice questions — "Is this an apple?"
  Product questions — "Where's John?" "What happened?"
  Process questions — "Why did he go?" "How did it happen?"
  Action requests — "Give it to me." "Put the toy down."
  Permission requests — "May I go?"

Assertives: report facts, state rules, convey attitudes, etc.
  Identifications — "That's a car."
  Descriptions — "The car is red."
  Internal reports — "I like it."
  Evaluations — "That's good."
  Rules — "We don't fight in school."

Performatives: accomplish acts (establish facts) by being said
  Claims — "That's mine."
  Protests — "Stop hitting me."
  Warnings — "Be careful."

Responsives: supply requested information or acknowledge remarks
  Choice answers — "Yes, it's a green light."
  Product answers — "John is here."
  Process answers — "I want to go."
  Clarifications — "I said no."

Regulatives: control personal contact and conversation flow
  Attention-getters — "Hey John! Look!"
  Speaker selections — "It's your turn, Lydia."
  Rhetorical questions — "You know what?"

Expressives: convey attitudes or repeat others
  Exclamations — "Wow!"
  Accompaniments — "There you go."

SOURCE: Dore, Gearhart, & Newman, 1979.

the door shut?" has the grammatical form of a request for information. But "Is the door shut?" may also be a request for action or a criticism. In these cases it is pragmatically equivalent to the sentences "Please shut the door" or "You have forgotten to shut the door again."

The ability to understand and use speech forms to accomplish actions is acquired at an early age. Shatz (1974, 1978) found that children as young as 2 years responded correctly to their mother's indirect commands, such as "Is the door shut?" Instead of responding to the surface grammatical form and answering "Yes" or "No," Shatz's toddlers went to shut the door. A 3-year-old observed by John Dore (1979) used three different ways to accomplish a single goal: "Get off the blocks!" "Why don't you stay away from my blocks?" and "You're standing on my blocks."

In the hope of getting a proper overall picture of language development, a number of scholars have attempted to catalog the full set of language functions that children have to master. This task has proven formidable because there is so much variety in the uses of speech, even by 3-year-olds. The 3- and 4-year-olds studied by Dore, Gearhart, and Newman (1979), for example, have come a long way from mere pointing or the use of idiosyncratic "words" such as *ha.* They can solicit information ("What happened?"), or action ("Put the toy down!"). They can assert facts and rules ("We have a boat"), utter warnings ("Watch out!"), and clarify prior statements. Some idea of the magnitude of young children's pragmatic skills can be obtained by an examination of Table 9.5, which shows a categorization by John Dore and his colleagues of the major classes of conversational acts used by 3- and 4-year-old children in only one setting, a nursery school.

Taking account of the listener   The core meaning of the word *communicate* is "to place in common." Language is said to communicate when speakers and listeners come to share a common interpretation of what is said. Yet a major limitation on early childhood language, as we have seen, is that it leaves so much of the interpretive work to the listener. In this sense, children's language is not fully communicative. Children's increasing knowledge of word meanings and mastery of syntactic rules reduces this problem but by no means eliminates it.

One of the major skills that children must master in order to make their language more communicative is to say things in such a way that the meaning will be clear from the listener's point of view. This skill is evident at an early age in rudimentary form. However, it develops very slowly in the years from 2½ to 7 or 8 and is rarely applied in a uniform way, even by adults.

Children as young as 4 years of age show that they can take the listener into account when they know they are talking to younger children whose language ability is more primitive than their own. In an often cited study, Shatz and Gelman (1973) found that when 4-year-olds play with 2-year-olds, the older children modify their speech to make it easier for the younger children to understand: the 4-year-olds' sentences are shorter, they speak more slowly, and they simplify both their vocabulary and their syntax. This ability is independent of the child's experience talking to little children; 4-year-olds with little brothers or sisters are no more likely to simplify their speech than only children. In another study, Sachs and Devin (1973) demonstrated that small children make the same kinds of simplifications when playing with a baby doll, but not when playing with a grownup doll.

Even four-year-olds adapt their language when speaking to younger children.

LANGUAGE AND THOUGHT

It is clear from the research reviewed in this chapter that language bears a complex relationship to events and ideas, and that children learn early how to use this relationship to influence their interactions with the world. How, then, is the development of language related to other aspects of children's development, particularly the development of their thought processes? Each major developmental approach offers its own answer to this question.

The Environmental-Learning Perspective

Learning theorists such as Bandura (1986) and Skinner (1957) agree that a great deal of human thought is linguistically based. They also believe that there are special advantages to thinking based on language. As Bandura points out,

> By manipulating symbols that convey relevant information, one can gain understanding of causal relationships, expand one's knowledge, solve problems, and deduce consequences of actions without actually performing them. The functional value of thought rests on the close correspondence between the symbolic system [e.g., language] and external events, so that the former can be substituted for the latter. (1986, p. 462)

Language, according to this view, is more than a means of communication with others. Words deepen a child's understanding of certain aspects of objects and of the subtle relations among various events. Associations among words provide a kind of mental map of the world, thus shaping how a child thinks. This view suggests that thinking should change markedly when children begin to acquire language and that if adults can accelerate linguistic development, they will thereby speed cognitive development as well.

Piaget's Interactionist Perspective

Piaget claimed that a new mode of representation, in which children begin to think in symbols, arises on the basis of sensorimotor schemas at the end of infancy, as discussed in Chapter 7 (p. 217). Language, he believed, is a verbal reflection of the individual's nonlinguistic understanding (Piaget, 1926, 1983). Since language reflects thought, language developments cannot cause cognitive development. Rather, cognition determines language.

As discussed in Chapters 5 to 7, Piaget believed that cognitive development arises from the child's attempts to assimilate the environment, which are modified through subsequent interactions. At the end of the sensorimotor period, children have developed a basic understanding that they are a part of a world that exists separately from them, but, as we will see in the next chapter, they still have difficulty adopting other people's points of view.

If language is determined by thought, it would follow that early speech, like early thought, would be egocentric and fail to take into account others' points of view. Early in his career, Piaget supported this hypothesis with data collected from preschool children's conversations. What struck him was that while preschoolers appear to be playing and conversing together, their remarks actually focus on what they are doing by themselves, with no real regard for their partner and with no apparent intention of actually communicating. Piaget (1926) called this type of language **collective monologues,** which he believed mirror a profoundly egocentric mode of thought. The following conversation between two American preschoolers illustrates his point:

Jenny: They wiggle sideways when they kiss.

Chris: (*vaguely*) What?

Jenny: My bunny slippers. They are brown and red and sort of yellow and white. And they have eyes and ears and these noses that wiggle sideways when they kiss.

Chris: I have a piece of sugar in a red piece of paper. I'm gonna eat it but maybe it's for a horse.

Jenny: We bought them. My mommy did. We couldn't find the old ones. These are like the old ones. They were not in the trunk.

Chris: Can't eat the piece of sugar, not unless you take the paper off.

Jenny: And we found Mother Lamb. Oh, she was in Poughkeepsie in the trunk in the house in the woods where Mrs. Tiddywinkle lives.

Chris: Do I like sugar? I do, and so do horses.

Jenny: I play with my bunnies. They are real. We play in the woods. They have eyes. We *all* go in the woods. My teddy bear and the bunnies and the duck, to visit Mrs. Tiddywinkle. We play and play.

Chris: I guess I'll eat my sugar at lunch time. I can get more for the horses. Besides, I don't have no horses now.

(Stone and Church, 1957, pp. 146–47)

Piaget noted that as children grow older, their ability to adopt others' points of view increases, and these collective monologues therefore give way to genuine dialogues.

Piaget's idea about the dependence of language on thought was tested in a study by Hermione Sinclair-de-Zwart (1967), who taught French-speaking preschoolers the correct meanings of the terms for *more* and *less,* then tested the children's ability to solve problems involving the relationships of *more* and *less.* Sinclair-de-Zwart's results showed that the children who had learned to use the words appropriately in the training situation showed no advantage over untrained children when these relationships were actually needed to solve a problem. This failure of language training to influence problem solving seems to confirm the theory that language does not affect thought.

The Structural-Innatist Perspective

Structural-innatist theorists such as Noam Chomsky explicitly deny that it is possible for language to grow out of sensorimotor schemas, declaring that there are no known similarities between the principles of language and the principles of sensorimotor intelligence (Chomsky, 1980). Rather, as explained earlier, Chomsky believes that language acquisition is made possible by a specifically human language acquisition device (LAD).

Chomsky (1980) has used the term *mental module* to signal the self-contained nature of the language-using capacity. A mental module is a highly specific mental faculty that is tuned to particular kinds of environmental input. In claiming that language forms a distinctive mental module, Chomsky seems to be declaring that language and thought do not depend on each other. As support for his position, Chomsky cites evidence that severely retarded children often have relatively advanced linguistic abilities even though their other intellectual abilities are extremely limited. However, Chomsky does not go so far as to say that there is *no* connection between these two domains of mind. When challenged on this issue by Piaget's colleague, Barbel Inhelder, Chomsky replied:

> I take it for granted that thinking is a domain that is quite different from language, even though language is used for the expression of thought, and for a good deal of thinking we really need the mediation of language. (1980, p. 174)

A Cultural-Context Perspective

The most prominent cultural theory of language and thought was developed by the Soviet psychologist Lev Vygotsky (1934/1987, 1978). Pointing out that children's development always occurs in a context organized and watched over by adults, Vygotsky insisted that children's experience of language is social from the outset. Instead of seeing children's gradual socialization with age, as Piaget maintained, Vygotsky held that children are social beings from the moment of their birth and that the social environment plays a crucial role in the acquisition of language as in all other aspects of development.

According to Vygotsky (1934/1987), even a child's initial words are communicative acts, mediating children's interactions with those around them. More generally, Vygotsky believed that new psychological functions will first be manifested while children are in interaction with others who can support and nurture their efforts. These shared efforts are gradually taken over by the child and transformed into individual abilities. Applied to the area of language, this sequence suggests a progression from social and communicative speech to internal dialogue, or inner speech, in which thought and language are intimately interconnected.

Vygotsky suggests that sometime after children begin to communicate, egocentric speech (speech primarily for oneself) splinters off from social speech and becomes the earliest form of individual, linguistically mediated thought. This type of speech is still a rudimentary form of thought because it is partially external and only some fragments of the fully formed thought find expression. But even egocentric speech influences the individual's behavior, in Vygotsky's view. This is just the opposite of the relation between language, cognition, and the social world that Piaget proposes, and, as might be expected, this opposition led Vygotsky to an interpretation of collective monologues (or "egocentric speech") that also differs from Piaget's.

Vygotsky and his colleagues conducted a series of studies to test Piaget's idea that egocentric speech serves no cognitive or communicative function (Vygotsky, 1934/1987). In one such study, they demonstrated the psychological functionality of egocentric speech; when children were faced with a difficulty in solving a problem, they increased their level of overt, self-regulatory speech, a finding replicated by Kohlberg, Yaeger, and Hjertholm (1968). In a second study, researchers demonstrated that egocentric speech retains a communicative function for others as well as oneself. In this case preschoolers were placed among deaf-mute children, with whom they had little chance of communicating. Vygotsky reasoned that if egocentric speech was really not intended to communicate, it would not be affected by potential listeners' inability to understand. Instead, the rate of egocentric speech decreased markedly in comparison with its level among hearing children (described in Wertsch, 1985).

A basic innovation in Vygotsky's approach was his assertion that the relationship between language and thought is not constant. Both language and thought develop, and so does the relationship between them. According to Vygotsky, during the first two years of life, language and thought develop more or less along parallel, relatively unrelated lines. Until the end of infancy, it is possible to encounter precursors of language that seem unrelated to any intellectual operation (such as babbling) and elements of thought that occur without any language (such as the sensorimotor schemas described by Piaget). However, beginning around 2 years of age there is a fundamental change in the relationship between language and thought. Up to this point, thought and language have been developing on more or less independent tracks, but now they begin to intermingle. This intermingling, wrote Vygotsky (1934/1987), fundamentally changes the na-

- -

BOX 9.2

FIGURATIVE LANGUAGE
...

A 2½-year-old runs up to his parents, points at his yellow plastic baseball bat, and says with delight, "Corn, corn!" A 1½-year-old sends a toy car twisting along his mother's arm and exclaims, "Nake" (snake). At first glance these children might appear to be overextending the meaning of their words. But a variety of evidence suggests that not long after children begin to name objects, they begin to use words figuratively as well as literally. They deliberately call objects by the name of something else to which it bears some striking resemblance. Such deliberate renamings are in fact deliberate metaphors (Winner, McCarthy, Kleinman, & Gardner, 1979). Significantly, the beginnings of metaphorical language coincide with the onset of symbolic play (described in Chapter 7, p. 220). In both forms of behavior, the 2-year-old child treats objects and events nonliterally.

Figurative use of words provides important evidence that language production is a creative process, not a simple imitative one. As Ellen Winner and her colleagues point out, in order to generate a metaphor,

children must recognize and express a similarity between two things in some novel way that they have never heard before.

Winner and her coworkers identify two distinct routes for the development of nonliteral, metaphoric speech. Some metaphors are closely tied to action: a 2-year-old rubs a fur teddy bear against a wooden armchair. He then holds up the teddy and says, "Zucchini." Then he points at the arm of the chair and calls it "grater." A teddy bear does not look at all like a zucchini and most wooden chair arms do not look like vegetable graters; the resemblance that makes these words meaningful depends upon the way that the objects fit into a typical action sequence.

By contrast, perceptual metaphors take on meaning from the physical similarities between the objects compared. When a little child exclaims, "Oh mommy, how balloony your legs look!" or "Can't you see, I'm barefoot all over!" she is using perceptual metaphors (Chukovsky, 1968). Because adults also base some of their metaphoric use of words on the same kinds of physical

- -

ture of both thinking and language, providing the growing child with a uniquely human form of behavior in which language becomes intellectual and thinking becomes verbal.

In Vygotsky's framework, language allows thought to be individual and social at the same time. It is the medium through which individual thought is communicated to others while at the same time it allows social reality to be converted into the idiosyncratic thought of the individual. This conversion from the social to the individual is never complete, even in the adult, whose individual thought processes continue to be shaped in part by the conventional meanings present in the lexicon and speech habits of the culture.

The relation between language and thought remains one of the most tangled and controversial issues dividing developmental psychologists. There appears to be reasonable agreement that language and thought are separable psychological functions; they are not reducible one to the other. There is also agreement that the two functions intermingle in normal development. However, the field is still far from agreeing on the extent to which development in one domain influences development in the other and on their combined roles in the development of the child as a whole. (For one interesting example of the intermingling of language and thought in early childhood, see Box 9.2, "Figurative Language.")

similarities as children do, adults are often able to figure out what the child means.

Although children between the ages of 2 and 6 years use a good deal of figurative language, they often fail to understand the figurative meaning of adult speech that does not depend upon simple actions or an object's perceptual characteristics. Kornei Chukovsky, a Russian linguist, translator, and children's poet, was especially impressed by the special intelligence revealed by children's misunderstandings of adult figurative speech. His examples are difficult to improve upon:

A woman . . . asked her 4-year-old Natasha:

"Tell me, what does it mean to say that a person is trying to drown another in a spoonful of water [a Russian expression]?"

"What did you say? In what kind of a spoon? Say that again."

The mother repeated the adage.

"That's impossible!" Natasha said categorically. "It can never happen!"

Right there and then she demonstrated the physical impossibility of such an act; she grabbed a spoon and quickly placed it on the floor.

"Look, here am I," and she stood on the spoon. "All right, drown me. There isn't enough room for a whole person—all of him will remain on top. . . .

"Let's not talk about it any more—it's such nonsense!"

Four-year-old Olia, who came with her mother to visit a Moscow aunt, looked closely at this aunt and her husband as they were all having tea, and soon remarked with obvious disappointment:

"Mama! You said that uncle always sits on Aunt Aniuta's neck [a Russian expression for being bossy and controlling] but he has been sitting on a chair all the time that we've been here." (Chukovsky, 1968, pp. 12–13)

As children begin to master their native language and approach the age when they will be expected to acquire adult skills, either as apprentices or in school, there is a noticeable decrease in their freewheeling use of figurative language. On the one hand, this narrowing of linguistic adventurism can be considered a good thing: children are learning what is conventional and acceptable in their community. On the other hand, a good deal of the creativity goes out of their speech. It may take some effort for them to regain their sense of delight in discovering new properties of the world through figurative language.

ESSENTIAL INGREDIENTS OF LANGUAGE ACQUISITION

Now that we have surveyed many of the basic facts of language acquisition, we can return to the central theoretical issue raised at the start of the chapter: What is required for an organism to acquire human language? To what extent must we assume that the issue is decided by innate predispositions? Which aspects of the environment play a role and how? Research on a series of special cases of language development helps to provide some answers to these questions.

Language and Other Species

For most of human history it has seemed obvious that the basic requirement for acquiring human language is that the learner be a human being. Many other species make a variety of communicative sounds and gestures, but none has evolved a communicative system as powerful and flexible as human language (Lieberman, 1984). At this rather crude level, virtually all developmental psychologists agree with Chomsky that there is a significant inherited component in the process of language development.

This chimp is signing "I want to hold" (top) "the cat" (bottom). (Courtesy of H. Terrace.)

One strategy for testing the hypothesis that only human beings can acquire language is to raise a creature from another species in the home along with one's own children. Several researchers have done just that with chimpanzees, hoping that these near phylogenetic neighbors would acquire oral language if they were treated just like human beings (Hayes & Hayes, 1951; Kellog & Kellog, 1933; Ladygina-Kots, 1935). Despite heroic efforts to treat human and chimpanzee infants alike, these experiments failed to produce more than the barest rudiments of vocal language (for example, in one case one chimp learned to make a sound corresponding to one word). More than a caring human family is apparently required for language acquisition, suggesting a fundamental discontinuity between *Homo sapiens* and other species in this respect.

In recent decades, the assumption of a total discontinuity between *Homo sapiens* and higher primates has been cast into doubt. Several investigators have suggested that earlier studies erred in requiring evidence of *oral* language, which is likely to be difficult for higher primates because of the structure of their vocal apparatus. In subsequent research it has been claimed that, with intensive training, chimpanzees can be taught to use a manual/visual system of communication, similar in its mode of operation to the sign language used by hearing-impaired people (Gardner & Gardner, 1969). These claims are still hotly disputed (Terrace, 1979), but the research that resulted from the ensuing controversy has revealed that at least some of the elements of human language exist among nonhuman species.

In the wild, chimpanzees and related species make a variety of different communicative sounds and gestures that are important to the social organization of their lives (Goodall, 1986; Marler, 1976). Certain of these sounds help to coordinate the group when it is foraging for food. Monkey and chimpanzee troops are organized so that if a predator appears, the males, who are on the outside of the troop, make a distinctive sound that sends the females and juvenile monkeys, who are in the center, heading for the trees. In some species there are different sounds for such different kinds of predators as leopards, eagles, and snakes; infant primates make these same sounds but may confuse a cheetah for a leopard or a hawk for an eagle (Seyfarth & Cheney, 1980). Additional sounds signal playfulness, submissiveness, social excitement, and a variety of other states (Cheney & Seyfarth, 1982).

In captivity, chimpanzees are capable of acquiring a store of nonvocal "words" which they use to get things they want. Several chimps have learned more than 100 "words" that are expressed by hand shapes or plastic chips provided by their human tutors (Gardner & Gardner, 1969; Premack & Premack, 1983). They can also learn to use their signs to make simple requests ("Give stick") not only of their trainer, but of other chimps (Savage-Rumbaugh, 1979; Savage-Rumbaugh, McDonald, Sevcik, Hopkins, & Rubert, 1986).

Results of these chimp studies suggest that there are evolutionary precursors of human language capacities. However, the continuity between human and subhuman language capacities should not be overstated. Current evidence (summarized in Lieberman, 1984) indicates that while languagelike behavior can be induced in chimps, the human language system is crucially different. After four years of hard work, chimps can learn several signs; but children with no special training learn several thousand. Chimps also learn to construct sequences of signs analogous to an infant's multiword utterances, but the internal complexity of these constructions is rudimentary; often a long sequence will consist of only a few unique elements and many repetitions ("Give banana, banana, banana") (Terrace, 1979). This pattern is very different from the telegraphic speech of small children.

As a consequence of their limitations, chimp uses of languagelike behaviors remain primitive and infrequent. Among humans, by contrast, even little children are able to use language to coordinate activities with each other and to understand their physical surroundings in ways that are qualitatively more complex and flexible than the communicative and knowledge systems possessed by any other kind of living creature, including chimpanzees raised by psychologists!

The Environment of Language Development

Evidence from studies of primate communicative abilities suggests an absolute biological precondition for language acquisition: one must be a human being. Evidence from cases such as that of Genie, the girl who grew up in total isolation from language and normal human interaction (described in Chapter 8), suggests the absolute precondition on the environmental side: one must grow up among humans. Between these requirements, important questions remain: Which aspects of the environment, in what configuration, are necessary to "trigger" language? What are the optimal conditions for ensuring that the language capacity is fully developed?

Partial deprivation   One way to answer such questions is to find cases where children are exposed to a great deal of language, but are cut off from normal interactions with the speakers. There have been a few reports, for example, of children who are left alone for long periods of time with a television set broadcasting in a language different than the language spoken in the home. Scenes on television portray routine interactions involving normal language, so they might support language acquisition through the association of sound and action. Yet children do not seem to acquire language from watching television alone. This would seem to contradict the idea that mere exposure is all that is required to develop language. Children must also test their ideas about language by interacting with other speakers (Snow, Arlman-Rupp, Hassing, Jobse, Joosken, & Vorster, 1976).

The crucial role of active participation in human interaction is demonstrated by cases in which children grow up in an environment without language but with human interaction: for example, deaf children whose hearing parents do not know sign language and discourage its use (Feldman, Goldin-Meadow, & Gleitman, 1978; Goldin-Meadow, 1982, 1985). In the families studied by Susan Goldin-Meadow and her colleagues, parents believed that their deaf children could learn to read lips and to vocalize sounds. As a consequence, at an age when other children are hearing (or seeing) language, these children received virtually no language input.

Earlier studies had shown that deaf children raised under these circumstances will spontaneously begin to gesture in *home sign,* a kind of communication through pantomime (Fant, 1972). Goldin-Meadow and her colleagues wanted to find out if the home sign systems developed by the deaf children displayed the characteristic features of language acquisition. They discovered that, indeed, the gestures developed by these children exhibited certain characteristics of language even though they had no one to show them the signs.

Home sign begins as pointing, with the children gesturing one sign at a time—at the same age when hearing children develop single-word utterances. Home sign gestures seem to refer to the same kinds of objects and to fulfill the same functions as the early words of hearing children, or deaf children with signing parents. Remarkably, home-signing children go on to make patterns of two, three, and more sign/gestures around their second birthdays, at about the same time that hearing children utter multiword sentences (see Figure 9.8).

Analysis of these multipart sign/gestures reveals ordering principles much like those seen at the two-word stage in hearing children. In addition, Goldin-Meadow

FIGURE 9.8 *This little girl is signing the word "sleep." (Copyright Ursula Bellugi, The Salk Institute for Biological Studies; reprinted with permission.)*

reports that these deaf children were embedding sign sentences within each other ("You/Susan give me/ Abe cookie which is round."). This is the property of *recursion,* which, as pointed out at the beginning of this chapter, is characteristic of all human languages and absent in the communicative system of chimpanzees or other creatures even after long periods of training.

Once deaf children in hearing homes are able to make two- to three-word signed "utterances" and begin to embed sign sentences within each other, their language development appears to come to an end. They fail to acquire grammatical morphemes or to master complex syntactic distinctions. The mere fact of being raised in an environment where the actions of all the other participants are organized by human language and culture is sufficient to allow the child to acquire the "basics" of linguistic structure. But only access to the additional information provided by the sights (or sounds) of language *as a part of that environment* allows the child to discover its more subtle features (Goldin-Meadow, 1982, 1985).

Remarkable confirmation of this conclusion comes from the case of a hearing child raised by deaf parents (Sachs, Bard, & Johnson, 1981). This child's parents exposed him neither to conventional oral nor to conventional manual language input. He heard English only on TV and during a brief time in nursery school.

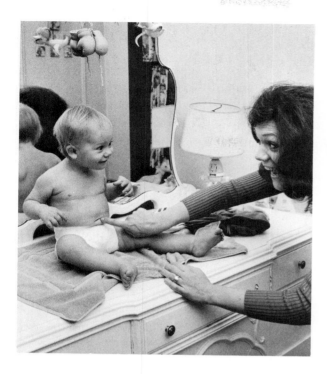 

Language is acquired in the context of ongoing activity. This mother is talking and playing with her baby as a routine part of getting him dressed.

The course of development for this child was precisely the same as for the deaf children of hearing parents: he developed the basic features of syntax, but not the more complex ones. After hearing adults began a language training program for the boy when he was 3 years and 9 months old, he quickly acquired normal language abilities.

Such research narrows the search for the critical environmental ingredients of language development. The rudimentary beginnings of language seem to appear during the second year of life even in the absence of direct experience of language, so long as children are included in the everyday life of their family. However, the kind of language that appears under such linguistically impoverished conditions is by no means fully developed, resembling instead the language behavior of children at the two-word phase.

Language and activity It seems an inescapable conclusion from the evidence presented thus far that in order for language acquisition to proceed beyond the rudiments, children must not only hear (or see) language, they must also participate in family or community activity. In the everyday lives of hearing children (or deaf children of signing parents) words are a part of the activity, filling in the gaps between actions, fine-tuning expectations and interpretations. Experience of the *co-variation* between language and action helps children in many small ways to coordinate their own actions with people around them. In the process of figuring out what is being asked of them and how to deal with other people effectively, children discover the vast range of meanings encoded in their language and find new ways to carry out their own intentions.

The close relationship between communication and action in language development is illustrated in research on vocabulary development by Elsa Bartlett (1977) and Susan Carey (1978) that was mentioned in Chapter 1 (p. 26). Bartlett and Carey used the normal routine of a preschool to find out what would happen if a totally new word was introduced into conversation with children. They chose to study the acquisition of color vocabulary. None of the 14 children in the classroom knew the name of the color that adults call olive; some of them called it brown, others called it green, and some didn't refer to the color by name at all.

Bartlett and Carey decided to give it an implausible name, *chromium,* just in case some children had partial knowledge of the real name that they had not revealed.

After the children had been tested to determine that they did not know the name of the color olive, one cup and one tray in the classroom were painted "chromium" (olive). While preparing for snack time, the teacher found an opportunity to ask each child something like the following: "Please bring me the chromium cup; not the red one, the chromium one" or "Bring me the chromium tray; not the blue one, the chromium one."

This procedure worked. All of the children succeeded in picking the correct cup or tray, although they were likely to ask for confirmation ("You mean this one?"). Some of the children could be noticed repeating the unfamiliar word (or some rough approximation) to themselves.

One week after this single experience with the new word, children were given a color-naming test with color chips. Two-thirds of the children showed that they had learned something about this odd term and its referents; when asked for chromium, they chose either the olive chip or a green one. Six weeks later many of the children still showed the influence of this single experience.

Bartlett and Carey's research illustrates the kind of ongoing involvement of adults in children's language acquisition that is emphasized by environmental learning theorists. However, their study does not support the idea that children acquire language because adults explicitly reward their efforts, nor does it support the idea that children seem to be learning by any simple process of imitation. Rather, when they hear an unfamiliar word in a familiar and highly structured situation that constrains how they are likely to interpret it, children seem to form a hypothesis about what the new word might mean and then actively fit it into their already existing repertoire. This is the kind of adult-guided constructive process emphasized by interactional theorists such as Bruner and Vygotsky. According to this view, adult reinforcement need not come in the form of explicit rewards. Instead, the reinforcement comes from the increased success of communication and the greater freedom children experience once they can use new words as instruments of their own actions.

Is there a role for deliberate instruction? As described thus far, language acquisition appears to re-

quire elements emphasized by several of the major theories:

1. A biologically programmed sensitivity to language present at birth, which develops as the child matures (Chomsky)

2. Imitation of the language behavior of others (environmental-learning theorists)

3. Acquisition of basic schemas for actions with objects and people (Piaget)

4. Interaction with caretakers who treat language as one of many spheres in which children need to become competent members of the community (Bruner, Vygotsky)

Missing from this list is any role for deliberate instruction with explicit rewards of the kind emphasized in some environmental-learning explanations of language acquisition. Are deliberate adult efforts to foster language development by teaching about language irrelevant?

In search of evidence that adults do in fact assist language acquisition directly, many investigators have noted that adults sometimes modify the way they speak when they talk to small children in order to make themselves better understood and to help children acquire language (Newport, 1977; Snow & Ferguson, 1977).

As can be seen in Table 9.6, middle-class parents in the United States simplify virtually every aspect of their language when speaking to their children.

Several studies have shown that the complexity of adult speech to children is carefully graded to the level of complexity in the child's speech (Pfuderer, 1969). Parents attempt to make sentence parts more obvious to the child by the partial sentences they use in helping children carry out actions. An example provided by Catherine Snow (1972) shows how this "highlighting" can work. A child is putting away toys under the mother's direction. Note the sequence of the mother's directions: "Put the red truck in the box now." "The red truck," "No, the red truck," "In the box," "The red truck in the box." Snow argues that this kind of language environment provides excellent tutoring in syntax because it isolates constituent phrases at the same time that it models the whole correct grammatical structure.

American adults not only simplify what they say as an aid to children's comprehension (and perhaps, to

TABLE 9.6 Simplifications when middle-class U.S. adults speak to small children

Phonological simplifications —
    Higher pitch and exaggerated intonation
    Clear pronunciation
    Slower speech
    Distinct pauses between utterances

Syntactic differences —
    Shorter and less varied utterance length
    Almost all sentences well formed
    Many partial or complete repetitions of child's
        utterances, sometimes with expansion
    Fewer broken sentences
    Grammatically less complex

Semantic differences —
    More limited vocabulary
    Many special words and diminutives
    Reference to concrete circumstances of here and now
    Middle level of generality in naming objects

Pragmatic differences —
    More directives, imperatives, and questions
    More utterances designed to draw attention to aspects
        of objects

SOURCE: deVilliers & deVilliers, 1978.

aid the process of discovering how to use language); they also *complicate* what children say in order to foster language acquisition. This phenomenon was pointed out by Roger Brown and Ursula Bellugi (1964), who called this kind of adult speech "expansion" because it seemed to expand the child's utterance into a grammatically correct adult version. For example, a child who says "Mommy wash" might be responded to with "Yes, Mommy is washing her face"; the declaration "Daddy sleep" might evoke the caution, "Yes, Daddy is sleeping. Don't wake him up." Although it is possible that these tailored modifications of speaking help children to master language, existing evidence suggests that such deliberate teaching actually has little impact.

One line of such evidence comes from studies that link forms of adult expansion to children's language development. When Courtney Cazden attempted to "force-feed" children with a heavy diet of expansions, no special effect on language development was obtained (Cazden, 1965). Only when adults combined selective rephrasing of their children's utterances with helpful expansions and comments about ongoing joint activity could some effect on language development be detected (Nelson, 1976).

A second line of evidence against the idea that explicit adult tutoring is necessary for children to acquire language comes from research in cultures where adults fail to provide such tutoring. Samoan parents, for example, do not think that their infants are interesting conversational partners, nor do they believe in simplifying what they say for children or in guessing at children's meanings. Instead, they wait for the children to make themselves clear. But the children nonetheless acquire language at the same time that Americans and Europeans do (Ochs, 1982).

Although the specific simplifying behaviors typical of middle-class American adults may not be necessary to language development, some attention may need to be given to children for language to develop normally. Although Samoans do not engage in American-style helping activities, they have their own ways of guiding language acquisition. Samoan adults and older children explicitly coach beginning speakers about how to address other people. They utter sentences that the youngster is supposed to repeat for a third party; children as young as 3 years of age are expected to be able to deliver messages for older family members verbatim. Other tutoring practices have been observed in as divergent groups as the Kaluli of New Guinea and working-class children in Baltimore (Miller, 1982; Schieffelin, 1986).

Overall, the evidence indicates that all cultural groups take into account the fact that small children do not understand language and make some provision for seeing that they have the opportunity to acquire it. But it has not been possible to prove that a particular adult practice that might be called "teaching the child to speak" has an important impact on language acquisition nor that one method of structuring children's language experience is universally essential. Rather, the necessary condition for language acquisition is the integration of children into a culturally organized world. As young children struggle to make use of their increasingly sophisticated understanding of objects and social relations in order to gain control over their environments and themselves, they naturally acquire language as an essential tool for further development.

Only as children begin to acquire specialized skills that will be needed to cope with adult life does deliberate teaching begin to play a conspicuous role in language development. Such specialized activities as reciting nursery rhymes, acting in a play, and writing an essay in school are all forms of language activity requiring practice and instruction.

SUMMARY

1. Despite intensive investigation, the nature of language acquisition remains elusive. No theory is able to explain satisfactorily how children acquire either word meaning or the rules of word arrangement (syntax).

2. Three theories dominate late twentieth-century explanations of language acquisition. *Learning theories* claim that words and patterns of words are learned through imitation, and through classical and operant conditioning. *Structural-innatist theories* claim that children are born with a language acquisition device (LAD) that is automatically activated by the environment when the child has matured sufficiently. *Interactional theories* emphasize the cognitive preconditions for language acquisition and the role of the social environment in providing support for the child's development of language.

3. In the transition from babbling to talking, children begin to conform to the restricted set of sounds of the language their parents speak. The basic sounds of a language (phonemes) are those sounds that distinguish one word from another.

4. Early words indicate children's emerging ability to operate on the world indirectly (in a mediated way), as well as directly.

5. Early word meanings correspond to an intermediate level of abstraction. As a consequence, they are often too broad (overextensions) or too narrow (underextensions) to conform to adult definitions.

6. As the child's basic stock of words (the lexicon) increases, the structure of word meanings changes fundamentally; meanings embedded in particular contexts of action are supplemented by meanings dominated by logical categories.

7. Children's first words are often nonconventional; interpretation depends to a great extent on the listener's knowledge of the context in which they are used.

8. Two-word utterances allow children to take advantage of word relationships within utterances to convey meaning, marking the birth of syntax. As the length of utterances increases, so does the complexity of the grammatical rules governing the arrangement of words within sentences and word elements (morphemes) within words.

9. The growth of children's lexicons and their increased ability to use complex syntax are accompanied by a corresponding growth in their ability to engage in conversational acts with a variety of language uses.

10. Central to successful language use is the ability to say things in a way that will be understandable to conversational partners. Children reveal at an early age their ability to tailor their language to their listeners' needs.

11. Different theories of language acquisition propose different views of the relationship between language and thought:
    a. According to Chomsky, language and thought are independent of each other.
    b. According to Piagetians, developments in thought are the preconditions for language development.
    c. According to Vygotsky, language and thought arise independently but fuse in early childhood to create specifically human modes of thinking and communication.

12. Language is a particularly human communicative ability, but aspects of languagelike communication can be found among chimpanzees and other primates.

13. Basic elements of human language are acquired with no language input if children are raised in normal speaking or signing homes where communication is appropriate to the hearing ability of the child. However, developing the full range of language abilities requires both participation in human activity and exposure to language as part of that activity.

14. Although simplification of adult language to suit children's level of ability is observed in some cultures, special teaching techniques do not seem to be necessary for children to acquire language.

KEY TERMS

Abstract modeling

Collective monologues

General nominals

Grammatical morphemes

Holophrase

Language acquisition device (LAD)

Language acquisition support system (LASS)

Lexicon

Morphemes

Overextension

Pragmatic use of language

Recursion

Specific nominals

Syntax

Underextension

SUGGESTED READINGS

BRUNER, JEROME. *Child's Talk: Learning to Use Language.* New York: Norton, 1983.

For Jerome Bruner, learning language means learning to use language. In this slim book, Bruner explores the central role of participation in scriptlike interactions between children and adults in the process of language acquisition. He calls the social structuring of children's talk by adults a "language acquisition support system," which is the necessary complement to the innate language-learning mechanisms posited by Chomsky.

CHUKOVSKY, KORNEI. *From Two to Five.* Berkeley: University of California Press, 1968.

A renowned Soviet children's writer and translator provides a wealth of detail and wisdom about the creative processes involved in language acquisition. The book is especially rich in concrete examples collected over a lifetime of thinking about children and language.

CHOMSKY, NOAM. *Reflections on Language.* New York: Pantheon, 1976.

This small book by the man who revolutionized the study of language in the latter half of the 20th century was written for a nonspecialist audience. It provides one of the most accessible summaries of his ideas about language and its relationship to human psychological processes.

MILLER, GEORGE A. *Language and Speech.* New York: W. H. Freeman and Company, 1981.

Probably more than any other psychologist, George Miller has been responsible for introducing fundamentally important concepts of linguistics to American psychology. The book includes discussions of the origin of language in the species, the biological bases of language, and each of the major topics covered in the present text.

TERRACE, HERBERT. *Nim: A Chimpanzee Who Learned Sign Language.* New York: Washington Square Press, 1979.

Professor Terrace's account of the training of Nim Chimpsky has the rare quality of a scientific monograph written with humor and a willingness to describe how research really gets done. The final judgment of Nim's linguistic prowess will disappoint those hoping for communication with other species, but a great deal is learned about the nature and acquisition of language along the way.

PARADOXES OF THE PRESCHOOL MIND

> In every sentence . . . , in every childish act, is revealed complete ignorance of the
> simplest things. Of course, I cite these expressions not to scorn childish absurdities. On the
> contrary, they inspire me with respect because they are evidence of the gigantic work that
> goes on in the child's mind which, by the age of 7, results in the conquest of this mental chaos.
>
> —Kornei Chukovsky, *From Two to Five*

. . . .

A group of 5-year-old children have been listening to *Stone Soup,* a folktale retold by Marcia Brown, which is about three hungry soldiers who trick some selfish peasants into feeding them by pretending to make soup out of stones. "Do stones melt?" asks Rose, one of the children. Master Teacher Vivian Paley reports the conversation that followed this question:

"Do you think they melt, Rose?"
"Yes."
". . . Does anyone agree with Rose?"
"They *will* melt if you cook them," said Lisa.
"If you *boil* them," Eddie added.
No one doubted that the stones in the story had melted and that ours too would melt.
"We can cook them and find out," I said. "How will we be able to tell if they've melted?"
"They'll be smaller," said Deana.

The stones are placed in boiling water for an hour and then put on the table for inspection.

Ellen: They're much smaller.

Fred: Much, much. Almost melted.

Rose: I can't eat melted stones.

Teacher: Don't worry, Rose. You won't. But I'm not convinced they've melted. Can we prove it?

Paley suggests weighing the stones to see if they lose weight from boiling. They weigh two pounds at the start. After they're boiled again, the following conversation ensues:

Eddie: Still two [pounds]. But they *are* smaller.

Wally: Much smaller.

Teacher: They weigh the same. Two pounds before and two pounds now. That means they didn't lose weight.

Eddie: They only got a *little* bit smaller.

Wally: The scale can't *see* the stones. Hey, once in Michigan there were three stones in a fire and they melted away. They were gone. We saw it.

Deana: Maybe the stones in the story are magic.

Wally: But not these.

(Adapted from Paley, 1981, pp. 16–18.)

To the inquiring parent or psychologist, children between the ages of 2½ and 6 present a bewildering patchwork of ability and vulnerability, logic and magic, insight and ignorance. For example, when the children in Paley's classroom are enticed into reconciling the world of the story book and the world of their senses, their explanations are a mixture of sound physical theory and magical thinking. The children fully understand the idea that "melted stones" should grow smaller and that small stones should be lighter than big ones. At the same time they are willing to believe that there really are such things as magical stones that melt, leading them to misinterpret the point of *Stone Soup.*

In the domain of memory, to take another example, it is quite common for preschool children to recall the details of trips to the museum or to remember the location of a favorite toy they have not seen for hours (DeLoache & Brown, 1979; Fivush, Hudson, & Nelson, 1984). They have difficulty, however, recalling a list of unrelated familiar words or a set of toy objects immediately after they are asked to remember them (Case & Khanna, 1981).

The complexity of children's thought increases considerably between the end of infancy and the beginning of middle childhood. When 2½-year-olds see steam come out of a kettle or watch rain fall, they are unlikely to understand much about the causes of such events. Most 6- and 7-year-olds may still be uncertain about the precise causes, but they are likely to have learned about the connection between heating water and the appearance of steam or between the appearance of clouds and subsequent rain. The growth of such knowledge is a major factor promoting increasingly complex intellectual behavior during the preschool years (Carey, 1983; Flavell, 1985; Siegler, 1986).

In addition to gaining more factual knowledge, children also appear to gain skills in reasoning and logic between the ages of 2½ and 6. If 3-year-old children are asked to explain where babies come from, they may display no understanding that a causal account is called for, offering instead such statements as "It just grows inside" or "It was there all the time. Mommy doesn't have to do anything. She waits until she feels it." At the age of 5 or 6, on the other hand, children may have been given facts about the mechanics of reproduction, for which they then offer their own interpretations: "The seed is planted inside mommy's tummy; the fluid from the daddy's penis waters it; then the seed grows in the soil in the mommy's tummy." The older children's explanations leave much to be desired from a scientific point of view, but they clearly reflect an attempt at cause–effect reasoning (Carey, 1985).

Developmental psychologists' attempts to explain the patchwork of ability and incompetence that characterizes preschoolers' thought raise in a new way the basic questions of developmental continuity versus discontinuity and nature versus nurture. Is the unevenness of preschool thinking a result of variable maturation rates for different areas of the brain or does it result from variations in preschoolers' experience? Is the logic used by preschool children basically different from that used by adults or do their "illogical" conclusions merely reflect their relative ignorance of the world and its ways?

In the middle decades of this century, Jean Piaget's descriptions of young children's thinking dominated explanations of preschoolers' mental development. In recent years Piaget's account of early childhood development has been increasingly questioned by a number of researchers. Fruitful alternative lines of research and theory have sprung up, each of which pursues a somewhat different strategy for achieving an improved understanding of the preschool mind.

In this chapter we begin by describing Piaget's views and the observations of young children that motivated them. Then we will discuss the changes in this view in light of the research conducted in recent decades. Notice that even when today's specialists disagree with Piaget they still use his observations as the starting point for their work.

PIAGET'S ACCOUNT OF THE PRESCHOOL MIND

In Piaget's framework, the period between 2½ and 6 years is a time of transition during which children gradually overcome various mental barriers to systematic, logical thinking (Piaget & Inhelder, 1969).

With completion of the final sensorimotor substage, children have acquired the rudiments of representational thought, as we saw in Chapter 7. Forever after they are able to use one thing to stand for another, the fundamental capacity upon which their newfound ability to use language is based. They no longer rely exclusively on overt trial and error to solve problems; they imitate actions that they have observed in quite different circumstances; they engage in pretend play.

Even as simple a pastime as blowing bubbles gives children the opportunity to explore cause-and-effect relations.

But the ways in which young children think about the world are still decidedly primitive. Piaget was fascinated with preschoolers' theories about such varied phenomena as the nature of thinking and the origin of dreams, names, the sun, the wind, and trees. Dreams, he was told, come from the sky or the street lamps outside the child's window; we think with our mouths or our ears; clouds are alive; and the sun follows us when we move (Piaget, 1929).

When at the age of 6 or 7 children reach the stage of concrete operations, they are finally able to engage in what Piaget considered "true" mental **operations**. When this occurs, children are able to combine, separate, and transform information mentally in a logical manner. They know that the sun does not follow them around to give them light and that dreams do not come from street lamps. They still have many inaccurate theories about the world (as do adults!), but their reasoning loses its make-believe quality.

Piaget's belief that preschoolers are led into error and confusion because they are still unable to engage in true mental operations is captured in the name that he gave to this period, the **preoperational stage**. The paradoxes of the preschool mind are implicit in this negative formulation of 3-, 4-, and 5-year-old children's thinking as *not yet operational*. Negative definitions provide no guide to understanding the mechanisms of developmental change, nor can they be used to organize educational programs. Consequently, Piaget and those who have built upon his ideas have attempted to characterize in positive terms the special properties of preschool thought.

Piaget hypothesized that the key feature of preschool thinking is that children this age are able to focus attention (or *center,* as he called it) on only a single, salient aspect of whatever they are trying to think about. Only after overcoming this limitation do children make the transition to the stage of concrete operations. Two classic examples from Piaget's work have greatly influenced all subsequent thinking about early childhood development; they illustrate the limitations of centering on a single aspect of a problem.

First, as may be recalled from Chapter 1 (p. 28), preschoolers appear to become confused about the relationship between a class of objects and its subclasses. When shown a set of wooden beads, most of which are brown and the rest of which are white, preschoolers fail to keep simultaneously in mind both the nature of the full set and its differently colored members. When asked "Which are there more of, brown beads or wooden beads?" they focus on the subsets only and claim that there are more brown beads. When Piaget conducted this experiment, he inferred that preschoolers could only center on one aspect of the problem at a time — in this case, color. In middle childhood, on the other hand, children can keep in mind more than one feature of the problem. They remember both that there are more brown beads than white beads, and that there are more wooden beads than either. Thus they are not led into error.

The second example is perhaps Piaget's most famous demonstration of the difference between preoperational and concrete operational thinking. Children are presented with two identical beakers, each filled with exactly the same amount of water. While the child watches, the water in one of the beakers is poured into a third, narrower and taller beaker, so that the level of the water in the new beaker is higher. From this change in level, 3- and 4-year-olds conclude that the amount of water has somehow increased.

Piaget maintained that preschoolers err because they center on only a single dimension of the problem: the height of the water in the beaker. They are unable to consider simultaneously the height and width of the beaker. Once children are capable of mental operations, they firmly deny that the amount has changed, presumably because their thinking has become decentered and they can consider several aspects of the problem at once. Thus they are able to think through what would happen if the water were poured back into its original beaker at the same time that they keep track of the information about the new beaker.

We will return to these examples in Chapter 13 because they play a central role in theories of thinking during middle childhood. Here, we will concentrate on the difficulties young children experience when asked to adopt multiple points of view, to make a clear distinction between appearances and reality, or to explain causal relations.

Egocentrism

A basic characteristic of preoperational thought, according to Piaget (1983), is its egocentric character. Recall from Chapter 6 that as a technical term within Piaget's theory, **egocentrism** has a narrower meaning than its use in everyday speech. It does not mean selfish or arrogant. Rather, it means to interpret the world

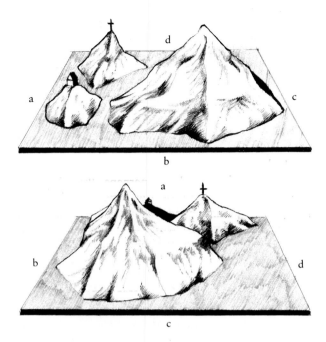

FIGURE 10.1 *Preschool children shown this diorama of three mountains with distinctive landmarks on each mountain were unable to say how the scene might look from perspectives other than the one they had adopted at the moment. (From Piaget & Inhelder, 1956.)*

from "ego's" point of view, the point of view of the self. Relative to young infants, who, according to Piaget, are totally centered on their own actions (thus, *ego-centric*), preschool children are far more anchored in external reality. However, they still have only a hazy idea of how their ideas and desires relate to the world around them, and they tend to assume that everyone else sees things just as they do. Piaget believed that as a consequence of this centering on themselves, preschoolers have distinctive difficulties in a variety of problem-solving situations. He described the source of these difficulties in the following way:

> In order to be objective, one must have become conscious of one's "I." Objective knowledge can only be conceived in relation to subjective, and a mind that was ignorant of itself would inevitably tend to put into things its own pre-notions and prejudices. . . . [O]riginally the child puts the whole content of consciousness on the same plane and draws no distinction between "I" and the external world. (Piaget, 1930, pp. 241–242)

The egocentric nature of preschool thought is revealed by the difficulty young children have adopting another person's perceptual point of view. The classic example of this form of egocentrism is the "three mountains problem" studied by Piaget and Inhelder (1956). In this task, preschoolers are confronted with a large diorama representing three distinctively marked mountains, each of which is a different size and shape (see Figure 10.1).

Children are first asked to walk around the diorama and to become familiar with the landscape. Once they have familiarized themselves with it, they are seated at one side and shown a doll. The doll is placed on a different side of the diorama from the children so that it has a "different view" of the landscape. The children are then shown pictures of the diorama from several different perspectives and asked to identify the picture that corresponds to the doll's point of view. Despite the fact that they have traveled around the diorama, preoperational children almost always choose the picture corresponding to their own point of view, not the doll's.

The egocentric quality of children's thought also appears in their speech. Recall from Chapter 9, for example, the tendency of young children to engage in "collective monologues" when playing together rather than true dialogues. This quality also becomes evident when two preschoolers are seated at a table and asked to communicate with each other about identical sets of toys arrayed before them. In experiments of this kind a small screen is placed between the children so that they cannot see each other (for a review of the literature on this type of experiment, see Glucksberg, Krauss & Higgins, 1975). The experimenter indicates one of the toys to a child and asks her to describe that toy to the other child, who must choose it from her own array. A typical experimental arrangement is shown in Figure 10.2.

Most 4- and 5-year-old children fail to include information that the other person needs to know in order to understand which toy is being described. It is not at all unusual to hear the following kind of dialogue:

Child 1: She has picked out this one [*child points at correct toy*].

Child 2: Do you mean this one [*pointing at one of the toys on her side of the barrier*]?

Child 1: Yes. I told you this one!

Speaker   Listener

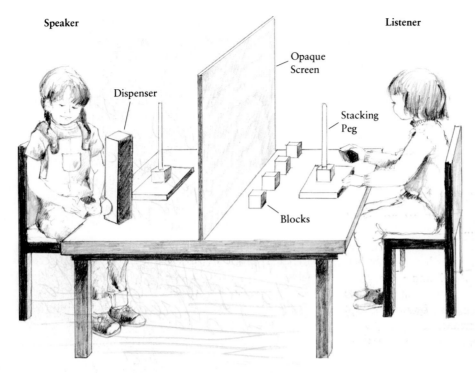

FIGURE 10.2 *The task of keeping in mind what someone else needs to be told in order to communicate with that person effectively often defeats preschoolers. In the drawing above, the children must describe the blocks they have, being careful to mention their distinguishing features, in order to stack them in the same order. (From Krauss & Glucksberg, 1969.)*

Evidently, these preoperational children are not able to imagine what information another person with a different point of view might need.

Distinguishing Appearance from Reality

Another distinctive feature of preschool thought is a tendency to focus attention on what is perceptually most striking, that is, on surface appearances. This makes it difficult for the preschooler to distinguish between the way things seem to be and the way they are (Flavell, 1985). An example of the appearance – reality distinction is the changed appearance of a straight stick when it is partially submerged in water: the stick looks bent, but adults know it is not (see Figure 10.5). Preschoolers, however, may believe the stick has actually changed. Likewise, because they have difficulty with the appearance – reality distinction, 2½-year-olds may become frightened at Halloween time when an older child puts on a mask, as if the

mask had actually changed the child into a witch or a dragon.

Rheta De Vries (1969) took advantage of small children's confusion over the reality behind masks to study the development of the appearance – reality distinction. In separate experimental sessions, each child was introduced to Maynard, an unusually well-behaved black cat. At the start of the experiment, each child was told, "I want to show you my pet. Do you know what it is?" All of the children were able to say that Maynard was a cat. Then they were encouraged to play with Maynard for a short while, after which De Vries hid Maynard's front half behind a screen while she strapped a realistic mask of a ferocious dog onto his head (see Figure 10.3a). The children were asked to keep their eyes on the cat's tail while the mask was put on so that they would be certain that she was not switching one animal for another. As she removed the screen, De Vries told each child, "Now this animal is going to look quite different. Look, it has a face like a dog."

De Vries went on to ask a set of questions designed

to assess the child's ability to distinguish between the animal's real identity and its appearance. She included such queries as the following: "What kind of animal is it now?" "Is it *really* a dog?" "Can it bark?" The strength of children's ability to distinguish appearance and reality was measured on an 11-point scale, whereby children who fully believed that the cat had turned into a dog were given a score of 1, while children who believed that the cat only appeared to become a dog but could never really become one were rated 11.

By and large, the 3-year-olds focused almost entirely on Maynard's appearance (see Figure 10.3*b*). They thought he had actually become a ferocious dog and some of them were afraid he would bite them. Most of the 6-year-olds scoffed at this idea, understanding that the cat only looked like a dog. The 4- and 5-year-olds showed considerable confusion. They didn't believe that a cat could become a dog, but they could not always keep the fact that Maynard remained a cat firmly enough in mind to answer DeVries' questions correctly.

Precausal Reasoning

Piaget believed that on some occasions young children reason in a loose and illogical manner. They seem indifferent to causal explanations or they seriously confuse cause and effect. On the basis of his observations Piaget (1930) termed preschool children's thinking **precausal.**

A clear example of a preschool child's confusion of cause and effect is provided by our own daughter. At the age of $3\frac{1}{2}$, Jenny happened to walk with us through an old graveyard. Listening to us read the inscriptions on the gravestones, she realized that somehow these old moss-covered stones represented people. "Where is she now?" she asked when we finished reading the inscription on one stone.

"She's dead," we told her.

"But where is she?" We tried to explain that after people die they are buried in the ground, in cemeteries. After that, Jenny steadfastly refused to go into cemeteries with us and would become upset when we were near one. At bedtime every evening, she repeatedly asked us about death, burial, and graveyards. We answered her questions as best we could, yet she kept asking the same questions. The reason for her fear

(a)

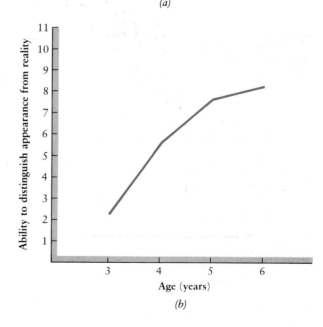

(b)

FIGURE 10.3 *(a) Maynard the cat, without and with a dog mask. (b) The growth of the ability to understand that Maynard remains a cat even when his appearance is changed so that he looks like a dog. (Adapted from DeVries, 1969.)*

became clear when we were moving to New York City. "Are there any graveyards in New York City?" she asked anxiously. We were exhausted by her insistent questions, and our belief that we should be candid and honest was crumbling.

"No," we lied. "There are no graveyards in New York City." At this response, she visibly relaxed.

"Then people don't die in New York," she said a couple of minutes later. In her confusion of cause and effect, Jenny had reasoned that since graveyards are

The idea of death is especially difficult for preschoolers to grasp.

places where dead people are found, graveyards must be the cause of death. This led her to the magical conclusion that if you can stay away from graveyards, you are not in danger of dying.

THE STUDY OF PRESCHOOL THINKING AFTER PIAGET

Piaget's great contribution to the study of early childhood thinking was to provide a theory to account for how all the different phenomena he studied fit together, and how all fit into the overall sequence of

With preschoolers' increased understanding and growing ability to imagine come new fears. (Top) A little girl is frightened by a bearded creature in a red suit, whom we know to be Santa Claus. (Bottom) A 5-year-old's drawing of the monster who wakes him up in the middle of the night. (Drawing courtesy of Dr. J. Welsh.)

cognitive development. His theory's comprehensive nature, plus the vivid and convincing reports of his interviews, won wide acceptance for his hypothesis about a stage of preoperational thinking for several decades, despite some criticism (Isaacs, 1966; Vygotsky 1934/1987).

In the past decade, however, several investigators have shown that when the problems presented are simplified, or when they deal with topics familiar to the children, preschoolers sometimes reveal themselves to be capable of the more sophisticated ways of thinking that Piaget had thought reserved for middle childhood (Gelman, 1978; Gelman & Baillargeon, 1983). This new evidence of effective thinking has inspired a broad reexamination of Piaget's theory of early childhood thought processes.

The Problem of Uneven Levels of Performance

A common problem for all post-Piagetian theories of early childhood thought is to account for the extreme unevenness of preschool children's performance when they are presented with different versions of what appear to be the same intellectual problem. Piaget himself realized that there was some variation in children's performance from one version of a problem to the next, a phenomenon that he labeled horizontal decalage. However, Piaget believed that, in general, a common set of underlying cognitive structures characterizes children's behavior in each stage. As a consequence, at each stage it should be possible to predict how a child will perform a wide variety of tasks that are believed to require a particular mode of thought (Flavell, 1985; Levin, 1986). Children in the sensorimotor stage are assumed to reason through overt action; children in the concrete operational phase are assumed to reason through logical manipulation of symbols. Preschoolers should manifest characteristics of preoperational thought: that is, they should fail to distinguish their point of view from that of others, become easily captured by surface appearances, and often be confused about causal relations.

No one, of course, would expect young children to be *totally* consistent in the way that they reason and solve problems. Common sense suggests that a child's performance might differ depending upon such factors as familiarity with the particular objects being

reasoned about or the way that experimenters frame their questions. It is equally reasonable to expect that children, as well as adults, will slip up from time to time and perform less maturely than expected.

However, the evidence of grossly uneven levels of performance by preschoolers who have been presented with what appear to be logically equivalent problems has become so pervasive as to cast doubt on Piaget's account of this period of development. The difficulties can be illustrated by research using modifications of the same kinds of problem situations that Piaget had used to conclude that early childhood thinking is egocentric, confuses reality and appearance, and is precausal.

Nonegocentric reasoning The presumed inability of preschoolers to comprehend another person's point of view provides a case that appears to put a great strain on the concept of horizontal decalage as a way of explaining variable levels of performance within

"Quick, hon. I think he's got it."

Psychologists are in disagreement about preschool children's ability to construct such a logical series. Were a preschooler to succeed, however, it would be on the basis of the pictures and not on the symbolic meaning the series has for adults. (Drawing by Lorenz; ©1987 The New Yorker Magazine, Inc.)

what is presumably a single stage of development (see Flavell, 1985; Gelman & Baillargeon, 1983, for reviews of this topic). In one study, Helen Borke (1975) replicated the original Piaget and Inhelder "three mountain" experiment, but included an alternative form of the problem. One version of the task was precisely like the Piaget and Inhelder problem; of three mountains, one was snow-capped, one had a church on it, and one had a house (see Figure 10.1). In the other version, there was a small lake with a boat on it, a horse and cow, and a building. These landmarks were placed in approximately the same locations on the diorama as the three mountains (see Figure 10.4).

In Borke's alternative version, Grover, a character from the television program *Sesame Street*, drove around the landscape in a car. From time to time he would stop and take a look at the view. The child's task was to indicate what Grover's view of the scene looked like. Children as young as 3 years old performed well on Borke's "farm scene" version of the problem, but their performance on the three-mountain version of the problem was poor, as Piaget and Inhelder's work had suggested. These contrasting levels of performance led Borke to conclude that when easily differentiated objects are used and care is taken to make it easy for preschoolers to express their understanding, they are able to imagine perspectives

FIGURE 10.4 *Borke's modification of Piaget's three-mountain perspective-taking task. When confronted with familiar objects in a diorama, preschoolers are more likely to be able to say how the scene looks from a point of view other than their own.*

other than their own. On the basis of similar results from similar experiments, Margaret Donaldson (1978) suggests that 3- to 5-year-old children can display a nonegocentric perspective, but the motives and intentions of the characters involved in the problem must be clear, so that the task makes what she calls "human sense."

Distinguishing appearance from reality   In a series of studies, John Flavell and his colleagues showed children various objects that appeared to be one thing but were really another: a sponge that appeared to be a rock, a stone that appeared to be an egg, and a small piece of white paper placed behind a transparent piece of pink plastic. The children were then asked to say what the object looked like and what it "really really" was under a variety of conditions (Flavell, Flavell, & Green, 1983; Flavell, Green, & Flavell, 1986).

Consistent with Piaget's claims about the difficulties that preschool children experience in distinguishing reality from appearance, these researchers found that American 3-year-olds were very likely to answer incorrectly. Chinese 3-year-olds experienced similar difficulties (Flavell, Zhang, Zou, Dong & Qi, 1983).

However, even 3-year-olds showed some ability to distinguish between the way the objects appeared and their real nature. The expression of this ability seemed to depend upon the objects used and the method for creating a misleading appearance. When the white paper was placed behind a pink plastic screen, most 3-year-olds said it only appeared to be pink. But when shown the "sponge-rock" object they said not only that it looked like a rock but that it "really really" was one too. Most 5-year-olds seemed to have the reality–appearance distinction well in hand in a variety of distorting conditions, but even they could be fooled in some circumstances. (For an example of how difficult it can sometimes be to distinguish between appearance and reality, see Figure 10.5.)

Confirmation that children begin to make the appearance–reality distinction at an earlier age than anticipated by Piaget is provided by an experiment that asked 4-year-olds to distinguish between how a character in a story really felt about a situation and how he or she behaved publicly (Harris, Donnelly, Guz, & Pitt-Watson, 1986). These researchers presented children with stories such as the following:

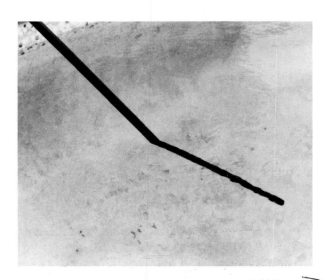

FIGURE 10.5 *A straight stick seen through water looks bent. The distinction between what a thing is really like and how it appears under certain circumstances is only partially mastered during early childhood.*

Diana wants to go outside, but she has a tummy ache. She knows that if she tells her Mom that she has a tummy ache, her Mom will say that she can't go out. She tries to hide the way she feels so that her Mom will let her go outside.

When the researchers asked "How did Diana really feel when she had a tummy ache?" and "How did she try to look on her face when she had a tummy ache?" Harris and his colleagues found that 4-year-olds were usually able to distinguish between real and displayed feelings. However, this ability, as in the case of the problems posed by Flavell and his colleagues, was fragile, and the 4-year-olds were generally unable to justify their correct judgments in a reasoned manner.

Effective causal reasoning   One of Piaget's best-known examples of precausal reasoning came from interviews with children about the causal mechanisms of bicycles. Piaget asked children to explain how a bicycle works and to draw a picture illustrating their explanations. During the interview a bicycle was propped against a chair in front of the child. The following interview with Grim, aged 5½, illustrates the kind of evidence that led Piaget to conclude that the

reasoning of preschoolers is precausal (Piaget, 1930, p. 206):

Piaget: How does the bicycle move along?
Grim: With the brakes on top of the bike.
Piaget: What is the brake for?
Grim: To make it go because you push.
Piaget: What do you push with?
Grim: With your feet.
Piaget: What does that do?
Grim: It makes it go.
Piaget: How?
Grim: With the brakes.

In the late 1920s Piaget visited the Malting House School in Cambridge, England, where Susan Isaacs was also conducting research on preschool children. Isaacs was skeptical about Piaget's ideas on preoperational thought. When she spotted one of her preschoolers riding by on a tricycle, she put her visitor's theory to the following impromptu test:

At that moment, Dan [aged 5 years, 9 months], happened to be sitting on a tricycle in the garden, back-pedaling. I went to him and said, "The tricycle is not moving forward, is it?" "Of course not, when I'm back-pedaling," he said. "Well," I asked, "how does it go forward when it does?" "Oh, well," he replied, "your feet press the pedals, that turns the crank round, and the cranks turn that round" (pointing to the cog-wheel), "and that makes the chain go round, and the chain turns the hub round, and then the wheels go round—and there you are!" (Isaacs, 1966, p. 44)

Isaacs offered this anecdote as evidence against Piaget's theory that preschool children are incapable of causal reasoning. Before accepting either conclusion, most developmental psychologists would require more information about how the striking difference between the reasoning of Grim and Dan arose. Is Dan simply an especially advanced preschooler? Is the difference in their performances the result of differences in the way the problems were posed to them? Systematic answers to such questions require experiments that deliberately vary the way in which the problems are presented.

FIGURE 10.6 *The apparatus used by Bullock and Gelman to test preschoolers' understanding that cause precedes effect. A marble was dropped into the one of the slots. Two seconds after the marble disappeared into the slot, a Snoopy doll popped out of the hole in the middle of the apparatus. At the same moment, a second marble was dropped into the other slot, where it disappeared with no further result. Preschoolers are generally able to indicate which marble caused Snoopy to jump up. (From Bullock & Gelman, 1979.)*

During the 1970s and 1980s experiments by developmental psychologists provided ample evidence to support the conclusion that, when the task is sufficiently simplified, preschoolers understand causation to an extent far beyond what Piaget thought typical (Bullock, 1984; Bullock & Gelman, 1979). Merry Bullock and Rochele Gelman, for example, tested the ability of 3- to 5-year-olds to understand the basic principle that causes come before effects, using the apparatus shown in Figure 10.6.

Children observed two sequences of events. In the first, a steel marble was dropped into one of the slots, which were both visible through the side of the box. Two seconds after the marble disappeared at the bottom of the slot, a Snoopy doll popped out of the hole in the apparatus's middle. At that moment, a second ball was dropped into the other slot where it too disappeared, with no further result. The children were asked which ball had made Snoopy jump up and to give a reason for their answer. Then they were given a ball and asked to drop it into the apparatus on the side that made Snoopy jump up.

Even the 3-year-olds were usually correct in selecting the side that caused Snoopy to jump up. The 5-year-olds had no difficulty with the task at all. However, there was a marked difference between the age groups in their ability to explain what had happened. Many of the 3-year-olds could give no explanation or said something completely irrelevant ("It's got big teeth"). Almost all of the 5-year-olds could provide at least a partial explanation of the principle that causes precede effects. This finding suggests one reason why Piaget underestimated the cognitive competence of preschoolers; his research techniques relied heavily on verbally presented problems and verbal justifications of reasoning, both of which put young preschoolers at a disadvantage (see Box 10.1 on preschoolers as court witnesses).

The search for alternatives The various lines of evidence that preschoolers are capable of thinking in ways previously assumed to be the province of older children has been the starting point for several attempts to improve on Piaget's approach. One group of psychologists, the **neo-Piagetians,** have reaffirmed Piaget's fundamental assumptions about the nature of development, but are refining Piaget's theory to account for modern evidence. A second group, those who adopt an **information-processing approach,** have taken an altogether different tack by studying the preschool child as a limited-capacity information processor whose thinking can best be understood through analogy with the digital computer. A third group of psychologists have suggested that the psychological developments that Piaget thought to be the result of constructive interaction between the child and the world are really a consequence of biological maturation. Finally, a fourth group of psychologists emphasizes the role of adults in constructing cultural contexts that foster children's development, as opposed to Piaget's view that development results from the child's independent cognitive inventions.

Neo-Piagetian Theories of Cognitive Development

There have been two major strands in neo-Piagetian attempts to account for preschool thought. One retains Piaget's idea that children construct knowledge through the interplay of assimilation and accommodation, but argues that stages of knowledge acquisition occur only within narrowly circumscribed spheres of activity, or domains, such as social reasoning, drawing, music, language, and mathematics (Damon, 1977; Feldman, 1980; Fischer, 1980; Gelman & Baillargeon, 1983; Karmiloff-Smith, 1986). The basic intuition of this approach is summarized by Jean Mandler: "It may well be that in many areas of thinking there is no generalized competence, only hard-won principles wrested anew from each domain as it is explored" (1983, p. 475). According to this way of thinking, there may be little correspondence between the level of development a child displays in one situation and the developmental level he or she displays in another because children's thinking may progress differently in different spheres of activity.

An example of this approach is provided by Malcom Watson and Kurt Fischer (1980), who tested children's ability to understand and act out two kinds of social relations. In the first case the roles they studied were *doctor*, *patient*, and *nurse*. Using dolls, an adult modeled a particular relationship that children were then asked to act out. At the age of 3½, children could make a doll doctor put a thermometer in the patient doll's mouth. At the age of 4, the children managed a relationship where both dolls are active: the doctor doll examined the patient doll and responded appropriately to the patient doll's complaints (e.g., examining the doll patient's ears for an earache and its stomach for a stomachache). At the age of 5, children could make the doctor doll relate simultaneously to a patient and a nurse doll.

The same children were asked to participate in an analogous role-playing game involving fathers and children. In this task children had to explain the concept of father under various conditions. At the simplest level, it was only necessary to say that a father is a man who has children; at the next, children had to say how a father can become a grandfather; at the next, how a father can be both a father and a grandfather, and so on.

In both of these tasks, the complications were mastered strictly in the order of complexity, illustrating the kind of stepwise progressions that are expected by Piagetian theory. However, there was little correspondence between the levels that individual children attained on the two tasks. Many children reached a high level on the "doctor" task, but a low level on the "father" task. This kind of discrepancy is the basis for neo-Piagetians' insistence that each domain must be examined separately.

A second line of neo-Piagetian work, adopted by Robbie Case and his colleagues, maintains that if researchers can gain a sufficiently precise understanding of the knowledge required by each cognitive domain,

they may eventually achieve Piaget's initial goal of defining global stages that apply to all domains (Case, 1985; Case, Marini, McKeough, Dennis, & Goldberg, 1986). According to this view, when task-specific knowledge is equally demanding in each domain and the logical structure of all the tasks is the same, a general quality of mind will appear across domains in the child's behavior.

To demonstrate the possibility of synchronous stages in different domains, Case and his colleagues constructed two sets of problems with identical logical structures. The first required children to calculate how "juicy" a drink made up of different mixtures of orange juice and water would taste. For example, would a mixture made up of five parts juice and three parts water taste as juicy as a mixture made up of four parts juice and one part water?

The second, logically equivalent, problem concerned two boys, each of whom was having a birthday party and each of whom wanted polished stones for his birthday (in the school where the investigators were conducting their research, polished stones were highly prized by the children). The children were shown how many stones each boy wanted and how many he actually received. Then they were asked, "Which child would be happier?" For 89 percent of the preschoolers tested, the estimated level of cognitive development for the two kinds of problems was either the same or only a single problem-solving stage off (Case, Marini, McKeough, Dennis, & Goldberg, 1986). The fact that the children reached virtually the same levels of reasoning on the two tasks supports the hypothesis that when enough care is taken to equate the logical structure of two problems with content from different domains, synchronous change across domains of the kind Piaget believed in can be observed.

Information-Processing Approaches

Some psychologists want to replace Piaget's vision with a view of humans as information-processing organisms whose thought processes can best be understood by analogy with the mechanisms of high-speed computers (Klahr & Wallace, 1976; Siegler, 1986).

BOX 10.1

PRESCHOOL WITNESSES

· · ·

The nature of preschoolers' thought processes becomes an important social issue when young children are called upon to give testimony in a court of law. In some cases, they may be witnesses to a crime, in others, suspected victims of a crime.

There is a long history of doubting the word of preschool children. Psychologists have viewed young children as suggestible (Stern, 1910); unable to distinguish fantasy from reality (Piaget, 1926, 1928; Werner, 1948); and prone to fantasize sexual events (Freud, 1905). Judges, lawyers, and prosecutors have also expressed reservations about children's reliability as witnesses (Goodman, 1984). Legal rulings on the admissibility of children's testimony reflect these long-standing doubts. In many states, for example, the judge determines whether a child below a certain age (which varies from state to state) is competent to testify (King & Yuille, 1987).

In recent years, however, due to growing concern over the prevalence of sexual and physical abuse of children, the legal community has re-examined the reliability of children's testimony. At the same time, psychologists are raising their own doubts about earlier evaluations of the inability of young children to testify about prior events (Ceci, Toglia, & Ross, 1987).

At the heart of the current discussion of child testimony are two questions: How good are children's memories at different ages? and How susceptible are young children to suggestions that change what they remember?

Reason for concern is provided both by children's behavior in actual trials and in experimental studies conducted by psychologists. For example, in a case in which the adults were eventually convicted of sexual abuse, children at first denied that anything unusual had happened. They then recounted tales of sexual abuse leading to conviction of their baby-sitter and her husband, but also said outrageous, fanciful things — for example, that after the assaults, the children were eaten for dinner by the baby-sitter and her husband (Goodman, Aman, & Hirschman, 1987).

Experimental evidence of preschoolers' vulnerability to suggestion is illustrated in an experiment where 3- and 4-year-old children first witnessed a staged incident involving three men and a woman, and were then interviewed by an experienced police officer about the woman's appearance. One session went as follows:

Q: Wearing a poncho and a cap?
A: I think it was a cap.
Q: What sort of a cap was it? Was it like a beret, or was it a peaked cap, or . . . ?
A: No, it had a sort of, it was flared with a little piece coming out. It was flared with a sort of button thing in the middle.
Q: What . . . Was it a peak like that, that sort of thing?
A: Ye – es.
Q: That's the sort of cap I'm thinking you're meaning, with a little peak out there.

David Klahr, a leading figure in this movement, expressed his dissatisfaction with Piagetian theorizing about development in the following colorful terms:

For 40 years now we have had *assimilation* and *accommodation,* the mysterious and shadowy forces of equilibration, the "Batman and Robin" of the developmental processes. What are they? How do they operate? Why is it after all this time, we know no more about them than when they first sprang upon the scene? What we need is a way to get beyond vague verbal statements of the nature of the developmental process.
(Klahr, 1982, p. 80)

A: Yes, that's the top view, yes.

Q: Smashing. Um—what colour?

A: Oh! Oh—I think it was black or brown.

Q: Think it was dark, shall we say?

A: Yes—it was dark colour I think, and I didn't see her hair.

(Dent, 1982, pp. 290–291)

In fact, the woman in the staged scene was wearing neither a poncho nor a hat. The child not only came to "remember" these items, but even added that the woman carried a dark purse to match her hat! As Elizabeth Loftus and Graham Davies (1984) point out, by persistent requests for details, the police officer leads the child into error.

Such results appear to support the common wisdom that young children are especially suggestible. But adult memories have also been shown to be highly susceptible to suggestion. For example, Loftus (1979) reports several studies in which adults are shown a film of a complex event such as a traffic accident and then asked a series of questions about it. Typically, some of the questions are misleading and some suggest the existence of objects that were not a part of the scene. In one such case, people were asked "How fast was the white car going when it passed the barn while traveling on the country road?" Later they were likely to report having seen the barn, even though there was no such barn in the film they were shown. As many as 80 percent of the people in Loftus' studies were influenced by misinformation introduced through questioning, so suggestibility definitely cannot be thought of as peculiar to preschool thinking.

A number of recent studies directly concerned with early childhood memory and child testimony have found that when preschoolers are simply allowed to retell an event, or to reenact it with props, their recall is relatively accurate, although they recall fewer details than adults (Cole & Loftus, 1987).

The weakest aspect of preschoolers' recall is locating events in time and being able to give specific examples of recurrent events. This weakness may make it difficult for adults to piece together children's accounts into a coherent story. However, adults' probing for more information may also lead to problems. For example, Katherine Nelson (1978) asked preschoolers about what happens when they eat lunch at school. She found that if she asked for information that children did not have (e.g., "Where did the lunch come from?") they would provide responses that appeared to come from other scripted events such as a restaurant or a market (e.g., "Mommy bought it"), rather than saying they did not know.

At present, there is no reliable way to overcome the pitfalls of preschoolers' legal testimony. By using the same kinds of techniques that have proved useful in supporting preschoolers' memory and problem solving (evoking scenes that make human sense to the child, providing props in the form of dolls and dioramas) it is possible that the investigator will bring to light memories that children do not spontaneously report. But insofar as these same techniques falsely suggest aspects of the original event to the child, the child may say things that have no basis in reality. Thus, it is still extremely difficult to determine the accuracy of young children's testimony.

Figure 10.7 contains a simplified schematic diagram of one influential information-processing approach. At the left-hand side is the presumed starting point of any problem-solving process. Some kind of stimulation ("input" in the language of computer programming) is attended to and "read into" the system's **sensory register.** Then it is stored in **short-term (working) memory,** where it can be retained for several seconds. The environmental information deposited in short-term memory is combined there with memory for past experiences (**long-term memory**). Short-term memory is continually monitored by control processes that determine how stored information is to be applied to the problem at hand—for example, whether new infor-

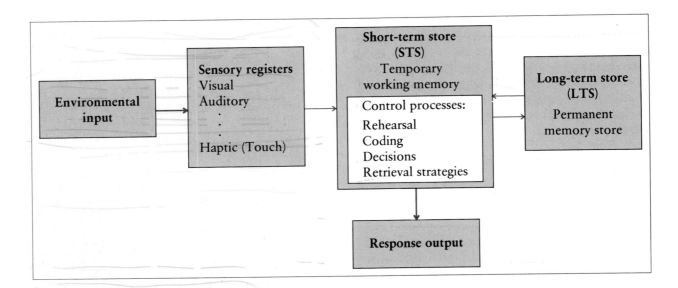

FIGURE 10.7 *A schematic summary of the major components in an information-processing model of mental actions. (Adapted from Atkinson & Shiffrin, 1971.)*

mation must be gathered from the environment, or whether long-term memory must be searched more thoroughly for a better response.

A pervasive assumption that unites information-processing psychologists, despite differences among them, is the belief that human beings, like computers, have limited information-processing capacities. From this perspective, cognitive development is a process whereby children *reduce limitations* on their ability to process information. In this view, young children's difficulties are caused by insufficient or uneven attention, limited memory, and limited strategies (Siegler, 1986).

These limitations take several forms. First, preschoolers' attention is easily captured by loud, flashy, stimuli, which means that they are likely to be easily distracted. When they lose their train of thought in the middle of doing something, their performance naturally suffers.

Second, even when they are not distracted, preschoolers are likely to explore an object in an unsystematic way. This aspect of preschool attention was demonstrated some years ago by Soviet psychologist Vladimir Zinchenko and his colleagues (Zinchenko, Chzhitsin, & Tarakanov, 1963), who asked 3- and 6-year-olds to examine various objects and become familiar with them. As shown in Figure 10.8, the 3-year-olds examined only a few points within the object, while the 6-year-olds gave it a thorough examination.

Third, preschoolers have difficulty focusing on the most relevant features of a task if there are no strong

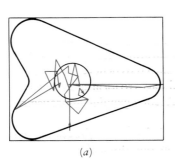

(a)

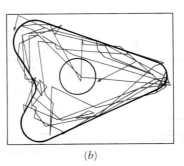

(b)

FIGURE 10.8 *Most 3-year-olds (a) asked to examine a novel figure for 20 seconds are less persistent and thorough than 6-year-olds (b) assigned the same task. (From Zinchenko, Chzhi-tsin, & Tarakanov, 1963.)*

hints from the environment. This limitation of pre-schoolers' attention was demonstrated by Eliane Vur-pillot (1968), who recorded the eye movements of children aged 3 to 10 while they examined pairs of line drawings of houses such as those shown in Figure 10.9. On some trials, children were shown identical houses, on some the houses differed in one or more ways. Children were asked to say whether or not the houses were identical.

Vurpillot found that all of the children responded correctly when the houses were identical, but that the preschoolers were likely to make mistakes when the houses differed, especially if they differed only in one way. Her recordings of eye movements pinpointed the difficulty. The preschoolers scanned several windows in haphazard order, rather than making a systematic comparison. The older children scanned the windows row by row or column by column until they had checked almost all of them, sometimes scanning back again to check themselves. Preschoolers thus seem to have only limited ability to select relevant details.

A variety of research has identified other limitations in the amount of information that preschoolers take in and their subsequent ability to store and manipulate it. For example, Chi and Klahr (1975) found that 5-year-olds could immediately perceive no more than three objects flashed briefly on a screen, while adults could take in six or seven objects at a glance. With respect to short-term memory, Case and Khanna (1981), among many others, have demonstrated age-related increases in the ability to hold several items of information in mind at one time. Thus older children and adults can work through various steps in complex problems without losing track of what they are doing, while young children cannot. Finally, older children and adults have generally accumulated more knowledge and developed more effective strategies for dealing with various problems than have preschoolers. This information is available in long-term memory storage and can be applied to new problems as they arise, leading to competent performance (Chi & Koeske, 1983; Siegler, 1986).

This view of preschoolers' information-processing limitations suggests that when children are interested in a task, when information is presented slowly, and when children have good background knowledge, their cognitive performance should be enhanced. These are precisely the circumstances arranged by ex-perimenters whose preschool subjects have demon-strated competence on the Piagetian tasks reviewed

FIGURE 10.9 *Stimuli used by Vurpillot to assess visual search. Preschoolers fail to scan systematically, which often leads them to claim that the top pair of houses are identical. (From Vurpillot, 1968.)*

earlier in this chapter. Information-processing psy-chologists are thus encouraged to believe that by shift-ing the focus from global stages to local circumstances, their approach may represent a genuine improvement on Piaget.

We will discuss the information-processing ap-proach in more detail in our discussion of middle childhood because very few explicit computer models of young children's thinking have been developed. However, it is worth pointing out here that adopting the information-processing perspective and the child-as-computer metaphor does not necessarily commit the investigator to a particular point of view about the nature of development itself. For example, some information-processing psychologists believe that development is a continuous process in which limitations on memory capacity are gradually overcome, long-term memory capacity gradually increases, behaviors are routinized, and strategies are developed to link input more effectively to output (Klahr & Wallace, 1976; Siegler, 1986). Others believe that gradual changes in one part of the cognitive system — for example, increased short-term memory capacity — lead to discontinuous, stage-like changes in the overall functioning of the child. This second group uses the information-processing metaphor in the service of Piagetian or neo-Piagetian theorizing (Case, 1985; Fischer, 1980).

Biological Accounts of Preschoolers' Mental Development

So far we have accounted for uneven preschool performances according to how tasks are presented: in a familiar and comfortable way or in a way that is unfamiliar or confusing. It is entirely possible, however, that preschool limitations are simply a reflection of preschoolers' relative physical immaturity, later to be overcome by the normal processes of growth.

As indicated by the growth charts presented in Chapter 6 (Figures 6.2 and 6.3), preschoolers undergo a steady process of growth in the years leading up to middle childhood; 5-year-olds are markedly larger and better coordinated than 2½-year-olds. In attempting to account for preschoolers' mental development, attention has naturally focused on developmental changes in the brain.

The growth of the brain   One promising line of research implicating biological growth in cognitive development during early childhood comes from evidence that developmental changes in the brain correspond to changes in behavior. We have already

reviewed evidence supporting such correspondences as part of the bio-social-behavioral shifts that occur during infancy (see Chapters 5, 6, and 7). Maturational changes in the brain have likewise been proposed to explain psychological changes between the ages of 2½ and 6 (Case, 1984; Fischer & Pipp, 1984; Milner, 1967).

At the start of the preschool period, the brain has attained about 50% of its adult weight. By the age of 6, the brain will have grown to 90 percent of its adult weight (Lecours, 1982; Tanner, 1978). Within this overall process of growth, myelination within and between several areas appears to play a particularly important role in preschoolers' cognitive development (see Figure 5.8 for an overview of major brain areas). First, the auditory system develops quite rapidly, which is consistent with the fact that the preschool period is a time of rapid language growth. Second, more effective connections are established between the temporal, occipital, and parietal areas, which are crucially important for the processing of temporal, visual, and spatial information. The increased connections among these different centers allows for more efficient synthesis of information about different aspects of a problem. At the same time, all of these areas are more firmly linked with the speech area of the brain, which fosters the growth of symbolizing and communication abilities. Other areas which undergo rapid myelination during the preschool period include the hippocampus, which is important to short-term memory; and the fibers linking the cerebellum to the cerebral cortex, which allow for the fine control of voluntary movements, such as those needed to tie a shoelace.

Mental modules   The major theoretical event that has brought changes in the brain to the forefront of recent psychological theorizing about mental development is Noam Chomsky's theory of language and its acquisition. As we saw in Chapter 9, children's use of human language is acquired without any special tutoring by adults. Chomsky (1980) and others have proposed that principles of language acquisition apply to many other cognitive phenomena as well.

Jerry Fodor (1983), for example, has suggested that the mind be considered a vast collection of **mental modules,** highly specific mental faculties tuned to particular kinds of environmental input. Face recognition, the concept of number, music perception, and elementary perception of causality have all been offered as examples of mental modules (Gardner, 1983; Leslie & Keeble, 1987). The concept of mental modules shares key characteristics with Chomsky's concept of a language faculty:

1. Psychological operations are domain-specific. The mental operations required to perceive a musical tune are different from those required to recognize a face, and both are different from the principles that govern talking about perceiving a tune or talking about seeing a face.

2. The psychological principles that organize the operation of each domain are *innately specified;* that is, they are coded in the genes.

3. Different domains do not interact directly; each represents a separate mental module. The separate modules are only loosely connected.

Modularity has been applied to psychological development by British psychologist Alan Leslie and his colleagues in their work on the early development of the concept of causality (Leslie, 1986; Leslie & Keeble, 1987). As we have seen, Piaget believed that understanding of causality was not constructed until middle childhood, but Gelman and her colleagues had shown that such understanding is present during early childhood. Leslie's goal was to show that some form of the concept of causality is present as near to birth as could be tested for; that is, he wanted to show that the perception of causality is an innate mental module.

Leslie and his colleagues studied the impression of a cause-effect relationship that people receive when a rolling billiard ball collides with a stationary billiard ball, which then begins to roll. So strong is this impression, that even when adults are shown a series of dots on a page where one dot draws closer to the other and eventually "bumps into it," they experience the illusion that the first dot "causes" the second to move, even though they know that neither dot is really moving.

When Leslie and his colleagues presented 6-month-old children with a computer display in which one dot appears to bump into another, causing it to move, the babies tracked the first and then the second object, showing by the sequence in which they looked that

they perceived the first dot as causing the second to move.

Leslie and Keeble (1987) suggest that this apparent perceptual capacity may serve as a template that children use to develop genuine causal understanding even before they have much real-world knowledge. Although this primitive capacity is a very rigid and low-level form of causal understanding, it points babies in the right direction when they attempt to interpret their experiences, and thereby supports the later development of more complex causal knowledge.

Other evidence supporting the modularity position comes from children whose overall level of development is exceptionally low but who possess islands of brilliance. Some of these children suffer from **autism,** a poorly understood condition that is primarily defined by an inability to relate to other people. Young autistic children rarely use language to communicate, often fail to make eye contact with others, and do not respond appropriately to other human beings (Frith, 1984).

A remarkable characteristic of some autistic children is their highly developed mental capacities in certain very specific domains. For example, some autistic children have been reported to be able to sing an entire opera at the age of $1\frac{1}{2}$, read text aloud at the age of 2 (without any apparent comprehension), or assemble complicated objects when they are 3 years old (Rimland, 1964).

Each of these extraordinary accomplishments appears to fit the idea of mental modules. Each falls within a domain that has its own distinctive structure (music, arithmetic, language). These are domains in which there have also been child prodigies, children who excel in some specific ability at a considerably earlier age than is normal. Performance in these domains does not seem to require much social support, nor does it affect the normal development of other domains.

Assessing modularity explanations The evidence that several mental capacities display the properties of modularity proposed by Fodor is too important to ignore. Variability in modular systems' rates of development almost certainly contribute to the unevenness of preschool children's behavior.

However, this theory has its shortcomings. First, there is no current way of delineating either the full set of mental modules or the boundaries between modules. Second, it is difficult to imagine how the modularity approach would explain many of the examples of uneven performance by preschoolers described earlier. It seems implausible, for example, that there would be separate modules for "taking another's point of view," that correspond to different kinds of task setting, or that there would be distinct modules for deductive reasoning, for appearance–reality distinctions, and so on.

Of course, such possibilities should not be dismissed out of hand. Baron-Cohen, Leslie, and Frith (1986), for example, appear to have discovered a very specific, module-like deficit among autistic children associated with the ability to impute mental states to other people.

However, given the present state of knowledge about mental modules, they do not seem to offer a full-fledged explanation of preschool mental development. Rather, they should be considered one important source of variability that a full theory of early childhood thought should take into account.

Culture and Preschoolers' Mental Development

The cultural-context view shares Piaget's emphasis on development as a process of construction, but differs in assigning the social environment a far greater role than Piaget gave it. This view shares a focus on specific domains of behavior with the various post-Piagetian approaches, but unlike them, it does not focus on individual achievement or maturation. Rather, it examines the way that adults promote development by creating a context that supports the child's efforts to master new forms of behavior. Examples of the process of context-specific social construction presented earlier in this text include the father who helped his little daughter achieve a slightly more sophisticated level of play by the way he positioned her toy (Chapter 6, p. 201) and the mother encouraging her toddler son to walk (Chapter 8, p. 245).

Up to this point, we have used the term *context* in a relatively commonsense way. In order to show how the social environment might both influence the overall course of children's development during the preschool period and contribute to the marked unevenness of their performance in different circumstances, it is now important to present a more precise explana-

tion of what context means and how it is involved in the process of developmental change.

Context comes from the Latin term *contexere*, which means "to weave together," "to join together," or "to compose." Context is the connected whole that gives coherence to its parts (*Oxford English Dictionary*). The intimate relationship between behavior and context can be illustrated by considering the single physical behavior of a child waving a hand. This single motion can mean very different things: that the child is waving goodby to grandma, petting the cat, patting down play-dough to make a pancake, or swatting a fly. Which meaning the action has, and its consequent significance for later behavior, will depend upon the relationship of that act to what preceded it, what is happening at the time, and what follows it. Thus *context* gives coherence to the hand-waving plus grandma, or the hand-waving plus the cat, uniting the various parts of the situation into a coherent whole.

Because they come from the historical experience of a group, cultural contexts will differ from society to society. Even where particular contexts are shared by two cultures (e.g., deer-hunting), contexts may differ in how often they occur, in the details of their structure, and in their meaning within the totality of a culture (Stocking. 1968).

Contexts and schemas In Piaget's theory of developmental change, the concept of *schema* refers to an organized pattern of individual knowledge that specifies what goes with what and how to behave. Schemas are also important in cultural-context explanations of development, but they are conceived of differently. Rather than being treated as exclusively individual knowledge structures, children's schemas are seen as intimately connected to the supporting behaviors of the people around them. To use the example in Chapter 5 (p. 167), by helping the neonate to suck under conditions that will nourish it, the mother is contributing to the development of the child's "nursing schema," which cannot develop entirely on its own. Thus the child's nursing behavior develops in a context.

In the cultural-context view of development, schemas and contexts develop together. The structure of an action and the schemas required to implement it have become far more complex at the age of 4 or 5 years than they were at 4 or 5 weeks or 4 or 5 months. At the age of 4 weeks, eating a meal, for example, requires only one action schema, nursing, which is constructed of a small set of elements with the collaboration of only one other person. At 4 years, eating a meal at nursery school is part of a context called "lunch." Lunches are contexts consisting of many actions (in our culture: drinking from a cup, sitting at the table on a chair, picking up food with a fork). Nursery-school lunches also require the coordination of several people in addition to the child.

While Piagetian schemas are elements of complex events such as building a block tower or eating at snack time, the overall knowledge needed to be a competent participant in such activities goes well beyond the schemas children form of their own actions, thus requiring adult support to ensure that the integrity of the whole event is maintained. Consider the activity we call "taking a bath." "Taking a bath" is done *to* a 2-month-old infant. An adult fills a sink or appropriate basin with warm water, lays out a towel, a clean diaper and clothing, then slips the infant into the water, while holding tightly to keep the baby from drowning.

By the age of 2 years, a child has "taken" many baths. Each time, roughly the same sequence is followed, the same objects are used, and the same cast of characters has participated. Water is poured in a tub, clothes are taken off, the child gets into the water, soap is applied and rinsed off, the child gets out of the water, dries off, and dresses. There may be variations —a friend might take a bath with the child, or the child may play with water toys before or after washing —but the basic sequence is constant. Initially, the only role played by the infant is to be there. Gradually, as bathing becomes familiar and as children become more competent, they assume a greater role in the activity. Joseph Church (1966), for example, reports the case of a 12-month-old girl who responded to the word *bath* by going to the bathroom, taking off her clothes, turning on the water, and climbing in.

During the preschool period, adults still play an important role in the context called "taking a bath." They initiate children's baths and come in to scrub their ears, to wash their hair, or to help them to dry off. Not until adulthood will the child be responsible for the entire event, including scouring the tub and worrying about clean towels, hot water, and the money that pays for them.

The changing structure of this simple activity provides one prototype for relating context to development. In some sense, "taking a bath" remains the same at all ages. What changes are the parts of the activity

The meaning of an activity such as weaving and the development of the skills needed to do it differ markedly from one culture to another.

for which the child is responsible and the role of others in helping to maintain the context.

The mental representation of contexts

Katherine Nelson (1981, 1986) suggests that as a result of their participation in routine contexts, children construct a kind of schema for events: generalized representations that specify the people who participate in an event, the social roles they play, the objects that are used during the event, and the sequence of actions that make up the event. She calls these schemas *generalized event representations*, or **scripts.**

Nelson points out that "children grow up inside of other people's scripts." As a consequence, human beings rarely, if ever, experience the natural environment "raw." Rather, they experience an environment that has been prepared ("cooked up"!) according to the recipes prescribed by their culture.

Nelson and her colleagues have studied the growth of scripted knowledge by interviewing children and by recording conversations while children play together. For example, when she asked children to tell her about "going to a restaurant" she obtained such reports as

"Well, you eat and then go somewhere." (Boy aged 3 years, 1 month)

"Okay. Now, first we go to restaurants at night-time and we, um, we, and we go and wait for a while, and then the waiter comes and gives us the little stuff with the dinners on it, and then we wait for a little bit, a half an hour or a few minutes or something, and, um, then our pizza comes or anything, and um, [interruption]. . . . [The adult says, "So then the food comes. . . ."] Then we eat it, and um, then when we're finished eating the salad that we order we get to eat our pizza when it's done, because we get the salad before the pizza's ready. So then when we're finished with all the pizza and all our salad, we just leave." (Girl aged 4 years, 10 months) (Nelson, 1981, p. 103)

Even these simple reports illustrate the way in which scripts represent generalized knowledge. First, the children *are* describing general content: they are clearly referring to more than a single, unique occasion. The 3-year-old uses the generalized form "You eat," rather than a specific reference to a particular time when he ate. The little girl's introduction ("First, we go to restaurants at nighttime") indicates that she, too, is speaking of restaurant visits in general.

Participation in scripted activities such as lunch at day care or a birthday party provides children with a more complex understanding of the culture's basic concepts and ways of doing things.

Besides containing general content, the scripts are also organized into a general structure similar to that of adult scripts. Children evidently abstract the idea of a script from many particular stories, then use the script form to organize their reports ("First, we do this, then we do that. . . ."). All that changes from one report to the other is the specifics of place, the particular contents, and the amount of detail.

The functions of scripts

First and foremost, scripts are guides to action. They are mental representations that tell children what is likely to happen next in familiar circumstances. Until they have acquired a large repertoire of scripted knowledge, children must use a lot of mental effort to construct scripts as they participate in unfamiliar events. Lacking scripted knowledge means that they must pay attention to the details of each new activity. As a consequence, they may be less likely to distinguish between the essential and the superficial features of a context. The little girl interviewed by Nelson, for example, seemed to think that eating pizza is a basic part of the "going to a restaurant" script, whereas paying for the meal was entirely absent. When the little girl grasps a script ahead of time, she will be free to attend to other things, which will provide the opportunity to gain a deeper understanding of the events she participates in.

A second function of scripts is to allow people within a given social group to coordinate more effectively. This function of scripts becomes possible because script knowledge is knowledge generally held in common. "Without shared scripts," Nelson says, "every social act would need to be negotiated afresh" (1981, p. 109). In this sense, as Nelson points out, "the acquisition of scripts is central to the acquisition of culture" (p. 110). When going to most restaurants in the United States, children learn that first you ask the host or hostess for a table and are assigned a seat. A somewhat different script applies to fast-food restaurants. Discoordination can result if the script is violated (for example, if the child were to enter a restaurant and to sit down at a table where an elderly couple was midway through their meal).

Script knowledge, although generalized, cannot be learned in a vacuum. It is still tied to particular events (birthday parties, building a block tower, lunchtime, etc.). Somehow children must also acquire abstract concepts (such as *gift, friend, play, balance, appetite,* and so forth) that are not tied to particular events or settings.

A third function of scripts is to provide a framework within which abstract concepts that apply to many kinds of events can be acquired. When, for example, children acquire scripts for *playing with blocks, playing in the sandbox,* and *playing house,* they have the opportunity to subsume the specific examples of *play* into a general category (Lucariello and Rifkin, 1986) (see Box 10.2 on Sociodramatic Play).

Cultural context and the unevenness of development

In the cultural-context view, the close relationship between contexts and scripts provides a natural explanation for the unevenness of development during the preschool period. Once children leave the confines of their caretakers' arms and their cribs, they begin to experience a variety of contexts that require a variety of scripts. The collection of scripts they develop will depend crucially on the contexts appropriate to their culture and the roles that they are expected to play within those contexts. When they encounter a familiar context in which they know the expected sequence of actions and can interpret the requirements of the situation in scripted terms they are familiar with, children are most likely to behave in a logical way, adhering to adult standards of thought. But when the contexts are unfamiliar, they may apply inappropriate scripts and display magical or illogical thinking.

Overall, there are four basic ways in which culture influences the unevenness of children's development (Laboratory of Comparative Human Cognition, 1983):

1. *By arranging the occurrence or nonoccurrence of specific contexts.* You cannot learn about something you do not experience. The 4-year-olds who grow up among the Bushmen of the Kalahari desert are unlikely to learn about taking baths or pouring water from one glass to another; children growing up in Seattle are unlikely to be skilled at tracking animals or finding water-bearing roots in a desert.

2. *By arranging the frequency of basic contexts.* Children growing up in Bali may be skilled dancers by the age of 4 (Mead & Macgregor, 1951), while Norwegian children are likely to become good skiers and skaters. In each case, adults arrange for children to practice these activities. Likewise, children growing up in a Mexican village famous for its pottery may work with clay day after day while children living in a nearby town, where the people are weavers, may encounter clay only rarely (Price-Williams, Gordon & Ramirez, 1969; Childs & Greenfield, 1980). Insofar as practice makes perfect, greater frequency of practice will foster higher levels of performance.

3. *By shaping the relationships among different contexts.* If molding clay is associated with making pottery, it may carry with it a whole host of related contexts: digging from a quarry, firing clay, glazing clay, selling the products. Molding clay as part of a nursery school curriculum will be associated with an entirely different pattern of experience and knowledge.

BOX 10.2

SOCIO-DRAMATIC PLAY

...

The ability to engage in make-believe play undergoes important transformations during the preschool period that reflect and perhaps promote advances in cognitive development. By the end of infancy, as we saw in Chapter 7 (p. 220), children are typically able to pretend that a matchbox is a car that can zoom around the sandbox, or that a block is an iron. However, such play is largely solitary; even when several children are in a room together, their play is unlikely to be interconnected (Bretherton, 1984).

Play among children between the ages of 2½ and 6 is both more social and more self-conscious than during infancy. Instead of solitary pretending, children begin to engage in *socio-dramatic* play — make-believe games involving other children where a variety of social roles are enacted. These games require shared understanding between the participants which must be negotiated as part of the game:

Four girls in the doll corner have announced that they will play house and agree upon the roles: mother, sister, baby, and maid.

Karen: I'm hungry. Wa-a-ah!
Charlotte: Lie down, baby.
Karen: I'm a baby that sits up.
Charlotte: First you lie down and sister covers you and then I make your cereal and *then* you sit up.
Karen: Okay.
Karen: (to Teddy, who has been observing) You can be the father.
Charlotte: Are you the father?
Teddy: Yes.
Charlotte: Put on a red tie.
Janie: (in the "maid's" falsetto voice) I'll get it for you honey.
Now don't that baby look pretty? This is your daddy, baby.

(Adapted from Paley, 1984, p. 1.)

Socio-dramatic play is a leading activity for children from the age of 2½ to 6.

Several features of preschoolers' play are illustrated in this transcript. The children are enacting social roles and using scripts that they have encountered numerous times, in their daily lives, on television, or in their favorite stories (Nelson & Seidman, 1984). Babies make stereotypic baby noises, maids get things for people, and fathers wear ties. At the same time that they are in the play world, the children are also outside it, giving stage directions to one another and commenting on their roles. The "baby" who sits up has to be talked into lying down and the boy is told what role he can play. Occasionally, however, the fantasy may become so real and threatening that children stop the game or refuse to join in (Garvey & Berndt, 1977).

Although children draw upon familiar scenes in their socio-dramatic play, the scripts and social facts that they use are not reproduced in anything resembling precise imitation. As Catherine Garvey (1977) notes, when a boy engaged in socio-dramatic play walks into the house and announces, "Okay, I'm all through with work, honey. I brought home a thousand dollars," he has probably never witnessed this scene before, but rather abstracted certain behaviors characteristic of husbands that are then embellished with fantasy.

In recent decades there has been intense interest in socio-dramatic play among developmental psychologists and a lively controversy about its significance for cognitive development (Bretherton, 1984; Ruben & Pepler, 1982; Yawkey & Pellegrini, 1984). The two main positions in this discussion are derived from the work of Piaget (1962) and Vygotsky (1978).

In Piaget's view, the special quality of play during the preoperational period derives directly from the characteristics of egocentrism. As he phrased it, "for egocentric thought, the supreme law is play" (Piaget, 1928, p. 401). Because he assumed that, in play, assimilation dominates over accommodation, Piaget minimized the significance of play for cognitive development. He predicted that when egocentric thought gives way to logical thought in middle childhood, pretend play should give way to the kind of rule-bound play evident in board games and organized sports.

A number of studies have traced the rise and decline of pretend play during the preschool years by observing children and coding the kinds of play they engage in (Rubin, Fein, & Vandenberg, 1983). While the results are not completely consistent, Piaget's belief that socio-dramatic play should peak some time in the preschool years and then begin to decline has generally been confirmed. However, whether the disappearance of socio-dramatic play really supports Piaget's view is in dispute. Douglas Hofstader (1979) suggests that throughout their lives people constantly create mental variants on the situations they face:

[The manufacture of "as-if worlds"] happens so casually, so naturally, that we hardly notice what we are doing. We select from our fantasy a world which is close, in some internal mental sense, to the real world. We compare what is real with what we perceive as *almost* real. In so doing what we gain is some intangible kind of perspective on reality (p. 643).

Lev Vygotsky (1978) believed that play provides children with an important mental support system that allows them to think and act in new ways. In real life, children depend on adults to help them by providing the rules and by filling in for them in little ways that Vygotsky called a *zone of proximal development* (see Chapter 6). The freedom to negotiate reality that is essential to symbolic play provides children with analogous support. As a consequence, wrote Vygotsky, "In play a child is always above his average age, above his daily behavior; in play it is as though he were a head taller than himself" (p. 102).

An example of how children use play to control their own behavior is provided in an experiment by Maniulenko (1975). He asked 4-year-olds to stand still with their hands at their sides for as long as they could. They understood the requirements of standing still well enough to strike a pose and begin to hold it. But they found it virtually impossible to stand still for more than a few seconds. Maniulenko then asked the children to pretend that they were part of the honor guard at the entrance to the tomb of Vladimir Lenin, the leader of the Russian revolution. Every Soviet child knows about these honor guards, who stand motionless at attention for hours on end. When this request was part of a pretend game, the children's ability to stand still increased dramatically.

Vygotsky's studies of play highlight Nelson's point that a great deal of preschoolers' pretend play is based upon common scripts taken from their everyday experience. As we shall see in Chapter 11, preschoolers are preoccupied with figuring out who they are and how they are supposed to act. They have many opportunities to watch adults as a source of clues to their own identities, but they remain uncertain of basic social categories and rules for a long time. A major challenge to contemporary research is to demonstrate the role of play in helping them come to grips with these uncertainties.

4. *By regulating the level of difficulty.* As in the example of taking a bath, adults decide how much responsibility the child will bear. For any context, there are likely to be gradations in the contributions that a child must make, beginning with mere presence in the scene and proceeding, as the child grows and gains experience in the context, to a central role with controlling responsibility.

Assessing the cultural-context explanation In contrast with the Piagetian emphasis on generalized transformations in the logic of action following infancy, the cultural-context view emphasizes the patchwork nature of children's changing competence. Magical thinking, failure to take another's perspective, confusion of appearance and reality are not seen as unique to preschoolers; they are also present among adults. If adults manifest these traits differently, this is in part because they have much greater direct experience of the world. Adults also have the benefit of knowing about the experiences and adaptive solutions of prior generations.

The combination of greater experience and more sophisticated theories may often, as Piaget emphasized, lead to qualitatively more sophisticated ways of thinking. But these qualitative changes will always be context-specific; rather than a general stage change following infancy, cultural-context theorists see the gradual accumulation of many restricted changes in many particular domains.

The cultural-context approach also adopts a different view toward the mechanism of developmental change. In place of the "lone child" puzzling out the world unaided, the cultural-context approach attaches great importance to the ways in which children are coordinated within adult scripts. At first they simply "go along" under adult control, because they comprehend the script only in a very undifferentiated, "holistic" way. Gradually, as they master the overall feel and fill in some of the details of the adult-controlled scripts, children begin to anticipate what script will apply to a situation. That script then becomes available to guide the child's future actions.

Like the biological modularity view, the cultural-context approach assumes that biological maturation is a basic prerequisite for development. However, the two approaches contrast markedly in how they conceive of the mechanisms of change and the sources of variability in behavior. Modularity theorists emphasize biological maturation and "triggering" by the environment. Development "just happens" when the organism is ripe for it and children's behavior varies based on changes in the central nervous system.

Cultural-context theorists, on the other hand, see change as at least partly organized from outside the child. Children's behavior varies based on the contexts that adults make available to them.

The strength of the cultural-context view is also its greatest weakness. It does explain why preschoolers' behavior varies, but it does not yet account for the combination of children's general and domain-specific abilities. This shortcoming has been summarized by Gustav Jahoda, who wrote of the cultural-context approach that it

appears to require extremely exhaustive, and in practice almost endless explorations of quite specific pieces of behavior, with no guarantee of a decisive outcome. This might not be necessary if there were a workable "theory of situations" at our disposal, but . . . there is none. What is lacking . . . are global theoretical constructs relating to cognitive processes of the kind Piaget provides, and which save the researcher from becoming submerged in a mass of unmanageable material. (1980, p. 126)

To complicate an already complicated picture, it seems most reasonable to assume that the context-specific organization of the child's environment is constantly interacting with the biological properties of the child which are themselves developing at different rates. When these two sources of variability, one from the social world and one from biology, are combined, we can appreciate more fully why unevenness is a central feature of early childhood development.

APPLYING THE THEORETICAL PERSPECTIVES

Each of the current theories of early childhood provides a different perspective from which to view development. By seeking cases in which two or more approaches attempt to explain the same phenomenon, we can more easily assess the strengths and weaknesses of the alternative views.

Development of the ability to draw, an activity that includes many cognitive components, provides an intriguing example. Children's drawing goes through a regular series of stages (consistent with Piaget's constructivist approach); these stages are domain-specific — children whose linguistic, mental, or social development is severely retarded may nonetheless draw at a high level of competence (consistent with the modularity approach); stages in drawing can in some cases be tied closely to the ability to hold several aspects of an object in mind at one time (consistent with an information-processing approach); and development depends upon the social organization of the child's activity (consistent with the cultural-context approach).

Constructing Stages

In every culture where children are given the opportunity to draw from an early age, their drawing appears to pass through the same sequence of stages (Gardner, 1980; Golomb, 1974; Kellogg, 1969). In the beginning they scribble. Children are not "making pictures" when they scribble. What seems to matter to them is not the "look of the product," but the joy of moving their hands and the trail of their movements.

Scribbling embodies both of the functions of art in a primitive form. It *expresses* a feeling — the exuberance of motion — and it leaves a trace of the movement, *re-presenting* it for later examination. Scribbling is considered primitive because its expression is uncontrolled and unplanned and because it represents only itself.

A major step beyond scribbling occurs about the age of 3 when children begin to recognize that lines can represent things. At about this time, children begin to draw circles and ellipses that are cleared of the whorls and lines that used to fill their scribble pictures. Most children interpret these circles as "things." Their circular line bounds an inside area which seems more solid to them than the field it is on.

As children continue to gain experience with drawing, they are likely to adopt stereotyped ways of depicting objects: a house is a pentagon, a sun is a circle with lines extending from its surface, a flower is a circle surrounded by ellipses, animals appear to be

tadpole figures turned on their side (see Figure 10.10). Eventually children begin to combine representations of people and things to make scenes and stories or to depict a variety of experiences.

Between the ages of 7 and 11, children increasingly strive to be realistic in their drawings. At the same time they become more skilled at composition and the techniques of drawing (see Figure 10.11).

Many of the developments reported for U.S. and European children can be found in all societies where drawing is an activity. The existence of such universals in the development of artistic representation provides an illustration of the kind of phenomenon central to Piaget's theory of cognitive development.

FIGURE 10.10 *Drawing the human figure develops through a sequence of steps. At first a child will draw a big circle that stands for a whole person. The child's global representation of a person soon evolves into a circle or an ellipse with the face in the upper part and two protruding lines underneath. This distinctive form is called a "tadpole figure." Gradually the circle comes to represent only the head, and the body descends between the two vertical lines. Some months later, the child adds a second circle to represent the body, with another pair of lines extending from it as arms. (From Goodnow, 1977.)*

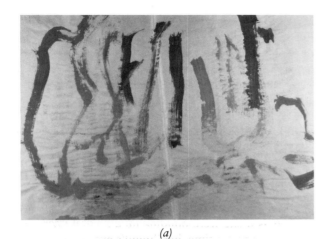

(a)

(b)

(c)

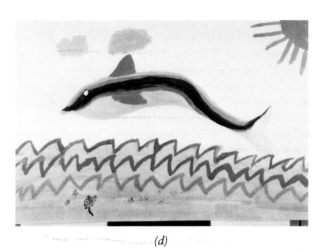

(d)

(e)

FIGURE 10.11 *A sequence of drawings by an American child: (a) at 2½ years, Carrie was drawing lines of different colors; (b) at 3½ years, she began to draw global representations of a person; (c) at 5 years, a body and legs have been added to the creatures she draws, and her main figure is set in a scene; (d) at 7½ years, motion, rhythm, and greater realism are evident in her drawings; (e) at 12 years, she was able to draw a cartoon of a realistic scene. (Courtesy of Carrie Hogan.)*

An Information-Processing Account

People drew objects for thousands of years before the ability to represent objects in three dimensions became fully understood and exploited (Arnheim, 1954). Modern children who grow up with three-dimensional representations all around them acquire at least a rudimentary ability to represent three dimensions in their drawings.

Figure 10.12 shows the developmental sequence that children go through in learning to draw a schematic house in three dimensions. The youngest children collapse three dimensions into two. Then the third dimension is partially added, but it is initially collapsed into one of the other two. Finally, different ways to represent the third dimension are acquired (Willats, 1987). From an information-processing perspective, this sequence follows directly from children's growing acquisition of drawing rules and their ability to remember the need to represent all three spatial coordinates in their drawings.

Drawing as a Mental Module

Although the development of children's ability to draw normally passes through the series of stages we have just described, some important exceptions suggest that drawing ability may be modular in certain respects. A compelling example is provided by Nadia, an autistic child in Nottingham, England (Selfe, 1977). At first Nadia seemed to develop normally, but by the

age of 3, she had forgotten the few words she had learned, her behavior was lethargic, and she did not engage in pretend play. At the age of 3½, Nadia began to display an unusual artistic ability. Without any apparent practice, she began to use perspective and other artistic techniques that are usually acquired only after years of experience in drawing (Figure 10.13). Nadia's dexterity when drawing was quite remarkable, yet her hand movements were otherwise uncoordinated.

Extensive testing showed that Nadia had an extraordinary ability to form and remember visual images. She would often study a drawing for weeks before producing a version from memory herself. It seemed as if she were building up a mental image so that at some later time, her "mind's eye" could guide her hands in recreating the image on paper. Howard Gardner, who has conducted research on the cognitive basis of art, uses terms reminiscent of Chomsky and Fodor's idea of mental modules in his discussion of Nadia's case:

> Nadia may have been operating with a high powered mental computational device — one seldom, if ever, exploited by others but perhaps available to at least a sample of the human species. (Gardner, 1980, pp. 186–187)

Lorna Selfe (1983) reports that Nadia's unusual development is not unique. She has found a number of children whose language ability and general mental functioning were quite low, but whose ability to create images and draw was exceptionally high. These cases

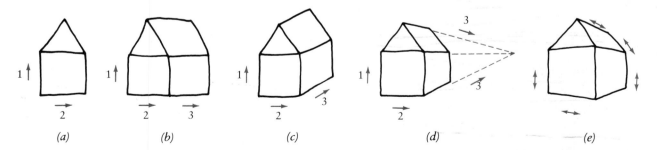

FIGURE 10.12 *The developmental sequence for drawing an object in three dimensions. Drawing (a) leaves out the third dimension. Drawings (b) and (c) introduce the third dimension in partially correct ways. Drawings (d) and (e) each represent the full three dimensions according to two different conventions. (Adapted from Willats, 1987.)*

FIGURE 10.13 *While a preschooler with only minimal exposure to models, Nadia displayed an uncanny ability to capture form and movement in her drawings.*

fit nicely with the idea that mental modules, such as language and perception, can develop in relative isolation from each other.

Evidence from less extreme cases also suggests that the ordinary sequence of stages is not necessary to mastery. Gardner (1980) reports that children deprived of the opportunity to draw during the preschool years may skip the initial stages of drawing altogether when they are finally given the opportunity to draw at an older age. If true, this finding would run counter to the Piagetian position that stages follow each other in an invariant sequence.

A Cultural-Context Account of the Development of Drawing

A cultural-context view of the development of drawing takes for granted both the existence of innate human representational potential and the fact that within any particular medium, such as drawing, representations may be constructed at differing levels of complexity. What a cultural approach adds to the previous accounts is some idea of the processes that transform children's potential for drawing into meaningful representations.

An important indicator of the culturally organized nature of children's drawing is to be found in the ways that adults talk to children about what they are doing. When American adults ask preschoolers, "What are you drawing?" the very form of the question assumes that there is some *thing* to be drawn and that the child is attempting to represent it. When questions of this kind are posed, children often go along by making up stories about what they have drawn after the fact. Initially, these stories are not tied to anything that can be perceived on the paper by adults. After children have gained some experience, their explanations may be connected to the discovery that the marks they have made resemble an actual object in the world. But this discovery is made only after the drawing is completed (Golomb, 1974).

The following dialogue between Roslyn and Don, recorded in a study of 3-year-old children in a U.S. preschool, illustrates the rudimentary nature of preschoolers' understanding of drawing as well as some of

The development of drawing depends on the traditions of the culture into which the child is born. This drawing was done by a Sri Lankan girl.

the ways that those understandings change (adapted from Gearhart & Newman, 1980, p. 172):

Rosyln: I got brown *(holds up her crayon).*

Don: I got another color *(draws short lines back and forth).*

Roslyn: I made a brown circle *(illustrates with counterclockwise gesture, holding crayon over the paper).*

Don: I got another color.

Roslyn: I, I, I made a big brown circ-er square *(repeats the illustrative gesture).*

Don: *(makes a counterclockwise form on his paper)* Look what I'm making, Roslyn.

Roslyn: Huh! Ehh! *(looks)*

Don: I, I went *rround* like this *(illustrates with larger counterclockwise movements).* . . .

Roslyn: Well . . . Now watch what I am making, I'm making *moun*tains *(immediately draws a series of short vertical lines).*

From their words and actions, it is clear that neither child has a fixed, individual drawing in mind. All of their talk refers either to something that they have just done ("I *made* a brown circle) or something they are doing ("I'm *making*"). There is little talk about future plans for their pictures. Each child imitates elements introduced by the other, with no overall plan of how that element might fit into the whole.

However, even these children's drawings have progressed beyond scribbling. As they show each other crayons and figures, swapping comments and ideas, they are talking *as if* the drawings represented something (circles, squares, mountains) even if the correspondence is by no means clear to outsiders.

The way in which the teacher arranged for a picture to be called "finished" was also important in helping the children to discover what it means to draw a picture. Before writing the child's name on the picture and pinning it up on the board, she asked open-ended questions about what the child had been drawing, again behaving *as if* the child had been drawing a particular "something."

Learning to draw and paint is an absorbing activity for pre-schoolers.

Teacher: Jeff? [Come] tell me about your picture. . . . (*Jeffrey comes and looks at his drawing.*)

Jeffrey: Uh it has two mountains on orange, two orange circles.

Teacher: Two orange circles (*as she writes his name on the drawing*). (Adapted from Gearhart & Newman, 1980, p. 182).

In this example the teacher selectively accepts that part of the child's account (two orange circles) that accords with her notion of "thingness." The scribbled "mountains" are ignored. As a consequence, Jeffrey learns something about what sort of marks count as a drawing of a mountain or circles in the eyes of adults and which do not.

The existence of scripted activities for drawing does not contradict the possibility that there is a mental module for drawing nor the idea that drawing goes through a series of increasingly complex stages. Rather, the ways in which adults organize instruction provide an essential medium within which modular potential can be "triggered" and stages "constructed." Over the course of a year or two, the teacher's assumptions become second nature to the children. They learn not only that it is possible to draw pictures of "things," but a good many techniques for how to make those things take shape on the page. Most importantly, they come to understand and share the teacher's concept of what "drawing a picture" means.

This common understanding then becomes the basis for further instruction.

RECONCILING ALTERNATIVE PERSPECTIVES

Scholarly explanations for the phenomena of preschool thought are reminiscent of the parable of the blind men feeling an elephant: the man who feels the trunk believes that the creature is a snake; the man who feels the leg believes that the creature is a tree; and the man who feels the tail is certain that he has hold of a rope. Lacking a coordinated understanding, each man mistakes his part for the whole, which is distinctively different from the parts.

Piaget's preschoolers are incomplete logicians. Having only recently learned to represent the world symbolically, they still labor to construct stable cause-effect schemas and to separate reality from appearance. Failing to distinguish their own point of view from the perspective of others, they are constantly led into error. It takes several years for them to translate conflicting information into action- and language-based schemas.

Neo-Piagetian explanations of preschool thinking have sought to revise the negative description of preschoolers as egocentric and prelogical. Neo-Piagetians show that preschoolers can reason logically in familiar circumstances as long as their still fragile verbal skills are not overstrained. Still very much at issue among this school of researchers, however, is the question of whether Piaget's idea of global transformations of mind should be retained, or replaced by a piecemeal, domain-specific picture of development.

The information-processing approach focuses on preschoolers' limited knowledge, attention, memory capacities, and lack of sophisticated problem-solving strategies to explain their characteristic thought processes. This theoretical framework may be viewed as either a rival theory or as an alternative strategy for research. In the hands of Robbie Case (1985), information-processing ideas are used to support a neo-Piagetian theory. In the hands of Robert Siegler (1986), similar ideas are used to arrive at a new theory, in which cognitive development is seen as a non-stagelike, continuous process of change arising from the accumulation of specific knowledge and strategies.

Among the major alternatives to Piaget and various neo-Piagetian approaches, modularity theorists deny that constructive interactions play a prominent role in promoting cognitive development. Viewing the child's mental processes as a collection of separate "computational modules," researchers in this tradition attribute the special characteristics of preschool thought primarily to the physical maturation of the brain. In some striking cases these researchers have shown that even infants display rudimentary forms of the cognitive abilities that Piaget denied to preschoolers. From this perspective, the unevenness of preschool behavior mirrors unevenness in the rate of physical maturation. As basic brain structures approach maturity, extreme variations among modules decrease, and greater consistency of behavior in line with adult norms results.

Like those who work within a Piagetian or neo-Piagetian framework, cultural-context theorists believe that complex cognitive processes are constructed in social interaction. However, this approach emphasizes that the process of construction, and hence the mechanism of cognitive development, is shared between children and older members of their communities in scripted activities organized, or at least supervised, by adults.

Perhaps these competing approaches are most usefully viewed as complementary. Certainly, the various phenomena they highlight would need to be included in any comprehensive explanation of preschool development, even if no single theoretical framework has yet been able to encompass them all.

A child's total psychological development encompasses far more than the restricted abilities described here. Still to be explored are the way that preschoolers think about themselves as members of their social worlds, their experiences in nursery school and day care (where they must learn to get along with children their own age under new circumstances), as well as their induction into the world of books and television. In the remaining chapters of this section, we will round out our picture of preschool children as they leave infancy further and further behind and move toward a new bio-social-behavioral shift marking the transition to middle childhood.

SUMMARY

1. Preschool children's thought processes are characterized by great unevenness; islands of sophistication exist in a sea of uncertainty and naiveté.

2. Piaget's explanation of preschoolers' thought stresses the absence of logical operations and thinking's *egocentric* nature. In his view, preschool children experience difficulty adopting others' perspectives, reasoning about cause and effect, and distinguishing appearance from reality.

3. Piaget's theory has difficulty accounting for the uneven level of children's thought within what he called the preoperational stage. Some developmental psychologists want to refine his theory, while others have suggested alternatives.

4. Neo-Piagetian accounts of preschool thought retain Piaget's theory of stages. Some neo-Piagetians restrict the applicability of stages to specific domains of activity, while others attempt to account for uneven development by citing differences in the requirements of specific tasks.

5. According to the information-processing view, cognitive development is a gradual process of expanding limited attentional, memory, and problem-solving capacities. The unevenness of preschool thought is explained by differences in children's familiarity with specific task settings, and by differences in the demands each setting makes.

6. Biologically oriented theories hold that the brain is organized into mental modules that are domain-specific, innately structured, and relatively isolated from each other. These theorists point to uneven changes in brain structure as the major cause of unevenness in preschool

thought. The mental capacity of prodigies (children who excel in a single domain at an early age) as well as pathological cases (such as childhood autism) support this hypothesis.

7. In the cultural-context view, contexts provide coherence to otherwise isolated actions. Contexts and schemas develop together. Increased complexity in the child's behavior is accompanied by, and helps to create, increased complexity in the behavior of those with whom the child interacts.

8. Contexts are represented mentally in the form of scripts —conceptual structures that are guides to action, a means of coordination between people, and a framework in which abstract concepts applicable across contexts are formed.

9. Culture mediates society's influence on mental development by:

a. Arranging for the occurrence of specific contexts and associated scripts

b. Arranging which contexts a child will frequently experience

c. Deciding which contexts are associated with particular activities

d. Regulating the level of the child's participation

10. Artistic development illustrates the complementary nature of the competing explanations. Learning to draw normally passes through a series of stages; these stages are domain-specific in ways that fit with neo-Piagetian and modularity themes. They follow a course of representing more aspects of an object, in line with an information-processing approach. Learning to draw is culturally organized in ways that fit with cultural-context theories.

KEY TERMS

Autism	Long-term memory	Precausal thinking
Context	Mental modules	Preoperational stage
Egocentrism	Neo-Piagetian approach	Scripts
Horizontal decalage	Operations	Sensory register
Information-processing approach		Short-term memory

SUGGESTED READINGS

DONALDSON, MARGARET *Children's Minds.* New York: Norton, 1978.

This British psychologist has conducted a number of the key studies suggesting that preschool children are capable of more sophisticated thinking than they had been given credit for by Piaget. This book summarizes both the basic research strategy for conducting experiments that make "human sense" and many important ideas about early childhood development.

FLAVELL, JOHN *Cognitive Development.* Englewood Cliffs, N.J.: Prentice Hall, 1985.

A leading interpreter of the psychology of Jean Piaget, John Flavell has long been a leader in the study of cognitive development among preschool children. This book contains especially useful discussions of the many factors that could account for the unevenness of pre-

school thought. It also ranges over the full course of cognitive development, and will be a useful reference for later chapters.

GARDNER, HOWARD *Artful Scribbles.* New York: Basic Books, 1980.

Howard Gardner has written widely on problems of cognitive development, specializing in the development of children's aesthetic sensibilities and modes of artistic expression. In this readable account of artistic development, Gardner includes discussions not only of the development of art among modern children, but also the development of art in human history and pre-history. Also included is a fascinating account of the artistic achievements of autistic children.

PALEY, VIVIAN *Walley's Stories.* Cambridge, Mass.: Harvard University Press, 1981.

This account of the irrepressible Walley and his class-mates by master teacher Vivian Paley is a joy to read and a treasure-trove of information about preschool thinking.

PIAGET, JEAN *The Child's Conception of the World.* New York. Harcourt-Brace, 1929.

Many of Piaget's books are highly theoretical and difficult to read. This relatively early book is an exception. It contains extensive transcripts of discussions with children about all matter of natural phenomena: the nature of thinking, the origin of names, the sources of dreams, and young children's conceptions of the nature of life, to name a few. Reading this book will help to explain why Piaget's ideas about preschool thought have had an enduring effect on developmental psychology.

SIEGLER, ROBERT S. *Children's Thinking.* Englewood Cliffs, N.J.: Prentice Hall, 1986.

This is the first general text about child development written from the perspective of information-processing theories. The book contains examples of different approaches to computer modeling of cognitive development, helping to explain why information-processing ideas have contributed to an understanding of cognitive development.

SOCIAL DEVELOPMENT IN EARLY CHILDHOOD

> The incorporation of the individual as a member of a community, or his adaptation to it, seems like an almost unavoidable condition which has to be filled before he can attain the objective of happiness. . . . Individual development seems to us a product of the interplay of two trends, the striving for happiness, generally called "egoistic," and the impulse towards merging with others in the community, which we call "altruistic."
>
> — Sigmund Freud, *Civilization and Its Discontents*

The process to which Sigmund Freud is referring is called **social development,** a double-sided process in which children simultaneously become integrated into the larger social community and differentiated as distinctive individuals. The first side of social development is called **socialization,** the process by which children acquire the standards, values, and knowledge of their society. The second side of social development is **personality formation** — the way in which individual children come to have a characteristic sense of themselves and a distinctive way of thinking and feeling (Damon, 1983).

Socialization begins as soon as the child is born and a mother says, "You're just like your dad" or a father remarks, "I will be worried to death when she is 18." It continues as part of getting the infant on a schedule, and as parents later admonish their children to be polite to their elders, cover their mouths when they cough, and never tell a lie.

Socialization during early childhood is especially important because this is when children construct their first understandings of their community. These early interpretations of adult roles and expectations form the foundation for those to follow.

The process of socialization requires the active participation of both adults and children. Adults tell children how they are expected to behave and reward or punish their behavior. Adults also select the social contexts within which children have the experiences from which they must abstract social categories and rules of behavior. But children do not automatically or passively absorb the lessons adults intend. What children learn depends upon how they interpret these lessons and what they select from the conflicting messages around them. When parents tell their 3-year-olds "You are my son" or "Be a responsible young lady,"

terms such as *son* and *responsible young lady* must somehow be interpreted by the children, who don't yet have clear concepts for these words. In addition, if preschooler Mark admires his older cousin Eric and wants to be like him, will he imitate Eric's socially appropriate style of dress, his inappropriate use of slang, or both?

Children need to understand social categories, roles, rules, and expectations in order to participate in a social world, but they must also acquire the abilities required by these roles. As children acquire their native language and participate in social activities, they also acquire knowledge of *when* to act like a nursery school student, *when* to behave like a friend, and *when* to act like a Japanese-American. Effective socialization assures that if they come to consider themselves girls, they will acquire the behavior appropriate to girls in their social group; if they consider themselves a friend, they will form some conception of what being a friend implies and learn how to behave accordingly.

The combination of characteristics that emerges from the second side of social development, the child's **personality,** is unique, because the particular mix of genetic endowment and personal experience that enters into the formation of each personality is never completely shared with another human being. Even if two children are both nursery school students, friends, nieces, and Japanese-Americans, they will not be precisely alike. Some elements of personality are discernible shortly after birth, when infants display their own characteristic levels of activity, responses to frustration, and other aspects of their temperament (see Chapter 4, p. 130). But personality is more than individual temperament. It also includes the way people conceive of themselves and their characteristic style of dealing with others.

Thus personality development is closely intertwined with socialization. Crucial to one's sense of self is all of the feedback that one receives from the social environment. This idea was expressed at the turn of the century by James Mark Baldwin, a pioneer psychologist:

> The development of the child's personality could not go on at all without the constant modification of his sense of himself by suggestions from others. So he himself, at every stage, is really in part someone else, even in his own thought of himself. (1902, p. 23)

Personality formation and socialization are in constant tension as children discover that their individual desires often conflict with their culture's rules. A 5-year-old boy who wants to wear a dress to school as his sister does is likely to be discouraged by his parents and, if his parents do not forbid it, mocked by his peers. A child who is jealous of the attention her baby brother receives must learn that she can't pinch him; she must find some socially acceptable way to gain her mother's attention.

Perhaps the most remarkable fact about social development is the extent to which children come to adopt as reasonable, and even necessary, the rules prescribed by their social group. By the time they are 6, children will have learned a great deal about the roles they are expected to play and how to behave in accordance with them, how to control anger and aggressive feelings, and how to respect the rights of others. How does this learning take place and what elements of nature and nurture enter into it?

ACQUIRING A SOCIAL IDENTITY

Psychologists agree that socialization requires **identification, a psychological** process that contributes to a sense of who one is and who one wants to be. Experts disagree, however, about the mechanisms by which identification is achieved. Four proposed mechanisms have figured most prominently in discussions of this basic developmental process: *differentiation; affiliation; imitation and social learning; and cognition.*

These preschool girls are participating (with varying degrees of enthusiasm) in a beauty contest. This kind of experience gives them an idea of what the adults in their community expect of girls.

Sex-Role Identity

The development of identification can be studied with respect to almost any social category — becoming a member of a family, a religious group, a neighborhood clique, or a nationality. However, the overwhelming majority of research on identification focuses on the acquisition of **sex roles.***

Sex is not a role in the sense that being a big sister, an airplane pilot, or a factory worker is a role. Rather, sex is an attribute that shapes many social roles, determining whether we are sons or daughters, husbands or wives, girlfriends or boyfriends. Sexual identity also influences our choice of work and our social status. Because sexual identity is so central to adult experience, the question of how children acquire the understanding that they are a boy or a girl and how they interpret that role is of great interest to developmental

* Some authors recommend using the word *gender* instead of *sex* when discussing this topic. These authors believe that the term *sex* implies that all sex-typed behavior is ultimately determined by biology. On the other hand, Maccoby (1980) argues against the term *gender,* which she sees as implying that sex-linked behavior is ultimately determined by the environment. In this book, we will continue to use the term *sex,* without intending to imply either that sex roles are basically biological or that they are basically environmental.

psychologists. The central issues in acquiring a sex-role identity are illustrated by the following anecdotes.

"When I grow up," says [4-year-old] Jimmy at the dinner table, "I'm gonna marry Mama." "Jimmy's nuts," says the sensible voice of 8-year-old Jane. "You can't marry Mama and anyway, what would happen to Daddy?" Exasperating, logical female! Who cares about your good reasons and your dull good sense! There's an answer for that too. "He'll be old," says the dreamer, through a mouthful of string-beans. "And he'll be dead." Then, awed by the enormity of his words, the dreamer adds hastily, "But he might not be dead, and maybe I'll marry Marcia instead. (Fraiberg, 1959, pp. 202–203)

The following conversation took place when our daughter, Jenny, was 4 years old. She was lying on her mother's side of her parents' bed, watching her mother comb her hair.

Jenny: You know, Mommy, when you die I am going to marry Daddy.

Sheila: I don't think so.

Jenny: (nodding her head gravely) I am, too.

Sheila: You can't. It's against the laws of God and man.

Jenny: (close to tears) But I want to.

Sheila: (going to comfort her) You'll have your own husband when you grow up.

Jenny: No, I won't! I want Daddy. I don't like you, Mommy.

Intuitively, these stories are easy to understand. Each of these children has had several years to observe the family life around them. Jimmy knows that he is a boy and Jenny knows that she is a girl. Although neither has a deep understanding of what these labels imply, they know that they want the things that big boys and big girls have. The "big girl" in Jenny's household has a special relationship with Daddy. The "big boy" in Jimmy's household has a special relationship with Mommy. At this early stage of sex-role identification, the best way children can think of to get what they want is literally to "take the place" of the person they want to be like.

Boys and girls in early childhood both tend to choose same-sex parents as models with whom to identify. Yet the developmental path that brings each

sex to its respective identity is different. During the first two years of life, the person who almost always looms largest in the lives of both boys and girls is their mother. She is likely to be the single, greatest source of physical comfort, food, and attention for the child. As children enter their third year, the behaviors that indicate the strong and obvious attachment of the second year tend to diminish (see Chapter 7, p. 226). During the preschool period, the feeling of "wanting to be near" that dominates infancy is supplanted by "wanting to be like." (See Figure 11.1.)

For boys, becoming like their father requires that they become different from the person with whom they have had the closest relationship: their mother. Thus for boys, development of sex-role identity requires *differentiation*. For girls, however, development requires that they become more similar to their mothers—identity through *affiliation*. The implications of this sex-linked difference in developmental tasks has sparked intense debate about both the process of identification and the issue of sexual equality.

Identification through Differentiation

By far the best-known account of identity formation is Sigmund Freud's (1921/1949, 1933/1964). Freud believed that early in life, perhaps late in the first year, infants recognize that some objects in the external world are like themselves. He called this primitive recognition **primary identification**. During the third year of life, **secondary identification** occurs. This identification is "the endeavor to mold a person's own ego after the fashion of one that has been taken as a model" (Freud, 1921/1949, p. 63). In other words, having noticed that a particular adult, or perhaps an older child, is somehow similar to themselves, children "identify *with*" that person, striving to take on his or her qualities.

By Freud's account, Jimmy is playing out the universal male predicament of boys around the age of 3 or 4, the dilemma of the *phallic stage* (see Box 11.1 for a summary of Freudian stages). This is the period during which children first begin to regard their own genitals as a major source of pleasure. Here's how Freud saw the conflict that these new pleasures evoke:

In a word, his early awakened masculinity seeks to take his father's place with [his mother]; his father has hitherto in any case been an envied model to the

(a)

(b)

FIGURE 11.1 *(a) Preschoolers still stay close to their parents when they feel uncertain or afraid. (b) In addition to wanting to be near their parents, preschoolers also want to be like them, especially the parent of the same sex.*

boy, owing to the physical strength he perceives in him and the authority with which he finds him clothed. His father now becomes a rival who stands in his way and whom he would like to get rid of. (1940/1964, p. 189)

These feelings cause Jimmy a lot of mental anguish. He is old enough to know that feelings like wanting your father to die are considered bad, yet young enough to believe that his parents, who are such powerful figures in his life, are always aware of what he is thinking. So he lives in fear of being punished and feels guilty about his bad thoughts.

According to Freud, in middle childhood male children reach the next level of sex role development, *latency,* by defending themselves against the perceived threats from angry fathers. The change to latency requires the simultaneous operation of two **defense mechanisms,** Freud's term for the psychological processes that people use to protect themselves from unpleasant thoughts. First, males use *identification,* a strong desire to look, act, and feel like their fathers. By literally "playing the role of Daddy" (helping to bring in kindling from the wood pile, pretending to shave) the boy banishes his feelings of hostility and fear. Now he is a powerful figure, too. Second, the boy *represses* his feelings toward his mother. He stops desiring total possession of her, thus removing the original source of guilty feelings.

Identification through Affiliation

Freud believed that female identification is also a defensive adaptation that propels girls into a latent stage, but that the defense mechanism is different for girls. He claimed that the key event in the development of a girl's sex identity is triggered by her discovery that she does not have a penis. According to this account, the girl is "mortified by the comparison with boys' far superior equipment" (1933/1964, p. 126). She blames her mother for this "deficiency" and transfers her love to her father. Then she competes with her mother for her father's affection.

As with masculine identification, though, the girl feels guilty. She is afraid that her mother knows what she is thinking and that she will be punished by losing her mother's love. She overcomes her fear and guilt by suppressing her feelings for her father and identifying

BOX 11.1

SIGMUND FREUD

• • •

Trained as a neurologist, Sigmund Freud (1856–1939) sought throughout his career to create a theory of human personality that would enable him to cure the patients who came to him with such symptoms as extreme fears, emotional trauma, or an inability to cope with everyday life. Although many of these symptoms appeared similar to neurological disorders, Freud found that he could best understand his patients' problems by tracing their symptoms back to traumatic, unresolved experiences in earlier childhood.

On the basis of his clinical data, Freud constructed a general theory of development that gave primacy to the manner in which children satisfy their basic drives as the necessary condition for their survival. However, survival of the individual child is not sufficient for survival of the species. Influenced by Charles Darwin's theory of evolution, Freud reasoned that whatever their significance for individual adaptation, all biological drives have but a single goal: the survival and propagation of the species. Since reproduction, the necessary condition for the continuation of the species, is accomplished through sexual intercourse, it followed for Freud, that starting from the earliest days of life, all biological drives must ultimately serve the fundamental sexual drive upon which the future of the species rests. Sex, he said, is the master motive of human behavior.

Although Freud believed the sexual nature of all gratification remains constant throughout life, the forms of that gratification change. Sexual gratification passes through an orderly series of stages defined in terms of the parts of the body that people use to satisfy their drives. At each stage, human beings strive to satisfy the drives that dominate that stage. Freud held that the way in which children experience the conflicts they en-

Sigmund Freud and his father.

counter in each of the early stages of development determines their later personality (1920/1955).

During the first year of life children experience the **oral stage,** in which the mouth is the primary source of pleasure. The mother's gratification of the baby's need to suck is critically important.

with her mother. As a result of this sequence, Freud said, a woman's psychological makeup never becomes as independent of its emotional wellsprings — her initial identification with her mother — as does a man's. This, he believed, rendered women an "underdeveloped" version of men. He concluded that women

show less sense of justice than men, that they are less ready to submit to the great exigencies of life, and that they are more often influenced in their judgment by feelings of affection or hostility. (1925/1961, pp. 257–258)

In the second year of life, the **anal stage,** the child is preoccupied with gaining control of the smooth muscles involved in defecation.

Around the age of 3, Freud believed children begin to focus their pleasure-seeking on the genital area. Freud held that during this, the **phallic stage,** development for boys and girls diverges. Boys become aware that they have a penis. They develop sexual feelings toward their mothers and become jealous of their fathers. Girls become aware that they do not have a penis and begin resenting their mothers for sending them out into the world "ill-equipped." Freud believed that resolution of these conflicts produces the most basic form of sexual identification.

At about the age of 6, the phallic stage is followed by the **latency stage,** which lasts until the beginning of puberty approximately 6 years later. During the latency stage sexual desires are suppressed and no new areas of bodily excitation emerge. Instead, sexual energy is channeled into the acquisition of technical skills for earning a living that will be needed during adulthood.

The physiological changes of *puberty,* or the onset of sexual maturity, cause the repressed sexual urges to reappear in full force—marking the beginning of the **genital stage.** Now sexual urges are no longer directed toward the parents or repressed but directed toward peers of the opposite sex to produce adult sexuality and, ultimately, reproduction.

Freud believed that from the preschool period onward the personality is made up of three mental structures that mediate between an individual's drives and his or her behavior. The **id** contains our basic desires and is the main source of mental energy. It is unconscious, energetic, and pleasure-seeking (1933/1964).

The **ego** is the intermediary between the id and the social world. The ego emerges out of the id as the infant is forced by reality to cope with the fact that simply desiring something will not satisfy its drives—action is necessary. The ego's task, therefore, is self-preservation, which it accomplishes through voluntary movement, perception, logical thought, adaptation, and problem solving. It performs its tasks by gaining control over instinctual demands, deciding where, when, and how they are to be satisfied.

The **superego,** which begins to form during the preschool period, becomes a major force in the personality during middle childhood. It represents the authority of the social group, embodied in the image of the father. The demands of the superego keep the ego in touch with reality while holding the energy of the id within bounds.

The three structures that make up human personality are rarely if ever in perfect equilibrium. Instead, dominance shifts as the superego and the id battle for control. The constant process of resolving these conflicts is the engine of developmental change, which is often spoken of in Freudian terms as *ego development.*

Summarized in this brief fashion, Freud's theory may appear to be fanciful. His theory of infantile sexuality provoked outrage early in this century when it was first proposed and remains controversial to this day. Freud's psychoanalytic method has been criticized as ineffective and unscientific. It must also be noted that although Freud makes many claims about infancy and early childhood, he made all of his observations on disturbed adults. Freud is certainly vulnerable to criticism on both methodological and theoretical grounds, yet he remains one of the most influential forces in contemporary developmental research and theorizing.

Freud's great achievement was to extend Charles Darwin's insights into the sphere of individual personality development. His insistence on the central role of sex and reproduction is a logical extension of Darwin's theory. His portrait of conflict and competition between the growing child and the social environment is not flattering, but it is extremely useful in shaping detailed research on development.

Not surprisingly, Freud's argument has evoked many attacks. In particular, Freud has been criticized for claiming that the lack of a penis makes girls feel inferior to boys and for assuming that sexual identification only occurs as a defense mechanism. Nancy Chodorow (1974), for example, acknowledges the difference in the two sexes' experience of early social interaction and their differing biological roles. But she draws another conclusion from these differences than did Freud.

Chodorow, unlike Freud, emphasizes the role of parents in their children's sex-role identification. She points out that while daughters identify with mothers, mothers likewise experience daughters as like themselves. In contrast, "mothers experience their sons as a male opposite" (Chodorow, 1974, pp. 166–167). In defining themselves as masculine, boys reinforce their mothers' reactions to them, aiding in the differentiation process. In defining themselves as feminine, daughters evoke further feelings of similarity in their mothers, reinforcing the fusion of attachment with the experience of sex-role identity. Because daughters do not have to go through the alienating experience of differentiating themselves from their mothers, they "emerge from this period with a basis for 'empathy' built into their primary definition of self in a way that boys do not" (p. 167). Put differently, because girls' identity is based upon affiliating with their mothers, girls have a built-in basis for understanding the needs of others.

In many respects Chodorow's formulation is similar to Freud's but the difference in emphasis is important, as Carol Gilligan (1982) points out. Freud assumed that because girls experience less differentiation from their mothers, they are less developed, whereas Chodorow does not equate differentiation with development. By her account, the two paths to sexual identity result in two complementary developmental endpoints, each with its own strengths and weaknesses. Males achieve identity through separation; as a result, males see themselves as threatened by intimacy. Females, on the other hand, achieve identity through attachment. They see themselves as threatened by separation.

Identification through Observation and Imitation

Freudian theories of identification assume that the process occurs indirectly: children are caught in hidden conflicts between their fears and their desires and resolve these conflicts through identification.

Social learning theorists have a very different perspective on how children adopt adult roles. They assume that the process of identification is not driven by inner conflict, but is simply a matter of observation and imitation. For example, as a 4-year-old, Sasha loved to run down the hallway and slide feet first into a pillow. He was not driven by desire for his mother, who disapproved strongly for fear that his sliding bothered the downstairs neighbors and from the cer-

tainty that he was wearing holes in his pants. Nor was his father's disapproval enough to stop him. Sasha was modeling his behavior on a baseball star who was being given prominence by the media at the time.

Albert Bandura (1969, 1986), Walter Mischel (1966), and other social learning theorists believe that behavior such as Sasha's is shaped by the environment, just as all behavior is. According to this view, children observe that male and female behavior differs. From this observation, children develop hypotheses about appropriate male and female behaviors (Perry & Bussey, 1984). Further, children learn that boys and girls are rewarded differently by adults for different kinds of behavior, so they choose to engage in sex-appropriate behaviors that will lead to rewards.

In Bandura's view, the ability to learn from observation depends upon several factors:

1. *Availability* The behavior to be learned must be available in the child's environment either directly or through a medium such as a book or television program.

2. *Attention* Children cannot learn from observation unless they pay attention to the model (the mother, the father, or the fictional character) and perceive the significant features of the behavior in question. A child often needs repeated observation before determining the significant features of a complex behavior. For example, a boy who watches Daddy shave may at first see the application of shaving cream as the salient feature; it may take several contacts before the boy realizes that using a razor is what signifies shaving.

3. *Memory* Observation will have no lasting effect if children immediately forget what they observe. Bandura believes that when children have a name for modeled events, their observation becomes especially effective and memorable. Significantly, early childhood is the time when children are acquiring *both* language *and* knowledge of basic social categories—and their memory capacities are also increasing (see Chapter 10).

4. *Motor reproduction process* Observation shows the child which behaviors to imitate. However, if a behavior is too complex (such as doing a backward flip), the child will usually not try to perform it.

5. *Motivation* For imitation and subsequent learning to occur, the observer must perceive some

payoff. Motivation, like learning, can occur by observing the experiences of others. When Ben, who wants to be thought well of by grownups, hears Daddy praise Lisa for taking her glass to the sink when she finishes her apple juice, he may be motivated to take his glass to the sink next time. If Daddy's good opinion means little to him, he probably will not be motivated to learn from this observation.

There is abundant evidence that parents not only provide models for children to imitate, but that they also reward what they consider sex-appropriate behavior and punish cross-sex behavior. For example, Beverly Fagot (1978), who spent many hours observing preschoolers and their parents in their homes, found that many parents rewarded their daughters with smiles, attention, and praise for dressing up, dancing, playing with dolls, and simply following them around the house. By contrast, parents rewarded boys more than girls for playing with blocks. These same parents criticized their girls for manipulating objects, running, jumping, and climbing, but criticized their boys for playing with dolls, asking for help, or volunteering to be helpful. Such findings support social-learning theorists' basic assumption: that sex-appropriate behaviors are shaped by the distribution of rewards and punishments in the environment.

Despite many attractive features, a social-learning theory has a serious problem in defining one of its central concepts—reward. To some degree, rewards, like beauty, are in the eye of the beholder. A 2-year-old boy and a 2-year-old girl may both be pleased when their grandparents give them a doll for good behavior. But two years later, while the girl might find another doll rewarding, the boy might turn away in disgust at "those girl things." Such incidents make it appear that children's prior conceptions about what is proper behavior for boys and girls determines their ideas of appropriate rewards for boys and girls. Where do these prior conceptions come from?

Identification through Cognition

The belief that a child's concepts are central to socialization is the cornerstone of the cognitive-developmental approach to sex-role acquisition proposed by Lawrence Kohlberg (1966). In contrast to the social-learning view, Kohlberg argued that "the child's sex-role concepts are the result of the child's active structuring of his own experience; they are not passive products of social training" (p. 85). In contrast to the Freudian view, Kohlberg claimed that the "process of forming a constant sexual identity is not a unique process determined by instinctual wishes and identifications, but a part of the general process of conceptual growth" (p. 98).

In Kohlberg's view, the crucial factor in sex-role identification is children's developing ability to categorize themselves as "boys" or "girls." This process typically begins about the age of 2, when children are acquiring a distinctive sense of themselves and beginning to form complex concepts. Once formed, children's conceptions of their own sex are difficult to reverse and are maintained regardless of the social environment.

A slightly different version of this cognitive view has been proposed by Sandra Bem (1981), who suggests that children acquire a **gender schema**, a network of associations embodying the culture's conception of sex roles, which children then use to guide their own behavior and which structures children's perceptions of their environment. In line with the way that scripts and schemas structure preschoolers' cognitive development (Chapter 10), Bem's view suggests that children learn their society's gender schemas through observing and participating in many events, which show them which attributes belong to their sex.

In the cognitive view, once children have acquired a concept or schema of themselves as girls or boys, they use that concept to choose actively from the options present in the environment. Whereas the social-learning theorists assume that the thought sequence of male children is "I want rewards, I am rewarded for doing boy things, therefore I want to be a boy," Kohlberg (1966, p. 89) proposed the following sequence:

I am a boy; therefore I want to do boy things; therefore the opportunity to do boy things (and to gain approval for doing them) is rewarding.

Kohlberg acknowledged that children need to feel that they can control their environment and that they are loved by others. But in his view, rewards come from behaving in a manner that be consistent with one's sexual identity. The key for the child in finding a sex-typed behavior rewarding is that it be consistent with maintenance of the appropriate identity, which itself is a cognitive judgment by the child.

Sex-role knowledge and sex-role behavior In order to decide among conflicting theories about how preschoolers form sex-role identities, psychologists have sought to trace the developing relationship between the earliest signs of sex-typed behavior and children's earliest concepts of what adults mean when they use the labels "girl" and "boy." The existing evidence suggests that during the preschool years children gradually develop a well-articulated concept of what it means to be a boy or girl in their culture, which then, as Kohlberg suggested, shapes their behavior. However, between the ages of 2½ and 6, children are still piecing this conceptual structure together. Both biological and social factors seem to play important roles in promoting both sex-appropriate behaviors and the development of basic sex-role categories themselves.

Well before children manifest knowledge of sexual stereotypes, boys and girls are apt to behave differently from each other. Carol Jacklin and Eleanor Maccoby (1978) observed distinctive styles of play among 2½-year-olds, in which children were likely to find partners of the same sex more compatible. For example, when boys played together and got into a tug of war over a toy, the tug of war was likely to become part of the game. But when a girl and boy got into the same kind of tug of war, the girl was likely to retreat and simply observe the boy playing. Maccoby is careful not to specify the origins of these differences, restricting herself to the conclusion that even at this early age, children "are already developing somewhat distinctive styles of play" (1980, p. 215).

Not only do boys and girls play differently from an early age, they often prefer to play with different things. When children aged 14 to 22 months were observed in their own homes, researchers found that boys were more likely to play with trucks and cars while girls chose dolls and soft toys (Smith & Daglish, 1977). The children spent more time playing with sex-identified toys than with equally available toys that were not sex-typed, suggesting that even at this young age, these children had developed sex-typed preferences. (See Figure 11.2.)

The source of these preferences is much debated. Social learning theorists emphasize the role of adults who give toddlers toys they consider sex-appropriate and reward children for playing with them (Rheingold & Cook, 1975; Sidorowicz & Lunney, 1980). Psychoanalytic theorists, such as Erik Erikson (1963), are

FIGURE 11.2 *Preschoolers often adopt an extreme, stereotyped version of adult sex-role behavior in their dress-up play.*

more likely to hypothesize a biological predisposition to various toy preferences.

Whatever the original source of sex differences, young preschoolers show no evidence that their behavior is guided by conceptual understanding. For example, 2-year-olds can identify their own sex in a photograph of themselves and are usually able to identify the sex of a stereotypically dressed man or woman in a photograph, according to the findings of S. K. Thompson (1975). But when asked to sort a photograph of themselves along with photographs of other children into "boys" and "girls," their accuracy is no better than chance. Moreover, they are unable to predict other children's toy preference on the basis of sex. In other words, children make sex-typed choices without expressing any conscious awareness of sexual identity. Hence, the kind of active selection proposed by Kohlberg cannot yet be considered a crucial factor.

At the age of 3, conceptual understanding is more in evidence. For example, Thompson found that 3-year-olds could separate pictures of boys and girls. However, many of these same children still could not say whether they themselves were going to be a mommy or a daddy. Not until they were 4 years old could most children choose which of two sex-typed dolls they most resembled.

Additional evidence that the concepts of *male* and *female* begin to influence personal preferences for same-sex behaviors around age 3 or 4 comes from a study by Nancy Eisenberg and her colleagues, who asked 3- and 4-year-olds which sex-typed toys they thought they themselves, another boy, or another girl would like or dislike (Eisenberg, Murray, & Hite, 1982). Although children's ability to apply these categories to other children's toy preferences was a little shaky, from 11 percent to 55 percent of the reasons each child gave for predicting that another child would like or dislike a particular toy were based on their prejudgments about boys' or girls' preferences. Moreover, most teachers agree that in fantasy play and other classroom interactions, 4- and 5-year-olds make their understanding that there are "girl" and "boy" behaviors abundantly clear

Sex-role constancy The ambiguous evidence about what exactly preschoolers understand reflects the fact that they are struggling to reconcile a great deal of information. A full concept of one's sexual identity goes well beyond predicting toy preferences or identifying key biological attributes. A sexual identity also includes many other characteristics that are a part of each culture's general conceptions of the categories *masculine* and *feminine*.

Regardless of the theory used to explain it, a good deal of evidence suggests that by the time children are about 6 or 7 years old, they have formed a stable concept of their own identity as male or female. At this point, almost all children strive to imitate behavior that they interpret as appropriate to their sex in the way that Kohlberg emphasized (Perry & Bussey, 1984).

Part of this greater conceptual stability reflects children's new understanding that their sexual identities are permanent. Children develop the idea that physical characteristics are permanent rather slowly (Marcus & Overton, 1978). In a study similar to De Vries' investigation of children's ability to distinguish between appearance and reality (described in Chapter 10, p. 313), Kohlberg asked children between the ages of 4 and 8 if a cat could become a dog if it wanted to, or if its whiskers were cut off. Most 4-year-olds said that this change in species was possible, while most 6-year-olds denied the possibility (Kohlberg, 1966). Kohlberg asked the same question about the possibility of changing sexes. Again, young children saw no difficulty in such a change, while older ones knew that it was impossible. The young children who claimed that a doll's sex could change explained their reasoning by saying such things as " 'Cause I want her to be a girl,"

There is often very marked sex-role stereotyping in preschoolers' play.

while older children explained that it was impossible because "She was born a girl" or "She doesn't have magic; she can't change without an operation."

A similar pattern was observed when these same children were asked about the apparent transformation of various physical objects (see also Chapter 10, p. 316). For example, Kohlberg showed children a piece of clay that was then pounded flat or pushed into different shapes. By and large, the children who knew that sex is a permanent feature of people also knew that the amount of clay had not been changed by transforming its appearance. Kohlberg interpreted this result as support for his cognitive approach to development, which led him to expect that the development of a stable concept of sex would reflect the children's overall cognitive development.

Theories of Identification Compared

Developmental psychologists do agree on two points concerning children's discovery of social categories and initial mastery of behavior that is appropriate to their sex: (1) children conduct some kind of mental "matching" operation that allows them to isolate key features that they share with others; (2) later ideas of sex-appropriate behavior are closely tied to children's ability to categorize, observe, and imitate.

Theorists differ, though, in their view of adults' power to shape the final outcome. For somewhat different reasons, both Freudian and cognitive-developmental theorists believe that the child's sexual identification and subsequent sex-role behavior are unlikely to be affected by any but the most drastic changes in environmental circumstances. In Freud's famous phrase, "biology is destiny"; males and females are biologically different forms of *Homo sapiens* that no cultural conditioning can change. In the cognitive-developmental view, sexual identity grows out of universal forms of experience; although cultural influence is not absent, it is not primary.

The social-learning view implies a far greater role for culture in shaping sexual identification and behavior, thus suggesting that changing the culture can produce significant changes in sexual identity. In this view, the essential requirement for changing behavior is changing the pattern of rewards.

Just how much flexibility exists for redefining *masculine* and *feminine* remains a matter of dispute (Huston, 1983). Cross-cultural research has shown that many attributes that are sex-typed one way in one society—including types of gestures, speech patterns, dress, activities, interests, and occupations—are typed quite differently in another (Rosaldo & Lamphere, 1974).

In many countries, for example, physicians are predominantly male and being a doctor is considered "men's work." But in the Soviet Union, most physicians are female, and this occupation is considered women's work. In various countries and at various times in history, men have worn robes; in the United States, this form of dress is currently associated with femaleness.

By whatever route, children of 5 or 6 have acquired the idea that they are members of one sex or the other. Simultaneously, children are learning a vast array of other roles: how to behave as a big sister, a visitor in someone else's home, a patient in a dentist's chair, or Mommy's helper at the market. They are also learning something about possible roles they may play in the future: farmer, nurse, daddy, or president.

DEVELOPING THE ABILITY TO REGULATE ONESELF

As children acquire a basic sense of identity, they are also learning which behaviors are considered good and bad. Their parents expect them not only to learn the rules of proper behavior, but to follow these rules without constant supervision. In short, children are expected to adopt the standards of conduct appropriate in their culture and to accept them so thoroughly that they "behave themselves."

Because children want to please those with whom they identify in addition to wanting to be like them, the ways in which the significant people in their lives respond to their behavior give children their first, primitive ideas of what is good and bad. The following discussion with several 5-year-olds clearly shows that adult evaluations are more than an external fact; they are the basis for children's self-evaluations.

Eddie: Sometimes I hate myself.

Teacher: When?

Eddie: When I'm naughty.

Teacher: What do you do that's naughty?

Eddie: You know, naughty words. Like "shit." That one.

Teacher: That makes you hate yourself?

Eddie: Yeah, when my dad washes my mouth with soap.

Teacher: What if he doesn't hear you?

Eddie: Then I get away with it. Then I don't hate myself.

Wally: If I'm bad, like take the food when it's not time to eat yet and my mom makes me leave the kitchen, then I hate myself because I want to stay with her in the kitchen.

Eddie: And here's another reason when I don't like myself. This is a good reason. Sometimes I try to get the cookies on top of the refrigerator.

Teacher: What's the reason you don't like yourself?

Eddie: Because my mom counts to ten fast and I get a spanking and my grandma gets mad at her.

Deana: Here's when I *like* myself: when I'm coloring and my mommy says, "Stop coloring. We have to go out." And I tell her I'm coloring and she says, "Okay, I'll give you ten more minutes."

Teacher: What if you have to stop what you're doing?

Deana: When she's in a big hurry. That's when she yells at me. Then I don't like myself.

(Paley, 1981, pp. 54–55)

As Vivian Paley comments, "Bad and good depended on the adult response. . . . An angry parent denoted a naughty child. To the adult, the cause of the punishment was obvious, but the child only saw the stick and judged himself accordingly" (1981, p. 55).

Paley is echoing the opinion of Jean Piaget (1932/1965), who called this pattern of thinking the "morality of constraint" or **heteronomous morality** (*heteronomous* means "from the outside"). According to Piaget, preschoolers' reasoning about moral issues is shaped by three considerations:

1. I should obey the rules set by more powerful people no matter what.

2. I should obey the letter of the rule, not its spirit.

3. What counts is the outcome of my actions. Even if my intentions are good, if the outcome is bad, then I am bad.

Piaget reached these conclusions about the moral reasoning of preschoolers by telling them pairs of stories and then asking them questions. One of his story pairs went as follows (1932/1965, p. 122):

Version A. There was a little boy called Julian. His father had gone out and Julian thought it would be fun to play with his father's ink-pot. First he played with the pen, and then he made a little blot on the table cloth.

Version B. A little boy who was called Augustus once noticed that his father's ink-pot was empty. One day that his father was away he thought of filling the ink-pot so as to help his father, and so he should find it full when he came home. But while he was opening the ink-bottle he made a big blot on the table cloth.

Piaget first asked the child to repeat each of the stories and then asked a series of questions. This kind of task proved too difficult to carry out with preschoolers, so Piaget interviewed somewhat older children who were still young enough, he believed, to retain the kind of moral reasoning characteristic of early childhood. The following is a conversation with a 7-year-old child (1932/1965, p. 126):

Piaget: Are they both equally naughty or not?

Child: No.

Piaget: Which is the most naughty?

Child: The one who made the big blot.

Piaget: Why?

Child: Because it was big.

Piaget: Why did he make a big blot?

Child: To be helpful.

Piaget: And why did the other make a little blot?

Child: Because he was always touching things. He made a little blot.

Piaget: Then which of them is the naughtiest?

Child: The one who made a big blot.

Piaget proposed that children's beliefs grew out of their experience of the restrictions placed on them by powerful elders. It had always been the child's experience that older people announce the rules, compel conformity, and decide what is right and wrong:

The morality of constraint is that of duty pure and simple and of heteronomy. The child accepts from the adult a certain number of commands to which it must submit whatever the circumstances may be. Right is what conforms with these commands; wrong is what fails to do so; the intention plays a very small part in this conception, and the responsibility is entirely objective. (1932/1965, p. 335)

According to Piaget, as children enter middle childhood and begin increasingly to interact with their peers outside of situations directly controlled by adults, the morality of constraint gives way to a more **autonomous morality,** one that is based on an understanding that rules are arbitrary agreements that can be challenged, and even changed, if those being governed by them agree.

Internalization

As we saw in Chapter 7, children at the end of infancy become sensitive to society's standards of good and bad even when they are not explicitly instructed or have not yet seen how those in authority will respond to a particular act. Instead, they begin to anticipate adults' reactions and plan their own actions accordingly. Once children both want to conform to adult wishes and are able to anticipate adult reactions, they are said to have **internalized** adult standards.

Freud describes the process of internalizing adult standards and the consequences of internalization for the development of self-control in the following way:

. . . about the age of 5. . . . A portion of the external world has, at least partially, been abandoned as an object and has instead, by identification, been taken into the ego and thus become an integral part of the internal world. This new psychical agency continues to carry on the functions which have hitherto been performed by the people [the abandoned objects] in the external world: it observes the ego, gives it orders, judges it and threatens it with punishments, exactly like the parents whose place it has taken. We call this agency the *super-ego* and are aware of it in its judicial functions as our *conscience.* (Freud, 1940/1964, p. 205)

Once the child has internalized adult standards, a new form of psychological tension begins to emerge —

guilt. Children experience guilt when they know what's right but feel unable to do it. In the view of Erik Erikson (see Box 11.2), the basic task of early childhood is to resolve the conflict between the need to take initiative and the negative feelings that arise when initiative leads to bad behavior (1968, p. 289):

Conscience . . . forever divides the child within himself by establishing an inner voice of self-observation, self-guidance, and self-punishment.

The words that psychologists use to describe the development of conscience reveal the important roles of language and culture in the process of internalization. As in the case of sex-role identification, culture enters in the form of rules, roles, activities, and beliefs —the *content* of the conscience. But culture also enters into the *process* of developing a conscience, in the internal dialogue between the child and authority figures. The very concept of conscience suggests that the child is imagining what those in authority will say (Vygotsky, 1978).

Self-Control

In order to resolve the tension between personal desire and internalized social standards, children must acquire the capacity to control their own behavior. Self-control includes both the ability to inhibit action and to carry through actions according to preestablished rules even when one does not feel like it.

Preschoolers are well known for their lack of self-control and the consequent need for supervision when their activities do not naturally engage their attention. The 4-year-old who sits in rapt attention while she is being read the story of Little Red Riding Hood is likely to squirm and whisper during a church sermon. The same child who finds it almost impossible to stand quietly when a teacher announces it is time to line up for recess will stand still for many minutes when playing the role of an honor guard (see Box 10.2, on sociodramatic play).

Insofar as children's behavior is simply a direct response to the environment, they are being controlled "from the outside." The direct response to being hit is to become angry and hit back. The direct response to taking bitter medicine is to spit it out. Children who inhibit the impulse to hit back by seeking an alternative response or who accept the rule to "follow the doctor's orders" are displaying self-control.

Eleanor Maccoby (1980) identifies four kinds of inhibition that preschoolers begin to master (although mastery can never be considered complete, even among adults!).

1. Inhibition of movement A number of studies have shown that it is easier for small children to start an action than to stop one already in progress (Luria, 1981). A child who does not know when or how to stop is likely, both literally and figuratively, to step on someone else's toes.

The same problem applies to verbal commands. Strommen (1973) investigated the way that children learned to inhibit movement in the familiar children's game "Simon Says." In this follow-the-leader game, the leader's command is supposed to be obeyed only when it is preceded by the phrase "Simon says." Preschoolers find it very difficult not to respond to the command, whether they hear the phrase or not. Even first-graders continue to make errors in this game.

2. Inhibition of emotions In the preschool period, children begin to gain control over the intensity of their emotions. Maccoby recounts an incident in which a mother found her 4-year-old with a cut on his hand that ordinarily would have led to tears. When she said to him, "Why, honey, you've hurt yourself! I didn't hear you crying," the youngster replied, "I didn't know you were home."

3. Inhibition of conclusions Before the age of 6, children presented with a difficult problem tend to respond quickly, failing to note that the task is more difficult than it seemed at first glance. For example, Messer (1976) asked children to match a familiar figure with its mate in a set of confusing alternatives (Figure 11.3). Young preschoolers respond quickly to this task, and they perform poorly. As they grow older, they slow down to reflect on the problem and improve their performance (Figure 11.4).

4. Inhibition of choice An important element of adult self-control is the knowledge that it is often better to pass up short-term gratification for a larger, long-term goal. Given a choice between eating a small candy bar immediately and a large candy bar the next day, kindergartners overwhelmingly take the small candy bar; not until they are about 12 years old do children choose to wait (Mischel, 1968).

Young children's growing ability to estimate the tradeoffs implied by a change from direct, immediate reactions to indirect, mediated, thoughtful ones is

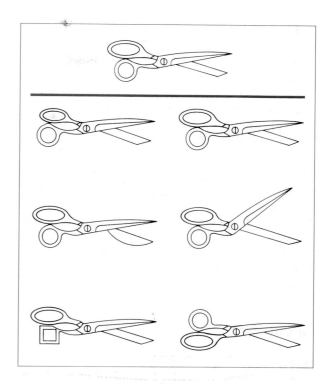

FIGURE 11.3 *An item from the Children's Matching Familiar Figures Test. Which pair of scissors from the six at the bottom of the figure matches the model at the top? (Courtesy of Jerome Kagan.)*

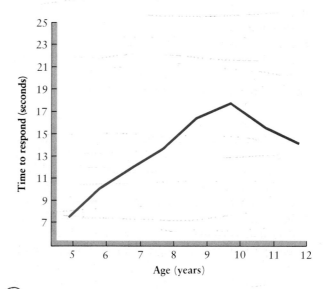

FIGURE 11.4 *Between the ages of 5 and 10, children become increasingly cautious in responding to the task of matching familiar figures. Children older than 10 respond more rapidly because the problems are relatively easy for them. (Adapted from Salkind & Nelson, 1980.)*

BOX 11.2

ERIK ERIKSON

• • •

Erik Erikson (1902–), a student of Freud's, has managed to combine a background in art, teaching, psychoanalysis, and anthropology in his approach to the process of development throughout the individual lifespan. Erikson is best known for adding an important social dimension to Freud's biological determinism.

Erikson's emphasis on the influence of society has expanded the scope of psychoanalysis, as has his addition of new methods for observing children, his cross-cultural comparisons, and his psychohistories. In his psychohistories he analyzes the psychological development of such well-known figures as Martin Luther and Mahatma Gandhi, basing his conclusions on their writings and on the reports of others (Erikson, 1958, 1969).

Erikson accepts many of Freud's basic ideas about development, including the importance of early childhood in the formation of personality, the existence of the three basic psychological structures (id, ego, and superego), and the existence of unconscious drives. He holds that the main theme of life is the quest for *identity,* a stable mental picture of the relation between the self and the social world. He sees identity formation as a lifelong process that goes through many stages. All throughout their lives people ask themselves "Who am I" and at each stage of life they arrive at a different answer (Erikson, 1963, 1968b).

While Freud's stages of development end in adolescence, Erikson proposes that human development has eight stages and continues throughout life. In formulating his stages of *psychosocial* development, he built upon Freud's *psychosexual* stages. A comparison of Freud's and Erikson's stages of development can be seen in the table on the facing page.

Each stage, Erikson believes, embodies a crisis that the individual must resolve in order to move on to the next stage of development. The individual's sense of identity is formed in the resolution of these crises; these crises are periods of great vulnerability but also of heightened potential. Thus, whether a 2- or 3-year-old girl is successful in acquiring control over her desires and her body will determine whether she feels proud of herself and autonomous or ashamed and doubtful of her ability to control herself. In each stage, maturation

Erik Erikson. Copyright © 1988 Jill Krementz.

opens up both new possibilities and increased social demands. For example, a young girl's pleasure at being able to play the role of flower girl at an aunt's wedding is matched by the psychosocial demands from those around her to be able to sit still and to follow directions without too much prompting.

Although development creates what Erikson describes as a "succession of potentialities," these potentialities are continuously being shaped by other individuals as well as by social institutions. The "widening circle" of significant individuals who interact with the child includes parents, siblings, peers, grandparents, aunts, uncles, teachers, teammates, mentors, colleagues, employers, employees, and grandchildren. As the circle widens, so does the individual's contact with social institutions.

Each individual's life cycle unfolds in the context of a specific culture. While physical maturation writes the general timetable in which a particular component of personality "comes to its ascendancy, meets its crises, and finds its solution," culture determines the situations in which the crises and resolutions must be worked out.

Comparison of psychosexual and psychosocial stages

Approximate Age	Freud (Psychosexual)	Erikson (Psychosocial)
First year	*Oral stage:* The mouth is the focus of the baby's pleasurable sensations as the baby sucks and bites.	*Trust vs. mistrust:* Infants learn to trust or mistrust others to care for their basic needs.
Second year	*Anal stage:* The anus is the focus of pleasurable sensations as the baby learns to control elimination.	*Autonomy vs. shame and doubt:* Children learn to exercise their will and to control themselves or they become uncertain and doubt that they can do things by themselves.
Third to sixth year	*Phallic stage:* Children develop sexual curiosity and obtain gratification when they masturbate. They have sexual fantasies about the parent of the opposite sex and feel guilt about their fantasies.	*Initiative vs. guilt:* Children learn to initiate their own activities, enjoy their accomplishments, and become purposeful. If they are not allowed to follow their own initiative, they feel guilty for their attempt to become independent.
Seventh year through puberty	*Latency:* Sexual urges are submerged. Children focus on mastery of skills valued by adults.	*Industry vs. inferiority:* Children learn to be competent and effective at activities valued by adults and peers or they feel inferior.
Adolescence	*Genital Stage:* Adolescents have adult sexual desires, and they seek to satisfy them.	*Identity vs. role confusion:* Adolescents establish a sense of personal identity as part of their social group or they become confused about who they are and what they want to do in life.
Early adulthood		*Intimacy vs. isolation:* Young adults find an intimate life companion or they risk loneliness and isolation.
Middle age		*Generativity vs. stagnation:* Adults must be productive in their work and willing to raise a next generation or they risk stagnation.
Old age		*Integrity vs. despair:* People try to make sense of their prior experience and to assure themselves that their lives have been meaningful or they despair over their unaccomplished goals and ill-spent lives.

made possible in part by their expanding time frame and their increased understanding of the scripts governing events in which they participate. Children who do not understand "short-term" versus "long-term" cannot measure "short-term versus long-term *gain*." As Maccoby points out, "Memory is the basis of anticipation" (1980, p. 163).

Up to this point, we have focused on the issues of conscience and self-control as more or less individual matters. However, as we pointed out at the beginning of this chapter, individual personality development and socialization are two sides of a single developmental coin. During the preschool era, children begin to spend significant amounts of time interacting with children their own age. As Freud reminds us in this chapter's opening quotation, children must somehow learn to gain acceptance by their social group. Sometimes they must inhibit their anger when their goals are thwarted; at other times they will have to subordinate their personal desires for the good of the group. Learning to control aggression and to help others are two of the central processes in preschool social development.

AGGRESSION AND PROSOCIAL BEHAVIOR

Children begin to display the rudiments of both aggression and socially constructive behavior shortly after birth. The earliest signs of aggression are the angry responses of newborns whose rhythmic sucking has been interrupted. The first signs of socially constructive behavior are manifested just as early, when newborns react to the cries of other babies by starting to cry themselves (Simner, 1971). It is widely believed that this "contagious crying" is the earliest form of empathy, the sharing of another's feelings, which is the basis for helping and for a variety of other behaviors referred to as **prosocial** (Radke-Yarrow, Zahn-Waxler, & Chapman, 1983; Sagi & Hoffman, 1976).

The Development of Aggression

Aggression is a difficult form of behavior to define. At the core of its meaning is the idea that one person commits an action that hurts another—but not all

ways in which one person hurts another count as aggression. A teething baby who bites the mother's breast while nursing causes pain, as does a toddler who slips and falls on a friend, but these actions aren't usually considered aggressive. To be counted as aggressive, a behavior must be intended to harm others (Parke & Slaby, 1983). Maccoby (1980) suggests that aggression begins only after children understand that they can be the cause of other's distress. To be aggressive, children must know that they can get others to do what they want by causing them distress. This understanding seems to take shape during early childhood.

As children mature, two forms of aggression appear (Hartup, 1974). **Instrumental aggression** is directed at obtaining something desirable; for example, threatening or hitting another child to obtain a toy. **Hostile aggression,** sometimes called "person-oriented" aggression, is more specifically aimed at hurting another

Teeth are a favorite weapon when preschoolers engage in person-oriented aggression.

Disputes over toys are frequently the occasion for aggression among preschoolers.

person, either for revenge, or as a way of establishing dominance, which, in the long run, may gain the aggressor possessions.

To trace the early development of aggressive behavior, Wanda Bronson (1975) invited three or four children to a playroom at one time. She gave them toys to play with, and she permitted their mothers to be present to give them a sense of security. As the children explored and played, Bronson watched for occasions when two children wanted the same toy.

Between the ages of 12 and 20 months, most antagonistic interactions observed by Bronson consisted of brief tussles in which one child tried to take a toy from another. Children in this age range showed no evidence of deliberately causing harm in order to obtain a toy. They became upset when something was taken from them or they couldn't get something they wanted, but it was easy to distract them by substituting another toy.

As children in the United States approach the age of 2 (just when a new and distinctive sense of self seems to emerge, as we saw in Chapter 7, p. 236), they begin to worry about "ownership rights." Taking toys then becomes a more serious affair. In fact, Bronson noted that often the 2-year-olds struggled over a toy that neither child had shown any interest in before and

which neither cared about once the conflict ended. The fact of possession itself, as well as the possibility of "winning out," were new elements in their interactions. Observations in other cultures suggest that similar changes are likely to appear in all societies (Kagan, 1981; Ochs & Schieffelin, 1984; Raum, 1940/1967).

A classic early study by Florence Goodenough (1931/1975) traced the emergence of what she called "true aggression" — anger directed at a specific person for a specific purpose. She asked 45 mothers to keep daily diaries of their children's angry outbursts and the circumstances surrounding them. She found that as children mature, there is a gradual shift from conflict evoked by desire for an object, which is not directed at another individual *per se*, to true aggression. Between 12 and 24 months of age, tantrums, which were not directed at anyone in particular, were children's most common expression of anger. But by 4 years of age, some 20 percent of the children's outbursts were directed at a particular person whom they perceived as doing them wrong.

Between the ages of 3 and 6, the expression of aggression undergoes several related changes. First, physical tussles over possessions decrease, while the amount of verbal aggression, such as threats or insults, increases. Second, "person-oriented" or "hostile" aggression, in which one child attempts to hurt another even though there are no possessions at stake, makes its appearance (Hartup, 1974).

Preschoolers are not only verbally aggressive to their peers, they may also abuse their parents when they are frustrated and angry.

Although the causes of the difference are uncertain, many studies show boys to be more aggressive than girls in a wide variety of circumstances. Seymour Feshbach (1970) suggested that boys are only more aggressive physically, but according to a later survey by Maccoby and Jacklin (1974), males are also more aggressive verbally.

What Causes Aggression?

During this century, more people have died in war than in all prior centuries combined. Our newspapers daily carry stories of people killing each other in search of money, to revenge a perceived wrong, or for no apparent reason at all. Among all the questions that can be asked about human social relations, none is more fraught with concern and uncertainty than the causes of aggression.

Some of these causes can be found in people's immediate circumstances. A common instigator of aggression is *frustration*, the emotional response to a goal being blocked. Because newborns' only response to an obstacle (for example, when a nipple is removed while they are feeding) is to cry and thrash around, their frustration does not result in aggression. But, as we have seen, no sooner are children able to direct their anger against the perceived obstacle than aggression appears. Other causes of aggression arise from the person's prior experience and learning. Still others appear to have their origins in our evolutionary past.

The argument from evolution Noting that no group in the animal kingdom is free from aggression, many students of animal behavior have proposed that aggression is an important mechanism of evolution (Lorenz, 1966). According to Darwin (1859/1959, see Chapter 2, p. 66), a species gradually comes to assume the characteristics of its most successful individuals. Darwin defined as "most successful" those individuals who manage to pass on their inborn characteristics to the next generation. Because each individual is, in some sense, competing with every other individual for the resources necessary for survival and reproduction, evolution would seem to favor competitive and selfish behaviors. Such animal behaviors as territorial defense, which insures a mating pair access to food, have been interpreted as survival-oriented competition (Wilson, 1975). According to this interpretation of evolution, aggression is natural and necessary; its appearance automatically accompanies biological maturation of the young.

Rewarding aggression A second explanation, generally associated with the social learning view, is that aggressive behavior is learned because it is often rewarding to the aggressor. G. R. Patterson and his colleagues spent many hours watching the aggressive behavior of nursery school children. For every aggressive incident that occurred during their observations, they noted who the aggressor was, who the victim was, and what the consequences were. They found that an aggressive action occurred several times an hour and that well over three-quarters of the aggressive acts they observed were followed by positive consequences for the aggressor: the victim either gave in or retreated. These victories increased the probability that the aggressor would repeat the attack on the same victim. However, if the aggression was followed by negative consequences, such as an aggressive response, the child was less likely to repeat the aggressive act (Patterson, Littman, & Bricker, 1967).

Modeling A third cause of aggression may be parents who inadvertently teach their children to behave aggressively by modeling aggressive behavior in the act of punishing them. Evidence for this mechanism comes from a famous series of experiments conducted by the social-learning theorist Albert Bandura and his coworkers (Bandura, Ross, & Ross, 1963; Bandura 1965; 1973). They arranged for several groups of preschool children to watch as an adult yelled at a large, inflatable "Bobo" doll, hit it on the head with a mallet, threw it across the room, punched it, and otherwise abused it (see Figure 11.5). In some cases the children watched a normally dressed adult model aggressing; in others, they saw a filmed version of the same events; in still another case, the model was costumed as a cartoon cat.

After the children watched the episodes of aggressive behavior, the experimenters arranged for them to engage in other activities for a while. Then they brought the children to a playroom containing a Bobo doll and invited them to play in order to see if they would imitate the adult they had observed. As expected on the basis of Bandura's social-learning theory, the aggressive behavior of children who had observed adult aggression was substantially higher than that of children in a control group who had

FIGURE 11.5 *The top row of photos shows an adult behaving aggressively toward a "Bobo" doll. In the two lower rows, youngsters imitate her aggressive behavior.*

watched nonaggressive interactions. Not only did the children who had been exposed to an aggressive model imitate specific forms of aggression, they also made up forms of their own, such as pretending to shoot the doll, or spanking it. It made little difference whether the adult models were live or filmed, but the children were somewhat less likely to imitate the aggression of the cartoon character. The conclusion seems inescapable; once children are old enough to understand that they can get their way by harming others, they learn from adults both specific types of aggression and the general idea that acting aggressively is acceptable (Figure 11.6).

As in so many other cases where psychologists attempt to ferret out a single cause of a particular behavior, there is a tendency to pose biological-evolutionary and environmental-learning theories of aggression against each other. Such either/or thinking is not sufficient to explain a complex form of behavior such as aggression, which grows out of the interactions between deep-seated biological characteristics and culturally organized environmental influences. Nor can aggression be understood without looking at the various mechanisms that counteract it, since aggression is just one among several factors that regulate social behavior.

Controlling Human Aggression

The same theories that attempt to explain aggression also point to mechanisms that are likely to be effective in controlling it. Two such mechanisms that have been extensively studied are the evolution of hierarchical systems of control and the use of reward and punishment.

Evolutionary theories While aggression is widespread among animal species, so are mechanisms that limit aggression. Changes in the aggressive behavior in litters of puppies provide an instructive example (James, 1951). These changes follow a maturational

FIGURE 11.6 *Among the Dani of New Guinea, boys are socialized to be aggressive and warlike from an early age through organized practice sessions and many opportunities to observe admired older males in battle.*

timetable. At about three weeks, young puppies begin to engage in rough and tumble play, mouthing and nipping one another. A week later the play has become rougher; there is growling and snarling when the puppies bite, and the victim may yelp in pain. A few weeks later, if littermates are left together, there is little doubt that serious attacks occur. Often the larger animals concentrate their attacks on the runts of the litter, and among some breeds, it is necessary to remove the small animals to keep them from being killed.

Once injurious attacks become really serious, a new form of social structure emerges, with some animals dominant and others subordinate in a hierarchy. After such a **dominance hierarchy** is formed, the dominant animal needs only to threaten, without attacking, to succeed in getting its way. At this point, the frequency of fighting diminishes (Cairns, 1979). Throughout nature, there are innumerable such hierarchies that regulate interactions among members of the same species (see Figure 11.7).

The developmental history of aggression and its control among puppies is similar in some interesting ways to development in human children. F. F. Strayer and his colleagues (Strayer & Strayer, 1976; Strayer, 1980) observed a close connection between aggression and the formation of dominance hierarchies among 3- and 4-year-olds in a nursery school. They identified a specific pattern of hostile interactions among children: when one child would aggress, the other child would almost always submit by crying, running away, flinching, or seeking help from an adult. These dominance encounters formed an orderly pattern of social relationships within the group. If one child dominated another, he or she also dominated all children below that one in the dominance hierarchy of that group.

As dominance hierarchies in the nursery school took shape, they influenced who would fight with whom, and under what circumstances. Once children knew their position in such a hierarchy, they only challenged those whom it was safe for them to challenge. They left others alone, thereby reducing the amount of aggression within the group.

FIGURE 11.7 *Many species of animals have innate mechanisms for signaling defeat to allow the establishment of a social dominance hierarchy without bloodshed. (From Eibl-Eibesfeldt, 1971.)*

The existence of some similarities across species in these patterns of aggression and its control should not blind us to some important differences. The young of other species often must rely entirely on dominance hierarchies, whereas human offspring are watched over by their parents and older siblings, who set limits to their initial expressions of aggression to keep them from harming others. These older members of the group also invoke rules about proper behavior which the children begin to internalize, thus helping to pave the way for self-control.

Frustration and the catharsis myth One of the most popular and persistent beliefs about aggression is that providing people with harmless ways to be aggressive will reduce their aggressive and hostile tendencies. This belief is based on the assumption that unless they are "vented" in a safe way, an individual's aggressive urges build up until they violently explode. Psychologists refer to this process of "blowing off steam" as **catharsis**. According to this theory, the way to control aggression is to arrange for "venting" before there is trouble (Quanty, 1976).

In spite of its popularity in folk beliefs and clinical practice, there is little convincing evidence to support catharsis as a means of controlling aggression. In a rare experimental study of the efficacy of catharsis, Shahbaz Mallick and Boyd McCandless (1966) asked two groups of third-grade boys to build a block house within a limited amount of time in order to win a cash prize. The activities of one group were interfered with by a boy who was a confederate of the experimenters. These children were angered because they lost the opportunity to win the prize. The other group was allowed to work uninterrupted. Some of the boys were then given the opportunity to shoot a play gun at animated targets of people and animals, or at a bull's-eye target. Others were asked to solve arithmetic problems. Next, the boys were asked to administer uncomfortable shocks to the boy who had interrupted their building task (actually, no shocks were received by the boy). The number of "shocks" delivered was used as the measure of aggression.

The experimenters found that frustration did appear to increase the children's aggression. The boys who had been interrupted administered more "shocks" than the other children. However, contrary to the catharsis hypothesis, the opportunity to blow off steam did not reduce the boys' aggressive behavior;

the boys who shot at targets delivered just as many "shocks" as the children who had solved arithmetic problems.

The ineffectiveness of catharsis contrasts sharply with a noncathartic treatment included as part of the experiment. Some of the boys were told that the boy who had interrupted their building was "sleepy and upset." This sympathetic reinterpretation was sufficient to dissipate their anger, emphasizing both the role of interpretation in human aggression and the specifically human possibilities of controlling aggression.

Punishment Another common belief about aggressive behavior is that it can be eliminated if it is punished whenever it occurs. Under some circumstances, this approach suppresses aggressive behavior, but often it does not. Several studies have found that parents who control their children's behavior by means of physical punishment, or by threats to apply raw power, actually create *more* aggressive children (Bandura & Walters, 1959; and Sears, Maccoby, & Levin, 1957).

Patterson and his colleagues have observed how this effect is produced under natural conditions. They observed two groups of children aged 3 to 13½ along with parents in their homes. The boys in the first group had been referred to the researcher's project for help by schools and clinics because of their excessively aggressive behavior. The second group of boys had not been referred for help. The investigators found that punitive child-rearing tactics were more frequent in the homes of the referred boys and that these tactics often increased the level of aggression in the family as a whole (Patterson, 1976, 1979, 1982). Based on Patterson's findings, such learning occurs in the following way:

A younger brother hits his older sister in order to obtain a toy. His sister hits him back. He shouts at her, and while pulling on the toy, hits her again. She resists. Their mother comes running to see what is the matter. She shouts at them to stop, but they do not listen. Exasperated, she lashes out and slaps her son, and roughly shoves her daughter. The boy withdraws, breaking the cycle for the moment. If matters stopped here, this would be a simple case of punishment. But now the mother's behavior has been modified. Since the mother's slaps successfully stopped the children's fighting, *she* is more likely to be aggressive at a later time. Since she models suc-

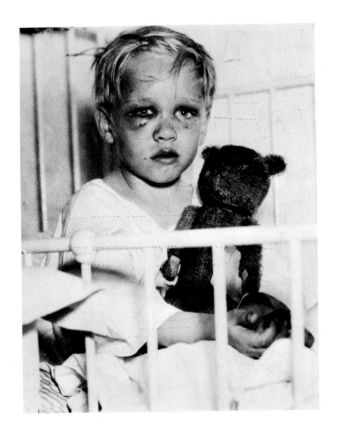

When a family adopts coercive child-rearing behaviors, the levels of violence may escalate to create serious patterns of abuse. Evidence suggests that such patterns may perpetuate themselves in the next generation when young parents who were abused as children abuse their own children (Crowell, Evans, & O'Donnell, 1987).

cessful aggression, her children may also learn to interact in that way.

Patterson points out that in interactions of this kind, which he calls "coercive," children may inadvertently train their parents to use physical punishment and make themselves still more aggressive as a result. Coercive situations such as this teach children both how to initiate aggression and how to be the victim.

If punishment is used as a means of socialization, it is most likely to suppress aggressive behavior when the child identifies strongly with the person who does the punishing (Eron, Walder, & Lefkowitz, 1971) and when it is employed consistently. Used inconsistently, punishment may provoke children to further aggression (Block, Block, & Morrison, 1981; Parke & Slaby, 1983).

Rewarding nonaggressive behaviors Since young children sometimes become aggressive in order to gain attention, one strategy is to ignore the aggression and to pay attention to children only when they are engaged in cooperative behavior. When teachers are trained to use this selective-attention technique, aggression in their classroom declines significantly (Brown & Elliot, 1965).

A closely allied technique was studied by Allen, Turner, and Everett (1970). They trained nursery school teachers to step in between the children involved in an altercation and to pay attention to the *victim,* while ignoring the aggressor. The attention to the victim included comforting the injured child, giving the child something interesting to do, or suggesting nonaggressive ways in which the victim might handle future attacks. For example, children were taught to say "No hitting," or "I'm playing with this now."

In such selective-attention techniques the aggressor is not rewarded either by adult attention or by the submission of the victim. The victim is taught how to deal with such attacks without becoming an aggressor, thus keeping the aggression from escalating. In addition, other children who may have observed the scene are shown that it is appropriate to be sympathetic to the victim of aggression, and that nonviolent assertion in the face of aggression can be effective.

Cognitive training Another way to control aggression is to use reason. Though it is sometimes difficult to hold a rational discussion with a 4-year-old who has just grabbed a toy away from a playmate, such discussions have been found to reduce aggression even at this early age.

Shoshana Zahavi and Steven Asher (1978) arranged for the most aggressive boys in a preschool program to be taken aside by their teacher, one by one, and engaged in a 10-minute conversation aimed at teaching the following three concepts: (1) aggression hurts another person and makes that person unhappy; (2) aggression does not solve problems, it only brings about the resentment of the other child; and (3) conflicts can often be solved by sharing, taking turns, and playing together. Each concept was taught by asking the child leading questions and encouraging the desired response. After these conversations, the boys' aggressive

behavior decreased dramatically and their positive behavior increased.

An important component in helping the children to control their aggression in the Zahavi and Asher study was that they were made aware of the feelings of those they aggressed against. All of the successful techniques for teaching self-control of aggression go beyond mere suppression of aggressive impulses. Instead, children are induced to stop their direct attacks and to consider another way to behave.

The Development of Prosocial Behavior

When Charles Darwin published *The Origin of Species,* the public's understanding of evolution was dominated by such famous phrases as "survival of the fittest" and "nature red in tooth and claw." In this one-sided version of evolution, behaviors that benefit the group with no direct reward for the benefactor are considered superfluous. Yet such *prosocial* behaviors, which include altruism, cooperation, helping, and empathy are common occurrences. When a preschooler offers her teddy bear to a friend who is crying because she scraped her knee or another brings candy to share with friends, they are engaging in prosocial behavior. Why do such behaviors occur and how do they develop?

Evolutionary explanations Prosocial behavior, like aggression, is not an exclusively human trait. Many animals, including social insects, hunting dogs, and chimpanzees, exhibit behaviors that at least appear similar to human altruism. The challenge to theories of biological evolution is to show how these behaviors have evolved and how they apply to human beings.

Edward O. Wilson, a biologist, has posed the problem and its solution as follows:

. . . how can altruism, which by definition reduces personal fitness, possibly evolve by natural selection? The answer is kinship: if the genes causing the altruism are shared by two organisms because of common descent, and if the altruistic act by one organism increases the joint contribution of these genes to the next generation, the propensity to altruism will spread through the gene pool. This occurs even though the altruist makes less of a solitary contribution to the gene pool as the price of its altruistic act. (1975, pp. 3–4)

Wilson reasoned that if natural selection "looked for" altruism among lower animals, there must also be a direct genetic basis for altruism among human beings.

Wilson's argument set off a controversy which is still in progress. Among the lower animals studied by Wilson, altruism seemed explicable because it was restricted to *kin,* those with a very similar gene pool. But among human beings, altruism extends well beyond kin to include total strangers. While the argument can be made that altruism to strangers may increase a person's chance for survival because it may eventually be reciprocated (a modern version of the notion of casting bread on the waters), to many investigators, such a connection to human behavior seems too remote to be useful (Kitcher, 1985).

Here we encounter the flip side of the arguments about aggression. There is no doubt that human beings have a biological potential for prosocial behavior; otherwise there would be none. But as with aggression, prosocial behavior is also influenced by immediate social circumstances and cultural traditions. How then does the biological predisposition for prosocial behavior manifest itself, and how is it modified by the social environment?

Empathy A major stimulus for human prosocial behavior is *empathy,* the sharing of another's emotional response. According to Martin Hoffman (1975), a child can feel empathy for another person at any age. However, as children develop, their ability to empathize broadens and they become better able to interpret and respond appropriately to the distress of others.

Hoffman has proposed four stages in the development of empathy. The first stage occurs during the first year of life, even before a baby appears to be aware of the existence of others. As noted earlier in this chapter, babies as young as two days cry at the sound of another infant's cries (Sagi & Hoffman, 1976). At this early age, these "empathic" behaviors are akin to innate reflexes, since babies can obviously have no *understanding* of the feelings of others. Yet they respond as if they were having those feelings themselves.

As children gradually become aware of themselves as distinct individuals during the second year of life, their responses to others' distress or laughter changes.

Now when babies are confronted by someone who is distressed, they are capable of understanding that it is the other person who is upset, not them. This realization allows children to turn their attention from concern with their own comfort to comforting others. However, since they have difficulty keeping other people's points of view in mind, some of their attempts to comfort or help may be inappropriate, such as giving a security blanket to a daddy who looks upset.

The third stage in the development of empathy, corresponding roughly to the preschool period, is brought on by the child's increasing command of language and other symbols. Language allows children to empathize with a wider range of feelings that are more subtly expressed, as well as with people who are not present. Indirect information gained through stories, pictures, or television permits children to empathize with people whom they have never met.

The fourth stage in the development of empathy occurs sometime between the ages of 6 and 9, when children can appreciate not only that others have feelings of their own, but that they occur within a larger set of experiences. Children at this stage begin to be concerned about the general conditions of others, their poverty, oppression, illness, or vulnerability, not just their momentary state. Since children in this age range are aware that there are classes of individuals, they are capable of empathizing with groups of people, which makes possible a budding interest in political and social issues.

It might be noted that Hoffman's theory of empathy is linked to Piaget's theory of cognitive development. Each new stage of empathy corresponds to a new stage of children's cognitive abilities which allow them better to understand themselves in relation to others.

A somewhat different explanation of empathy was proposed by Freud, who emphasized the importance of identification in children's internalization of social values. Identification, Freud wrote, "results among other things in a person limiting his aggressiveness toward those with whom he has identified himself, and in his sparing them and giving help" (1921/1955, p. 110). This approach to prosocial behavior also differs from Hoffman's by locating its origins not in infancy but in the preschool period, when, as we have seen, processes of identification come to the fore.

Evidence on the development of prosocial behaviors Several studies document the development of such prosocial behaviors as sharing, helping, caregiv-

ing, and showing compassion even before the preschool era (see Figure 11.8). For example, Carolyn
Zahn-Waxler and Marion Radke-Yarrow (1982) studied the development of prosocial action over a 9-
month period among three groups of children, who
were 10, 15, and 20 months of age at the start of the
observations. Their findings were based on mothers'
reports of occasions when their children expressed
sympathy for others.

When confronted with someone else's distress, the
youngest children responded by crying themselves. As
the children grew older, crying decreased and was replaced by worried attention. At the age of 1, most of
the children were observed to comfort a person who
was crying or who was in pain by patting her, hugging
her, or presenting her with an object. In the period
between 12 and 18 months of age, the majority of
children had progressed from diffuse emotional responses to active caregiving and comforting behavior
in response to another's distress. Among 1½- and 2-
year-olds comforting behavior was sometimes quite
elaborate. Children this age did such things as try to
put a Band-Aid on someone's cut or cover their resting
mother with a blanket. They also began to express
their concern verbally and to give suggestions about
how to deal with the problem (see Box 11.3).

(b)

(a)

(c)

FIGURE 11.8 *(a) This preschool girl is sharing a bottle of
soap bubble mixture with her little sister. (b) One twin brother
shows his sympathy for the other as he tries to comfort him.
(c) Fastening each other's clothes is one way that preschoolers
help each other.*

BOX 11.3

SIBLINGS AND SOCIALIZATION

•••

Most theories of socialization concentrate on relations between one child and two parents in addressing such questions as the development of sex-role identity, aggression, and prosocial behavior. But actual families—and actual socialization—are more complex. Single-child families are a distinct minority the world over. In the United States, most families include at least two children.

A number of recent studies show that although parents are of primary importance in children's socialization, siblings also play a significant role. The role of siblings is most obvious in nonindustrial, agricultural societies where much of the child care is performed by older siblings or by the mother's younger sisters. It is through these child caretakers, who are sometimes no more than five years older than their charges, that many of the behaviors and beliefs of the social group are passed on (Whiting & Whiting, 1975). In industrialized societies, which tend to have fewer children in a family and in which children attend school from the age of 5, boys and girls have less responsibility for their younger siblings. Nevertheless, siblings still play an important role in each other's socialization (Lamb, 1978).

Judy Dunn and Carol Kendrick (1979) studied the influence of siblings by observing 40 lower-middle class English families in their homes from late in the mother's second pregnancy through the infancy of the second child. They visited the family again when the first child

was 6 years old. Their observations, supplemented by reports from the mothers, illustrate many of the ways in

Siblings play an important role in each other's lives.

As young children follow their parents through their daily rounds of activities, they often try to help. Harriet Rheingold (1982) invited parents and their 18-, 24-, and 30-month-old children into a laboratory setting that simulated a home. The setting included several undone chores, including a table to set, scraps to sweep up, dusting to be done, a bed to be made, and laundry to fold. The parents and other adults were instructed to do these chores without asking the children for help. Yet in a 25-minute session, all the 2-year-olds helped their mothers, and 18 out of the 20 helped an unfamiliar woman. While they were helping,

the children said things that indicated that they knew the goals of the tasks and were aware of themselves as working with others to accomplish these goals. They worked spontaneously, eagerly, and went well beyond imitation in their helpfulness.

Promoting prosocial behavior Adults are, of course, anxious to encourage children's prosocial behavior. Research has identified many strategies that adults use to promote this goal, most notably rewarding children for prosocial activity.

However, using explicit rewards like a piece of

which siblings are prominent persons in each other's lives.

One of the most obvious indications that the newcomer makes a difference is the fact that in fully 78 percent of the occasions when one of the parents interacted with the new baby, the older sibling joined in. Sometimes their participation was friendly and cooperative; at other times they were openly disruptive. There were also many instances observed in which the older sibling responded to signs that the baby was upset or was engaged in a forbidden act.

New babies are not only charges to be taken care of, they are people to play with (Abramovitch, Corter, & Lando, 1979). A lot of the play is imitative. During the first year, it is the firstborn who imitates the new baby; then the tables are turned and it is the little sibling who becomes the imitator (Abramovitch, Pepler, & Corter, 1982).

The sexes of the siblings play an important role in their relationship. The interactions between brothers are characterized by relatively high levels of aggression, while those of sisters reveal more prosocial features. In cross-sex relationships, older sisters are consistently more nurturing when interacting with their little brothers than are big brothers with their little sisters.

Sibling relationships are often ambivalent ones; it is not possible to characterize them as either consistently friendly or consistently hostile. The obvious explanation for this ambivalence is that children compete for their parents' love and attention.

The birth of a second child is often upsetting for firstborns, especially if they are less than 4 years old. Considering that until the second child arrived on the scene the firstborn had no competition, this is understandable. In many families the added demands on the mother's attention reduce the amount of time she interacts with her firstborn child. The firstborn may respond to the mother's inattentiveness by being demanding and showing more negative behavior, by becoming more independent, by taking a larger role in initiating conversations and play, or by becoming more detached from the mother (Dunn, 1985; Dunn & Kendrick, 1979).

The reactions of an older child to a new birth depend on several factors, including the sex of the baby, the age difference between the two children, and the parents' response to the new child. In families in which the mother had a particularly playful and intense relationship with her firstborn daughter before the birth of the second child, for example, Dunn and Kendrick found that the older sibling was unlikely to be friendly to the newcomer. And after a year, the baby was hostile to the older sister. However, in families in which the mother was tired or depressed after the new birth, the sibling relationship developed in a particularly friendly fashion.

An important factor influencing how well siblings get along with each other seems to be the way the mother includes the older child in the care of the younger ones. In families in which the mother drew the first child into discussion of the baby's care as an equal, asking the older child's help in interpreting the baby's cries and deciding what to do, the siblings were observed to be significantly more friendly with one another 14 months later (Dunn & Kendrick, 1979).

candy or a gold star might well create a situation where children behave prosocially *only* if they are rewarded. This unwanted consequence of explicit rewards was demonstrated by Mark Lepper and his colleagues (Lepper & Greene, 1978). These researchers knew that 3- to 5-year-old children enjoy drawing with colored felt pens. They promised one such group of children a special certificate if they would draw a picture for a visiting adult, while others were allowed simply to draw on their own. They found that during free-play periods, a week or two later, the children who had made their drawings "under contract" and had been rewarded for their efforts spent only half as much time drawing with pens as the nonrewarded comparison group.

As a consequence of such findings, developmental psychologists suggest less direct means of promoting prosocial behavior. Two methods that have been shown effective by recent research are **explicit modeling,** in which adults behave in ways they desire the child to imitate, and **induction,** giving explanations that appeal to children's pride, their desire to be grownups, and their concern for others (Eisenberg, 1982).

Most studies of explicit modeling contrast the behavior of two groups of children. In the "nonmodeling" group, no special arrangements are made for teachers to model prosocial behaviors such as helping and sharing. In the "modeling" group, teachers are told to stage periodic training sessions in which sharing and helping behaviors are demonstrated: candies are shared among the children with explicit fairness, books are read about helping a child who is feeling sad or who is being teased, and so on. When such techniques have been used with preschool children, they produce an increase in prosocial behavior among the children who have been exposed to explicit models over those who have not (Fukushima & Kato, 1976; Yarrow, Scott, & Waxler, 1973). The study by Marion Yarrow and her colleagues also found that when the training was carried out in a nurturant, loving way, children showed the effects of the training as long as two weeks later, providing some evidence that the effects of modeling can last for some time.

Application of induction strategies, in which adults attempt to reason with children, has usually been carried out with older children. However, a study of early prosocial behaviors in the home found that the children of mothers who attempted to induce prosocial behavior did in fact perform more prosocial acts (Zahn-Waxler, Radke-Yarrow, & King, 1979). Reason by itself, however, was not the crucial factor in modifying the children's behavior; the most effective mothers combined reason with a loving feeling of concern.

It is worth remembering that in real life outside of research settings, the strategies to increase prosocial behavior do not occur in isolation from efforts to decrease aggressive behavior. Rather, a great variety of techniques are likely to occur in combination with each other, creating diverse overall patterns of socializing influences. (This patterning of socialization will be further discussed in Chapter 12.)

TAKING ONE'S PLACE IN THE SOCIAL GROUP

The kindergarteners in Vivian Paley's classroom are discussing the fate of Tico, a wingless bird who is cared for by his black-winged friends. Their discussion reveals considerable sophistication about the dilemmas of achieving happiness, indicating the vast amount these children have learned about social life since infancy.

In the story, the wishingbird visits Tico one night and grants him a wish. Tico wishes for golden wings. In the morning his friends are angry. They abandon him because he wanted to make himself better than they. Tico is upset by his rejection and wants to gain readmission to the group. He discovers that he can exchange his golden feathers for black ones by performing good deeds. When at last he has replaced all the golden feathers with black ones, he is granted readmission by the flock, who comment, "Now you are just like us" (Leoni, 1964).

Teacher: I don't think it's fair that Tico has to give up his golden wings.

Lisa: It *is* fair. See, he was nicer when he didn't have any wings. They didn't like him when he had gold.

Wally: He thinks he's better if he has golden wings.

Eddie: He *is* better.

Jill: But he's not supposed to be better. The wishingbird was wrong to give him those wings.

Deana: She *has* to give him his wish. He's the one who shouldn't have asked for golden wings.

Wally: He could put black wings on top of the golden wings and try to trick them.

Deana: They'd sneak up and see the gold. He should just give every bird one golden feather and keep one for himself.

Teacher: Why can't he decide for himself what kind of wings he wants?

Wally: He *has to* decide to have black wings.

(Paley, 1981, pp. 25–26)

This conversation shows that the children understand that by wishing for golden wings, Tico has wished himself a vision of perfection. Each child has done the same thing countless times: "I'm the beautiful princess"; "I'm Superman. I will save the world." For the blissful, magic moments when the world of play holds sway, perfection is attainable, even by a lowly bird or a preschool child.

Wally and his friends also appreciate the dilemmas of perfection. In their eyes, Tico not only thinks he is better, he *is* better — but he is not *supposed* to be. Try as they might to conceive of a way for Tico to retain his prized possessions, the children realize that conformity is unavoidable. Wally's summary is difficult to improve upon: Tico has to choose to conform.

Note too that the children are able to see an individual's responsibility for regulating social relations. Since wishingbirds grant wishes, it is not the wishingbird's fault that Tico wished himself better than the others. Tico should have known better. He should have been able to control *himself* and make a reasonable wish. These children have by no means completed the socialization process, but they demonstrate great sensitivity to the social world and a readiness to engage it with all the intelligence and energy that their developing cognitive and physical abilities permit.

The material in this chapter indicates the close connection between children's developing cognitive and linguistic skills, as discussed in Chapters 9 and 10, and children's development as social beings. Before we turn in Part IV to the wide range of new roles and rules that children encounter in middle childhood, we need to round out the discussion of early childhood by investigating the range of contexts and social influences that make up the world of the young child. As we shall see in Chapter 12, even during early childhood, children are exposed to a great variety of social influences, complicating the already complicated process of social development.

SUMMARY

1. Social development is the double-sided process in which children become integrated into their community while differentiating themselves as distinct individuals.

2. Socialization, the first side of social development, is the process by which children acquire the standards, values, and knowledge of their society.

3. Personality formation, the second side of social development, is the process by which children acquire a characteristic sense of themselves and characteristic ways of interacting with other people.

4. Identification, a process that contributes to children's distinctive sense of themselves, follows a different course for males and females: Male identification requires differentiation from the mother, while female identification requires continued affiliation with the mother.

5. Competing theories of identification emphasize four different mechanisms:
   a. Identification as a process of differentiating oneself
   b. Identification as a process of empathy and attachment
   c. Identification resulting from observation and imitation of powerful others, and from being rewarded for appropriate behaviors
   d. Identification resulting from the cognitive capacity to recognize oneself as a member of a social category

6. Early ability to identify oneself as a boy or girl does not depend on anatomical knowledge of sex differences.

Not until the end of the preschool period do boys and girls fully understand that sex is a permanent characteristic.

7. Sex-role categories serve as an important basis for acquiring other roles that contribute to the child's personality.

8. The social standards displayed by adult models with whom children identify become the basis for children's initial judgments of good and bad behavior.

9. Internalizing social roles and standards of behavior provides children with a framework for gaining control of their own impulses.

10. Self-control requires persistence and inhibition of action. Categories of inhibition include:
    a. Inhibition of motion
    b. Inhibition of emotion
    c. Inhibition of conclusions
    d. Inhibition of choice

11. Children display the rudiments of both aggression and altruism shortly after birth.

12. Aggression in the sense of an act that is intended to hurt others does not appear until late in the second year of life.

13. Aggression is observed among animals of many species. From some evolutionary perspectives, aggression is seen as a natural consequence of competition for resources.

14. *Instrumental* aggression is directed at obtaining desirable resources. *Hostile* aggression may also gain resources, but it is more directly aimed at causing pain to another.

15. Aggressive behavior may be increased among children either because they are directly rewarded for it or because children imitate the aggressive behavior of others.

16. The development of aggression is accompanied by the development of social dominance hierarchies that control aggression.

17. Among humans, additional effective means for controlling aggression include rewarding nonaggressive behav-

iors and cognitive training that induces children to consider the negative consequences of aggressive behaviors.

18. Prosocial behavior, no less than aggression, is a characteristic of our species. Empathy—the ability to feel what another person is feeling—may be the basis for the development of prosocial behavior.

19. The development of the ability to hurt other people is paralleled by the ability to help others. Helping, sharing, and other prosocial behaviors can be observed as early as the first three years of life.

KEY TERMS

Aggression
Anal stage
Autonomous morality
Catharsis
Defense mechanism
Dominance hierarchy
Ego
Empathy
Explicit modeling
Gender schema

Genital stage
Heteronomous morality
Hostile aggression
Id
Identification
Induction
Instrumental aggression
Internalization
Latency stage
Oral stage

Personality
Personality formation
Phallic stage
Primary identification
Prosocial behaviors
Secondary identification
Sex role
Social development
Socialization
Superego

SUGGESTED READINGS

BANDURA, ALBERT. *Social Learning Theory.* Englewood Cliffs, N.J.: Prentice-Hall, 1977.

A major figure in the development of social-learning theory provides a thorough introduction to its major ideas and their application to many important aspects of children's early social development including aggression, prosocial development, and the development of self-control.

DUNN, JUDY. *Sisters and Brothers.* Cambridge, Mass.: Harvard University Press, 1985.

By studying children as they interact with their brothers and sisters in everyday settings, Judy Dunn reveals the important influences that siblings have on each other, including their ways of talking, thinking about themselves and their families, and their abilities to make friends.

EISENBERG, NANCY (Ed.) *The Development of Prosocial Behavior.* New York: Academic, 1982.

A collection of essays on the development of prosocial behavior representing several different research traditions and theoretical positions. Included are discussions of the socialization of prosocial behavior and the role of cognition, emotion, and mood in prosocial behavior.

ERIKSON, ERIK. *Childhood and Society.* New York: Norton, 1963.

This early and classic statement of Erikson's theory of development includes extended case studies of development in different cultural circumstances, making clear both Erikson's indebtedness to Freud and the ways in which he accorded culture a larger role in development than did Freud.

FREUD, SIGMUND. *An Outline of Psychoanalysis.* In J. Strachey (Ed. and Trans.), *The Standard Edition of the Complete Psychological Works of Sigmund Freud* (Vol. 17). London: Hogarth 1964; New York: Norton, 1970.

This series of lectures provides an excellent introduction to Freud's theory of personality development, particularly his view of sexuality as a fundamental source of development.

PALEY, VIVIAN. *Boys and Girls.* Chicago: University of Chicago Press, 1984.

The preschool classroom is the setting for this book about the development of sex-role identity during early childhood. To an unusual degree, the children are allowed to speak for themselves by the author, a teacher who believes that an understanding of preschool development requires that adults listen with great care and sympathy to what children are trying to say.

C H A P T E R

12

...

SOCIALIZATION: CONTEXTS AND MEDIA

CULTURAL VARIATIONS IN FAMILY SOCIALIZATION
Modal Patterns of Parenting in the United States
Factors Influencing Family Interaction Patterns
Socialization and Social Inequality

MEDIA LINKING COMMUNITY AND HOME
Television: What Is Real? What Is Pretend?
Books

THE CHILD IN THE COMMUNITY
Varieties of Day Care
Developmental Effects of Day Care
Nursery School

ON THE THRESHOLD

> A new level of organization is in fact nothing more than a new relevant context.
>
> —C. H. Waddington, *Organizers and Genes*

. . . .

With the wages she earned as an auto mechanic in Buena Park, California, Patricia Ridge could not afford a babysitter to pick up her 5-year-old son, Patrick Mason, from kindergarten and watch him until she came home from work every day. Instead, she decided to keep the boy home from school, locked in the bedroom of their apartment, while she worked.

In the late afternoon of March 3, 1983, a police officer responded to a call from a friend of Ms. Ridge's who said she had not been able to contact the family for two weeks. The officer knocked on the door of the Ridge apartment and, when no one responded, used a passkey to enter the dark apartment. Because the apartment was dusty and sparsely furnished, he thought it had been burglarized or that its occupants had moved out.

While searching the premises, he heard a noise coming from the bedroom. The officer called out twice, identifying himself as a policeman. When no one responded, he kicked in the door, his gun drawn. The room was dark except for the light from the television set. He saw a figure three feet away pointing what he thought was a gun. He fired, killing Patrick Mason, who had been holding a toy pistol (Dolan, 1983).

The story of Patrick Mason's death shocked the country. Authorities investigated both the mother's and the police officer's conduct, but it was difficult to assign blame to people who were doing the best they could under difficult circumstances. In the editorials, television commentaries, and letters to the editor that followed, some people said the tragedy was an example of what can occur when a family disintegrates, leaving small children to live in poverty with a single parent. Others blamed the boy's death on the lack of affordable day-care services for working mothers. Still others linked the events in the dark apartment to government cuts in services for children and the poor.

Implicit in almost all of the commentaries about Patrick Mason's death was a recognition that children's lives are profoundly influenced by events that occur in the world outside of their homes. This recognition finds its scientific counterpart in Urie Bronfenbrenner's ecological approach to children's development (see Chapter 1, p. 20). Bronfenbrenner (1979, p. 22) suggests that in order to understand both the obvious and the subtle ways in which children interact with their environment, the environment of development should be thought of as a "nested arrangement of concentric structures, each contained within the next" (see Figure 1.6, p. 21).

Each relationship in Bronfenbrenner's model is reciprocal. Children are influenced by parents; they also influence their parents. Parental behavior at home is influenced by the experiences parents have at work and in their communities, while the society, of which the community is a part, both shapes and is shaped by its members.

The environment that has the most direct impact on young children's development is the home. Within the home, parents influence their children's development in two ways. First, they shape children's personalities by the ways in which they respond to particular behaviors, the values they promote, and the patterns of behavior that they model. But that is only part of the story. As anthropologist Beatrice Whiting (1980) has observed, parents also influence their children's development by selecting the contexts to which they expose them, the settings outside the home they arrange for them to frequent, the television programs they permit them to watch, and the other children they permit them to play with.

This chapter describes the influence of different contexts on early childhood development. These contexts take on a new importance in early childhood because children during this period begin to have many more experiences outside the home with peers and adults from other families. These people may have different social backgrounds, beliefs, and values than the parents. Consequently, when young children are introduced to the complex world outside the family, they are likely to be faced with serious challenges in figuring out how to behave.

We begin by describing the ways that different family patterns of child rearing are shaped by the economic and cultural characteristics of the community. These different child-rearing patterns, in turn, influence children's behavior and cognitive abilities. Research in this field includes evidence from a variety of the world's cultures as well as from a variety of families within the United States.

Next, we examine the influence of books and television—two media that link the family to the larger context of the society. Finally, we discuss the socializing effects of two institutions designed to serve young children and their families: day care, which substitutes for parental care at home; and nursery schools, which go beyond "minding" children to fostering development.

CULTURAL VARIATIONS IN FAMILY SOCIALIZATION

In the 1950s, Beatrice and John Whiting (1975) organized teams of anthropologists to observe child rearing in six different locales, including towns in New England and India and villages in Kenya and Mexico. The families studied thus came from societies that differed in social complexity, economic development, cultural belief systems, and domestic living arrangements.

When families are small and have their own homes, preschoolers often play alone. Their caretakers are usually not far off.

The contrasts between two groups, the Gussi of Nyansongo, Kenya, and Americans from a small New England town, illustrate the importance of culturally organized contexts for individual development. Such contrasts show how differences in life circumstances produce variations in basic economic activities and family life, influencing the way that parents treat their children, which in turn affects the children's development.

The Gussi, who were once herders, were an agricultural people living in the fertile highlands of western Kenya at the time of the Whitings' work. Women were the main farm laborers. Men, no longer active as cattle herders, sometimes took wage-earning jobs but also spent a lot of time in local politics. The community had no specialized occupations, few specialized buildings, and almost no differences in social rank or wealth among its inhabitants.

Because of their farm work, Gussi mothers were often separated from their infant children, who were left to play in the care of their older siblings and elderly family members. Beginning at the age of 3 or 4, children were expected to start helping their mothers with simple household tasks. By the age of 7, their economic contributions to the family were indispensable.

New England's Orchard Town represents the opposite extreme in terms of family organization and social complexity. Most of the adult men of Orchard Town were wage- or salary-earners who lived in single-family dwellings, each with its own yard. A few of the mothers had part-time jobs outside the home, but most of them spent their time caring for their children, their husbands, and their property. There were many specialized buildings in the town (see Figure 12.1) and a wide variety of specialized occupations, including doctors, fire fighters, auto mechanics, teachers, librarians, and merchants.

Children in Orchard Town were observed to spend more time in the company of adults than did the children of Nyansongo. At home, Orchard Town children played in the house or the yard within earshot of their mothers. At school, they were constantly supervised by their teachers. In contrast to the Gussi, Orchard Town children were rarely asked to do chores. Instead, they often sought their parents' help and attention for activities of their own choosing.

When the Whitings inquired into children's behavior patterns, they found that children in the two societies behaved in both prosocial and aggressive ways.

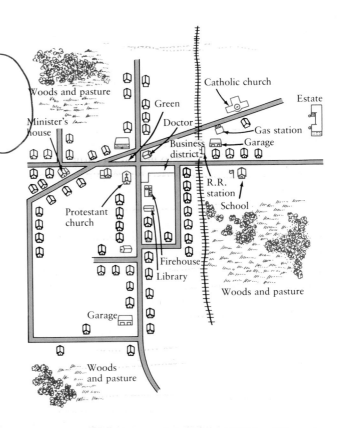

FIGURE 12.1 *A map of the village of Orchard Town in the United States. Husbands and wives live with their children in their own houses. (From Whiting & Whiting, 1975.)*

However, the overall patterns of children's behavior were different. Gussi children were more likely to engage in "nurturant-responsible" behaviors—offering help and support, and making responsible suggestions to others. Orchard Town children were less prone to such prosocial behaviors and were often observed seeking help and attention, or trying to dominate other children, in what the Whitings called a "dependent-dominant" pattern of behavior.

The Whitings' data, summarized in Table 12.1, do not allow us to conclude simply that the Gussi are prosocial and the U.S. children are self-centered. Gussi children also reprimanded and assaulted others, behavior that the Whitings characterized as "authoritarian-aggressive." The Orchard Town children, by contrast, were found to be more "sociable and intimate" with others. In order to obtain an adequate picture of the social behavior of children in the two societies, both the "nurturant-responsible" vs. "dependent-dominant" and the "sociable-intimate" vs. "authoritrian-aggressive" dimensions of their behavior need to be related to conditions of family life in the two societies.

The Whitings believed that children of preindustrial societies like the Gussi were more nurturant and responsible because the nature of their parents' work made it necessary for them to help at an early age. As early as 3 to 5 years of age, Gussi children did economically vital work. Children of industrialized societies, like those in Orchard Town, were found less nurturant and responsible because their chores were less clearly related to their family's economic welfare and may even have seemed arbitrary. Orchard Town children also spent their days in school where, rather than helping others, they competed with them for good grades and were encouraged to think of themselves as individuals, rather than as members of a group.

The same set of factors helps to explain why the Orchard Town children were found more "sociable-intimate" than the children from Nyansongo. Orchard Town children lived in nuclear households (Figure 12.1). Their fathers ate at the same table with their wives and children, slept with their wives, were likely to have been present when the children were born, and helped to care for them. These conditions, made possible and even necessary by the economic demands and

TABLE 12.1 Patterns of social behavior distinguishing Gussi and U.S. children

Specific Kinds of Behavior	Category of Behavior	Cultural Group
Offers help Offers support Makes responsible suggestions	Nurturant-responsible	Gussi
Seeks help Seeks dominance Seeks attention	Dependent-dominant	U.S.
Acts sociably Engages in horseplay Touches	Sociable-intimate	U.S.
Reprimands Assaults Insults	Authoritarian-aggressive	Gussi

SOURCE: Whiting & Whiting, 1975.

Whereas children in traditional rural communities are socialized to cooperate and to care for younger family members, children in industrialized societies are more likely to compete with each other for adult attention and approval.

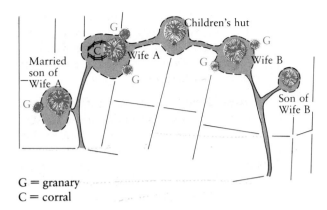

G = granary
C = corral

FIGURE 12.2 *The household plan of a typical residence in the village of Nyansongo, Kenya. Each wife lives in her own house. Older children also live in separate houses. Husbands may live in the same house as their wives but do not share their beds with them. (From Whiting & Whiting, 1975.)*

cultural traditions of modern New England, helped create the intimacy within U.S. families.

The "authoritarian-aggressive" aspect of Gussi children's behavior had also been shaped by their household arrangements, which in turn reflected their society's strategy for dealing with their physical environment. The Gussi lived in extended families, headed by a grandfather, but with property owned by the family as a group. Clans were continued through male descendants, so that the father lived in the village where he grew up, surrounded by his parents, brothers and other kinsmen, while young girls left their home communities when they married. As shown in Figure 12.2, each wife had her own house. Her husband may have slept in the same house with her, but not in the same bed, and the preferred pattern was for him to sleep in a separate house. By American standards, there was little intimacy between husbands and wives or fathers and children, in part because many Gussi men had several wives, each of whom lived in her own hut and sent the husband food to eat in his.

From a middle-class American point of view, these arrangements may appear strange, even unpleasant. But to the Gussi, these patterns were proper and desirable. The behavior of Gussi children fit Gussi expectations and the Gussi way of life, illustrating the power of culture to shape the socialization of new members. Likewise, U.S. children learn the behavior that fits the cultural expectations of their society.

Modal Patterns of Parenting in the United States

The Whitings' six-culture study provides a broad picture of how cultural differences in patterns of family life are shaped by economic demands and, in turn, shape children's personalities and behavior. The six-culture study does not, however, take up the differences in child rearing that exist between individual families within a single society.

A considerable body of research conducted in the United States has shown that while child-rearing behaviors differ in many ways, parenting styles can be usefully thought of as varying along two major dimensions (Schaefer, 1959). The first dimension refers to the degree to which parents try to control how their children behave—are they strictly controlling or do they allow a good deal of autonomy? The second di-

TABLE 12.2 Sample items from the Baumrind rating scale for preschool behavior grouped into statistically related clusters

Hostile-Friendly	{ Selfish Understands other children's position in interaction
Resistive-Cooperative	{ Impetuous and impulsive Can be trusted
Domineering-Tractable	{ Manipulates other children to enhance own position Timid with other children
Dominant-Submissive	{ Peer leader Suggestible
Purposive-Aimless	{ Confident Spectator
Achievement-Oriented– Not Achievement-Oriented	{ Gives best to play and work Does not persevere when encounters frustration
Independent-Suggestive	{ Individualistic Stereotyped in thinking

SOURCE: Baumrind, 1971.

mension refers to the amount of affection that parents display toward their children—are they warm and loving, or cool and indifferent?

How do these different styles affect children's development? And what mix of control, autonomy, and expression of affection is most supportive of healthy development?

One of the best-known research programs on the consequences of different parenting styles was conducted by Diana Baumrind (1967, 1971, 1972, 1980). Baumrind arranged for trained observers to record children's behavior during routine activities in a nursery school. The observers rated the children's behavior using a 72-item scale. These ratings were then correlated with each other to obtain seven clusters of scores, representing seven dimensions of preschool behavior (e.g., hostile vs. friendly, resistive vs. cooperative, domineering vs. tractable) (Table 12.2).

Another investigator interviewed each of the children's parents, first separately and then together, about their child-rearing beliefs and practices (Table 12.3). This investigator also visited the children's homes twice, staying from just before dinner until after the child went to bed.

When the interviews and observations were scored and analyzed, Baumrind and her colleagues found that the child care in 77 percent of their families fit into one of three patterns:

1. **Authoritarian parents** try to shape, control, and evaluate the behavior and attitudes of their children according to a set standard. These parents stress the importance of obedience to authority. They favor punitive measures to curb their children's "willfulness" whenever their children's behavior conflicts with what they believe to be correct.

2. **Authoritative parents** take it for granted that they have more knowledge and skill, control more resources, and have more physical power than their children, but they believe that the rights of parents and children are reciprocal. Compared to authoritarian parents, authoritative parents are less likely to use physical punishment and less likely to stress obedience to authority as a virtue in itself. Instead, these parents attempt to control their children by explaining their rules or decisions, and by reasoning with

them. They are willing to listen to their child's point of view, even if they do not always accept it. Authoritative parents set high standards for their children's behavior and encourage them to be individualistic and independent.

3. **Permissive parents** exercise less explicit control over their children's behavior than do authoritarian or authoritative parents, either because they believe children must learn how to behave through their own experience or because they do not take the trouble to provide discipline. They give their children a lot of leeway to determine

TABLE 12.3 Sample of Baumrind behavior-rating items from home-observation scale

Set regular tasks

Demand child put toys away

Provide intellectually stimulating environment

Set standards of excellence

Many restrictions on TV watching

Fixed bedtime hour

Mother has independent life

Encourage contact with other adults

Demand mature table behavior

Clear ideals for child

Stable, firm views

Cannot be coerced by child

Use negative sanctions when defied

Force confrontation when child disobeys

Parents' needs take precedence

Regard themselves as competent people

Encourage independent action

Solicit child's opinions

Give reasons with directives

Encourage verbal give and take

Inhibit annoyance or impatience when child dawdles or is annoying

Become inaccessible when displeased

Lack empathetic understanding

SOURCE: Baumrind, 1971.

their own schedules and activities, and often consult them about family policies. They demand less achievement and put up with less mature behavior than do authoritative or authoritarian parents.

Baumrind found that, on the average, each style of parenting was associated with a different pattern of children's behavior in the preschool:

1. Children of *authoritarian* parents tended to lack social competence in dealing with other children. They frequently withdrew from social contact and rarely took initiative. In situations of moral conflict, they tended to look to outside authority to decide what was right. These children were often characterized as lacking spontaneity and intellectual curiosity (Baumrind, 1971; Hoffman, 1970).

2. Children of *authoritative* parents seemed to be more self-reliant, self-controlled, and willing to explore, as well as more content than those raised by permissive or authoritarian parents. Baumrind believes that this difference is a result of the fact that, while authoritative parents set high standards for their children, they explain to them why they are being rewarded and punished. These explanations improve children's understanding and acceptance of the social rules.

3. Children of *permissive* parents tended to be relatively immature; they had difficulty controlling their impulses, accepting responsibility for social actions, or acting independently.

Baumrind reported a number of differences in the way that girls and boys responded to the major parenting patterns. For example, boys from authoritarian families seemed to show more pronounced difficulties with social relations than did girls. "Authoritarian" boys were also more likely than other boys to show anger and defiance toward those in authority. Girls from authoritative families were more likely to be independent than their boy counterparts; while the boys from such families were more likely to be socially responsible than the girls. Recently Sanford Dornbusch and his colleagues (Dornbusch, Ritter, Leiderman, Roberts, & Fraleigh, 1987) have shown that Baumrind's basic findings also apply to older children. Authoritative parenting is associated with better

school performance and better social adjustment among high school students, just as it is among preschoolers.

Despite the consistency of these findings, it is important to remember the limitations of this type of research (see Maccoby & Martin, 1983, for a comprehensive review). One limitation is that Baumrind's families were not representative of American families as a whole: the children were from suburban, white, largely middle-class, two-parent families. Different family configurations, ethnic heritages, or socio-economic backgrounds might have led to other findings (see Box 12.1, "Growing Up in a Single-Parent Family").

Baumrind (1972) herself notes the possibility of different outcomes when the same parenting styles are associated with other ethnic and class backgrounds. In observations of 16 black children who were attending the preschools where her study was located, she found that contrary to the pattern for daughters of white authoritarian parents, daughters of black authoritarian parents tended to be dominant and assertive in the preschool. Baumrind was particularly impressed that these girls played aggressively and enthusiastically in the preschool, but were able to sit quietly and attentively when they accompanied their mothers to an evening meeting at the nursery school. Although the sample was too small to warrant full-scale comparisons, Baumrind speculates that the meaning of authoritarian behaviors is different in the black households. Dornbusch and his colleagues (1987) confirmed the existence of such ethnic differences in the consequences of parenting styles with a much larger sample of older children.

A second limitation that is endemic to observational studies that rely on correlational data is that there can be no certainty that differences in parenting styles are what produced the differences in children's behavior (see Chapter 1, pp. 24–25, for a general discussion of this problem). Michael Lamb (1982), among others, has pointed out that, in fact, preexisting differences among children may influence parents' choice of child-rearing strategies. For example, a particularly active and easily frustrated child might elicit authoritarian responses from parents who might respond differently to another type of child.

In support of this latter view, recent research on the personalities of biologically unrelated children growing up in the same household has shown these children to be quite different from one another, despite the fact that they were raised by the same parents (Rowe & Plomin, 1981). Such findings imply either that patterns of caretaking do not have much effect on a child's behavior pattern, or that parents' patterns of caretaking differ from one child to the next. Researchers are currently pursuing a variety of strategies to allow them to assess the effects of parental beliefs and patterns of child care more accurately (Goodnow, 1984; Sigel, 1985).

Baumrind is well aware of these difficulties, but maintains that while individual differences among children may affect parenting styles, there is still solid evidence that parenting styles have a significant impact on children's personalities (Baumrind, 1980).

Factors Influencing Family Interaction Patterns

Apart from individual differences in children's temperaments, what causes parents to use one style of child rearing as opposed to others? One obvious answer is the psychological characteristics of the parents. Adults who are subject to depression, who feel insecure, or who have unreasonable outbursts of temper are most likely to use an authoritarian parenting style, to hit or to shout at their children, and to treat them inconsistently (Becker, Peterson, Luria, Shoemaker, & Hellmer, 1962).

However, a parent's personality is not the only influence. The Whitings' cross-cultural data and Bronfenbrenner's ecological framework remind us that we must also take into consideration the circumstances in which the family finds itself in addition to the characteristics of the family members.

It seems plausible that parents' child-rearing styles would vary with the stress they are under from circumstances having nothing to do with bringing up children. An experiment by John Zussman (1978) demonstrated the influence of even minor stress on the parenting styles of middle-class adults such as those in Baumrind's study. Zussman invited parents with two children, a preschooler and a toddler, to come to an observation room where there were both play materials and opportunities to get into mischief. Some parents were simply allowed to watch and help their children. Others were given a paper-and-pencil problem to solve while keeping an eye on their young-

sters. Under even this very mild stress, the preoccupied parents played less with their children, ignored attention-getting initiatives they might otherwise have responded to, and used more peremptory control strategies.

This same pattern appears in real-life conditions, according to observational evidence and interviews. Forgatch and Wieder (summarized in Patterson, 1982) periodically observed interactions between mothers and their children in the home and obtained daily reports from mothers about such stressful events in their lives as unexpectedly large bills, the illness of a family member, and quarrels with their husbands. The investigators found that a mother's irritability usually increased when things outside her relationship with her children were going badly. When a mother was irritable, she was more likely to hit or scold her children and more likely to refuse their requests.

When adults feel preoccupied or pressured, their tempers may flair and they are more likely to adopt an authoritarian style when dealing with their children.

BOX 12.1

GROWING UP IN A SINGLE-PARENT FAMILY
···

The U.S. Census Bureau has estimated that at some time during their childhood as many as 60 percent of U.S. children will live in a single-parent household. Divorce is the most prevalent cause of single-parent families. Of the 14.8 million children living with only one parent in 1985, 42 percent were the children of divorced parents, 27 percent had parents who had never married, 24 percent had parents who were married and separated, and 7 percent had a widowed parent (U.S. Census Bureau, 1988).

What difference does it make to a child to live with only one parent? First, single-parent households headed by women (which constitute 90 percent of all single-parent families) often undergo financial strains. Over half the children growing up in such households are living on a family income that is below the poverty level (Weinraub & Wolf, 1983). (In 1987, the U.S. Census Bureau defined a family of four as poor if its annual income fell below $11,203.) Second, a mother raising children alone is trying to accomplish by herself what is usually a demanding job for two adults. Third, the mother in a single-parent household is often socially isolated and lonely (Hetherington, Cox, & Cox, 1982). She has no one to support her when her children question her authority, nor does anyone act as a buffer between her and her children when she is not functioning well as a parent.

Most research on single-parent households has been devoted to those created through divorce. Both children's initial reaction and their long-term responses to a divorce depend upon how old they are at the time and on their sex, according to a longitudinal study of 60 California families whose 131 children ranged in age from 2½ to 18 years old when their parents divorced (Wallerstein, 1983, 1984, 1987). Judith Wallerstein (1984) found that, initially, preschoolers tended to worry about being abandoned by both parents. They felt responsible for causing the divorce, had sleep disturbances, and became irritable, tearful, and aggressive. They also did not play as much as other children.

Children whose parents divorced when they were 7 or 8 years old were likely to be depressed. They tended to be preoccupied with their father's departure, to long for his return, and to fear their mother's remarriage. These children desperately wanted their parents to reconcile and felt a conflict of loyalty between their mother and father.

The effects of divorce and the marital disharmony that precedes it seem, according to some studies, to be greater for boys than for girls (Kurdek, Blisk, & Siesky, 1981). Even in the period before their parents separate, boys are already showing more signs of behavioral disruption than girls (Block, Block, & Gjerde, 1986). Girls also seem to recover from the social and emotional disturbances brought on by their parents' divorce by the time 2 years have elapsed, while boys continue to

Sources of stress are clearly evident in the following interview with a working-class mother raising a 3-year-old child while holding a full-time job:

We don't have any kind of life. When you work, you're constantly racing around back and forth. There's never any relaxation. Work, come home and work, go to bed . . . , etc., over and over. No respite. It's not my idea of living. . . . There's no way you can cram seven days of housework into less than two days [the weekend]. . . . Seems like I'm always running around on my lunch hour. There's so little time. (Bronfenbrenner, Alvarez, & Henderson, Jr., 1984, p. 1367)

Because the frequency of such stressful events tends to be greater among poor families than well-to-do ones (Brown, Ní Bhrocháin, & Harris, 1975), we

show signs of emotional problems well after this period (Hetherington, Cox, & Cox, 1982; Wallerstein & Kelly, 1980). Boys are particularly likely to be angry with their mothers, whom they blame for the loss of their fathers.

In general, a divorce is likely to be followed by lowered academic performance and various problems of social development (Hetherington, Camara, & Featherman, 1983; Hetherington, Cox, & Cox, 1982). Some researchers suggest that children from one-parent households do poorly in school because their lack of self-control leads them to be disruptive in the classroom (Guidubaldi, Perry, Cleminshaw, & McLoughlin, 1983; Hetherington et al., 1982). Mavis Hetherington attributes this alleged lack of self-control to the breakdown in maternal control over children that follows divorce. She and her colleagues observed that in the year following divorce, divorced mothers exercise less control over their children than they did before, made fewer demands on them, and did not communicate as often as previously (Hetherington, Cox, & Cox, 1982).

In addition, some researchers have noted that children in single-parent families receive less adult attention and are involved in fewer joint activities with adults than is true for children who live with two parents (Medrich, Roizen, Rubin, & Buckley, 1982). As a consequence, children of divorce lose out on important kinds of social and intellectual stimulation in addition to obtaining less guidance and assistance.

How long-lasting are the effects of divorce? Many of the young people interviewed by Wallerstein (1984, 1987) 10 years after their parents' divorce said that the

divorce still influenced their lives. Children who were preschoolers when their parents divorced seemed to have fared best. Many said they had no memory of their family before the divorce. School-aged children, on the other hand, still had vivid memories of their parents' conflicts. Several were preoccupied with the idealized family of their fantasies and with their fathers, whom they felt they had lost. They expressed concern about the unreliability of relationships and feared disappointment in their own love relationships.

Findings also show that some children are more vulnerable than others to the effects of family conflict and the stresses brought on by divorce (Hetherington, Cox, & Cox, 1982; Wallerstein, 1983, 1984, 1987). A recent review of studies of children in divorced families found that family discord before and after divorce constitutes one of the most important risk factors for children (Wolkind and Rutter, 1985). They hasten to add that parents who cannot live amicably together should not necessarily maintain a tension-ridden, discordant marriage "for the sake of the children," but note that divorce may not bring the conflict to an end. Frequently, it makes things worse for parents and children, at least in the short run. Children fare best when parents strive to establish harmony and cooperation. Among older children particularly, siblings provide important sources of support and affection. For both parents and children, good relationships outside of marriage as well as other sources of self-esteem were found to be helpful in adapting successfully to single-parent households.

might expect that authoritarian and inconsistent styles of child rearing would be more frequent in lower socio-economic households. This is exactly what sociologists and psychologists have observed in the United States and in Britain (Baumrind, 1972; Bernstein, 1971; Kohn, 1977).

Comparisons of family structures in different parts of the world indicate that in relatively affluent populations independence and autonomy are valued over

obedience, while in populations with scarce resources, parents place a higher value on children's obedience (LeVine, 1974). In families living close to the subsistence level, as Robert LeVine has noted,

parents see obedience as the means by which their children will be able to make their way in the world and particularly to establish themselves economically in young adulthood when the basis must be laid for the economic security of their nascent families. (1974, p. 63)

These conclusions are also applicable to poor families in the United States and other industrial countries (Kohn, 1977; Kohn & Schooler, 1978). Melvin Kohn and his colleagues have found a direct relationship between the kinds of work engaged in by fathers and parental emphasis on obedience.

Middle-class occupations place a premium on the ability to work without close supervision. The content of such work is often complex and the flow of work is nonroutinized; therefore workers must be self-directed. By contrast, working-class occupations demand obedience and punctuality. The flow of work is often so routinized that a robot can—and increasingly does—carry out the job just as efficiently as a human being (assembly-line jobs are a classic example). Entrance to middle-class jobs often requires high levels of schooling, which also demand long periods of self-directed work, whereas entrance to working-class jobs requires far less formal education (Berg, 1970; Braverman, 1974).

The association across many societies between kinds of work and relative income on the one hand, and family socialization patterns on the other, suggests that researchers should be cautious about applying value judgments to the parenting practices of working-class and poor populations. Kohn states the need for such caution quite clearly:

> Since social scientists understand (and largely share) middle-class values, we find middle-class parental behavior [which emphasizes independence and self-direction] self-evidently reasonable. But, because many of us have not had an adequate grasp of working-class values, it has been less apparent that working-class parental behavior is also reasonable. . . . Working-class parents are as concerned as are middle-class parents about their children's futures. (1977, p. 197)

Research by Kohn and others illustrates the importance of an ecological perspective. Family patterns cannot be completely accounted for either by the parents' personalities or by parent-child interactions. Patterns of socialization are also shaped by parents' experiences in other settings, the resources they can draw on, and the accumulated beliefs of their community.

Children raised in poverty may be socialized to behave in ways that perpetuate their poverty.

Socialization and Social Inequality

The research on socialization indicates that it tends to support whatever social arrangements exist at the time. On the one hand, parents raise their children to adapt to the world as they understand it on the basis of their own experiences. On the other hand, children's tendency to identify with the powerful people in their lives leads them to adopt the patterns of behavior that their parents try to instill. Thus, despite parents' best efforts to provide their children with a better life, children of the poor are likely to be socialized to remain poor. Kohn again pinpoints the issue:

The family, then, functions as a mechanism for perpetuating inequality. At lower levels of the stratification order, parents are likely to be ill-equipped and often will be ill-disposed to train their children in the skills needed at higher class levels. (1977, pp. 200–201)

These dilemmas occur in all industrialized countries. But in the United States, which is founded on the belief that all people are created equal and should have equal opportunity, the role of the family in perpetuating its class position is an especially serious issue, even though this issue cannot be resolved entirely within the family.

MEDIA LINKING COMMUNITY AND HOME

Parents are by no means the only ones in the home to shape children's behavior. Children are affected by their brothers and sisters, and sometimes by their grandparents, aunts, uncles, and cousins, as well as by people from the surrounding community who come into the home as visitors, to perform a service, or to bring news of the world outside. In modern societies like our own, the outside world also enters the home through letters, magazines, newspapers, television, radio, and books. The sheer magnitude of children's exposure to modern media makes it important to understand the media's impact on child development.

Both the content of what children encounter in the media (fairy tales, adventure stories, advertisements, or news programs) and the form in which the information is presented (brief images flashed on a screen or stories read aloud by a parent or grandparent) are widely claimed to exert lasting effects on the development of children's interests, cognitive skills, and social behavior (Greenfield, 1984). Here we will discuss the claims for watching television and being read to.

Television: What Is Real? What Is Pretend?

Most 3- and 4-year-olds are easily fooled about the distinction between reality and appearance, as we saw in Chapter 10 (p. 312). This difficulty is particularly severe when children are watching television.

Television programming is generally presented in a realistic format, depicting real people engaged in behavior and events that could be happening. A fictitious story about a cowboy who goes to Dallas and rides in a rodeo may be acted out by real cowboys at a real rodeo in Dallas.

Aimee Dorr (1983) reports that children under the age of 7 years often have difficulty understanding that on television, when a bad guy is shot, the actor isn't really dead, or when a husband beats his wife, the actress isn't really hurt. Even 7- and 8-year-olds will claim that actors and actresses who play married couples must be friends and that actors wear bullet-proof vests in case the bullets are real.

Susceptibility to confusion about the reality of television is not restricted to children. From time to time, for example, one reads of an irate adult assaulting an evil character in a soap opera. But the problem is more acute for preschool children because they have little independent knowledge of the world against which to compare the "reality" of what they see on television. Some physical features of the medium and the way it is used may also cause confusion for preschoolers.

The problem of television form Television, like film, allows extraordinary flexibility in the way realistic visual images can be made and sequenced. Human beings' attention is attracted by movement, changes in sound, and other unexpected changes. Television plays on this characteristic by using quick cuts from one scene — or one camera angle — to another, jolting expectations to maintain attention. The popular children's program *Sesame Street,* for example, uses a new cut on the average of every 30 seconds (Lesser, 1974).

Many techniques of television production help to focus viewers' attention and highlight the central message: close-up shots pick out essential details, camera placement gives hints about point of view, flashbacks fill in prior parts of the story. These thought-shaping techniques are a great resource for producing meaning, but they have their negative side as well, particularly for young children.

Preschool children do not understand special television techniques (Singer, 1980; Smith, Anderson, & Fischer, 1985). They become confused by scene changes without transitions; they need both long shots and closeups to understand the action; and they fail to

FIGURE 12.3   *An item from the space construction test, which assesses children's ability to recreate an entire setting on the basis of partial glimpses that correspond to the various camera angles used in making films and television programs. (From Greenfield, 1984.)*

infer the location of one aspect of the action from seeing another (see Figure 12.3).

In an evaluation of a number of standard shows watched by preschoolers, Andrew Collins found that children could keep track of less than 50 percent of the content (Collins, 1975). When they were tested for memory of the content of what they had seen, they might recall as little as 30 percent of the central events (Friedlander, Whetstone, & Scott, 1974). Although comprehension improves markedly during middle childhood, even 9- and 10-year-olds have difficulty understanding fast-paced programs that do not clearly show the continuity of action from one sequence to the next (Wright et al., 1984).

To the extent that television techniques are successful, they raise a different concern. Television provides a prefabricated, alternative world that requires little mental effort to comprehend once a viewer has sufficient background knowledge and mastery of its forms. Furthermore, its fast pace makes it impossible to stop and ponder what is being presented. Do these characteristics affect children's responses to the world off the air? Evidence that they do has been reported by Gabriel Salomon (1984). He found that children socialized to learn from television had lower than normal expectations about the amount of mental work required to learn from written texts.

The problem of television content   In an advertisement about the portrayal of people in business, media analysts working for the Mobil Oil Corporation make explicit a widespread feeling that television's depiction

of reality may sometimes overpower reality itself (Mobil Oil Corporation, 1981). Television entertainment, the advertisement tells us, "impacts powerfully and directly on people's *underlying attitudes* almost without challenge from other sources" (italics ours). According to this argument, to the extent that people believe in the reality of what is portrayed on television, they will be influenced by its content.

There is ample evidence that the content of television does differ systematically from the reality of people's everyday lives. The Mobil advertisement, for example, cited a survey of prime-time programming showing that two out of three business people on television are portrayed as foolish, greedy, or criminal and that almost half of all work activities performed by businessmen involved illegal acts. On the basis of these and other findings, the surveyors conclude, "If American business has redeeming social value, it is not visible on prime time television." Similar complaints have been lodged on behalf of other groups; women and minorities are rarely shown positively in positions of power; Italians are stereotyped as gangsters, Latin Americans as lazy, and Orientals as inscrutable (Liebert, Sprafkin, & Davidson, 1982).

Such unrepresentative portrayals on television are believed to work their way into children's basic assumptions about the world and from there into their behavior by substituting false beliefs for true ones. Later, when children find themselves in a new situation where they are uncertain what to think and how to act, they will look to their past experience for guidance. Insofar as the experiences that come to mind are made up of images from television, images that may be false, these experiences may lead to actions which are contrary to the best interests of the child and the society.

One of the best-documented cases that television offers models for behavior in real life comes from research on the effects of children watching violent episodes. Fully 80 percent of the television programs that young children watch in the United States include at least one violent episode and many contain more. Evidence has been accumulated in recent decades that watching violence on television increases violent behavior among many viewers, not just among those "predisposed" to be violent (Murray, Rubenstein, & Comstock, 1972; Pearl, Bouthilet, & Lazar, 1982; Phillips, 1982; Potts, Huston, & Wright, 1986; Singer & Singer, 1980).

Many researchers believe that violence caused by television viewing is learned through observation. As we saw in Chapter 11, young children in the laboratory learn to act aggressively from observing filmed models (Bandura, Ross, & Ross, 1963; Potts, Huston, & Wright, 1986). Such results are not restricted to laboratory studies. Jerome Singer and Dorothy Singer (1980) have demonstrated a significant relationship between frequent television viewing at home and the level of overt aggression at preschool. Lynette Friedrich and Althea Stein (1973) pinpointed violence in programming as the key to such effects. Preschoolers who watched *Batman* and *Superman* became more aggressive in their preschool play, whereas those who watched episodes of *Mister Rogers' Neighborhood,* a children's program noted for its positive values, did not.

Family influences The evidence that television affects children's behavior is complemented by equally strong evidence that the family affects the way that television influences children. Singer and Singer (1980), for example, studied patterns of family viewing in a working-class community in the eastern United States. They found that the homes of highly aggressive preschoolers who watched a lot of television had relatively few books or records. These children were often permitted to stay up late to watch whatever programs they wanted to. Their parents rarely took them out of the house, except to the market or to the movies.

In contrast, the families of less aggressive children tended to keep tighter control on how their children spent their time. They restricted their children's television viewing to educational and children's programs. Their children were more likely than those in the more aggressive group to go to bed early and to be taken to parks, museums, and cultural events.

When parents watch television with their children and talk about what they see, children learn more of the content (Ball & Bogartz, 1979). The parents can provide connections that the children miss and remind children of related events in their own lives, helping them to make sense of what they are seeing.

The message of these results is that parents concerned about the negative effects of television on their children's behavior should restrict the amount of time that their children spend watching television and increase the amount of time they spend with their children while they are watching television. To help parents with such concerns, researchers have written guides informing them how to get the most out of watching television (see Figure 12.4) (Dorr, Graves, & Phelps, 1980; Singer, Singer, & Zuckerman, 1981).

Parents often use television as a baby-sitter. Research shows, however, that children get more out of television viewing when their parents are there to discuss the programs with them.

EDITING: THE BIONIC PUZZLE

Here are three pictures showing how a bionic jump is done. How does the bionic jump look on TV? You can find out by cutting out the three small pictures at the bottom of the page and pasting them onto the big TV screen.

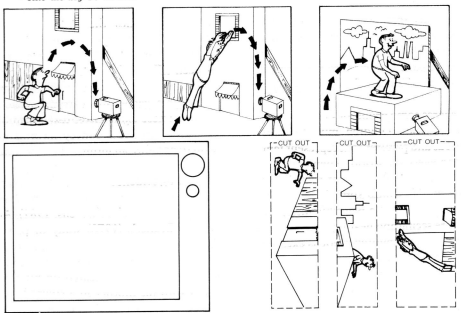

MATCHING CAMERA EFFECTS

Here are four different pictures taken with a TV camera. Draw a line from each TV set to the TV camera that is taking that picture.

FIGURE 12.4 *Sample exercises to help people interpret the conventions of editing used in television production. (From Singer, Singer, & Zuckerman, 1981.)*

Books

While there is concern that extensive television viewing may impede children's development, there is an equally pervasive belief that reading enhances it. In part, the positive evaluation of reading comes from a belief that reading to children stimulates their cognitive development; in part, it comes from general approval of the content of stories that parents read to their children.

Being read to shares some properties with watching television. In both cases, children must construct meaning from words and pictures that represent familiar elements of the everyday world. They encounter difficulties with both media because of their limited experience of the world, which sometimes makes it difficult for them to construct a plausible interpretation of what they are seeing and hearing. The evidence on the effects of reading to children is not as extensive as that on television viewing, but what data there are provide an instructive contrast between the two media.

This little boy has acquired part of the idea of what it means to read just by watching those around him, but there are many crucial elements still to be learned.

The form of early literacy experiences U.S. preschoolers from every social class are involved with print in some way almost every day, even if only for a few minutes (Anderson & Stokes, 1984; Brice-Heath, 1982). Sometimes the children are just "hanging around" while their parents read a letter or discuss big sister's homework. But preschoolers are also likely to be seen talking about the messages on cereal boxes, asking for help with a television schedule or instructions for a game, and carrying notes from nursery school. These experiences teach them that the marks on paper somehow convey information. Thus they begin to acquire an intuitive feel for some functions of literacy.

Existing evidence indicates that young children who are often read to at home learn to read relatively easily once they start school (Wells, 1981). Anat Ninio and Jerome Bruner's (1978) study of parents reading to their 1- to 2-year-old children suggests how such experiences might help children's later reading. For example, Richard, who is seated on his mother's lap, engages with his mother in a stylized, cyclical form of dialogue focused on the picture in a book. With few exceptions, each cycle in their conversation goes something like this:

Mother: (*pointing to picture on the page*) Look at this!
Child: (*touches picture or gives some other indication of attention*)
Mother: What is it?
Child: A doggy.
Mother: Right! (*turns pages and initiates a new round*)

Once children begin to attend school, the vast majority of their instructional experience will occur in a similar format:

Teacher: Who knows the capital city of France?
Student: Paris.
Teacher: That's right! (*after which, teacher initiates a new round*)

When children are young, adults may fill in the labels for objects and accept any sort of contribution from the child as an adequate turn. As the child's knowledge increases, adults supply less help in keeping the game going. Instead they raise the stakes by providing more complex texts and pictures, or by asking more complicated questions about old favorites (De Loache, 1984). This kind of tailored support that keeps changing to fit children's growing competence illustrates the "zone of proximal development" discussed in earlier chapters.

One reason to expect such early experiences to influence children's cognitive development is that parents who introduce their children to books in the way Ninio and Bruner described also talk to their children about book contents at odd times of the day when no books are present (Brice-Heath, 1982; Crago & Crago, 1983). These parents make it clear to their children that the pictures and text in books are relevant to the world at large, thus helping them to acquire more powerful cognitive schemas.

In homes where picture- and story-book reading is infrequent, Shirley Brice-Heath (1982, 1984) has found that the whole structure and purpose of reading to preschoolers is likely to be different from that described by Ninio and Bruner. In some families she observed, for example, being read to was more an occasion for the children to learn to sit still than an occasion to make meaning of pictures and words. Children who learn that kind of lesson well may have trouble learning to read once they begin school, even if they sit very quietly and behave themselves in class.

The content of early reading Perhaps the most crucial difference between television viewing and being read to for small children is the relative degree to which adults exercise control over the content their children are exposed to. Adults choose the books they deem appropriate for children, and because few preschoolers can read, adults must be present to read to them. By contrast, once small children can toddle over to the television set and push the correct buttons, they are likely to be exposed to content that was not designed for preschool children, such as adult programs with relatively high levels of sex and violence.

Although adults have more control over the books that the children are exposed to, some of the books they choose to read to children have come under fire for being potentially harmful to a child's view of the world. A case in point is fairy tales and myths. Most of these were created in the centuries before childhood was considered a special period of life and before there was a literature specifically for children (Sale, 1979). Adults have occasionally argued (echoing arguments

One of the most effective ways of giving children both a love of books and basic reading skills is to read to them.

about television) that fairy tales should not be read to children because they are brutal, cruel, frightening, and are not realistic portrayals of the world. They are condemned as not sensible or "educational." Others, such as the psychoanalyst Bruno Bettelheim, insist that children need fairy tales. "Like all great art, fairy tales both delight and instruct; their special genius is that they do so in terms which speak directly to children" (Bettelheim, 1977, p. 56). Bettelheim argues that the very unreality of such stories allows children to use them to find solutions to their own inner conflicts; it is certainly less threatening to think about a storybook evil stepmother than to think consciously about real negative feelings toward an actual mother or father (see Box 12.2, "The Sense of Nonsense Verse").

BOX 12.2

THE SENSE OF NONSENSE VERSE
...

Kornei Chukovsky, a Soviet author of poems for children, was sometimes accused of damaging children by his use of fantasy. The following letter is typical of such criticism.

> Shame on you, Comrade Chukovsky, for filling the heads of our children with all kinds of nonsense, such as that trees grow shoes. I have read with indignation in one of your books such fantastic lines as:
>
> *Frogs fly in the sky,*
> *Fish sit in fishermen's laps,*
> *Mice catch cats*
> *And lock them up in*
> *Mousetraps.*
>
> Why do you distort realistic facts? Children need socially useful information and not fantastic stories about white bears who cry cock-a-doodle-doo. That is not what we expect from our children's authors. We want them to clarify for the child the world that surrounds him, instead of confusing his brain with all kinds of nonsense.

The following is Chukovsky's defense of his nonsense verse. Speaking of the man who sent the critical letter, he wrote:

> Had he had other resources than "common sense," he would have realized that the nonsense that seemed to him so harmful not only does not interfere with the child's orientation to the world that surrounds him, but, on the contrary, strengthens in his mind a sense of the real; and that it is precisely in order to further the education of children in reality that such nonsense verse should be offered to them. For the child is so constituted that in the first years of his existence we can plant realism in his mind not only directly, by acquainting him with the realities in his surroundings, but also by means of fantasy. (1968, pp. 89–90)

In recent decades in the United States and elsewhere, concern like that shown over television has been expressed that some children's books present children with a distorted view of reality. Claims that these books ignore or misrepresent certain ethnic and racial groups, women, or working-class and poor people have frequently been supported by surveys of the contents of children's books (Council on Interracial Books for Children, 1976; Tanyzer & Karl, 1972; White, 1976).

Whether in the form of a television situation comedy, an evening news bulletin, or a story about a beautiful princess, the larger world of adult relationships enters the homes of children in great variety. Existing evidence supports the conclusion that the influence of a particular form of mediated experience is neither "good" nor "bad" in any abstract sense. How one assesses the value of, say, reading fairy tales, or Bible stories, or watching adult programming on television, depends upon how one sees the social values of the home and the community, and the future life for which the child is being prepared.

THE CHILD IN THE COMMUNITY

As long as parents remain at home with their children, they retain relatively direct control over outside influences, even the influence of television. But when the parents leave their children in the care of others for several hours a day, the nature of children's experiences—as well as the nature of parental control—changes in a decisive way. In the United States and other industrialized countries, one of the most important tasks parents face is to select the day-care arrangement or nursery school that will supervise the upbringing of their children during those hours.

Varieties of Day Care

In 1987, more than 50 percent of U.S. mothers with preschool-aged children were working and using some form of day care for their children (U.S. Department of Labor, 1987). The most popular arrangement is *family day-care*, in which children go to the home of someone who is not a family member. The least-used arrangement—although it has attracted the most public attention—is to take the child to a *day-care center.* In between is *home care,* in which children are cared for in their own home by either a relative or a babysitter (U.S. Dept. of Agriculture, 1988). Choices between different kinds of care are usually based on availability, cost, parental judgments about quality of care, the age of the children that require care, and the number of children involved (Belsky, Steinberg, & Walker, 1982) (see Figure 12.5).

Home care Because it is so private, relatively little is known about child care in the home. One study comparing various types of care confirmed what one might expect on common-sense grounds (Clarke-Stewart, 1982). Children cared for at home experience the least

change from normal routine: they eat food provided by their parents and take naps in their own beds. They also come in contact with relatively few children their own age.

Family day care Family day care exposes children not only to caretakers from outside the family circle, but also to new settings and, often, to children from other families. The children in a family day-care home may range widely in age, exposing the child to a more diverse social group than is likely to exist at home. The routine of activities in family day-care centers, however, is usually very similar to the routine at home (Clarke-Stewart & Fein, 1983).

State, county, or local government agencies grant licenses to family day-care homes when they meet basic health and safety requirements and maintain acceptable adult-child ratios. However, most family day-care homes are unlicensed. Observations of licensed and unlicensed family day-care providers have found that unlicensed providers are less likely than licensed ones to give comfort, verbal stimulation, and guidance to the children in their care (Carew, 1980).

Day-care centers Licensed day-care centers tend to offer a wider variety of formal learning experiences than family or home day care, and are likely to employ at least one trained caretaker. However, waiting lists for places in day-care centers tend to be long, since the demand far exceeds the available places.

Because licensed day-care centers often receive public financing, they have been more accessible to researchers, who have studied both the characteristics of different centers and how these characteristics affect children's development. Some of their findings are:

1. Day-care centers with populations of more than 60 children place more emphasis on rules, are relatively inflexible in their scheduling, and offer children fewer opportunities to initiate or control their own activities, as compared to smaller centers. Teachers in large centers tend to show less sensitivity to the needs of individual children, perhaps because there are so many children for them to supervise (Clarke-Stewart & Fein, 1983; Heinicke, Friedman, Prescott, Puncell, & Sale, 1973).

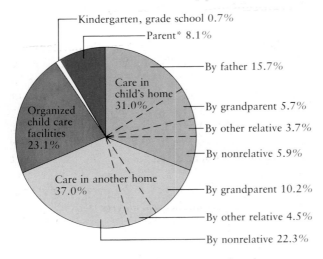

Kindergarten, grade school 0.7%
Parent* 8.1%
By father 15.7%
Care in child's home 31.0%
By grandparent 5.7%
By other relative 3.7%
Organized child care facilities 23.1%
By nonrelative 5.9%
Care in another home 37.0%
By grandparent 10.2%
By other relative 4.5%
By nonrelative 22.3%

*Includes mothers working at home or away from home.

FIGURE 12.5 *Primary child-care arrangements used by working mothers for children under 5 years of age. The data are from 1984–1985 U.S. Census Bureau figures. (From U.S. Department of Agriculture, 1988.)*

These children at a day-care center in Czechoslovakia are obtaining the kind of experience in getting along in groups that is one of the major features of the day-care experience.

2. According to the studies of day care, the most important factor for 3- to 5-year-old children is the size of the day-care group the children are in (Travers & Ruopp, 1978). Groups of less than 15 to 18 children allow for more individual contact and more verbal interaction between children and adults, and for more active involvement by children in group activities (McCartney, Scarr, Phillips, & Grajek, 1985; Ruopp, Travers, Glantz, & Coelen, 1979).

The programs offered by day-care centers vary in style and philosophy. Some offer an academic curriculum, emphasize discipline, and have a school-like atmosphere. Others emphasize social development and allow children to exercise more initiative in their activities. Consistent with the class differences in modes of parenting discussed earlier in this chapter, most lower-class parents have been found to prefer the more school-like day-care centers, while middle-class parents are likely to choose the less structured centers (Joffe, 1977).

Developmental Effects of Day Care

Psychologists disagree sharply about the developmental impact of day care on young children just as they do about the impact of day care on infants (see Box 8.1). Some notable figures in the field of child development such as Selma Fraiberg (1977) and Burton L. White (1975) claim that prolonged daily separation of young children from their mothers is detrimental to their development. Other experts conclude that as long as it is of high quality, day care is not bad for preschool-aged children and can even make positive contributions to their later intellectual and social development (Clarke-Stewart & Fein, 1983; McCartney, 1984).

Shortcomings of the evidence These disagreements are difficult to resolve because intensive research on day care is still in its infancy, and existing research is subject to some important limitations. First, a great deal of the early research on the effects of day care was conducted in university-affiliated day-care centers of high quality. The experience of children in these centers is probably not representative. This problem is being redressed by research such as recent comparative studies of day care in Bermuda, (McCartney, 1984; McCartney, Scarr, Phillips, & Grajek, 1985), but caution must be exercised when attempting to generalize across programs that differ both in the backgrounds of the families involved and the quality of care offered (Howes & Olenick, 1986).

Second, most research has looked only at the immediate effects of day care, leaving open the question of possible long-term effects. Finally, the families of children in day care are not a random sample of all families with young children. The lack of clear data comparing families that do and don't use day care raises the possibility that differences between children found at the end of the program were there at the beginning, and were not the result of day care but of other aspects of the family situation (Belsky & Steinberg, 1978; Howes

& Olenick, 1986). Despite these limitations, a number of suggestive findings have emerged from existing studies.

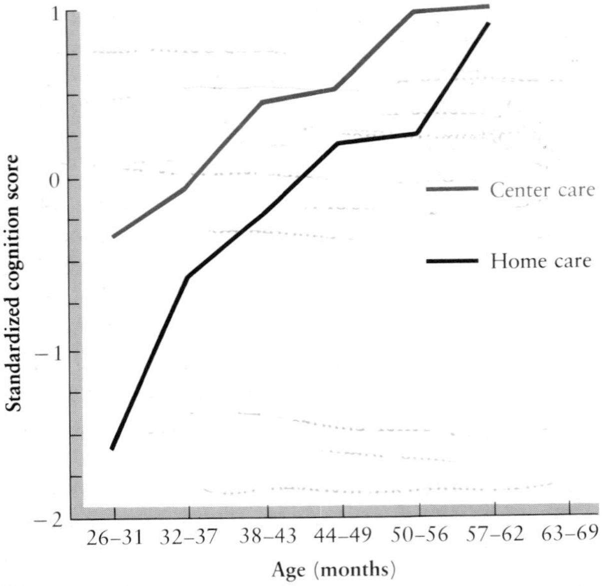

Intellectual effects The intellectual development of middle-class children in adequately staffed and equipped day-care centers is at least as good as that of children raised at home by their parents (Clarke-Stewart, 1982; Clarke-Stewart & Fein, 1983; Kagan, Kearsley, & Zelazo, 1978) (see Figure 12.6). In some cases it may actually be accelerated (Clarke-Stewart, 1984). Among children from low-income homes with poorly educated parents, experience in day-care enrichment programs seems in some cases to ameliorate the decline in intellectual performance that sometimes occurs after the age of 2 when such children remain at home. In other cases, enrichment programs may lead to marked gains in language and cognitive development among these children (Golden et al., 1978; McCartney, 1984; McCartney, Scarr, Phillips, & Grajek, 1985; Ramey & Haskins, 1981).

Impact on social development The most clear-cut influence of day care is in the realm of social development. Children who attend day-care centers in the United States tend to be more self-sufficient and more independent of parents and teachers, more helpful and cooperative with peers and mothers, more verbally expressive, more knowledgeable about the social world, and more comfortable in new situations. In some cases they also tend to be less polite, less agreeable, less compliant with adults, and more aggressive than children who do not attend day-care centers (Clarke-Stewart & Fein, 1983; Haskins, 1985; Howes & Olenick, 1986). These effects may vary with the quality of day care and the involvement of the child's parents. Children in low-quality day care often come from families with more stressful lives and consequently less involvement in their children's lives than children who attend high-quality day-care centers (Howes & Olenick, 1986).

It isn't necessary to look far for an explanation of day care's effects on a preschooler's social development. At home the wishes and needs of small children are often anticipated, their social incompetence overlooked, and their failures at communication filled in. Care outside of the home requires the child to get along with adults who do not know their special likes and dislikes and who must fit several children into a common schedule. In addition, children in day care

FIGURE 12.6 *A comparison of the performance on tests of intellectual development by children cared for in day-care centers with those cared for at home. The tests were specially constructed to assess children's ability to use language, form concepts, and remember information. (From Clarke-Stewart, 1984.)*

must learn to interact successfully with a variety of other children, often when relatively few adults are present.

Compared to children who do not attend day care, those that do often have more opportunities to turn to one another for companionship, affection, amusement, and a sense of identity and belonging. Experience with groups their own age helps children to learn about their strengths and weaknesses by comparing themselves to others. The flowering of language at the end of the second year and the beginning of the third adds an important dimension to children's social interactions that influences their experiences in day care. By the time children are 2½,

> they are able to manage interactions with one another that contain, in fledgling form, all the basic features of social interactions among older children or adults — sustained attention, turn-taking, and mutual responsiveness. (Rubin, 1980, p. 17)

Children's experiences with each other in day-care centers and nursery schools usually occurs around a shared activity to which the members are committed, such as playing fantasy games or building with blocks. Observations conducted by William Corsaro (1981) at a state university child study center indicate that most voluntary interactions among groups of 3- and 4-year-olds are extremely fragile. Such group interactions usually last less than 10 minutes and often end abruptly when a playmate leaves the play area without warning. The fragility of such groups requires that children learn how to gain access to another group — or face the prospect of playing alone.

Attempting to enter a preexisting group poses a problem: Group members may react fiercely to the outsider, especially if the group is made up of good friends. In his study Corsaro (1981) observed the outcome of 128 bids to gain access to a group's ongoing activities. More than 50 percent met with initial resistance. Typical of the reasons children gave for refusing admission to a newcomer are "We don't like you today" or "We only want boys here."

The key to success in entering a group seems to lie in understanding what is going on in the group, what its structure is, who is doing what, and then using that knowledge to "go with the flow" as if one were already a member of the group. Children who ask questions about what is going on, criticize what group members are doing, or tell the others how they feel are more

It requires a good sense of the game and good timing to gain entry into someone else's ongoing activity. Most children spend some time hovering on the periphery watching before they try.

likely to be rejected when they try to join a group (Putallaz & Gottman, 1981).

Fearing rejection, most young children hover around the periphery of the group before making their first attempt to gain access to it (Corsaro, 1981). As their experience increases, they are less likely to be found playing by themselves or hovering on the periphery of a group (Schindler, Moely, & Frank, 1987).

In the later preschool years, popular children (those with whom the other children most often choose to play) do not require as much time as those who are unpopular to gain entry to a group composed of popular children. However, it is more difficult for them to enter a group composed of unpopular children. The situation is just the opposite for children who are not well-liked by other children. They have a more difficult time gaining admittance to an activity in which popular children are involved, but an easier time when the group is composed of other unpopular children.

No matter how socially skillful a girl is, she can expect to have particular difficulty gaining entry to a group composed of boys. A preschool-aged girl who asks to join two boys who are playing on the swings is likely to be told "No! We don't want girls here." In the early preschool years, boys have a somewhat easier time joining a group of girls, but as they grow older they encounter more resistance from the girls.

Such exclusive behavior may be cruel, but according to Corsaro, it functions to preserve existing groups. By excluding others, the members of a group give themselves a special identity. They become "we," as against those outsiders who are "them." Their rejections protect their ongoing interactions from the disruption of a newcomer, especially one who plays differently than they do.

It is these kinds of experiences—gaining access to group activities, learning to become desirable companions, and dealing with rejection—that are the most likely social benefits of day care. On the negative side, some of the behavior children learn in day care may conflict with parents' standards for how children should behave at home and in other community settings.

Making friends at the day-care center.

Nursery School

Day care originated in response to the needs of adults who wanted their children supervised while they worked or went to school. By contrast, the purpose of *nursery schools* (sometimes termed *preschools*) is primarily educational. Nursery schools came into being early in the twentieth century out of educators' and physicians' concern that the complexities of urban life were overwhelming children and stunting their development. The nursery school was conceived as "a protected environment scaled to [children's] developmental level and designed to promote experiences of mastery within a child-sized manageable world" (Prescott & Jones, 1971, p. 54).

The basic intuition justifying nursery schools as environments for development is contained in the botanical metaphor of the child as a budding flower. At the age of 5 many children "graduate" from nursery school to kindergarten, a "garden for children" (from the German term *kinder* [children] *garten* [garden]). According to this same intuition, 3- and 4-year-old children are not ready for the rigors of this garden where rain falls, wind blows, and birds forage for seeds. Like the seedlings at a local garden store (a nursery!), they are most likely to develop healthily if they are specially protected until ready for transplanting.

A typical nursery school's layout and schedule reveal prevalent ideas of how best to foster development from the age of 2½ to 6. There are likely to be several kinds of play areas: a sandbox, a water-play table, a doll corner, a block area, a large area with a rug where children can gather to listen to stories or sing songs, a cluster of low tables used for doing arts and crafts projects and eating snacks, and an outdoor area with jungle gyms, slides, and swings. Each area provides an environment for developing a different aspect of children's overall potential: their ability to understand physical transformations in play materials; to control their own bodies; to create representations in language, song, clay, and paint; to adopt various social roles; and to get along with other children.

During the 2½ to 3 hours that children may spend in a nursery school, they are guided from one activity area to another. The developmental spirit of nursery schools is reflected in their lack of pressure on children to perform correctly on preassigned tasks and in their emphasis on exploration.

Preschools and the "War on Poverty"   In the 1960s, a variety of scientific and social factors combined to create great interest in nursery schools' potential to increase the educational chances of the poor. On the scientific side was a growing belief that environmental influence during the first few years of life is crucial to all later abilities, especially intellectual ones (see Chapter 8). This belief coincided with broader historical pressures for improved status among ethnic and racial minorities and with widespread political concern that social barriers between the rich and the poor and between whites and blacks were creating a dangerous situation for the United States. For example, in 1963, Michael Harrington warned that the United States was creating

> an enormous concentration of young people who, if they do not receive immediate help, may well be the source of a kind of hereditary poverty new to American society. If this analysis is correct, then the vicious circle of poverty is, if anything, becoming more intense, more crippling, and problematic. (1963, p. 188)

This combination of social, political, and scientific factors led the U.S. Congress to declare a "War on Poverty" in 1964. One of the key programs in this "war" was Project Head Start. The purpose of Project Head Start was to intervene in the cycle of poverty at a crucial time in children's lives to provide them with important learning experiences that they might have missed. Federal support allowed Head Start programs to offer early educational experience at no charge to children who would not otherwise have been able to afford it.

This strategy of social reform through preschool education rested on three crucial assumptions:

1. The environmental conditions of poor homes are insufficient to prepare children to succeed in school.

2. Schooling is the social mechanism that permits children to succeed in our society.

3. Poor children could succeed in school, and thereby overcome their poverty, if given extra assistance in the preschool years.

When President Lyndon Johnson initiated Head Start, he declared that because of it, "thirty million man years—the combined life span of these youngsters—will be spent productively and rewardingly, rather than wasted in tax-supported institutions or welfare-supported lethargy."

Originally conceived of as a summer program, Head Start had become by 1967 a year-round program serving approximately 200,000 preschool children (Consortium for Longitudinal Studies, 1983). More than 20 years later, nursery school education continues to play an important role for U.S. children, although changes in the political climate have curtailed Head Start activities (Clarke-Stewart & Fein, 1983).

What difference does preschool make? Because nursery schools have gained considerable social acceptance since the 1960s it might be assumed that the preschool experience has proven to have positive benefits for children. The facts are more complicated.

Planners of Project Head Start and other preschool programs were sensitive to the need for scientific demonstrations of the usefulness of nursery schools (Zigler & Valentine, 1979). The logical requirements for proving the effectiveness of preschool were clear enough: select a large sample of children; give half of them, chosen at random, the experimental treatment (in this case, the nursery school experience); and let the other half of the sample stay at home. But the demand for nursery school was so great that everyone who could be given access to a program received it. No parents wanted their children to be part of a control group, so the logic of experimental design was bypassed. As a consequence, there has been a great deal of controversy over the developmental consequences of preschool education.

The first reports were promising. Children attending the summer program showed marked gains in standardized test scores. Hundreds of thousands of parents were involved in their children's school lives for the first time, as members of Head Start planning boards, through special training programs for parents, or as classroom helpers. A great many children received improved nutrition and health care (Condry, 1983).

Doubts about the effectiveness of the program were soon heard, however. In 1969, it was reported that the effects of Head Start slowly disappeared during the first three years of elementary school (Grotberg, 1969). A widely publicized evaluation by the Westinghouse Learning Corporation (1969) concluded that although "full-year Head Start appears to be a more effective compensatory education program than summer Head Start, its benefits cannot be described as satisfactory" (p. 11).

People who had never favored Head Start programs felt their doubts had been confirmed by the Westinghouse report. But supporters were by no means persuaded. They pointed out that the Westinghouse study lacked any proper control groups and included a variety of doubtful statistical substitutes for them.

In 1983, a consortium of researchers published a study of 11 experimental nursery school programs, including follow-up evaluations of children, some of whom were already in high school (Consortium for

Longitudinal Studies, 1983). Whereas early evaluations had focused narrowly on changes in children's intelligence-test scores and school grades, the long-term follow-up permitted researchers to test more adequately the initial belief that Project Head Start would reduce school failure and increase productive social participation.

The results of this long-term evaluation support many of the program's hopes (Royce, Darlington, & Murray, 1983, p. 450). On the average, children who attended a preschool program contrasted with those who did not in the following ways:

1. They had higher intelligence-test scores upon entering school.

2. They performed better in mathematics and reading during the third and sixth grades.

3. They were less likely to be placed in remedial classes or to be retained in their grade during junior or senior high school.

4. They had higher occupational aspirations while in high school.

These conclusions are far more optimistic than those provided by previous large-scale studies, and are based on a more solid scientific foundation. The evidence indicates that nursery school experience for children from low-income families does make a difference in their later school achievement.

The future of compensatory nursery school programs
Despite broad public support for the idea of nursery school education and evidence that these programs enhance later school performance, preschool programs face an uncertain future in the United States. Concern for equal access to education has been swamped by other issues.

Two major objections have been raised to compensatory preschool programs. Daniel Patrick Moynihan, a U.S. senator from New York with a long record of interest in social welfare policies, argues that even the successful programs are not successful enough. In his opinion, the failure rates, joblessness, and criminal records of the children who have participated in such programs are still "unacceptably high" (*New York Times*, October 9, 1984). Other critics argue that federal money is misspent: educational programs cannot compensate for the damage caused by poor housing, inadequate nutrition, discrimination, and parental un-

employment. From this point of view, President Johnson and those involved in Project Head Start were misleading the public. Giving the children of the poor a "head start" would not reduce their poverty.

This controversy shows that even when great care is taken to ensure that evidence is properly gathered, the facts may not be able to speak for themselves. Rather, social reality is likely to undermine the logic of experimental design. Consequently, the same facts speak differently depending upon the prior theories and social priorities of those who interpret them.

ON THE THRESHOLD

This chapter has by no means surveyed all of the contexts that significantly influence early childhood development: preschoolers also learn from trips to the beach, attendance at houses of worship, and visits to the doctor's office. Each new context brings with it new cognitive and social challenges as young children gradually piece together a deeper understanding of their world and their place in it.

Adding the influence of contexts to the picture of preschool development helps to make sense of the variable picture that preschoolers present to the world. In familiar contexts, where children know the appropriate scripts and their roles in accompanying events, they may display mature reasoning and surprising competence. But often they find themselves novices in new settings, where they do not know the appropriate scripts, where they are expected to work out social relationships with strangers, and where they are set new tasks, requiring them to master new concepts. In these circumstances, their powers of self-expression and self-control are put under great strain, and their thought processes may be inadequate to the heavy demands placed upon them.

The problem of being a novice is by no means restricted to preschoolers; it faces people throughout life. But the difficulties are particularly acute for young children at the beginning of the preschool era because they have accumulated relatively little general knowledge about how their culture works. Consequently, children need almost constant supervision at this age. When they play together, they need some powerful organizing activity, like pretend play, to support their fragile abilities to coordinate with other preschoolers.

By the end of the preschool era, children's vocabularies and command of grammatical forms have grown immensely. They have greater knowledge about a wider variety of contexts and a more complicated sense of themselves; and they are vastly more competent in their ability to think about the world, to control themselves, and to deal with other children. In these and many other ways they have indicated that they are ready to venture into new settings, to take on new social roles, and to accept the additional responsibilities that await them as they enter middle childhood.

SUMMARY

1. The factors that influence children's lives can be usefully thought of as a nested set of contexts: individual – family – community – society – larger world.

2. Different levels of context have reciprocal influences on one another.

3. The family influences children's development in two ways: by shaping their behavior within the family context and by selecting other contexts for them to inhabit.

4. Cross-cultural comparisons of family life and personality configurations reveal that children develop to fit the overall demands of economic activity and community life in their society.

5. Family socialization patterns differ within societies, depending upon such factors as values, beliefs, education, income, and the personalities of family members.

6. Patterns of socialization can be grouped for purposes of comparison. The following three patterns can be used to describe child-rearing patterns in the United States:
   a. Authoritarian families use set standards and emphasize conformity.
   b. Authoritative families emphasize control through reasoning and discussion.
   c. Permissive families avoid overt control and believe that children should make their own decisions.

7. Among white middle-class families, authoritative child-rearing practices are associated with children who are more self-reliant, self-controlled, and willing to explore than those raised by permissive or authoritarian parents.

8. Patterns of parenting are influenced by several factors at different levels of context:
   a. Parents who are subject to depression, insecurity, and other personality characteristics that render them inconsistent negatively influence their children's development.
   b. Stressful family circumstances increase parents' irritability and decrease their consistency. These circumstances are often associated with lower socioeconomic status.
   c. Obedience is more highly valued by families who are close to the subsistence level, while autonomy is valued by more well-to-do families.

9. Parents raise their children to confront the world as they, the parents, understand it. Consequently, family socialization patterns tend to perpetuate society's class structure.

10. Influences from the community enter the family context through such media as newspapers, television, radio, and books. Each medium is assumed to influence children's development in specific ways.

11. A major contributor to television's influence on children is the great amount of time they spend watching it.

12. Television's potential for realism makes it difficult for children to distinguish reality from fiction in television content. Preschoolers also have difficulty understanding such cinematic techniques as rapid transitions and zoom shots.

13. Television content influences people's underlying beliefs about the world. Insofar as reality is distorted by television content, children who watch television are given false beliefs about the world.

14. A variety of evidence indicates that violence depicted on television increases children's aggressive behavior.

15. Parents can influence television's impact on their children by controlling what their children watch and by watching with them.

16. Reading to young children provides an early model of reading activities that will be important in school. Reading to children provides parents with far greater control over the pace and the content of the material that the child encounters than does watching television.

17. Once children begin to spend time outside of the home, their experience changes in fundamental ways.

18. Day-care centers differ widely in social settings, philosophy, and physical facilities. Small-group sizes are especially important to the quality of day care.

19. The most clear-cut effects of day care in the United States are on children's social behavior rather than on

their cognitive behavior. Major effects include
   a. Increased self-sufficiency and decreased compliance with adult wishes
   b. Increased ability to engage in peer-led group activity

20. Nursery schools developed during the twentieth century as a means of promoting the development of children who had to cope with the complexities of urban life.

21. Since the early 1960s, nursery school education has been promoted as a means of combating school failure among poor populations.

KEY TERMS

Authoritarian parenting pattern   Authoritative parenting pattern   Permissive parenting pattern

SUGGESTED READINGS

THE CONSORTIUM FOR LONGITUDINAL STUDIES. *As the Twig Is Bent: The Lasting Effects of Preschool Programs.* Hillsdale, N.J.: Erlbaum, 1983.

The history and background of modern preschool programs is presented through important case studies and pooled analyses across programs. An excellent entry point into research that attempts to apply developmental theories as a means of promoting development.

CLARKE-STEWART, ALISON. *Daycare.* Cambridge, Mass.: Harvard University Press, 1982.

Alison Clarke-Stewart, who has extensive experience in day-care research, provides both a concise discussion of the critical scientific issues surrounding day care and practical advice about evaluating day-care facilities.

GREENFIELD, PATRICIA M. *Mind and Media.* Cambridge, Mass.: Harvard University Press, 1984.

Too often discussion of the effects of television on children's development neglect other forms of media that children begin to encounter, such as radio, books, and computers. Greenfield surmounts this problem by drawing interesting comparisons between different forms of mediation and their implications for development.

MACCOBY, ELEANOR E., and JOHN MARTIN. "Socialization in the Context of the Family: Parent-Child Interaction."

In P. H. Mussen (Ed.), *Handbook of Child Psychology.* Vol. 4: E. M. Hetherington (Ed.), *Socialization, Personality, and Social Behavior.* New York: Wiley, 1983.

An authoritative summary of research on the special quality of families as contexts for development.

MONTESSORI, MARIA. *The Montessori Method.* New York: Shocken, 1964.

Maria Montessori was the first Italian woman M.D. and a pioneer in the study of intellectual development and early childhood education. This comprehensive summary of her ideas includes both statements of her general theory and detailed descriptions of her program for a "scientific pedagogy." In one form or another, many of Montessori's ideas remain influential in early childhood education today.

WHITING, BEATRICE and WHITING, JOHN W. M. *Children of Six Cultures.* Cambridge, Mass.: Harvard University Press, 1975.

This volume pulls together evidence from many parts of the world to provide a convincing account of the ways that ecological and historical factors shape adult economic activities, which in turn shape the socialization practices of adults, and eventually the personalities of their children.

IV

...

Middle Childhood

In societies around the world, adults behave as if children enter a new stage of development that begins between the ages of 5 and 7 and lasts until about age 12 (Harkness & Super, 1985; Rogoff, Sellers, Pirrotta, Fox, & White, 1975).

Among the Ngoni of Malawi in central Africa, for example, adults believe that the loss of milk teeth and the acquisition of second teeth (which begins around the age of 6) signals that children are ready for a different kind of life. When this physical change occurs, adults expect children to begin to act more independently. Children of both sexes are held accountable for being discourteous. They are supposed to stop playing childish games and to start learning skills that will be essential when they grow up. The boys leave the protected control of women and move into dormitories, where they must adapt to a system of male dominance and male life. Margaret Read describes the associated stresses for Ngoni boys:

> There was no doubt that this abrupt transition, like the sudden weaning [several years earlier], was a shock for many boys between six-and-a-half and seven-and-a-half. From having been impudent, well fed, self-confident, and spoiled youngsters among the women many of them quickly became skinny, scruffy, subdued, and had a hunted expression. (1960/1968, p. 49)

In the United States and most industrialized societies, the onset of middle childhood is currently marked by the beginning of formal schooling in literacy and arithmetic. In his book on the history of the idea of childhood, Philippe Ariès tells us that a change in children's status at around age 7 has a long history in European society, reaching back to even before the advent of industrialization and compulsory schooling:

> In the Middle Ages, at the beginning of modern times, and for a long time after that in the lower classes, children were mixed with adults as soon as they were considered capable of doing without their mothers or nannies, not long after a tardy weaning (in other words, at about the age of seven). They immediately went straight into the great community of men, sharing in the work and play of their companions, old and young alike. (1962, p. 411)

Even the brief descriptions provided by Read and Ariès indicate one universal feature of middle childhood: children are no longer restricted to the home or to settings where they are carefully watched by adults. They are now responsible for behaving themselves in a variety of new contexts.

The new contexts that children in this stage enter can be divided into three principal types: *solitary* contexts, where children are expected to carry out chores on their own; *instructional* contexts, which are controlled by one or a few adults; and *peer* contexts, which are controlled by others of their own age. There are important differences within and among societies in the particular mix of contexts that children begin to inhabit in middle childhood as well as in the nature of the activities that go on there.

Cultural variation can be seen most clearly by comparing societies that expect children to work with those that expect children to submit to deliberate instruction. In the highlands of Guatemala, boys go out to herd cattle, a solitary activity that takes them well beyond the range of watchful adults, while girls spend more time at home helping their mothers and the older women of the village (Rogoff, 1978). In the United States, boys and girls alike spend long hours in school with their peers under the supervision of adults.

At first glance, time spent with peers may appear less important to development than time spent in instructional contexts; much peer interaction is taken up with games, gossip, or simply "hanging out." But this appearance is almost certainly deceiving; as we shall see, peer groups provide children with important opportunities for exploring social relationships and moral feelings and for the development of personal identities.

These changes in the social contexts of development would be impossible if children did not also acquire new cognitive capacities to support their newly granted autonomy. Evidence from experiments and clinical interviews makes clear that a defining characteristic of middle childhood is a greatly increased ability to think more deeply and logically, to follow through on a problem once it is undertaken, and to keep track of more than one aspect of a situation at a time.

This section has been divided into three chapters: Chapter 13 describes changes in biological and cognitive capacities that occur between ages 5 and 7. Chapter 14 examines the relationship between schooling and development, paying particular attention to the unique way that school activities are organized, and to the intellectual capacities that schooling both demands and fosters. Chapter 15 focuses on the new social relations that emerge during middle childhood, particularly among peers.

13

...

COGNITIVE AND BIOLOGICAL ATTAINMENTS OF MIDDLE CHILDHOOD

Walking was my project before reading. The text I read was the town; the book
I made up was a map. . . .

I pushed at my map's edges. Alone at night I added newly memorized streets and blocks to
old streets and blocks, and imagined connecting them on foot. . . . I felt that my life
depended on keeping it all straight — remembering where on earth I lived, that is, in
relation to where I walked. It was dead reckoning. On darkened evenings I came home
exultant, secretive, often from some exotic leafy curb a mile beyond what I had known at
lunch, where I had peered up at the street sign, hugging the cold pole, and fixed the
intersection in my mind. What joy, what relief, eased me as I pushed open the heavy front
door! — joy and relief because, from the very trackless waste, I had located home, family, and
the dinner table once again.

An infant watches her hands and feels them move. Gradually she fixes her own boundaries
at the complex incurved rim of skin. Later she touches one palm to another and tries for a
game to distinguish each hand's sensations of feeling and being felt. What is a house but a
bigger skin, and a neighborhood map but the world's skin ever expanding?

— Annie Dillard, *An American Childhood*

. . . .

One of the best ways to gain a sense of middle child-hood is to observe what goes on in children's everyday lives. Roger Barker and Herbert Wright (1951) arranged for a team of observers to follow every minute in the waking day of one child living in Midwest, a small community in the United States. The resulting minute-by-minute portrait of 7-year-old Raymond Birch illustrates the new independence, the greater responsibility, and the new variety of contexts that characterize middle childhood. The following account has been adapted from Barker and Wright's *One Boy's Day:*

Raymond gets up, dresses himself (although his clothes have been laid out for him by his mother), and takes care of his own grooming. He eats breakfast with his mother and father. Then he helps his father to clear the dishes. He negotiates with his mother about the need to wear a jacket to school and grudgingly accepts her judgment that a jacket is in order. He decides on his own not to take his bike to school because it might rain.

After spending a few minutes casting a fishing rod with his father in the backyard (he is the only one who caught fish on their last outing), he accompanies his mother to the courthouse where she works. At the courthouse he greets adults politely, and holds the door open for a man who is going out at the same time he is. He plays by himself outside while his mother works. When it is time for him to go to school, he walks the few blocks by himself, crossing the street cautiously. On the playground, he and the other children are unsupervised. A few minutes before 9 A.M. he enters his classroom, which the second-graders share with the first grade. While waiting for school to begin, he draws on the board, looks at a book with a friend, and chats quietly with other children. When the teacher comes into the room promptly at 9 A.M., he turns in his seat (all the seats are arranged in rows, facing front). While the teacher readies the first-graders to go to music, Raymond, who has become worried that he left his coat on the playground, asks permission to search for it. He has forgotten that he has hung it in the cloakroom. When he discovers this, he comes back and makes May baskets out of paper strips with the rest of the second-graders. He goes to music, listens to other children's stories, and goes outside for recess.

In the afternoon he does poorly on the spelling test. When asked by another boy "What did you get on your spelling?" he blushes and looks down at his desk. In a swift hoarse whisper he tells the boy that his grades are his own business. He seems embarrassed when he speaks. Close to dismissal time, the class searches for the money another boy has reported lost. When it turns out to have been in his desk the entire time, Raymond smiles companionably at him and leans back to pat his hand. Then the boy pats Raymond's hand. They pat harder and harder, grinning broadly, until the teacher intervenes with a directive for the entire class.

While his mother is preparing dinner after work, Raymond pushes the lawn mower for a minute. He then joins his 11-year-old neighbor Stewart Evarts, and Clifford, Stewart's 3½-year-old nephew, in the vacant lot across the street. Playing with their trucks in a pit that was once the basement of a house, Raymond discovers a dilapidated wooden crate about five feet long buried in the weeds. He drags the crate out, and the boys devise several different ways to play with it, despite its unwieldy size. They lift it out of the pit and send it crashing back in, get in the crate and pretend it is a cage and that they are monkeys, and hang on with their hands and feet as it rocks and tumbles over and over. At the same time, the older boys are careful that Clifford is not harmed by their games.

From such observations carried out with many children, Barker and Wright (1954) concluded that out of more than 200 different activity settings in which Midwest's children might have participated, on an average weekday they actually participated in about a dozen settings, such as the street, the classroom, the playground, and the grocery store, each requiring its own special set of skills, expectations, values, and attitudes.

Adults were present in many of these places. But generally, the amount of time that children like Raymond Birch spend unsupervised by adults increases markedly during the course of middle childhood (see Figure 13.1). In about one-third of the settings where

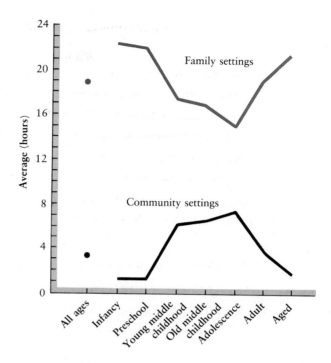

FIGURE 13.1 *The average number of hours a day that residents of "Midwest" of different ages spent in family and community settings (From Wright, 1956.)*

children Raymond Birch's age spent their time— walking to school or playing around the empty lot, for example—there was no adult supervision. Similar increases in unsupervised time have been reported for urban centers as well as the rural midwest, and for quite different societies from several parts of the world (Ellis, Rogoff, & Cromer, 1981; Whiting & Whiting, 1975).

The new independence and responsibility that adults around the world confer on children between 5 and 7 suggest how much more adults expect of them than of preschoolers. These expectations are supported both by cultural traditions and by parents' observations of how well their children cope with these new demands (Goodnow, 1984; Sigel, 1985). Raymond Birch's parents, for example, would not have allowed him to play around the courthouse unattended if they did not expect him to behave appropriately. If he were to become so fascinated with a playground game that he lost his jacket, he would be held responsible for his mistake because he was supposed to know better. He was expected by his teacher and his parents to have learned his spelling words and he knew enough to be embarrassed when he did not do well on his test.

Children entering middle childhood can meet adult expectations because they have increased physical capacities, can perform tasks independently, and can formulate goals and resist temptation in meeting them. Children of this age are strong and agile enough to catch a runaway goat or to carry their little sister on their hip. They know enough not to let the baby crawl into the fire. They can wait for the school bus without wandering off. They can, sometimes under duress, sit still for several hours at a time while adults attempt to instruct them, and they can carry out their chores in an acceptable manner.

In this chapter we will investigate the changes in children's biological and psychological functioning that justify adults' new demands. Are these changes the same all over the world or do they differ from one society to the next? Are they a sign of a distinctive new stage of development or can they be accounted for on the basis of continuous buildup of capacities already present in early childhood?

BIOLOGICAL DEVELOPMENTS

One reason for what appears to be a universal change in children's status is their physical maturation (Gesell & Ilg, 1943). In many cultures the first loss of baby teeth, which occurs at about age 6, is used both as an index of a child's age and as a sign of new capacities that permit a new status (Rogoff, Sellers, Pirotta, Fox, & White, 1975) (see Fig. 13.2). While the loss of baby teeth is clearly a sign of physical maturation, there is no reason to believe that the arrival of new teeth is the cause of changes in children's behavior or in their parents' expectations. Other biological changes—increases in physical size and strength and brain developments that support better coordination and more complex thinking—are more likely sources of new capacities.

FIGURE 13.2 *The loss of one's front teeth is a widely accepted sign that middle childhood is beginning.*

Physical Growth

Children's size and strength increase significantly during middle childhood, although more slowly than in earlier years. Average 6-year-olds in the United States are about 3½ feet tall and weigh about 50 pounds. At the start of adolescence, six or seven years later, their average height will have increased to almost five feet and their weight to approximately 100 pounds (see Figure 6.2). Strength increases even more dramatically than size. Most boys double their muscular strength during this period and girls become significantly stronger as well (Tanner, 1978).

As in other periods of development, children's growth depends upon both nutritional and genetic factors. Margaret Janes (1975) investigated nutritional factors by comparing the sizes of Nigerian boys from well-off families with those of poor boys. During middle childhood, the children from poor families were, on the average, almost 4 inches shorter than their well-off counterparts.

When groups of children whose nutrition is equivalent and adequate are compared, the genetic contribution to differences in size can be clearly seen. Phyllis Eveleth and J. M. Tanner (1976) compared the sizes of European, Asian, and Afro-American children from the ages of 1 to 18. The Asian boys and girls, even those who received better than average care, were found to be distinctively shorter than children in the other two groups.

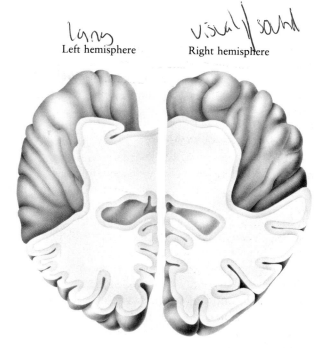

Left hemisphere   Right hemisphere

FIGURE 13.3 *Anatomical differences between the two hemispheres of the brain are clearly visible when comparing the two halves of the temporal lobe, which are not symmetrical. Perception of language-related sounds, letters, words, and verbal memory are generally controlled by the left hemisphere of the brain. Perception of music, of other nonspeech sounds, of visual patterns, as well as visual memory are generally controlled by the right hemisphere. (From Kolb & Whishaw, 1985.)*

Brain Developments

Increases in size and strength are only two ingredients in children's increased competence during middle childhood. Children in this period also become more agile and finely coordinated (enabling them to ride bikes, weave on looms, and write legibly with a pencil) and capable of solving more complex problems.

Some researchers have suggested that these new skills are made possible by a change in the working relationship between the two halves of the brain (Brown & Jaffe, 1975; Lenneberg, 1967). This hypothesis is based on the idea that at birth the two halves of the brain are not specialized. As children grow older, however, psychological functions become controlled by one hemisphere which "dominates" the other, a

process known as **lateralization** (see Figure 13.3). According to this line of reasoning, the onset of middle childhood is accompanied by an increase in lateralization, which supports more subtle and coordinated action and more complex thought.

Evidence in favor of this idea comes from research showing that lateralization of such complex behaviors as writing, throwing, or kicking a ball increases during middle childhood (Coren, Porac, & Duncan, 1981). Researchers have also noted that in cultures around the world, it is not until about age 6 that children are punished for violating social norms that require them to use their right hand for such functions as eating and shaking hands (Rogoff, Sellers, Pirotta, Fox, & White, 1975).

However, recent research has cast doubt on the idea that lateralization is responsible for developments seen

Middle childhood is a time when a combination of physical changes and extended practice enables children to acquire complex, culturally valued skills.

between the ages of 5 and 7. First, it has been shown that even during the first few months of life, the two halves of the brain manifest different electrical patterns, an indication that they are already functioning differently (Kinsbourne & Hiscock, 1983). Moreover, infants, like older children and adults, display dominance of the right ear over the left ear in perceiving speech sounds (Best, Hoffman, & Glanville, 1982) and hand preferences in reaching (Mischel, 1981). Thus, if lateralization plays a role in the advent of middle childhood, it is only part of the story.

Other biological changes associated with middle childhood include an increase in brain size and changes in the brain pattern of electrical activity. The rate of growth in the surface area of the brain's frontal lobes rises sharply around age 2 with another increase between ages 5 and 7, after which the rate of growth remains level, as can be seen in Figure 13.4 (Luria, 1973). The growth spurt in head circumference at age 6 or 7 also indicates a growth in brain size (Eichorn & Bayley, 1962). This age also sees the near completion of the myelination of the cortex (Lecours, 1982). (Recall from Chapter 5 that myelination provides each cortical neuron with an insulating sheath tissue to speed neural transmission.)

The change in the interconnections between different parts of the brain, which myelination helps induce, is accompanied by a fundamental shift in the pattern of waking brain-wave activity (Corbin & Bickford, 1955). As shown in Figure 13.5, until the age of 5, awake children's EEGs (electroencephalograms) display more theta activity (characteristic of adult sleep states) than alpha activity (characteristic of engaged attention). Between 5 and 7 years the amount of theta and alpha activity is about equal, after which alpha activity (engaged attention) predominates.

Generally, by the age of 5 or 7, children's brains have achieved a level of complexity that is similar to that of

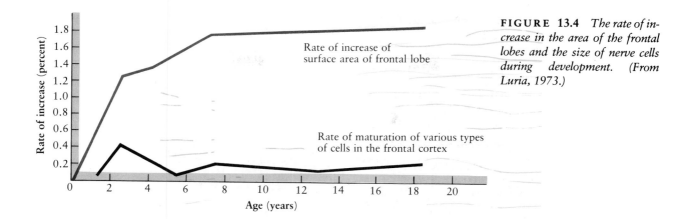

FIGURE 13.4 *The rate of increase in the area of the frontal lobes and the size of nerve cells during development. (From Luria, 1973.)*

adults. This might be sufficient by itself to support the new and more complex behaviors that are said to characterize middle childhood.

This conclusion is adopted by several researchers who have attempted to explain the relationship between the brain and cognitive development (Epstein, 1980; Milner, 1967). Alexander Luria, for example, has argued that frontal lobes coordinate the activity of other brain centers when people form explicit plans, one of the behaviors that appears to undergo important developments in middle childhood (Luria, 1973; Pribram & Luria, 1973). Luria's view is supported by the fact that when human and animal adults suffer damage to the frontal lobes their behavior deteriorates in specific ways: they are unable to maintain goals; their behavior becomes fragmentary and uncontrolled; they respond to irrelevant stimuli and are easily thrown off track by interruptions and pauses. These deficits are very similar to the deficits attributed to preschool children (see Chapter 10), making it plausible that a greater role for frontal lobes in the overall brain organization of children's behavior might account for the behavioral changes of middle childhood.

Despite these documented changes in the brain, we must be cautious about inferring direct causal links between particular changes in the brain and specific changes in behavior. Much of the evidence cited above is correlational—as children grow older, we observe changes in their brains and changes in their behavior. But the direction of causation is uncertain. Do children perform in more sophisticated ways because of prior changes in their brains, or have their brains become larger and more complicated because they are put in more challenging situations? (For further discussion of this possibility, see Box 5.2.)

Caution is also necessary because attempts to link biological and behavioral changes have often failed. For example, Robert McCall and his colleagues tested the hypothesis that spurts in head growth precede spurts in cognitive development. But they found no relation between physical and psychological changes (McCall, Meyers, Harman, & Roche, 1983). Perhaps such tests have failed because either the measures of brain change or those of behavioral change have not been adequate (see Fischer, 1987). Whatever their

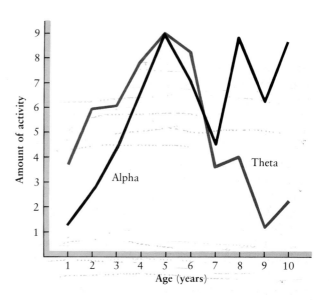

FIGURE 13.5 *Changes in the amount of theta (sleeplike) and alpha (alert) EEG activity during development. Note that alpha waves come to predominate over theta waves around the age of 7. (From Corbin & Bickford, 1955.)*

cause, it is essential to look more closely at the behavioral changes themselves.

In the remainder of this chapter we will review research on children's memory and problem-solving abilities with several interlocking questions in mind: To what extent are the new forms of cognitive activity that become prominent during middle childhood qualitatively distinct from those seen during early childhood, and to what extent are they just a firming up of already existing abilities? Insofar as new abilities do arise in middle childhood, what are their key features? Finally, to what extent are changes universal across cultures? Answers to these questions are, as we will see, hotly disputed.

A NEW QUALITY OF MIND?

During the middle decades of this century there was a broad consensus that children's thought processes undergo a qualitative change between preschool and middle childhood. However, based in part on the evidence surveyed in Chapter 10 about the cognitive abilities of preschool children, there is currently considerable doubt about whether middle childhood constitutes a distinctive stage of cognitive development or is merely a collection of gradual advances in cognitive developments that first appeared at the end of infancy (Flavell, 1985; Gelman & Baillargeon, 1983; Piaget & Inhelder, 1969).

New Forms of Remembering

As long as children remain in the company of their parents or other caretakers, their behavior can be guided step by step. Once they begin to spend time on their own, they must be able to follow directions without being constantly reminded. According to a variety of evidence, once children reach middle childhood, they are increasingly able to carry out tasks based on a preliminary set of adult instructions (Luria, 1961; Miller, Shelton, & Flavell, 1970. For example, in Africa and Central America a number of chores are commonly assigned to children in middle childhood —gathering wood or kindling, bringing food to parents working in the fields, guarding crops from pigs or

birds, bringing a horse in from the field, running errands, making small purchases at the store, shelling and husking corn. All these tasks require the execution of a series of actions often performed without supervision (Nerlove, Roberts, Klein, Yarbrough, & Habicht, 1974).

It requires self-control to do these chores.

Changes in the ability to follow instructions were studied by Oleg Tikhomirov (1978), who asked children to squeeze a rubber bulb according to different preliminary instructions; for example, "Squeeze when the green light flashes" or "Squeeze twice each time a light flashes." Tikhomirov reported that when preschoolers were asked to squeeze whenever a green light flashed and to not squeeze when they saw a red light, they quickly became confused and pressed every time a light flashed, regardless of its color. They could cope with the task only if the experimenter presented one light at a time and specified each time what should be done. Eight-year-olds, however, quickly mastered the task on the basis of preliminary instructions alone.

Perhaps the most obvious interpretation of the difficulties preschoolers have in following directions is that they simply forget what has been asked of them. This conclusion is bolstered by a vast experimental literature about children's information-processing capacities, which shows that there are marked increases in memory performance between the preschool era and middle childhood (Kail, 1984). In light of this evidence, psychologists often link improvements in memory to other forms of increased cognitive competence that appear during middle childhood (Case, 1985; Siegler, 1986).

Four factors appear to account for differences in memory performance between preschoolers and children in middle childhood: (1) an increase in memory capacity; (2) the development of strategies for remembering; (3) an increase in knowledge about the topic under consideration; and (4) the development of knowledge about one's own memory processes (Siegler & Richards, 1982).

Memory capacity As was noted in Chapter 10 (p. 323), during childhood there is a steady increase in the number of random digits that a person can keep in mind at one time. Several investigators propose that this increase reflects an underlying maturation of the child's capacity to hold information in short-term (or "working") memory (Pascual-Leone, 1970; White & Pillemer, 1979; see Figure 10.7, which illustrates a general model of memory. According to this view, 5- to 7-year-olds' new ability to keep track of a task while carrying it out can be explained by increases in their ability to execute actions and hold information in working memory at the same time.

Not all developmental psychologists agree with this explanation. Robbie Case (1984, 1985), for example, believes that the absolute size of children's memory storage capacity does not increase with age. What does increase, he contends, is children's efficiency at using their mental capacities. For example, in order to remember several randomly presented numbers, children must somehow represent each number to themselves, perhaps by silently repeating "10, 6, 8, 2." Case and his colleagues have shown that young children take longer than older children simply to repeat a number such as "10" or "2," indicating that they must use much of their information-processing capacities on this part of the task alone. By contrast, older children name individual numbers quite quickly, which means that more of their information-processing resources are left for the task of actually retaining the numbers in memory (Case, Kurland, & Goldberg, 1982).

Memory strategies A second factor that might lead to increased memory is the appearance of **memory strategies,** patterned ways of learning effectively (Brown, Bransford, Ferrara, & Campione, 1983; Baron, 1978). Two such strategies are rehearsal and reorganization of information.

Rehearsal refers to the repetition of material that the person is trying to memorize, such as a list of words, a song, or a poem. In order to study the development of rehearsal strategies in children, Keeney, Canizzo, and Flavell (1967) presented 5- and 10-year olds with seven pictures of objects to be remembered. The children were asked to wear a "space helmet" with a visor that was pulled down over their eyes during the 15-second interval between presentation of the pictures and the test for recall. The visor prevented the children from seeing the pictures and allowed the experimenter to watch their lips to see if they repeated to themselves what they had seen. Few of the 5-year-olds rehearsed, but almost all of the 10-year-olds did. Within each age group, children who rehearsed the pictures recalled more than children who did not. When those who had not rehearsed were later taught to, they did as well on the memory task as those who had rehearsed on their own. More recent research shows that, under some conditions, preschoolers use some of the same memory strategies as children in middle childhood use, but less frequently. Jill Weissberg and Scott Paris (1986), for example, observed rehearsal among 43 percent of the 3- to 4-year-olds they tested and 79 percent of the 6- to 7-year-olds.

There are also marked changes in the use of another strategy, called **memory organization,** associated with the advent of middle childhood. First, 7- and 8-year-olds are more likely than preschoolers to impose their own ordering principles on what they have to remember by grouping items to be remembered according to easy-to-remember categories (Kail, 1984). Second, the kinds of groupings that children impose on lists of things to be remembered changes. Preschool children often use sound features, such as rhyme (*cat-sat*) or situational associations (*cereal-milk*), to link words they are trying to remember. In middle childhood, children are more likely to link words according to the categories to which they belong, such as *animals:* cat-dog-horse; *plants:* tree-flower-grass; or *geometric figures:* triangle-square-circle (Hasher & Clifton, 1974). The consequence of these changes is an enhanced ability to store and retrieve information deliberately and systematically.

Knowledge base In general, children in middle childhood are likely to know more about any given topic than preschoolers do simply by virtue of having accumulated more experience in the world. Their relatively greater knowledge may thus partly account for their relatively good performance when faced with a memory task (Cole & Means, 1981; Lange, 1978). To the extent that this is true, it suggests that increases in memory may result neither from increased biological capacity nor more powerful strategies, but from an accumulation of experience that provides older children with a richer **knowledge base,** or store of information upon which to draw in a new situation.

Two studies conducted by Michelene Chi dramatically illustrate how a child's knowledge base influences memory performance. In one experiment Chi (1978) compared memory for the arrangement of chess pieces among 10-year-old chess buffs with the memory abilities of college-age chess amateurs. The 10-year-olds recalled the chess arrangements better than the college students, although when the two groups were compared on their ability to recall a random series of numbers, the college students' performances were far superior.

A second study (Chi & Koeske, 1983) compared a 4½-year-old boy's memory for different dinosaur names. Chi and Koeske first elicited the names of all the dinosaurs the child knew (46 in all for this unusually well-versed child!) by questioning him on different occasions. They selected the 20 most frequently men-

Skill at cards requires the ability to remember the cards that have been previously dealt and the relative values of different hands, as well as the ability to use strategies to defeat your opponent.

tioned and 20 least frequently mentioned dinosaurs in order to study how the child's comparative knowledge influenced his memory of each group.

The child's knowledge about these 40 dinosaurs was probed in a game in which the experimenter and the child took turns generating clues from which the other had to guess the dinosaur in question ("lives in forest, eats plants, moves on four legs, is very big— what is it?"). The child was more familiar with the dinosaurs he most frequently mentioned, and these were also more closely associated with each other in his mind.

Chi and Koeske subsequently read the two lists of dinosaurs to the child three times each and asked him to remember them after each presentation of a list. He recalled twice as many items from the list he knew more about (an average of 9.7) than from the less well-known list (an average of 5.0), leading the researchers to conclude that the more one knows about a topic, the easier it is to recall items that pertain to it. Since a great deal of a person's knowledge base is stored as concepts in memory, and these concepts are likely to be richer and more elaborate the more one knows, children's experiences once they reach middle childhood are likely to account for at least a part of their increased memory performance.

Metamemory Most 7- and 8-year-olds not only have more elaborate knowledge about the world than preschoolers, they are also likely to possess more knowledge about the process of remembering itself (called **metamemory**). Even 5-year-olds have some understanding of the process of remembering. In one study, for example, they knew that it is easier to remember a short list of words than a long one, to relearn something you once knew than to learn it from scratch, and to remember something that happened yesterday than something that happened last month (Kreutzer, Leonard, & Flavell, 1975).

Most 8-year-olds have a much better understanding of the limitations of their own memories than most 5-year-olds, however. When shown a set of 10 pictures and asked if they could remember them all, most of the 5-year-olds, but only a few of the 8-year-olds, claimed that they could. The 5-year-olds also failed to evaluate correctly how much progress they had made in remembering. Given unlimited time to master the set of pictures, the 5-year-olds announced that they were ready right away, even though they succeeded in remembering only a few of the items. The 8-year-olds, by contrast, knew enough to study the materials and to test themselves on their ability to remember (Flavell, Friedrichs, & Hoyt, 1970).

The combined picture The data on development of memory capacity, the use of remembering strategies, an increased knowledge base, and metamemory all attest to the growth of memory between preschool age and the age of 8. Considered one domain at a time, these data undermine the hypothesis that a *qualitatively* new form of remembering arises in middle childhood. When familiar materials are presented to preschoolers in a simplified fashion that supports their limited understanding of what is being asked of them, preschool children display many of the strategies common in middle childhood, as well as displaying impressive levels of performance.

But the similarity between the memory abilities of preschoolers and 7- or 8-year-olds should not be overstated. Older children's propensity to remember well in a wide variety of circumstances contrasts sharply with preschoolers' fleeting and fragile demonstration of sophisticated remembering in highly restricted contexts (Brown, Bransford, Ferrara, & Campione 1983).

New Forms of Reasoning: Concrete Operations

Without denying that changes in memory contribute to the new behaviors observed in middle childhood,

Piaget believed that the key to children's new behavior in this period lay in the crystallization of a new form of thought based on **concrete operations** (Piaget, 1983; Piaget & Inhelder, 1969; Piaget, 1952). An *operation*, in Piaget's terminology, is an internalized (mental) action that fits into a logical system (see Chapter 10, p. 310). When the laws of logic begin to structure children's thought processes, children become capable of mentally combining, separating, ordering, and transforming information and objects.

Preschoolers can physically manipulate objects, but they cannot do so mentally, in Piaget's view, leaving them at the mercy of current appearances. Most 8-year-olds, by contrast, can think about manipulations with blocks, or clay, or glasses full of water. These mental operations are termed *concrete* because, during middle childhood, children still cannot manipulate ideas in the absence of the objects being thought about. When the ability to manipulate abstract ideas and symbols makes its appearance during adolescence, it will mark the most complex level of thought in Piaget's theory, the stage of *formal* operations (Inhelder & Piaget, 1958).

During middle childhood, changes in the logic underpinning thought transform all aspects of psychological functioning, according to Piaget. The world becomes more predictable to children when they achieve concrete operations because they understand that such physical aspects of objects as size, quantity, and number remain the same even when certain aspects of their appearances have changed. Children's thinking also becomes more flexible. They can think about alternatives when solving problems, or mentally retrace their steps if they want to, as Raymond Birch did when he thought he had left his coat on the playground and asked permission to search for it (see page 411).

With the advent of concrete operational thinking, children's social behavior changes: they gain an understanding of how to play games with rules, and, as we shall see in Chapter 15, they can better understand social and moral rules. Children also become less susceptible to being caught in their own point of view and more skilled at interpreting other people's intentions, which increases the scope of their social relations.

Piaget invented a number of problems to discuss with children in order to study the emergence of concrete operational thinking. His problems of conservation of quantities and logical classification provide especially clear examples of how mastering concrete operations increases the power of thought (Inhelder & Piaget, 1964; Piaget & Inhelder, 1973). **Conservation** was Piaget's term for the understanding that properties of an object or substance remain the same even though its appearance may be altered in some superficial way.

Conservation   In the most famous version of the conservation task, touched on briefly in Chapter 10, children are presented with two identical glass beakers, each containing the same amount of liquid (see Figure 13.6). The experimenter begins by asking, "Is there the same amount of liquid in the two glasses?" If the child does not think so, the amounts are adjusted until the child agrees that the two glasses contain exactly the same amount. Then the experimenter pours the contents of one of the beakers into a third beaker, which is taller and thinner. Naturally, the liquid rises higher in the new beaker. Now the experi-

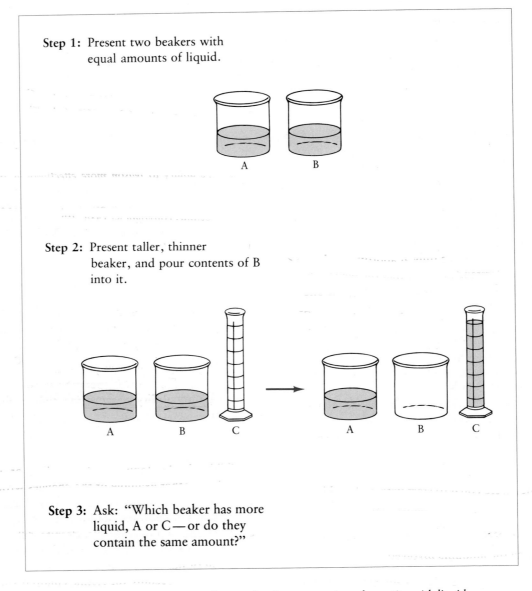

Step 1: Present two beakers with equal amounts of liquid.

Step 2: Present taller, thinner beaker, and pour contents of B into it.

Step 3: Ask: "Which beaker has more liquid, A or C—or do they contain the same amount?"

FIGURE 13.6   *The procedure used to test for the conservation of quantity with liquids.*

menter asks the child, "Does the new beaker contain more liquid than the old beaker, does it contain the same amount, or does it contain less?"

Most 3- and 4-year-old children focus their attention on a single aspect of the new beaker — its height. (Focusing on a single attribute of an object is the phenomenon of "centering" introduced in Chapter 10, p. 310.) They apparently believe that the amount of liquid has changed as a consequence of being poured into a taller container. Even when the experimenter points out that no liquid was added or subtracted, and even following a demonstration that the amount is the same when the liquid is poured back into the original beaker, 3- and 4-year-olds claim that there is more liquid in the taller beaker. When asked why, they explain, "There's more because it's higher," or "There's more because it's bigger," or even, "There's more because you poured it."

When Piaget conducted these observations, he found that sometime between the ages of 5 and 6 children's understanding of conservation goes through a transitional stage. At this point they seem to realize that it is necessary to consider both the height and the circumference of the beakers, but they have difficulty keeping both in mind simultaneously so that they can properly compare them.

According to Piaget, children begin to master the principle of conservation fully at approximately age 8, when they understand not only that the new beaker is both taller and thinner, but that a change in one dimension of the beaker is accompanied by a change in the other. Children who have acquired the concept of conservation of liquid recognize that it is *logically necessary* for the amount of liquid to remain the same despite the change in appearances. When asked the reasons for their judgment they make such statements as "The liquid *can't* change just because you poured it." When pressed further, they offer several arguments showing that they understand the logical relationships involved:

1. "They were equal to start with and nothing was added, so they are the same." This mental operation is called **identity** because the child realized that changes in outward appearance did not change the amounts involved.

2. "The liquid is higher, but the glass is thinner." This mental operation is called **compensation**

Children's ability to reason more effectively as they grow older complicates the kinds of questions they begin to ask and the kinds of mischief they can get into. (From Love Is Hell by Matt Groening, copyright © 1984, 1985 by Matt Groening. Reprinted by permission of Pantheon Books, a Division of Random House, Inc.)

because changes in one aspect of a problem are compared and compensated for by mental calculations of changes in the other.

3. "If you pour it back you will see that it is the same." This mental operation is called **negation** or **reversibility** because the child realizes that one operation will negate, or reverse, the effects of another.

Children's developing understanding of number provides another example of the changes wrought by their acquisition of concrete operations. Piaget called the ability to recognize one-to-one correspondence between two rows of objects, despite differences in the size of the objects or their spatial positions, "conservation of number" (Piaget, 1952b).

The basic procedure for testing children's ability to conserve numbers is to present them with two rows of

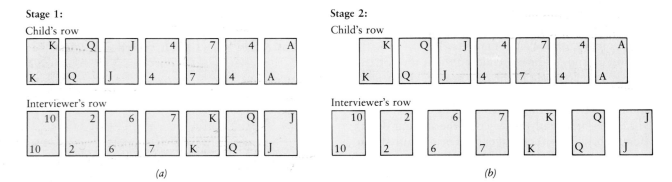

FIGURE 13.7 *The procedure used by Ginsburg (1977) to test for the conservation of number. (a) In Stage 1, the child's and the interviewer's seven cards are arrayed at equal intervals. (b) In Stage 2, the interviewer spreads out his cards and asks the child if she and the interviewer still have the same number of cards. (From Ginsburg, 1977.)*

objects such as those shown in Figure 13.7(*a*). Both the number of objects and the lengths of the two lines are equal and children are asked to affirm this. Then one of the rows is spread out as shown in Figure 13.7(*b*), and children are asked if there is still an equal number of objects in each row. Usually preschool-aged children fail to realize that number is conserved despite changes in objects' location, while older children realize that the number remains the same.

Piaget claimed that preschoolers are incapable of conservation owing to their presumed inability to engage in concrete operations. Nevertheless, when they are given some training and a small number of objects is used, children as young as 3 or 4 years can recognize one-to-one correspondence and conserve numbers (Gelman & Baillargeon, 1983). This does not mean that Piaget was totally wrong. Consistent with his observations, children as old as 6 or 7 can still become confused if asked to make number conservation judgments about a relatively large number of objects (Cowan, 1987). However, his argument that preschool-aged children are *unable* to conserve numbers appears to be overstated.

The following interview with 6-year-old Deborah illustrates the typical pattern of confusion experienced by children who have not fully mastered concrete operations. In this case, one attribute that Deborah perceives—length—overpowers her ability to use logic.

The interviewer (I) placed seven playing cards in a line on the table in front of Deborah (D):

I: How many cards?

D: Seven.

I: Make another line of cards that's the same number.

Deborah counted out seven cards—"one, two, three, four, five, six, seven"—and placed them directly above the interviewer's. The interviewer pointed to the bottom row, saying it was his, and to the top row, identifying it as Deborah's.

I: Now does your line have just as many as my line? Is it just as many cards?

D: Yes.

I: All right, now watch what I do with my line.

The interviewer spread out his row of cards as Deborah watched. This is the "conservation" problem. The question is whether Deborah will *conserve* the initial equivalence despite the change in the appearance of the array.

I: See. Now do we both have as many cards? Does this line have as many cards as this line?

Deborah shook her head to indicate no.

I: Which line has more?

Deborah pointed to the interviewer's line.

I: Why does this line have more?

D: Because it is out here [meaning the interviewer's line was longer than hers].

I: O.K. I see . . . but how many cards are in my line?

D: Seven.

I: How many cards are in your line?

D: Seven.

I: How come this one has more if they both have seven?

D: Because you spread them out.

(Adapted from Ginsburg, 1977, pp. 26–27.)

In the first part of this interview, Deborah shows that she grasps the principle of one-to-one correspondence, which she uses to create a row equal in number to the row created by the experimenter. However, when the length of the rows is made unequal because the experimenter spreads out his cards, the child fails to conserve the property of row number and instead makes her judgment on the basis of row length.

In Piaget's view, once the child is capable of thinking operationally, individual bits of knowledge are no longer isolated or merely juxtaposed in the mind, as they were earlier. The capacity to perform concrete operations permits children to unify their experience into a coherent logical structure, which in turn enables them to think more systematically and effectively. In particular, the ability to perform the crucial operation of reversing something in their minds allows children to coordinate their representations of present and future states of objects and people. They can "think ahead" to see how actions might change the objects and "think back" to the scene before them. If Deborah were able to apply concrete operations to the number conservation task, she would be able to say to herself, in effect, "There must be the same number of cards, because if the experimenter moved the cards in his row back to where they were at the beginning, nothing would have changed."

Logical classification Another important way in which children grasp relationships among events and unify their experiences into logical wholes is by classifying objects according to a variety of attributes. As we saw in Chapter 7, even in the third year of life children are able to separate a collection of objects into two categories (e.g., blue objects and red objects), even when other attributes differ (e.g., some of the blue objects are toy boats, others are wooden dolls). The ability to classify increases during early childhood, but it remains fragile and breaks down quickly as soon as the situation is made more complex (Gelman & Baillargeon, 1983).

During middle childhood, the ability to create categories increases in ways that support Piaget's ideas about children's emerging capacity to engage in mental operations. When children begin to collect stamps or baseball cards, for example, they often organize their collections according to multiple criteria. Stamps come from different countries, are issued in different

Systematic cataloguing of a rock collection requires the ability to classify according to multiple criteria.

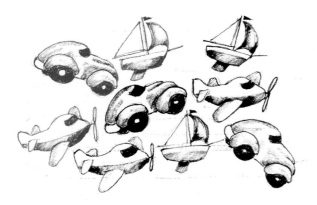

FIGURE 13.8 *The typical stimuli used to determine whether children are capable of systematically categorizing objects according to two or more dimensions simultaneously. Initially the objects are arrayed randomly. The child is then asked to place them in the two-dimensional matrix.*

denominations and in different years. There are stamps depicting insects, animals, sports, heroes, and space exploration. Children who organize their stamps according to type of animal and country of origin (so that, for example, within "France," all the tigers are together, all the rabbits are together, and so on) are creating a multiple classification for their collections. Similarly, grouping baseball cards according to league, team, and position creates a multiple classification.

When psychologists seek to demonstrate the changes that take place between early and middle childhood in children's ability to group objects into categories, they often ask children to classify objects such as those depicted in Figure 13.8. Unlike the very simple materials presented to 1- and 2-year-olds (Chapter 7, p. 223), the three kinds of objects (cars, boats, and airplanes) in Figure 13.8 come in three colors — red, blue, and yellow — permitting multiple possibilities for grouping.

Preschool-aged children are unlikely to create a consistent classification of the objects (Frith & Frith, 1978). Instead, they usually create a number of small groups, each according to its own principle (a red and a blue airplane in one group, three yellow objects in a second group, a row of alternating boats and cars in a third group, etc.). Children over the age of 8 quickly figure out the underlying principle of cross-classification and create classification matrices like the one shown in Figure 13.8. They also are able to combine

classes of objects, such as *cat, dog, rabbit,* into more general categories, such as *animals.*

The contrast in classifying abilities between middle and early childhood becomes apparent when children are asked to think simultaneously about the relationship between a category and its members, as depicted in Figure 13.9 (Inhelder & Piaget, 1964). In order to

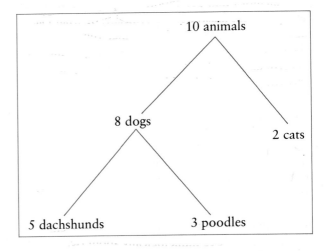

FIGURE 13.9 *A class inclusion problem. Before middle childhood, children find it difficult to keep in mind such facts as that there are more dogs than dachshunds and more animals than dogs, even when concrete objects embodying these objects are there for them to see.*

make the task concrete, the different animals in Figure 13.9 are usually presented to the child as toy figurines. Suppose, for example, that children are presented with ten figurines, five of which are dachshunds, three of which are poodles, and two of which are cats. The children are asked a series of preliminary questions to make certain that they can identify each of the figurines and that they understand the words being used. Once the investigator is satisfied that the children are able to discuss the objects in question, they are asked the key question designed to reveal their comprehension of the relationship between a category and its parts: *Are there more dogs or more dachshunds?*

Children who are about 8 years old may find it peculiar to be asked such a question but they quickly figure out how to respond appropriately; preschoolers are likely to affirm that there are more dachshunds than dogs, and that there are more dogs than animals. This confusion about the relationship of parts to wholes makes it difficult for preschoolers to reason systematically about objects or to communicate effectively with other people. (For another example of this problem, see Chapter 1, p. 28.)

Considering Two Things at a Time

The relative ease with which 7- and 8-year-olds solve conservation and classification problems compared to the difficulties that preschoolers experience with the same problems illustrates the centrality of what Piaget calls concrete operational thinking, the process in which elements of a problem are mentally combined, ordered, and reordered in a systematic way that preserves the actual relationships among the objects being thought about.

The common element underlying the many different manifestations of concrete operations is the two-sided nature of reversible mental operations. In effect, children begin to think simultaneously about two aspects of a thing at a time. This common element influences children in a variety of ways.

Perceiving two things at a time Clearly children would not be able to think logically about two aspects of a problem at once if they had not perceived each aspect in the first place. It has been suggested that as children reach middle childhood, their reasoning improves not only because they use mental operations, but also because they perceive more of the elements of

a problem (Elkind, 1978; O'Bryan & Boersma, 1971). By contrast, preschoolers often fail to notice more than a single aspect of the problem, centering on only one of its salient features.

David Elkind (1978) showed children the pictures depicted in Figure 13.10, each of which is either ambiguous or made up of several elements. Those over 8 were generally able to see the alternative possibilities in the drawings right away, but the 6-year-olds rarely gave more than one interpretation of each drawing unless the alternatives were pointed out to them. Among 4- and 5-year-olds the tendency to latch on to a single interpretation was so strong that they did not perceive the alternative possibilities even when they were pointed out.

Research by Kenneth O'Bryan and Frederic Boersma (1971) suggests a relationship between preschoolers' tendency to fasten on to only one attribute of a problem and their difficulty in the conservation task discussed on p. 420. Using a camera that records eye movements, O'Bryan and Boersma found that children who did not understand the principle of con-

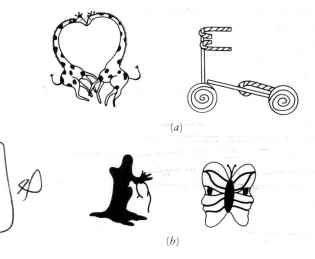

FIGURE 13.10 *(a) Parts and wholes: These figures depict objects constructed from other objects such as a heart made of giraffes or a scooter made of candy canes and lollipops. (b) Ambiguous figures: a tree/swan and a butterfly/face. Until middle childhood the double significance of these kinds of figures is unlikely to be perceived. (From Elkind, 1978.)*

servation failed to look systematically at different parts of the display. It is as if their gaze was captured by—or centered on—a single attribute, which they used to guide their answer about the amount of liquid.

Declining egocentricism   The preschooler's bias toward interpreting events only from one's own point of view never completely disappears. John Flavell, who has conducted a great deal of research on children's developing thought, comments:

> I believe we are "at risk" (almost in a medical sense) for egocentric thinking all of our lives, just as we are for certain logical errors. The reason lies in our psychological designs in relation to the jobs to be done. We experience our own points of view more or less directly, whereas we must always attain the other person's in more indirect manners. Our own points of view are more cognitively "available" to us than another person's. (1985, p. 125)

Despite continuing slips and difficulties, children's reasoning becomes less egocentric in a broad range of situations during middle childhood. No longer is it necessary to create a friendly farm scene with a puppet driving around in a car for children to know how things look from the other side of the diorama in the "three mountain problem," for example (see Chapter 10, p. 316). Children can now more easily keep two perspectives in mind, which allows them to communicate more effectively, to consider the views of others, and to anticipate how other people will behave.

The growth of effective communication   A series of studies begun by Robert Krauss and Sam Glucksberg (1969), subsequently replicated with many variations (see Shatz, 1983, for a summary), shows that decreased egocentrism among children during middle childhood can promote effective communication. As described in Chapter 10 (p. 311), these studies have children seated at opposite sides of a table with a barrier preventing them from seeing one another. Each has the same set of figures on the table before them. One child is asked to describe one figure at a time so that the other child can pick it out.

In the Krauss and Glucksberg experimental arrangement, children are often shown novel figures that are difficult to describe with simple labels (see Figure 13.11). Children under the age of 7 typically respond

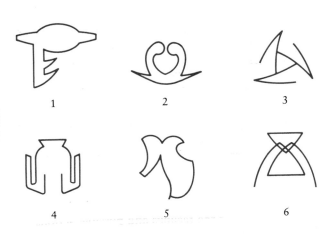

FIGURE 13.11   *Six novel figures used by Krauss and Glucksberg to study the development of communication skills. (From Krauss & Glucksberg, 1969.)*

to this task by choosing labels that are peculiar to their own experience ("It looks like my mommy's hat"). In middle childhood, children realize that they must choose features and labels that will mean something to their listener. They might say, for example, "It looks like a flying saucer with a saw hanging off it." (The reader might check to see if this description is adequate!) Between the ages of 6 and 10, children double the number of features they mention to identify the target item for listeners (Rubin, 1973), indicating their growing ability to take their listeners into account.

Social perspective-taking   Both tests of spatial perspective-taking—such as the "three mountain problem"—and tests of communication require children to think about how objects will be perceived by others. Children must also learn to think about how their actions and ideas will be perceived by others.

Children's understanding of others' social perspectives has been studied by Robert Selman (1976, 1980). Selman asked children to listen to a brief story and then to answer questions posed in a clinical interview format. The following is one of the stories Selman used:

> Holly is an 8-year-old girl who likes to climb trees. She is the best tree climber in the neighborhood. One day while climbing down from a tall tree she falls off the bottom branch but does not hurt her-

self. Her father sees her fall. He is upset and asks her to promise not to climb trees any more. Holly promises.

Later that day, Holly and her friends meet Sean. Sean's kitten is caught up in a tree and cannot get down. Something has to be done right away or the kitten may fall. Holly is the only one who climbs trees well enough to reach the kitten and get it down, but she remembers her promise to her father. (1980, p. 36)

Once the story is read, children are asked to make judgments about the feelings and possible actions of the various characters. The contrasting comments of two children, one a preschooler, one in middle childhood, illustrate these age groups' differing understandings of people's points of view.

A preschooler's understanding:
Q. What do you think Holly will do, save the kitten or keep her promise?
A. She will save the kitten because she doesn't want the kitten to die.
Q. How will her father feel when he finds out?
A. Happy, he likes kittens.
(Selman, 1976, p. 303)

A 9-year-old's understanding:
Q. What punishment does Holly think is fair if she climbs the tree?
A. None.
Q. Why not?
A. She knows that her father will understand why she climbed the tree so she knows that he won't want to punish her at all.
(Selman, 1976, p. 305)

The preschooler clearly fails to take into account that Holly and her father might not have the same point of view. The 9-year-old is aware that each person in the story has a distinct point of view. Moreover, the 9-year-old's answers coordinate the points of view of Holly and her father in a plausible way. Note, however, that the older child still does not systematically take both persons' points of view into account. When children achieve the ability to be systematic, sometime in adolescence, they will find it difficult to say for

certain how Holly's father would react. They will begin to realize that while the father may see Holly's perspective, he may not accept it.

The increase in children's social perspective-taking skills depends in part on their growing ability to consider both behavior and psychological states. This developmental change is evident in a study by Dorothy Flapan (1968), who showed 6- to 12-year-old children an edited version of the commercial film *Our Vines Have Tender Grapes.*

In a key episode of this film, a father punishes his daughter because she refuses to share her roller skates with a neighbor boy. But the father feels uncomfortable about the harshness of his punishment. Later, he seeks to make it up to his daughter by taking her to the circus.

Once the children had viewed the film, Flapan asked them to explain what happened in a scene that takes place after the father has punished his daughter but before he tries to make up for his harshness. Contrast the account of a 6-year-old with that of a 12-year-old.

The 6-year-old's-account:
At the beginning, her daddy was sitting in the chair in the living room looking at the paper, and the little girl got out of her bed and said, "Pa, will you kiss me goodnight?" And the daddy said, "Go to bed," and the little girl went to bed crying. And he tore up the paper and he threw it down on the floor. Then he went into the kitchen and was getting ready to go out to the barn. And the lady said, "Where are you going?" And he said, "Out to the barn." And the lady said, "At this time of the night?" And the man said, "Yes."

The 12-year-old's account:
The father was reading the newspaper, but he was thinking about something else. He couldn't really read it. And the little girl was looking down and asked her father if he didn't want to kiss her good night. The father wanted to say good night, but then he thought she did something bad, so he said, "No. Go back to bed." And the girl was crying and did go back to bed. And the father tried to read the newspaper again, but he couldn't read it, so he threw it away. He wanted to go up to her and say it wasn't so bad. But he decided he better not. So he went to the kitchen and said to his wife he was going out. And the mother said, "I think you just want to be by

yourself." And he said, "Yes." And the mother said, "There is a circus coming to town tonight." I think he is going to go to the circus with the girl now. (Flapan, 1968, pp. 31–32)

The two accounts show a striking difference in their quality. The 6-year-old makes virtually no reference to psychological states, while the 12-year-old provides a plausible interpretation of the father's internal conflict and explains the film's actions in psychological terms.

Cultural Variations in Cognitive Change

So far we have seen that middle childhood brings with it both a change in the complexity of the tasks that adults demand of their children and more sophisticated forms of problem solving in which different aspects of a problem or different points of view are weighed simultaneously. However, we have remained cautious about concluding that such achievements signal a qualitatively new level of cognitive development because even preschoolers demonstrate similar abilities in some circumstances. In addition, researchers have raised questions about the universality of the presumed cognitive changes described in this chapter.

So far, we have concentrated on studies of children in industrialized societies like our own. When psychologists use their standard procedures to test the performance of children from nonindustrial societies,

where literacy and schooling are either absent or have been introduced only in recent decades, they often fail to discover the cognitive changes that appear to be characteristic of the transition to middle childhood in industrialized societies (Dasen, 1972, 1977; Jahoda, 1980).

The possibility that the development of problem solving and memory among nonliterate children follows a different course than among children raised in industrial societies raises a new set of problems about cognitive development in middle childhood. Are the cultural conditions of industrialized countries necessary for the development of the cognitive abilities said to characterize middle childhood? Or do cultural circumstances merely influence the rate at which children proceed through universal stages? Or does the evidence from nonindustrial cultures require a reevaluation of the whole idea of a universal stage of middle childhood (Laboratory of Comparative Human Cognition, 1983)?

Figure 13.12 summarizes the kinds of developmental growth patterns that might be found relating age to cognitive development during childhood. The curves refer specifically to concrete operations, but equivalent curves could be drawn for metamemory, egocentricism, or any cognitive process. The curve labeled *w* (for "Western, technologically sophisticated") represents performance for a sample of children such as those Piaget worked with in Geneva. As these children grow older, more and more of them show that they understand the concepts being tested until the curve levels off at 100 percent.

FIGURE 13.12 *Hypothetical development curves representing the percentage of children who have acquired the concept of concrete operations at varying ages. Curve w is assumed to be the developmental curve for a sample of children from a Western, technological background. Curves a, b, c, and d are possible developmental curves from cross-cultural studies; their interpretation is discussed in the text. (From Dasen & Heron, 1981.)*

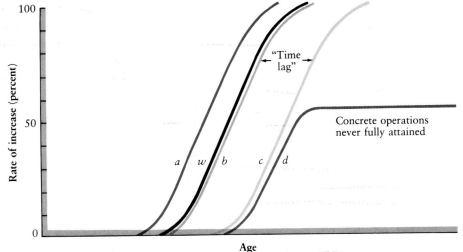

Curves *a, b, c,* and *d* represent possible patterns that one might observe in other cultures. Curves *a, b,* and *c* differ from curve *w* only in the rate of change: curve *a* represents the early acquisition of the concept; *b* represents development at essentially the same rate as the Western norms; *c* represents delayed development by Western standards. Curve *d* is different from the other curves in that not only does the rate vary, but the final level of performance is significantly lower than 100 percent. Were curve *d* to reflect accurately the pattern of acquisition of concrete operations in a society, it would counter the hypothesis that concrete operations are universal, since many people in the hypothetical society represented by curve *d* never reach this stage of understanding at all.

Curves *a, b,* and *c* were the results that Piaget anticipated when he reviewed the meager data available in the mid-1960s, a time when research in other cultures on his theory was just gaining momentum. Piaget (1966) assumed that, owing to their common phylogenetic heritage, people everywhere would eventually attain the level of concrete operations.

A great deal of research has been conducted in other cultures to test these speculations, not only as they apply to concrete operations, but to other cognitive abilities as well (Dasen, 1977; Laboratory of Comparative Human Cognition, 1983). Two of the most frequently studied cognitive abilities are conservation and free recall memory, each of which raises important questions about universal stagelike changes in children's development, the role of culture in development, and standard psychological methods of assessment.

Studies of concrete operations By far the greatest amount of research on cultural variations in cognitive development has been conducted using Piaget's conservation tasks (Dasen, 1977; Dasen & Heron, 1981). In general, this research has found that children from traditional, nonindustrial societies show pattern *c*, a lag of one or more years in the age at which they achieve the stage of concrete operations as compared to children in Western industrialized societies (Dasen, 1972). But in several cultures, investigators have encountered 12- and 13-year-old children and even adults who demonstrated no understanding of the principles underlying conservation in the Piagetian tasks (Dasen, 1977, 1982).

One example is provided by Patricia Greenfield (1966), who conducted a series of conservation studies among Wolof children in the West African nation of Senegal. Following the classical procedure, Greenfield first presented children with two beakers containing equal amounts of liquid, then poured the contents of one beaker into a taller, thinner beaker. Although children did improve somewhat with age, only 50 percent of those 10 to 13 years old showed that they understood that the amount of liquid was not changed when it was poured from one beaker to another.

Greenfield concluded that in traditional Wolof society "intellectual development, defined as *any* qualitative change, ceases shortly after age nine" (1966, p. 234, italics in original). Similar conclusions were drawn from the results of a great many studies of other societies, including studies with adults from cultures as varied as those found in central Australia, New Guinea, the Amazon jungle region of Brazil, and rural Sardinia (Dasen, 1977). Reviewing the evidence available in the early 1970s, Dasen wrote, "It can no longer be assumed that adults of all societies reach the concrete operational stage" (1972, p. 31).

This conclusion was immediately challenged because of its wide-reaching implications. If adults lacked concrete operations, they would be severely handicapped in everyday life. Like preschool-aged children, they would not be able to think through the implications of their actions and would believe that objects changed simply because of their spatial distribution. They would be unable to understand another person's social perspective or to engage in causal reasoning. It would also justify the belief, popular in the nineteenth and early twentieth centuries, that "primitives think like children" (Hallpike, 1979).

Such implications led Gustav Jahoda (1980), a leading cross-cultural psychologist, to reject outright the possibility that in some cultures children did not eventually achieve the ability to think operationally. As Jahoda points out, it is difficult to see how a society could survive if its members were indifferent to causal relations, incapable of thinking through the implications of their actions, or unable to adopt the point of view of others. He concluded that

. . . no society could function at the preoperational stage, and to suggest that a majority of any people are at that level is nonsense almost by definition. (1980, p. 116)

Despite Jahoda's strong statement, words alone do not suffice to settle the questions posed by such research as Greenfield's. If Greenfield and Dasen were incorrect, it would have to be shown that their methods of observation, which seemed straightforward enough, were misrepresenting the state of children's mental capacities.

One plausible source of difficulty in studying other cultures is that the people being tested fail to understand what is expected of them, either because they are unfamiliar with the test situation or because the experimenters do not make their intentions clear in the unfamiliar culture and language. Dasen and his colleagues tackled this problem by training subjects to deal with conservation tasks (Dasen, Ngini, & Lavallée, 1979). They reasoned that if subjects were truly able to engage in concrete operational thinking but did not display it because of unfamiliarity with the tests, training on similar tasks should be sufficient to change their performance.

In a series of studies, the researchers demonstrated that by the end of middle childhood, relatively brief training in procedures similar to the standard conservation task was sufficient to change the pattern of performance on the conservation task itself. One such result is shown in Figure 13.13, taken from the work of Dasen, Ngini, & Lavallée (1979), in which rural aboriginal Australian children are compared with children from the city of Canberra. Without training, half of the aboriginal children appear not to acquire the concept of conservation of quantity at all (curve *d* in Figure 13.12). But when they are sufficiently trained, their test results show that they do understand the basic concept of conservation of quantity. Even with training, the aboriginal children exhibit curve *c* in Figure 13.12: they lag behind children from Canberra, in their acquisition of the concept of conservation by approximately 3 years, suggesting that their culture does not provide practice that is relevant to this concept.

Research by African psychologists suggests that specialized training may actually be unnecessary and that no lags will appear if the researchers are from the same culture as the children they are testing and know the local language well. Psychologists native to the culture are able to follow the flexible questioning procedures that are the hallmark of Piaget's clinical interviews, procedures that seem to be more effective in bringing out children's best performance than are training studies.

Raphael Nyiti (1982) for example, compared performances on a conservation task of 10- and 11-year-old children from two different cultural groups, both living on Cape Breton, Nova Scotia. Some of the children were from English-speaking European backgrounds and some were from Micmac Indian backgrounds. The Indian children all spoke Micmac in the home, but they had spoken English in school since the

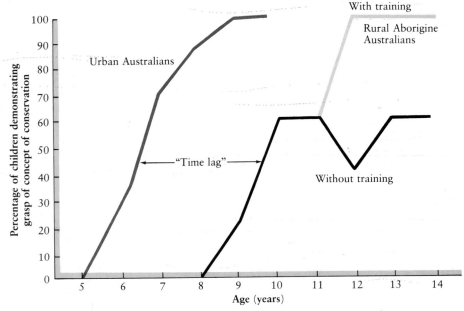

FIGURE 13.13 *Actual development curves for the development of the concept of conservation of liquid, showing that rural Aborigine Australians lag behind urban children from European backgrounds. Without training, 50 percent of the aboriginal children as old as 14 years failed to demonstrate a grasp of the concept of conservation. (From Dasen, Ngini, & Lavalleé, 1979.)*

first grade. The children from European backgrounds were all interviewed in English by an English speaker of European background. The Indian children were interviewed in English once and Micmac once.

The results of Nyiti's experiment clearly suggest that inadequate communication between researchers and children can be the source of apparent developmental lags in children of some cultures. When all children were interviewed in their native languages, there was no difference at all in the results of the two cultural groups. But when the Indian children were interviewed in English, they seemed to understand the concept of conservation only half as often as the children from European backgrounds, creating a large gap in performance between the two cultural groups. Nyiti (1976) obtained similar results in a study of children in his native Tanzania as did other researchers in the West African country of Sierra Leone (Kamara & Easley, 1977).

There are also cases in which children from nonindustrial societies appear to make a cognitive transition *earlier* than the industrialized norm (curve *a* in Figure 13.12). This occurs when the tasks used to assess cognitive development tap more closely into the nonindustrialized society's experience. For example, Jahoda (1983) studied the development of the concept of profit, which has been shown to develop through several Piagetian-like stages. Jahoda arranged for 107 fourth- to sixth-graders from the central African country of Zimbabwe and 48 Scotch children the same age to act as shopkeepers in several mock business transactions. This task was assumed to be closer to the experience of the Zimbabwean children, who all had helped their parents with marketing and for whom trading was part of their way of life.

Some transactions given in the hypothetical problems involved selling goods such as cloth or rice from a "store"; others required buying goods from a supplier. The main question was whether the children would know that they needed to sell the goods for more than they had paid for them, thereby demonstrating their understanding of the concept of profit. Jahoda hypothesized that the Scotch children would lag behind the children from Zimbabwe because they had had less experience buying and selling at a profit. This was exactly what he found: fully 84 percent of the Zimbabwean children displayed full or partial understanding of the concept, compared to only 45 percent of the Scottish children.

Taken as a whole, recent evidence appears to dem-

Children who are potters gain an understanding of the concept of conservation of quantity earlier than children the same age who do not have experience manipulating a material like clay. These children live in India.

onstrate that when Piaget's clinical procedures are properly applied, concrete operations *are* a universal cognitive achievement of middle childhood, just as Piaget (1966) assumed they were. However, there are quite dramatic cultural variations in children's familiarity with content and testing procedures, and these variations clearly influence children's performances (Greenfield, 1976; Jahoda, 1980; Laboratory of Comparative Human Cognition, 1983).

Studies of memory Cross-cultural studies of memory call the universality of cognitive developments into question in a somewhat different way (Rogoff, 1982). As in the conservation studies, research on memory shows that children's familiarity with materials and procedures influences their performance. But unlike the conservation studies, when familiarity is arranged for, there still remains a difference in the kind of remembering that takes place.

For example, Michael Cole and his colleagues (Cole, Gay, Glick, & Sharp, 1971; Cole & Scribner, 1974) studied the development of memory among tribal people living in rural Liberia. To overcome the barriers of language and culture, these researchers observed everyday cognitive activities before conducting their experiments and worked closely with the college-educated local people who acted as the experimenters. Even with these precautions, they found striking cultural differences in the way that tribal people went about remembering and problem solving in their experimental tasks.

The nature of these cultural differences can be illustrated by studies of the development of *free recall* memory. In a free recall task people are shown a large number of objects, one at a time, and then asked to remember them. This kind of memory is called "free" recall because people are free to recall the items in any order they wish.

Below is a list of a set of objects used in several of these studies. The list shows that the objects appear to fall into four distinct categories. To make certain that this appearance was not simply the imposition of American categories on Liberian reality, preliminary investigations were made to ensure that Liberian subjects were familiar with the items used and that they readily grouped these items into the four categories indicated in the list (Cole, Gay, Glick, & Sharp, 1971).

Plate	Cutlass
Calabash	Hoe
Pot	Knife
Pan	File
Cup	Hammer
Potato	Trousers
Onion	Singlet
Banana	Headtie
Orange	Shirt
Coconut	Hat

The researchers found that compared to children in industrial societies, there was no regular increase in memory performance over the middle childhood years among the Liberians — unless they had attended several years of school. Among the nonschooled people, there was little improvement in performance on these tasks after the age of 9 or 10. These subjects remembered approximately 10 items on the first trial, which only increased to about 12 items after 15 practice trials. By contrast, the Liberian children who were attending school learned the materials rapidly in a manner similar to that of schoolchildren the same age in the United States.

Important clues about the sources of this variation came from detailed analyses of the order in which words were recalled. Educated children from Liberia and the United States not only learned the list rapidly,

they used the categorical similarities of items in the list to aid their recall. Following the first trial, they clustered their responses, recalling first, say, the items of clothing, then the items of food, and so on. The nonschooled Liberian subjects displayed very little such clustering, indicating that they were not using the categorical structure of the list to help them remember.

To track down the source of this difference, the researchers varied aspects of the task. They found that if, instead of a list of objects presented in random order, the same objects were presented in a meaningful way as part of a story, their nonschooled Liberian subjects recalled them easily, clustering the objects according to the role that they played in the story.

Similar results on tests of children's memorization skills have been obtained in research among Mayan people of rural Guatemala. When presented with a free recall task, Mayan children's performance lagged considerably behind the performance levels of age-mates living in the United States (Kagan, Klein, Finley, Rogoff, & Nolan, 1979). However, their performance changed dramatically when Barbara Rogoff and Kathryn Waddell (1982) gave them a memory task that was meaningful in local terms.

Rogoff and Waddell constructed a diorama of a Mayan village located near a mountain and a lake, similar to the locale in which the children lived. Each child watched as a local experimenter selected 20 miniature objects from a set of 80 and placed them in the diorama. The objects included cars, animals, people, and furniture — just the kinds of things that would be found in a real town. Then the 20 objects were returned to the group of 60 others remaining on the table. After a few minutes, the children were asked to reconstruct the full scene they had been shown. Under these conditions, the memory performance of the Mayan children was slightly superior to that of their United States counterparts.

These memory studies have a different implication than do the cross-cultural studies of concrete operational thinking. The basic mental operations studied by Piaget and his followers are presumed to reflect the logic underlying everyday actions in any culture. Being able to remember is also a universal intellectual requirement, but specific forms of remembering are not universal. Those forms of memory most often studied by psychologists are more or less associated with formal schooling.

Schooling presents children with specialized information-processing tasks such as committing large amounts of information to memory in a short time, learning to manipulate abstract symbols in one's head and on paper, using logic to conduct experiments, and many more tasks that have few if any analogies in societies without formal schooling. The free recall task that Cole and his colleagues initially used to assess memory among Liberian tribal people has no precise analogy in traditional Liberian cultures, so it is not surprising that the corresponding way of remembering would not be acquired.

The same conclusion applies to the vast majority of tasks psychologists use to assess other mental transformations that occur in middle childhood. Such tasks embody forms of activity that are specific to certain kinds of settings, especially schools and the modern technological workplace, settings that occur only in certain cultures. Performance on these tasks can be expected to be closely related to children's experience in school, but the relationship of these tasks to other contexts of development is still poorly understood (Rogoff & Lave, 1984).

Is middle childhood a universal stage of development? The evidence presented thus far provides a mixed picture with respect to middle childhood as a distinctive stage of development. The changes in adult behavior toward children that propel them into new activity contexts and an increase in biological capaci-

ties (including greater physical strength, dexterity, and perhaps a more complex brain structure) seem to occur during the years from 5 to 7 everywhere. However, because the kinds of contexts into which children are put and the skills that they are expected to acquire there differ markedly from one culture to the next, it is more difficult to determine whether the cognitive changes associated with middle childhood in some cultures are universal.

These complexities require us to withhold judgment on the competing views about the distinctiveness of middle childhood. First, it is necessary to examine the special context of schooling, which is so important to growing up in industrialized countries. What are the cognitive demands specific to schooling? Is it possible that mastery of school-based tasks is essential to produce basic changes in the way children think? Second, it is necessary to look into the kinds of activities that go on in peer groups, where children in middle childhood begin to spend so much of their time. Piaget, among others, argued that experiences in peer groups are crucial to the cognitive changes he associated with middle childhood. What is the evidence to support such a claim? Once we have a more well-rounded picture of children's experience in these different contexts, we can return to examine the central issue of the distinctiveness of middle childhood and the forms of thought that characterize it.

SUMMARY

1. The bio-social-behavioral shift that signals the onset of middle childhood is seen in cultures around the world when adults begin to assign children tasks that take them away from adult supervision and hold them responsible for their own actions. This reorientation in adult behavior implies an increase in children's physical capacities, in their ability to follow instructions, and in their ability to keep track of what they are doing.

2. Around the start of middle childhood, the cerebral cortex reaches approximately adult size. This increase in growth is accounted for in part by myelination of pathways between different brain areas, which is accompanied by changes in the basic electrical activity patterns of the brain.

3. Increased lateralization of complex behaviors during middle childhood may play a role in the improvement of children's motor coordination.

4. It is widely speculated that changes in brain capacity are associated with distinctive cognitive changes during middle childhood, but there is little direct evidence to confirm these speculations.

5. Changes in memory associated with middle childhood are manifested in children's increased capacity to hold several items of information in mind at one time (storage capacity), the use of mental strategies such as rehearsal and organization of the material to be remembered into meaningful chunks, the ability to think about remem-

bering, and the development of a relevant knowledge base.

6. Evidence of a discontinuous change in the quality of remembering between early and middle childhood is accompanied by evidence that many of the accomplishments of middle childhood can be seen during early childhood in simplified and carefully supported contexts.

7. Piaget believed that around the age of 7 children begin to think in terms of concrete operations, which permit them to combine, separate, reorder, and transform objects mentally. The advent of concrete operations is said to be manifested in the following ways:

   a. The performance of conservation tasks in which the appearance of objects is changed, although their quantity, or some other feature, remains the same.

   b. The classification of objects according to multiple criteria. Multiple classification enables children to think more systematically about the relation of one object to another.

   c. The ability to perceive multiple objects in specially constructed pictures in which the objects in question are made up of many distracting elements.

   d. The ability to adopt another person's perceptual point of view.

   e. The ability to communicate effectively about objects not visible to the person who is receiving the message.

   f. The ability to adopt other people's social perspectives and to understand their intentions.

8. Cross-cultural research often reveals cases in which children in middle childhood fail to display the changes in mental abilities that are characteristic of children in industrialized societies.

9. Cross-cultural differences on Piagetian conservation problems disappear when the subjects are provided special training or when the studies are conducted by experimenters who are familiar with the language and culture of the people studied.

10. There are sizable variations in memory performance differentiating nonschooled people from those who attend school. These differences are most evident when the materials to be remembered are randomly constructed lists of things, or items whose relationship to each other does not fit everyday patterns of activity. However, when memory is tested using materials organized in meaningful ways, there is no discernible difference in performance across cultures.

11. Cross-cultural evidence on cognitive development indicates that culture-specific contexts are important contributors to development during middle childhood. Study of schooling and peer groups is key to resolving questions about development in middle childhood.

KEY TERMS

Compensation	Lateralization	Rehearsal
Concrete operations	Memory organization	Reversibility
Conservation	Memory strategies	Social perspective-taking
Identity	Metamemory	
Knowledge base	Negation	

SUGGESTED READINGS

COLLINS, W. ANDREW (Ed.). *Development During Middle Childhood.* Washington, D.C.: National Academy Press, 1984.

This volume summarizing the status of basic research on children from 6 to 12 years of age was produced for the National Research Council. Individual essays focus on biological, behavioral, and social factors in development, as well as the important contexts of middle childhood—the family, the school, and the peer group.

KAIL, ROBERT. *The Development of Memory in Children,* Second Edition. New York: W. H. Freeman and Company, 1984.

A clear description of such important issues in the development of memory as the use of strategies, the growth of the ability to think about and monitor one's own memory, and the role of increasing knowledge of the ability to remember.

LABORATORY OF COMPARATIVE HUMAN COGNITION. "Culture and Cognitive Development." In P. Mussen (Ed.), *Handbook of Child Development. Vol. 1: History, Theory, and Methods.* New York: Wiley, 1983.

A thorough review of research on cognitive development in different cultures, focusing on middle childhood. In addition to information on cultural variability in cognitive development, the work explores the methodological problems of assessing memory and problem solving when children do not share a common cultural heritage with the experimenter and test constructor.

PIAGET, JEAN. *The Child's Conception of Number.* New York: Humanities Press, 1952.

The classic discussion of the logic of the conservation experiments as crucial evidence in the transformation from preoperational to concrete operational thinking. In addition, the book provides rich detail on Piaget's use of the clinical method as a means of studying cognitive development.

ROGOFF, BARBARA, and LAVE, JEAN (Eds.). *Everyday Cognition: Its Development in Social Context.* Cambridge, Mass.: Harvard University Press, 1984.

Essays by psychologists and other social scientists examining the impact of context on the process of cognitive development. The book also contains suggestions for ways to modify methods for studying children in order to take the role of context into account for the purpose of psychological assessments.

SCHOOLING AND DEVELOPMENT IN MIDDLE CHILDHOOD

I spent that first day picking holes in paper, then went home in a smoldering temper.

"What's the matter, Love? Didn't he like it at school, then?"

"They never gave me the present."

"Present? What present?"

"They said they'd give me a present."

"Well, now, I'm sure they didn't."

"They did! They said: 'You're Laurie Lee, aren't you? Well you just sit there for the present.' I sat there all day but I never got it. I ain't going back there again."

— Laurie Lee, *Cider with Rosie*

. . . .

In the United States, where going to school is a legal obligation from age 6 to 16, the activities that children engage in at school have a central role in defining the characteristics of their middle childhood. For nine months of the year, five days a week, children spend five to seven hours listening to teachers, answering questions, reading from books, writing essays, solving arithmetic problems in workbooks, taking tests, and generally "being educated." Before they take their places as adult workers, most young Americans will have spent more than 15,000 hours in classrooms.

In order to determine the influence of schooling on children's overall development, we need to address a series of important questions:

1. What is the nature of school as a context for children's development and under what historical conditions do schools arise?

2. How does learning in school differ from learning in other contexts?

3. How does schooling influence cognitive development?

4. What special abilities does schooling require and what factors account for school success?

Answers to these questions have far-reaching significance in modern societies. In terms of individual development, children who fail to thrive in school or who drop out must look forward to less interesting and less secure work as well as to substantially lower incomes than children who meet our society's expectations by completing high school (Sexton, 1961). De-spite the importance of adequate education, many millions of young people in the United States do not thrive in school. In the opinion of policy makers, the resulting low levels of literacy and mathematics skills jeopardize the country's ability to compete effectively in the international arena (Educational Testing Service, 1988; U.S. Department of Education, 1983). As a result of these concerns, the study of learning and development in school contexts is one of the most active areas of research in developmental psychology.

THE CONTEXTS IN WHICH SKILLS ARE TAUGHT

In Chapter 11 we examined socialization in the family, concentrating on the ways that young children are raised to acquire the basic knowledge, skills, and beliefs essential in their community. Socialization is a universal human process; as far as anyone knows, it has always been a part of human experience everywhere. That some form of preparation in the skills necessary to adult life begins in the years between 5 and 7 also appears to be universal. What is not universal is the specific content of the preparation and the way in which it is organized. Although formal schooling is an enduring fact of life in the United States and other industrialized countries, it is only one of several ways in which societies have transmitted adult skills to their young.

Education refers to a form of socialization in which adults engage in *deliberate teaching* of the young to ensure the acquisition of specialized knowledge and skills. It is not known if education existed among the hunter-gatherer people who roamed the earth tens of thousands of years ago, but in contemporary hunter-gatherer cultures, deliberate teaching is not a conspicuous part of socialization (LeVine, 1974). Among the !Kung Bushmen of Africa's Kalahari desert, for example, basic skill training is embedded in everyday activity:

> [T]here is . . . very little explicit teaching. . . . What the child knows, he learns from direct interaction with the adult community, whether it is learning to tell the age of the spoor left by a poisoned kudu buck, to straighten the shaft of an arrow, to build a fire, or to dig a spring hare out of its burrow. . . . It is all implicit. (Bruner, 1966, p. 59)

When societies achieve a certain degree of complexity in the tools they use and in the ways they secure food and housing, socialization for certain occupations is likely to take the form of an apprenticeship, in which a novice spends an extended period of time working for an adult master and learning the trade on the job (Childs & Greenfield, 1980; Goody, 1978; Lave, 1977). Unlike modern schools, the settings in which apprenticeship education occurs are not organized primarily for the purposes of teaching. Rather, instruction and productive labor are combined; from the beginning, apprentices contribute to the work process.

Several of apprenticeship's distinctive features follow directly from the fact that the apprentice participates in the work. For example, in a study of apprentice tailors in Monrovia, Liberia, Jean Lave (1977) found that apprentices might have a hand in producing complex forms of clothing, with the level of their contribution scaled to the level of their expertise. The novice begins by cleaning the shop, running errands, and learning how to use a needle, thread, tape measure, and other tools. Practice is then ordered by the master in easy stages to include sewing buttonholes, cutting cloth for inexpensive items like hats and shorts, and finally, the more difficult jobs of making gowns and suits.

Apprenticeship for tailoring is likely to contain little explicit instruction. Instead, the novices are given ample opportunity to observe others who are more

Apprenticeship remains an important form of education, despite the spread of classroom-based formal schooling.

skilled and to practice specific tasks. As the novices gain skills, the master turns over responsibility for more and more of the work until they are ready to go out on their own and become masters.

In many societies, the apprentice's relationship with the master is part of a larger web of family relationships. Sometimes the master is a relative who takes on the training of the novice in exchange for the novice's parents training one of the master's children. Often the child lives with the master and does farming or household chores to help pay for his upkeep. In this way the tasks of socialization, community-building, and education are woven together.

Although on-the-job-training remains important in the industrialized world, it has been surpassed by formal schooling as the primary form of education. Schooling differs both from informal instruction in family settings and from apprenticeship training in four main ways (Greenfield & Lave, 1982; Scribner & Cole, 1973).

First, the *motives* for learning are different. When students begin school, they must work for years to perfect their skills before these are put to any practical use. By contrast, apprentice tailors are present for the entire process of making a garment. They do not go through a long period of training without any notion of how the skills they are learning fit into the overall logic of the activity.

Second, the *social relations* of child and teacher differ from those of apprentice and master. Schoolteachers are assigned a carefully prescribed role in their pupils' upbringing that separates education from real-life economic contributions. The teacher is likely to be a stranger who has been hired as an "educational expert." In the United States, for example, it is not uncommon to find a white, middle-class adult from the suburbs teaching in an inner-city classroom with predominantly Hispanic pupils. The social background and values of the teacher may thus differ substantially from those of the families who send their children to school.

Third, the *social organization* of schooling also differs from that of a workshop in which there are people of diverse ages passing through and more skilled people working by the apprentice's side who can assist at crucial junctures. At school, children usually find themselves in large rooms in the company of other children all about the same age and with only one adult present. They are expected to work individually, rather than cooperatively, or risk being labeled as "cheaters."

Mastery of written symbol systems is the focus of most early education.

Fourth, the *medium* of formal schooling is distinctive. Instruction outside of school is usually conducted in spoken language in the context of the everyday activities of life. Although oral language remains important to formal schooling, the essence of schooling is learning about the world through the manipulation of *written symbols*.

In order to gain a deeper understanding of the distinctive nature of formal schooling as a context for development during middle childhood we need to examine more closely the historical development of literacy, numeracy, and schooling, as well as the special language of schooling. Knowing more about the social conditions that give rise to schooling and the distinctive ways that children learn about the world through written symbols in such contexts will help us to understand what the developmental consequences of schooling might be and why many children have so much trouble in school settings.

THE NATURE OF SCHOOL LEARNING

Literacy and numeracy are direct extensions of the mediating capacity of language. Sounds disappear as soon as they are spoken and even the loudest speakers can only project their voices over a short distance. The essential advantage shared by all written notation systems is that they extend the power of language in time and space (Goody, 1977, 1987). Words that are written down can be carried great distances with no change in their physical characteristics. Writing freezes words in time; once written down, ideas and events can be returned to and thought about time and again in their original form. In this respect, written notations are a form of memory. Available evidence indicates that writing systems are a recent human achievement that is closely associated historically with the rise of large civilizations (Larsen, 1986; Pfeiffer, 1977).

The Development of Literacy and Schooling

The remains of some of the earliest permanent settlements of human beings are found in that part of the world now called the Middle East. A settled life per-

FIGURE 14.1 *These tokens, found in the Middle East and dating from 10,000 B.C., are believed to be the earliest precursors of literacy. The shapes of the tokens and the marks on them indicate the identity and quantity of different objects. (From Schmandt-Besserat, 1978.)*

sides themselves. This fact made possible a substantial division of labor and the development of city-states.

With the development of early cities, token-based record-keeping systems rapidly expanded, allowing kings to monitor the wealth of their lands, the size of their armies, and the tax payments of their subjects. As the number of tokens increased, the entire system became cumbersome. To solve this problem, people began to draw pictures of the tokens on clay tablets, instead of using the tokens themselves (see Figure 14.2). This practice gave rise to *cuneiform writing* (cuneiform means, literally, "wedge-shaped," referring to the shape of the symbols etched in clay) (Larson, 1986; Schmandt-Besserat, 1978).

This transformation in the medium of recording made possible a crucial change in how people began to relate inscribed symbols to objects. The tokens literally stood for objects, and the earliest cuneiform writing retained pictures of the tokens as part of its nota-

mitted people to accumulate surplus goods to trade for things they could not grow or make themselves (Pfeiffer, 1977). In such early, predominantly agricultural villages, archeologists discovered the first precursors of modern literacy: small clay tokens, such as those depicted in Figure 14.1.

In a primitive way, these tokens served the fundamental purposes of writing systems. They regulated people's interactions with the physical world and with each other (Schmandt-Besserat, 1978). Because the tokens stood for actual objects, they enabled people to keep track of their goods over time without having to count them over and over again; because the tokens were small and sturdy, they could be carried from place to place as a kind of "promissory note" for purposes of trade. In either case, they were artificial signs that represented natural objects, allowing people to keep track of their economic and social activities more effectively.

The system of tokens remained unchanged for several thousand years until about 4,000 B.C., when people discovered a means of smelting bronze that revolutionized their economic and social lives. With bronze, plows could be used to till the earth more deeply, extensive irrigation canals could be built, and armies could be equipped with more effective weapons. For the first time, one portion of a population could grow enough food to support a large number of others be-

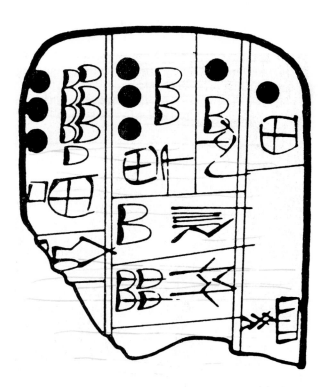

FIGURE 14.2 *The earliest writings were symbols etched on clay tablets. This tablet records information about a herd of sheep. It is thought to be the annual account of a shepherd, who records that of the 33 sheep in the herd, 12 gave birth to lambs, 2 were taken away for some reason, and 4 died. (From Strauss, 1988.)*

tion system. But when complicated transactions began to occur in the newly complex political and economic conditions of cities, the need arose to represent *relationships* among objects (such as "owe" or "paid") as well as objects themselves. In these conditions, a revolutionary discovery was made: It is possible to represent the sounds of language using marks in clay just as it is possible to represent objects.

The new system of cuneiform writing that resulted from this discovery could only be mastered after long and systematic study. But so important was this new system of written communication that societies began to devote resources to support selected young men with the explicit purpose of making them *scribes*, people who could write. The places where young men were brought together for this purpose were the earliest schools.

Activities in these early schools were in some ways specific to the societies in which they arose, and in other ways startlingly modern. As in modern schools, students were asked to copy out lists containing the names of various objects their teachers deemed important (see Table 14.1). In addition to learning the rudiments of writing and reading, these early students learned the record-keeping procedures they would use as civil servants once they graduated.

Children in modern elementary schools still make lists, although they are more likely to be lists of U.S. presidents or the spelling words in which *e* comes before *i*. But the purposes to which this practice is put, and the presumed advantages to be gained from such education, remain much the same as they were in the schools of ancient Babylonia. In addition to the financial benefits that derive from schooling, the ancients also believed that there was power to be had from the knowledge it produced. The basis of this knowledge is the ability to read, write, and solve problems in the economic and social spheres of life. As one father admonished his son, several thousand years ago,

I have seen how the belaboured man is belaboured —thou shouldst set thy heart in pursuit of writing. . . . Behold, there is nothing which surpasses writing. . . .

I have seen the metalworker at his work at the mouth of his furnace. His fingers were somewhat like crocodiles; he stank more than fish-roe. . . .

The small building contractor carries mud . . . . He is dirtier than vines or pigs from treading under his mud. His clothes are stiff with clay. . . .

Behold, there is no profession free of a boss— except for the scribe: he is the boss. . . .

Behold, there is no scribe who lacks food from the property of the House of the King—life, prosperity, health! . . . (Quoted in Donaldson, 1978, pp. 84–85)

TABLE 14.1   List-learning in school: ancient and modern

Ancient Lists		Modern Lists	
Subject	Number of Items	Subject	Number of Items
Trees	84	Presidents of the U.S.	40
Stones	12	States of the union	50
Gods	9	Capitals of the states	50
Officials	8	Elements in the periodic table	105
Cattle	8	Planets in the solar system	9
Reeds	8		
Personal names	6		
Animals	5		
Leather objects	4		
Fields	3		
Garments	3		
Words compounded with *gar*	3		
Chairs	3		

SOURCE: Goody, 1977.

Literacy and Schooling in Modern Times

Evidence from the Middle East and other ancient civilizations indicates that once literacy and numeracy become central to the functioning of society, schooling arises as a means of ensuring that children master the new technologies for representing and communicating information (Gelb, 1963; Goody, 1987).

For centuries, the tradition of literacy and schooling in the Western world spread only slowly beyond the children of the elite. Not until the nineteenth century, in response to the industrial revolution, did nations begin to institute mandatory schooling and mass literacy.

The spread of schooling in the past two centuries has created a distinctive set of problems. Two hundred years ago, when mass literacy programs were in their infancy, there were two kinds of education. "Higher education" included some mastery of classical literature and the rudiments of geometry and algebra; it was intended for a small elite. A tutor was hired to see that the children of the wealthy gained a degree of learning equal to their status in life. These children received individual attention and as much explanation as the tutor could provide.

The education provided to the mass of people was quite different. It enabled them to recite from the Bible or the Koran and to calculate simple sums, but it was not intended to provide them with a general education as we understand that term today. The fact that teachers were confronted by 20, 40, or, in some cases, 50 students instead of one or two produced a quite different form of instruction, one based largely on drill and practice combined with oral imitation of the teacher (Resnick & Resnick, 1977). Today, many societies expect all their children to attain a level of education that was once reserved for small elites, but these children are still expected to do so in large classes in which there is little if any individual instruction.

In two respects, the task facing children in the modern classroom is far more difficult than the task faced by their ancient predecessors in the Middle East. First, owing to the advent of literacy some six thousand years ago, human knowledge has been accumulating far more rapidly than in all the prior history of *Homo sapiens*. While civilizations waxed and waned, science and technology continued to accumulate, adding immeasurably to the lessons that children were asked to master as part of "the basics." Second, the mode of representing knowledge has undergone fundamental

INFANT CLASS AT THE FIVE POINTS MISSION, NEW YORK CITY—RECEIVING LUNCH.

In the early decades of mass education, schools were motivated by a desire to control the children of the poor and to teach them habits of piety and industry, in addition to teaching basic numeracy and literacy skills.

changes that have made reading and writing a more complex undertaking.

Development of the Alphabet

When the practice of cuneiform writing began to take hold, pictures representing objects came to be supplemented by written symbols representing language (Larsen, 1986). Since, as noted in Chapter 9, language is a representation of reality, writing became a representation of a representation of reality.

Methods of representing language have developed differently in different parts of the world. In some societies symbols were developed to correspond to each distinct concept, while in other societies the system of representation focused on units of sound (Gelb, 1963). Each representational strategy has certain costs and benefits to users (Hatano, 1987). Here we will concentrate on the system in use in most of the world's societies, a system that is descended from cuneiform and that focuses on the representation of sound.

The first written symbols that stood for units of sound corresponded to syllables. Thus, a word such as "lackadaisical" would be written using six symbols corresponding to "lack-a-dai-si-cal." This kind of writing continued in use for about 2000 years. The process of creating a representation system for language sounds reached what many consider its height around the seventh century B.C. when the Greeks hit upon a system to represent each significant sound variant *(phoneme)* with a single symbol (Havelock, 1982; Logan, 1986).

A phoneme-based writing system might seem very inconvenient. The word "lackadaisical," for example, is written using a total of 13 symbols. But in fact the system, which came to be called the *alphabet* (after two alphabetic characters representing two phonemes in the Greek language, *alpha* and *beta),* enabled spoken language to be represented using only 26 basic symbols and a few punctuation marks. By contrast, there are more than 8000 basic syllables in English. Representing each with its own symbol would make mastery of written English a formidable task indeed! However, phonemes are themselves abstractions; they cannot easily be pronounced in isolation, but only in combinations that we perceive as syllables.

Learning to Read

How do today's children master such a complex representational system? Jean Chall (1983), a leading authority on reading, suggests that children go through six stages in learning to incorporate the system of representation we know as alphabetic writing into the process of gaining information about the world.

Stage 0. Prereading: Birth to age 6 Children arrive at school already skilled in many of the elements of reading. For several years they have been "reading" in the broad sense of being able to interpret events on the basis of partial signs. They know that when they see the car in the driveway, their mother is home from work, and that the stormy look on their father's face means they should stay out of the way until his mood brightens. They can also "read" in the more conventional sense of identifying the logo of their favorite fast-food restaurant, and they may have acquired knowledge about some properties of words, such as that some words have the same beginnings or endings (alliteration, rhyme); that words can be broken into parts; and that word parts can be put together in various combinations. If they are read to, children may

also learn that books are the source of good stories and adult attention. But with few exceptions, preschoolers cannot read in the sense of scanning alphabetic print and interpreting what it says.

Stage 1. Decoding: Grades 1 – 2, ages 6 – 7 The basic task of Stage 1 is to learn the arbitrary set of letters and to "decode" the way in which they correspond to the sounds of spoken language, (e.g., that the symbol *a* stands for the sound *a).* This process is far more complex than it may appear. Although even very small children can say their ABC's, that is not the same as knowing how alphabets represent languages. When children recite the alphabet, they are pronouncing the names of letters; they are not making sounds that they recognize as representing parts of words.

One difficulty in teaching children to read stems from the fact that although teachers can illustrate properties of word sounds by pronouncing whole words or syllables, they cannot communicate directly about phonemes. Suppose, for example, that you ask a child to say the multisyllabic word *cat-er-pil-lar.* After each attempt, ask for a slower pronunciation. The result will be something like this:

caterpillar
caaaterrpiiilarr
caaaaaat   eerrrr   piiiiiiil   laaarrrrrrr

Learning letter-sound correspondences so that written symbols can be decoded to find the corresponding sounds is one of the essential tasks confronting beginning readers.

The word takes longer and longer to say, but most significantly, it breaks down into parts corresponding to syllables. It does not, and cannot, break down in such a way that *c* is pronounced separately from *a*, which is pronounced separately from *t* and so on.

Faced with this problem, the teacher may start out with a short word such as *cat* and attempt to illustrate the sounds corresponding to the pattern of letters. Although children may have learned the names of each of the letters, "cee" "aaa," and "tee," this learning may not help much. No matter how quickly the children pronounce these *names* in sequence, the result will not be the sound blend that renders *c-a-t* into *cat*.

Somehow, the child must grasp the fact that while *t* remains *t*, it is not pronounced the same way when encountered in the words *tea* and *both,* while such seemingly different letters as *g* and *f* can be used to produce very similar sounds, as in *muff* and *tough*.* Similar lessons must be mastered for the entire alphabet.

Stage 2. Confirmation, fluency, ungluing from print: Grades 2–3, ages 7–8 During this stage, new readers confirm and solidify the gains of the previous stage. They move from relatively halting and uncertain application of their decoding skills to rapid and fluent decoding. They no longer read letter by letter or word by word, and they can begin to think about the topic while they are reading about it, the process that Chall refers to as "ungluing." However, their reading is restricted to texts that they know well.

Stage 3. Reading for learning something new: Grades 4–8, ages 9–14 According to Chall, children in the primary grades learn to read, while in secondary school they read to learn:

> During Stages 1 and 2 what is learned concerns more the relating of print to speech while Stage 3 involves more the relating of print to ideas. Very little new information about the world is learned from reading before Stage 3; more is learned from listening and watching. It is with the beginning of Stage 3 that

reading begins to compete with these other means of knowing. (1983, pp. 20–21)

Early in the twentieth century, reading at Stage 3 was believed to occur from the "bottom up": letters that compose words are first sounded out, thereby giving access to individual word meanings; these are then added together to produce the meaning of phrases, sentences, paragraphs, and so on. A good deal of research in recent years has demonstrated that such "bottom up" processes are only half of the story (Chall, 1983; National Academy of Education, 1985; Resnick & Weaver, 1979). In order to read at the Stage 3 level, information from words and phrases must simultaneously be integrated with the reader's prior knowledge. Interpretation based upon prior knowledge is often referred to as "top down" processing because it begins with general knowledge that becomes increasingly focused as the reader combines it with "bottom up" information from letters and words.

The kind of "top down" information needed for meaningful reading is illustrated by the following two passages. Although the words in each are of roughly equivalent difficulty (i.e., the "bottom" components are similar), note how much more difficult it is to understand the second passage:

Passage 1: When Mary arrived at the restaurant, the woman at the door greeted her and checked for her name. A few minutes later, Mary was escorted to her chair and was shown the day's menu. The attendant was helpful but brusque, almost to the point of being rude. However, her meal was excellent, especially the main course. Later she paid the woman at the door and left.

Passage 2: The procedure is really quite simple. First you arrange items into different groups. Of course, one pile may be sufficient depending on how much there is to do. If you have to go somewhere else due to lack of facilities that is the next step, otherwise you are pretty well set. It is important not to overdo things. That is, it is better to do too few things at once than too many. In the short run this may not seem important but complications can easily arise. A mistake can be expensive as well. . . . After the procedure is completed, one arranges the materials into different groups again. Then they can be put into their appropriate places.

---

* A famous example of the alphabet's complex relationship to spoken English is attributed to the British writer George Bernard Shaw (1963), who suggested that the word "fish" be written *ghoti*. This apparently peculiar spelling is derived as follows: pronounce *gh* as in "cough"
    pronounce *o* as in "women"
    pronounce *ti* as in "nation"

Eventually they will be used once more and the whole cycle will then have to be repeated. (Bransford, 1979, p. 135)

The first passage is easy to comprehend because we realize that it is about a restaurant. We have well-worked-out scripts for restaurants (see Chapter 10) that allow us to anticipate what is happening, thereby providing "top down" constraints on our reading of the passage. The second passage is harder to read because it lacks a "top down" specification of what it is about. You can verify this difference by trying to remember, without looking back, what the second passage says. However, as soon as you are told that the passage is about "washing clothes" the separate sentences fall into place and the passage is easily interpreted. If readers cannot imagine what a passage is

about, even if they can decode all of the words, the act of interpretation that is crucial to true reading does not occur.

When children are just learning to read, all three aspects of the process — "low-level" text information, "high-level" general information, and the act of combining the two to produce an interpretation — can be serious sources of difficulty. If children do not know how to assign letters to sounds, they may struggle over the interpretation of specific words letter by letter ("c-c-che-check"). As the child struggles with the letter-sound correspondences, the knowledge that the passage is about a restaurant experience may be momentarily forgotten, allowing children to substitute, for example, *cheek* for *check*. It takes few such misreadings to cause a child to become confused and discouraged, making further reading difficult indeed.

Stage 4. Multiple viewpoints: Grades 9–12, ages 15–18 This is the kind of reading expected in high school courses. Various theories and facts are juxtaposed and the reader must reconcile the different viewpoints in order to interpret a text's meaning.

Stage 5. Construction and reconstruction: Post-secondary level At this stage, readers are doing more than learning what the writer has to say. They are engaged in their own process of knowledge construction in which written texts become aids in solving problems. At this stage, readers know when to skim, when to reread, and when to take notes. As Chall phrases it, this highest level of reading entails "a struggle to balance one's comprehension of the ideas read, one's analysis of them, and one's own ideas about them" (1983, p. 24).

Once children catch on to reading, it can become a source of pleasure. This boy's comic book promises him not only the adventures of Tarzan, but knowledge of the world of zoology as well.

Learning Arithmetic

Just as learning to read in school builds upon a prior ability to interpret situations and to make inferences from partial information, so does doing mathematics in school build upon prior practical ability with numbers. As we saw in Chapters 10 and 13, by the age of 6 or 7, children around the world have the ability to engage in the primitive mathematical operation of counting, as well as in the rudiments of addition and subtraction (Gelman & Baillargeon, 1983; Gelman & Gallistel, 1978).

When children begin school their use of the vocabulary of number and of actual number operations such

Counting on their fingers is a universal strategy for beginning arithmetic students.

as counting may be poorly coordinated. In arranging instruction, adults need to remember that although children may use the same words adults do ("There are seven cards in each row," for example), they do not necessarily share the same word meanings, as we saw in the discussion of language acquisition in Chapter 9 and the discussion of number conservation in Chapter 13.

Early in their developing understanding of numbers, youngsters hit upon the use of their bodies as aids in keeping track of quantity. Throughout the ages and in many cultures children have used their fingers when they begin to count (Conant, 1896); in some societies much more elaborate counting systems using the body have been devised. The Oksapmin of New Guinea, for example, use a system involving 27 body parts (Saxe, 1981) (see Figure 14.3). Other societies have used conventional counters such as kola nuts or cowry shells (Gay & Cole, 1967; Zaslavsky, 1973). Such systems can be more powerful than one might imagine. West Africans who traded in cowry shells with Portuguese merchants in the seventeenth century could do arithmetic using cowry-shell counters for sums running into the tens of thousands.

However, the kind of mathematical knowledge that children are required to learn in school demands a far greater range and degree of complexity than the human body can provide, a more flexible notation system than piles of seashells. A partial list of the accomplishments demanded of sixth-graders in San Diego, California, in the mid-1980s includes the following:

- Know common properties of numbers and place value through hundred billions

- Add, subtract, multiply, and divide fractions and mixed numbers with unlike denominators, renaming the answer in simplest terms

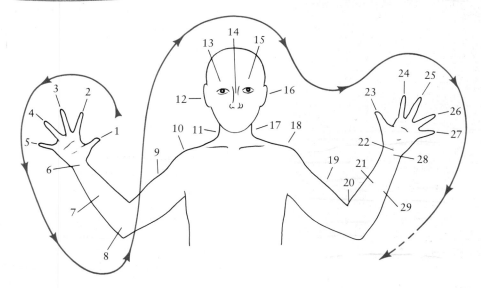

FIGURE 14.3 *The Oksapmin of New Guinea do their arithmetic using a basic set of 29 numbers corresponding to a conventionalized sequence of body parts. (From Saxe, 1981.)*

- Add and subtract with decimals to thousandths, renaming as necessary

- Identify points, lines, line segments, rays, and angles, and know their common geometric properties

- Determine the area of rectangles, parallelograms, and triangles using formulas

- Write a function rule and graph ordered pairs for the rule

- Find the mean, median, mode, and range of a list of numbers

- Determine the relationship of decimals and fractions to percents (San Diego City Schools, 1984, p. 479)

This curriculum is based upon more than 2000 years of developments in the science of mathematics. When children arrive at school, this is the highly developed form of mathematical knowledge that they confront.

One of the first tasks facing children when they encounter mathematics at school is to learn to write the first 10 digits. Since it is only a cultural convention that the symbol 9 should stand for the spoken word "nine," the first stage of this process is memorization.

Once the initial 10 digits are learned, children must learn the conventions for writing larger quantities and the concept of place value that underpins our notation system. The required correspondences are not intuitively obvious. Some first-graders, for example, have written "23" as "203" (Ginsburg, 1977). This representation, although erroneous, follows the conventions of our way of speaking ("twenty-three") and our

Learning the proper ways to behave in the classroom is an important part of children's school experience.

TABLE 14.2 Initiation-reply-evaluation sequence

Initiation	Reply	Evaluation
T [Teacher]: . . . what does this word say? Beth.	**Beth:** One.	*T:* Very good.
T: What does this word say? Jenny.	**Jenny:** One.	*T:* Okay.
T: Now look up here. What does this word say? Ramona.	**Ramona:** Umm.	
T: Kim.	**Kim:** First.	*T:* Okay.

SOURCE: Mehan, 1979.

system for representing spoken language in print. Unfortunately from the child's point of view, conventions for representing place value in arithmetic do not follow the conventions of the writing system. While numbers like 203 ("two hundred and three") are, so to speak, pronounced from left to right, they are actually constructed using the decimal point as the point of origin. So, for example, "Two hundred and three and forty-five hundredths" is written 203.45.

It takes most children several years to master these complexities, a fact that influences their ability to carry out such basic operations as addition and subtraction. Common mistakes include adding numbers in the way the words for them are pronounced — from left to right — and lining up numbers from the left. Misunderstandings of this kind produce such errors as

$$\begin{array}{r} 123 \\ +1 \\ \hline 223 \end{array}$$

Children who produce such answers are behaving as they are expected to in school in one important respect: they are applying previously acquired knowledge to solve new problems. As long as they don't become discouraged, they are eventually likely to catch on to the system underlying the written number system their teachers present to them (see Box 14.1, "Teaching the Basics").

The Special Language of Schooling

As we have seen, schooling is a distinctive form of socialization in which children are expected to learn how to gain information about the world by manipulating symbols — while sitting at their desks. Instead of learning by doing, children must learn by reading, writ-

ing, and calculating. The "real world" to which their learning applies is outside the classroom. In addition to reading, writing, and calculating, children must also learn a way of using language that is peculiar to the classroom.

Studies of the way that language is used in schools reveal a distinctive pattern known as **instructional discourse**. Instructional discourse differs in both structure and content from other ways in which adults and children speak. The central goals of instructional discourse are to give children information about the curriculum's content and feedback about their own efforts while providing teachers with information about their students' progress (Mehan, 1979; Shuy & Griffin, 1978; Sinclair & Coulthard, 1975).

One of the distinctive characteristics of instructional discourse is the presence of the initiation-reply-evaluation sequence. In this pattern, the teacher initiates an exchange, usually by asking a question; a student replies; and then the teacher provides an evaluation. Table 14.2 demonstrates this kind of exchange.

The initiation-reply-evaluation sequence includes a form of question-asking that is rarely encountered outside of school, the "known-answer question" (Searle, 1969). When the teacher asks Beth "What does this word say?" that teacher is seeking information about Beth's ability to read. Children can ask questions just as they would at home, but when the teacher asks a question it is often a covert way to evaluate the student's progress. Learning to respond easily to known-answer questions, in addition to learning about the academic content of the curriculum, is an important early lesson of schooling (Mehan, 1979).

The initiation-reply-evaluation sequence can be used quite flexibly. When Ramona hesitates, the teacher immediately calls on Kim, who provides the answer. This arrangement provides an opportunity for Ramona to learn, by observing what Kim says and the

BOX 14.1

TEACHING THE BASICS

• • •

Children are taught reading and arithmetic from materials that are specifically created for those purposes, which thus embody theories about how children learn. Uncertainties about the process of learning and development combined with chronic failures of a significant proportion of children to master "the basics" have generated an ongoing debate about the best methods of school instruction.

Reading Instruction

In the early years of this century, educational reformers believed that failure to learn how to read arose because instruction focused on letter-sound correspondence rather than on whole words (Mathews, 1966). Educators then developed the "look-say" approach to reading instruction, reasoning that if students learned to "say" words having "looked at them," the way adult readers seem to do, they would learn more rapidly to interpret novel combinations of these words. The "look-say" method of teaching reading became the standard of instruction until the 1960s.

The adoption of a look-say approach had a large impact on the content of children's learning. The "old-fashioned" sounding-out method of the nineteenth century used books valued by the culture, primarily famous literature. The adoption of a look-say approach led to the creation of novel texts with radically simplified vocabulary that built up a core "sight vocabulary" of frequently encountered words, adding new words in a measured way.

In the 1950s, continuing evidence of instructional failure in the early school grades led Rudolph Flesch (1955) to write *Why Johnny Can't Read,* a scathing attack on look-say instruction. Flesch maintained that the older methods, with their emphasis on teaching "word attack" skills based on principles of phonetics, were the best way to ensure that children learned to read. A decade later Jean Chall (1983) brought together the existing evidence pitting the look-say approach

against more traditional phonics instruction. She concluded that programs that include phonics instruction, especially in the early grades, are superior to those that do not.

Color the part brown if the word ends like 🗄 . What is the surprise?

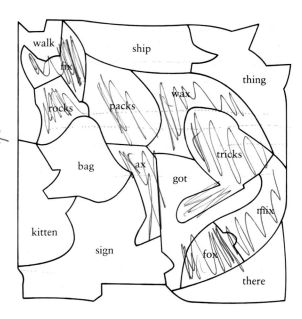

A great deal of reading instruction in the elementary school grades is carried out in workbook exercises like this one on building decoding skills.

When reading instruction switched from the look-say method back to an emphasis on phonics, the strategy of using simplified texts remained. However, the simplifications were now designed to help children "crack the code" instead of building up a large sight vocabulary (see the illustration above for a sample exercise). The result was sometimes very painful to read because classic stories were molded to allow children to solve the problem of decoding *before* they interpreted new materials. Aesop's tale of the tortoise and the hare, for example, was presented as follows:

> Rabbit said, "I can run. I can run fast. You can't run fast."
> Turtle said, "Look Rabbit. See the park. You and I will run. We'll run to the park."
> Rabbit said, "I want to stop. I'll stop here. I can run, but Turtle can't. I can get to the park fast."
> Turtle said, "I can't run fast. But I will not stop. Rabbit can't see me. I'll get to the park." (Quoted in Green, 1984, p. 176)

This kind of text did not exist long before it, too, attracted critics. They complained that such texts made it impossible for children to read for meaning, the actual purpose of reading. In effect, the experience children were getting was all "bottom up" with no "top down" information necessary to the full act of reading (Goodman & Goodman, 1979). At present, theories of how reading should be taught advocate balancing a "code emphasis," which drills children on phonetic analysis, with reading for meaning (National Academy of Education, 1985).

Teaching Mathematics

The problems of teaching formal mathematics, like the problems of teaching reading, have been the subject of intense investigation during most of this century. Recommendations for effective pedagogy vacillate between two poles, analogous to the "code emphasis" versus the "meaning emphasis" dichotomy in reading instruction. At one end are psychologists who believe that instruction is best carried out through intensive drill and practice on small parts of the overall process; at the other end are psychologists who believe that learning should begin with understanding and then proceed to practice (Resnick & Ford, 1981).

The drill and practice approach is exemplified by the work of E. L. Thorndike (1922), an earlier pioneer in educational research. Thorndike believed that learning arithmetic was a matter of building up the strength of a large number of specific habits orchestrated within a single system. Once automated, the individual parts could fit into a total problem-solving organization "as a soldier fighting together with others," to produce the correct answer (Thorndike, 1922, p. 139).

Although Thorndike's emphasis on drill to create automatic knowledge became a standard part of educational practice, it met with strenuous objections from psychologists and educators who believed that drill would promote only a low level of arithmetic competence. The alternative approach, learning with understanding, was championed by William Brownell (1928), who believed that it is important to make problems more meaningful to children so that their drill and practice would achieve the desired level of automaticity without sacrificing understanding. Proper understanding, Brownell claimed, would enable students to go beyond the narrow confines of the practice problems and apply their knowledge in novel situations.

Research has supported Brownell's view. For example, McConnell (1934/1958) compared a strict drill method to meaningful instruction. The drill method simply repeated number facts ($5 + 7 = 12$, $4 + 5 = 9$, etc.). The meaningful instruction presented number facts in conjunction with pictures and objects, which allowed students to verify their answers against real-world knowledge. McConnell found that straight drill was an efficient way to acquire rapid and automatic responses to the training materials, but when the students were tested on novel combinations, the meaningful approach led to significantly better results. Similar evidence in favor of meaningful instruction in basic number facts was obtained in other research (Swenson 1949/1958).

In recent decades there has been intensive research on elementary mathematics instruction (Resnick & Ford, 1981). It is now generally agreed that both drill in computation and practice in generalizing computations to a variety of meaningful new problems are necessary. While there is no generally agreed-upon procedure for mixing these two aspects of instruction, a variety of effective instructional procedures have been worked out for specific content domains (Bruner, 1960; Dienes, 1966; Rasmussen, Hightower, & Rasmussen, 1964).

TABLE 14.3 Lesson on use of prepositions

Initiation	Reply
T [Teacher]: Make a red flower under the tree. *(pause)* Okay, let's look at the red flower. Can you tell me where the red flower is?	*Children:* Right here, right here.
T: Dora?	*Dora:* Under the tree.
T: Tell me in a sentence.	*Dora:* It's under the tree.
T: What's under the tree, Dora?	*Children:* The flower.
T: Tell me, the flower . . .	*Dora:* The flower is under the tree.
T: Where is the red flower, Richard?	*Richard:* Under the tree.
T: Can you tell me in a sentence?	*Richard:* The flower is under the tree.
T: Cindy, where is the red flower?	*Cindy:* The red flower is under the tree.
Richard: [noticing that Cindy actually drew the "red" flower with a yellow crayon] Hey, that's not red.	

SOURCE: Mehan, 1979.

teacher's evaluation, at the same time that it allows the teacher to assess Ramona's need for more instruction.

The special nature of school-based language is also evident in the emphasis that teachers place on the linguistic form of their students' replies. This can be seen in the lesson on the use of prepositions shown in Table 14.3.

There are several interesting aspects to the interchange shown in Table 14.3. First, note that the teacher gradually builds an understanding of the linguistic form that she considers appropriate by using the turn-taking rules of classroom discourse. Second, note that the truth of what the children say is less important, for purposes of this lesson, than the form of their responses. Cindy gave the full answer the teacher was looking for but, as Richard noticed, Cindy had used a crayon of a different color! She was correct in school terms, although what she said did not match the presumed referent of her talk.

In everyday discourse, there is usually ample opportunity to check one's expectations against reality. But in the closed world of the classroom, in which feedback depends on the manipulation of language and symbols, the everyday processes of interpretation are blocked. Consequently, children must learn to focus on language itself as the vehicle of information in order to master the specialized knowledge taught in school.

THE COGNITIVE CONSEQUENCES OF SCHOOLING

It seems reasonable to assume that many thousands of hours sitting in classrooms learning about the world through reading and writing should have considerable impact on cognitive development during middle childhood and beyond. After all, schooling expands children's knowledge base, provides massive experience in deliberate remembering, and trains children in systematic problem-solving, all of which, as we saw in Chapter 13, are areas of cognitive functioning that appear to undergo fundamental changes in middle childhood. Insofar as the experience of schooling does have an impact on cognitive development, it suggests that important aspects of cognitive development are not universal because schooling is not universal.

The possibility that schooling engenders some cognitive changes that might be mistakenly attributed to universal laws of development has been tested by conducting experiments in societies where many children do not attend school. By comparing the cognitive performances of children who have attended school with those who have not, it is possible to begin to specify the special contributions of schooling to cognitive development. Four cognitive domains have figured widely in this research: concrete operations, the relation between language and thought, memory, and metacognitive skills (the ability to reflect upon one's own thought processes).

Concrete Operations

As discussed in Chapter 13, studies of children's performance on tests of concrete operations (the ability to engage in internalized, mental actions tied to objects and events in the child's immediate environment) are more or less evenly split between studies that find an advantage for children who have attended school and those who have not (Rogoff, 1981). When schooling does seem to accelerate the development of concrete operations, test results may well depend on schoolchildren's greater familiarity with the circumstances of testing (including the forms of question-asking), their greater ease in speaking to unfamiliar adults, and their greater ability to speak the language when testing is not conducted in their native language. This evidence suggests that the development of concrete operations is relatively unaffected by schooling, consistent with Piaget's belief that concrete operations are a universal accomplishment of middle childhood.

The Organization of Word Meanings

In comparison to children who are assigned to tend the sheep, to care for their younger siblings, or to weave rugs to be sold in the market, children attending school spend vastly more time learning through talking and listening than through doing. The content of this talk and the way that words are used also differ between the children who attend school and those who do not. Not only does talk in school require the mastery of abstract concepts, it requires that mastery to be used in isolation from the context of the actions being referred to. A biology lesson about the way that sunlight influences plant growth, for example, may take place in a windowless room with no plants in it. As a consequence, children must learn to create meaning from subtle differences in the way that words are used in conjunction with other words. This feature of schooling has led some psychologists to suggest that

the underlying organization of children's *lexicons* — the total store of words in their vocabulary — is changed by schooling (Luria, 1976; Olson, 1978).

The impact of schooling on lexical organization was demonstrated by Donald Sharp and his coworkers in a study of Mayan Indians living in the Yucatan peninsula of Mexico (Sharp, Cole, & Lave, 1979). When adolescents who had attended one or more years of high school were asked which words they associated with the word "duck," they responded with other words in the same category, such as "fowl," "goose," "chicken," and "turkey." When adolescents from the same area who had not attended school were presented with the same word, their responses were dominated by words that describe what ducks do ("swim," "fly") or what one does with ducks ("eat").

The results of the Sharp study, and findings from other parts of the world (e.g., Cole, Gay, Glick, & Sharp, 1971), suggest that schooling sensitizes children to the abstract, categorical meanings of words, in addition to building up their general knowledge. This does not imply, however, that word meaning among those who have not attended school fails to develop. For example, nonliterate Mayan farmers studied by Sharp and his colleagues knew perfectly well that ducks are a kind of fowl. Although they did not demonstrate this knowledge in the artificial circumstances of the free-association task, they readily displayed it when talking about kinds of animals on their farms.

Memory

In Chapter 13 we saw that during middle childhood children in some cultures do not display the same increase in memory skills that U.S. children do when tested on the standard tasks that psychologists generally use. Research comparing schooled and nonschooled children has shown that schooling is the crucial experience underlying these cultural differences. When children in other cultures have had the opportunity to go to school, their tested memory performance on these standard tests is more similar to their American counterparts in the same grade than it is to their age-mates from the same village (Cole, Gay, Glick, & Sharp, 1971).

A study by Daniel Wagner (1974) suggests the kind of information-processing skills that children acquire as a consequence of schooling. Wagner conducted his

FIGURE 14.4   *Cards used to test short-term memory. Seven cards are selected and then turned face down. The person being tested is then shown a duplicate of one of the cards (a rooster in this example) and asked to select the card that corresponds to it from the seven cards that are face down. (From Wagner, 1974.)*

study among educated and noneducated Mayans living in the Yucatan. He asked 248 people varying in age from 6 years to adulthood to recall the positions of picture cards, laid out in a linear array (see Figure 14.4). The items were all taken from a popular local game called *lotteria,* so Wagner could be certain the pictures were all well known. On each trial, each of seven cards was displayed for two seconds and then turned face down. As soon as all seven cards had been presented, a duplicate of one card was shown and people had to point to the position where they thought that it was located. By selecting cards in different positions, Wagner in effect manipulated the length of the time between when the card to be remembered had been presented and when it was to be recalled.

Research in the United States had previously demonstrated a marked increase in the ability of children to remember the location of cards once they reach middle childhood (Hagen, Meacham, & Mesibov, 1970). This increased capacity has been attributed to the older children's ability to rehearse each card's location as it is presented. Two key results from Wagner's study, which he replicated successfully several years later in Morocco (Wagner, 1978), suggest that it is schooling that leads to improved memory for the location of objects during middle childhood. First,

performance increased only if the children tested were attending school (see Figure 14.5). Second, the pattern of improvement for the educated children as they grew older was the pattern to be expected if they were using rehearsal strategies.

As in the case of changes in lexical organization, the outcomes of studies of schooling's impact on memory should not be interpreted to mean that the psychological function in question simply fails to develop among children who have not attended school. Superiority of educated children in memory experiments is most noticeable in cases, such as Wagner's experiment, in which the materials to be learned are not connected to each other according to any everyday script. In studies where the to-be-remembered materials are part of a meaningful setting, such as Rogoff and Wadell's study of memory for objects placed in a diorama of the subjects' town (see Chapter 13, p. 432), the effects of schooling on memory performance disappear (see also Mandler, Scribner, Cole, & DeForest, 1980). It appears that the effect of schooling is to teach children specialized strategies for remembering, enhancing their ability to commit arbitrary material to memory for purposes of later testing. There is no evidence to support the conclusion that schooling increases an individual's memory capacity in general.

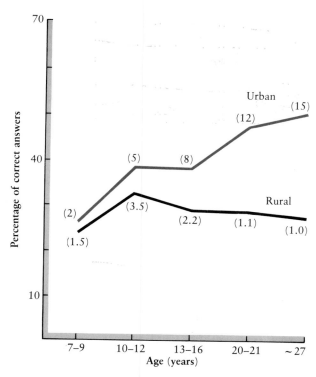

FIGURE 14.5 *Short-term memory performance as a function of age and number of years of education. In the absence of further education, performance does not improve with age, implicating schooling as a key factor in how well one does on this task. (Numbers in parentheses are the average number of years of education for the designated group.) (From Wagner, 1978.)*

Metacognitive Skills

A third area in which schooling appears to influence cognitive development is the degree to which children can reflect on and talk about their own thought processes (Luria, 1976; Rogoff, 1981; Scribner & Cole, 1973). When children have been asked to explain how they arrived at the answers to problems, or which strategies they used to remember in a particular experiment, those who have not attended school are likely to say something like, "I did what my sense told me" or to fail to offer any description at all. Schoolchildren, on the other hand, seem better able to describe the mental activities and logic that underpin their problem-solving activities. This ability is called **metacognition.**

Attendance at school also seems to affect children's ability to think about their own language-using skills (referred to as *metalinguistic awareness*). For example, Sylvia Scribner and Michael Cole (1981) asked educated and noneducated Vai people from Liberia to judge the grammatical correctness of several phrases spoken in Vai. Some of the sentences were grammatical; some were not. Education had no impact on the ability to identify the ungrammatical phrases. However, those who had not attended school could not identify the basis for their judgments, while those who were educated could generally explain just what it was about the phrase that made it ungrammatical.

These Liberian boys are learning to read passages from the Koran by an early morning fire.

The Evidence in Overview

Overall, the picture that emerges from recent decades of intense research on schooling provides only minimal support for the idea that schooling changes the basic cognitive processes associated with middle childhood in a general way. With the possible exception of the ability to think about one's own thinking processes, those who have attended school are typically shown to outperform those who have not, primarily when presented with materials or procedures that are closely related to school activity (Rogoff, 1981).

This conclusion in no way detracts from the importance of schooling in modern life. Schooling need not produce a generalized increase in the level of cognitive ability to be of great significance for children's development. To focus entirely on generalized cognitive change may lead one to overlook the fact that the central goal of schooling is not to transform mental machinery but to make people more effective problem solvers and rememberers when they have pencils and books at hand. If reading, writing, and calculating have real importance outside of school, and they do, the impact of schooling may be more appropriately sought in the new activities that people engage in because they have been to school than in any general mental transformations that schooling may produce.

Perhaps the most important effect of schooling for most people is that it may become a gateway to economic power and social status (see Table 14.4). Most work in modern industrial societies requires the level of literacy a high school education usually provides, and most highly paid jobs require a college-level education and perhaps specialization beyond that. The associations between years of schooling, income, and job status are very strong (Jencks, 1972); on the average, the more years of schooling children complete, the higher their incomes are and the more likely they are to obtain white-collar and professional jobs.

Developmental psychologists and educators have therefore investigated the factors that account for success in school, with particular attention to the possibility that some children come equipped with a special "aptitude for schooling" while others do not. There has also been considerable research on the role of the home, the community, and the school itself in influencing school success.

APTITUDE FOR SCHOOLING

In *The Mill on the Floss*, the nineteenth century novelist George Eliot provides a particularly clear account of the difficulties facing a poor student:

"You feel no interest in what you are doing sir," [Tom's teacher] Mr. Stelling would say, and the re-

TABLE 14.4 School enrollment in selected countries

Country	Percentage in Primary School		Percentage Who Enter Grade 1 and Complete Primary School	Percentage in Secondary School	
	Male	Female	Male and Female	Male	Female
Afghanistan	16	8	54	11	5
Senegal	50	34	86	17	8
Sierra Leone	46	32	48	23	10
Nicaragua	72	74	27	38	47
Indonesia	97	93	68	42	31
Phillipines	97	98	71	61	66
Hungary	100	100	93	74	73
France	97	97	95	83	95
Japan	98	99	100	93	95

SOURCE: United Nations Children's Fund, 1987.

proach was painfully true. Tom had never found any difficulty in discerning a pointer from a setter, when once he had been told the distinction, and his perceptive powers were not at all deficient. I fancy they were quite as strong as those of the Rev. Mr. Stelling, for Tom could predict with accuracy what number of horses were cantering behind him, he could throw a stone right into the center of a given ripple, he could guess to a fraction how many lengths of his stick it would take to reach across the playground, and could draw almost perfect squares on his slate without any measurement. But Mr. Stelling took no note of these things; he only observed that Tom's faculties failed him before the abstractions hideously symbolized to him in the pages of the Eton Grammar and that he was in a state bordering on idiocy with regard to the demonstration that two given triangles must be equal, though he could discern with great promptitude and certainty the fact that they *were* equal.

Although Tom's teacher attributed his difficulties either to "natural idiocy" or to deliberate efforts to avoid learning, neither proved true. A few years later, when his family lost its middle-class standing, Tom demonstrated both his ability to learn and his diligence as a businessman.

While cases where children struggle in school but are later successful are by no means restricted to fiction, in the real world of today thousands of youngsters leave school without having acquired the basic reading and arithmetic skills that they will need to be successful later. In the United States alone, it is estimated that as many as 25 percent of adults read so poorly that their ability to cope with the demands of everyday life is undermined (Kozol, 1985).

Why is it that some children experience exceptional difficulty learning in their schools while others don't? And what can be done to promote development in school settings? All during this century, discussion of these questions has been influenced by the idea that people vary in an aptitude called "intelligence" that explains the variations in their school performance.

At the level of common sense, the concept of intelligence is very widespread. All languages have terms that describe individual differences in the way that people solve problems and the kinds of problems that they are good at solving (Nerlove, Roberts, Klein, Yarbrough, & Habicht, 1974; Serpell, 1977). But the precise meaning of these terms differs among cultures and it

has proved difficult—some would say impossible—to define intelligence so that it can be measured as precisely as weight or height. Nonetheless, almost all children growing up today in the United States can expect to take an intelligence test at some time before completing their education. Such tests are used to make important decisions about the kind of education they will receive, which in turn will influence the kind of lives they will lead as adults. It is thus important to understand the nature of intelligence as a factor in children's development as well as the nature of intelligence testing.

The Origins of Intelligence Testing

Wide interest in measuring intelligence began at the turn of the century when mass education was becoming the norm in Europe and the United States. While most children seemed to be able to profit from the instruction they were given, some seemed virtually unable to learn in school. Concerned educational officials sought to determine the causes and cures for these difficulties.

In 1904 the French Minister of Public Instruction named a commission to ensure the benefits of instruction for what he termed "defective" children. Alfred Binet, a professor of psychology at the Sorbonne and Theodore Simon, a doctor, were asked by the commission to create a means of examining children to identify those who needed special instruction. Binet and Simon set out to construct a psychological examination to diagnose mental subnormality that would have all the precision and validity of a medical examination. They were especially concerned about children *incorrectly* diagnosed as subnormal because, as they put it, "to be a member of a special class can never be a mark of distinction" (Binet & Simon, 1916, p. 10).

The diagnostic strategy adopted by Binet and Simon was to present children with a series of problems considered indicative of intelligence in the culture of their time. The problems were tailored to differentiate between children at each age, so that children who were far behind could be identified and given special instruction. For example, Binet and Simon surmised that one aspect of intelligence is the ability to follow directions while keeping several task components in mind at once. To test for this ability, they presented children aged 4 to 6 with the following task:

Do you see this key? You are to put it on the chair over there (pointing to the chair); afterwards shut the door; afterwards you will see near the door a box which is on a chair. You will take that box and bring it to me. (1916, p. 206)

At 4 years of age, few children could carry out all parts of this task without help. At 5 years, about half the children responded adequately, and at 6 years, almost all children passed. This age-graded regularity provided Binet and Simon with the test characteristics they needed. A 4-year-old who passed the test was considered precocious while a 6-year-old who failed was considered retarded with respect to this ability.

Other tasks required children to identify the missing parts of a picture, to name colors, to copy geometric figures, to remember strings of random digits, to count backward from 20, to make change for 20 francs, and so on. After extensive pretesting, Binet and Simon gave such test items (a different set to each age level) to slightly more than 200 children ranging in age from 3 to 12 years. As they had hoped, almost precisely 50 percent of these children scored at the expected age level. Of the remainder, 43 percent were within one

year of expectation and only 7 percent deviated above or below the norm by as much as two years.

Binet and Simon concluded that they had succeeded in constructing a scale of intelligence. They called the basic index of intelligence for this scale **mental age (MA)**. A child who did as well on the test as an average 7-year-old was said to have an MA of 7; a child who did as well as an average 9-year-old was said to have an MA of 9, and so on. The MA provided Binet and Simon with a convenient way to characterize mental subnormality. A "dull" 7-year-old child was one who performed like a normal child one or more years younger.

To verify that their scale reflected more than a lucky selection of test items, Simon and Binet tested their conclusions against teachers' judgments. Their success in picking out the children judged most and least able by teachers confirmed their hopes.

Binet and Simon offered two explanations for school failure: a child might be lacking either the "natural intelligence" (the "nature") needed to succeed in school, or the cultural background (the "nurture") presupposed by the school.

A very intelligent child may be deprived of instruction by circumstances foreign to his intelligence. He may have lived far from school; he may have had a long illness . . . or may be some parents have preferred to keep their children at home, to have them rinse bottles, serve the customers of a shop, care for a sick relative or herd the sheep. In such cases . . . it suffices to pass lightly the results of tests which are of a notably scholastic character, and to attach the greatest importance to those which express the natural intelligence. (1916, pp. 253–254)

This approach may appear intuitively plausible, but in fact it contains a crucial ambiguity: nowhere do Binet and Simon offer a definition of "natural intelligence" that would allow them to separate tests of natural intelligence from tests of a "scholastic character." Instead of defining natural intelligence in a manner that is distinct from cultural experience (which they refer to as a problem of "fearful complexity") they contented themselves with pointing out that whatever natural intelligence means, it is *not* equivalent to being successful in school. In their view, not only is there more to intelligence than schooling, there is also more to schooling—and to life—than intelligence:

The jigsaw puzzle that this 10-year-old is trying to complete is part of a standard IQ test.

Information (30 items)

How many legs does a dog have?
In what direction does the sun set?

Picture Completion (26 items)

What is the missing part of each picture?

Similarities (17 items)

In what way are a cat and a mouse alike?
In what way are liberty and justice alike?

Picture Arrangement (12 items made up of
3 to 5 picture cards each)

These pictures tell the story of a fire. Put
them in the right order so that the picture
makes sense.

Comprehension (17 items)
What are some reasons why we need
policemen?
Why do we have to put stamps on letters?

FIGURE 14.6 *Sample items from the Wechsler Intelligence Scale for Children. (Adapted from Wechsler, 1974.)*

Our examination of intelligence can not take account of all these qualities, attention, will, regularity, continuity, docility, and courage which play so important a part in school work, and also in after-life; for life is not so much a conflict of intelligences as a combat of characters. (1916, p. 256)

The Legacy of Binet and Simon

Educators immediately adopted Binet and Simon's tests, and their use spread rapidly. By 1916, more than 20,000 translated test booklets had been distributed by a single American institution devoted to education of the retarded. This was only the beginning. The tests were subsequently translated and used in such far-flung locations as Australia, China, the Soviet Union, and South Africa, in addition to Europe and the United States.

Many refinements of the original tests have been made in the past 80 years. In the United States, Lewis Terman at Stanford University modified the original scales to create the Stanford-Binet Intelligence Scale in an attempt to determine the origins of mental giftedness (Terman, 1925), and David Wechsler devised tests for use with both adults and children (Wechsler, 1939) (see Figure 14.6). Updated versions of these tests are still widely used today.

William Stern (1912), a German developmental psychologist, introduced an important refinement in the way tests were thought about and applied. He suggested that intelligence be considered the ratio of children's mental age to their actual, or chronological, age (CA). Thus was born the unit of measurement that we use today, the "intelligence quotient" **(IQ)**, where $IQ = MA/CA \times 100$. The stratagem of multiplying the relative magnitude of MA/CA by 100 is simply a convenience. Calculating IQ in this fashion ensures that when children are performing precisely as expected for their age, the resulting score will be 100, making 100 an "average IQ" by definition (see Figure 14.7). For example, a 9-year-old child with a mental age of 10 is credited with an IQ of 111 ($\frac{10}{9} \times 100 = 111$), while a 10-year-old child with a mental age of 10 is credited with an IQ of 100.

Stern's IQ score was quickly adopted as the basic unit for comparison of mental performance. It provided psychologists and educators with a convenient index that could specify the correlation between intel-

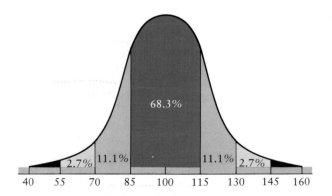

FIGURE 14.7 *An idealized bell-shaped curve of the distribution of IQ scores. A bell-shaped curve is a distribution of scores on a graph in which the most frequent value, the mode, is in the center and the less frequent values are distributed symmetrically to either side. By definition, the modal IQ score is 100 (see text).*

ligence test scores and grades in school. (See Chapter 1, pp. 24–25 for an additional discussion of correlation). In recent decades, the method of calculating IQ has been refined to compensate for the fact that people's mental age reaches a plateau in their mid-twenties, but the underlying logic of calculating IQ remains the same.

Despite various revisions, the procedures invented by Binet and Simon remain the basis of standardized intelligence testing. The key elements are:

1. Create a set of test items that produces a range of performances among children within the same age level.

2. Select items that form a sequence of difficulty, so that as children grow older, they are more likely to pass a given item.

3. Make certain that performance on the test corresponds to performance in school.

Only part of the legacy of Binet and Simon is to be found in the adoption and refinement of their testing methods. Equally important have been the questions they left unresolved, three of which have dominated research on intelligence since their pioneering efforts. The first question focuses on the nature of intelligence itself: How is intelligence to be defined? Is it a general characteristic of a person's entire mental life or is it a bundle of relatively specific abilities? Second is the "nature–nurture" question: What causes variations in intelligence test scores? Third, why do variations in IQ scores predict variations in school performance?

The nature of intelligence: general or specific?
Although Binet and Simon were skeptical about the possibility of defining intelligence, the nature of their assignment forced them to attempt to characterize the quality of mind they were seeking to test for. In their monograph on the subject, they offered the following characterization:

> It seems to us that in intelligence there is a fundamental faculty, the alteration or lack of which is of the utmost importance for practical life. This faculty is judgment, otherwise called good sense, practical sense, initiative, the faculty of adapting oneself to circumstances. To judge well, to comprehend well, to reason well, these are the essential activities of intelligence. (1916, p. 43)

This definition served to motivate the items that Binet and Simon chose for their test, but it did not by any means settle the question of the essential properties of intelligence.

Following World War I, when the use of intelligence testing by educators was spreading rapidly, the editors of the *Journal of Educational Psychology* asked a number of experts to give their views on the nature of intelligence. The characteristics offered by most of the contributors are represented by the following sample:

1. The power to think one's way to the truth or facts of a situation

2. The ability to think abstractly

3. The ability to learn and adjust oneself to the environment

4. The ability to adapt to new situations in life

5. The capacity to inhibit instinctive judgment

As John Carroll (1982) comments, the variety of these definitions is sufficiently great to make one wonder whether the different experts in 1921 were talking about the same thing. But in one respect, these

TABLE 14.5 Howard Gardner's idea of multiple intelligences

Kind of Intelligence	Characteristics	Kind of Intelligence	Characteristics
Linguistic	Special sensitivity to language allowing person to choose precisely the right word or turn of phrase and to catch onto new meanings easily	Spatial	Ability to perceive relations among objects, to transform mentally what one sees, and to re-create visual images from memory
Musical	Sensitivity to pitch and tone allowing person to detect and produce musical structure	Bodily–kinesthetic	Ability to represent ideas in movement; characteristic of great dancers or mimes
Logical–mathematical	Ability to engage in abstract reasoning and manipulate symbols	Personal	Ability to gain access to one's own feelings and to understand the motivations of others

respondents agreed with Binet and Simon's early definition. Intelligence, whatever it is, is a *general* characteristic of a person's behavior. This view has been supported over the years by statistical evidence that the separate tasks on the test are highly correlated with one another; people who score high on one task tend to score high on the others (Jensen, 1980; Spearman, 1927).

One participant in the 1921 symposium on intelligence, V. A. C. Henmon, disagreed with his colleagues. He believed that intelligence tests measure only "the special intelligence upon which the schools place a premium" (1921, p. 197). The idea that intelligence tests measure only school-specific aptitudes has been championed in recent years by a number of scholars.

Several characteristics seem to distinguish the intellectual tasks demanded by schools from tasks encountered in many other settings, as we have seen in the earlier sections of this chapter (see also Neisser, 1976; Scribner & Cole, 1973; Wagner & Sternberg, 1985). They include the following:

1. School tasks are formulated by other people.

2. School tasks are of little or no intrinsic interest to the learner.

3. All the needed information is present at the start of school tasks.

4. School tasks are separate from everyday experience.

5. School tasks are usually well defined, with a single correct answer.

6. There is often only one method for finding the solution to school tasks that is considered correct.

7. School tasks are usually presented in written symbols (words, numbers).

These characteristics of school tasks have led several modern investigators to follow Henmon's suggestion that there is a special form of intelligence that is specific to such tasks. Ulric Neisser (1976) speaks of "academic" versus "everyday" intelligence. Robert Sternberg (1985) distinguishes academic and practical intelligence, both of which are said to be different from a third kind of intelligence, which he calls wisdom.

The search for separate intelligence factors by no means stops at two or three types. The psychologist Louis Thurstone (1938) proposed the existence of seven "primary mental abilities": verbal comprehension, word fluency, number, space, memory, perceptual speed, and reasoning. J. P. Guilford (1967) went further. He proposed 120 separate mental abilities, all of which could be tapped by appropriate test items.

More recently, Howard Gardner (1983) has proposed a theory of multiple intelligences, each of which follows a different developmental path (see Table 14.5). Musical intelligence often appears at an early age; logical mathematical intelligence seems to peak in late adolescence and early adulthood; while the kind of spatial intelligence upon which artists rely may reach its peak much earlier or later.

There is at present no firm agreement on the best way to characterize intelligence. Part of the problem arises because different statistical techniques for assessing the correlations among different subtests of IQ tests yield different answers (Gould, 1981). But researchers' personal intuitions about what intelligence is also play a role in their theorizing on this topic. Should great musical ability be called a form of intelligence, or is it better thought of as a "talent"? Conversely, couldn't the ability to solve IQ test problems be considered a talent, or is there really something fruitful about identifying it as intelligence? There is no obvious right answer to these questions.

Population differences and the nature–nurture controversy Disagreements over general intelligence versus specific intelligences coincide with disagreements about reasons why people's test performance varies. As mobilization for World War I was beginning, Robert Yerkes proposed that all recruits be given an intelligence test to determine their fitness to serve in various military capacities as well as to generate data about the intelligence of the U.S. population as a whole. Approximately 1.75 million men were tested using group-administered written tests for those who could read English, and a picture completion test for those who could not (see Figure 14.8). Men who failed were given an individually administered version of the Binet and Simon scales (Yerkes, 1921). Never before had IQ tests been administered to such large groups of people at one time, nor to people for whom the language of testing differed from their native languages.

Both because of the chaotic conditions of testing and because of the results, Yerkes' research began a controversy that has continued to the present time (Gould, 1981). Two results appeared to be particularly problematic. First, the average score of native-born white Americans was assessed at a mental age of 13 years. Since, by the standards of the time, a mental age of 8 to 12 years was considered mentally subnormal for an adult, it appeared that a substantial part of the white population were "morons."

Second, there was a substantial difference between the scores obtained from European immigrants and Afro-Americans. Overall, the average for recruits of European origin was a mental age of 13.7 years, although the recruits whose families came from southern and eastern Europe scored lower than northern Europeans, with an average mental age of about 11 years. Afro-Americans scored lowest of all, with an average tested mental age of slightly more than 10 years.

Several of the pioneer mental testers interpreted such differences as the result of innate, immutable differences in natural intelligence ("nature"). For example, Terman's book on mental giftedness bore the title, *Genetic Studies of Genius*. Cyril Burt (1883–1971) was another early test developer who exercised great influence on the field, although some of his data have subsequently been shown to be fraudulent (Hearnshaw, 1978). Burt believed both that intelligence is an innate quality and that each person has one general "intelligence," rather than a set of specific intelligences:

By intelligence the psychologist understands inborn, all-round intellectual ability. It is inherited, or at least innate, not due to teaching or training; it is intellectual, not emotional or moral, and remains uninfluenced by industry or zeal; it is general, not specific, i.e., it is not limited to any particular kind of work, but enters into all we do or say or think. Of all our mental qualities, it is the most far-reaching. (Quoted in Carroll, 1982, p. 90)

In short, according to this **innatist hypothesis of intelligence,** some people are born generally smarter than others and no amount of training or variation in the environment can alter this fact. Many psychologists of the 1920s rushed to embrace this conclusion. In an address entitled "Is America Safe for Democracy," the then head of the Harvard University psychology department, William McDougall, stated, "The results of the Army tests indicate that about 75 percent of the population has not sufficient innate capacity for intellectual development to enable it to complete the usual high school course" (quoted in Chase, 1977, p. 226). The generally lower test scores of members of ethnic minority groups and the poor (who often, but not always, were the same people) were thus widely interpreted to mean that such groups were innately inferior, a condition that could not be altered by changes in their life experiences.

During the 1930s and 1940s scholarly opinion was seriously divided on this issue (Cronbach, 1975). The general-intelligence, innatist position championed by Terman, Burt, and others was balanced by an **environmentalist hypothesis of intelligence** as both specific and heavily dependent upon experience (Klineberg, 1980). It was demonstrated, for example, that when people moved from rural areas to the city, intelligence test scores rose (Klineberg, 1935) and that when or-

FIGURE 14.8 *Items from the picture-completion test used by Yerkes and his colleagues to test recruits during World War I. Each picture is incomplete in some way; the task is to identify what is missing. (From Yerkes, 1921.)*

phans were removed from very restricted early environments, their intelligence test scores improved markedly (see Chapter 8).

In the 1960s, the scientific and social debates about ethnic and social class differences in tested intelligence erupted again when Arthur Jensen (1969) published an article with the provocative title "How Much Can We Boost IQ and Scholastic Achievement?" Jensen was disenchanted with the federally sponsored Head Start program (see Chapter 12). He suggested that it was a mistake to expect scholastic improvements from Head Start because poor and minority children were genetically less capable of the mental processes demanded by school. His provocative thesis fueled a heated controversy. Jensen's critics charged that he used biased tests, misused statistical techniques, and misrepresented the data, charges that Jensen has disputed (Block & Dworkin, 1981; Gould, 1981; Jensen, 1980).

environment + genes

IQ performance and school success: current research

At the present time, no responsible scholar believes that the variation in intelligence test scores from person to person can be attributed entirely to either environmental or genetic factors, or that school success is caused entirely by inherited differences in intelligence (Sternberg & Powell, 1983). Rather, it is accepted that all behavior, including performance on IQ tests and in school, reflects the individual's *phenotype* (the child's observable characteristics), which arises from interactions between the *genotype* (the set of genes a child inherits) and the environment.

As was pointed out in Chapter 2, the study of gene–environment interactions among human beings is especially difficult for several reasons. First, for ethical reasons, it is impossible to study the full range of reaction. To do so would mean to expose some newborn children to environments known to threaten human survival only to satisfy scientific curiosity. Second, almost all human characteristics are *polygenic*—that is, they are shaped by several genes acting in combination with each other in a given set of environmental conditions. Thus, even when an estimate of the genetic contribution to a trait is obtained, little can be said about precisely which genes are interacting with the environment in what way. Third, the fact that human beings grow up in a cultural environment means that parents contribute to both the genetic material of their children and their children's environment, complicating the process of separating different influences on the phenotype. Finally, children are active shapers of their own environments, further complicating an already complicated situation (see Figure 2.9 for a reminder of these complexities).

Attempts to understand how genetic and environmental factors combine to create the phenotypic behavior called "intelligence" face another, even greater difficulty. As was noted earlier, psychologists disagree profoundly about what, precisely, they are measuring when they administer an intelligence test. All they can say with any degree of confidence is that these tests predict later school performance to a moderate degree. (The typical correlation between test performance and school performance is .50 [Snow & Yalow, 1982]). We can better understand this uncertainty by comparing the genetic–environmental interactions that might determine intelligence with those that determine height.

To determine how environmental variation influences height, we might study sets of monozygotic (identical) and heterozygotic (fraternal) twins. Suppose, for example, that the twins to be studied were all born in Minnesota. Suppose further that some of the twins were separated, with the second member of each pair sent to live among the !Kung Bushmen of the Kalahari desert. Although these environments do not represent the most extreme variations compatible with human life, they are sufficiently different in climate, diet, daily activities, and other relevant factors to represent a plausible test of the relative importance of genetic and environmental contributions to height.

If, within this environmental range, genetic factors dominate the expression of the phenotype (measured height), then we would expect two facts to emerge:

1. The heights of identical twins should be roughly as similar to each other when raised far apart as they are when raised in the same family.

2. The similarity between heights of identical twins should be greater than the similarity of heights of the fraternal twins. In fact, the similarity of the heights of identical twins raised in very different environments might be greater than that of fraternal twins raised in the same environment.

One of the keys to making these comparisons is that whether the children are in Minnesota or the Kalahari desert, we can be pretty confident about our measure of height. Whether we use a yardstick or a metric scale, there is a standardized measure relating the length of a ruler to the height of a person, regardless of the context in which they are measured. At first glance IQ tests may appear to be standard measures logically similar to measuring height. But this appearance is an illusion.

Precisely because intelligence tests take their meaning from their correlation with schoolwork, they are inherently bound to the schooled society in which they are developed. As we have seen, central to all schooling are graphic systems of representation. But these modes of representation are generally absent in nonliterate societies. To be administered to a !Kung child, every existing intelligence test would thus require some modification, if only translation from English to !Kung. If, for example, a !Kung child were asked how many fingers are on two hands, the modification seems minimal, but caution is still necessary. The number system used by the !Kung is not the same

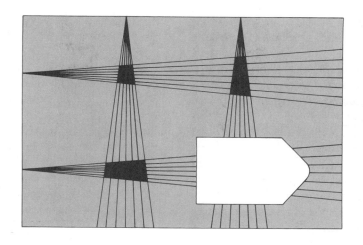

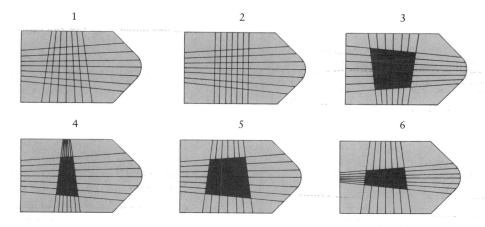

FIGURE 14.9 *Items from a "culture-free" intelligence test. Note that these test items, while not requiring elaborate verbal formulation, assume that the test-taker is familiar with two-dimensional representations of figures, a convention that does not exist in many cultures. (From Raven, 1962.)*

as that used by Minnesotans, and it plays a different role in their lives. What in !Kung society is the relative importance of knowing the number of fingers on a hand versus, say, knowing how to tie knots with those fingers?

When it comes to the tests that require interpretation of pictures or copying from written figures, even more serious difficulties arise. The !Kung have no tradition of either drawing or writing. Research with young children in the United States (Klapper & Birch, 1969) and nonliterate peoples in several parts of the world (Deregowski, 1980) shows that people do not

automatically interpret two-dimensional pictures as they would the objects depicted. So the tests that use pictures and require copying are inappropriate, as are any tests that depend upon the ability to read. We thus cannot assume that an IQ test is like a ruler, yielding equivalent measures across cultural environments.

Various attempts to create "culture-free" tests have been proposed to deal with this challenge (Cattell, 1949; Davis, 1948). But to date, no generally satisfactory solution has been found: all tests of intelligence draw on a background of learning that is culture-specific (Cole, 1985) (see Figure 14.9).

The fact that intelligence cannot be tested independently of the culture that gives rise to the test greatly limits the conclusions that can be drawn from cross-cultural testing. A good deal of research uses comparisons of identical and fraternal twins to distinguish genetic from environmental contributions to intelligence. However, these studies suffer an important limitation. According to the logic of twin studies, the environmental variations for separated twins ought to be great enough to allow environmental influences to be visible. But if the environmental variation is too great, such as in the case of children from Minnesota and the Kalahari desert, comparable testing methods will be unsuitable. It seems that the crucial requirements for estimating the heritability of IQ cannot be met: if the environments of separated twins are too different, the tests won't be applicable, but if they are not very different, the contributions of genes and the environment cannot be differentiated.

Despite these difficulties, a large literature has grown up around studies of twins' IQ test performance, along with studies of children from interethnic marriages and of children adopted across ethnic-group lines (Mackenzie, 1984; Scarr, 1981). Controversy continues to attend this work, but the following conclusions appear most defensible:

1. There is some inherited component to individual differences in IQ test performance. The degree of heritability is in dispute: some claim that it is very high (Jensen, 1980); some claim that it is very low or indeterminate (Lewontin, Rose, & Kamin, 1984). One influential recent summary estimates that perhaps 50 percent of the variation in test performance *within groups* is controlled by genetic factors (Plomin & DeFries, 1980).

2. Taken as a whole, there are significant differences between the average IQ scores of black and white Americans. Whites score approximately 15 points higher than blacks, with other ethnic groups such as Native Americans and Hispanics scoring at some intermediate level (Jensen, 1980).

3. There is *no evidence* that the average difference in scores between ethnic groups is the result of inherited differences in intelligence, however defined. Nonetheless, great uncertainty remains

about precisely what environmental factors are involved in producing the group differences.

At first glance, these three facts may appear to be in conflict with each other: if there is a large inherited component to individual differences in tested intelligence, and if there are large group differences in tested intelligence, why wouldn't it be reasonable to conclude that the source of the group differences is the same as the source of the individual differences?

There are two answers to this question, one logical and the other empirical. The logical answer was provided by Richard Lewontin (1976). It can be illustrated simply by using an example from plant genetics (see Figure 14.10). Suppose that a farmer has two fields, one fertile and the other barren. He randomly takes corn seed from a bag containing several genetic varieties and plants them in the two fields. He cares for

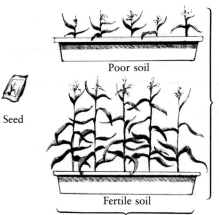

FIGURE 14.10 *An illustration of the reason why differences within groups do not explain differences between groups. In this case, the difference in the height of the plants within each box reflects genetic variations in the seeds planted in them. The difference between the average heights of the plants in the two boxes is best explained by the quality of the soil, an environmental factor. The same principle holds true for IQ test scores of different human groups. (Adapted from Gleitman, 1983.)*

them equally. When the plants have reached maturity he will discover that *within* each field some plants have grown taller than others. Since all the plants within each field experienced roughly the same environment by comparison with the differences *between* fields, their variation can be attributed to genetic factors. But the farmer will also discover variation between the fields; the plants grown in the fertile field will be taller than the plants grown in the barren field. The explanation for this average difference in the heights of the plants depends on their environments, even though within each field, there may be equal degrees of heritability.

This same argument applies to ethnic group variations in test performance. Even though the heritability of intelligence *within* groups from different ethnic backgrounds may be the same, the average difference in performance *between* groups may still be caused not by their genetic endowment but by differences in the environments within which the children have been raised.

Lewontin's example illustrates another important point about heritability that applies equally to IQ. Heritability is a *population statistic*. It applies to groups, not to individuals. If the heritability statistic for a field of corn or a set of IQ scores is .50, it does *not* mean that 50 percent of the height of each corn plant or each IQ score is determined by genetic factors. Instead, it means that 50 percent of the *variation* in a field of corn or a group of IQ scores can be traced to genetic differences. The other 50 percent of the variation must be explained in another way.

The evidence (summarized by Mackenzie, 1984) also speaks strongly against the idea that ethnic and class differences in tested IQ can be explained by inheritance. In a particularly important study, Sandra Scarr and Richard Weinberg (1976, 1983) evaluated the impact on children from black working-class families of being adopted into white, middle-class homes. Had the black children remained at home, they would be expected to achieve an average IQ score of 85. Raised in white, middle-class families, these children had an average IQ score of 97, almost precisely the national average, despite the fact that they had been adopted more than a year after birth. Children adopted close to birth had even higher scores. This kind of evidence points squarely at children's environment as a major factor in promoting the abilities tapped by standardized intelligence tests, abilities that are important to success in school.

The research described in Chapters 8 and 12 suggests some of the home characteristics that are likely to be influential (Baumrind, 1967; White & Watts, 1973). Parents who encourage exploration, who take care to explain what they are doing and to listen to their children, and who tailor the difficulty of the environment to their children's abilities and interests tend to raise academically more successful children. Such results are not restricted to the United States. Similar patterns of parental influence mediated by distinctive patterns of communication are found in Japan as well (Stevenson, Lee, & Stigler, 1986).

THE SCHOOL AND THE COMMUNITY

As important as they are, inherited ability and the home environment in which it develops are not sufficient to ensure school success. A great deal also depends upon the quantity and quality of available education and the importance attached to education by the community. Two different lines of evidence illustrate how community and school factors influence the likelihood that children will succeed in school.

Peer Influence

William Labov and Clarence Robbins (1969) studied the way that children's participation in peer groups may interfere with their success in school. Their research, carried out in central Harlem, focused on groups of boys in grades 4 to 10. Although these groups were not "gangs," in the sense that they did not fight other groups as a unit, fighting was common and intergroup conflict was an important source of group cohesion.

The major values of group members were incompatible with those of the school, according to Labov and Robbins:

> Sources of prestige within the group are physical size, toughness, courage and skill in fighting; skill with language in ritual insults, verbal routines with girls, singing, jokes and story-telling; knowledge of nationalist lore; skill and boldness in stealing. . . .

BOX 14.2

TEACHER EXPECTATIONS AND SCHOOL SUCCESS
...

Every reader of this book has spent a dozen or more years in classrooms. Everyone knows from personal experience that teachers' attitudes toward students vary and that teachers expect some students to do better than others in mastering academic material. What modern research has shown is that these attitudes and expectations influence students' performance in a variety of ways.

Perhaps the most famous, and certainly the most controversial, research on the effect of teacher expectations was initiated in the 1960s by Robert Rosenthal and his colleagues (Rosenthal, 1987; Rosenthal & Rubin, 1980). These researchers reported that a teacher's expectations about a child's academic ability may become a self-fulfilling prophecy, even when these expectations are groundless.

In order to demonstrate the power of teacher expectations, Rosenthal and Jacobsen (1968) gave children in all six elementary grades a test which, they told the teachers, would identify children who were likely to "bloom" intellectually during the coming year. After the testing, teachers were given the names of those children who, the researchers said, would show a spurt in intellectual development during the school year. In fact, the names of the presumed "bloomers" were chosen at random.

At the end of the school year the children were tested again. This time the researchers found that there was in fact a difference between the two groups at the first and second grade levels; the children who had been randomly identified as likely candidates for rapid intellectual growth really did grow. They gained an average of 15 points on their IQ scores over their scores at the beginning of the school year, while their classmates' IQ scores remained unchanged. In this study, the IQs of

Teachers' expectations about children's academic abilities affect in complex ways how they pay attention to their students, encourage them, and discipline them.

children in the upper grades did not change, but in a follow-up study Rosenthal and his colleagues found that older schoolchildren could also be influenced by teacher expectations (Rosenthal, Baratz, & Hall, 1974).

Since the children identified as those likely to bloom intellectually were chosen at random, Rosenthal and his colleagues concluded that teachers' expectations influence their students' behavior, making teachers more effective with children whom they believe are more academically able.

A particularly provocative finding in Rosenthal and Jacobsen's (1968) study concerned ethnic and class differences in academic performance. Teachers often have lower expectations for the academic performance of minority group and poor children than they do for their

Success in school is irrelevant to prestige within the group, and reading is rarely if ever used outside of school. (1969, p. 55)

By comparing the reading scores of group members and nonmembers at different grade levels, Labov and

Robbins could assess the influence of participation in certain peer groups on academic achievement. They found that as nongroup members progressed through the grades, their reading scores became higher and higher, while there was virtually no improvement for group members.

Anglo, middle-class counterparts (Minuchin & Shapiro, 1983). To test the possibility that these lowered expectations actually contribute to minority and poor children's lower academic performance, Rosenthal and Jacobsen included a group of poor Mexican-American children among those they identified as likely to bloom during the coming year. These children made particularly large gains in IQ test performance. In fact, the children that the teachers identified as most "Mexican-looking" made the largest gains, perhaps because they were the ones from whom the teachers would ordinarily have expected the least.

Such results immediately attracted the attention of researchers and the public at large. At present there have been more than 500 studies of the role of teacher expectations on academic performance (Wineberg, 1987). Many school districts even have special training programs for their teachers to ensure that they are sensitive to the ways in which their expectations might negatively affect some children.

Despite general acceptance of the idea that teacher expectations are a significant factor in children's academic performance, some psychologists and educators remain skeptical (Wineberg, 1987). One basis for doubt is that the effects of teacher expectations are only found on the average; there are many studies which fail to find them. Whey do some studies fail to find such effects?

In an attempt to answer this question, researchers observed teachers and children interacting in classrooms. They found that not all teachers behave the same way toward the children for whom they have low expectations. Some teachers ignore those that they expect little from academically and focus their attention on the children whom they believe to be more capable. But other teachers seem to compensate by giving extra help and encouragement to the children for whom they have low expectations, while still others are even-handed (Good, Sikes, & Brophy, 1973). This classroom

observation research also makes it clear that children are not passive recipients of teachers' expectations. Children influence the very expectations that are shaping them by their own classroom behavior (Brophy, 1983).

Research by Carol Dweck and her colleagues has shown one way in which the interplay between teachers' expectations and children's behavior may shape academic development. Dweck's research has focused on teachers' differing expectations for boys and girls. In general, girls are better behaved than boys during the elementary school years. Consequently, teachers expect boys to challenge classroom decorum, and girls to support it. Dweck and her colleagues found that these differences in children's behavior and teacher expectations led teachers to respond differently to boys and girls (Dweck & Bush, 1976; Dweck, Davidson, Nelson, & Enna, 1978; Dweck & Goetz, 1978). Overall, teachers criticize boys more than girls. Often this criticism focuses on boys' lack of decorum, their failure to do their work neatly, or their inattentiveness. By contrast, when teachers criticize girls, their criticism is likely to focus on ability and intellectual performance. At the same time, when teachers praise girls it is likely to be for their cooperative social behavior, while their praise for boys is more likely to focus on their intellectual accomplishments.

These differences in teachers' expectations for boys and girls and in the kind of feedback they give them has been found to be related to the kinds of expectations that children form about their own behavior (Dweck & Elliott, 1983). When girls are told by teachers that they have failed, they usually believe that the teacher has correctly assessed their ability. As a result of such criticism, they tend to stop trying. Boys interpret such criticism differently. Instead of concluding that they are unable to do well academically, they blame someone else or their situation for their poor performance and retain faith in their own ability to do better next time.

School Atmosphere

It might be concluded from Labov and Robbins's results that the schools are helpless in the face of community and peer-group pressures, but research in recent years demonstrates convincingly that the quality

of experience within the school can make a decisive difference in promoting educational success. For example, Michael Rutter and his colleagues carried out a large-scale study of secondary schools in central London, where housing conditions are poor, there is high unemployment, a high crime rate, low levels of education among adults, and high rates of handicapping psychiatric disorders (Rutter, Maughan, Mortimore, & Ouston, 1979). These are just the community conditions that one might expect would lead to poor educational achievement, and in many cases, they do. What makes the research by Rutter and his colleagues important is their demonstration that the school *can* make a difference. The most successful school in their sample was more than four times more successful in educating pupils than the least successful school.

The most expected explanations for why some schools succeeded and some failed turned out to be wrong. The successful schools were not more modern, did not have better trained or better paid teachers, nor did they take in students with higher IQs or more favorable family conditions. The differences were instead caused by educational processes within the schools. Among the processes found most important were the following:

1. *Academic emphasis*   Schools that clearly demonstrated their expectation that students were in school to master academic subjects produced higher levels of achievement. These expectations were manifested in a variety of ways, such as assignment of homework and regular displays of excellent work on classroom bulletin boards. Figure 14.11 displays the relationship between the amount of homework assigned and the average examination score pupils achieved. (See also Box 14.2, "Teacher Expectations and School Success.")

2. *Teacher behaviors*   When teachers must stop to discipline individual children, everyone tends to lose the thread of the lesson. Successful classrooms were those where teachers could coordinate the entire class at one time; often these teachers expected their students to work silently, on their own.

3. *Distribution of rewards and punishments*   The most successful classrooms were those where punishment was given less frequently than praise.

4. *Student conditions*   Schools in which students were given freedom to use the buildings during breaks and lunch time, given access to a telephone, and expected to accept responsibility for keeping the classroom clean and pleasant pro-

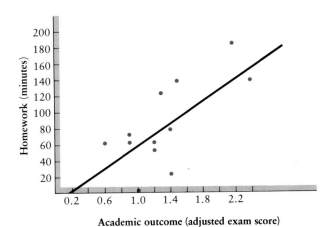

FIGURE 14.11 *As the amount of homework assigned each week increases (a measure of the academic emphasis of the school), so do student grades. (From Rutter, Maughan, Mortimore, & Ouston, 1979.)*

duced better student achievement than schools that were entirely adult run.

The most intriguing finding was that in the successful schools, each individual factor seemed to feed the others, creating an overall favorable environment, or "school atmosphere" that produced success. This positive school atmosphere cannot be legislated; it must be created by the staff and the students together. Each successful school was successful in a different way, using a different mixture of approaches.

Out of School

Although success at schooling has come to define a successful passage through middle childhood in literate societies, it should not be forgotten that there is more to life than school. On weekday afternoons and evenings, on weekends and holidays, 6- to 12-year-old children are likely to be found among friends, engaged in activities of their own choosing. Participation in these peer groups provides a kind of preparation for adult life that is quite different from that organized by adults in classrooms or in the home. A full understanding of the nature of middle childhood requires investigation of this context as well, to which we turn in the next chapter.

SUMMARY

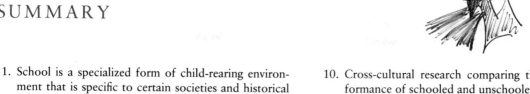

1. School is a specialized form of child-rearing environment that is specific to certain societies and historical eras. Formal education in schools differs from traditional training, such as apprenticeship, in the motives for learning, as well as in the social relations, the social organization, and the medium of instruction.

2. Schooling arose as a means of training large numbers of scribes in order to transmit writing and record-keeping skills from one generation to the next.

3. Essential to formal education is the use of written notation systems. The technology of writing has undergone a long evolution. The early notation systems that represented objects gave way to the use of symbols representing language. The evolution of the written notation system called an alphabet decreased the number of symbols that people need to learn but increased the abstractness of the resulting system for representing sounds.

4. Reading acquisition goes through a number of stages. The transition at around third or fourth grade from decoding individual words to reading in order to learn something new is particularly difficult for many children.

5. Reading instruction has undergone changes in response to demands for higher levels of proficiency: current curricula seek to balance an emphasis on analysis of letter–sound correspondences with an emphasis on reading for meaning.

6. Children arrive at school with a good deal of knowledge about practical arithmetic, including the idea of one-to-one correspondence and the ability to count. Early school mathematics builds on these abilities, requiring mastery of a notation system and such mathematical operations as addition, subtraction, and multiplication.

7. Some children fail to link formal mathematics with their practical knowledge. Current teaching techniques attempt to balance drill with explanation.

8. A special kind of talk characterizes classroom instruction. Children must learn to acquire knowledge through verbal exchanges, in which teachers ask questions, children reply, and teachers evaluate.

9. The great emphasis placed on using correct linguistic forms in classroom discourse reinforces the hypothetical, "as if" nature of classroom problem solving.

10. Cross-cultural research comparing the cognitive performance of schooled and unschooled children reveals that in several domains — including the organization of the lexicon, memory, and metacognitive skills — formal schooling appears to enhance the development of certain cognitive skills during middle childhood. Positive cognitive consequences of schooling turn out to be restricted to materials and procedures that closely match classroom practices. There is no evidence for any consequences of schooling on *general* cognitive development.

11. Tests of aptitude for schooling arose when public education became a mass phenomenon. The earliest tests were designed to identify children who needed special support to succeed in school.

12. The key innovation in Binet and Simon's test of school aptitude was to scale test items in terms of the age at which typical children could cope with them, thus producing a scale of "mental age."

13. The aptitude measure called IQ represents a child's mental age (as determined by the age at which average children pass each test item) divided by chronological age (IQ = MA/CA × 100). This ratio yields an average IQ of 100 by definition.

14. IQ test scores have been found to correlate significantly with later school success.

15. An important, unresolved question about intelligence tests is the degree to which the aptitudes they tap are general across all domains of human activity versus being closely related to specialized activities such as those involved in schooling, music, and so on.

16. Persistent class and ethnic differences in IQ test performance have caused fierce debates about the degree to which some ethnic groups and classes are genetically inferior.

17. Modern research comparing IQs of identical and fraternal twins indicates that there is a genetic contribution to IQ, accounting for perhaps 50 percent of variation in test performance *within* ethnic groups.

18. Black children adopted into white, middle-class homes develop normal IQs, indicating that there are no differ-

ences in genetic endowment to explain why children from some ethnic groups do so poorly in school.

19. Peer-group values contradictory to the school can exert a powerful negative effect on student achievement.

20. Schools with a strong academic emphasis, teachers skilled in classroom management, an emphasis on praise over punishment, and a welcoming attitude toward students make a positive difference to student achievement in school.

KEY TERMS

Apprenticeship

Education

Environmentalist hypothesis of IQ

Innatist hypothesis of IQ

Initiation-reply-evaluation sequence

Instructional discourse

IQ

Mental age (MA)

Metacognition

SUGGESTED READINGS

CHALL, JEAN. *Stages of Reading Development.* New York: McGraw-Hill, 1983.

As the director of a reading clinic at the Harvard School of Education, Jean Chall brings many years of clinical practice to her account of the process of learning to read. The result is a book that combines theoretical sophistication in the study of cognitive development with the practical wisdom of long experience.

GINSBURG, HERBERT. *Children's Arithmetic: The Learning Process.* New York: Van Nostrand, 1977.

This book analyses the development of mathematical reasoning, focusing primarily on the struggles that children face when they come up against school arithmetic tasks. It is particularly rich in its detailed descriptions of individual children's reasoning as their intuitive ways of thinking about number confront the written notation system of mathematics.

GOULD, STEPHEN J. *The Mismeasure of Man.* New York: Norton, 1981.

Professor of biology, geology, and the history of science, Stephen J. Gould here surveys the historical origins of the idea that intelligence is a single entity, located in the brain, that can be legitimately used to rank people along a single dimension of ability.

HOLT, JOHN. *How Children Fail.* New York: Dell, 1964.

A first-hand account of the dynamics of children's lives that make failure in school an integral part of the experience of a large percentage of the world's children during middle childhood.

ROGOFF, BARBARA. "Schooling and the Development of Cognitive Skills." In H. C. Triandis and A. Heron (Eds.), *Handbook of Cross-Cultural Psychology* (Vol. 4). Boston: Allyn & Bacon, 1981.

A review of the evidence concerning schooling's impact on cognitive development, based primarily on cross-cultural research in societies in which many children do not attend school.

STERNBERG, ROBERT J. *Handbook of Intelligence.* New York: Cambridge University Press, 1983.

An authoritative compendium of essays on the history and theory of intelligence testing.

STEVENSON, HAROLD, HIROSHI AZUMA, and KENJI HAKUTA. *Child Development and Education in Japan.* New York: W. H. Freeman and Company, 1986.

The educational and economic achievements of the Japanese have won widespread admiration. This book describes the cultural values and social policies that underlie recent Japanese educational successes and that shape the experience of middle childhood in Japan.

WARDLE, DAVID. *The Rise of the Schooled Society.* London: Routledge & Kegan Paul, 1974.

This history of the rise of schooling in England touches on many themes of importance to the study of middle childhood: the changing relationship of children to their families once a society adopts schooling as a means of instruction, transformations in social concepts of childhood, and the new relationship of education to work.

THE SOCIAL RELATIONS OF MIDDLE CHILDHOOD

We went home and when somebody said, "Where were you?" we said, "Out," and when

somebody said, "What were you doing until this hour of the

night," we said, as always, "Nothing."

But about this doing nothing: we swung on the swings. We went for walks. We lay

on our backs in backyards and chewed grass . . . and when we were done, he [my

best friend] walked me home to my house, and when we got there I

walked him back to his house, and then he —.

We watched things: we watched people build houses, we watched men fix cars, we

watched each other patch bicycle tires with rubber bands . . . [we watched] our

fathers playing cards, our mothers making jam, our

sisters skipping rope, curling their hair. . . .

We sat in boxes; we sat under porches; we sat on roofs; we sat on limbs of trees.

We stood on boards over excavations; we stood on tops of piles of leaves; we

stood under rain dripping from the eaves; we stood up to our ears in snow.

We looked at things like knives . . . and grasshoppers

and clouds and dogs and people.

We skipped and hopped and jumped. Not going anywhere — just skipping

and hopping and jumping and galloping.

We sang and whittled and hummed and screamed.

What I mean, Jack, we did a lot of nothing.

— Robert Paul Smith, *Where Did You Go? Out. What Did You Do? Nothing.*

. . . .

Between the ages of 6 and 12, children spend an average of over 40 percent of their waking hours in the company of **peers**, children of their own age and status. This figure is more than double the percentage of time that they spent with their peers when they were preschoolers. This increase in time spent among peers is accompanied by a complementary decrease in the time spent with parents (Baldwin, 1955; Barker & Wright, 1955; Hill & Stafford, 1980).

Comparisons of children's behavior in different settings suggest two obvious differences between contexts where adults supervise and contexts dominated by peers. First, the content of the activity is different. When adults preside over the activities of children, some form of instruction is likely to be involved; when several children get together with no adults present, they are likely to play a game or "just hang out."

Second, the forms of social control are different. When children are under the watchful eye of adults, either at home or in school, the adults provide the mechanism for maintaining the social order. If Sarah takes more than her share of the ice cream, or if Tom and Jimmy refuse to let Sam play on the swings, the adult is there to invoke the rules ("Share and share alike"; "Everyone gets a turn") and to settle disputes. But when children are on their own in peer groups, the distribution of authority has to be established by the children themselves. Sometimes "might makes right" when an especially strong child dominates the group. By and large, however, authority is established through negotiation, compromise, and discussion (Youniss, 1980). Sources of power within the group may also change, depending upon what the children are doing. A leader in making mischief may not be the leader in organizing a trip to the Saturday afternoon movies (Sherif & Sherif, 1956).

The increased time that children spend among their peers is both a cause and an effect of their development. Adults begin to allow their children to spend extensive time with friends and assign them new responsibilities because they recognize their children's greater ability to think and act for themselves. At the same time, the new peer groups challenge children to master new cognitive and social skills to complement

the skills they learn in school and in other instructional settings (Damon, 1983; Harter, 1983; Hartup, 1984).

Children's sense of themselves also changes in middle childhood. So long as children spend their time primarily among family members, their place in the social world is determined for them. They are accepted as "Mrs. Smith's little girl, Suzie," or "Juan Lopez's brother, Tony." When, during middle childhood, children spend more time among their peers, the sense of self they acquired in their families no longer

Learning to get along without fighting is a difficult task, especially when a smaller child is threatened and one's honor is at stake.

suffices and they must learn to reconcile their old identities with the new ones they begin to form in the new contexts they inhabit. The responsible older sibling who watches the baby, the classroom comedian, the star volleyball player, and the kid who spends a lot of time reading adventure stories may well be one and the same person.

Children's new status during middle childhood influences the quality of their relationships with their parents. Parents can no longer easily pick up their children and physically remove them from danger or from sibling squabbles. Parents must rely on their children's greater understanding of the consequences of their actions and on their desire to comply with adult standards. Socialization techniques must become more indirect: parents increasingly use discussion and explanation rather than physical force to influence their children's behavior.

Unfortunately, psychological research methods cannot always do justice to the greatly increased diversity of experience during middle childhood. In studying preschoolers, scientific generalizations are impeded because the children are just learning to talk and it is difficult to distinguish fact from fancy in their reports. On the other hand, preschoolers, whether at home or in a day-care center, are restricted to relatively few environments, where adults can keep an eye on them and record what they do. Most 8- and 9-year-olds are perfectly capable conversationalists, but when they are spending time with their peers and an adult observer appears on the scene, the nature of the interactions immediately changes.

Scientific knowledge about middle childhood is therefore fragmentary in several respects. There is extensive information about children's behavior in school, but not about their life in other contexts. There are a great many studies of how children respond to questions about hypothetical moral dilemmas, their explicit conceptions of friendship, and the manner in which they attempt to solve a variety of intellectual puzzles adults pose for them. But there is little systematic information about their actual moral behavior, their qualities as friends, or their ability to recognize and solve problems in everyday life.

Despite these gaps in knowledge, research in recent decades has illuminated some important ways in which peer interactions contribute to development: fostering increased understanding of social rules, improving the ability to resolve conflicts and get along with others, and developing a more complex concept of oneself.

GAMES AND GROUP REGULATION

The appearance of peer groups among children raises a central question about middle childhood: how do children acquire the ability to regulate their social relations by themselves? While uncertainty remains about the precise psychological mechanisms involved, it appears that one important arena for this development is game-playing (Piaget, 1967; Sutton-Smith, 1979).

Games and Rules

Like preschoolers, children who have entered middle childhood engage in fantasy play based on roles in which each child takes a part in an imaginary situation: cops chase robbers; treehouses become havens for shipwrecked families; and forts hide runaway children. But now a new form of play comes into prominence—games based upon rules.

Both the rules and styles of interaction that these games promote vary from culture to culture. In West Africa children divide into teams and challenge each

These !Kung children are enjoying a game in which they imitate a local animal.

other to remember the names of leaves gathered in the forest. Children in the United States are more likely to play "Twenty Questions" or "Trivial Pursuit." Throughout many cultures we find variations on games where a ball is kicked, hit, or thrown as part of a team sport, or games that resemble tag or hopscotch (Rubin, Fein, & Vandenberg, 1983; Schwartzman, 1980). But even in cultures in which children are more likely to begin to work rather than attend school, middle childhood is distinguished as a time when games with explicit rules make their appearance.

Although fantasy play is based on *roles* and games are based on *rules*, rules are not totally absent from preschoolers' fantasy play; nor are roles totally absent from rule-based play. Rules are a part of preschool play in two ways. First, when children perform their roles, they typically follow several implicit social rules. The pretend teacher tells the pretend children to sit quietly, rather than the children telling the teacher what to do.

Second, preschoolers use rules to negotiate the roles they adopt and to maintain the make-believe context: "Only girls are allowed to be Superwoman"; "Go away, Darth Vader, we're having a birthday party and spacemen are not allowed at birthday parties" (Paley, 1984).

Rules enter into the play of older children in quite a different way. At about the age of 7 or 8, rules become the essence of many games while roles and imaginary situations fade into the background. The content of preschool fantasy play can change from moment to moment, allowing children constantly to merge their whims with their play. But in the games characteristic of middle childhood, participants must agree ahead of time about the rules that will govern their activity. To change the rules without common consent will be called "cheating."

Rule-based games seem to require the same kind of mental abilities that were described in Chapter 13 as the basis for adult assignment of new responsibilities to 6- and 7-year-olds. Children must be able to keep in mind the overall set of conditions specified ahead of time as they pursue the goals of the moment. At the same time, they need to engage in social perspective-taking, understanding the relation between the thoughts of the other players and their own actions ("If I move my checker piece into this opening, my opponent will double-jump me").

Rule-based games also differ in purpose from fantasy play. In fantasy play, "the play's the thing." Satisfaction comes from exercising the imagination in the company of others. In rule-governed play, the objective is more likely to be to win through competition based on rules. The following description of an attempt to involve a preschooler in a rule-based game captures beautifully this difference in orientation:

> The experimenter is playing hide-and-seek with a 3-year-old child. When the child has hidden, the experimenter does not "find" it immediately, but deliberately waits near the child for a minute or two pretending not to be able to find it. Then the tot cannot restrain itself from breaking the rule, and almost immediately begins to shout: "Uncle, here I am!" A 6-year-old plays hide-and-seek quite differently. For it, the main thing is to stick to the rules. The experimenter conceived the idea of telling both children (the 3-year-old and the 6-year-old) to hide together. He again pretended that he could not find them. Soon the children's excited voices were heard, and then a muffled noise. The little one was trying to give itself up while the 6-year-old was preventing it from doing so. Exclamations were heard: "Quiet, keep still!" Finally the older child tried to stop the little one's mouth — matters came to very vigorous measures to make the younger child observe the rule. (Leontiev, 1981, p. 381)

The shift from role-based fantasy play to rule-based games greatly expands both the number of children who can play together and the likely duration of their joint activity. In a typical preschool setting, only two or three children play together at a time and their play episodes are likely to last less than 10 minutes (Corsaro, 1981). When larger groups gather, it is almost certainly because the teacher has taken the trouble to coordinate their activity, which is unlikely to be fantasy play. By contrast, school-age children can often be seen playing for hours in groups ranging up to 20 or so children (Hartup, 1984). The increased duration and complexity of children's play provides evidence that at least under some conditions, children who have entered middle childhood are capable of regulating their own behavior according to agreed-upon social rules.

Games and Life

The link between preschoolers' play and their social surroundings is fairly obvious because they use adult roles to structure their activity. How a game of hopscotch or checkers relates to adult life is less evident. Nonetheless, there are good reasons to believe that rule-based games help children to coordinate extended interactions with their peers, enabling them to get along with others in the absence of adult authority.

Piaget (1965) believed that the appearance of rule-based games in middle childhood has a double significance for children's development. First, he saw the ability to engage in rule-based games as a manifestation of concrete operations in the social sphere, corresponding to the appearance of conservation and other cognitive abilities discussed in Chapter 13. Second, he believed that games and other rule-based activities contribute to development by creating structured circumstances within which children obtain practice balancing their own desires against the rules of their society.

Rule-based games are a model of society for children in two closely related respects, Piaget argued. First,

> Games with rules are social institutions in that they remain the same as they are transmitted from one generation to the next and they are independent of the will of the individuals who participate in them. (Piaget & Inhelder, 1969, p. 119)

Like other social institutions—a school lesson, for example—games provide an already existing structure of rules about how to behave in specific social circumstances.

Second, like social institutions, rule-based games can only exist if people agree to their existence. In order to play a game such as checkers or hide-and-seek, children must learn to subordinate their behavior to a socially agreed-upon system. Piaget linked this ability to their acquisition of a respect for rules and a new level of moral understanding:

> All morality consists in a system of rules, and the essence of all morality is to be sought for in the respect which the individual acquires for these rules. . . . The rules of the game of marbles are handed down, just like so-called moral realities, from one generation to another, and are preserved solely by the respect that is felt for them by individuals. (1965, pp. 13–14)

In Piaget's view, it is through the give and take of negotiating plans, settling disagreements, making and

enforcing rules, and keeping and breaking promises that children come to develop an understanding that social rules provide a structure within which cooperation with others can take place (Piaget, 1965).

Based upon his observations of the way children play games, Piaget proposed a developmental progression in children's understanding of social rules. The game upon which he based most of his discussion is marbles. He maintained that preschool-aged children play marbles with little regard for the rules and with no notion of competition. Young children pile marbles up or roll them around as suits their fancy. At this stage, marbles is not a true game at all.

In middle childhood, children begin trying to win according to preexisting rules. At first they tend to believe that the rules of the game have been handed down by such authority figures as older children, adults, or even God; therefore, they are sacred and cannot be changed. For example, Piaget asked one $5\frac{1}{2}$-year-old if it would be all right to allow little children to shoot their marbles from a position closer to the marbles they were trying to hit.

> "No," answered Leh, "that wouldn't be fair." — "Why not?" — "Because God would make the little boy's shot not reach the marbles and the big boy's shot would reach them." (1965, p. 58)

Piaget suggested to Ben, age 10, that he might invent a new version of marbles. Ben agreed reluctantly that it would be possible to think up new rules. Piaget then asked if such a new rule would be acceptable:

> *Piaget:* Then people could play that way?
>
> *Ben:* Oh, no, because it would be cheating.
>
> *Piaget:* But all your pals would like to, wouldn't they?
>
> *Ben:* Yes, they all would.
>
> *Piaget:* Then why would it be cheating?
>
> *Ben:* Because I invented it: it isn't a rule! It's a wrong rule because it's outside of the rules. A fair rule is one that is in the game.
>
> (1965, p. 63)

Sometime between the ages of 9 and 11, according to Piaget, most children begin to treat the rules of games with less awe. They realize that game rules are social conventions resulting from mutual consent. The

Games with rules are prominent in the lives of children during middle childhood.

rules must be respected if you want to play together, "but it is permissible to alter the rules as long as general opinion is on your side" (1965, p. 28).

Although he focused his attention on the game of marbles, which in Geneva was played almost exclusively by boys, Piaget wanted to show that the developmental progression he had encountered was a universal one. However, he reported that he could not find any collective games played by girls that used as many rules and as many fine-grained codifications as marbles had. After observing many girls playing hopscotch, he remarked that girls seemed more interested in inventing new configurations of hopscotch squares than in elaborating the rules.

Piaget's observation that boys and girls not only play different games but play games differently has generated a good deal of subsequent research. José Linaza (1984), for instance, observed English and Spanish boys and girls playing marbles. He found that while the boys might play marbles more often and more skillfully than girls, there were no marked sex differences in boys' and girls' understanding of the rules of the game. On the other hand, Janet Lever (1978) used observational methods to confirm Piaget's finding that rules enter into the play of boys and girls differently (see Box 15.1, "Boys' Games, Girls' Games"). Overall, the research suggests that, despite some observed sex differences, middle childhood is a time when play based upon explicit rules begins to occupy a prominent role in the interactions of both sexes.

REASONING AND ACTION IN DIFFERENT RULE DOMAINS

In the transition to middle childhood, children must come to understand several different domains of rules, each with its own nature and content. The various types of social rules are distinguishable from each other by their importance, their apparent permanence, and their generality (Turiel, Killen, & Helwig, 1987) (see Table 15.1). At the most general level are **moral rules,** obligatory social regulations based on principles of justice and welfare—such as the prohibition against killing another human being or the obligation to take care of one's children. Such moral rules define

obligations necessary to the maintenance of the social group. They are found in some form in all societies (Rawls, 1971).

At the next level of generality are *social norms,* or **social conventions** — rules that are particular to a single society — such as prescriptions about the kinds of behavior appropriate for males and females or the kind of clothes people should wear in public, as well as rules about who has authority over other people, how authority is exercised, and how it is acknowledged (Turiel, 1983). Social conventions coordinate the behavior of individuals within a social system, but differ from society to society (see Table 15.1). A more restricted kind of social norm, known as **group norms,** apply to small groups such as peer groups. They include special modes of greeting (such as secret handshakes) and styles of dress.

TABLE 15.1 The domains of conventional and moral reasoning

Conventional events

Sample Event Types	Examples of Event Type
School rules	Chewing gum in class; boys entering girls' bathroom; talking back to the teacher
Forms of address	Calling teacher by first name
Attire and appearance	Not wearing school uniform; dressing casually in a business office
Sex roles	Boy wears barrette to keep his hair out of his eyes while playing football; girl gets a crew cut
Etiquette	Eating with hands; swearing

Moral events

Physical harm	Hitting; pushing; killing
Psychological harm	Hurting feelings; ridiculing a cripple
Fairness and rights	Stealing, breaking a promise; slavery, turn-taking
Prosocial behaviors	Donating to charity; sharing; helping people in distress

SOURCE: Turiel, Killen, & Helwig, 1987.

BOX 15.1

BOYS' GAMES, GIRLS' GAMES

· · ·

Piaget's observation that during middle childhood boys are more likely than girls to engage in competitive games based on explicit rules was corroborated many years later by Janet Lever (1978). Lever observed children in the United States on playgrounds, interviewed them, and had them keep diaries of their after-school play. She then rated the children's play according to its complexity. She defined as complex games that require each player to take a different role (such as baseball); have a relatively large number of participants; are competitive based on explicit goals, such as scoring a goal in soccer or checkmating an opponent; have a number of specified rules that are known by all the players before the game begins and whose violations are penalized; and require teams.

According to Lever's data (see the accompanying table), both boys and girls engage in a wide variety of play activities, including complex games. But, on the average, girls play less complex games with fewer participants than boys. Boys are almost twice as likely to engage in competitive games than girls, even when they are not playing team sports. Girls, by contrast, tend to play cooperatively. When their games allow competition, as do jump-rope and jacks, it is indirect: each player acts independently of the others, competing by turn against the others' scores, rather than competing in face-to-face confrontations as boys do.

Boys and girls not only play different games, they participate in different-sized play groups. Boys tend to play in larger groups than girls. Team sports, which they are more likely to engage in than girls, require from 10 to 25 participants to be played properly. Lever rarely observed girls playing in groups as large as 10 persons. Instead, she found them playing games such as hopscotch and tag, which can be played with as few as two people and seldom include more than six. Some girls talked more than they played.

Sex differences in percent of time children observed playing different kinds of games

	Girls	Boys
Complexity Score 0 roller-skating, bike-riding, listening to records	42%	27%
Complexity Score 1 singing, playing catch, bowling, racing electric cars	7%	12%
Complexity Score 2 indoor fantasy, jump rope, tag, simple card games	31%	15%
Complexity Score 3 board games, checkers	8%	15%
Complexity Score 4 capture the flag	2%	1%
Complexity Score 5 team sports	10%	30%

SOURCE: Lever, 1978.

Lever conjectures that such differences provide girls and boys with a markedly different set of socialization experiences and social skills. Boys' games, she contends, provide them with the opportunity to deal with diversity, to coordinate with a large number of people, to cope with impersonal rule systems, and to work for collective as well as personal goals. In particular, participation in team sports furnishes boys with the opportunity to be rewarded for improving their skills, to gain experience in leadership positions, and to deal with competition in a depersonalized fashion, as well as to maintain self-control. Most girls' play activities tend instead to recreate primary human relationships and to concentrate on intimacy.

At the most specific level are **personal rules** governing particular events, such as "Do homework before watching TV" or "Brush teeth before going to bed every night." Personal rules are often created by individuals to regulate their own behavior.

As early as the age of 5 years, children appear to recognize the differences between moral principles and social conventions (Much & Shweder, 1978; Nucci & Turiel, 1978). For example, Donna Weston and Eliot Turiel (1980) told children a series of stories in which a young protagonist hit another child, undressed on the playground, left toys on the classroom floor, and refused to share a snack. All of the children, who ranged in age from 5 to 11 years, considered hitting another child and other moral transgressions wrong even if there were no specific rules against them at their school, while only 20 percent of the children considered breaches of social convention (such as undressing in public) wrong in the absence of explicit rules against such behavior.

Larry Nucci (1981) demonstrated that at least from middle childhood on, children distinguish the different kinds of rules according to their importance. He presented cartoon strips depicting violations of moral, conventional, or personal rules to children and adolescents (see Figure 15.1). Asked to judge the seriousness of each incident, subjects at all ages ranked moral violations as more serious, then violations of social convention, and finally violations of personal rules.

Although children seem to understand the distinction between rule types from an early age, their understanding of each type continues to develop all during childhood. A major research goal is to determine the extent to which development within one rule domain affects development within others, and to grasp how understanding rules relates to children's behavior in everyday life.

Moral Rules

As children begin to spend extensive time with their peers beyond the constraints of adult authority, the way in which they think about moral rules changes (Smetana, 1981, 1985; Turiel, 1983). As described briefly in Chapter 11 (p. 356), Piaget linked changes in reasoning about moral issues to children's new forms of peer interaction as well as to their increased cognitive abilities. This belief was supported by his observation that during late middle childhood children begin to realize that game rules are social conventions that can be changed if everyone agrees. At the same time, they begin to make judgments of "good" and "bad" behavior based on autonomous moral reasoning rather than on externally imposed authority.

Piaget's hypothesis was modified by Lawrence Kohlberg, whose influential research program of more than 20 years has evoked both friendly and critical

responses (Gilligan, 1977; Hoffman, 1983; Kagan & Lamb, 1987; Kohlberg, 1969, 1976, 1984; Kurtines & Gewirtz, 1984; Lickona, 1976; Rest, 1983). Kohlberg's approach to assessing moral reasoning was to create a series of story-dilemmas, each of which embodies traditional questions of moral philosophy: the value of human life and property, people's obligations to each other, and the meaning of laws and rules. The story-dilemmas pose these abstract issues in a concrete, dramatic way to engage the subjects' interest.

Kohlberg's most famous story is called the "Heinz dilemma." In the manner of Piaget's clinical interview technique, Kohlberg would read the story, ask the child's opinion, and then probe the reasoning behind that opinion with a set of questions tailored to the individual child's answer.

> In Europe, a woman was near death from cancer. One drug might save her, a form of radium that a druggist in the same town had recently discovered. The druggist was charging $2,000, ten times what the drug cost him to make. The sick woman's husband, Heinz, went to everyone he knew to borrow the money, but he could get together only about half of what it cost. He told the druggist that his wife was dying and asked him to sell it cheaper or let him pay later. But the druggist said no. The husband got desperate and broke into the man's store to steal the drug for his wife. Should the husband have done that? Why? (Kohlberg, 1969, p. 379)

Kohlberg (1976, 1984) proposed that reasoning about moral issues generally progresses through five stages. He also believed in the existence of a sixth, ideal stage based upon what he called "universal moral principles," but he encountered this stage so rarely that he gave up trying to score it.

Kohlberg's six stages are grouped according to three levels of moral judgment corresponding to the three major Piagetian stages of cognitive development from age 3 to adulthood. At the *preconventional* level (corresponding to the stage of preoperational thinking), moral judgments are based on the direct physical consequences of the action in question and on the child's own desires. At the *conventional* level (corresponding to the stage of concrete operations), moral judgments depend on what other people think; acts that violate social standards are bad. At the *postconventional* level

(a)

Kathy is playing with her doll. | Meg comes over and takes Kathy's doll away from her. | Kathy is upset. Meg is not supposed to take things away from other children.

(b)

Karen is watching her very favorite TV program, "The Mickey Mouse Club." | Her big sister tells her, "Karen, you're not allowed to stay inside on sunny days. Mom says you have to go outside and play." | "Those are the rules."

(c)

Larry is eating lunch in the school cafeteria. He is eating with his fingers. | Laura tells Larry, "You shouldn't eat meat with your fingers." | "You should use a knife and fork when you're eating in the cafeteria."

FIGURE 15.1 *Cartoon strips used to evaluate the relative importance that children attach to (a) moral infractions, (b) infractions of personal rules, and (c) infractions of social conventions. (Courtesy of L. Nucci.)*

TABLE 15.2 Kohlberg's six moral stages

Level and Stage	What Is Right	Reasons for Doing Right	Social Perspective of Stage
Level I — Preconventional			
Stage 1 — Heteronomous morality	To avoid breaking rules backed by punishment, obedience for its own sake, and avoiding physical damage to persons and property.	Avoidance of punishment, and the superior power of authorities.	Egocentric point of view: Doesn't consider the interests of others or recognize that they differ from the actor's; doesn't relate two points of view. Actions are considered physically rather than in terms of psychological interests of others. Confusion of authority's perspective with one's own.
Stage 2 — Individualism, instrumental purpose, and exchange	Following rules only when it is to someone's immediate interest, acting to meet one's own interests and needs and letting others do the same. Right is also what's fair, what's an equal exchange, a deal, an agreement.	To serve one's own needs or interests in a world where you have to recognize that other people have their interests, too.	Concrete individualistic perspective: Aware that everybody has his own interests to pursue and these conflict, so that right is relative (in the concrete individualistic sense).
Level II — Conventional			
Stage 3 — Mutual interpersonal expectations, relationships, and interpersonal conformity	Living up to what is expected by people close to you or what people generally expect of people in your role as son, brother, friend, etc. "Being good" is important and means having good motives, showing concern about others. It also means keeping mutual relationships, such as trust, loyalty, respect and gratitude.	The need to be a good person in your own eyes and those of others. Your caring for others. Belief in the Golden Rule. Desire to maintain rules and authority which support stereotypical good behavior.	Perspective of the individual in relationships with other individuals: Aware of shared feelings, agreements, and expectations which take primacy over individual interests. Relates points of view through the concrete Golden Rule, putting yourself in the other guy's shoes. Does not yet consider generalized system perspective.
Stage 4 — Social system and conscience	Fulfilling the actual duties to which you have agreed. Laws are to be upheld except in extreme cases where they conflict with other fixed social duties. Right is also contributing to society, the group, or institution.	To keep the institution going as a whole, to avoid the breakdown in the system "if everyone did it," or the imperative of conscience to meet one's defined obligations (easily confused with Stage 3 belief in rules and authority).	Differentiates societal point of view from interpersonal agreement of motives: Takes the point of view of the system that defines roles and rules. Considers individual relations in terms of place in the system.

(Continued)

TABLE 15.2 Kohlberg's six moral stages *(Continued)*

Level and Stage	What Is Right	Reasons for Doing Right	Social Perspective of Stage
Level III — Postconventional, or principled			
Stage 5 — Social contract or utility and individual rights	Being aware that people hold a variety of values and opinions, that most values and rules are relative to your group. These relative rules should usually be upheld, however, in the interest of impartiality and because they are the social contract. Some nonrelative values and rights like *life* and *liberty,* however, must be upheld in any society and regardless of majority opinion.	A sense of obligation to law because of one's social contract to make and abide by laws for the welfare of all and for the protection of all people's rights. A feeling of contractual commitment, freely entered upon, to family, friendship, trust, and work obligations. Concern that laws and duties be based on rational calculation of overall utility, "the greatest good for the greatest number."	Prior-to-society perspective: Perspective of a rational individual aware of values and rights prior to social attachments and contracts. Integrates perspectives by formal mechanisms of agreement, contract, objective impartiality, and due process. Considers moral and legal points of view; recognizes that they sometimes conflict and finds it difficult to integrate them.
Stage 6 — Universal ethical principles	Following self-chosen ethical principles. Particular laws or social agreements are usually valid because they rest on such principles. When laws violate these principles, one acts in accordance with the principle. Principles are universal principles of justice: the equality of human rights and respect for the dignity of human beings as individual persons.	The belief as a rational person in the validity of universal moral principles, and a sense of personal commitment to them.	Perspective of a moral point of view from which social arrangements derive. Perspective is that of any rational individual recognizing the nature of morality or the fact that persons are ends in themselves and must be treated as such.

SOURCE: Kohlberg, 1976.

(corresponding to the stage of formal operations, which typically emerges after the middle childhood years), moral judgments are based on abstract, universal principles. (See Table 15.2 for a summary of Kohlberg's stages.)

According to Kohlberg (1984), attaining increasingly higher levels of moral development depends upon increases in both the ability to engage in logical reasoning and in sophisticated perspective-taking. Thus a person whose logical development is low is limited to Stages 3 and 4 in this sequence. Similarly, people who have difficulty interpreting the thoughts

and feelings of others will be restricted to lower levels of moral development (Kohlberg, 1976).

Since children in middle childhood rarely go beyond Stage 3, we will describe only the initial three stages in Kohlberg's moral development theory here. The remaining three stages will be discussed in Chapter 17. Stage 1 coincides with the end of the preschool period and the beginning of middle childhood. In this stage, children adopt an egocentric point of view in which they do not recognize the interests of others as distinct from their own. Their judgments about the rightness and wrongness of an action are based on its objective outcome, which in this case is how author-ities respond to it. Stage 1 children might assert that Heinz must not steal the medicine because he will be put in jail. Or they might reason that he might as well take the medicine because it is not worth much money, so no one will get very upset. In either case, the Stage 1 child focuses on the likely consequences of the man's actions.

At Stage 2, which ordinarily appears at around 7 to 8 years, children continue to adopt a concrete self-inter-ested (egocentric) perspective but can recognize that different people have different needs and perspectives. Justice is seen as an exchange system (sometimes dubbed a "market mentality" or an agreement that "if you'll scratch my back, I'll scratch yours") in which you give equally to what you receive. Kohlberg also used the term "instrumental morality" to refer to the moral reasoning of children in this stage, because they believe it is perfectly acceptable to use others for their own interests. For example, children at this stage might answer the Heinz dilemma by saying that Heinz should steal the drug, because he might need someone to steal it for him some day.

At Stage 3, people make their judgments on the basis of a social-relational perspective. They see shared feel-ings and agreements, especially with people close to them, as more important than individual self-interest. For example, one child quoted by Kohlberg (1984, p. 629) said,

> If I was Heinz, I would have stolen the drug for my wife. You can't put a price on love, no amount of gifts make love. You can't put a price on life either.

Stage 3 is often equated with the kind of moral reasoning associated with the "golden rule." In Jewish tradition, this precept is attributed to Rabbi Hillel, who lived in the decades just preceding the birth of Christ. Rabbi Hillel phrased this injunction as "Do not unto others what you would not have them do unto you." This same idea was expressed in positive form in the Sermon on the Mount when Jesus exhorted his followers to "Do unto others as you would have them do unto you."

Robert Selman (1971) showed that differences be-tween Stages 2 and 3 are revealed by the way that children interpret the golden rule. Those in Stage 2 interpreted the rule to mean that you should treat others well so that they would treat you well at a later time. Those in Stage 3 correctly interpreted the rule to mean that you should treat others as if they were your-self.

While Stage 3 is undoubtedly a more humane way of thinking about morality than either stages 1 or 2, Stage 2 is the key transition associated with the new ability to get along without adult supervision that appears during middle childhood. No longer do children de-pend upon a strong external source to define right and wrong; instead, reciprocal relations between group members regulate behavior. Adults may not find the resulting behaviors desirable ("I won't tell your mom you went to see that R-rated movie, if you won't tell mine"), but at least this form of thinking allows children to regulate their actions with each other.

It should be noted that the vast majority of research on moral development during middle childhood fo-cuses on children's reasoning processes, not on how they actually behave. Fortunately, some research has been done on the links between behavior and the de-velopment of the idea of fairness.

Rules of Fairness

William Damon (1975, 1977, 1980) took a somewhat different approach to the study of moral development than did Kohlberg. Instead of examining situations that concerned breaking rules, Damon investigated children's conceptions of positive justice: how to di-vide resources or distribute rewards. Damon also stud-ied the ways that children's reasoning is related to their actions.

In order to study age-related changes in forms of reasoning, Damon adopted the popular technique of telling a story and then posing a series of questions. One of his stories went as follows:

> A classroom of children spent a day drawing pic-tures. Some children made a lot of drawings; some made fewer. Some children drew well; others did not draw as well. Some children were well-behaved and worked hard; others fooled around. Some chil-dren were poor, some were boys, some were girls, and so on. The class then sold the drawings at a school bazaar. How should the proceeds from the sale of the drawings be fairly distributed? (Adapted from Damon, 1975)

The answers given by children 4 to 12 years old to such questions were probed extensively, challenged, and followed up to determine the reasoning behind them. Damon found that children's conceptions of positive justice, like the moral judgments studied by Kohlberg, develop through a sequence of levels as children grow older (see Table 15.3).

Before the age of 4, children do not give objective reasons for their choices; they simply state their wants.

TABLE 15.3 Levels of positive reasoning about justice

Level 0-A: (age 4 and under):

Positive-justice choices derive from wish that an act occur. Reasons simply assert the wishes rather than attempting to justify them ("I should get it because I want to have it").

Level 0-B: (ages 4 to 5):

Choices still reflect desires but are now justified on the basis of external, observable realities such as size, sex, or other physical characteristics of persons (e.g., we should get the most because we are girls). Such justifications, however, are invoked in a fluctuating, after-the-fact manner, and are self-serving in the end.

Level 1-A: (ages 5 to 7):

Positive-justice choices derive from notions of strict equality in actions (i.e., that everyone should get the same). Equality is seen as preventing complaining, fighting, "fussing," or other types of conflict.

Level 1-B: (ages 6 to 9):

Positive-justice choices derive from a notion of reciprocity in actions: that persons should be paid back in kind for doing good or bad things. Notions of merit and deserving emerge.

Level 2-A: (ages 8 to 10):

A moral relativity develops out of the understanding that different persons can have different, yet equally valid, justifications for their claims to justice. The claims of persons with special needs (e.g., the poor) are weighed heavily. Choices attempt quantitative compromises between competing claims.

Level 2-B: (ages 10 and up):

Considerations of equality and reciprocity are coordinated such that choices take into account the claims of various persons and the demands of the specific situation. Choices are firm and clear-cut, yet justifications reflect the recognition that all persons should be given their due (though, in many situations, this does not mean equal treatment).

SOURCE: Damon, 1980.

Most 4- and 5-year-olds are still primarily focused on gratifying themselves, but now they begin to justify their decisions with appeals to such arbitrary characteristics as size or sex. They offer such judgments as "The biggest should get the most" or "We should all get some because we're girls."

Between the ages of 5 and 7, children begin to believe that all participants have a claim to the rewards. They usually assert that the way to resolve conflict is to give everyone an equal share. There are no mitigating circumstances in their arguments; the only fair treatment is equal treatment.

From approximately the age of 8 onward, children seem to believe that some individuals within the group may have a legitimate claim to more than an equal share of the group's rewards if they contributed more to the group's work or if they were handicapped in some way, such as by poverty or by a physical disability. However, it is still difficult for 8-year-olds to balance all of the competing considerations to produce a fair outcome. Changes after the age of 8 reflect children's increased sophistication at logically weighing all of the relevant factors. Damon (1983), whose initial studies were in the United States, reports that this same progression has been found in a number of other countries, including Israel, Puerto Rico, and parts of Europe (see Table 15.4).

How is children's reasoning about positive justice related to their actions in a real situation where there are rewards to be distributed? To answer this question, Damon arranged for 144 children to be divided into groups of four. Each group was asked to make bracelets for which the group would be rewarded. After they had been at work for a while, he brought the work period to a close and gave each group 10 candy bars to divide among themselves as payment for their work. In order to ensure that the relevant issues of positive justice arose as a problem for the children, Damon arranged the composition and working conditions of each group so that there would be several different claims: for example, one of the children would have made more bracelets than the others while another might be noticeably younger.

Damon compared hypothetical reasoning of children with their actual behavior in this real situation. In half the cases, the children's behavior matched their reasoning. About 10 percent of the children actually exhibited more advanced reasoning when faced with a real task, while almost 40 percent scored lower in reality than in their reasoning. When faced with real

TABLE 15.4 Excerpts from Damon's transcripts comparing 6- and 10-year-olds' reasoning about positive justice

Three 6-year-olds: Jay, Juan, and Susan	Three 10-year-olds: Craig, Norman, and Bonnie
Experimenter: So what Jay said is he put them out, three for him and three for Juan, two for Susan and two for Jennifer *[not present]*. And Susan said that's OK too. That's the way she did it.	*E:* . . . What do you think is the best way to give it out?
Jay: *[To Juan]* You should think that's fair too. You have three, and I have three, and they have two.	*Craig:* Would Dennis *[the younger child]* get some?
Juan: I dont't think that's fair.	*E:* If you think so.
Jay: Why?	*Norman:* He has to be here too.
Juan: We shouldn't give the boys more than the girls. We should break them in half and give the girls two, the boys two, and then . . .	*E:* Well, you all decide among you.
Jay: No. No. No. I said ours were the prettiest, that's why we get more.	*Bonnie:* I was thinking, we could give out one a bracelet, because Dennis did one and we all did three. Or give two and a half to everybody. That way everybody gets the same thing.
Juan: Wait a second. Whose is this?	*Craig:* Maybe he *[Dennis]* should get one and we get three.
Jay: Yours.	*Norman:* No. It ain't fair.
Juan: No, it isn't.	*Bonnie:* Also, Dennis is younger and he left earlier.
Jay: See, we made the prettiest. I say we made the prettiest. Do you think that's a nice one? And you made nice ones, and we made the prettiest. I think that's fair because we made the prettiest. . . .	*E:* Well, what do you think? Is that the best way?
	Norman: No.
E: What do you think, Susan? Didn't you at one point say you thought we should split them in half?	*E:* Why not, Norman?
Susan: That's what I said. Now I say . . . *[Susan gives them out—three, three, two, two, as Jay wishes.]*	*Norman:* Because if he were here too, and he's a child too, so he should get even.
E: What? This way?	*Bonnie:* Yeah, well lookit. His was bigger so it would have taken longer. And he used more black, but that made it shorter. But he left earlier, he's younger and, you know, didn't do it neat.
Jay: Yeah. Because she thinks that we made the prettiest.	*Norman:* I know. That's beside the point. That means we don't expect much from him. . . .
Juan: She got some in her lunch box. Do you have candy? . . .	*Craig:* Or give three to her *[Bonnie]*, three for Norman, and three for me, and one for Dennis.
E: Susan says it's OK. How about Jennifer?	*E:* And why do you think that is the best way, Craig?
Jay: I think she would say it's OK.	*Craig:* *[No reply.]*
Juan: If she didn't leave, I think it wouldn't be OK. . . .	*Norman:* You're not putting his *[Dennis's]* mind into your little mind. . . .
Jay: Think that would be fair! She would have three, and we would all have three.	*Craig:* Yes, I am.
E: We don't have eleven, we have ten.	*Norman:* Well, you're not reasoning about him. If we did that he would say *[mimics child's whining voice]* "Come, come, you guys got this and I only got this" and he'd start bawling his brains out.
Jay: But she only made one, and it's not pretty.	*Bonnie:* Well, his isn't that neat or anything.
Juan: It's good. She's only in kindergarten. She would think it's fair, I think. Yeah, she would.	*Norman:* I know, but he is younger.
E: What are you guys going to do?	*Bonnie:* Well, wouldn't you say, supposing that you had a younger dog and an older dog, right? You could teach them both the same tricks. And if you had a box of dog bones, you'd give them a bone for every trick. Supposing the little one or even the big one just wanted the dog bones and he wouldn't do any tricks. You wouldn't give him one for that.
Jay: If you think it's fair, and Susan thinks it's fair, and I think it's fair, she *[Jennifer]* might think it's fair.	
E: Well let's see what Juan thinks. What do you suggest, Juan? What's the best way? What's the best thing to do with the candy bars?	*Norman:* I know, but he did something. It's not like he didn't do anything. Least he did one. You're getting on the point like he didn't do anything.
Juan: I think that's *[three, three, two, two]* the best way, if she's only in kindergarten. . . .	*Bonnie:* No, I know he did something. He did the best he could.
Jay: She had two, and we have three. . . .	
Juan: You made the most.	

(Continued)

TABLE 15.4 Excerpts from Damon's transcripts comparing 6- and 10-year-olds' reasoning about positive justice (Continued)

Three 6-year-olds: Jay, Juan, and Susan	Three 10-year-olds: Craig, Norman, and Bonnie
Jay: You see I had four bracelets.	*Norman:* Yeah, so he should get as much as we do.
Juan: I had the second most. Give these two candy bars to her.	
Jay: You see, what I was thinking was, Juan and I get three 'cause we, ours are pretty and I made the most. Susan already has one in her lunch box.	
Juan: And Jennifer's only in kindergarten.	
Jay: She doesn't get more, 'cause she just made one and it's not pretty.	
E: Do you agree, Susan?	
Susan: OK.	

SOURCE: Damon, 1977.

candy bars, these children were likely to give in to temptation and claim more than they would consider their due based on their reasoning in the hypothetical situation.

Reasoning about Social Conventions

According to Kohlberg's account of moral development, true moral reasoning grows out of an earlier kind of reasoning based on social conventions. However, as we saw from the work of Elliot Turiel and his colleagues (Nucci & Turiel, 1978; Turiel, 1983), preschoolers evaluate the consequences of moral infractions, such as hurting someone, differently from violations of social conventions, such as dress codes. These results led Turiel to the conclusion that moral reasoning and reasoning about social conventions are independent domains. In a series of studies, Turiel and his colleagues have provided evidence that each domain —moral rules and social conventions— undergoes its own sequence of developmental transformations (Turiel, 1983; Turiel, Killen, & Helwig, 1987).

Turiel, like other researchers who have probed children's reasoning about social rules, told brief stories and then used clinical interviewing to investigate children's reasoning processes. One story was about a young boy who wants to become a nurse caring for infants when he grows up, but his father thinks he shouldn't do so.

The following interview based on the nurse story illustrates the earliest stage of reasoning about social conventions. The child seems to believe that conventions reflect the natural order of things. Violating the convention would mean behaving unnaturally.

Joan (6 years, 5 months): (Should he become a nurse?) *Well, no, because he could easily be a doctor and he could take care of babies in the hospital.* (Why shouldn't he be a nurse?) *Well, because a nurse is a lady and the boys, the other men would just laugh at them.* (Why shouldn't a man be a nurse?) *Well, because it would sort of be silly because ladies wear those kind of dresses and those kind of shoes and hats. . . .* (Do you think his father was right?) *Yes, because, well, a nurse, she typewrites and stuff and all that.* (The man should not do that?) *No, because he would look silly in a dress.* (Turiel, 1978, pp. 62–63)

At the second level of reasoning about social conventions, reached around 8 or 9 years, children realize that just because most doctors are men and most nurses are women, the empirical association of activities, roles, and modes of dress does not mean that other combinations are impossible. At this level, children reject the need for social conventions; they see no necessity for such rules in the coordination of people with each other. They are even sophisticated enough to realize that traditional social conventions may be misleading to others:

> Emily (8 years, 11 months): (Why do you think his parents see that job as for women only?) *Being a nurse — because not many men are nurses so they get used to the routine. I know a lot of ladies who are doctors, but I don't know a man who is a nurse, but it is okay if they want to.* (Turiel, 1978, p. 64)

At Level 3, children display a dawning awareness that social conventions, despite their arbitrary nature, have a legitimate role in the regulation of social life. Eventually, sometime in early adulthood, they come to view social conventions as a positive force in facilitating coordination of social interactions, which is essential to the functioning of any social group.

At present it is not clear whether children around the world think about moral rules and social conventions in the same way that children in the United States do. Using culturally appropriate versions of Turiel's stories, some studies have replicated his basic findings in a wide variety of societies (Nucci, Turiel, & Encarnación-Gawrych, 1983; Song, Smetana, & Kim, 1987). However, when anthropologists have studied children's moral reasoning in naturally occurring situations or have used somewhat different techniques to elicit judgments, it appears that, at least in some cultures, people are more likely to consider breaches of social convention to be moral issues than they do in the United States (Shweder, Mahapatra, & Miller, 1987).

A more serious source of uncertainty about developmental sequences in reasoning about social rules is the generally low level of correspondence between the levels children reach when they are asked to reason about different rule types. They often, for example, think at one level about moral rules, at another about fairness, and at still another about social conventions. (Turiel & Davidson, 1986; Shweder, 1987). While it is clear that children's thinking about different aspects of social life becomes more complicated as they grow older, the existing data raise considerable doubt about whether a unitary process governs the kinds of games children play, the kinds of rules they invoke, and the way they reason about morality.

Both social-learning theorists and those who adopt a cultural-context perspective suggest that children's moral evaluations depend upon a variety of factors, including cultural norms and the particular situation children face (Bandura, 1986; Edwards, 1986; Shweder, 1987). This may be the reason there often appears to be a very loose relationship between the way children reason about moral aspects of behavior in a formal interview and the way they actually behave.

RELATIONS WITH OTHER CHILDREN

Once children begin to spend significant amounts of time among their peers, they must learn to create a special place for themselves within the social group. Their greater appreciation of social rules, along with their increased ability to consider other people's points of view, are essential resources for this new task. But no matter how sophisticated or sensitive they are, there is no guarantee that they will be accepted by their peers. Children must still seek out friends, come to terms with the possibility that they may not be liked, learn to compete for social status, and deal with the conflicts that inevitably arise.

Friendship

Even preschool children experience intense friendships characterized by strong feelings of empathy, affection, jealousy, anger, and competitiveness. What appear to distinguish friendships during middle childhood from earlier relations are the kinds of behavior that count as friendly and children's conceptions of what a friend is (Berndt, 1981; Bigelow, 1977; Hayes, 1978; Rubin, 1980).

Among 3- and 4-year-olds the word "friend" is often used in place of the word "playmate" in such phrases as "We're friends, aren't we, Josh?" or "I won't be your friend anymore if you won't give me the hammer." Preschoolers who are friends typically live near each other, are the same age and sex, are from similar backgrounds, and like to do the same things (Doyle, 1981).

Some of these factors are also important in determining one's friends during middle childhood. But as the following excerpt from the description of an 11-year-old girl makes clear, by the end of middle childhood, friendship and children's conceptions of it have become quite complicated:

What a wrong day! Lindsey is getting me more and more irritated every day. I think we're both beginning a *bad* relationship. She bothers me a lot. We kind of made a commitment to tell each other everything. But no, she had just recently started to tell me things, about her and Alan, and that she hated me during the summer. I wonder if she still does hate me, maybe. . . I always have to listen to how she feels but she won't listen to how I feel. I hate her as of the present moment, but I will never take off the bead ring I have that she gave me. I love her a lot and never want to part as a friend, but there are times I just can't stand when she does things like this. (Rubin, 1980, p. 74)

To trace the changing nature of friendships during middle childhood, James Youniss and his associates interviewed boys and girls ranging in age from 6 to 14 about their conceptions of friendship and their ideas of how friends are made (Youniss, 1980; Youniss & Volpe, 1978). They found that 6- and 7-year-olds spoke of friends as playmates with whom they share activities and things. In answer to the question, "What is a best friend?" they say, "When they play together" or "Play with them and give them stuff."

By the time they are 9 and 10 years old, children no longer view friends as just anyone you play with. Friends are people you have interacted with enough to know well, people who have common interests, similarities in abilities, and compatible personalities. Asked how one makes friends, 9- and 10-year-olds say such things as "They'll play around on the playground and talk to each other," or "They might find out they like the same things." They believe that a friend is "someone who really cares about you and doesn't

Being with a friend is one of life's special pleasures.

want to betray you . . . a person who would want to help out when you need his help." These older children in the Youniss studies believed that friendship transcends momentary interactions and is an ongoing relationship whose continued existence depends upon mutual responsibility, support, caring, and commitment.

Friendship and perspective-taking In the opinion of Robert Selman, the key to developmental changes in the basis of friendship is the ability to take another's perspective (Selman, 1976, 1980). Recall from the discussion of perspective-taking in Chapter 13 (the story of Holly the tree-climber and her father, p. 426) that 8- to 10-year-olds are able to coordinate the perspectives of two characters in a story, while most preschoolers are not. In one set of studies, Selman (1981) tested his theory by comparing children's social perspective-taking skills (as revealed in their interpretations of stories) with their understanding of friendship (as revealed in structured, clinical interviews). As he predicted, he found that children who respond at a high level to perspective-taking problems are also likely to have more sophisticated ideas about friendship. Table 15.5 illustrates Selman's view of how perspective-taking is related to levels of friendship.

From Table 15.5 it can be seen that there is an interesting parallel between developmental changes in children's understanding of friendship and their understanding of social perspective-taking. Children's reasoning in each domain moves through a progression from uncoordinated, individualistic understanding, to an understanding that coordinates two perspectives, and then to a stage in which individual perspectives are viewed in the context of a more complex system. This sequence fits closely with Piaget's theory that young children's egocentricity restricts them to their own point of view, while older children can keep two aspects of a problem in mind at the same time (see Chapter 10, p. 261, and Chapter 13, p. 425).

To see if there was any connection between children's conceptions of friendship and their actual behavior as friends, Selman undertook research on interpersonal relations at a clinic for emotionally disturbed children. A notable characteristic of emotionally disturbed children is that they have difficulty getting along with others and often behave immaturely. Selman (1981) found a very complex range of relationships between children's understanding of friendship and their actual relationships. As expected, the children with low levels of understanding as manifested in clinical interviews had difficulties forming and maintaining friends because they failed to take their partner's point of view or to understand the motives of the partner's behavior. However, intellectually precocious children also ended up at the clinic because of interpersonal difficulties with their peers, caused in their cases by the fact that they reasoned significantly above the children in their school class and were disliked for being bossy or hard to understand.

Insofar as forms of reasoning about friendship correlate with the quality of actual friendships, it might be tempting to conclude that the friendships of very young children are shallow or less meaningful than friendships among cognitively more mature people. This conclusion would not only be premature, it would probably be wrong. Observations of preschool children (Gottman and Parkhurst, 1980) and of severely retarded adults (MacAndrew & Edgerton, 1966) make it clear that cognitively immature people may display the characteristics of true friendship, including a caring regard for each other as well as the ability to anticipate and fulfill each other's desires. These observations strongly suggest that genuine friendships can exist separately from the ability to talk about them systematically in conceptual terms.

However, it appears that higher levels of reasoning about interpersonal relationships, including friendships, provide children with **social repair mechanisms,** strategies that allow friends to remain friends even when serious differences temporarily drive them apart. When serious disputes arise among young children or those whose development is delayed, there is usually a caretaker present to intervene and help the children settle them. In friendship, as in other domains of social interaction, increased understanding permits freedom from the need for supervision. By middle childhood, increased cognitive and social sophistication makes it easier for friends to reconstruct their relationship after a breach without the aid of adult intervention.

Boys, girls, and friends During middle childhood, children in all cultures tend to be segregated sexually. In nonindustrialized societies, this sexual cleavage fits with the kinds of chores that children are assigned by adults. The girls help their mothers around the village by fetching water, doing the wash, sweeping, and helping with the preparation of food, while the boys watch the herds, hunt, and fish (Harkness & Super, 1985; Weisner, 1984; Whiting & Whiting, 1975).

TABLE 15.5 Selman's developmental levels of perspective-taking and stages of friendship

Developmental Level in the Coordination of Relations between Perspectives of Self and Others	Stages of Reflective Understanding of Close Dyadic Friendships
Level 0 (approximately ages 3 to 7)	*Stage 0*
Egocentric or undifferentiated perspective. Children do not distinguish their own perspective from that of others. They do not yet recognize that others may interpret the same social experience or course of action differently from the way they do.	Momentary playmates. A close friend is someone who lives close by and with whom one is playing.
Level 1 (approximately ages 4 to 9)	*Stage 1*
Subjective or differentiated perspectives. The child understands that others' perspectives may differ from her own.	One-way assistance. Conceptions of friendship are one way in the sense that a friend does what one wants. A close friend is someone who shares the same dislikes and likes.
Level 2 (approximately ages 6 to 12)	*Stage 2*
Self-reflective or reciprocal perspective. The child is now able to view his own thoughts and feelings from another's perspective.	Fair-weather cooperation. With their new awareness of the reciprocal nature of personal perspectives, children become concerned with coordinating their thoughts and actions, rather than adjusting them to a fixed standard as they had before. Relationships depend upon adjustment and cooperation and fall apart over arguments.
Level 3 (approximately 9 to 15)	*Stage 3*
Third person or mutual perspective. The child at this level can step outside of an interaction and take the perspective of a third party.	Intimate and mutually shared relationships. Friendships are seen as the basic means of developing mutual intimacy and mutual support. At this stage friendship transcends momentary interactions including conflicts. The primary limitation of this stage is possessiveness and jealousy.
Level 4 (approximately age 12 to adulthood)	*Stage 4*
Societal or in-depth. Children at this level are able to take the generalized perspective of society, the law or morality.	Autonomous, interdependent friendships. This stage is characterized by an awareness of the interdependence of friends for support and a sense of identity and at the same time an acceptance of the others' need to establish relations with other people.

SOURCE: Adapted from Selman, 1981.

Sex segregation is not total during middle childhood, as Willard Hartup (1983) points out. In industrialized societies there are often ritualized meetings between the two sexes in schoolyards, parks, and on neighborhood streets. Some of these meetings have the characteristics of forays into enemy territory. Others, such as chase-and-kiss games and teasing, have sexual overtones. But there are also occasions where the two sexes easily merge together in joint activities, as they do when family friends get together, when there is a large project such as a school play to be put on, or when they are simply "playing on the block" (Ellis, Rogoff, & Cromer, 1981).

On the basis of their observations in a rural Kenyan (Kipsigi) town, Harkness and Super (1985) also caution against overstating the degree of sex segregation that occurs in middle childhood. In the Kipsigi community where the researchers worked, companions were often kin from nearby homesteads, who might vary widely in age and sex. Boys and girls are more likely to

Although the extent of sex segregation increases during middle childhood, boys and girls often play with each other on the playground and around the neighborhood.

be found playing together when the supply of potential companions is limited, as it is likely to be both in a Kenyan village and when playing around a U.S. neighborhood.

Studies of sex-segregated peer groups show that boys' and girls' experiences with peers are often quite different. Girls tend to have fewer friends than boys and to make friends less rapidly (Eder & Hallinan, 1978). They seem to be more sensitive to the boundaries between close friends and acquaintances and to discourage interactions with those who are not close friends. Girls' friendships are more often intimate ones than is true for boys (Waldrop & Halverson, 1975). Their friendships are characterized by the sharing of feelings, exchange of presents and compliments, and lengthy discussions about likes and dislikes, embarrassments and triumphs. By comparison, boys are more likely to have larger groups of friends and more friends of different ages. They are also more likely than girls to play physical, boisterous, competitive games with their friends and to interact with one another in places where there is no direct adult supervision.

Thus a strong pattern of sex-role socialization emerges. Boys appear to be socialized for competition with one another in activities bound by rule systems, while girls are socialized for cooperation and interpersonal sensitivity in circumstances with only implicit rules. In the United States, this pattern may be changing as more women enter the modern workplace to compete with men. Girls may be socialized more for competition than they have been in the past, but if such a change is occurring, it is not yet visible in the social relations among peers during middle childhood.

Popularity

Most people care deeply about how their peers feel about them. However, not everyone in a group is equally well-liked. Whenever a group exists for a while, a social structure emerges. There are a few people whose friendship is sought after, a few people who are not sought out or who are actively rejected, and an intermediate position between these two poles. Developmental psychologists study popularity as an element of both the development of interpersonal relationships and children's personalities.

Researchers who study the relative popularity of members of a group usually begin by constructing a sociogram of friendship choices in the group. The sociogram is a graphic representation of how each child feels about every other child in the group (Asher & Dodge, 1986; Hayden-Thomson, Rubin, & Hymel, 1987) (see Figure 15.2). The investigators ask the group members to name the children they would like to sit near, to play with, to work with, or simply to name their friends in the group. By plotting all of the children's choices, it becomes possible to investigate the relation between children's individual characteristics and their group standing. The children named the most often are assumed to be the most popular in the group, while those who are not named by anyone are assumed to be either neglected or rejected.

One of the most pervasive findings of such research is that the degree of popularity within a group is related to a person's physical attractiveness (summarized in Hartup, 1983). In one such study, boys were categorized into five subgroups on the basis of their popularity as indicated by a sociogram of their standing among their peers. Then adult raters who did not know the boys were asked to judge their attractiveness from photographs. The less attractive the boys were rated, the lower the popularity standing of their subgroup (Dodge, 1983).

There is more to popularity than good looks, however. Popular children tend to be friendlier, more out-

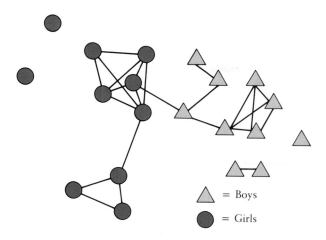

FIGURE 15.2 *A sociogram of the relationships among a group of 5th grade boys and girls. Note that the one boy having mutual relationships with girls is also the boy who has the most relationships with other boys. Similarly, the girl who is the link between a trio of girls and the main subgroup of girls is the one with the largest number of mutual relationships with other girls. Two girls and one boy are social isolates, while a pair of boys have chosen each other in isolation from the group. (Adapted from Gronlund, 1959.)*

△ = Boys

● = Girls

going, and more helpful than other children; they also tend to be brighter and more socially skilled (Dodge, 1983; Hartup, 1983). These findings suggest that social skillfulness is also a cause of popularity, but since sociogram studies rely on observation and correlation, no firm conclusions about the *causes* of popularity can validly be drawn from them. They can only tell us what traits are associated with a particular social status in a group.

A study by Martha Putallaz (1983) helps to pinpoint some of the reasons — other than attractiveness — that some children are more popular than others. Instead of beginning with an already formed group, Putallaz began her study the summer before children entered first grade in an attempt to see if social skills demonstrated in a totally different setting could be used to predict popularity at a later time. In the first phase of her study, 22 boys were invited, one at a time, to play with two unfamiliar children who were the researcher's confederates. The two confederates were already playing a game when the child being studied arrived on the scene. The experimenter introduced the children and told them that later on they would be asked to tell her how they liked the game. Then she left them alone to observe the new boy's attempts to join the ongoing game. The two confederates were instructed to engage in several preplanned social interactions that were designed to cause problems for the newcomer. For example, at one point one of the confederates asked for help. In another case, the two confederates pretended to have an argument.

The social interactions occurring in these episodes were videotaped and then used to predict the boy's popularity in his first-grade classroom four months later. Putallaz found that the boys later rated as most popular by their classmates were those who had been able to fit into the experimental group by making constructive contributions to the ongoing conversation, to adopt the group's frame of reference, and to understand the rules of the social interaction.

Other attempts to analyze the relationship between social skills and popularity have brought together unacquainted school-aged boys in play groups (Coie & Kupersmidt, 1983; Dodge, 1983). At first, of course, no one in these groups could be considered to be more popular since none of the boys knew the others. The experimenters observed the emergence of group structures and the behaviors that led to popularity, neglect, or rejection. They found that the boys who became popular were helpful, reminded others of the rules, provided suggestions in ambiguous and difficult situations, and were almost never aggressive. The rejected boys, on the other hand, were more talkative, active, and verbally and physically aggressive than the other members of the group. The rejected boys were also less likely than the popular ones to stay at work or at play with the rest of the group and often wandered off on their own. Boys who were neglected by the others interacted with their peers the least but rarely offended anyone.

From these descriptions, it seems that popular children are those who somehow pick up implicitly on the things that other people are trying to do. They are able to understand what is happening and to behave in a way that fits the ongoing flow of interaction in the group. They use common understandings to facilitate common goals, which makes others feel good.

Socialization Practices and Peer Relations

Peer group interactions are never entirely free of adult influence. Even when no adult is actually present, social norms accepted by the adult community are likely to influence children's behavior. These influences are most readily seen in studies of how adult norms shape patterns of cooperation, competition, and conflict among peers.

Competition and cooperation   Millard Madsen and his colleagues (Kagan & Madsen, 1971; Madsen & Shapira, 1970; Shapiro & Madsen, 1969) studied the way that small peer groups chose cooperation or competition to solve a problem. The purpose of the studies was to contrast problem-solving strategies of children whose cultures emphasize cooperation with those whose cultures emphasize competition.

In one of the early studies in this series, two groups of Israeli children were contrasted (Shapira & Madsen, 1969). One group was composed of children from agricultural communes, or kibbutzim; the other group was made up of children from a middle-class urban neighborhood. Middle-class urban children in Israel, like their U.S. counterparts, are encouraged by their parents to achieve as individuals. Kibbutzim, by contrast, prepare children from an early age to cooperate and work as a group. Kibbutz adults deliberately reward cooperation while punishing the failure to cooperate (Spiro, 1965). Competition is so discouraged in

kibbutz classrooms that children may feel ashamed if they are at the top of their class (Rabin, 1965).

Children from both communities ranging in age from 6 to 10 were brought together, four at a time, to play a game using the apparatus depicted in Figure 15.3. At the start of each round of the game four children were seated at the corners of the board. In the center of the board was a pen connected to each corner of the board by a string which each child could pull to move the pen. The board itself was covered with a clean piece of paper upon which the pen left a mark as it moved.

The game consisted of the children moving the pen to specific places on the game board marked by four small circles. To make the pen cross one of these circles, the children had to cooperate in pulling the strings, or the pen would remain in the center or move erratically.

The children were asked to play this game six times. For the first three trials Madsen and Shapira told them that the aim of the game was to draw a line over the four circles in one minute. If they succeeded in doing this, each of them would get a prize. If they covered the four circles twice, they were promised two prizes, and so on. But if they covered fewer than four circles, no one would receive a prize. Children from the two kinds of communities responded similarly, in a generally cooperative manner under these circumstances (see Figure 15.4).

After they had completed the three trials, the experimenters changed the way in which rewards were given. Now, whenever the pen crossed the circle nearest a child, that child received a reward. Under these new conditions, a cultural difference quickly became apparent. The urban children changed tactics and started pulling the pen toward themselves. They persisted in competing even on the fifth trial, by which time they had ample opportunity to see that they were getting nowhere. In some cases the children would agree to cooperate, but the cooperation would break down as soon as one child pulled a little too hard on the string. As a result, their rate of success was greatly reduced.

The children from kibbutzim responded quite differently to the new condition. They quickly set up cooperative rules, saying such things as "Okay gang, let's go in turns." They also directed one another during the game with such suggestions as "We'll start here, then here. . . ." The kibbutz children were concerned that no one be rewarded more than the others

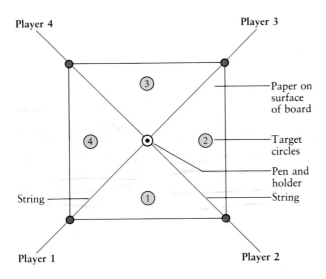

Player 4   Player 3

Paper on surface of board

Target circles

Pen and holder

String   String

Player 1   Player 2

FIGURE 15.3   *Diagram of apparatus used to assess children's predispositions to compete or cooperate. The pen at the center of the board must be moved to the target circles, an act that requires changes in the length of the strings manipulated by all four players. (From Shapira and Madsen, 1969.)*

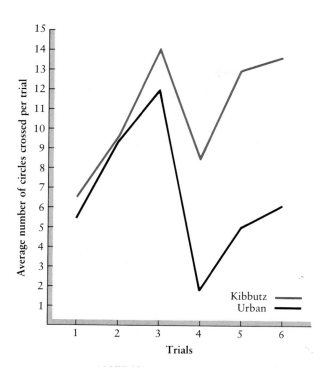

FIGURE 15.4 *The average number of successful attempts to cross a target circle for Israeli urban children and Israeli children raised in a kibbutz. On the first three trials, children were rewarded for cooperating. On the second three trials, rewards were distributed for individual achievement. Children raised on a kibbutz continued to cooperate and succeeded, but urban children began to compete, lowering their success rate. (From Shapira and Madsen, 1969.)*

and they set up rules to see that everyone shared equally in the prizes.

Madsen's studies, which have been repeated in different countries under varying conditions (Kagan & Madsen, 1971; Madsen & Shapira, 1970) show that different patterns of socialization fostered in different cultures significantly influence how peers work together. Cultures that emphasize group cohesion over individualism produce children with a greater readiness to cooperate for the mutual benefit of the group.

Competition and conflict Except in small, widely separated communities, peer groups are unlikely to be isolated from each other. In a single urban neighborhood there might be several groups based on common interest, membership in the same church, the same athletic team, or simply residence on the same block. In some locales, children may become involved in street gangs in middle childhood.

When we turn from the study of peer group interaction within a single group to peer interaction between two groups, many of the issues repeat themselves in a new form. Just as children must learn to get along with each other without strict adult control, so must groups find a way to regulate their interactions with each other.

A classic series of studies by Muzafer and Carolyn Sherif (1953) provides the best evidence on the conditions that foster different kinds of interaction between peer groups. In the most famous of these studies, 11-year-old boys were brought to one of two separate summer camp locations in Robbers Cave State Park in Oklahoma. The boys all came from stable, middle-class homes. They were all in the upper halves of their class in academic standing, and all were judged to be physically healthy and well-adjusted.

The boys in the two encampments went canoeing, swam, played ball, and engaged in other typical summer camp activities. To ensure that the boys at each encampment, who had not known one another previously, formed a cohesive group, the adults arranged for them to encounter problems that could only be solved cooperatively. For example, they made ingredients for dinner available to the boys, but left it to the boys themselves to assume responsibility for preparing and dividing the food. For the first week of the experiment the two groups lived in ignorance of each other.

At the end of the week, friendships had formed and leaders had emerged within each of the groups. Each had adopted a name, "Rattlers" and "Eagles." They

Cats' cradle requires a high level of cooperation for success.

had made their own group flags, constructed their own hide-outs, and claimed particular swimming holes as their own.

When it was clear that both the Rattlers and the Eagles had formed a stable pattern of group interactions, the adults let it be known that there was another group in the area. The boys expressed a keen desire to compete and immediately issued a challenge to the other group.

The adults arranged for a tournament, with prizes going to the winners. At the end of the first day of competition, the Eagles lost a tug of war. Stung by their defeat, they burned one of the Rattlers' flags which had been left behind. When the Rattlers returned the next morning and discovered the burned flag, they immediately seized the Eagles' flag. Scuffling and name-calling ensued.

For the next five days, hostilities escalated. The Rattlers staged a raid on the Eagles' camp, causing the Eagles a good deal of inconvenience and frustration. The Eagles retaliated with a destructive raid of their own. At the end of this period the two groups disliked each other intensely.

Once the intergroup hostility had reached a high level, the experimenters took steps to reverse the sad state of affairs. First they arranged for the boys to get together in a series of pleasant social circumstances, including joint meals, attendance at a movie together, and shooting firecrackers in the same area. These arrangements all failed miserably. The boys used their physical proximity to escalate hostilities by throwing food and calling names.

Next, the experimenters introduced a series of *superordinate* problems that affected the welfare of both groups equally, requiring them to combine efforts to reach a solution. The most successful application of this technique occurred during an overnight camping trip. The adults arranged for the truck that was to bring food to get stuck in a position where it could not be pushed. The boys came up with the idea of using their tug-of-war rope to pull the truck out of its predicament. Now, instead of pulling against each other, the boys were pulling together for a burning common reason — hunger. Here is how the Sherifs describe the outcome.

It took considerable effort to pull the truck. Several tries were necessary. During these efforts, a rhythmic chant of "Heave, heave" arose to accent the times of greatest effort. This rhythmic chant of "Heave, heave" had been used earlier by the Eagles during the tug-of-war contests in the period of intergroup competition and friction. Now it was being used in a cooperative activity involving both groups. When, after some strenuous efforts, the truck moved and started there was jubilation over the common success. (1956, pp. 322–323)

After this success, there seemed no point in preparing meals separately. The two groups cooperated without much discussion and with no outbreaks of name-calling or food throwing. The experimenters arranged for the truck to get stuck again. This time the boys knew what to do and the two groups mixed freely when organizing the rope pull.

At the end of the series of joint activity problems, the boys' opinions of each other had changed significantly. Mutual respect had mostly replaced the hostility, and several of the boys had formed friendships in the opposite group.

The Sherif experiments carry an important lesson. Cooperation and competition are not fixed biological characteristics of individuals or groups. They are forms of interaction that can be found at some time in all social groups and all individuals; they can be, and are, arranged for.

Developmental Consequences of Peer Interaction

Several lines of research suggest that peer interaction in middle childhood is important to the development of social-cognitive skills and to later social well-being (Doise, Mugny, & Perret-Clermont, 1975; Piaget, 1965; Sullivan, 1953). One relevant line of research was initiated by Marida Hollos (Hollos, 1975; Hollos & Cowan, 1973), who studied children growing up in three distinctive social settings in Norway and Hungary: isolated farm homesteads, villages, and towns. Hollos sought to determine if differences in the peer interaction children experience lead to distinctive patterns and rates of cognitive development.

In Norway, for example, many children live on remote farms that are difficult to reach, especially during the winter. Consequently these children experience relatively little peer interaction. When they are small, except for holidays, farm children rarely interact with other children aside from their brothers and sisters.

Once they begin school at the age of 7, they are bused to a neighboring community three times a week and bused home again immediately afterward, so they have no free time to play with other children. When they are at home, these children spend most of their time playing alone or observing their mothers at work. Communication within these families is often simple and direct, perhaps because so much time is spent in each others' company and there is not much new to talk about.

By contrast, the village and town children start early to spend most of their free time playing with other children. They bicycle through the streets, go down to the waterfront, visit each other's homes, ski together in winter, and play out on the streets at all times of the year. They also interact with a number of adults in shops, on the street, and in their friends' homes. Village children encounter a smaller number of people than the town children do, but the type of peer interaction is similar. Although the particulars were different, the circumstances for the Hungarian children Hollos studied were similar.

To assess the impact of peer experience on development, Hollos presented 7-, 8-, and 9-year-old children from these settings with a battery of tests drawn from two Piagetian categories. The first set consisted of classification and conservation tasks, designed to test the development of logical operations. The second set was designed to measure social perspective-taking and communication skills.

In one perspective-taking task, the child was presented with a seven-picture cartoon sequence suggesting an obvious story that the child had to recount. Then three of the pictures were removed. The remaining four pictures suggested a different story. A second experimenter then entered the room and the child was asked to pretend to take the first experimenter's place and tell the story that the experimenter would tell. The key question was whether children would simply repeat the first story or adjust to the new circumstances.

Hollos obtained similar results among the Norwegian and Hungarian children (Hollos, 1975). As shown in Figure 15.5 for the Hungarian data, the scores of the children from the three different settings were about

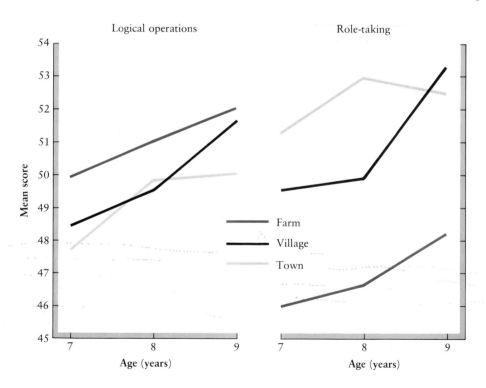

FIGURE 15.5 *The cognitive development of Hungarian children from isolated farms, villages, and towns. The graph on the left depicts their performance on tests of logical operations. The graph on the right depicts their performance on role-taking tasks. (From Hollos, 1975.)*

equal on the test of logical operations. All groups improved with age. On the social perspective-taking tasks however, the farm children, who spent little time interacting with others, did less well than the village and town children. In a study conducted in Iceland, other researchers also found that urban children's performance on social perspective-taking tests was superior to that of rural children (Edelstein, Keller, & Wahlen, 1984).

Further evidence that peer interaction helps develop the ability to take others' perspectives comes from a study conducted in the United States, which found that those elementary school children who played with their peers on the playground less often than their agemates also scored lower on social perspective-taking tests (Le Mare & Rubin, 1987).

A quite different kind of evidence comes from the work of the psychiatrist Harry Stack Sullivan (1892–1949), who believed that the experience of friendship during middle childhood is an essential precursor to adult intimacy, with which it shares some important features:

> If you will look very closely at one of your children when he finally finds a chum . . . you will discover something very different in the relationship—namely, that your child begins to develop a new sensitivity to what matters to another person. And this is not in the sense of "what should I do to get what I want," but instead "what should I do to contribute to the happiness or to support the prestige and feeling of worth-whileness of my chum." So far as I have been ever been able to discover, nothing remotely like this appears before the age of, say, 8½, and sometimes it appears decidedly later. (1953, pp. 245–246)

Sullivan believed that the tendency of children to pick out one or a few other children with whom they feel this kind of special affinity is the childhood precursor of the need for interpersonal intimacy that will be called love when it is encountered again in adolescence. He further claimed that the failure to form such friendships in childhood creates a social deficit that is difficult to remedy later. As evidence, he cites several of his psychiatric patients who had failed to form friendships as children and who, as adults, were extremely uncomfortable in their business or social dealings with others. (See Figure 15.6 for one person's interpretation of the consequences of failing to participate in peer groups.)

DEAR DR

I read the report in the Oct. 30 issue of _____ about your study of only children. I am an only child, now 57 years old and I want to tell you some things about my life. Not only was I an only child but I grew up in the country where there were no nearby children to play with. My mother did not want children around. She used to say 'I don't want my kid to bother anybody and I don't want nobody's kids bothering me.'

. . . From the first year of school I was teased and made fun of. For example, in about third or fourth grade I dreaded to get on the school bus to go to school because the other children on the bus called me 'Mommy's baby.' In about the second grade I heard the boys use a vulgar word. I asked what it meant and they made fun of me. So I learned a lesson —don't ask questions. This can lead to a lot of confusion to hear talk one doesn't understand and not be able to learn what it means . . .

I never went out with a girl while I was in school—in fact I hardly talked to them. In our school the boys and girls did not play together. Boys were sent to one part of the playground and girls to another. So, I didn't learn anything about girls. When we got into high school and the boys and girls started dating I could only listen to their stories about their experiences.

I could tell you a lot more but the important thing is I have never married or had any children. I have not been very successful in an occupation or vocation. I believe my troubles are not all due to being an only child, but I do believe you are right in recommending playmates for preschool children and I will add playmates for the school agers and not have them strictly supervised by adults. I believe I confirm the experiments with monkeys in being overly timid sometimes and overly aggressive sometimes. Parents of only children should make special efforts to provide playmates for [their children].

Sincerely yours,

FIGURE 15.6 *A letter from a friendless man giving his account of the importance of childhood friendships for development. (From Hartup, 1978.)*

Some children are required to come straight home from school so that their working parents can know where they are. The consequences of such safety rules can be loneliness and boredom.

Statistical studies of psychiatric patients for whom records of childhood social behavior are available lend support to Sullivan's belief that children who fail to make friends are indeed more likely to experience psychiatric problems in later life (Cowen, Pederson, Babigian, Izzo, & Trost, 1973; Roff, Sells, & Golden, 1972). However, this evidence needs to be treated with some caution. As in all correlational studies, it may be that the failure of psychiatric patients to form friendships in early childhood is the result of preexisting psychiatric problems rather than a cause of later interpersonal difficulties.

Despite some weaknesses, the existing data support the belief that peer interactions and childhood friendships play an important part in development during middle childhood. However, it would be a mistake to attribute all of social development during this period to peer interactions. Children's relationships with their parents continue to play an important role.

CHANGING RELATIONS WITH PARENTS

When Alfred Baldwin (1946) compared the parent-child relationships of 3-year-old American children with those of 9-year-olds, he found that parents of 9-year-olds were less warm to their children, more severe, and more critical of them. By the time their children are 8 or 9, most parents are no longer willing to shelter them as they had when the children were younger. Parental standards for their children's behavior continue to increase throughout middle childhood, in line with the belief that by the time their children reach the end of this period, they should be capable of nearly adult standards of behavior (Rogoff, Newcombe, Fox, & Ellis, 1980).

Related to this change in expectations is a change in the issues that arise between parents and children, according to Eleanor Maccoby (1980). Parents of preschool children have to deal with establishing daily routines, controlling temper tantrums and fights, and teaching children to care for, dress, feed, and groom themselves. Some of the salient issues of early childhood, such as fights among siblings, are still of concern during the years from 6 to 12. In addition, a whole new set of issues arises when children start to attend school, to work, and to spend increasing amounts of time away from adult supervision (see Box 15.2, "Maternal Employment and Child Welfare").

In economically developed countries, parents become concerned with their children's industriousness and achievement, even though it may have no immediate economic consequences for the family. In such cases, school is the arena in which a child's achievement is most prominently judged. Parents worry about how much they should become involved in their child's schoolwork, what they should do if a child has academic problems at school, and how to deal with behavior problems. Other concerns that emerge during middle childhood include whether to require children to do chores and what standards of performance should be expected of them, whether children should be paid for work they do around the house, and the extent to which parents should monitor their children's social life (Maccoby, 1984). In less developed countries, where family survival often depends on putting children to work once they enter middle childhood, analogous concerns arise (Weisner, 1984). In those societies, adults worry about their children's ability to take care of younger kin in the absence of adult supervision and to carry out important economic tasks such as the care of livestock or the hoeing of weeds.

As children grow bigger and spend increasing amounts of time out of adult sight, it becomes difficult for parents to remove them from dangerous or forbid-

BOX 15.2

MATERNAL EMPLOYMENT AND CHILD WELFARE
... ...

Although all parents must rely on their children's good sense and behavior as they leave direct adult supervision, such reliance becomes an urgent necessity in those families where working mothers are unavailable to their children for long periods of time each day. In the United States in the 1980s, this is the case for nearly 60 percent of all mothers of school-aged children (Hayes & Kamerman, 1983) (see the accompanying table). Because large numbers of children have mothers who are employed, the National Research Council formed a panel of scholars to review the research on how children are affected.

Contrary to popular belief, this report concludes that available research "has not demonstrated that mothers' employment per se has consistent direct effects, either positive or negative, on children's development . . ." (Hayes & Kamerman, 1983, p. 221). The effects of a mother's employment on her children depend on how the mother's work interacts with other factors, including the family's socioeconomic situation, race, family structure (married, divorced, single, etc.), and parents' attitudes toward work and housework, as well as where the family lives (rural, suburban, city, near relatives, etc.). Although the data permit no

Women in the labor force

Ethnicity	Percent of All Women Working	Percent with Children under 18	Percent with Children 14 to 17	Percent with Children 6 to 13	Percent with Children 3 to 5	Percent with Children under 3
White	54.4	62.2	72.1	68.7	58.7	50.4
Black	56.6	66.3	72.8	73.0	64.2	54.3
Hispanic	48.9	48.6	58.4	54.6	48.2	39.8

SOURCE: U.S. Department of Labor, 1987.

den activities as they had when they were small. Instead, parents reason with their children more, appeal to their self-esteem ("You wouldn't do anything that stupid") or to their sense of humor, and seek to arouse their guilt. They remind children that they are responsible for themselves. When school-aged children break rules, they are not as likely to be punished as they were when they were younger (Clifford, 1959). But when they are punished, their parents are most likely to deprive them of privileges and confine them to the house or their room rather than to spank them (Newson & Newson, 1976).

Along with the changes in parental behavior, there are also changes in how children interact with their parents. They do not openly express their anger toward their parents as often as they did when they

were younger (Goodenough, 1931, 1975). They are less likely to use such coercive behaviors as whining, yelling, hitting, or ignoring others' overtures (Patterson, 1982). Instead, children argue with their parents, sometimes (to their parents' consternation) at great length, even going so far as to point out the inconsistencies in their parents' arguments. When conflict breaks out, however, or when they become angry, children do not recover as quickly as they did when they were younger. Parents report that their children are often sulky, depressed, passively noncooperative, or that their children avoid them after an angry conflict (Clifford, 1959).

In sum, parents in middle childhood increasingly share the responsibility for controlling their children with the children themselves. Maccoby (1984) terms

sweeping generalizations, some specific findings are of interest.

As might be expected, school-aged children with working mothers spend less time in their parents' presence than children whose mothers are not employed. What might not be expected is that although they spend less time with their parents, the amount of time that they spend actively doing things with their parents does not vary significantly from the amount of time spent by children whose mothers are not employed (Hayes & Kamerman, 1983). Children of working mothers do, however, spend somewhat more time on household chores than do their peers whose mothers do not hold jobs (Medrich, Roizen, Rubin, & Buckley, 1982). Several studies suggest that such responsibilities can have a positive effect on development (Elder, 1974; Woods, 1972). Beyond this, one can only speculate about how children are affected by the amount of time they spend with their parents, and whether it matters if the time is spent actively doing something together or just in one another's company.

Socioeconomic status influences this situation in several ways. The children of single, impoverished, poorly educated mothers in many cases appear to benefit from their mother's holding a job not only because of the increase in income, but also because there is some improvement in the mother's social circumstances, her morale, and her self-confidence (Bronfenbrenner, 1986).

Overall, it appears that maternal employment has a positive influence on girls. Daughters of working mothers are reported to be more "independent, outgoing, higher achievers, to admire their mothers more, to have more respect for women's competence, and to show better social and personal adjustment" (Hoffman, 1984, p. 116).

Boys do not fare as well when their mothers hold jobs. In poor families, the evidence suggest that the sons of employed women are less well-adjusted than the sons of mothers who do not work outside of the home; in middle-class families, the sons of employed mothers do not perform as well in school (Hoffman, 1980).

Since there is a general social trend toward full and part-time maternal employment in industrialized countries, considerable attention has been devoted to the evidence suggesting that, under some conditions, boys are at risk if the mother works outside the home (Hoffman, 1984). However, there is as yet no clear agreement about the precise conditions under which maternal employment has a negative impact on boys' psychological development.

this sharing coregulation. Coregulation is built on parent-child cooperation. It requires parents to work out methods of monitoring, guiding, and supporting their children when adults are not present, using the time that they are together to reinforce their children's understandings of right and wrong, what is safe and unsafe, and when they need to come to adults for help. For coregulation to succeed, children must be willing to inform their parents of their whereabouts, their activities, and their problems.

These changes in child-parent interaction are consistent with Freud's characterization of middle childhood as a time when the superego becomes dominant, causing children to be preoccupied with mastering adult standards. To recall Freud's words, it is a time when the superego "observes the ego, gives it orders, judges it and threatens it with punishments, exactly like the parents whose place it has taken" (Freud, 1940/1964, p. 205) (see Chapter 11, p. 349). As a result, children want to conform to parental expectations and feel distressed when they fail to meet them. They blame this distress partially on their parents, and partially on themselves, which causes both interpersonal and psychological conflict.

A NEW SENSE OF SELF

As a result of the changes in their physical size, their relationships with their peers and parents, and their developing cognitive abilities, children come to have a new, more complex understanding of themselves during middle childhood. Research on changes in children's sense of themselves has focused on the ways in which they define themselves, the emergence of sensitivity to their relative standing among their peers, and their resulting efforts to maintain a sense of self-esteem.

Self-Definition

Using interviews, story dilemmas, and questionnaires, researchers have been able to probe developmental changes in the way that children think about the nature of the self. Although results vary slightly depending upon the procedure used, the general picture that emerges is that, at the start of middle childhood, children think of themselves as defined by their physical bodies and the activities they engage in (Broughton, 1978; Keller, Ford, & Meacham, 1978; Secord & Peevers, 1974; Selman, 1980). Later in middle childhood they distinguish between the mental and the physical aspects of themselves, and their view of the relationship between self and activity becomes more complex.

Selman (1980), for example, obtained evidence about the changing sense of self by posing story dilemmas such as the following:

> Eight-year-old Tom is trying to decide what to buy his friend Mike for a birthday party. By chance, he meets Mike on the street and learns that Mike is extremely upset because his dog, Pepper, has been lost for two weeks. In fact, Mike is so upset that he tells Tom, "I miss Pepper so much that I never want to look at another dog again." Tom goes off, only to pass a store with a sale on puppies: only two are left, and these will soon be gone. (1980, p. 94)

After telling the story, Selman asked whether Tom should buy a puppy for Mike and followed up this question with probes about the child's ideas concerning the self and others. Sample questions included "Is there an inside and an outside to a person?" and "Can you ever fool yourself into thinking that you feel one way when you really feel another?"

Prior to middle childhood, children take Mike's statement that he never wants to look at another dog at face value. They deny that what people say can be different from what they think. Selman calls this conception of the self *physicalistic* because the self is equated with specific body parts. Children at this level, Selman writes, will report that their mouth tells their hand what to do or that their ideas come from their tongue (Selman, 1980).

At about the age of 6, the children in Selman's study believed that psychological and physical experience are different but claimed that they must be consistent with each other. Then, about the age of 8, they realized that there can be a discrepancy between inner experience and outer appearance; the self can fool itself. Thus, Mike might really want another puppy (the psychological experience) even though he says that he doesn't (outer appearance). At this point, children have developed the idea that each person has a private, subjective self that is not always easily read from behavior.

Using a different technique, Keller, Ford, and Meachum (1978) asked preschool children to complete the following sentence stems such as: "I am a boy/girl who _____." When asked to define themselves in this way, preschoolers described themselves in terms of what they did: "I am a girl who walks to school" or "I am a boy who plays baseball." These activity-based answers undergo a subtle change during middle childhood (Secord & Peevers, 1974). Whereas preschoolers might answer such questions by stating, "I ride a bike," third-graders were more likely to respond, "I ride a bike better than Sammy." In short, during middle childhood, children begin to define themselves by comparison with other children.

The way one looks is often central to self-definition.

Social Comparison

There is no mystery as to why social comparison plays a role in children's sense of themselves during middle childhood. Their activities with their peers and the knowledge that their behavior is being critically evaluated by others — including their parents — leads children to engage in a new kind of questioning about themselves. If the setting is the playground, they must decide "Am I good at sports?" "Am I a good friend?" "Do the other kids like me?" If the setting is the classroom, the comparison is likely to be along academic lines ("Am I good at math?"). Such questions have no absolute answer because there are no absolute criteria of success. Rather, adequacy is defined by one's relationship to the social group. Consequently, the process of self-definition resulting from such experiences is called **social comparison.** From specific comparisons in many different settings, children begin to formulate a new overall sense of themselves.

Of course, most preschoolers are not complete strangers to social comparison. When cookies are being distributed at snack time in a day-care center, preschoolers can be seen making certain that they get the same amounts as their peers. And certainly jealousy among siblings reflects awareness of comparing the level of attention from parents. But around the age of 8 or 9 years, children's sensitivity to themselves in relation to others their own age increases significantly (Broughton, 1978; Damon, 1983; Selman, 1980).

A study by Diane Ruble and her colleagues illustrates how one common form of social comparison, the extent of athletic ability, arises in middle childhood (Ruble, Boggiano, Feldman, & Loebl, 1980). The researchers arranged for 5-, 7-, and 9-year-old children to play a modified game of basketball, the objective of which was to throw the ball into a basketball hoop that was concealed behind a curtain. Because the children could not see for themselves if they were successful, they had to depend upon what they were told by the experimenter. The unusual procedure was explained to the children as a test of their ability to *remember* the location of the hoop when it was no longer visible. To make this story plausible, the children were given a brief practice session with the hoop visible.

Once the experimenters were convinced that the children knew what was expected of them, each child was given four chances to throw the ball through the hoop. All the children were told that they were suc-

cessful on the second and fourth throws. This part of the procedure set the stage for the social comparison manipulation to follow.

Each of three groups of children at each age level was provided with different information about how they performed relative to a hypothetical group of other children their own age. To make the comparison clear, the experimenter pasted paper symbols on a large cardboard scorecard to mark the child's performance. Each child saw two balls and two Xs pasted on the board to mark his or her two "hits" and two "misses," respectively. Children in the relative success group also saw the hypothetical scores of eight other children, only one of whom scored as many as one "hit." Children in the relative failure group saw scores of eight children all of whom scored three or more "hits." Children in a control group saw only their own scores. The children were asked both how good they were at this game, and how pleased they were with their performance.

If the children assessed their own performance by comparing their scores with others', one would expect that those who experienced relative failure would have low self-assessment, and those who experienced relative success would assess themselves highly. This is exactly what Ruble and her associates observed among the 9-year-olds. Children in the relative success group had the highest self-assessment, followed by those in the control group, with those in the failure group having the lowest self-assessment. But these findings did not hold true for the 5- and 7-year-olds. The younger children did not seem to assess their own performance in relation to those of others. They were equally pleased with their performance regardless of whether they had experienced relative failure, relative success, or no social comparison at all.

In real-life situations, in which children have a great deal of experience evaluating their relative abilities, the process of social comparison can be quite complex. The following example is taken from an interview with an aspiring ballet dancer. Gwen, who is $12\frac{1}{2}$ years old, is in a special class from which members of a leading national ballet company are chosen. Gwen knows that she is constantly being graded, much as she might be in school.

Partly because she is so much younger, Gwen is smaller and doesn't have as much strength and stamina as the other girls in her class. They also have more experience on toe than she does and she takes fewer classes than they do. "Mostly it doesn't really bother me that much," she says. "But sometimes I think I'm doing really badly and I start comparing myself to them. Then I say, 'Hey, look, I'm not as old.' But I like having people a little bit older than me because that way I can look up to them and see what they're doing and then try to work up to that, instead of having kids my own age. Because when I was with the kids my own age I was always better than they were," she states matter-of-factly. Then, catching herself, she adds, "I feel badly saying that, but it's true." (Cole, 1980a, p. 159)

From the existing evidence, it appears that deliberate and pervasive social comparison becomes important around 8 years of age, although its rudiments reach back into the preschool years (Ruble, 1983). By the end of middle childhood, most children will develop a more complex sense of themselves as a consequence of social comparisons.

These girls have compared themselves to boys, and found that there is something that boys have that they also want — paper routes.

Self-Esteem

Erik Erikson's theory of personality development emphasizes the special importance of the new adult expectations that 7- and 8-year-old children encounter. As mentioned in Chapter 11 (p. 358), Erikson (1963) thought of middle childhood as the time when children have to resolve the crisis of industry versus inferiority. The "industry" side of this formulation was discussed at length in Chapters 13 and 14, which described the new assignments adults give children who work or go to school. Here we focus on the "inferiority" side of the crisis by considering the challenges to self-esteem that arise from children's efforts to demonstrate that they are capable and worthy of others' love and admiration.

Self-esteem is considered to be a critical index of mental health (Jahoda, 1958). High self-esteem has been linked to later life satisfaction (Crandall, 1973) and happiness (Bachman, 1970), while low self-esteem has been linked to depression, anxiety, and maladjustment, both in school and in children's social relations (Damon, 1983).

Self-esteem is often measured by questionnaires asking children to respond to such statements as "On the whole, I am satisfied with myself," "At times I think I am no good at all," "I am popular with kids my own age," or "I find it difficult to talk in front of the class." As crude as this method may appear to be, it does yield scores of self-esteem that remain stable for several years (Coopersmith, 1967; Rosenberg, 1979).

By the time they are 8 years old, schoolchildren in the United States evaluate themselves in terms of their overall feelings of self-worth and their competencies in three areas: cognitive competence, social competence, physical competence, according to research conducted by Susan Harter (1982).

Harter obtained her measures of self-esteem by presenting children with 28 items that required them to select the one of two statements that is "most like me" and then to indicate whether the statement is "really true for me" or only "sort of true for me" (see Table 15.6 for examples in each category). These individual judgments were scored from one to four. A score of one was given if the child marked the far left-hand box in Figure 15.7, indicating low self-evaluation; four was given for a mark in the far right-hand box, indicating high self-evaluation. Then the scores for individual items were added together to determine a child's overall self-evaluation in each area.

TABLE 15.6 Harter self-esteem scale

Area of Self-evaluation	Content of Sample Items
Cognitive competence	Good at schoolwork, can figure out answers, remember easily, remember what is read
Social competence	Have a lot of friends, popular, do things with kids, easy to like
Physical competence	Do well at sports, good at games, chosen first for games
General self-worth	Sure of myself, do things fine, I am a good person, I want to stay the same

SOURCE: Harter, 1982.

Children's evaluations of themselves using this method were found to coincide reasonably well with the way they were evaluated by others. When asked to rate children using the same questions that the children used to rate themselves, Harter found that teachers' ratings were significantly correlated with the children's ratings. For example, children rated highly in physical skills by their teachers were likely to be both those who were chosen by their peers for team games and those who rated themselves highly on physical competence. In addition, children were found to be sensitive to the fact that how competent they felt depended on the context they were in. A particularly tall girl might feel confident on the basketball court but self-conscious at junior high dances.

Self-esteem has also been linked in some research to patterns of child rearing (Coopersmith, 1967; Loeb, Horst, & Horton, 1980). For example, in an extensive study of 10- to 12-year-old boys, Stanley Coopersmith found that parents of boys with high self-esteem (as determined by their answers to a questionnaire and

their teachers' ratings) employed a style of parenting strikingly similar to the "authoritative" pattern described by Diana Baumrind in her study of parenting (see Chapter 12). It may be recalled that authoritative parents were distinguished by their mixture of firm control, promotion of high standards of behavior, encouragement of independence, and willingness to reason with their children. Coopersmith's data, taken from a significantly older group of children, suggest that three parental characteristics combine to produce high self-esteem in late middle childhood:

1. *Acceptance of their children*. The mothers of sons with high self-esteem had closer, more affectionate relationships with their children than mothers of children with low self-esteem. The children seemed to appreciate this approval and to view their mothers as favoring and supportive. They also tended to interpret her interest as an indication of their personal importance, as a consequence of which they came to regard themselves favorably. "This is success in its most personal expression — the concern, attention, and time of significant others" (Coopersmith, 1967, p. 179).

2. *Clearly defined limits*. When parents impose strict limits on their children's activities, they make it clear when deviations are likely to evoke action; enforcement of limits gives the child a sense that norms are real and significant, and contributes to the child's self-definition.

3. *Respect for individuality*. Within the limits set by the parents' sense of standards and social norms, the children were allowed a good deal of individual self-expression. Parents showed respect for their children by reasoning with them and taking their points of view into account.

Really true for me	Sort of true for me	Some kids often forget what they learn	but	Other kids can remember things easily	Sort of true for me	Really true for me
☐	☐				☐	☐

FIGURE 15.7 *A sample item from Harter's scale of self-esteem. Choices to the left of center indicate degrees of poor self-esteem; choices to the right indicate degrees of positive self-esteem. (From Harter, 1982.)*

Taken together, these data suggest that the key to high self-esteem is the feeling, transmitted in large part by the family, that one has some ability to control one's own future, both by controlling oneself and one's environment (Harter, 1983). This feeling of control is not without bounds. As the second point indicates, children who have a positive self-image know their boundaries, but this does not detract from their feeling of effectiveness. Rather, it sets clear limits within which the person feels considerable freedom of action and assurance.

A good start in the family cannot completely shield children against buffeting from their peers, but it does provide a secure foundation for the trials they undergo when they are on their own.

MIDDLE CHILDHOOD RECONSIDERED

With the evidence about children's development during middle childhood before us, it is appropriate to return to the question of whether middle childhood is a universal stage of development with its own unique psychological characteristics.

A universal social contribution to the changes that occur in middle childhood is the rise of the peer group as a major context for development. For the first time, children are in the position of achieving their status within a group of those with relatively equal power and status without the intervention of adults. The skills they acquire for building enduring social relations will be essential to their effectiveness and happiness as adults. Equally important is children's mastery of the social conventions and moral rules that regulate their communities.

The new cognitive capacities that develop at this time are less accessible to observation, but no less important in creating a qualitatively distinct stage of development. As we saw in Chapter 13, thought processes in middle childhood become more logical, deliberate, and consistent. Children become more capable of thinking through actions and their consequences; they are able to engage in concentrated acts of deliberate learning with no tangible rewards; and

they keep in mind the points of view of other people in a wider variety of contexts.

Least visible are the biological changes that underpin children's apparent new mental capacities. The fact that children are bigger, stronger, and better coordinated is obvious enough. But only recently has modern anatomical and neurophysiological research permitted observation of such subtle changes as the proliferation of brain circuitry and the new influence of the brain's frontal lobes in guiding behavior.

If we were to consider each element in the construction of middle childhood separately, it would be difficult to sustain the argument that it constitutes a discontinuous, stagelike change from earlier periods. After all, preschoolers are often found in neighborhood groups with older children when no adults are present, they have been shown to exhibit logical thinking and the use of memory strategies, and the evidence of discontinuous biological change (except for the loss of baby teeth) is still disputable.

However, when we survey the world's cultures, it is clear that adults everywhere assign 6- and 7-year-olds to a new social category and require them to behave themselves in new (and often stressful) contexts. Whether individual children are fully prepared or not, change they must or face the displeasure of their parents and the scorn of their peers. This process of social categorization introduces discontinuity simultaneously into children's experiences and adult expecta-

TABLE 15.7 The bio-social-behavioral shift initiating middle childhood

Biological domain

Loss of baby teeth and gain of permanent teeth
Growth spurt in frontal lobes and in overall brain size
Alpha activity begins to predominate over theta in the EEG

Behavioral domain

Increased memory capacity; strategic remembering
Concrete operations
Logical classification
Decreased egocentrism and improved perspective-taking

Social domain

Peer group participation; games with rules
Deliberate instruction
"Golden Rule" morality
Coregulation of behavior between parents and child
Social comparison

tions of how they should behave. The consequence of the changes in adult expectations and the demands of the contexts that children begin to inhabit is the formation of a distinctive constellation of biological, behavioral, and social factors corresponding to the everyday notion of middle childhood (See Table 15.7).

Within the universal pattern of changes associated with middle childhood, it is important to keep in mind that different cultures create marked variations in spe-

cific cognitive skills and forms of social behavior. Particularly important in this regard is the institution of schooling, which provides children with powerful means of manipulating information about their environment. The kinds of chores that adults assign to children are also important, as these shape distinctive patterns of nurturant and egoistic interpersonal behavior. With the advent of adolescence, these cultural variations will become even more prominent.

SUMMARY

1. Middle childhood, the years from 6 to 12, is a time when children begin to spend significant amounts of time beyond direct adult control in the company of children roughly their own age.

2. During middle childhood, the nature of children's play changes from role-based fantasy to games that require adherence to rules.

3. Social rules are of several types—moral rules, social conventions, and personal rules. Especially important for the conduct of peer groups are basic moral rules and social conventions.

4. The distinction between moral rules and social conventions is understood during early childhood. Within each domain of rules, children's thinking goes through a sequence of developmental stages.

5. Moral reasoning changes during middle childhood from a belief that moral authority resides naturally in a more powerful other ("heteronomous morality"), to a "market mentality" based on mutual support and, in some cases, to a belief in reciprocal responsibility ("the golden rule").

6. Concepts of the fair distribution of resources change from the use of arbitrary criteria to a recognition of the rights of all to share in group resources. Further development consists of children's increasingly sophisticated ability to calculate the legitimacy of distributing resources unequally under certain conditions.

7. Reasoning about social conventions begins with children treating conventions as more or less equivalent to natural laws. With increased sophistication they begin to separate empirical associations ("Most nurses are

women") from necessity. Finally, children come to appreciate the usefulness of social conventions in regulating social interaction.

8. Children's conceptions of friendship develop from an emphasis on participating in joint activities to an emphasis on sharing interests, building mutual understanding, and creating trust.

9. The development of conceptions of friendship is closely associated with an increased ability to adopt other people's points of view, and to repair misunderstandings when they occur.

10. Middle childhood is a period of relative segregation of the sexes. Boys tend to have more friends than girls, but girls' friendships tend to be more intimate than boys'.

11. Social differentiation in peer groups creates preference patterns for who likes to spend time with whom. Physical attractiveness is a major factor in popularity. However, relevant social skills—such as making constructive contributions to group activity, adopting the group's frame of reference, and understanding social rules—also play an important role in popularity.

12. There are marked cultural variations in the values placed on cooperation versus competition in peer interactions.

13. When conflicts arise between peer groups, involvement in solving common problems is the most likely path to reducing intergroup tensions.

14. Participation in peer groups is important to later development because it fosters the ability to communicate, to understand others' points of view, and to get along with others.

15. As children begin to participate in peer groups, their relationship with their parents undergoes significant changes.
    a. During middle childhood, parents become more demanding of their children, with respect to both their domestic duties and their achievement in school.
    b. At this time, parental control shifts from direct to indirect methods, which include reasoning, humor, appeals to self-esteem, and the arousal of guilt.

16. Increased time spent among peers poses challenges to children's sense of themselves. Their basic conceptions of the self change from a fusion of the physical and the mental toward a recognition that people can feel one way and behave another.

17. Special challenges to the sense of self arise from the process of social comparison, which occurs when children compete in games and in school.

18. A strong sense of self-esteem is important to mental health. Family practices that emphasize acceptance of children, clearly defined limits, and respect for individuality are most likely to give rise to a firm sense of self-worth.

19. Social development is an essential part of the bio-social-behavioral shift occurring in the years between 5 and 7. Understood as a unique configuration of biological, social, and behavioral characteristics, middle childhood appears to be a universal stage of human development.

KEY TERMS

Coregulation

Group norms

Moral rules

Peers

Personal rules

Positive justice

Rule-based games

Social comparison

Social conventions

Social repair mechanisms

Sociogram

SUGGESTED READINGS

COLES, ROBERT. *The Moral Life of Children.* Boston: Atlantic Monthly Press, 1986.

Child psychiatrist Robert Coles provides many examples of children's moral thinking about important issues: school segregation, social inequality, and the threat of nuclear annihilation.

DAMON, WILLIAM. *Social and Personality Development.* New York: Norton, 1983.

An excellent summary of many topics treated in this chapter: changing senses of the self, friendship, the roles of parents and peers in social and personality development, and the importance of cultural context.

GOLDING, WILLIAM. *The Lord of the Flies.* New York: Putnam, 1954.

A terrifying fantasy of what might happen if a group of boys were marooned on an island with no supervision.

RUBIN, ZICK. *Children's Friendships.* Cambridge, Mass.: Harvard University Press, 1980.

Beginning with an examination of the question "Do friends matter?" this book describes the evolution of children's friendships in a nontechnical and readable fashion, with special emphasis on middle childhood.

SOYINKA, WOLE. *Ake, the Years of Childhood.* New York: Random House, 1981.

This is a fascinating autobiographical account of growing up in an African village by a Nobel Prize-winning playwright, poet, and novelist. It gives a glimpse into a different culture that provides its children with their own distinctive ways of making sense of the world.

YOUNISS, JAMES. *Parents and Peers in Social Development.* Chicago: University of Chicago Press, 1980.

Drawing on the theories of Jean Piaget and Harry Stack Sullivan, James Youniss examines the nature of social development, having conducted hundreds of interviews with children about the nature of their interactions with other people.

V

...

Adolescence

Among the major developmental transitions that follow birth, none is so clearly marked by a change in the biological constitution of the individual as that between childhood and adolescence. Around the end of the first decade of life, a cascade of biochemical events begins that will alter the size, the shape, and the functioning of the human body. The most revolutionary of the changes that will occur is the development of the entirely new potential of individuals to engage in biological reproduction. These biological changes have profound social implications for the simple reason that reproduction cannot be accomplished by a single human being. As their reproductive organs reach maturity, boys and girls begin to engage in new forms of social behavior because they begin to find the opposite sex attractive.

There is more to human reproduction than sex, however. The process of *biological* reproduction, by itself, is not sufficient for the continuation of our species. It must be complemented by a social process, an extended period of *cultural* reproduction, which ensures that the "designs for living" evolved by the group will be transmitted to the next generation. Robert Havighurst (1967), an educational sociologist, has summarized the many developmental tasks that young people who have reached biological maturity must accomplish before they can take their places as adult members of their societies. In addition to mastering the basic skills necessary for economic survival, these include achieving new and more mature relations with age-mates of both sexes, learning the appropriate masculine or feminine social roles, developing emotional independence from parents and other adults, acquiring a set of values and an ethical system to guide behavior, and learning to behave in a socially responsible manner.

In the United States and other industrialized societies, a gap of 7 to 9 years typically separates the biological changes that mark the onset of sexual maturity and the social changes that confer adult status (such as the right to marry without parental consent or to run for elective office). This lengthy period is necessary because of the time it takes to acquire the many skills that will ensure economic independence and cultural reproduction. It is in such societies that a well-formed concept of adolescence as an intermediate stage of development between middle childhood and adulthood is most likely to be found.

In some societies, there is little or no gap between the beginning of sexual maturity and the beginning of adulthood (Whiting, Burbank, & Ratner, 1982). These are usually societies in which the level of technology is relatively low and in which biological maturity occurs relatively late by our standards. By the time biological reproduction becomes possible, which is about the age of 15 in many nonindustrial societies, young people already know how to farm, weave cloth, prepare food, and care for children. In such societies, there may be no commonly acknowledged stage of development equivalent to adolescence.

The variations among societies in the interval between the achievement of sexual maturity and the attainment of adult status raise the possibility that adolescence is not a universal stage of development. Historians of childhood such as Philippe Ariès (1962) and John and Virginia Demos (1969) argue that the existence of adolescence as a distinct stage of development depends on a society's need for prolonged education. Alternatively, some scholars argue that there is a period in every society during which children strive to attain adult status and that this striving produces similar experiences and hence a common stage of development in all cultures (Bloch & Niederhoffer, 1958). They believe, therefore, that adolescence should be considered a universal developmental stage.

We will return to the question of the universality of adolescence at the end of Chapter 17. First, however, we must examine some of the relevant factors involved. Chapter 16 describes the advent of biological maturity and its intimate links with changes in social life, including changes in the nature of peer group interactions, friendships, and relationships with one's family, as well as entry into the work force. Chapter 17 concentrates on what have traditionally been thought of as the psychological characteristics that develop during adolescence: the new modes of thought that are needed to perform the economic tasks and fulfill the social responsibilities of adulthood, the changed sense of personal identity that is occasioned by a transformed physique and altered social relationships, and the new beliefs about morality and the social order that accompany preparation for adulthood.

Although we will examine the social, biological, and psychological aspects of adolescence separately, it should be kept in mind that they are part of the single process of development. From their interaction in particular cultural contexts will emerge adult people, who are ready to take their places in society and begin the cycle of development over again by creating the next generation.

BIOLOGICAL AND SOCIAL FOUNDATIONS OF ADOLESCENCE

> How is it that, in the human body, reproduction is the only function to be performed by an organ of which an individual carries only one half so that he has to spend an enormous amount of time and energy to find another half?
>
> — François Jacob, *The Possible and the Actual*

. . . .

One of the clearest accounts of what it feels like to enter adolescence appears in the diary of Anne Frank, a Jewish girl who lived in Holland during the German occupation of World War II. Unable to leave her hiding place and go outside for fear of being captured, Anne communicated with her diary, until she and her family were discovered and sent to their deaths in a concentration camp.

Wednesday, 5 January, 1944

Yesterday I read an article about blushing by Sis Heyster. This article might have been addressed to me personally. Although I don't blush very easily, the other things in it certainly all fit me. She writes roughly something like this — that a girl in the years of puberty becomes quiet within and begins to think about the wonders that are happening to her body.

I experience that, too, and that is why I get the feeling lately of being embarrassed about Margot, Mummy, and Daddy. Funnily enough, Margot, who is much more shy than I am, isn't at all embarrassed.

I think what is happening to me is so wonderful, and not only what can be seen on my body, but all that is taking place inside. I never discuss myself or any of these things with anybody; that is why I have to talk to myself about them.

Each time I have a period — and that has only been three times — I have the feeling that in spite of all the pain, unpleasantness, and nastiness, I have a sweet secret, and that is why, although it is nothing but a nuisance to me in a way, I always long for the time that I shall feel that secret within me again. . . . (1975, pp. 116–117)

Thursday, 6 January, 1944

My longing to talk to someone became so intense that somehow or other I took it into my head to choose Peter.

Sometime if I've been upstairs into Peter's room during the day, it always struck me as very snug, but because Peter is so retiring and would never turn anyone out who became a nuisance, I never dared stay long, because I was afraid he might think me a bore. I tried to think of an excuse to stay in his room and get him talking, without it being too noticeable, and my chance came yesterday. Peter has a mania for crossword puzzles at the moment and hardly does anything else. I helped him with them and we sat opposite each other at his little table, he on the chair and me on the divan.

It gave me a queer feeling each time I looked into his deep blue eyes, and he sat there with that mysterious laugh playing round his lips. I was able to read his inward thoughts. I could see on his face that look of helplessness and uncertainty as to how to behave, and at the same time, a trace of his sense of manhood. I noticed his shy manner and it made me feel very gentle; I couldn't refrain from meeting those dark eyes again and again, and with my whole heart I almost beseeched him: oh, tell me, what is going on inside you, oh can't you look beyond this ridiculous chatter?

But the evening passed and nothing happened, except that I told him about blushing — naturally not what I have written, but just that he would become more sure of himself as he grew older. (p. 118)

These diary entries, written less than 24 hours apart when Anne was $14\frac{1}{2}$ years old, poignantly illustrate the intimate connection between the physical changes of puberty and the social characteristics of adolescence. They touch on many different aspects of the bio-social-behavioral shift that marks the end of middle childhood. First, there are the biological changes of puberty, which transform the size and shape of young people's bodies and evoke new, initially strange feelings. These changes are accompanied by changes in social life: After many years of relatively little interest in the opposite sex, boys and girls begin to find each other attractive, which brings about changes in the nature of peer group interactions and personal friendships. Simultaneously, their relationships to their parents change, as if in recognition of the fact that independence, work, and the responsibility of caring for others must replace reliance on parental support. Last, the combination of biological and social developments requires changes in the way young people think about themselves and the world.

In attempting to gain a comprehensive picture of psychological development during adolescence, developmental psychologists face several difficulties. On the one hand, adolescents are able to talk more reflectively about their feelings and thought processes than are younger children. On the other hand, more of what they think is socially awkward to talk about, and more of what they do cannot be observed directly, so the actual facts of adolescent behavior are difficult to doc-

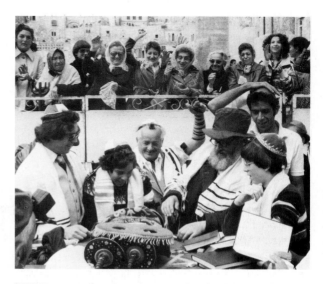

Every society has evolved customs that mark the end of childhood and the transition to adult status. Clockwise from the upper left: puberty rites for a girl among the Apache; a Jewish boy's Bar Mitzvah ceremony at the Western Wall in Jerusalem; aboriginal boys in Australia undergoing a painful circumcision ceremony; a confirmation ceremony in Santa Fe, New Mexico.

ument. Despite these difficulties, the nature of adolescence has long excited the interest of scholars, who have sought to understand its special characteristics both as a transition from middle childhood to adulthood and as a stage of development in its own right. Conceptions of adolescence are of vital importance to adolescents because they determine the demands made of them and the rights they are accorded by society. If they live in a society that considers puberty to be the onset of adulthood, they will be expected to maintain themselves economically and to care for others, and they are subject to the full sanctions of the law should they break it. Conversely, if 15- and 16-year-olds are still considered to be children, they will be cared for by others and will remain free of many of the responsibilities adults must face, but they will also be expected to bend to adult demands as the price for their dependence.

TRADITIONAL CONCEPTIONS OF ADOLESCENCE

Present-day conceptions of adolescence are still heavily influenced by the eighteenth- and nineteenth-century scholars who wrote about it as a distinct period of life. The first great theorist of adolescence was Jean-Jacques Rousseau (see Chapter 1, p. 13). In *Emile* (1762/1911), his treatise on human nature and education, Rousseau suggested three characteristics of adolescence.

1. Adolescence is a period of heightened instability and emotional conflict that is brought on by biological maturation. As Rousseau phrased it:

As the roaring of the waves precedes the tempest so the murmur of rising passions announces this tumultous change, a suppressed excitement warns us of the approaching danger. A change of temper, frequent outbreaks of anger, a perpetual stirring of the mind, make the child almost ungovernable. He becomes deaf to the voice he used to obey; he is a lion in a fever; he distrusts his keeper and refuses to be controlled. (p. 172)

2. In important respects, adolescence recapitulates — repeats in concise form — the earlier stages of life through which the child has passed. As

Rousseau expressed this idea: "We are born, so to speak, twice over; born into existence, and born into life; born a human being and born a man" (p. 172). (See Box 16.1, "Recapitulation and Development.")

3. The biological and social changes that figure prominently in adolescence are accompanied by a fundamental change in cognitive processes. The transition to adolescence, Rousseau believed, brought with it self-conscious thought and the ability to reason logically.

When developmental psychologists began to turn their attention to the phenomenon of adolescence at the end of the nineteenth century, Rousseau's ideas were picked up by, among others, G. Stanley Hall, the first president of the American Psychological Association and a major figure in the shaping of developmental psychology (Cairns, 1983; Kessen, 1965). Hall's goal was to construct a theory of individual development based on Darwin's ideas about the evolution of the species. Hall proclaimed that

Adolescence is a new birth, for the higher and more completely human traits are now born. The qualities of body and soul that now emerge are far newer. The child comes from and harks back to a remoter past; the adolescent is neo-atavistic, and in him the later acquisitions of the race become prepotent. Development is less gradual and more saltatory, suggestive of some ancient period of storm and stress when old moorings were broken and a higher level attained. (1904, p. xiii)

This key passage contains two controversial ideas, both of which can be traced to Rousseau. One is that adolescence is characterized by a heightened state of emotionality, stress, intense states of mind, and love of excitement. The other is that adolescence is a period of rebirth following childhood. In the flush of late nineteenth-century Darwinism, this idea fit a fashionable theory: that each child's individual development repeats the entire evolutionary history of the *species*, which was expressed in the aphorism "Ontogeny recapitulates phylogeny." For example, according to Hall, middle childhood corresponds to an ancient period of historical development when human reason, morality, feelings of love toward others, and religion were presumably underdeveloped by modern standards. As he put it, the end of childhood was once, and for a very protracted and relatively stationary period, the age of maturity in the remote, perhaps pigmoid, stage of human evolution, when in a warm climate the young of our species once shifted for themselves independently of further parental aid. (1904, pp. ix–x)

Adolescence was seen by Hall as a time for the development of the highest human capacities and as the period during which human progress could be promoted.

Modern texts on adolescence tend to present Hall as a figure of purely historical interest. His insistence that the young recapitulate the entire history of the human species is now assumed to be wrong (Gould, 1977b), and his portrait of adolescence as a period of emotional excess is now considered to be exaggerated (Lerner & Foch, 1987). But Hall's ideas, like Rousseau's, live on as a cultural stereotype of modern adolescence, and they appear in modified form in the ideas of several influential twentieth-century psychologists, including Freud, Gesell, Piaget, and Erikson.

MODERN THEORIES OF ADOLESCENCE

The challenge to modern theorists of adolescence is to explain how biological, social, behavioral, and cultural factors contribute to adolescent development and how they are woven together to shape the transition from childhood to adulthood. Each of the four theoretical perspectives we have already encountered repeatedly offers insights to development during this age period. However, there is as yet no widely accepted unified theory of adolescence.

The Biological-Maturation Perspective

Biological-maturation theories of adolescence, like similar theories of development during earlier periods, emphasize that development is primarily the unfolding of inherited biological potentials. Two leading adherents of this view have been Arnold Gesell and Sigmund Freud.

Arnold Gesell Gesell admitted that the environment may exert a more powerful influence during ado-

lescence than it did during infancy, but he still maintained that different environmental conditions do not alter the *basic* pattern of development during adolescence in any fundamental way:

[N]either he [the adolescent] nor his parents in their zeal can transcend the basic laws of development. He continues to grow essentially in the same manner in which he grew as he advanced from the toddling stage of two years through the paradoxical stage of two and a half, and the consolidating stage of three. (Gesell & Ilg, 1943, p. 256)

Gesell agreed with Hall and others, holding that the child recapitulates the history of the species during the course of development. He asserted that the "higher human traits," such as abstract thinking, imagination, and self-control, make their appearance late in the development of the individual because they were acquired late in the history of the species. Although Gesell may be criticized for overstating the degree to which maturational changes can explain adolescent behavior, his insistence on the importance of biological factors in determining the basic pattern of adolescent psychological functioning currently enjoys considerable support.

Sigmund Freud As mentioned in Chapter 1 (p. 16), Freud's ideas are often best thought of as reflecting an interactionist position with respect to the sources of development, although he attributed great importance to biological factors in developmental change. Here we include him as a biological theorist because adolescence, according to Freud, is a distinctive stage of development during which human beings can at last fulfill the biological imperative to reproduce themselves and hence the species. This evolutionary assumption underlay Freud's emphasis on sex as *the* master motive for all human behavior, even behavior in the earliest stages of life. He called adolescence the *genital stage* because this is the period during which sexual intercourse, which is dependent upon mature genitals, becomes the dominant motive of behavior.

In Freud's theory, the emotional storminess that accompanies the adolescent stage is the culmination of the psychological struggle among the three parts of the personality: the id, the ego, and the superego (see Chapter 11, p. 350). As Freud saw it, the upsurge in sexual excitation that accompanies puberty reawakens primitive instincts, increases the power of the id, and upsets the psychological balance achieved during mid-

BOX 16.1

RECAPITULATION AND DEVELOPMENT

···

In their attempts to understand the laws governing the evolution of life, nineteenth-century scholars revived an idea that can be traced back to antiquity: that the development of an individual organism *recapitulates* the entire evolutionary history of the species. In the decades prior to the publication of Darwin's *The Origin of Species* (1859), this debate focused not on human beings but on lower species whose origins could be traced in readily available fossils (Gould, 1977b).

For example, Louis Agassiz, a geologist who believed that "ontogeny recapitulates phylogeny," offered the development of the tail of the fish *Pleuronectes* as a prime example. As shown in the left half of the illustration there is a regular progression in the growth of *Pleuronectes'* tail as individual fish develop. First the tail is symmetrical and pointed, then the top half extends well beyond the lower half, and finally symmetry is reestablished when a new and more complex structure connects the tail to the fish's spinal cord.

This same progression describes the evolution of *Pleuronectes* as a species as shown in the right half of the illustration. This sequence depicts the adult tails of three kinds of fish that represent three stages in the evolution of *Pleuronectes* as shown by the fossil record. Comparison of the left and right sides of the illustration reveals that the sequence of changes in the lifetime of individual *Pleuronectes* parallels the evolutionary history of the species.

Once Darwin made the claim that the evolutionary laws that apply to lower species apply to human beings

as well, the idea that human children recapitulate earlier stages of human evolution during their development became enormously popular (Gould, 1977b; Kessen, 1965). The heyday of speculations about parallels be-

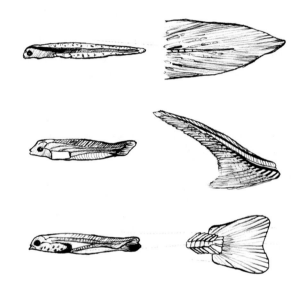

Parallels between individual development and evolutionary change provided key evidence for the hypothesis that ontogeny recapitulates phylogeny. On the left are changes in the tail of a single Pleuronectes as it develops. On the right is fossil evidence of three stages in the evolution of the species Pleuronectes. (From Gould, 1977b.)

dle childhood. This imbalance produces psychological conflict and erratic behavior. The main developmental task of adolescence is therefore to reestablish the balance of psychological forces by reintegrating them in a new and more mature way that is compatible with the individual's new sexual capacities.

Freud, like Hall, was greatly influenced by the doctrine of recapitulationism (Gould, 1977b; Sulloway, 1979). For example, he argued that when sexual maturation reawakens the oedipal urges that were repressed

at the start of middle childhood, the young person must rework this "old" conflict under these new conditions.

Although the Freudian theory of adolescence is rooted in biology because of its assumption that the imperative to reproduce is the engine of individual development, it does not ignore the social world. The superego is, after all, the internal representation of society, and the ego mediates between the social world embodied in the superego on the one hand and the

tween human origins and individual development coincided with the flowering of developmental psychology. Consequently, many early developmental psychologists believed in some form of the recapitulationist theory and applied it in their work.

In the early twentieth century, the doctrine of recapitulationism came under heavy attack within the scientific community. It was not that scholars suddenly decided that ontogeny and phylogeny were totally unrelated. However, as biological knowledge expanded at the turn of the century, it became evident that the evidence upon which recapitulationists had drawn was selective—there were many examples that did not fit the law of recapitulation. Even more damaging, the mechanism of heredity that recapitulationists relied on required them to assume that acquired characteristics were inherited, an assumption that was totally rejected in biology once the genetic basis of evolution became established (see Chapter 2, p. 64, for a discussion of the idea that acquired characteristics are inherited).

Despite its demise as a scientific theory, the idea of recapitulationism has been a major influence on professionals who have concerned themselves with child development throughout the twentieth century. As recently as 1968, Dr. Benjamin Spock, whose book on child rearing influenced generations of parents and their children, wrote:

Each child as he develops is retracing the whole history of mankind, physically and spiritually, step by step. A baby starts off in the womb as a single tiny cell, just the way the first living thing appeared in the ocean. Weeks later, as he lies in the amniotic fluid in the womb, he has gills like a fish. Towards the end of the first year of life, when he learns to clamber to his feet, he's celebrating that period millions of years ago when man's ancestors got up off all fours. . . . The child in the years after six gives up part of his dependence on his parents. He makes it his business to find out how to fit into the world outside the family. . . . He is probably reliving that stage of human history when our wild ancestors found it was better not to roam the forest in independent family groups but to form larger communities. (p. 229)

One of the areas where recapitulationist ideas have continued to be important is in education, where they are still used to organize the early classroom experience of many children. It was to help children "traverse the path of human development" that Maria Montessori (1912/1964), whose methods of preschool education are still in wide use, recommended that young children be shown how to grow plants and tend animals. She believed that by discovering how to intensify "the production of the soil," young children, like their remote ancestors, would "obtain the reward of civilization" (p. 160). John Dewey (1916), perhaps the most influential of all American educational theorists, adopted recapitulationist ideas in advocating active participation of children in farming, building houses, and the like as a way to break through the abstract, formal nature of much school instruction. He insisted that the goal of allowing children to learn about and thus vicariously experience prior epochs in human history was to help them to understand better their current circumstances.

demands of the id on the other. Consequently, personality development during adolescence, as in earlier periods, involves social as well as biological factors.

The Environmental-Learning Perspective

Beginning with the ascendance of behaviorist explanations of human behavior in the 1920s, biologically oriented accounts of development were criticized for underestimating the degree to which the social environment shapes children's behaviors and overestimating the degree of discontinuity that distinguishes adolescence from middle childhood. For example, Albert Bandura and Richard Walters (1959) argued in one study that the aggressiveness, which is often associated with male behavior in adolescence is not biological in nature but a product of societal reinforcement. They found that aggressive boys were encouraged by their parents to be aggressive outside the home — to "stick up for their rights" and to use their fists. The fathers of aggressive boys even seemed to get vicarious enjoyment from their sons' aggressive behavior, which meant that by being aggressive, the boys could have the satisfaction of pleasing their fathers.

Arguing that the same principles of learning can be used to explain human development in all periods, Bandura (1964) has been skeptical about claims that adolescence is a distinctive stage of development. He has been particularly critical of the idea that adolescence is inevitably a period of stress, tension, and rebellion, citing evidence that the rate of emotional difficulties among adolescents is no higher than it is for adults.

A favorite strategy of those who give primary weight to the environmental causes of development has been to seek out societies in which teenagers do not display the presumably universal characteristics of adolescence to support their claim that the social environment shapes the nature of adolescent behavior. One of the most famous examples of such cross-cultural research was undertaken by the anthropologist Margaret Mead (1901–1978), who went to the Pacific island of Samoa in 1926. Mead posed the question to be answered by her research in a characteristically straightforward manner:

Is adolescence a period of mental and emotional stress for the growing girl as inevitably as teething is a period of misery for the small baby? Can we think of adolescence as a time in the life history of every girl child which carries with it symptoms of conflict and stress as surely as it implies a change in the girl's body? (1928/1973, p. 109)

Her conclusion was equally straightforward:

Following the Samoan girls through every aspect of their lives we have tried to answer this question and we found throughout that we had to answer it in the negative. The adolescent girl in Samoa differed from her sister who had not reached puberty in one chief respect, that in the older girl certain bodily changes were present which were absent in the younger girl. There were no other great differences to set off the group passing through adolescence from the group which would become adolescent in two years or the group which had become adolescent two years earlier. (1928/1973, p. 109)

Mead attributed the tranquility of Samoan adolescence to the general casualness of Samoan society, particularly its relaxed attitude toward sexual relationships among adolescents, in contrast with the wide variety of conflicting attitudes and choices that confront young people in the United States and in western European societies.

Although subsequent investigators have claimed that there was a much higher level of conflict and stress among the Samoan girls Mead studied than she had recognized (Freeman, 1983; Raum, 1940/1967), Mead's work has exerted an enormous influence on our basic ideas about adolescence. She forced psychologists to pay serious attention, for the first time, to the cultural and social factors that contribute to the characteristics of adolescence proposed by Hall, Freud, and other biologically oriented psychologists.

The Interactional Perspective

Two of the most influential theorists of adolescence, Erik Erikson and Jean Piaget, sought to reconcile the biological and environmental-learning explanations of adolescence by showing how the distinctive qualities of this stage of development arise from the interaction of biological and social factors found in all societies, irrespective of their cultural organization. Although they approached the problem in different ways, their theories of adolescent psychology are similar in many important respects (Kegan, 1982; Kohlberg, 1984).

Jean Piaget At the core of Piaget's theory of adolescence is the idea that as young people begin to take on adult roles they must simultaneously begin to plan ahead and to think more systematically about the world. As we will see in Chapter 17, Barbel Inhelder and Jean Piaget (1958) believed that the systematic nature of adolescent thinking is evidence of an advance from the *concrete* operational to the *formal* operational level. They argued that this new mode of thinking changes all aspects of psychological functioning, including adolescents' relations with their peers, their ability to work, and their attitudes toward social ideals.

Erik Erikson As mentioned in Chapter 1 (p. 16), Erik Erikson's theory of development is difficult to classify with respect to the nature-nurture issue; in some ways it fits into the cultural-context approach, and in other ways it more closely approximates an interactional approach. Although he is a student of Freud, Erikson is as concerned as Mead was with showing that the development of human personality is not totally controlled by biological instincts; in this respect he is similar to the environmental-learning and cultural-context theorists. Yet he accepts Freud's emphasis on the role of biological factors in shaping the characteristics of adolescence, and he also maintains that adolescence is a universal, qualitatively distinct period of development.

Erikson believes that the task for young people about to enter adulthood is to incorporate their new sexual drives and the social demands placed upon them into a fully integrated and healthy personality. The result of this integration is what Erikson calls identity, which he defines as a "sense of personal sameness and historical continuity" (1968a, p. 17). Phrased a little differently, our identity tells us how we "fit in" with the people around us and with ourselves in the past and future. Identity is not a single trait or belief. Rather, it is a *pattern* of beliefs about the self constructed by adolescents that reconciles the many ways in which they are like other people with the ways in which they differ from them.

The formation of identity becomes crucial during adolescence, in Erikson's view, because this is the time when the child's beliefs, abilities, and desires must be reconciled with adult norms; that is, individual identity and social identity must be made compatible. For this reason, Erikson characterized the central crisis of adolescence as one of "identity versus identity confusion" (1968a, p. 94). The alternative to identity, identity confusion, leads to social deviance and conflict.

Among the developmental theorists of adolescence, Erikson's approach is notable in that it does *not* view adolescence as the end point of development. Rather, adolescence sets the stage for the later development of intimacy, generativity, and commitment (see Box 11.2, p. 359 for a summary of the Eriksonian stages).

The Cultural-Context Perspective

The theories of adolescence discussed so far have differed from one another in several respects: whether or not they consider the end of adolescence to be the end point of development, the emphasis they place on biological versus social factors in determining the psychological characteristics of the period, and the extent to which they assume that adolescence involves distinctive psychological characteristics. The biological-maturation and Piagetian views are alike in that they assume that adolescence is a universal period of development that encompasses some part of the teenage years. Social-learning theorists also accept the idea that adolescence is a universal period of life but deny its stagelike qualities. In contrast to all these views, psychologists who take the cultural-context perspective contend that in some cultural circumstances adolescence will appear to be a distinct stage and in some it will not (Laboratory of Comparative Human Cognition, 1983; Whiting, 1980). The critical factors that determine whether or not adolescence will be recognized in a society as a distinct stage are the kinds of activities required of adults and the age at which young people are given full access to (and responsibility for) these activities.

For example, among traditional !Kung San of the Kalahari desert there is no delay between puberty and marriage. During middle childhood, !Kung San children become sufficiently competent in carrying out hunting and gathering activities to sustain themselves. When they become ready for biological reproduction, they are also ready to engage in the tasks of cultural reproduction; they can sustain a family economically and can bring their children up to deal with the world as they know it (Lee & Devore, 1976; Shostak, 1981). By contrast, when 13- or 14-year-olds in the United States have children, both the parents and the children face great hardships because the parents cannot sustain either themselves or their children (Furstenberg, 1976).

Differences in the kinds of activities that must be mastered to carry out the full process of human reproduction in a society have an important impact on the psychological characteristics that are developed at the end of childhood. For example, a teenage girl from an industrialized society who spends 7 hours a day in classrooms studying mathematics, the natural sciences, and literature will likely develop different intellectual skills than one from a preliterate society who spends the same number of hours a day helping her mother-in-law with farming, cooking, and child-rearing chores.

As we have found for each of the earlier periods of development, data supporting one theoretical perspective do not necessarily discredit rival perspectives. In some cases, when the facts to be accounted for are similar and have been generated in similar ways, theoretical disputes can be settled by further observation. But often the aspects of development that rival theories address are too different from one another to permit direct comparisons or choices among them.

With these words of caution, we will now turn to the major phenomena of the adolescent period that the alternative theories of adolescence attempt to explain. We will start with a description of puberty, the biological changes that initiate the capacity for sexual reproduction. We will then turn to the reorganization of social life that the potential for biological reproduction requires as an essential part of the transition to adulthood.

PUBERTY

During the second decade of life, a revolutionary series of biological developments called **puberty** transforms individuals from a state of physical immaturity to one in which they are biologically mature and capable of sexual reproduction. Puberty begins with a signal from the hypothalamus, located at the base of the brain, that activates the pituitary gland, a pea-sized organ appended to the hypothalmus. As a result, the pituitary increases its production of growth hormones, which in turn stimulate the growth rate of all body tissue. The pituitary also releases hormones that trigger a great increase in the manufacture of the two gonadotrophic (gonad-seeking) hormones. In females, these hormones stimulate the ovaries to manufacture the hormones estrogen and progesterone, which trigger the numerous physical events, including the release of mature ova from the ovaries, that eventually allow for reproduction. In males, they stimulate the testes and adrenal glands to manufacture the hormone testosterone, which brings about the manufacture of sperm (Katchadourian, 1977) (see Figure 16.1).

The Growth Spurt

One of the first visible signs of puberty is a spurt in the rate of physical growth, during which boys and girls

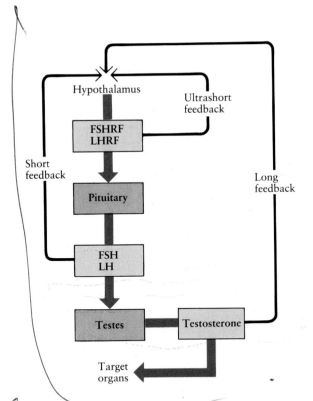

FIGURE 16.1 *Puberty in males is initiated by complex interactions among the hypothalamus, the pituitary gland, and the testes. When the hypothalamus releases gonadotropin-releasing factors (FSHRF, LHRF), it causes the pituitary to discharge the gonadotropins FSH and LH into the blood. These stimulate the testes, promoting the production of testosterone, which in turn stimulates changes in other body organs and provides feedback to the hypothalamus. (From Katchadourian, 1977.)*

grow at a faster rate than at any time since they were babies. A boy may grow as much as 9 inches taller and a girl as much as 6 to 7 inches taller during the 2 to 3 years of the growth spurt. Although adolescents continue to grow throughout puberty, they reach 98 percent of their ultimate adult height by the end of the growth spurt (Tanner, 1978).

Some parts of the body spurt ahead of others in violation of the cephalocaudal (from the head down) and proximodistal (from the center to the periphery) patterns of growth. As a rule, leg length reaches its peak first, followed 6 to 9 months later by trunk length. Shoulder and chest breadths are the last to reach their peak. This trend is characterized by J. M.

Tanner with the quip "A boy stops growing out of his trousers (at least in length) a year before he stops growing out of his jackets" (1978, p. 69).

Even the head, which has grown little since the age of 2, participates in the growth spurt. The skull bones increase in thickness, making adolescents' heads longer and wider than children's. The brain, which attains 90 percent of its adult weight by the age of 5, grows little during this period (Tanner, 1978).

Changes in physical size are accompanied by changes in overall shape. During puberty, males and females acquire the distinctive physical features that characterize the two sexes. Girls develop breasts and have a marked spurt in the growth of their hips. Boys acquire wide shoulders and a muscular neck. They also lose fat during adolescence, which makes them appear more muscular and angular than girls, who retain their fat and so have a higher proportion of fat to muscle, giving them a rounder, softer look.

Most boys not only appear to be stronger than girls after puberty, they are stronger (see Figure 16.2). Before puberty, there is little difference in the strength of boys and girls of similar size. But by the end of this period, boys can exercise for longer periods and can exert more force per ounce of muscle than girls of the same size. Contributing to males' greater strength and their greater capacity for exercise are the relatively larger hearts and lungs they develop. These give them higher blood pressure when their heart muscles contract, a lower resting heart rate, and a greater capacity for carrying oxygen in the blood and neutralizing the chemicals that lead to fatigue during physical exercise (Katchadourian, 1977).

The physiological differences between males and females may help to explain why males have traditionally been the warriors, hunters, and heavy laborers throughout human history. They also help to explain why most superior male athletes can outperform superior female athletes. In some important respects, however, females exhibit greater physical prowess than males: they are, on the average, healthier, longer lived, and better able to tolerate long-term stress (Tavris & Offir, 1977).

Sexual Development

During puberty, all the **primary sexual organs,** those organs involved in reproduction, enlarge and become

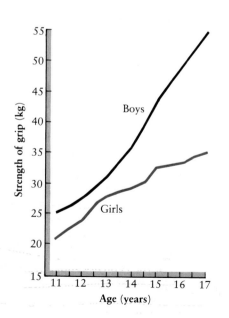
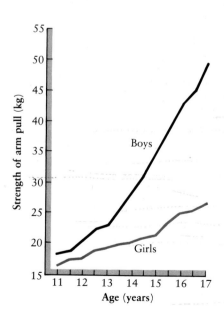

FIGURE 16.2 *Following the onset of puberty there is a steady increase in the difference in strength between males and females. (Adapted from Katchadourian, 1977.)*

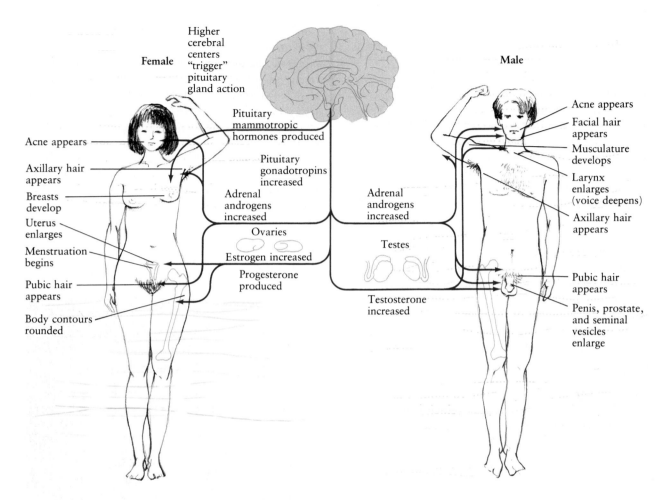

FIGURE 16.3 *The hormonal changes that accompany puberty cause a wide variety of physical changes in both females and males. (Adapted from CIBA Pharmaceutical Company, 1965.)*

functionally mature. In males, the testes begin to produce sperm cells and the prostate begins to produce semen. Males gain the capacity to ejaculate the semen, which contains the sperm. In females, the ovaries begin to release mature ova into the fallopian tubes. When there is no conception, menstruation occurs. **Secondary sexual characteristics,** the anatomical and physiological signs that outwardly distinguish males from females, appear as the primary sexual organs are maturing (see Figure 16.3).

The first signs that boys are entering puberty are an enlargement of the testes, a thickening and reddening of the skin of the scrotum, and the appearance of

pubic hair. These changes usually occur about a year before boys begin their growth spurt. About the time the growth spurt begins, the penis begins to grow; it continues to do so for about 2 years. About a year after the penis begins to grow, boys become able to ejaculate. The first ejaculation of semen often occurs spontaneously during sleep and is called a *nocturnal emission*. At first, the sperm in the semen are not numerous nor as fertile as they will be during early adulthood (Katchadourian, 1977).

Underarm and facial hair appear about 2 years after a boy's pubic hair begins to grow, but in some individuals underarm and facial hair may appear first. Generally, men do not develop a hairy chest until late adolescence or early adulthood. A boy's voice usually does not deepen until late in puberty. This deepening takes place gradually as the larynx increases in size and the vocal cords lengthen. While it is occurring, often embarrassing cracks in a boy's voice announce to the world the changes that are taking place in his body.

The first visible sign that a girl is beginning to mature sexually is often the appearance of a small rise around the nipples called the *breast bud*. Pubic hair usually appears a little later, just before the growth spurt begins, but sometimes it appears first. At about the same time that girls' outward appearance is beginning to change, their ovaries enlarge and the cells that will eventually evolve into ova begin to ripen. The uterus begins to grow and the vaginal lining thickens.

Girls' secondary sexual characteristics develop throughout puberty. The breasts continue to grow with the development of the mammary glands, which allow for lactation, and the accumulation of adipose (fatty) tissue, which gives them their adult shape. The external genitalia also enlarge during adolescence. **Menarche** — the first menstrual period — occurs relatively late in puberty, about 18 months after the growth spurt has reached its peak velocity. Early menstrual periods tend to be irregular, and they often occur without *ovulation* — the release of a mature egg. Ovulation typically begins about 12 to 18 months after menarche (Boxer, Tobin-Richards, & Petersen, 1983).

The Timing of the Events of Puberty

A glance around a seventh-grade classroom is sufficient to remind even the most casual observer of the wide variations in the age at which puberty begins. Some of the 12- and 13-year-old boys may look much as they did at the age of 9 or 10, whereas others may have the gangly look that often characterizes the growth spurt. Among the girls, who on the average begin to mature sexually somewhat earlier, some may look like mature women with fully developed breasts and rounded hips, some may still have the stature and shape of little girls, and some may be somewhere in between. Figure 16.4 shows typical variations in the maturity of two adolescent girls.

The timing of the changes of puberty depend, as do all events in development, on a complex interaction between genetic and environmental factors. The im-

portance of genetic factors is demonstrated by comparisons of identical and fraternal twins. The average difference in the age at which menarche occurs for identical twin sisters is only two months, whereas the average difference for fraternal twin sisters is 8 months (Marshall & Tanner, 1974).

Environmental factors, such as nutrition, stress, physical exercise, family size, and socioeconomic background, also influence the age of menarche. Girls from higher socioeconomic classes have been found to go through menarche as much as 11 months earlier than girls from poor families (Marshall & Tanner,

FIGURE 16.4 *Differences in the timing of puberty can result in startling differences in size between adolescents who are close in age. The shorter girl in this photograph is 14 years old, while the taller girl is only 13 years old.*

1974). Researchers believe that better nutrition, especially higher protein intake, is primarily responsible for this difference, but since such factors as health care and stress are closely intertwined with socioeconomic class, the specific factors have not been completely isolated (Frisch, 1978; Tanner, 1978).

Even more striking than class differences in the age at which menarche is reached are historical changes. In industrialized countries and in some developing countries as well, the age of onset of menstruation has been decreasing among all social groups (see Figure 16.5). In the 1840s the average age of menarche among European women was between 14 and 15 years of age, whereas today it is between 12 and 13 (Bullough, 1981). A similar trend has occurred in the United

States, where menarche now occurs about a year and a half earlier than it did in 1905.

The onset of puberty among males also seems to be occurring earlier, but the evidence for this change is less direct. Fifty years ago, the average American male gained his maximum height at the age of 26; now this marker of the end of puberty occurs at the age of 18 (Marshall & Tanner, 1974).

Studies of the physical changes associated with puberty indicate that it ordinarily lasts about 4 years (Tanner, 1978). However, individual differences in the duration of puberty are as variable as the age at which puberty begins. For instance, one boy may go through all the events of puberty in the time it takes another's genitals to develop.

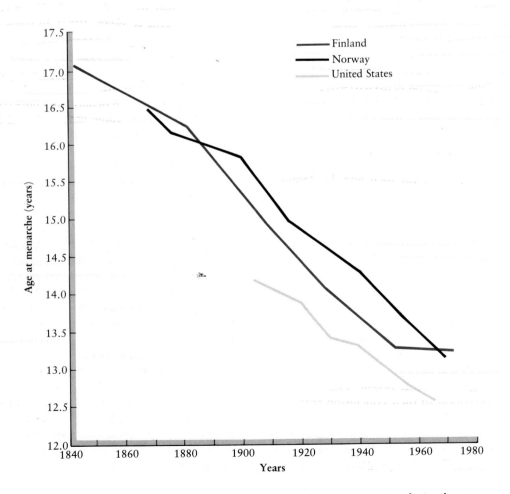

FIGURE 16.5 *The age of menarche has been declining in many countries during the past 150 years. (Adapted from Katchadourian, 1977.)*

Consequences of Early and Late Maturation

Several studies have sought to determine how early or late sexual maturation relative to their peers might influence young people's peer relations, personality, and social adjustment. This research has produced a mixed picture (Brooks-Gunn & Petersen, 1983; Lerner & Foch, 1987; Simmons & Blyth, 1987).

One of the earliest of these studies, conducted by Mary Cover Jones and Nancy Bayley (1950), reported different consequences for early- and late-maturing boys in the United States. Using data from an ongoing longitudinal study of growth and development, these researchers identified 16 adolescent boys who were late maturing and 16 who were early maturing, based on x-ray analyses of their bone growth. They then asked adults and peers who knew the boys to rate them on a variety of social and personality scales to see if the boys' state of physical maturation affected other people's perceptions of them.

The early-maturing boys were rated by both adults and their peers as more psychologically and socially mature. They did not appear to need to strive for status among their peers, and they were the group from among whom school leaders were chosen. By contrast, the boys who were slower to mature physically were rated as less mature psychologically and socially. Both adults and their peers thought that they often sought attention to compensate for their late development and that in some cases, they tended to withdraw from social interaction.

Other studies have confirmed some parts of this picture. In general, early-maturing boys seem to have a more favorable attitude toward the way their bodies have matured, largely because their greater size and strength make them more capable athletes, which in turn brings them a good deal of social recognition (Brooks-Gunn & Petersen, 1983; Simmons & Blyth, 1987). Apparently, however, not all the effects are positive. Based on data from a different longitudinal study than Jones's and Bayley's and a personality test instead of ratings from other people, Harvey Peskin (1967) took exception to their conclusion that clear advantages follow from early maturation. Peskin found that early-maturing boys become significantly more somber, temporarily more anxious, less exploratory, less intellectually curious, and less active following the onset of puberty than do late-maturing boys. He argued that early-maturing boys are actually handicapped by the early termination of latency because

they are less prepared for the hormonal and social changes they are undergoing. This makes the experience of puberty more intense and less manageable than it is for those who have a longer latency period. In Peskin's view, early-maturing boys also pay a price for their social acceptance because they tend to cling too rigidly to the patterns that bring them early success.

Peskin's conclusions are supported by recent research showing that early sexual maturation is associated with lower self-control and less emotional stability as measured by psychological tests (Sussman et al. 1985). Boys who reach puberty at a relatively early age are also more likely to smoke, drink, use drugs, and get in trouble with the law during adolescence (Duncan, Ritter, Dornbusch, Gross, & Carlsmith, 1985).

The picture for girls is also mixed, but the overall effect of early maturation appears to be less positive for girls than for boys (Brooks-Gunn & Petersen, 1983; Simmons & Blyth, 1987). In some cases, early maturation brings greater social prestige based on sexual attractiveness. Although their fuller figures may attract attention from older boys, early-maturing girls are also larger than other children of the same age, especially boys, who generally enter puberty later. This may be the reason some early-maturing girls report dissatisfaction with their height and weight (Simmons & Blyth, 1987). Furthermore, when girls go through puberty early, they may experience social difficulties because their physical development leads boys to pressure them into sexual relationships they are not ready for psychologically (Clausen, 1975).

Perhaps as a consequence of the increased uncertainties and social pressures that early-maturing girls experience, recent research has found that they tend to have somewhat lower emotional stability and self-control (Petersen & Crockett, 1985). They are also more likely to get into trouble with adults because of increased truancy, smoking, drinking, and defiant behavior and to have fewer years of schooling (Magnusson, Stattin, & Allen, 1985).

A relatively late passage through puberty may initially be a negative experience for girls. Late-maturing sixth-grade girls, for example, report dissatisfaction with their appearance and their lack of popularity. But later in adolescence, the later-maturing girls may actually be more satisfied with their appearance and more popular than their early-maturing peers (Simmons & Blyth, 1987).

Unfortunately, evidence concerning the impact of early or late puberty on later life is quite skimpy. Jones

(1965) followed groups of early-maturing and late-maturing boys into their early thirties. On the basis of psychological tests and interviews, she concluded that, for males, early maturation has positive psychological benefits that continue into adulthood. She found the early maturers to be poised, cooperative, and responsible; they held good positions at work and were leaders in their social organizations. She found the late developers more likely to be impulsive, touchy, and nonconforming; they were not as successful, and some felt rejected and inferior. However, when John A. Clausen (1975) tested these men at the age of 38, he could find only two differences between the groups: the early maturers took more pride in being objective and in being seen as conventional than did the later maturers.

Overall, it is risky to generalize about the impact of early or late sexual maturation on the experience of adolescence. There appear to be some advantages for young people who mature early because of the social success that such maturity may bring and the self-confidence that goes with such success, but there appear to be some drawbacks as well. Early maturation may cut short the time that young people have for such important developmental tasks of adolescence as developing a more mature sense of self and preparing to become economically productive.

THE REORGANIZATION OF SOCIAL LIFE

The biological events that herald the end of middle childhood have a profound impact on young people's social development. Not only their concepts of themselves but also their relationships with their peers, their families, and others with whom they come in contact are reorganized as a result of their new biological capacities.

A New Relationship to Peers

Adolescent peer relationships reflect more than a continuation of the social patterns established during middle childhood. In place of an almost exclusive reliance on same-sex social groups, young people begin to gather in groups that are increasingly heterosexual. Friendships, too, undergo important changes, attaining new levels of complexity and intensity.

During adolescence, the relations that young people have with their parents change both emotionally and physically. As part of this process, they question adult standards and authority on a wide range of issues (Coleman, 1980; Douvan & Adelson, 1966), as the following quote from Anne Frank's diary illustrates:

> Things improved slightly in the second half of the year, I became a young woman and was treated as more of a grownup. I started to think, and write stories, and came to the conclusion that the others no longer had the right to throw me about like an india-rubber ball. I wanted to change in accordance with my desires. But *one* thing that struck me even more was when I realized that even Daddy would never become my confidant over everything. I didn't want to trust anyone but myself any more. (1975, p. 153)

The tendency to bypass parents is amplified in the case of sex, which has historically been a taboo subject in European and American households. Instead of turning to their parents for advice and information, adolescents often rely on their friends, who are facing the same uncertainties and who are having similar experiences (Coleman, 1980). So important can such contacts be that Elizabeth Douvan and Joseph Adelson (1966), two leading researchers on adolescent friendship, have commented "All in all, it would seem that the adolescent does not choose friendship, but is driven into it" (p. 179).

Friendship   The increased importance of friends as sources of advice and self-confirmation is associated with a change in the nature of friendship. A variety of evidence indicates that adolescents, more than children in middle childhood, place special emphasis on the qualities of intimacy, mutual understanding, and loyalty in their friendships (Douvan & Adelson, 1966; Selman, 1980; Youniss, 1980). Each of these characteristics is tightly bound up with the others.

Intimacy among adolescents entails a close association over a long period of time and the sharing of personal information. Furthermore, true intimacy requires mutual understanding (Youniss, 1980). In early adolescence, mutual understanding increases as young people develop a fascination with their friends' life histories, interests, and personalities. They also develop the corresponding need to be appreciated in the same way. They begin to see that friends complement one another — that their differences, combined with the feelings they share, help to legitimate each partner in the friendship.

Loyalty is an outgrowth of both the mutual understanding and the intimacy that friends share. It is reflected in friendships in two main ways. First, friends should be trustworthy — able to keep to themselves what they hear. It is a betrayal of friendship to pass on knowledge of someone else's intimate feelings and actions. Second, friends should be accepting and helpful, regardless of whether they share the same feelings or would participate in the same actions.

Several large-scale studies conducted in the United States support this general view of adolescent friendship (Bigelow & La Gaipa, 1975; Douvan & Adelson, 1966; Selman, 1980; Youniss, 1980). In addition, they reveal qualitative differences in the way in which boys and girls structure their relationships with their closest friends. Table 16.1 shows the changing expectations children and adolescents have for their best friends.

Note the shifts in dominant expectations that come with age. It is not until grades 7 and 8 (12 to 13 years of age) that loyalty and intimacy become the most important attributes of friendship.

At about the age of 11 or 12, when girls are on the threshold of adolescence, they focus primarily on doing things together in their close friendships (Douvan & Adelson, 1966). Around the age of 14, their conception of friendship undergoes a shift toward greater emphasis on their friends' responses to them, which frequently coincides with an increase in their relations with boys. Girls this age want a friend to be "loyal, trustworthy and a reliable source of support in any emotional crisis. She should not be the kind of person who will abandon you or who gossips behind your back" (Douvan & Adelson, 1966, p. 188). This new emphasis on intimacy and loyalty may be linked to girls' growing erotic interests. Intensely loyal friendships help girls to negotiate the transition to active sexuality by providing them with a confidante with whom they can check the acceptability of their fantasies and behaviors.

During the late teen years, girls' friendships seem to lose the feverish, jealous qualities that characterize them during the middle phase of adolescence. "Need-

TABLE 16.1 Percentage incidence of different types of friendship, by grade level

Type	Grade Level*							
	1	2	3	4	5	6	7	8
Help (friend as giver)	5	12†	14	7	14	25	33	35
Common activities	3	7	32	52	24	40	60	60
Propinquity	7	5	9	12	12	20	38	32
Stimulation value	2	3	12	23	30	51	52	61
Organized play	2	0	15	26	9	10	17	20
Demographic similarity	0	3	7	35	15	15	10	23
Evaluation	2	5	13	13	17	33	21	30
Acceptance	3	0	5	9	9	18	18	38
Admiration	0	0	5	23	17	24	32	41
Incremental prior interaction	2	7	4	10	10	17	32	34
Loyalty and commitment	0	0	2	5	10	20	40	34
Genuineness	0	3	0	2	5	12	10	32
Help (friend as receiver)	2	5	3	5	2	12	13	25
Intimacy potential	0	0	0	0	0	0	8	20
Common interests	0	0	5	7	0	5	30	18
Similarity of attitudes and values	0	0	0	0	2	3	10	8

* At each grade level, the number of subjects *(n)* = 60.
† Underlined scores represent grade levels when the incidence of the type of friendship first becomes significant.
SOURCE: Bigelow & La Gaipa, 1975.

ing friendship less, they are less haunted by fears of being abandoned and betrayed," Douvan and Adelson suggest (1966, p. 192). When they were younger, girls tolerated differences in their friends only when these differences allowed them to work out instinctual dilemmas, but by the time they are in their late teens most girls show a greater capacity to tolerate friends' differences. These findings are consistent with Selman's developmental stages of friendship (see Chapter 15, p. 495). According to Selman's (1981) evidence, there is a shift during adolescence from stage 3 (in which friendships are seen as a means of developing mutual intimacy and support) to stage 4 (which is characterized by a new acceptance of a friend's need to establish relations with other people).

Boys between the ages of 14 and 16 years are less likely to form friendships as close as those of girls, according to Douvan and Adelson. These researchers suggest that this difference arises because boys are more concerned with their relations to authority than girls are. To assert and maintain their independence from control by parents and other adults, boys need the alliance of a group of friends.

Boys are generally less articulate than girls about the nature and meaning of friendship, perhaps because they are less concerned with the relational aspects of friendship. Like girls who are 11 to 13 years old, the 14- to 16-year-old boys studied by Douvan and Adelson (1966) said that they wanted their friends to be amiable, cooperative, and able to control their impulses and to share a common interest with them. Like girls in their late teens, they said they expected their friends to help them in times of trouble. What differed between the sexes was the kind of trouble they expected and therefore the kind of friendly support they sought. Girls wanted someone they could confide in about their relations with boys, whereas boys wanted support when they got into trouble with authority.

Adolescent friendships for both boys and girls play a developmental role similar in certain respects to the role of attachment in infancy. During infancy babies engage in "social referencing" — continually looking to their mothers to see how they evaluate what is going on — and they use their mothers as a "secure base" to which they can retreat when they feel threatened as they explore their environments (see Chapter 6, p. 203 and Chapter 7, p. 229). During adolescence, friends help each other to confront and make sense of uncertain and often anxiety-provoking situations. The first time a boy calls up a girl for a date, his best friend may well be standing at his elbow. And no sooner has the girl hung up than she is likely to call her best friend. Together, the two pairs of friends will decide if the call was a success or a failure and lay plans for the next move. For both the infant and the adolescent, successful interaction with the world "out there" modifies the attachment bond; eventually the baby will leave the mother and the adolescent will begin to depend less on the best friend.

Popularity   In the world of the American high school, some friends are more desirable than others because they have more status. James S. Coleman (1962) conducted a classic study of the factors determining individual status and membership in high prestige groups among U.S. high school students. He based his conclusions on the analysis of questionnaires distributed to thousands of students at 10 high schools chosen to represent small towns, small cities, large cities, and suburbs. His main findings have been replicated several times in subsequent decades (Eitzen, 1975; Sebald, 1981).

In every school he studied, Coleman found that students could identify a "leading crowd" in terms of which they evaluated themselves. The responses he obtained to the question "What does it take to get into the leading crowd in this school?" reveal some of the values of American adolescent society and the characteristics that are considered important to be a success within it:

Calling a boy is likely to be a group project at first.

High school athletic events are an important context for winning popularity for both boys and girls.

Girls

Money, clothes, flashy appearance, date older boys, fairly good grades.

Be a sex fiend, dress real sharp, have own car and money, smoke and drink, go steady with a popular boy.

Have pleasant personality, good manners, dress nicely, be clean, don't swear, be loads of fun.

Hang out at _____'s, don't be too smart, flirt with boys, be cooperative on dates.

(1962, p. 37)

Boys

Money, cars, the right connections, and a good personality.

Be a good athlete, have a good personality, be in everything you can, don't drink or smoke, don't go with bad girls.

Prove you rebel [against] the police officers, dress sharply, go out with sharp freshman girls, ignore senior girls.

Good in athletics, "wheel" type, not too intelligent. (Adapted from Coleman, 1962, pp. 40–41)

When Coleman tabulated the responses to his questionnaires, he found that both boys and girls said a good personality was the most important characteristic of people in the leading group. For boys, the next most important characteristics were having a good reputation, being a good athlete, being good looking, wearing good clothes, and getting good grades. For girls, the most important characteristics after a good personality were good looks, good clothing, and a good reputation.

The leading crowd seemed to have great influence in adolescents' lives, Coleman discovered. When he asked for responses to the statement "If I could trade, I would be someone different from myself," he found that one out of five boys and girls expressed a desire to change themselves so that they would be accepted by

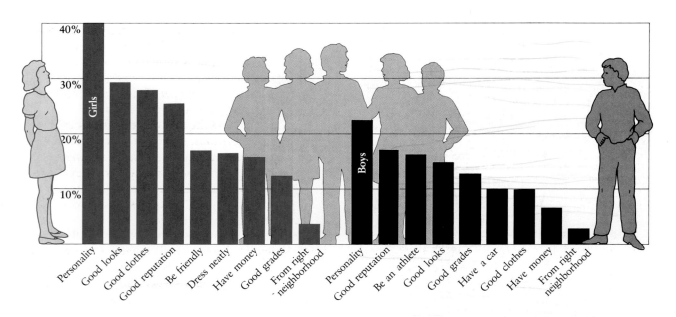

FIGURE 16.6 *The average ranks given by boys and girls to major criteria for popularity. (Adapted from Coleman, 1962.)*

the leading crowd. The importance of membership in the leading crowd was also reflected in the answers to Coleman's questions about popularity (see Figure 16.6).

Largely absent from Coleman's study was a consideration of the influence of socioeconomic class on adolescent social relations. Another classic study, carried out in the late 1940s and followed up in the 1970s by August Hollingshead (1975), adds this dimension to the picture of adolescent social relations. Hollingshead found that at every grade level adolescents tended to form friendships and cliques with others from the same socioeconomic background. Only rarely did adolescents date or have friends whose socioeconomic backgrounds diverged widely from their own, and when they did, they were usually censured by their parents and other adults in the community. For example, when a lower-class girl dated a boy from the highest class, not only did his parents object but the townspeople predicted trouble. They made such remarks as: "She's flying too high"; "After high school she is going to take a fall"; and "Ten years from now she will be taking in laundry like her sister on Beacon Street" (p. 158).

The transition to sexual relationships Often it is the popular boys and girls, those who are members of

the leading crowd in high school, who lead their peers in making the transition from participation in same-sex peer groups to participation in heterosexual groups. A classic study by Dexter Dunphy (1963), an Australian sociologist, traced the way adolescent peer groups helped to organize the development of heterosexual relationships among a group of Australian adolescents in the late 1950s. Dunphy observed and interviewed 303 young people between the ages of 13 and 21 over a 2-year period in largely middle-class areas of Sydney. He supplemented this information with data from questionnaires and diaries kept by his subjects.

Cliques and crowds Dunphy distinguished between two kinds of adolescent peer groups, which he labeled *cliques* and *crowds*. Cliques are small groups (six to seven members) of select friends; they are about the size of a two-child family with the grandparents present. "Their similarity in size to a family," Dunphy wrote, "facilitates the transference of the individual's allegiance to them and allows them to provide an alternative center of security" (p. 233).

Cliques differ from families in an important respect. They are voluntary groups that adolescents are free to leave, whereas membership in a family is not normally a matter of choice for adolescents. The element of choice in peer group membership reflects the in-

When cliques initially form they are likely to consist only of members of the same sex.

creased control adolescents have in choosing the settings in which they find themselves, the people they associate with, and the things they do.

Cliques exist as a part of a larger social unit, the crowd. In Dunphy's study, crowds ranged in size from 15 to 30 members, with an average size of about 20. Like cliques, crowds are, by and large, voluntary groups. Also like cliques, much of what goes on in the crowd is under the control of its members. But unlike the cliques studied, which were at least, initially, composed of young people of the same sex, the crowds were generally heterosexual groups in which the fact of heterosexuality *was* the issue.

As the adolescents Dunphy studied grew older, the relationship between their participation in cliques and

crowds changed in a way that supported the transition to heterosexual intimacy. Dunphy diagramed the stages of this transition as shown in Figure 16.7.

At stage 1, there are as yet no crowds, only isolated same-sex cliques. These are, in effect, a carryover from the days of latency in middle childhood.

Stage 2 represents the first movement toward heterosexual peer relations. At first the cliques come together to form crowds at places like ice skating rinks, football games, swimming pools, and ice cream parlors, where boys and girls get together under conditions in which anonymity precludes the danger of too much intimacy, which they fear.

In stage 3, the members of the crowd with the highest status initiate heterosexual contacts across cliques while still maintaining membership in their same-sex cliques. At this stage, adolescents start going to parties and the movies with members of the opposite sex, but

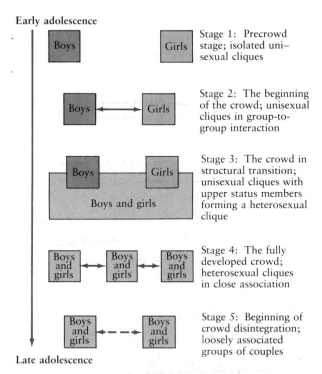

FIGURE 16.7 *A graphic representation of the stages of group development during adolescence. At the start of this period, peer group interactions are largely segregated by sex; at the end, there is far more heterosexual peer group interaction. (Adapted from Dunphy, 1963.)*

they continue to spend a great deal of time with same-sex peers.

During stages 2 and 3, social events that require more intimate interaction, like dances and parties, come to prominence. Here again the size of the crowd is important. There is safety in numbers! The presence of others makes it less likely that anyone would step over the bounds of propriety.

Eventually cross-clique pairing begins to transform the peer group structures. In stage 4, same-sex cliques are transformed into heterosexual cliques in which the members are often paired. These arrangements allow a greater degree of intimacy, should the pair want it, but also provide a group of co-conspirators with whom an individual can talk about what is going on.

Stage 5 sees the slow disintegration of the crowd and the formation of loosely associated groups of couples who are going steady or are engaged to be married. It coincides with the transition to marriage and the reorganization of social life that is associated with adulthood and parenting.

The crowds Dunphy observed were themselves connected in a loose hierarchy of prestige that depended upon the relative ages of their members. The most prestigious crowds were those with the oldest members. The crowds emerged as part of a loosely structured cultural system in which the oldest, most mature, and most knowledgeable members of the social group modeled in their behavior the "next developmental steps" for the members of each crowd below them on the status/age hierarchy.

Peer group leaders The leaders of cliques and crowds were likely to be the most sexually active members of the group as well as those who were the most popular and who set the standards for others to emulate. According to Dunphy, the leaders of adolescent groups facilitated the transition of other members to heterosexual relations because they simultaneously participated in both the clique and the crowd. Their dual membership gave them wider and more frequent contact with those outside the clique than their followers had. Clique leaders were better informed than their followers about what was going on in the generally older and more sexually active crowd. Other members of the cliques came to rely on them for information about people in other cliques and crowds and their activities.

Taken together, the intimate friendship, the clique, and the crowd constituted a sequence of social mechanisms that orchestrated the adolescents' transitions from same-sex to heterosexual pairings. They provided an interlocking set of social relations that sequentially linked the individual to the social (friendship), the friendship dyad to the same-sex friendship group (clique), the same-sex group to the heterosexual group (crowd), and finally, the individual back to a dyad, this time a heterosexual friendship, which in its institutionalized form is called first *going steady* and eventually *marriage*.

The young people that Dunphy identified as leaders by virtue of their positions in the interlocking social relationships just described literally "led" their followers in being the first people admitted to the crowd of the next higher age bracket; they were the people whose behavior was expected to be heterosexual earlier than that of their followers.

The social arrangements that are a part of the transitions from small, same-sex friendship groups to large, heterosexual groups and eventually back to exclusive relationships are strikingly analogous to the zone of proximal development that was introduced in Chapter 6 (p. 202) as a useful characterization of the way adults support young children's cognitive development. In the case of adolescent social development, this zone is created by the hierarchy of group arrangements and the group leaders who have, so to speak, one foot in the future and one foot in the present. It allows young people to learn something about what the future has in store for them before they are responsible for behaving in a more advanced way themselves.

As plausible as this description of the social mechanisms that facilitate the transition to sexual relationships may be, it should be kept in mind that the pattern described by Dunphy may well differ from one society or one era to another because of variations in such factors as geographic mobility, education, and the timing of marriage. Unfortunately, no research of a similar type has been reported for other societies, so there is no way to judge cultural variability in the way peer group interactions are modified over the course of adolescence.

Sexual Activity

It should be clear from this and preceding chapters that a great deal of the social behavior associated with sex roles must be learned from observation and practice. Less obvious, perhaps, is the fact that behaviors appropriate to the physical act of two individuals uniting sexually also require a good deal of learning. Moreover, because the biological roles and social histories of boys and girls are different, the processes by which they learn to engage in sexual intercourse — often referred to as *coitus,* from a Latin word meaning "to join together" — differ in important respects.

One line of evidence about the role of prior social experience in sexual intercourse comes from the studies of monkeys raised in isolation by Harry Harlow and his colleagues. As we saw in Chapter 8 (p. 258), monkeys deprived of the opportunity to interact with their mothers and peers for the first 6 months of life were incapable of engaging in intercourse (Harlow & Novak, 1973).

A second line of evidence for the importance of social learning in sexual activity comes from the wide variations in social behaviors that lead up to and accompany sexual intercourse. Social learning, for example, appears to play some role even in the choice of the sex of the partner (see Box 16.2, "Homosexuality"). In heterosexual activity, the changing incidence of *petting* — erotic caressing that does not include the union of male and female genitals — provides another good illustration of the role of social experience in sexual behavior. According to Dr. Alfred Kinsey and his associates, who conducted famous surveys of sexual behavior that were published at midcentury (Kinsey, Pomeroy, & Martin, 1948; Kinsey, Pomeroy, Martin, & Gebhard, 1953), there was a substantial increase in the practice of petting among people born after 1900 in the United States. The incidence of petting has continued to increase in the decades since Kinsey and his colleagues conducted their surveys, leading some researchers to suggest that an increase in petting represents the greatest change in premarital sexual experience in the twentieth century (Scanzoni & Scanzoni, 1976).

Sex as scripted activity Petting is often part of a larger sequence of actions that make up sexual behavior in our culture. John Gagnon and William Simon (1973) use the concept of scripts to describe this sequence, which goes from lip kissing to tongue kissing to touching breasts through clothing to touching breasts under the clothing to touching the genitals through clothing to, finally, genital contact.

In Chapter 10, we saw that the concept of scripts is important in understanding the mental development of preschool children. Scripts allow very small children, who clearly do not understand fully what is expected of them, to participate with adults in such ac-

BOX 16.2

HOMOSEXUALITY

• • •

Although the dominant form of sexual behavior centers around the union of male and female, a sizable number of people exhibit *homosexual* preferences — that is, a preference for members of their own sex as sexual partners — at various times in their lives. Because of the social stigma attached to homosexuality in many societies and the resulting reticence to talk about such matters, there is no way to know for sure how many people have engaged in homosexual practices. Still, that homosexuality is common is borne out by survey data collected almost 40 years ago by Alfred Kinsey and his colleagues (Kinsey, Pomeroy, & Martin, 1948; Kinsey, Pomeroy, Martin, & Gebhardt, 1953). These researchers found that 37 percent of males and 13 percent of females reported having reached homosexual orgasm at least once in their lives. However, only 3 to 16 percent of the males and 1 to 3 percent of the females sampled reported exclusively homosexual experience. These findings have led some researchers to view exclusive heterosexuality and exclusive homosexuality as poles on a continuum (Bermant & Davidson, 1974).

In the Western world, homosexuality has long been controversial. In recent times, this controversy has revolved around two interrelated questions: Is homosexual behavior normal or abnormal? And why do some people prefer to have sexual relations with members of their own sex?

Until 1973 the American Psychiatric Association included homosexuality on its list of pathological behaviors. Although homosexuality no longer appears on that list, whether or not homosexual behavior is normal is still being debated by psychiatrists, clinical psychologists, and clergymen, as well as by the general public. In part, the answer depends on the answer to the question about the causes of homosexuality. But only in part, since the question of normalcy is a question of cultural values as well as scientific fact.

For a number of years biological and social-learning theorists have competed in attempting to provide a comprehensive explanation for how some individuals come to prefer members of their own sex as sexual partners. Proponents of a biological explanation claim that homosexual preferences are the result of hormonal imbalances at some crucial time in development that predispose children to a same-sex preference in their sexual relations (Hoffman, 1977). Supporters of social-learning explanations believe that learning experiences are the crucial determinants for such preferences (Money & Ehrhardt, 1972).

An extensive interview study of 1456 homosexual and heterosexual men and women living in the San Francisco area was conducted by Alan Bell and his colleagues in 1969 and 1970 (Bell, Weinberg, & Hammersmith, 1981). These researchers concluded that there may be different causes for different patterns of homosexual involvement. They found no support for the popular psychiatric theory that male homosexuals have dominant mothers and ineffective fathers (Bieber, 1962). Nor did they find that unfortunate experiences with members of the opposite sex or seduction by an older person of the same sex were likely causes of later homosexuality. However, poor relationships with fa-

---

tivities as eating in a restaurant, birthday parties, and drawing lessons. A similar use of scripts is evident among adolescent boys and girls who are encountering sexual relations for the first time. Their peer group experiences, their observations of adults, and their general cultural knowledge provide them with a rough idea of the script they are supposed follow and the roles they are supposed to play. (Box 16.3 "The Traditional Kikuyu Script for Adolescent Sex" provides a glimpse of a very different way of organizing the transition to heterosexual behavior.) In the United States, for example, the male is traditionally active and controls the interaction and the female responds.

A script also gives sexual meaning to individual acts that might not have sexual meaning in other contexts. Hand holding, kissing, and unzipping one's pants are

thers did seem to increase the likelihood of later homosexuality for both sexes.

Bell and his colleagues classify homosexuals into two main types based on the apparent influence of two kinds of social-learning factors on their behavior: those who have relations exclusively with members of their own sex, and those who engage in both heterosexual and homosexual relations, called *bisexuals* by the researchers. Among those whose sexual preference is exclusively homosexual, the researchers concluded that learning factors play a minor role. They report that, very early in life, exclusive homosexuals experience a feeling of "gender nonconformity," which they found to be the single strongest predictor of adult homosexuality. The people in this group reported feeling and acting differently from others of their sex well before they had any sexual experience, as the following remarks by some male homosexuals indicate:

> About the only interest boys had was playing ball, and I didn't like to play ball. I frequently stayed indoors during recess. (p. 75)
>
> I wasn't as aggressive as other boys, not as active as they were, not rambunctious and boisterous. (p. 78)
>
> I was more emotional. I was too "goody-goody" to be one of the boys. (p. 78)
>
> I began to get the feeling I was gay. I'd notice other boys' bodies in gym and masturbate excessively. (p. 86)
>
> I had a keener interest in the arts. (p. 86)
>
> (Bell, Weinberg, & Hammersmith, 1981)

The bisexual interviewees did not report such feelings of gender nonconformity.

"Exclusive homosexuality," Bell and his colleagues conclude, "tends to emerge from a deepseated predisposition, while bisexuality is more subject to influence by social and sexual learning" (p. 201). They suggest that participating in homosexual activities during childhood and adolescence may teach bisexuals homosexual responsiveness but that it does not cause them to abandon completely their heterosexual feelings or behaviors.

Some highly controversial evidence regarding the "deepseated predisposition" of exclusive homosexuals to which Bell and his colleagues refer comes from research showing that some exclusively homosexual men respond metabollically as women typically do when they are injected with estrogen (a female hormone) whereas the response of heterosexual men is quite different (Dorner, 1976; Gladue, Green, & Hellman, 1985). Other researchers have noted differences between the sleep patterns, blood chemistry, and physical structures of homosexual and heterosexual men (Evans, 1972). Homosexual and heterosexual women have been found to differ with respect to their physical structures and physiological indicators of aging (Gartell, Loriaux, & Chase, 1977).

The difficulty of reaching a firm conclusion about the causes of homosexuality is reflected in the very careful way that Bell and his colleagues summarize their results: "Our findings *are not inconsistent with what one would expect to find if, indeed, there were a biological basis for sexual preference*" (Bell, Weinberg, & Hammersmith, 1981, p. 216, italics in original). But they do not rule out social-learning factors, declaring that there is "no reason to believe that all homosexuals . . . are so much alike that one causal model does equally well for all of them" (p. 192).

---

not inherently sexual acts. Each occurs often in nonsexual contexts. It is only within the context of the larger script of dating or of coitus that these acts take on sexual meanings and give rise to sexual excitement.

Sexual expectations Evidence from a wide variety of sources indicates that males and females come to sexual activity with different expectations as a result of

their different histories (Gagnon & Simon, 1973; Sorenson, 1973). To begin with, biological differences between the two sexes set the stage for males and females to have divergent experiences with the erotic potential of their bodies.

Sexual arousal is more obvious in males than in females because of its expression in clearly visible penile erections. Among newborns erections are reflexive.

BOX 16.3

THE TRADITIONAL KIKUYU SCRIPT FOR ADOLESCENT SEX
. . .

Among the Kikuyu people living in central Kenya at the turn of the century, boys and girls underwent an initiation ceremony, or *rite of passage,* just before the start of puberty, after which the boys were considered to be junior warriors and the girls were considered to be maidens (Worthman & Whiting, 1987). For the next several years, approved sexual relations between the young men and women followed a script that differed in many ways from those typically followed by teenagers in the United States.

In addition to helping their mothers with household chores and gardening, Kikuyu maidens were expected to strengthen the social cohesion of the group by entertaining the bachelor friends of their older brothers. The entertainment included not only dancing and feasting, but a kind of love making called *ngweko.* Jomo Kenyatta (1938), the first president of Kenya following its independence in 1962, described *ngweko* in his autobiography.

> The girls visit their boy-friends at a special hut, *thingira,* used as a rendezvous by the young men and women. . . .
>
> Girls may visit the *thingira* at any time, day or night. After eating, while engaged in conversation with the boys, one of the boys turns the talk dramatically to the subject of *ngweko.* If there are more boys than girls, the girls are asked to select whom they want as their companion. The selection is done in the most liberal way. . . . In such a case it is not neces-

sary for girls to select their most intimate friends, as this would be considered selfish and unsociable. . . .

> After the partners have been arranged, one of the boys gets up, saying *"ndathie kwenogora"* (I am going to stretch myself). His girl partner follows him to the bed. The boy removes all his clothing. The girl removes her upper garment . . . and retains her skirt, *motheru,* and her soft leather apron, *mwengo,* which she pulls back between her legs and tucks in together with her leather skirt, *motheru.* The two V shaped tails of her *motheru* are pulled forward between her legs from behind and fastened to the waist, thus keeping the *mwengo* in position and forming an effective protection of her private parts. In this position, the lovers lie together facing each other, with their legs interwoven to prevent any movement of their hips. They begin to fondle each other, rubbing their breasts together, whilst at the same time engage in love-making conversation until they gradually fall asleep. (pp. 157–158)

Sexual intercourse was explicitly not allowed as a part of this premarital sexual activity. In fact, both the boys and the girls were taught that if either of them touched directly the genitals of the other, they would become polluted and have to undergo a costly purification rite. Boys who did not adhere to this restriction were ostracized by their peers. Not until marriage was sexual intercourse sanctioned.

Just when and how this reflexive response becomes sexual is still a mystery (Katchadourian & Lunde, 1975). Erections continue to occur during childhood, making it easy for boys to discover that stimulating their penises gives pleasure. At puberty, there is a dramatic increase in the frequency of erections and the sensitivity of the genitals. Within 2 years after puberty, most males experience orgasm, usually through masturbation (Gagnon & Simon, 1973). According to Kinsey and his coworkers 82 percent of the men they surveyed reported they had masturbated to orgasm by

the age of 15 years (Kinsey, Pomeroy, & Martin, 1948).

In females, sexual arousal is more ambiguous. The clitoris, the center of female sexual pleasure, is small and hidden within the vulva. As a result, girls are less likely to discover the erotic possibilities of their own bodies. In fact, Kinsey and his colleagues found that only 20 percent of the females they surveyed reported having masturbated to orgasm by the time they were 15.

According to Gagnon and Simon (1973), differences in the masturbatory behavior of boys and girls have a number of consequences for later sexual behavior. First, masturbating to orgasm reinforces males' commitment to sexual behavior early in adolescence. Second, experience with masturbation tends to focus the male's feelings of sexual desire on the penis, whereas most females, lacking such experiences, do not localize their erotic responses in their genitals until much later, and then primarily as a result of sexual contacts with males.

Differences in the socialization of males and females give rise to differences in the fantasies that accompany masturbation. Male gender training in our culture emphasizes aggressive, competitive, and achievement-oriented behaviors. Correspondingly, males report having masturbatory fantasies that involve sexual aggression, unattainable excesses (such as a harem at one's command), and sexual dominance. Their fantasies are rich in specific sexual behaviors and are seemingly devoid of affiliative emotions (Gagnon & Simon, 1973). In contrast, female gender training emphasizes affiliation and pleasing others — parents when they are young and males as they grow older (Chodorow, 1974). Although fewer females than males report masturbating during adolescence, those who do so report having fantasies that are limited to the sexual acts they have already performed and are set in a context that emphasizes love, marriage, and, in some cases, mild forms of masochism (Gagnon & Simon, 1973).

These differences between male and female experience, taken together, have led Gagnon and Simon to suggest that when males and females come together in later adolescence, the males are committed to sexuality but are relatively untrained in the rhetoric of romantic love, whereas the females are committed to romantic love but are relatively untrained in sexuality. "Dating and courtship may well be considered processes in which persons train members of the opposite sex in the meaning and content of their respective commitments" (1973, p. 74).

Initial responses to sexual intercourse Boys and girls differ in the ways they approach and respond to sexual intercourse, according to interviews Robert Sorenson (1973) conducted with more than 400 American adolescents. The girls, far more than the boys, chose someone they knew well and liked as a first partner for sexual intercourse; 85 percent of the girls but only 56 percent of the boys reported that their first intercourse was with someone they knew well. Girls are also likely to repeat intercourse over a long period

of time with their first partner, whereas boys are much more likely to change partners.

First intercourse is less likely to be a positive experience for girls than it is for boys. As shown in Table 16.2, girls most often report being afraid, guilty, and worried, whereas boys most often say they are excited, satisfied, and thrilled.

Research in the United States reveals a hesitant emergence of active sexuality in midadolescence that only gradually becomes transformed into sustained intimate sexual relations (Sorenson, 1973; Miller & Simon, 1980). According to a national survey of women between the ages of 15 and 19, for example, those who were sexually active said they had had intercourse less than three times a month; most said they had not had coitus during the preceding month (Zelnik, Kantner, & Ford, 1981).

Changing sexual habits Conventional social wisdom has it that a "sexual revolution" occurred in the 1960s that markedly changed the sexual habits of young Americans. In this view, the advent of birth

TABLE 16.2 Adolescents' immediate reactions to their first intercourse (%)*

	All	Boys	Girls
Excited	37	46	26
Afraid	37	17	63
Happy	35	42	26
Satisfied	33	43	20
Thrilled	30	43	13
Curious	26	23	30
Joyful	23	31	12
Mature	23	29	14
Fulfilled	20	29	8
Worried	20	9	35
Guilty	17	3	36
Embarrassed	17	7	31
Tired	15	15	14
Relieved	14	19	8
Sorry	12	1	25
Hurt	11	0	25
Powerful	9	15	1
Foolish	8	7	9
Used	7	0	16
Disappointed	6	3	10
Raped	3	0	6

* Percentages add up to more than 100% because most respondents reported more than one reaction.

SOURCE: Sorenson, 1973.

control pills combined with the social unrest surrounding the civil rights and anti–Vietnam War movements created a new climate of social permissiveness. Liberated by these new conditions, teenagers were believed to be initiating their sexual careers earlier, to be more open in expressing their sexuality, and to be less concerned about exclusive sexual relationships.

Evidence to support these beliefs comes from a variety of sources, most notably questionnaire studies of sexual activity and attitudes. In 1953, Kinsey and his colleagues reported that 3 percent of 14-year-old girls and 20 percent of college-age young women had experienced sexual intercourse (Kinsey, Pomeroy, Martin, & Gebhard, 1953). Harold Christensen and Christina Gregg (1970) obtained similar figures for college-age women in 1958. By 1968, however, the percentage of college-age women reporting sexual intercourse had increased to 34 percent. Evidence for a continuing change comes from Melvin Zelnik and John Kantner (1980) and from a U.S. Department of Health and Human Services survey of family growth conducted in 1982. As shown in Table 16.3, the percentage of

never-married females between the ages of 15 and 19 living in metropolitan areas who had experienced sexual intercourse was higher in 1971 than that reported by Kinsey in the 1950s. The percentage increased significantly until 1979 and then decreased slightly in the early 1980s. There is also some evidence that having sex with more than one partner was becoming increasingly acceptable in the 1960s and 1970s (Reiss, 1972).

However, the idea that the changes wrought since the 1960s have totally reorganized teenage sexual relations appears to be overstated in several respects. To begin with, the data in Table 16.3 indicate that more than half of all teenage girls do *not* engage in sexual intercourse and that the others do so too infrequently to fit the picture of sexual license evoked by the idea of a sexual revolution. It is also important to realize that changes in the sexual habits of Americans were not restricted to the 1960s. The most dramatic increase in premarital sexual intercourse in this century occurred around the time of World War I, when the number of nonvirgins at the time of marriage doubled (Reiss, 1972).

Although the greater availability of contraceptive devices probably played some role in the more recent increases in teenage sexual activity, contraception is unlikely to have been the decisive factor. Most teenagers make no attempt to prevent conception when they first have sexual intercourse (Zelnik & Shah, 1983). The average delay between the initiation of sexual activity and the first use of prescription methods of birth control, which are the most effective, is about 1 year. Of the adolescents who use birth control, many use contraceptives inconsistently, and they tend to choose the least reliable ways of preventing pregnancy (National Research Council, 1987).

The relatively inconsistent use of contraception among teenagers does not reflect a general lack of concern about pregnancy, although it may contribute to the rate of pregnancy among unmarried teenagers. (Nearly 50 percent of those who use no contraception become pregnant within 2 years of becoming sexually active.) Fully 89 percent of the boys and 71 percent of the girls surveyed by Sorenson (1973) reported that they worried about pregnancy. The greater concern of boys than girls in Sorenson's survey is intriguing in light of another fact that is underplayed in most discussions of a sexual revolution. When rates of sexual activity are charted for boys (note that most of the preceding discussion has been about girls), change is far less than it is for girls. What has changed most

TABLE 16.3 Percentage of never-married girls ages 15 to 19 living in metropolitan areas experiencing sexual intercourse, 1971 to 1982

Race and Age	1982	1979	1976	1971	Percent Change 1971–1982
All races*	42.2	46.0	39.2	27.6	52.9
15	17.8	22.5	18.6	14.4	23.6
16	28.1	37.8	28.9	20.9	34.4
17	41.0	48.5	42.9	26.1	57.0
18	52.7	56.9	51.4	39.7	32.7
19	61.7	69.0	59.5	46.4	33.0
Whites	40.3	42.3	33.6	23.2	73.7
15	17.3	18.3	13.8	11.3	53.1
16	26.9	35.4	23.7	17.0	58.0
17	39.5	44.1	36.1	20.2	95.5
18	48.6	52.6	46.0	35.6	36.5
19	59.3	64.9	53.6	40.7	45.7
Blacks	52.9	64.8	64.3	52.4	1.0
15	23.2	41.1	38.9	31.2	−15.6
16	36.3	50.4	55.1	44.4	−18.2
17	46.7	73.3	71.0	58.9	−20.7
18	75.7	76.3	76.2	60.2	25.7
19	78.0	88.5	83.9	78.3	−0.4

* Includes blacks, whites, and other races.

SOURCES: Zelnik & Kantner, 1980; NCHS National Survey of Family Growth, 1982; unpublished tabulations, 1984.

dramatically for boys is not the rate of their participation in sexual intercourse but the fact that they are having sexual intercourse with a larger number of girls.

Instead of a single factor accounting for changing sexual habits or the influence of a hypothesized sexual revolution, the evidence suggests that the pattern of increasing sexual activity among unmarried people, teenagers in particular, is part of a long-term trend that reflects many interlocking factors. Ira Reiss provides an excellent overview of this trend:

> In the 50 years from World War I to the late 1960's the predominant change was not in the proportion of women non-virginal but rather in the attitudes of women and men toward premarital sexuality. During that half century, guilt feelings were reduced, the public discussion of sex increased radically, probably the number of partners increased, and the closeness to marriage required for coitus to be acceptable decreased. For males, other changes were occurring. Males were becoming more discriminate; they were beginning to feel that sex with someone they felt affection for, person-centered sex, was much to be preferred to body-centered coitus. (1972, p. 169)

Recently, with the advent of AIDS (Acquired Immune Deficiency Syndrome) and the spread of venereal diseases and genital infections in the United States, there has been some indication that the trends toward initiating sexual activity earlier in life and toward having multiple sexual partners may be slowing (U.S. Department of Health and Human Services, 1982). But the evidence regarding the effect of AIDS on sexual behavior, which is derived from surveys, has been at best contradictory (Kolata, 1988; Steinbrook, 1987).

Teenage pregnancy According to a survey of 37 countries, the United States leads nearly all other developed nations in its incidence of pregnancy among girls between the ages of 15 and 19 (National Research Council, 1987). Though the survey found that U.S. teenagers were no more sexually active than those in the other countries surveyed, they were far more likely to become pregnant. The rate of pregnancy for U.S. teenagers is nearly double that of British and French teenage girls and six times that of Dutch girls.

Of the girls between the ages of 15 and 19 who become pregnant, an estimated 40 percent choose to terminate their pregnancy by having an abortion; among girls under the age of 15, over 50 percent of all

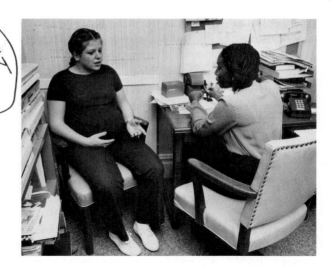

This pregnant teenager is being counseled to help her deal effectively with the complexities of her situation.

pregnancies end in abortion (National Research Council, 1987). Of the girls who go on to give birth, an increasing number are unmarried (see Figure 16.8). Unlike unwed mothers of previous decades, these unmarried mothers are more likely to keep and raise their babies than to give them up for adoption (National Research Council, 1987).

Race, social class, education, and the strength of religious beliefs all affect a teenager's decision about

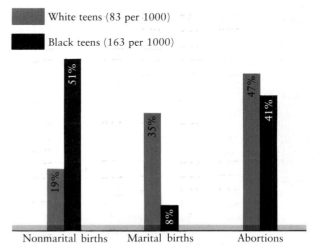

FIGURE 16.8 *The rates of nonmarital and marital births and abortions among black and white teenagers in the United States in 1985. (From* Time, *December 9, 1985.)*

whether or not to have and keep her child. Black teenagers are more likely than white teenagers to become single mothers, particularly if their families are receiving welfare. White teenagers are more likely to choose to have an abortion or to get married before the baby is born. The more education a pregnant teenager's mother has (which is an indirect measure of her social class) and the better the teenager is doing in school, the more likely she is to decide to abort the pregnancy. Teenagers with strong religious convictions are likely to have and keep their babies, no matter what their race or social class (Eisen, Zellman, Leibowitz, Chow, & Evans, 1983).

Several studies have found that teenage motherhood usually imposes lasting hardships on both the mother and the child (see National Research Council, 1987, for a summary of this research). Teenage mothers are, on the average, more likely to drop out of high school, to be poor, and to be dependent on welfare. Of the women under the age of 30 who receive welfare benefits from Aid to Families with Dependent Children, 71 percent had their first child as a teenager (National Research Council, 1987). The babies of teenage mothers also have higher rates of mortality and illness than do babies born to older women.

Parents and Peers

Psychologists agree that the far-reaching changes in young people's interactions with their peers and their greater independence are accompanied by important changes in their relationships with their parents. But they disagree about the basic nature of these changes. The disagreement focuses on two questions:

1. What is the major source of change? Is it primarily the result of factors operating within the family or does the peer group play the major role?

2. Are changes in parent-child relations best thought of as a process of "breaking away" from the family or as one of renegotiating an ongoing relationship?

The relative influence of parents and peers Traditional ideas about the rebelliousness of youth have given rise in recent decades to the idea that adolescents, especially those growing up in the last decades of this century, are part of a distinctive "youth culture" that is separated from the culture of their parents

by a "generation gap" (Eisenstadt, 1963; Roszak, 1972). In *The Adolescent Society* (1962), James Coleman has made perhaps the stongest case for a distinctive society of adolescence among American teenagers:

[The adolescent] is "cut off" from the rest of society, forced inward toward his own age group, made to carry out his whole social life with others his own age. With his fellows, he comes to constitute a small society, one that has most of its important interactions *within* itself, and maintains only a few threads of connection with the outside adult society. In our modern world of mass communication and rapid diffusion of ideas and knowledge, it is hard to realize that separate subcultures can exist right under the very noses of adults—subcultures with languages all their own, with special symbols, and, most importantly, with value systems that may differ from adults'. (p. 3)

Evidence for the existence of a separate youth culture can be obtained by visiting any "Main Street" on a Saturday night. One is likely to find traffic lanes full of cars that have been carefully (and often expensively) modified to fit prevailing styles. The young people riding in those cars or strolling in suburban shopping malls are no less self-consciously decked out in styles that systematically deviate from, and outrage, adult tastes. The jargon that these teenagers speak and the music trumpeting from their cars or hand-held radios are distinctive and may seem to have been chosen because they are incomprehensible to adults or offend those who have authority.

Despite the plausibility of claims for a discontinuous, self-contained youth culture, research by psychologists and sociologists reveals considerable continuity between the culture of adolescents and that of their parents as well as agreement about most important issues (Bandura, 1964; Brittain, 1963; Brown, 1982; Douvan & Adelson, 1966; Youniss & Smollar, 1985). Writing a decade after the publication of Coleman's book, psychologists Denise Kandel and Gerald Lesser (1972) summarized their extensive study of high school students in the United States and Denmark with an outright rejection of Coleman's ideas:

We find no evidence, in the two societies we studied, for the alienation of the young . . . or for the segregation and isolation of adolescents from the adult world proposed by Coleman. . . . Most adolescents have a close relationship with their parents. (p. 7)

Based on data from questionnaires filled out by more than a thousand teenagers and their mothers, Kandel and Lesser found that most teenagers respect their parents. Dialogue rather than outright conflict or rejection was the major method of resolving disagreements. When asked how they felt about their parents, approximately 60 percent of the adolescents in Kandel and Lesser's study said that they were "extremely" or "quite" close, and only 11 percent denied that they felt close at all. Almost 60 percent also said that they wanted to be like their parents in many or most ways.

Adolescents are conspicuous for their unusual styles of dress and behavior, which change from one generation to the next. The only constant in these styles is their deviation from adult norms.

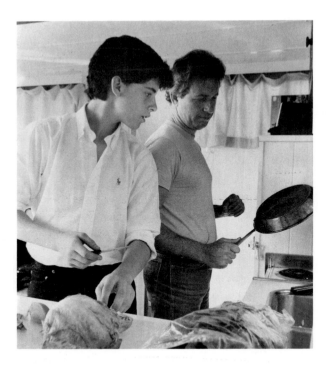

Contrary to stereotype, adolescents generally continue to maintain close relationships with their parents and to share in household activities.

Kandel and Lesser's conclusions are supported by and have been extended to additional topics by a number of other studies. Ian Chand, Donald Crider, and Fern Willits (1975), for example, report that adolescents and their parents tend to agree on issues related to religion and marriage, although they disagree about issues related to drugs and sex. Similarly, Robert Kelley (1972) found that parents and adolescents are in basic agreement about moral issues, but not about dress styles, hair length, and hours of sleep.

Studies reveal that adolescents' interactions with their parents differ depending on the parent (Gjerde, 1986; Kandel & Lesser, 1972; Steinberg, 1981; Youniss & Smollar, 1985). James Youniss and Jacqueline Smollar describe a "family division of labor" in which fathers are authority figures who are responsible for providing their adolescent children with long-range goals. They are brought into personal matters only when special advice is needed. By contrast, adolescents talk to their mothers about personal topics both to obtain practical advice and to validate their feelings and impressions. This talk may be argumentative. The adolescents interviewed by Kandel and Lesser, for example, reported that they disagreed with their mothers about the value of academic success, dating, involvement in athletics, financial independence, and popularity. On a great many issues, however, mothers and teenagers agreed: it is important to plan for the future, to have a good reputation, and to respect one's parents. Overall, the relationships of adolescents with their mothers were found to be considerably more intimate than those with their fathers.

Young people not only frequently consult their parents during adolescence but also continue to spend time with them. From telephone interviews with 64 young adolescents, ranging in age from 12 to 15, Raymond Montemayer (1982) found that adolescents spend equal amounts of time with their parents and their peers, but their activities in the two contexts are so different that Montemeyer called them "contrasting social worlds." Time spent with parents is largely devoted to eating, shopping, and household chores, whereas relaxation and play are the leading activities they participate in with their peers. That adolescents find time they spend with their parents important is evidenced by the fact that when they get into disagreements with one parent, they are not driven to spending more time with their peers. Instead, they spend more time with the other parent.

Overall, the studies just discussed make a convincing case that extreme forms of the "generation gap" hypothesis are an oversimplification.

Peer pressure to conform   No less widespread than the idea of a generation gap is the belief that adolescents are especially susceptible to peer pressure (Cole-

When peer pressure to conform results in the use of addictive drugs, young people are put at serious risk.

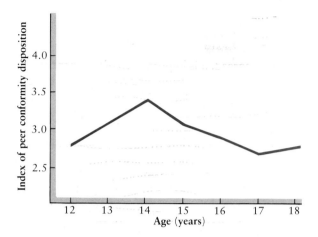

FIGURE 16.9 *Susceptibility to peer pressure increases during early adolescence and then begins to decline. (Adapted from Berndt, 1979.)*

man, 1980). Adults worry that peer pressure may lead adolescents to engage in antisocial behaviors (Glynn, 1981; Huba & Bentler, 1980). The evidence suggests that young people are especially sensitive to peer pressures during early adolescence, but their willingness to go along with the group depends greatly on the particular issue involved.

Thomas Berndt (1979) addressed the question of special susceptibility of young people to peer pressure at different ages. Overall, he found that children who had just entered adolescence were more likely to report that they were willing to follow their peers than were younger children. In a later study, B. Bradford Brown, Donna Rae Clasen, and Sue Ann Eicher (1986) found that this general pressure for participation in peer activities was especially strong for sixth- through twelfth-grade students. This sensitivity to pressure to participate in peer group activities confirms Erikson's assertion that adolescents feel a need to affiliate with groups (Erikson, 1968). Some, but not all, studies have found that susceptibility to peer pressure increases to the age of 15 and then decreases (Coleman, 1980). (See Figure 16.9.)

Evidence that the effectiveness of peer pressure varies according to the kind of activity involved comes from a variety of questionnaire studies (Berndt, 1979; Brittain, 1963; Brown, Clasen, & Eicher, 1986; Brown, Lohr, & McClenahan, 1986; Larson, 1972). To a certain extent, these studies confirm adult concerns that adolescents are susceptible to antisocial peer pressure. Brown, Clasen, and Eicher (1986), for example, found that the more pressure adolescents feel to engage in misconduct, the more likely they were

Outraging public decorum doesn't necessarily spoil an adolescent's future, although it might, in this case, be disconcerting to others.

to do so. On the whole, however, adolescents reported that they were more likely to give in to peer pressure that was prosocial than to pressure to misbehave.

Unlike peer pressure in other domains, Brown, Clasen and Eicher (1986) found that peer pressure to smoke, drink alcoholic beverages, and engage in sexual intercourse increases with age. However, it should be noted that adults consider many of these same behaviors acceptable for themselves. This fact has led Richard Jessor and Shirley Jessor (1977) to argue that age-related increases in adolescent drinking should be viewed as an attempt to model adult behavior rather than as social deviance. This argument may also apply to some of the other behaviors considered to be antisocial during adolescence, such as sexual intercourse and smoking. In line with this reasoning, Brown, Clasen, and Eicher (1986) suggest that the increased pressure on adolescents to engage in such activities as they grow older may simply reflect their efforts to prepare themselves for assuming adult roles.

The content and severity of adolescent-parent conflict   From the studies of adolescent relations with parents and peers reviewed so far, it appears that the cultural stereotype of intergenerational conflict is somewhat exaggerated. A difficulty with this conclusion is that the evidence depends heavily on self-reports and questionnaires. These techniques clearly do not provide data that are representative of everyday parent-adolescent interactions.

A study by Mihaly Csikszentmihalyi and Reed Larson (1984) provides a partial solution to the problems with typical questionnaire studies and fills an important gap in our knowledge. Csikszentmihalyi and Larson asked adolescents to carry an electronic beeper with them for a week from the time they got up in the morning until they went to sleep at night. At a randomly chosen moment every 2 hours or so, the subjects were "beeped," at which point they filled out a standard report about what they were doing and experiencing (see Figure 16.10). This technique provided detailed information about the kinds of activities adolescents engage in at home as well as their moods and their thoughts. The following is a sample of the responses to the question "As you were beeped, what were you thinking about?" It gives some sense of the conflicts that occurred between the subjects and their parents:

Why my mother manipulates the conversation to get me to hate her.
How much of a bastard my father is to my sister.
How ugly my mom's taste is.
How incompetent my mom is.
My bitchy mom.
How pig-headed my mom and dad are.
About my mom getting ice cream all over her.
How f——g stupid my mom is for making a big f——g fuss.

Notice that such issues as the importance of grades or the undesirability of drinking that are highlighted in the survey studies of Coleman or Kandel and Lesser are missing from this sample of adolescent complaints. Csikszentmihalyi and Larson report that, for their sample as a whole, the conflicts between adolescents and their parents often seem to center on seemingly unimportant matters of taste. But the appearance of triviality is deceiving:

Asking a boy who has spent many days practicing a song on the guitar Why are you playing that trash? might not mean much to the father, but it can be a great blow to the son. The so-called "growth pains" of adolescence are no less real just because their causes appear to be without much substance to adults. In fact, this is exactly what the conflict is all about: What is to be taken seriously? (1984, p. 140)

Adults naturally try to structure adolescents' realities to correspond to their notions about how the world works. However, adolescents, who are at the threshold of adulthood themselves, can see the shortcomings of their parents' realities. In large and small ways, they resist having their realities defined for them on their parents' terms and seek to assert their own preferences. At the same time, adolescents realize they are dependent on their parents. When Sorenson (1973) asked his national sample of adolescents between the ages of 13 and 19 to respond to the statement "I am not a child anymore, but I'm not an adult yet," 73 percent agreed with it. Approximately 50 percent agreed with the statement "If I had to go out into the world on my own right now, I think I would have a pretty hard time of it."

Here we see the real dilemma of adolescence and the major source of conflict between adolescents and their parents. Teenagers are caught between two worlds, one of dependence, the other of responsibility. Quite naturally, they would like to have the best of both worlds. But their parents, who pay the bills and pick up the clothing tossed on the floor, demand that independence be matched by responsibility. Once we realize that conflicts over "little things" are also disagreements about the major issue of growing up — the power to decide for oneself — the issue of adolescent-parent conflict is brought into proper focus.

Overall, the data on the role of parents and peers in shaping changes in adolescent behavior speak against strong forms of a "generation gap" hypothesis. In some cases, adolescents really do "break away" and establish relationships outside the family that remove them from their parents physically and emotionally. The more common pattern, however, is a process of individuation, whereby adolescents and their parents negotiate a new form of interdependence that grants the adolescent a more equal role and more nearly equal responsibilities (Youniss, 1983). Neither the peer group nor the family can be assigned the primary role in this process. Instead, the two different social con-

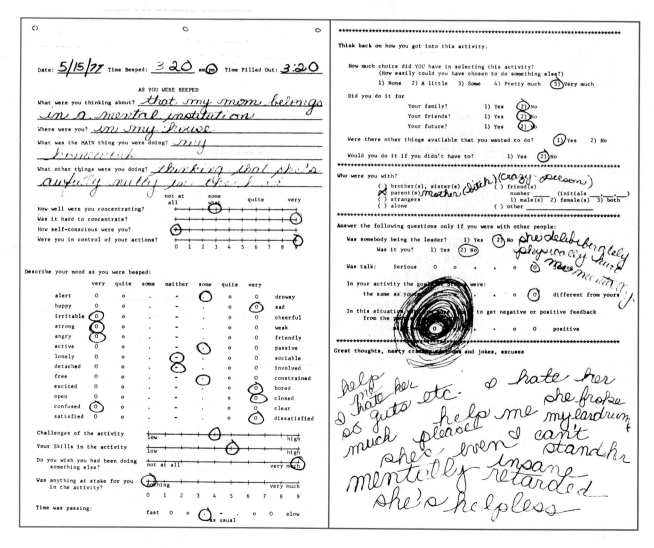

FIGURE 16.10 *A sample self-report filled out by a teenager at the time she was "beeped." (From Csikszentmihalyi & Larson, 1984.)*

texts play complementary roles in reorganizing adolescent social life.

Work

A vital factor in rearranging adult-child relations is the young person's ability to make the transition to adult work responsibilities. Until young people can participate in adult work — work that sustains them and the family of which they are a part — they will not gain adult status.

In many societies, including our own, access to adult jobs and adult status comes only after a long period of preparation during which young people learn to work and learn the skills that are required by particular jobs (Greenfield & Lave, 1982; Taggart, 1980). In the United States, children's first work experience often consists of doing household chores such as setting the table, washing dishes, and caring for pets, usually without pay. About the age of 12 years, many children begin to work at odd jobs around the neighborhood — babysitting, delivering newspapers, mowing lawns. In most households, the money they earn from these jobs is theirs to spend with a minimum of adult supervision (Cole, 1980a). By the age of 15, many adolescents have progressed from working in casual jobs to regular part-time employment. (Taggart, 1980). A number of adolescents drop out of high school and plunge directly into full-time work. The most conservative estimate is the 10.5 percent of students leave school before graduating, but the drop out rate in inner-city neighborhoods has been estimated as high as 50 percent (U.S. Bureau of the Census, 1988).

The work available to most adolescents is neither glamorous nor secure, but it provides knowledge and experience about what it means to hold a job, as well as a highly valued margin of independence.

Because many teenagers work in jobs that are not counted by the U.S. Department of Labor and because some are paid "off the books" by employers who are seeking to avoid paying the minimum wage or Social Security taxes, there is no accurate count of how many high school students work. Recent studies estimate that more than 50 percent of all high school seniors and juniors and as many as 40 percent of all tenth graders are employed at some time during the school year. Many of these teenagers work more than 14 hours a week in addition to attending school full time (D'Amico, 1984). During the summer, when school is not in session, many work longer hours.

It has been widely believed that extensive work experience during adolescence is all for the good. This opinion has been supported by government policy advisers who are concerned with the problems of youth. They have contended that work is a good complement to school. Holding a job, so the argument goes, teaches adolescents responsibility, develops positive attitudes toward work, provides on-the-job training, brings youngsters into contact with adults from whom they can learn, and keeps them out of trouble (Carnegie Commission on Policy Studies in Higher Education, 1980; National Commission on Youth, 1980; National Panel on High School and Adolescent Education, 1976; President's Science Advisory Committee, 1973).

Working is a way for young people to acquire practical knowledge that will ease their transition into adulthood. Their work experience teaches them how to find and hold a job, how to manage money, and how the business world functions (Cole, 1980a). In addition, working requires that adolescents learn to budget their time and to assess their goals: Do they have the time to see their favorite television program and also get their homework done? Which is more important, working a few more hours a week or getting good grades?

When they handle work situations well, youngsters often feel the pride and self-confidence that comes from a sense of accomplishment. Not surprisingly, even when they dislike their jobs, most adolescents enjoy the sense of power and independence they get from earning their own money. For most boys and for some girls, earning their own money is an essential prerequisite for dating and participating in many heterosexual activities, which can be expensive.

Contrary to the beliefs of many advocates of adolescent work experience, however, part-time jobs do not typically provide students with on-the-job training that will prove useful in adulthood, nor do they usually bring adolescents into contact with many adults. The vast majority of U.S. adolescents who are employed work in jobs that pay the minimum wage, offer no job protection, and provide few opportunities for advancement (Cole, 1980a). Few adults can afford to work in such jobs. As a result, adolescents frequently work with other adolescents in segregated sections of the labor market. They work primarily in food service, retail sales, clerical and manual laboring jobs — all jobs that offer little formal instruction in work-related skills (Greenberger & Steinberg, 1981).

To complicate matters further, part-time employment does not, as its advocates assume, keep teenagers out of trouble. Ellen Greenberger, Laurence Steinberg, and Mary Ruggiero (1982) found that holding a job is associated with higher rates of alcohol and marijuana use. Many adolescent part-time workers also admitted taking goods from their employers, which they usually gave friends and family either free or at a discount.

Given the close correlation between years of schooling and the ability to find work as an adult, the data with perhaps the most serious negative implications for the future are those showing that adolescents who work part-time are generally less involved in school than their nonworking classmates (D'Amico, 1984). The employed adolescents surveyed by Greenberger and Steinberg (1981) reported being absent more and enjoying school less than their nonworking classmates. This distaste for school typically increases the more a youngster works, perhaps because holding a job gives youngsters a chance to compare school (where some report they are not permitted to do the things they feel they do best) with other environments. More than 27 percent of the teenagers in the Greenberger and Steinberg study reported a decline in their grades after they began working, whereas only 16 percent reported an improvement.

It is not the mere fact of working that causes the grades of teenage workers to fall but rather the number of hours they work. For tenth graders, a drop in grades occurs if a student works an average of more than 14 hours a week; eleventh graders can, on the average, work up to 20 hours a week before their grades begin to decline (Steinberg, 1982). Those adolescents who work more than 20 hours a week during the school year when they are in the tenth and eleventh

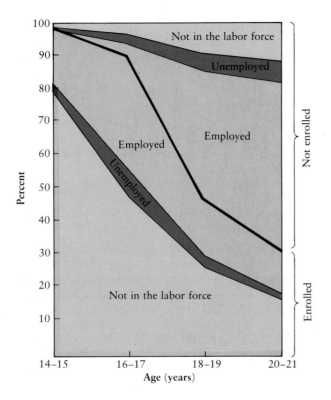

FIGURE 16.11 *Increases in participation in the work force over the course of adolescence. (From U.S. Department of Labor, 1978.)*

grades are more likely to drop out of school than are their classmates who do not work as much (D'Amico, 1984). However, less intensive commitment to work during the tenth and eleventh grades is associated with an increase in the probability of completing high school.

Even as late as the high school years, many U.S. adolescents know little about available occupations in their geographic region, the content of people's work, or their earnings (DeFleur & Menke, 1975). Adolescents' information about the labor force increases slowly as they begin to work themselves and as their network of friends who work grows. Only gradually do they develop some sense of what work they want to do as adults.

Each subsequent job that adolescents hold tends to be more substantial, more responsible, and to provide greater exposure to the options in the labor market (see Figure 16.11). In the period after high school,

many adolescents gradually enter jobs in which they stay long enough to learn a skill, either formally or informally. Others seek career training in professional schools, colleges, public programs, or the military. By the time they are in their midtwenties, most young people have acquired vocational competency and are beginning to work in an adult career (Taggart, 1980).

The Bio-Social Frame and Adolescent Development

The information presented in this chapter describes the basic bio-social dilemma of adolescence. In all societies where adult rights and responsibilities are delayed well beyond puberty, young people must cope with bodies that allow mature sexual activity but social circumstances that keep them in a state of dependence and immaturity. These circumstances complicate a developmental transition that could be expected to be difficult in any event because biological maturity fundamentally changes the power relations between children and their parents. In a phrase, the child becomes "too big to be spanked." Parents continue to exert an important influence over their children, but this influence must be organized differently.

The difficulties of adolescents in modern, industrialized societies are further complicated owing to two interrelated sets of facts. First, the increasingly earlier onset of puberty and the increasingly longer years of education required for economic productivity have combined to increase the length of adolescence in these societies. Second, the ways that schooling and work are organized separate adolescents and adults, increasing the influence of peers and dividing generations.

Taken together, the biological and social reorganizations that define modern adolescence create essential conditions for the unique psychological changes that characterize this developmental period. In this chapter, we have touched only briefly on the psychological contributions to this process or the cultural conditions that lead to the social recognition of adolescence as a distinctive stage. In the next chapter, we will examine the special qualities of mind that develop as young people struggle to understand their new circumstances and to master the complex systems of technical knowledge that will structure their adult work lives. When we consider all three domains of developmental change—the biological, the social, and the psychological—simultaneously as an interacting system of influences in a cultural context, we will be led to a deeper understanding of both the universal and the culture-specific aspects of adolescence. We will also be better able to evaluate the success of competing theories in accounting for the transition to adulthood.

SUMMARY

1. From the time of Rousseau, three key issues have preoccupied theorists of adolescence:
   a. The degree to which rapid biological changes increase behavioral instability
   b. The possibility that adolescent development recapitulates earlier stages in achieving an integration appropriate to adulthood
   c. The relation of biological and social changes to cognitive changes

2. Common to all theories of adolescence is recognition of the child's need to integrate new biological capacities with new forms of social relations. Theories differ from each other in ways described for earlier periods:
   a. Biological theories emphasize the universal physical changes in children's bodies as the central causes of adolescent behavior.
   b. Environmental-learning theories emphasize the continuity of adolescence with earlier periods and the power of society to shape its psychological characteristics.
   c. Interactionist theories emphasize the discontinuity of adolescence from earlier periods and the complementary roles of biological and social factors in provoking the emergence of a new level of psychological organization.
   d. Cultural-context theories do not assume that adolescence is a universal stage of development. Instead, they emphasize that it will appear only under conditions that create a delay between biological maturity and adulthood.

3. Puberty, the biological changes that lead to sexual maturity, is accompanied by a growth spurt during which boys and girls attain approximately 98 percent of their adult size. During puberty the bodies of males and females take on their distinctive shapes.

4. Menarche, or the first menstrual period, usually occurs late in a girl's puberty, after her growth spurt has reached its peak. Among males, the ability to ejaculate semen signals the maturation of the primary sex organs.

5. The age at which biological maturation occurs influences a child's social standing with peers and adults.

6. The dominant mode of peer relations at the start of adolescence is same-sex friendship in which the focus is on shared activities. As adolescence proceeds, same-sex friendship is increasingly characterized by an emphasis on trust, loyalty, and mutual understanding.

7. Social standing within one's peer group depends upon social factors, such as membership in a leading crowd, and personal factors, such as physical attractiveness for girls and athletic ability for boys.

8. The transition to two-person, heterosexual relations goes through a number of stages. It begins with membership in small, same-sex cliques and participation of the members of these cliques in social events that are attended by heterosexual crowds. Within these crowds, heterosexual cliques are formed as couples begin the process of pairing off preparatory to going steady, becoming engaged, and marrying.

9. Achieving an intimate, mutually satisfactory heterosexual relationship requires learning as well as biological maturation.

10. The transition to heterosexual relations proceeds in opposite directions for males and females in our culture because of differences in their prior histories. Males begin with the highly developed goal of sexual satisfaction and only gradually learn to include deeper social and emotional commitments in their heterosexual relations. Females begin with the highly developed goal of social and emotional affiliation and only gradually acquire the goal of sexual satisfaction.

11. Biological maturation and the increasing time spent with peers bring about important changes in parent-child relations during adolescence. Parental authority, which decreases relative to the influence of peers, must now be exercised more through persuasion.

12. Contrary to the hypothesis of a separate youth culture, most adolescents share their parents' values. Dialogue, rather than outright conflict or rejection, is the major method of resolving adolescent-parent disagreements.

13. Conflicts with parents during adolescence ostensibly seem to center on matters of taste. Often such disagreements are actually about larger issues of control.

14. Most U.S. adolescents have considerably more intimate relationships with their mothers than with their fathers.

15. Sensitivity to peer pressure seems to peak at around the age of 15. Most adolescents report that they are more likely to go along with peer pressure that is prosocial than with pressure to misbehave. However, the more

pressure adolescents feel to engage in antisocial behavior, the more likely they are to do so.

16. Evidence concerning the developmental impact of adolescent work experience in the United States is mixed. Moderate amounts of work enhance feelings of independence and efficacy, but too much work reduces school achievement.

17. The bio-social-behavioral shift to adulthood is complicated by the fact that sexual maturity does not necessarily coincide with adult status. The resulting conflict between biological and social forces in development gives this transition its unique psychological characteristics.

KEY TERMS

Identity
Menarche

Puberty
Primary sexual organs

Recapitulate
Secondary sexual characteristics

SUGGESTED READINGS

FRANK, ANNE. *Diary of a Young Girl*. New York: Pocket Books, 1975.

The classic self-description of the experience of early adolescence. The very normalcy of this account, written when the author was in fearful circumstances, attests to universal psychological features evoked by coming of age.

KATCHADOURIAN, HERANT. *The Biology of Adolescence*. New York: W. H. Freeman and Company, 1977.

A wide-ranging and readable account of the biological changes associated with adolescence. The author does an especially good job of presenting information about the biology of development in a way that connects with students' everyday knowledge.

KETT, JOSEPH F. *Rites of Passage: Adolescence in America, 1790 to the Present*. New York: Basic Books, 1977.

This historical account is full of information about the quality of adolescence since the founding of the United States. In addition to providing glimpses of very different kinds of lives in progress, the book provides insights about universal and historically determined characteristics of adolescence as a stage of development.

MEAD, MARGARET. *Coming of Age in Samoa: A Psychological Study of Primitive Youth*. New York: American Museum of Natural History, 1973.

The book that is a high-water mark of the idea that the stressful characteristics of adolescence are created through cultural practices that inhibit sexual activity and restrict adolescent autonomy. Not only an important document in the anthropological study of child development, this book continues to exert an influence on our basic conceptions of human nature.

NATIONAL RESEARCH COUNCIL. Panel on Adolescent Pregnancy and Childbearing. C. Hayes (Ed.). *Risking the Future: Adolescent Sexuality, Pregnancy, and Childbearing.* Vol. I. Washington, D.C.: National Academy Press, 1987.

An up-to-date summary of the complex issues surrounding teenage pregnancy.

YOUNISS, JAMES and **JACQUELINE SMOLLAR.** *Adolescent Relations with Mothers, Father, and Friends.* Chicago: University of Chicago Press, 1985.

This book provides a picture of the reorganization in social life that is fundamental to adolescence through extensive interviews.

17

...

THE PSYCHOLOGICAL ACHIEVEMENTS OF ADOLESCENCE

Now I look into myself and see the I of me, the weak and aimless thing which makes me. I is not strong and needs be, I needs to know direction, but has none. My I is not sure, there are too many wrongs and mixed truths within to know. I changes and does not know. I knows little reality and many dreams. What I am now is what will be used to build the later self. What I am is not what I want to be, although I am not sure what this is which I do not want.

But then what is I? My I is an answer to every all of every people. It is this which I have to give to the waiting world and from here comes all that is different.

I is to create.

—John D., age 17, quoted in Peter Blos *On Adolescence*

· ·

There is broad agreement among theorists of development, dating back at least to Rousseau, that the transition from middle childhood to adulthood requires the development of a new quality of mind. The basic logic behind this consensus is similar to that of a bio-social-behavioral shift: changes in children's capacity for biological reproduction are necessarily accompanied by changes in social relations that propel them into a different social status, with new rights and responsibilities; these changed circumstances, in turn, require of them more complex forms of thinking.

One manifestation of this new mode of thinking is the special sensitivity toward adult opinions and toward the proprieties of adult behavior that adolescents express. They become critical of received wisdom and even more critical of the differences between adult ideals and adult behavior.

The adolescent

seeks out among [adults] models to imitate; heroes to worship. He also seeks out heroes of history and of biography. . . . Literature, art, religion take on new meanings and may create new confusions in his thinking. He has a strangely novel interest in abstract ideas. He pursues them in order to find himself. (p. 256)

Eventually, neither slavish adherence to, nor rejection of, existing cultural expectations will suffice; rather, young people must reconcile their own desires and ways of doing things with satisfying the requirements of their community to be economically productive and good citizens. This process of reconciliation requires a level of systematic thought that strains or exceeds the capacity of younger children. This new level of adolescent thinking is both a result of the process of reconciling competing social demands and the most important psychological means available to the adolescent to forge the new kinds of psychosocial resolutions that are necessary for effective adult functioning.

We begin this chapter with an examination of the experimental evidence that the thought processes of young people exhibit a new level of systematicity and logic as they begin to make the transition to adulthood. This evidence raises a number of important questions: Does the quality of thinking exhibited in scientific experiments also describe the way that young people think about such pressing issues as the laws that govern their society, their rights and obligations as citizens, and their own personal sense of identity? Is the new quality of mind observed among young people who grow up in technologically advanced societies universal or does it result from their extended education? And finally, does the entire pattern of changes constituted of biological, social, and cognitive factors, when examined in different cultural contexts, support the idea of adolescence as a universal stage of development? Although these questions are closely intertwined, we will approach their answers one at a time, beginning as we so often have with Piaget's account of the cognitive changes that characterize this age period.

RESEARCH ON ADOLESCENT THOUGHT

On the basis of an extensive review of the existing research, Daniel Keating (1980) suggested five basic characteristics of adolescent thinking that distinguish it from thought during middle childhood:

1. *Thinking about possibilities* Compared with younger children, who are more at ease reasoning about what they can directly observe, adolescents are more likely to think about alternative possibilities that are not immediately present to their senses.

2. *Thinking ahead* Adolescence is a time when young people start thinking about what they will do when they grow up. Adolescents by no means always plan ahead, but they do so more often and more systematically than younger children. Contemplating the upcoming summer holiday, an adolescent might think, "Well, I could go to Montana and work on a ranch. Or I could stay at home and make up that 'D' in algebra, which isn't going to look too good when I apply to college." A younger child would more likely focus only on having a good time and forget other responsibilities.

3. *Thinking through hypotheses* Relative to younger children, adolescents are more likely to engage in thinking that requires them to generate and test hypotheses and to think about situations that are contrary to fact. In thinking about going to a beach party with a boy she does not know well, a teenage girl might reason, "What if they get drunk and rowdy? What will I do? I guess if things get out of hand, I can always ask someone to take me home. But then they'll think I'm a drag." A younger child would make a decision without contemplating the wide range of possible scenarios.

4. *Thinking about thought* During adolescence, thinking about one's own thought processes — "metacognitive thinking," as described in Chapter 13 — becomes increasingly complex. Adolescents also acquire the ability to engage in **second-order thinking;** that is, they can develop rules about rules, holding two disparate rule systems in mind while mulling them over. At the same time, they can think more systematically and deeply than younger children about other people's points of view, a development illustrated in the changing nature of adolescent friendships (see Chapter 16, p. 533).

5. *Thinking beyond conventional limits* Adolescents use their newly sophisticated cognitive abilities to rethink the fundamental issues of social relations, morality, politics, and religion — issues that are debated by the adults in their community and that have perplexed human beings since the dawn of history. Now acutely aware of the discrepancies between the ideals of their community and the behavior of the people around them, adolescents are highly motivated to figure out how to "do it right." Gesell and Ilg, in the passage quoted above, link this aspect of adolescent thought to youth's idealism and search for heroes.

One can certainly find many examples in the United States of the characteristics of adolescent thinking that Keating describes. In addition, evidence from standardized IQ tests and similar tests shows that American adolescents can routinely solve problems that younger children cannot. For example, when asked to solve analogies such as "*under* is to *beneath* as *pain* is to [*pleasure, doctor, feeling, hurt*]," adolescents err very little, while 9- and 10-year-olds have considerable difficulty (Sternberg & Nigro, 1980). Disagreements arise, however, when psychologists try to explain the source of these differences and to expand the scope of their research to determine whether these differences are universal. As we shall see, recent research on adolescent thinking has raised basic questions about the distinctiveness and the universality of cognitive development during adolescence.

A good deal of the current debate about adolescent thought revolves around Piaget's notion of formal operations, which has inspired much of the existing research in this area. In assessing the nature of adolescent thought, we will first examine Piaget's theory and research and then look at alternative approaches to the study of adolescent thinking.

Formal Operations

It was Piaget's contention that changes in the way adolescents think about themselves, their personal relationships, and the nature of the society in which they live have a common source: the development of a new kind of thought, based on a new logical structure that Piaget called **formal operations.** As you will recall from Chapter 13, an *operation* in Piaget's terminology is a mental action that fits into a logical system. Inhelder and Piaget distinguished formal operations, which they believed emerge by age 12, from concrete operations, which are characteristic of middle childhood, in the following way:

> Although concrete operations consist of organized systems (classifications, serial ordering, correspondences, etc.), [children in the concrete operational stage] proceed from one partial link to the next in step-by-step fashion, without relating each partial link to all the others. Formal operations differ in that all of the possible combinations are considered in each case. Consequently, each partial link is grouped in relation to the whole; in other words, reasoning moves continually as a function of a "structured whole." (Inhelder and Piaget, 1958, p. 16)

In this view formal operational thinking is the kind of thinking needed by anyone who has to solve problems systematically. This new ability would be needed by the owner of a gasoline station who, in order to make a profit, has to take into account the current price he pays for gasoline, the kinds of customers that pass by his station, the kinds of services he needs to

offer, the hours he needs to stay open, and the cost of labor. Or it might apply to a lawyer, who lays out a course of action that takes into account a wide variety of complications and who develops a far-reaching scenario for her client.

In Inhelder and Piaget's classic series of studies, children were asked to combine chemicals or reason about a balance beam, problems that required them to hold one variable of a complex system constant while systematically searching mentally through all the other variables. The children in these experiments were aged 6 through 14, permitting the investigators to clarify the contrast between childhood and adolescent thought.

The "combination of chemicals" problem illustrates both the idea of combination of variables and the idea of a "structured, psychological whole" that Inhelder and Piaget believed to be the key characteristics of formal operational thinking. At the start of the task, four large bottles, one indicator bottle, and two beakers are arrayed on a table in front of the child, as shown in Figure 17.1. Each bottle contains a different clear liquid. The liquids are chosen so that when (1) and (3) are combined in a beaker and then a drop of the chemical from the indicator bottle (*g*) is added, the liquid turns yellow. If the chemical in (2) is added to a beaker containing liquid from both (1) and (3), the solution remains yellow, but if (4) is then added, the liquid turns clear again.

The experimenter begins with two of the beakers already full of liquid. One contains liquid from bottles (1) and (3), the other contains liquid from bottle (2). He puts a drop from the indicator bottle (*g*) in each beaker, demonstrating that it produces a yellow color in one case, but not the other. Now the child is allowed to try out different combinations and to attempt to determine which combination of chemicals will transform the color of the liquid.

Interviews with two of Inhelder and Piaget's subjects are shown in the bottom of Figure 17.1: one with a 7-year-old boy who does not have the kind of overall conceptual grasp of the problem that indicates the presence of a structured whole, (a system of relationships that can be logically described and thought about) and one with a 14-year-old boy who does. The first child is unsystematic in his sampling of possible combinations, even with hints from the experimenter. The second, an adolescent, sets about his task systematically. He starts with the simplest possibility (one of the chemicals, when combined with *g*, turns yellow) then proceeds to combining pairs of chemicals and

These girls are encountering a task that requires them to combine variables as part of their high school curriculum.

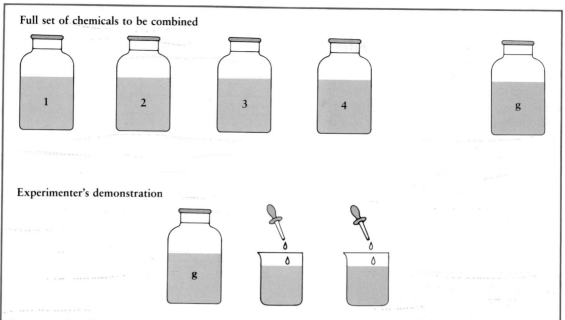

Full set of chemicals to be combined

Experimenter's demonstration

[Ren (7.1 years old) tries 4 × g, then 2 × g, and 3 × g.]

Ren: I think I did everything. I tried them all.

Exp [Experimenter]: What else could you have done?

Ren: I don't know. *[He is given the glasses again. He repeats 1 × g, etc.]*

Exp: You took each bottle separately. What else could you have done?

Ren: Take two bottles at a time? *[He tries 1 × 4 × g, then 2 × 3 × g, thus failing to cross over between the two sets of bottles. When we suggest that he add others, he puts 1 × g in the glass already containing 2 × 3, which results in the appearance of the color.]*

Exp: Try to make the color again.

Ren: Do I put in two or three? *[He tries 2 × 4 × g, then adds 3, then tries it with 1 × 4 × 2 × g.]*

Ren: No, I don't remember any more.

[Eng (14.6 years old) begins with 2 × g, 1 × g, 3 × g, and 4 × g.]

Eng: No it doesn't turn yellow. So you have to mix them. *[He goes on to the six two–by–two combinations and at last hits 1 × 3 × g.]*

Eng: This time I think it works.

Exp: Why?

Eng: It's 1 and 3 and some water

Exp: You think it's water?

Eng: Yes, no difference in odor. I think that it's water.

Exp: Can you show me? *[He replaces g with some water: 1 × 3 × water.]*

Eng: No, it's not water. It's a chemical product: it combines with 1 and 3 and then it turns into a yellow liquid. *[He goes on to three–by–three combinations beginning with the replacement of g by 2 and by 4 — i.e., 1 × 3 × 2 and 1 × 3 × 4.]*

Eng: No, these two products aren't the same as the drops: they can't produce color with 1 and 3 *[Then he tries 1 × 3 × g × 4.]*

Eng: It turns white again: 4 is the opposite of g because 4 makes the color go away while g makes it appear.

FIGURE 17.1 *Examples of how children of different ages cope with the combination-of-chemicals task. Note that the 7-year-old starts by testing only one chemical at a time. When it is suggested that he try working with two chemicals at a time, he becomes confused. The 14-year-old also starts with one chemical at a time but quickly realizes that he must create more complicated combinations, which he does in a systematic way until he arrives at the solution to the problem. (From Inhelder & Piaget, 1958.)*

finally triplets. When combining pairs, he discovers that when *g* is added to a mixture of (1) and (3), the yellow color appears, but because he is methodical in exploring all the logical possibilities, he also discovers that (4) counteracts *g*, thereby arriving at a systematic understanding of the miniature chemical system that Inhelder and Piaget had arranged for him. The adolescent is exhibiting formal operational thinking *par excellence*.

In a second problem, which highlights somewhat different features of formal operations, Inhelder and Piaget asked children to make judgments about the conditions under which a balance beam would be in equilibrium (see Figure 17.2).

The youngest children fail to understand the problem at all. The 8-year-olds concentrate on the weights on each side of the fulcrum: if the weights are equal, they predict that the beam will balance, disregarding the distance of the weights from the fulcrum. Only the adolescents consistently consider both weight and distance in solving the problem (Inhelder & Piaget, 1958; Siegler, 1976).

The correct solution to the balance beam problem exemplifies the key properties of formal operational thinking because this problem requires that the values of both variables—width and distance from the fulcrum—be systematically varied and combined. Equally important is the fact that the solution general to the problem requires the development of logical and mathematical principles. The adolescent can now use those principles to solve an infinite variety of combinations of weight and distance problems.

Although Inhelder and Piaget selected these problems from specific scientific domains, they claimed that the quality of reasoning needed to solve them was quite general. Formal operations, they declared, are "like a center from which radiate the various more visible modifications of thinking which take place in adolescence" (Inhelder & Piaget, 1958, p. 335).

Are formal operations universal? Casual readings of Inhelder and Piaget's 1958 monograph on adolescent thought processes or of standard texts on adolescence can easily lead one to conclude that formal operational thinking is universal. These writings suggest both that formal operational thinking suffuses all domains of adolescent thought, and that the social conditions that give rise to formal operational thinking—the requirement that the young person adopt adult roles and responsibilities—are as universal a part of

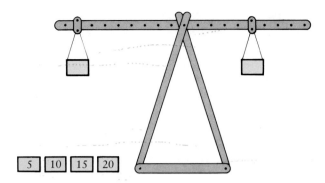

FIGURE 17.2 *The balance beam used by Inhelder and Piaget. On each trial of the experiment, weights of varying magnitude are hung at varying distances from the fulcrum. It is the child's task to determine if the beam will be in balance, and if not, to predict which side will be the heavier. (From Inhelder & Piaget, 1958.)*

adolescence as puberty. One would thus expect to see formal operations organizing adolescent and adult thought in all societies and in all cultural contexts. The actual evidence tells a far more complicated story.

In studies among well-educated American teenagers, as few as 30 to 40 percent have solved such problems as the combination of chemicals and the balance beam that require formal thinking according to Piaget's criteria (Capon & Kuhn, 1979; Keating, 1980; Linn, 1983; Neimark, 1975; Siegler & Liebert, 1975). Such widespread failure among adolescents who ought to be manifesting formal operational thinking raises serious doubts as to whether this kind of thought process is universally acquired. A good deal of research has been carried out to determine if formal operational thinking is, or is not, a universal achievement of adolescence, and what kinds of factors promote or block its development and expression.

Studies among U.S. subjects Robert Siegler and Robert Liebert (1975) designed a combination-of-variables problem in which children ranging in age from 10 to 13 were asked to find the combination of open and closed positions on four switches needed to make a model train go along a track. This arrangement made the problem logically similar to Inhelder and Piaget's combination-of-chemicals problem.

Siegler and Liebert compared the performance of children on the problem as Inhelder and Piaget would have presented it with the performance of children who were tutored using one of two supplementary procedures. In the first supplementary procedure, the children were shown a systematic way to check through the various combinations of open and closed switches. In the second procedure, the children were shown the checking method and were also coached on two problems that were logically equivalent to the one they would be asked to solve.

The tutoring helped. With no tutoring, none of the 10-year-olds and only 20 percent of the 13-year-olds searched systematically through all the alternatives as formal operational thinkers are supposed to do. With training in checking, the 13-year-olds showed only modest improvement and the 10-year-olds showed none at all. When both training and analogous problems were provided, all the children solved the problem correctly. (Similar findings are reported by Stone and Day, 1980).

These results suggest that children on the threshold of adolescence are capable of the systematic, logical manipulation of variables that is the hallmark of formal operations if they are taught how to carry out systematic searches and if the benefits of doing so are made clear. But such coached performance cannot be considered evidence for the spontaneous development of a new mode of thought in early adolescence.

Difficulties with formal operational thinking do not disappear in later adolescence, nor do they show up only on laboratory problems. Noel Capon and Deanna Kuhn (1979) approached adult shoppers at a supermarket and asked them to judge which of two sizes of garlic powder was a better buy: a 67-gram bottle at 77 cents or a 35-gram bottle at 41 cents. The shoppers were provided with paper and pencil to help them reach a solution.

Only 20 percent of the shoppers followed the formal operational procedure of determining the ratio of amount to price; most shoppers relied instead on the conventional belief that the bigger bottle must be a better buy. These results led Capon and Kuhn to conclude that "there does in fact exist significant variability in the level of logical reasoning among an adult population" (p. 421).

Sex differences in formal operations A good deal of research in recent decades has sought to determine whether there are sex differences in children's performance on formal operational tasks. The reasons for this interest are social as well as scientific. If formal operations are a universal capacity, acquisition of this kind of reasoning should eventually be achieved by

Even such everyday adult tasks as shopping may require the kind of systematic thinking that Piaget referred to as formal operations.

both sexes. Yet there is a pervasive popular belief that men have greater talent in such areas as mathematics, science, and engineering, fields that appear to require formal operational thinking. This stereotype is bolstered by (and bolsters) the fact that more men than women currently work in these fields in many industrialized societies. Researchers have sought to determine whether there is any validity to the belief that men have greater talent in these areas and are superior in their ability to engage in formal operational thought.

Anita Meehan (1984) surveyed 150 studies in which both males and females solved the same formal operational problems. In many of the studies she surveyed, no differences were found between the performances of males and females, but in those cases where sex differences were found, they generally favored males.

Several attempts have been made to discover why males sometimes perform better than females on experimental tasks that require formal operations. J. Pes-

How well you reason depends, in part, on how interested you are in the subject matter and how much you know about it.

kin (1980) found that female high school students who took little interest in science performed better on "female-oriented" tasks in which the content captured their interest than on standard, science-oriented Piagetian tasks. By contrast, female students interested in science performed no better on the special "female-oriented" problems than on the standard Piagetian tasks. Since in contemporary American schools fewer females than males are interested in science, these findings suggest that sex differences such as those Meehan documented may be caused by boys' greater interest in the content of the standard Piagetian tasks that require formal operations, as well as by their greater familiarity with the procedures.

Many tasks using formal operational reasoning require the exercise of spatial abilities. Since males, on average, out perform girls on tasks in which spatial abilities play a large role (Hyde, 1981), it may be that the difference between males and females on some formal operational tasks is simply the result of sex-linked differences in spatial abilities (Linn & Sweeney, 1981). However, a clear link between spatial abilities and formal reasoning performance has not been established (Linn & Pulos, 1983).

Current evidence favors the idea that the capacity to solve formal operational problems develops equally in males and females, but the realization of this ability in solving particular problems depends upon a person's past experience. This conclusion, as we will see, is supported by evidence from the other main line of research on the universality of formal operations, which compares the performance of children from different cultural environments.

Cultural variations in formal operations In our review of research on cultural variability in the development of concrete operations in Chapter 13, we found that there is considerable variability across cultures in the age at which children display the ability to engage in concrete operational reasoning when confronted with conservation tasks. However, we saw that this variability appears to be the result of relatively superficial difficulties in understanding the task because of the way it is presented. Concrete operational abilities do appear to be universal.

Evidence across cultures on the development of formal operations offers a far sterner challenge to the idea that this stage is universal. People from small, technologically unsophisticated societies rarely demonstrate formal operations when tested with Piagetian methods (Dasen, 1977; Jahoda, 1980; Laboratory of Comparative Human Cognition, 1983; Rogoff, 1981).

At different times in his career, Piaget adopted different positions on the universality of formal operational thinking. Within his general framework, the acquisition of formal operations should be universal, reflecting universal properties of biological growth and social interaction. Nonetheless, he entertained the notion that "in extremely disadvantageous conditions, [formal operational thought] will never really take shape" (Piaget, 1972, p. 7). This is the position that Inhelder and Piaget adopted in their monograph on formal operations:

The age of about 11 to 12 years, which in our society we found to mark the beginning of formal thinking, must be extremely relative, since the logic of the so-called primitive societies appears to be without such structures (1958, p. 337).

In such statements we see explicit rejection of formal operations as a universal cognitive ability by Piaget, coupled with a claim about differences in development between cultures.

An alternative possibility, which Piaget also entertained,

is to envisage a difference in speed of development without any modification of the order of succession of the stages. These different speeds would be due to the quality and frequency of intellectual stimulation received from adults or obtained from the possibilities available to children for spontaneous activity in their environment. (1972, p. 7)

The conclusion that Piaget preferred toward the end of his life was that all normal people attain the level of formal operations. "However," he wrote,

they reach this stage in different areas according to their aptitudes and their professional specializations (advanced studies or different types of apprenticeship for the various trades): the way in which these formal structures are used, however, is not necessarily the same in all cases. (1972, p. 10)

In common-sense terms, a lawyer might think in a formal manner about law cases but not when sorting the laundry, or a baseball manager might employ formal operational thinking to choose his batting lineup, but fail to do so in the combination-of-chemicals task.

We will return later to consider in more detail the importance of formal operations for adolescent cognitive development. First, however, it is useful to consider the evidence from other research traditions on the universality of the psychological processes required to solve complex logical problems.

Alternative Approaches to Adolescent Thought

Those who question Piaget's account of adolescent cognition have sought alternative explanations along three dimensions. First, those working in the information-processing tradition have explained performance on logical reasoning tasks in terms of cumulative

changes in memory capacities, strategies, and metacognitive understanding, much in the same way that they attempted to explain thinking at earlier ages. Second, researchers from a number of traditions have suggested that adolescence brings with it a new relation between thought and language that is the key to cognitive development during this period. Third, those who emphasize the importance of cultural context have pursued the path suggested by Piaget himself, concentrating on the way that specialized practice in particular domains of experience gives rise to the kind of systematic thought that appears to underlie the new quality of adolescent cognition.

Information-processing theories In recent years psychologists working within the information-processing tradition have provided provocative alternative analyses to Piaget's. These scholars disagree with Piaget's position that children develop a qualitatively different mode of thought during adolescence. Instead, they maintain that characteristics of adolescent thought are best accounted for by an increasing capacity to process information. According to this view, adolescents develop more efficient strategies for solving problems and become better able to retain information in memory while relating the components of a task to one another (Siegler, 1983).

Using an information-processing perspective, Siegler (1976), for example, analyzed the different ways in which Inhelder and Piaget's balance beam problem (see p. 564) can be posed. The impression one

Programming a computer requires the kinds of logical reasoning skills that come to prominence in adolescence.

gets from Inhelder and Piaget's account is that the balance beam problem is a single logical puzzle that older children come to master by the application of more powerful logic.

However, by carefully examining the different ways in which the balance beam can be arranged, Siegler demonstrated that what seems like a single logical problem is really several different tasks, each of which makes somewhat different cognitive demands. For example, he contrasted 5- to 17-year-old children's performance on balance beam problems in which the weights were equal but distributed at different distances from the fulcrum with children's performance on problems in which both the weights and their distances from the fulcrum were unequal (see Figure 17.3).

Siegler found that the older children were much more likely than the younger children to give correct responses to the problem in which the weights were equal but the distances were unequal. In this problem, the youngest children took only weight into account and hence incorrectly concluded that the beam was balanced. However, for the problem in which both weight and distance could be varied and the larger weight had been placed closer to the fulcrum, the youngest children in the experiment, who were 5 years old, performed *better* (89 percent correct) than the oldest ones, who were 17 years old (51 percent correct). But the *reason* for their correct answers was itself incorrect: Since they continued to concentrate only on weight, they correctly predicted that the side with the greater weight would go down. The 17-year-olds considered both weight and distance, but since they had not arrived at the rule for solving this problem, they simply "muddled through," performing better than chance, but not very well.

These results pose two challenges to Piagetian explanations of adolescent thinking. First, they suggest that rather than a global, discontinuous, qualitative change in modes of thinking, the increased problem-solving skills of adolescents are better described as the gradual acquisition of more powerful rules that can be applied to particular problem-solving situations with increasing reliability. Second, only a quarter of the 17-year-olds demonstrated an ability to solve the balance beam problem in all its forms, whereas if they had acquired formal operations, the whole group would have been expected to find the solution. These results therefore call into question the notion that adolescents achieve a general new mode of thought.

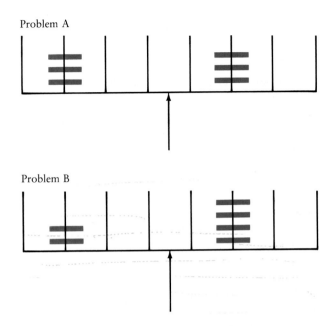

Problem A

Problem B

FIGURE 17.3 *The balance beams used by Siegler and his colleagues to demonstrate the development of different problem-solving strategies. In* (a) *the weights are equal but distance is varied; in* (b) *both weight and distance from the fulcrum are varied. Surprisingly, 5-year-olds, who use faulty reasoning, outperform adolescents on problem B (see text). (From Siegler, 1976.)*

A changing relation of thought to language

Scholars associated with several theoretical traditions believe that an increased ability to use abstract verbal concepts is central to such characteristics of adolescent thought as the ability to think about alternative worlds and plan future ways of life (Vygotsky, 1934/1987; Werner & Kaplan, 1952). This new level of ability is evident both in the way that children make sense of unfamiliar words and in the way they make inferences from relations among familiar words.

Heinz Werner and Bernard Kaplan (1952) devised a clever way to show how children figure out the meanings of unfamiliar words. The researchers made up a series of sentences, each of which contained a nonsense word whose meaning the child had to figure out from the sentence context. For example:

1. You can't fill anything with a *contavish*.

2. The more you take out of a *contavish* the larger it gets.

3. Before the house is finished, the walls must have *contavishes*.

4. You can't feel or touch a *contavish*.

5. A bottle has only one *contavish*.

6. John fell into a *contavish* in the road.

These sentences were presented one at a time. Each time a definition for *contavish* was decided on, the next sentence was presented, until the whole set was included. The 9- and 10-year-olds were more likely to try to figure out each sentence as a separate entity, ignoring the fact that the same word was present in all the previous sentences. So, for example, a 9-year-old might respond to sentence (3) by saying that before the house is finished the walls must have *paint* and to sentence (4) by saying that you can't feel or touch *air*. Such children were unlikely to come up with a common definition for *contavish* that could be used in all of the sentences.

By contrast, 11- and 12-year-old children often had difficulty coming up with a good definition of *contavish* in the first sentence or two (as did we when we first encountered this research), but they were able to compare the possible meanings in each sentence, eventually finding a meaning that fit all of the cases (*hole* in the case of *contavish*).

The complementary ability to build analogies such as "day is to night as _____ is to dark" also seems to develop during adolescence (Levinson & Carpenter, 1974; Lunzer, 1965). This kind of problem is often encountered on IQ tests, and on the Miller Analogies Test, a test made up of verbal analogies that is widely used in the United States as one of the criteria for evaluating candidates for admission to graduate school.

Philip Levinson and Robert Carpenter (1974) presented children who were 9 through 15 years old with two kinds of analogies in order to distinguish between abstract and concrete modes of thinking about words. The first kind of analogy, which they referred to as "true" analogies, were of the form "Bird is to air as fish is to _____." The second kind of analogy, which they referred to as quasi-analogies, were of the form "A bird uses air; a fish uses _____."

The 9-year-olds found the quasi-analogies significantly easier to grasp than the real analogies. In fact they were almost as good at the quasi-analogies as the 15-year-olds. The 15-year-olds found quasi-analogies and real analogies equally easy to solve. Thus the ability to coordinate meanings from isolated words into a single logically consistent system seems to be a key achievement of adolescent thought.

The experiments on the development of verbal concepts suggest that new structures of word meaning begin to take shape during adolescence (Sternberg & Powell, 1983; Vygotsky, 1934/1987). These studies do not contradict the idea that a new form of logic contributes to adolescent thinking, but they demonstrate that changes in the structure and use of language, as well as changes in the logic of problem solving, are important aspects of adolescent cognitive development.

The cultural-context perspective The cultural-context approach to understanding adolescent thought begins from a starting point similar to Inhelder and Piaget's: qualitatively new modes of thought become prominent in adolescence as teenagers prepare to adopt adult roles. Both approaches start from an analysis of the structure of adult activity. However, while Piaget sought a single new logic underlying all adult thought, the cultural-context theorists emphasize variation among the contexts of adult activity and the consequent heterogeneity of adult thought processes. Thus these theorists believe that it is necessary to analyze the different kinds of settings that adults frequent, each setting's structure of activity, and each setting's scripts. (See Box 17.1 on formal reasoning in a nonliterate culture.)

To the extent that different contexts require different degrees of systematic thought, the cultural-context perspective would lead one to expect variability in thinking from context to context; in particular, variability in the likelihood that someone would use formal operational thought. In this respect, the cultural-context position is similar to the approach Piaget (1972) adopted when he proposed that systematic, theoretically precise thinking will most likely appear where it is most often demanded. This perspective differs from Piaget, however, in assuming that all cultures have some contexts that require the use of some variant of formal operational thinking; thus adolescents in all cultures should be expected to use formal operational thought in some contexts. What is universal from this perspective is the acquisition of the ability to think systematically about systems. What is variable is the contexts in which such abilities will be used.

This approach emphasizes that Inhelder and Piaget's experiments are based on the kinds of activity that scientists are assumed to engage in and that school-

BOX 17.1

FORMAL OPERATIONS IN A NONLITERATE CULTURE

...

A great many of the situations that seem to call for the use of formal operations in our everyday lives are also cases in which problem solvers, left to their own devices, would probably also need to keep notes. Even scientists, who are likely candidates for having achieved the stage of formal operations, routinely resort to such "tools of thought" as paper and pencil, or a computer, when they have to sort through a large number of variables to solve a problem. Only rarely, such as in the context of a chess game or a psychological test, does the thinking have to go on entirely inside one's head.

In attempting to determine the universality of a new mode of thinking associated with the transition to adulthood, standard psychological tests of formal operational reasoning are of limited use because they are so closely modeled on procedures used in scientific experiments, procedures that are completely alien forms of activity in many cultures of the world. Fortunately, however, recent research by anthropologists familiar with psychological theories has begun to provide evidence on complex adult problem solving in a variety of activity settings (Hutchins, 1980; Rogoff & Lave, 1984).

An interesting example of this kind comes from studies of navigation in the South Seas (Goodenough, 1953; Gladwin, 1970). Until such devices as magnetic compasses became readily available following World War II, natives of Polynesia and Micronesia, islands northeast of New Guinea, sailed their small outrigger canoes over many miles of ocean to get from one tiny island to another without the help of conventional instruments. Even very experienced sailors from other parts of the world would not presume to sail such distances without

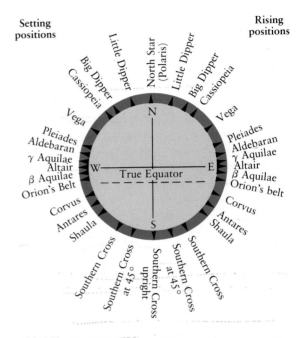

A *schematic representation of the star compass used by navigators in the Caroline Islands to guide their outrigger canoes from one island to another. (From Goodenough, 1953.)*

a compass for fear of sailing off into the South Pacific and probable death.

The skill necessary to engage in such navigation requires an external record-keeping system, a hypothetical reference point, and constant estimates of speed —

children are exposed to when they are taught principles of science. This use of scientific procedures as the standard means to assess "formal operations in general" is inappropriate from the cultural-context perspective, which sees formal operational thinking as dependent on specific properties of activity and context. Instead, this approach would start by analyzing actual activities, finding occasions when formal operational thinking is required and therefore when it is likely to be manifested.

For example, a common occasion that may require formal operational thought is the event called "planning a holiday meal." The following example concerning this activity was provided by Peg Griffin, a sociolinguist, who obtained it from a 40-year-old college-educated woman who declared on the basis of

all combined in a single problem-solving process that lasts as long as the voyage itself. Instruction in how to navigate begins in adolescence and continues for several years. Experienced navigators have learned to use a system that depends heavily on 14 distinctive "star paths"; that is, a set of stars that always rise from the same point on the eastern horizon and set at the same place in the west, traveling the same arc as they appear to move across the sky. A practiced navigator is able to construct the entire "star compass" mentally from a glimpse of two or three stars on the horizon. As Edwin Hutchins phrases it, "The star compass is an abstraction which can be oriented as a whole by determining the orientation of any part" (1983, p. 195).

This star compass is only one part of the navigator's mental model of the voyage. An essential additional element is a "reference island," whose bearing on the star compass is known for any island from which a boat might set out (see the illustration). The term "reference island" is placed in quotation marks because in many cases it is a purely hypothetical entity, needed only to make calculations of relative distance from the destination.

In the actual process of sailing, navigators mentally combine the information about the star paths, the location of the reference island, and information about their rate of speed in order to discover their current position and distance from their destination. So skillful are they at doing this that they can tack away from their destination when the wind conditions require it, but still calculate their location and find their destination.

In some of the earlier research on this kind of navigation, it was believed that navigators could not talk logically about the system they were using (Gladwin, 1970). Their explanations seemed to be inconsistent with the analysis that the anthropologist had made of their navigational system. If true, this inability to describe their own thought processes would weaken the claim that their problem solving illustrates formal operations.

Hutchins (1983), however, showed that the navigators' explanations were perfectly logical for the system they were using. The apparent illogicality arose from a basic cultural difference in the way that people think about compasses and relative motion. It seemed obvious to Gladwin that the canoe moved across the water while the islands remained still. The natives, however, had developed their system by imagining that the boat stood still while the reference island moved. When Hutchins took native accounts completely seriously, he was able to show that the anthropologists had simply failed to work out the full native system.

Although Micronesian navigators show that they can engage in formal operational thought when sailing, they showed no such ability when they were presented with a standard Piagetian combination-of-variables task (Gladwin, 1970). Gladwin presented adolescents and adults with stacks of poker chips of different colors. He asked them to find all combinations of colors. Even adult expert navigators responded to this task at a very low level within Piaget's framework; most paired only a few colors, falling far short of the formal operational ideal. Only a few young men who had attended high school succeeded in displaying some aspects of systematic combinatorial activity. These young men, however, could not use the native system of navigation!

These results suggest that formal operational thinking may occur far more widely than the evidence from typical experiments suggests, making it plausible that this type of thinking is universal among human groups. At the same time, the data make it clear that formal operations do not uniformly replace earlier modes of thought. Their use remains highly restricted to contexts in which they are appropriate, and for which individuals have the greatest experience.

reading Piaget that she "did not have formal operations."

On the holiday in question it is customary to eat one of several main dishes: turkey, goose, lamb, or ham. The choice of the main course depends on several variables: What is available? How expensive is each of the alternatives? Is anyone coming who has a low-cholesterol diet? Does anyone keep kosher? Is anyone a vegetarian? Do the guests have exotic tastes, or are they "meat and potatoes" people? If turkey is on sale and there are a lot of people, turkey can seem very tempting. Goose, on the other hand, is rather exotic but also fatty, which may bother the low-cholesterol people.

These calculations do not stop with the main course. If there is turkey, there has to be cranberry sauce; with lamb, mint sauce is essential. What about starches? Stuffing? Rice? Potatoes? Sweet potatoes? What about the soup? Clam chowder goes with turkey, but will it go with goose, or would a clear broth be better?

Social factors also have to be taken into account. First, who is coming to dinner? The choice will differ if all the guests are old friends who expect a turkey or if some are guests of guests who happen also to be a visiting symphony conductor and his wife. Social factors also include such elements as what to wear and how to plan to keep everyone happy—for example, who will sit next to chatty Aunt Betty?

The ability of women and men to engage in such thinking while standing in front of the meat counter on the eve of a holiday illustrates several essential features of formal operational thinking. First, the person must sort through several variables, holding one constant while working on the others ("Hmmm, ham, candied sweet potatoes, cranberries . . . uh-oh, no cranberries, gotta start over again. . . . Besides, Johnny keeps begging for lamb, but will one leg be enough for 12 people? Two would make dinner too expensive. Well, let's see. . . ."). Second, this kind of thinking clearly is a form of planning. Third, the plan must result in a "structured whole" organized by concepts significant to our hypothetical shopper, for example, the concept *holiday meal*. Finally, the shopper in this case was perfectly capable of reflecting on, and describing, her thought processes.

This example differs from Inhelder and Piaget's characterization of formal operations in that the shopper fails to consider literally *all* of the possible combinations of relevant factors. Instead, she pursues each of the variables in her problem only long enough to come up with a usable solution. Nevertheless, the process of planning the meal clearly requires the use of formal operations.

Several recent experimental studies suggest that it is quite common for people to reason differently in everyday situations than they do in formal experiments designed as logical puzzles (Linn, 1983; Rogoff & Lave, 1984; Tschirgi, 1980). For example, a study by Marcia Linn, Tina de Benedictus, and Kevin Delucchi (1982) compared reasoning performance for Piagetian-style problems with reasoning about the truthfulness of advertising. The level of formal reasoning was rather low in both cases, casting doubt in the first place on the universality of this mode of thought among adults. The researchers also questioned Piaget's hy-

pothesis that once individuals can engage in formal reasoning, it becomes a *general* characteristic of their thinking. They found virtually no correlation between the quality of reasoning for the Piagetian problems and that for the advertising problems, suggesting that participants did not use one single characteristic mode of thinking.

Judith Tschirgi (1980) found that even when the same kinds of problem materials were used, the kind of reasoning differed depending upon whether the outcome of the situation was one that the subject viewed as positive (and hence, wanted to maintain) or negative (and hence, wanted to change). An example is given in Figure 17.4. The boy has baked a cake with margarine, honey, and whole wheat flour, and the cake is a great success because it is so moist. The boy hypothesizes that the cause of the success is the use of honey. The question is, what should he change when he bakes another cake to check his hypothesis? In the negative case, the cake is too runny and the boy again hypothesizes that honey is the crucial factor. The question remains, what must be done to test this hypothesis?

The logic of these problems is the same. In each case, the best way to test the hypothesis is to hold the kind of shortening and flour constant while varying the kind of sweetener. But in this experiment, only when the cake was a failure did participants agree that the boy should substitute sugar for honey. When the cake was a success, they kept honey constant and changed other factors. College students were as likely to follow this pattern as second-graders, indicating that this illogical pattern may be a general characteristic of human reasoning.

As Tschirgi comments, when confronted with an everyday problem, people's expectations about the outcome, rather than underlying cognitive competencies, control the way they reason (see also Linn, 1983).

The shortcuts taken by Griffin's shopper and the participants in Tschirgi's study do not manifest the idealized scientific solution embodied in Piaget's procedures, but studies of how experts solve problems suggest that such shortcuts represent the typical way in which adults engage in problem solving (Chi, Glaser & Kees, 1982). In fact, the systematic reasoning shown by the shopper displays more aspects of formal operations than are found in many kinds of skilled adult thinking where formal operations might be thought appropriate. Expert chess players, for example, do not usually run through all possible combinations of

John decided to bake a cake. But he ran out of some ingredients. So:

He used margarine instead of butter for the shortening

He used honey instead of sugar for the sweetening and

He used brown whole wheat flour instead of regular white flour.

The cake turned out great because it was so moist.

John thought that the reason the cake was so great was the honey. He thought that the type of shortening (butter or margarine) or the type of flour really didn't matter.

 = Great cake

What should he do to prove this point?

He can bake the cake again but use sugar instead of honey, and still use margarine and brown whole wheat flour.

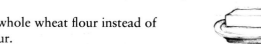

He can bake the cake again but this time use sugar, butter, and regular white flour.

He can bake the cake again still using honey, but this time using butter and regular white flour.

FIGURE 17.4 *An example of a combination-of-variables task using an everyday situation. Children were asked to choose one of the three hypothetical problem-solving strategies. When the outcome of the hypothetical event was positive, as in this case, neither children nor adults used rigorously logical testing procedures. (From Tschirgi, 1980.)*

moves, preferring instead to match the overall board pattern to a successful pattern they recall from past experience (Chase & Simon, 1973). Similarly, scientists take shortcuts based on their intuitions that clearly violate the canons of scientific reasoning (Latour, 1987).

These data fit with Piaget's final speculation (1972) that formal operations are acquired in a context-specific manner, casting doubt on his and Inhelder's earlier description of formal operational thinking as a totally systematic pattern that comes into routine use during adolescence.

Both the information-processing and the cultural-context approaches blur the discontinuity between middle childhood and adolescence that is central to traditional Piagetian theory (Flavell, 1982, 1985). According to these approaches, the transition in thinking between these ages may appear either continuous or discontinuous, depending upon the depth of knowledge that the young person has about a particular context or problem content. Consequently, in order to resolve uncertainties about whether thinking undergoes a stagelike change in adolescence, we must assess to what extent adolescent thinking in a variety of contexts is systematic. Only if a qualitatively new mode of thinking appears across a broad range of contexts is it legitimate to conclude that a stagelike change has taken place.

ADOLESCENT THINKING ABOUT THE SOCIAL ORDER

Still unknown is whether the characteristics of adolescent thought observed in specially organized experiments explain the actual thought processes of adolescents when they are thinking about issues of vital concern to them: their relations with their peers and parents; what they like and dislike; who they are; why the world is organized as it is; what might be done to improve the way things work; what they are going to do today, tomorrow, and 10 years from now.

Thinking About Politics

Although children as young as 9 think seriously about the nature of society (Furth, 1980), they still have little understanding of political issues, according to Joseph Adelson and his colleagues. Based on interviews with hundreds of children and adolescents in the United States, Germany, and England, Adelson writes

> Unable to imagine social reality in the abstract, he [the child] enters adolescence with only the weakest sense of social institutions, of their structure and functions, or of that invisible network of norms and principles which link these institutions to each other. Furthermore, the failure to achieve abstractness does not permit him to understand, except in a most rough and ready way, those concepts essential to political thought—such ideas as authority, rights, liberty, equity, interests, representation, and so on. (1972, p. 109)

Adelson and his colleagues investigated how young people's reasoning about politics changes during the course of adolescence. To overcome national differences in knowledge about political figures and the fact that adolescents may have little specific knowledge about their political system, they asked teenagers to imagine that a thousand people move to a Pacific Island where they have to set up a new society. The researchers then posed a series of questions about how the new society should be organized. Some questions required the young people to choose among different forms of government or to decide upon the laws governing personal freedom and the rights of minorities. Others posed such hypothetical problems as should a dissenting religious group be allowed to avoid vaccinations?

Adelson and his colleagues found that a major change in adolescents' reasoning about politics occurs sometime around the age of 14 (Adelson & O'Neil, 1966; Adelson, Green, & O'Neil, 1969). This change was so little affected by such factors as gender, social class, and nationality that Adelson declared: "A twelve-year-old German youngster's ideas of politics are closer to those of a twelve-year-old American than to those of his fifteen-year-old brother" (Adelson, 1972, p. 108).

The change was particularly evident in three areas: the way adolescents reason about politics, the level of social control that they think appropriate, and the frequency of their appeal to overarching political ideals when expressing their views.

Reasoning processes Whereas 12- to 13-year-olds respond to questions about society in terms of concrete people and events, 15- to 16-year-olds respond in terms of abstract principles, as shown by their answers to the question "What is the purpose of laws?"

> [12- to 13-year-olds:] They do it, like in school, so that people don't get hurt. If we had no laws, people could go around killing people. So people don't steal or kill.

> [15- to 16-year-olds:] To ensure safety and enforce the government. To limit what people can do. They are basically guidelines for people. . . . (Adelson, 1972, p. 108)

In their responses to questions about a law on the right of government to take private property for public use, the older adolescents demonstrated that they could reason hypothetically, taking many aspects of the problem into account. Adelson presented them with the case of a government wanting to build a highway through land that an owner refused to sell. An older adolescent answers:

If it's a strategic point like the only way through a mountain maybe without tunneling, then I'm not too sure what I'd do. If it's a nice level stretch of plain that if you didn't have it you'd have to build a curve in the road, I think that the government might go ahead and put a curve in the road. (1972, p. 114)

Social control The way that 12- to 13-year-olds think about social control becomes evident when they are asked about crime, punishment, and retribution. In response after response, the youngest adolescents suggest that severe punishment is the best way to deal with law-breaking, leading Adelson to conclude that "the young adolescent's authoritarianism is omnipresent" (1972, p. 119). For example, when asked how to teach people not to commit crimes in the future, a young adolescent answered:

Jail is usually the best thing, but there are others. . . . In the nineteenth century they used to torture people for doing things. Now I think the best place to teach people is in solitary confinement. (1972, p. 116)

As adolescents grow older, ideas of reform and rehabilitation begin to enter into their answers. Older adolescents also conceive of the beneficial side of laws, whereas younger ones think of laws only as a way of keeping people from behaving badly. When a law seems not to be working, older adolescents suggest that perhaps the law should be changed, while younger adolescents tend to say that the level of punishment should be increased.

Younger adolescents seem to find it difficult to conceive of social and political regulation as ongoing processes, assuming instead that "What is, has been; what is, will be." What "has been" for them is a world in which they were told what to do, so they project this regime onto the future. By contrast, older adolescents have experienced situations in which they were responsible for their own good behavior; thus they can reason about a world in which they must provide their own rules and regulations voluntarily.

Adelson points out that this mid-adolescent shift in reasoning about politics corresponds to changes that Inhelder and Piaget found in their studies of scientific problem solving. The thinking of the younger adolescents, with its emphasis on the one right answer, doesn't require formal operational thinking, while conceptions of modifiable, flexible, well-balanced po-

litical systems do. Younger adolescents are only beginning to engage in real formal operational thinking and their thinking does not include some of the more difficult operations, while older adolescents are more likely to explore all possibilities.

Political idealism In this century, adolescents have been prominent among those who have been attracted to political and religious ideologies and who have been active on their behalf. For example, young people were active participants in the uprising in the Warsaw ghetto during World War II, and in the civil rights protests of the 1960s. According to many scholars of adolescence, young people are both "pushed" and "pulled" toward ideologies (Coles, 1967; Erikson, 1963; Inhelder & Piaget, 1958). They are pushed by their desire to become independent of their parents and to show that they can govern their own affairs; they are pulled by the attractiveness of a seemingly coherent system that offers an alternative to the adult world.

Adolescents' new ability to search for inconsistencies among long-held beliefs comes with the ability to think logically, which also increases their interest in ideal systems of thought. Jerome Kagan (1972) suggests that as part of the process of becoming independent, adolescents use the following syllogism to question long-held beliefs about their parents:

1. Parents are omnipotent and omniscient.

2. My parent has lost a job, or failed to understand me, or behaved irrationally (or any other liability the teenager cares to select).

Their increased understanding makes teenagers critical of society and eager to suggest better ways of doing things.

3. If my parents were omniscient, they would not be tainted with failure and vulnerability.

Now more capable of thinking hypothetically, adolescents note the contradictions in their previous belief in their parents' omniscience. Having reached the conclusion that their parents are not perfect, they confront a new psychological problem. Parents have been their role models. The adolescent has identified with them and been attached to them since early infancy. What is to replace them? Identification with a person or system that *is* ideal is one possible answer. Since no ideal person or political system has yet made an appearance on earth, an adolescent's adoption of an ideology is frequently accompanied by the adoption of a utopian political project or a new sense of religion. This adolescent proclivity was especially visible in the civil rights and commune movements of the 1960s, both of which drew heavily for support on adolescents who saw in them a consistent alternative to the imperfections of the society in which they lived (see Figure 17.5) (Berger, 1981; Coles, 1967).

Although adolescents have traditionally been viewed as idealistic and may have the ability to think about ideal systems, most teenagers have not worked out any systematic alternatives to the existing political order for themselves. With rare exceptions, when asked directly to imagine an ideal society, teenage respondents came up with such platitudes as the following:

A society that everyone gets along and knows each other's problems and try to sit down and figure out each other's problem and get along like that.

I think right now that the only society I would have would be the exact same one as we have now, although it does have its faults, I think we do have a good government now.

Well, I would set up a society of helping out people like when there would be crime, like I said before, I would put these criminals in there for life because when they get out they would want to do it again and all that. (Adelson, 1975, pp. 74–75)

These not-very-utopian interview responses are accompanied by evidence that many young people become increasingly cynical about political processes during adolescence. They are able to see the problems

FIGURE 17.5 *Chanting adolescents seek an end to war.*

and inconsistencies in political life but they are unable to work out practical solutions. Table 17.1 shows adolescents' responses to the question "Would it ever be possible to eliminate . . . (crime, poverty, racial prejudice)?" In general, the older adolescents are pretty certain that political solutions to the world's ills are unlikely. At the same time, since they are in the process of defining themselves in contrast to their parents' generation, they are still attracted to the promises of someone who declares that, given the right beliefs and behavior, a more rational organization of life on earth *is* possible.

TABLE 17.1 Percentage of pessimistic responses to the question "Would it ever be possible to eliminate . . . ?", according to age

Age	Crime	Poverty	Racial Prejudice
12	48	9	45
14	66	40	80
16	72	54	85
18	75	53	76

SOURCE: Adelson, 1975.

Thinking About Moral Issues

Among the questions that preoccupy adolescents when they think about their own and others' behavior are the following: What is right? What is wrong? What principles should I base my behavior on and use to judge the behavior of others? According to some evidence, the processes that young people use to think about such questions, like the processes they use to think about science problems or politics, also change during adolescence.

Recall from Chapter 15 that Kohlberg, elaborating on Piaget's ideas, posited six stages in the development of moral reasoning (see Table 17.2 for a summary of these stages; a more detailed description of them appears in Table 15.2). During middle childhood, children make the transition from stage 2 reasoning ("instrumental morality"), in which they understand being moral as behaving well in return for others' good behavior) to stage 3 reasoning, in which being moral means to do unto others as you would have others do unto you.

Stage 4 reasoning begins to appear during adolescence, but it is rarely seen in those who have not gone beyond a high school education. Stage 3 is still the dominant mode of reasoning about moral questions during adolescence (Colby, Kohlberg, Gibbs, & Lie-

berman, 1983). Reasoning at the level of stage 4 is like reasoning at the level of stage 3 in that people are aware that there are two points of view about moral issues. But stage 4 moral reasoning focuses on relations between the individual and the group, while stage 3 reasoning focuses on relations between individuals. People who reason at stage 4 believe that the point of view of society is primary and accept its existing laws and customs. Moral behavior from this point of view is behavior that maintains the social order. For this reason, stage 4 is sometimes referred to as the "law and order" stage within Kohlberg's theory (Brown & Herrnstein, 1975, p. 289).

Moral thinking in stages 3 and 4 depends on partial attainment of the ability to engage in formal operational reasoning, in particular the ability to consider simultaneously all *existing* relations, according to Kohlberg (1984). However, Kohlberg believed that people who are reasoning at these stages still do not consider all *possible* relations, nor do they form abstract hypotheses about what is moral.

Kohlberg referred to the perspective used in stage 5 moral reasoning as *prior-to-society*. Individuals who think about moral issues at this level accept and value the social system, but instead of insisting on maintaining the existing social order, they focus on democratic processes, continually seeking possibilities for im-

TABLE 17.2 Kohlberg's stages of moral reasoning

	What Is Right		What Is Right
Stage 1 — Heteronomous morality	To avoid breaking rules backed by punishment; obedience for its own sake.	Stage 4 — Social system and conscience	Fulfilling the actual duties to which you have agreed. Laws are to be upheld except in extreme cases where they conflict with other fixed social duties.
Stage 2 — Individualism, instrumental purpose, and exchange	Following rules only when it is to someone's immediate interest, acting to meet one's own interests and needs and letting others do the same.	Stage 5 — Social contract or utility and individual rights	Being aware that people hold a variety of values and opinions, that most values and rules are relative to your group.
Stage 3 — Mutual interpersonal expectations, relationships, and interpersonal conformity	Living up to what is expected by people close to you or what people generally expect of people in your role as son, brother, friend, etc.	Stage 6 — Universal ethical principles	Following self-chosen ethical principles. Particular laws or social agreements are usually valid because they rest on such principles.

SOURCE: Kohlberg, 1976.

proving upon the existing social contract. They believe that laws are sometimes in conflict with moral principles. Recognition of this conflict drives them to be "law creators" as well as "law maintainers." Stage 5 moral reasoning does not appear until early adulthood, and then only rarely.

The final achievement in Kohlberg's system of moral reasoning, stage 6, occurs when a person adopts a point of view that places certain moral principles above the rules of society. The idea that human life is of supreme value and cannot be taken by another under any circumstances is an example of such a universal moral principle. A person who reasons at the level of stage 6 believes that certain precepts are sacrosanct no matter what the personal consequences of holding such a view, since fundamental to this kind of reasoning is the idea that moral laws apply equally to everyone, including oneself. The philosophies and policies of civil disobedience practiced by Mahatma Gandhi in India and Martin Luther King, Jr. in the United States serve as examples of behavior based on Kohlberg's stage 6 reasoning.

As noted in Chapter 15, stage 6 reasoning is rarely encountered. But under extraordinary circumstances, otherwise ordinary people will put their own lives at risk because of moral beliefs guided by stage 6 reasoning. Such was the case during World War II, for example, when many Europeans rescued Jews scheduled for extermination. According to Samuel and Pearl Oliner (1988), most of those who took an active part in helping Jews were motivated by ethical principles that apply to all of humanity, the hallmark of stage 6 moral reasoning.

Despite its comprehensiveness and its ability to inspire research, Kohlberg's theory of moral development has had a somewhat stormy history (see Kurtines & Gewirtz, 1984; and Shweder, 1982, for representative discussions; an extended reply to critics is contained in Kohlberg, 1984). Although several studies have confirmed that children progress through Kohlberg's stages of moral reasoning in the predicted order (Walker, 1986), others have failed to support the idea that Kohlberg's stages follow each other in an invariant sequence from lower to higher. Instead of a steady progression upward, subjects sometimes regress in their development or seem to skip a stage (Kuhn, 1976; Gilligan & Murphy, 1979; Kohlberg & Kramer, 1969; Kurtines & Grief, 1974).

Another controversial assumption of Kohlberg's

TABLE 17.3   Parallel stages of cognitive and moral development

Cognitive Stage	Moral Stage
Preoperations: The "symbolic function" appears but thinking is marked by centration and irreversibility.	Stage 1 — Heteronomy The physical conseqences of an action and the dictates of authorities define right and wrong.
Concrete operations: The objective characteristics of an object are separated from action relating to it: and classification, seriation, and conservation skills develop.	Stage 2 — Exchange Right is defined as serving one's own interests and desires, and cooperative interaction is based on terms of simple exchange.
Beginning formal operations: There is development of the ability to use propositional logic.	Stage 3 — Expectations Emphasis is on good-person stereotypes and concern for approval.
Early basic formal operations: The hypothetico-deductive approach emerges, involving the abilities to develop possible relations among variables and to organize experimental analyses.	Stage 4 — Social system and conscience Focus is on the maintenance of the social order by obeying the law and doing one's duty.
Consolidated basic formal operations: Operations are now completely exhaustive and systematic.	Stage 5 — Prior rights and social contract Right is defined by mutual standards that have been agreed upon by the whole society.

SOURCE: Walker, 1980.

theory is that there is a correspondence between the levels of cognitive development as described by Piaget and levels of moral reasoning (a summary of expected correspondences is contained in Table 17.3). The expected correspondences between cognitive and moral development have been found by some researchers (Colby, Kohlberg, Gibbs, & Lieberman, 1983; Walker, 1986). But others report failure to find such correspondences (Haan, Weiss, & Johnson, 1982). Some investigators have taken these failures as evidence that Kohlberg's stage theory was incorrectly formulated (e.g., Hoffman, 1980), while others argue that the problem lies in the way that the theory is related to the data (Walker, 1986).

One problem in relating Kohlberg's data to his theory arises from the procedures used to score the answers to his questions. Recall from Chapter 15 that Kohlberg presented dilemmas in the form of stories and asked children to reason about them in a give-and-take interview session. Some investigators report having trouble sorting interview answers reliably into the correct categories (Kurtines & Grief, 1974). Unreliable scoring makes it difficult to evaluate predictions from the theory. In response to this criticism, Colby and Kohlberg (1984) created a standardized scoring scheme that they claim is both easy to use and reliable. Using the revised procedures, Lawrence Walker (1986) found improved correspondence between the theory and the data. (For further discussion of alternative scoring methods and their implications for understanding moral development, see Kurtines & Gewirtz, 1984.)

A second problem in evaluating Kohlberg's theory is that there is considerable uncertainty about how moral reasoning in response to a hypothetical moral dilemma is related to actual moral behavior (Gilligan & Belenky, 1980; Kohlberg, Hickey, & Scharf, 1972). It is a commonplace observation that perfectly respectable, law-abiding citizens, who are likely to score at stages 3 or 4 on Kohlberg's scale, sometimes fail to help strangers in need, or riot at football games, causing great pain and loss to others. Clearly, the ability to argue about moral dilemmas does not inevitably lead to moral behavior.

One well-known study supporting a positive relationship between moral reasoning and action was conducted with young people who participated in the free speech movement at the University of California in the 1960s (Haan, Smith, & Block, 1968). By their participation in the free speech movement, these people risked being arrested for civil disobedience. Moral dilemmas were presented both to people who actually engaged in sit-ins to support their beliefs and to those who did not. As shown in Table 17.4, students who risked arrest by sitting in scored at higher moral stages than those who did not, providing support for Kohlberg's claim that levels of moral reasoning should be related to levels of moral action.

Sex differences in moral reasoning Piaget located the origins of a new, autonomous form of moral reasoning in middle childhood in the ways that children play games with their peers (see Chapter 15). He also claimed that there were clear sex differences in children's play; girls seemed to be more interested in elaborating social relations in their play, while boys seemed to be more interested in rules and litigation about infractions. Insofar as the kinds of games played by boys are conceived of as more advanced cognitively (as Piaget thought), this line of reasoning leads naturally to the inference that there are sex differences in moral development. Both this line of reasoning and the evidence from research are hotly disputed (Baumrind, 1986; Walker, 1984, 1986; Walker, de Vries, & Trevethen, 1987).

In some early tests of moral reasoning among adolescents it appeared that males score higher than females (Holstein, 1976; Haan, Langer, & Kohlberg,

TABLE 17.4 Percentage of subjects sitting in, by moral stage and attitude toward the free speech movement

	Attitude toward Free Speech Movement											
	Sitting in Is Right				Mixed Attitude				Sitting in Is Wrong			
Kohlberg Stage	3	3/4	4	4/5	3	3/4	4	4/5	3	3/4	4	4/5
Percent participating	23	54	63	75	11	17	12	60	0	0	0	0
Percent at each stage	7	37	40	16	13	44	35	7	19	52	28	1

SOURCE: Haan, Smith, and Block, 1968.

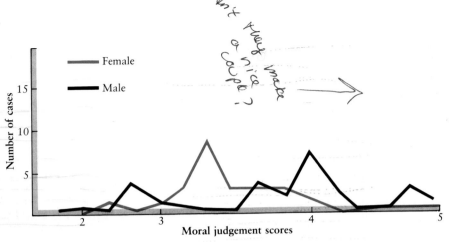

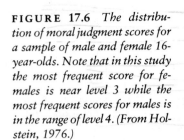

FIGURE 17.6 *The distribution of moral judgment scores for a sample of male and female 16-year-olds. Note that in this study the most frequent score for females is near level 3 while the most frequent scores for males is in the range of level 4. (From Holstein, 1976.)*

1976). The data in Figure 17.6, taken from Constance Holstein's study of moral reasoning, display the pattern of results around which controversy has focused. As shown, adolescent boys were most frequently found to be in stage 4, while adolescent girls most frequently scored in stage 3. Among adults, males virtually never gave answers based on stage 3 reasoning, while females hardly ever responded with stage 5 reasoning.

Data such as Holstein's spurred Carol Gilligan (1977, 1982) to question whether Kohlberg's description had left out a dimension of morality of great concern to females. She argued that female responses to moral dilemmas are lower on Kohlberg's scale than are those of males because moral thinking among women is oriented toward interpersonal relationships coupled with an ethic of caring and responsibility for other people. This difference in what she referred to as "moral orientation" inclines women to suggest altruism and self-sacrifice, rather than invoking rights and rules as the solution to interpersonal problems and moral dilemmas.

In effect, Gilligan was arguing that males and females are really using different moral criteria. According to criteria of importance to females, as judged by Gilligan, stage 3, which emphasizes mutual caring, should be ranked more highly than Kohlberg's stage 4.

Gilligan illustrated this difference in moral orientation by contrasting adult male and female responses to questions about morality:

[A 25-year-old man's response to the question "What does the word *morality* mean to you?"]

Nobody in the world knows the answer. I think it is recognizing the right of the individual, the rights of other individuals, not interfering with those rights. Act as fairly as you would have them treat you. I think it is basically to preserve the human being's right to existence. I think that is the most important. Secondly, the human being's right to do as he pleases, again without interfering with somebody else's rights.

[A 25-year-old woman's response to the question "Is there really some correct solution to moral problems or is everybody's opinion equally correct?"]

No, I don't think that everyone's opinion is equally right. I think that in some situations there may be opinions that are equally valid, and one could conscientiously adopt one of several courses of action. But there are other situations in which I think there are right and wrong answers, that sort of inhere in the nature of existence, of all individuals here who need to live with each other to live. We need to depend upon each other, and hopefully it is not only a physical need but a need of fulfillment in ourselves, that a person's life is enriched by cooperating with other people and striving to live in harmony with everybody else, and to that end, there are right and wrong, there are things which promote that end and that move away from it. . . . (1982, pp. 19–20)

In Gilligan's view, these answers capture the difference between male moral reasoning, which is focused on individual rights, and female moral reasoning, which is based on a sense of responsibility for other people.

At present, there is no consensus with respect to male–female differences in moral development, and no simple resolution to the disputes about them appears to be in sight. Contrary to expectations based on either Piaget's analysis of game playing or Gilligan's hypothesis about two different paths to the development of moral reasoning, sex differences in moral reasoning performance show up relatively rarely, and when they do appear they are small (Nunner-Winkler, 1984; Rest, 1979; Snarey, 1985; Walker, 1984, 1986). In a review of 80 studies of moral reasoning involving 152 different groups of subjects, Walker and deVries (1985) found only 22 that showed significant sex differences, nine of which indicated that females scored higher than males on Kohlberg's scale. Beyond the test data there remains the unanswered question of whether these or other differences in reasoning about morality manifest themselves in actual moral behavior.

A well-developed sense of empathy is an important element in the moral development of adolescents.

Cultural variation in moral reasoning? Standard studies of cross-cultural variability in moral reasoning, like those of tests of formal operational reasoning, reveal far greater differences between cultural groups than between the two sexes (Snarey, 1985). Although there are some exceptions (Shweder, Mahopatra, & Miller, 1987), most studies show that people from technologically unsophisticated societies who continue to live in relatively small, face-to-face communities rarely reason beyond stage 3 on Kohlberg's scale and often justify their decisions at the level of stage 1 or 2 (Edwards, 1982; Harkness, Edwards, & Super, 1981; Kohlberg, 1969; Tietjen & Walker, 1985) (see Figure 17.7).

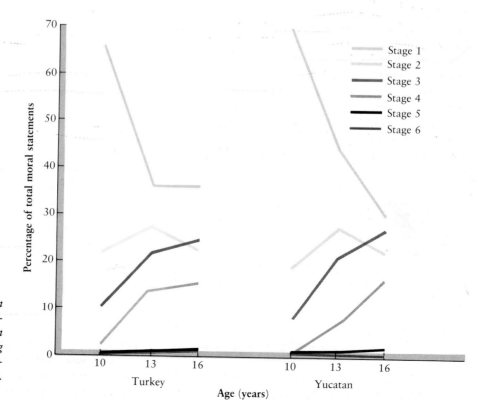

FIGURE 17.7 *Age trends in the moral judgments of boys living in small isolated villages in two nations. Note the continuing high incidence of level-1 responses even by 16-year-olds. (From Kohlberg, 1969.)*

Kohlberg explained cross-cultural data such as those shown in Figure 17.7 by suggesting that cultural differences in social stimulation produce differences in the ability to engage in formal operational reasoning, which, in turn, explains differences in moral reasoning:

> . . . an absence of cognitive stimulation necessary for developing formal logical reasoning may be important in explaining ceilings on moral level. In a Turkish village, for example, full formal operational reasoning appeared to be extremely rare (if the Piagetian technique for intellectual assessment can be considered usable in that setting). Accordingly, one would not expect that principled (Stage 5 or 6) moral reasoning, which requires formal thinking as a base, could develop in that cultural context. (1984, p. 198)

A number of critics have pointed out the unfortunate implications that follow from Kohlberg's willingness to accept the validity of Piagetian techniques and to apply his own moral standards to different cultures. Anthropologist Richard Shweder (1982), for example, claims that there are culture-specific value judgments built directly into the stage sequence itself, which make it no more than a justification for the special cultural perspective of Anglo males, inheritors of the political ideology of liberal democracy. Are we to believe, such critics ask, that people growing up in a small, traditional Third World village are less moral than city residents of industrially advanced countries (Simpson, 1974)? Isn't it more reasonable to assume that because the Turkish villagers live in face-to-face contact with the people who govern their fate, the Golden Rule, a morality of caring and responsibility, should be given the greatest moral value?

The same doubts are expressed in a different way by historian Howard Kaminsky (1984):

> Is a Stage 6 refusal to support a friend who is wrong superior to a Stage 3 loyalty to that friend? A medieval nobleman would say no, and history suggests to us that if we repudiate the nobleman's sense of right, we are also repudiating the civilization created in resonance with his mentality, as well as those elements of the aristocratic ideal that have formed the modern sense of individuality. . . . [P]ersonal loyalty has obvious virtues that are lost when friendship or affection is made conditional on abstract rightness. (p. 410)

Kohlberg denied claims that bias in his scales fosters the conclusion that some societies, including the United States, are more moral than others. He echoed the classical position of modern anthropology, that cultures should be thought of as unique configurations of beliefs and institutions that help the social group to adapt to both local conditions and universal aspects of life on earth (Boas, 1911; Geertz, 1984). Consistent with this relativistic view of cultures, Kohlberg wrote that "We do not understand how a 'moral ranking' of cultures could either be done or be scientifically useful" (1984, p. 311). In this view, a culture in which stage 3 was the height of moral reasoning would be considered morally equivalent to a culture dominated by stage 5 or 6 reasoning, even though the specific reasoning practices could be scored as less developed according to Kohlberg's universal criteria.

Kohlberg's position on cultural levels of moral development would be logically consistent, whatever else one thought of it, were it not for the nagging problem that he had already proposed that people living in other cultures are at a lower level of *cognitive* development, which is not relative. As a result of this crucial link between formal operational thinking and moral judgment, Kohlberg's view is vulnerable to his critics' claims that higher scores on his scale of moral development really do imply "moral superiority" at both the individual and cultural level (e.g., Liebert, 1984; Simpson, 1974).

Despite many uncertainties arising from disagreements about how data should be gathered and interpreted, the evidence collected around the world indicates that by the time they become adolescents, young people are capable of reasoning at least at a level corresponding to the Golden Rule. That they often fail to live up to this basic moral tenet reflects the wry wisdom contained in the old aphorism "Do as I say, not as I do."

INTEGRATION OF THE SELF

One of the most widely held ideas about adolescence is that the individual forges the basis for a stable adult personality during this period. The ability to reason about society, to tell right from wrong, and to examine the basis for one's moral principles are all important to establishing an integrated adult sense of identity.

Two aspects of forming an integrated sense of self have dominated discussions of adolescent personality development: the need to come to terms with the problems brought on by sexual maturity and the need to cope with the new social relations of work and responsibility in the adult community.

The Psychosexual Resolution

In the years of middle childhood, most young people strongly prefer to spend time with members of their own sex (Hayden-Thompson, Rubin, & Hymel, 1987). During this time, a girl's sense of self depends upon how other girls respond to her. Following puberty, as we saw in Chapter 16, a girl's sense of self must also include what boys think of her. Boys, too, must include the opinions of the opposite sex in arriving at a sense of self. As a result of the changes brought on by puberty, the childhood sense of self must change from one based on opposition to the other sex to one based on interdependence of the sexes.

The process of readjustment that begins when the biological events of puberty disrupt the delicate psychological balance of middle childhood (latency) is the focus of Freud's theory of adolescent personality formation. In the Freudian view, adolescence is a period when children recapitulate the conflicts of earlier stages in new guises. These problems must be worked through and resolved, or a distorted adult personality will result.

Central among the early developmental problems that must be reworked, according to Freud, is the primitive desire of young children to possess the parent of the opposite sex. The earlier resolution of this conflict, which Freud called the *oedipus conflict,* was to repress illicit desire by identifying with the same-sex parent. Freud maintained that this infantile resolution was essential to proper sex-role identification (see Chapter 11, p. 349).

When these early oedipal feelings are encountered again in adolescence, repression and identification with members of the same sex are no longer the adaptive responses that they were at the end of infancy. The reawakening of sexual desires during puberty comes at a time when adolescents are fully capable both of carrying out the forbidden acts and of understanding the incest taboos that deny them the parent as a sexual partner.

The combination of awakened desire and social constraint leads the adolescent to seek people outside the family to love. The basis for this search has been established in the peer group experience of middle childhood, but the adolescent's reorientation is nonetheless fraught with difficulties. To begin with, the young person has had little experience of friendship with opposite-sex peers and virtually no experience interacting with peers as sexual partners; new modes of social behavior will have to be learned. Secondly, a shift in the object of affection from a parent to a peer requires emotional disengagement from the family, which has been the bedrock of emotional security since birth. Recognizing the difficulty of this task, Freud referred to the adolescent's reorientation of affection as "one of the most painful psychical achievements of the pubertal period" (Freud, 1905/1953, p. 227).

Painful or not, the adolescent's reorientation from family to peers is viewed as essential by Freudian scholars. If, for example, a girl refuses to give up her dependence on her parents' love and authority, she may lack the capacity to love her husband. She may also, Freud (1905/1953) claimed, become a sexually cold wife because she is fixated at a level of development where love is asexual. Similarly, a young man who fails to reorient his affections may find himself attracted only by older women, and may later involve his mother too intimately in his marriage, evoking the anger and alienation of his wife. Successful adolescent adjustment, therefore, should both reawaken old conflicts and provide a new equilibrium within socially acceptable constraints.

Freud believed that these competing demands and the stress that they induce make adolescent personality especially susceptible to disorders that may have lasting effects. Freud's daughter, Anna, an important psychoanalyst in her own right, concentrated on the period of adolescence because of her concern about its special dangers. As she conceived it, to regain psychological balance the ego must avoid overassociation with either the superego or the id. If the ego "allies itself too closely with the superego" (to use her terminology), the resulting adult will be inflexible in personal relations, a slave to social rules. Such a person will experience difficulty in forming attachments to the opposite sex. At the other extreme, if the ego sides too much with the id, "no trace will be left of the previous character of the individual and the entrance into adult life will be marked by a riot of uninhibited gratification of instinct" (A. Freud, 1946, p. 163).

Resolving the Identity Crisis

Erik Erikson also believes that the process of development during adolescence requires a reworking of previously resolved developmental crises. He explains the idea of a **developmental crisis as follows:**

> At a given age, a human being, by dint of his physical, intellectual and emotional growth, becomes ready and eager to face a new life task, that is, a set of choices and tests which are in some traditional way prescribed and prepared for him by his society's structure. A new life task presents a *crisis* whose outcome can be a successful graduation, or alternatively, an impairment of the life cycle which will aggravate future crises. Each crisis prepares the next, as one step leads to another; and each crisis also lays one more cornerstone for the adult personality. (1958, p. 254; italics in original)

The earlier developmental crises that adolescents must rework, according to Erikson, are the following:

1. *Establishing trust,* the problem that infants encounter as part of the attachment process, reappears in adolescence as the search for people to have faith in, people to whom one can prove one's own trustworthiness. This search goes on at several levels simultaneously. First, one seeks trustworthy and admirable friends. At the beginning of adolescence these are friends of the same sex who can be trusted to share your anxieties without making fun of you. Later, the focus shifts to partners of the opposite sex who will find you attractive and love you.

   The need to establish trust extends to the larger social world, where it takes the form of a search for political causes and leaders worth supporting. To succeed at this level, adolescents must think through a system of ideas about human nature and society (an *ideology*) in which to place their trust. The difficulties of this search are often expressed in mistrust and cynical expressions of indifference about adult social institutions.

2. *Establishing autonomy* was expressed at the end of infancy as the 2-year-old's demand to "do it myself!" Now autonomy means the opportunity to choose one's own path in life instead of going along with decisions imposed by parents.

3. *Taking initiative,* which was expressed as pretend play during early childhood, now means setting goals for what one might become, rather than settling for the limited reality that adults have arranged. The imaginary situations of preschool play find their counterparts in new dreams of greatness that the adolescent can seek to act on in the real world.

4. *Industry* takes on a new meaning toward the end of adolescence quite different from its meaning during middle childhood. No longer will the tasks be set by the teacher; the relative independence of adulthood carries with it the duty to take responsibility for setting goals and for the quality of one's work.

Recall from Chapter 16 that Erikson sees the fundamental task of adolescence as the need to achieve a secure sense of identity or confront the problem of identity confusion. The process of **identity formation** during adolescence requires the simultaneous integration of the resolutions of all four previous crises if a healthy adult personality is to result. What is special about the process of identity formation during adolescence is that for the first time physical maturation, cognitive skills, and social expectations come together in a manner that makes it possible for young people to "sort through and synthesize their childhood identifications in order to construct a viable pathway toward adulthood" (Marcia, 1980, p. 160).

For Erikson, the integration process of adolescent identity formation involves more than the individual personality. In order to forge a secure identity, adolescents must resolve their identities in both the individual and the social spheres or, as Erikson put it, establish "the identity of these two identities" (1968a, p. 22). Some idea of the intellectual complexity of this task can be gleaned from Erikson's attempt to specify the thought processes required to achieve identity formation:

Adolescence is a time when young people must confront adult stereotypes and come to their own decisions about who they are and what kind of identity they want to achieve.

. . . in psychological terms, identity formation employs a process of simultaneous reflection and observation, a process taking place on all levels of mental functioning, by which the individual judges himself in the light of what he perceives to be the way in which others judge him in comparison to themselves and to a typology significant to them; while he judges their way of judging him in the light of how he perceives himself in comparison to them and to types that have become relevant to him. (1968a, pp. 22–23)

The complicated language of this passage is worth careful study because it fits very nicely with cognitive psychologists' theories about the new complexity of thought that becomes possible during adolescence. Erikson's core idea is that each person's identity-forming processes depend on the following:

1. How you judge others

2. How others judge you

3. How you judge the judgment process of others

4. The ability to keep in mind social categories ("typologies") available in the culture when making judgments about other people

Moreover, it is not enough to take only one or two of these elements into account—say, how you judge others using social categories of importance to you ("Sam is a jerk for allowing himself to be caught smoking behind the gym"). Rather, to produce an integrated sense of identity, you must simultaneously consider both your own and other people's judgments, plus the perspective of society (embodied in the linguistic categories used to formulate the judgments) if your judgment of Sam is to be complete with respect to your own identity. It may be that Sam was caught smoking behind the gym, but if you also smoke, or if you also cut class, does that make you a "jerk" too? Or is "getting caught" the only way to be a jerk? And wouldn't Sam think you were a jerk for attending a dumb civics lesson just because you are the "teacher's pet"? And what would your teacher think if he knew whom you had been with at 11:30 last night and what you were doing?

Erikson's characterization of the developmental tasks of adolescence makes it clear that the process of identity formation is likely to be difficult for families and friends as well as for the adolescents themselves. Young people suffering from identity confusion sometimes take out their feelings on others, resulting in antisocial, sometimes criminal behavior (see Figure 17.8).

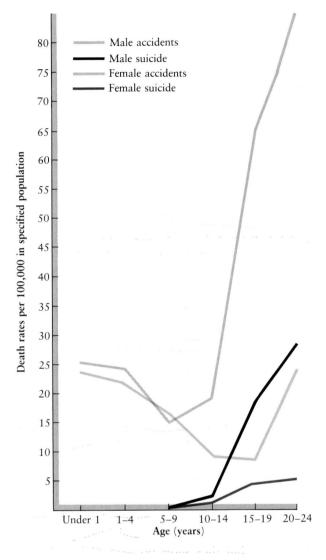

FIGURE 17.8 *Adolescence is a time when young people are at increasing risk of dying accidentally or from suicide. Especially striking is the precipitous increase in adolescent male mortality caused by accidents or suicide. Researchers contend that many suicides are reported as accidents because of the social stigma attached to suicide. Experts estimate that there are at least 50 suicide attempts for every successful suicide (U.S. Select Panel for the Promotion of Child Health, 1981). While girls attempt suicide more often than boys, they are less likely to be successful.*

Youth after youth, bewildered by the incapacity to assume a role forced on him by the inexorable standardization of American adolescence, runs away in one form or another, dropping out of school, leaving jobs, staying out all night, or withdrawing into bizarre and inaccessible moods. (Erikson, 1968a, p. 132)

Here we have the Eriksonian version of Hall's and Freud's vision of an emotionally stormy adolescence, clothed in modern terminology and modern examples.

Evaluating Erikson's ideas about identity It has proven difficult to create explicit, objective methods

for testing Erikson's ideas about identity. Not only do many different threads enter into the process of establishing an identity, but each person must create a unique synthesis of all the disparate parts (Marcia, 1980; Waterman, 1985).

One of Erikson's favorite methods for testing his ideas was the biographical case study, such as his famous biographies of Martin Luther and Mahatma Gandhi (Erikson, 1958, 1969). These studies produced fascinating interpretations of these great men's psychological states. But applying such a method to the everyday problems of contemporary teenagers who are experiencing identity confusion is time-consuming, expensive, and difficult.

The great popularity of Erikson's ideas about identity has created a demand for psychodiagnostic techniques that bypass the laborious process of constructing biographical accounts (Constantinople, 1969; Grotevant, 1986; Marcia, 1966; Waterman, 1985). James Marcia, for example, devised a relatively brief interview in which 86 male college students were asked about their choice of occupation as well as the nature of their beliefs about religion and politics. Harold Grotevant, William Thorbecke, and Margaret Meyer (1982) extended Marcia's interview questions to include the interpersonal domains of friendship, dating, and sex roles. The questions in these interviews are designed to elicit information on the degree to which individuals have adopted and fully committed themselves to a well-thought-out point of view.

On the basis of interview answers, Marcia (1966) identified four patterns of coping with the task of identity formation:

1. *Identity achievers* These adolescents show that they have experienced a decision-making period about their choice of occupation, for example, or their political or religious commitment. They are now actively pursuing their own goals. When people in this group were asked about their political beliefs, for instance, they would respond with answers such as "I have thought it over, and I have decided to be a _____. Their program is the most sensible one for the country to be following."

2. *Foreclosers* These young people are also committed to occupational and ideological positions, but they show no signs of having gone through an identity crisis. In a sense they never really undergo a personality reorganization. Instead, they just take over patterns of identity from their parents. They respond to questions about their political beliefs with such answers as "I really never gave the question of politics any thought. Our family always votes _____, so that's how I vote."

3. *Moratoriums* This is the label Marcia gives to adolescents who are currently experiencing an adolescent identity crisis. They would be likely to answer a question about their political beliefs by saying "I'm not sure. Both parties have their good points, but neither one seems to offer a better chance for my economic future."

Some teenagers become upset because they cannot reconcile themselves to the identity that they perceive for themselves. Running away is one response to such psychological conflicts.

4. *Identity diffusions* These adolescents have tried out several identities without being able to settle on one. They are likely to take a cynical attitude toward the issues confronting them, so they might answer questions about political commitment by declaring "I stopped thinking about politics ages ago. There are no parties worth following."

If Erikson's ideas about identity formation are successfully captured by Marcia's categories, there ought to be a consistent shift away from identity diffusion toward identity achievement as children grow older. This expectation is confirmed by a large number of studies summarized by Alan Waterman (1985). The proportion of identity achievers increases steadily from the years preceding high school to the late college years, while the proportion manifesting identity diffusion decreases (see Table 17.5, which shows the relevant data on occupational choice). Consistent with Erikson's belief that identity formation is a process

TABLE 17.5 Percent manifesting difference identity statuses in the domain of vocational choice

| Age Group | Identity Achievement | Identity Status | | Identity Diffusion |
		Moratorium	Foreclosure	
Pre-high school years	5.2	11.7	36.6	46.4
High school underclass years	9.0	14.6	37.1	39.3
High school upperclass years	21.3	13.5	36.0	29.2
College underclass years	22.8	28.3	25.7	23.2
College upperclass years	39.7	15.5	31.3	13.5

SOURCE: Waterman, 1985.

rather than a trait, researchers find a general shift toward identity achievement well into adulthood as individuals readjust their understandings of themselves in terms of their experiences (Waterman & Waterman, 1971). In addition, Waterman (1985) reports that the level of identity achievement differs according to the domain in question; the level of identity achievement is considerably lower for political ideology than for vocational choice.

A number of studies have explored the influence of experiences within the family on identity achievement. Harold Grotevant and Catherine Cooper (1985), for example, examined the way in which family interactions in a specially constructed "family interaction task" correlated with scores for identity achievement.

The identity that one adopts is influenced by the admired role models in one's community.

In the family interaction task, a mother, father, and their adolescent are asked to make plans for a two-week vacation together. Twenty minutes are given for them to arrive at a day-by-day plan, including both the location and the activity for each day. The discussions are scored for the way in which family members express their individuality (for example, through stating their own point of view or through disagreeing with another family member) and their connectedness (for example, through their responsiveness and sensitivity to others' points of view).

Grotevant and Cooper interviewed the adolescents in these families to find out how much they had explored a variety of options for their futures. They hypothesized that identity exploration would be related to individuality — the adolescent had to learn how to develop a distinctive point of view — as well as to connectedness — the family had to provide a secure base from which the adolescent could explore. In their study of middle-class Anglo families, these researchers found that adolescents' interactions with their parents were associated with identity exploration, but in different ways for sons and daughters. For sons, greater identity exploration was associated with a willingness on the part of their fathers to allow disagreement, to compromise, and to modify their own suggestions in light of what adolescents said. This did not mean that the fathers were pushovers; rather, they were willing to engage in genuine give and take. For daughters, a higher degree of identity exploration was associated with family communication that involved daughters disagreeing and showing assertiveness in making suggestions. Despite the different patterns, it appears safe to say that a family system that both encourages the

When adolescents are struggling to achieve a stable identity, they often prefer to spend time by themselves to think through their problems.

adolescent to create a distinct identity and offers support and security appears to be most effective in promoting identity achievement.

Sexual and cultural variation in identity formation Investigations of possible sex differences and cultural variations in identity formation have raised problems similar to those encountered in attempts to understand adolescent modes of thinking. Freud (1905) claimed that the psychosexual dynamics of development are universal across cultures but different for the two sexes. In contrasting the adolescent resolution of males and females, Freudian psychoanalyst Peter Blos has claimed that

> [a boy's] energies are directed outward toward control of and dominance over the physical world. The girl, in contrast, turns — either in fact or fantasy — with deep-felt emotionality, mixed of romantic tenderness, possessiveness, and envy, to the boy. While the boy sets out to master the physical world, the girl endeavors to deal with relationships. (1972, p. 61)

Erikson also believes that there are significant sex differences in the process of forming an identity. Like Freud, Erikson asserts that "anatomy is destiny." According to this view, a woman's biological makeup determines her social role as an adult, when she has greater responsibility for child rearing and homemaking. At times Erikson has softened his stance by noting that "nothing in our interpretation . . . is meant to claim that either sex is doomed to one . . . mode or another; rather . . . these modes "come more naturally.' . . ." (1968a, p. 273). Within the limits set by the norms of the social group, adolescent females, like adolescent males, try out various roles and modes of life.

Recent research provides mixed evidence on Erikson's claims about sex differences. Waterman (1985) summarized several studies in which interviews of the type designed by Marcia (1966) were used. He found only "weak and inconsistent evidence" that males and females follow different paths to identity achievement in the domains of vocational choice, religious belief, political ideology, and sex roles. However, Thorbecke and Grotevant (1982), using similar interviews, found

TABLE 17.6   Views of adolescent girls and boys on family and career priorities

Views of Girls	Views of Boys
I might be a mother and not a wife. Having a husband is just like your father. You can't go out, can't do anything. You have to cook, clean, take care of the children and still work.	If I was into sports, my wife and kids would have to travel and stay in a little room — but there's nothing that couldn't be worked out.
If I have a career and a husband who doesn't want me to work, I'll do what I want.	If I am a musician, on tour, my wife's going to get worried. I wouldn't try to bring it home. We'd talk and just give it some time. Sometimes it shouldn't interfere.
I intend to have a career. Being a wife is okay; it's not so much of a strain. Kids are a strain. Maybe I can talk him into adopting a 5-year-old; or stop my career. If I am into my career, especially at my peak, it would really hurt.	I would enjoy something like marriage and family. I'd love to have my own kid at the right time. I look forward to it. You have a wife to be with and share time with. Helping each other out. But you're tied down. Can't go out with the guys.

SOURCE: Archer, 1985.

that adolescent females score higher than males in the domain of friendship, while Archer (1985) found that females score higher in the domain of choices about combining career and family. Archer's interviews also provide illustrations of female ambivalence and confusion as adolescent girls in the United States confront the dilemmas that are inherent in the cultural expectations and standard social roles that await them (see Table 17.6).

A difficult problem facing many young women in their search for identity is to find a satisfactory way to reconcile vocational choice and sex roles.

In comparison to the shaky evidence for sex differences, cultural differences in identity formation seem a virtual certainty (Fogelson, 1982; Geertz, 1984; Hallowell, 1955; Rosaldo, 1984). Consider, for example, Marcia's assertion that for healthy identity formation to occur, adolescents must, at a minimum, make a "commitment to a sexual orientation, an ideological stance, and a vocational choice" (1980, p. 160). It makes sense to think of identity formation as a difficult "crisis" in the context of the contemporary United States, where questions of choice abound, especially for adolescents. But it almost certainly does not apply among people whose cultures adhere to long-held, unified world views and prescribe both eventual marriage partners and occupations. Unfortunately, knowledge of identity formation in such circumstances is too limited to enable scholars to gauge the extent to which the processes observed to occur in our own culture are universal.

THE TRANSITION TO ADULTHOOD

As we commented in the introduction to the discussion of adolescence, no developmental transition following birth is so well marked as the end of middle childhood. Profound changes in the size and shape of children's bodies are an unmistakable sign that they are "ripening." However, certainty about the end of middle childhood is not the same as certainty that a distinctive stage called adolescence is beginning. Is adolescence really a stage in the same way that infancy or middle childhood is, or is it more like an uneven transition between stages, as Piaget sometimes conceived early childhood to be?

We have seen that in at least two key respects, the period between middle childhood and adulthood does not fit the pattern of earlier stages. First, since in many societies the onset of puberty coincides closely with marriage and the adoption of adult roles, it is by no means certain that adolescence—considered as the stage *before* adulthood—is universal. Second, in societies such as our own in which there is an extended delay between puberty and adult status, the factors that make up a bio-social-behavioral shift do not seem to converge in the relatively well-coordinated manner of earlier stages. Consequently, it is important to reconsider the nature of adolescence and to take seriously the possibility that adolescence is not a stage of development but reflects instead a slow transition between childhood and adulthood in which aspects of the two stages commingle (Fox, 1977).

Is Adolescence a Distinctive Stage of Development?

A first step toward resolving uncertainties about adolescence as a distinctive stage is to note that we have been using two phrases, *the transition from middle childhood to adulthood* and *adolescence* as if they were more or less synonyms for each other. In fact, as ordinarily used by psychologists, *transition* and *stage* are not synonyms. A stage is a more or less stable, patterned, and enduring system of interactions between the organism and the environment; a transition is a period of flux, when the "ensemble of the whole" that makes up one stage has disintegrated and a new stage is not firmly in place. The transition from middle childhood to adulthood is universal, but what part of the phenomenon called adolescence should also be considered universal?

Bloch and Niederhoffer (1958) suggest one of the universal features shared by both the notion of a "transition to adulthood" and "adolescence": a struggle for adult status. In all societies, the old eventually give way to the young. It is not easy for those in power to give it up, so it is natural to expect that to some degree, the granting of adult status, and with it, adult power, will involve a struggle. Freud's focus on the difficulties of making the transition from latency to mature sexuality identifies a second universal feature, one that arouses tension but that is necessary for the continuation of human society. It is not easy for children, who have long identified strongly with members of their own sex, to become attached to a member of the opposite sex. Whether or not these necessary changes require an entire stage of development for their realization remains, however, to be demonstrated.

Often the argument for the universality of adolescence as a stage of development is based on historical evidence such as the following:

> The young are in character prone to desire and ready to carry any desire they may have formed into action. Of bodily desires it is the sexual to which they are most disposed to give way, and in regard to sexual desire they exercise no self-restraint. They are changeful too, and fickle in their desires, which are as transitory as they are vehement. . . . They are passionate, irascible, and apt to be carried away by their impulses. . . . They regard themselves as omniscient and are positive in their assertions; this is, in fact, the reason for their carrying everything too far. . . . Finally, they are fond of laughter and consequently facetious, facetiousness being disciplined insolence. (quoted in Kiell, 1964, pp. 18–19)

This description has a certain timeless quality to it. It could be a description of members of a high school clique in almost any modern city or town, or it might be a description of Romeo and his friends in medieval Verona. In fact, it is a description of youth in the fourth century B.C., written by the Greek philosopher Aristotle. Combining such historical evidence with similar accounts from a tribal village in Africa or a Winnebago Indian village in Nebraska leads naturally enough to a belief that the experience of adolescence is universal. However, the universality of adolescence as a unified stage is by no means clearly established on the basis of these data.

First, there is a noticeable shortcoming in the evidence cited from ancient societies; women are largely excluded. In Aristotle's description of adolescents and in similar descriptions from other ancient societies

(Kiell, 1964), the people being talked about are clearly males. Moreover, they are urban males of the monied classes who did indeed undergo a period of extended training, often including formal schooling, which created a delay between puberty and full adult status. Generally speaking, women and most members of the lower classes did not undergo such specialized training, nor is there evidence that they were ever included in the category of adolescents.

Second, the evidence from other cultures may support the idea that the transition to adult status is universally fraught with anxiety and uncertainty, but it provides equally strong evidence that adolescence, as the term is used in modern industrialized societies, exists only under particular cultural circumstances (Whiting, Burbank, & Ratner, 1986). When researchers make the assumption that adolescence exists in societies that have no concept for it and no set of social practices corresponding to it, they do violence to the facts.

Among the Inuit Eskimos of the Canadian Arctic at the turn of the century, for example, special terms were used to refer to boys and girls when they entered puberty, but these terms did not coincide with the usual notion of adolescence (Condon, 1987). Young women were considered fully grown (adult) at menarche, a change in status marked by the fact that they were likely to be married by this time and ready to start bearing children within a few years. Young men were considered fully grown as soon as they were able to build a snowhouse and hunt large game unassisted. This might occur shortly after the onset of puberty, but it was more likely for boys to achieve adult status somewhat later because they had to prove first that they could support themselves and their families. In view of the different life circumstances of these people, it is not surprising that they developed no special concept corresponding to adolescence which applied to boys and girls alike; such a concept did not correspond to their reality.

Adolescence in Modern Societies

Granted that a social category corresponding to adolescence may arise only in certain cultural circumstances, we are still left with the problem of understanding the developmental dynamics of young people who fit this category in our own society. If we want to claim that adolescence is a stage of development in modern societies, does it adhere to the same rules of stage organization and stage transition as earlier stages, or is it unique in important respects?

When the roots of adolescence in the United States and other modern industrialized societies are traced, it appears to be closely associated with the existence of apprenticeship training or formal schooling; that is, with a period of waiting until the designated adult role becomes available, through a marriage proposal or an inheritance, for instance (Ariès, 1962; Fox, 1977; Gillis, 1974; Kett, 1977). Although scattered examples of the concept of adolescence can be found in ancient civilizations, it was only during the nineteenth century, when formal schooling was introduced on a mass basis for both sexes, that adolescence became a generally recognized and pervasive category defining children of a certain age regardless of sex and social class.

The crucial factors introduced by formal schooling are a long delay in achieving economic self-sufficiency and prolongation of socialization in contexts that are institutionally separated from the real processes of production and adult life. In the United States, for example, young people are required to attend school for 12 or more years and are expected to abstain from starting a family during that period.

Consequently, some but not all aspects of the bio-social-behavioral shift that defines adolescence in modern societies coincide in the manner that characterized earlier stages. To be sure, biological maturation simultaneously gives rise to new desires and emotions, and to new forms of social relationship. Intimate friendships with peers of the same sex are supplemented by, and in some cases supplanted by, intimate love relationships with members of the opposite sex. These intimate sexual relationships are accompanied by a loosening of family ties, as if in anticipation of the new family configuration to come. Although different theorists dispute the details (they argue, for example, about how much conflict and discontent the process of change engenders), they agree about the overall pattern of change during adolescence since the observed connections between the biological and social domains seem to occur in a logical fashion. (See Table 17.7 for a summary of the elements in the transition to adulthood.)

However, an important element in the "social" part of the bio-social-behavioral shift that defines the tran-

TABLE 17.7 The bio-social behavioral transition to adulthood

Biological domain

Capacity for biological reproduction
Development of secondary sexual characteristics
Attainment of adult size

Behavioral domain

Achievement of formal operations in some areas (systematic thinking)
Formation of identity

Social domain

Sexual relations
Shift toward primary responsibility for oneself
Beginning of responsibility for next generation

tional cognitive abilities that are supposed to make their appearance at this time. In many other situations, however, both their social roles and their thought processes can be expected to remain distinctly "adolescent."

In summary, the historical and cross-cultural evidence, when combined with what we know about the transition from childhood to adulthood in our own society, suggests the following formulation: The transition to adulthood universally engenders conflict as young people come to terms with sexual maturity and the need to adopt adult roles. However, adolescence, as a recognized stage of development during which the young person is prepared for adult roles, is not universal. Consequently, the transition to adulthood will be experienced differently according to one's cultural circumstances.

sition to adulthood for Piaget and other stage theorists is the partial failure of part of the social system to change at the expected time. With some exceptions, such as participation in adult work, modern young people are offered carefully arranged substitutes for real adult roles. Instead of the responsibility for conducting real chemistry experiments, students are given exercises that model the ideal practice of chemists. Instead of responsibility for running their own school, students are given a student government with elected officers, laws, and legislatures, but no power. Instead of responsibility for informing the community of important events, students are allowed to run student newspapers whose topics are carefully circumscribed by rule and custom.

Thus, if modern adolescence is to be considered a separate stage of development, we must admit that it combines biological, social, and behavioral factors in a way unlike that of any of the stages that preceded it. In place of a full bio-social-behavioral shift, some of the changes in the social sphere are replaced by simulated forms of adult social activities.

The uneven character of adolescent thinking that makes the special psychological characteristics of this age period so difficult to pin down grows directly out of the artificial nature of some of the changes occurring in the social sphere. When adolescents throw themselves into an activity as if it were "for real" or in those rare cases where they are allowed or required to take on adult roles (e.g., in certain work situations, or if a mother falls ill), they may display the formal opera-

Looking Ahead

The modern trend toward extension and intensification of adolescence comes from the same forces that created this concept in the first place. It is a virtual certainty that in the decades to come, young people will be expected to achieve higher levels of educational knowledge than ever before (U.S. Department of Education, 1984). In part, this increased achievement will be sought through intensification of education in the lower grades, longer school hours, and more days of schooling per year. But to gain access to higher paying and more secure jobs, young people will also be ex-

pected to spend more years in school, which will further delay their independent working lives and prolong their economic dependence. These economic factors suggest that either we will see further extensions of adolescence or, as psychologist Kenneth Keniston (1970) has suggested, we will see the invention of a new stage of development occupying a place somewhere between the current stages of adolescence and adulthood, during which young people will achieve some forms of autonomy not currently accorded to adolescents, but will still stop short of the full responsibilities of adults.

SUMMARY

1. When compared with the thinking of younger children, adolescent thinking is typified by five characteristics:
   a. Thinking about possibilities
   b. Thinking through hypotheses
   c. Thinking ahead
   d. Thinking about thought
   e. Thinking beyond conventional limits

2. Piagetian theory attributes these characteristics to the emergence of formal operations, in which all possible logical aspects of a problem are thought about as a structured whole. The core of Piaget's evidence comes from observations of problem solving modeled on scientific experiments.

3. Contrary to classical Piagetian theory, not everyone proves capable of solving Piagetian formal operational tasks, even in adulthood. In some societies, virtually no adults can solve these problems. However, non-Piagetian versions of formal operational thinking occur in some contexts in all societies.

4. Difficulties with Piaget's explanations of adolescent thought processes have inspired attempts at alternative explanations.
   a. Information-processing approaches hypothesize that increased memory capacity, increased efficiency in the use of strategies and rules, and the ability to form abstract verbal concepts — rather than changes in the logic of thought — account for adolescents' new thought processes.
   b. Theorists of several persuasions have suggested that developments in the domain of language are crucial to the emergence of new cognitive abilities during adolescence.
   c. Cultural-context theorists propose that involvement in new activities creates the conditions for a new level of systematic thought. This achievement is assumed to occur in all societies but is always bound to the demands of particular contexts.

5. The more powerful thought processes manifest themselves in new ways of thinking about the social world, including moral problems and politics.

6. While some psychologists assume that increased intellectual capacities result in higher levels of moral and political behavior, the evidence linking reasoning ability with actual behavior shows that many other factors are involved.

7. Variability in the way that sex and culture affect adolescents' and adults' reasoning about moral standards has led some theorists to propose that there are a variety of moral orientations, rather than a single sequence of moral development.

8. Personality development during adolescence requires the integration of new sexual capacities and new social relations with the personality characteristics accumulated since birth.

9. According to Freud, this reintegration is set off because new sexual desires upset the balance of id, ego, and superego; the resolution requires that the individual find an appropriate person to love, bringing to a close the oedipal conflict of infancy.

10. According to Erikson, adolescence is the time when the person recapitulates and resolves all earlier developmental crises in order to form an adult identity.

11. According to both Freudian and Eriksonian theories of adolescent personality, failure to resolve past crises leads to neurotic adult personalities.

12. Both Freudian and Eriksonian theories hypothesize that there are sex differences in adolescent personality formation, but both offer relatively weak evidence about the course of female development. Evidence on whether there are cultural variations in adolescent personality formation is generally lacking.

13. The extent of cultural variability in the psychological characteristics of young people following the end of middle childhood raises the possibility that in some so-cieties adolescence is better thought of as a transitional period between childhood and adulthood rather than as a distinct developmental stage.

KEY TERMS

Developmental crisis

Formal operations

Identity formation

Second-order thinking

Structured whole

SUGGESTED READINGS

ADELSON, JOSEPH (Ed.). *Handbook of Adolescence.* New York: Wiley, 1980.

Chapters by leading experts in the field survey all of the major issues currently under investigation.

DRAGASTIN, SIGMUND and GLEN H. ELDER, JR. (Eds.). *Adolescence in the Life Cycle,* New York: Wiley, 1974.

This book, edited by a science administrator and by one of the early champions of a life-span approach to the study of development, places adolescence in historical and social context. Individual articles are particularly effective in treating adolescence as an integral part of the life cycle.

ERIKSON, ERIK H. *Identity: Youth in Crisis.* New York: Norton, 1968.

This is the classic monograph by perhaps the most influential theorist of adolescent psychology in the twentieth century.

GILLIGAN, CAROL. *In a Different Voice: Psychological Theory and Women's Development.* Cambridge, Mass.: Harvard University Press, 1982.

A major statement on sex differences in psychological development. Gilligan argues that women have a different orientation to the social world, and hence to themselves, than men do. This in turn leads to a different basis for the development of moral reasoning for each sex.

INHELDER, BARBEL and JEAN PIAGET. *The Growth of Logical Thinking from Childhood to Adolescence.* New York: Basic Books, 1958.

This is the classic monograph on formal operational thinking. In order to obtain an overall grasp of the Piagetian view of adolescent thought patterns, it is helpful to read the final chapter before plunging into the details of particular studies.

KOHLBERG, LAWRENCE. *The Psychology of Moral Development: The Nature and Validity of Moral Stages.* New York: Harper and Row, 1984.

This volume brings together many of Kohlberg's seminal papers on moral development. It includes theoretical papers that give the overall approach, and important empirical papers that provide the basic evidence for and against the theory.

STERNBERG, ROBERT J. *Intelligence Applied: Understanding and Increasing Your Intellectual Skills.* San Diego: Harcourt Brace Jovanovich, 1986.

In addition to providing an up-to-date discussion of theories of intelligence and their implications for adult functioning, this book is filled with interesting examples of problems that call upon the kinds of intellectual processes that come into prominence during adolescence.

DEVELOPMENT
AND
LATER LIFE

The Discovery of Adulthood

Theoretical Approaches to Adulthood and Old Age

The Biological, Social, and Behavioral Course of Later Life

Social Factors and Later Psychological Change

Decline or Continuing Development?

We leave childhood without knowing what youth is, we marry without knowing what it is to be married, and even when we enter old age, we don't know what it is we're heading for: the old are innocent children of their old age. In that sense, man's world is a planet of inexperience.

— Milan Kundera, *The Art of the Novel*

· · ·

We shall not cease from exploration
And the end of all our exploring
Will be to arrive where we started
And know the place for the first time.

— T. S. Eliot, "Little Gidding"

· ·

With the end of the transitional period from childhood to adulthood, known as adolescence, people begin to support themselves economically and to take on new roles, often marrying and founding new families. In common-sense terms, the process of "growing up" has come to an end and the individual is recognized as an adult — "one who has grown up."

Although this way of talking about adulthood is widely accepted in the folk beliefs of many cultures, it poses a new problem for students of human development. When we examined the years from conception through adolescence, we could feel certain that we were dealing with *development*, a sequence of regular age-linked changes in the nature of human beings as they grow toward adulthood. But if adulthood is thought of as the endpoint of development, it follows that once adulthood is reached, development is over. As we looked at earlier periods of life, the conviction that we were dealing with developmental change was supported by the fact that many of the changes under study could in some respect be considered "advances" because they involved a change from less (smaller, weaker, less self-sufficient) to more (larger, stronger, more independent). Generally speaking, change during adulthood does not have a clearly "progressive," upward direction, which raises further doubts about the developmental nature of psychological change in later life.

Questions about psychological change during adulthood might seem to have limited significance for understanding the psychological development of children. However, they are in fact illuminating because they force one to confront basic questions about development in general. Must development be a rapid rise to full individual, physical maturity, followed by a period of equilibrium or decline? Or might it be that development is really a lifetime process, during which we are constantly children in the world of inexperience who return again and again to our starting point, only to know it for the first time?

We will address these questions by applying the same analytic strategy that we used to investigate earlier periods of life. To begin with, we will examine the historical and cultural conditions that lead societies to recognize periods of life after adolescence. As we shall see, the demarcation of adulthood as a stage of life is itself a cultural phenomenon, the boundaries of which vary according to sociohistorical circumstances. Next, we will discuss briefly the major theories of psychological change following adolescence; some of these theories claim that development effectively comes to a close, while others posit a sequence of developmental transformations up to the time of death. With this information as background, we will briefly review evidence concerning biological, social, and behavioral changes as these interact through later life. In light of our previous analyses, we will pay special attention to the applicability of the idea of bio-social-behavioral shifts to the pattern of later life changes.

The Discovery of Adulthood

People in all cultures at all times have known perfectly well that some individuals are grownups and others are children. However, they have differed about the degree to which they have explicitly conceived the period following childhood to be a period of life possessing its own psychological characteristics. They have also differed about the ages at which they expect significant transitions to occur.

As we have seen in previous chapters, the explicit belief that a particular age range constitutes a stage of life depends upon a combination of social and historical factors. Thus, well-articulated conceptions of childhood and adolescence grew up in Europe and the United States in the eighteenth and nineteenth centuries in close conjunction with the origins of schooling and the changing demands of the workplace. The most recent age period to be conceived of explicitly as a life stage is **adulthood,** a period bounded on one side by adolescence and on the other by old age. In adulthood the individual has reached full maturity and responsibility before the law. It was not until the middle of the twentieth century that adult psychological change began to command the attention that had been devoted to infancy and childhood a century earlier.

The first stirrings of social awareness that adulthood might be considered a distinct period of life can be traced back to nineteenth-century Europe and the United States. At that time, social concern was focused on the two social categories that would come to provide the boundaries of adulthood: adolescence, marked by concerns about the need for extended education and the fear that failure to integrate young people properly into the society would lead to crime and social disintegration; and old age, marked by concerns for maintaining people who could no longer care for themselves.

Adolescence was institutionalized several decades before old age was institutionalized as a distinct period. Extended schooling and the passage of child labor laws near the turn of the century created a separate status for adolescents that the elderly did not enjoy. To be sure, it had long been recognized that old age was a time of reduced physical capacities that might cause the elderly to be dependent. Caring for old people had always been a significant family issue; however, it only began to be seen as an important social problem in the late nineteenth century as urbanization separated a growing number of elderly people from the support of their families. However, relatively few people survived into old age, thus, while a problem was acknowledged to exist, it did not seem to constitute a serious threat to the social order.

This situation changed rather abruptly in industrially advanced countries during the early twentieth century due to a dramatic shift in the demographic composition of society brought about by improved health conditions and modern medicine (Uhlenberg, 1980). For example, when the United States was being formed, at the end of the eighteenth century, only 20 percent of the population lived to the age of 70 years; now more than 80 percent do. In 1900 the average life expectancy in the United States was 49 years; today it is approximately 75 years, a 50 percent increase in life expectancy in less than a century.

This increase in life expectancy meant a dramatic increase in the number of people surviving into old age. Their presence placed a great burden of support and care on younger adults. At the same time, their growing numbers increased their political power, so that they made the special needs of the elderly a part of national consciousness.

A critical event that helped mark the boundary between adulthood and old age was the Great Depression of the 1930s, when massive unemployment meant that many adults had no way to maintain themselves as they grew older. The combined factors of greatly in-

Congressman Claude Pepper of Florida is seen here visiting a home for the aged in New York City. Congressman Pepper has gained renown for his legislative efforts on behalf of the elderly.

creased longevity and massive unemployment crystallized public perception of the elderly as a severe social problem. Public consciousness of this problem led to the passage of legislation that stipulated 65 as the official age of retirement and provided the financial assistance of social security.

Once old age was recognized as a distinct period of life, the conditions for a more finely honed awareness of adulthood were achieved; adulthood came into being as a social category referring to the period of life bounded by old age on the one side and by adolescence on the other.

Theoretical Approaches to Adulthood and Old Age

While chronological age clearly advances and people continue to change as they grow older, it is by no means obvious that the psychological changes associated with the process of aging should be considered developmental in the same way that changes earlier in life are. From a purely biological point of view, the endpoint of adult development is death; and biologically speaking, there is a clear sense that once humans can reproduce biologically, change is on a downward course. However, when we include *cultural* reproduction as one of the goals of human development, developmental change is seen as a lifelong process to which the elderly and dying can contribute just as the robust and active do.

Since psychologists are sharply divided over the relative roles of biology and culture in the process of development, it is only natural that they should be sharply divided on the question of whether development continues into adulthood. For example, those who focus on biological maturation as the engine of development are most likely to believe that the process of development ceases by age 30 as biological growth comes to a halt and the process of decay begins.

For example, according to G. Stanley Hall (1922), whose influential book on adolescence was discussed in Part V, the period from puberty to death should be divided into only two parts: adolescence and senescence. Adolescence, he believed, lasted for a long time, into the 30s and 40s, while senescence began where adolescence ended. As he wrote, "all that we have thought characteristic of middle life consists of only

When the mandated age arrives, it is time to retire, regardless of how alert and active one feels. Here a retiring college professor is congratulated by her students.

the phenomena which are connected with the turn of the tide" (1921, p. 294).

Interactionists like Piaget and Freud, who focus on universal aspects of mind, also assume that the process of change itself undergoes a change after adolescence. But rather than seeing adulthood as a slow deterioration, they see it as a long plateau, during which the mature psychological equipment continues to function unchanged so long as the necessary biological support is available.

Freud believed that once young people reach the genital stage and complete the process of sexual reproduction, they have fulfilled their fundamental biological role — to ensure the continuation of the species. To be sure, adults must care for their offspring until they are sufficiently mature to repeat the cycle, but Freud did not attribute any particular developmental significance to the activities of parenting.

In Piagetian theory, formal operations are the logical endpoint of development because they provide an exhaustive logical apparatus that allows a person to maintain a state of cognitive equilibrium. Piaget did recognize that pure logic is an insufficient basis for mature action, pointing out that some of the less attractive aspects of teenage behavior result from adolescents' new discovery of the power of logic, which leads them to act "as though the world should submit itself to idealistic schemes rather than systems of reality" (1967, p. 64). Experience brings about a more realistic balance between the adolescent's newfound powers of systematic thinking and the messiness of life. "Just as experience reconciles formal thought with the reality of things," Piaget wrote, "so does effective and enduring work, undertaken in concrete and well-defined situations, cure dreams" (1967, pp. 68–69).

However, coming to terms with reality did not imply *developmental* change for Piaget; in his view, there existed no stage of thought beyond formal operations. At best, according to this view, changes after adolescence represent a process of consolidation and an increase in judgment about how to employ one's — fundamentally unchanged — cognitive resources.

It is those psychologists who assign a significant role to culture in development who are likely to believe that development is a lifelong process. Instead of concluding that change ends, or even begins a downward spiral in adulthood, these theorists believe that the task of cultural reproduction creates a sequence of new stagelike configurations of psychological processes during adulthood. As in the case of earlier stages, these adult stages are held to apply to an entire population of a particular age period in conjunction with particular sociohistorical circumstances.

For example, followers of L. S. Vygotsky have written about the years from 18 to 30 as a time when psychological processes are organized to achieve competence at productive work activity, and the years from 30 to 60 as "the period of real creativity, when the individual enriches and perhaps reorders" the nature of social life in the community (Markova, 1979, p. 26). Old age, according to this approach, is a time when the individual has the time to look back over a long span of experience, to theorize productively about life itself, and to pass on the results of such theoretical activity to the next generation.

The developmental view of adulthood and old age is most fully elaborated in the writings of Erik Erikson, who has proposed three additional stages beyond adolescence. According to Erikson (1980; Erikson, Erikson, & Kravnik, 1986), **early adulthood** — the years between the ages of 20 and 35 — is a period when adults commit themselves to a love relationship or else develop a sense of isolation. **Middle adulthood** — roughly ages 35 to 65 — is a time when adults must commit themselves to productive work, including the raising of a next generation, or become stagnant and self-centered. **Old age** — 65 years and beyond — is a time when people attempt to make sense out of life and to incorporate the choices they have made in the past. Failure at this stage leads to despair; success results in that elusive quality known as wisdom.

Within the past twenty years, a great deal of scholarly attention has been focused on psychological change during adulthood and old age by medical researchers, historians, anthropologists, and sociologists, in addition to psychologists (Harevan, 1982). New approaches within psychology, such as the study of "life-span" or "life-course" development, have begun to provide detailed accounts of the biological, behavioral, and social changes that influence post-adolescent development (Baltes & Schaie, 1973; Hareven, 1978; Neugarten, 1968; Smelser & Erikson, 1980). Although similar in many respects, these approaches differ somewhat in emphasis. For example, in the **life-span approach,** central phenomena like the sense of self or problem-solving abilities are traced from infancy through old age to determine how they are transformed as a result of both psychological and social change (Baltes & Brim, 1979). The **life-course approach** is more concerned with the relationship between individual change and the timing of major life events, such as the onset of schooling, the time at which someone leaves home, the beginning of childbearing, and retirement from the labor force (Elder, 1974; Hareven, 1982).

While theoretical disagreements remain about whether adult change should be considered "develop-

Although no longer actively working, the elderly have a significant role to play in passing on their knowledge to the younger generation.

ment," empirical knowledge about such changes has burgeoned. We will first review the results of this research and then summarize its implications for understanding human development as a whole.

The Biological, Social, and Behavioral Course of Later Life

Where developmental psychologists once saw adulthood as a featureless plateau, many have now come to see it as a complex landscape with its own special qualities. The scientific challenge is to find a way to describe this newly perceived complexity. The task is a difficult one because change during adulthood does not seem to follow the apparently orderly transformations of earlier years. As Bernice Neugarten and Gunhild Hagestad (1976) point out,

> Ours seems to be a society that has become accustomed to 70-year-old students, 30-year-old college presidents, 22-year-old mayors, 35-year-old grandmothers, 50-year-old retirees, 65-year-old fathers of preschoolers, 60-year-olds and 30-year-olds wearing the same clothing styles and 85-year-old parents caring for 65-year-old offspring. (p. 52)

Despite these difficulties, some major trends are discernible in the ways that adult human beings function as they age.

Biological change In earlier chapters we charted biological growth from conception through adolescence. At every step we encountered *increases* — for example, growth in the size of the body, increased myelination of the brain, improved visual acuity, and greater strength. By about the age of 20 years, this general pattern of increase levels off and biological capacities gradually begin to decrease (see Figure 18.1) (Shock, 1977; Timiras, 1972).

It may be many years before the decreases in biological functioning make themselves felt because the capacity of our various organs is greater than required. However, for people who engage in heavy labor or who are athletes, aging begins to be felt in the early 30s. Muscles no longer have the elasticity and recuperative power they once did; reaction times have begun to slow owing to aging of the brain; and eyesight begins to wane owing to a loss of elasticity in the muscles that focus the lens of the eye.

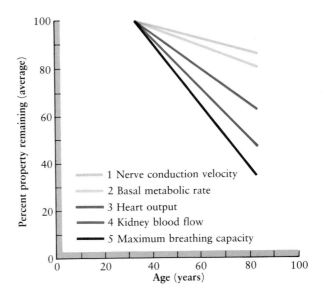

FIGURE 18.1 *The capacity of various bodily organs declines in a linear fashion following the age of 35. (From Shock, 1960.)*

By the age of 50, the decline in biological functioning becomes more evident for most people. It is rare for athletes to continue competing with younger men or women when they enter their fifth decade. Workers engaged in heavy labor or assembly-line jobs find that they can no longer keep up with those who are younger.

Perhaps the only measurable discontinuity in adult biological functioning before the age of 65 or 70 occurs in women, who usually stop ovulating and menstruating sometime between the ages of 45 and 55, a process called **menopause**. At one time, menopause was considered a major turning point in a woman's life because it signaled a change in hormonal output and meant that she could no longer bear children. However, contemporary research has shown that women who are going through menopause or have already gone through it are less concerned about it than younger women who have yet to experience it (Neugarten, Wood, Krames, & Loomis, 1963).

Some researchers have speculated that men also undergo a rapid decrease in hormonal output, a form of "male menopause." However, the dominant view is that men continue to produce testosterone and sperm throughout life, although in progressively smaller quantities (Katchadourian, 1987).

For both sexes, the body's functioning begins to deteriorate markedly sometime after age 65, although there are wide individual differences in the age at which a precipitous decline in biological functioning sets in. As in other periods of life, the organism's condition depends both upon the individual's biological makeup (nature) and upon the healthiness of the individual's environment and way of life (nurture). In some cases, deterioration may reflect the accumulation of small defects, such as when the buildup of residue inside veins and arteries triggers a heart attack or stroke. But even in the absence of any detectable diseases, the body's cells eventually stop dividing, and the individual dies (Hayflick, 1980).

Overall, scientists agree on a picture of biological function that matches many aspects of G. Stanley Hall's image of adulthood as a plateau of peak capacity followed by a gradual decline. However, adulthood may include as little as a decade of "level ground" at

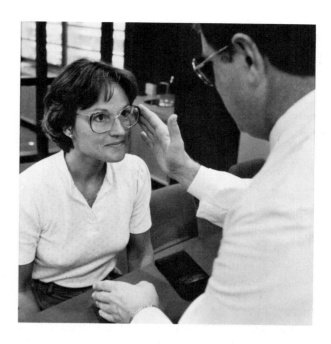

One of the early signs of aging is the deterioration of eyesight, which often begins in one's 40s.

Decreasing physical capacities do not preclude the elderly from participating in athletic events, but they can no longer compete on an equal basis with younger adults, so special categories of competition are created for them.

Declining physical strength makes it necessary for the elderly to obtain help with previously simple daily chores.

top capacity, with a sharp rather than a gradual downward turn at the end of life.

Cognitive changes For most of this century, it appeared that cognitive capacity ran along the same time line as biological capacity: rapid development from birth to adolescence; relatively unchanging capacity during adulthood; and then a decline in old age that ended with senility, or "mindlessness."

While most experts acknowledge the eventual decline of some cognitive capacities, there is considerable uncertainty about which capacities change and in what ways. This uncertainty can be explained by the fact that the extent of cognitive change in adults is more difficult to assess than biological change. Two reasons for this difficulty are: (1) the course of change differs for different cognitive functions, and (2) methods of measurement often influence the estimate of cognitive change.

Two kinds of cognitive change On some kinds of intellectual tasks, performance appears to decline during adulthood, while on others it appears to remain about the same or even to improve. Starting with the curve at the bottom of Figure 18.2, we see that tasks that require the subject to construct novel analogies from common words such as "sonata is to composer as portrait is to ?" (answer: painter), or to complete a series such as 32 11 33 15 34 19 35 —— —— —— (answer: 23 36 27), or to memorize a list of unrelated words—all decrease markedly after the age of 30. However, the ability to recall information from the distant past improves slightly into middle age and by the age of 60 shows only a slight decline. The ability to interpret a spoken or written communication actually increases markedly up to the age of 60 before it too begins to decline.

John Horn and Gary Donaldson (1980) explain the varying course of performance on these different cognitive tasks as the result of two fundamentally different kinds of intelligence. The kinds of performance that improve over the course of adulthood, they argue, arise from **crystallized intelligence**—intelligence that is built up over a lifetime on the basis of experience. The kinds of performance that begin to decrease during adulthood they see as depending on **fluid intelligence**—intelligence that requires the manipulation of new information in order to solve a problem.

In Horn and Donaldson's view, fluid intelligence is largely an inherited biological predisposition that parallels other biological capacities in its growth and decline. Crystallized intelligence, by contrast, depends

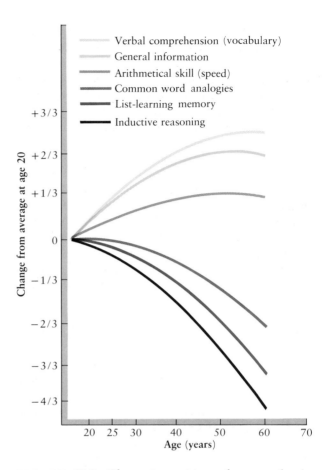

FIGURE 18.2 *Changes in cognitive performance after the age of 20 for various intellectual abilities. Performance that depends upon the manipulation of novel information declines with age; highly practiced mental operations such as arithmetic calculation increase slightly; performance that depends upon accumulation of culturally transmitted knowledge continues to increase up to old age. (Adapted from Horn & Donaldson, 1980.)*

upon culturally organized experience; thus it continues to increase until the biological foundations that support all behavior have markedly deteriorated.

Paul Baltes and his colleagues offer a similar "dual process" explanation of cognitive change during adulthood. They suggest that a person's growing knowledge base actually compensates for the brain's declining efficiency (Baltes, Dittman-Kohli, & Dixon, 1984).

Problems of measurement Firm conclusions about adult cognitive change are complicated by several problems of measurement. For example, many real-life problems seem to demand mixtures of the two kinds of abilities distinguished by Horn and Donaldson and by Baltes, which makes it difficult to predict how actual performance will change over time. For example, to obtain a driver's license, it is necessary to pass a written test of one's knowledge of the law. Often such tests require the application of fluid intelligence to decide between two plausible alternatives, or to figure out what the examiner is getting at with a particular question. This aspect of the test may put older people at a disadvantage. But these same older people have long experience with such laws and a great deal of general knowledge to draw on to pick the correct answers in uncertain cases. Consequently, they may do better than younger people with more fluid intelligence but less background knowledge.

Another difficulty of measurement can be seen in criticisms of studies such as Horn and Donaldson's because they employ cross-sectional designs, which compare people of different ages at a single point in time (Baltes & Schaie, 1973; Labouvie-Vief, 1982; Schaie, 1981). Recall from Chapter 1 (p. 30) that cross-sectional designs are especially vulnerable to confounding by sociocultural factors such as changes in average levels of education, economic conditions, and exposure to information through the mass media. A study conducted in 1985, for example, might compare the cognitive performances of 20-, 30-, 40-, 50-, 60-, and 70-year-olds, showing few differences for those below 40 and marked declines thereafter. Would age be the cause of the decline? Or might it be that the poor performance of the 50-year-olds resulted from their birth during the Great Depression of the 1930s, when their mothers were ill fed and poorly educated, while the 60- and 70-year-olds' performances suffered owing to a lack of education caused by their having to go to work during the Depression?

A useful, although still not trouble-free, method of overcoming these weaknesses is to conduct a longitudinal study, wherein the same people are tested several times over several years. When longitudinal studies of adult cognitive change are compared with cross-sectional ones, or when cross-sectional designs are supplemented with follow-up observations, much of the apparent decline of cognitive functions disappears (Kliegl & Baltes, 1987; Labouvie-Vief, 1982; Schaie & Strother, 1968). For example, Warner Schaie and Gisela Labouvie-Vief (1974) report results from administering the Thurstone test of primary mental abilities to three groups ranging in age from the early 20s to the 80s. The first group was initially tested in 1956 and then again in 1963 and 1970. The second group was tested in 1963 and again in 1970. The third group was tested in 1970. Comparisons of the first test given to each group provided the researchers with a cross-sectional experiment. The repeated testing of the first and second groups at seven-year intervals provided evidence of cognitive changes over time.

The results of these comparisons are shown in Figure 18.3. As can be seen in the left half of the figure, when the cross-sectional data for the 1956, 1967, and 1970 samples are plotted, a steady decline of performance as a function of age is observed. However, when

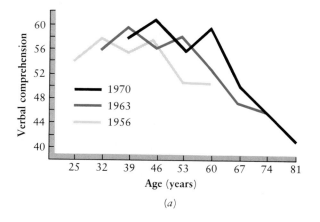

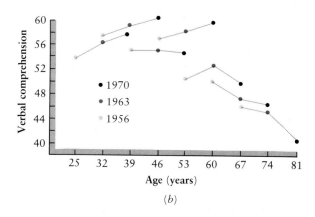

FIGURE 18.3 *Graph (a) shows performance on a test of verbal comprehension given to groups of people varying in age from 25 to 81 years at three different times: 1956, 1963, and 1970. Note that in this cross-sectional approach, the generally downward slope of the curves begins as early as age 40. Graph (b) presents the initial tests and retests for groups tested in 1956, again in 1963, and again in 1970. For these longitudinally tested groups, performance begins to deteriorate only after the age of 65 years. (From Schaie & Labouvie-Vief, 1974.)*

the data from repeated testing of the same subjects are considered — shown in the right half of Figure 18.3 — little or no decline in functioning is evident except among the oldest subjects. Such results strongly suggest that at least part of the decline in function during adulthood found by those using cross-sectional designs is an artifact of the methods of observation.

There are other reasons for caution in reaching conclusions about cognitive changes during adulthood. When one considers the fact that everyday intellectual activity is rarely carried out under tightly constrained laboratory circumstances, there is good reason to question the practical significance of the data reported so far. Moreover, the content of laboratory tasks is often trivial by everyday standards; remembering a list of nonsense words, creating verbal analogies outside of any recognizable context, or mentally rotating geometric figures scarcely constitutes the kind of challenge that would motivate a worldly 70-year-old to think hard. When elderly subjects are asked to memorize interesting material relevant to their lives and allowed to use the memory strategies they have developed over their lifetimes, excellent performance has been reported (Kliegl & Baltes, 1987). Consequently, laboratory studies may systematically underestimate the abilities of older people simply by virtue of the testing materials themselves.

As a result of these difficulties, there is presently a lively debate among psychologists about the nature of cognitive changes during adulthood and old age (Horn & Donaldson, 1980; Labouvie-Vief, 1982). Perhaps the best that can be concluded is that the extreme picture of inevitable, steady intellectual decline is overdrawn, except near the very end of life. While certain aspects of intellectual function may decline — for example, the flexibility to deal rapidly with novel problems — this loss is compensated for in most everyday tasks by skills, knowledge, and a lifetime of experience. However, before attempting to gain closure on these issues, we must still consider the role of social, cultural, and historical circumstances in adult cognitive change.

Social Factors and Later Psychological Change

The changes observed in the biological and cognitive spheres do not count as reflecting development in the sense in which we applied that term to early life, be-

cause (with the exception of a sharp downturn as death approaches) these changes appear to accumulate gradually and continuously, with no hint of stagelike discontinuities or bio-social-behavioral shifts. Consequently, it is important to examine the possibility that stagelike changes and discontinuities during adulthood and old age arise not from the biological or cognitive, but from the social domain.

One useful method for tracing social events that mark discontinuities in development over the entire life span has been proposed by Robert Atchley (1975), who focused on the influence of age-related changes in family life, occupational status, and economic power. At the top of Figure 18.4 is a time line, marked in ten-year periods, against which to evaluate the parallel influences of various age-graded aspects of the life course. The second time line depicts the normative life stages for modern industrialized societies as these stages are portrayed by a number of contemporary theorists (e.g., Baltes & Brim, 1979; Baltes, Featherman, & Lerner, 1988; Erikson, 1968). The next three lines chart important landmarks in an individual's changing social life.

In this view, birth to mid-adolescence is a time of preparation for an occupational role. The individual's work life, once it begins, goes through its own stages: experimentation, settling on a choice of jobs, a period of heavy involvement in work, and then, around the age of 50, a gradual phasing out followed by retirement and removal from the workplace.

The family cycle roughly parallels the work cycle. The individual starts out life "at home," in the family setting. Then, after a period "on one's own," family life once again becomes important, but this time as a parent. In late middle age, when the children are grown and begin to leave the house, the individual's family shrinks in size (the "empty nest" situation) and finally, through the loss of one's spouse, disappears, unless the individual is absorbed into one of the children's families or remarries.

The economic cycle is characterized in terms of one's dependence on others; until an occupational choice has been made and the power to earn a living is secure, the individual is dependent on others for a livelihood. A long period of relative economic independence during adulthood is then followed by decreased earning power and, in old age, dependence once again.

As a number of theorists see it, when all the social factors are added up, they produce a typical "develop-

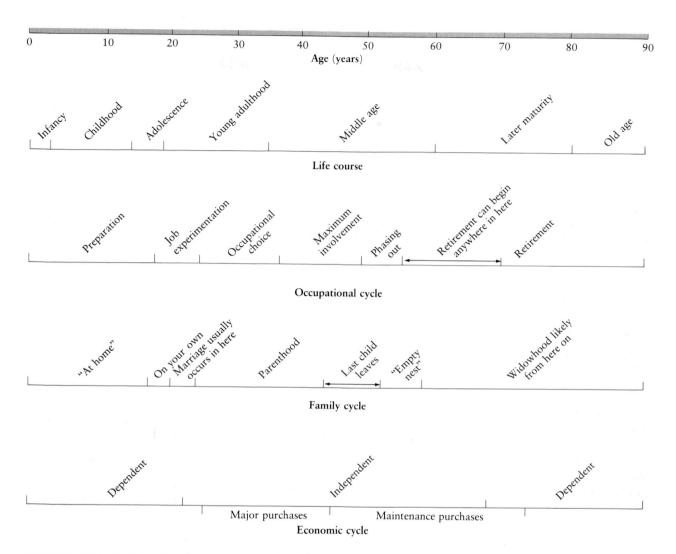

FIGURE 18.4 *Relationships between age, standard developmental periods, and major socially determined life events. As discussed in the text, these relationships vary widely according to sex, social class, culture, and historical era. (From Atchley, 1975.)*

mental contour," a social life cycle of heavy involvement in many domains during youth and middle age, followed by decreased activity (Barker & Barker, 1968; Frankel-Brunswik, 1968; Smelser, 1980) (see Figure 18.5; see also Figure 13.1, p. 411). During their late 30s, 40s, and 50s, most people are simultaneously building a family, making major purchases such as a house, and becoming involved in the most responsible

and time-demanding aspects of their chosen occupation. This pattern does not go unnoticed in American popular culture, where it has been ironically noted that the convergence of social involvements in middle age results in a kind of "mid-life bulge" not unlike the propensity of people in their 40s to put on weight.

In a general way, the contour of social involvements parallels the buildup and decline of biological and

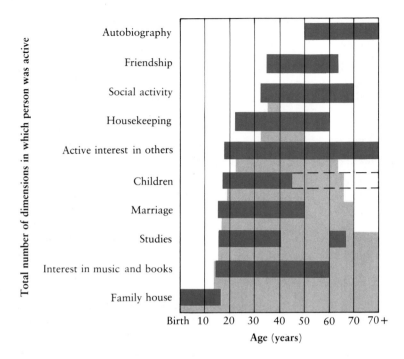

FIGURE 18.5 *An example of the growth and decline of involvement in different activities over the life course. The bars indicate the different kinds of activity engaged in by Elizabeth Textor Goethe, mother of the 18th century German poet and writer, John Wolfgang von Goethe. The shaded background represents a summation of the number of activities simultaneously engaged in. (From Frankel-Brunswik, 1968.)*

cognitive capacities described earlier. In one respect, however, social changes during adulthood differ sharply from biological and cognitive changes at this time; unlike cognitive and biological changes, changes in the social sphere are marked by clear *discontinuities* in individual experience. These discontinuities have two major sources. First, a change in social category is often associated with a change in the contexts that one encounters and the roles that one plays. Second, a change in social categories means that one is treated differently by others; because we experience ourselves so much in terms of how others treat us, the sense of self is likely to change quite suddenly with a change in social category.

For example, consider the transition from the period of job preparation (which in technologically advanced societies is often synonymous with formal schooling) to a permanent full-time job. A young person entering an office, a factory, or some other workplace is immediately confronted with the need to learn a new set of skills and to get along with a group of strangers. In place of a group of classmates of similar age and perhaps similar background and adults who

set the rules "for your own good," there are co-workers and supervisors of many different ages and backgrounds and employers who set rules "for the good of the company." Similarly, the act of getting married and setting up housekeeping with another person requires a reorientation of authority relationships and responsibility. The appearance of children introduces an even more dramatic discontinuity into one's social identity and responsibilities.

Changes in social category bear a complicated relationship to psychological change. It is often quite a shock when a young adult who has been attending college to become a teacher first walks into a classroom and is addressed as Miss Jones or Mr. Smith, receiving somewhat anxious deference from the children. It may be even more disconcerting, and an even more powerful stimulus to psychological change, for new teachers to realize that, no longer students themselves, they must now exert authority over their students, who may prefer talking with their friends to learning the day's spelling words. Similarly, young adults may experience a sharp discontinuity when marriage causes a sudden decrease in the amount of

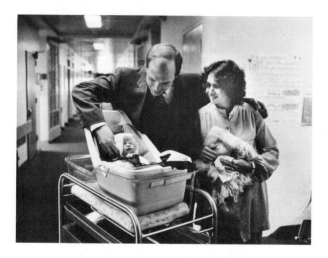

The transitions marked by marriage, the birth of a first child, and the death of a spouse all bring about a marked change in young adults social and economic circumstances, creating a discontinuity in experience.

attention and open admiration they receive from members of the opposite sex.

At the other end of the adult spectrum, the chairperson of the board who retires and is no longer in a position to exert authority may not only find it difficult to keep herself occupied, but also to adjust to a long-forgotten state of relative powerlessness that accompanies the social category "retired person." Likewise, a man whose wife dies after many years of married life may be surprised to find himself once again the object of attention from female acquaintances now that he again fits the social category of "bachelor."

These socially engendered changes in life experience ensure that the aging individual is confronted with qualitatively new experiences, demanding the kind of active adaptation that also marks development early in life.

Variability in the social structuring of the life course Although family, occupational, and economic timetables must be considered along with chronological age when studying adult development, the particular set of relationships depicted in Figure 18.4 is far from universal, as Atchley himself points out.

To begin with, Atchley's important life events inadequately represent the conditions of adult women. Until the twentieth century, there was no question of occupational choice for most women; the normative adult career was to be a mother and housewife. In such cases, there was no "time on one's own," and no period of economic independence. When women's life paths did deviate from this norm, it was seldom in the direction taken by men. For example, it was often expected that the youngest daughter would forgo marriage and a family of her own altogether in order to remain at home and help her parents (Hareven, 1982). Meanwhile, those who married often bore several children, and were faced with severe economic hardships when their husbands began to lose earning power or die. Since the average life expectancy was much lower than today, many women died before their youngest children had "left the nest."

To some extent these conditions have been mitigated by improved health care, changing occupational roles, and social security legislation. But the social circumstances of elderly women remain difficult —and different in many ways from those of men.

The normative picture presented by Atchley is also oriented toward the highly educated middle class, and in this way misrepresents the life course of working-class and poor people of both sexes (Espenshade & Braun, 1983). Those in our society who are born into families with few financial resources are also those who are likely to drop out of school early, and those whose jobs are likely to require physically demanding labor. For these workers, whose health care is also likely to be rudimentary and housing inadequate, problems arise because their bodies are no longer capable of sustaining "maximum involvement" at work into their 50s and 60s. By their mid-50s, they may be relegated to sweeping up or running errands, the kinds of jobs that used to be assigned to 10- or 12-year-olds just entering the work force. This suggests a very different life trajectory from the one projected by Atchley.

Finally, Atchley is providing a picture of people living in modern industrialized societies (see Figure 18.6). When we turn to nonindustrial societies, we find enormous variability in the culturally accepted stages of adult development (Falk, Falk, & Tomashevich, 1981; Fry, 1988; Holmes, 1983) and in the social significance assigned to various age periods. Despite this great variability, nonindustrialized societies generally seem to have no social institutions comparable to what we call retirement (Jacobs, 1975). Old people in these societies are likely to continue to play active roles.

The continued importance of old people in such societies grows out of their importance to the process

In many traditional, nonliterate societies, the elders retain high status because of the store of knowledge they have accumulated over a life time.

of cultural reproduction. Most such societies lack writing systems to retain the prior experiences of the group. Consequently, the elders are repositories of vital information. Old people in general, and old men in particular, often occupy respected roles that allow them to wield power in many spheres. As repositories of the culture's most important knowledge, the old increase rather than decline in status. For example, among the Ashanti of West Africa,

> The grandparents . . . on both sides are the most honored of one's kinsfolk. Their position and status are of very great importance in the social system. In Ashanti it is the grandparents who are the prototypes of persons and institutions commanding reverence and submission to the norms of tradition. (Fortes, 1950, p. 276)

The situation of the elderly in nonindustrialized societies should not, however, be overly romanticized. In agricultural societies, the elderly are generally expected to contribute to the economic well-being of the household until they die. In many subsistence hunter–gatherer societies, the old and feeble suffer a loss of prestige, and if the group is put under extreme pressure, they may be killed or left to die (Falk et al., 1981).

The particular patterns of individual lives vary according to a person's sex, social class, culture, and historical period. They also vary in response to irregu-

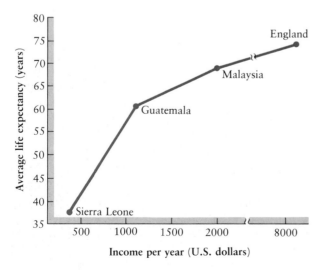

FIGURE 18.6 *In many parts of the world, life expectancy is still relatively short. As a nation's income increases, so does the average life expectancy. (From United Nations Children's Fund, 1988.)*

lar events that affect whole generations and their progeny, such as the severe worldwide economic depression of the 1930s and World War II. In a longitudinal study of the impact of these events on people living in Oakland, California, Glen Elder (1974) showed that the Depression and the war affected people differently, depending upon how old they were, their economic status at the start of the Depression, and the severity of the Depression's impact on family income. Elder found that the people who became teenagers at the time of the Depression experienced the fewest difficulties. Although they were required to help their families by finding odd jobs and doing housework, these added responsibilities gave them a sense of usefulness and spurred them to greater efforts. Although the males faced the terrors of war, those who survived returned to a booming economy and a period of unexcelled material well-being. The females entered the work force in record numbers, during the war, and after the war they, together with the returning men, started the baby boom.

By contrast, the Depression was particularly difficult for younger children, who experienced family disruption all during their childhoods—first because their fathers were out of work, often causing their families to lose their homes and to accept difficult living conditions; then because their fathers went to war while their mothers went to work.

In a study of these same families when the participants had entered old age, Elder (1982) found that the effects of these early experiences often lingered. For example, women from middle-class households that had experienced only mild economic difficulties reported that they found the transition to retirement and lowered income less difficult because they had learned to cope successfully with such circumstances as young mothers. However, women who had decided not to have children because of their experience of serious economic deprivation in the 1930s found themselves in very difficult circumstances in the 1970s when their husbands had died and there were no adult children to help them deal with their old age.

Such complexities in actual lives suggest caution in drawing conclusions from simplified schemas of the life course. While Atchley's overall approach has merit, it must be continually modified to take actual historical and cultural contexts into account.

The influence of social factors on cognition and biology
In assessing the nature of psychological

change in later life, it is important to keep in mind a principle that was central to our understanding of early development: experience shapes biology as well as the other way around (see Chapter 5, p. 156). As applied to adulthood and old age, this principle alerts us to the strong possibility that variations in experience produced by socially mandated life changes such as retirement can also affect development in the biological and cognitive spheres.

For example, a variety of evidence indicates that the disengagement that accompanies retirement, the loss of a spouse, or placement in an old-age home—all events that change one's social world—contribute substantially to biological and cognitive decline (Schooler & Schaie, 1987). Even when elderly people are placed in an institution that is fully satisfactory from the point of view of health care, the quality of the food, and material comforts, the mere fact of being placed in such an environment seems to increase their chances of dying sooner (Lawton, 1977).

Precisely which features of that environment exert such negative effects? The answer seems to be that when elderly people are confronted by new and unfamiliar social contexts, they lose the courage to engage in the kind of active adaptation necessary to allow them to develop. Echoing the problem caused by learned helplessness during infancy (Chapter 8, p. 248),

The transition to life in an institution that cares for the elderly and disabled can be a source of severe stress, even if there is adequate provision of basic necessities.

such a response leads people simply to give up on life, and their development comes to an abrupt end.

But just as learned helplessness can be overcome by rearranging the newborn's environments, the negative impact of social changes in adulthood can be mitigated by deliberate intervention to change the social environment (Langer & Rodin, 1976; Rodin & Langer, 1977).

For example, Ellen Langer and her colleagues intervened in a nursing home in an attempt to reverse the intellectual decline reported for those who enter such institutions (Langer, Rodin, Beck, Weinman, & Spitzer, 1979). The researchers focused on memory function. First, they gave a memory pretest to all residents who participated in the study. They visited the home four or five times over a six-week period, and posed simple, readily understandable questions to the residents, explaining that they were interested in learning more about life in such institutions. For example, they asked about what was going on in the home that day, what residents had eaten for breakfast or dinner the night before, and so on. They also asked about the residents' former lives — their families, jobs, and earlier life experiences.

These interviews were carried out in two different ways, creating two groups of subjects. In one group, the researcher talked about his or her own life experiences in addition to asking about the residents' experiences, a procedure that Langer and her colleagues called "reciprocal self-disclosure." On the basis of prior research, the researchers believed that when they reciprocated the residents' trust by talking honestly about their own lives, they would build interest and motivation, leading to residents' enhanced readiness to engage in mental work. In the second group, the researchers asked the same questions and showed the same level of interest in answers but did not reciprocate by talking about themselves.

Despite its apparent simplicity, this manipulation had a significant impact. On the basis of nurses' estimates of the residents' level of awareness, sociability, health, and other measures of well-being, as well as on the basis of formal memory testing, the residents who engaged in reciprocal discussions outscored those who were engaged in a less interactive way. Such results provide evidence that environmental arrangements that promote development early in life continue to do so when appropriately applied later on.

As Ronald Abeles and Matilda Riley (1987) point out, these and similar results demonstrate that aging is

As simple an act as taking the time to chat with elderly people living in a home for the aged has been shown to increase their mental alertness and improve their overall health.

not determined solely by biology; rather, like development at the start of life, it reflects complex interactions between social, behavioral, and biological processes. To this we would add the reminder that these interactions are themselves shaped by and help to shape the cultural contexts in which they occur.

Decline or Continuing Development?

It is now time to return to the question with which we opened this chapter: Does development continue throughout life or do the principles of psychological change themselves undergo a change following the transition to adulthood? On the one hand, a plausible case can be made for seeing psychological change during adulthood and old age as a gradual process of decline, much like the retreat of the tide from its high-water mark on a beach. From birth through puberty and a few years more, the tide rises, sometimes with a rush, sometimes with a smooth, imperceptible advance along the beach. At some vaguely definable time, the high-water mark is reached, and the tide slowly retreats.

Although the data are not unequivocal, the growth of biological capacities to the age of approximately 30 years and their subsequent slow decline appear to follow such a course. So do the cognitive abilities of individuals encountering totally new kinds of information under unusual and highly constrained circumstances, whether in a psychological experiment or in any unusual life event for which they have no ready script. There is a similar pattern replicated in the social domain: infants begin life confined entirely to contexts where they can be watched over and protected by parents; the range of contexts where the growing person can act as an independent agent grows steadily into middle age; then the contexts for independent action begin to shrink, until life ends as it began, with the elderly person heavily dependent on others within a restricted range of contexts.

On the other hand, this picture of gradual growth and decline often fails to correspond to individuals' actual experience of psychological change. Instead of a subjective feeling of gradual decline, what emerges from studies of adult development is an intricate, shifting mosaic in which gradual change and expectable experiences are mixed with sudden, unexpected events — new insights, conceptual reintegrations, and

Later life can hold a variety of surprises, including the opportunity to form new, intimate relationships.

triumphs as well as disappointments, loss of power, and decline. Even as one's physical powers decrease, the accumulated experiences of a lifetime provide adults with resources for dealing with life completely beyond the reach of the young.

This perception of later life as a form of development comes through very clearly in interviews with middle-aged and elderly people conducted by Bernice Neugarten:

> There is a difference between wanting to *feel* young and wanting to *be* young. Of course, it would be pleasant to maintain the vigour and appearance of youth; but I would not trade those things for the authority or autonomy I feel — no, nor the ease of interpersonal relationships nor the self-confidence that comes from experience.

> You feel you have lived long enough to have learned a few things that nobody can learn earlier. That's the reward . . . and also the excitement. I now see things in books, in people, in music that I couldn't see when I was younger. . . . It's a form of ripening that I attribute largely to my present age.

An active, engaged elderly person is more likely to retain her good health.

It's as if there are two mirrors before me, each held at a partial angle. I see part of myself in my mother who is growing old, and part of her in me. In the other mirror, I see part of myself in my daughter. I have had some dramatic insights, just from looking in those mirrors. . . . It is a set of revelations that I suppose can only come when you are in the middle of three generations. (1968, pp. 97–98)

Nor is life any more predictable as one grows into middle and old age than it was during middle childhood or adolescence. Biological changes such as menopause or social changes such as retirement or widowhood may bring unexpected and dramatic changes in social identity, and exciting opportunities to pursue some long-desired goal, or simply the time to discover new insights about the past.

As the novelist Milan Kundera reminded us at the beginning of this chapter, the old, no less than the young, are innocent of the experiences yet to come. Except for the unavoidable fact of death, little can be known for certain about the new experiences that await us each day. Consequently, as long as one actively engages the environment, one has the possibility of gaining new insights even into the most familiar of life's experiences, feeling the pleasure of knowing one's life in a fresh way each time. In this sense, development shares common features at all ages; it is always a process of becoming.

SUMMARY

1. The study of adulthood poses a major problem for students of development: Does development continue after the transition to adulthood, or does it cease and some other process of change begin?

2. Adulthood is the last major period of the lifespan to attract detailed scholarly study. Analysis of adulthood followed institutionalization of the period of old age, which forms its upper boundary.

3. Concern with old age and adulthood was spurred by changes in public health and medicine that resulted in a major shift in society's age profile. During the past century, average life expectancy has increased by 50 percent.

4. Major theoretical approaches to the study of child development have offered three basic theories of adult development:
   a. Development ceases and a period of gradual decline ensues — the biological maturation approach.
   b. Development ceases but does not decline until shortly before death — the interactionist view.
   c. Development continues throughout life, but the par-

ticular mix of biological, social, and behavioral factors that become reintegrated at successive stages differ both as a function of age and as a function of cultural and historical circumstances — the cultural-context view.

5. Physiological indicators of organ capacity decline steadily from approximately the age of 30.

6. Among women, menopause represents a biological discontinuity in the ability to bear children; there is no comparable biological discontinuity among men.

7. Sometime after the age of 65, a period of rapid deterioration in biological capacity occurs, ending in death.

8. It is widely believed that different cognitive abilities follow different paths of change during adulthood and old age. Tasks calling upon crystallized intelligence see an increase in performance, while task performance depending upon fluid intelligence declines.

9. Firm conclusions about cognitive change are complicated by problems of measurement. Longitudinal designs often fail to confirm the decline in performance suggested by cross-sectional designs. The performance of the elderly is also susceptible to improvement through changes in materials and conditions of testing, indicating that low performance does not always reflect low ability.

10. Changes in life experiences associated with events in the family and work spheres introduce major discontinuities into the process of change during adulthood and old age. These changes also confront adults with qualitatively new experiences that require the kind of active adaptation associated with earlier development.

11. The particular pattern of individual life events differs according to sex, social class, culture, and historical era, making it difficult to specify a single pattern for adult development. Generalization is further impeded by irregular life events, which exert a major impact on development.

12. Causal relations among biological, behavioral, and social factors in adulthood, as in early life, are multi-directional: behavioral and social factors influence biology, as well as the other way around.

13. At the level of individual psychological experience, development appears to be a lifelong process of encountering the new and unexpected, creating greater insight into human experience through a process of active adaptation.

KEY TERMS

Adulthood
Crystallized intelligence
Early adulthood

Fluid intelligence
Life-course approach
Life-span approach

Menopause
Middle adulthood
Old age

SUGGESTED READINGS

ERIKSON, ERIK H. (Ed.). *Adulthood*. New York, Norton, 1978.

A seminal series of essays by leading students of adult development from many scientific disciplines. Erikson himself uses Ingmar Bergman's classic film *Wild Strawberries* as an exemplary case study of development during adulthood and old age.

ERIKSON, ERIK H., JOAN M. ERIKSON, and HELEN Q. KIVNICK. *Vital Involvement in Old Age*. New York: Norton, 1986.

The leading proponent of development as a lifelong process, his wife and co-worker, and another co-worker summarize a lifetime of reflections about development through interviews with the surviving participants in a longitudinal study begun 60 years earlier.

FRIES, JAMES F., and LAWRENCE M. CRAPO. *Vitality and Aging*. New York: W.H. Freeman and Company, 1981.

A readable and comprehensive survey of the aging process.

HAREVEN, TAMARA K. *Family Time and Industrial Time.* Cambridge: Cambridge University Press, 1982.

A detailed account of the links between family life and work in a New England mill town after the turn of the century, showing the intimate links between the social organization of people's lives and their experience of lifelong development.

SKINNER, B. F. and **BARBARA E. VAUGHN.** *Enjoy Old Age.* New York: Norton, 1988.

An informal, engaging, and well-informed view of how to cope with aging that combines personal experience with insights gained from a half-century of research about the behavior of organisms.

Glossary

· · ·

ABSTRACT MODELING A kind of modeling in which children abstract general linguistic principles from specific utterances. According to Bandura, this is one of the main ways in which children acquire language.

ACCOMMODATION In Piaget's theory, the process by which children modify their existing schemas in order to incorporate or adapt to new experiences.

ADULTHOOD From the Latin word meaning "one who has grown up." A period bounded on one side by adolescence and on the other by old age. In adulthood the individual has reached full maturity and responsibility before the law.

AGGRESSION An act in which someone intentionally hurts another.

ALLELE An alternate form of a gene coded for a particular trait.

ALPHA-FETOPROTEIN TEST A blood test used mainly to detect prenatal defects of the neural tube.

AMNIOCENTESIS A medical procedure in which a long, hollow needle is inserted through the mother's abdomen into the amniotic sac surrounding the fetus and amniotic fluid is withdrawn for later analysis. It is one of the principle techniques for discovering whether a fetus suffers from certain genetic defects.

AMNION One of the membranes that arises out of the trophoblast. The amnion is the thin, tough, transparent membrane that holds the amniotic fluid surrounding the prenatal organism. It is sometimes called the amniotic sac.

ANAL STAGE In Freudian theory, the period during the second year of life when the child is preoccupied with gaining control of the smooth muscles involved in defecation.

ANIMAL MODEL Research conducted on animals whose patterns of behavior serve as models for the explanation of human behaviors, such as attachment.

A NOT B ERROR A characteristic of stage 4 of Piaget's six stages of object permanence; babies will look for a hidden object where they first found it even after they have seen it moved to a new location.

APGAR SCALE A quick, simple test used to diagnose the physical state of newborn infants.

APPRENTICESHIP A special process of training in which a novice spends an extended period of time working for a master in a particular trade or craft while learning on the job.

ASSIMILATION In Piaget's theory, the process by which children incorporate new experiences into their existing schemas.

ATTACHMENT An enduring emotional bond that infants form with specific people, usually beginning with their mothers, sometime between the ages of 7 and 9 months. Children are said to be attached to someone when they seek to be near that person, are distressed when they are separated from the person, are happy when they are reunited with the person, and orient their actions to the person even in the person's absence.

AUTHORITARIAN PARENTING PATTERN Authoritarian parents try to shape and evaluate the behavior and attitudes of their children according to a set standard. They stress the importance of obedience to authority and favor punitive measures to bring about their children's compliance.

AUTHORITATIVE PARENTING PATTERN Authoritative parents try to control their children by explaining their rules or decisions, and by reasoning with their children. They are willing to listen to their children's point of view, even if they do not always accept it. They set high standards for their children's behavior and encourage them to be individualistic and independent.

AUTISTIC In Piagetian terms, a form of thinking that is undirected, pleasure-seeking, and oblivious to reality, characteristic of neonates. *Autistic* also refers to children suffering from an illness, autism, in which they are unable to interact with others normally, their language development is retarded, and their behavior is often ritualistic and compulsive.

AUTONOMOUS MORALITY Morality based on the belief that rules are arbitrary agreements that can be changed if those governed by them agree.

AVERSIVE CONDITIONING Learning to anticipate unpleasant events. Infants cannot form expectations for aversive events until a few months after birth.

BABBLING A form of vocalizing that includes consonant and vowel sounds like those used in speech. Babies begin to babble at approximately 4 months of age.

BABY BIOGRAPHY A parent's detailed record of an infant's behavior over a period of time.

BABYNESS The combination of physical features that ethologists believe attracts adults to the young of the species. Babyness includes a large head relative to body size; a large and protruding forehead in relation to the rest of the face; eyes that are positioned below the horizontal midline of the face; and round, protruding cheeks.

BIOLOGICAL DRIVES Aroused states, such as hunger and thirst, that urge the organism to obtain the basic requirements for survival.

BIO-SOCIAL-BEHAVIOR SHIFT The process of change arising from the convergence and reorganization of biological, social, and behavioral elements of development in which distinctively new and significant forms of behavior emerge.

BLASTOCYST The hollow sphere of cells that results from the differentiation of the cells in the morula into trophoblast cells on the outside and the inner cells mass on the inside.

BRAIN STEM A central nervous system structure located at the upper end of the spinal cord. It becomes active during the fetal period. At birth, it is one of most highly developed areas of the brain and controls such vital functions as breathing, sleeping, the inborn reflexes, emotions, and states of alertness.

BRAZELTON NEONATAL ASSESSMENT SCALE A scale used to assess the newborn's neurological condition. Included in it are tests of infants' reflexes, motor capacities, muscle tone, capacity for responding to objects and people, and capacity for controlling their own behavior and attention.

CANALIZED CHARACTERISTICS Characteristics that are relatively invulnerable to environmental influence during their development.

CATEGORIZE To perceive objects or events that differ in various ways as similar because they share common aspects.

CATHARSIS The reduction of an urge, or an emotional release.

CEPHALOCAUDAL PATTERN The sequence of body development from head to foot.

CEREBRAL CORTEX The uppermost part of the central nervous system. Within the cortex there are specialized regions for the analysis of time, space, and language; as well as for motor functions and sensory discriminations.

CHORION One of the membranes that develops out of the trophoblast. It forms the placenta.

CHORIONIC VILLUS SAMPLING A medical procedure in which cells are taken from the villi (hairlike projections) on the chorion. This procedure can reveal the presence of chromosomal defects.

CHROMOSOME A threadlike structure made up of genes; in humans there are 46 chromosomes in the nucleus of each cell.

CLASSICAL CONDITIONING The process by which an organism learns which events in its environment go with others. It is the establishment of a connection between a response (such as salivation) and a previously neutral stimulus (such as a tone), resulting from the neutral stimulus being paired with an unconditional stimulus (such as food).

CLEAVAGE The initial mitotic divisions of the zygote into several cells as it travels down the fallopian tube into the uterus.

CLINICAL METHOD A method of observation in which questions are tailored to the individual, with each successive response of the individual determining what the investigator will ask next.

CODOMINANCE A trait that is determined by two alleles but is distinctively different than the trait produced by either of the contributing alleles alone.

COEVOLUTION The combined process that emerges from the interaction of biological and cultural evolution.

COHORT A group of persons the same age who are therefore likely to share some common experiences that are different from those of younger or older groups.

COLLECTIVE MONOLOGUES The speech that occurs when several children are playing near each other and each of them is talking as if he or she were addressing others, but no one seems to pay attention to what anyone else is saying.

COMPENSATION A mental operation that allows the child to consider how changes in one aspect of a problem are related to (and potentially compensated for by) changes in another.

COMPLEMENTARY GENES Genes that can only produce their phenotypical effect if they work in combination with other genes.

CONCRETE OPERATIONS In Piaget's theory, internalized mental actions that fit into a logical system. Such operations are termed concrete because they are restricted to objects and events actually present in the child's environment.

CONDITIONAL RESPONSE In classical conditioning, a response that occurs following a previously neutral stimulus as a result of pairing the neutral stimulus with an unconditional stimulus.

CONDITIONAL STIMULUS In classical conditioning, a stimulus that evokes no particular response by itself but which can come to elicit a response after training. For example, a tone can become the conditional stimulus for salivation if it is repeatedly sounded before food is presented.

CONSERVATION Piaget's term for the understanding that the properties of an object or a substance remain the same even though its appearance may have been altered in some superficial way.

CONTEXT The combination of factors in the environment, individual actions, and interpretations that give coherence to behavior as a whole.

CONTROL GROUP The persons in an experiment who are treated as much as possible like the persons in the experimental group except that they do not undergo the experimental manipulation.

COREGULATION The sharing between parent and child of responsibility for the child's behavior.

CORRELATION Two factors are said to be correlated with one another when changes in one are associated with changes in the other.

CRITICAL PERIODS Periods in the growth of the organism during which specific biological or environmental events must occur for development to proceed normally.

CROSSING OVER The process during the first phase of meiosis in which genetic material is exchanged between chromosomes containing genes for the same characteristic.

CROSS-SECTIONAL DESIGN A research design in which children of different ages are studied at a single time.

CRYSTALIZED INTELLIGENCE Problem-solving ability built up from prior experience.

CULTURE The humanmade part of the environment. It includes artifacts, such as tools and clothing; knowledge of how to construct and use those artifacts; beliefs about the world; and values about what is worthwhile—all of which guide people in the ways they behave.

DEFENSE MECHANISM Freud's term for psychological processes, such as repression, that people use to protect themselves from unpleasant thoughts.

DEFERRED IMITATION In Piagetian terms, the imitation of actions that have occurred at another time under different circumstances.

DEVELOPMENTAL CRISIS In Erikson's theory, a set of choices and tests that an individual faces as he or she becomes ready to face a new life task. The outcome of a crisis can be either successful transition to the next stage or failure and an impairment of the life cycle.

DISHABITUATION To begin paying attention again when some aspect of the stimulus situation has been changed.

DIZYGOTIC TWINS Twins that result from the fertilization by two sperm of two eggs that are released at the same time; also called "fraternal" twins.

DOMINANCE HIERARCHY A hierarchical social structure in which some individuals are dominant and others subordinate to them.

DOMINANT ALLELE The allele that is expressed when there are two different alleles for the same trait.

EARLY ADULTHOOD In Erikson's theory, the years between 20 and 35 when adults commit themselves to a love relationship or else develop a sense of isolation.

ECOLOGY In developmental psychology, the range of situations in which people are actors; the roles they play; and the predicaments they encounter.

ECTODERM One of the layers of cells that develops out of the inner cell mass of the blastocyst. The ectoderm eventually develops into the outer surface of the skin, the nails, part of the teeth, the lens of the eye, the inner ear, and the central nervous system.

EDUCATION A specialized form of socialization in which adults engage in deliberate teaching of the young to ensure the acquisition of specialized knowledge and skills required in adult life.

EGO In Freud's theory, the mental structure that emerges out of the id. Its major task is self-preservation, which it accomplishes through voluntary movement, perception, logical thought, adaptation, and problem-solving, and by gaining control over the instinctual demands of the id.

EGOCENTRISM The interpretion of the world from one's own (ego's) point of view without taking into consideration alternative perspectives.

EMBRYONIC PERIOD The period of prenatal development that begins with implantation and lasts for about 6 weeks until all the major organs take shape and ossification begins.

EMOTION The feeling tone, or affect, with which people respond to their circumstances.

EMPATHY The sharing of another's emotional response.

ENDODERM The inner layer cells that develops from the inner cell mass of the blastocyst. The endoderm eventually develops into the digestive system and the lungs.

ENDOGENOUS CAUSES Causes of development arising from the child rather than from the environment; part of the child's biological heritage.

ENVIRONMENTALIST HYPOTHESIS OF IQ The position that intelligence is both specific and heavily dependent on experience.

EPIGENETIC HYPOTHESIS The hypothesis that new forms emerge through the process of the organism's interaction with the environment.

EQUILIBRATION The term Piaget used for the back-and-forth process of seeking a balance between existing psychological structures and new environmental experiences. When the child achieves a balance between accommodation and assimilation, he or she enters a new stage of development.

ETHOLOGY The study of behavior and its evolutionary bases.

EXOGENOUS CAUSES Causes of development arising from the "outside" as a result of the child's interaction with the environment.

EXPERIMENTAL GROUP The persons whose environment is changed as part of an experiment.

EXPERIMENTS Research procedures in which the investigator introduces some change in the person's experience and then measures the effect of that change on the person's behavior.

EXPLICIT MODELING A method of increasing prosocial behavior in which adults behave in the ways they desire children to imitate.

FETAL GROWTH RETARDATION The term used to describe the conditions of babies who are especially small for their gestational age at birth.

FETAL PERIOD The period from about 9 weeks after conception until birth. During this period, the primitive organs grow in size and complexity until the baby can exist outside the mother without medical support.

FLUID INTELLIGENCE Problem-solving ability that enables a person to manipulate new information.

FORMAL OPERATIONS The ability to think in a systematic manner about all logical relations within a problem. Piaget hypothesized that formal operational thinking emerges at about the age of 12. It is the final stage in his theory of development.

GENDER SCHEMA According to Sandra Bem, a network of associations embodying the culture's conception of sex roles, which children use to guide their own behavior, and which structures their perceptions of the various scenes they inhabit.

GENERAL NOMINALS Words that label things and classes of things at the same time; for example, "dog" or "rock."

GENE POOL The total genetic information possessed by a sexually reproducing population.

GENES The molecules that transmit the hereditary blueprints for the development of the individual from one generation to the next.

GENITAL STAGE In Freudian theory, the period of mature sexuality that begins with adolescence, in which sexual urges are no longer directed toward the parents but are transferred to peers of the opposite sex.

GENOTYPE The total complement of genes that an individual inherits.

GERM CELLS Sperm and ova; the cells specialized for sexual reproduction that have only half the number of chromosomes normal for a species (23 in humans).

GERMINAL PERIOD The period from conception to implantation, which occurs about 8 to 10 days after conception.

GESTATIONAL AGE The elapsed time between conception and birth.

GRAMMATICAL MORPHEMES Words and parts of words that create meaning by elaborating relations among elements in a sentence.

GROUP NORMS Rules that apply only to particular groups, such as peer groups or professional groups.

HABITUATION The gradual decrease of attention paid to a repeated stimulus.

HETERONOMOUS MORALITY The morality of constraint, according to Piaget. Such morality is characterized by unquestioning obedience to rules and to more powerful individuals; by attention to the letter of the law, rather than its spirit; and by a conception of responsibility in which outcomes are crucial and motives irrelevant.

HETEROZYGOUS Having inherited two genes of different allelic forms for the same attribute.

HOLOPHRASE A term for babies' single-word utterances; the term indicates a belief that these single words stand for entire sentences.

HOMOZYGOUS Having inherited two genes of the same allelic form for a single attribute.

HORIZONTAL DECALAGE Piaget's term for a child's uneven performance at a given stage of development when the same logical problem is presented in different forms.

HOSTILE AGGRESSION An act aimed at hurting another, either for revenge or to establish dominance.

HUMAN DEVELOPMENT The sequence of changes in human beings that begins after conception and continues throughout life.

ID In Freudian theory, the first mental structure. It is the part of ourselves responsible for our innate desires and is the main source of mental energy. It is unconscious, energetic, and pleasure-seeking.

IDENTIFICATION A process that provides individuals with a sense of who they are and who they want to be. In Freudian terms, identification is the strong desire to look, act, and feel like another person of the same sex.

IDENTITY According to Erikson, an individual's sense of personal sameness and historical continuity. It is a pattern of beliefs about the self that reconciles the many ways in which one is like other people with the ways in which one differs from others. According to Piaget, *identity* refers to the ability of children to realize that objects and quantities remain invariant when surface appearances change.

IDENTITY FORMATION According to Erikson, the developmental crisis faced by adolescents. To forge a secure identity, adolescents must bring about a resolution of the identity crisis in both the individual and the social spheres. They must establish the "identity of these two identities."

IMPLANTATION The process by which the blastocyst becomes attached to the uterus.

INDUCTION A method of increasing children's prosocial behavior through the use of explanations that appeal to their pride, concern for others, and their desire to be grownup.

INFORMATION-PROCESSING APPROACH A strategy of explaining development using the analogy of a modern computer. Research in this tradition is greatly concerned with a detailed analysis of each intellectual task and each step in solving a problem.

INITIATION–REPLY–EVALUATION SEQUENCE A pattern within instructional discourse that begins when the teacher initiates an exchange, a student replies, and the teacher provides an evaluation of the student's reply.

INNATIST HYPOTHESIS OF IQ The position that some people are born generally smarter than others and no amount of training or normal variation in the environment can alter this fact.

INNER CELL MASS The knot of cells inside the blastocyst that eventually becomes the embryo.

INSTRUCTIONAL DISCOURSE A specialized use of language within the context of the classroom that is designed to give students information about the content of the curriculum and feedback about their efforts, while providing teachers with information about student progress.

INSTRUMENTAL AGGRESSION Aggression committed in order to obtain a goal.

INTERNALIZATION The process by which children become sensitive to society's standards without being explicitly instructed or needing to wait for those in authority to respond.

IQ A score on a test of intelligence; a child's mental age (as determined by the age at which average children pass the test items) divided by chronological age, multiplied by 100 ($IQ = MA/CA \times 100$). By definition, this ratio yields an average IQ of 100.

JARGONING Vocalizations of strings of syllables that have the intonation and stress of actual utterances in the language that the baby will eventually speak.

KINSHIP STUDIES Studies in which members of the biological family are compared to see how similar they are in one or more attributes.

KNOWLEDGE BASE A store of information upon which the child can draw in a new situation.

LANGUAGE ACQUISITION DEVICE (LAD) According to Chomsky, the LAD is an innate language-processing capacity that is programmed to recognize the universal grammar common to all languages. The LAD is realized in the particulars of the language the child hears.

LANGUAGE ACQUISITION SUPPORT SYSTEM (LASS) According to Bruner, the LASS is the set of parental behaviors that structure children's language environment to support the development of language.

LATENCY In Freudian theory, the stage of development that lasts from about the age of 6 years until the beginning of puberty. During this period, sexual desires are suppressed and sexual energy is channeled into acquiring the technical skills that will be needed during adulthood.

LATERALIZATION The process by which one side of the brain takes the lead in organizing a particular mental process or behavior.

LEARNED HELPLESSNESS People's perception that their behavior does not matter because of their inability to effect events, as a consequence, they lose the desire to act and become passive.

LEARNING A relatively permanent change in behavior brought about by the experience of events in the environment.

LEXICON The store of words in an individual's vocabulary. The structure of the lexicon (e.g., the relationships among words) develops over time.

LIFE-COURSE APPROACH An approach to development from birth to death that focuses on influences of major life events (onset of schooling, retirement, etc.) on development.

LIFE-SPAN APPROACH A framework for studying development that assumes it to be a lifelong process arising from the interaction of biological, social, and historical influences on the individual.

LOGICAL THOUGHT According to Piaget, thought that is directed, self-controlled, and finely tuned to reality.

LONGITUDINAL DESIGN A research design in which data are gathered from the same group of people at several ages, making it possible to trace change over time.

LONG-TERM MEMORY Memory from past experience.

LOW BIRTH WEIGHT A baby's weight of 2500 grams or less at birth.

MASKING GENE A gene that masks the normal expression of another gene.

MATURATION The genetically determined patterns of change that occur as individuals age from conception through adulthood.

MEIOSIS The reduction division process that produces sperm and ova, each of which contain only half of the parent cell's original complement of chromosomes (23 in humans).

MEMORY STRATEGIES Patterned ways of learning and remembering effectively.

MENARCHE A girl's first menstrual period.

MENOPAUSE The cessation of ovulation and menstruation in women, signaling the end of the period of biological reproduction.

MENTAL AGE The basic index of intelligence for an age-graded scale such as that developed by Binet and Simon. A child who does as well on such a test as an average 9-year-old is said to have a mental age of 9.

MENTAL MODULES Highly specific mental faculties tuned to particular kinds of environmental input. Mental modules are specific to particular domains such as music and language, and are only loosely connected to one another. The psychological principles that organize the operation of each domain are often claimed to be innate.

MESODERM The middle layer of cells that develops from the inner cell mass of the blastocyst. It eventually becomes the muscles, the bones, the circulatory system, and the inner layers of the skin.

METACOGNITION The ability to describe one's own mental activities and the logic underpinning one's attempts to solve problems.

METAMEMORY Knowledge about one's own memory processes.

MIDDLE ADULTHOOD In Erikson's theory, the years between 35 and 65 when adults must engage in productive work and raise the next generation or else become stagnant and self-centered.

MITOSIS The process of cell duplication and division that generates all an individual's cells except sperm and ova.

MODIFIER GENE A gene that influences the action or expression of other genes.

MONOZYGOTIC TWINS Twins that come from the same zygote and therefore have identical genotypes; also called "identical" twins.

MORAL RULES Obligatory social regulations based on principles of justice and welfare.

MORO REFLEX In response to an abrupt noise or to the sensation of being dropped, very young babies fling their arms out with their fingers spread and then bring their arms back toward their bodies with their fingers bent as if to hug something.

MORPHEMES The parts of a word that carry meaning. A word may contain more than one morpheme; for example, "*act*" + "*or*" or "*un*" + "*manage*" + "*able*."

MORULA A solid ball of cells that results from the cleavage of the zygote as it moves through the fallopian tube.

MUTATION An error in the process by which a gene is replicated that results in a change in the molecular structure of the genetic material itself.

MYELIN The sheath of fatty cells that covers the neurons, stabilizing them and speeding the transmission of impulses along the neurons.

MYELINATION The process by which myelin covers nerve cells.

NATURALISTIC OBSERVATIONS A research method for obtaining detailed evidence about the actual behavior of people in the real world settings they inhabit, including home, school, and community.

NATURE The inborn, genetically coded biological capacities and limitations of individuals.

NEGATION The mental operation that allows the child to think back and imagine undoing or reversing—negating—an action.

NEO-PIAGETIAN A theoretical approach that accepts Piaget's basic framework but seeks to reform it in order to account for facts about development that Piaget's original account does not encompass.

NEURONS Nerve cells.

NURTURE The influence of the environment exerted on the individual by the social group, particularly the family, the school, and the community.

OBJECTIVITY A requirement that the information on which scientific knowledge is based not be distorted by the investigator's preconceptions.

OBJECT PERMANENCE The understanding that objects have substance, are external to oneself, and continue to exist when out of sight. Piaget maintained that we cannot infer that babies understand object permanence until they begin to search actively for an object they no longer see.

OLD AGE A time late in life (usually 65 years or older) of reduced physical capacities and (in many societies) reduced social responsibilities, often producing a state of dependence. In Erikson's theory, a stage of life leading either to integration and wisdom, or to despair.

ONTOGENY The course of development during an individual's lifetime.

OPERANT CONDITIONING Sometimes called instrumental conditioning, this is the modification of behavior as a consequence of the rewards or punishments that the behavior produces.

OPERATION Piaget's term for an internalized (mental) action that fits into a logical system, allowing children to combine, separate, order, reorder, and transform information and objects in their minds.

ORAL STAGE In Freudian theory, the first stage of development, in which the mouth is the primary source of pleasure.

OSSIFICATION The conversion of cartilage into bone.

OVEREXTENSION A term used for the error of applying verbal labels too broadly. Young children commonly overextend the meaning of words when they are learning to talk; for example, using "*cat*" to mean all four-legged animals.

PEER An individual of comparable age and status to other individuals; the term is often used to refer to children of about the same age as one another.

PERMISSIVE PARENTING PATTERN Permissive parents exercise less explicit control over their children's behavior than do other parents. They give their children a lot of leeway to determine their own schedules and activities and often consult them about family policies. They make fewer demands on their children for achievement or mature behavior than do other parents.

PERSONALITY The pattern of characteristic behaviors that results from each person's unique mix of genetic endowment and personal experience. It also includes the way one conceives of oneself and one's characteristic style of dealing with others, as well as the idiosyncracies that make one distinctive.

PERSONALITY FORMATION The way in which individuals come to have a characteristic sense of themselves and a distinctive way of thinking, feeling, and seeking happiness for themselves.

PERSONAL RULES Rules created by individuals to regulate their own behavior.

PHALLIC STAGE According to Freud, a stage in development during which children begin to regard their own genitals as a major source of pleasure.

PHENOTYPE The organism's observable characteristics that result from the interaction of the genotype with the environment.

PHONEMES The sounds that signal differences among words in a language. Phonemes differ from language to language.

PHYLOGENY The evolutionary history of a species.

PLACENTA A complex organ made up of tissue from both the mother and the fetus that serves as both a barrier and a filter. As a barrier, it keeps the bloodstreams of the mother and the fetus separate. As a filter, it converts nutrients carried in the mother's bloodstream into nourishment for the fetus and it enables the fetus's waste products to be absorbed by the mother's bloodstream.

POLYGENIC TRAITS A genetic trait that is determined by the interaction of several genes. Most human traits are polygenic.

POSITIVE JUSTICE Damon's term for the process of reaching a decision about how to divide resources or distribute rewards fairly.

PRAGMATIC USE OF LANGUAGE The ability to select words and word orderings that do in fact convey what the speaker intends to communicate.

PRECAUSAL REASONING According to Piaget, a form of thinking observed in young children in which they are indifferent to causal explanation and fail to distinguish cause from effect.

PREFORMATIONIST HYPOTHESIS The hypothesis that the adult form is present in some way in the cells out of which it develops.

PREMATURE Born before the thirty-seventh week of gestation.

PREOPERATIONAL STAGE In Piagetian theory, the period between 2½ and 6 years, during which the child's thought does not have the clear-cut properties of the sensorimotor stage that precedes it or the stage of concrete operations that follows. During this period children often fail to distinguish their point of view from that of others, become easily captured by surface appearances, and are often confused about causal relations.

PREPARED CHILDBIRTH Special training in which pregnant women learn about the process of labor and are taught various techniques intended to reduce the sensation of pain.

PREREACHING A reflexlike movement in which newborns reach toward an object that catches their attention and si-

multaneously, but independently, make grasping movements.

PRIMACY The idea that the earliest experiences of children determine their later development.

PRIMARY CIRCULAR REACTION Behavior characteristic of the second substage of Piaget's sensorimotor period, which lasts from about 1 to 4 months, in which the baby repeats simple actions for their own sake.

PRIMARY IDENTIFICATION Freud's term for infants' recognition that some objects in the external world are like themselves.

PRIMARY MOTOR AREA The area of the cerebral cortex that controls voluntary movement.

PRIMARY SENSORY AREA Those areas of the brain that are responsible for the initial analysis of sensory information.

PRIMARY SEXUAL ORGANS Those organs that are involved in reproduction.

PROSOCIAL BEHAVIORS Behaviors that benefit the group with no direct reward for the benefactor. Prosocial behaviors include empathy, sharing, helping, and cooperation.

PROXIMODISTAL PATTERN The sequence of body development from the middle outward.

PUBERTY A revolutionary series of biological developments that transforms individuals from a state of physical immaturity to one in which they are biologically mature and capable of reproduction.

RANGE OF REACTION / NORM OF REACTION All the possible phenotypes for a single genotype that are compatible with life.

RECAPITULATE To repeat in concise form. The idea that human children recapitulate earlier stages of human evolution during their development was popular in the period when the study of child development began.

RECESSIVE ALLELE The allele that is not expressed when there are two different alleles for the same trait.

RECURSION A term for the embedding of sentences within each other.

REFLEXES Specific, well-integrated responses; behaviors that are automatically elicited by specific aspects of the environment.

REHEARSAL A strategy for remembering that involves repetition of material.

REINFORCEMENT In operant conditioning, reinforcement refers to the consequences of a behavior that makes the behavior either more or less likely to be repeated.

RELIABILITY A requirement of scientific knowledge that the phenomenon under study can be observed repeatedly and that different observers agree on what that they observe.

REPLICATION A study is replicated when the same procedures are used on another occasion and the same results are obtained.

REPRESENTATION The capacity to go beyond actions in a present world to "present" the world to oneself mentally.

REPRESENTATIVE SAMPLE A sample of individuals included in a study who are representative of the population to which the conclusions of the observations are to be applied.

REVERSIBILITY Piaget's term for mental operations in which children can think through an action and then reverse it.

RULE-BASED GAMES Games in which the rules are agreed upon ahead of time, and in which the objective of the game is to win by competing within the confines of the rules.

SCHEMA The structure, or organized pattern, of action that remains the same in similar or analogous circumstances.

SCRIPTS Generalized event representations developed by individuals as a result of their repeated participation in routine activities. Scripts specify the appropriate people who participate in an event, the social roles they play, the objects that are used, and the sequence of actions that occur. Scripts serve as guides to action for the participants, and help them to coordinate themselves with one another.

SECONDARY CIRCULAR REACTIONS The diligent repetition of an action by a baby in order to produce an interesting change in its environment. This is a characteristic behavior of the third substage of Piaget's sensorimotor period, which occurs approximately between the ages of 4 and 8 months.

SECONDARY IDENTIFICATION Freud's term for the endeavor to mold one's own ego to be like one that has been taken as a model.

SECONDARY SEXUAL CHARACTERISTICS The anatomical and physiological signs that outwardly distinguish males from females. These characteristics make their appearance as the primary sexual organs are maturing.

SECOND-ORDER THINKING The ability to develop rules about rules and to hold competing thoughts in mind while mulling over both thoughts.

SECURE BASE Bowlby's term for the source of security provided by the persons to whom a child is attached. The secure base helps to regulate the baby's explorations of the world.

SELF-REPORT A method of gathering data through diaries, interviews, or questionnaires, in which people report on their own psychological states and behaviors.

SENSORIMOTOR STAGE The first of Piaget's four developmental stages, during which the behaviors that develop involve coordination between infant's sensory experiences and simple motor behaviors. Piaget distinguished six substages in this period, which lasts for the first 2 years of life.

SENSORY RECEPTOR A neuron that is specialized to receive sensory input from the environment.

SENSORY REGISTER The term used by information processing psychologists to refer to the earliest stages of a cognitive act in which information from the environment is detected and becomes available for further processing.

SEX-LINKED CHARACTERISTIC An attribute determined by genes that are found on the X chromosome.

SEX ROLE A basic attribute of individuals that shapes many of their social roles. An individual's sex role is usually based on his or her biological gender, but there are exceptional cases.

SHORT-TERM MEMORY Working memory that retains new information for a period of several seconds; as opposed to long-term memory, in which information is held in storage.

SOCIAL COMPARISON A process in which children come to define themselves by comparing themselves with their peers. Social comparison comes to prominence in middle childhood.

SOCIAL CONVENTIONS Rules that are specific to a society, such as rules about who has authority over people and how it is exercised.

SOCIAL DEVELOPMENT A double-sided process in which children simultaneously become integrated into the larger social community and differentiated as distinctive individuals.

SOCIALIZATION The process by which children acquire the standards, values, and knowledge of their society.

SOCIAL PERSPECTIVE-TAKING The ability to think about how one person's actions and ideas will be perceived by others.

SOCIAL REFERENCING The communicating behavior in which babies keep a watchful eye on their mother's expression to see how they should interpret unusual events.

SOCIOGRAM The graphic representation of how each child feels about every other child in a group. A sociogram is derived from children's answers to questions about which children in a particular group they would like to be with or sit near, or about which children they like the most.

SOMATIC CELLS All the cells in the body except for the germ cells (ova and sperm).

SPECIFIC NOMINALS A term for words that label particular objects and people, rather than categories; for example, *Rover* rather than *dog*. Many of children's early words are specific nominals.

STAGE A distinctive period of development that is qualitatively different from the periods that come before and after.

STEPPING REFLEX The rhythmic leg movements newborn infants make when they are held in an upright position with their feet touching a flat surface.

STRANGE SITUATION A procedure designed by Mary Ainsworth to assess children's responses to a stranger when they are with their mothers, when they are left alone, and when they are reunited with their mothers.

STRUCTURED WHOLE A system of relationships that can be logically described and thought about.

SUPEREGO Freud's term for the part of the psyche that represents the authority of the social group.

SYMBOLIC PLAY Play in which one object stands for another. Children begin to participate in symbolic play during their second year.

SYNAPSE The small space between neurons across which nerve impulses must flow.

SYNTAX A term for the rules that govern both the sequence of words and the ordering of word parts within a sentence.

TEMPERAMENT The basic style with which an individual responds to the environment, as well as his or her dominant mood.

TERATOGENS Environmental agents that can cause deviations in normal development and lead to serious abnormalities or death.

TERTIARY CIRCULAR REACTIONS Piaget's term for the behaviors characteristic of substage 5 of the sensorimotor period in which infants become capable of performing varied action sequences, thereby making their explorations of the world more complex. Piaget referred to tertiary circular reactions "as experiments in order to see." They are typical of babies from about 8 to 18 months of age.

THEORY A broad framework or body of principles used to interpret a set of facts.

TOP-DOWN READING Reading in which the interpretation of what is being read is controlled by prior knowledge.

TRANSACTIONAL MODEL Models of development that trace the ways the characteristics of the child and the characteristics of the child's environment interact across time to determine developmental outcomes.

TROPHOBLAST The outer cells of the blastocyst that eventually develop into the membranes that support and protect the embryo.

UMBILICAL CORD A soft tube containing blood vessels that connects the embryo to the placenta.

UNCONDITIONAL RESPONSE A response that occurs unconditionally whenever a particular stimulus is present. Salivation, for example, is the unconditional response to food in the mouth.

UNCONDITIONAL STIMULUS In classical conditioning, a stimulus that always elicits a particular response without prior training. For example, food placed in the mouth is an unconditional stimulus for the salivary response.

UNDEREXTENSION A term for applying verbal labels too narrowly. Young children learning language commonly underextend the meaning of some words, using "*cat*" to apply only to black kittens, for example.

VALIDITY The scientific requirement that a description of behavior correctly reflect the underlying psychological process that the investigator claims it does.

VILLI The hairlike projections of the chorion that burrow into the lining of the uterus.

X CHROMOSOME The larger of the two chromosomes that determine the sex of the individual. Normal females have two X chromosomes, while normal males have only one.

Y CHROMOSOME The smaller of the two chromosomes that determine the sex of the individual. Normal males have one Y chromosome inherited from their fathers and one X inherited from their mothers. Normal females do not have a Y chromosome.

ZONA PELLUCIDA The thin, delicate envelope that surrounds the zygote and later the morula.

ZONE OF PROXIMAL DEVELOPMENT The kind of support provided by adults and more competent others that permits children to accomplish with assistance actions that they will later learn to accomplish independently.

ZYGOTE The single cell formed at conception by the union of the genetic material of the sperm and the ovum.

References

. . .

ABBOUD, T. K., KHOO, S. S., MILLER, F., DOAN, T., & HENRIKSEN, E. H. (1982). Maternal, fetal, and neonatal responses after epidural anesthesia with Bupevacaine, 2-Chloraprocaine, or Zedocaine. *Anesthesia and Analgesia, 61,* 638–643.

ABELES, R. P., & RILEY, M. W. (1987). Longevity, social structure and cognitive aging. In C. Schooler & K. W. Schaie (Eds.), *Cognitive functioning and social structure over the life course.* Norwood, N.J.: Ablex.

ABRAMOVITCH, R., CORTER, C., & LANDO, B. (1979). Sibling interaction in the home. *Child Development, 50,* 997–1003.

ABRAMOVITCH, R., PEPLER, D., & CORTER, C. (1982). Patterns of sibling interaction among pre-school-aged children. In M. Lamb & B. Sutton-Smith (Eds.), *Sibling relationships: Their nature and significance across the lifespan.* Hillsdale, N.J.: Erlbaum.

ABRAVANEL, E., LEVAN-GOLDSCHMIDT, E., & STEVENSON, M. B. (1976). Action imitation: The early phase of infancy. *Child Development, 47,* 1032–1044.

ABRAVANEL, E., & SIGAFOOS, A. D. (1984). Exploring the presence of imitation during early infancy. *Child Development, 55,* 381–392.

ACREDOLO, L. (1978). Development of spatial orientation in infancy. *Developmental Psychology, 14,* 224–234.

AD HOC DAY CARE COALITION (1985). *The crisis in infant and toddler care.* Washington, D.C.: Author.

ADELSON, J. (1972). The political imagination of the young adolescent. In J. Kagan & R. Coles (Eds.), *Twelve to sixteen: Early adolescence.* New York: Norton.

ADELSON, J. (1975). The development of ideology in adolescence. In S. E. Dragastin & G. H. Elder, Jr. (Eds.), *Adolescence in the life cycle.* Washington, D.C.: Hemisphere.

ADELSON, J., GREEN, B., & O'NEIL, R. P. (1969). Growth of the idea of law in adolescence. *Developmental Psychology, 1,* 327–332.

ADELSON, J., & O'NEIL, R. P. (1966). Growth of political ideas in adolescence: The sense of community. *Journal of Personality and Social Psychology, 4,* 295–306.

AINSWORTH, M. D. S. (1967). *Infancy in Uganda; Infant care and the growth of love.* Baltimore: Johns Hopkins Press.

AINSWORTH, M. D. S. (1982). Attachment: Retrospect and prospect. In C. M. Parkes & J. Stevenson-Hinde (Eds.), *The place of attachment in human behavior.* New York: Basic Books.

AINSWORTH, M. D. S., & BELL, S. M. (1969). Some contemporary patterns of mother-infant interaction in the feeding situation. In A. Ambrose (Ed.), *Stimulation in Early Infancy.* New York: Academic Press.

AINSWORTH, M. D. S., BELL, S. M., & STAYTON, D. J. (1971). Individual differences in strange-situation behavior of one-year-olds. In H. R. Schaffer (Ed.), *The origins of human social relations.* New York: Academic Press.

AINSWORTH, M. D. S., BLEHAR, M. C., WATERS, E., & WALL, S. (1978). *Patterns of attachment: A psychological study of the strange situation.* Hillsdale, N.J.: Erlbaum.

AINSWORTH, M. D. S., & WITTIG, B. A. (1969). Attachment and exploratory behavior of one-year-olds in a strange situation. In B. M. Foss (Ed.), *Determinants of infant behavior* (Vol. 4). London: Methuen.

ALDRICH, C. A., & HEWITT, E. S. (1947). A self regulating feeding program for infants. *Journal of the American Medical Association. 35,* 341.

ALEKSANDROWICZ, M. K. (1974). The effect of pain relieving drugs administered during labor and delivery on the behavior of the new born: A review. *Merrill-Palmer Quarterly. 20,* 121–141.

ALLEN, K. E., TURNER, K. D., & EVERETT, P. M. (1970). A behavior modification classroom for headstart children with problem behavior. *Exceptional Children, 37,* 119–127.

ALLISON, A. C. (1954). Protection afforded by sickle-cell trait against subtertian malarial infection. *British Medical Journal, 1,* 290–294.

ALLPORT, G. (1937). *Personality: A psychological interpretation.* New York: Holt, Rinehart and Winston.

AMES, B. N. (1979). Identifying environmental chemicals causing mutations and cancer. *Science, 204,* 587–593.

ANDERSON, A., & STOKES, S. (1984). Social and institutional influences on the development and practice of literacy. In H. Goelman, A. Oberg, & F. Smith (Eds.), *Awakening to literacy.* Exeter, N.H.: Heinemann.

ANGLIN, J. (1977). *Word, object, and conceptual development.* New York: Norton.

ANTONOV, A. N. (1947). Children born during the siege of Leningrad in 1942. *Journal of Pediatrics, 30,* 250.

APGAR, V. (1953). A proposal for a new method of evaluation of the newborn infant. *Current Researches in Anesthesia and Analgesia, 32,* 260–267.

ARCHER, S. L. (1985). Identity and the choice of social roles. In A. S. Waterman (Ed.), *Identity in adolescence: Processes and contents (New directions for child development,* No. 30). San Francisco: Jossey-Bass.

AREY, L. B. (1974). *Developmental anatomy: A textbook and laboratory manual of embryology* (7th ed.) Philadelphia: Saunders.

ARIÈS, P. (1962). *Centuries of childhood: A social history of family life.* New York: Vintage Books.

ARNHEIM, R. (1954). *Art and visual perception*. Berkeley: University of California Press.

ASCHER, M., & ASCHER, S. R. (1981). *Code of the quipu*. Ann Arbor: University of Michigan Press.

ASHER, S. R., & DODGE, K. A. (1986). Identifying children who are rejected by their peers. *Developmental Psychology, 22*, 444–449.

ASHMEAD, D. H., & PERLMUTTER, M. (1980). Infant memory in everyday life. In M. Perlmutter (Ed.), *Children's memory (New directions for child development*, No. 10). San Francisco: Jossey-Bass.

ASLIN, R. N. (1987). Visual and auditory development in infancy. In J. D. Osofsky (Ed.), *Handbook of Infant Development* (2nd ed.). New York: Wiley.

ATCHLEY, R. C. (1975). The life course, age grading, and age-linked demands for decision making. In N. Datan & L. H. Ginsberg (Eds.), *Life-span developmental psychology: Normative life crises*. New York: Academic Press.

ATKINSON, J. & BRADDICK, O. (1982). Sensory and perceptual capacities in the neonate. In P. Stratton (Ed.), *Psychology of the human newborn*. Chichester, Eng.: Wiley.

ATKINSON, R. C., & SHIFFRIN, R. M. (1980). The control of short-term memory. In R. L. Atkinson & R. C. Atkinson (Eds.), *Mind and behavior: Readings from Scientific American*. New York: W. H. Freeman.

AUSTIN, C. R., & SHORT, R. V. (Eds.). (1972). *Reproduction in mammals: Embryonic and fetal development*. Cambridge: Cambridge University Press.

AUSTIN, C. R., & SHORT, R. V. (Eds.) (1972). *Embryonic and fetal development*. Cambridge: Cambridge University Press.

AZUMA, H., KASHIWAGI, K., & HESS, R. (1981). *The influence of maternal teaching style upon the cognitive development of children*. Tokyo: University of Tokyo Press. (Text in Japanese).

BACHMAN, J. G. (1970). *The impact of family background and intelligence on tenth grade boys: Vol. 2. Youth in transition*. Ann Arbor, Mich.: Survey Research Center, Institute for Social Research.

BAILLARGEON, R. (1987). Object permanence in 3½- and 4½-month old infants. *Developmental Psychology, 23*, 655–664.

BAILLARGEON, R., SPELKE, E., & WASSERMAN, S. (1985). Object permanence in five-month-old infants. *Cognition, 20*, 191–208.

BALDWIN, A. L. (1946). Differences: Parent behavior toward three and nine year old children. *Journal of Personality, 15*, 143–165.

BALDWIN, A. L. (1947). Changes in parent behavior during pregnancy: An experiment in longitudinal analysis. *Child Development, 18*, 29–39.

BALDWIN, A. L. (1955). *Behavior and development in childhood*. New York: Dryden Press.

BALDWIN, J. M. (1902). Social and ethical interpretations in mental development (3rd ed.). New York, Macmillan.

BALL, S., & BOGATZ, G. A. (1972). Summative research of Sesame Street: Implications for the study of preschool children. In A. D. Pick (Ed.), *Minnesota Symposia on Child Psychology* (Vol. 6). Minneapolis: University of Minnesota Press.

BALTES, P. B., & BRIM, O. G., JR. (Eds.). (1979). *Life-span development and behavior* (Vol. 2). New York: Academic Press.

BALTES, P. B., DITTMAN-KOHLI, F., & DIXON, R. A. (1984). New perspectives on the development of intelligence in adulthood: Toward a dual-process conception and a model of selective optimization with compensation. In P. B. Baltes & O. G. Brim, Jr. (Eds.), *Life-span development and behavior* (Vol. 6). New York: Academic Press.

BALTES, P. B., FEATHERMAN, D. L., & LERNER, R. M. (Eds.) (1988). *Life-span development and behavior* (Vol. 8). Hillsdale, N.J.: Erlbaum.

BALTES, P. B., & SCHAIE, K. W. (Eds.). (1973). *Life-span developmental psychology: Personality and socialization*. New York: Academic Press.

BANDURA, A. (1964). The stormy decade: Fact or fiction. *Psychology in the School, 1*, 224–231.

BANDURA, A. (1965). Influence of models' reinforcement contingencies on the acquisition of imitative responses. *Journal of Personality and Social Psychology, 1*, 587–595.

BANDURA, A. (1969). Social-learning theory of identificatory processes. In D. A. Goslin (Ed.), *Handbook of socialization theory and research*. Chicago: Rand McNally.

BANDURA, A. (1973). *Aggression: A social learning analysis*. Englewood Cliffs, N.J.: Prentice-Hall.

BANDURA, A. (1977). *Social learning theory*. Englewood Cliffs, N.J.: Prentice-Hall.

BANDURA, A. (1986). *Social foundations of thought and action: A social cognitive theory*. Englewood Cliffs, N.J.: Prentice-Hall.

BANDURA, A., ROSS, D., & ROSS, S. A. (1963). Imitation of film-mediated aggressive models. *Journal of Abnormal and Social Psychology, 66*, 3–11.

BANDURA, A., & WALTERS, R. H. (1959). *Adolescent aggression*. New York: Ronald Press.

BANDURA, A., & WALTERS, R. H. (1963). *Social learning and personality development*. New York: Holt, Rinehart and Winston.

BANKS, M. S., & SALAPATEK, P. (1983). Infant visual perception. In P. H. Mussen (Ed.), *Handbook of child psychology: Vol. 2. Infancy and developmental psychobiology.* New York: Wiley.

BARGLOW, P., VAUGHN, B. E., & MOLITOR, N. (1987). Effects of maternal absence due to employment on the quality of infant-mother attachment in a low-risk sample. *Child Development, 58, 945–953.*

BARKER, R. G., & BARKER, L. S. (1968). The psychological ecology of old people in Midwest, Kansas, and Yoredale, Yorkshire. In B. L. Neugarten (Ed.), *Middle age and aging.* Chicago: University of Chicago Press.

BARKER, R. G., & WRIGHT, H. F. (1951). *One boy's day: A specimen record of behavior.* New York: Harper Brothers.

BARKER, R. G., & WRIGHT, H. F. (1955). *Midwest and its children.* New York: Harper & Row.

BARON, J. C. (1978). Intelligence and general strategies. In G. Underwood (Ed.), *Strategies of information processing.* London: Academic Press.

BARON-COHEN, S., LESLIE, A. M., & FRITH, U. (1985). Does the autistic child have a "theory of mind"? *Cognition, 21, 37–46.*

BARON-COHEN, S., LESLIE, A. M., & FRITH U. (1986). Mechanical behavioral and intentional understanding of picture stories in autistic children. *British Journal of Developmental Psychology, 4, 113–125.*

BARRETT, K. C., & CAMPOS, J. J. (1987). Perspectives on emotional development: II. A functionalist approach to emotions. In J. D. Osofsky (Ed.), *Handbook of Infant Development* (2nd ed.). New York: Wiley.

BARTLETT, E. (1977). The acquistion of the meaning of color terms. In P. T. Smith & R. N. Campbell (Eds.), *Proceedings of the Sterling conference on the psychology of language.* New York: Plenum Press.

BATES, E. (1976). *Language and context: The acquisition of pragmatics.* New York: Academic Press.

BATES, E., BENIGNI, L., BRETHERTON, I., CAMAIONI, L., & VOLTERRA, V. (1979). *The emergence of symbols: Cognition and communication in infancy.* New York: Academic Press.

BATES, E., & MACWHINNEY, B. (1982). A functionalist approach to grammatical development. In L. Gleitman and E. Wanner (Eds.), *Language acquisition: The state of the art.* Cambridge: Cambridge University Press.

BATES, E., & SNYDER, Z. (1987). The cognitive hypothesis in language development. In I. Uzgiris & J. McV. Hunt (Eds.), *Infant performance and experience: New findings with the ordinal scales.* Champagne: University of Illinois Press.

BATES, J. E. (1987). Temperament in infancy. In J. D. Osofsky (Ed.), *Handbook of Infant Development* (2nd ed.). New York: Wiley.

BATES, J. E., MASLIN, C. A., & FRANKEL, K. A. (1985). Attachment, security, and temperament as predictors of behavior: Problem ratings at three years. In I. Bretherton & E. Waters (Eds.) Growing points in attachment theory. *Monographs of the Society for Research in Child Development, 50,* (Serial No. 209).

BAUMRIND, D. (1967). Child care practices anteceding three patterns of pre-school behavior. *Genetic Psychology Monographs, 75, 43–88.*

BAUMRIND, D. (1971). Current patterns of parental authority. *Developmental Psychology Monographs, 4* (1, Part 2).

BAUMRIND, D. (1972). An exploratory study of socialization effects on Black children: Some Black-White comparisons. *Child Development, 43, 261–267.*

BAUMRIND, D. (1980). New directions in socialization research. *American Psychologist, 35, 639–652.*

BAUMRIND, D. (1986). Sex differences in the development of moral reasoning: A response to Walker's (1984) conclusion that there are none. *Child Development, 57, 511–521.*

BECK, N. C., & HULL, D. (1978). Natural childbirth: A review and analysis. *Obstetrics and Gynecology, 52, 371–379.*

BECKER, W. C., PETERSON, D. R., LURIA, Z., SHOEMAKER, D. J., & HELLMER, L. A. (1962). Relations of factors derived from parent interview ratings to behavior problems of five-year-olds. *Child Development, 33, 509–535.*

BELL, A. P., WEINBERG, M. S., & HAMMERSMITH, S. K. (1981). *Sexual preference: Its development in men and women.* Bloomington: Indiana University Press.

BELL, R. Q., WELLER, G., & WALDROP, M. F. (1971). Newborn and preschooler: Organization of behavior and relation between periods. *Monographs of the Society for Research in Child Development, 36* (1–2, Serial No. 142).

BELL, S. M., & AINSWORTH, M. (1972). Infant crying and maternal responsiveness. *Child Development, 43, 1171–1190.*

BELSKY, J. (1986). Infant day care: A cause for concern. *Zero to three, 6(5), 1–9.*

BELSKY, J. (1987). Risks remain. *Zero to three, 7(3), 22–24.*

BELSKY, J., & MOST, R. K. (1982). Infant exploration and play. In J. Belsky (Ed.), *In the beginning.* New York: Columbia University Press.

BELSKY, J., & ROVINE, M. (1987). Temperament and attachment security in the strange situation: An empirical rapprochement. *Child Development, 58, 787–795.*

BELSKY, J. & STEINBERG, L. D. (1978). The effects of day care: A critical review. *Child Development, 49, 929–949.*

BELSKY, J., STEINBERG, L. D., & WALKER, A. (1982). The ecology of day care. In M. E. Lamb (Ed.), *Nontraditional families: Parenting and child development.* Hillsdale, N.J.: Erlbaum.

BEM, S. L. (1981). Gender schema theory: A cognitive account of sex-typing. *Psychological Review, 88,* 354–364.

BERG, I. (1970). *Education and jobs: The great training robbery.* New York: Praeger.

BERG, W. K., & BERG, K. M. (1987). Psychophysiological development in infancy: State, startle, and attention. In J. D. Osofsky (Ed.), *Handbook of infant development* (2nd ed.). New York: Wiley.

BERGER, B. M. (1981). *The survival of a counter culture: Ideological work and everyday life among rural communards.* Berkeley: University of California Press.

BERGSMA, D. (Ed.). (1979). *Birth defects compendium* (2nd ed.). New York: Alan R. Liss.

BERMANT, G., & DAVIDSON, J. M. (1974). *Biological bases of sexual behavior.* New York: Harper & Row.

BERNAL, J. F. (1972). Crying during the first few days, and maternal responses. *Developmental Medicine and Child Neurology, 14,* 362–372.

BERNDT, T. J. (1979). Developmental changes in conformity to peers and parents. *Developmental Psychology, 15,* 608–616.

BERNDT, T. J. (1981). Relations between social cognitive, nonsocial cognitive, and social behavior: The case of friendship. In J. H. Flavell & L. Ross (Eds.), *Social cognitive development: Frontiers and possible futures.* Cambridge: Cambridge University Press.

BERNSTEIN, B. (1971). *Class, codes, and control: Vol. 1. Theoretical studies toward a sociology of language.* London: Routledge and Kegan Paul.

BERTENTHAL, B. I., CAMPOS, J. J., & BARRETT, K. C. (1984). Self-produced locomotions: An organizer of emotional, cognitive and social development in infancy. In R. Emde & R. Harmon (Eds.), *Continuities and discontinuities in development.* New York: Plenum Press.

BERTENTHAL, B. I., & FISCHER, K. W. (1978). Development of self-recognition in the infant. *Developmental Psychology, 14,* 44–50.

BEST, C. T., HOFFMAN, H., & GLANVILLE, B. B. (1982). Development of infant ear asymmetries for speech and music. *Perception and Psychophysics, 31,* 75–85.

BETTELHEIM, B. (1977). *The uses of enchantment: The meaning and importance of fairytales.* New York: Vintage Books.

BIEBER, I., DAIN, H. J., DINCE, P. R., DRELLICH, M. G., GRAND, H. G., GUNDLACH, R. H., KREMER, M. W., RIFKIN, A. H., WILBUR, C. B., & BEIBER, T. B. (Society of Medical Psychoanalysts). (1962). *Homosexuality: A psychoanalytic study.* New York: Basic Books.

BIGELOW, B. J., & LAGAIPA, J. J. (1975). Children's written descriptions of friendship: A multi-dimensional analysis. *Developmental Psychology, 41,* 857–858.

BIGELOW, B. J. (1977). Children's friendship expectations: A cognitive developmental study. *Child Development, 48,* 246–253.

BIJOU, S. W., & BAER, D. M. (1966). *Child development: Vol. 2. The universal stage of infancy.* New York: Appleton-Century-Crofts.

BINET, A., & SIMON, T. (1916). *The development of intelligence in children.* Vineland, N.J.: Publications of the Training School at Vineland. (Reprinted by Williams Publishing Co., Nashville, Tenn., 1980)

BIRNHOLZ, J. C., & BENACERRAF, B. R. (1983). The development of human fetal hearing. *Science, 222,* 516–518.

BITTMAN, S. J. & ZALK, S. R. (1978). *Expectant fathers.* New York: Hawthorn Books.

BLAKEMORE, C., & MITCHELL, D. E. (1973). Environmental modification of the visual cortex and the neural basis of learning and memory. *Nature, 241,* 467–468.

BLASS, E. M., GANCHROW, J. R, & STEINER, J. E. (1984). Classical conditioning in newborn humans 2–48 hours of age. *Infant Behavior and Development, 7,* 223–235.

BLEICHFELD, B., & MOELY, B. (1984). Psychophysiological response to an infant cry: Comparison of groups of women in different phases of the maternal cycle. *Developmental Psychology, 20,* 1082–1091.

BLOCH, H. A., & NIEDERHOFFER, A. (1958). *The gang: A study in adolescent behavior.* New York: Philosophical Library.

BLOCK, J. H., BLOCK, J., & GJERDE, P. (1986). The personality of children prior to divorce: A prospective study. *Child Development, 57,* 827–840.

BLOCK, J. H., BLOCK, J., & MORRISON, A. (1981). Parental agreement-disagreement on child-rearing orientations and gender-related personality correlates in children. *Child Development, 52,* 965–974.

BLOCK, N. J., & DWORKIN, G. (Eds.). (1976). *The I.Q. controversy.* New York: Pantheon.

BLOMBERG, S. (1980). Influences of maternal distress during pregnancy on complications in labor and delivery. *Acta Psychiatria Scandinavia, 62,* 399–404.

BLOS, P. (1962). *On adolescence.* New York: Free Press.

BLOS, P. (1972). The child analyst looks at the young adolescent. In J. Kagan & R. Coles (Eds.), *Twelve to sixteen: Early adolescence.* New York: Norton.

BOAS, F. (1911). *The mind of primitive man.* New York: Macmillan.

BOLTON, P. J. (1983). Drugs of abuse. In D. F. Hawkins (Ed.), *Drugs and pregnancy: Human teratogenesis and related problems*. Edinburgh: Churchill Livingston.

BONVILLIAN, J. D., ORLANSKY, M. D., & NOVACK, L. L. (1983). Developmental milestones: Sign language and motor development. *Child Development, 54,* 1435–1445.

BORKE, H. (1975). Piaget's mountains revisited: Changes in the egocentric landscape. *Developmental Psychology, 11,* 240–443.

BORNSTEIN, M. H. (1976). Infants are trichomats. *Journal of Experimental Child Psychology, 21,* 425–445.

BORNSTEIN, M. H., & SIGMAN, M. D. (1986). Continuity in mental development from infancy. *Child Development, 57,* 251–274.

BOUKYDIS, C. F. Z., & BURGESS, R. L. (1982). Adult physiological response to infant cries: Effects of temperament of infant, parental status, and gender. *Child Development, 53,* 1291–1298.

BOWER, T. G. R. (1979). *Human Development.* New York: W. H. Freeman.

BOWER, T. G. R. (1982). *Development in human infancy.* New York: W. H. Freeman.

BOWER, T. G. R., & WISHART, J. G. (1972). The effects of motor skill on object permanence. *Cognition, 1,* 165–171.

BOWLBY, J. (1969). *Attachment and loss: Vol. 1. Attachment.* New York: Basic Books.

BOWLBY, J. (1973). *Attachment and loss: Vol. 2. Separation.* New York: Basic Books.

BOWLBY, J. (1980). *Attachment and loss: Vol. 3. Loss, sadness, and depression.* New York: Basic Books.

BOXER, A. M., TOBIN-RICHARDS, M., & PETERSEN, A. C. (1983). Puberty: Physical change and its significance in early adolescence. *Theory into Practice, 22,* 85–90.

BRACKBILL, Y. (1971). Culmulative effects of continuous stimulation on arousal level in infants. *Child Development, 42,* 17–26.

BRACKBILL, Y. (1979). Obstetrical medication and infant behavior. In J. D. Osofsky (Ed.), *Handbook of infant development.* New York: Wiley.

BRACKBILL, Y., MCMANUS, K., & WOODWARD, L. (1985). *Medication in maternity: Infant exposure and maternal information.* Ann Arbor: University of Michigan Press.

BRADLEY, R. M., & MISTRETTA, C. M. (1975). Fetal sensory receptions. *Physiological Review, 55,* 352–382.

BRAINE, M. D. S. (1963). The ontogeny of English phrase structure: The first phase. *Language, 39,* 3–13.

BRANSFORD, J. D. (1979). *Human cognition: Learning, understanding, and remembering.* Belmont, Ca.: Wadsworth.

BRAVERMAN, H. (1974). *Labor and monopoly capital: The degradation of work in the twentieth century.* New York: Monthly Review Press.

BRAZELTON, T. B. (1973). *Neonatal behavior assessment scale.* London: Spastics International Medical Publications.

BRAZELTON, T. B. (1978). Introduction. In A. Sameroff (Ed.), Organization and stability of newborn behavior: A commentary on the Brazelton neonatal behavior assessment scale. *Monograms of the Society for Research in Child Development, 43*(5–6, Serial No. 177).

BRAZELTON, T. B., KOSLOWSKI, B., & MAIN, M. (1974). The origin of reciprocity: The early mother-infant interaction. In M. Lewis & L. Rosenblum (Eds.), *The effect of the infant on its caretaker.* New York: Wiley.

BRAZELTON, T. B., NUGENT, K. J., & LESTER, B. M. (1987). Neonatal behavioral assessment scale. In J. D. Osofsky (Ed.), *Handbook of Infant Development* (2nd ed.). New York: Wiley.

BRETHERTON, I. (1984). Representing the social world in symbolic play: Reality and fantasy. In I. Bretherton (Ed.), *Symbolic play: The development of social understanding.* New York: Academic Press.

BRETHERTON, I. (1985). Attachment theory: Retrospect and prospect. In I. Bretherton & E. Waters (Eds.), Growing Points in Attachment Theory. *Monographs of the Society for Research in Child Development. 50* (1–2, Serial No. 209).

BRETHERTON, I., & BATES, E. (1985). The development of representation from 10 to 28 months: Differential stability of language and symbolic play. In R. N. Emde & R. J. Harmon (Eds.), *Continuities and discontinuities in development.* New York: Plenum Press.

BRETHERTON, I., & WATERS, E. (Eds.). (1985). Growing points in attachment theory. *Monographs of the society for research in child development, 50,* (1–2, Serial No. 209).

BRITTAIN, C. V. (1963). Adolescent choices and parent-peer cross pressures. *American Sociological Review, 28,* 385–391.

BRONFENBRENNER, U. (1979). *The ecology of human development.* Cambridge: Harvard University Press.

BRONFENBRENNER, U. (1986). Ecology of the family as a context for human development: Research perspectives. *Developmental Psychology, 22,* 723–742.

BRONFENBRENNER, U., ALVAREZ, W. F., & HENDERSON, C. R., JR. (1984). Working and watching: Maternal employment status and parents' perceptions of their three-year-old children. *Child Development, 55,* 1362–1373.

BRONFENBRENNER, U., DEVEREUX, E. C., JR., SUCI, G. J., & ROGERS, R. R. (1965, April). Adults and peers as sources of conformity and autonomy. Paper presented at conference on Socialization for Competence, Cornell University.

BRONSON, W. C. (1975). Development of behavior with age-mates during the second year of life. In M. Lewis & L. A. Rosenblum (Eds.), *The origins of behavior: Friendship and peer relations.* New York: Wiley.

BROOKS,-GUNN, J., & PETERSEN, A. (Eds.). (1983). *Girls at puberty: Biological and psychosocial perspectives.* New York: Plenum Press.

BROPHY, J. E. (1983). Research on the self-fulfilling prophecy and teacher expectations. *Journal of Educational Psychology, 75,* 631–661.

BROUGHTON, J. (1978). Development of concepts of self, mind, reality, and knowledge. In W. Damon (Ed.), *Social Cognition (New Directions for Child Development,* No. 1). San Francisco: Jossey-Bass.

BROWN, A. L., BRANSFORD, J. D., FERRARA, R. A., & CAMPIONE, J. C. (1983). Learning, remembering, and understanding. In P. Mussen (Ed.), *Handbook of child psychology: Vol. 3. Cognitive development.* New York: Wiley.

BROWN, B. B. (1982). The extent and effects of peer pressure among high school students: A retrospective analysis. *Journal of Youth and Adolescence, 11,* 121–133.

BROWN, B. B., CLASEN, D. R., & EICHER, S. A. (1986). Perception of peer pressure, peer conformity dispositions, and self reported behavior among adolescents. *Developmental Psychology, 22,* 521–530.

BROWN, B. B., LOHR, M. J. L., & MCCLENAHAN, E. L. (1986). Early adolescents' perceptions of peer pressure. *Journal of Early Adolescence, 6,* 139–154.

BROWN, G. W., NI BHROCHLÁIN, M., & HARRIS, T. O. (1975). Social class and psychiatric disturbance among women in an urban population. *Sociology, 9,* 225–254.

BROWN, J. W., & JAFFE, J. (1975). Hypothesis on cerebral dominance. *Neuropsychologia, 13,* 107–110.

BROWN, P., & ELLIOT, R. (1965). Control of aggression in a nursery school class. *Journal of Experimental Child Psychology, 2,* 103–107.

BROWN, R. (1973). *A first language: The early stages.* Cambridge: Harvard University Press.

BROWN, R., & BELLUGI, U. (1964). Three processes in the child's acquisition of syntax. *Harvard Educational Review, 34,* 133–151.

BROWN, R., & HERRNSTEIN, R. J. (1975). *Psychology.* Boston: Little, Brown.

BROWNE, SIR THOMAS (1642/1964). *Religio Medici.* London: Oxford University Press.

BROWNELL, W. A. (1928). *The development of children's number ideas in the primary grades.* Chicago: University of Chicago Press.

BRUNER, J. S. (1960). *The process of education.* Cambridge: Harvard University Press.

BRUNER, J. S. (1966). On cognitive growth. In J. S. Bruner, R. R. Olver, & P. M. Greenfield (Eds.), *Studies in cognitive growth.* New York: Wiley.

BRUNER, J. S. (1968). *Process of cognitive growth: Infancy.* Worcester, Mass: Clark University Press.

BRUNER, J. S. (1972). The nature and uses of immaturity. *American Psychologist, 27,* 687–708.

BRUNER, J. S. (1983). *Child's talk.* New York: Norton.

BRUNER, J. S. (1986). Actual minds, possible worlds. Cambridge: Harvard University Press.

BULLOCK, M., & GELMAN, R. (1979). Preschool children's assumptions about cause and effect: Temporal ordering. *Child Developmental, 50,* 89–96.

BULLOUGH, V. (1981). Age of menarche: A misunderstanding. *Science, 213,* 365–366.

BURLINGHAM, D., & FREUD, A. (1942). *Young children in wartime.* London: Allen and Unwin.

BUSHNELL, I. W. R. (1982). Discrimination of faces by young infants. *Journal of Experimental Child Psychology, 33,* 298–308.

BUSHNELL, I. W. R. (1985). The decline of visually guided reaching. *Infant Behavior and Development, 8,* 139–155.

BUSS, A. H., & PLOMIN, R. (1975). *A temperament theory of personality development.* New York: Wiley.

BUTTERFIELD, E. L., & SIPERSTEIN, G. N. (1972). Influence of contingent auditory stimulation upon nonnutritional sucking. In J. Bosma (Ed.), *Oral sensation and perception: The mouth of the infant.* Springfield, Ill.: Charles C. Thomas.

CAIRNS, R. B. (1979). *Social development: The origins of interchanges.* New York: W. H. Freeman.

CAIRNS, R. B. (1983). The emergence of developmental psychology. In P. H. Mussen (Ed.), *Handbook of child psychology: Vol. 1. History, theory and methods.* New York: Wiley.

CALDWELL, B. M., & BRADLEY, R. H. (1978). *Manual for the home observation for measurement of the environment.* Little Rock: University of Arkansas.

CAMPOS, J. J., BENSON, J., & RUDY, L. (1986). The role of self-produced locomotion in spatial behavior. Poster-paper presented at the meeting of the International Conference for Infant Studies. Beverly Hills, California.

CAMPOS, J. J., BARRETT, K. C., LAMB, M. E., GOLDSMITH, H. H., & STENBERG, C. (1983). Socioemotional development. In P. H. Mussen (Ed.), *Handbook of child psy-*

chology: Vol. 2. Infancy and developmental psychobiology. New York: Wiley.

CAMPOS, J. J., & STENBERG, C. R. (1981). Perception, appraisal, and emotion: The onset of social referencing. In M. E. Lamb & L. R. Sherrod (Eds.), *Infants social cognition: Empirical and social considerations.* Hillsdale, N.J.: Erlbaum.

CAPON, N., & KUHN, D. (1979). Logical reasoning in the supermarket: Adult females' use of proportional reasoning strategy in an everyday context. *Developmental Psychology, 15,* 450–452.

CAREW, J. V. (1980). Experience and the development of young children at home and in day care. *Monographs of the Society for Research in Child Development, 45(6–7,* Serial No. 187).

CAREY, S. (1978). The child as word learner. In M. Halle, J. Bresnan, & G. A. Miller (Eds.), *Linguistic theory and psychological reality.* Cambridge: MIT Press.

CAREY, S. (1983). Cognitive development: The descriptive problem. In M. Gazzaniga (Ed.), *Handbook for cognitive neurology.* Hillsdale, N.J.: Erlbaum.

CAREY, S. (1985). *Conceptual change in childhood.* Cambridge: MIT Press.

CARMICHAEL, L. (1926). The development of behavior in vertebrates experimentally removed from the influence of external stimulation. *Psychological Review, 33,* 51–58.

CARMICHAEL, L. (1970). Onset and early development of behavior. In P. H. Mussen (Ed.), *Carmichael's manual of child psychology: Vol. I, Part I. Infancy and early experience.* New York: Wiley.

CARNEGIE COMMISSION ON POLICY STUDIES IN HIGHER EDUCATION (1980). *Giving youth a better chance.* San Francisco: Jossey-Bass.

CARRAHER, T. N., & CARRAHER, D. W. (1981). Do Piagetian stages describe the reasoning of unschooled adults? *Quartly Newsletter of the Laboratory of Comparative Human Cognition, 3,* 61–68.

CARROLL, J. B. (1982). The measurement of intelligence. In R. J. Sternberg (Ed.), *The handbook of human intelligence.* Cambridge: Cambridge University Press.

CASE, R. (1984). The process of stage transition: A neo-Piagetian view. In R. J. Sternberg (Ed.), *Mechanisms of cognitive development.* New York: W. H. Freeman.

CASE, R. (1985). *Intellectual development: A systematic reinterpretation.* New York: Academic Press.

CASE, R., & KHANNA, F. (1981). The missing links: Stages in children's progression from sensorimotor to logical thought. In K. W. Fischer (Ed.), *Cognitive development (New directions for child development,* No. 12). San Francisco: Jossey-Bass.

CASE, R., KURLAND, D. M., & GOLDBERG, J. (1982). Operational efficiency and growth of short-term memory span. *Journal of Experimental Child Psychology, 33,* 386–404.

CASE, R., MARINI, Z., MCKEOUGH, A., DENNIS, S., & GOLDBERG, J. (1986). Horizontal structure in middle childhood: Cross domain parallels in the course of cognitive growth. In I. Levin (Ed.), *Stage and structure: Reopening the debate.* Norwood, N.J.: Ablex.

CATTELL, R. B. (1949). *The culture free intelligence test.* Champaign, Ill.: Institute for Personality and Ability Testing.

CAZDEN, C. (1965). *Environmental assistance to the child's acquisition of grammar.* Unpublished doctoral dissertation. Harvard University.

CECI, S. J., TOGLIA, M. P., & ROSS, D. F. (Eds.). (1987). *Children's eyewitness memory.* New York: Springer Verlag.

CHALL, J. (1983). *Stages of reading development.* New York: McGraw-Hill.

CHAND, I. P., CRIDER, D. M., & WILLITS, F. K. (1975). Parent-youth disagreement as perceived by youth: A longitudinal study. *Youth and Society, 6,* 365–375.

CHASE, A. (1977). *The legacy of Malthus.* New York: Knopf.

CHASE, W.G., & SIMON, H. A. (1973). Perception in chess. *Cognitive Psychology, 4,* 55–81.

CHASE-LANSDALE, L. P., & OWEN, M. T. (1987). Maternal employment in a family context: Effect on infant-mother and infant-father attachments. *Child Development, 58,* 1505–1512.

CHENEY, D. L., & SEYFARTH, R. M. (1982). How vervet monkeys perceive their grunts: Field playback experiments. *Animal Behavior, 30,* 739–751.

CHESS, S., & THOMAS, A. (1982). Infant bonding: Mystique and reality. *American Journal of Orthopsychiatry, 52,* 213–221.

CHI, M. T. H. (1978). Knowledge structures and memory development. In R. S. Siegler (Ed.), *Children's thinking: What develops?* Hillsdale, N.J.: Erlbaum.

CHI, M. T. H., GLASER, R., & REES, E. (1982). Expertise in problem solving. In R. J. Sternberg (Ed.), *Advances in the psychology of human intelligence* (Vol. 1). Hillsdale, N.J.: Erlbaum.

CHI, M. T. H., & KLAHR, D. (1975). Span and rate of apprehension in children and adults. *Journal of Experimental Child Psychology, 19,* 434–439.

CHI, M. T. H., & KOESKE, R. D. (1983). Network representation of a child's dinosaur knowledge. *Developmental Psychology, 19,* 29–39.

CHILDS, C. P., & GREENFIELD, P. M. (1980). Informal modes of learning and teaching: The case of Zinacanteco learning. In N. Warren (Ed.), *Studies in cross-*

cultural psychology (Vol. 2). New York: Academic Press.

CHODOROW, N. Family structure and feminine personality. In M. Z. Rosaldo & L. Lamphere (Eds.), *Women, culture and society*. Stanford: Stanford University Press.

CHOMSKY, C. (1969). *Acquisition of syntax in children from 5 to 10*. Cambridge: MIT Press.

CHOMSKY, N. (1965). *Aspects of a theory of syntax*. Cambridge: MIT Press.

CHOMSKY, N. (1975). *Reflections on language*. New York: Pantheon.

CHOMSKY, N. (1980). Initial states and steady states. In M. Piatelli-Palmerini (Ed.), *Language and learning: The debate between Jean Piaget and Noam Chomsky*. Cambridge: Harvard University Press.

CHRISTENSEN, H. T., & GREGG, C. F. (1970). Changing sex norms in America and Scandinavia. *Journal of Marriage and the Family, 32*, 616–627.

CHUKOVSKY, K. (1968). *From two to five*. Berkeley: University of California Press.

CHURCH, J. (1966). *Three babies*. New York: Random House.

CHURCH, R. M. (1974). Refelx action. *The world book encyclopedia* (Vol. 16). Chicago: Field Enterprises.

CIANFRANI, T. (1960). *A short history of obstetrics and gynecology*. Springfield, Ill.: Charles Thomas.

CIBA PHARMACEUTICAL COMPANY. (1965). *The CIBA collection of medical illustrations*, illustrated by Frank H. Netter, M. D.

CLARK, E. V. (1973). What's in a word? On the child's acquisition of semantics in his first language. In T. E. Moore (Ed.), *Cognitive development and the acquisition of language*. New York: Academic Press.

CLARKE, A. M., & CLARKE, A. D. B. (1986). Thirty years of child psychology: A selective review. *Journal of Child Psychology and Psychiatry, 27*, 719–759.

CLARKE-STEWART, A. (1984). Day-care: A new context for research and development. In M. Perlmutter (Ed.), *Parent-child interaction and parent-child relations in child development: The Minnesota Symposia on Child Psychology* (Vol. 17). Hillsdale, N.J.: Erlbaum.

CLARKE-STEWART, A. (1978). And daddy makes three: The father's impact on mother and young child. *Child Development, 49*, 466–479.

CLARKE-STEWART, A. (1982). *Daycare*. Cambridge: Harvard University Press.

CLARKE-STEWART, A., & FEIN, G. G. (1983). Early childhood programs. In P. H. Mussen (Ed.), *Handbook of child psychology: Vol. 2. Infancy and developmental psychobiology*. New York: Wiley.

CLAUSEN, J. A. (1975). The social meaning of differential physical and sexual maturation. In S. E. Dragastin & G. E. Elder, Jr. (Eds.), *Adolescence in the life cycle*. Washington, D.C.: Hemisphere Press.

CLIFFORD, E. (1959). Discipline in the home: A controlled observational study of parental practices. *Journal of Genetic Psychology, 95*, 45–82.

COHEN, J. E., & PARMALEE, A. H. (1983). Prediction of five-year Stanford-Binet scores in preterm infants. *Child Development, 54*, 1242–1253.

COIE, J. D., & KUPERSMIDT, J. B. (1983). A behavioral analysis of emerging social status in boys' groups. *Child Development, 54*, 1400–1416.

COLBY, A., KOHLBERG, L., GIBBS, J., & LIEBERMAN, M. (1983). A longitudinal study of moral development. *Monographs of the Society for Research in Child Development, 48*, (1–2, Serial No. 200).

COLE, C. B., & LOFTUS, E. F. (1987). The memory of children. In S. J. Ceci, M. P. Toglia, & D. F. Ross (Eds.), *Children's eyewitness memory*. New York: Springer Verlag.

COLE, M. (1985). Mind as a cultural achievement: Implications for IQ testing. In E. Eisner (Ed.), *Learning and teaching the ways of knowing*. Chicago: National Society for the Study of Education.

COLE, M., GAY, J., GLICK, J. A., & SHARP, D. W. (1971). *The cultural context of learning and thinking*. New York: Basic Books.

COLE, M., & MEANS, B. (1981). *Comparative studies of how people think*. Cambridge: Harvard University Press.

COLE, M., & SCRIBNER, S. (1974). *Culture and thought*. New York: Wiley.

COLE, S. (1980a). *Working kids on working*. New York: Lothrop, Lee and Shepard

COLE, S. (1980b). Send our children to work? *Psychology Today, 14*, 44–68.

COLEMAN, J. C. (1980). *The nature of adolescence*. London: Methuen.

COLEMAN, J. S. (1962). *The adolescent society*. Glencoe, Ill.: Free Press.

COLEMAN, P. D., & RIESEN, A. H. (1968). Environmental effects on cortical dendritic fields: I. Rearing in the dark. *American Journal of Anatomy, 102*, 363–374.

COLES, R. (1967). *Children of crisis: A study of crisis and fear*. Boston: Atlantic–Little, Brown.

COLLINS, A. (1975). The developing child as viewer. *Journal of Communication, 25*, 35–43.

CONANT, L. L. (1896). *The number concept*. New York: Macmillan.

CONDON, R. G. (1987). *Inuit youth*. New Brunswick, N.J.: Rutgers University Press.

CONEL, J. L. (1939–1967). *The postnatal development of the human cerebral cortex* (8 vols.). Cambridge: Harvard University Press.

CONNELL, D. B. (1976). *Individual differences in attachment: An investigation into stability, implications, and relationships to the structure of early language development.* Unpublished doctoral dissertation, Syracuse University.

CONSORTIUM FOR LONGITUDINAL STUDIES (1983). *As the twig is bent.* Hillsdale, N.J.: Erlbaum.

CONSTANTINOPLE, A. (1969). An Eriksonian measure of personality development in college students. *Developmental Psychology, 1*, 357–372.

COOPERSMITH, S. (1967). *The antecedents of self esteem.* New York: W. H. Freeman.

CORBIN, P. F., & BICKFORD, R. G. (1955). Studies of the electroencephalogram of normal children. *Electroencephalography and Clinical Neurology, 7*, 15–28.

COREN, S., PORAC, C. E., & DUNCAN, P. (1981). Lateral preference behaviors in preschool children and young adults. *Child Development, 52*, 443.

CORNELL, E. H., & MCDONNELL, P. M. (1986). Infants' acuity at twenty feet. *Investigative Opthalmology and Visual Science, 27*, 1417–1420.

CORSARO, W. A. (1981). Friendship in the nursery school: Social organization in a peer environment. In S. R. Asher & J. M. Gottman (Eds.), *The development of children's friendships.* Cambridge: Cambridge University Press.

CORTER, C. M., ZUCKER, K. J., & GALLIGAN, R. F. (1980). Patterns in infants' search for mother during brief separation. *Developmental Psychology, 16*, 62–70.

COUNCIL ON INTERRRACIAL BOOKS FOR CHILDREN. (1976). *Human (and anti-human) values in children's books.* New York: Racism and Sexism Resource Center for Educators.

COWAN, R. (1987). Assessing children's understanding of one-to-one correspondence. *British Journal of Developmental Psychology, 5*, 140–153.

COWAN, W. M. (1979). The development of the brain. *Scientific American, 241*, 112–133.

COWEN, E. L., PEDERSON, A., BABIGIAN, H., IZZO, L. D., & TROST, M. A. (1973). Long term follow-up of early detected vulnerable children. *Journal of Consulting and Clinical Psychology, 41*, 438–446.

CRAGO, M., & CRAGO, H. (1983). *Prelude to literacy.* Carbondale: Southern Illinois University Press.

CRANDALL, R. (1973). The measurement of self-esteem and related concepts. In J. P. Robinson & P. R. Shaver (Eds), *Measures of social psychological attitudes* (rev. ed.). Ann Arbor, Mich: Institute for Social Research.

CRAVIOTO, J., DELICARDIE, E. R., & BIRCH, H. G. (1966).

Nutrition, growth and neurointergrative development: An experimental and ecological study. *Pediatrics, 38*, 319–372.

CRNIC, K. A., RAGOZIN, A. S., GREENBERG, M.T., ROBINSON, N. M., & BASHAM, R. R. (1983). Social interaction and developmental compliance of preterm and fullterm infants during first year of life. *Child Development, 54*, 1199–1210.

CRONBACH, L. J. (1975). Beyond the two disciplines of scientific psychology. *American Psychologist, 30*, 116–127.

CROWELL, D., EVANS, I., & O'DONNELL, C. (Eds.). (1987). *Childhood aggression and violence: Sources of influence, prevention, and control.* New York: Plenum Press.

CSIKSZENTMIHALYI, M., & LARSON, R. (1984). *Being adolescent: Conflict and growth in the teenage years.* New York: Basic Books.

CURTIS, H. (1979). *Biology.* New York: Worth.

CURTISS, S. (1977). *Genie: A psychological study of a modern-day wild child.* New York: Academic Press.

D'AMICO, R. (1984). Does employment during high school impair academic progress? *Sociology of Education, 57*, 152–164.

D'ANDRADE, R. G. (1974). Memory and assessment of behavior. in H. M. Blalock, Jr. (Ed.), *Measurement in the social sciences.* Chicago: Aldine.

DAMON, W. (1975). Early conceptions of positive justice as related to the development of logical operations. *Child Development, 46*, 301–312.

DAMON, W. (1977). *The social world of the child.* San Francisco: Jossey-Bass.

DAMON, W. (1980). Patterns of change in children's social reasoning: A two-year longitudinal study. *Child Development, 51*, 1010–1017.

DAMON. W. (1983). *Social and personality development: Infancy through adolescence.* New York: Norton.

DARWIN, C. (1877). A biographical sketch of an infant. *Mind, 2*, 286–294.

DARWIN, C. (1958). *The origin of species.* New York: Penguin. (Originally published in 1859)

DASEN, P. R. (1972). Cross-cultural Piagetian research: A summary. *Journal of Cross-cultural Psychology, 3*, 29–39.

DASEN, P. R. (1977). Are cognitive processes universal? A contribution to cross-cultural Piagetian psychology. In N. Warren (Ed.), *Studies in cross-cultural psychology* (Vol. 1). London: Academic Press.

DASEN, P. R. (1977). *Piagetian psychology: Cross cultural contributions.* New York: Gardner.

DASEN, P. R. (1982). Cross-cultural data on operational development: Asymptotic development curves. In T. G. Bever (Ed.), *Regressions in Development*. Hillsdale, N.J.: Erlbaum.

DASEN, P. R., & HERON, A. (1981). Cross-cultural tests of Piaget's theory. In H. Triandis & A. Heron (Eds.), *Handbook of cross-cultural psychology: Vol. 4. Developmental psychology*. Boston: Allyn and Bacon.

DASEN, P. R., NGINI, L., & LAVALÉE, M. (1979). Cross-cultural training studies of concrete operations. In L. H. Eckenberger, W. J. Lonner, & Y. H. Poortinga (Eds.), *Cross-cultural contributions to psychology*. Amsterdam: Swets & Zeilinger.

DAVID, H. P. (1981). Unwantedness: Longitudinal studies of Prague children born to women twice denied abortions for the same pregnancy and matched controls. In P. Ahmed (Ed.), *Pregnancy, childbirth, and parenthood*. New York: Elsevier.

DAVIS, A. (1948). *Social class differences in learning*. Cambridge: Harvard University Press.

DECARIE, T. G. (1969). A study of the mental and emotional development of the thalidomide child. In B. M. Foss (Ed.), *Determinants of infant behavior* (Vol. 4). London: Methuen.

DE CASPER, A. J., & FIFER, W. P. (1980). Of human bonding: Newborns prefer their mother's voices. *Science, 208,* 1174–1176.

DE CASPER, A. J., & SIGAFOOS, A. D. (1983). The intrauterine heartbeat: A potent reinforcer for newborns. *Infant Behavior and Development, 6,* 19–25.

DE CASPER, A. J. & SPENCE, M. J. (1986). Prenatal maternal speech influences newborn's perception of speech sounds. *Infant Behavior and Development, 9,* 133–150.

DE CHATEAU, P. (1987). Parent-infant socialization in several Western European countries. In J. D. Osofsky (Ed.), *The handbook of infant development* (2nd ed.). New York: Wiley.

DE FLEUR, L., & MENKE, B. (1975). Learning about the labor force: Occupational knowledge among high school males. *Sociology of Education, 48,* 324–345.

DE LOACHE, J. (1984). What's this? Maternal questions in joint picture book reading with toddlers. *Quarterly Newsletter of the Laboratory of Comparative Human Cognition, 6,* 87–95.

DE LOACHE, J. S. (1987). Rapid change in the symbolic functining of very young children. *Science, 238,* 1556–1557.

DE LOACHE, J. S. & BROWN, A. L. (1979). Looking for Big Bird: Studies of memory in very young children. *Quarterly Newsletter of the Laboratory of Comparative Human Cognition, 1,* 53–57.

DEMOS, J., & DEMOS, V. (1969). Adolescence in historical

perspective. *Journal of Marriage and the Family, 31,* 632–638.

DENNIS, W. (1973). *Children of the creche*. New York: Appleton-Century-Crofts.

DENNIS, W., & DENNIS, M. (1940). The effect of cradling practices upon the onset of walking in Hopi children. *Journal of Genetic Psychology, 56,* 77–86.

DENT, H. R. (1982). The effects of interviewing strategies on the results of interviews with child witnesses. In A. Trankell (Ed.), *Reconstructing the past*. Deventer, the Netherlands: Kluwer.

DEREGOWSKI, J. B. (1980). *Illusions, patterns, and pictures: A cross-cultural perspective*. London: Academic Press.

DESCARTES, R. (1985). Lettre à Morus 5/2/1649. In R. Descartes, *Oeuvres et lettres*. Paris: Gallimard.

DE VILLIERS, J. G., & DE VILLIERS, P. A. (1978). *Language acquisition*. Cambridge: Harvard University Press.

DE VILLIERS, J. G., & DE VILLIERS, P. A. (1979). *Early language*. Cambridge: Harvard University Press.

DE VRIES, R. (1969). Constancy of genetic identity in the years three to six. *Monographs of the Society for Research in Child Development, 34,* (Serial No. 127). Chicago: University of Chicago Press.

DE VRIES, M. W., & DE VRIES, M. R. (1977). The cultural relativity of toilet training readiness: A perspective from East Africa. *Pediatrics, 60* (2), 170–177.

DIAMOND, A. (1985). Development of the ability to use recall to guide action, as indicated by infants' performance on AB. *Child Development, 56,* 868–883.

DICK-READ, G. (1933). *Childbirth without fear*. New York: Harper & Row.

DIENES, Z. P. (1966). *Mathematics in the primary school*. London: Macmillan.

DILLARD, A. (1987). *An American childhood*. New York: Harper & Row.

DODGE, K. A. (1983). Behavioral antecedents of peer social status. *Child Development, 54,* 1386–1399.

DOISE, W., MUGNY, G., & PERRET-CLERMONT, A. N. (1975). Social understanding and the development of cognitive operations. *European Journal of Social Psychology, 5,* 367–383.

DOLAN, M. (1983, March 5). Boy with toy gun shot, killed by Stanton officer. *Los Angeles Times*, Part 1, pp. 1, 28,

DONALDSON, M. (1978). *Children's minds*. New York: Norton.

DORE, J. (1978). Conditions for acquisition of speech acts. In I. Markova (Ed.), *The social concept of language*. New York: Wiley.

DORE, J. (1979). Conversational acts and the acquisition of

language. in E. Ochs & B. B. Schieffelin (Eds.), *Developmental Pragmatics*. New York: Academic Press.

DORE, J., GEARHART, M., & NEWMAN, D. (1979). The structure of nursery school conversation. In K. E. Nelson (Ed.), *Children's language* (Vol 1). Hillsdale, N.J.: Erlbaum.

DORNBUSCH, S. M., RITTER, P. L., LEIDERMAN, P. H., ROBERTS, D. F., & FRALEIGH, M. J. The relation of parenting style to adolescent school performance. *Child Development, 58,* 1244–1257.

DORNER, G. (1976). *Hormones and brain differentiation.* Amsterdam: Elsevier.

DORR, A. (1983). No shortcuts to judging reality. In P. E. Bryant & S. Anderson (Eds.), *Watching and understanding T.V.: Research on children's attention and comprehension.* New York: Academic Press.

DORR, A., GRAVES, S. B., & PHELPS, E. (1980). Television literacy for young children. *Journal of Communication, 30,* 71–83

DOTT, A., FORT, B., & ARTHUR, T. (1975). The effects of maternal demographic factors on infant mortality rates: Summary of the findings of the Louisiana Infant Mortality Study: Part 1. *American Journal of Obstetrics and Gynecology, 123,* 847–853.

DOTT, A., FORT, B., & ARTHUR, T. (1975). The effects of availability and utilization of prenatal care and hospital services of infant mortality rates: Summary of the findings of the Louisiana Infant Mortality Study: Part 2. *American Journal of Obstetrics and Gynecology, 123,* 854–860.

DOUVAN, E., & ADELSON, J. (1966). *The adolescent experience.* New York: Wiley.

DOYLE, A. B. (1981). Friends, acquaintances, and strangers: The influence of familiarity and ethnolinguistic background on social interaction. In S. R. Asher & J. M. Gottman (Eds.), *The development of children's friendships.* Cambridge: Cambridge University Press.

DREYFUS-BRISAC, C. (1978). Ontogenesis of brain bioelectrical activity and sleep organization in neonates and infants. In F. Falkner & J. M. Tanner (Eds.), *Human Growth: Vol. 3 Neurobiology and Nutrition.* New York: Plenum Press.

DUNCAN, P. D., RITTER, P. L., DORNBUSCH, S. M., GROSS, R. T., & CARLSMITH, J. M. (1985). The effects of pubertal timing on body image, school behavior, and deviance. *Journal of Youth and Adolescence, 14,* 227–235.

DUNN, J. (1977). *Distress and comfort.* Cambridge: Harvard University Press.

DUNN, J. (1984). *Sisters and brothers.* Cambridge: Harvard University Press.

DUNN, J., & KENDRICK, C. (1979). Young siblings in the context of family relationships. In M. Lewis & L. A. Rosenblum (Eds.), *The child and its family.* New York: Plenum Press.

DUNPHY, D. C. (1963). The social strucure of urban adolescent peer groups. *Sociometry, 26,* 230–246.

DURRETT, M. E., OTAKI, M., & RICHARDS, P. (1984). Attachment and mothers' perception of support from the father. *Journal of the International Society for the Study of Behavioral Development, 7,* 167–176.

DWECK, C. S., & BUSH, E. S. (1976). Sex differences in learned helplessness: I. Differential debilitation with peer and adult evaluators. *Developmental Psychology, 12,* 147–156.

DWECK, C. S., DAVIDSON, W., NELSON, S., & ENNA, B. (1978). Sex differences in learned helplessnes: II. The contingencies of evaluative feedback in the classroom. III. An experimental analysis, *Developmental Psychology, 14,* 268–276.

DWECK, C. S., & ELLIOTT, E. S. (1983). Achievement motivation. In P. H. Mussen (Ed.), *Handbook of child psychology:* Vol. 4. *Personality and social development.* New York: Wiley.

DWECK, C. S., & GOETZ, T. E. (1978). Attributions and learned helplessness. In J. H. Harvey, W. Ickles, & R. F. Kidd (Eds.), *New directions in attribution research* (Vol. 2). Hillsdale, N.J.: Erlbaum.

ECKERMAN, C. D., STURM, L. A., & GROSS, S. J. (1985). Different developmental courses for very-low-birth-weight infants differing in early hand growth. *Developmental Psychology, 21,* 813–827.

EDELSTEIN, W., KELLER, M., AND WAHLEN, K. (1984). Structure and content in social cognition: Conceptual and empirical analysis. *Child Development, 55,* 1514–1526.

EDER, D. & HALLINAN, M. T. (1978). Sex differences in children's friendships. *American Sociological Review, 43,* 237–250.

EDGERTON. R. B. (1979). *Mental retardation.* Cambridge: Harvard University Press.

EDUCATIONAL TESTING SERVICE. National Assessment of Educational Progress (1988). *The mathematics report card: Are we measuring up?* Princeton, N.J.: Author.

EDWARDS, C. P. (1982). Moral development in comparative cultural perspective. In D. Wagner & H. Stevenson (Eds.), *Cultural perspectives on child development.* New York: W. H. Freeman.

EDWARDS, C. P. (1986). Another style of competence: The caregiving child. In A. Fogel & G. F. Melson (Eds), *Origins of nurturance.* Hillsdale, N.J.: Erlbaum.

EGELAND, B., & BRUNQUETTE, D. (1979). An at-risk approach to the study of child abuse: Some preliminary findings. *Journal of the American Academy of Psychiatry, 18*, 219–235.

EGELAND, B., & SROUFE, L. A. (1981). Attachment and early maltreatment. *Child Development, 52*, 44–52.

EHRHARDT, A. A., & MEYER-BAHLBERG, H. F. L. (1979). Prenatal sex hormones and the developing brain: Effects on psychosexual differentiation and cognitive function. *Annual Review of Medicine, 30*, 417–430.

EIBL-EIBESFELDT, I. (1970). *Ethology: The biology of behavior.* New York: Holt, Rinehart & Winston.

EICHORN, D. H. (1979). Physical development: Current foci of research. In J. Osofsky (Ed.), *The handbook of infant development.* New York: Wiley.

EICHORN, D. H., & BAYLEY, N. (1962). Growth in head circumference from birth through young adulthood. *Child Development, 33*, 257–271.

EIMAS, P. D. (1985). The perception of speech in early infancy. *Scientific American, 204*, 66–72.

EIMAS, P. D., SIQUELAND, E., JUSCZYK, P., & VIGORITO, J. (1971). Speech perception in infants. *Science, 171*, 303–306.

EISEN, M., ZELLMAN, G. I., LEIBOWITZ, A., CHOW, W., K., & EVANS, J. R. (1983). Factors discriminating pregnancy resolution decisions of unmarried adolescents. *Genetic Psychology Monographs, 108*, 69–95.

EISENBERG, N. (1982). *The development of prosocial behavior.* New York: Academic Press.

EISENBERG, N., MURRAY, E., & HITE, T. (1982). Children's reasoning regarding sex-typed toy chices. *Child Development, 53*, 81–86.

EISENSTADT, S. N., (1963). Archetypal patterns of youth. in E. H. Erikson (Ed.), *The challenge of youth.* Garden City, N.Y.: Doubleday.

EITZEN, D. S. (1985). Athletics in the status system of male adolescents: A replication of Coleman's *The adolescent society. Adolescence, 10*, 267–275.

EKMAN, P., & FRIESEN, W. (1972). Constants across cultures in the face and emotion. *Journal of Personality and Social Psychology, 117*, 124–129.

EKMAN, P., SORENSON, E., & FRIESEN, W. (1969). Pan-cultural elements in the facial expression of emotion. *Science, 164*, 86–88.

ELDER, G. H. (1974). *Children of the great depression.* Chicago: University of Chicago Press.

ELDER, G. H., JR. (1982). Historical experiences in the later years. In T. K. Hareven & K. J. Adams (Eds.), *Aging and life course transitions: An interdisciplinary perspective.* New York: Guilford Press.

ELDREDGE, N., & GOULD, S. J. (1972). Punctuated equilibria: An alternative to phyletic gradualism. In T. J. M. Schopf

(Ed.), *Models in paleobiology.* New York: W. H. Freeman.

ELIOT, G. (1965). *The mill on the floss.* New York: New American Library. (Original work published 1860)

ELIOT, T. S. (1971). Little Gidding. In *The complete poems and plays: 1909 to 1950.* Orlando, Fla.: Harcourt Brace Jovanovich.

ELIOT, T. S. (1971). East Coker. In *The complete poems and plays: 1909 to 1950.* Orlando, Fla.: Harcourt Brace Jovanovich.

ELKIND, D. (1978). *The child's reality: Three developmental themes.* Hillsdale, N.J.: Erlbaum.

ELLIS, S., ROGOFF, B., CROMER, C. (1981). Age segregation in children's interactions. *Developmental Psychology, 17*, 399–407.

EMDE, R. N., GAENSBAUER, T. J., & HARMON, R. J. (1976). Emotional expression in infancy: A behavioral study. *Psychological Issues Monograph Series, 10*, (1, Serial No. 37). New York: International Universities Press.

EMDE, R. N., & HARMON, R. J. (1972). Endogenous and exogenous smiling systems in early infancy. *Journal of the American Academy of Child Psychiatry, 11*, 77–100.

EMDE, R. N., & HARMON, R. J. (1984). Entering a new era in the search for developmental continuities. In R. N. Emde and R. J. Harmon (Eds.), *Continuities and discontinuities in development.* New York: Plenum Press.

EMDE, R. N., & ROBINSON, J. (1979). The first two months: Recent research in developmental psychobiology and the changing view of the newborn. In J. Noshpitz & J. Call (Eds.), *Basic handbook of child psychiatry.* New York: Basic Books.

ENDSLEY, R. C., HUTCHERS, M. A., GARNER, A. P., & MARTIN, M. J. (1979). Interrelationships among selected maternal behaviors, authoritarianism, and preschool children's verbal and non-verbal curiosity. *Child Development, 50*, 331–339.

ENGEN, T., LIPSITT, L. P., & KAYE, H. (1963). Olfactory responses and adaptation in the human neonate. *Journal of Comparative and Physiological Psychology, 56*, 73–77.

EPSTEIN, H. T. (1980). EEG developmental stages. *Developmental Psychobiology, 13*, 629–631.

ERIKSON, E. H. (1958). *Young man Luther.* New York: Norton.

ERIKSON, E. H. (1963). *Childhood and society* (2nd ed.). New York: Norton.

ERIKSON, E. H. (1968a). *Identity: Youth and crisis.* New York: Norton.

ERICKSON, E. H. (1968b). Life cycle. in D. L. Sills (Ed.), *Inter-*

national encyclopedia of the social sciences (Vol. 9). New York: Crowell, Collier.

ERIKSON, E. H. (1969). *Gandhi's truth*. New York: Norton.

ERIKSON, E. H. (1980). *Identity and the life cycle*. New York: Norton.

ERIKSON, E. H., ERIKSON, J. M., & KIVNICK, H. Q. (1986). *Involvement in old age*. New York: Norton.

ERIKSON, M. F., SROUFE, A. L., & EGELAND, B. (1985). The relationship between the quality of attachment and behavior problems in preschool in a high-risk sample. In I. Bretherton and E. Waters (Eds.), Growing points of attachment theory and research. *Monographs of the Society for Research in Child Development, 50,* (1-2, Serial No. 209).

ERON, L., WALDER, L., & LEFKOWITZ, M. (1971). *Learning of aggression in children*. Boston: Little, Brown.

ESPENSHADE, T. J., & BRAUN, R. E. (1983). Economic aspects of an aging population and the material well-being of older persons. In M. W. Riley, B. B. Hess, K. Bond (Eds.), *Aging in society: Selected reviews of recent research*. Hillsdale, N.J.: Erlbaum.

ETZEL, B. C. & GEWIRTZ, J. L. (1976). Experimental modification of caregiver maintained high-rate operant crying in a 6 week and a 20 week old infant (Infant tyrannotearus): Extinction of crying with reinforcement of eye contact and smiling. *Journal of Experimental Child Psychology, 5,* 303–317.

EVANS, H. E., & GLASS, L. (1976). *Perinatal medicine*. Hagerstown, Md.: Harper & Row.

EVANS, H. E., MOODIE, A. D., & HANSEN, J. D. L. (1971). Kwashiorkor and intellectual development. *South African Medical Journal, 45,* 1413–1426.

EVANS, R. B. (1972). Physical and biochemical characteristics of homosexual men. *Journal of Consulting Psychology, 39,* 140–147.

EVELETH, P. B., & TANNER, J. M. (1976). *Worldwide variation in human growth*. Cambridge: Cambridge University Press.

FAGOT, B. I. (1978). The influence of sex of child on parental reactions to toddler children. *Child Development, 49,* 459–465.

FAGOT, B. I. (1978). Reinforcing contingencies for sex role behaviors: Effect of experience with children. *Child Development, 49,* 30–36.

FALK, G., FALK, U., & TOMASCHEVICH, G. V. (1981). *Aging in America and other cultures*. Saratoga, Ca.: Century Twenty-one Publishing.

FANT, L. (1972). *Ameslan*. Silver Springs, Md.: National Association for the deaf.

FANTZ, R. L. (1961). The origins of form perception. *Scientific American, 204,* 66–72.

FANTZ, R. L. (1963). Pattern vision in newborn infants. *Science, 140,* 296–297.

FANTZ, R. L., ORDY, J. M., & UDELF, M. S. (1962). Maturation of pattern vision in infants during the first six months. *Journal of Comparative Physiological Psychology, 55,* 907–917.

FELDMAN, D. (1980). *Beyond universals in cognitive development*. Norwood, N.J.: Ablex.

FELDMAN, H., GOLDIN-MEADOW, S., & GLEITMAN, L. (1978). Beyond Herodotus: The creation of language by linguistically deprived, deaf children. In A. Lock (Ed.), *Action, symbol, and gesture: The emergence of language.* New York: Academic Press.

FENSON, L., & RAMSAY, D. S. (1980). Decentration and integration of child's play in the second year. *Child Development, 51,* 171–178.

FENSON, L., & RAMSAY, D. S. (1981). Effects of modelling action sequences on the play of twelve, fifteen, and nineteen month old children. *Child Development, 52,* 1028–1036.

FESBACH, S. (1970). Aggression. In P. H. Mussen (Ed)., *Carmichael's manual of child psychology: Vol. 2, Part 4. Socialization* (3rd ed.). New York: Wiley.

FIELD, T. M., COHEN, D., GARCIA, R., & GREENBERG, R. (1984). Infant response to facelike patterns under fixed-trial and infant-control procedures. *Child Development, 54,* 172–177.

FIELD, T. M., & GOLDSON, E. (1984). Pacifying effects of nonnutritive sucking on term and preterm neonates during heelstick procedures. *Pediatrics, 74,* 1012–1015.

FIELD, T. M., SOSTEK, A. M., VIETZE, P., & LIEDERMAN, P. H. (Eds.). (1981). *Culture and early interactions*. Hillsdale, N.J.: Erlbaum.

FIELD, T. M., WOODSON, R., GREENBERG, R., & COHEN, D. (1982). Discrimination and imitation of facial expressions by neonates. *Science, 218,* 179–182.

FINCHAM, F.D., & CAIN, K. M. (1986). Learned helplessness in humans: A developmental analysis. *Developmental Review, 6,* 301–333.

FINKELSTEIN, N. W., & RAMEY, C. T. (1977). Learning to control the environment in infancy. *Child Development, 48,* 806–819.

FISCHER, K. W. (1980). A theory of cognitive development: The control and construction of hierarchies of skills. *Psychological Review, 87,* 477–531.

FISCHER, K. W. (1987). Commentary—Relations between brain and cognitive development. *Child Development, 58,* 623–632.

FISCHER, K. W., & PIPP, S. L. (1984). Processes of cognitive development: Optimal level and skill acquisition. In

R. J. Sternberg (Ed.), *Mechanisms of cognitive development*. San Francisco: W. H. Freeman.

FISHBEIN, H. D. (1976). *Evolution, development and children's learning*. Pacific Palisades, Ca.: Goodyear.

FIVUSH, R., HUDSON, J., & NELSON, K. (1984). Children's long-term memory for a novel event: An exploratory study. *Merrill-Palmer Quarterly, 30,* 303–315.

FLAPAN, D. (1968). *Children's understanding of social interaction.* New York: Teachers College Press, Columbia University.

FLAVELL, J. H. (1971). Stage-related properties of cognitive development. *Cognitive Psychology, 2,* 421–453.

FLAVELL, J. H. (1982). Structures, stages and sequences in cognitive development. In W. A. Collins (Ed.), *The concept of development: Minnesota Symposia on Child Psychology* (Vol. 15). Hillsdale, N.J.: Erlbaum.

FLAVELL, J. H. (1985). *Cognitive development* (2nd ed.). Englewood Cliffs, N.J.: Prentice Hall.

FLAVELL, J. H., FLAVELL, E. R. & GREEN, F. L. (1983). Development of the appearance-reality distinction. *Cognitive Psychology, 15,* 95–120.

FLAVELL, J. H., FRIEDERICHS, A. G., & HOYT, J. D. (1970). Developmental changes in memorization processes. *Cognitive Psychology, 1,* 324–340.

FLAVELL, J. H., GREEN, F. L., & FLAVELL, E. R. (1986). Development of knowledge about the appearance-reality distinction. *Monographs of the Society for Research in Child Development, 51,* (1, Serial No. 212).

FLAVELL, J. H., ZHANG, X. D., ZOU, H., DONG, Q., & QI, S. (1983). A comparison between the development of the appearance-reality distinction in the People's Republic of China and the United States. *Cognitive Psychology, 15,* 459–466.

FLESCH, R. (1955). *Why Johnny can't read, and what you can do about it.* New York: Harper & Row.

FODOR, J. (1983). *The modularity of mind.* Cambridge: MIT Press.

FOGELSON, R. D. (1979). Person, self, and identity: Some anthropological retrospects, circumspects, and prospects. In B. Lee (Ed.), *Psychosocial theories of the self.* New York: Plenum Press.

FORGAYS, D. G., & FORGAYS, J. W. (1952). The nature of the effect of free-environmental experience in the rat. *Journal of Comparative and Physiological Psychology, 45,* 322–328.

FORTES, M. (1950). Kinship and marriage among the Ashanti. In A. R. Radcliffe-Brown & D. Forde (Eds.), *African systems of kinship and marriage.* London: Oxford University Press.

FOX, N. (1977). Attachment of Kibbutz infants to mother and metapelet. *Child Development, 48,* 1228–1239.

FOX, N., KAGAN, J., & WESIKOPF, S. (1979). The growth of memory during infancy. *Genetic Psychology Monographs, 99,* 91–130.

FOX, V. C. (1977). Is adolescence a phenomenon of modern times? *Journal of Psychohistory, 5,* 271–295.

FRAIBERG, S. H. (1959). *The magic years: Understanding and handling the problems of early childhood.* New York: Scribner.

FRAIBERG, S. H. (1974). Blind infants and their mothers: An examination of the sign system. In M. Lewis & L. Rosenblum (Eds.), *The effect of the infant on its caregiver.* New York: Wiley.

FRAIBERG, S. H. (1977). *Every child's birthright: In defense of mothering.* New York: Basic Books.

FRANCIS, P. L., SELF, P. A., & HOROWITZ, F. D. (1987). The behavioral assessment of the neonate: An overview. In J. D. Osofsky (Ed.), *Handbook of infant development* (2nd ed.). New York: Wiley.

FRANK, A. (1975). *The diary of a young girl.* New York: Pocket Book.

FRANKENBURG, W. K., & DODDS, J. B. (1967). The Denver developmental screening test. *The Journal of Pediatrics, 71,* 181–191.

FREED, K. (1983, March 14). Cubatao—a paradise lost to pollution. *Los Angeles Times,* pp. 1, 12, 13.

FREEDMAN, D. (1974). *Human infancy: An evolutionary perspective.* Hillsdale, N.J.: Erlbaum.

FREEMAN, D. (1983). *Margaret Mead and Samoa.* Cambridge: Harvard University Press.

FREEMAN, H. E., KLEIN, R. E., TOWNSEND, J. W., & LECHTIG, A. (1980). Nutrition and cognitive development among rural Guatemalan children. *American Journal of Public Health, 70.* 1277–1285.

FREGE, G. (1960). On sense and reference. In P. Geach & M. Black (Eds.), *Translations from the philosophical writings of Gottlieb Frege.* Oxford: Basil Blackwell.

FREMGEN, A., & FAY, D. (1980). Overextensions in production and comprehension: A methodological clarification. *Journal of Child Language, 7,* 201–2111.

FRENKEL-BRUNSWIK, E. (1963). Adjustments and reorientation in the course of the life-span. In R. E. Kuhlen & G. G. Thompson (Eds.), *Psychological studies of human development.* New York: Appleton-Century-Crofts.

FREUD, A. (1958). Adolescence. *Psychoanalytic study of the child* (Vol. 8). New York: International Universities Press.

FREUD, S. (1905/1953). Three essays on the theory of sexuality. In J. Strachey (Ed. and Trans.), *The standard edition of the complete psychological works of Sigmund Freud* (Vol. 7). London: Hogarth Press.

FREUD, S. (1905/1953). The transformation of puberty. In J. Strachey (Ed. & Trans.), *The standard edition of the complete psychological works of Sigmund Freud* (Vol. 7). London: Hogarth Press.

FREUD, S. (1920/1924). The psychogenesis of a case of homosexuality in a woman. (B. Low and R. Gabler, Trans.). *Collected Papers* (Vol. 2). London: Hogarth Press.

FREUD, S. (1920/1955). Beyond the pleasure principle. In J. Strachey (Ed. and Trans.), *The standard edition of the complete psychological works of Sigmund Freud* (Vol. 18). London: Hogarth Press.

FREUD, S. (1921/1949). Group psychology — The analysis of the Ego. In J. Strachey (Ed. and Trans.), *The standard edition of the complete psychological works of Sigmund Freud* (Vol. 18). London: Hogarth Press.

FREUD, S. (1925/1961). Some psychical consequences of the anatomical distinctions between the sexes. In J. Strachey (Ed. & Trans.), *The standard edition of the complete psychological works of Sigmund Freud* (Vol. 19). London: Hogarth Press.

FREUD, S. (1930). Civilization and its discontents. In J. Strachey (Ed. and Trans.), *The standard edition of the complete psychological works of Sigmund Freud* (Vol. 21). London: Hogarth Press.

FREUD, S. (1933/1964). *New introductory lectures in psychoanalysis* (J. Strachey, Ed. and Trans.). New York: Norton.

FREUD, S. (1937/1953). Analysis terminable and interminable. In J. Strachey (Ed.), *The standard edition of the complete psychological works of Sigmund Freud.* (Vol. 5). London: Hogarth Press.

FREUD, S. (1940/1964). An outline of psychoanalysis. In J. Strachey (Ed. and Trans.), *The standard edition of the complete psychological works of Sigmund Freud* (Vol. 23). London: Hogarth Press.

FREUD, S. (1946). *The ego and the mechanisms of defense* (C. Baines, Trans.). New York: International Universities Press.

FRIEDLANDER, B. Z., WHETSTONE, S., & SCOTT, L. (1974). Suburban preschool children's comprehension of an age-appropriate information television program. *Child Development, 45*, 561–565.

FRIEDMAN, S. L., & SIGMAN, M. (Eds.). (1980). *Preterm birth and psychological development.* New York: Academic Press.

FRIEDRICH, L. K., & STEIN, A. H. (1973). Aggressive and prosocial television programs and the natural behavior of preschool children. *Monographs of the Society for Research in Child Development, 38*, (4, Serial No. 151).

FRISCH, R. E. (1978). Menarche and fatness. *Science, 200*, 1509–1513.

FRITH, C. D., & FRITH, U. (1978) Feature selection and classification: A developmental study. *Journal of Experimental Child Psychology, 25*, 413–428.

FRITH, U. (1984). A new perspective on research in autism. In ARPI (Eds.), *Contributions à la recherche scientifique sur l'autisme: Aspects cognitifs.* Paris: Association pour la Recherche sur l'Autisme et les Psychoses Infantiles.

FRODI, A. M., LAMB. M. E., LEAVITT, L. A., & DONOVAN, W. L. (1978). Fathers' and mothers' responses to the faces and cries of normal premature infants. *Developmental Psychology, 14*, 490–498.

FROST, R. (1969). The road not taken. In E. C. Lathem (Ed.), *The poetry of Robert Frost.* New York: Holt Rinehart & Winston Inc. (Original work published 1916)

FRY, C. I. (1988). Theories of age and culture. in J. Berren & V. Bingtson (Eds.), *Emergent theories of aging.* New York: Springer.

FUKUSHIMA, O., & KATO, M. (1976). The effects of vicarious experiences on children's altruistic behavior. *Bulletin of Tokyo Gakuge University, 27* (Series 1), 90–94.

FULLARD, W., & REILING, A. M. (1976). An investigation of Lorenz's babyness. *Child Development, 47*, 1191–1193.

FURMAN, W., RAHE, D. F., & HARTUP, W. W. (1979). Rehabilitation of socially withdrawn preschool children. Through mixed-age and same-age socialization. *Child Development, 50*, No. 4, 915–922.

FURSTENBERG, F., & CRAWFORD, A. (1978). Family support: Helping teenage mothers to cope. *Family Planning Perspctives, 10.*

FURSTENBERG, F. F. (1976). *Unplanned parenthood: The social consequences of teenage childbearing.* New York: Free Press.

FURTH, H. G. (1980). *The world of grownups: Children's conceptions of society.* New York: Elsevier.

GAGNON, J. H., & SIMON, W. (1973). *Sexual conduct: The social sources of human sexuality.* Chicago: Aldine.

GALLUP. G. G., JR. (1970). Chimpanzees: Self-recognition. *Science, 167*, 86–87.

GAMBLE, T., & ZIGLER. E. (1986). Effects of infant day care: Another look at the evidence. *American Journal of Orthopsychiatry, 56*, 26–42.

GAMPER, E. (1926/1959). In J. Field, H. W. Magoun, & V. E. Hall (Eds.), *Handbook of physiology* (Vol. 2). Washington, D.C.: American Physiological Society.

GARDNER, H. (1980). *Artful scribbles: The significance of children's drawings.* New York: Basic Books.

GARDNER, H. (1983). *Frames of mind: The theory of multiple intelligences.* New York: Basic Books.

GARDNER, J, & GARDNER, H. (1970). A note on selective imitation by a six-week-old infant. *Child Development, 41,* 1209–1213.

GARDNER, R. A., & GARDNER, B. T. (1969). Teaching sight language to a chimpanzee. *Science, 165,* 664–672.

GARMEZY, N., & TELLEGEN, A. (1984). Studies of stress resistant children: Methods, variables, and preliminary findings. in F. J. Morrison, C. Lord, & D. P. Keating (Eds.), *Applied developmental psychology* (Vol 1.). Orlando, Fla.: Academic Press.

GARTELL, E., LORIAUX, D. L., & CHASE, T. N. (1977). Plasma testosterone in homosexuals and heterosexual women. *American Journal of Psychiatry, 134,* 1117–1118.

GARVEY, C. (1977). *Play.* Cambridge: Harvard University Press.

GARVEY, C., & BERNDT, R. (1977). Organization of pretend play. Paper presented at the meetings of the American Psychological Association in Chicago.

GAY, J., & COLE, M. (1967). *The new mathematics and an old culture.* New York: Holt, Rinehart and Winston.

GEARHART, M., & NEWMAN, D. (1980). Learning to draw a picture: The social context of individual activity. *Discourse Processes, 3,* 169–184.

GEERTZ, C. (1973). *The interpretation of cultures.* New York: Basic Books.

GEERTZ, C. (1984). From the native's point of view: On the nature of anthropological understanding. In R. Shweder & R. Levine (Eds.), *Culture theory.* Cambridge: Cambridge University Press.

GELB, I. J. (1963). *A study of writing.* Chicago: University of Chicago Press.

GELMAN, R. (1978). Cognitive development. *Annual Review of Psychology, 29,* 297–332.

GELMAN, R., & BAILLARGEON, R. (1983). A review of some Piagetian concepts. In P. Mussen (Ed.), *Handbook of child development: (Vol. 3). Cognitive development.* New York: Wiley.

GELMAN, R., & GALLISTEL, C. R. (1978). *The child's understanding of number.* Cambridge: Harvard University Press.

GESELL, A. (1929). *Infancy and human growth.* New York: Macmillan.

GESELL, A. (1940). *The first five years of life.* (9th ed.). New York: Harper & Row.

GESELL, A. (1945). *The embryology of behavior.* New York: Harper & Row.

GESELL, A., & AMATRUDA, C. S. (1947). *Developmental diagnosis: Normal and abnormal child development* (3rd ed.). Hagerstown, Md.: Harper & Row.

GESELL, A., ILG, F. L., & AMES, L. (1956). *Youth: the years from ten to sixteen.* New York: Harper & Row.

GESELL, A., & ILG, F. L. (1943). *Infant and child in the culture of today.* New York: Harper & Row.

GILLIGAN, C. (1982). *In a different voice: Psychological theory and women's development.* Cambridge: Harvard University Press.

GILLIGAN, C. (1977). In a different voice: Women's conceptions of the self and of morality. *Harvard Educational Review, 47,* 481–517.

GILLIGAN, C., & BELENKY, M. (1980). A naturalistic study of abortion practices. In R. Selman & R. Yondo (Eds.), *Clinical developmental psychology* (*New directions for child development,* No. 7). San Francisco: Jossey-Bass.

GILLIGAN, C., & MURPHY, J. M. (1979). Development from adolescence to adulthood: The philosopher and the "dilemma of the fact." In D. Kuhn (Ed.), *Intellectual development beyond childhood* (*New directions for child development,* No. 5). San Francisco: Jossey-Bass.

GILLIS, J. R. (1974). *Youth and history: Tradition and change in European age relations 1770–present.* New York: Academic Press.

GINSBURG, H. (1977). *Children's arithmetic.* New York: Van Nostrand.

GJERDE, P. F. (1986). The interpersonal structure of family interaction settings: Parent-adolescent relations in dyads and triads. *Developmental Psychology, 22,* 297–304.

GLADUE, B. A., GREEN, R., & HELLMAN, R. E. (1985). Neuroendocrine response to estrogen and sexual orientation. *Science, 225,* 1496–1499.

GLADWIN, E. T. (1970). *East is a big bird.* Cambridge: Harvard University Press.

GLEITMAN, H. (1963). *Psychology.* New York: Norton.

GLUCKSBERG, S., KRAUSS, R., & HIGGINS, E. T. (1975). The development of referential communication skills. In F. D. Horowitz (Ed.), *Review of Child Development Research* (Vol. 4). Chicago: University of Chicago Press.

GLYNN, T. J. (1981). From family to peer: A review of transitions of influence among drug using youth. *Journal of youth and adolescence, 10,* 363–383.

GOLBUS, M. S. (1980). Teratology for the obstetrician: Current status. *Journal of the American College of Obstetricians and Gynecologists, 55,* 269–276.

GOLDBERG, S., & DIVITTO, B. A. (1983). *Born too soon: Premature birth and early development.* New York: W. H. Freeman.

GOLDEN, M., ROSENBLUTH, L., GROSSI, M. T., POLICARE, H. J., FREEMAN, H., & BROWNLEE, L. M. (1978). *The New*

York City Infant Day Care Study: A comparative study of licensed group and family day care programs and the effects of these programs on children and their families. New York: Medical and Health Research Association of New York City.

GOLDIN-MEADOW, S. (1982). The resilience of recursion: A study of a communication system developed without a conventional language model. In E. Wanner & L. R. Gleitman (Eds.), *Language acquisition; The state of the art.* New York: Norton.

GOLDIN-MEADOW, S. (1985). Language development under atypical learning conditions. In K. E. Nelson (Ed.), *Children's language* (Vol. 5). Hillsdale, N.J.: Erlbaum.

GOLDMAN-RAKIC, P. S. (1987). Development of cortical circuitry and cognitive function. *Child Development, 58,* 601–622.

GOLDSMITH, H. H. (1987). Roundtable: What is temperament? *Four Approaches in Child Development, 58,* 505–529.

GOLDSMITH, H. H., & CAMPOS, J. J. (1982). Toward a theory of infant temperament. In R. N. Emde & R. Harmon (Eds.), *The development of attachment and affiliative systems.* New York: Plenum Press.

GOLDSMITH, H. H., & GOTTESMAN, I. I. (1981). Origins of variation in behavior style: A longitudinal study of young twins. *Child Development, 52,* 91–103

GOLINKOFF, R. M., & AMES, G. J. (1979). A comparison of fathers' and mothers' speech with their young children. *Child Development, 50,* 28–32.

GOLOMB, C. (1974). *Young children's sculpture and drawing.* Cambridge: Harvard University Press.

GOOD, T. L., SIKES, J., & BROPHY, J. (1973). Effects of teacher sex and student sex on classroom interaction. *Journal of Educational Psychology, 65,* 74–87.

GOODALL, J. (1986). *The chimpanzees of Gombe: Patterns of behavior.* Cambridge: Harvard University Press.

GOODENOUGH, F. L. (1975). *Anger in young children.* Minneapolis: University of Minnesota Press. (Original work published in 1931)

GOODENOUGH, W. H. (1953). Native astronomy in the Central Carolines. *Museum Monographs.* Philadelphia: University Museum, University of Pennsylvania.

GOODMAN, G. (1984). Children's testimony in historical perspective. *Journal of Social Issues, 40,* 9–31.

GOODMAN, G. S., AMAN, C., HIRSCHMAN, J. (1987). Child's sexual and physical abuse: Children's testimony. In Ceci, S. J., Toglia, M. P., & Ross, D. F. (Eds.) *Children's eyewitness memory.* New York: Springer-Verlag.

GOODMAN, K. S. & GOODMAN, Y. M. (1979). Learning to read is natural. in L. B. Resnick & P. A. Weaver, *Theory and practice of early reading.* Hillsdale, N.J.: Erlbaum.

GOODNOW, J. (1984). Parents' ideas about parenting and development. In A. L. Brown & B. Rogoff (Eds.), *Advances in developmental psychology* (Vol. 3). Hillsdale, N.J.: Erlbaum.

GOODNOW, J. J. (1977). *Children drawing.* Cambridge: Harvard University Press.

GOODY, E. N. (Ed.). (1978). *Questions and politeness: Strategies in social interaction.* Cambridge: Cambridge University Press.

GOODY, J. (1977). *Domestication of the savage mind.* Cambridge: Cambridge University Press.

GOODY, J. (1987). *The interface between the written and the oral.* Cambridge: Cambridge University Press.

GORDON, J. S., & HAIRE, D. (1981). Alternatives in childbirth. In P. Ahmed (Ed.), *Pregnancy, childbirth, and parenthood.* New York: Elsevier.

GOREN, C C., SARTY, J., & WU, P. Y. (1875). Visual following and pattern discrimination of face-like stimuli by newborn infants. *Pediatrics, 56,* 544–549.

GOTTESMAN, I. I., & SHIELDS, J. (1973). Genetic theorizing and schizophrenia. *British Journal of Psychology, 122,* 17–18.

GOTTLIEB, G. (Ed.). (1973). *Behavioral embryology.* New York: Academic Press.

GOTTLIEB, G. & KRASNEGOR, N. A. (1985). *Measurement of audition and vision in the first year of postnatal life: A methodological overview.* Norwood, N.J.: Ablex Press.

GOTTMAN, J. M., & PARKHURST, J. T. (1980). A developmental theory of friendship and acquaintanceship processes. In W. A. Collins (Ed.), *Development of cognition, affect, and social relations. Minnesota Symposia on Child Psychology* (Vol. 13). Hillsdale, N.J.: Erlbaum.

GOULD, S. J. (1977a). *Ever since Darwin.* New York: Norton.

GOULD, S. J. (1977b). *Ontogeny and phylogeny.* Cambridge: Harvard University Press.

GOULD, S. J. (1980). The episodic nature of evolutionary change. In S. J. Gould (Ed.), *The panda's thumb: More reflections in natural history.* New York: Norton.

GOULD, S. J. (1981). *The mismeasure of man.* New York: Norton.

GRAHAM, F. K., MATARAZZO, R. G., & CALDWELL, B. M. (1956). Behavioral differences between normal and traumatized newborns: II. Standardization, reliability, and validity. *Psychological Monographs, 70* (21, Serial No. 428).

GRAHAM, P., RUTTER, M., & GEORGE, S. (1973). Temperamental characteristics as predictors of behavior disorders in children. *American Journal of Orthopsychiatry, 43,* 328–339.

GRAVES, Z., & GLICK, J. A. (1978). The effect of context on mother-child interaction: A progress report. *Quarterly*

Newsletter of the Laboratory of Comparative Human Cognition, 2, 41–46.

GREEN, G. (1984). On the appropriateness of adaptations in primary-level basal readers: Reactions to remarks by Bertram Bruce. In R. C. Anderson, J. Osborn, & R. J. Tierney (Eds.), *Learning to read in American schools.* Hillsdale, N.J.: Erlbaum.

GREENBERGER, E., STEINBERG, L., & RUGGIERO, M. (1982). A job is a job is a job . . . or is it? Behavioral observations in the adolescent work place. *Work and Occupations, 9,* 79–96.

GREENFIELD, P.M. (1966). On culture and conservation. In J. S. Bruner, R. P. Olver, & P. M. Greenfield (Eds.), *Studies in cognitive growth.* New York: Wiley.

GREENFIELD, P. M. (1976). Cross-cultural Piagetian research: Paradox and progress. In K. F. Riegel and J. A. Meacham (Eds.), *The developing individual in a changing world: Historical and cultural issues* (Vol. 1). Chicago: Aldine.

GREENFIELD, P. M. (1982). The role of perceived variability in the transition to language. *Journal of Child Language, 9,* 1–12.

GREENFIELD, P. M. (1984). *Mind and media: The effects of television, video, games and computers.* Cambridge: Harvard University Press.

GREENFIELD, P. M., & LAVE, J. (1982). Cognitive aspects of informal education. In D. A. Wagner & H. E. Stevenson (Eds.), *Cultural perspectives on child development.* New York: W. H. Freeman.

GREENFIELD, P. M., & SMITH, J. H. (1976). *The structure of communication in early language development.* New York: Academic Press.

GREGG, N. M. (1941). Cogenital cataracts following German measles in mothers. *Transcripts of the Opthalmological Society of Australia, 3,* 35.

GREENOUGH, W. T., BLACK, J. E., & WALLACE, C. S. (1987). Experience and brain development. *Child Development, 58,* 539–559.

GRIFFIN, P. (1983). Personal communication.

GRIMWADE, J. C., WALKER, D. W., BARTLETT, M., GORDON, S., & WOOD, C. (1970). Human fetal heartrate change and movement-response to sound and vibration. *American Journal of Obstetrics and Gynecology, 109,* 86–90.

GRONLUND, N. E. (1959). *Sociometry in the classroom.* New York: Harper & Bros.

GROSSMANN, K. FREMMER-BOMBIK, E., RUDOLPH, J., & GROSSMANN, K. (1987). Maternal attachment in relation to patterns of infant-mother attachment and maternal care during the first year. Paper presented at Conference of Intrafamilial Relationships. Cambridge, England: January, 1987.

GROSSMANN, K., GROSSMANN, K. E., SPANGLER, S., SUESS, G., & UNZNER, L. (1985). Maternal sensitivity and newborn orientation responses as related to quality of attachment in Northern Germany. In I. Bretherton & E. Waters, Growing points of attachment theory. *Monographs of the Society for Research in Child Development, 50* (1–2 Serial No. 209).

GROTBERG, E. (1969). *Review of Head Start research, 1965–1969.* Washington, D.C.: OEO Pamphlet 1608:13 (ED02308).

GROTEVANT, H. (1986). Assessment of identity development: Current issues and future directions. *Journal of Adolescent Research, 1,* 175–181.

GROTEVANT, H. & COOPER, C. (1985). Patterns of interaction in family relationships and the development of identity exploration in adolescence. *Developmental Psychology, 56,* 415–428.

GROTEVANT, H. D., THORBECKE, W., & MEYER, M. L. (1982). An extension of Marcia's identity status interview in the interpersonal domain. *Journal of Youth and Adolescence, 11,* 33–47.

GUIDUBALDI, J., PERRY, J. D., CLEMINSHAW, H. K. & MCLOUGHLIN, C. S. (1983). The impact of parental divorce on children: Report of the nationwide NASP study. *School Psychology Review, 12*(3), 300–323.

GUILFORD, J. P. (1967). *The nature of human intelligence.* New York: McGraw-Hill.

GUTTMACHER, A. (1973). *Pregnancy, birth and family planning: A guide for expectant parents.* New York: Viking.

HAAF, R. A., SMITH, P. H., & SMITELY, S. (1983). Infant response to facelike patterns under fixed-trial and infant-control procedures. *Child Development, 54,* 172–177.

HAAN, N., LANGER, J., & KOHLBERG, L. (1976). Family patterns of moral reasoning. *Child Development, 47,* 1204–1206.

HAAN, N., SMITH, B., & BLOCK, J. (1968). The moral reasoning of young adults. *Journal of Personality and Social Psychology, 10,* 183–201.

HAAN, N., WEISS, R., & JOHNSON, V. (1982). The role of logic in moral reasoning and development. *Developmental Psychology, 18,* 245–256.

HAFEZ, E. S. E., & EVANS, T. N. (Eds.). (1973). *Human reproduction.* New York: Harper & Row.

HAGEN, J. W., MEACHAM, J. A., & MESIBOV, G. (1970). Verbal labeling, rehearsal, and short-term memory. *Cognitive Psychology, 1,* 47–58.

HAITH, M. N., BERMAN, T., & MOORE, M. J. (1977). Eye contact and face scanning in early infancy. *Science, 198,* 853–855.

HALL, G. S. (1904). *Adolescence: Its psychology and its relations to psychology, anthropology, sociology, sex, crime, religion, and education.* New York: Appleton.

HALL, G. S. (1921). The dangerous age. *Pedagogical Seminary, 28,* 275–294.

HALL, G. S. (1922). *Senescence: The last half of life.* New York: Appleton.

HALLOWELL, A. I. (1955). The self and its behavioral environment. In A. I. Hallowell (Ed.), *Culture and experience.* Philadelphia: University of Pennsylvania Press.

HALLPIKE, C. R. (1979). *The foundations of primitive thought.* Oxford: Clarendon Press.

HALPERN, D. F. (1986). *Sex differences in cognitive abilities.* Hillsdale, N.J.: Erlbaum.

HALVERSON, H. M. (1931). An experimental study of prehension in infants by means of systematic cinema records. *Genetic Psychology Monographs, 10*(2–3), 107–286.

HAMBURGER, V. (1957). The concept of "development" in biology. In D. B. Harris (Ed.), *The concept of development.* Minneapolis: University of Minnesota Press.

HANSON, J. W., STREISSGUTH, A. P., & SMITH, D. W. (1978). The effects of moderate alcohol consumption during pregnancy on fetal growth and morphogenesis. *Journal of Pediatrics, 92,* 457–460.

HAREVEN, T. K. (1978). The last stage: Historical adulthood and old age. In E. H. Erikson (Ed.), *Adulthood.* New York: Norton.

HAREVEN, T. K. (1982). *Aging and life course transitions: An interdisciplinary perspective.* New York: Guilford.

HARKNESS, S., EDWARDS, C. P., & SUPER, C. M. (1981). Social roles and moral reasoning: A case study in a rural African community. *Developmental Psychology, 17,* 595–603.

HARKNESS, S., & SUPER, C. M. (1985). The cultural context of gender segregation in children's peer groups. *Child Development, 56,* 219–224.

HARLOW, H. F., & HARLOW, M. K. (1962). Social deprivation in monkeys. *Scientific American, 207,* 136–146.

HARLOW, H. F., & HARLOW, M. K. (1969). Effects of various mother-infant relationships on rhesus monkey behaviors. In B. M. Foss (Ed.), *Determinants of infant behavior* (Vol. 4). London: Methuen.

HARLOW, H. F., & NOVAK, M. A. (1973). Psychopathological perspectives. *Perspectives in Biology and Medicine,* Spring 1973, 461–478.

HARLOW, H. F., ZIMMERMAN, R. R. (1959). Affectional responses in the infant monkey. *Science, 130,* 421–432.

HARRINGTON, M. (1963). *The other America: Poverty in the United States.* New York: Macmillan.

HARRIS, B. (1979). Whatever happened to little Albert? *American Psychologist, 34,* 151–160.

HARRIS, P. L. (1983). Infant cognition. In P. H. Mussen (Ed.), *Handbook of child psychology: Vol. 2. Infancy and developmental psychobiology.* New York: Wiley.

HARRIS, P. L., DONNELLY, K., GUZ, G. R., & PITT-WATSON, R. (1986). Children's understanding of the distinction between real and apparent emotion. *Child Development, 57,* 895–909.

HARTER, S. (1982). The perceived competence scale for children. *Child Development, 53,* 87–97.

HARTER, S. (1983). Development perspectives on the self-system. In P. M. Mussen (Ed.), *Handbook of Child Psychology: Vol. 4. Socialization, personality, and social development.* New York: Wiley.

HARTUP, W. W. (1974). Aggression in childhood. Developmental perspectives. *American Psychologist, 29,* 336–341.

HARTUP, W. W. (1978). Children and their friends. In H. McGurk (Ed.), *Issues in childhood social development.* London: Methuen.

HARTUP, W. W. (1983). Peer relations. In P. H. Mussen (Ed.), *Handbook of child psychology: Vol. 4. Socialization, personality, and social development.* New York: Wiley.

HARTUP, W. W. (1984). The peer context in middle childhood. In A. Collins (Eds), *Development during middle childhood: The years from six to twelve.* Washington, D.C.: National Academy Press.

HASHER, L., & CLIFTON, D. (1974). A developmental study of attribute encoding in free recall. *Journal of Experimental Child Psychology, 1,* 332–346.

HASKINS, R. (1985). Public school aggression among children with varying day-care experience. *Child Development, 56,* 687–703.

HATANO, G. (1987). How do Japanese children learn to read ?: Orthographic and eco-cultural variables. In B. R. Foorman & A. W. Siegel (Eds.), *Acquisition of reading skills: Cultural constraints and cognitive universals.* Hillsdale, N.J.: Erlbaum.

HAVELOCK, E. A. (1982). The literate revolution in Greece. Princeton: Princeton University Press.

HAVIGHURST, R. J. (1967). *Developmental tasks and education.* New York: David McKay.

HAYDEN-THOMSON, L., RUBIN, K. H., & HYMEL, S. (1987). Sex preferences in sociometric choice. *Developmental Psychology, 23,* 558–562.

HAYES, C. D., & KAMERMAN, S. B. (Eds.). (1983). *Children of working parents: Experiences and outcomes.* Washington, D.C.: National Academy Press.

HAYES, C. D., & WATSON, J. S. (1981). Neonatal imitation:

Fact or artifact. *Developmental Psychology, 17,* 655–660.

HAYES, D. S. (1978). Cognitive basis for liking and disliking among preschool children. *Child Development, 49,* 906–909.

HAYES, K. & HAYES, C. (1951). The intellectual development of a home-raised chimpanzee. *Preceedings of the American Philosophical Society, 95,* 105–109.

HAYFLICK, L. (1980). The cell biology of human aging. *Scientific American, 242,* 58–65.

HEATH, S. B. (1984). *Ways with words: Language, life, and work in communities and classrooms.* Cambridge: Cambridge University Press.

HEATH, S. B. (1982). What no bedtime story means: Narrative skills at home and school. *Language in Society, 11,* 49–77.

HEARNSHAW, L. S. (1979). *Cyril Burt, psychologist.* London: Hudder & Stanghton.

HECOX, K., & DEEGAN, D. M. (1985). Methodological issues in the study of auditory development. In G. Gottlieb & N. A. Krasnegor (Eds.), *Measurement of audition and vision in the first year of postnatal life: A methodological overview.* Norwood, N.J.: Ablex Publishing.

HEINICKE, C., FRIEDMAN, D., PRESCOTT, E., PUNCELL, C., & SALE, I. (1973). The organization of day care: Considerations relating to the mental health of child and family. *American Journal of Orthopsychiatry, 43,* 8–22.

HELD, R. (1965). Plasticity in sensory-motor systems. *Scientific American, 213*(5), 84–94.

HELD, R., & HEIN, A. (1963). Movement-produced stimulation and the development of visually guided behaviors. *Journal of Comparative and Physiological Psychology, 56,* 872–876.

HENMAN, V. A. C. (1921). Intelligence and its measurement: A symposium. *Journal of Educational Psychology, 12,* 195–198.

HERSKOVITZ, M. J. (1948). *Man and his works: The science of cultural anthropology.* New York: Knopf.

HETHERINGTON, E. M., CAMARA, K. A., & FEATHERMAN, D. L. (1983). Achievement and intellectual functioning of children from one-parent households. In J. Spence (Ed.), *Achievement and achievement motives.* New York: W. H. Freeman.

HETHERINGTON, E. M., COX, M., & COX, R. (1982). Effects of divorce on parents and children. In M. E. Lamb (Ed.), *Nontraditional families: Parenting and child development.* Hillsdale, N.J.: Erlbaum.

HICKS, L. E., LANGHAM, R. A., & TAKENAKA, J. (1982). Cognitive and health measures following early nutritional supplementation: A sibling study. *American Journal of Public Health, 72,* 1110–1118.

HILL, R. C., & STAFFORD, F. P. (1980). Parental care of children: Time diary estimates of quantity, predictability, and variety. *Journal of Human Research, 15,* 219–239.

HINDE, R. (1982). Attachment: Some conceptual and biological issues. In C. Parkes & J. Stevenson-Hinde (Eds.), *The place of attachment in human behavior.* New York: Basic Books.

HINER, N. R., & HAWES, J. M. (Eds.) (1985). *Growing up in America: Children in historical perspective.* Champaign: University of Illinois Press.

HIRSCH, H. V. B., & SPINELLI, D. N. (1970). Visual experience modifies distribution of horizontally and vertically assisted receptive fields in cats. *Science, 168,* 869–871.

HIRSCH, H. V. B., & SPINELLI, D. N. (1971). Modification of the distribution of receptive field orientation in cats by selective visual exposure during development. *Experimental Brain Research, 13,* 509–527.

HOFER, M. A. (1981). *The roots of human behavior: An introduction to the psychobiology of early development.* New York; W. H. Freeman.

HOFFMAN, L. W. (1980). The effects of maternal employment on the academic attitudes and performance of school-age children. *School Psychology Reveiw, 9,* 319–335.

HOFFMAN, L. W. (1984). Maternal employment and the young child. In M. Perlmutter (Ed.), *Parent-child interactions and parent-child relations in child development. Minnesota Symposia on Child Psychology* (Vol. 17). Hillsdale, N.J.: Erlbaum.

HOFFMAN, M. (1977). Homosexuality. In F. A. Beach (Ed.), *Human sexuality in four perspectives.* Baltimore: Johns Hopkins University Press.

HOFFMAN, M. L. (1970). Conscience, personality, and socialization techniques. *Human Development, 13,* 90–126.

HOFFMAN, M. L. (1970). Moral development. In P. H. Mussen (Ed.), *Carmichael's manual of child psychology: Vol. 2, Part 4. Socialization* (3rd ed.). New York: Wiley.

HOFFMAN, M. L. (1975). Developmental synthesis of affect and cognition and its implications for altruistic motivation. *Developmental Psychology, 11,* 605–622.

HOFFMAN, M. L. (1975). Altruistic behavior and the parent-child relationship. *Journal of Personality and Social Psychology, 31,* 937–943.

HOFFMAN, M. L. (1980). Moral development in adolescence. In J. Adelson (Ed.), *Handbook of adolescent psychology.* New York: Wiley.

HOFFMAN, M. L. (1981). The development of empathy. In P. Rushton & R. M. Sorrentino (Eds.), *Altruism and helping behavior: Social, personality, and developmental perspectives.* Hillsdale, N.J.: Erlbaum.

HOFFMAN, M. L. (1983). Affective and cognitive processes in moral internalization. In E. T. Higgins, D. N. Ruble, &

W. W. Hartup (Eds.), *Social cognition and social behavior: Developmental perspectives.* Cambridge: Cambridge University Press.

HOFSTADER, D. (1979). *Gödel, Escher, Bach: An eternal golden braid.* New York: Basic Books.

HOLLINGSHEAD, A. B. (1949). *Elmtown's youth.* New York: Viking.

HOLLINGSHEAD, A. B. (1975). *Elmtown's youth and Elmtown revisited.* New York: Wiley.

HOLLOS, M. (1975). Logical operations and role-taking abilities in two cultures: Norway and Hungary. *Child Development, 46,* 638–649.

HOLLOS, M., & COWAN, P. A. (1973). Social isolation and cognitive development: Logical operations and role-taking abilities in three Norwegian social settings. *Child Development, 44,* 630–641.

HOLMES, L. D. (1983). *Other cultures, elder years: An introduction to cultural gerontology.* Minneapolis: Burgess Publishing Company.

HOLMES, S. T., & HOLMES, T. H. (1969). Short-term intrusions into the life style routine. *Journal of Psychosomatic Research, 14,* 1–7.

HOLSTEIN, C. (1976). Development of moral judgment: A longitudinal study of males and females. *Child Development, 47,* 51–61.

HOOKER, D. (1952). *The prenatal origins of behavior.* New York: Hafner.

HORN, J. L., & DONALDSON, G. (1980). Cognitive development in adulthood. In O. G. Brim & J. Kagan (Eds.), *Constancy and change in human development.* Cambridge: Harvard University Press.

HOWELLS, W. H. (1960). The distribution of man. *Scientific American, 203,* 112–127.

HOWE, P. E., & SCHILLER, M. (1952). Growth responses of the school child to changes in diet and environmental failures. *Journal of Applied Physiology, 5,* 51–61.

HOWES, C., & OLENICK, M. (1986). Family and childcare influences on toddlers' compliance. *Child Development, 57,* 202–216.

HSIA, D. Y., DRISCOLL, K. W., TROLL, W., & KNOX, W. E. (1956). Detection of phenylalanine tolerance tests heterozygous carriers of phenylketonuria. *Nature, 176,* 1239–1240.

HUBA, G. J., & BENTLER, P. M. (1980). The role of peer and adult models for drug taking at different stages of adolescence. *Journal of Youth and Adolescence, 9,* 449–468.

HUBEL, D. H., & WIESEL, T. N. (1979). Brain mechanisms of vision. *Scientific American, 241,* 130–139.

HUNT, J. V., & RHODES, L. (1977). Mental development of preterm infants during the first year. *Child Development, 48,* 204–210.

HURLEY, L. S. (1980). *Developmental nutrition.* Englewood Cliffs, N.J.: Prentice Hall.

HUSTON, A. C. (1983). Sex typing. In P. H. Mussen (Ed.), *Handbook of child psychology: Vol. 4. Socialization, personality, and social development.* New York: Wiley.

HUTCHINS, E. (1980). *Culture and inference.* Cambridge: Harvard University Press.

HUTCHINS, E. (1983). Understanding Micronesian navigation. In D. Gentner & A. Stevens (Eds.), *Mental models.* Hillsdale, N.J.: Erlbaum.

HYDE, J. S. (1981). How large are cognitive gender differences? A meta-analysis using W and D. *American Psychologist, 36,* 892–901.

INHELDER, B., & PIAGET, J. (1958). *The growth of logical thinking from childhood to adolescence.* New York: Basic Books.

INHELDER, B., & PIAGET, J. (1964). *The early growth of logic in the child.* New York: Harper & Row.

ISAACS, S. (1966). *Intellectual growth in young children.* New York: Schocken.

ISTOMINA, A. Z. (1975). The development of voluntary memory in pre-school-age children. *Soviet Psychology, 13,* 5–64.

ITARD, J. M. G. (1801). *De l'education d'un homme sauvage ou des premiers développements physiques et moraux du jeune sauvage de l'Aveyron.* Paris: Gouyon. (G. Humphrey & M. Humphrey, Trans., 1982. *The wild boy of Aveyron.* New York: Appleton-Century-Crofts)

IZARD, C. E., HUEBNER, R. R., RISSER, D., MCGINNES, G. C., & DOUGHERTY, L. M. (1980). The young infant's ability to produce discrete emotion expressions. *Developmental Psychology, 16,* 132–140.

JACKSON, E., CAMPOS, J. J., & FISCHER, K. W. (1978). The question of decalage between object permanence and person permanence. *Development Psychology, 14,* 1–10.

JACOBS, F. (1982). *The possible and the actual.* New York: Pantheon Books.

JACOBS, J. (1975). *Older persons and retirement communities.* Springfield, Ill: Charles C. Thomas.

JAHODA, M. (1958). *Current concepts of positive mental health.* New York: Basic Books.

JAHODA, G. (1980). Theoretical and systematic approaches in mass-cultural psychology. In H. C. Triandis & W. W. Lambert (Eds.), *Handbook of cross-cultural psychology* (Vol. 1). Boston: Allyn and Bacon.

JAMES, W. T. (1890). The principles of psychology. New York: Holt.

JAMES, W. T. (1951). Social organization among dogs of different temperaments: Terriers and beagles, reared together. *Journal of Comparative and Physiological Psychology, 44,* 71–77.

JAMESON, S. (1986, July 11). South Korean parents tip birth ratio. *Los Angeles Times.* p. 1, 18.

JANES, M. D. (1975). Physical and psychological growth and development. *Environmental Child Health, 121,* 26–30.

JEANS, P. C., SMITH, M. B., & STEARNS, G. (1955). Incidence of prematurity in relation to maternal nutrition. *Journal of the American Dietary Association, 31,* 576–581.

JENCKS, C. (1972). *Inequality: A reassessment of the effect of family and schooling in America.* New York: Basic Books.

JENKINS, J. B. (1979). *Genetics* (2nd ed.). Boston: Houghton Mifflin.

JENSEN, A. R. (1969). How much can we boost I.Q. and scholastic achievement? *Harvard Educational Review, 29,* 1–123.

JENSEN, A. R. (1980). *Bias in mental testing.* New York: Free Press.

JERRISON, H. J. (1982). The evolution of biological intelligence. In R. J. Sternberg (Ed.), *Handbook of human intelligence.* Cambridge: Cambridge University Press.

JESSOR, R., & JESSOR, S. L. (1977). *Problem behavior and psychosocial development: A longitudinal study of youth.* New York: Academic Press.

JOFFE, C. (1977). *Friendly intruders: Child care professionals and family life.* Berkeley: University of California Press.

JOHNSON, W., EMDE, R. N., PANNABECKER, B., STENBERG, C., & DAVIS, M. (1982). Maternal perception of infant emotion from birth through 18 months. *Infant Behavior and Development, 5,* 313–322.

JOHNSON, F. E., BORDEN, M., & MACVEAN, R. B. (1973). Height, weight, and their growth velocities in Guatemalan private school children of high socioeconomic class. *Human Biology, 45,* 627–641.

JONES, M. C. (1965). Psychological correlates of somatic development. *Child Development, 36,* 899–911.

JONES, M. C., & BAYLEY, N. (1950). Physical maturing among boys as related to behavior. *Journal of Educational Psychology, 41,* 129–184.

KAGAN, J. (1972). A conception of early adolescence. In J. Kagan & R. Coles (Eds.), *Twelve to sixteen: Early adolescence.* New York: Norton.

KAGAN, J. (1981). *The second year.* Cambridge: Harvard University Press.

KAGAN, J. (1982). *Psychological research on the human infant: An evaluative summary.* New York: William T. Grant Foundation.

KAGAN, J. (1984). *The nature of the child.* New York: Basic Books.

KAGAN, J., & HAMBURG, M. (1981). The enhancement of memory in the first year. *Journal of Genetic Psychology, 138,* 3–14.

KAGAN, J., KEARSLEY, R. B., & ZELAZO, P. (1978). *Infancy: Its place in human development.* Cambridge: Harvard University Press.

KAGAN, J., KLEIN, R. E., FINLEY, G. E., ROGOFF, B., & NOLAN, E. (1979). A cross-cultural study of cognitive development. *Monographs of the Society for Research in Child Development, 44*(5, Serial No. 180).

KAGAN, J., & LAMB, S. (1987). *The emergence of morality in young children.* Chicago: University of Chicago Press.

KAGAN, J., & MOSS, H. A. (1962). *Birth to maturity.* New York: Wiley.

KAGAN, J., REZNICK, J. S., CLARKE, C., SNIDMAN, N., & GARCIA-COLE, C. (1984). Behavioral inhibition to the unfamiliar. *Child Development, 55,* 2212–2225.

KAGAN, S., & MADSEN, M. C. (1971). Cooperation and competition of Mexican, Mexican-American, and Anglo-American children of two ages under four instructional sets. *Developmental Psychology, 5,* 32–39.

KAIL, R. (1984). *The development of memory in children* (2nd ed.). New York: W. H. Freeman.

KAIL, R., & PELLEGRINO, J. W. (1986). *Human intelligence.* New York: W. H. Freeman.

KAMARA, A. I., & EASLEY, J. A., JR. (1977). Is the rate of cognitive development uniform across cultures? A methodological critique with new evidence from Themne children. In P. R. Dasen (Ed.), *Piagetian psychology: Cross-cultural contributions.* New York: Gardner.

KAMINSKY, H. (1984). Moral development in historical perspective. In W. M. Kurtines & J. L. Gewirtz (Eds.), *Morality, moral behavior, and moral development.* New York: Wiley.

KANDEL, D. B., & LESSER, G. S. (1972). *Youth in two worlds: United States and Denmark.* San Francisco: Jossey-Bass.

KARMILOFF-SMITH, A. (1986). On the structure-dependent nature of stages of development. In I. Levin (Ed.), *Stage and structure: Reopening the debate.* Norwood, N.J.: Ablex.

KATCHADOURIAN, H. A. (1987). *Fifty: Midlife in perspective.* New York: W. H. Freeman.

KATCHADOURIAN, H. A., & LUNDE, D. T. (1975). *Fundamentals of human sexuality* (2nd ed.). New York: Holt, Rinehart and Winston.

KATCHADOURIAN, H. A. (1977). *The biology of adolescence.* New York: W. H. Freeman.

KAWAI, M. (1965). Newly-acquired pre-cultural behavior of the natural troop of Japanese monkeys on Koshima Island. *Primates, 6,* 1–30.

KAY, D. A., & ANGLIN, J. H. (1982). Overextension and underextension in the child's experience and receptive speech. *Journal of Child Language, 9,* 83–98.

KAYE, K. (1982). *The mental and social life of babies.* Chicago: University of Chicago Press.

KEATING, D. (1980). Thinking processes in adolescence. In J. Adelson (Ed.), *Handbook of adolescent psychology.* New York: Wiley.

KEENEY, T. J., CANNIZZO, S. D., & FLAVELL, J. H. (1967). Spontaneous and induced verbal rehearsal in a recall task. *Child Development, 38,* 935–966.

KEETON, W. T. (1980). *Biological science* (3rd ed.). Norton.

KEGAN, R. (1982). *The emerging self: Problem and process in human development.* Cambridge: Harvard University Press.

KELLER, A., FORD, L. H., & MEACHUM, J. A. (1978). Dimensions of self concept in preschool children. *Developmental Psychology, 14,* 483–489.

KELLEY, R. K. (1972). The premarital sexual revolution: Comments on research. *Family Coordinator, 21,* 334–336.

KELLOGG, R. (1969). *Analyzing children's art.* Palo Alto: National Press Books.

KELLOGG, W. N., & KELLOGG, L. A. (1933). *The ape and the child: A study of environmental influences upon early behavior.* New York: Whittlesey House.

KENNELL, J. H., JERAULD, R., WOLFE, H., CHESTER, D., KREGER, N., MCALPINE, W., STEFFA, M., & KLAUS, M. H. (1974). Maternal behavior one year after early and extended post-partum contact. *Developmental Medicine and Child Neurology, 16,* 172–179.

KENNELL, J. H., VOOS, D. K., & KLAUS, M. H. (1979). Parent-infant bonding. In J. D. Osofsky (Ed.), *Handbook of infant development.* New York: Wiley.

KENISTON, K. (1970). Youth: As a stage of life. *American Scholar, 39,* 631–654.

KENYATTA, J. (1938). *Facing Mt. Kenya: The tribal life of the Kikuyu.* London: Secker and Warburg.

KESSEN, W. (1965). *The child.* New York: Wiley.

KETT, J. F. (1977). *Rites of passage: Adolescence in America 1790 to the present.* New York: Basic Books.

KIELL, N. (1964). *The universal experience of adolescence.* New York: International Universities Press.

KIERKEGAARD, S. quoted in **L. A. SROUFE.** (1979). Socioemo-

tional development. In J. D. Osofsky (Ed.), *Handbook of infant development.* New York: Wiley.

KING, M. A., & YUILLE, J. C. (1987). Suggestibility and the child witness. In S. J. Ceci, M. P. Toglia, & D. F. Ross (Eds.), *Children's eyewitness memory.* New York: Springer-Verlag.

KING, M. C., & WILSON, A. C. (1975). Evolution at two levels in humans and chimpanzees. *Science, 188,* 107–115.

KINSBOURNE, M., & HISCOCK, M. (1983). Development of lateralization of the brain. In P. Mussen (Ed.), *Handbook of child development: Vol. 2. Infancy and developmental psychobiology.* New York: Wiley.

KINSEY, A. C., POMEROY, W. B., & MARTIN, C. E. (1948). *Sexual behavior in the human male.* Philadelphia: Saunders.

KINSEY, A. C., POMEROY, W. B, MARTIN, C. E., & GEBHARD, P. H. (1953). *Sexual behavior in the human female.* Philadelphia: Saunders.

KITCHER, P. (1985). *Vaulting ambition: Sociobiology and the quest for human nature.* Cambridge: MIT Press.

KLAHR, D. (1982). Nonmonotone assessment of monotone development: An information processing analysis. In S. Strauss (Eds.), *U-shaped behavioral growth.* New York: Academic Press.

KLAHR, D., & WALLACE, J. G. (1976). *Cognitive development: An information processing view.* Hillsdale, N.J.: Erlbaum.

KLAPPER, Z. S., & BIRCH, H. G. (1969). Perceptual and action equivalence of objects and photographs in children. *Perceptual and Motor Skills, 29,* 763–771.

KLAUS, M. H., & KENNELL, J. H. (1976). *Maternal-infant bonding: The impact of early separation or loss on family development.* St. Louis: Mosby.

KLAUS, M. H., KENNELL, J. H., PLUMB, N., & ZUEHLKE, S. (1970). Human maternal behavior at the first contact with her young. *Pediatrics, 46,* 187.

KLEIN, R. E., ARENALES, P., DELGADO, H., ENGEL, P., GUZMAN, G., IRWIN, M., LASKY, R., LECHTIG, A., MARTORELL, R., MEJIA PIVARAL, V., RUSSELL, P., & YARBROUGH, C. (1976). Effect of maternal nutrition of fetal growth and infant development. *Pan American Health Organization Bulletin, 10,* 301–306.

KLEITMAN, N. (1963). *Sleep and wakefulness.* Chicago: University of Chicago Press.

KLIEGL, R., & BALTES, P. (1987). Theory-guided analysis of mechanisms of development and aging through test-the-limits and research on expertise. In C. Schooler & K. W. Schaie (Eds.), *Cognitive functioning and social structure over the life course.* Norwood, N.J.: Ablex.

KLINEBERG, O. (1935). *Race differences.* New York: Harper & Row.

KLINEBERG, O. (1980). Historical perspectives: Cross-cultural psychology before 1960. In H. Triandis and W. Lambert (Eds.), *Handbook of cross-cultural psychology* (Vol 1.). Boston: Allyn and Bacon.

KLOPFER, P. H., ADAMS, D. K., & KLOPFER, M. S. (1964). Maternal imprinting in goats. *Proceedings of the National Academy of Sciences, 52*, 911–914.

KLUCKHOHN, C., & KELLY, W. H. (1945). The concept of culture. In R. Linton (Ed.), *The science of man in the world crisis.* New York: Columbia University Press.

KOHLBERG, L. (1966). A cognitive-developmental analysis of childrens' sex role concepts and attitudes. In E. E. Maccoby (Ed.), *The development of sex differences.* Stanford: Stanford University Press.

KOHLBERG, L. (1969). Stage and sequence: The cognitive-developmental approach to socialization. In D. A. Goslin (Ed.), *Handbook of socialization theory and research.* Chicago: Rand McNally.

KOHLBERG, L. (1976). Moral stages and moralization: The cognitive-developmental approach. In J. Lickona (Ed.), *Moral development behavior: Theory, research and social issues.* New York: Holt, Rinehart and Winston.

KOHLBERG, L. (1984). *The psychology of moral development: The nature and validity of moral stages* (Vol. 2). New York: Harper & Row.

KOHLBERG, L., & CANDEE, D. (1984). The relationship of moral judgment to moral action. In W. M. Kurtines & J. L. Gewirtz (Eds.), *Morality, moral behavior, and moral development.* New York: Wiley.

KOHLBERG, L., HICKEY, J., & SCHARF, P. (1972). The justice structure of the prison: A theory and intervention. *Prison Journal, 51*, 3–14.

KOHLBERG, L., & KRAMER, R. (1969). Continuities and discontinuities in childhood and adult moral development. *Human Development, 12*, 93–120.

KOHLBERG, L., YAEGER, J., & HJERTHOLM, E. (1968). Private speech: Four studies and a review of theories. *Child Development, 39*, 691–736.

KOHN, M. L. (1977). *Class and conformity* (2nd ed.). Chicago: University of Chicago Press.

KOHN, M. L., & SCHOOLER, C. (1978). The reciprocal effects of the substantive complexity of work and intellectual flexibility: A longitudinal assessment. *American Journal of Sociology, 84*, 24–52.

KOLATA, G. (1987, Sept. 22). Flaws reported in new prenatal test. *New York Times*, Section I, p. 12.

KOLB, B., & WHISHAW, I. Q. (1985). *Fundamentals of human neuropsychology* (2nd ed.). New York: W. H. Freeman.

KOLUCHOVA, J. (1972). Severe deprivation in twins: A case study. *Journal of Child Psychology and Psychiatry, 13*, 107–114.

KOLUCHOVA, J. (1976). A report on the further development of twins after severe and prolonged deprivation. In A. M. Clarke & A. D. B. Clarke (Eds.), *Early experience: Myth and evidence.* London: Open Books.

KONNER, M. (1977). Evolution in human behavior development. In P. H. Leiderman, S. Tulkin, & A. Rosenfeld (Eds.), *Culture and infancy: Variations in human experience.* New York: Academic Press.

KOPP, C. B. (1983). Risk factors in development. In P. H. Mussen (Ed.), *Handbook of child development: Vol. 2. Infancy and developmental psychobiology.* New York: Wiley.

KOPP, C. B., & KRAKOW, J. B. (1983). The developmentalist and the study of biological risk: A view of the past with an eye toward the future. *Child Development, 54*, 1086–1108.

KOPP, C. B., & MCCALL, R. B. (1982). Predicting later mental performance for normal, at-risk, and handicapped infants. In P. B. Baltes & O. G. Brim (Eds.), *Life span development and behavior* (Vol. 4). New York: Academic Press.

KOPP, C. B., & PARMALEE, A. H. (1979). Prenatal and perinatal influences on behavior. In J. D. Osofsky (Ed.), *Handbook of infant development.* New York: Wiley.

KORNER, A. F. (1987). Preventive intervention with high-risk newborns: Theoretical conceptual and methodological perspectives. In J. D. Osofsky (Ed.), *Handbook of infant development.* (2nd ed.). New York: Wiley.

KORNER, A. F., & GROBSTEIN, R. (1966). Visual alertness as related to soothing in neonates. *Child Development, 37*, 867–876.

KORNER, A. F., KRAEMER, H. C., HAFFNER, E., & COSPER, L. N. (1975). Effects of waterbed flotation on premature infants: A pilot study. *Pediatrics, 56*, 361–366.

KORNER, A. F., & THOMAN, E. (1970). Visual alertness in neonates as evoked by maternal care. *Journal of Experimental Child Psychology, 10*, 67–78.

KOTELCHUCK, M. (1976). The infant's relationship to the father: Experimental evidence. In M. E. Lamb (Ed.), *The role of the father in child development.* New York: Wiley.

KOTELCHUK, M., SCHWARTZ, J. B., ANDERKA, M. T., & FINISON, K. S. (1984). WIC participation and pregnancy outcomes: Massachusetts statewide evaluation project. *American Journal of Public Health, 74*, 1086–1091.

KOZOL, J. (1985). *Illiterate America.* Garden City, N.Y.: Doubleday.

KRAMER, L. I., & PIERPONT, H. E. (1976). Rocking waterbed and auditory stimuli to enhance growth of preterm infants. *Journal of Pediatrics, 88*, 297–299.

KRASNOGORSKI, N. I. (1907/1967). The formation of artificial conditioned reflexes in young children. In Y. Brackbill & G. G. Thompson (Eds.), *Behavior in infancy and early childhood: A book of readings*. New York: Free Press.

KRAUSS, R. M., & GLUCKSBERG, S. (1969). The development of communication: Competence as a function of age. *Child Development, 42,* 255–266.

KREUTZER, M. A., LEONARD, S. C., & FLAVELL, J. H. (1975). An interview study of children's knowledge about memory. *Monographs of the Society for Research in Child Development, 40* (1, Serial No. 159).

KUHL, P. K. (1978). Predispositions in the perception of speech-sound catogories: A species-specific phenomenon? In F. D. Minifie & L. L. Lloyd (Eds.), *Communicative and cognitive abilities: Early behavioral assessment*. Baltimore: University Park Press.

KUHL, P. K., & MILLER, J. D. (1978). Speech perception by the chinchilla: Identification functions for synthetic VOT stimuli. *Journal of the Acoustical Society of America, 63,* 905–917.

KUHN, D. (1976). Short-term longitudinal evidence for the sequentiality of Kohlberg's early stages of moral judgment. *Developmental Psychology, 12,* 162–166.

KUHN, T. (1962). *The structure of scientific revolutions*. Chicago: University of Chicago Press.

KUNDERA, M. (1988). *The art of the novel*. New York: Grove Press.

KURDEK, L. A., BLISK, D., & SIESKY, A. E., JR. (1981). Correlates of children's long-term adjustment to their parents' divorce. *Developmental Psychology, 17,* 565–579.

KURTINES, W. M., & GEWIRTZ, J. L. (1984). Certainty and morality: Objectivistic versus relativistic approaches. In W. E. Kurtines & J. L. Gewirtz (Eds.), *Morality, moral behavior, and moral development*. New York: Wiley.

KURTINES, W. M., & GRIEF, E. B. (1974). The development of moral thought: Review and evaluation of Kohlberg's approach. *Psychological Bulletin, 81,* 453–470.

LABORATORY OF COMPARATIVE HUMAN COGNITION. (1983). Culture and cognitive development. In P. Mussen (Ed.), *Handbook of child psychology*: Vol. 1. W. Kessen (Ed.), *History, theory, and methods*. New York: Wiley.

LABOUVIE-VIEF, G. (1982). Individual time, social time, intellectual aging. In T. Hareven, & K. Adams (Eds.), *Aging and life course transitions: An interdisciplinary perspective*. New York: Guilford Press.

LABOV, W., & ROBBINS, C. (1969). A note on the relation of reading failure to peer-group status in urban ghettos. *Florida Language Reporter, 167,* 54–57.

LADYGINA-KOTS, N. N. (1935). *Infant, ape, and human child*. Moscow: Darwin Museum.

LAGERCRANTZ, H., & SLOTKIN, T. A. (1986). The "stress" of being born. *Scientific American, 254,* 100–107.

LAMAZE, F. (1970). *Painless childbirth*. Chicago: Henry Regnery.

LAMB, M. E. (1978). The development of sibling relationships in infancy: A short term longitudinal study. *Child Development, 49,* 1189–1196.

LAMB, M. E. (1978). Qualitative aspects of mother- and father-infant attachments. *Infant Behavior and Development, 1,* 265–275.

LAMB, M. E. (1982). What can "research experts" tell parents about effective socialization? In E. Zigler, M. E. Lamb, & I. L. Child (Eds.), *Socialization and personality development*. Oxford: Oxford University Press.

LAMB, M. E., & CAMPOS, J. J. (1982). *Development in infancy: An introduction*. New York: Random House.

LAMB, M. E., & HWANG, C. P. (1982). Maternal attachment and mother-neonate bonding: A critical review. In M. E. Lamb & A. L. Brown (Eds.), *Advances for developmental psychology* (Vol. 2). Hillsdale, N.J.: Erlbaum.

LAMB, M. E., THOMPSON, R. A., GARDNER, W. P., CHARNOV, E. L., & ESTES, D. (1984). Security of infantile attachment as assessed in the 'strange situation.' *Behavioral and Brain Sciences, 7,* 127–171.

LANE, H. (1976). *The wild boy of Aveyron*. Cambridge: Harvard University Press.

LANGE, G. (1978). Organization-related processes in children's recall. In P. A. Ornstein (Ed.), *Memory development in children*. Hillsdale, N.J.: Erlbaum.

LANGER, E. J., & RODIN, J. (1976). The effects of choice and enhanced personal responsibilities for the aged: A field experiment in an institutional setting. *Journal of Personality and Social Psychology, 34,* 191–198.

LANGER, E. J., RODIN, J., BECK, P., WEINMAN, C., & SPITZER, L. (1979). Environmental determinants of memory improvement in late adulthood. *Journal of Personality and Social Psychology, 37,* 2003–2013.

LARSEN, M. T. (1986). Writing on clay: From pictograph to alphabet. *Quarterly Newsletter of the Laboratory of Comparative Human Cognition, 8,* 3–9.

LARSON, L. E. (1972). The influence of parents and peers during adolescence; The situational hypothesis revisited. *Journal of Marriage and the Family, 34,* 67–74.

LATOUR, B. (1987). *Science in action*. Cambridge: Harvard University Press.

LAVE, J. (1977). Tailor-made experiments and evaluating the intellectual consequences of apprenticeship training.

Quarterly News Letter of the Institute of Comparative Human Development, 1, 1–3.

LAVE, J., MURTAUGH, M., & DE LA ROCHA, O. (1984). The dialectic of arithmetic in grocery shopping. In B. Rogoff & J. Lave (Eds.), *Everyday cognition.* Cambridge: Harvard University Press.

LAVIK, N. J. (1977). Urban-rural differences in rates of disorder. A comparative psychiatric population study of Norwegian adolescents. In P. T. Graham (Ed.), *Epidemiological approaches in child psychiatry.* London: Academic Press.

LAVIGNE, M. (1982). Rubella's disabled children: Research and rehabilitation. *Columbia, 7,* 10–17.

LAWSON, A. E. (1975). Sex differences in innate and formal reasoning ability as measured by manipulation tasks and written tasks. *Science Education, 59,* 397–405.

LAWTON, M. P. (1977). The impact of the environment on aging and behavior. In J. E. Birren & K. W. Schaie (Eds.), *Handbook of the psychology of aging.* New York: Van Nostrand Reinhold.

LAZER, I. (1983). Discussion and implications of the findings. In The Consortium for Longitudinal Studies (Ed.), *As the twig is bent . . . lasting effects of preschool programs.* Hillsdale, N.J.: Erlbaum.

LECOURS, A. R. (1975). Mylogenetic correlates of the development of speech and language. In E. H. Lenneberg & E. Lenneberg (Eds.), *Foundations of language development* (Vol. 1). New York: Academic Press.

LECOURS, A. R. (1982). Correlates of developmental behavior in brain maturation. In T. Bever (Ed.), *Regressions in mental development.* Hillsdale, N.J.: Erlbaum.

LEE, L. (1965). *Cider with Rosie.* London: Hogarth Press.

LEE, R. B. & DEVORE, I. (Eds.). (1976). Kalahari hunter-gatherers. Cambridge: Harvard University Press.

LEGG, C., SHERICK, I., & WADLAND, W. (1974). Reaction of preschool children to the birth of a sibling. *Child Psychiatry and Human Development, 5,* 3–39.

LEIBENBERG, B. (1967). Expectant fathers. *American Journal of Orthopsychiatry, 37,* 358–359.

LE MARE, L. J., & RUBIN, K. H. (1987). Perspective taking and peer interaction: Structural and developmental analyses. *Child Development, 58,* 306–315.

LENNEBERG, E. H. (1967). *The biological foundations of language.* New York: Wiley.

LENNEBERG, E. H., REBELSKY, F. G., & NICHOLS, I. A. (1965). The vocalizations of infants born to hearing and deaf parents. *Human Development, 8,* 23–27.

LEONARD, L. B., CHAPMAN, K., ROWAN, L. E., & WEISS, A. L. (1983). Three hypotheses concerning young children's imitations of lexical items. *Developmental Psychology, 19,* 591–601.

LEONI, L. (1964). *Tico and the golden wings.* New York: Pantheon.

LEONTIEV, A. N. (1981). *Problems of the development of the mind.* Moscow: Progress Publishers.

LEOPOLD, W. F. (1949). *Speech development of a bilingual child: A linguist's record: Vol. 2 Diary from age two.* Evanston, Ill.: Northwestern University Press.

LEPPER, M. R., & GREENE, D. (Eds.). (1978). *The hidden costs of reward.* Hillsdale, N.J.: Erlbaum.

LERNER, M. I. & LIBBY, W. J. (1976). *Heredity, evolution, and society.* New York: W. H. Freeman.

LERNER, R. M., & FOCH, T. T. (Eds.). (1987). *Biological-psychosocial interactions in early adolescence.* Hillsdale, N.J.: Erlbaum.

LESLIE, A. M. (1986). Getting development off the ground: Modularity and the infant's perception of causality. In P. van Geert (Ed.), *Theory building and development.* Amsterdam: Elsevier.

LESLIE, A. M., & KEEBLE, S. (1987). Do six month old infants perceive causality? *Cognition, 25,* 265–288.

LESSER, G. S. (1974). *Children and television.* New York: Random House.

LESTER, B. M. (1984). A biosocial model of infant crying. In L. P. Lipsitt (Ed.), *Advances in infancy research.* New York: Academic Press.

LESTER, B. M., ALS, H., & BRAZELTON, T. B. (1982). Regional obstetric anesthesia and newborn behavior. A reanalysis towards synergistic effects. *Child Development, 53,* 687–692.

LESTER, B. M., & ZESKIND, P. S. (1982). A biobehavioral perspective on crying in early infancy. In H. Fitzgerald, B. Lester, & M. Yogman (Eds.), *Theory and research in behavioral pediatrics* (Vol 1). New York: Plenum Press.

LEVER, J. (1978). Sex differences in the complexity of children's play and games. *American Sociological Review, 43,* 471–483.

LEVIN, I. (Ed.). (1986). *Stage and structure: Reopening the debate.* Norwood, N.J.: Ablex.

LEVINE, R. A. (1974). Parental goals: A cross cultural view. In H. J. Leichter (Ed.), *The family as educator.* New York: Teachers College Press.

LEVINSON, P. J., & CARPENTER, R. L. (1974). An analysis of analogical reasoning in children. *Child Development, 45,* 857–861.

LEWIS, M., & BROOKS-GUNN, J. (1979). *Social cognition and the acquisition of self.* New York: Plenum Press.

LEWIS, M., & STARR, M. (1979). Developmental continuity.

In J. Osofsky (Ed.), *Handbook of infant development*. New York: Wiley.

LEWIS, M., & WEINRAUB, M. (1974). Sex of parent versus sex of child: Socio-emotional development. In R. C. Friedman, R. M. Richart, R. C. Friedman, & R. Vande Wiele (Eds.), *Sex differences in behavior*. New York: Wiley.

LEWONTIN, R. (1982). *Human diversity*. New York: Scientific American Books.

LEWONTIN, R., ROSE, R., & KAMIN, L. (1984). *Not in our genes*. New York: Pantheon.

LEWONTIN, R. C. (1976). Race and intelligence. In N. J. Block & G. Dworkin (Eds.), *The IQ controversy*. New York: Pantheon.

LICKONA, T. (Ed.). (1976). *Moral development and behavior: Theory, research and social issues*. New York: Holt, Rinehart, and Winston.

LIEBERMAN, P. (1984). *The biology and evolution of language*. Cambridge: Harvard University Press.

LIEBERT, R. M. (1984). What develops in moral development? In W. K. Kurtines & J. L. Gewirtz (Eds.), *Morality, moral behavior, and moral development*. New York: Wiley.

LIEBERT, R. M., SPRAFKIN, J. N., & DAVIDSON, E. S. (1982). *The early window: Effects of television on children and youth*. New York: Pergamon Press.

LINAZA, J. (1984). Piaget's marbles: The study of children's games and their knowledge of rules. *Oxford Review of Education, 10*, 271–274.

LINN, M. C. (1983). Content, context, and process in reasoning. *Journal of Early Adolescence, 3*, 63–82.

LINN, M. C., DE BENEDICTUS, T., & DELUCCHI, K. (1982). Adolescent reasoning about advertisements: Preliminary investigations. *Child Development, 53*, 1599–1613.

LINN, M. C., & PULOS, S. (1983). Male-female differences in predicting displaced volume: Strategy usage, aptitude relationships, and experience influences. *Journal of Educational Psychology, 75*, 86–96.

LINN, M. C., & SWEENEY, S. F., JR. (1981). Individual differences in formal thought: Role of expectations and attitudes. *Journal of Educational Psychology, 73*, 274–286.

LIPSITT, L. P. (1977). Taste in human neonates: Its effects on sucking and heart rate. In J. M. Weiffenbach (Ed.), *Taste and development: The genesis of sweet preference*. Washington, D.C.: U.S. Government Printing Office.

LIPSITT, L. P., & LEVY, N. (1959). Electrotactual threshold in the neonate. *Child Development, 30*, 547–554.

LOCK, A. (1980). *The guided reinvention of language*. New York: Academic Press.

LOCKE, J. (1699/1938). *Some thoughts concerning education*. London: Churchill.

LOEB, R. C., HORST, L., & HORTON, P. J. (1980). Family interaction patterns associated with self-esteem in preadolescent boys and girls. *Merrill-Palmer Quarterly, 26*, 203–217.

LOFTUS, E. F. (1979). *Eyewitness testimony*. Cambridge: Harvard University Press.

LOFTUS, E. F., & DAVIS, G. M. (1984). Distortions in the memory of children. *Journal of Social Issues, 40*, 51–67.

LOGAN, R. K. (1986). *The alphabet effect*. New York: Morrow.

LOMAX, E. M., KAGAN, J., & ROSENKRANTZ, B. G. (1978). *Science and patterns of child care*. New York: W. H. Freeman.

LORENZ, K. (1966). *On aggression*. New York: Harcourt, Brace and World.

LORENZ, K. Z. (1943). Die Angebornen Formen mögicher Erfahrung. *Zeitschrift für Tierpsychologie, 5*, 233–409.

LUCARIELLO, J., & RIFKIN, A. (1986). Event representations as the basis of categorical knowledge. In K. Nelson (Ed.), *Event knowledge: Structure and function in development*. Hillsdale, N.J.: Erlbaum.

LUMSDEN, C. J., & WILSON, E. O. (1981). *Genes, mind, and culture*. Cambridge: Harvard University Press.

LUNZER, E. A. (1965). Problems of formal reasoning in test situations. In P. H. Mussen (Ed.), *Handbook of child psychology: Vol. 3. Cognitive development*. New York: Wiley.

LURIA, A. R. (1973). *The working brain*. New York: Basic Books.

LURIA, A. R. (1976). *Cognitive development*. Cambridge: Harvard University Press.

LURIA, A. R. (1981). *Language and cognition*. New York: Wiley.

MAAS, H. (1963). The young adult adjustment of twenty wartime residential nursery children. *Child Welfare, 42*, 57–72.

MACANDREW, C., & EDGERTON, R. (1966). On the possibility of friendship. *American Journal of Mental Deficiency, 70*, 612–621.

MACCOBY, E. E. (1980). *Social development: Psychological growth and the parent-child relationship*. New York: Harcourt Brace Jovanovich.

MACCOBY, E. E. (1984). Middle childhood in the context of the family. In W. A. Collins (Ed.), *Development during middle childhood: The years from six to twelve*. Washington D.C.: National Academy Press.

MACCOBY, E. E., & JACKLIN, C. N. (1974). *The psychology of sex differences*. Stanford: Stanford University Press.

MACCOBY, E. E., & MARTIN, J. A. (1983). Socialization in the context of the family: Parent-child interaction. In P. H. Mussen (Ed.), *Handbook of child psychology: Vol. 4. Socialization, personality, and social behavior*. New York: Wiley.

MACFARLANE, A. (1977). *The psychology of childbirth*. Cambridge: Harvard University Press.

MACKENZIE, B. (1984). Explaining race differences in I.Q. *American Psychologist, 39,* 1214–1233.

MACLUSKY, N. J., & NAFTOLIN, F. (1981). Sexual differentiation in the central nervous system. *Science, 211,* 1294–1303.

MADSEN, M .C., & SHAPIRA, A. (1970). Cooperative and competitive behavior of urban Afro-American, Anglo-American, Mexican-American, and Mexican village children. *Developmental Psychology, 3,* 16–20.

MAGNUSSON, D., STATTIN, H., & ALLEN, V. L. (1985). Biological maturation and social development: A longitudinal study of some adjustment processes from mid-adolescence to adulthood. *Journal of Youth and Adolescence, 14,* 267–283.

MAIN, M. (1973). *Play, exploration, and competence as related to child-adult attachment*. Unpublished doctoral dissertation, John Hopkins University.

MAIN, M., & WESTON, D. (1981). The quality of the toddler's relationship to mother and father: Related to conflict behavior and the readiness to establish new relationships. *Child Development, 52,* 932–940.

MALLICK, S. K., & MCCANDLESS, B. R. (1966). A study of catharsis of aggression. *Journal of Personality and Social Psychology, 4,* 590–596.

MANDLER, J. (1983). Representation. In P. H. Mussen (Ed.), *Handbook of child psychology: Vol 3. Cognitive development*. New York: Wiley.

MANDLER, J. (1984). Representation and recall in infancy. In M. Moscovitch (Ed)., *Infant memory*. New York: Plenum Press.

MANDLER, J., SCRIBNER, S., COLE, M., & DE FOREST, M. (1980). Cross-cultural invariance in story recall. *Child Development, 51,* 19–26.

MANIULENKO, Z. V. (1975). The development of voluntary behavior in pre-school-age children. *Soviet Psychology, 13,* 65–116.

MARATSOS, M. (1983). Some issues in the study of the aquisition of grammar. In P. Mussen (Ed.), *Handbook of child psychology: Vol 3. Cognitive development*. New York: Wiley.

MARCIA, J. E. (1966). Development and validation of ego identity status. *Journal of Personality and Social Psychology, 3,* 551–558.

MARCIA, J. E. (1980). Identity in adolescence. In J. Adelson (Ed.), *Handbook of adolescent psychology*. New York: Wiley.

MARCUS, D. E., & OVERTON, W. E. (1978). The development of cognitive gender constancy and sex role preferences. *Child Development, 49,* 434–444.

MARKOVA, A. K. (1979). *The teaching and mastery of language*. White Plains, N.Y.: M. E. Sharpe.

MARLER, P. (1976). An ethological theory of the orgin of vocal learning. *Annals of the New York Academy of Science, 280,* 386–395.

MARQUIS, D. (1931). Can conditioned reflexes be established in the newborn infant? *Journal of Genetic Psychology, 39,* 479–492.

MARSHALL, W. A., & TANNER, J. M. (1974). Puberty. In J. A. Davis & J. Dobbing (Eds.), *Scientific foundations of pediatrics*. Philadelphia: Saunders.

MATAS, L., AREND, R., & SROUFE, L. A. (1978). Continuity of adaptation in the second year. The relationship between quality of attachment and later competence. *Child Development, 49,* 547–556.

MATHENY, A. P., RIESE, M. L., & WILSON, R. S. (1985). Rudiments of infant temperament: Newborn to 9 months. *Developmental Psychology, 21,* 486–494.

MATHEWS, M. (1966). *Teaching to read: Historically considered*. Chicago: University of Chicago Press.

MATTHEWS, K. A., BATESON, C. D., HORN, J., & ROSENMAN, R. H. (1981). Principles in his nature which interest him in the fortune of others. . . . The heritability of empathic concern for others. *Journal of Personality, 49,* 237–247.

MCCALL, R. B. (1979). *Infants*. Cambridge: Harvard University Press.

MCCALL, R. B. (1981). Nature, nurture and the two realms of development: A proposed integration with respect to mental development. *Child Development, 52,* 1–12.

MCCALL, R. B. (1983). Exploring developmental transitions in mental performance. In K. W. Fischer (Ed.), *Levels and transitions in children's development (New Directions for Child Development, No. 21)*. San Francisco: Jossey-Bass.

MCCALL, R. B., EICHORN, D. H., & HOGARTY, P. S. (1977). Transitions in early mental development. *Monographs of Society for Research Child Development, 42* (3, Serial No. 171).

MCCALL, R. B., MEYERS, E. D., JR., HARTMAN, J., & ROCHE, A. F. (1983). Developmental changes in head-circumference and mental-performance growth rates: A test of Epstein's phrenoblysis hypothesis. *Developmental Psychology, 20,* 244–260.

MCCARTNEY, K., SCARR, S., PHILLIPS, D., & GRAJEK, S. (1985). Day care as intervention: Comparisons of varying quality programs. *Journal of Applied Development Psychology, 6,* 247–260.

MCCONNELL, T. M. (1934/1958). Discover or be told! Reprinted in C. W. Hunnicutt & W. J. Iverson (Eds.). (1958). *Research in the three R's.* New York: Harper & Row.

MCCUNE-NICOLICH, L., & BRUSKIN, C. (1982). Combinatorial competency in symbolic play and language. In D. J. Pepler & K. H. Rubin, *The play of children: Current theory and research.* Basal: S. Krieger.

MCGRAW, M. B. (1943). *The neuromuscular maturation of the human infant.* New York: Columbia University Press.

MCGRAW, M. B. (1975). *Growth: A study of Johnny and Jimmy.* New York: Arno Press. (Original work published 1935)

MCKUSICK, V. A. (1975). *Mendelian inheritance in man: Catalog of autosomal dominant, autosomal recessive, and x-linked phenotypes* (4th ed.). Baltimore: John Hopkins University Press.

MCMILLEN, M. M. (1979). Differential mortality by sex in fetal and neonatal deaths. *Science, 204,* 89–91.

MCNEIL, D. (1970). *The acquisition of language: The study of developmental psycholinguistics.* New York: Harper & Row.

MEAD, M. (1973). *Coming of age in Samoa: A psychological study of primitive youth.* New York: American Museum of Natural History. (Original work published 1928)

MEAD, M., & MACGREGOR, F. C. (1951). *Growth and culture.* New York: Putnam.

MEAD, M., & NEWTON, N. (1967). Cultural patterning of perinatal behavior. In S. Richardson & A. Guttmacher, *Childbearing: Its social and psychological aspects.* Baltimore: Williams & Wilkins.

MEDRICH, E. A., ROIZEN, J., RUBIN, V., & BUCKLEY, S. (1982). *The serious business of growing up.* Berkeley: University of California Press.

MEEHAN, A. M. (1984). A meta-analysis of sex differences in formal operational thought. *Child Development, 55,* 1110–1124.

MEHAN, H. (1979). What time is it, Denise? Asking known informtion questions in classroom discourse. *Theory into Practice, 18,* 285–294.

MEHLER, J., LAMBERTZ, G., JUSCZYK, P., & AMIEL-TISON, C. (1986). Discrimination de la langue maternelle par le nouveau-né. *Comptes rendus de l'Académie de Science, 303,* Serie III, 637–640.

MELTZOFF, A. N., & MOORE, M. K. (1983a). The origins of imitation in infancy: Paradigm, phenomena, and theories. In L. Lipsitt & C. Rovee-Collier (Eds.), *Advances in infancy research* (Vol 2). Norwood, N.J.: Ablex.

MELTZOFF, A. N., & MOORE, M. K. (1983b). Newborn infants imitate adult facial gestures. *Child Development, 54,* 702–709.

MESSER, S. B. (1976). Reflection-impulsivity: A review. *Psychological Bulletin, 83,* 1026–1052.

MICHEL, G. F. (1981). Right handedness: A consequence of infant supine head orientation preference. *Science, 212,* 385–387.

MILLER, G. A. (1981). *Language and speech.* New York: W. H. Freeman.

MILLER, N. E., & DOLLARD, J. (1941). *Social learning and imitation.* New Haven: Yale University Press.

MILLER, P. (1982). *Amy, Wendy and Beth: Learning language in south Baltimore.* Austin: University of Texas Press.

MILLER, P., & SIMON, W. (1980). The development of sexuality in adolescence. In J. Adelson (Ed.), *The handbook of adolescent psychology.* New York: Wiley.

MILLER, S. A., SHELTON, J., & FLAVELL, J. H. (1970). A test of Luria's hypothesis concerning the development of verbal self-regulation. *Child Development, 1970, 41,* 651–665.

MILNER, E. (1967). *Human neural and behavioral development.* Springfield, Ill: Charles C. Thomas.

MINUCHIN, P. P., & SHAPIRO, E. K. (1983). The school as a context of social development. In P. H. Mussen (Ed.), *Handbook of child psychology: Vol. 4. Socialization, personality, and social development.* New York: Wiley.

MINTON, H L. & SCHNEIDER, F. W. (1980). *Differential psychology.* Monterey, Ca: Brooks/Cole.

MISCHEL, W. (1966). A social learning view of sex differences in behavior. In E. M. Maccoby (Ed.), *The development of sex differences.* Stanford: Stanford University Press.

MISCHEL, W. (1968). *Personality and assessment.* New York: Wiley.

MISCHEL, W. (1981). Metacognition and the rules of delay. In J. H. Flavell & L. Ross (Eds.), *Social cognitive development: Frontiers and possible futures.* Cambridge: Cambridge University Press.

MIYAKE, K., CHEN, S. & CAMPOS, J. J. (1985). Infant temperament, mother's mode of interaction, and attachment in Japan. An interm report. In I. Bretherton & E. Waters (Eds.), *Growing points of attachment theory and research: Monographs of the Society for Research in Child Development, 50,* (1–2, Serial No. 209).

MOBIL OIL CORPORATION. (1981, May 19). Does the TV camera distort society? Mobil Oil advertisement. *Los Angeles Times,* Part I, p. 5.

MONEY, J. & EHRHARDT, A. A. (1972). *Man and woman, boy and girl.* Baltimore: Johns Hopkins Press.

MONTEMAYOR, R. (1982). The relationship between parent-adolescent conflict and the amount of time adolescents spend alone and with their parents and peers. *Child Development, 53,* 1512–1519.

MONTESSORI, M. (1964). *The Montessori method.* New York: Schocken Books. (Original publication New York: Frederick A. Stokes, 1912)

MOORE, K. L. (1982). *The developing human: Clinically oriented embryology* (3rd ed.). Philadelphia: Saunders.

MOORE, T. R., ORIGEL, W., KEY, T. C., & RESNIK, R. (1986). The perinatal and economic impact of prenatal care in a low socio-economic population. *American Journal of Obstetrics and Gynecology, 154,* 29–33.

MOWBRAY, C. T., LANIR, S., & HULCE, M. (1982). Stress, mental health, and motherhood. *Birth Psychology Bulletin, 3,* 10–33.

MOWRER, O. H. (1950). *Learning theory and personality.* New York: Ronald Press.

MUCH, N., & SCHWEDER, R. (1978). Speaking of rules: The analysis of culture in breach. In W. Damon (Ed.). *Moral development (New directions for child development,* No. 2). San Francisco: Jossey-Bass.

MUIR, D., & FIELD, J. (1979). Newborn infants orient to sounds. *Child Development, 50,* 431–436.

MURRAY, J. P., RUBENSTEIN, E. A., & COMSTOCK, G. A. (Eds.). (1972). *Television and social behavior* (Vol. 2). Washington, D.C.: Government Printing Office.

NAEYE, R. L. (1978). Effects of maternal cigarette smoking on the fetus and placenta. *Journal of Obstetrics and Gynaecology of the British Commonwealth, 85,* 732–735.

NATIONAL ACADEMY OF EDUCATION. COMMISSION ON READING. (1985). *Becoming a nation of readers: The report of the Commission on reading.* Washington, D.C.: U.S. Department of Education.

NATIONAL CENTER FOR HEALTH STATISTICS. (1982). *Monthly Vital Statistics Report, 31,* No. 6 supplement. Washington, D.C.: Author.

NATIONAL CENTER FOR HEALTH STATISTICS. (1987). *Monthly Vital Statistics Report. Table 4. Infant deaths, infant mortality rate, and births and marriages: United States, June 1984–June, 1985.* Washington, D.C.: Author.

NATIONAL COMMISSION ON YOUTH. (1980). *The transition of youth to adulthood: A bridge too long.* Boulder, Co.: Westview Press.

NATIONAL PANEL ON HIGH SCHOOL AND ADOLESCENT EDUCATION. (1976). *The education of adolescents.* HEW Publication (OE) 76-00004. Washington, D. C.: U. S. Government Printing Office.

NATIONAL RESEARCH COUNCIL (U. S.). PANEL ON ADOLESCENT PREGNANCY AND CHILDBEARING. (1987). C. Hayes (Ed.), *Risking the future: Adolescent sexuality, pregnancy and childbearing.* Washington, D.C.: National Academy Press.

NEEDHAM, J. (1968). *Order and life.* Cambridge: MIT Press.

NEIMARK, E. D. (1975). Longitudinal development of formal operational thought. *Genetic Psychology Monographs, 91,* 171–225.

NEISSER, U. (1976). *General, academic, and artificial intelligence.* Hillsdale, N.J.: Erlbuam.

NELSON, K. (1973). Structure and strategy in learning to talk. *Monographs of the Society for Research in Child Development, 38,* (2, Serial No. 149).

NELSON, K. (1977). The syntagmatic-paradigmatic shift revisited: A review of research and theory. *Psychological Bulletin, 84,* 93–116.

NELSON, K. (1978). Semantic development and the development of semantic memory. In K. E. Nelson (Ed.), *Children's language* (Vol. 1). New York: Gardner Press.

NELSON, K. (1979). Exploration in the development of a functional system. In W. Collins (Ed.), *Children's language and communication. The Minnesota Symposia on Child Psychology:* Vol. 12. Hillsdale, N.J.: Erlbaum.

NELSON, K. (1981). Social cognition in a script framework. In J. H. Flavell & L. Ross (Eds.), *Social cognitive development.* Cambridge: Cambridge University Press.

NELSON, K. (1986). Event knowledge: Structure and function in development. Hillsdale, N.J.: Erlbaum.

NELSON, K., & S. SEIDMAN. (1984). Playing with scripts. In I. Bretherton, *Symbolic play: The development of social understanding.* New York: Academic.

NELSON, K. E. (1976). Facilitating syntax acquisition. *Developmental Psychology, 13,* 101–107.

NERLOVE, S. B., MUNROE, R. H., & MUNROE, R. L. (1971). Effects of environmental experience on spatial ability: A replication. *Journal of Social Psychology, 84,* 3–10.

NERLOVE, S. B., ROBERTS, J. M., KLEIN, R. E., YARBROUGH, C., & HABICHT, J. P. (1974). Natural indicators of cognitive ability. *Ethos, 2,* 265–295.

NEUGARTEN, B. L. (Ed.) (1968). *Middle age and aging.* Chicago: University of Chicago Press.

NEUGARTEN, B. L., & HAGISTAD, G. O. (1976). Age and the life course. In R. H. Binstock & E. Shanas (Eds.), *Handbook of aging and the social sciences.* New York: Van Nostrand Reinhold.

NEUGARTEN, B. L., WOOD, V., KRAMAS, R. J., & LOOMIS, B. (1963). Women's attitudes toward menopause. *Vita Humana, 6,* 140–151.

NEWPORT, E. L. (1977). Motherese. The speech of mothers to young children. In N. J. Castillan, D. B. Pisoni, & G. R. Potts (Eds.), *Cognitive theory* (Vol. 2). Hillsdale, N.J.: Erlbaum.

NEWSON, J., & NEWSON, E. (1976). *Seven years old in the home environment.* New York: Wiley.

NEWTON, N., & NEWTON, M. (1972). Lactation: Its psychological component. In J. G. Howells (Ed.), *Modern perspectives in psycho-obstetrics.* New York: Brunner/Mazel.

NIGHTINGALE, E. O., & MEISTER, S. B. (1987). *Prenatal screening, policies and values: The example of neural tube defects.* Cambridge: Harvard University Press.

NINIO, A., & BRUNER, J. (1978). The achievement of antecedents of labelling. *Journal of Child Language, 5,* 1–5.

NISWANDER, K. R. (1981). *Obstetrics: Essentials of clinical practice* (2nd ed.). Boston: Little, Brown.

NEW YORK TIMES (1984, Oct. 9). Society's stake in preschool teaching of poor. Section C, p. 10.

NUCCI, L., TURIEL, E., & ENCARNACION-GAWRYCH, G. E. (1983). Children's social interactions and social concepts: Analyses of morality and convention in the Virgin Islands. *Journal of Cross-cultural Psychology, 14,* 469–487.

NUCCI, L. P., & TURIEL, E. (1978). Social interactions and the development of social concepts in pre-school children: Methods, issues, and illustrations. *Child Development, 49,* 400–407.

NUNNER-WINKLER, G. (1984). Two moralities: A critical discussion of an ethic of care and responsibility versus an ethic of rights and justice. In W. M. Kurtines & J. L. Gewirtz (Eds.), *Morality, moral behavior, and moral development.* New York: Wiley.

NYHAN, W. L. (1976). *The heredity factor: Genes, chromosomes and you.* New York: Grosset & Dunlap.

NYITI, R. M. (1976). The development of conservation in the Meru children of Tanzania. *Child Development, 47,* 1122–1129.

NYITI, R. M. (1982). The validity of "cultural differences explanations" for cross-cultural variation in the rate of Piagetian cognitive development. In D. Wagner & H.

Stevenson (Eds.), *Cultural perspectives on child development.* New York: W. H. Freeman.

O'BRYAN, K. G. & BOERSMA, F. T. (1971). Eye movement, perceptual activity, and conservation development. *Journal of Experimental Child Psychology, 12,* 157–169.

OCHS, E. (1982). Talking to children in Western Samoa. *Language in Society, 11,* 77–104.

OCHS, E., & SCHIEFFELIN, B. (1984). Language acquisition and socialization. Three developmental stories and their implications. In R. Shweder & R. LeVine, *Culture theory.* Cambridge: Cambridge University Press.

OLINER, S. B., OLINER, P. (1988). *The altruistic personality: Rescuers of Jews in Nazi Germany.* New York: Macmillan.

OLLER, D. K. (1978). The emergence of the sounds of speech in infancy. In G. H. Yeni-Komshian, J. F. Kavanaugh, & C. A. Ferguson (Eds.), *Child Phonology: Perception and production.* New York: Academic Press.

OLSON, D. R. (1978). The language of instruction. In S. Spiro (Ed.), *Schooling and the acquisition of knowledge.* Hillsdale, N.J.: Erlbaum.

OPPEL, W. C., HARPER, P. A., & REDER, R. V. (1968). The age of attaining bladder control. *Pediatrics, 42,* (4), 614–626.

OPPENHEIM, R. W. (1981). Ontogenetic adaptation and retrogressive processes in the development of the nervous system and behavior: A neuroembryological perspective. In K. J. Connolly & H. F. R. Prechtl (Eds.), *Maturation and development: Biological and psychological perspectives.* Philadelphia: Lippincott.

OSTREA, E. M., & CHAVEZ, C. J. (1979). Perinatal problems (excluding neonatal withdrawal) in maternal drug addiction: A study of 830 cases. *Journal of Pediatrics, 94,* 292–295.

PALEY, V. G. (1981). *Wally's stories.* Cambridge: Harvard University Press.

PALEY, V. G. (1984). *Boys and girls.* Chicago: University of Chicago Press.

PARKE, R. D. (1978). Parent-infant interaction: Progress, paradigms, and problems. In G. P. Sackett (Ed.), *Observing behavior.* Baltimore: University Park Press.

PARKE, R. D. (1981). *Fathers.* Cambridge: Harvard University Press.

PARKE, R. D., & SLABY, R. G. (1983). The development of aggression. In P. H. Mussen (Ed.), *Handbook of child psychology: Vol. 4. Socialization, personality, and social behavior.* New York: Wiley.

PARKE, R. D., & SAWIN, D. B. (1975). Infant characteristics and behavior as initiators of maternal and paternal responsivity. Paper presented at the Biennial Meeting of the Society for Research in Child Development, Denver, Colorado.

PARKES, C. M., & STEVENSON-HINDE, J. (Eds.). (1982). *The place of attachment in human behavior.* New York: Basic Books.

PARMALEE, A. H., JR., AKIYAMA, Y., SCHULTZ, M. A., WENNER, W. H., SCHULTE, F. J., & STERN, E. (1968). The electroencephalogram in active and quiet sleep in infants. In P. Kellaway & I. Petersen (Eds)., *Clinical electroencephalography of children.* New York: Grune and Stratton.

PASCUAL-LEONE, J. (1970). A mathematical model for the transition rule in Piaget's developmental stages. *Acta Psychologia, 32,* 301–345.

PATTEN, B. M. (1968). *Human embryology* (3rd ed.). New York: McGraw-Hill.

PATTERSON, G. R. (1979). A performance theory of coercive family interaction. In R. Cairns (Ed.), *Social Interaction: Methods.* Hillsdale, N.J.: Erlbaum.

PATTERSON, G. R. (1976). The aggressive child: Victim and architect of a coercive system. In E. J. Marsh, L. A. Hamerlynk, & L. C. Handy (Eds.), *Behavior modification and families: Vol. 1. Theory and research.* New York: Brunner/Mazel.

PATTERSON, G. R. (1982). *Coercive family processes.* Eugene, Ore.: Castalia Press.

PATTERSON, G. R., LITTMAN, R. A., & BRICKER, W. (1967). Assertive behavior in young children: A step toward a theory of aggression. *Monographs of the Society for Research for Child Development, 32* (Serial No. 113).

PAVLOV, I. P. (1927). *Conditioned reflexes.* Oxford: Oxford University Press.

PEARL, D., BOUTHILET, L., & LAZAR, J. (Eds.) (1982). *Television and behavior: Ten years of scientific progress and implications for the eighties.* Washington, D.C.: U. S. Government Printing Office.

PEIPER, A. (1963). *Cerebral function in infancy and childhood.* New York: Consultants Bureau.

PERCY, W. (1975). *The message in the bottle.* New York: Farrar, Straus & Giroux.

PERRY, D. G., & BUSSEY, K. (1984). *Social development.* Englewood Cliffs, N.J.: Prentice-Hall.

PERSAUD, T. V. N. (1977). *Problems of birth defects: From Hippocrates to thalidomide and after.* Baltimore: University Park Press.

PESKIN, H. (1967). Pubertal onset and ego functioning. *Journal of Abnormal Psychology, 72,* 1–15.

PESKIN, J. (1980). Female performance and Inhelder's and Piaget's tests of formal operations. *Genetic Psychology Monographs, 101,* 245–256.

PETERSEN, A. C., & CROCKETT, L. (1985). Pubertal timing and grade effects on adjustment. *Journal of Youth and Adolescence, 14,* 191–206.

PFEIFFER, J. (Ed.). (1964). *The cell.* New York: Time Inc.

PFEIFFER, J. (1977). *The emergence of society: A prehistory of the establishment.* New York: McGraw-Hill.

PFUDERER, C. (1969). Some suggestions for a syntactic characterization of baby talk (Working Papers, No. 14). Language-Behavior Laboratory, University of California, Berkeley.

PHILLIPS, D., MCCARTNEY, K., SCARR, S., & HOWES, C. (1987). Selective review of infant day care research: A cause for concern! *Zero to Three, 1*(3), 18–21.

PHILLIPS, D. P. (1982). The behavioral impact of violence in the mass media: A review of the evidence from laboratory and non-laboratory investigations. *Sociology and Social Research, 66,* 387–388.

PIAGET, J. (1926). *The language and thought of the child.* New York: Meridian Books.

PIAGET, J. (1928). *Judgment and reasoning in the child.* London: Routledge and Kegan Paul.

PIAGET, J. (1929). *The child's conception of the world.* New York: Harcourt Brace.

PIAGET, J. (1930). *The child's conception of physical causality.* New York: Harcourt Brace.

PIAGET, J. (1952). *The origins of intelligence in children.* New York: International Universities Press.

PIAGET, J. (1952). *The child's conception of number.* New York: Norton.

PIAGET, J. (1954). *The construction of reality in the child.* New York: Basic Books.

PIAGET, J. (1962). *Play, dreams and imitation.* New York: Norton.

PIAGET, J. (1965). *The moral judgment of the child.* New York: Free Press. (Original work published 1932)

PIAGET, J. (1967). *Six psychological studies.* New York: Random House.

PIAGET, J. (1972). Intellectual evolution from adolescence to adulthood. *Human Development, 15,* 1–12.

PIAGET, J. (1973). *The psychology of intelligence.* Totowa, N.J.: Littlefield & Adams.

PIAGET, J. (1977). The development of thought: Equilibration of cognitive structure. New York: Viking.

PIAGET, J. (1983). Piaget's theory. In P. H. Mussen (Ed.), *Handbook of child psychology: Vol 1. History, theory and methods.* New York: Wiley.

PIAGET, J., & INHELDER, B. (1956). *The child's conception of space.* London: Routledge and Kegan Paul.

PIAGET, J., & INHELDER, B. (1969). *The psychology of the child.* New York: Basic Books.

PIAGET, J., & INHELDER, B. (1973). *Memory and intelligence.* New York: Basic Books.

PIATTELLI-PALMERINI, M. (1980). *Language and learning.* Cambridge: Harvard University Press.

PITTMAN, R., & OPENHEIM, R. W. (1979). Cell death of motor neurons in the chick embryo spinal cord: IV. Evidence that a functional neuromuscular interaction is involved in the regulation of naturally occurring cell death and the stabilization of synapses. *Journal of Comparative Neurology, 187,* 425–446.

PLATH, D. W. (1980). *Long engagements: Maturity in modern Japan.* Stanford: Stanford University Press.

PLATO. (1945). *The republic.* (F. M. Cornford, Trans.) London: Oxford University Press.

PLOMIN, R. (1952). Childhood temperament. In B. Lahey & A. Kazdin (Eds.), *Advances in clinical child psychology* (Vol. 6). New York: Academic Press.

PLOMIN, R. (1986). *Developmental genetics and psychology.* Hillsdale, N.J.: Erlbaum.

PLOMIN, R., & DE FRIES, J. C. (1980). Genetics and intelligence: Recent data. *Intelligence, 4,* 15–29.

PLOMIN, R., & DE FRIES, J. C. (1983). The Colorado adoption project. *Child Development, 54,* 276–289.

PLOMIN, R., & DE FRIES, J. C. (1985). *Origins of individual differences in infancy.* New York: Academic Press.

PLOMIN, R., DE FRIES, J. C., & LOEHLIN, J. C. (1977). Genotype-environment interaction and correlation in the analysis of behavior. *Psychology Bulletin, 84,* 309–322.

PLOMIN, R., DE FRIES, J. C., & MCCLEARN, G. (1980). *Behavioral genetics: A primer.* New York: W. H. Freeman.

POTTS, R., HUSTON, A., & WRIGHT, J. (1986). The effects of television form and violent content on boys' attention and social behavior. *Journal of Experimental Child Psychology, 41,* 1–17.

PRATT, K. C. (1954). The neonate. In L. Carmichael (Ed.), *Manual of child psychology* (2nd ed.). New York: Wiley.

PRECHTL, H. (1977). *The neurological examination of the full-term newborn infant* (2nd ed.). Philadelphia: Lippincott.

PREMACK, D., & PREMACK, A. J. (1983). *The mind of an ape.* New York: Norton.

PRESCOTT, E., & JONES, E. (1971). Day care of children — assets and liabilities. *Children, 18,* 54–58.

PRESIDENT'S SCIENCE ADVISORY COMMITTEE (1974). *Youth: Transition to adulthood.* Chicago: University of Chicago Press.

PRIBRAM, K. H., & LURIA, A. R. (Eds.). (1973). *Psychophysiology of the frontal lobes.* New York: Academic Press.

PRICE-WILLIAMS, D., GORDON, W., & RAMIREZ, M. (1969). Skill and conservation: A study of pottery-making children. *Developmental Psychology, 1,* 769.

PRITCHARD, J. A., & MACDONALD, P. C. (1980). *Williams' Obstetrics* (16th ed.). New York: Appleton-Century-Crofts.

PUTALLAZ, M. (1983). Predicting children's sociometric status from their behavior. *Child Development, 54,* 1417–1426.

PUTALLAZ, M., & GOTTMAN, J. M. (1981). Social skills and group acceptance. In S. R. Asher & J. M. Gottman (Eds.), *The development of children's friendships.* Cambridge: Cambridge University Press.

QUANTY, M. B. (1976). Aggression catharsis: Experimental investigations and implications. In R. G. Green & E. C. O'Neal (Eds.), *Perspectives on aggression.* New York: Academic Press.

QUINTON, D., & RUTTER, M. (1976). Early hospital admissions and later disturbances of behavior: An attempted replication of Douglas' findings. *Developmental Medicine and Child Neurology, 18,* 447–459.

QUINTON, D., & RUTTER, M. (1985). Parenting behavior of mothers raised "in care." In A. R. Nicol (Ed.), *Longitudinal studies in child psychology and psychiatry: Practical lessons from research experience.* New York: Wiley.

RABIN, A. J. (1965). *Growing up in the kibbutz.* New York: Springer.

RABINOWICZ, T. (1979). The differentiate maturation of the human cerebral cortex. In F. Falkner & J. M. Tanner (Eds.), *Human growth: Vol. 3. Neurobiology and nutrition.* New York: Plenum Press.

RADER, N., BAUSANO, M., & RICHARDS, J. (1980). On the nature of the visual-cliff avoidance response in human infants. *Child Development, 51,* 61–68.

RADKE-YARROW, M., SCOTT, P. M., & ZAHN-WAXLER, C. (1973). Learning concern for others. *Developmental Psychology, 8,* 240–260.

RADKE-YARROW, M., ZAHN-WAXLER, C., & CHAPMAN, M. (1983). Children's prosocial dispositions and behavior. In P. H. Mussen (Ed.), *Handbook of child psychology: Vol. 4. Socialization, personality, and social behavior.* New York: Wiley.

RAMEY, C. T. & HASKINS, R. (1981). The modification of

intelligence through early experience. *Intelligence, 5,* 5–19.

RANK, O. (1929). *The trauma of birth.* New York: Harcourt Brace.

RASMUSSEN, L., HIGHTOWER, R., & RASSMUSSEN, P. (1964). *Mathematics for the primary school teacher.* Chicago: Learning Materials.

RAWLS, J. (1971). *A theory of justice.* Cambridge: Harvard University Press.

RAUM, O. F. (1967). *Chaga childhood.* Oxford: Oxford University Press. (Original work published 1940)

RAUSCH, W. A., BARRY, R. K., HERTEL, R. K., & SWAIN, M. A. (1974). *Communication, conflict, and marriage.* San Francisco: Jossey-Bass.

READ, M. (1960/1968). *Children of their fathers: Growing up among the Ngoni of Malawi.* New York: Holt, Rinehart and Winston.

REISS, I. L. (1972). Premarital sexuality: Past, present and future. In I. L. Reiss (Ed.), *Readings on the family system.* New York: Holt, Rinehart and Winston.

RESCORLA, L. (1980). Overextension in early language development. *Journal of Child Language, 7,* 321–335.

RESNICK, D. P., & RESNICK, L. B. (1974). The nature of literacy: A historical exploration. *Harvard Educational Review, 47,* 370–385.

RESNICK, L. B., & FORD, W. W. (1981). *The psychology of mathematics instruction.* Hillsdale, N.J.: Erlbaum.

RESNICK, L. B., & WEAVER, P. A. (1979). *Theory and practice of early reading.* Hillsdale, N.J.: Erlbaum.

REST, J. R. (1979). *Development in judging moral issues.* Minneapolis: University of Minnesota Press.

REST, J. R. (1983). Morality. In P. H. Mussen (Ed.), *Handbook of child psychology: Vol. 3. Cognitive development.* New York: Wiley.

REZNICK, S. J., KAGAN, J., SNIDMAN, N., GERSTEN, M., BAAK, K., & ROSENBERG, A. (1986). Inhibited and uninhibited children: A follow up study. *Child Development, 57,* 660–680.

RHEINGOLD, H. L. (1982). Little children's participation in the work of adults, a nascent prosocial behavior. *Child Development, 53,* 114–125.

RHEINGOLD, H. L., & COOK, K. V. (1975). The content of boys' and girls' rooms as an index of parent behavior. *Child Development, 46,* 459–463.

RICHARDS, J., & RADER, N. (1981). Crawling-onset age predicts visual cliff avoidance in infants. *Journal of Experimental Psychology: Human Perception and Performance, 7,* 382–387.

RIESEN, A. H. (1950). Arrested vision. *Scientific American, 183,* 16–19.

RIMLAND, B. (1964). *Infantile autism; The syndrome and its implications for a neural theory of behavior.* New York: Appleton-Century-Crofts.

ROBBINS, L. C. (1963). The accuracy of parental remembering of aspects of child development and of child rearing practices. *Journal of Abnormal and Social Psychology, 66,* 261–270.

ROBBINS, W. J., BRODY, S., HOGAN, A. G., JACKSON, C. M., & GREEN, C. W. (Eds.). (1929). *Growth.* New Haven: Yale University Press.

ROBSON, K. S., & MOSS, H. A. (1970). Patterns and determinants of maternal attachment. *Journal of Pediatrics, 77,* 976–985.

RODEN, J., & LANGER, E. J. (1977). Long-term effects of a control-relevant intervention with the institutionalized aged. *Journal of Personality and Social Psychology, 35,* 897–902.

ROFF, M., SELLS, B., & GOLDEN, M. M. (1972). *Social adjustment and personality development in children.* Minneapolis: University of Minnesota Press.

ROGOFF, B. (1978). Spot observation: An introduction and examination. *Quarterly Newletter of the Laboratory of Comparative Human Cognition, 2,* 21–26.

ROGOFF, B. (1981). Schooling and the development of cognitive skills. In H. C. Triandis & A. Heron (Eds.), *Handbook of cross-cultural psychology* (Vol. 4). Boston: Allyn and Bacon.

ROGOFF, B. (1982). Integrating context and cognitive development. In M. E. Lamb & A. L. Brown (Eds.), *Advances in developmental psychology* (Vol. 2). Hillsdale, N.J.: Erlbaum.

ROGOFF, B., & LAVE, J. (1984). *Everyday cognition.* Cambridge: Harvard University Press.

ROGOFF, B., NEWCOMBE, N., FOX, N., & ELLIS, S. (1980). Transitions in children's roles and capabilities. *International Journal of Psychology, 15,* 181–200.

ROGOFF, B., SELLERS, M. J., PIRROTTA, S., FOX, N., & WHITE, S. H. (1975). Age of assignment of roles and responsibilities to children. A cross-cultural survey. *Human Development, 18,* 353–369.

ROGOFF, B., & WADDELL, K. J. (1982). Memory for information organized in a scene by children from two cultures. *Child Development, 53,* 1224–1228.

ROSALDO, M. Z. (1984). Toward an ethnography of self and feeling. In R. Shweder & R. A. LeVine (Eds.), *Culture theory: Essays on mind, self, and emotion.* Cambridge: Cambridge University Press.

ROSALDO, M. Z., & LAMPHERE, L. (Eds.). (1974). *Women, culture, and society.* Stanford: Stanford University Press.

ROSE, S. A. (1983). Differential rates of visual information processing in full-term and preterm infants. *Child Development, 54,* 1189–1198.

ROSENBERG, M. (1979). *Conceiving the self.* New York: Basic Books.

ROSENBLITH, J. F. & SIMS-KNIGHT, J. E. (1985). *In the beginning: development in the first two years of life.* Monterey, Calif.: Brooks/Cole.

ROSENTHAL, R. (1987). Pygmalian effects: Existence, magnitude, and social importance. *Educational Researcher, 16*(9), 37–41.

ROSENTHAL, R., BARATZ, S. S., & HALL, C. M. (1974). Teacher behavior, teacher expectations, and gains in pupils' rated creativity. *Journal of Genetic Psychology, 124,* 115–121.

ROSENTHAL, R., & JACOBSEN, L. (1968). *Pygmalion in the classroom: Teacher expectation and pupils' intellectual development.* New York: Holt, Rinehart and Winston.

ROSENTHAL, R., & RUBIN, D. B. (1978). Interpersonal expectancy effects: The first 345 studies. *Behavioral and Brain Sciences, 3,* 377–415.

ROSENZWEIG, M. R. (1984). Experience, memory, and the brain. *American Psychologist, 39,* 365–376.

ROSENZWEIG, M. R., BENNETT, E. L., & DIAMOND, M. C. (1972). Brain changes in response to experience. *The nature and nurture of behavior: Development psychobiology.* New York: W. H. Freeman.

ROSZAK, T. (1969). *The making of a counter culture; reflections on the technocratic society and its youthful opposition.* Garden City, N.Y.: Doubleday.

ROUSSEAU, J. J. (1911). *Emile; or On education.* London: Dent. (Original work published 1762)

ROVEE-COLLIER, C. K. (1984). The ontogeny of learning in infancy. In R. V. Kail, Jr. & N. E. Spear (Eds.), *Comparative perspectives on the development of memory.* Hillsdale, N.J.: Erlbaum.

ROVEE-COLLIER, C. K. (1987). Learning and memory. In J. D. Osofsky (Ed.), *Handbook of infant development* (2nd ed.). New York: Wiley.

ROVEE-COLLIER, C. K., & SULLIVAN, M. W. (1980). Organization of infant memory. *Journal of Experimental Psychology: Human Learning and Development, 6,* 798–807.

ROVEE-COLLIER, C. K., SULLIVAN, M. W., ENRIGHT, M., LUCAS, D., & FAGAN, J. W. (1980). Reactivation of infant memory. *Science, 208,* 1159–1161.

ROVET, J., & NETLEY, C. (1982). Processing deficits in Turner's syndrome. *Developmental Psychology, 18,* 77–94.

ROWE, D. C., & PLOMIN, R. (1981). The importance of non-shared (E1) environmental influences in behavioral development. *Developmental Psychology, 17,* 517–531.

ROYCE, J. M., DARLINGTON, R. B., & MURRAY, H. W. (1983). Pooled analysis: Findings across studies. In The Consortium for Longitudinal Studies, *As the twig is bent . . . Lasting effects of preschool programs.* Hillsdale, N.J.: Erlbaum.

RUBIN, J. Z., PROVEZANO, F. J., & LURIA, Z. (1974). The eye of the beholder: Parents' view on sex of newborns. *American Journal of Orthopsychiatry, 44,* 512–519.

RUBIN, K. H. (1973). Egocentrism in childhood: A unitary construct? *Child Development, 44,* 102–110.

RUBIN, K. H., FEIN, G. G., & VANDENBERG, B. (1983). Play. In P. H. Mussen (Ed.), *Handbook of child psychology: Vol. 4. Socialization, personality, and social behavior.* New York: Wiley.

RUBIN, K. H., & PEPLER, D. J. (1980). The relationship of child's play to social-cognitive development. In H. Foot, T. Chapman, & J. Smith (Eds.), *Friendship and childhood relationships.* London: Wiley.

RUBIN, Z. (1980). *Children's friendships.* Cambridge: Harvard University Press.

RUBLE, D. N., BOGGIANO, A. K., FELDMAN, N. S., & LOEBL, J. H. (1980). Developmental analysis of the role of social comparison in self-evaluation. *Developmental Psychology, 16,* 105–115.

RUBLE, D. N. (1983). The development of social-comparison processes and their role in achievement-related self-socialization. In E. T. Higgins, D. Ruble, & W. W. Hartup (Eds.), *Social cognition and social development: A sociocultural perspective.* Cambridge: Cambridge University Press.

RUFF, H. (1978). Infant recognition of the invariant form of objects. *Child Development, 49,* 293–306.

RUOPP, R., TRAVERS, J., GLANTZ, F., & COELEN, C. (1979). *Children at the center. Final report of the national day care study.* Cambridge: Abt Books.

RUOPP, R., & TRAVERS, J. (1982). Janus faces day care: Perspectives on quality and cost. In E. F. Zigler & E. W. Gordon (Eds.), *Day care: Scientific and social policy issues.* Boston: Auburn House.

RUTTER, M. (1976). Parent-child separation: Psychological effects—Addendum: December 1975. In A. M. Clarke & A. D. B. Clarke (Eds.), *Early experience: Myth and evidence.* London: Open Books.

RUTTER, M. (1976). Maternal deprivation 1972–1978: New findings, new concepts, new approaches. *Child Development, 50,* 283–305.

RUTTER, M. (1981). *Maternal deprivation, reassessed* (2nd ed.). New York: Penguin Books.

RUTTER, M. (1985). Psychopathology and development: Links between childhood and adult life. In M. Rutter & L. Hersov (Eds.), *Child and adolescent psychiatry: Modern approaches* (2nd ed.). Oxford: Oxford University Press.

RUTTER, M. (1987). Continuities and discontinuities from infancy. In J. D. Osofsky (Ed.), *Handbook of infant development*. New York: Wiley.

RUTTER, M., & GARMEZY, N. (1983). Developmental psychopathology. In P. H. Mussen (Ed.), *Handbook of child psychology: Vol. 4. Socialization, personality, and social development*. New York: Wiley.

RUTTER, M., MAUGHAN, B., MORTIMORE, P., & OUSTON, J. (1979). *Fifteen thousand hours: Secondary schools and their effects on children*. Cambridge: Harvard University Press.

RUTTER, M., YULE, B., QUINTON, D., ROWLAND, O., YULE, W., & BERGER, M. (1975). Attainment and adjustment in two geographical areas: III. Some factors accounting for area differences. *British Journal of Psychiatry, 126,* 520–533.

SACHS, J., BARD, B., & JOHNSON, M. I. (1981). Language learning with restricted input; Case studies of two hearing children of deaf parents. *Applied Psycholinguistics, 2,* 33–54.

SACHS, J., & DEVIN, J. (1973). Young children's knowledge of age-appropriate speech styles. Paper presented to Linguistic Society of America.

SAGI, A., & HOFFMAN, M. L. (1976). Empathetic distress in the newborn. *Developmental Psychology, 12,* 175–176.

SAGI, A., LAMB, M. E., LEWKOWICZ, K. S., SHOHAM, R., DVIR, R., & ESTES, D. (1985). Security of infant-mother, -father, and metapelet attachments among kibbutz-reared Israeli children. In. I. Bretherton & E. Waters (Eds.), Growing points of attachment theory and research. *Monographs of the Society for Research in Child Development, 50,* (1–2, Serial No. 209).

SALAPATEK, P. (1975). Pattern perception in early infancy. In L. B. Cohen & P. Salapatek (Eds.), *Basic visual processes: Vol. 1. Infant perception: From sensation to cognition*. New York: Academic Press.

SALAPATEK, P. & KESSEN, W. (1966). Visual scanning of triangles by the human newborn. *Journal of Experimental Child Psychology, 3,* 155–167.

SALE, R. (1978). *Fairy tales and after*. Cambridge: Harvard University Press.

SALK, L. (1973). The role of the heartbeat in the relationship between mother and infant. *Scientific American, 228,* 3, 24–29.

SALKIND, N. J., & NELSON, C. F. (1980). A note on the developmental nature of reflection-impulsivity. *Developmental Psychology, 16,* 237–238.

SALOMON, G. L. (1984). Television is "easy" and print is "tough": The differential investment of mental effort in learning as a function of perceptions and attributions. *Journal of Educational Psychology, 76,* 647–658.

SAMELSON, R. (1980). J. B. Watson's little Albert, Cyril Burt's twins, and the need for a critical science. *American Psychologist, 35,* 619–625.

SAMEROFF, A. J. (1978). Organization and stability of newborn behavior: A commentary on the Brazelton Neonatal Behavior Assessment Scale. *Monographs of Society for Research in Child Development, 43,* (5–6, Serial No. 177).

SAMEROFF, A. J. (1983). Developmental systems; Contexts and evolutions. In P. H. Mussen (Ed.), *Handbook of child psychology: Vol. 1. History, theory and methods*. New York: Wiley.

SAMEROFF, A. J., & CAVANAUGH, P. J. (1979). Learning in infancy: A developmental perspective. In J. D. Osofsky (Ed.), *Handbook of infant development*. New York: Wiley.

SAMEROFF, A. J., & CHANDLER, M. J. (1975). Reproductive risk and the continuum of caretaking casualty. In F. D. Horowitz (Ed.), *Review of child development research* (Vol. 4). Chicago: University of Chicago Press.

SAN DIEGO CITY SCHOOLS. (1984). *Course of study*. San Diego: Author.

SAVAGE-RUMBAUGH, S. (1979). Symbolic communication—its origins and early development in the chimpanzee. In W. Wolf (Ed.), *Early symbolization (New Directions for Child Development,* No. 3). San Francisco: Jossey-Bass.

SAVAGE-RUMBAUGH, S., MCDONALD, K., SEVCIK, R. A., HOPKINS, W. D., & RUBERT, E. (1986). Spontaneous symbol acquisition and communication use by pygmy chimpanzees. *Journal of Experimental Psychology: General, 115,* 211–235.

SAXE, G. B. (1981). Body parts as numerals: A developmental analysis of numeration among the Oksapmin in Papua New Guinea. *Child Development, 52,* 306–316.

SCANZONI, L., & SCANZONI, J. (1976). *Men, women and change: A sociology of marriage and family*. New York: McGraw-Hill.

SCARR, S. (1981). Testing for children: Assessment and the many determinants of intellectual competence. *American Psychologist, 36,* 1159–1166.

SCARR, S. (1981). *Race, social class and individual differences in I.Q.*. Hillsdale, N.J.: Erlbaum.

SCARR, S., & MCCARTNEY, K. (1983). How people make their own environments: A theory of genotype-environment effects. *Child Development, 54*, 424–435.

SCARR, S., & WEINBERG, R. A. (1976). IQ performance of black children adopted by white families. *American Psychologist, 31*, 726–739.

SCARR, S., & WEINBERG, R. (1977). Intellectual similarities within families of both adopted and biological children. *Intelligence, 2*, 170–191.

SCARR, S. & WEINBERG. R. A. (1983). The Minnesota adoption studies: Genetic differences and malleability. *Child Development, 54*, 260–267.

SCHACTER, D. L., & MOSCOVITCH, M. (1984). Infants, amnesics, and dissociable memory systems. In M. Moscovitch (Ed.), *Infant Memory.* New York: Plenum Press.

SCHAFFER, H. R. (1974). Cognitive components of the infant's response to strangeness. In M. Lewis & L. Rosenblum (Eds.), *The origins of fear.* New York: Wiley.

SCHAEFER, E. S. (1959). A circumplex model for maternal behavior. *Journal of Abnormal and Social Psychology, 59*, 226–235.

SCHAFFER, H. R., & EMERSON, P. E. (1964). The development of social attachments in infancy. *Monographs of the Society for Research in Child Development, 29* (3, Serial No. 94).

SCHAIE, K. W. (Ed.). (1981). *Longitudinal studies of adult psychological development.* New York: Guilford Press.

SCHAIE, K. W., & LABOUVIE-VIEF, G. (1974). Generational versus ontogenetic componets of change in adult cognitive behavior. *Developmental Psychology, 10*, 305–320.

SCHAIE, K. E., & STROTHER, C. R. (1968). A cross-sectional study of age changes in cognitive behavior. *Psychological Bulletin, 70*, 671–680.

SCHEINFELD, A. (1972). *Heredity in humans.* Philadelphia: Lippincott.

SCHEPER-HUGHES, N. (1985). Culture, scarcity, and maternal reasoning. *Ethos, 13*, 291–317.

SCHIEFFELIN, B. B. (1986). *How Kaluli children learn what to say, what to do and how to feel.* New York: Cambridge University Press.

SCHINDLER, P. J., MOELY, B., & FRANK, A. L. (1987). Time in day care and social participation of young children. *Developmental Psychology, 23*, 255–261.

SCHMANDT-BESSERAT, D. (1978). The earliest precursor of writing. *Scientific American, 283*, 50–59.

SCHNEIDER-ROSEN, K., BRAUNWALD, K., CARLSON, V., & CICCHETTI, D. (1985). Current perspectives in attachment theory: Illustration from the study of maltreated infants. In I. Bretherton & E. Waters (Eds.), Growing

points of attachment theory and research. *Monographs of the Society for Research in Child Development, 50,* (1-2, Serial No. 209).

SCHOOLER, C., & SCHAIE, K. W. (Eds.). (1987). *Cognitive functioning and social structure over the life course.* Norwood, N.J.: Ablex.

SCHWARTZMAN, H. B. (1980). *Play and culture.* West Point, N.Y.: Leisure Press.

SCRIBNER, S., & COLE, M. (1973). Cognitive consequences of formal and informal education. *Science, 182*, 553–559.

SCRIBNER, S., & COLE, M. (1981). *The psychology of literacy.* Cambridge: Harvard University Press.

SEARLE, J. (1969). *Speech acts.* Cambridge: Cambridge University Press.

SEARS, R., MACCOBY, E., & LEVIN, H. (1975). *Patterns of childrearing.* Evanston, Ill.: Row, Peterson.

SEBALD, H. (1981). Adolescent's concept of popularity and unpopularity: Comparing 1960 with 1976. *Adolescence, 16*, 187–193.

SECORD, P., & PEEVERS, B. H. (1974). The development and attribution of person concepts. In T. Mischel (Ed.), *Understanding other persons.* Totowa, N.J.: Rowman and Littlefield.

SELFE, L. (1977). *Nadia: A case of extraordinary drawing ability in an autistic child.* New York: Academic Press.

SELFE, L. (1983). *Normal and anomalous representational drawing ability in children.* New York: Academic Press.

SELIGMAN, M. (1975). *Helplessness: On depression, development, and death.* New York: W. H. Freeman.

SELMAN, R. L. (1976). Social cognitive understanding. In T. Lickona (Ed.) *Moral development and behavior: Theory, research, and social issues.* New York: Holt, Rinehart and Winston.

SELMAN, R. L. (1976). Toward a structural-developmental analysis of interpersonal relationship concepts: Research with normal and disturbed adolescent boys. In A. Pick (Ed.), *Minnesota Symposia on Child Psychology* (Vol. 10). Minneapolis: University of Minnesota Press.

SELMAN, R. L. (1980). *The growth of interpersonal understanding: Developmental and clinical analysis.* New York: Academic Press.

SELMAN, R. L. (1981). The child as a friendship philosopher. In S. R. Asher & J. M. Gottman (Eds.), *The development of children's friendships.* Cambridge: Cambridge University Press.

SENDAK, M. (1967). *Higglety, pigglety, pop! or There must be more to life.* New York: Harper & Row.

SEPKOWSKI. C. (1985). Maternal obstetric medication and newborn behavior. In J. W. Scanlon (Ed.). *Prenatal anesthesia.* London: Blackwell.

SERBIN, L. A., O'LEARY, K. D., KENT, R. N., & TONICK, I. J. (1973). A comparison of teacher response to the pre-academic and problem behavior of boys and girls. *Child Development, 44,* 796–804.

SERPELL, R. (1977). Strategies for investigating intelligence in its cultural context. *Quarterly Newsletter of the Laboratory of Comparative Human Cognition, 1,* 11–15.

SEXTON, P. C. (1961). *Education and income.* New York: Viking Press.

SEYFARTH, R. M., & CHENEY, D. L. (1980). The ontogeny of monkey alarm calling behavior: A preliminary report. *Z. Tierpsychologie, 54,* 36–56.

SHAFFER, D. R. (1985) *Developmental psychology: Theory, research, and applications.* Monterey, Calif.: Brooks/Cole.

SHAPIRA, A., & MADSEN, M. C. (1969). Cooperative and competitive behavior of kibbutz and urban children in Israel. *Child Development, 4,* 609–617.

SHARP, D. W., COLE, M., & LAVE, C. (1979). Education and cognitive development: The evidence from experimental research. *Monographs of the Society for Research in Child Development, 4,* (1–2, Serial No. 178).

SHATZ, M. (1974). The comprehension of indirect directives: Can you shut the door? Paper presented at Linguistics Society of America. Amherst, Mass.

SHATZ, M. (1978). Children's comprehension of question-directives. *Journal of Child Language, 5,* 39–46.

SHATZ, M. (1983). Communication. In P. H. Mussen (Ed.), *Handbook of child psychology: Vol. 3. Cognitive development.* New York: Wiley.

SHATZ, M., & GELMAN, R. (1973). The development of communication skills: Modification in the speech of young children as a function of listener. *Monographs of the Society for Research in Child Development, 38,* (5, Serial No. 152).

SHAW, G. B. (1963). *George Bernard Shaw on language.* A. Tauben (Ed.). London: Peter Owen.

SHERIF, M., & SHERIF, C. W. (1953). *Groups in harmony and tension.* New York: Harper & Row.

SHERIF, M., & SHERIF, C. W. (1956). *An outline of social psychology.* New York: Harper & Row.

SHERROD, L. R. (1979). Social cognition in infants: Attention to the human face. *Infant Behavior and Development, 2,* 279–294.

SHOCK, N. (1977). Systems integration. In L. Hayflick & C. E. Finch (Eds.), *Handbook of the biology of aging.* New York: Van Nostrand Reinhold.

SHOPEN, T. (1980). How Pablo says "love" and "store." In T. Shopen and J. M. Williams (Eds.), *Standards and dialects in English.* Cambridge: Winthrop.

SHORT, R. V. (1972). Sex determination and differentiation. In C. R. Austin & R. V. Short (Eds.), *Embryonic and fetal development.* Cambridge: Cambridge University Press.

SHOSTAK, M. (1981). *Nissa: The life and words of a !Kung Woman.* Cambridge: Harvard University Press.

SHUY, R., & GRIFFIN, P. (Eds.) (1986). The study of children's functional language and education in the early years. *Final report to the Carnegie Corporation of New York.* Arlington, Va.: Center for Applied Linguistics.

SHWEDER, R. (1982). Liberalism as destiny. *Contemporary Psychology, 27,* 421–424.

SHWEDER, R., MAHAPATRA, M., & MILLER, J. G. (1987). Culture and moral development. In J. Kagan & S. Lamb (Eds.), *The emergence of morality in young children.* Chicago: University of Chicago Press.

SIDOROWICZ, L. S., & LUNNEY, G. S. (1980). Baby X revisited. *Sex Roles, 6,* 67–73.

SIEGLER, R. S. (1976). Three aspects of cognitive development. *Cognitive Psychology, 8,* 481–520.

SIEGLER, R. S. (1983). Information processing approaches to development. In P. H. Mussen (Ed.), *Handbook of child psychology: Vol. 1. History, theory and methods.* New York: Wiley.

SIEGLER, R. S. (1986). *Children's thinking.* Englewood Cliffs, N.J.: Prentice-Hall.

SIEGLER, R. S., & LIEBERT, R. M. (1975). Acquisition of formal scientific reasoning by 10- and 13-year olds: Designing a factorial experiment. *Developmental Psychology, 11,* 401–402.

SIEGLER, R. S., & RICHARDS, D. D. (1982). The development of intelligence. In R. J. Sternberg (Ed.), *Handbook of human intelligence.* Cambridge: Cambridge University Press.

SIGEL, I. E. (Ed.). (1985). *Parental belief systems.* Hillsdale, N.J.: Erlbaum.

SIGMAN, M., & PARMALEE, A. H. (1979). Longitudinal evaluation of the preterm infant. in T. M. Field, A. M. Sostek, S. Goldberg, & H. H. Shuman (Eds.). *Infants born at risk: Behavior and development.* Jamaica, N.Y.: Spectrum.

SIMMONS, R. G., & BLYTH, D. A. (1987). *Moving into adolescence: The impact of pubertal change in school context.* New York: A. de Gruyter.

SIMNER, M. L. (1971). Newborn's response to the cry of another infant. *Developmental Psychology, 5,* 136–150.

SIMPSON. E. L. (1974). Moral development research: A case of scientific cultural bias. *Human Development, 17,* 81–106.

SINCLAIR, J. MCH., & COULTHARD, R. M. (1975). *Towards an analysis of discourse: The English used by teachers and pupils.* Oxford: Oxford University Press.

SINCLAIR DE ZWART, H. (1976). *Acquisition du langage et développement de la pensée.* Paris: Dunod.

SINGER, D. G., SINGER, J. L., & ZUCKERMAN, D. M. (1980). *Getting the most out of TV.* Santa Monica: Goodyear.

SINGER, J. L. (1980). The powers and limitations of television. In P. Tannenbaum (Ed.), *The entertainment functions of television.* Hillsdale, N.J.: Erlbaum.

SINGER, J. L., & SINGER, D. G. (1980). Television viewing, family style and aggressive behavior in preschool children. In M. Green (Ed.), *Violence and the family: Psychiatric, sociological and historical implications.* Boulder, Col: Westview Press.

SIQUELAND, E. (1970). Basic learning processes: 1. Classical conditioning. In H. W. Reese & L. P. Lipsitt (Eds.), *Experimental child psychology.* New York: Free Press.

SIQUELAND, E. R. (1968). Reinforcement patterns and extinction in human newborns. *Journal of Experimental Child Psychology, 6,* 431–432.

SKINNER. B. F. (1938). *The behavior of organisms.* New York: Appleton-Century-Crofts.

SKINNER, B. F. (1957). *Verbal behavior.* New York: Appleton-Century-Crofts.

SKUSE, D. (1984a). Extreme deprivation in early childhood — I. Diverse outcomes for three siblings from an extraordinary family. *Journal of Child Psychology and Psychiatry, 25,* 523–541.

SKUSE, D. (1984b). Extreme deprivation in early childhood — II. Theoretical issues and a comparative review. *Journal of Child Psychology and Psychiatry, 25,* 543–572.

SMELSER, N., & ERIKSON, E. H. (Eds.). (1980). *Themes of work and love in adulthood.* Cambridge: Harvard University Press.

SMELSER, N. J. (1980). Issues in the study of work and love in adulthood. In N. J. Smelser & E. H. Erikson (Eds.), *Themes of work and love in adulthood.* Cambridge: Harvard University Press.

SMETENA, J. (1981). Preschool children's conceptions of moral and social rules. *Child Development, 52,* 1333–1336.

SMETENA, J. (1985). Preschool children's conceptions of transgressions: The effects of varying moral and conventional domain-related attributes. *Developmental Psychology, 21,* 18–29.

SMITH, A. (1984). *The mind.* New York: Viking.

SMITH, M. E. (1926). An investigation of the development of the sentence and the extent of vocabulary in young children. *University of Iowa Studies in Child Welfare, 3* (No. 5).

SMITH, N. V. (1971, Oct. 2). How children learn to speak. *The Listener.*

SMITH, P. K. (1982). Does play matter: Functional and evolutionary aspects of animal and human play. *Behavioral and Brain Sciences, 5,* 139–184.

SMITH, P. K., & DAGLISH, L. (1977). Sex differences in parent and infant behavior in the home. *Child Development, 48,* 1250–1254.

SMITH, R., ANDERSON, D. R., & FISCHER, C. (1985). Young children's comprehension of montage. *Child Development, 56,* 962–971.

SNAREY, J. R. (1985). Cross-cultural universality of social-moral development: A critical review of Kohlbergian research. *Psychological Bulletin, 97,* 202–232.

SNOW, C. E. (1972). Mother's speech to children learning language. *Child Development, 43,* 549–565.

SNOW, C. E., ARLMAN-RUPP, A., HASSING, Y., JOBSE, J., JOOSKEN, J., & VORSTER, J. (1976). Mother's speech in three social classes. *Journal of Psycholinguistic Research, 5,* 1–20.

SNOW, C. E., & FERGUSON, C. A. (Eds.). (1977). *Talking to children.* Cambridge: Cambridge University Press.

SNOW, R. E., & YALOW, E. (1981). Education and intelligence. In R. J. Sternberg (Ed.), *Handbook of human intelligence.* Cambridge: Cambridge University Press.

SONG, M., SMETANA, J. G., & KIM, S. Y. (1987). Korean children's conceptions of moral and conventional transgressions. *Developmental Psychology, 23,* 577–582.

SONTAG. L. W. (1941). The significance of fetal environmental differences. *American Journal of Obstetrics and Gynecology, 42,* 996–1003.

SONTAG, L. W. (1944). War and fetal-maternal relationship. *Marriage and Family Living, 6,* 1–5.

SONTAG, L. W., & WALLACE, R. F. (1935). The movement response of the human fetus to sound stimuli. *Child Development, 6,* 253–358.

SORENSON, R. C. (1973). *Adolescent sexuality in contemporary America.* New York: World.

SPEARMAN, C. (1927). *The abilities of man.* New York: Macmillan.

SPELKE, E. S. (1976). Infants' intermodal perception of events. *Cognitive Psychology, 8,* 553–560.

SPELKE, E. S. (1984). The development of intermodal perception. In L. B. Cohen & P. Salapatek (Eds.), *Handbook of infant perception.* New York: Academic Press.

SPELKE, E. S., & OWSLEY, C. (1979). Intermodal exploration and knowledge in infancy. *Infant Behavior and Development, 2,* 13–24.

SPIRO, M. E. (1965). *Children of the kibbutz.* New York: Schocken.

SPITZ, R. (1965). *The first year of life.* New York: International Universities Press.

SPOCK, B. (1968). *Baby and child care* (rev. ed.). New York: Pocket Books.

SPRUNGER, L., BOYCE, W. T., & GAINES, J. A. (1985). Family-infant congruence: Routines and rhythmicity in family adaptations to a young infant. *Child Development, 56,* 564–572.

SROUFE. L. A. (1979). Socioemotional development. In J. Osofsky (Ed.), *Handbook of infant development.* New York: Wiley.

SROUFE. L. A., & FLEESON, J. (1985). Attachment and the construction of relationships. In W. W. Hartup & Z. Rubin (Eds.), *Relationships and development.* Hillsdale, N.J.: Erlbaum.

STAATS, A. W. (1968). *Learning, language, and cognition.* New York: Holt, Rinehart & Winston.

STARKEY, D. (1981). The origins of concept formation: Object sorting and object preference in early infancy. *Child Development, 52,* 489–497.

STATISTICAL ABSTRACTS OF THE UNITED STATES. (1985). (106th edition). Washington, D.C.: U. S. Government Printing Office.

STEIN, Z., SUSSER, M., SAENGER, G., & MAROLLA, F. (1975). *Famine and development: The Dutch hunger winter of 1944–1945.* Oxford: Oxford University Press.

STEINBERG, L. D. (1981). Transformations in family relations at puberty. *Developmental Psychology, 17,* 833–840.

STEINBERG, L. D. (1982). Jumping off the work experience bandwagon. *Journal of Youth and Adolescence, 11,* 183–205.

STEINBROOK, R. (1987, July 30). AIDS threat changes life style of one in five. *Los Angeles Times,* Part 1, p. 1.

STEINER, J. E. (1977). Facial expressions of the neonate infant indicating the hedonics of food related chemical stimuli. In J. N. Weiffenbach (Ed.), *Taste and development: The genesis of sweet preference.* Washington D.C.: U.S. Government Printing Office.

STEINER, J. E. (1979). Human facial expressions in response to taste and smell stimulation. In H. W. Reese & L. P. Lipsitt (Ed.), *Advances in child development and behavior* (Vol. 13). New York: Academic Press.

STEPHAN, C. W., & LANGLOIS, J. H. (1984). Baby beautiful: Adult attributions of infant competence as a function of infant attractiveness. *Child Development, 55,* 576–585.

STERN, D. (1977). *The first relationship.* Cambridge: Harvard University Press.

STERN, D. (1985). *The interpersonal world of the infant: A view from psychoanalysis and developmental psychology.* New York: Basic Books.

STERN, L. (1973). Prematurity as a factor in child abuse. *Hospital Practices, 8,* 117–123.

STERN, W. (1910). Abstracts of lectures on the psychology of testimony and on the study of individuality. *American Journal of Psychology, 21,* 273–282.

STERN, W. (1912). *Psychologische methoden der intelligenzprüfung.* Leipzig: Barth.

STERNBERG, R. J. (Ed.). (1985). *Human abilities: An information processing approach.* New York: W. H. Freeman.

STERNBERG, R. J., & NIGRO, G. (1980). Developmental patterns in the solution of verbal analogies. *Child Development, 51,* 27–38.

STERNBERG, R. J., & POWELL, J. S. (1983). The development of intelligence. In P. H. Mussen (Ed.), *Handbook of child psychology: Vol. 3. Cognitive development.* New York: Wiley.

STEVENSON, H. W., LEE, S., & STIGLER, J. W. (1986). Mathematics achievement of Chinese, Japanese, and American children. *Science, 231,* 693–699.

STEVENSON, R. (1977). *The fetus and newly born infant: Influence of the prenatal environment* (2nd ed.). St. Louis: Mosby.

STOCKING, G. W., JR. (1968). *Race, culture, and evolution.* New York: Free Press.

STONE, C. A., & DAY, M. C. (1980). Competence and performance models and the characterization of formal operational skills. *Human Development, 23,* 323–353.

STONE, J. L., & CHURCH, J. (1957). *Childhood and adolescence: A psychology of the growing person.* New York: Random House.

STOUT, D. B. (1974). *San Blas Cuna acculturation: An introduction.* New York: Viking Fund Publications.

STRAUSS, S. (Ed.). (1988) *Ontongeny, phylogeny and history.* Norwood, N.J.: Ablex.

STRAYER, F. F. (1980). Social ecology of the preschool peer group. In W. A. Collins (Ed.), *Development of cognition, affect, and social relations: Minnesota Symposia in Child Development* (Vol. 13). Hillsdale, N.J.: Erlbaum.

STRAYER, F. F., & STRAYER, J. (1976). An ethological analysis of social agonism and dominance relations among preschool children. *Child Development, 47,* 980–987.

STROMMEN, E. A. (1973). Verbal self-regulation in a children's game: Impulsive errors on "Simon Says." *Child Development, 44,* 849–853.

SUGERMAN, S. (1983). *Children's early thought.* Cambridge: Cambridge University Press.

SULLIVAN, H. S. (1953). *The interpersonal theory of psychiatry.* New York: Norton.

SULLIVAN, M. W., ROVEE-COLLIER, C. K., & TYNES, D. M. (1979). A conditioning analysis of infant long-term memory. *Child Development, 50,* 152–162.

SULLOWAY, F. J. (1979). *Freud, biologist of the mind: Beyond the psychoanalytic legend.* New York: Basic Books.

SUOMI, S. J., & HARLOW, H. F. (1972). Social rehabilitation of isolate-reared monkeys. *Developmental Psychology, 6,* 487–496.

SUOMI, S. J., HARLOW, H. F., & MCKINNEY, W. T., JR. (1972). Monkey psychiatrists. *American Journal of Psychiatry, 128,* 927–932.

SUPER, C. M. (1976). Environmental effects on motor development: A case of African infant precocity. *Developmental Medicine and Child Neurology, 18,* 561–567.

SUPER, C. M. (1981). Behavioral development in infancy. In R. H. Munroe, R. L. Munroe, & B. B. Whiting (Eds.), *Handbook of cross-cultural human development.* New York: Garland.

SUPER, C. M., & HARKNESS, S. (1972). The infant's niche in rural Kenya and metropolitan America. In L. Adler (Ed.), *Issues in cross-cultural research.* New York: Academic Press.

SUSSMAN, E. J., NOTTELMANN, E. D., INHOFF-GERMAIN, G. E., DORN, L. D., CUTLER, G. B., JR., LORIAUX, D. L., & CHROUSOS, G. P. (1985). The relation of development and social-emotional behavior in young adolescents. *Journal of Youth and Adolescence, 14,* 245–264.

SUTTON-SMITH, B. (1979). *Play and learning.* New York: Gardner.

SWENSON, E. J. (1922). How to teach for memory and application. Reprinted in C. W. Hunnicutt & W. J. Iverson (Eds.), *Research in the three R's.* (1958). New York: Harper & Row.

SWIFT, J, (1970). *Gulliver's travels.* New York: Norton. (Original work published 1726)

TAGGART, R. (1980). Youth knowledge development report 2:12. *Youth employment policies and programs for the 1980's: Background analysis for the Department of Labor Employment and Training Components of the Youth Act of 1980.* Washington D.C.: U.S. Department of Labor.

TANNER, J. M. (1978). *Fetus into man: Physical growth from conception to maturity.* Cambridge: Harvard University Press.

TANNER, N. M. (1981). *On becoming human.* Cambridge: Cambridge University Press.

TANYZER, H., & KARL, J. (1972). *Reading, children's books,* and our pluralistic society. Newark, Del.: International Reading Association.

TAVRIS, C., & OFFIR, C. (1977). *The longest war: Sex differences in perspective.* San Diego: Harcourt Brace Jovanovich.

TELLER, D. Y., PEEPLES, D. R., & SEKEL, M. (1978). Discrimination of chromatic from white light by two-month-old human infants. *Vision Research, 18,* 41–48.

TELZROW, R. W., CAMPOS, J. J., SHEPHERD, A., BERTENTHAL, B. I., & ATWATER, S. (1987). Spatial understanding in infants with motor handicaps. Unpublished manuscript.

TELZROW, R., CAMPOS, J. J., & BERTENTHAL, B. I. (1987) Studies on self-produced locomotion: An overview. Paper presented at the Meetings of the MacArthur Network on the transition from infancy to early childhood, Durango, Co.

TERMAN, L. M. (1925). *Genetic studies of genius.* Stanford: Stanford University Press.

TERRACE, H. S. (1979). *Nim.* New York: Knopf.

THELAN, E. (1984). Learning to walk: Ecological demands and phylogenetic constraints. In L. P. Lipsitt and C. Rovee-Collier (Eds), *Advances in infancy research* (Vol. 3). Norwood, N.J.: Ablex.

THELAN, E. (1986). Treadmill-elicited stepping in seven month old infants. *Child Development, 57,* 1498–1506.

THELAN, E., & FISHER, D. M. (1982). Newborn stepping: An explanation for a disappearing reflex. *Child Development, 18,* 760–775.

THOMAS, A., & CHESS, S. (1977). *Temperament and development.* New York: Brunner/Mazel.

THOMAS, A., & CHESS, S. (1984). Genesis and evaluation of behavioral disorders: From infancy to early adult life. *American Journal of Psychiatry, 141,* 1–9.

THOMAS, A., CHESS, S., BIRCH, H. G., HERTZIG, M. E., & KORN, S. (1963). *Behavioral individuality in early childhood.* New York: New York University Press.

THOMPSON, S. K. (1975). Gender labels and early sex role development. *Child Development, 46,* 339–347.

THORBECKE, W., & GROTEVANT, H. D. (1982). Gender differences in adolescent interpersonal identity formation. *Journal of Youth and Adolescence, 11,* 479–492.

THORNDIKE, E. L. (1911). *Animal intelligence: Experimental studies.* New York: Macmillan.

THORNDIKE, E. L. (1922). *The psychology of arithmetic.* New York: Macmillan.

THURSTONE, L. L. (1938). Primary mental abilities. *Psychometric Monographs, 1,* (1).

TIETJEN, A. M., & WALKER, L. J. (1985). Moral reasoning and leadership among men in a Papua New Guinea society. *Child Development, 21*, 982–992.

TIKHOMIROV, O. K. (1978). The formation of voluntary movements in children of preschool age. In M. Cole (Ed.), *The selected writings of A. R. Luria*. White Plains, N.Y.: Merle Sharp.

TIMARAS, P. S. (1972). *Developmental physiology and aging*. New York: Macmillan.

TIME MAGAZINE. (1984, Dec. 9). Children having children: Teenage pregnancy in America 78–90.

TIZARD, B., & HODGES, J. (1978). The effect of early institutional rearing on the development of eight year old children. *Journal of Child Psychology and Psychiatry, 19*, 99–118.

TIZARD, B., & REES, J. (1975). The effect of early institutional rearing on the behavioral problems and affectional relationship of four year old children. *Journal of Child Psychology and Psychiatry, 16*, 61–73.

TOLSTOY, L. (1950). *Anna Karenina*. (C. Garnett, Trans). New York: Modern Library. (Original work published 1875–1877)

TRAVERS, J., & RUOPP, R. (1978). *National day care study: Preliminary findings and their implications*. Cambridge: Abt.

TRETHOWAN, W. H., & CONLON, M. F. (1965). The couvade syndrome. *British Journal of Psychiatry, 111*, 57–66.

TREVARTHEN, C. (1982). Basic patterns of psychogenetic change. In T. Bever (Ed.), *Regressions in development*. Hillsdale, N. J.: Erlbaum.

TSCHIRGI, J. E. (1980). Sensible reasoning: A hypothesis about hypotheses. *Child Development, 51*, 1–10.

TUCHMANN-DUPLESSIS, H. (1975). *Drug effects on the fetus*. Acton, Mass.: Publishing Science Group Inc.

TUCHMANN-DUPLESSIS, H., DAVID, G., & HAEGEL, P. (1971). *Illustrated human embryology* (Vol. 1). New York: Springer-Verlag.

TURIEL, E. (1978). Social regulation and domains of social concepts. In W. Damon (Ed.), *Social cognition (New directions for child development*, No. 1). San Francisco: Jossey-Bass.

TURIEL, E., & DAVIDSON, P. (1986). Heterogeneity, inconsistency, and asynchrony in the development of cognitive structures. In I. Levin (Ed.), *Stage and structure: Reopening the debate*. Norwood, N.J.: Ablex.

TURIEL, E., KILLEN, M., & HELWIG, C. C. (1987). Morality: Its structure, functions, and vagaries. In J. Kagan & S. Lamb (Eds.), *The emergence of morality*. Chicago: Chicago University Press.

UHLENBERG, P. (1980). Death and the family. *Journal of Family History, 5*, 313–320.

U.S. CENSUS BUREAU. (1975). *Historical statistics of the United States: Colonial times to 1970, Part 1*. Washington, D.C.: U.S. Government Printing Office.

U.S. CENSUS BUREAU, POPULATION DIVISION. (1988, March). Marital status and living arrangements: March 1987. *Current Reports*, Series P-20, No. 423. Washington, D.C.: U.S. Government Printing Office.

U.S. CONGRESS, SENATE COMMITTEE ON HUMAN RESEARCH. (1978). *Obstetrical practices in U.S.* Washington, D.C.: U.S. Government Printing Office.

U.S. DEPARTMENT OF AGRICULTURE. FAMILY ECONOMICS RESEARCH GROUP. AGRICULTURAL RESEARCH SERVICE. (1988, Jan.) Child care arrangements of working women. *Family Economics Review*. Hyattsville, Md.: U.S. Government Printing Office.

U.S. DEPARTMENT OF EDUCATION. NATIONAL COMMISSION ON EXCELLENCE IN EDUCATION. (1983). *A nation at risk: The imperative for educational reform*. Washington, D.C.: U.S. Government Printing Office.

U.S. DEPARTMENT OF LABOR. (1987, Aug.). Office of Information, Publication and Reports. Over half of mothers with children one year or under in labor force in March 1987. *Women and Work*. Washington, D.C.: U.S. Government Printing Office.

U.S. SELECT PANEL FOR THE PROMOTION OF CHILD HEALTH. (1981). *Better health for our children: A national strategy: Report of the Select Panel for the Promotion of Child Health to the U.S. Congress*. Washington, D.C.: U.S. Government Printing Office.

UNITED NATIONS CHILDREN'S FUND (UNICEF). (1987). *The state of the world's children 1987*. Oxford: Oxford University Press.

UNITED NATIONS CHILDREN'S FUND (UNICEF). (1988). *The state of the world's children 1988*. Oxford: Oxford University Press.

UZGIRIS, I. C., & HUNT, J. (1975). *Assessment in infancy: Ordinal scales of psychological development*. Champaign: University of Illinois Press.

VANDER LINDE, E., MORRONGIELLO, B. A., & ROVEE-COLLIER, C. K. (1985). Determinants of retention in 8-week-olds. *Developmental Psychology, 21*, 601–613.

VAUGHN, B., EGELAND, B., SROUFE, L. A., & WATERS, E. (1979). Individual differences in infant-mother attachment at twelve and eighteen months: Stability and change in families under stress. *Child Development, 50*, 971–975.

VERNY, T., & KELLY, J. (1981). *The secret life of the unborn child*. New York: Summit Books.

VINTER, A. (1986). The role of movement in eliciting early imitation. *Child Development, 57,* 66–71.

VON HOFSTEN, C. (1984). Developmental changes in the organization of prereaching movements. *Developmental Psychology, 20,* 369–382.

VORHEES, C. V., & MOLLNOW, E. (1987). Behavior teratogenesis: Long-term influences on behavior. In J. D. Osofsky (Ed.), *Handbook of infant development* (2nd ed.). New York: Wiley.

VURPILLOT, E. (1968). The development of scanning strategies and their relation to visual differentiation. *Journal of Experimental Child Psychology, 6,* 632–650.

VYGOTSKY, L. S. (1978). *Mind in society.* Cambridge: Harvard University Press.

VYGOTSKY, L. S. (1987). Thinking and speech. In *The collected works of L. S. Vygotsky: Vol 1. Problems of general psychology.* (N. Minick, Trans.). New York: Plenum Press.

WADDINGTON, C. H. (1947). *Organizers and genes.* Cambridge: Cambridge University Press.

WADDINGTON, C. H. (1962). *New patterns in genetics and development.* New York: Columbia University Press.

WADDINGTON. C. H. (1966). *Principles of development and differentiation.* New York: Macmillian.

WAGNER, D. A. (1974). The development of short-term and incidental memory: A cross cultural study. *Child Development, 48,* 389–396.

WAGNER, D. A. (1978). Memories of Morocco: The influence of age, schooling, and environment on memory. *Cognitive Psychology, 10,* 1–28.

WAGNER, R. K., & STERNBERG, R. J. (1985). Practical intelligence in real-world pursuits: The role of tacit knowledge. *Journal of Personality and Social Psychology, 49,* 436–458.

WALDROP, M. R., & HALVERSON, C. F. (1975). Intensive and extensive peer behavior. *Child Development, 46,* 19–26.

WALKER, L. J. (1984). Sex differences in the development of moral reasoning: A critical review. *Child Development, 55,* 677–691.

WALKER, L. J. (1986). Sex differences in the development of moral reasoning: A rejoinder to Baumrind. *Child Development, 57,* 522–526.

WALKER, L. J., & DE VRIES, B., (1985). Moral stages/moral orientations: Do the sexes really differ? In C. Black (Ed.), *Gender differences in research in moral development.* Symposium conducted at the meetings of the American Psychological Association, Los Angeles.

WALKER, L. J., DE VRIES, B., & TREVETHAN, S. D. (1987). Moral stages and moral orientations in real-life and hypothetical dilemmas. *Child Development, 58,* 842–858.

WALLERSTEIN, J. S., & KELLY, J. B. (1982). *Surviving the breakup: How children and parents cope with divorce.* New York: Basic Books.

WALLERSTEIN, J. S. (1983). Children of divorce: Stress and developmental tasks. In N. Garmezy & M. Rutter (Eds.), *Stress, coping and development in children.* New York: McGraw Hill.

WALLERSTEIN, J. S. (1984). Parent-child relations following divorce. In J. Anthony & C. Chiland (Eds.), *Clinical parenthood* (Vol. 8). The Yearbook of the International Association of Child and Adolescent Psychiatry. New York: Wiley.

WALLERSTEIN, J. S. (1987). Children of divorce: Report of a ten-year follow-up of early latency-age children. *American Journal of Orthopsychiatry, 57* (2), 199–211.

WANNER, E., & GLEITMAN, L. R. (Eds.) (1982). *Language acquisition: State of the art.* Cambridge: Cambridge University Press.

WASZ-HÖCKERT, O., LIND, J., VUORENKOSKI, V., PARTANEN, T., & VALANNÉ, E. (1968). *The infant cry: A spectographic and auditory analysis.* Clinics in developmental medicine, No. 29. Lavenham, Suffolk: Spastics International Medical Publications and William Heinemann Medical Books, Ltd.

WATERMAN, A. S. (1985). Identity in the context of adolescent psychology. In A. S. Waterman (Ed.), *Identity in adolescence: Progress and contents: (New directions for child development,* No. 30). San Francisco: Jossey-Bass.

WATERMAN, A. S., & WATERMAN, C. K. (1971). A longitudinal study of changes in ego identity status during the freshman year at college. *Developmental Psychology, 5,* 167–173.

WATERS, E. (1978). The reliability and stability of individual differences in infant-mother attachment. *Child Development, 49,* 483–494.

WATERS, E., WIPPMAN, J., & SROUFE, L. A. (1979). Attachment, positive affect, and competence in the peer group: Two studies in construct validation. *Child Development, 50,* 821–829.

WATSON, J. B. (1930). *Behaviorism.* Chicago: Chicago University Press.

WATSON, J. B., & RAYNER, R. (1920). Conditioned emotional reactions. *Journal of Experimental Psychology, 3,* 1–14.

WATSON, J. S. (1971). Cognitive-perceptual development in infancy: Setting for the seventies. *Merrill-Palmer Quarterly, 17,* 139–152.

WATSON, J. S. (1972). Smiling, cooing and "the game." *Merrill-Palmer Quarterly, 18,* 323–340.

WATSON, J. S. (1984). Memory in learning: Analysis of the momentary reactions of infants. In R. Kail & N. E. Spear (Eds.), *Comparative perspectives on the development of memory*. Hillsdale, N.J.: Erlbaum.

WATSON, M. W., & FISCHER, K. W. (1977) A developmental sequence of agent use in late infancy. *Child Development, 48*, 828–835.

WATSON, M. W., & FISCHER, K. W. (1980). Development of social roles in elicited spontaneous behavior during the preschool years. *Developmental Psychology, 16*, 483–494.

WEBER, D. J., REDFIELD, R. R., & LEMON, S. M. (1986). Acquired immunodeficiency syndrome: Epidemiology and significance for the obstetrician and gynecologist. *American Journal of Obstetrics and Gynecology, 155*(2), 235–239.

WECHSLER, D. (1939). *The measurement of adult intelligence*. Baltimore: Williams & Wilkins.

WECHSLER, D. (1974). *Manual for the Wechsler intelligence scale for children*. New York: Psychology Corporation.

WEINRAUB, M., & WOLF, B. M. (1983). Effects of stress and social supports on mother-child interactions in single and two-parent families. *Child Development, 54*, 1297–1311.

WEILL, B. C. (1930). Are you training your child to be happy? *Lesson material in child management*. Washington, D.C.: U.S. Government Printing Office.

WEISNER, T. S. (1984). Ecocultural niches of middle childhood. In W. A. Collins (Ed.), *Development during middle childhood: The years from six to twelve*. Washington D.C.: National Academy Press.

WEISSBERG, J. A., & PARIS, S. G. (1986). Young children's remembering in different contexts: A reinterpretation of Istomina's study. *Child Development, 57*, 1123–1129.

WELLS, G. (Ed.). (1981). *Learning through interaction*. Cambridge: Cambridge University Press.

WERNER, E., & SMITH, R. S. (1982). *Vulnerable but invincible: A longitudinal study of resilient children and youth*. New York: McGraw-Hill.

WERNER, H. (1948). *Comparative psychology of mental development*. New York: International Universities Press.

WERNER, H., & KAPLAN, B. (1952). The acquisition of word meanings: A developmental study. *Monographs of the Society for Research in Child Development, 15*, (1, Serial No. 51).

WERNER, J. S., & LIPSETT, L. P. (1981). The infancy of human sensory systems. In E. S. Gollin (Ed.), *Developmental plasticity: Behavioral and biological aspects of variations in development*. New York: Academic Press.

WERNER, J. S., & WOOTEN, B. R. (1979). Human infant color vision and color perception. *Infant Behavior and Development, 2*, 241–273.

WERTSCH, J. (1985). *Vygotsky and the social formation of mind*. Cambridge: Harvard University Press.

WESTINGHOUSE LEARNING CORPORATION. (1969). *The impact of Head Start: An evaluation of the effects of Head Start on children's cognitive and affectional development*. Executive summary, Ohio University report to the Office of Economic Opportunity. Washington, D.C.: Learning House for Federal Scientific and Technical Informations (ED036321).

WESTON, D. R. & TURIEL, E. (1980). Act-rule relations: Children's concepts of social rules. *Developmental Psychology, 16*, 417–424.

WHITE, B. L. (1975). *The first three years of life*. Englewood Cliffs, N.J.: Prentice-Hall.

WHITE, B. L., & WATTS, J. C. (1973). *Experience and environment: Major influences on the development of the young child*. Englewood Cliffs, N.J.: Prentice-Hall.

WHITE, L. A. (1949). *The science of culture*. New York: Grove Press.

WHITE, L. A. (1959). The concept of culture. *American Anthropologist, 61*, 227–251.

WHITE, M. J. D. (1978). *Modes of speciation*. New York: W. H. Freeman.

WHITE, M. L. (1976). *Children's literature: Criticism and response*. Columbus, Ohio: Charles E. Merrill.

WHITE, R. W. (1959). Motivation re-considered: The concept of competence. *Psychological Review, 66*, 279–333.

WHITE, S. H., & PILLEMER, D. B. (1979). Childhood amnesia and the development of a socially accessible memory system. In J. F. Kihlstrom & F. J. Evans (Eds.), *Functional disorders of memory*. Hillsdale, N.J.: Erlbaum.

WHITING, B. (1980). Culture and social behavior: A model for the development of social behavior. *Ethos, 8*, 95–116.

WHITING, B. B., & WHITING, J. W. M. (1975). *Children of six cultures: A psycho-cultural analysis*. Cambridge: Harvard University Press.

WHITING, J. W. M., BURBANK, V. K., & RATNER, M. S. (1982). The duration of maidenhood. A paper presented at the Social Science Conference on School Age Pregnancies and Parenthood. Elkridge, Maryland.

WIDMAN, M. V., & SINGER, J. E. (1984). The role of psychological mechanisms in preparation for childbirth. *American Psychologist, 39*, 1357–1369.

WILCOX, A. J., WEINBERG, C. R., O'CONNER, J. F., BAIRD, D. D., SCHLATTERER, J. P., CANFIELD, R. E., ARMSTRONG, E. G., & NISULA, B. C. (1988). Incidence of early loss in pregnancy. *New England Journal of Medicine, 319* (4), 189–194.

WILLATS, J. (1987). Marr and pictures: An information processing account of children's drawings. *Archives de Psychologie, 55,* 105–125.

WILSON, E. O. (1975). *Sociobiology: The new synthesis.* Cambridge: Harvard University Press.

WILSON, J. D., GEORGE, F. W., & GRIFFIN, J. E. (1981). The hormonal control of sexual development. *Science, 211,* 1278–1284.

WILSON, J. G. (1977). Current status of teratology. In J. G. Wilson & F. C. Fraser (Eds.), *Handbook of teratology* (Vol. 1). New York: Plenum Press.

WINCHESTER, A. M. (1972). *Genetics.* Boston: Houghton Mifflin.

WINEBERG, S. S. (1987). The self-fulfillment of the self-fulfilling prophecy. *Educational Researcher, 16,* 28–36.

WINNER, E., MCCARTHY, M., KLEINMAN, S., & GARDNER, H. (1979). First metaphors. In D. Wolfe (Ed.), *Early symbolization (New directions for child development,* No. 3). San Francisco: Jossey-Bass.

WINNICOTT, D. W. (1971). *Playing and reality.* London: Tavistock Publications.

WOLFENSTEIN, M. (1953). Trends in infant care. *American Journal of Orthopsychiatry, 33,* 120–130.

WOLFF, P. H. (1966). The causes, controls, and organization of behavior in the neonate. *Psychological Issues, 5,* 1–105.

WOLFF, P. H. (1969). The natural history of crying and other vocalizations in infancy. In B. M. Foss (Ed.), *Determinants of infant behavior* (Vol. 4). London: Methuen.

WOLKIND, S., & RUTTER, M. (1985). Separation, loss and family relationships. In M. Rutter & L. Hersov (Eds.), *Child and adolescent psychiatry.* Oxford: Blackwell.

WOODS, M. B. (1972). The unsupervised child of the working mother. *Developmental Psychology, 6,* 14–25.

WORTHMAN, C. M. & WHITING, J. W. M. (1987). Social change in adolescent sexual behavior, mate selection, and premarital pregnancy rates in a Kikuyu community. *Ethos, 15,* 145–165.

WRIGHT, H. F. (1956). Psychological development in Midwest. *Child Development, 27,* 265–286.

WRIGHT, J. C., HUSTON, A. C., ROSS, R. P., CALVERT, S. L., ROLANDELL, I. D., WEEKS, L. A., RAESSI, P., & POTTS, R. (1984). Pace and continuity of television programs: Effects on children's attention and comprehension. *Developmental Psychology, 20,* 653–666.

YAKOVLEV, P. I., & LECOURS, A. P. (1967). The myelogenetic cycles of regional maturation of the brain. In A. Menkowski (Ed.), *Regional development of the brain in early life.* Oxford: Blackwell.

YARROW, M. R., SCOTT, P. M., & WAXLER, C. Z. (1973). Learning concern for others. *Developmental Psychology, 8,* 240–260.

YAWKEY, T. D., & PELLEGRINI, A. D. (1984). *Child's play: Developmental and applied.* Hillsdale, N.J.: Erlbaum.

YERKES, R. M. (Ed.). (1921). Psychological examining in the United States Army. *Memoirs of the National Academy of Sciences, 15.*

YOUNG, W. W., GOY, R., & PHOENIX, C. (1964). Hormones and sexual behavior. *Science, 143,* 212–218.

YOUNGER, B., & COHEN, L. B. (1986). Developmental change in infants' perception of correlation among attributes. *Child Development, 57,* 803–813.

YOUNISS, J. (1980). *Parents and peers in social development.* Chicago: University of Chicago Press.

YOUNISS, J. (1983). Social construction of adolescence by adolescents and their parents. In H. D. Grotevant & C. R. Cooper (Eds.), *Adolescent development in the family (New directions for child development,* No. 22). San Francisco: Jossey-Bass.

YOUNISS, J., & SMOLLAR, J. (1985). *Adolescent relations with mothers, fathers, and friends.* Chicago: University of Chicago Press.

YOUNISS, J., & VOLPE, J. (1978). A relational analysis of friendship. In W. Damon (Ed.), *Social cognition (New directions for child development,* No. 1). San Francisco: Jossey-Bass.

ZAHAVI, S., & ASHER, S. R. (1978). The effects of verbal instruction on preschool children's aggressive behavior. *Journal of School Psychology, 16,* 146–153.

ZAHN-WAXLER, C., & RADKE-YARROW, M. (1982). The development of altruism: Alternative research strategies. In N. Eisenberg (Ed.), *The development of prosocial behavior.* New York: Academic Press.

ZAHN-WAXLER, C., RADKE-YARROW, M., & KING, R. (1979). Child rearing and children's prosocial initiations toward victims of distress. *Child Development, 50,* 319–330.

ZASLAVSKY, C. (1973). *Africa counts.* Boston: Prindle, Weber, and Schmidt.

ZEGIOB, L. E., ARNOLD, S., & FOREHAND, R. (1975). An examination of observer effects in parent child interaction. *Child Development, 46,* 509–512.

ZELAZO, P. R. (1983). The development of walking: New findings and old assumptions. *Journal of Motor Behavior, 15*, 99–137.

ZELAZO, P. R., ZELAZO, N. A., & KOLB, S. (1972). Walking in the newborn. *Science, 179*, 314–315.

ZELNIK, M., & KANTNER, J. F. (1980). Sexual activity, contraceptive use, and pregnancy among metropolitan area teens, 1971–1979. *Family Planning Perspectives, 12*(2), 69–76.

ZELNIK, M., KANTNER, J. F., & FORD, K. (1981). *Sex and pregnancy in adolescence.* Beverly Hills: Sage Publications.

ZELNIK, M., & SHAH, F. K. (1983). First intercourse among young Americans. *Family Planning Perspectives, 15*, 64–72.

ZESKIND, P. S. (1983). Cross-cultural differences in maternal perceptions of cries of low- and high-risk infants. *Child Development, 54*, 1119–1128.

ZESKIND, P. S., & RAMEY, C. T. (1978). Fetal malnutrition: An experimental study of its consequences in two caregiving environments. *Child Development, 49*, 1155–1162.

ZESKIND, P. S., & RAMEY, C. T. (1981). Preventing intellectual and interactional sequelae of fetal malnutrition: A longitudinal, transactional and synergistic approach to development. *Child Development, 52*, 213–218.

ZESKIND, P. S., SALE, J., MAIO, M. C., HUNTINGTON, L., & WEISEMAN, J. R. (1985). Adult perceptions of pain and hunger cries: A synchrony of arousal. *Child Development, 56*, 549–554.

ZIGLER, E., & VALENTINE, J. (Eds.). (1979). *Project Head Start: A legacy of the war on poverty.* New York: Free Press.

ZINCHENKO, V.P., VAN CHZHI-TSIN, & TARAKANOV, V. V. (1963). The formation and development of perceptual activity. *Soviet Psychology, 2*, 3–12.

ZUSSMAN, J. N. (1978). Relationship of demographic factors in parental discipline techniques. *Developmental Psychology, 14*, 683–686.

Sources of Photographs

• • •

CHAPTER 1

Opener: © George Ancona 1982/International Stock Photo; p.2: Jean-Loup Charmet, Paris; p.5: The Granger Collection; p.6: The Bettmann Archive; p.7: © John Bini Moss/Black Star; p.10: Thomas McAvoy, LIFE Magazine © 1955 Time, Inc.; p.14: Herbert Gehr, LIFE Magazine © Time, Inc.; p.15: Yves de Braines/Black Star; p.17: *(top left)* © James Carroll, *(top right)* Yves Jeanmougin/Woodfin Camp & Associates, *(middle left)* © Burk Uzzle 1984/Archive Pictures, *(middle right)* © Chris Perkins 1981/VIVA/ Woodfin Camp & Associates, *(bottom left)* WHO photo by E. Schwab, *(bottom right)* © George Cohen/Stock Boston; p.20: Copyright Down House and The Royal College of Surgeons of England; p.23: courtesy Joseph Campos, University of Illinois

CHAPTER 2

Opener: from Lennart Nilsson, *How Was I Born*. Copyright © 1975 Penguin Books Ltd. Photograph courtesy Lennart Nilsson, Bonnier Fakta, Stockholm; pp.46–47: from the collection of Kathryn Abbe and Frances McLaughlin-Gill; p.47: *(top right)* courtesy Barbara Rogoff; p.49: *(left)* The Bettmann Archive, *(right)* from Philip Morrison and Phylis Morrison and The Office of Charles and Ray Eames, *Powers of Ten*. Copyright © 1982 by Scientific American Books, Inc.; p.56: *(top)* © Frank Siteman/Stock Boston, *(middle)* UNICEF photo by Joan Liftin, *(bottom)* © Eastfoto; p.57: © Scheler/Black Star; p.61: Omikron/Photo Researchers; p.62: © Bruce Roberts/Photo Researchers

CHAPTER 3

Opener: © Petit Format, Nestle, Science Source/Photo Researchers; p.73 from Lennart Nilsson, *Behold Man*. Copyright © 1974 Little, Brown and Company. Photographs courtesy Lennart Nilsson, Bonnier Fakta, Stockholm; p.75: *(top left)* © Petit Format, Nestle, Science Source/Photo Researchers, *(top right and bottom left and right)* © Dan McCoy/Rainbow; p.80: *(left)* from Lennart Nilsson, *A Child is Born*. Copyright © 1978 Delacorte Press. Photograph courtesy Lennart Nilsson, Bonnier Fakta, Stockholm, *(right)* © Petit Format, Nestle, Science Source/Photo Researchers; p.85: from Lennart Nilsson, *A Child is Born*. Copyright © 1978 Delacorte Press. Photograph courtesy Lennart Nilsson, Bonnier Fakta, Stockholm; p.88: courtesy Anthony De Casper, photo Walter Salinger; p.89: © Eastfoto; p.95: *(left)* AP/Wide World Photos, *(right)* © Erika Stone; p.96: from Ann Pytkowicz Streissguth et al., "Teratogenic effects of alcohol in humans and laboratory animals," *Science,* 18 July 1980, *209,* 353–361, figs. 2, 3, 4. Copyright © 1980 by the American Association for the Advancement of Science. Pho-

tographs courtesy University of Washington, School of Medicine; p.99: © 1975 Aileen & W. Eugene Smith/Black Star

CHAPTER 4

Opener: © Joel Gordon 1984; p.108: © Ulrike Welsch/ Photo Researchers; p.109: © Mariette Pathy Allen/Peter Arnold, Inc.; p.111: © Nancy Durrell McKenna from *The Pregnancy and Birth Book* by Miriam Stoppard, Dorling Kindersley, U.K., 1985/Photo Researchers; p.114: © Thomas Bergman, Solna, Sweden; p.116: © Monkmeyer Press Photo Service; p.117: © Phiz Mezey/Taurus Photos, p.122: © David Linton, *Scientific American, 204,* 66–72. p.124: © James Kilkelly, *Scientific American, 252,* 46–52. p.127: courtesy Jacob E. Steiner, The Hebrew University-Hadassah School of Dental Medicine, Tel Aviv; p.129: courtesy Carroll Izard; p.132: © Hella Hammid/Photo Researchers

CHAPTER 5

Opener: UNICEF photo by Bernard Wolff; p.145: *(top left)* © Herlinde Koelbl/Betty Dornheim Picture Service, *(top right)* © Ellan Young/Photo Researchers, *(bottom left)* UNICEF photo by John K. Isaac, *(bottom right)* © B. Grunzweig/Photo Researchers; p.148: © Erika Stone 1985/Photo Researchers; p.150: UNICEF photo by Ray Witlin; p.155: from E. Gamper, *Zeitschrift für der gesamte Neurologie und Psychiatrie,* 1926, *104,* 65, fig. 14; p.158: *(left)* © Lew Merrim/Monkmeyer Press Photo Service, *(right)* © Leonard Lessin/Peter Arnold, Inc.; pp.160–161: from Tiffany M. Field et al, "Discrimination and imitation of facial expressions by neonates," *Science, 218,* 179–182. Copyright © 1980 by the American Association for the Advancement of Science. p.163: courtesy Einar R. Siqueland, Brown University; p.166: © Grete Mannheim/DPI; p.169: *(top left)* © M. Konner/Anthro-Photo, *(top right)* © Barbara Rios/Photo Researchers, *(bottom left)* courtesy of the Institute for Intercultural Studies, Inc., photo Library of Congress, *(bottom right)* © Erika Stone; p.172: *(top)* © Suzanne Szasz/Photo Researchers, *(bottom)* © Beryl Goldberg; p.173: *(top)* from D. G. Freedman, *Human Infancy; An Evolutionary Perspective,* Erlbaum, 1974, *(bottom)* © Michael Hayman 1983/ Photo Researchers

CHAPTER 6

Opener: © Alice Kandell/Photo Researchers; p.181: © Suzanne Szasz 1981/Photo Researchers; p.184: *(left)* © Lew Merrim/Monkmeyer Press Photo Service, *(right)* © Joel

Gordon 1983; p.186: *(left)* courtesy of the Institute for Inter-cultural Studies, Inc., photo Library of Congress, *(right)* © Beryl Goldberg; p.187: © James Chisalm/Anthro-Photo; p.188: *(left)* © Ray Ellis 1983/Photo Researchers, *(right)* © Randy Taylor/Sygma; p.190: © Doug Goodman/Monkmeyer Press Photo Service; p.191: courtesy T. G. R. Bower; p.200: © Charles Gatewood/The Image Works; p.202: © Jan Lukas/Photo Researchers; p.204: courtesy Mary D. Ainsworth; p.205: © Suzanne Szasz/Photo Researchers; p.206: UNICEF photo; p.207: © Erika Stone

CHAPTER 7

Opener: © Sybil Shelton/Peter Arnold, Inc.; p.213: © Michael Hayman/Black Star; p.214: UNICEF photo by Hewett; p.215: © Erika Stone; p.216: © Fred Mayer 1978/Woodfin Camp & Associates; p.219: © George S. Zimbel/Monkmeyer Press Photo Service; p.220: © Lawrence Manning 1981/Click/Chicago Ltd.; p.223: © James Carroll; p.229: © Erika Stone 1987; pp.230–231: Harlow Primate Laboratory, University of Wisconsin; p.232: © Joel Gordon 1978; p.233: David M. Grossman; p.234: © Erika Stone 1984; p.235: © Hella Hammid/Photo Researchers; p.237: © Susan Lapides 1981/Design Conceptions; p.238: © Elizabeth Crews/Stock Boston; p.239: © Erika Stone 1985

CHAPTER 8

Opener, © Nik Wheeler/Sygma; p.247: © Ellan Young 1980/Photo Researchers; p.249: UNICEF photo by Ed Rice; p.250: © Shirley Zeiberg/Taurus Photos; p.253: © Paul Sequeira/Photo Researchers; pp.259–260: Harlow Primate Laboratory, University of Wisconsin; p.261: © Alice Kandell/Photo Researchers; p.264: © W. Eugene Smith/Black Star

CHAPTER 9

Opener, © Eastfoto; p.276: courtesy Noam Chomsky, MIT; p.278: © Teresa Zabala/Monkmeyer Press Photo Service; p.280: © Phiz Mezey/Taurus Photos; p.281: © Beryl Goldberg; p.283: *(left)* ©Erika Stone, *(right)* © Jacques Jangoux 1978/Peter Arnold, Inc.; p.289: © Jean Gaumy/Magnum Photos; p.291: © Erika Stone 1987; p.293: Novosti from Sovfoto; p.301: © Erika Stone 1985

CHAPTER 10

Opener: © Eastfoto; p.309: © Tony Triolo/Black Star; p.313: courtesy Rheta De Vries; p.314: *(left)* © Mimi For-syth/Monkmeyer Press Photo Service, *(right)* © Joel Gordon 1978; p.316: courtesy Helene Borke; p.237: *(top)* © Bernard Wolff/Omni-Photo Communications, *(bottom)* © Karen R. Preuss 1982/Taurus Photos; p.328: *(top)* © Beryl Goldberg; *(bottom)* © Ray Ellis 1985/Photo Researchers; p.330: © Eastfoto p.336: from Lorna Selfe, *Nadia: A Case of Extraordinary Drawing Ability in an Autistic Child.* Copyright © 1977 Academic Press, plates 20 and 27. p.337: © Eastfoto; p.338: © Karen Gilborn/Omni-Photo Communications

CHAPTER 11

Opener: © Eastfoto; p.345: © Polly Brown/Archive Pictures; p.347: *(top)* © Bernard Pierre Wolff/Photo Researchers, *(bottom)* © Lynn Johnson 1987/Black Star; p.348: The Granger Collection; p.352: © Erika Stone 1985; p.353: *(top)* © David M. Grossman, *(bottom)* © Richard Frieman/Photo Researchers; p.360: © Herlinde Koelbl/Betty Dornheim Picture Service; p.361: *(top)* © Barbara Rios/Photo Researchers, *(bottom)* © Ed Lettau 1984/Photo Researchers; p.363: courtesy Albert Bandura, Stanford University; p.364: Film Study Center, Harvard; p.366: UPI/Bettmann Newsphotos; p.369: *(left)* © Erika Stone 1988, *(top right)* © David M. Grossman, *(bottom right)* © Lynn Johnson 1987/Black Star; p.370: © Erika Stone/Peter Arnold, Inc.

CHAPTER 12

Opener: © David M. Grossman; p.379: *(left)* © Susan Lapides 1980/Design Conceptions, *(right)* © Erika Stone 1986/Photo Researchers; p.381: *(top)* © Renate Jope/Photo Researchers, *(bottom)* © Hella Hammid/Photo Researchers; p.385: © Erika Stone 1985; p.388: © Cary Wolinsky/Stock Boston; p.391: © Joel Gordon 1979; p.393: © Barbara Rios/Photo Researchers; p.394: © Erika Stone 1987; p.397: © Eastfoto; p.399: © Elizabeth Crews/Stock Boston; p.400: © Suzanne Szasz 1981/Photo Researchers

CHAPTER 13

Opener: © Bernard Wolff/Omni-Photo Communications; p.412: *(top)* © Suzanne Szasz/Photo Researchers, *(bottom)* © R. Lee/Anthro-Photo; p.414: *(top)* © Erika Stone/Peter Arnold, Inc., *(bottom)* © Suzanne Szasz 1981/Photo Researchers; p.416: *(top)* © Beryl Goldberg, *(bottom)* © Barbara Rios/Photo Researchers; p.418: © Phiz Mezey/Taurus Photos: p.423: © Beryl Goldberg; p.431: UNICEF photo by Sean Sprague

CHAPTER 14

Opener: © Sovfoto; p.439: © Beryl Goldberg; p.440: © Cornell Capa/Magnum Photos; p.443: The Granger Collection; p.444: © Eastfoto; p.446: © Ulrike Welsch 1982/Photo Researchers; p.447: © David M. Grossman; p.448: UNICEF photo by Anthony Hewett; p.455: courtesy Michael Cole; p.458: © Suzanne Szasz 1981/Photo Researchers; p.468: © David M. Grossman

CHAPTER 15

Opener: © Edouard Boubat/Rapho/Photo Researchers; p.477: © Shirley Zeiberg/Taurus Photos; p.478: © R. Lee/Anthro-Photo; p.481: *(top left)* © Ira Berger 1982/Woodfin Camp & Associates, *(top right)* UN photo by John Isaac, *(bottom left)* © Ellis Herwig/Taurus Photos, *(bottom right)* © Erika Stone 1988; p.493: © Michael Hayman/Black Star; p.496: © Beryl Goldberg; p.499: © Vivienne della Grotta 1982/Photo Researchers; p.503: © Michael Austin/Photo Researchers; p.506: © Shirley Zeiberg/Taurus Photos; p.508: © Bettye Lane/Photo Researchers

CHAPTER 16

Opener: © Jim Richardson/Black Star; p.519: *(top left)* © Martin Etter/Anthro-Photo, *(top right)* © Paul Conklin/Monkmeyer Press Photo Service, *(bottom left)* © Mimi Forsyth/Monkmeyer Press Photo Service, *(bottom right)* Fritz Goro, LIFE Magazine 1955 © Time, Inc.; pp.529 and 534: © Joel Gordon 1988; p.535: © Chris Sheridan/Monkmeyer Press Photo Service; p.537: © Susan Lapides 1982/Design Conceptions; p.538: © Eastfoto; p.539: © Pierre Baisclair/Black Star; p.545: © Erika Stone 1985; p.547: *(top and bottom right)* UPI/Bettmann Newsphotos, *(bottom left)* © Robert Kalman/The Image Works, p.548: *(top)* © Danielle B. Hayes/Omni-Photo Communications, *(bottom)* © Harriet

Gans 1986/The Image Works; p.549: © Joel Gordon 1972; p.552: © Bill Owens/Archive Pictures

CHAPTER 17

Opener: © Ken Karp/Omni-Photo Communications; p.562: © Novosti from Sovfoto; p. 565: © Ann Hagan Griffiths/Omni-Photo Communications; p.566: *(top)* © Karen Preuss/Taurus Photos, *(bottom)* © Joel Gordon 1988; p.567: © John Lei/Omni-Photo Communications; p.575: © Susan Lapides 1981/Design Conceptions; p.576: © Bettye Lane/Photo Researchers p.581: © Joel Gordon 1988; p.585: *(left)* © Susan Lapides 1986/Design Conceptions, *(right)* © James Carroll; p.585: © Hays/Monkmeyer Press Photo Service; p.587: © Daemmrich/Click/Chicago Ltd.; p.588: © Alan Carey/The Image Works; p.589: *(top)* © Elizabeth Crews/The Image Works; *(bottom)* Gabe Palmer © Mug Shots™ 1987/The Stock Market; p.590: © David M. Grossman; p.593: © Steve and Mary Skjold/The Image Works

CHAPTER 18

Opener: © Elizabeth Crews/The Image Works; p.599: © Irene Bayer/Monkmeyer Press Photo Service; p.600: © Will McIntyre 1984/Photo Researchers; p.601: © Barbara Rios/Photo Researchers; p.603: *(top)* © Bohdan Hrynewych/Stock Boston, *(bottom left)* © Ulrike Welsch/Photo Researchers, *(bottom right)* © Rhoda Sidney/Monkmeyer Press Photo Service; p.609: *(top)* © Martine Franck/Magnum Photos, *(middle)* © Ulrike Welsch/Stock Boston, *(bottom)* © Bernard Pierre Wolff/Photo Researchers; p.610: © Owen Frankin/Stock Boston; p.611: © Martin M. Rotker/Taurus Photos; p.612: © Shirley Zeiberg/Taurus Photos; p.613: *(top)* © David S. Strickler/Monkmeyer Press Photo Service, *(bottom)* © David Hurn/Magnum Photos; p.614: © Lynn Johnson 1987/Black Star

Name Index

...

Subject Index

...